CONNECTIONIST PSYCHOLOGY

Connectionist psychology:
A text with readings

Rob Ellis

University of Plymouth, UK

Glyn W. Humphreys

University of Birmingham, UK

Psychology Press
a member of the Taylor & Francis group

Psychology Press, Publishers
27 Church Road
Hove
East Sussex, BN3 2FA
UK

EXCEPT:
Pages 75–105: Copyright © 1985 by the American Psychological Association. Reprinted with permission.
Pages 107–138: Copyright © 1992 by the American Psychological Association. Reprinted with permission.
Pages 181–186: Copyright © (1988) Macmillan Magazines Limited. Reprinted with permission.
Pages 187–236: Copyright © Academic Press (1993). Reprinted with permission.
Pages 259–288: Copyright © Academic Press (1992). Reprinted with permission.
Pages 289–312: Copyright © Cognitive Science Society Incorporated (1990), used by permission.
Pages 367–454: Copyright © (1996) by the American Psychological Association. Reprinted with permission.
Pages 487–526: Copyright © (1991) Elsevier Science – NL. Reprinted with Kind permission.
Pages 577–604: Copyright © (1994) Cambridge University Press. Reprinted with permission.
Pages 641–658: Copyright © (1992) by the Massachusetts Institute of Technology. Reprinted with permission.

British Library Cataloguing in Publication Data
A catalogue record for this title is available from the British Library

ISBN 0–86377–786–4 (Hbk)
ISBN 0–86377–787–2 (Pbk)

Typeset by Graphicraft Limited, Hong Kong
Printed and bound in the United Kingdom by Bookcraft Ltd, Midsomer Norton, Somerset

For Joe and Thomas Ellis
and
Katie Humphreys

Contents

Figure and table acknowledgements

Figure

1.1   Beatty, J. (1995). *Principles of behavioral neuroscience*. London: Brown & Benchmark Publishers. This material is reproduced with the permission of The McGraw-Hill Companies.

1.2   Carlson, N. R. (1986). *Physiology of behavior* (2nd ed.). Hemel Hempstead, UK: Allyn & Bacon. Copyright © (1986) by Allyn & Bacon. Reprinted with permission.

1.4   McClelland, J. L. & Rumelhart, D. E. (1981). An interactive activation model of context effects in letter perception: Part 1. An account of basic findings. *Psychological Review, 88*, 375–407. Copyright © (1981) by the American Psychological Association. Reprinted with permission.

1.5   Julesz, B. (1971). *Foundations of cyclopean perception*. Chicago: University of Chicago Press. Copyright © (1971) University of Chicago Press. Reprinted with permission.

1.6   Frisby, J. (1979). *Seeing: Illusion, brain and mind*. Milton Keynes, UK: Oxford University Press. Reprinted by permission of Oxford University Press.

2.9   Hinton, G. E. & Sejnowski, T. J. (1986). Learning and relearning in Boltzmann machines. In D. E. Rumelhart, & J. L. McClelland (Eds.), *Parallel distributed processing: Explorations in the microstructure of cognition* (Vol. 1, pp. 282–317). Cambridge, MA: MIT Press. Copyright © (1986) MIT Press. Reprinted with permission.

2.11a/b/c   Rumelhart, D. E., Hinton, G. E., & Williams, R. J. (1986). Learning internal representations by error propagation. In D. E. Rumelhart & J. L. McClelland (Eds.), *Parallel distributed processing: Explorations in the microstructure of cognition* (Vol. 1). Cambridge, MA: MIT Press. Copyright © (1986) MIT Press. Reprinted with permission.

2.13   Rumelhart, D. E., & Zipser, D. (1985). Feature discovery by competitive learning. *Cognitive Science, 9*, 75–122. Copyright © (1985) Cognitive Science Society, Inc.

2.14a/b   Rumelhart, D. E., & Zipser, D. (1985). Feature discovery by competitive learning. *Cognitive Science, 9*, 75–122. Copyright © (1985) Cognitive Science Society, Inc.

2.16   Grossberg, S. (1987). Competitive learning: From interactive activation to adaptive resonance. *Cognitive Science, 11*, 23–63. Copyright © (1987) Cognitive Science Society, Inc.

3.1   McClelland, J. L., & Rumelhart, D. E. (1986). A distributed model of human learning and memory. In J. L. McClelland & D. E. Rumelhart (Eds.). *Parallel distributed processing: Explorations in the microstructure of cognition* (Vol. 2). Cambridge, MA: MIT Press. Copyright © (1986) MIT Press. Reprinted with permission.

3.2   McClelland, J. L., & Rumelhart, D. E. (1986). A distributed model of human learning and memory. In J. L. McClelland & D. E. Rumelhart (Eds.). *Parallel distributed processing: Explorations in the microstructure of cognition* (Vol. 2). Cambridge, MA: MIT Press. Copyright © (1986) MIT Press. Reprinted with permission.

3.3   Marr, D. (1969). A theory of cerebellar cortex. *Journal of Physiology, 202*, 437–470. Copyright © (1969) The Physiological Society. Reprinted with permission.

3.4   Charniak, E., & McDermott, D. (1985). *Introduction to artificial intelligence*. Reading, MA: Addison-Wesley. Copyright © (1985). Reprinted with permission.

3.5   Hinton, G. E. (1989a). Learning distributed representations of concepts. In R. G. M. Morris (Ed.), *Parallel distrib-*

uted processing: Implications for psychology and neurobiology. Oxford: Oxford University Press. Reprinted by permission of Oxford University Press.

3.6   Hinton, G. E. (1989a). Learning distributed representations of concepts. In R. G. M. Morris (Ed.), *Parallel distributed processing: Implications for psychology and neurobiology*. Oxford: Oxford University Press. Reprinted by permission of Oxford University Press.

3.7a/b   Hinton, G. E. (1989a). Learning distributed representations of concepts. In R. G. M. Morris (Ed.), *Parallel distributed processing: Implications for psychology and neurobiology*. Oxford: Oxford University Press. Reprinted by permission of Oxford University Press.

3.8   Rumelhart, D. E., & Todd, P. M. (1993). Learning and connectionist representations. In D. E. Meyer & S. Kornblum (Eds.), *Attention and performance XIV*. Cambridge, MA: MIT Press. Copyright © (1993) MIT Press. Reprinted with permission.

3.9   Hinton, G. E., & Sejnowski, T. J. (1986). Learning and relearning in Boltzmann machines. In D. E. Rumelhart, & J. L. McClelland (Eds.), *Parallel distributed processing: Explorations in the microstructure of cognition* (Vol. 1, pp.282–317). Cambridge, MA: MIT Press. Copyright © (1986) MIT Press. Reprinted with permission.

3.10a/b   McCloskey, M., & Cohen, N. J. (1989). Catastrophic interference in connectionist networks: The sequential learning problem. In G. H. Bower (Ed.), *The psychology of learning and motivation*, 24. New York: Academic Press. Copyright © (1989) Academic Press. Reprinted with permission.

3.11   Kruschke, J. K. (1992). ALCOVE: An exemplar-based connectionist model of category learning. *Psychological Review, 99*, 22–44. Copyright © (1992) by The American Psychological Association. Reprinted with permission.

3.12a/b/c   Kruschke, J. K. (1992). ALCOVE: An exemplar-based connectionist model of category learning. *Psychological Review, 99*, 22–44. Copyright © (1992) by The American Psychological Association. Reprinted with permission.

3.13a/b   Kruschke, J. K. (1993). Human category learning: Implications for back propagation models. *Connection Science, 5*, 3–36. This material is reproduced with the permission of Carfax Publishing Limited, P.O. Box 25, Abingdon, Oxfordshire, OX14 3UE.

3.14   Dienes, (1992). Connectionist and memory-array models of artificial grammar learning. *Cognitive Science, 16*(1), 41–79. Copyright © (1992) Cognitive Science Society, Inc.

3.15   Murre, J. M. J. (1997). Implicit and Explicit memory in amnesia: Some explanations and predictions by the TraceLink model. *Memory, 5*, 213–232. Hove, UK: Psychology Press. Reprinted with permission.

4.1a/b/c   Marr, D., & Hildreth, E. (1982). Theory of edge detection. *Proceedings of the Royal Society, London, B207*, 187–216. Copyright © (1982) The Royal Society.

4.2a/b/c   *Vision* by David Marr © 1982 by W. H. Freeman and Company. Used with permission.

4.3a/b/c/d   Marr, D., & Hildreth, E. (1982). Theory of edge detection. *Proceedings of the Royal Society, London, B207*, 187–216. Copyright © (1982) The Royal Society.

4.4a/b/c   Marr, D., & Hildreth, E. (1982). Theory of edge detection. *Proceedings of the Royal Society, London, B207*, 187–216. Copyright © (1982) The Royal Society.

4.5a/b   Grossberg, S. (1973). Contour enhancement, short term memory and constancies in reverberating neural networks. *Studies in Applied Mathematics, 52*, 217–257. Copyright © (1973) by Blackwell Publishers. Reprinted with permission

4.6a/b   Kohonen, T. (1990). The self-organizing map. *Proceedings of the IEEE, 78*, 1464–1480. Copyright © (1990) IEEE.

4.7a/b/c   Kohonen, T. (1990). The self-organizing map. *Proceedings of the IEEE, 78*, 1464–1480. Copyright © (1990) IEEE.

4.8   Kohonen, T. (1990). The self-organizing map. *Proceedings of the IEEE, 78*, 1464–1480. Copyright © (1990) IEEE.

4.9a–g   Lehky, S. R., & Sejnowski, T. J. (1988). Network model of shape-from-shading: Neural function arises from both receptive field and projective fields. *Nature, 333*, 452–454. Reprinted with permission from Nature. Copyright © (1988) Macmillan Magazines Limited.

4.10   Lehky, S. R., & Sejnowski, T. J. (1988). Network model of shape-from-shading: Neural function arises from both receptive field and projective fields. *Nature, 333*, 452–454. Reprinted with permission from Nature. Copyright © (1988) Macmillan Magazines Limited.

4.11   Lindsay, P. H., & Norman, D. A. (1977). *Human information processing* (2nd ed.). New York: Academic Press. Copyright © (1977) Academic Press. Reprinted with permission.

4.12   McClelland, J. L. (1986). The programmable blackboard model of reading. In D. E. Rumelhart & J. L. McClelland (Eds.), *Parallel distributed processing: Explorations in the microstructure of cognition* (Vol. 1). Cambridge, MA: MIT Press. Copyright © (1986) MIT Press. Reprinted with permission.

4.14a/b   Hummel, J. E., & Biederman, I. (1992). Dynamic binding in a neural network for shape-recognition. *Psychological Review, 99*(3), 480–517. Copyright © (1992) by The American Psychological Association. Reprinted with permission.

4.15   Phaf, R. H., Van der Heijden, A. H. C., & Hudson, P. T. W. (1990). SLAM: A connectionist model for attention in visual selection. *Cognitive Psychology, 22*(3), 273–341. Copyright © (1990) Academic Press. Reprinted with permission.

4.16   Humphreys, G. W., & Heinke, D. (1998). Spatial representation and selection in the brain: Neuropsychological and computational constraints. *Visual Cognition, 5*, 9–47. Reprinted with permission.

4.17   Humphreys, G. W., & Heinke, D. (1998). Spatial representation and selection in the brain: Neuropsychological and computational constraints. *Visual Cognition, 5*, 9–47. Reprinted with permission.

4.18   Humphreys, G. W., & Müller, H. J. (1993). Search via recursive rejection (SERR): A connectionist model of visual search. *Cognitive Psychology*, 25(1), 43–110. Copyright © (1993) Academic Press. Reprinted with permission.

4.19   Humphreys, G. W., & Müller, H. J. (1993). Search via recursive rejection (SERR): A connectionist model of visual search. *Cognitive Psychology, 25*(1), 43–110. Copyright © (1993) Academic Press. Reprinted with permission.

4.20 Humphreys, G. W., Lamote, C., & Lloyd-Jones, T. J. (1995). An interactive activation approach to object processing: Effects of structural similarity, name frequency and task in normality and pathology. *Memory, 3*, 535–586. Reprinted with permission.

4.21 Humphreys, G. W., Lamote, C., & Lloyd-Jones, T. J. (1995). An interactive activation approach to object processing: Effects of structural similarity, name frequency and task in normality and pathology. *Memory, 3*, 535–586. Reprinted with permission.

4.22 Burton, A. M., & Bruce, V. (1993). Naming faces and naming names: Exploring an interactive activation model of person recognition. *Memory, 1*, 457–480. Reprinted with permission.

4.23 Martinez, T. M., Ritter, H. J., & Schulten, K. J. (1990). Three dimensional neural net for learning visuomotor co-ordination of a robot arm. *IEEE Transactions on Neural Networks, 1*, 131–136. Copyright © (1990) IEEE.

4.24a/b Martinez, T. M., Ritter, H. J., & Schulten, K. J. (1990). Three dimensional neural net for learning visuomotor coordination of a robot arm. *IEEE Transactions on Neural Networks, 1*, 131–136. Copyright © (1990) IEEE.

5.1 Rumelhart, D. E., & Norman, D. A. (1982). Simulating a skilled typist: A study of skilled motor performance. *Cognitive Science, 6*, 1–36. Copyright © (1982) Cognitive Science Society, Inc., used by permission.

5.2a/b Rumelhart, D. E., & Norman, D. A. (1982). Simulating a skilled typist: A study of skilled motor performance. *Cognitive Science, 6*, 1–36. Copyright © (1982) Cognitive Science Society, Inc., used by permission.

5.3 Burgess, N., & Hitch, G. J. (1992). Toward a network model of the articulatory loop. *Journal of memory and Language, 31*, 429–460. Copyright © (1992) Academic Press. Reprinted with permission.

5.4 Hitch, G. J., Burgess, N., Towse, J. N., & Culpin, V. (1996). Temporal grouping effects in immediate recall: A working-memory analysis. *Quarterly Journal of Experimental Psychology, 49A*(1), 116–139. Copyright © (1996) The Experimental Psychology Society.

5.5 Burgess, N., & Hitch, G. J. (1992). Toward a network model of the articulatory loop. *Journal of memory and Language, 31*, 429–460. Copyright © (1992) Academic Press. Reprinted with permission.

5.6 Hinton, G. E. (1984). Parallel computations for controlling an arm. *Journal of motor behaviour, 16*, 171–194. Reprinted with permission of the Helen Dwight Reid Educational Foundation. Published by Heldref Publications, 1319 Eighteenth Street., N.W., Washington, D.C. 20036–1802. Copyright © 1984.

5.7 Cohen, J. D., Dunbar, K., & McClelland, J. L. (1990). On the control of automatic processes: A parallel distributed processing account of the Stroop Effect. *Psychological Review, 97*(3), 332–361. Copyright © (1990) by The American Psychological Association. Reprinted with permission.

5.8 Cohen, J. D., Dunbar, K., & McClelland, J. L. (1990). On the control of automatic processes: A parallel distributed processing account of the Stroop Effect. *Psychological Re-view, 97*(3), 332–361. Copyright © (1990) by The American Psychological Association. Reprinted with permission.

5.9 Cohen, J. D., Dunbar, K., & McClelland, J. L. (1990). On the control of automatic processes: A parallel distributed processing account of the Stroop Effect. *Psychological Review, 97*(3), 332–361. Copyright © (1990) by The American Psychological Association. Reprinted with permission.

5.10 Grossberg, S. (1982). *Studies of mind and brain: Neural principles of learning, perception, development, cognition and motor control.* Amsterdam: Reidel Press. Reprinted with kind permission from Kluwer Academic Publishers.

5.11 Grossberg, S. (1982). *Studies of mind and brain: Neural principles of elarning, perception, development, cognition and motor control.* Amsterdam: Reidel Press. Reprinted with kind permission from Kluwer Academic Publishers.

5.12 Elman, J. L. (1990). Finding structure in time. *Cognitive Science Society, 14*, 179–211, Copyright © (1990) Cognitive Science Society, Inc., used by permission.

5.13 Elman, J. L. (1990). Finding structure in time. *Cognitive Science Society, 14*, 179–211, Copyright © (1990) Cognitive Science Society, Inc., used by permission.

5.14 Elman, J. L. (1990). Finding structure in time. *Cognitive Science Society, 14*, 179–211, Copyright © (1990) Cognitive Science Society, Inc., used by permission.

6.2 McClelland, J. L., & Rumelhart, D. E. (1981). An interactive activation model of context effects in letter perception: Part 1. An account of basic findings. *Psychological Review, 88*, 375–407. Copyright © (1981) by the American Psychological Association. Reprinted with permission.

6.4 McClelland, J. L., & Rumelhart, D. E. (1986). A distributed model of human learning and memory. In J. L. McClelland & D. E. Rumelhart (Eds.). *Parallel distributed processing: Explorations in the microstructure of cognition* (Vol. 2). Cambridge, MA: MIT Press. Copyright © (1986) MIT Press. Reprinted with permission.

6.5 McClelland, J. L. (1985). Putting knowledge in its place: A scheme for programming parallel processing structures on the fly. *Cognitive Science, 9*, 113–146. Copyright © (1985) Cognitive Science Society, Inc., used by permission.

6.6 McClelland, J. L. (1985). Putting knowledge in its place: A scheme for programming parallel processing structures on the fly. *Cognitive Science, 9*, 113–146. Copyright © (1985) Cognitive Science Society, Inc., used by permission.

6.7 Mozer, M. C. (1987). Early parallel processing in reading: A connectionist approach. In M. Coltheart (Ed.), *Attention and performance XII.* Hove, UK: Lawrence Erlbaum Associates Ltd. Reprinted with permission.

6.8 Behrman, M., Moscovitch, M., & Mozer, M. C. (1991). Directing attention to words and nonwords in normal subjects and in a computational model: Implications for neglect dyslexia. *Cognitive Neuropsychology, 8*, 213–248. Reprinted with permission.

6.9 Humphreys, G. W., & Evett, L. J. (1985). Are there independent lexical and nonlexical routes in work processing? An evaluation of the dual-route theory of reading. *Behavioral and Brain Sciences, 8*, 689–740. Copyright © (1985) by Cambridge University Press. Reprinted with permission.

6.10 Sejnowski, T. J., & Rosenberg, C. R. (1987). Parallel networks that learn to pronounce English text. *Complex Systems, 1*, 145–168. CUP

6.11 Sejnowski, T. J., & Rosenberg, C. R. (1987). Parallel networks that learn to pronounce English text. *Complex Systems, 1*, 145–168. CUP

6.12 Seidenberg, M. S., & McClelland, J. L. (1989). A distributed, developmental model of word recognition and naming. *Psychological Review, 96*, 523–568. Copyright © (1989) by the American Psychological Association. Reprinted with permission.

6.13 Seidenberg, M. S., & McClelland, J. L. (1989). A distributed, developmental model of word recognition and naming. *Psychological Review, 96*, 523–568. Copyright © (1989) by the American Psychological Association. Reprinted with permission.

6.14 Plaut, D. C., McClelland, J. L., Seidenberg, M. S., & Patterson, K., (1996). Understanding normal and impaired word reading: Computational principles in quasi-regular domains. *Psychological Review, 103*(1), 56–115. Copyright © (1996) by the American Psychological Association. Reprinted with permission.

6.15 Masson, M. E. J. (1991). A distributed memory model of context effects in word identification. In D. Besner & G. W. Humphreys (Eds.) Basic Processes in reading: *Visual word recognition*. Hillsdale, NJ: Lawrence Erlbaum Associates Inc. Copyright © (1991) by Lawrence Erlbaum Associates Inc. Reprinted with permission.

6.16 McClelland, J. L., & Rumelhart, D. E. (1986). A distributed model of human learning and memory. In J. L. McClelland & D. E. Rumelhart (Eds.). *Parallel distributed processing: Explorations in the microstructure of cognition* (Vol. 2). Cambridge, MA: MIT Press. Copyright © (1986) MIT Press. Reprinted with permission.

6.17 McClelland, J. L., & Rumelhart, D. E. (1986). A distributed model of human learning and memory. In J. L. McClelland & D. E. Rumelhart (Eds.). *Parallel distributed processing: Explorations in the microstructure of cognition* (Vol. 2). Cambridge, MA: MIT Press. Copyright © (1986) MIT Press. Reprinted with permission.

6.18 McClelland, J. L., & Rumelhart, D. E. (1986). A distributed model of human learning and memory. In J. L. McClelland & D. E. Rumelhart (Eds.). *Parallel distributed processing: Explorations in the microstructure of cognition* (Vol. 2). Cambridge, MA: MIT Press. Copyright © (1986) MIT Press Reprinted with permission.

6.19 Norris, D. (1994b). Shortlist: A connectionist model of continuous speech recognition. *Cognition, 52*, 189–234. Reprinted with kind permission from Elsevier Science — NL, Sara Burgerhartstraat 25, 1055 KV Amsterdam, The Netherlands.

6.20 Brown, G. D. A., & Loosemore, R. P. W. (1994). Computational approaches to normal and impaired spelling. In G. D. A. Brown & N. C. Ellis (Eds.), *Handbook of spelling*. Chichester, UK: Wiley. Copyright © (1994) John Wiley & Sons Ltd. Reproduced with permission.

6.21 Brown, G. D. A., & Loosemore, R. P. W. (1994). Computational approaches to normal and impaired spelling. In G. D. A. Brown & N. C. Ellis (Eds.), *Handbook of spelling*. Chichester, UK: Wiley. Copyright © (1994) John Wiley & Sons Ltd. Reproduced with permission.

6.22 Houghton, G., Glasspool, D., & Shallice, T. (1994). Spelling and serial recall: Insights from a competitive queueing model. In G. D. A. Brown & N. C. Ellis (Eds.), *Handbook of spelling: Theory, process and intervention*. Chichester, UK: Wiley. Copyright © (1994) John Wiley & Sons Ltd. Reproduced with permission.

6.23 Houghton, G., Glasspool, D., & Shallice, T. (1994). Spelling and serial recall: Insights from a competitive queueing model. In G. D. A. Brown & N. C. Ellis (Eds.), *Handbook of spelling: Theory, process and intervention*. Chichester, UK: Wiley. Copyright © (1994) John Wiley & Sons Ltd. Reproduced with permission.

6.24 Dell, G. S. (1986). A spreading-activation theory of retrieval in sentence production. *Psychological Review, 93*, 283–321. Copyright © (1986) by the American Psychological Association. Reprinted with permission.

6.25 Hartley, T., & Houghton, G. (1996). A linguistically constrained model of short-term memory for non-words. *Journal of memory and language*. Copyright © (1996) Academic Press. Reprinted with permission.

6.26 Hartley, T., & Houghton, G. (1996). A linguistically constrained model of short-term memory for non-words. *Journal of memory and language*. Copyright © (1996) Academic Press. Reprinted with permission

6.27 Harley, T., & MacAndrew, S. B. G. (1992). Modelling paraphasias in normal and aphasic speech. *Proceedings of the 14th Annual Conference of the Cognitive Science Society* (pp.378–383). Hillsdale, NJ: Lawrence Erlbaum Associates Inc. Copyright © (1992) by Lawrence Erlbaum Associates Inc. Reprinted with permission.

6.28 Dell, G. S., Juliano, C., & Govindjee, A. (1995). Structure and content in language production: A theory frame contraints in phonological speech errors. *Cognitive Science, 17*, 149–195. Copyright © (1985) Cognitive Science Society, Inc.

Table 6.1 Plaut, D. C., McClelland, J. L., Seidenberg, M. S., & Patterson, K. (1996). Understanding normal and impaired word reading: Computational principles in quasi-regular domains. *Psychological Review, 103*(1), 56–115. Copyright © (1996) by the American Psychological Association. Reprinted with permission.

7.1 McClelland, J. L., & Rumelhart, D. E. (1986). A distributed model of human learning and memory. In J. L. McClelland & D. E. Rumelhart (Eds.). *Parallel distributed processing: Explorations in the microstructure of cognition* (Vol. 2). Cambridge, MA: MIT Press. Copyright © (1986) MIT Press. Reprinted with permission.

7.2 McClelland, J. L., & Rumelhart, D. E. (1986). A distributed model of human learning and memory. In J. L. McClelland & D. E. Rumelhart (Eds.). *Parallel distributed processing: Explorations in the microstructure of cognition* (Vol. 2). Cambridge, MA: MIT Press. Copyright © (1986) MIT Press. Reprinted with permission.

7.3 McClelland, J. L., & Rumelhart, D. E. (1986). A distributed model of human learning and memory. In J. L. McClelland & D. E. Rumelhart (Eds.). *Parallel distributed processing: Explorations in the microstructure of cognition* (Vol. 2). Cambridge, MA: MIT Press. Copyright © (1986) MIT Press. Reprinted with permission.

7.4 Hare, M., Elman, J. L., & Daugherty, K. G. (1995). Default generalization in connectionist networks. *Language and Cognitive Processes, 10*(6), 601–630. Reprinted with permission.

7.5 McClelland, J. L., & Kawamoto, A. H. (1986). Mechanisms of sentence processing: Assigning roles to constituents. In J. L. McClelland & D. E. Rumelhart (Eds.). *Parallel distributed processing: Explorations in the microstructure of cognition* (Vol. 2). Cambridge, MA: MIT Press. Copyright © (1986) MIT Press. Reprinted with permission.

7.6 Elman, J. L. (1990). Finding structure in time. *Cognitive Science Society, 14*, 179–211, Copyright © (1990) Cognitive Science Society, Inc., used by permission.

7.7 Blank, D. S., Meeden, L. A. & Marshall, J. B. (1992). Exploring the symbolic/subsymbolic continuum: A case study of RAAM. In J. Dinsmore (Ed.) T*he symbolic and connectionist paradigms: Closing the gap*, Hillsdale, NJ: Lawrence Erlbaum Associates Inc. Copyright © (1992) by Lawrence Erlbaum Associates Inc. Reprinted with permission.

7.8 Blank, D. S. Meeden, L. A., & Marshall, J. B. (1992). Exploring the symbolic/subsymbolic continuum: A case study of RAAM. In J. Dinsmore (Ed.) *The symbolic and connectionist paradigms: Closing the gap*, Hillsdale, NJ: Lawrence Erlbaum Associates Inc. Copyright © (1992) by Lawrence Erlbaum Associates Inc. Reprinted with permission.

7.9 Blank, D. S. Meeden, L. A., & Marshall, J. B. (1992). Exploring the symbolic/subsymbolic continuum: A case study of RAAM. In J. Dinsmore (Ed.) *The symbolic and connectionist paradigms: Closing the gap*, Hillsdale, NJ: Lawrence Erlbaum Associates Inc. Copyright © (1992) by Lawrence Erlbaum Associates Inc. Reprinted with permission.

7.10a/b Shastri, L., & Ajjanagade, V. (1993). From simple associations to systematic reasoning: A connectionist representation of rules, variables, and dynamic bindings using temporal synchrony. *Behavioral and Brain Sciences, 16*, 417–541. Copyright © (1993) Cambridge University Press. Reprinted with the permission of Cambridge University Press.

7.11 Shastri, L., & Ajjanagade, V. (1993). From simple associations to systematic reasoning: A connectionist representation of rules, variables, and dynamic bindings using temporal synchrony. *Behavioral and Brain Sciences, 16*, 417–541. Copyright © (1993) Cambridge University Press. Reprinted with the permission of Cambridge University Press.

7.12 Shastri, L., & Ajjanagade, V. (1993). From simple associations to systematic reasoning: A connectionist representation of rules, variables, and dynamic bindings using temporal synchrony. *Behavioral and Brain Sciences, 16*, 417–541. Copyright © (1993) Cambridge University Press. Reprinted with the permission of Cambridge University Press.

7.13 Shastri, L., & Ajjanagade, V. (1993). From simple associations to systematic reasoning: A connectionist representation of rules, variables, and dynamic bindings using temporal synchrony. *Behavioral and Brain Sciences, 16*, 417–541. Copyright © (1993) Cambridge University Press. Reprinted with the permission of Cambridge University Press.

7.14 Holyoak, K. J. (1990). Problem solving. In D. N. Osherson & E. E. Smith (Eds.), *Thinking: An Invitation to cognitive science* (Vol. 3). Cambridge, MA: MIT Press. Copyright © (1990) MIT Press. Reprinted with permission.

7.15 Lamberts, K. (1990). A hybrid model of learning to solve physics problems. *European Journal of Cognitive Psychology, 2*(2), 151–170. Reprinted with permission.

Table 7.1 Plunkett, K., & Marchman, V. A. (1991). U-shaped learning and frequency effects in a multi-layered perception. *Cognition, 38*, 43–102. Reprinted with kind permission from Elsevier Science — NL, Sara Burgerhartstraat 25, 1055 KV Amsterdam, The Netherlands.

8.1 Mayall, K. A., & Humphreys, G. W. A connectionist model of alexia: Covert recognition and case mixing effects. *British Journal of Psychology*, (1996), *87*, 355–402 © The British Psychological Society.
   Mayall, K. A., & Humphreys, G. W. (1996). Covert recognition in a connectionist model of pure alexia. In J. Reggia, E. Ruppin, & R. S. Berndt (Eds.), *Neural modelling of brain and cognitive disorders*. London: World Scientific.

8.2 Plaut, D. C., McClelland, J. L., Seidenberg, M. S., & Patterson, K., (1996). Understanding normal and impaired word reading: Computational principles in quasi-regular domains. *Psychological Review, 103*(1), 56–115. Copyright © (1996) by the American Psychological Association. Reprinted with permission.

8.3 Hinton, G. E., & Shallice, T. (1991). Lesioning an attractor network. Investigations of acquired dyslexia. *Psychological Review, 98*, 74–96. Copyright © (1991) by the American Psychological Association. Reprinted with permission.

8.4a/b Plaut, D. C., & Shallice, T. (1993a). Deep dyslexia: A case study of connectionist neuropsychology. *Cognitive Neuropsychology, 10*, 377–500. Reprinted with permission.

8.5 Plaut, D. C., & Shallice, T. (1993a). Deep dyslexia: A case study of connectionist neuropsychology. *Cognitive Neuropsychology, 10*, 377–500. Reprinted with permission.

8.6 Plaut, D. C., & Shallice, T. (1993a). Deep dyslexia: A case study of connectionist neuropsychology. *Cognitive Neuropsychology, 10*, 377–500. Reprinted with permission.

8.7 Martin, N., Dell, G. S., Saffran, E. M., & Schwartz, M.F. (1994). Origins of paraphasias in deep dysphasia: Testing the consequences of a decay impairment to an interactive spreading activation model of lexical retrieval. *Brain and Language, 47*(4), 609–660. Copyright © (1994) Academic Press. Reprinted with permission.

8.8 Brown, G. D. A., & Loosemore, R. P. W. (1994). Computational approaches to normal and impaired spelling. In G. D. A. Brown & N. C. Ellis (Eds.), *Handbook of spelling*. Chichester, UK: Wiley. Copyright © (1994) John Wiley & Sons Ltd. Reproduced with permission.

8.9a/b Humphreys, G. W., Freeman, T. A. C., & Müller, H.J. (1992b). Lesioning a connectionist network of visual search: Selective effects on distractor grouping. *Canadian Journal of Psychology, 46*(3), 417–460. Copyright © Canadian Psychological Society.

8.10 Humphreys, G. W., & Müller, H. J. (1993). Search via recursive rejection (SERR): A connectionist model of visual search. *Cognitive Psychology, 25*(1), 43–110. Copyright © (1993) Academic Press. Reprinted with permission.

8.11 Farah, M. J., & McClelland, J. L. (1991). A computational model of semantic memory impairment: Modality specificity and emergent category specificity. *Journal of Experimental*

Psychology: General, 120(4), 339–357. Copyright © (1991) Cambridge University Press. Reprinted with permission.

8.12 Farah, M. J., & McClelland, J. L. (1991). A computational model of semantic memory impairment: Modality specificity and emergent category specificity. *Journal of Experimental Psychology: General, 120*(4), 339–357. Copyright © (1991) Cambridge University Press. Reprinted with permission.

8.14 Plaut, D. C., & Shallice, T. (1993b). Preservative and semantic influences on visual object naming errors in optic aphasia: A connectionist account. *Journal of Cognitive Neuroscience, 5*, 89–117. Copyright © (1993) by the Massachusetts Institute of Technology. Reprinted with permission.

8.15 Plaut, D. C., & Shallice, T. (1993b). Preservative and semantic influences on visual object naming errors in optic aphasia: A connectionist account. *Journal of Cognitive Neuroscience, 5*, 89–117. Copyright © (1993) by the Massachusetts Institute of Technology. Reprinted with permission.

8.16 Farah, M. J. (1994). Neuropsychological inference with an interactive brain: A critique of the "locality" assumption. *Behavioral and Brain Sciences, 17*, 43–104. Copyright © (1994) Cambridge University Press. Reprinted with the permission of Cambridge University Press.

8.17 Farah, M. J. (1994). Neuropsychological inference with an interactive brain: A critique of the "locality" assumption. *Behavioral and Brain Sciences, 17*, 43–104. Copyright © (1994) Cambridge University Press. Reprinted with the permission of Cambridge University Press.

8.18 Farah, M. J. (1994). Neuropsychological inference with an interactive brain: A critique of the "locality" assumption. *Behavioral and Brain Sciences, 17*, 43–104. Copyright © (1994) Cambridge University Press. Reprinted with the permission of Cambridge University Press.

8.19 Humphreys, G. W., Lamote, C., & Lloyd-Jones, T. J. (1995). An interactive activation approach to object processing: Effects of structural similarity, name frequency and task in normality and pathology. *Memory, 3*, 535–586. Reprinted with permission.

8.20a/b Humphreys, G. W., Lamote, C., & Lloyd-Jones, T. J. (1995). An interactive activation approach to object processing: Effects of structural similarity, name frequency and task in normality and pathology. *Memory, 3*, 535–586. Reprinted with permission.

8.21 McClelland, J. L., McNaughton, B. L., & O'Reilly, R. C. (1995). Why there are complimentary learning systems in the hippocampus and neocortex: Insights from the successes and failures of connectionist models of learning and memory. *Psychological Review, 102*, 419–457. Copyright © (1995) by the American Psychological Association. Reprinted with permission.

8.22 Plaut, D. C. (1992). *Relearning after damage in connectionist networks: Implications for patient rehabilitation.* Paper presented to the Cognitive Science Society, March. This material is reproduced with the permission of the author.

8.23 Plaut, D. C. (1992). *Relearning after damage in connectionist networks: Implications for patient rehabilitation.* Paper presented to the Cognitive Science Society, March. This material is reproduced with the permission of the author.

9.1 *Fundamentals of Human Neuropsychology* (4th ed.) by Bryan Kolb and Ian Q. Whishaw. Copyright © 1980, 1985, 1990, 1996 by W. H. Freeman. Used with permission.

9.2 *Fundamentals of Human Neuropsychology* (4th ed.) by Bryan Kolb and Ian Q. Whishaw. Copyright © 1980, 1985, 1990, 1996 by W. H. Freeman. Used with permission.

9.3 Rolls, E. T. (1989). Parallel distributed processing in the brain: Implications of the functional architecture of neuronal networks in the hippocampus. In R. G. M. Morris (Ed.), *Parallel distributed processing: Implications for psychology and neurobiology*. Oxford: Oxford University Press. Reprinted by permission of Oxford University Press.

9.4 Marr, D. (1969). A theory of cerebellar cortex. *Journal of Physiology, 202*, 437–470. Copyright © (1969) The Physiological Society. Reprinted with permission.

9.5 Rueckl, J. G., Cave, K. R., & Kosslyn, S. M. (1989). Why are "what" and "where" processed by separate cortical visual systems? A computational investigation. *Journal of Cognitive Neuroscience, 1*, 171–186. Copyright © (1989) by the Massachusetts Institute of Technology. Reprinted with permission

9.6 Rueckl, J. G., Cave, K. R., & Kosslyn, S. M. (1989). Why are "what" and "where" processed by separate cortical visual systems? A computational investigation. *Journal of Cognitive Neuroscience, 1*, 171–186. Copyright © (1989) by the Massachusetts Institute of Technology. Reprinted with permission.

9.7 Jacobs, R. A., & Jordan, M. I. (1992). Computational consequences of a bias towards short connections. *Journal of Cognitive Neuroscience, 4*(4), 323–336. Copyright © (1992) by the Massachusetts Institute of Technology. Reprinted with permission.

9.8a/b Plunkett, K., & Sinha, C. (1992). Connectionism and developmental theory. *British Journal of Developmental Psychology, 10*, 209–254. Copyright © (1992) The British Psychological Society.

9.9 Plunkett, K., & Sinha, C. (1992). Connectionism and developmental theory. *British Journal of Developmental Psychology, 10*, 209–254. Copyright © (1992) The British Psychological Society.

Preface

Connectionism is one of the strongest growth points in psychology. In about 15 years it has emerged from relative obscurity to become one of the handful of prominent perspectives on mental phenomena, with the promise of becoming a unified theory for the discipline. The first, heady phase of the spread of connectionist ideas was marked by an emphasis on the general properties of brain-like computing architectures and the startling behavioural repertoire of even crude models of this sort. This phase has probably passed, and we are now in, or entering, a period in which the development of connectionism consists of its application to the myriad problems in our science, and the consequent evaluation of its utility over a broad range of issues. This book has the twin aims of introducing the basic concepts, and the general properties of models that incorporate them, while demonstrating the developing maturity of connectionism by describing its application to specific classes of mental function. It is the attempt to fit connectionist models to specific, and detailed, aspects of behaviour that will finally determine connectionism's worth. For the most part, the book contains our evaluation of the literature on connectionist models and their contribution to psychological theory. In addition, to provide some source material at first hand, we also include one or two examples of primary papers from the field. We hope both that readers will find these useful when reading our text and that the text will help to throw new light on the papers. The choice of which papers to include and which to exclude is of course extremely difficult and, to some extent, arbitrary. We hope to have included papers that capture something of the range of models employed in the literature, and especially models that relate directly to psychological issues. From the many authors of the undoubtedly excellent papers not included, we beg forgiveness.

We are grateful to the many people who helped shape this book. Our colleagues and students in two departments have suffered much as a result of our infection with connectionist ideas, and we thank them for their patience. Nevertheless, we hope that at least a little of this virus has been transmitted! Several individuals read earlier versions of the text, and their comments have undoubtedly improved it. Thank you to Liz Styles, Trevor Harley, and Jane Riddoch. Our readers will understand that all the faults that remain are our responsibility alone.

1

Basic issues and concepts

This book is about the relevance of computation to aspects of intelligent behaviour. In the main it will attempt to introduce and evaluate the claims that one particular class of computation is more relevant than others. This class we will refer to as connectionist. In this first chapter the basic ideas of connectionism will be introduced, while comparing it in a variety of ways with more conventional computational models. In this chapter we review some of the basic properties of connectionist models that might make them attractive for people interested in modelling cognitive processes. We begin by discussing the relations between connectionist models and real neuronal systems, before proceeding to discuss functional properties of the models that link them to psychological issues such as the nature of learning, memory, and perception.

One basis for the claim that connectionist styles of computation are of special interest to brain and behavioural scientists is quite simply that it is intended that they should be "brain-like". The similarity is said to exist at several levels including that of physical structure.

1.1 PHYSICAL STRUCTURES

What is entailed by being similar to the brain in physical structure? The way we describe a nervous system depends on the techniques of observation. The naked eye and an electron microscope give very different impressions of physical structure. However our initial interest here is the features that are most striking at a resolution somewhere between these two. That is roughly the structure described vividly by Cajal as long ago as 1888 when he successfully applied the Golgi staining technique to nervous tissue. Shepherd (1988, p.40) quotes Cajal's description:

Against a clear background stood black threadlets, some slender and smooth, some thick and thorny, in a pattern punctuated by small dense spots, stellate or fusiform. All was sharp as a sketch with Chinese ink on transparent Japan-paper.

Such features may be seen in Fig. 1.1. The work of Cajal and others established the neuronal doctrine of the nervous system in which the central elements are independent, specialised cells or neurons which pass signals to each other via their rich interconnections — the "black threadlets" seen by Cajal and in Fig. 1.1.

A single neuron, of which there are many types, has three main components: the cell body, the axon, and the dendrites. Examples are shown in Fig. 1.2. The cell body is the "power plant": encapsulating within its membrane the processes that maintain the cell and provide the chemical resources needed for its various functions. The axon is the neuron's output channel along which an electrical pulse or action potential may be propagated. The cell is said to "fire" when such a pulse occurs. Axons branch repeatedly ending in terminal buttons, which are in close proximity to, but not actually touching, parts of other neurons. An action potential will result in the release of chemicals across these junctions or synapses, which modify the behaviour of the recipient neuron. Many of the synapses are found at the junction of axon terminal buttons and the dendrites of other neurons, the other, tree-like component of neurons. But synapses are found at other types of junction too: axon to cell body, axon to axon, and dendrite to dendrite.

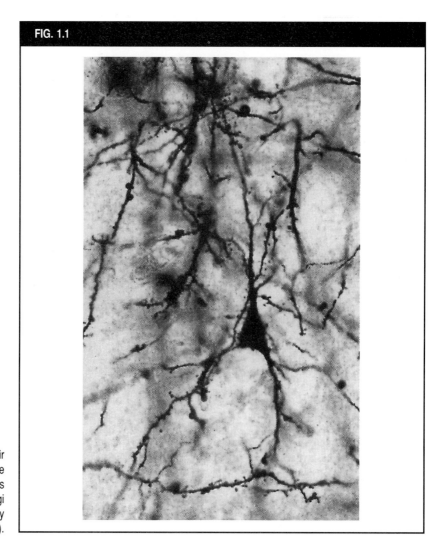

FIG. 1.1

Neurons and their interconnections in the visual cortex of the cat as revealed by the Golgi method. From Beatty (1995).

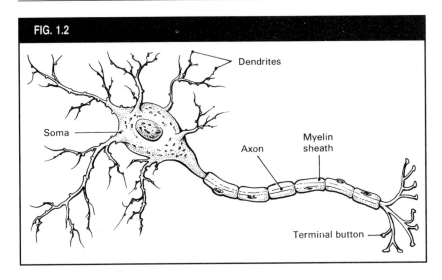

FIG. 1.2

Dendrites

Soma

Axon

Myelin
sheath

Terminal button

The main parts of a
neuron illustrated with a
multipolar cell. From
Carlson (1986).

Processes within the cell membrane seek to maintain a chemical (ionic) imbalance between the cell interior and its immediate surrounds. This imbalance results in a small, negative electrical gradient or potential across the membrane when the cell is at rest. The release of neurotransmitter chemicals into the synaptic gap modifies the post-synaptic membrane structure in a manner that effects the ionic imbalance and therefore membrane potential at the synaptic site. One of two effects is observed at a given synapse. At one type of synapse an increase in the polarisation of the membrane potential is seen, at the other type of synapse a decrease in polarisation is found. Both effects spread along the membrane but, mostly, decline with distance from the synaptic site and in time.

An action potential is generated whenever the membrane potential at the junction of the cell body and axon, the axon hillock, is depolarised to a threshold value. An individual neuron is therefore summing together, or integrating, the effects of changes in polarity at the synaptic sites distant in space and time, firing if their summed effect at the axon hillock exceeds some threshold. It follows from the foregoing that some synapses will inhibit the firing of a neuron, others will excite it. Also the frequency of firing of a neuron is a function of the relative number of stimulations of excitatory and inhibitory synaptic sites.

Any single neuron has anything from a few hundred to tens of thousands of synaptic junctions. A central thesis of what is to follow in this book is that it is these rich connections that make the brain, and similar devices, powerful computers. A single neuron is very simple and capable, in isolation, of only a very limited function. However it can affect, and may be affected by, many thousands of other neurons. These effects taken together allow functions of great complexity to be performed.

Our description of the physical structure of the brain may be summarised as follows:

It consists of many functionally simple, but richly connected, cells. Each of these receives many inputs; some are excitatory, others are inhibitory. The inputs are summed and if a threshold of excitation is exceeded a single output is broadcast to many other cells.

Let us call this the connectionist brain description. Notice that it has wide application: just about anything that could reasonably be called a brain meets such a description. Also notice that it certainly does not do justice to the complexity of the central nervous system, even at this level of neurons and their connections. Neurons have other means of influencing each other's behaviour and there is much that is simply not understood (see Crick & Asanuma, 1986; Sejnowski, 1986a,b; Shepherd, 1979). We intend the connectionist brain description to be a working hypothesis about the appropriate level for understanding the brain as a processor of information.

What is the comparable description of the physical structure of a conventional digital computer? Again one is confronted with a variety of possible levels of description. The most general we shall refer to as the von Neumann description or design. Almost all computers in production, and almost certainly all the computers the reader has ever encountered, are examples of the von Neumann design at the level of hardware or physical structure. Two components are essential to the design: a central processing unit (cpu) and a memory. The cpu is some mechanism that can perform a set of arithmetic or logical operations. The set of operations may be small or large, but only one may be performed at an instance. A von Neumann computer is therefore a sequential machine at the level we are descibing here. The items upon which the operations are performed are stored in the memory. The memory may be thought of as a set of locations each of which may store an item. Items can be accessed only by reference to the address of its location. A typical operation would be to add together the items stored at locations x and y, and place the result of the addition in location z. The nature and sequence of such events is determined by a set of instructions: the program. This is also stored in memory.

We will now provide a preliminary, very general description of the physical structure of a connectionist computer:

A connectionist computer consists of a set of simple, but richly connected, processing units. Each unit receives a number of inputs which it sums. A single output is derived from the latter sum and broadcast to other units.

It should be no surprise that the connectionist brain is an example of a connectionist computer. But notice that many other variants are possible.

The most striking differences between the physical structure of von Neumann and connectionist computers are these. First, operations in a von Neumann machine are essentially serial, one at a time in a sequence; in contrast, operations in a connectionist machine are parallel, with very many components simultaneously active. Second, memory in the connectionist computer does not consist of a register of locations as in the von Neumann machine. Quite what it does consist of should become clear shortly. Third, activities in von Neumann computers are coordinated or controlled by means of a set of instructions, whereas in connectionist machines no such overall orchestration is apparent.

Do these differences matter for the purposes of explaining or understanding intelligent behaviour?

1.2 DO DIFFERENCES IN PHYSICAL STRUCTURE MATTER?

If the brain is a type of connectionist computer, what implications does this have for understanding what brains do? For instance might the brain's physical structure condition or constrain basic cognitive processes? It does seem perfectly plausible that this should be the case. If it were, of course, it would seem sensible for cognitive scientists to develop an understanding of connectionist computation. There are, however, a set of highly respectable, and respected, arguments which conclude that, for the purpose of understanding cognition, differences in physical structure, between brains and computers on which we attempt to model aspects of cognition, do not matter. We will briefly review two (related) arguments here.

1.2.1 Turing machines

The most general definition of computation and computers is given by the Turing notion of computability. Turing's thesis was that any deterministic formal system could be realised by a so-called Turing machine (Turing, 1937 and 1950; and see Haugeland, 1985, for an introduction). A Turing machine is a notional computer of very simple design. It consists of a tape divided into sections or cells, each of which may contain a symbol, and a head that is able to read the symbols as well as write new ones. At any instant the machine is in one of a finite set of states which represent its entire repertoire. What it does next is determined by its present state and the symbol in the tape cell currently being scanned. Three things will be determined in this way: what new symbol to over-write at the current tape cell; what new tape cell to move to; and what new internal state to enter into. The new symbol or cell or state may be the same as the old. Turing's thesis states that some machine having this design is capable of realising any single deterministic formal system and there-fore any single computer. Moreover it can be shown that a universal Turing machine is possible which will realise all possible computers. Turing's thesis has the effect of defining computation.

It follows from this that a connectionist com-puter may be realised by a Turing machine. All connectionist computers could be realised by a universal Turing machine. If machines of such different physical architectures can perform the same computations then physical structure cannot matter — at least to those who regard cognition as essentially a form of computation.

Von Neumann computers are also universal: given unlimited memory a von Neumann design can realise any other type of computer. With a suit-able program it can be made to produce exactly the same outputs, for given inputs, as some other machine with a very different hardware architec-ture. The hybrid of real machine and program which behaves as if it were some other real machine is called a virtual machine. All the con-nectionist models described in this book are in fact simulations performed on von Neumann com-puters. They are virtual connectionist computers.

1.2.2 Physical symbol systems

The description of the Turing machine is an account of symbol manipulation. It is obviously related to Physical Symbol Systems (PSSs) which are characterised by Newell and Simon (1980, p.40) in the following way:

. . . a set of entities, called symbols, which are physical patterns that can occur as com-ponents of another type of entity called an expression (or symbol structure). Thus, a

symbol structure is composed of a number of instances (or tokens) of symbols related in some physical way (such as one token being next to another) . . . beside these struc-tures the system also contains a collection of processes that operate on expressions to produce other expressions: processes of creation, modification, reproduction and destruction. A physical symbol system is a machine that produces through time an evolving collection of symbol structures.

Such systems, Newell and Simon argue, have the necessary and sufficient conditions for intel-ligent behaviour. That is, all intelligent systems may be shown to be examples of PSSs; and any PSS could in principle be organised so as to sup-port intelligent behaviour. Clearly according to this Physical Symbol System Hypothesis the essen-tial feature of intelligence is symbol manipulation. Intelligent action arises from the formal properties of a system rather than its physical properties.

Clark (1989) has pointed out that two inter-pretations of the PSS hypothesis are possible. First the weak interpretation, in which a PSS is taken to include any universal computer, and therefore the essential feature of intelligence is computa-tion in the general sense discussed earlier. The second interpretation is stronger (and, Clark, 1989 claims, the one intended by the authors of the PSS hypothesis). It is that in which a PSS is taken to refer to devices in which von Neumann type operations on symbols take place. So to have the architecture of a von Neumann virtual machine is to have the necessary and sufficient conditions for intelligence.

Both Turing's thesis and the PSS hypothesis support the view that the physical structure of the brain may have little bearing on its computational abilities. A connectionist brain may be used to realise a von Neumann virtual machine! A cent-ral tenet of connectionism amounts to a simple denial of such views in that a connectionist brain is taken to entail a connectionist mind.

There is a fascinating tangle of issues here, many of which lie within the scope of the philo-sophy of mind, rather than psychology. It is suffi-cient to note at this point that connectionist models may be applied to the brain itself or its functions. Much of the work we will present can be best described as seeking to understand the virtual machinery of cognitive processes. Its interest is in abstract computational structures whose neural implementation is left unspecified. This sentiment can be detected in the following passage from McClelland, Rumelhart, and Hinton (1986 p.11):

> Though the appeal of PDP models is definitely enhanced by their physiological plausibility and neural inspiration, these are not the primary bases for their appeal to us. We are, after all, cognitive scientists, and PDP models appeal to us for psychological and computational reasons. They hold out the hope of offering computationally sufficient and psychologically accurate mechanistic accounts of the phenomena of human cognition which have eluded successful explication in conventional computational formalisms . . .

We will return to the issue of the neural basis of connectionism at the end of this chapter and in the final chapter. In the next two sections we consider some of its computational and psychological bases.

1.3 COMPUTATIONAL STRUCTURES

The basic computational process in a von Neumann machine, real or virtual, is a sequence of logical operations on symbols fetched from locations in memory, with the results of these operations being other symbols which are placed back in memory. A string of symbols at specified memory locations may be designated a solution or result.

How may the basic computational processes in a connectionist machine be best characterised? We will begin to answer this question by describing a very simple example of a so-called relaxation network. Consider the small network in Fig. 1.3a. Several computational units are connected together by excitatory and inhibitory connections.

Each of the units may be in one of two states: its level of "activity" can be 1 or 0. They can also sum their net input, turning on or remaining on if this is zero or greater, otherwise they turn or remain off. This we will call our activation rule. The net input to a unit is a simple sum thus:

$$\text{Net}_i = \Sigma_i W_{ij} A_j. \tag{1}$$

Where Net_i is the net input to the ith unit; A_j is the activity level of the jth unit and W_{ij} is the weighting of the connection between the ith and jth unit. The weighting term may be regarded as a factor (in fact a number) by which the effects of a signal from one unit to another are amplified or attenuated. The significance of weighting factors will become clearer as we proceed. In our simple example all the excitatory connections have a weight of 1 and all the inhibitory connections have a weight of −1.

Imagine some arbitrary initial state of the network arrived at by switching on just two units at random. Suppose we started with the first configuration shown on the left in Fig. 1.3b. As all units receive both excitatory and inhibitory inputs, the network will change its pattern of activity over time. The reader should confirm to themselves, by applying the activation rule successively to the results of equation (1), that in fact the network will change state just twice and then remain

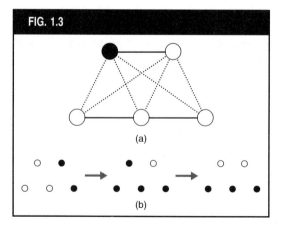

FIG. 1.3

(a) A very simple relaxation network of binary units with excitatory (solid lines) and inhibitory (dotted lines) connections. (b) The sequence of states reached when the network is initiated with just two units active.

in the stable configuration shown on the right in Fig. 1.3b. The process of converging from some arbitrary unstable pattern of activation to a stable pattern will be referred to as a relaxation process. Relaxation is a characteristic style of computation in connectionist systems. It is both parallel and cooperative. That is, the processes are simultaneously active and communicate with each other in order to reach some global state. For a given network with a given set of weightings there may be several possible stable patterns of activation. Which is reached will depend on the initial pattern configuration. In our small example there is a second stable state. Can the reader find it? It is the trivial case of just the two uppermost units being active, which can only be reached from a starting point of the very same pattern: in effect if the network is initiated with just those particular two units active it will stick there. From any other starting point it will relax into the state shown in Fig. 1.3b.

There is another class of network that differs significantly from the examples discussed so far. In these, activation can be passed in only one direction along the weighted connections. Typically a set of units are designated as inputs and the activation of these is fed forward, sometimes via intermediate units, to other units designated as outputs. These will be refered to as feed-forward networks. They do not have the same dynamic properties as relaxation networks in that activation states do not cycle through a series of intermediate states to a final, stable configuration of activations. Instead activation is "one-shot": the activation states of the inputs determine the activation states of the outputs in a single pass. However, they do share with relaxation networks the property of finding global configurations or patterns of activation on the basis of purely local computations. The activation of any single unit is calculated from the inputs of its neighbours to which it is directly connected. It is "blind" to the states of all other units in the network, yet the set of local calculations yield a global pattern which in many cases, as we shall see, constitutes a useful solution.

Relaxation and feed-forward networks are useful computational devices because they relax to or arrive at stable pattern configurations and these

patterns can be designated as results or solutions. This should become very clear as we proceed. They also appear to be potential solutions to some interesting general problems in psychology. This potential is discussed and illustrated in the next section.

1.4 PSYCHOLOGICAL STRUCTURES

One assumption of the connectionist endeavour is that brain-like structure (physical or computational) will lead to brain-like capacities. There are some very general requirements or features of psychological processes that are, it is argued, captured by connectionist networks in a very natural manner. That is, they do not have to be contrived, but appear as intrinsic properties of such networks. In this section we deal with two such properties: simultaneous multiple constraint satisfaction and content-addressable memory.

Simultaneous multiple constraint satisfaction may be described as the generation of a solution which meets some set of, perhaps disparate or competing, criteria at a single instance. Some theorists see this class of problem as a highly pervasive and possibly critical aspect of biological information processing (see McClelland et al., 1986, for an example of this viewpoint). For example, interactive models of language comprehension assume that rich communication between processes at lexical, syntactic, and semantic levels is needed to explain many aspects of natural language use (examples are Marslen-Wilson & Tyler, 1980; Rumelhart, 1977; Winograd, 1972; see Chapter 6). It has required great ingenuity to implement this type of scheme in von Neumann architectures, but the problem seems a natural application for relaxation networks, where interactions between processing levels can enable a network to converge on a solution. This "naturalness" of the network solution is apparent in the interactive activation model of word recognition (McClelland & Rumelhart, 1981; Rumelhart & McClelland, 1982) which we will now outline and will discuss in greater detail in Chapter 6 (section 6.2).

A relaxation network is shown in Fig. 1.4, in which each unit is designated as standing for or representing either elements or features of letters, letters, or words. The feature and letter units are specific to their position in a word, and the system shown can only handle four-letter words. The activity level of a given unit may be regarded as the strength of the hypothesis that the thing represented by that unit is present in the input. A pattern of excitatory and inhibitory connections implements the constraints that actually exist between the three levels. Thus, as an example, the presentation of the word "TRIP" will activate the feature units for horizontal and vertical lines for the first letter position, which in turn will attempt to activate the unit standing for "T" in the first letter position and turn off all others. The active first-position T-unit will also inhibit the other first-position letter units. The active T-unit will attempt to activate all the units for words with a T in the first position, and suppress the others. The active word units will now activate their corresponding

letter units. Further constraints are of course provided by the second, third, and fourth letter positions, leading to a relaxation process which will result in a stable pattern of activity over the appropriate units following the presentation of a word. The network at that point meets simultaneously all the constraints that exist between the elements of a four-letter word.

It turns out that this way of solving the word-recognition problem has some interesting spin-offs. It seems to account for a number of quite puzzling experimental findings. For instance it has been shown that single letters can be recognised more easily when embedded in pronounceable nonwords than in non-pronounceable nonwords. So it is easier to spot the "E" in "TRET" than in "QAEV". If "TRET" is presented to the network it tends to relax to a state in which several candidate words are partially active; say: "TROT", "TREE", "TREK" and so forth. Such partial activity will tend to reinforce the activity in the appropriate "T", "R", and "E" units. In contrast,

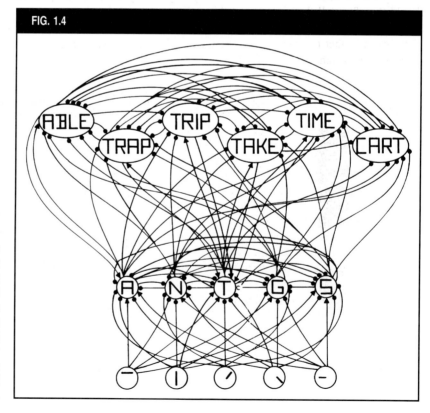

FIG. 1.4

Part of the network of the interactive activation model of word recognition showing the inhibitory and excitatory connections between the various levels. The letter and feature units are those for the first letter position only. From McClelland and Rumelhart (1981).

"QAEU" tends not to activate word units, so there is less top-down support for individual letters. Thus one obtains facilitation of letter recognition in "TRET" compared to the case when little or no activation occurs at the word level, when "QAEV" is presented for instance. The relationship between the model and data from empirical studies of word recognition will be discussed in more detail in Chapter 6.

The constraints discussed in these examples are largely transparent. It is obvious that the letter sequence "W–O–R–D" together uniquely specifies a particular word. Other constraints may be at work in other psychological processes which are not so obvious. Consider the case of stereopsis in human vision. The position of our eyes is such that the two images falling on the two retina are slightly different. The geometry of the situation results in each point in the visual field projecting to a slightly different location on the two retina, except at the point of fixation. The degree of retinal disparity is a function of the distance of points in the visual field from the viewer. Retinal disparity should therefore tell the viewer something about the relative distance of regions of the visual field. That this is in fact the case is vividly illustrated by the effects of random dot stereograms (Julesz,

1971) an example of which is shown in Fig. 1.5. In these cases two random dot patterns are created so as to be identical except for a central region which is shifted a small distance laterally in one pattern relative to the other. If the pair are arranged so that one pattern is viewed by the right eye and the other by the left, two surfaces are seen with the displaced central region behind or in front of its surround (which occurs depends on the direction of the lateral displacement of the central region). The implication of this effect is simple: the visual system is able to derive distance information from retinal disparity alone (mimicked in the stereograms by the displacement of a region in one pattern relative to the other). This is a profound achievement, for if distance is to be estimated retinal disparity must be measured and, it follows, points in one image matched with corresponding points in the other. In the case of the random dot stereograms this seems to be a potential nightmare, as any candidate match is surrounded by others that in principle are equally possible.

How can the correct matches be found among all the possible matches? Marr and Poggio (1976) described a relaxation network to solve this problem. An essential part of their solution was the

FIG. 1.5

An example of a random-dot stereogram. The two patterns are identical except for a central region which is shifted slightly. If viewed stereoscopically the central region will be seen as being at a different distance from the viewer than its surround. This may be seen if the reader focuses on a distant surface and then moves the stereogram into their visual field. From Julesz (1971).

formulation of a number of physical constraints which could be derived from an analysis of the geometry of surfaces and applied to the matching problem. The constraints and their justifications were these:

1. The points to be matched should be compatible, so in the case of stereograms a black dot can only match another black dot.
2. Any single point can only be in one location at any instant (except in rare coincidences

arising from oblique lines of sight), so any dot may match only one other dot.

3. Changes in surfaces are mostly continuous. Discontinuities, although significant, are rare. Thus the disparity of matches should mostly vary smoothly.

A network that implements these constraints is illustrated in Fig. 1.6. Each logically possible match between a pair of dots is represented in the network by a unit. A unit may assert a match

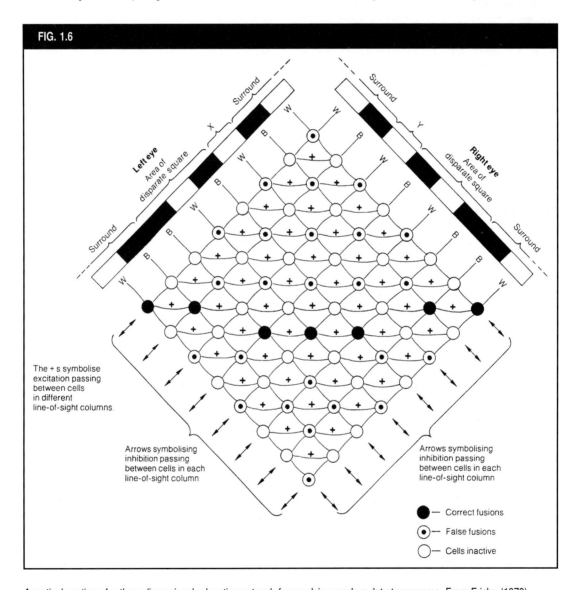

A vertical section of a three-dimensional relaxation network for resolving random-dot stereograms. From Frisby (1979).

between the pair of dots it represents by having an activity level of 1, otherwise it is 0. The first constraint is obviously met in that the only matches allowed are between similar objects: black dots. The other two constraints are implemented in the connections. The matching of one dot in one pattern with several in the other is discouraged by having inhibitory links between units representing such multiple matches: all the diagonal connections in Fig. 1.6. Smooth variation in disparity is encouraged by having units representing matches corresponding to similar disparity values excite each other: all the horizontal connections in Fig. 1.6. Marr and Poggio (1976) demonstrated that the simultaneous satisfaction of these three simple constraints led to a unique, and correct, solution to random dot stereograms. The network is initiated by setting to 1 all the units representing possible matches between a particular pair of random dot patterns, and the rest to 0. It will then relax, via a number of intermediate states, to a stable configuration which effectively represents the correct disparity values and therefore the surface information implicit in the stereo pair.

We do not intend that the reader regard the network models of word recognition and stereopsis as entirely adequate to their domain. The two examples are simply meant to show that a relaxation style of computation has broad application: from natural language understanding to low-level vision. In particular they show that any problem that can be expressed as a simultaneous multiple constraint satisfaction may be amenable to a relaxation solution. We hope that by the end of this book the reader will agree that a surprisingly large number of problems in biological information processing may be expressed as simultaneous multiple constraint satisfaction. Our examples also illustrate the power of cooperative processes: a global solution can be derived from cooperative but purely local processes.

We now turn to the issue of content-addressable memory. This notion can be simply illustrated by observing aspects of human memory. For instance if the reader is asked to name a group of four musicians who began their career playing in a cellar in Liverpool, they would almost certainly respond: "The Beatles". Again this is a profound achievement. You have been able to "find" a memory by reference to its contents or at least some of its contents. Notice that it would be very difficult to find an item in a conventional library using this method: that is, finding a particular book using just a part of its contents. The only possible method in such a circumstance would be to search all the books for a match to the partial contents, unless the library kept an index providing sufficient details of the contents of all the books it stored. Fortunately for the users of libraries, items are in fact found by reference to a location specified by an address. We have already described conventional von Neumann computers as having a memory which stores items at locations found by reference to their address. It should be obvious therefore that, like conventional libraries, conventional computers are not easily made content-addressable.

Relaxation networks may be regarded as memory devices. When so regarded they are content-addressable. Consider Fig. 1.7 which attempts to illustrate these claims. Each unit represents a concept or object. Items that are associated together are linked by excitatory connections. The strength of the association may be represented by the weighting on the connection. Items that are disassociated or mutually exclusive are linked by inhibitory connections. Together this system knows some things about groups of people. If we activate the "four", "musicians", "cellar", and "Liverpool" units the network will relax to a state in which "Beatles" is also active. This rather bizarre memory demonstrates the important general properties of knowledge representation in relaxation networks which are as follows. First the system is by nature content-addressable, as activation in any subset of memory units leads to the rest of the members in the set also becoming active. Second, memories are not stored at any particular "place", so memory does not have to be "searched" in order to "find" a piece of information. A better way of talking is to describe memories as being stored in the pattern of connectivity and "evoked" by appropriate cues. Third, the system is highly robust in the sense that misleading cues may still evoke appropriate memory structures. For instance in our example the probe "Five musicians from

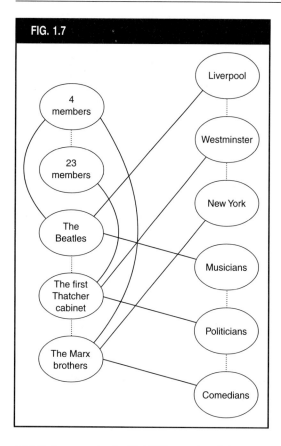

FIG. 1.7

A small memory network with inhibitory and excitatory connections among a set of items.

Liverpool who began their career playing in a cellar in Liverpool" will evoke a pattern in which "Beatles" is active. Naturally there are limits to this immunity: the level of activity of "Beatles" and its related memory structure will decrease as the cues become poorer, or some other structure entirely may be evoked if the misleading cues take the network closer to another memory. This ability to continue to provide useful information despite errors in the enquiries is an example of "graceful degradation".

Similar properties are also possessed by memory systems implemented as feed-forward networks. We will have a lot more to say about these particular properties of networks when we examine memory in detail in Chapter 3. For the moment we would wish to emphasise how difficult they are to arrange using von Neumann computational models.

1.5 LEARNING MECHANISMS

Our descriptions of network behaviour thus far have demonstrated some of their utility as computational devices. They can do at least some of the things we have come to expect of computers, such as solving well specified problems and storing information. The next chapter will show that in fact they, as a class, are general-purpose computers: they can compute anything that is computable in the Turing sense. But, first, how may the networks be programmed so that they compute useful functions?

Connectionist computers cannot be programmed in any conventional sense. That is, they do not follow a set of explicit instructions which may be constructed so as to implement any computable function. Instead the connectivity, the way in which units are connected and the values of the weightings on those connections, is manipulated. In the examples given earlier the connectivity was arranged or contrived in order to produce the desired behaviour. Such networks may be termed "hardwired" as their connectivity is predetermined by the experimenter. In many others we are to consider, the weights are variables. Their values may be determined by the inputs to the network, so that in a sense the network learns through experience. For many this ability to learn is one of the most remarkable features of connectionist computers.

In almost all cases the value of variable weights is determined by a simple rule. A great many such rules are currently being investigated and a subset of these are described in the next chapter. Here we will describe a simple, and trivial, example that gives something of the flavour of connectionist learning rules. Consider the network in Fig. 1.8a. The units are binary (they take an activation level of 1 or 0) and the weights on the connections are set to 0. The activation rule for the units is that they take a value of 1 if and only if their net input is greater than 1. The net input to a unit is given by equation (1). Suppose, for some strange reason, we wanted to associate together the patterns shown in Fig. 1.8b: whenever the activation levels on the left are applied to the left-hand

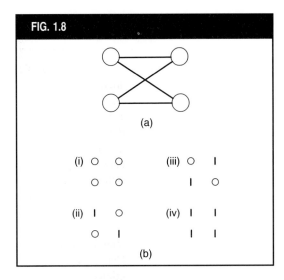

FIG. 1.8

(a) A simple network having excitatory, bilateral connections to be trained to associate the activity patterns shown in (b) such that after training the application of the left-hand pattern will elicit the right-hand pattern for each of the four cases.

The example is trivial yet illustrates significant aspects of conectionist learning. First, a set of weightings has been acquired as a result of exposure to some population of inputs. Second, the information needed by the learning rule is available locally: for a given connection the rule only needs to know the activity levels of the units that the connection links directly. Third, despite the local nature of the weight change rule, a set of weightings may be found which together fulfil a global function such as associating sets of patterns or performing a logical operation or representing abstract information. Chapter 2 will show various learning rules, having these characteristics, which have quite striking, and often counterintuitive, power.

units (for each example (i) through (iv)), the right-hand units should take on the activation levels shown on the right, and vice versa. With weights of zero this of course will not be achieved. In order to evolve a suitable set of weights a learning phase is required during which each of the four patterns is applied to the network in turn and a simple learning rule is used to modify the weights. The learning rule has the following form:

$$\Delta W_{ij} = A_i . A_j \qquad (2)$$

where ΔW_{ij} is the change in weighting on the connection between units i and j, which have activity levels of A_i and A_j respectively. In other words the weighting on each line is changed by an amount equal to the product of the activation levels of the connected units. This rule is applied after each pattern has been imposed on the network. Following this learning phase the network will have acquired weights that yield the desired association. The reader could "simulate" the learning phase, using pencil and paper, and satisfy themselves that this is the case. They should arrive at weightings of 1 on the horizontal connections (as shown in Fig. 1.8a) and 2 on the diagonal.

1.6 SO WHAT IS CONNECTIONISM?

Wittgenstein famously pointed out that an attempt to provide a definitive list of the attributes of some categories is misguided. Connectionist computation is one such category. It is more useful to regard connectionism as referring to a set of models among which there are strong family resemblances. The description of a connectionist computer in section 1.1 gives one strong clue to family membership. Two of the most important other resemblances have also been introduced in this chapter: a particular style of computation, and weight change as a result of exposure to a learning environment.

Several things follow from adopting this very general approach which also serve to distinguish the connectionist endeavour from others in cognitive science. We have discussed some of these already and will return to all of them a number of times in a number of different ways throughout this book. At this point they will simply be highlighted.

1. Connectionism is an attempt to explore the computational properties of brain-like mechanisms. As indicated earlier the intended similarity may be of various sorts. Some workers regard themselves as modelling real networks of real neurons (Ballard,

1986; Sejnowski, 1981). Others see their investigations as directed at understanding the computational structure directly (Smolensky, 1988). Their networks are abstract and how they map onto brain structure is not specified. In fact most of the work we report here is of the latter variety. Both approaches share the assumption that, at least in principle, the physical properties of the brain have a bearing on its computational and psychological functions. Indeed this assumption alone sharply distinguishes connectionism from the recently dominant views in cognitive science. It must be remembered, however, that our knowledge of the central nervous system is very slight. Certainly connectionist networks are highly idealised models of real neural networks. Perhaps crude is a better description! It is also possible that they are entirely misleading models: sets of highly connected neurons may not be the physical basis of information processing.

2. Connectionist schemes are well suited to the solution of problems that involve multiple simultaneous constraint satisfaction. Moreover multiple simultaneous constraint satisfaction is a ubiquitous feature of cognition. The latter claim is clearly empirical and the few examples we have provided thus far do not establish its truth. Readers may become more persuaded as we proceed. Or they may not!

3. Connectionism has a theory of learning. Or in more precise terms: it is able to describe simple mechanisms which appear to explain how elaborate knowledge or control structures can be acquired through exposure to an environment. The problem of learning has not received much attention within cognitive science. Those exceptional attempts to deal with it (e.g. Samuel, 1963) have dealt with learning in a very limited domain. A characteristic feature of connectionist learning is that it aims to be general-purpose: what is learned depends on the environment not the learning mechanism. The extent to which connectionist models achieve this aim is a controversial and important issue.

4. The organisation of memory in connectionist networks is highly distinctive. A memory is a particular pattern of activity which may be evoked by some cue. Effective cues may be the partial contents of the memory or a degraded version of a part of the contents. Memories are stored in the pattern of connectivity, so cannot be regarded as being spatially located. Memories are also superimposed on each other, in that a single unit in a network may participate in several memories, for instance in our example the "musician" unit serves in several memory structures.

5. Units in connectionist networks can represent or stand for things in the world. Representation may be "distributed" or "local". In the model of memory we had each unit designated as standing for some aspect of a particular object: the Beatles were represented by units that stood for their name, occupation, city of origin and so forth. The representation of the Beatles may be thought of as being distributed over a set of units each of which stands for some microfeature. The representation of micro-features is said to be local: one unit for each feature. However the micro-features could also, in principle, be represented in a distributed fashion as patterns of activity over sets of units.

6. Rule-following behaviour may be realised in connectionist networks without any need to have the rules represented explicitly in the network.

7. The performance of connectionist models breaks down gracefully rather than in an all-or-none fashion, when the models are damaged. This form of breakdown mimics at a functional level the behaviour of real neural systems.

Much of the rest of this book is concerned with specific members of the connectionist family and their adequacy in accounting for specific psychological phenomena. The next chapter will describe the formal properties of a number of different connectionist models, and Chapters 3 to

8 illustrate how these, and related, models may be applied to particular psychological processes. It is these chapters that carry the main burden of demonstrating the utility of connectionism to the cognitive sciences. The reader who is primarily interested in the application of the models to psychological issues, and who is not interested in the activation and learning functions that characterise particular models, may wish to proceed straight to Chapter 3.

2

Models

The characteristic properties of connectionist networks described in the previous chapter define a family of models. It is now a large family: something in the order of 50 different sorts of networks are currently under investigation. The purpose of this chapter is to describe a subset of these. Our selection is intended to serve two ends. First it will provide a (very) roughly chronological description of the major developments in connectionist ideas. Following the order in which the ideas were developed and elaborated should allow the reader a similar, gradual elaboration of their knowledge. The second goal is to describe those models that will be used in the remainder of the book where we discuss issues in psychology and cognitive science.

A model of a network will be taken to refer to its formal properties. These will be described in prose and, where it helps, with equations. For the most part we present only the results of mathematical derivations, but even these may be skipped without great loss to the reader.

2.1 ON THE WRITING OF HISTORY

Winners write history! As a consequence, losers often disappear from the accounts of historical events. Anyone who studied psychology or cognitive science as an undergraduate between the early 1970s and the early 1980s can be forgiven for not being familiar with the early varieties of connectionism. Rather like Trotsky disappearing from the photographs of the early Bolshevik leadership, connectionism cannot be found, without great effort, among the histories or textbooks of our disciplines for that period. Now history is being rewritten as part of the rehabilitation of connectionism. But a word of caution: the new "official" version may be just as misleading as the old.

In fact like all good ideas the origins of connectionism may be clearly seen in earlier work. Among the earliest were efforts to explore the computational abilities of networks of simplified neurons.

2.2 LOGIC AND NEURONS

McCulloch and Pitts (1943) explored the formal properties of neuron-like devices. What could neurons compute or what logical operations could they perform when linked by weighted connections in a network? To this end they devised a model of a simplified neuron based on the (then) known properties of real ones. Five assumptions form the basis of the McCulloch–Pitts neuronal network:

1. The activity of a neuron is "all-or-none". Or in latter day terms, a neuron is a binary unit.
2. Each neuron has a fixed threshold, in that a certain number of synapses must be excited within a specified time period before the neuron will itself be excited. This implies that the excitatory inputs have identical weights.
3. Synaptic action causes a time delay. This time delay corresponds to the period for synaptic integration.
4. Inhibition is absolute: a single active inhibitory synapse prevents the excitation of a neuron irrespective of the number of active excitatory synapses.
5. The physical structure of a network of neurons does not change with time. Both connections and the weights on those connections are fixed.

With these assumptions it should be clear that a given neuron will only fire if, during the integration period, an above-threshold number of excitatory inputs are active and no inhibitory inputs are active. This behaviour is illustrated in Fig. 2.1a.

McCulloch and Pitts (1943) were able to demonstrate several interesting properties of their model neural networks by deductive proofs in logic. The most significant result for our purposes here is that such networks are able to perform any (finite) logical function. It follows therefore that some network can be found that can realise any given effective procedure (see the discussion of the Turing machine in Chapter 1). Very simple devices are shown to have effectively unbounded computational potential. An informal demonstration of this may be obtained by inspection of the networks illustrated in Figs. 2.1b to 2.1d. The reader is invited to discover a (finite) logical expression that cannot be realised by some concatenation of the three networks!

This work was perhaps the earliest attempt to explore the potential of connectionist computational architectures in any detail. It is hard to exaggerate its subsequent influence on computational sciences. Ironically it can be seen to have

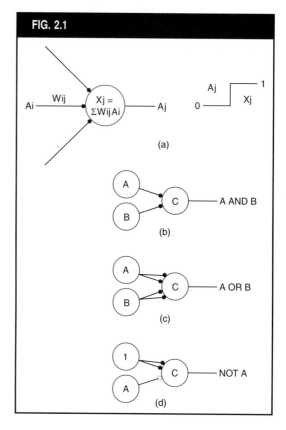

FIG. 2.1

(a) A schematic representation of the McCulloch–Pitts neuron with only excitatory inputs. The input to unit j is simply the sum of the products of the weights by activation levels of all units to which it is connected. Unit j has an activation level of 1 when this sum exceeds some threshold. (b), (c), and (d) show implementations of the logical functions "AND", "OR" and "NOT" using McCulloch–Pitts neurons connected by excitatory (filled circles) and inhibitory (unfilled circles) connections.

had an influence on the development of the conventional digital computer (see von Neumann, 1958). More to our point here, its mark is very apparent in subsequent developments of the connectionist idea. In section 2.4 it will be shown that if weight adaptation is added to the McCulloch–Pitts model it becomes possible for a network to function as, among other things, a pattern recogniser. Before considering this, however, we will describe an early model of synaptic change or weight adaptation.

2.3 CELL ASSEMBLIES AND HEBBIAN LEARNING

Hebb (1949) set himself the goal of making explicit the links between aspects of human behaviour and aspects of brain behaviour. In the attempt to achieve his goal he developed a speculative theory of neural activity that described intra-cerebral events mediating between sensory stimuli and the response of the organism. A central notion in this theory is the "cell-assembly". This consists of a diffuse network linking neurons in the cortex and other brain regions. Neurons in an assembly tend to be jointly active for transient periods. An assembly may be excited by a preceding assembly or a sensory event. Sequences of activation among different assemblies constitute the neural basis of the mental processes that mediate between stimulus and response. Hebb's (1949, p.xix) description of what sort of theory this is clearly identifies it as a precursor to the connectionist notion:

> The theory is evidently a form of connectionism, one of the switchboard variety, though it does not deal in direct connections between afferent and efferent pathways: not an "S–R" psychology, if R means muscular response. The connections serve rather to establish autonomous central activities, which are then the basis of further learning ... It (the theory) does not, further, make any single nerve cell or pathway essential to any habit or perception.

Whereas the McCulloch–Pitts model was concerned with the formal properties that followed from their assumptions, Hebb (1949) aimed to set out the psychological implications of a particular neural model. For instance some aspects of perceptual integration were said to result from the types of connectivity that were possible in the association areas of the cortex (see later). He also proposed a physiological theory of learning which accounted for the development of cell assemblies. The theory supposes that neuronal activity resulting from, for instance, sensory stimulation may be sustained for very short durations (milliseconds) as a result of reverberatory excitation among the active neurons. Repeated activity in such a reverberatory circuit will lead to physical changes in the connections (the synapses between the cells) such that the mutual excitability of the neurons is increased. According to Hebb (1949, p.62) synaptic modification occurs such that:

> When an axon of cell A is near enough to excite a cell B and repeatedly or persistently takes part in firing it, some growth process or metabolic change takes place in one or both cells such that A's efficiency, as one of the cells firing B, is increased.

This may be stated more formally as follows. In Hebbian learning, the change on the weight (ΔW) connecting two units, i and j, will be:

$$\Delta W_{ij} = \eta a_i \cdot a_j$$

where a_i and a_j are the activation values in units i and j, and η is a learning parameter. According to this rule, the weight between two units is increased if the units are both excited (e.g. +1), but it will be decreased if one unit is excited and the other inhibited (−1). Thus the "Hebb learning rule" is sensitive to correlated firing between units, and it will alter the weights within a network according to patterns of correlation between stimuli in the training set. The learning parameter, η, typically operates so that weight changes saturate (say to 1) and do not keep increasing when inputs are constantly presented.

As a simple example of the consequence of Hebbian learning consider the following case. Neurons at neighbouring locations x, y, and z in the primary visual cortex of the brain (known as area V1) tend to come on together and provide input to neuron a in the next cortical area responding to visual input (area V2). This would be the case if neurons x, y, and z each fire maximally to edges of the same orientation, so that neuron a will be activated by a long edge falling across the receptive fields for neurons x, y, and z (a receptive field, in vision, is the area on the retina from which a given cell at a higher level in the nervous system receives input). As the V1 neurons will tend to come on together — reflecting the properties of edges in the world — there will be a strengthening of the connections between each V1 neuron and the V2 neuron, as a result of Hebbian learning. As a consequence, it may be possible to activate neuron a in V2 when input is present only in the receptive fields of neurons x and z. In such a case, neuron a would respond "as if" activity were present at y — it would complete the edge as if it were there in the real world, and integrate the activity from neurons x and z. Interestingly, cells in area V2 of the monkey's visual cortex have been found with just this integrative property (Peterhans & von der Heydt, 1989).

Hebbian learning principles have influenced many of the subsequent developments in connectionist learning procedures, as we shall see.

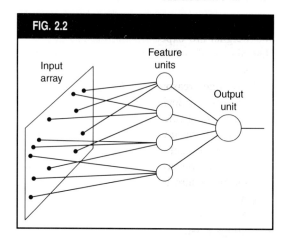

FIG. 2.2

A typical perceptron architecture: the input units are arranged as a two-dimensional array connected randomly, with fixed weights, to feature units which in turn have adaptive connections to an output unit that is to signal the class of the input pattern.

2.4 PERCEPTRONS AND THEIR LIMITATIONS

The McCulloch–Pitts neuron may be regarded as a linear threshold device. It sums its inputs and is turned on if the sum exceeds a certain threshold. Rosenblatt (1958, 1962) explored the properties of networks of such devices in which at least some of the connections could be modified by learning. The family of models that result from such an approach are referred to as perceptrons. As their name suggests, they appear to be good at pattern recognition (Nilsson, 1965; Rosenblatt, 1962).

The perceptron most commonly discussed in the literature is shown in Fig. 2.2. A set of input units are linked to a smaller set of linear threshold units by connections having fixed weights. Each threshold unit will be active if the sum of its weighted input exceeds some value. If the input units are thought of as constituting a retina-like, two-dimensional array, the threshold units may be regarded as visual feature detectors. An active threshold unit is asserting the presence of a particular feature on the retina. All the feature detectors are connected to a single output unit, which is itself a linear threshold device. The weight on these connections may be adapted in a manner that ensures that the output unit can be regarded

as performing binary classification of the retinal input. For instance whether a particular character is present or not in the input array.

How can the weightings on the connections between the feature units and the output unit be adapted so that the perceptron acts as a pattern classifier? Assume that a given population of patterns can be divided into two categories. For instance a useful division might be between all patterns that were examples of the letter "A" and all patterns that were "non-A"s. We want the output unit of the perceptron to be active only if the input is an "A". During learning, a sample of the population will serve as input to the perceptron. At first the output unit will give an arbitrary output to any input, because the initial weights are a random set of values. If this output happens to be correct then nothing is done to the weights. If it is wrong then the weights are modified, but only on those connections between active feature units and the output units. The rule governing weight change in such cases is simple: if the output unit is on when it should be off, then decrease the weights by some constant amount; if the output unit is off when it should be on, then increase the weights by the same constant amount. This learning rule is known as the perceptron convergence procedure. Given a sufficiently large training set, the weights are expected to converge to a state that allows all subsequent patterns drawn from the population to be correctly classified.

Now one reason for being interested in perceptron-type devices is that it can be shown that the learning rule is effective: for many populations of patterns it will lead to a stable classification scheme. In fact Rosenblatt (1962) has proved a perceptron convergence theorem which shows that the procedure is guaranteed to discover the weightings that lead to stable classification for a given population — providing such a set of weightings exist.

What populations of patterns are suitable for classification by perceptron-like devices? Or rather for what classifications do suitable weighting sets exist? One requirement is that the desired classifications must be linearly separable. To understand what this means we need to think about properties of vectors. A vector is simply a finite, ordered set of numbers. A two-component vector defines a point in two-dimensional vector space. The vectors [0 0], [0 1], [1 0], and [1 1] are represented graphically in Fig. 2.3. Consider the regions into which this particular vector space could be divided by a single straight line, and note that in none of these divisions are [0 0] and [1 1] in one region, while [0 1] and [1 0] are in the other. That is to say, those two pairs of vectors are not linearly separable. This being the case, no perceptron of the sort described here could perform this classification. This particular example is frequently referred to in the literature as the exclusive-or problem because the relationship between inputs and desired outputs is isomorphic with that logical function. In short, perceptrons cannot compute the exclusive-or ("XOR") problem. The requirement of linear separability is general: a perceptron may only divide an n-dimensional vector space into regions that can be divided by an n-dimensional plane. Unfortunately it can be shown that as the number of inputs increases the proportion that are linearly separable reduces!

In a very powerful formal analysis of the properties of perceptrons Minsky and Papert (1969) revealed several other fundamental limitations. One type of limitation is concerned with the detection of certain global properties of input patterns. For instance consider Figs. 2.4a to 2.4d. A perceptron cannot learn to distinguish the two patterns that are connected (c and d) from the two that are disconnected (a and b). To see that this is so, imagine a perceptron in which each of the feature units is connected to only a circular region of the input array, with the diameter of the regions being less than the full extent of the figure. This arrangement is illustrated in Fig. 2.4e. If our perceptron is to signal connectivity, the weighted output of the active feature units must sum to a value less than the threshold of the output unit given the figure shown in 2.4a. It is also a requirement that the net output of the feature units must increase for the case of 2.4c which is a connected figure. As the two figures differ only in the right-hand region of the array, it follows that the feature units connected to that part of the array (group 3 in 2.4e) must increase their output when presented with 2.4c. For the same reasons it is the group 1 feature units that must increase their output given connected Fig. 2.4d. But these two requirements are incompatible with a below-threshold output of the feature units for the unconnected Fig. 2.4b. That is, the combined increase in group 1 and group 3 outputs, each of which is required for correct responses to the connected figures, will result in the perceptron classifying

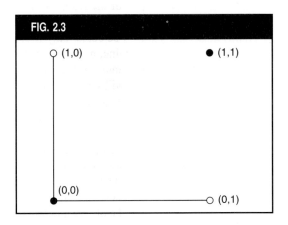

FIG. 2.3

A spatial representation of four vectors demonstrating that the two pairs [0 0], [1 1] and [0 1], [1 0] are not linearly separable. That is, the pairs cannot be segregated in vector space by a single, straight line.

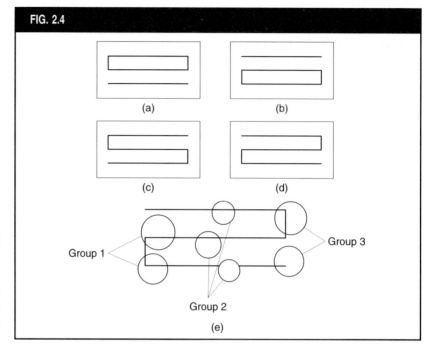

FIG. 2.4

(a) and (b) show two patterns that are not fully connected, and (c) and (d) show two that are. (e) illustrates the difficulty faced by a perceptron in using only local measures to compute connectivity.

the unconnected figure in 2.4b as connected. Thus no perceptron with limited-diameter receptive fields can learn to classify the four figures in terms of their connectivity. But what if the feature units are not diameter-limited? What if a given feature unit can be connected to any arbitrary subset of the input array? Still it can be shown that connectivity cannot be computed as long as the number of units in the input array to which any given feature unit is connected is significantly less than the total number of input units (for a proof see Minsky & Papert, 1969, pp.74–75). Similar conclusions apply to the determination of parity; that is, the determination of whether the same number of input units are on as are off. It can be shown (Minsky & Papert, 1969, pp.56–57) that the computation of this global property of an input pattern requires a feature detector that is connected to all the input units.

These demonstrations are more important than they perhaps seem on a first reading. They appear to show that no local computation, or set of local computations, is sufficient for a decision about certain global properties of patterns. In Chapter 1

we claimed that relaxation networks were natural methods for finding global solutions by local computations! What has gone wrong? We will be in a better position to answer this question when we have described other models which, as suggested in section 2.1, are said to overcome some of the objections to perceptrons.

The foregoing shows that some functions, such as connectivity and parity, cannot be computed by a perceptron. But even those functions that can in principle be computed may not be realisable. Minsky and Papert (1969) suggested that such functions may be unrealisable in two senses. First, the number and the magnitude of weights needed on the feature units to output unit connections may become hopelessly large. For example in some cases the weights may need to be so large that the memory needed to store the numbers exceeds that needed to store the entire set of figures defined by the function! Second, the learning time may become hopelessly long. Although the perceptron convergence procedure is guaranteed to find a set of weights that will separate groups that are linearly separable, it is not guaranteed to do so in an efficient manner. In some instances it may be no more efficient than a random but exhaustive search of all possible weights. As Rumelhart and Zipser (1985, p.158) have remarked:

> . . . parallel recognizing elements, such as perceptrons, are beset by the same problems of scale as serial pattern recognizers. Combinatorial explosion catches you sooner or later, although sometimes in different ways in parallel than in serial.

These are also issues we must return to at the end of this chapter.

2.5 ASSOCIATIVE NETWORKS

Perceptrons classify inputs by having an output signal one of a small number (usually two) of possible states. We will now describe a family of models that associate an input with a particular pattern of activity over a number (usually large) of units. In short, such a network is able to associate pattern pairs. Consider the simple network illustrated in Fig. 2.5a. This has two sets of units: A and B. We want it to associate patterns of activity over A units with patterns of activity over B units. To see how this can be arranged a short excursion into matrix algebra is needed. Stay calm!

A matrix is a two-dimensional array of real numbers. Here is a three by two matrix: $\begin{vmatrix} 3 & 7 \\ 2 & 4 \\ 6 & 1 \end{vmatrix}$.

A matrix may be multiplied by a vector provided the dimensionality of the vector is the same as the number of columns in the matrix. For instance our example matrix may be multiplied by the vector $\begin{vmatrix} 2 \\ 5 \end{vmatrix}$ in the following manner:

$$\begin{vmatrix} 3 & 7 \\ 2 & 4 \\ 6 & 1 \end{vmatrix} \times \begin{vmatrix} 2 \\ 5 \end{vmatrix} = \begin{vmatrix} (3 \times 2 + 7 \times 5) \\ (2 \times 2 + 4 \times 5) \\ (6 \times 2 + 1 \times 5) \end{vmatrix} = \begin{vmatrix} 41 \\ 24 \\ 17 \end{vmatrix}$$

Notice that each component of each row of the matrix has been multiplied by the comparable component of the vector and the results summed. Each such sum is said to be an inner product of two vectors. It follows that multiplying a n by m matrix with an m-dimensional vector yields a n-dimensional vector.

Now inspect Fig. 2.5b which illustrates the connectivity of the network shown in 2.5a in the form of a matrix. Let the activity pattern on the A units be regarded as a two-dimensional vector $\begin{vmatrix} a1 \\ a2 \end{vmatrix}$, the activity pattern on the B units a three-dimensional vector: $\begin{vmatrix} b1 \\ b2 \\ b3 \end{vmatrix}$ and the set of six weightings on the connections a three by two matrix: $\begin{vmatrix} w11 & w12 \\ w21 & w22 \\ w31 & w32 \end{vmatrix}$ For a simple linear association network the activity of a single unit is simply the sum of its weighted input; for example $b1 = (w11 \times a1 + w12 \times a2)$. This sum is of course

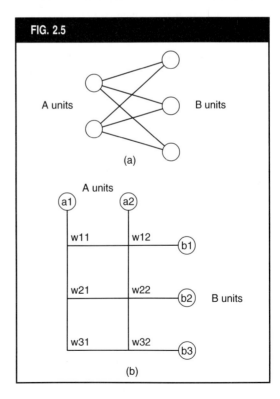

FIG. 2.5

A simple associative network is illustrated in (a) and the same network is expressed as a weight matrix in (b).

the inner product of two vectors. It should now be clear that, following our example of the multiplication of a matrix by a vector:

$$
\begin{vmatrix} b1 \\ b2 \\ b3 \end{vmatrix} = \begin{vmatrix} w11 & w12 \\ w21 & w22 \\ w31 & w32 \end{vmatrix} \times \begin{vmatrix} a1 \\ a2 \end{vmatrix}.
$$

Thus it is that a particular weight matrix will allow the association of two vectors or patterns of activity. Presentation $\begin{vmatrix} a1 \\ a2 \end{vmatrix}$ on the A units will result in the pattern $\begin{vmatrix} b1 \\ b2 \\ b3 \end{vmatrix}$ on the B units. How is the appropriate weight matrix to be found? We need to know a little more about matrix algebra to grasp the answer. In particular we need to note that:

1. The transpose of a matrix is another matrix in which the rows of one are the same as the columns of the other. Thus the transpose of the weight matrix given earlier would be:

   $$
   \begin{vmatrix} w11 & w21 & w31 \\ w12 & w22 & w32 \end{vmatrix}.
   $$

   By implication the transpose of an n-dimensional vector is a one by n matrix. For example the transpose of the vector $\begin{vmatrix} b1 \\ b2 \\ b3 \end{vmatrix}$ is denoted by bsT and is $\begin{vmatrix} b1 & b2 & b3 \end{vmatrix}$.
2. A unit vector is one whose inner product with itself is equal to one.
3. Matrix multiplication is noncommutative. In other words, the order of multiplication matters: $|M| \times |V|$ is not equal to $|V| \times |M|$. Having understood the previous example of multiplication the reader should be able to see that the result of $|3 \ 2| \times \begin{vmatrix} 3 \\ 4 \end{vmatrix}$ is $|3 \times 3 \ 3 \times 2| = |9 \ 6|$. However $\begin{vmatrix} 3 \\ 4 \end{vmatrix} \times |3 \ 2|$ is equal to $|4 \times 3 \ 4 \times 2|$, that is $|12 \ 8|$.

We are now in a position to see how to find the weight matrix, W, which will allow the association of the vector a, on the A units, with the vector b, on the B units. It was shown earlier that:

$$b = W \times a. \tag{1}$$

Our problem is to find the unknown given the knowns of a and b. It can be shown that provided a is a unit vector, then:

$$W = b \times asT. \tag{2}$$

This can be seen to be true by substituting this expression for W thus:

$$
\begin{aligned}
W \times a &= (b \times asT) \times a \\
&= b \times (asT \times a) \\
&= b
\end{aligned}
$$

because a is a unit vector and therefore $(asT \times a)$ is equal to one. Thus equation (1) can be derived from the substitution and equation (2) is thereby verified.

Returning to the example of Fig. 2.5 from equation (2) we get:

$$
W = \begin{vmatrix} b1 \\ b2 \\ b3 \end{vmatrix} \times \begin{vmatrix} a1 \\ a2 \end{vmatrix} sT
$$

$$
= \begin{vmatrix} b1 \\ b2 \\ b3 \end{vmatrix} \times |a1 \ a2| = \begin{vmatrix} b1 \times a1 & b1 \times a2 \\ b2 \times a1 & b2 \times a2 \\ b3 \times a1 & b3 \times a2 \end{vmatrix}.
$$

If you have followed the argument you should now be excited! For the appropriate weight on each connection has been shown to be simply the product of the activity of the two units connected. This is a version of the Hebbian learning rule: connections between units are strengthened as a consequence of correlated activity. It is also a local learning rule, as it depends only on the state of those units adjacent to the connection to be modified.

It can be further shown that a single weight matrix is sufficient for several pairs of associations provided the set of vectors, a, on the A units are orthogonal to each other (and thus do not overlap in their on/off activation values). Imagine n such vectors a1, a2, ... ai ... an. The weight matrix for any member of this set is given by equation (2):

Wi = bi × aisT.

Each of these terms may be combined in a single weight matrix thus:

W = W1 + W2 + . . . Wi . . . +Wn.

This combined matrix has the same dimensions as each of the individual ones and allows each of the members of the vector set a to be associated with the appropriate member of the vector set b; as can be seen thus:

W × ai = (W1 + . . . Wi . . . + Wn)ai
     = (b1 × a1sT + . . . bi × aisT . . . +
     bn × ansT)ai
     = b1(ai × a1sT) + . . . bi(ai × aisT) . . . +
     bn(ai × ansT),

and as, by definition, for orthogonal vectors (ai × ajsT) is zero, all the multiplication terms on the right-hand side of the equation are zero, except for (ai × aisT) which is one for unit vectors. Thus:

W × ai = bi.

In summary, our simple associative network will find, using a Hebbian learning procedure, a set of weightings for a population of orthogonal vectors which will associate each vector a with another unique vector b. We have a pattern associator or associative memory system. Models of this general type have been discussed by Willshaw, Buneman, and Longuet-Higgins (1969), Hinton and Anderson (1981), Marr (1969), Anderson (1970), and Kohonen (1984). In Chapter 3 the implications of this work for theories of memory and learning will be discussed. For now we simply point to two remarkable properties of such networks. First, they are tolerant of distortions of the input: a partial version of a "known" vector, or a distorted version of it, on the A units will elicit the complete or near complete associated vector on the B units. Second, they are robust when damaged: units may be lost without serious loss of information.

2.6 NETWORKS THAT MINIMISE ENERGY

Some of the networks we have described are useful devices for the storage and processing of information because they are capable of achieving, or converging to, a number of stable states in the space of possible states. Each of these states can be said to stand for something: it signifies the presence of a particular pattern in an input for instance. Moreover the stable states may be thought of as "attractors". If a network is close to one of its stable states it will tend to "be attracted" towards it. This property is the basis of the ability to respond correctly to imperfect inputs or to recognise different instances of the same classification. Hopfield (1982) described a network that was multistable in this way, and for which any prescribed set of states could be made the stable states. The Hopfield net has connections that allow activation to pass forward or backward: unit i sends activation to unit j, but j also sends activation to i. Importantly the weights are symmetrical in that wij is equal to wji. A novel feature of the Hopfield net is its asynchronous changes in the activation states of units. Each unit will adjust its state randomly in time at some average attempt rate. The activation rule is simple: unit i will be on and have an output of 1 only if the sum of its weighted input exceeds a threshold, otherwise it will have an output of 0. The weights are assumed to have been derived by the application of a version of the Hebbian learning rule. The learning rule is not the major focus of interest. Hopfield (1982) was primarily concerned to show that the collective action of the units, given some set of weightings, can be understood as analogous to energy minimisation, when energy is expressed by some global measure. One such global energy measure is defined by the function (for units having a threshold of zero):

$$E = -\sum W_{ij}A_iA_j.$$

Now the change in the total "energy" E of the system that would result from a change in activation of unit i is given thus:

$$\Delta E = -\Delta A_i \cdot \sum W_{ij} A_j. \qquad (3)$$

The repeated application of the activation rule described earlier effectively reduces E to a minimum, as each application of the rule will either leave E unchanged or reduce it. To see that this is so consider the three possible results of equation 3 for any particular unit. If there is no change of activation state the global energy remains constant. If the activation state changes from 1 to 0 (ΔA_i is -1) this implies its total input ($\sum W_{ij} A_j$) is negative, thus the product of these two terms is positive and by equation (3) there is a reduction in E. If the unit changes from an activation of 0 to 1 (ΔA_i is 1) its total input must be positive, again the product of these terms is positive and again by equation (3) E is reduced.

One way of understanding the process of energy minimisation in a Hopfield net is to visualise an energy landscape or surface. The network may be set to some initial arbitrary state of activation (a pattern of 1s and 0s over the units) which will correspond to a particular value of E. This initial state will correspond to a point on the energy surface, with E given by the height of the surface at that point. The activation rule will cause the network to move from state to state, therefore from point to point on the surface. But remember the rule only allows changes that keep E constant or reduce it. In other words it only allows moves that traverse a plateau or go downhill on the surface. Over time therefore the system will tend to find itself in one of the troughs: a local energy minimum. And here it will stay, because the only way out is to move uphill which is not allowed by the activation rule. Our illustration covers only three dimensions, but the principles hold for the multiple-dimensional surface that describes the state-space of a network having a large number of units. Hopfield (1982) demonstrated that such a state-space has a number of stable local energy minima which act as attractors in that if the network is initially at some point close to a particular minimum it will tend to "climb down" to it. The minima serve as information or memory states, which can be evoked from nearby states. The other networks we have described received sustained input on designated input units, in response to

which they relaxed to some stable state. In contrast, communication with the Hopfield net consists of setting the entire network to some state, in response to which it relaxes to a state corresponding to a nearby energy minimum.

The Boltzmann machine is a network that also seeks minimum energy states (Ackley, Hinton, & Sejnowski, 1985; Hinton & Sejnowski, 1986). However in its case the minimum sought is global rather than local. Clearly the ability to find a global minimum entails the ability to escape from local minima. The only way out of a local minimum is uphill on the energy surface. Thus the Boltzmann machine uses an activation rule that will usually move the system from low to higher energy states. The rule is similar to the one we described for the Hopfield net. The (symmetrical) binary units adjust their states randomly in time, but now the decision about whether a particular unit is placed into an on or off state is probabilistic. A unit is switched on with a probability, p, that depends on the energy change, ΔE, that would result from its activation (as calculated in equation 3) and a parameter referred to as temperature, T thus:

$$p = \frac{1}{(1 + e^{-\Delta E/T})}. \qquad (4)$$

The temperature term effectively sets the probability of energy jumps of particular magnitudes. Equation (4) entails that at high temperatures the likelihood of a state change which results in a large increase in energy is greater than that at low temperatures, and that, in general, small energy jumps are more likely than big ones, but at low temperatures this difference is far more pronounced. Figure 2.6 illustrates the form of this probability function as the temperature parameter varies. Under high-temperature conditions there is effectively more noise in the way units operate, as, relative to when there is a low temperature, units are more likely to be placed into an "on" state even when the supporting evidence is below a standard threshold level (note that, to the left of the threshold in Fig. 2.6, the probability of a unit coming on is greater than 0); likewise units that should be placed into an "on" state given the supporting evidence may not be (note that, to the

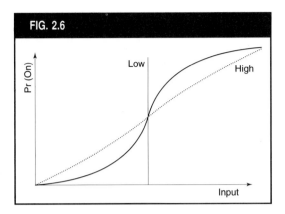

FIG. 2.6

The probability of a unit coming into an "on" state as a function of the "temperature" of the system.

right of the threshold in Fig. 2.6, the probability of a unit coming on is less than 1).

Now consider the energy landscape shown in Fig. 2.7, in particular the minima marked a and b. To get to a from b requires a bigger energy jump than to get from b to a. At low temperatures, therefore, it is far more probable that the system would fall into a than b. But as even the small energy jump would be rare, the system would take a long time to reach "thermal equilibrium". That is, to reach the state in which the probability of being in any particular state depends only on the height of the energy surface at that point. In our example it should be obvious that at thermal equilibrium the ratio of probabilities would favour the deeper

minimum. In contrast, at high temperatures both energy transitions would be relatively frequent, thus the system would rapidly approach the ratio of probabilities. However the ratio would be less favourable to the deeper minimum than the low-temperature case.

Perhaps an easier way of understanding this is to conceive of the situation in terms of a physical analogy. Imagine the energy surface in Fig. 2.7 to be a real surface on which a small ball-bearing moves. The problem is to have the ball-bearing move to the lowest point on the surface. Shaking is one way of achieving this. Gentle shaking, analogous to low values of T in equation (4), will far more likely move the ball-bearing from a to b, but both transitions will be rare and arriving at the lowest point would take a long time. Violent shaking, analogous to high values of T in equation (4), will allow both sorts of transition to occur frequently but the final state of the system is less likely to be one in which the ball-bearing is at the lowest point on the surface.

A solution to this dilemma may be to start with violent shaking, gradually reducing to gentle shaking during the adaptation phase. Kirkpatrick, Gellat, and Vecchi (1983) in effect achieved this by using a technique they referred to as simulated annealing, suggesting a further analogy with the annealing of metals. Simulated annealing consists of gradually reducing the temperature of a system from some initial high value to a low end value. At high temperatures the system explores state spaces in roughly the right region; as the temperature is reduced the system becomes sensitive to smaller energy differences. It has been shown that if the temperature reduction is very gradual the network will settle to a global minimum with a probability close to certainty (Kirkpatrick et al., 1983).

How does the Boltzmann machine learn? The answer is quite complicated, but intriguing. Imagine the units divided into two sorts: visible units and hidden units. The visible units serve to receive input from the environment or signal an output of the system. As an illustration of the learning process imagine a network with just three visible units: two designated as input and one as output, plus one hidden unit. Suppose we want

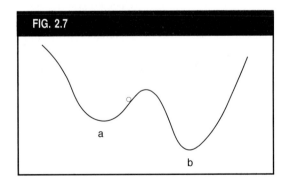

FIG. 2.7

A section of an energy landscape for a Boltzmann machine. Clearly a bigger energy "jump" is required to move from minima a to b, than from b to a.

the system to solve the problem described in section 2.4 and illustrated in Fig. 2.3a. That is, the output unit should be on only if just one of the input units is on. Or, in vector notation, the only legal states of the visible units should be (0,0,0), (1,1,0), (0,1,1), and (1,0,1), where the third component represents the state of the output unit. In an initial phase of learning the visible units are "clamped": their states are fixed to one of the four vectors. When clamped the network is allowed to reach thermal equilibrium using some schedule of annealing. The network is then allowed to run a little longer, during which measures are made of how frequently pairs of directly connected units are active at the same time. This procedure is repeated for each of the vectors, possibly several times. Co-occurrence statistics can then be calculated: the probability of two (directly connected) units being on together, p_{ij}, can be estimated from the average frequencies of co-activations after the various annealings. In a second learning phase the network is allowed to run freely with no clamped units. Again co-occurrence statistics are collected, using the same annealing schedule the same number of times. At this point the weights are changed according to the rule:

$$\Delta w_{ij} = c . \Delta p_{ij} \qquad (5)$$

where c is a constant and Δp_{ij} is equal to the value of p_{ij} in the second learning phase subtracted from its value in the first phase. In words: if the probability of two units being on together is greater when the network is clamped than when free running then increase the weight between them. The reader should note the Hebbian flavour of this learning rule; also that it works! If the training schedule just described is repeated a sufficiently large number of times, a set of weightings will evolve that solves our problem. The Boltzmann machine solves problems that could not be solved by perceptrons (see section 2.4).

Why does it work? There are two sorts of answer to this question. First a mathematical answer concerned with the derivation of the learning algorithm. This will be discussed in the next paragraph. Second, a conceptual answer concerned with the role of hidden units. This will be dis-

cussed in the paragraphs following the next one. The mathematically timid may go straight to the conceptual answer without losing too much.

The activation rule expressed in equation (4) has general application to physical systems consisting of particles having two energy states. In such systems, when in thermal equilibrium, the relative probabilities of two global states follow the Boltzmann distribution thus:

$$\frac{Pa}{Pb} = e^{-(Ea-Eb)/T} \qquad (6)$$

where Pa is the probability of state a and Ea is its energy. As the aim of the learning procedure we have described is to have the visible units behave when free-running in a similar manner to when clamped, some measure of the difference between the two conditions would be useful. One such measure is:

$$G = \Sigma_i P(Vi) \ln \frac{P(Vi)}{P\sim(Vi)} \qquad (7)$$

where $P(Vi)$ is the probability of the ith state of the visible units when clamped and $P\sim(Vi)$ is its probability when the network is free-running. The G term is zero only when the free-running states exactly match the clamped states, thus learning may be expressed as finding a global minimum for G. The way to change G, of course, is to change $P\sim(Vi)$ which in turn depends on changing the weights. In effect we need to know how G will change as a weight is changed. This could be a nightmare in a highly interactive network! One might suppose that the effect of changing one weight would depend on all the other weights. Ackley et al. (1985) were able to show that in fact this is not the case for the Boltzmann machine. Because at thermal equilibrium the probability of global states is a function of only their energies (equation 6) and because these energies are function of weights, the following can be derived from equation 7:

$$\frac{dG}{dw_{ij}} = -\frac{1}{T}(P_{ij} - P_{\tilde{i}j}). \qquad (8)$$

In words: the rate of change of G due to the change in any individual weight (w_{ij}) depends only, at a given value of T, on the difference between the probability of the two connected units being on together when some units are clamped (P_{ij}) and the probability of their being on together when the network is free-running ($P_{\bar{ij}}$). So once more we have discovered that a global measure can be minimised using local information: the way to reduce G is, as shown in equation 5, to change weights by an amount proportional to the difference between the co-activation probabilities in the clamped and free-running states. Another counterintuitive consequence of equation 8 is that this rule applies to any sort of connection: between hidden units, between visible units or between a hidden unit and a visible unit.

What is the role of hidden units? The various answers to this question turn out to be of profound general importance to the viability of the connectionist approach.

Consider again the problem illustrated in Fig. 2.3a. The problem is, as was mentioned, a familiar one in the connectionist literature, where it is usually expressed in its logical form. As can be seen in Fig. 2.8, the two inputs together with the appropriate output may be thought of as an implementation of the exclusive-or logical operator. Any network that attempts to implement such an operator by connecting the input directly to the output will fail. Single-layer networks of this sort, such as the perceptron described in the earlier sections of this chapter, will successfully map similar inputs to similar outputs. The exclusive-or implementation requires, however, that the least similar inputs are mapped to similar outputs. For instance whereas the pairwise correlation within each input category is 0, across categories it is 0.5. A solution is possible with a hidden unit because this is able to act as a sort of feature detector: for example it could detect the case where both inputs are on, as in the implementation illustrated in Fig. 2.8. Or in statistical terms the hidden unit can serve to represent aspects of the input population that are latent in the higher-order statistics of that population — at least higher order than pairwise correlations. The significance of the Boltzmann learning algorithm is that it is able to discover the weights that allow the hidden units to serve their feature-detection or representational role. Another example should serve to convince the reader of its power in this respect.

The so-called shift register problem has been described by Hinton and Sejnowski (1986) and implemented as a network. Three sorts of visible units were used. There were eight group A units, any number of which may be jointly active, arranged as a one-dimensional array. The group B units copied the activity states of the group A units, except that the pattern could be shifted to the right or left. For example in a right shift the fact that unit 5 is on in group A determined that unit 6 was on in group B. Wrap-around was allowed: in a left shift, for example, unit 1 being on in group A determined that unit 8 is on in Group B. The role of the three group C visible units was to signal the type of shift: right, left, or none. This is a hard problem in the sense that it is the high-order relations between group A and B units that must be discovered in order to signal the type of shift. Hinton and Sejnowski (1986) were able to show that a Boltzmann machine could develop feature-detecting hidden units that were sensitive to the appropriate high-order relations. They trained a network that in addition to the visible units had 24 hidden units. The visible units were clamped to an appropriate state, representing the two patterns and their shift, while the network was annealed to thermal equilibrium, when co-occurrence statistics were collected. This was repeated for 20 different clamped patterns,

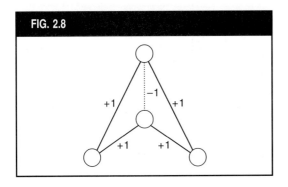

FIG. 2.8

A multilayer network implementation of the exclusive-or (XOR) function.

allowing P_{ij} to be estimated from the average co-occurrences. With the network free-running the annealing schedule was repeated, co-occurrence statistics collected, and $P_{\bar{ij}}$ estimated from 20 repetitions of the annealing. After each "sweep" of the 40 annealings each weight was changed by the amount $5(P_{ij} - P_{\bar{ij}})$ minus a small decay factor. After many such sweeps one can examine the behaviour of the hidden units. One outcome is illustrated in Fig. 2.9 in which the weights achieved after learning are displayed. Inspection of these reveals that at least some of the hidden units have indeed evolved into the sort of feature detectors one might imagine would be useful in a solution to the shift-register problem. For instance a hidden unit that has a strong positive weighting with the right-shift unit in group C, also has strong positive weightings with the fourth unit in group A and the fifth unit in group B. The top left-hand unit in Fig. 2.9 illustrates this case. But the network has also found solutions that one might not have immediately imagined! One way of detecting

no-shift would be to have hidden units with strong positive weights for the corresponding units in group A and group B. The network found an even better solution: have strong negative weightings for corresponding units, flanked by small excitatory weightings. Several examples of this strategy can be observed among the examples in Fig. 2.9.

The performance of the network is far from perfect. In the example shown its error rate varies from 50% when only one unit is active in each of A and B, to an optimum of 11% when five units are active. Also learning is very, very slow. The weights shown in Fig. 2.9 were arrived at after 9000 sweeps. However what is perhaps of greater significance is that a learning technique has been described that (perhaps) has the potential to overcome some of the limitations in earlier models highlighted by Minsky and Papert (1969). A connectionist solution to the exclusive-or problem, for example, was known to require a multilayer network for reasons discussed earlier. That is, a network in which there were mediating units

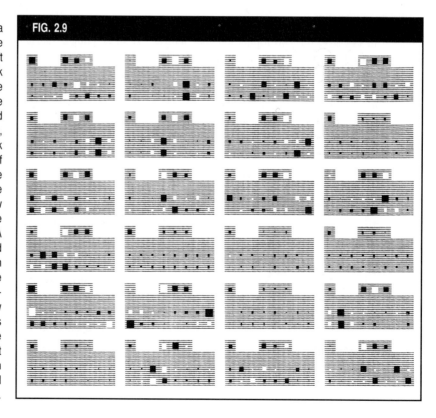

The weight structure of a Boltzmann machine trained on the shift register. Each large block represents one of the hidden units. Positive weights are represented by white squares, negative weights by black squares, and the size of the square represents the value of the weight. The bottom two rows show the weights on the connections from the A and B units (see text) and the three middle units in the upper row to the three output, C, units. The left-hand unit in the upper row indicates the hidden unit's threshold. In this example the hidden units were not interconnected with each other. From Hinton and Sejnowski (1986).

FIG. 2.9

between input and output, and, as a consequence, more than one layer of modifiable connections. At the time of their writing Minsky and Papert could rightly claim that the problem of learning in multilayer systems was profound and unsolved. The Boltzmann learning algorithm is a putative solution to learning in multilayer networks. In the next two sections we discuss others.

2.7 BACK-PROPAGATION IN MULTILAYER NETWORKS

A technique for learning in multilayer networks of perceptron-like units has recently been developed independently by several people (le Cun, 1985; Parker, 1985; Rumelhart, Hinton, & Williams, 1986). The description we include here is taken from Rumelhart, Hinton and Williams (1986). Consider the network shown in Fig. 2.10a. Input units are connected to one or more layers of hidden

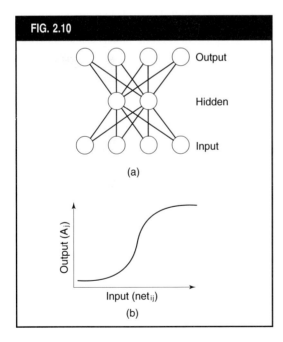

FIG. 2.10

(a)

Output (A$_j$)

Input (net$_{ij}$)

(b)

(a) A simple feed-forward network with three layers: input units, one layer of hidden units, and output units. (b) The semilinear activation function described by equation (9) in the text.

units which in turn connect to output units. The connections are asymmetrical in that activation flows in only one direction: from the input units to the output units. The system is called, therefore, a feed-forward network. The units are deterministic rather than stochastic (i.e. their activation values do not vary across different occasions). They are also perceptron-like in the sense that each unit sums its weighted input from the other units to which it is connected in order to determine what its output should be. The reader will remember that the output of a perceptron unit was 1 if the total input exceeded some threshold and 0 otherwise. In our new case here however the output for a given unit, j, is a continuous function of the input (from units i . . . n), for example:

$$A_j = \frac{1}{1 + e^{(-\Sigma_i W_{ij} A_i + T_j)}} \qquad (9)$$

where T_j is, in effect, a fixed threshold. This function, which Rumelhart et al. (1986a) describe as semilinear, is shown in Fig. 2.10b. This difference has important consequences for learning which we will now discuss.

Suppose the aim is to have a feed-forward multilayer network associate together a set of input and output patterns. After learning, each input should elicit some specified "target" output. Prior to learning, the output to a given input will be arbitrary. The aim of learning is to reduce this error between the actual and target outputs for the whole set of input/output pairs. If it were possible to compute a global measure of error, say E, learning could be regarded as finding an error minimum in an error landscape akin to the energy minimisation procedure discussed in relation to Hopfield networks (section 2.6). Rumelhart, Hinton and Williams (1986) developed a learning technique, called back-propagation of error, that appears to solve this problem. The next several paragraphs describe the mathematical results that underpin back-propagation. The reader uninterested in such issues may again skip this material. They should rejoin the text at the paragraph marked [HERE].

What then is a suitable global measure of error? A common statistic used to assess the difference between two sets of data is the sum of the squares of their differences (squaring the difference makes the measure insensitive to the direction of the differences). This can be calculated in the case of the difference between an actual and target output thus:

$$E_x = \frac{1}{2}\sum_j (T_{xj} - A_{xj})^2 \qquad (10)$$

where E_x is the error in the case of input pattern x, T_{xj} is the target activation state of the jth output unit for that pattern, and A_{xj} its actual state. A global measure of error, E, may be calculated by summing this statistic over all values of x, that is for all input patterns.

How can the minimum value of E be found? Rumelhart, Hinton and Williams (1986) have shown that an elaboration of a well known learning procedure, which they refer to as the delta rule, can be effective. The standard delta rule states that:

$$\Delta w_{ij} = c(T_j - A_j)A_i = c \cdot e_j \cdot A_i \qquad (11)$$

where Δw_{ij} is the change in the weighting on the connection between unit i which is sending activation to unit j, c is a constant, T_j is the target output for unit j, A_j is its actual output, and A_i is the activation state of the unit i. The value of $(T_j - A_j)$ may be thought of as the error term for an individual unit j which is denoted by e_j.

The formal basis of the effectiveness of a modified delta rule is a proof that the rate of decrease of the error in the total output pattern with respect to a change in any single connection weight is equal to the error term for the individual unit multiplied by the activation state of the unit to which it is connected. In notation for any input pattern x:

$$-\frac{dE_x}{dw_{ij}} = e_{xj} \cdot A_{xi}. \qquad (12)$$

It follows that a change in any weight will reduce the error in the output pattern provided the value of the change is proportional to the e_{xj} by A_{xi} product. This is of course precisely the change specified by the delta rule. Moreover, as

the global error, E, is simply the sum of E_x for all patterns, applying the delta rule to all connections in a training sequence involving all the patterns will tend to reduce the global error term to a minimum. The repeated application of the delta rule is an approximation to finding the minimum value of E by the method of gradient descent on the error surface: akin to the Hopfield rule which only allows changes that lead to a lower position on the energy surface or, as in the present case, the error surface.

There is a complication: the error term for individual units, e_j, is not simply the difference between some target activation value and its current value, as in the standard delta rule in equation (11). This can only apply to networks without hidden units and using a simple linear activation function of the form: $A_j = \sum_i w_{ij} \cdot A_i$. A suitable error term for our case here must deal with the non-linearities in the activation function, and with hidden units that have no obvious target activation levels from which to calculate an error. The most significant contribution of Rumelhart, Hinton and Williams (1986) is to demonstrate that a suitable error term can be derived for the output units, from which one can, by recursion, calculate errors for units in any number of hidden layers. They show that for the output units:

$$e_{xj} = (T_{xj} - A_{xj}) \cdot f_j' (\sum_i w_{ij} \cdot A_i) \qquad (13)$$

where $f_j'(\sum_i w_{ij} \cdot A_i)$ is the first derivative of the activation function. Also the error term for a hidden unit is given thus:

$$e_{xi} = f_j' \cdot (\sum_i w_{ij} A_i) \cdot \sum_j e_{xj} \cdot w_{ij} \qquad (14)$$

where the $\sum_j e_{xj}$ term stands for the errors calculated at the level of units above unit i. Together therefore equations (13) and (14) provide a method for computing the error terms for all the units of the network. From these error terms the weight increments can be calculated using the modified delta rule thus:

$$\Delta w_{ij} = e_j \cdot A_i. \qquad (15)$$

[HERE] It follows from the foregoing that there are two phases in learning by the back-propagation of error. In the first phase an input pattern is applied and the activation propagated forward through the network to the output units. Error calculations are made for each output unit based on the difference between the actual and desired activation state multiplied by a function of the net input to the unit. Using these error terms the weights on all connections to the output layer can be adjusted. This process can then be repeated on the penultimate layer, and recursively back through the entire network: the error term for each unit being calculated from the error terms of the units in the layer above to which it is connected and a function of its net input. In this manner the error can be back-propagated from the output to the first layer of hidden units and the appropriate weight changes made throughout the network. If this is repeated for each input pattern many times the process is a good approximation to error minimisation by gradient descent.

This is a very neat solution to a tough problem. As in other cases we have encountered it is not obvious, at the outset, which weights to change and by how much. In order to make such decisions we seem to have to answer questions like: to what degree is a hidden unit deep inside the network responsible for an erroneous output? This is often termed the "credit assignment" problem. Also, as we have seen before, it is not obvious that one can devise a rule that makes decisions about weight changes using only local information. Yet the back-propagation procedure is a further example of such a learning rule.

One reason for the technique's success is to do with the activation function used. If a binary threshold function had been applied, the credit assignment problem would have become intractable, as only small weight changes at one level may have led to profound and large changes at the next level. This is surely a major reason for the failure to invent a learning rule for multilayer perceptrons. The activation function described by equation (9), however, allows small increments in weights that do not have dire consequences for events at subsequent levels. The precise form of the function is not critical. What is required is a change in output that is a continuous function of each unit's input.

Back-propagation of error will approximate to a gradient descent in error space. But is it an efficient gradient descent technique? Also are the error spaces such that only local minima are found? Rumelhart, Hinton and Williams (1986) claim that back-propagation is an efficient method of error reduction which is not plagued by local minima. In a number of simulations they show that networks are able to learn solutions to some of the hard problems, for instance implementing the exclusive-or and discovering parity. Local minima were rarely encountered, leading the authors (1986, p.361) to conclude that:

> Although our learning results do not guarantee that we can find a solution for all solvable problems, our analyses and results have shown that as a practical matter, the error propagation scheme leads to solutions in virtually every case. In short, we believe that we have answered Minsky and Papert's challenge and have found a learning mechanism sufficiently powerful to demonstrate that their pessimism about learning in multilayer machines was misplaced.

Brave men! This issue of the power of the various learning rules for multilayer systems is of critical importance for the development of the connectionist idea. We shall return to it several times, in particular at the end of this chapter and in the final chapter of the book. In the meantime we illustrate some of the properties of back-propagation by describing one of Rumelhart, Hinton and Williams' (1986) simulations.

Consider the set of stimuli shown in Fig. 2.11a. Two characters, a "T" and a "C", are represented by active cells in a two-dimensional array of cells. The things to notice about the set of stimuli are these. Each pattern consists of exactly five cells, and the Ts differ from the Cs by only one cell. There is no simple measure which is rotation-independent that would serve to distinguish Ts from Cs. For instance the set of distances between all possible pairings of cells within each figure is clearly independent of the figure's orientation. Unfortunately it is identical for Ts and Cs (see Minsky & Papert, 1969, p.102). The T–C problem is hard and therefore interesting. Can a multilayer

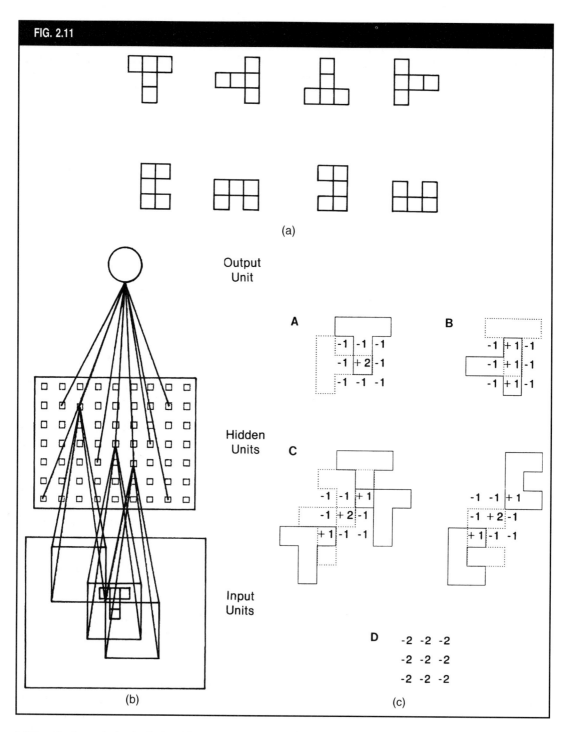

FIG. 2.11

(a)

Output Unit

Hidden Units

Input Units

(b)

(c)

A

-1	-1	-1
-1	+2	-1
-1	-1	-1

B

-1	+1	-1
-1	+1	-1
-1	+1	-1

C

-1	-1	+1
-1	+2	-1
+1	-1	-1

-1	-1	+1
-1	+2	-1
+1	-1	-1

D

-2	-2	-2
-2	-2	-2
-2	-2	-2

(a) The stimuli constituting the T–C problem, (b) the network architecture used to solve the T–C problem, and (c) examples of the weight structures that evolved during learning. From Rumelhart, Hinton, and Williams (1986).

network develop high-order feature-detecting hidden units sufficient to discriminate between the characters?

The network illustrated in Fig. 2.11b learned to solve the T–C problem. The input layer is arranged as a two-dimensional array with each unit representing a cell in two-dimensional visual space. The single layer of hidden units is also arranged spatially: each unit is connected to nine input units, the latter forming a three by three array. Each hidden unit, therefore, can be considered to have a particular receptive field: an area of the input array to which it responds, while ignoring input outside this region. The receptive fields overlap. All hidden units connect to a single output unit which, after learning, is to signal the presence of a T or a C. There are strong echoes of the particular perceptron model we discussed in section 2.4 in this architecture. The significant difference is that in this new case both layers of connections are modifiable.

To ensure that learning was independent of position on the input array, each hidden unit learned the same set of weights. This simplifies the problem somewhat but approximates to a much longer training phase in which all the stimuli are presented many times and with equal frequency at each location. Note also that this short cut does not help to achieve rotational independence. In several simulations the network we have described arrived at solutions to the T–C problem that are best understood by considering the four types of weight pattern displayed in Fig. 2.11c. Each pattern of numbers illustrates the weight pattern that each hidden unit evolved and represents a different solution to the problem. In effect the weight patterns specify a set of feature-detecting units, each of which is sufficient to distinguish a T from a C. In the first case a centre-on surround-off receptive field will signal the presence of a T as this stimulus is capable of overlying the receptive while covering only one cell having a negative weight. A C must cover at least two such inhibitory cells. Given a suitable threshold in the activation function, just one hidden unit will be turned on by a T input, and none by a C. The vertical bar detector constituted by the second weight pattern has similar properties. The third pattern is

interestingly different: a T will activate five hidden units (remember the receptive fields overlap), whereas a C will turn on only three. Notice this differs from the two previous cases in that the presence of a letter is signalled by activity distributed across a set of hidden units. The fourth pattern of weights also leads to a distributed representation of letter identity. In this case the weights are such that a letter will turn off any hidden unit upon whose receptive field it impinges. It turns out that because a C is a more compact form it turns off only 20 units compared to 21 for a T.

This work has touched on important issues which we will return to many times. First, it seems to indicate, again, that learning in multilayer networks is possible. Second, it demonstrates, also again, the representational role of hidden units. Third, in the case of the T–C problem, it has illustrated the difference between local and distributed representation.

2.8 RECURRENT NETWORKS

One adaption of the standard multilayer network, trained using back-propagation, is the recurrent network, which has been used to date mostly to model aspects of language function (discussed extensively in Chapters 5 and 7). In these networks, activation is not just fed-forward through the model on one pass, but it is also re-cycled back so that part of the network's response to a stimulus of trial N becomes part of the input given to the network on trial N + 1. An example of a recurrent network is given in Fig. 2.12.

In this network, an input on trial N first activates the set of hidden units, and from there activation is passed on to the output units. Activity in the hidden units on trial N is also re-cycled to provide part of the input on trial N + 1. This is achieved by having unchanging weights of 1 on the connections from the hidden units to the specific input units they link to (these are sometimes known as the context units). In this way, a network can become sensitive to the temporal order in which inputs are given, because the network's response on any trial is partly determined by its

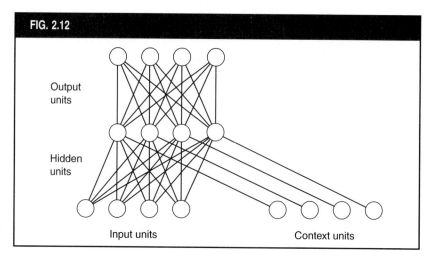

FIG. 2.12

Output units

Hidden units

Input units

Context units

Architecture of a recurrent network.

response on the previous trial. Training can be conducted using back-propagation. Recurrent networks can provide powerful tools for incorporating temporal information into networks.

2.9 LEARNING BY COMPETITION

The Boltzmann and back-propagation learning procedures are forms of supervised learning. That is, learning requires some comparison with a teaching input. We will now describe an unsupervised learning procedure known as competitive learning which can, in principle, be applied to multilayer networks. An early formulation of competitive learning was by von der Malsburg (1973), but it has been discussed in most detail in the work of Stephen Grossberg (see as examples Grossberg, 1976a,b).

The basis of a competitive learning mechanism is illustrated in Fig. 2.13. Each unit in an input layer is connected to each of the output units. The output units are also connected to each other. The input is normalised so that the activation levels of the input units sum to one, thus:

$$A_i = \frac{I_i}{\Sigma_k I_k} \qquad (16)$$

where I_i is a component of the input vector. The layer of output units is a "winner-take-all" net-

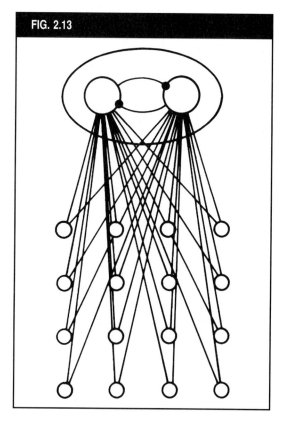

FIG. 2.13

An illustration of a competitive learning network architecture, this example having an array of input units but just a single competitive layer which serves as output. From Rumelhart and Zipser (1985).

work. That is, each unit sums its total weighted input and the unit receiving the greatest takes an activation value of one, while all the other (losing) units are zero. The learning rule involves changes in the weights on the connections to only the winning unit. Thus if the jth output unit wins, the changes in the weights are given by:

$$\Delta w_{ij} = C \cdot A_j \cdot (-w_{ij} + A_i) \qquad (17)$$

where C is a constant. In Grossberg (1976b) there is a proof that this learning regime will classify input patterns with each output unit representing a particular category. This finding is qualified by the number of input patterns needing not to be too many relative to the number of output units, or the number of categories among the input population needing not to be too great.

Such a finding is more profound than perhaps it seems at first. It implies that a competitive learning network is capable of discovering the underlying structure of a population, without any supervision. It can be shown that very subtle or high-order statistical regularities may be discovered, as simulations reported in Rumelhart and Zipser (1985) illustrate. Sixteen input units, shown as a four by four array, were each connected to two output units which were linked together in a winner-take-all manner (as in the example shown in Fig. 2.13). The stimulus population was simply the set of activation states of the input array in which just two adjacent units were active (dipole units). Using a competitive learning rule that was essentially the same as the one described earlier (see Grossberg, 1987, for a comparison of the two), Rumelhart and Zipser (1985) found that their network had invented an interesting way of dividing the stimuli set into two groups. This can be seen in Fig. 2.14 which shows the weight configurations before and after learning. The colour of the circles show which of the two output units had the greater weighting for a particular input unit. The links between the circles indicate which of the two output units was activated given an input pattern in which just the two units indicated by the circles were active: a thick line means unit 1, a thin line indicates unit 2. Before learning, as one would expect, the distribution of weights was

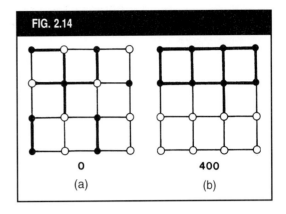

FIG. 2.14

The weight structure (a) before learning and (b) after learning in the dipole experiment (see text). From Rumelhart and Zipser (1985).

unordered. After learning a clear spatial arrangement was found, in which active pairs in one part of the array activated output unit 1, while those in another part activated output unit 2. Yet the network knew nothing about the spatial properties of the inputs! The four by four array is to be found only in the illustrations — and in our imaginations. What the network received is simply a 16-element vector in which neighbouring units in the two-dimensional array bear no more special relationship to one another than do non-neighbouring units. In effect it discovered the statistics of the set of vectors that underlie or map onto the spatial properties from which the set was generated. The network tuned itself to a particular environment of stimuli. This would seem a very sensible facility for any organism that has to adapt to uncertain worlds. We will have more to say on this later.

How may competitive learning be extended to multilayer systems? We have seen that the units in the winner-take-all network can become feature detectors or classifiers. These units may serve as the input to others which use combinations of features to signal the identity of the input to the system. Thus inputs that are not linearly separable are decomposed into components that can be successfully analysed at a higher level. Another network architecture, that of Kohonen's (1984b) self-organising feature map, uses this technique and will be described in Chapter 4.

2.10 RADIAL BASIS FUNCTION AND ART NETWORKS

In standard feed-forward networks (section 2.7), activation value in units in a hidden layer is a non-decreasing nonlinear function of the product of the input (in the feeding layer) and the connection weight. This is shown in Fig. 2.15a, which has x and y axes corresponding to the activation values in two input units (x and y) and a z axis corresponding to the magnitude of activation in a hidden unit. In Fig. 2.15b, the activation profile for a different form of network, a Radial Basis

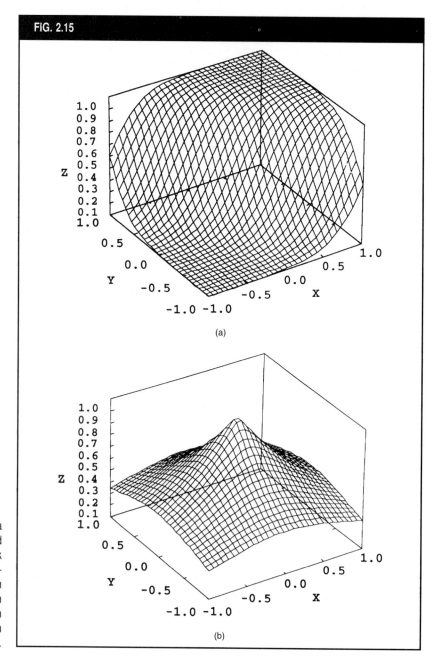

FIG. 2.15

(a)

(b)

(a) activation profile of a hidden unit in a standard feed-forward network trained using back-propagation (b) activation profile of a hidden unit in a Radial Basis Function (RBF) network (when $r = 2$).

Function (RBF) net, is given. Note that hidden units in RBF nets use a form of local "receptive field", in which a unit is maximally excited if the input is at a particular position in the "activation space", and the degree of activity in the unit decreases as the input activation moves from the preferred position. In contrast to this, hidden units in a standard feed-forward net respond to a broad range of inputs across the activation space. In such feed-forward networks, learning involves setting a boundary across the activation space; for example, given the activation profile in Fig. 2.15a, the network will assign low input values (from input units x and y) to one output category (high z score) and high input values to another (with a low z score) — the boundary is set between low and high activation values coming in across both input units. In contrast to this, RBF nets attempt to tune the activation profiles of the hidden units so that particular units respond maximally to particular patterns in the input set. In Fig. 2.15b, the hidden unit responds maximally to inputs of zero on the x and y input units, but responds much less as the x and y values each move away from zero.

The activation function for hidden unit j in an RBF network is as follows:

$$a_j^{hid} = \exp(-c(\Sigma_i w_i |h_{ji} - a_i^{in|r})^{q/r}) \qquad (18)$$

where c is a positive constant, and r and q are constants determining the nature of the similarity relation computed between the input and the hidden unit and the gradient of this relationship (e.g. when $r = 2$, the relation will correspond to the Euclidean distance where excitation of the hidden unit is maximal if the input falls at the centre of its "receptive field" in the activation space, and excitation decreases monotonically if the input falls further from the centre of this receptive field; as q increases in value, so the gradient becomes sharper for the fall-off in activation from the centre of the hidden unit's receptive field). Learning in such networks operates in a somewhat different way from that involved in standard feed-forward nets trained using back-propagation. For example, in a standard feed-forward model, learning involves setting and re-setting the same set of weights as all the inputs in a training set are sampled, and hidden units may represent more than input exemplar. However, in an RBF network, there may be as many hidden units as there are exemplars. Learning can involve an error-correction procedure to "tune" one hidden unit to respond maximally to an exemplar. If exemplars are similar to one another, and so activate more than one hidden unit, weights to and from these hidden units are adjusted to favour one unit in future over the other; in this way, learning is competitive, and hidden units tend to develop more local representations than in standard feed-forward nets trained using back-propagation. Indeed, hidden units representing similar inputs tend to have their receptive fields pushed in opposite directions in the input space as learning proceeds (to maximise dissimilarity). These properties (of representing one exemplar via one hidden unit and of pushing in opposite directions units responding to similar inputs, as learning proceeds) have particular consequences for modelling human learning, and in Chapter 3 (section 3.3) we discuss one application of an RBF network to category learning. In Chapter 4, we discuss an application relating to object recognition (section 4.3).

Another model that can learn local representations of stimuli is the ART network developed by Grossberg and colleagues (Carpenter & Grossberg, 1987a,b; Grossberg, 1976a,b, 1987). ART stands for Adaptive Resonance Theory. ART networks operate using a resonance process in which initial activation values on a set of "output" classifier units are adjusted by continued recycling of input through sets of trained weights. The networks also have arousal or orienting units which, if activated, lead to inhibition and re-setting of the classifier units; in learning, this re-setting can enable new units to come into play to represent unfamiliar inputs. A cycle of activity through an ART network is shown in Fig. 2.16. Input activates a particular pattern of activation (X) in a set of input units (F_1), and this activity in the input units also has the effect of inhibiting the arousal unit (A). Activation is then mapped from the input units through a set of learned weights to classifier units (F_2), where one pattern of activity may be generated (Y). The classifier units are competitive, so

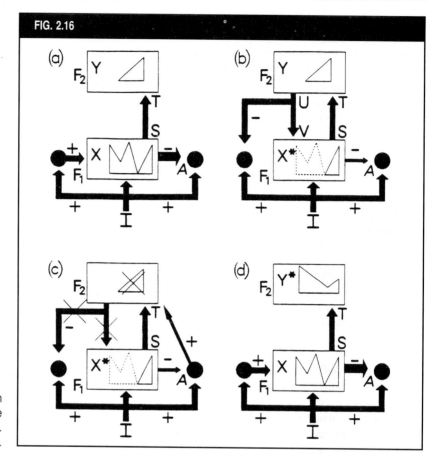

FIG. 2.16

Cycle of activity through
an Adaptive Resonance
Theory (ART) network.
From Grossberg (1987).

tending to favour a local representation of the input pattern. Activity in the classifier units is subsequently recycled down through an additional set of weights to adjust activity in the input units (F_1), with there being inhibition of activity that mis-matches that generated from the classifier units (F_2). If there is no mis-match, a stable pattern of activity is generated in which the model "resonates" to the input. Normally, there are some changes over time in the activity values in the two sets of units (so that different representations, X^* and Y^*, are respectively generated in the input and classifier units). If the initial representation (Y) in the classifier units does not provide a good match to the input representation (X), then the top-down feed-back will inhibit the input representation. When this occurs, the arousal unit (A) is re-activated. This provides a non-specific signal that re-sets the classifier units, enabling a different

classifier unit to "win" any competition if the same stimulus is subsequently presented.

Learning in ART networks involves changing the two sets of weights, from the input (F_1) to the classifier units (F_2), and from the classifier units (F_2) back to the input units (F_1): the bottom-up and the top-down weights. The weights are changed at a rate that reflects the activation values in (respectively) either the input or the output units (for the bottom-up and top-down weights) (using a procedure similar to Hebbian learning). These changes operate relatively slowly (determined by a "rate of change" parameter), and so only come into effect when the network reaches a stable (resonating) state.

ART networks have several interesting properties. They use an unsupervised learning scheme, and by incorporating an "arousal" mechanism, they have relatively automatic procedures for ensuring that learning is "spread" around the classifier units (when there is a mis-match between an input and stored representations); also, due to competitive interactions between the classifier units, units are biased towards developing sparse representations of input. To date, however, these networks have not been used extensively to mimic psychological data at a detailed level. One application is discussed in Chapter 6 (section 6.9).

2.11 CLASSIFYING AND ASSESSING THE MODELS

The reader may be rather perplexed by the variety of models we have introduced, and may want to know how to choose between them. What are the important differences between models? What significance do the differences have? Are the models, in fact, in competition with each other? How are they to be assessed?

The nine main networks discussed in this chapter are shown classified on four dimensions in Table 2.1. We will discuss the implications for network performance of each dimension and, in doing so, demonstrate their inter-relations.

1. Three major differences in the activation rule have arisen in our discussion: those between rules that are linear or non-linear, deterministic or stochastic, and synchronous or asynchronous.

    Perhaps the most significant of these three is the broad contrast between linear and non-linear activation functions. The associative network illustrates the use of a simple linear function: the activity level of an output unit is simply equal to its summed weighted input. The strong constraint that follows from the adoption of such a rule is that classifications can only be made if the input patterns are orthogonal. So for instance the exclusive-or function could not be implemented. As we have seen, units that take linear values of input activation states multiplied by the weights, but then pass them

through a threshold, to create a form of non-linear output, can be arranged into networks capable of computing functions like the exclusive-or. But learning rules exist for only single-layer networks of this type. Thus there is a paradox: linear threshold units can compute more interesting functions, but these require more than one layer and so networks of linear threshold units can learn to compute only what can in fact be computed by networks of linear units. We saw that the back-propagation solution to this difficulty depended in part on the use of a continuous, semi-linear activation function.

Of the networks discussed, only the Boltzmann machine used a stochastic activation rule. In this case, this allowed, among other things, an elegant solution to the problem of local energy minima in multilayer networks, as the probability of escaping from them could be manipulated in the process of simulated annealing.

Both the Hopfield network and the Boltzmann machine had asynchronous update of the activation values. This tends to produce more stable systems in which unhelpful variations in the network's state are avoided.

2. Two significant variations in learning regime should be noted: supervised or unsupervised and error reduction or stochastic. Some people have argued that supervised learning is rather unbiological. It seems, to them, that there are no known brain mechanisms that could provide the sort of teaching input that is generally required by a supervised learning procedure. We will evaluate this issue in the next chapter on learning and memory.

    Again the Boltzmann machine is unique, among the networks considered here, in having a stochastic learning procedure. Just as a stochastic activation function allows escape from local minima in energy landscapes, so a stochastic learning rule allows escape from local minima in error landscapes. In theory this should provide an important advantage over those deterministic techniques that allow only reductions

TABLE 2.1

Classification of different types of network

	Activation rule	Learning style	Layers	Connections
Perceptron	Threshold Synchronous Deterministic	Supervised Deterministic	Single	Asymmetric
Associative	Linear Synchronous Deterministic	Supervised Deterministic	Single	Asymmetric
Hopfield	Linear Asynchronous Deterministic	Supervised Deterministic	Single	Symmetric
Boltzmann	Semi-linear Asynchronous Stochastic	Supervised Stochastic	Multi	Symmetric
Back-propagation	Semi-linear Synchronous Deterministic	Supervised Deterministic	Multi	Asymmetric
Recurrent	Semi-linear Synchronous Deterministic	Supervised Deterministic	Multi	Asymmetric
Competitive	Winner-take-all Synchronous Deterministic	Unsupervised Deterministic	Multi	Asymmetric
Radial Basis Function (RBF)	Non-linear, receptive field Synchronous Deterministic	Supervised Deterministic	Multi	Asymmetric
Adaptive Resonance Theory (ART)	Semi-linear Synchronous Deterministic	Unsupervised	Single	Asymmetric

in error, such as perceptron convergence and back-propagation. Clearly if a rule states that only weight changes that reduce the global error are allowed, then there can be no escape from local minima into which the network happens to fall. This is something we will return to shortly.

3. We have already indicated that the distinction between single and multilayer systems is a central issue in the development of connectionism. We will return to it a great deal!

4. An issue we have not mentioned, however, is to do with how information is transmitted within a network. In some, information transmission is one-way: activation can only pass forward from input to output, perhaps via hidden units, once learning has taken place. In others, though, there is a 2-way flow of information (in Hopfield networks, Boltzmann machines, recurrent and ART networks). We will discuss other examples in Chapters 5, 6, and 7, where they have been

applied to psychological phenomena in language comprehension and production. Such systems can be very difficult to analyse because of the highly dynamic or interactive relationships between inputs and output. As the input of one unit will affect the output of another, and this in turn can affect the input of the first unit, such architectures can be very unstable (indeed some would say chaotic in the mathematical sense). Fortunately for our concerns here it has been proven by Cohen and Grossberg (1983) that a certain sub-class of recurrent networks are stable: those in which $w_{ij} = w_{ji}$ and $w_{ii} = 0$. This is of course precisely the case with the Boltzmann machine and the Hopfield network.

These are not the only dimensions on which networks can vary. Nor are the particular variants of the four dimensions we have discussed the only significant ones. More will be introduced in subsequent chapters. The interested reader also has a number of sources available which will provide a more comprehensive review: Kohonen (1984a,b), Amari (1977), Feldman and Ballard (1982), Rumelhart, Hinton, and Williams (1986), and Wasserman (1989).

How to assess the networks? As a major purpose of this book is to assess the utility of connectionism for work in cognitive science and psychology, we should indicate what criteria are relevant to this purpose. We will now consider three candidate criteria: computational properties, biological plausibility, and behavioural properties. In our discussion of them that follows it will be clear that the distinctions are rather arbitrary.

2.11.1 Computational properties

Minsky and Papert (1969) provide the paradigm example of an analysis of the computational properties of connectionist systems. They prove various theorems which show what particular networks can and cannot do — in principle. It is generally accepted that this is the most underdeveloped area in the current work on connectionism. We badly need some formal analysis of the limitations of the

various new learning rules for multilayer systems. For example, as back-propagation is an error-reduction procedure it should be threatened by local minima. Rumelhart et al. (1986a) show that this is not a problem for the limited number of cases they have simulated. But this is not good enough, as Minsky and Papert (p.261 of the 1988 expanded edition of *Perceptrons*) point out:

> . . . the pretence that problems do not exist can deflect us from valuable insights that could come from examining things more carefully. As the field of connectionism becomes more mature, the quest for a general solution to all learning problems will evolve into an understanding of which types of learning processes are likely to work on which classes of problems . . . We will really need to know a great deal more about the nature of those surfaces for each specific realm of problems that we want to solve.

What is needed is a formal assessment of the nature of the minima problem in multilayer networks and the limitations of the various learning procedures applied to them. In general such work will be regarded as beyond the scope of this book.

2.11.2 Biological plausibility

We argued in the first chapter that one great attraction of the connectionist approach was its gross similarities with aspects of biological computation. The descriptions of the models in this chapter should convince the reader of just how gross are the similarities! For instance back-propagation does not seem to map onto any known brain mechanism, requiring as it does a "teacher" who computes precise error signals and passes them back down the network. This may or may not matter. Not all connectionist networks are intended to be neural networks. There are some important conceptual issues tied up with the question of biological plausibility which we will be in a better position to discuss after we have considered the application of the models to problems in psychology and cognitive science. Consequently we will postpone this discussion until the final chapter.

2.11.3 Behavioural properties

The main criterion for validating the models on which we focus in this book is their behavioural properties. What are "behavioural properties"? They are clearly related to computational properties. Or at least we hope they are, as our aim is to formulate computational explanation of behaviours! However the methods of analysis are not, in large part, those of the logician or mathematician. Also obviously, the behaviours of interest will be closely related to the behaviours commonly investigated by psychologists and cognitive scientists. These are more likely to concern how well a particular network can respond to, say, visual input than whether it can compute an exclusive-or. Just as we illustrated what we meant by computational properties by pointing to an example, we illustrate the meaning of behavioural properties by providing examples. The next six chapters are devoted to those examples.

3

Learning and memory

The categories into which we divide mental processes are more a product of the intellectual history of our disciplines than a reflection of the natural categories of mind. Or at least that is how it seems to us! A typical psychology textbook will have sections on perception, memory, language and so forth. This book also conforms to this pattern. Yet of course the distinctions are not clear. In particular memory, in its various senses, is implicated in all mental functions. Language use, for example, obviously depends on long-term memory for linguistic entities such as meanings, word forms, and pronunciations. It is appropriate therefore to begin our description of explicitly psychological connectionist models with simulations of long-term memory. Models of more immediate memory processes are introduced in Chapter 5.

This chapter begins by examining issues to do with associative memory, into which connectionism seems to have injected new life.

3.1 ASSOCIATIVE MEMORY

Recall our discussion of simple linear associative networks in section 2.5 of the previous chapter. We demonstrated that a network, consisting of two layers of units, whose activity is simply the weighted sum of their inputs, can associate patterns of activity over the two layers. Weightings appropriate for associating together several pattern pairs can be found by the repeated application of a Hebbian-like learning rule, provided the input patterns are orthogonal and each are unit vectors. In such circumstances recall is perfect for each of n pairs in a network of n units. However if the input patterns are not orthogonal there will be interference or "cross-talk" between pattern pairs, increasing as the number of associations approach n. In such cases the differences between the desired and actual outputs may be quantified, for instance using the sum of the squares of these differences. In section 2.7 we described a learning rule that could find the minimum mean squares error in a set of outputs. This delta rule can also be applied to simple linear associative memories so as to escape the constraint of inputs having to be orthogonal.

Kohonen (1984a) derived proofs that error-reduction techniques applied to linear associative memories would lead to weight matrices that represented the "optimal linear associative mapping", by which is meant a set of weights that minimises the output errors for a set of associated inputs. He was able to show that for a set of inputs that were linearly independent (where no one input could be expressed as a linear combination of some of the others) the technique would result in error-free associations, and where the linear independence criterion was not met, the matrix yielding the minimum error in outputs would be arrived at. Some of the properties of such systems are illustrated by the performance of a simple associative network which was trained to classify images of faces by optimal associative mapping. The network was trained to classify pictures of 10 individual faces using a training set consisting of 10 individuals, each shown from several viewpoints. The inputs consisted of vectors whose components represented the average grey level for specified regions of a particular photograph. The outputs were patterns of activity on 10 units, with each unit standing for a different face. The network, after training, was able to classify faces correctly, even when given a novel viewpoint not presented in the training phase. The network can be said to have generalised. More precisely: it discovered statistical regularities among a complicated data set which allow it to categorise or divide the data set into prescribed classes. The statistical properties were clearly robust enough to handle novel cases.

Autoassociation is a special case of associative memory. Quite simply the input patterns are associated with a copy of themselves on the output units. This may seem an odd thing to do, but it gives rise to interesting properties in networks. Kohonen associated 100 faces using an error-reduction technique similar to that in the previous example. After training, incomplete inputs, with large sections of the image missing, continued to elicit the complete version on the output units. Similarly, a degraded or noisy input evoked the undegraded version on the output units.

Neither of Kohonen's examples of associative memory should be regarded as an attempt to model human face recognition or classification (if they were they would be discussed in the next chapter rather than here!). What they do is demonstrate two important general characteristics of simple linear associative memories. First they show an ability to generalise by correctly classifying examples that were not part of the training set. In a sense the weight matrix embodies a prototype of each category, abstracted from the examples presented

in the training phase, which is sufficient for categorisation of new exemplars. Second they are robust in the face of incomplete or degraded cues. Human associative memory is transparently robust, content-addressable, and abstractive (recall the example in Chapter 1). So our network models are psychologically valid at a very general level. However we want finer-grained comparisons than this. We aim where possible to fit models to behavioural data derived from experimental studies rather than anecdote. In the case of human associative memory McClelland and Rumelhart (1985, 1986) illustrated this finer-grained comparison of model and data.

Consider the simple network of eight units shown in Fig. 3.1. Each unit had a single external input and a single output which was broadcast to the other seven units in addition to the outside world. The activation level of each unit was a function of its net input and was a real number in the range -1 to $+1$. The net input to a unit was the external input received on the input line plus the internal input from the other seven units, with this internal input being given by:

$$\text{Internal}_i = \Sigma_j A_j \cdot W_{ij}. \tag{1}$$

That is the now familiar sum of the weighted activation levels of the other units. If the net input to a unit was positive, its activity level was increased by an amount proportional to the difference between its present value and the maximum value of $+1$ (the constant of proportionality). In the case of a negative net input, the unit's activity was decreased by an amount proportional to the difference between its present value and the minimum value of -1. In both cases a decay factor was added which had the effect of pulling all values back towards a resting state of zero, once an external stimulus was removed. These two parameters, the constants of proportionality and the decay factor, were the same for all the units.

Each input line could be clamped to a particular value within the prescribed range of $+1$ to -1 so that the set of eight values constituted an input pattern to the system. In these circumstances the network iterated to reach a stable configuration of

FIG. 3.1

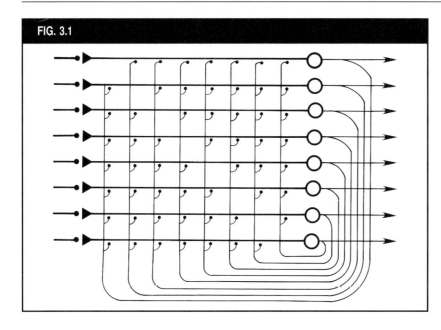

A simple network of eight interconnected units which may be trained to associate patterns of input with patterns of output as described in the text. From McClelland and Rumelhart (1986).

activity in which the increment in activity level entailed by the net input to a given unit was exactly balanced by the decay factor. In short, the network "relaxed", in the sense described in Chapter 1, to a final state. In fact McClelland and Rumelhart (1985) reported that stability was always achieved in less than 50 cycles in networks of this type with up to 24 units. They also showed that application of a form of the delta rule to the relaxed states of the network would serve to store several patterns in the form of an autoassociative memory. Recall that the delta rule minimised the difference between two sets of patterns of activation: a target pattern and an actual pattern (see equation 11 in Chapter 2). In our present example the rule was used to reduce the difference between the net external input to a single unit and the net input from the other units in the system, employing the external input as a "supervisor" and changing the internal weights between units. In this way the internal inputs received by any unit came to model its external input for any input pattern it has learned. This network is therefore another example of an autoassociator. As a consequence the system tended to "fill-in" missing or distorted components of a learnt input. The learning rule may be stated thus:

$$\Delta W_{ij} = C(E_i - I_i)A_j \qquad (2)$$

where ΔW_{ij} is the change in the connection strength between the ith and jth unit, C is a constant, E_i is the external input to the ith unit, Ii is its internal input, and A_j is the activation level of the jth unit.

This learning rule is powerful in the sense that it will discover the set of weightings that reduce the term $(E_i - I_i)$ to zero for all inputs provided such a set of weightings exists for that population of inputs. In fact solutions exist for only those populations that conform to the linear predictability constraint. This entails that the input to any single unit must be predictable from a linear combination of the activations of all the other units.

As in the earlier examples, McClelland and Rumelhart (1985, 1986) showed that the network could learn to classify. Using a 24-unit network, they generated three arbitrary prototypes consisting of an ordered pattern of 16 +1 and −1 values. Patterns one and two were correlated (r = 0.5) and pattern three was orthogonal to the others. Each prototype was given a name, "dog", "cat", or "bagel", which was represented by an eight-component pattern each of which was orthogonal to the others. During training, exemplars of each prototype were presented in combination with the appropriate name: units one to eight received the name pattern, units nine to twenty-four received the exemplar. The exemplars were all minor distortions of their prototype constructed by changing the sign of some values in a pattern — with a 10% probability of any single value being changed. For each of the three categories 50 name–exemplar pairs were presented with the weights being adjusted after each presentation. In order to test what had been learned, the network was subsequently presented with each of the three names alone and with each of the three prototypes alone. The prototype patterns and test results are summarised in Fig. 3.2.

Given only a name, the network responded with a good approximation to the appropriate prototype pattern on units nine to twenty-four. Given only a prototype, units one to eight relaxed to a good approximation to the appropriate name pattern. There are several aspects of this performance that deserve emphasis. First it is clear that the network is capable of storing or remembering a number of non-orthogonal categories of pattern. Obviously as the number of patterns increase and as their similarity increases so performance will degrade. However given what may be achieved with just 24 units the reader is invited to imagine the performance of a system with say 10^{10} units (such as the brain!). Second, the network is capable of pattern completion: it fills in missing parts of inputs. This is shown by its ability to recall the name, given only the visual prototype, or its ability to recall the prototype given only the name. It is therefore a basis for a content-addressable memory. Third, the network has in effect extracted a prototype representation from a set of exemplars — note that the network was trained only on the exemplars, not the prototype. Fourth, it also captures some specific information about the exemplars themselves. For instance those cases that are frequent during the learning phase will leave a greater "impression" in the set of weights than those that are infrequent. This is illustrated by a

---

FIG. 3.2

	Name Pattern	Visual Pattern
Pattern for dog prototype	+ − + − + − + −	+ − + + − − − − + + + + + − − −
Response to dog name		+3 −4 +4 +4 −4 −4 −4 −4 +4 +4 +4 +3 +4 −4 −4 −3
Response to dog visual pattern	+5 −4 +4 −5 +5 −4 +4 −4	
Pattern for cat prototype	+ + − − + + − −	+ − + + − − − − + − + − + + − +
Response to cat name		+4 −3 +4 +4 −4 −3 −3 −4 +4 −4 +4 −4 +4 +4 −4 +4
Response to cat visual pattern	+5 +4 −4 −5 +4 +4 −4 −4	
Pattern for bagel prototype	+ − − + + − − +	+ + − + − + + − + − − + + + + −
Response to bagel name		+3 +4 −4 +4 −4 +4 +4 −4 +4 −4 −4 +4 +3 +4 +4 −4
Response to bagel visual pattern	+4 −4 −4 +4 +4 −4 −4 +4	

Note: Decimal points have been suppressed for clarity; thus, an entry of +4 represents an activation value of +.4.

The activation states of the associative network for the prototypes and its response to the name and object patterns for the three items. From McClelland and Rumelhart (1986).

further simulation described by McClelland and Rumelhart (1985, 1986). Precisely as in the last example, a 24-unit network was taught to associate a name pattern with a prototype pattern using different exemplars of the prototype for each training presentation. In addition during training the network was presented repeatedly with two particular exemplars, each derived in the usual manner from the prototype and paired with a unique name pattern. With this regime the network learned to respond with the prototype name pattern whenever presented with a pattern of that category, except in the case of the two repeated exemplars when it would respond with their particular name patterns. Conversely, when given the names, it would produce the appropriate category patterns. As the authors point out, this is akin to learning to categorise dogs correctly, while also learning to name correctly two particular dogs, say "Fido" and "Rover". Because of the salience of Fido and Rover during the learning phase each was represented independently, among the weights, despite their patterns being very close to those of all other dogs.

The ability to represent both prototypical information and information about specific instances is the basis of the network's success in modelling some well established experimental effects; that is, so-called familiarity and repetition effects. The former refers to the fact that, in most circumstances, familiar objects are easier to recognise than unfamiliar ones. In the network we have been considering, patterns that are familiar are quite simply those that have been presented previously and therefore are represented individually in the weightings. The response of the autoassociative network to such patterns will therefore be stronger than to patterns that have not been presented previously and are therefore not represented in the weightings. Repetition priming effects refer to the response facilitation that may be observed when a stimulus is repeated. For example Scarborough, Cortese, and Scarborough (1977) reported a facilitation in deciding that a letter string was a word or not when the same word appeared earlier in a sequence of such trials. Warren and Morton (1982) found a facilitation in the recognition of line drawings if there had been a prior presentation of a drawing of a different object of the same name;

two different chairs, say. If the two drawings were in fact identical the facilitation was larger. Similar findings, but in the field of face recognition, have been reported by Ellis, Young, Flude, and Hay (1987b). They observed substantial priming effects on the recognition of an identical face, reduced priming for a similar photograph of the same face, and a further reduced priming effect for a dissimilar photograph of the same face (although all priming effects were reliable relative to recognition performance in an unprimed baseline).

Repetition priming effects of this sort can be accounted for by a system that is being constantly "tuned" by environmental inputs, as in the case of the network we are considering here. In a simulation of priming experiments, McClelland and Rumelhart (1985, 1986) had a 24-unit network learn eight prototypes by presenting exemplars as in the previous simulations. Priming was simulated by presenting the network with new examples of four of the previously learned prototypes, applying the delta rule to the relaxed network in each case. The system's responses were then tested with three classes of stimuli: patterns identical to the primes, patterns that were new exemplars of primed prototypes, and exemplars of the unprimed prototypes. In a manner analogous to the Warren and Morton (1982) findings, the network's strongest response was to identical patterns, next strongest to new exemplars of the primes, and weakest to unprimed patterns. Moreover if in the priming phase entirely new, unlearned, patterns were presented in addition to the new examples of learned ones, interesting effects were observed. The priming effect was found to be greater for the new patterns than for the previously learned ones. This is consistent with human experimental data which shows greater priming for non-words compared to words when subjects were having to identify the letters in letters strings (Feustel, Shiffrin, & Salasoo, 1983; Salasoo, Shiffrin, & Feustel, 1985). McClelland and Rumelhart's model is presented at the end of this chapter, and the reader may find it useful to work through the points we have covered in detail.

The foregoing shows that not only do associative networks have coarse properties that capture some of the flavour of human memory systems, but the similarity continues at finer resolutions. Some of the observed effects of familiarity and repetition priming arise in associative networks because of the intrinsic nature of information storage in such devices. Obviously there are models other than associative networks which can account for repetition priming effects. In Chapter 4, we review the interactive activation and competition (IAC) model of face recognition, proposed by Burton, Bruce, and colleagues (Burton, 1994; Burton & Bruce, 1993; Burton, Bruce, & Johnston, 1990), which explicitly deals with repetition priming of faces, using a Hebbian learning scheme. An older psychological account is provided by Morton's (1969, 1979) logogen model. In the original formulation a logogen was an internal recognition device for a word. Associated with each logogen was a level of activity which increased as evidence accumulated, from the senses or from the context, for the presence of the word for which it stood. When a threshold of activation was passed, the word was recognised in the sense that it was available for response purposes. Activation then returned to a resting level. Note that words that are presented frequently will come to have a higher level of activation within their logogens than will words presented infrequently. In effect it is as if the threshold for low-frequency words was higher than for high-frequency words, the result is that familiarity effects occur (low-frequency words being harder to recognise). According to this account, repetition effects are just a shorter-term version of familiarity effects. Repetition effects reflect the temporary activation within a logogen before the activation decomposes to resting level. Notice that aspects of this theory are derived from what is known about word recognition and the human experimental data. The changes in threshold are postulated because of what is known. It is therefore rather post-hoc. This is not the case with the network account: familiarity and repetition effects are truly predicted or "drop-out" of the way the network learns. Notice too that the graded nature of priming effects is expected in a system that stores information as a composite in a set of weights: related primes will produce some facilitation but not as much as identical primes; whereas the logogen account of such graded effects requires

additional assumptions about the manner in which logogens may be activated. For instance, if partial activation can be transmitted between logogens, then similar stimuli may partially activate each other's stored representations, enabling graded priming effects to occur.

Perhaps the two accounts are not in competition, however, they may simply be explanations at different levels. The network story may be an account of how logogens might be implemented in hardware. Or indeed an account of the implementation of any theory that is consistent with the experimental facts, such as those in which the representation of specific instances, rather than prototypes, result from learning (Hintzman, 1986; Medin & Schaffer, 1978). The issue of levels of explanation is important and controversial (Broadbent, 1985; Rumelhart & McClelland, 1985). We will return to it in the final chapter in detail and again in this chapter in passing.

There are some important limitations to the network explanation we have described, however. Perhaps most seriously, in an elaborated form it fails to account for the precise details of repetition effects. It is silent, for instance, as to why priming tends to be larger between stimuli presented in the same modality than between stimuli presented in different modalities (pictures and words, for instance; Warren & Morton, 1982). We might assume that, within McClelland and Rumelhart's distributed memory system, associations are formed between stimuli from all modalities (indeed, just this approach has been taken in some models of semantic memory that we will review in Chapter 8; Farah & McClelland, 1991, being an example). In this case, effects of updating the weights by the earlier presentation of a picture (say) should carry over to affect the subsequent recognition of a word. Psychological evidence suggests that such effects, if present, are relatively weak. One solution to this is to use a more complex model in which both modality-specific as well as modality-independent memory stores are represented. The IAC model of Burton, Bruce, and colleagues does this, although as a formal model of face recognition it will be dealt with in Chapter 4.

Associative networks are not confined to storing information about objects and concepts. Marr

(1969) has proposed a theory in which the cerebellum is viewed as a type of associative network whose properties underlie the acquisition and execution of motor skills. The network is said to consist of a number of different types of unit, with each type corresponding to one of the five types of neuron found in cerebellar cortex. It is illustrated in Fig. 3.3. The function of the network is to learn sequences of motor actions, or elements of actions, so that after training a partial or simple signal will elicit complex behavioural sequences. The output of the system is the pattern of activity of the Purkinje neurons. The latter receive excitatory input, via the climbing fibres, from olivary neurons, each of which encodes an "elemental movement" and which together comprise a dictionary of elemental movements. A given motor action will consist of a particular sequence of elemental movements, and the dictionary of elements is such that all possible actions can be composed out of some subset of them. Each olivary neuron is connected to just one Purkinje neuron. Thus the output of the Purkinje neurons may be viewed as a set of instructions for the execution of a motor action or, in other words, a motor program. However the Purkinje output may be associated with the activity signalled by another set of connections: the mossy fibre projections. These provide information about context such as what action elements are appropriate given the preceding element.

In the model, the cerebellum is, in effect, trained by other parts of the brain in the following manner. Instructions for specific sequences of action elements from elsewhere in the cerebrum result in activity in the olivary and hence Purkinje neurons. Appropriate actions are initiated as a result of this neural activity. When stimulated by the olivary activity the Purkinje neurons are also receiving input via the mossy fibres, which signal the context in which the olivary activity is occurring. The mossy fibre input is associated with the Purkinje output by the methods similar to those we have already described for simple associative networks. After training, explicit instructions are no longer needed for particular action sequences because the cerebellum will "recognise" known contexts indicated by the activity state of the mossy fibres and respond with appropriate Purkinje output. In effect the cerebellum now takes care of or

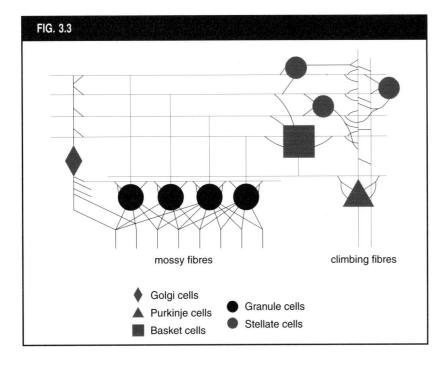

FIG. 3.3

mossy fibres   climbing fibres

◆ Golgi cells
▲ Purkinje cells   ● Granule cells
■ Basket cells   ● Stellate cells

The architecture of Marr's (1969) model of the cerebellum. The text describes how the mossy fibre and climbing fibre activity patterns are associated.

controls learned action sequences in familiar contexts. The cerebrum has delegated responsibility to the cerebellum.

This attractive theory is made more compelling by the manner in which certain general requirements of learning in associative networks appear to be met by the neurophysiology of the cerebellum. For example, as we have already indicated, learning in associative networks is strongly affected by the relationships between members of the input population. Highly correlated inputs would tend to limit the efficiency of learning. Marr (1969) suggests that the function of the granule cells (see Fig. 3.3) is to decorrelate the mossy fibre inputs. This ability to separate patterns may be understood in terms of the following analysis. The activity in the mossy fibres may be represented by elements, termed codons by Marr, which correspond to small subsets of active fibres. Assume that granule neurons are fired only by codons, with each neuron being so wired that it may be fired by several codons. In these circumstances the granule neurons can be said to be vehicles for a codon representation of the mossy fibre input. The overlap between two mossy fibre activity patterns may be expressed by the ratio W/L where W is the number of elements in common and L the number of active fibres. The overlap between the codons representing the same two patterns can be shown to be less: it tends towards $(W/L)^R$ where R is the codon size. For example if codons consisted of just five active fibres, inputs having an overlap of 0.5 (half of all elements in common) would result in an overlap of only 0.03 between their codon representations. So very similar input patterns can have significantly less similar representations as activity patterns among granule neurons, and associating the latter with the Purkinje outputs is likely to produce more efficient learning. A very neat solution! Note also that the size of codon that will fire a given granule neuron will depend on that neuron's threshold. If the threshold is low, codons of small size will suffice to fire granule neurons; hence many of these will be active if lots of mossy fibres were active. Unfortunately it can be shown that as the number of active granule neurons increases, the number of patterns that can be learned by a

Purkinje neuron falls sharply: Marr (1969) estimates that up to 480 patterns could be learned by a single cell when each pattern consists of 500 active elements, but only 11 when the number of active elements is 20,000. This problem is solved by the activity of the golgi neurons (again see Fig. 3.3) which raise the thresholds of the granule neurons and are themselves driven by mossy fibre activity. Thus memory overload is avoided because the threshold of granule cells increases as the number of active mossy fibres grows. A similar mechanism aids retrieval: the basket and stellate neurons seen in Fig. 3.3 inhibit Purkinje neurons so as to prevent spurious outputs from the latter as the number of active elements arising from the granule cells increases.

The theory of cerebellar cortex illustrates the use of an associative network model at a very different level of explanation to those described earlier in this chapter. We will have cause to return to the issue of levels of explanation at several places in this book.

3.2 SEMANTIC MEMORY AND HIDDEN UNITS

Associative memory does not exhaust the possibilities of human memory of course! Indeed within cognitive science associative memory has been largely ignored in favour of investigations of more structured types of memory system. Any standard text on artificial intelligence or cognitive science will quickly introduce notions such as propositional representation or semantic networks or schema (examples are Charniak & McDermott, 1985; Johnson-Laird, 1989). All are structures that can carry information and are easily implemented in symbol-manipulating von Neumann computers. For the purpose of illustration consider the blocks world scene in Fig. 3.4 and the semantic network description of it. Each node of the network stands for an object or a concept. The links represent the relationship between two nodes. In a conventional computer the links would be implemented by a system of pointers: the memory item "block1" would include the addresses of all the items to which it is linked: "block" and "white". Associated

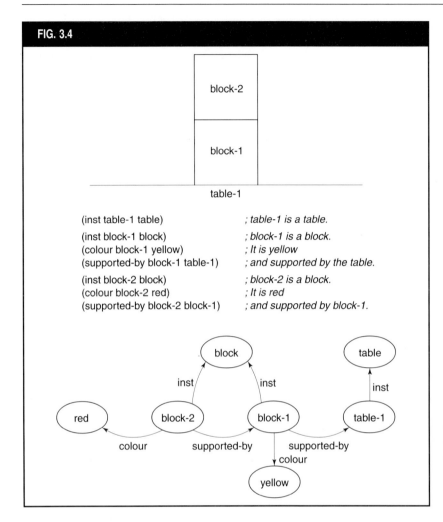

FIG. 3.4

(inst table-1 table)   ; *table-1 is a table.*

(inst block-1 block)   ; *block-1 is a block.*
(colour block-1 yellow)   ; *It is yellow*
(supported-by block-1 table-1) ; *and supported by the table.*

(inst block-2 block)   ; *block-2 is a block.*
(colour block-2 red)   ; *It is red*
(supported-by block-2 block-1) ; *and supported by block-1.*

A simple scene of two blocks on a table described in a propositional format and by a semantic network. From Charniak and McDermott (1985).

with the pointer will be specification of the type of relationship: "block1" will include an "isa" pointer to the address of "block". This is a highly efficient method of storing information. The pointer system allows easy access to parts of the structure and the "isa" relationship provides for the inheritance of properties. The latter refers to the fact that, for example, the "isa" link between "elephant" and "animal" warrants the inference that elephants share the characteristic features of all other animals.

At first glance the semantic network is rather like a connectionist network. Indeed connectionist implementations of semantic networks have been proposed (Fahlman, 1981; Feldman, 1981)

in which the nodes are simple units with their connections representing the relations between the nodes. Clearly such schemes are forced to rely on local rather than distributed representation. Each unit stands for a single concept. Hinton (1981a) argues for an alternative distributed scheme in which concepts are represented by patterns of activity over a set of units. He claims (1981a, pp.161–162) that this:

> . . . is a more promising model of how concepts are represented in the nervous system and that an understanding of the particular patterns of activity used for particular concepts (their microstructure) is important

because the interactions between concepts that are formalised as a single link in a semantic net are actually generated by millions of simultaneous interactions at the level of their microstructures. An understanding of these microcomputations is the key to understanding how existing concepts are recalled appropriately, how relationships between concepts change, and how new concepts arise.

This claim is best assessed by considering in detail a model of semantic memory in which concepts are represented in a distributed manner. Hinton (1989a) devised a distributed memory system with the aim of storing the family-tree structures shown in Fig. 3.5. Notice that the information in the tree may be expressed as a set of propositions of the form [person1, relationship, person2]. Such propositions may be realised in a network with units that are specific to each of the three roles, as may be seen by an examination of Fig. 3.6. The latter shows two sets of input units: there is a unit for each of the person1 role fillers, and a unit for each of the relationship fillers. Similarly each of the output units designates a filler for person2. Given some combination of person1 and relationship as input, the system is expected to signal the appropriate person2 (or set of such individuals) which fits this description. For example

given "Victoria" and "mother", the output units for "Colin" and "Charlotte" should be active. There are also three layers of hidden units. In the first of these there are twelve units, six of which are directly connected to each of the person1 input units and six to each of the relationship input units. Their function is to form distributed representations of the fillers for the two roles: so, for example, the input "Victoria" and "mother" will result in a unique pattern of activity across the twelve units in the first hidden layer. Individual units will code features rather than individuals, and the latter will be represented as coalitions of those features. Each of these units is connected in turn to all twelve units in a second hidden layer. The function of this second layer is very interesting: to detect and represent high-order relationships that may occur between the features represented in the first layer of hidden units. What this means should become clear when we describe Hinton's (1989a) simulation results in the next paragraph. These units are all connected to six units in a third and final hidden layer. These units form a distributed encoding of the fillers for person2 and serve to activate the appropriate outputs.

The crucial question is clearly: can the network learn the representations needed to store the information in the family trees? Hinton (1989a) put this to the test in the following manner. Taking the twelve relationships [father, mother, husband,

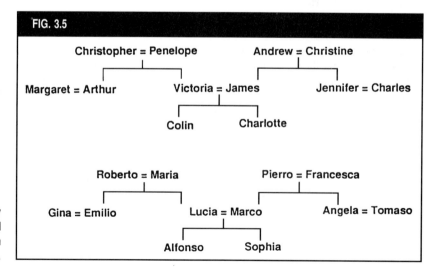

FIG. 3.5

Christopher = Penelope   Andrew = Christine

Margaret = Arthur   Victoria = James   Jennifer = Charles

Colin   Charlotte

Roberto = Maria   Pierro = Francesca

Gina = Emilio   Lucia = Marco   Angela = Tomaso

Alfonso   Sophia

Two isomorphic family trees, one English and one Italian. From Hinton (1989a).

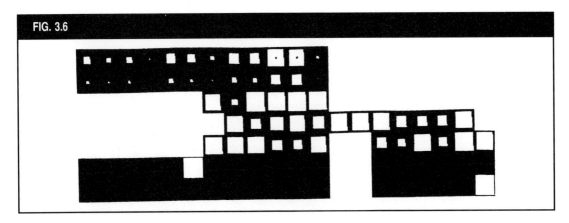

FIG. 3.6

A five-layer network trained to encode the family trees of Fig. 3.5. The first layer has 24 units for a local encoding of a person and 12 units for a local encoding of a relationship. Each group of input units is connected to 6 hidden units which form a distributed representation of the input items. These connect to 12 further hidden units and these to a penultimate hidden layer of 6 units that form distributed representations of a second person which activates the correct output units, each of which, like the input units, stands for a different person. In the figure, active units are shown by white squares with the size indicating the magnitude of activation. The example shows the network's correct reponse to the input "Colin" and "aunt-of" — in this case, the two individuals marked by the black dots on the output units. From Hinton (1989a).

wife, son, daughter, uncle, aunt, brother, sister, nephew, niece] together with the individuals in the family tree yields 104 different propositions of the general form [person1, relationship, person2]. The network was trained on 100 of these using the back-propagation learning procedure described in section 2.7 of the previous chapter. That is, an input [person1, relationship] pair would be presented to the network by clamping the input units to the appropriate states. The resultant activity would be fed forward through the successive layers, culminating in some activity in the output units. This activity would be compared with that required to signal the appropriate [person2]. This comparison allows error terms to be derived for the output units and, recursively, for the hidden units, from which the weight changes may be calculated (see equations 13 and 14 in Chapter 2 for the derivation of suitable error terms). The cumulative weight changes resulting from sweeping through all 100 training pairs were determined and applied only at the end of a sweep. There were 1500 such sweeps, at which point the weights were found to be changing only very slightly. After this training the outputs were correct: when presented with any one of the 100 pairs it had learned,

the activity of the output units for the correct answers was always greater than 0.8, and less than 0.2 for the others. The network also demonstrated some ability to generalise to the four cases that it had not seen during learning. Two entire simulations were run, starting from a different, random set of initial weights. In one the network gave correct responses to all four new cases, in the other it was correct in three of the new cases.

The ability of the network to generalise is very important. It suggests that what has been learned is not some arbitrary set of weights that is capable of storing the training items. The ability to respond correctly to new cases indicates that the network has found a way of representing, in its weights, the relationships among the family members. This may be glimpsed in some of the weight configurations that actually arose in the simulations we have described, as shown in Fig. 3.7. Examine 3.7a which shows the weights on the connections from the 24 input units representing the fillers of [person1] to the six hidden units expected to represent those individuals by a distributed pattern of activity. It should be obvious that one unit, number one, represented nationality: Italians tend to turn this unit off, the English

FIG. 3.7

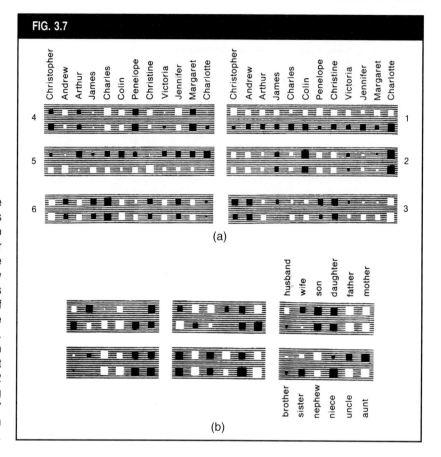

The weight structure from the 24 input units representing persons to the first 6-unit hidden layer is shown in (a). White squares indicate excitatory weights, black squares inhibitory, and the size of the square indicates the magnitude of the weight. In a similar fashion (b) shows the weight structure from the 12 input units representing relationships to the "it's" 6-unit hidden layer. From Hinton (1989a).

turn it on. The second unit effectively coded the generation of the individual: most distant generations turn the unit on, most recent generations turn it off, and intermediate generations lead to intermediate levels of activity. In a similar manner the sixth unit came to represent the family branch to which an individual belonged, although it seems a little muddled about the most recent generation. An inspection of Fig. 3.7b reveals that among the six units that are fed by the [relationship] input units, one codes gender.

Representing concepts by distributed patterns of micro-features in this way brings with it certain important advantages compared to localist and some distributed encodings. A consequence of having items represented by coalitions of features is that similar items will have similar representations. This is clearly not true of localist schemes in which each item is represented by a

single different unit, nor in distributed schemes in which items are coded by arbitrary sets of units, as for example in the Hopfield net described in the previous chapter. The great virtue of having similar representations for similar concepts is that it allows generalisation to new cases. As an example of this effect Hinton (1989a) asks us to suppose that one of the units in the second hidden layer responds whenever [person1] is old and [relationship] requires that both individuals have the same age. If this unit is connected so as to activate a unit that encodes the feature old in the penultimate layer which represents [person2] in a distributed manner, then the system is able to "infer" that the filler of [person2] must also be old. The unit in the second hidden layer is said to encode a micro-inference. So if Mary is to be added to the knowledge structure and Mary is old, when probed with [Mary, husband] the network will tend to complete the proposition with a filler for [person2] who is also old. The network's rather conservative view of such relationships arises as a result of the higher-order regularities that it finds in the training set! The network simply conforms to those regularities.

This work is an interesting preliminary exploration of distributed semantic memory. More recently, Rumelhart and Todd (1993) examined the knowledge captured in a three-layer network trained using back-propagation to learn the relations between input concepts (e.g. robin has) and output sets of properties (e.g. feathers and wings). Inspection of the hidden units showed that they came to represent conceptual distinctions (e.g. a unit in a positive state might represent *plant* while in a negative state it might represent *animal*) (see later for further discussion of the hidden unit representations in this model) and, similar to the network of Hinton (described earlier), the model as a whole showed the property of "inheritance" in which the properties of a learned concept were transferred to a new item sharing a subset of those properties. For example, even when trained only that a sparrow is a bird it could infer properties common to other birds (e.g. flies and has feathers) by dint of the representation of sparrow overlapping with that of other birds. Other extended models of semantic memory have been used to simulate neuropsychological disorders of semantic knowledge; we consider these models in detail in Chapter 8. The models of semantic memory also illustrate a number of issues that have general implications for the future development of connectionism. We wish to dwell on three of those in the final part of this section. All will be returned to in the final chapter.

3.2.1 Level of explanation
The first issue is to do with the various claims about the level of explanation for which connectionist models are most appropriate. In the final chapter we will discuss claims that connectionist theories are theories of implementation: that is, they explain how the higher-level functional theories may be implemented in brain-like mechanisms. The connectionist accounts are therefore fully compatible with the higher-level accounts

and not alternatives to them. It seems to us that the description of Hinton's (1989a) distributed semantic memory shows that this must be wrong — at least in some cases. The distributed model cannot be viewed as simply an implementation of, say, a traditional semantic network. There are important aspects of its behaviour, such as its ability to generalise to new cases, which depend on the distributed nature of its encodings. To explain some aspects of semantic memory performance one is forced to talk about interactions at the level of the connectionist model.

3.2.2 Connectionist methodology
The second general issue on which we wish to remark is to do with a novel methodology that connectionism seems to provide. One remarkable aspect of the learning in Hinton's (1989a) example is the way in which the network was able to extract and represent useful features, such as generation and family branch, which were only implicit in the examples provided for learning. Higher-order relationships between such features may be assumed to have been encoded in the penultimate, hidden layer given the orderly generalisation discussed in the previous paragraph. We think this ability of networks to discover adequate internal representation is startling and novel. It seems to open up a methodology in cognitive science for the "discovery" of forms of representation sufficient for the solution of a given problem. Other examples will be highlighted elsewhere in this book.

3.2.3 Interpreting network behaviour
The third general issue may be illustrated by reference to the family tree problem and is concerned with the problems in interpreting the behaviour of hidden units. Hinton (1989a) does not provide any description of the weights on the connections between the fist and second hidden layers, therefore it is not clear precisely what high-order relationships are encoded by the second hidden layer. In other cases, however, attempts to understand network behaviour have used cluster analyses to assess the representations developed at the hidden unit level. Typically, within a hierarchical

cluster analysis, stimuli that produce similar hidden unit values are grouped together within a "branch" of the overall tree, and branches divide between stimuli that produce dissimilar hidden units values. This enables the experimenter to visualise the similarity relationships between items at this level of coding in the model. The results of one such analysis performed by Rumelhart and Todd (1993) are shown in Fig. 3.8. Remember that this network was presented with input representing either plant and animal exemplars (e.g. robin) and a particular relationship (e.g. has) and output units represented properties of the stimuli (e.g. wings). The cluster analysis showed that, overall, animals clustered into one branch and plants into another, that trees formed a separate branch from other plants and so forth. In learning the properties for objects, the network has developed a semantic organisation which distinguishes super-ordinate terms from terms specific to particular exemplars, perhaps much as people do (cf. Rosch et al., 1976). Such analyses provide one way to peer inside the "black box" of a network.

3.3 MEMORY AND REPRESENTATION

We have used the term "representation" frequently in this chapter. The attentive reader will have noticed that it has been used to refer to different things (e.g. from a pattern of activation in a distributed memory system, re-created by passing an input through a set of weights, to the use of units within a model of semantic memory to stand for a particular micro-feature). It is time to clarify matters a little.

How things are represented in connectionist networks is clearly different from how things are represented in most conventional, symbol-based models of cognition. The crucial difference is perhaps that in the latter, symbol structures are intended as explicit vehicles for representation. That is, they are designed so that aspects of their structure or behaviour (or both) map neatly onto semantic features of the external world. Systems that have explicit representational structures in this sense are said to be "semantically transparent" (Clark, 1989; Smolensky, 1988). It should be clear

Hierarchical clustering of the hidden unit values generated to the inputs used by Rumelhart and Todd (1993). Note that, although the model correctly groups together most plants and most animals, it incorrectly groups sparrow (orig_sprrw) with the plants. This is because, in this example, the network was already trained (on the other items) and then presented with sparrow, for which it had not learned any features. In this instance, the representation of sparrow was determined simply by the initial random setting of the input values.

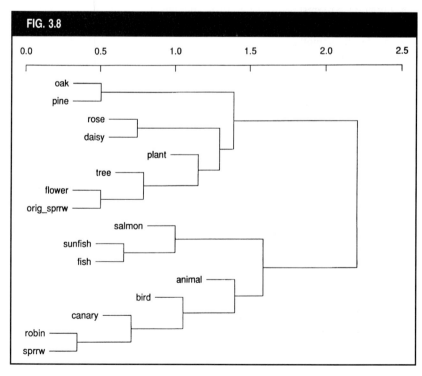

FIG. 3.8

from the models we have described thus far that connectionist memory systems are not semantically transparent. Although some of the features to which the hidden units responded in Hinton's (1989a) model were interpretable in terms of the semantics of the domain, none corresponded in a simple manner with the rules or syntax of the family trees. Moreover some of the hidden units may have behaved in ways that simply had no expression in the semantics of the domain. The rules and semantics of family trees arose as emergent properties of the behaviours of the system taken as a whole. Such systems may be said to be semantically opaque and to have the property of "informational holism" (Clark, 1989). A lot more needs to be said about these difficult issues and, once again, we will return to them in the final chapter. In a system that exhibits informational holism, the things that it "knows" and the relations between those things may be thought of as being embodied in its pattern of connectivity, its set of weights, and the activation properties of its units. Clearly, however, this does not exhaust the issue of representation in connectionist networks. At several places we have talked of hidden units as if they were representational or coding devices. That is, a single hidden unit can be conceived of as standing for something. Indeed one of the primary reasons for the explosion of interest among psychologists and other cognitive scientists in connectionism is to do with the representational properties of hidden units.

There are two significant aspects to this matter which relate to memory performance. First, networks without hidden units are limited in terms of the sorts of population of inputs they can handle. We saw in section 3.1 that, for interference-free storage, the inputs need to be orthogonal, if a simple Hebbian-style learning rule is applied, and linearly independent if an iterative learning procedure, such as the delta rule, is used. A little thought should convince the reader that even the latter case is far too restrictive for most, psychologically interesting, examples. Typically the size of the input population is far greater than the number of components in the input vector, thus ruling out linear independence. Also typically the required mapping between the input and output is

often complex and of a high order. For instance in Hinton's (1989a) example of a family tree structure (section 3.3) there was no direct correlation between the inputs and outputs among the items used for the test of generalisation. Indeed the fillers of [person1] and [person2] used during the generalisation trials had a negative correlation: in the learning phase they never appeared together but the same [person1]s did appear with different [person2]s. Thus high-order relationships must be discovered and coded by the hidden units, they simply cannot be represented as direct correlations between the input and output patterns. So hidden units can be regarded as devices for recoding inputs in ways that escape the various limitations of single-layer networks. They may also be thought of as devices that represent the features that support generalisation: they represent the family characteristics among category members so that new instances are categorised correctly.

We have suggested that the training of multi-layer networks is in some sense a new research methodology for the cognitive sciences. The form of representation sufficient for a given input–output mapping may be discovered by simulation. This is very important because the question of what to represent is fundamental to the concerns of cognitive science. However in some ways the technique is rather haphazard, and not just because the network solution may be difficult to interpret. What we do not have is a theory of learning in the sense of being able to specify the general conditions that will result in concept formation and hence the ability to generalise. As Hinton (1989a) has pointed out, until a such a "computational theory" of learning (Marr, 1982) is invented, one is confined to simulations in which reasonable generalisation may be demonstrated in some particular domain. The reader will encounter more examples of this methodology as they proceed.

Distributed representations can do things that local ones cannot. Or at least, as was argued earlier, there are some aspects of human memory that can most naturally be accounted for on the basis of interactions within a network of simple units in which items are represented by stable patterns of activity across those units (see Hinton, McClelland, & Rumelhart, 1986). We have already argued, when discussing Hinton's (1989a) model of a distributed semantic memory, that one advantage of having distributed representations of concepts is that it becomes possible to have similar concepts represented by patterns that are themselves similar. This provides for sensible generalisation as we saw in Hinton's (1989a) example. We will now discuss four more aspects: (1) the constructive character of recall, (2) concept learning, (3) the effects of damage, and (4) the effects of later learning on earlier learning.

3.3.1 The constructive character of recall

There is a long established theoretical approach in the psychology of memory which treats recall as a form of reconstruction. For example Bartlett (1932) showed that implausible stories were recalled as more plausible versions of themselves. The drift towards plausibility is thought to reveal the involvement of prior knowledge in the recall of specific materials. Memory for Bartlett (1932, p.213) is ". . . an imaginative reconstruction, or construction, built out of the relation of our attitude towards a whole active mass of organised past reactions or experience."

In a sense we have already shown connectionist memories to be reconstructive in this way when we explained how it was that they could be content-addressable. Their ability to fill-in a partial cue is derived from a connectivity that mirrors the relations among the components of a memory. One way of expressing this is to regard each active unit as representing a micro-feature of a memory item and a connection with another unit as a plausible inference from that micro-feature. For example activity in the micro-feature "claw" might lead to activity in the micro-feature "fur" thus expressing the reasonable inference that something that has claws also has fur. However it might also activate "shell" as some things with shells, in the sense that a lobster has a shell, also have claws. A useful network will arrive at a state in which implausible or contradictory inferences, such as something having a shell and fur, are minimised. That is, the stable patterns are stable precisely because they minimise inference violations to a greater extent than neighbouring patterns. In memories of this sort construction and retrieval are

truly the same process: both involve finding the best fit to a set of constraints by relaxation. The only sense in which veridical and non-veridical recall may be distinguished is to do with the history of the weights. In the case of veridical recall, the recalled pattern is stable because of weight changes that resulted from its previous occurrence. In the case of non-veridical recall the pattern's stability depends on weight changes attendant on the occurrence of other, related patterns. In either case, recall is constituted by the same process of relaxation or one-shot activation change.

3.3.2 Concept learning

A theory of knowledge representation should, ideally, include some account of how knowledge may be acquired. Knowledge acquisition in a network in which patterns of activity represent items is relatively straightforward. Or at least we have shown it to be when armed with the various learning rules that have been devised. In a distributed semantic network, for example, new concepts are acquired as a result of weight changes which allow a new stable configuration of activity. If concepts were locally represented, a unit would have to be added or found to be dedicated to the new concept. This way of doing things does not allow graduated learning: the new concept cannot emerge as the result of a number of different learning situations or the gradual differentiation of a single concept into two or more related ones.

3.3.3 The effects of damage

Distributed representations break down in very different ways to local ones. That is, there are characteristic consequences of damage to parts of a distributed memory system. This was nicely illustrated in a simulation of a Boltzmann machine which learned a distributed representation of the semantic properties of three-letter words (Hinton & Sejnowski, 1986). The network, which is sketched in Fig. 3.9, had three types of unit: 30 units represented letters in a specific positions within a word, 30 units represented particular semantic features, and 20 intermediate units were connected to all units in the other two groups which were not directly connected to each other. The Boltzmann learning procedure (see section 2.6 in the previous

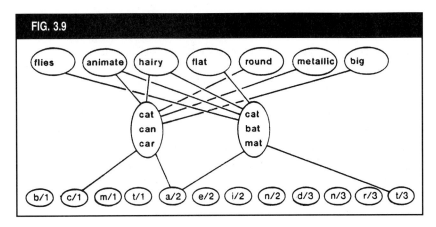

FIG. 3.9

An illustration of the network used by Hinton and Sejnowski (1986) to associate words with semantic features.

chapter) was used to associate together patterns of activity in the letter units with patterns in the semantic units. In a preliminary phase an energy landscape had been created among the semantic units by disconnecting them from the rest of the network and getting them to learn 20 clamped states which were designated as 20 word meanings. In the fully connected network these 20 patterns were associated with 20 arbitrary patterns among the letter units. After 5000 learning sweeps, each of which involved 80 annealings, network performance was 99.3% accurate, in that the appropriate semantic features would be activated given a particular letter string presented to the letter units.

After learning, words were represented in a distributed manner on the 20 intermediate units. What would be the effect of deleting intermediate units? Had the representation been local the answer would be clear: the loss of a unit would result in the "forgetting" of a word. When loss of a single unit was simulated with the distributed representations, Hinton and Sejnowski (1986) found that their network was still 98.3% accurate! This is typical of distributed representation: it is highly resistant to damage. Moreover the system recovers from the damage in a remarkable manner. If five of the twenty intermediate units are removed performance drops to about 65% accurate, but relearning is rapid: performance is back to about 90% accurate after only about ten learning sweeps. In the original learning phase at a comparable level of performance, 30 learning

sweeps were required for just a 10% improvement in accuracy. Similar rapid relearning was found after adding noise to a proportion of the connections or reducing the weights on some to zero. We will have a lot more to say about the consequences of damage to connectionist networks for their behaviours in Chapter 8.

3.3.4 The effects of later learning on earlier learning

Distributed representations do have one inherent weakness which threatens their utility in models of human memory. Ratcliff (1990) simulated memory in feed-forward networks trained by back-propagation. The networks were trained to autoassociate, typically, 32 component vectors of 0s and 1s. In a subsequent recognition phase the training set was represented along with a new set of vectors. A measure of the distance between the observed output and the desired output (in fact the dot product of the two vectors) allowed the discriminability between old and new patterns to be calculated. The finding of prime interest was that memories of previously learned patterns, which were discriminable from new patterns in a recognition memory test, were massively disrupted by the learning of a subsequent pattern. Both the match of a learned pattern with the output and its discriminability from entirely new (unlearned) patterns declined dramatically when a single new pattern was learned. The decline was so marked that the effect has come to be called "*catastrophic interference*". Various modifications of the network, such as adding hidden units and modifying only the small weights, during the learning of the new pattern failed to greatly reduce the interference effect.

Similar problems were noted in simulations by McCloskey and Cohen (1989). They trained three-layer networks using back-propagation to carry out simple addition problems. Input vectors represented two numbers plus the operation (add), and output vectors represented the resultant number. First networks learned "+1" additions ("Ones" problems), and they were subsequently trained on "+2" additions ("Twos" problems). McCloskey and Cohen found that, as the networks learned to produce the correct outputs for "+2" additions, so they "forgot" the correct outputs for "+1" additions. More formally, as on "+2" additions the difference between the output produced by the model and the correct output decreased (the measure taken was the mean of this difference [or error], across all output units), so the error score increased dramatically for the previously learned "+1" additions. This is illustrated in Fig. 3.10.

Interference effects of this form have long been known to occur in human memory. For example, Barnes and Underwood (1959) had subjects learn associations between nonsense syllables (e.g. dax) and adjectives (e.g. regal). Having learned a first set of associations, subjects were then trained to associate the nonsense syllables with a different set of words (a so-called A–B, A–C design). They found that as learning of the new associations increased, so recall of the old associations decreased (from 100%, at initial training, to around 45% after 20 learning trials with the new associations). However, in networks trained to about the same level as the subjects in Barnes and Underwood's study on (new) A–C associations, McCloskey and Cohen showed that recall of the A–B associations was practically zero. Thus, although interference effects are found in humans, they do not seem nearly so severe as those in these networks.

It is not difficult to understand why such effects can occur in networks. Essentially, the networks are attempting to learn the new relationships using the weights established for the old relationships. In changing the weights for the new relationships there is naturally some movement of the weights away from their old positions, which were optimised for the first relationships; the result is interference in the recall of the old stimuli. This problem of catastrophic interference has led theorists to argue that networks of this type cannot be adequate models of aspects of human memory (McCloskey & Cohen, 1989; Ratcliff, 1990). However, the problem may not be in the general connectionist approach, but in the way learning has been instantiated in the critical examples. We now consider three different remedies that maintain the use of back-propagation learning and a fourth that uses other forms of learning in networks.

One approach is to reduce the plasticity in a network as it learns. Essentially, if weights used to represent "old" memories are held constant, then they will not be over-written by new memories. One example of this is a model of "calendar calculation" reported by Norris (1993a). Some humans are able to calculate in a few seconds the day of the week on which any date fell, and, interestingly, this ability can be found in individuals with otherwise limited intellectual and arithmetic capacities — an example of an "island" of modular performance. Norris documented an attempt to simulate calendar calculation in a three-layer network trained using back-propagation. The task was to generate the day of the week on which a particular date fell (where the date, month, and year was given as input). Although the model could learn individual date–day relationships, it showed no signs of generalising; this held across variations in the number of hidden units involved. Generalisation was found, however, when different parts of a network were trained separately on individual parts of the problem. The first part of the problem involves learning, for a base month (e.g. January) in a base year (e.g. 1995) an association between the date (say 1 January 1995) and a day (Sunday). Once learned, the weights in this sub-network were "frozen" and its output used as input for a further sub-network which received (i) the day for a date in the base month (January) generated from the first sub-network, along with (ii) the same date for a new month. This sub-network was trained to produce as output the date in the new month. This essentially corresponds

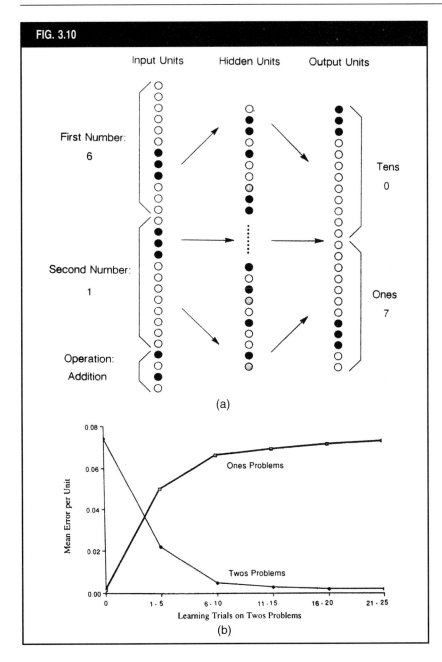

FIG. 3.10

(a)

(b)

(a) The network used by McCloskey and Cohen (1989) in their study of catastrophic interference in networks. (b) Error scores per unit in the McCloskey and Cohen model as a function of training on "Twos" problems. Performance starts after "Ones" problems have already been learned (so they start with a low error score).

to learning a rule such as: if it was Sunday on 15 January 1995 (output from sub-network 1) then it was Wednesday on 15 February (input to sub-network 2 = Sunday [for 15 January 1995] + February; output = Wednesday). This second sub-network was then frozen, but its output served as input for a final sub-network. This final sub-network learned a year-based association such that, if it was Wednesday on 15 February 1995 (from sub-network 2), it was Monday on the same date in 1993 (input to sub-network 3 = Wednesday [for 15 February 1995] + 1993). An overall model, with three such sub-networks, not only learned day–date relationships, it also generalised when given dates it has not been previously trained on. Generalisation occurred because the sub-networks had learned particular rules for separate parts of the problem — learning day–date relations for a base month in one year, the association for day–date relations for other months in that year, and the association for day–date relations in one year to other years. Note that, with back-propagation, the learning achieved for the first part of the association would be over-written as the other parts are learned, unless the first weights were "frozen". Of course, this requires some process that determines both the structure of learning and the plasticity of the network across different stages of learning, and at present there are no known automatic procedures for this. Nevertheless it may be that physiological changes in the plasticity of learning in real neural networks plays an important role in structuring learning in biological systems.

A second remedy may be to reduce the overlap in the representations of the items being learned. French (1992) argued that catastrophic forgetting tends to occur when new and old patterns have similar representations. It follows that the overlap in representations must be reduced to lessen forgetting. But there is a problem on the other side of this, which is that, by eliminating overlap between representations, so a network's generalisation ability may be reduced. To overcome these difficulties, French proposed a technique termed "activation sharpening" which involved robbing the least active units of some of their activity and giving it to the most active units, and using the resulting activities as the basis of weight calculation. This led to so-called semi-distributed representations which reduced forgetting without greatly affecting generalisation. The result, although promising, is highly provisional. It is not clear under what conditions semi-distributed representations are effective or how local they can become without producing degenerate generalisation (although see also McRae & Hetherington, 1993, and Murre, 1992, for similar approaches).

A third approach uses the idea that catastrophic interference may be reduced if old memories continue to be interleaved during the learning of new input–output relationships. Essentially the idea here is that old memories can be retained

in such networks if the original input–output relationships are continuously reinforced as new items are learned, so that something of the old "weight space" is retained. McClelland, McNaughton, and O'Reilly (1995) suggested that, in humans, a specific neural structure (the hippocampus) may provide this function, of regularly "reminding" other networks (in the cerebral cortex) of past events so that these old memories are not over-written as representations of new events are laid down in the cortex (see also Robins, 1995). This idea is considered in more detail in Chapter 8, where we review its application to cases of memory disorder.

A fourth approach is to use other forms of learning that naturally preserve old weights and that tend to develop sparse internal representations. Examples of this are RBF and ART networks (section 2.10, Chapter 2). In ART networks, learning takes place using weights to new classifier units when an input does not match stored representations, so preserving learning on the weights connecting to previously used classifier units. Also, the competition between classifier units leads to non-overlapping representations across learned patterns. In RBF nets, hidden units are tuned to represent each exemplar in an input set, so reducing catastrophic interference, as shown in studies of a model of human categorisation proposed by Kruschke (1992, 1993).

Kruschke's model, ALCOVE, was used to model human learning of simple categories of stimuli. ALCOVE used a RBF-approach in which hidden units (Kruschke termed these "exemplar nodes") had "receptive fields" tuned to discriminate the values of different exemplars in an input set (see Fig. 3.11). In a simple example he assessed a task in which stimuli were defined on two dimensions and were assigned to either of two categories. Learning first involved assigning the inputs 0, −1 to category 0, 1, and the inputs −1, 0 to category 1, 0. Subsequently, learning involved assigning the inputs 0, +1 to category 0, 1 and inputs +1, 0 to category 1, 0. A standard three-layer feedforward model trained with back-propagation showed catastrophic interference. When trained on phase 1 exemplars, the weights moved away from those required for the responses in phase 2, actually decreasing correct categorisations for

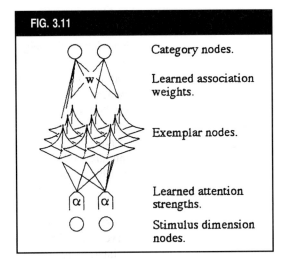

FIG. 3.11

Category nodes.

Learned association
weights.

w

Exemplar nodes.

Learned attention
strengths.

α   α

Stimulus dimension
nodes.

The architecture of ALCOVE (Kruschke, 1992). Input units respond to values of stimuli along set perceptual dimensions (the "stimulus dimension nodes"). The hidden units have weight structures that form receptive fields around the position of each exemplar in the input space (the "exemplar nodes"). The output units categorise the input (the "category nodes"). Weights from the input units to the hidden units represent learned biases towards certain stimulus dimensions ("learned attentional strengths"). Weights from the hidden units to the output units represent learned biases from particular exemplars to certain categories ("learned association weights").

phase 2 stimuli relative to when no training had taken place! When phase 2 learning was undertaken, however, the gain in categorisation for phase 2 exemplars was at the cost of a decrease in correct categorisations for phase 1 stimuli. This is shown in Fig. 3.12. In contrast, for ALCOVE there was no shift in the weights away from phase 2 stimuli during phase 1 learning (relative to an untrained baseline), and no interference on phase 1 "memories" when phase 2 exemplars were learned. Essentially the receptive fields developed for the phase 1 exemplars were independent of those developed for phase 2 exemplars, eliminating catastrophic interference. At the end of this chapter, Kruschke's paper introducing the ALCOVE model is presented. This paper illustrates how this class of model differs from back-propagation models, and how the model may usefully be applied to simulate human data.

Catastrophic interference is clearly a limitation for learning in simple feed-forward networks. Nevertheless, in attempting to overcome the problems, modellers have posed questions that are relevant to our understanding of learning in biological systems — such as: How does plasticity in learning vary across time? How might overlap in representations be reduced? How do different memory modules interact in learning (e.g. a hippocampal "reminding" module and a cortical module where memories are laid down over the longer term)? Hence even given the limitations currently apparent, we conclude that the connectionist enterprise, of using models to frame new questions that may be given empirical answers, is useful.

3.4 THEORIES OF LEARNING AND LEARNING THEORY

Associationism has continued to influence work in animal learning in the form of behaviourism. It should be obvious to anyone familiar with the latter tradition that it has some aspects that are similar to aspects of connectionist learning procedures. In particular we will examine here the claim that Pavlovian or classical conditioning has properties that appear to be shared by some types of connectionist learning.

Classical conditioning refers to the effects of the pairing of a conditioned stimulus (CS), such as a bell or light, with some established or unconditioned stimulus (US), such as food or electric shock. The typical effects are the subsequent production of the response previously elicited by the US, such as salivation or fear, in the presence of the CS alone. This learned response to the CS is the conditioned response (CR). Such associative learning depends not only on the CS and US being presented together, close in time and space, but also on the predictive power of the CS. This can be observed in the so-called blocking of conditioning reported by Kamin (1969) and illustrated in the following example. An animal has a shock paired with a light so that on subsequent presentations of the light alone a fear response, such as

FIG. 3.12

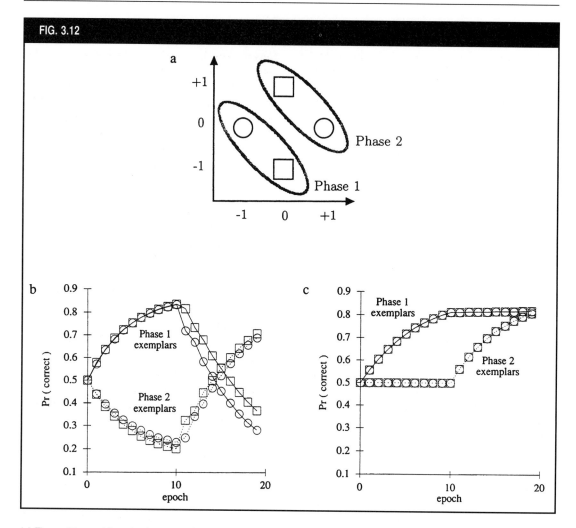

(a) The problem set for a back-propagation model of categorisation and for ALCOVE. The squares represent input values assigned to one output category and the circles the input values assigned to the second category. (b) and (c) show the probability of correctly classifying phase 1 and phase 2 exemplars, as a function of training. Phase 1 finished after 10 epochs (where 1 epoch = a complete presentation of the training set). (b) is for a back-propagation model; (c) is for ALCOVE. Only the back-propagation model shows interference on recall of phase 1 exemplars as phase 2 training progresses.

suppression of feeding behaviour, is elicited. If half of the animals now have a light and a tone paired with a shock, then after training, a tone alone will fail to elicit a fear response. The light will continue to do so. In contrast if the other half of the animals have a tone paired with a shock, both the tone and the light will come to elicit the fear response. The implication seems clear: conditioning will only occur to non-redundant stimuli.

Because in training the light always predicted the shock, the tone did not add any information and was not therefore associated with shock. One way of describing this outcome is in terms of expectancies developed by the animal on the basis of the predictive power of the various stimuli. This is of course a dangerously cognitive account! Learning theorists have therefore preferred an alternative, theoretically neutral view known as the Rescorla–Wagner model (Rescorla & Wagner, 1972; Wagner & Rescorla, 1972). The model assumes that the degree of conditioning to a given US on any learning trial depends on several factors: (1) how near to the asymptote conditioning is, (2) how big the effect of the US is, and (3) how much conditioning to other stimuli present on the trial has already occurred. These relationships can be expressed in the following equation:

$$\Delta V_a = B(C - \Sigma V_x) \qquad (3)$$

where ΔV_a is the amount of conditioning to stimulus a on the trial, B is some constant that determines the rate of conditioning, C is the upper limit of conditioning for the particular US, ΣV_x is the conditioning already achieved both to the stimulus a and to all other incidental stimuli. This model accounts for the blocking of conditioning in the following simple way. During the initial learning phase the light became strongly associated with the shock response: its strength of association may be assumed to have approached the limiting value of C. In the second learning phase when light and tone were paired the term $(C - \Sigma V_x)$ would have approached zero because of the high association between the CR and the light. Therefore no conditioning to the tone would be expected. Whereas when the tone alone was presented the $(C - \Sigma V_x)$ term would have been greater than zero and conditioning would occur.

The reader may have already noticed a similarity, noted by Sutton and Barto (1981), between the Rescorla–Wagner model as expressed in equation (1) and the Delta learning rule described in equation (11) of the last chapter: $\Delta W_{ij} = c(T_j - A_j) \cdot A_i$. If the weight-change term in the latter equation is seen as the change in association resulting from presentation of a CS, A_i is taken to be one whenever CS is present and T_j is taken to be equal to the upper limit on conditioning for a given US, the Delta rule for associating together a CS and a CR is simply equivalent to the Rescorla–Wagner model. One obvious thought is this: does the Delta rule/Rescorla–Wagner learning model capture the regularities of human learning as well as it appears to do so for animal learning? Gluck and Bower

(1988) have attempted to answer this question by investigating category learning in human subjects.

In the Gluck and Bower (1988) study subjects were asked to decide which of two fictitious diseases 250 imaginary patients were suffering from based on the presence or absence of four symptoms S1 to S4. After each response a subject was told whether they were correct or, if not, what the correct response should have been. At the end of the series subjects were asked to provide an estimate of the probability of each of the diseases given the presence of one of each of the symptoms. The 250 imaginary cases were constructed so that the probability of one disease was three times that of the other. Moreover it was arranged that a patient having the rarer disease would exhibit symptom S1 with a probability of 0.6; S2 with a probability of 0.4; S3 with a probability of 0.3; and S4 with a probability of 0.2. The corresponding probabilities for the more common disease were simply the inverse of those for the rare one. Given these figures one can work out the objective probabilities of the two diseases given the presence of a particular symptom. Note that the objective probability of both diseases is 0.5 given the presence of symptom S1.

After the 250 learning trials what have the subjects learned of the relationships between symptoms and diseases? Certainly not the objective probabilities. In particular, contrary to the conclusions of the previous paragraph, they came to believe that a patient exhibiting symptom S1 was more likely to be suffering the rare disease than the common one. Despite this symptom being paired with the common disease as frequently as the rare one, during learning subjects came to view it as having a greater association with the rare disease. In effect, subjects have paid insufficient attention to the relative frequencies of the two diseases. Similar effects have been reported in other contexts. For instance Kahneman and Tversky (1973) had subjects judge the likely academic discipline of each of a group of subjects from their personal descriptions. Despite being told that the group was drawn from a class 80% of whom were English students, subjects judgements were strongly influenced by the degree to which descriptions matched stereotypes of particular sorts of student.

These sorts of effects are examples of so-called base-rate neglects because in arriving at a probability of an outcome the underlying population distribution of probabilities is ignored.

What is very interesting for our purposes here is the fact that a network trained using the Delta rule/Rescorla–Wagner model of learning may exhibit similar base-rate neglect! It is a very simple matter to simulate an appropriate network: four input units connected in a feed-forward manner to a single output unit will suffice. The output unit signals the disease (on for rare, off for common) and the input units the presence or absence of the four symptoms. Gluck and Bower (1988) calculated the asymptotic weightings that would result in such a network from application of the Delta rule and presentation of learning trials comparable to those undergone by the human subjects. The weightings were positive only for the connection between the S1 input unit and the output, the other three were all negative. In a sense, then, the network behaves just like the human subjects in coming to associate symptom S1 strongly with the rare disease despite it being equally often presented in association with the common disease during learning. (But see Shanks, 1990 and Gluck & Bower, 1990 for a discussion of the most appropriate way of interpreting what the subjects are doing in making their probability estimates and relating this to the weightings in the network.) The associations formed by the network are explicable in the light of the following argument. Although S1 appears as many times paired with the common disease as the rare disease, when accompanying the common disease the other three symptoms were also likely to be present. When S1 accompanied the rare disease however, the three other symptoms were far less likely to be present. In the terms of the Rescorla–Wagner (1972) model of learning, S1 is a better predictor of the rare disease, but a relatively worse predictor of the common disease than the other symptoms. The weightings or association strengths reflect the relative validity of a symptom for a disease.

Other phenomena reported in the animal learning literature can also be explained by a connectionist model. McLaren, Kaye, and Mackintosh (1989) do so for the effects known as perceptual learning and latent inhibition. Perceptual learning refers to the increment in learning to discriminate between two stimuli which results from the earlier mere presence of the stimuli in the animal's environment. For example Gibson and Walk (1956) showed that rats raised with circles and triangles in their cages were able to learn to discriminate between the two shapes more rapidly than control animals. In contrast, latent inhibition refers to the decrement in learning that occurs with a stimulus that has previously been presented repeatedly (Lubrow, 1973). In general a novel stimulus conditions rapidly, whereas a familiar one does so only slowly. How may these two, seemingly contradictory, effects of perceptual learning and latent inhibition be reconciled? A starting point is to recognise that they are measures of different things: one reflects the discrimination between two objects, the other the conditioning to one. The effects can thus be disassociated within a single experiment. McLaren et al. (1989) report on studies where rats were first exposed to vertical and horizontal gratings, conditioned to one of these stimuli and then tested to judge whether that conditioning had generalised to the other stimuli. The prior exposure decreased conditioning and generalisation. In other words, prior exposure decreases the associability of an object while also increasing its discriminability (and hence reducing generalisation to other objects).

McLaren et al. (1989) provide rather a neat connectionist account of these phenomena. Assume that any object is constituted by a set of elements, each of which is represented by a unit in a network. In any single presentation of the object only a subset of the elements will be sampled by the network/animal and the subset will vary from trial to trial. With repeated presentations and application of the Delta rule, elements that are most commonly sampled will be associated together. In time therefore the network will come to represent the central components of each object so that any sampled subset will tend to elicit activity in the entire set of units which together represent that object. Now consider the case where objects are presented in pairs, as in discrimination learning.

Suppose the elements together making up each object are two partially overlapping sets: they have common and unique elements. On any given presentation only a subset of elements will be sampled. If the subject is naive, a presentation of the two objects to be discriminated will result in some unique elements of one object being associated with reinforcement, some unique elements of the other being associated with non-reinforcement, and some common elements being associated with both reinforcement and non-reinforcement. Given that the elements sampled will vary from trial to trial, the subject will be slow to learn the discrimination. However prior exposure of the objects would have resulted in associative connections between unique elements within a set; thus, on any trial during discrimination learning, unsampled unique elements will be activated by sampled ones. The result of which is that discrimination learning would be enhanced, as a greater proportion of unique elements would be active and available for association on any given trial. Moreover, prior exposure will have tended to lead to inhibitory connections between the two sets of unique elements: the objects will typically not be sampled simultaneously and the Delta rule will be sensitive to the negative correlation between the two sets. During discrimination learning these inhibitory connections will mitigate the positive associations that would form between unique elements in the different sets as a result of their being similarly associated with the common elements. Compared to a naive subject, therefore, learning of the discrimination is speeded. A third reason for prior exposure producing perceptual learning is that the common elements would have been sampled at a greater frequency than the unique elements during those prior exposures, and hence subject to greater latent inhibition. It follows that the unique elements would associate more readily than the common elements during learning and discrimination would be improved. In summary, prior exposure of stimuli may be expected to result in enhanced discrimination learning of those same stimuli because it: (1) increases the association between the elements that together constitute a single object; (2) decreases the association

between elements belonging to different objects; and (3) increases the latent inhibition of elements common to the objects to be discriminated.

What is the mechanism underlying latent inhibition? McLaren et al. (1989) suggest that it is the discrepancy between the input to a unit from other units in the network and the input it receives from sources external to the network (the CS and the reinforcer) that determines its associability. To see that this is so, imagine an animal learning the association between a tone and food. It should be clear that the Delta rule of equation (2) will act to reduce the difference between the internal and external input to a network unit in just the same manner as when learning to associate the name "bagel" with instances of bagels in our earlier example from McClelland and Rumelhart (1985). Thus the change in weights on the connections from tone units to food units will depend on the difference between the external and internal input to the food units. But notice also that the size of the weight change depends on the activation level of the tone unit. The more active a tone unit is the more associable it is. If, as McLaren et al. (1989) propose, the activity level of a unit is also increased in proportion to the difference between its external and internal inputs, latent inhibition would be expected. In the case of a naive animal the tone would have no internal representation, there would be a relatively large difference between the two sources of input leading to high activation levels in the tone units, and hence rapid association with the food units. Prior exposure to the tone would have led to the formation of connections among units representing elements of it, thereby reducing the tone's associability.

There may, however, be some aspects of human learning for which non-linear associative learning rules, such as the generalised Delta rule used in back-propagation, turn out to be too powerful. To illustrate this point, we return to Kruschke's (1992, 1993) ALCOVE model (Fig. 3.11, section 3.3). Remember that ALCOVE is a radial basis function (RBF)-type network in which hidden units have "receptive fields" tuned to match the activation patterns generated by particular exemplars. Kruschke (1993) examined performance with a simple training set varying on two stimulus dimensions (say line orientation and colour). If examples in a training set are aligned with the dimensions of the input space (e.g. if all right-sloping lines are assigned to category 1 and all left-sloping lines to category 2), ALCOVE can learn the categorisation fairly easily. This is illustrated by the input set shown in Fig. 3.13. In learning, weights are biased to push exemplars in one category away from those in the other, so that stimuli marked in black in Fig. 3.13a are pushed to the right and stimuli in white are pushed to the left, in the activation space for the hidden units. This facilitates the separate classification of the two categories of input.

However, consider a case now in which the categories do not align with the dimensions of the input space, as shown in Fig. 3.13b. Categorisation here might involve assigning very green stimuli that slope right to one category, but all other right-sloping stimuli to the other category;

likewise, all left-sloping stimuli would go to category 1 bar those that are very red, which belong to the second category! Correct learning here ought to push the exemplars apart from one another along the diagonal axis of the input space, as illustrated in Fig. 3.13b. However this turns out to be difficult for models such as ALCOVE, because the receptive fields are aligned along the dimensions of the input space. Consider the black and the white stimuli that lie on the fringes of their own categories and so are neighbours in the input space in Fig. 3.13b. Tuning the receptive field of (say) the fringe black stimulus to put the activation value it generates closer to those of the other black stimuli (e.g. moving the leftmost black stimulus to the right), will push the neighbouring white stimulus away from the other members of its category (pushing it left instead of left and down), disrupting its categorisation. Hence ALCOVE finds the first type of problem much easier than the second. Humans, given equivalent problems,

Example of the effects of learning on ALCOVE (a) when the assignment of categories (white vs. black) aligns with the perceptual dimensions encoded by the input units, learning pushes exemplars from each category apart, facilitating performance; (b) when the assignment of categories is not congruent with the encoded perceptual dimensions, ALCOVE cannot learn to push the exemplars apart along a new axis within the input space (in this example, the diagonal), because the receptive fields of the hidden units are always aligned along the input dimensions — see the text for details. Adapted from Kruschke (1993).

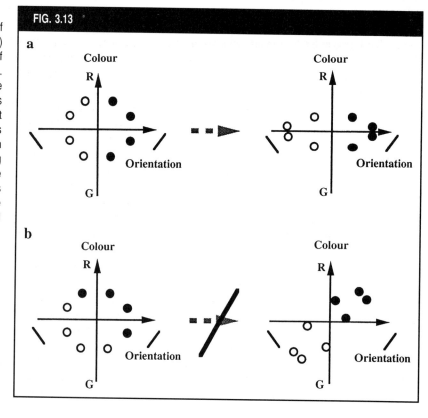

FIG. 3.13

show a similar pattern. However, networks trained using back-propagation do not. In Chapter 2, we discussed how back-propagation networks learn by aligning the sigmoid activation profiles of hidden units along boundaries in an input space (sections 2.7 and 2.10). For such models, a diagonal boundary can be found as easily as boundaries aligned with the dimensions of the input space. It may be that, in humans, there is a bias to align learning along the boundaries of perceptual dimensions which is not captured by models for which the dimensions of the input space carry no special significance. Models using receptive-field type structures, tuned to the dimensions of the input space, may show more plausible learning in this respect.

In summary, the work reported in this section has shown the utility of associative networks in providing plausible accounts of aspects of behaviours as diverse as diagnosis and perceptual discrimination. In so doing it has been necessary to emphasise both associative learning rules such as the Delta/Rescorla–Wagner formulation and the consequences for such learning on the representational properties of internal units. We have also noted that forms of back-propagation learning may be too powerful to capture all aspects of human learning, which shows a bias to be tuned to the dimensions of perceptual input. To capture all aspects of human data it may well turn out to be important to incorporate certain constraints on the input space so that, for example, it is tuned to certain dimensions prior to learning taking place; human learning, after all, does not take place on a *tabula rasa*. Overall though, the work illustrates a very important virtue of connectionism; namely that it has the potential of drawing together work in what had been very disparate traditions within psychology!

3.5 IMPLICIT AND EXPLICIT MEMORY

Much of the research we have dealt with in this chapter has been concerned with aspects of memory that in humans seem to operate in a relatively automatic way. Models of associative memory,

for instance, capture occasions such as when the smell of a flower evokes an episode from childhood — an event that seems to happen in an automatic and uncontrolled manner. However, in other circumstances memory is used to judge between an event that may have occurred and one that did not but might have — as when we have to judge which of two suspects was at the scene of a crime. In psychological experiments, such judgements are typically required in "recognition memory" experiments, in which subjects have to discriminate between a target and a distractor stimulus, only one of which was seen in an earlier list. Performance in such experiments can dissociate from that in other memory experiments, in which subjects are not required to judge whether they remember a stimulus but may use their memory to help perform the task. An example would be identifying a degraded picture, which is facilitated if people have seen an undegraded version earlier. Perhaps most dramatically, amnesic patients can show severe impairments on recognition memory judgements, but can nevertheless demonstrate learning in perceptual identification tasks (see Schacter, Chiu, & Ochsner, 1993, for one review). Such results suggest that different memory structures may support performance in the two types of task. The terms "explicit" and "implicit" memory are sometimes used to capture this distinction. In tasks such as perceptual identification, memory processes are used implicitly in the performance of another task, and some other system does not need to evaluate (explicitly) the content of the memory representation itself.

Dienes (1992) evaluated the performance of connectionist models directly in relation to studies of implicit memory in humans. The task chosen was "artificial grammar learning". In such a task, subjects are presented with a series of letter strings generated from a small finite-state grammar or a series of strings generated at random, and they are asked to memorise them (see Fig. 3.14 for an example grammar). Subsequently, subjects who have seen the grammatical strings are required to perform a grammaticality test in which they have to discriminate between novel strings that fit the "rules" and those that do not. Usually subjects perform well above chance at such judgements,

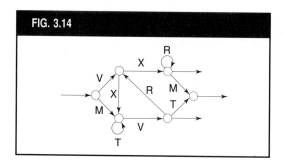

FIG. 3.14

The finite state grammar used by Dienes (1992) to study artificial grammar learning. This grammar generates grammatical strings such as VXTTTV, MVRXVT, VXVRXV; however it would not generate a string such as VXRRT, which is hence "ungrammatical".

yet they are unable to report on the rules they have learned. Indeed, subjects can be as confident about their incorrect grammaticality judgements as their correct ones, yet still show reliable classification performance (Dienes & Perner, 1994). The rules seem to have been extracted "implicitly" from the original data set (see Reber, 1967, for an early example).

Dienes (1992) tested the performance of an autoassociative network consisting of a single layer of units that were fully interconnected with one another. There were five units (one for each letter used in the grammar) at each of six string positions. The model was trained on 20 strings shown to human subjects, using either a Hebbian learning rule or the delta rule. Grammaticality judgements were tested by presenting the network with grammatical or random new exemplars. If the model reproduced the input string successfully, the string was judged grammatical; if it could not (i.e. if there was a high error value), the string was judged ungrammatical. The model trained using the delta rule performed well. It scored at a high level on the grammaticality judgement task, and, critically, its "ranking" of the grammaticality of the test strings correlated highly with the rankings made by human subjects. The model trained using the Hebb rule did not perform so well.

Such results suggest that connectionist models, which are sensitive to frequency and co-occurrence statistics in training sets, can capture aspects of

human implicit memory at quite a fine-grained level (distinguishing between the more and less grammatical strings). The models, like humans, appear to extract the rules of the grammar, although in the case of the models this is simply a matter of associative learning. However, whether the same networks can also capture aspects of explicit memory (and in particular the dissociations between explicit and implicit memory) has been much less explored. It may be that such dissociations are difficult to simulate within single networks, and that some form of metacognitive structure is required. That is, there may need to be layers of memory networks, with the job of some networks being to assimilate what the other networks are learning; the metacognitive net may then provide an explicit representation of what has been learned by the first network.

One way in which such an explicit representation could be developed is suggested by Murre (1997). Murre distinguishes between the effects of learning in a "trace" system, where long-term memories are held, and learning by associating activation patterns in the trace system with a "link" system (see Fig. 3.15). The link system serves to associate together different activations in the trace system (e.g. if the activations were generated by different modalities of input), and to maintain activation in the trace system by strengthening connections between trace and link units on a Hebbian basis. A slower form of learning is also presumed to take place between units in the trace system, based on those units activated over the longer term. Activation in the trace system is thus sensitive to prior learning, as well as to new input, and it will reflect a memory event implicitly. The link system can provide a separate record of the event, and codes "explicitly" the memory otherwise represented only in the states of the trace units. The link system may thus facilitate decisions between which stimuli have been presented earlier, even if both activate the trace system to some degree. Murre proposes that the trace system simulates processes in the cortex of the brain, and the link system processes in the hippocampus. We return to this idea in Chapter 8 (section 8.9), when we assess simulations of memory disorders.

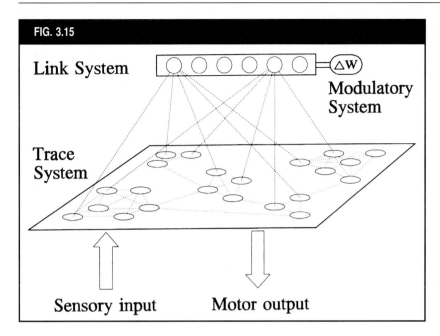

FIG. 3.15

Link System

Modulatory System

Trace System

Sensory input   Motor output

The TraceLink model proposed by Murre (1997). The "trace" system receives sensory input and directs motor output. Connections within this system are mostly local. The "link" system connects extensively with the trace system, and so can associate together different units in the trace system. The "modulatory" system moderates learning, and can increase "plasticity" (the speed of making weight changes) in the connections between the link and trace systems. From Murre (1997).

3.6 LEARNING IN NETWORKS: FORMAL PROPERTIES

We have used the term "learning" to apply to several different activities. Much of this chapter has been concerned with what is learned in networks when various learning rules are used in various networks. We now wish to focus on some general matters to do with how the learning rules learn (see Hinton, 1989b for a more comprehensive discussion of some of these issues).

The simple matrix memory we described in section 2.5 of the previous chapter has the great virtue of being able to learn a new association with a single application of a learning rule. However what it can learn is very limited. The other types of network we have described can learn more interesting things but at the cost of needing iterative learning procedures: the learning rule must be repeatedly applied to find a useful set of weights. An important question for such methods is how many iterations are needed? We will consider the Delta rule once again so as to better understand the force of this question.

Application of the Delta rule over all the units in a single-layer network may be thought of as reducing the mean square of the error value, E, between the actual and desired activation level of the output units. We explained in section 2.7 of Chapter 2 how the error term may be expressed as the height of an axis in a multi-dimensional space having one dimension for each of the weights in the network. In the case of a single-layer network with just two weights, the shape of this error surface is bowl-like with just one minimum, as shown in Fig. 3.16. In the case shown in Fig. 3.16a each of the two weights contribute equally to changes in the global measure of error E, which allows relatively large learning increments (that is, a big C value in equation 2) and hence rapid learning. But what if the weights have very different effects on E as in the case illustrated in Fig. 3.16b? Here the weight represented on the x-axis has far less effect on E than the weight represented on the y-axis, resulting in a valley or ravine in the error surface. Choosing an appropriate learning increment in this circumstance is difficult: small steps would be appropriate for descending the steep sides of the valley but conceal the gentle slope of

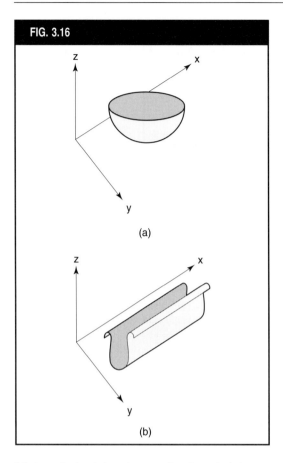

FIG. 3.16

(a)

(b)

(a) shows the bowl-shaped error surface for a single-layer network having just two weights, each of which has a similar effect on the error; (b) shows a ravine-shaped error surface in which one weight has a far greater effect on error than the other. Stable learning is more difficult in the latter case than the former.

the valley floor. Large steps would produce oscillations across the valley. Either way the network would take a long time to converge to the required configuration of weightings. A number of ways of dealing with this sort of problem have been suggested. Rumelhart et al. (1986a) used a "momentum" term in the generalised Delta rule for back-propagation. This term has the following effect, that each time a weight is changed a proportion of the immediately previous weight-change

is added in. This produces a damping down of the oscillations across the valley while allowing sufficiently large learning increments to traverse the valley.

Other techniques adjust the learning increment during the learning phase in attempts to make learning more sensitive to the system's location in weight space (examples are Jacobs, 1988 and Wasserman, 1988). Despite these various attempts, the rate of learning continues to be a general problem in connectionist architectures. As yet it is not possible to judge how serious this might be, but it should be remembered that the learning rate is likely to get worse as larger scale networks are developed. Minsky and Papert (p.253 of the epilogue to the 1988 expanded edition of *Perceptrons*) have said this of the ability of the back-propagation procedure to discover weightings to recognise symmetry in an input array:

> . . . the learning procedure required 1,208 cycles through each of the 64 possible examples — a total of 77,312 trials (enough to make us wonder if the time for this procedure to determine suitable coefficients increases exponentially with the size of the retina). PDP does not address this question. What happens when the retina has 100 elements? If such a network required on the order of 2^{200} trials to learn, most observers would lose interest.

As was noted in Chapter 2, similar remarks regarding the effects of scaling-up connectionist models apply to the problem of local minima. It should be clear that what determines whether problems of local minima or slow speed of convergence are likely to be encountered in a particular case depends on the nature of the error surface for that case. Who knows what nasty surprises lie in wait on highly convoluted n-dimensional error surfaces! Certainly not, as yet, the mathematicians. In this regard, then, connectionism is an empirical science, one aim of which is to show by simulation what particular learning procedures can do in particular domains.

Distributed memory and the representation of general and specific information

James L. McClelland and David E. Rumelhart
University of California, San Diego

We describe a distributed model of information processing and memory and apply it to the representation of general and specific information. The model consists of a large number of simple processing elements which send excitatory and inhibitory signals to each other via modifiable connections. Information processing is thought of as the process whereby patterns of activation are formed over the units in the model through their excitatory and inhibitory interactions. The memory trace of a processing event is the change or increment to the strengths of the interconnections that results from the processing event. The traces of separate events are superimposed on each other in the values of the connection strengths that result from the entire set of traces stored in the memory. The model is applied to a number of findings related to the question of whether we store abstract representations or an enumeration of specific experiences in memory. The model simulates the results of a number of important experiments which have been taken as evidence for the enumeration of specific experiences. At the same time, it shows how the functional equivalent of abstract representations — prototypes, logogens, and even rules — can emerge from the superposition of traces of specific experiences, when the conditions are right for this to happen. In essence, the model captures the structure present in a set of input patterns; thus, it behaves as though it had learned prototypes or rules, to the extent that the structure of the environment it has learned about can be captured by describing it in terms of these abstractions.

In the late 1960s and early 1970s a number of experimenters, using a variety of different tasks, demonstrated that subjects could learn through experience with exemplars of a category to respond better — more accurately, or more rapidly

Preparation of this article was supported in part by a grant from the Systems Development Foundation and in part by a National Science Foundation Grant BNS-79-24062. The first author is a recipient of a Career Development Award from the National Institute of Mental Health (5-K01-MH00385).

This article was originally presented at a conference organized by Lee Brooks and Larry Jacoby on "The Priority of the Specific." We would like to thank the organizers, as well as several of the participants, particularly Doug Medin and Rich Shiffrin, for stimulating discussion and for empirical input to the development of this article.

Requests for reprints should be sent to James L. McClelland, Department of Psychology, Carnegie-Mellon University, Pittsburgh, Pennsylvania 15213 or to David E. Rumelhart, Institute for Cognitive Science, C-015, University of California — San Diego, La Jolla, California 92093.

Journal of Experimental Psychology: General 1985, Vol. 114, No. 2, 159–188

— to the prototype than to any of the particular exemplars. The seminal demonstration of this basic point comes from the work of Posner and Keele (1968, 1970). Using a categorization task, they found that there were some conditions in which subjects categorized the prototype of a category more accurately than the particular exemplars of the category that they had previously seen. This work, and many other related experiments, supported the development of the view that memory by its basic nature somehow abstracts the central tendency of a set of disparate experiences, and gives relatively little weight to the specific experiences that gave rise to these abstractions.

Recently, however, some have come to question this "abstractive" point of view, for two reasons. First, specific events and experiences clearly play a prominent role in memory and learning. Experimental demonstrations of the importance of specific stimulus events even in tasks which have been thought to involve abstraction of a concept or rule are now legion. Responses in categorization tasks (Brooks, 1978; Medin & Shaffer, 1978), perceptual identification tasks (Jacoby, 1983a,

1983b; Whittlesea, 1983), and pronunciation tasks (Glushko, 1979) all seem to be quite sensitive to the congruity between particular training stimuli and particular test stimuli, in ways which most abstraction models would not expect.

At the same time, a number of models have been proposed in which behavior which has often been characterized as *rule-based* or *concept-based* is attributed to a process that makes use of stored traces of specific events or specific exemplars of the concepts or rules. According to this class of models, the apparently rule-based or concept-based behavior emerges from what might be called a conspiracy of individual memory traces or from a sampling of one from the set of such traces. Models of this class include the Medin and Shaffer (1978) context model, Hintzman's (1983) multiple trace model, and Whittlesea's (1983) episode model. This trend is also exemplified by our interactive activation model of word perception (McClelland & Rumelhart, 1981; Rumelhart & McClelland, 1981, 1982), and an extension of the interactive activation model to generalization from exemplars (McClelland, 1981).

One feature of some of these exemplar-based models troubles us. Many of them are internally inconsistent with respect to the issue of abstraction. Thus, though our word perception model assumes that linguistic rules emerge from a conspiracy of partial activations of detectors for particular words, thereby eliminating the need for abstraction of rules, the assumption that there is a single detector for each word implicitly assumes that there is an abstraction process that lumps each occurrence of the same word into the same single detector unit. Thus, the model has its abstraction and creates it too, though at slightly different levels.

One logically coherent response to this inconsistency is to simply say that each word or other representational object is itself a conspiracy of the entire ensemble of memory traces of the different individual experiences we have had with that unit. We will call this view the *enumeration of specific experiences* view. It is exemplified most clearly by Jacoby (1983a, 1983b), Hintzman (1983), and Whittlesea (1983).

As the papers just mentioned demonstrate, enumeration of specific experiences can work quite well as an account of quite a number of empirical findings. However, there still seems to be one drawback. Such models seem to require an unlimited amount of storage capacity, as well as mechanisms for searching an almost unlimited mass of data. This is especially true when we consider that the primitives out of which we normally assume one experience is built are themselves abstractions. For example, a word is a sequence of letters, or a sentence is a sequence of words. Are we to believe that all of these abstractions are mere notational conveniences for the theorist, and that every event is stored as an extremely rich (obviously structured) representation of the event, with no abstraction?

In this article, we consider an alternative conceptualization: a distributed, superpositional approach to memory. This view is similar to the separate enumeration of experiences view in some respects, but not in all. On both views, memory consists of traces resulting from specific experiences; and on both views, generalizations emerge from the superposition of these specific memory traces. Our model differs, though, from the enumeration of specific experiences in assuming that the superposition of traces occurs at the time of storage. We do not keep each trace in a separate place, but rather we superimpose them so that what the memory contains is a composite.

Our theme will be to show that distributed models provide a way to resolve the abstraction–representation of specifics dilemma. With a distributed model, the superposition of traces automatically results in abstraction though it can still preserve to some extent the idiosyncrasies of specific events and experiences, or of specific recurring subclasses of events and experiences.

We will begin by introducing a specific version of a distributed model of memory. We will show how it works and describe some of its basic properties. We will show how our model can account for several recent findings (Salasoo, Shiffrin, & Feustel, 1985; Whittlesea, 1983), on the effects of specific experiences on later performance, and the conditions under which functional equivalents of abstract representations such as prototypes or logogens emerge. The discussion considers generalizations of the approach to the semantic-episodic distinction and the acquisition of linguistic rule systems, and considers reasons for preferring a distributed-superpositional memory over other models.

Previous, related models. Before we get down to work, some important credits are in order. Our distributed model draws heavily from the work of Anderson (e.g. 1977, 1983; Anderson, Silverstein, Ritz, & Jones, 1977; Knapp & Anderson, 1984) and Hinton (1981a). We have adopted and synthesized what we found to be the most useful aspects of their distinct but related models, preserving (we hope) the basic spirit of both. We view our model as an exemplar of a class of existing models whose exploration Hinton, Anderson, Kohonen (e.g. Kohonen, 1977; Kohonen, Oja, & Lehtio, 1981), and others have pioneered. A useful review of prior work in this area can be obtained from Anderson and Hinton (1981) and other articles in the volume edited by Hinton and Anderson (1981). Some points similar to some of these we will be making have recently been covered in the papers of Murdock (1982) and Eich (1982), though the distributed representations we use are different in important ways from the representations used by these other authors.

Our distributed model is not a complete theory of human information processing and memory. It is a model of the internal structure of some components of information processing, in particular those concerned with the retrieval and use of prior experience. The model does not specify in and of itself how these acts of retrieval and use are planned, sequenced, and organized into coherent patterns of behavior.

A distributed model of memory

General properties

Our model adheres to the following general assumptions, some of which are shared with several other distributed models of processing and memory.

Simple, highly interconnected units. The processing system consists of a collection of simple processing units, each interconnected with many other units. The units take on activation values, and communicate with other units by sending signals modulated by weights associated with the connections between the units. Sometimes, we may think of the units as corresponding to particular representational primitives, but they need not. For example, even what we might consider to be a primitive feature of something, like having a particular color, might be a pattern of activation over a collection of units.

Modular structure. We assume that the units are organized into modules. Each module receives inputs from other modules, the units within the module are richly interconnected with each other, and they send outputs to other modules. Figure 1 illustrates the internal structure of a very simple module, and Fig. 2 illustrates some hypothetical interconnections between a number of modules. Both figures grossly underrepresent our view of the numbers of units per module and the number of modules. We would imagine that there would be thousands to millions of units per module and many hundreds or perhaps many thousands of partially redundant modules in anything close to a complete memory system.

The state of each module represents a synthesis of the states of all of the modules it receives inputs from. Some of the inputs will be from relatively more sensory modules, closer to the sensory end-organs of one modality or another. Others will come from relatively more abstract modules, which themselves receive inputs from and send outputs to other modules placed at the abstract end of several different modalities. Thus, each module combines a number of different sources of information.

Mental state as pattern of activation. In a distributed memory system, a mental state is a pattern of activation over the units in some subset of the modules. The patterns in the different modules capture different aspects of the content of the mental states in a partially overlapping fashion. Alternative mental states are simply alternative patterns of activation over the modules. Information

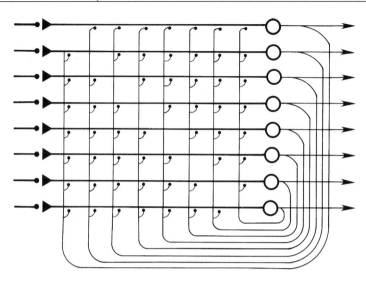

FIG. 1. A simple information processing module, consisting of a small ensemble of eight processing units. [Each unit receives inputs from other modules (indicated by the single input impinging on the input line of the node from the left; this can stand for a number of converging input signals from several nodes outside the module) and sends outputs to other modules (indicated by the output line proceeding to the right from each unit). Each unit also has a modifiable connection to all the other units in the same module, as indicated by the branches of the output lines that loop back onto the input lines leading into each unit. All connections, which may be positive or negative, are represented by dots.]

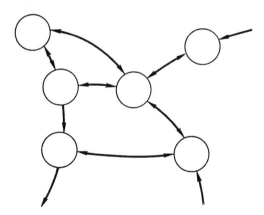

FIG. 2. An illustrative diagram showing several modules and interconnections among them. (Arrows between modules simply indicate that some of the nodes in one module send inputs to some of the nodes in the other. The exact number and organization of modules is of course unknown; the figure is simply intended to be suggestive.)

processing is the process of evolution in time of mental states.

Units play specific roles within patterns. A pattern of activation only counts as the same as another if the same units are involved. The reason for this is that the knowledge built into the system of recreating the patterns is built into the set of interconnections among the units, as we will explain later. For a pattern to access the right knowledge it must arise on the appropriate units. In this sense, the units play specific roles in the patterns. Obviously, a system of this sort is useless without sophisticated perceptual processing mechanisms at the interface between memory and the outside world, so that similar input patterns arising at different locations in the world can be mapped into the same set of units internally. Such mechanisms are outside the scope of this article (but see Hinton, 1981b; McClelland, 1985).

Memory traces as changes in the weights. Patterns of activation come and go, leaving traces behind when they have passed. What are the traces? They are changes in the strengths or *weights* of the connections between the units in the modules.

This view of the nature of the memory trace clearly sets these kinds of models apart from traditional models of memory in which some copy of the "active" pattern is generally thought of as being stored directly. Instead of this, what is actually stored in our model is changes in the connection strengths. These changes are derived from the presented pattern, and are arranged in such a way that, when a part of a known pattern is presented for processing, the interconnection strengths cause the rest of the pattern to be reinstated. Thus, although the memory trace is not a copy of the learned pattern, it is something from which a replica of that pattern can be recreated. As we already said, each memory trace is distributed over many different connections, and each connection participates in many different memory traces. The traces of different mental states are therefore superimposed in the same set of weights. Surprisingly enough as we will see in several examples, the connections between the units in a single module can store the information needed to complete many different familiar patterns.

Retrieval as reinstatement of prior pattern of activation. Retrieval amounts to partial reinstatement of a mental state, using a cue which is a fragment of the original state. For any given module, we can see the cues as originating from outside of it. Some cues could arise ultimately from sensory input. Others would arise from the results of previous retrieval operations fed back to the memory system under the control of a search or retrieval plan. It would be premature to speculate on how such schemes would be implemented in this kind of a model, but it is clear that they must exist.

Detailed assumptions

In the rest of our presentation, we will be focusing on operations that take place within a single module. This obviously oversimplifies the behavior of a complete memory system because the modules are assumed to be in continuous interaction. The simplification is justified, however, in that it allows us to focus on some of the basic properties of distributed memory that are visible even without these interactions with other modules.

Let us look, therefore, at the internal structure of one very simple module, as shown in Fig. 1. Again, our image is that in a real system there would be much larger numbers of units. We have restricted our analysis to small numbers simply to illustrate basic principles as clearly as possible; this also helps to keep the running time of simulations in bounds.

Activation values. The units take on activation values which range from -1 to $+1$. Zero represents in this case a neutral resting value, toward which the activations of the units tend to decay.

Inputs, outputs, and internal connections. Each unit receives input from other modules and sends output to other modules. For the present, we assume that the inputs from other modules occur at connections whose weights are fixed. In the simulations, we treat the input from outside the module as a fixed pattern, ignoring (for simplicity) the fact that the input pattern evolves in time and might be affected by feedback from the module under study. Although the input to each unit might arise from a combination of sources in other modules, we can lump the external input to each unit into a single real valued number representing the combined effects of all components of the external input. In addition to extra-modular connections, each unit is connected to all other units in the module via a weighted connection. The weights on these connections are modifiable, as described later. The weights can take on any real values, positive, negative, or 0. There is no connection from a unit onto itself.

The processing cycle. Processing within a module takes place as follows. Time is divided into discrete ticks. An input pattern is presented at some point in time over some or all of the input lines to the module and is then left on for several ticks, until the pattern of activation it produces settles down and stops changing.

Each tick is divided into two phases. In the first phase, each unit determines its net input, based on the external input to the unit and activations of all of the units at the end of the preceding tick modulated by the weight coefficients which determine the strength and direction of each unit's effect on every other.

For mathematical precision, consider two units in our module, and call one of them unit i, and the other unit j. The input to unit i from unit j, written i_{ij} is just

$$i_{ij} = a_j w_{ij},$$

where a_j is the activation of unit j, and w_{ij} is the weight constant modulating the effect of unit j on unit i. The total input to unit i from all other units internal to the module, i_i, is then just the sum of all of these separate inputs:

$$i_i = \sum_j i_{ij}.$$

Here, j ranges over all units in the module other than i. This sum is then added to the *external* input to the unit, arising from outside the module, to obtain the net input to unit i, n_i:

$$n_i = i_i + e_i,$$

where e_i is just the lumped external input to unit i.

In the second phase, the activations of the units are updated. If the net input is positive, the activation of the unit is incremented by an amount proportional to the distance left to the ceiling activation level of $+1.0$. If the net input is negative, the activation is decremented by an amount proportional to the distance left to the floor activation level of -1.0. There is also a decay factor which tends to pull the activation of the unit back toward the resting level of 0.

Mathematically, we can express these assumptions as follows: For unit i, if $n_i > 0$,

$$\mathring{a}_i = En_i(1 - a_i) - Da_i.$$

If $n_i \leq 0$,

$$\mathring{a}_i = En_i[a_i - (-1)] - Da_i.$$

In these equations, E and D are global parameters which apply to all units, and set the rates of excitation and decay, respectively. The term a_i is the activation of unit i at the end of the previous cycle, and $\mathring{a}_i$ is the change in a_i; that is, it is the amount added to (or, if negative, subtracted from) the old value a_i to determine its new value for the next cycle.

Given a fixed set of inputs to a particular unit, its activation level will be driven up or down in response until the activation reaches the point where the incremental effects of the input are balanced by the decay. In practice, of course, the situation is complicated by the fact that as each unit's activation is changing it alters the input to the others. Thus, it is necessary to run the simulation to see how the system will behave for any given set of inputs and any given set of weights. In all the simulations reported here, the model is allowed to run for 50 cycles, which is considerably more than enough for it to achieve a stable pattern of activation over all the units.

Memory traces. The memory trace of a particular pattern of activation is a set of changes in the entire set of weights in the module. We call the whole set of changes an *increment* to the weights. After a stable pattern of activation is achieved, weight adjustment takes place. This is though of as occurring simultaneously for all of the connections in the module.

The Delta rule. The rule that determines the size and direction (up or down) of the change at each connection is the crux of the model. The idea is often difficult to grasp on first reading, but once it is understood it seems very simple, and it directly captures the goal of facilitating the completion of the pattern, given some part of the pattern as a retrieval or completion cue.

To allow each part of a pattern to reconstruct the rest of the pattern, we simply want to set up the internal connections among the units in the module so that when part of the pattern is presented, activating some of the units in the module, the internal connections will lead the active units to tend to reproduce the rest. To do this, we want to make the internal input to each unit have the same effect on the unit that the external input has on the unit. That is, given a particular pattern to be stored, we want to find a set of connections such that the internal input to each unit from all of the other units matches the external input to that unit. The connection change procedure we will describe has the effect of moving the weights of all the connections in the direction of achieving this goal.

The first step in weight adjustment is to see how well the module is already doing. If the network is already matching the external input to each unit with the internal input from the other units, the weights do not need to be changed. To get an index of how well the network is already doing at matching its excitatory input, we assume that each unit i computes the difference Δ_i between its external input and the net internal input to the unit from the other units in the module:

$$\Delta_i = e_i - i_i.$$

In determining the activation value of the unit, we added the external input together with the internal input. Now, in adjusting the weights, we are taking the difference between these two terms. This implies that the unit must be able to aggregate all inputs for purposes of determining its activation, but it must be able to distinguish between external and internal inputs for purposes of adjusting its weights.

Let us consider the term Δ_i for a moment. If it is positive, the internal input is not activating the unit enough to match the external input to the unit. If negative, it is activating the unit too much. If zero, everything is fine and we do not want to change anything. Thus, Δ_i determines the magnitude and direction of the overall change that needs to be made in the internal input to unit i. To achieve this overall effect, the individual weights are then adjusted according to the following formula:

$$\mathring{w}_{ij} = S\Delta_i a_j.$$

The parameter S is just a global strength parameter which regulates the overall magnitude of the adjustments of the weights; $\mathring{w}_{ij}$ is the change in the weight to i from j.

We call this weight modification rule the *delta rule*. It has all the intended consequences; that is, it tends to drive the weights in the direction of the right values to make the internal inputs to a unit match the external inputs. For example, consider the case in which Δ_i is positive and a_j is positive. In this case, the value of Δ_i tells us that unit i is not receiving enough excitatory input, and the value of a_j tells us that unit j has positive activation. In this case, the delta rule will increase the weight from j to i. The result will be that the next time unit j has a positive activation, its excitat-

ory effect on unit i will be increased, thereby reducing Δ_i.

Similar reasoning applies to cases where Δ_i is negative, a_j is negative, or both are negative. Of course, when either Δ_i or a_j is 0, w_{ij} is not changed. In the first case, there is no error to compensate for; in the second case, a change in the weight will have no effect the next time unit j has the same activation value.

What the delta rule can and cannot do. The delta rule is a continuous variant of the perceptron convergence procedure (Rosenblatt, 1962), and has been independently invented many times (see Sutton & Barto, 1981, for a discussion). Its popularity is based on the fact that it is an error-correcting rule, unlike the Hebb rule used until recently by Anderson (1977; Anderson et al., 1977). A number of interesting theorems have been proven about this rule (Kohonen, 1977; Stone, 1985). Basically, the important result is that, for a set of patterns which we present repeatedly to a module, if there is a set of weights which will allow the system to reduce Δ to 0 for each unit in each pattern, this rule will find it through repeated exposure to all of the members of the set of patterns.

It is important to note that the existence of a set of weights that will allow Δ to be reduced to 0 is not guaranteed, but depends on the structure inherent in the set of patterns which the model is given to learn. To be perfectly learnable by our model, the patterns must conform to the following *linear predictability constraint*:

> Over the entire set of patterns, the external input to each unit must be predictable from a linear combination of the activations of every other unit.

This is an important constraint, for there are many sets of patterns that violate it. However, it is necessary to distinguish between the patterns used inside the model, and the stimulus patterns to which human observers might be exposed in experiments, as described by psychologists. For our model to work, it is important for patterns to be assigned to stimuli in a way that will allow them to be learned.

A crucial issue, then, is the exact manner in which the stimulus patterns are encoded. As a rule of thumb, an encoding which treats each dimension or aspect of a stimulus separately is unlikely to be sufficient; what is required is a *context sensitive* encoding, such that the representation of each aspect is colored by the other aspects. For a full discussion of this issue, see Hinton, McClelland, and Rumelhart (1986).

Decay in the increments to the weights. We assume that each trace or increment undergoes a decay process though the rate of decay of the increments is assumed to be much slower than the rate of decay of patterns of activation. Following a number of theorists (e.g. Wickelgren, 1979), we imagine that traces at first decay rapidly, but then the remaining portion becomes more and more resistant to further decay. Whether it ever reaches a point where it is no longer decaying at all we do not know. The basic effect of this assumption is that individual inputs exert large short-term effects on the weights, but after they decay the residual effect is considerably smaller.

The fact that each increment has its own temporal history increases the complexity of computer simulations enormously. In all of the particular cases to be examined, we will therefore specify simplified assumptions to keep the simulations tractable.

Illustrative examples

In this section, we describe a few illustrative examples to give the reader a feel for how we use the model, and to illustrate key aspects of its behavior.

Storage and retrieval of several patterns in a single memory module. First, we consider the storage and retrieval of two patterns in a single module of 8 units. Our basic aim is to show how several distinct patterns of activation can all be stored in the same set of weights, by what Lashley (1950) called a kind of algebraic summation, and not interfere with each other.

Before the first presentation of either pattern, we start out with all the weights set to 0. The first pattern is given at the top of Table 1. It is an

TABLE 1
Behavior of an 8-Unit Distributed Memory Module

Case	Input or response for each unit							
Pattern 1								
The Pattern:	+	−	+	−	+	+	−	−
Response to Pattern before learning	+.5	−.5	+.5	−.5	+.5	+.5	−.5	−.5
Response to Pattern after 10 learning trials	+.7	−.7	+.7	−.7	+.7	+.7	−.7	−.7
Test Input (Incomplete version of Pattern)	+	−	+	−				
Response	+.6	−.6	+.6	−.6	+.4	+.4	−.4	−.4
Test Input (Distortion of Pattern)	+	−	+	−	+	+	−	+*
Response	+.6	−.6	+.6	−.6	+.6	+.6	−.6	+.1
Pattern 2								
The Pattern:	+	+	−	−	−	+	−	+
Response to Pattern with weights learned for Pattern 1	+.5	+.5	−.5	−.5	−.5	+.5	−.5	+.5
Response to Pattern after 10 learning trials	+.7	+.7	−.7	−.7	−.7	+.7	−.7	+.7
Retest of response to Pattern 1	+.7	−.7	+.7	−.7	+.7	+.7	−.7	−.7

arrangement of +1 and −1 inputs to the eight units in the module. (In Table 1, the 1s are suppressed in the inputs for clarity). When we present the first pattern to this module, the resulting activation values simply reflect the effects of the inputs themselves because none of the units are yet influencing any of the others.

Then, we teach the module this pattern by presenting it to the module 10 times. Each time, after the pattern of activation has had plenty of time to settle down, we adjust the weights. The next time we present the complete pattern after the 10 learning trials, the module's response is enhanced, compared with the earlier situation. That is, the activation values are increased in magnitude, owing to the combined effects of the external and internal inputs to each of the units. If we present an incomplete part of the pattern, the module can complete it; if we distort the pattern, the module tends to drive the activation back in the direction it thinks it ought to have. Of course, the magnitudes of these effects depend on parameters; but the basic nature of the effects is independent of these details.

Figure 3 shows the weights our learning procedure has assigned. Actual numerical values have been suppressed to emphasize the basic pattern of excitatory and inhibitory influences. In this example, all the numerical values are identical. The pattern of + and − signs simply gives the pattern

of pairwise correlations of the elements. This is as it should be to allow pattern enhancement, completion, and noise elimination. Units which have the same activation in the pattern have positive weights, so that when one is activated it will tend to activate the other, and when one is inhibited it will tend to inhibit the other. Units which have different activations in the pattern have negative weights, so that when one is activated it will inhibit the other and vice versa.

What happens when we present a new pattern, dissimilar to the first? This is illustrated in the lower portion of Table 1. At first, the network responds to it just as though it knew nothing at all: The activations simply reflect the direct effects of the input, as they would in a module with all 0 weights. The reason is simply that the effects of the weights already in the network cancel each other out. This is a result of the fact that the two patterns are maximally dissimilar from each other. If the patterns had been more similar, there would not have been this complete cancellation of effects.

Now we learn the new pattern, presenting it 10 times and adjusting the weights each time. The resulting weights (Fig. 3) represent the sum of the weights for Patterns 1 and 2. The response to the new pattern is enhanced, as shown in Table 1. The response to the old, previously learned pattern is not affected. The module will now show enhancement, completion, and noise elimination for both patterns though these properties are not illustrated in Table 1.

Thus, we see that more than one pattern can coexist in the same set of weights. There is an effect of storing multiple patterns, of course. When only one pattern is stored, the whole pattern (or at least, a pale copy of it) can be retrieved by driving the activation of any single unit in the appropriate direction. As more patterns are stored, larger subpatterns are generally needed to specify the pattern to be retrieved uniquely.

Learning a prototype from exemplars

In the preceding section, we considered the learning of particular patterns and showed that the delta rule was capable of learning multiple patterns, in the same set of connections. In this section, we consider what happens when distributed models

	Pattern 1								Pattern 2							
	+	−	+	−	+	+	−	−	+	+	−	−	−	+	−	+

	Weights for Pattern 1								Weights for Pattern 2								Composite Weights for Both Pattern							
	1	2	3	4	5	6	7	8	1	2	3	4	5	6	7	8	1	2	3	4	5	6	7	8
1		−	+	−	+	+	−	−		+	−	−	−	+	−	+				−−		++	−−	
2	−		−	+	−	−	+	+	+		−	−	−	+	−	+			−−		−−			++
3	+	−		−	+	+	−	−	−	−		+	+	−	+	−		−−			++			−−
4	−	+	−		−	−	+	+	−	−	+		+	−	+	−	−−					−−	++	
5	+	−	+	−		+	−	−	−	−	+	+		−	+	−		−−	++					−−
6	+	−	+	−	+		−	−	+	+	−	−	−		−	+	++			−−			−−	
7	−	+	−	+	−	−		+	−	−	+	+	+	−		−	−−			++		−−		
8	−	+	−	+	−	−	+		+	+	−	−	−	+	−			++	−−		−−			

FIG. 3. Weights acquired in learning Pattern 1 and Pattern 2 separately, and the composite weights resulting from learning both. (The weight in a given cell reflects the strength of the connection from the corresponding column unit to the corresponding row unit. Only the sign and relative magnitude of the weights are indicated. A blank indicates a weight of 0; + and − signify positive and negative, with a double symbol, ++ or −−, representing a value twice as large as a single symbol, + or −.)

using the delta rule are presented with an ensemble of patterns that have some common structure. The examples described in this section illustrate how the delta rule can be used to extract the structure from an ensemble of inputs, and throw away random variability.

Let us consider the following hypothetical situation. A little boy sees many different dogs, each only once, and each with a different name. All the dogs are a little different from each other, but in general there is a pattern which represents the typical dog: each one is just a different distortion of this prototype. (We are not claiming that the dogs in the world have no more structure than this; we make this assumption for purposes of illustration only.) For now we will assume that the names of the dogs are all completely different. Given this experience, we would expect that the boy would learn the prototype of the category, even without ever seeing any particular dog which matches the prototype directly (Posner & Keele, 1968, 1970; Anderson, 1977, applies an earlier version of a distributed model to this case). That is, the prototype will seem as familiar as any of the exemplars, and he will be able to complete the pattern corresponding to the prototype from any part of it. He will not, however, be very likely to remember the names of each of the individual dogs though he may remember the most recent ones.

We model this situation with a module consisting of 24 units. We assume that the presentation of a dog produces a visual pattern of activation over 16 of the units in the hypothetical module (the 9th through 24th, counting from left to right). The name of the dog produces a pattern of activation over the other 8 units (Units 1 to 8, counting from left to right).

Each visual pattern, by assumption, is a distortion of a single prototype. The prototype used for the simulation simply had a random series of +1 and −1 values. Each distortion of the prototype was made by probabilistically flipping the sign of randomly selected elements of the prototype pattern. For each new distorted pattern, each element has an independent chance of being flipped, with a probability of .2. Each name pattern was simply a random sequence of +1s and −1s for the eight name units. Each encounter with a new dog

is modeled as a presentation of a new name pattern with a new distortion of the prototype visual pattern. Fifty different trials were run, each with a new name pattern–visual pattern pair.

For each presentation, the pattern of activation is allowed to stabilize, and then the weights are adjusted as before. The increment to the weights is then allowed to decay considerably before the next input is presented. For simplicity, we assume that before the next pattern is presented, the last increment decays to a fixed small proportion of its initial value, and thereafter undergoes no further decay.

What does the module learn? The module acquires a set of weights which is continually buffeted about by the latest dog exemplar, but which captures the prototype dog quite well. Waiting for the last increment to decay to the fixed residual yields the weights shown in Fig. 4.

These weights capture the correlations among the values in the prototype dog pattern quite well. The lack of exact uniformity is due to the more recent distortions presented, whose effects have not been corrected by subsequent distortions. This is one way in which the model gives priority to specific exemplars, especially recent ones. The effects of recent exemplars are particularly strong, of course, before they have had a chance to decay. The module can complete the prototype quite well, and it will respond more strongly to the prototype than to any distortion of it. It has, however, learned no particular relation between this prototype and any name pattern, because a totally different random association was presented on each trial. If the pattern of activation on the name units had been the same in every case (say, each dog was just called *dog*), or even in just a reasonable fraction of the cases, then the module would have been able to retrieve this shared name pattern from the prototype of the visual pattern and the prototype pattern from the name.

Multiple, nonorthogonal prototypes. In the preceding simulation we have seen how the distributed model acts as a sort of signal averager, finding the central tendency of a set of related patterns. In and of itself this is an important property of the model, but the importance of this property increases when we realize that the model

Prototype pattern:

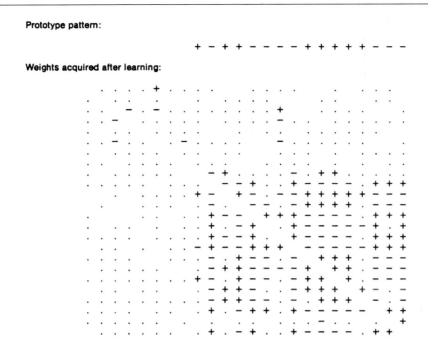

FIG. 4. Weights acquired in learning from distorted exemplars of a prototype. (The prototype pattern is shown above the weight matrix. Blank entries correspond to weights with absolute values less than .01; dots correspond to absolute values less than .06; pluses or minuses are used for weights with larger absolute values.)

can average several different patterns in the same composite memory trace. Thus, several different prototypes can be stored in the same set of weights. This is important, because it means that the model does not fall into the trap of needing to decide which category to put a pattern in before knowing which prototype to average it with. The acquisition of the different prototypes proceeds without any sort of explicit categorization. If the patterns are sufficiently dissimilar, there is no interference among them at all. Increasing similarity leads to increased confusability during learning, but eventually the delta rule finds a set of connection strengths that minimizes the confusability of similar patterns.

To illustrate these points, we created a simulation analog of the following hypothetical situation. Let us say that our little boy sees, in the course of his daily experience, different dogs, different cats, and different bagels. First, let's consider the case in which each experience with a dog, a cat, or a bagel is accompanied by someone saying *dog*, *cat*, or *bagel*, as appropriate.

The simulation analog of this situation involved forming three *visual* prototype patterns of 16 elements, two of them (the one for dog and the one for cat) somewhat similar to each other (r = .5), and the third (for the bagel) orthogonal to both of the other two. Paired with each visual pattern was a name pattern of eight elements. Each name pattern was orthogonal to both of the others. Thus, the prototype visual pattern for cat and the prototype visual pattern for dog were similar to each other, but their names were not related.

Stimulus presentations involved presentations of distorted exemplars of the name–visual pattern pairs to a module of 24 elements like the one used in the previous simulation. This time, both the name pattern and the visual pattern were distorted, with each element having its sign flipped with an independent probability of .1 on each presentation. Fifty different distortions of each name–visual pattern pair were presented in groups of three consisting of one distortion of the dog pair, one distortion of the cat pair, and one distortion of the bagel pair. Weight adjustment occurred after each presentation, with decay to a fixed residual before each new presentation.

At the end of training, the module was tested by presenting each name pattern and observing the resulting pattern of activation over the visual nodes, and by presenting each visual pattern and observing the pattern of activation over the name nodes. The results are shown in Table 2. In each case, the model reproduces the correct completion for the probe, and there is no apparent contamination of the cat pattern by the dog pattern, even though the visual patterns are similar to each other.

In general, pattern completion is a matter of degree. One useful measure of pattern completion is the dot product of the pattern of activation over the units with the pattern of external inputs to the units. Because we treat the external inputs as +1s and −1s, and because the activation of each node can only range from +1 to −1, the largest possible value the dot product can have is 1.0. We will use this measure explicitly later

when considering some simulations of experimental results. For getting an impression of the degree of pattern reinstatement in the present cases, it is sufficient to note that when the sign of all of the elements is correct, as it is in all of the completions in Table 2, the average magnitude of the activations of the units corresponds to the dot product.

In a case like the present one, in which some of the patterns known to the model are correlated, the values of the connection strengths that the model produces do not necessarily have a simple interpretation. Though their sign always corresponds to the sign of the correlation between the activations of the two units, their magnitude is not a simple reflection of the magnitude of their correlation, but is influenced by the degree to which the model is relying on this particular correlation to predict the activation of one node from the others. Thus, in a case where two nodes (call them i and j) are perfectly correlated, the strength of the connection from i to j will depend on the

TABLE 2
Results of Tests After Learning the Dog, Cat, and Bagel Patterns

	Input or response for each unit	
Case	Name units	Visual pattern units
Pattern for dog prototype	+ − + − + − + −	+ − + + − − − − + + + + + − − −
Response to dog name		+3 −4 +4 +4 −4 −4 −4 −4 +4 +4 +4 +3 +4 −4 −4 −3
Response to dog visual pattern	+5 −4 +4 −5 +5 −4 +4 −4	
Pattern for cat prototype	+ + − − + + − −	+ − + + − − − − + − + − + + − +
Response to cat name		+4 −3 +4 +4 −4 −3 −3 −4 +4 −4 +4 −4 +4 +4 −4 +4
Response to cat visual pattern	+5 +4 −4 −5 +4 +4 −4 −4	
Pattern for bagel prototype	+ − − + + − − +	+ + − + − + + − + − − + + + + −
Response to bagal name		+3 +4 −4 +4 −4 +4 +4 −4 +4 −4 −4 +4 +3 +4 +4 −4
Response to bagel visual pattern	+4 −4 −4 +4 +4 −4 −4 +4	

Note. Decimal points have been suppressed for clarity; thus, an entry of +4 represents an activation value of +.4.

number of other nodes whose activations are correlated with j. If i is the only node correlated with j, it will have to do all the work of predicting j, so the weight will be very strong; on the other hand, if many nodes besides i are correlated with j, then the work of predicting j will be spread around, and the weight between i and j will be considerably smaller. The weight matrix acquired as a result of learning the dog, cat, and bagel patterns (Fig. 5) reflects these effects. For example, across the set of three prototypes, Units 1 and 5 are perfectly correlated, as are Units 2 and 6. Yet the connection from 2 to 5 is stronger than the connection from 1 to 4 (these connections are *d in Fig. 5). The reason for the difference is that 2 is

one of only three units which correlate perfectly with 5, whereas Unit 1 is one of seven units which correlate perfectly with 4. (In Fig. 5, the weights do not reflect these contrasts perfectly in every case, because the noise introduced into the learning happens by chance to alter some of the correlations present in the prototype patterns. Averaged over time, though, the weights will conform to their expected values.)

Thus far we have seen that several prototypes, not necessarily orthogonal, can be stored in the same module without difficulty. It is true, though we do not illustrate it, that the model has more trouble with the cat and dog visual patterns earlier on in training, before learning has essentially

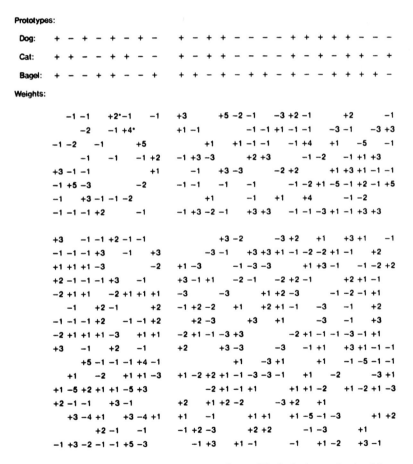

FIG. 5. Weights acquired in learning the three prototype patterns shown. (Blanks in the matrix of weights correspond to weights with absolute values less than or equal to .05. Otherwise the actual value of the weight is about .05 times the value shown; thus +5 stands for a weight of +.25. The gap in the horizontal and vertical dimensions is used to separate the name field from the visual pattern field.)

reached asymptotic levels as it has by the end of 50 cycles through the full set of patterns. And, of course, even at the end of learning, if we present as a probe a part of the visual pattern, if it does not differentiate between the dog and the cat, the model will produce a blended response. Both these aspects of the model seem generally consistent with what we should expect from human subjects.

Category learning without labels. An important further fact about the model is that it can learn several different visual patterns, even without the benefit of distinct identifying name patterns during learning. To demonstrate this we repeated the previous simulation, simply replacing the name patterns with 0s. The model still learns about the internal structure of the visual patterns, so that, after 50 cycles through the stimuli, any unique subpart of any one of the patterns is sufficient to reinstate to the rest of the corresponding pattern correctly. This aspect of the model's behavior is illustrated in Table 3. Thus, we have a model that can, in effect, acquire a number of distinct categories, simply through a process of incrementing connection strengths in response to each new stimulus presentation. Noise, in the form of distortions in the patterns, is filtered out. The model does not require a name or other guide to distinguish the patterns belonging to different categories.

Coexistence of the prototype and repeated exemplars. One aspect of our discussion up to this point may have been slightly misleading. We may have given the impression that the model is simply a prototype extraction device. It is more than this, however; it is a device that captures whatever structure is present in a set of patterns. When the set of patterns has a prototype structure, the model will act as though it is extracting prototypes; but when it has a different structure, the model will do its best to accommodate this as well. For example, the model permits the coexistence of representations of prototypes with representations of particular, repeated exemplars.

Consider the following situation. Let us say that our little boy knows a dog next door named Rover and a dog at his grandma's house named Fido. And let's say that the little boy goes to the park from time to time and sees dogs, each of which his father tells him is a dog.

The simulation-analog of this involved three different eight-element name patterns, one for Rover, one for Fido, and one for Dog. The visual pattern for Rover was a particular randomly generated distortion of the dog prototype pattern, as was the visual pattern for Fido. For the dogs seen in the park, each one was simply a new random distortion of the prototype. The probability of flipping the sign of each element was again .2. The learning regime was otherwise the same as in the dog–cat–bagel example.

At the end of 50 learning cycles, the model was able to retrieve the visual pattern corresponding

TABLE 3
Results of Tests After Learning The Dog, Cat, and Bagel Patterns Without Names

Case								*Input or response for each visual unit*								
Dog visual																
pattern	+	−	+	+	−	−	−	−	+	+	+	+	+	−	−	−
Probe									+	+	+	+				
Response	+3	−3	+3	+3	−3	−4	−3	−3	+6	+5	+6	+5	+3	−2	−3	−2
Cat visual																
pattern	+	−	+	+	−	−	−	−	+	−	+	−	+	+	−	+
Probe									+	−	+	−				
Response	+3	−3	+3	+3	−3	−3	−3	−3	+6	−5	+6	−5	+3	+2	−3	+2
Bagel visual																
pattern	+	+	−	+	−	+	+	−	+	−	−	+	+	+	+	−
Probe									+	−	−	+				
Response	+2	+3	−4	+3	−3	+3	+3	−3	+6	−6	−6	+6	+3	+3	+3	−3

to either repeated exemplar (see Table 4) given the associated name as input. When given the Dog name pattern as input, it retrieves the prototype visual pattern for dog. It can also retrieve the appropriate name from each of the three visual patterns. This is true, even though the visual pattern for Rover differs from the visual pattern for dog by only a single element. Because of the special importance of this particular element, the weights from this element to the units that distinguish Rover's name pattern from the prototype name pattern are quite strong. Given part of a visual pattern, the model will complete it; if the part corresponds to the prototype, then that is what is completed, but if it corresponds to one of the repeated exemplars, that exemplar is completed. The model, then, knows both the prototype and the repeated exemplars quite well. Several other sets of prototypes and their repeated exemplars could also be stored in the same module, as long as its capacity is not exceeded; given large numbers of units per module, a lot of different patterns can be stored.

Let us summarize the observations we have made in these several illustrative simulations. First, our distributed model is capable of storing not just one but a number of different patterns. It can pull the central tendency of a number of different patterns out of the noisy inputs; it can create the functional equivalent of perceptual categories with or without the benefit of labels; and it can allow representations of repeated exemplars to coexist with the representation of the prototype of the categories they exemplify in the same composite memory trace. The model is not simply a categorizer or a prototyping device; rather, it captures the structure inherent in a set of patterns, whether it be characterizable by description in terms of prototypes or not.

The ability to retrieve accurate completions of similar patterns is a property of the model which depends on the use of the delta learning rule. This allows both the storage of different prototypes that are not completely orthogonal and the coexistence of prototype representations and repeated exemplars.

TABLE 4
Results of Tests with Prototype and Specific Exemplar Patterns

Case	Name units								Visual pattern units															
																Input or response for each unit								
Pattern for dog prototype	+	−	+	−	+	−	+	−	+	−	+	+	−	−	−	−	+	+	+	+	+	−	−	−
Response to prototype name									+4	−5	+3	+3	−4	−3	−3	−3	+3	+3	+4	+3	+4	−3	−4	−4
Response to prototype visual pattern	+5	−4	+4	−4	+5	−4	+4	−4																
Pattern for "Fido" exemplar	+	−	−	−	+	−	−	−	+	−	(−)	+	−	−	−	−	+	+	+	+	+	(+)	−	−
Response to Fido name									+4	−4	−4	+4	−4	−4	−4	−4	+4	+4	+4	+4	+4	+4	−4	−4
Response to Fido visual pattern	+5	−5	−3	−5	+4	−5	−3	−5																
Pattern for "Rover" exemplar	+	−	−	+	+	+	−	+	+	(+)	+	+	−	−	−	−	+	+	+	+	+	−	−	−
Response to Rover name									+4	+5	+4	+4	−4	−4	−4	−4	+4	+4	+4	+4	+4	−4	−4	−4
Response to Rover visual pattern	+4	−4	−2	+4	+4	+4	−2	+4																

Simulations of experimental results

Up to this point, we have discussed our distributed model in general terms and have outlined how it can accommodate both abstraction and representation of specific information in the same network. We will now consider, in the next two sections, how well the model does in accounting for some recent evidence about the details of the influence of specific experiences on performance.

Repetition and familiarity effects

When we perceive an item — say a word, for example — this experience has effects on our later performance. If the word is presented again, within a reasonable interval of time, the prior presentation makes it possible for us to recognize the word more quickly, or from a briefer presentation.

Traditionally, this effect has been interpreted in terms of units that represent the presented items in memory. In the case of word perception, these units are called *word detectors* or *logogens*, and a model of repetition effects for words has been constructed around the logogen concept (Morton, 1979). The idea is that the threshold for the logogen is reduced every time it *fires* (that is, every time the word is recognized), thereby making it easier to fire the logogen at a later time. There is supposed to be a decay of this priming effect, with time, so that eventually the effect of the first presentation wears off.

This traditional interpretation has come under serious question of late, for a number of reasons. Perhaps paramount among the reasons is the fact that the exact relation between the specific context in which the priming event occurs and the context in which the test event occurs makes a huge difference (Jacoby, 1983a, 1983b). Generally speaking, nearly any change in the stimulus — from spoken to printed, from male speaker to female speaker, and so forth — tends to reduce the magnitude of the priming effect.

These facts might easily be taken to support the enumeration of specific experiences view, in which the logogen is replaced by the entire ensemble of experiences with the word, with each experience capturing aspects of the specific context in which it occurred. Such a view has been

championed most strongly by Jacoby (1983a, 1983b).

Our distributed model offers an alternative interpretation. We see the traces laid down by the processing of each input as contributing to the composite, superimposed memory representation. Each time a stimulus is processed, it gives rise to a slightly different memory trace: either because the item itself is different or because it occurs in a different context that conditions its representation. The logogen is replaced by the set of specific traces, but the traces are not kept separate. Each trace contributes to the composite, but the characteristics of particular experiences tend nevertheless to be preserved, at least until they are overridden by cancelling characteristics of other traces. And the traces of one stimulus pattern can coexist with the traces of other stimuli, within the same composite memory trace.

It should be noted that we are not faulting either the logogen model or models based on the enumeration of specific experiences for their physiological implausibility here, because these models are generally not stated in physiological terms, and their authors might reasonably argue that nothing in their models precludes distributed storage at a physiological level. What we are suggesting is that a model which proposes explicitly distributed, superpositional storage can account for the kinds of findings that logogen models have been proposed to account for, as well as other findings which strain the utility of the concept of the logogen as a psychological construct. In the discussion section we will consider ways in which our distributed model differs from enumeration models as well.

To illustrate the distributed model's account of repetition priming effects, we carried out the following simulation experiment. We made up a set of eight random vectors, each 24 elements long, each one to be thought of as the prototype of a different recurring stimulus pattern. Through a series of 10 training cycles using the set of eight vectors, we constructed a composite memory trace. During training, the model did not actually see the prototypes, however. On each training presentation it saw a new random distortion of one of the eight prototypes. In each of the distortions, each of the 24 elements had its value flipped with a probability of .1. Weights were adjusted after every presentation, and then allowed to decay to a fixed residual before the presentation of the next pattern.

The composite memory trace formed as a result of the experience just described plays the same role in our model that the set of logogens or detectors play in a model like Morton's or, indeed, the interactive activation model of word preception. That is, the trace contains information which allows the model to enhance perception of familiar patterns, relative to unfamiliar ones. We demonstrate this by comparing the activations resulting from the processing of subsequent presentations of new distortions of our eight familiar patterns with other random patterns with which the model is not familiar. The pattern of activation that is the model's response to the input is stronger, and grows to a particular level more quickly, if the stimulus is a new distortion of an old pattern than if it is a new pattern. We already observed this general enhanced response to exact repeti-

tions of familiar patterns in our first example (see Table 1). Figure 6 illustrates that the effect also applies to new distortions of old patterns, as compared with new patterns, and illustrates how the activation process proceeds over successive time cycles of processing.

Pattern activation and response strength. The measure of activation shown in the Fig. 6 is the dot product of the pattern of activation over the units of the module times the stimulus pattern itself, normalized for the number n of elements in the pattern: For the pattern j we call this expression α_j. The expression α_j represents the degree to which the actual pattern of activation on the units captures the input pattern. It is an approximate analog to the activation of an individual unit in models which allocate a single unit to each whole pattern.

To relate these pattern activations to response probabilities, we must assume that mechanisms exist for translating patterns of activation into overt responses measurable by an experimenter. We will

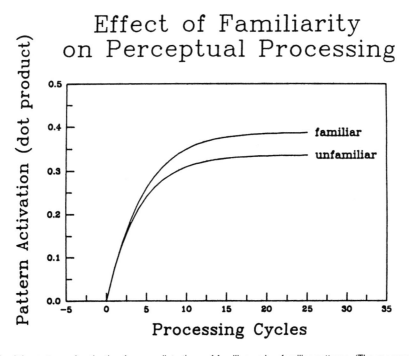

FIG. 6. Growth of the pattern of activation for new distortions of familiar and unfamiliar patterns. (The measure of the strength of the pattern of activation is the dot product of the response pattern with the input vector. See text for an explanation.)

assume that these mechanisms obey the principles stated by McClelland and Rumelhart (1981) in the interactive activation model of word perception, simply replacing the activations of particular units with the α measure of pattern activation.

In the interactive activation model, the probability of choosing the response appropriate to a particular unit was based on an exponential transform of a time average of the activation of the unit. This quantity, called the *strength* of the particular response, was divided by the total strength of all alternatives (including itself) to find the response probability (Luce, 1963). One complication arises because of the fact that it is not in general possible to specify exactly what the set of alternative responses might be for the denominator. For this reason, the strengths of other responses are represented by a constant C (which stands for the competition). Thus, the expression for probability of choosing the response appropriate to pattern j is just $p(r_j) = e^{k\bar{\alpha}_j}/(C + e^{k\bar{\alpha}_j})$, where $\bar{\alpha}_j$ represents the time average of α_j, and k is a scaling constant.

These assumptions finesse an important issue, namely the mechanism by which a pattern of activation give rise to a particular response. A detailed discussion of this issue will appear in Rumelhart and McClelland (1986). For now, we wish only to capture basic properties any actual response selection mechanism must have: It must be sensitive to the input pattern, and it must approximate other basic aspects of response selection behavior captured by the Luce (1963) choice model.

Effects of experimental variables on time-accuracy curves. Applying the assumptions just described, we can calculate probability of correct response as a function of processing cycles for familiar and unfamiliar patterns. The result, for a particular choice of scaling parameters, is shown in Fig. 7. If we assume performance in a perceptual identification task is based on the height of the curve at the point where processing is cut off by masking (McClelland & Rumelhart, 1981), then familiarity would lead to greater accuracy of perceptual identification at a given exposure

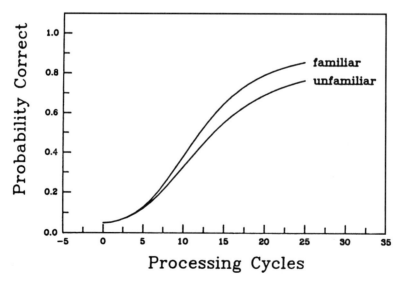

FIG. 7. Simulated growth of response accuracy over the units in a 24-unit module, as a function of processing cycles, for new distortions of previously learned patterns compared with new distortions of patterns not previously learned.

duration. In a reaction time task, if the response is emitted when its probability reaches a particular threshold activation value (McClelland, 1979), then familiarity would lead to speeded responses. Thus, the model is consistent with the ubiquitous influence of familiarity both on response accuracy and speed, in spite of the fact that it has no detectors for familiar stimuli.

But what about priming and the role of congruity between the prime event and the test event? To examine this issue, we carried out a second experiment. Following learning of eight patterns as in the previous experiment, new distortions of half of the random vectors previously learned by the model were presented as primes. For each of these primes, the pattern of activation was allowed to stabilize, and changes in the strengths of the connections in the model were then made. We then tested the model's response to (a) the same four distortions; (b) four new distortions of the same patterns; and (c) distortions of the four previously learned patterns that had not been presented as primes. There was no decay in the

weights over the course of the priming experiment; if decay had been included, its main effect would have been to reduce the magnitude of the priming effects.

The results of the experiment are shown in Fig. 8. The response of the model is greatest for the patterns preceded by identical primes, intermediate for patterns preceded by similar primes, and weakest for patterns not preceded by any related prime.

Our model, then, appears to provide an account, not only for the basic existence of priming effects, but also for the graded nature of priming effects as a function of congruity between prime event and test event. It avoids the problem of multiplication of context-specific detectors which logogen theories fall prey to, while at the same time avoiding enumeration of specific experiences. Congruity effects are captured in the composite memory trace.

The model also has another advantage over the logogen view. It accounts for repetition priming effects for unfamiliar as well as familiar stimuli.

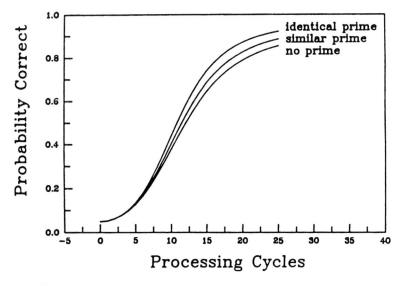

Priming and Prime Similarity Effects

FIG. 8. Response probability as a function of exposure time for patterns preceded by identical primes, similar primes, or no related prime.

When a pattern is presented for the first time, a trace is produced just as it would be for stimuli that had previously been presented. The result is that, on a second presentation of the same pattern, or a new distortion of it, processing is facilitated. The functional equivalent of a logogen begins to be established from the very first presentation.

To illustrate the repetition priming of unfamiliar patterns and to compare the results with the repetition priming we have already observed for familiar patterns, we carried out a third experiment. This time, after learning eight patterns as previously, a priming session was run in which new distortions of four of the familiar patterns and distortions of four new patterns were presented. Then, in the test phase, 16 stimuli were presented: New distortions of the primed, familiar patterns; new distortions of the unprimed, familiar patterns; new distortions of the primed, previously unfamiliar patterns; and finally, new distortions of four patterns that were neither primed nor familiar. The results are shown in Fig. 9. What we find is that long-term familiarity and

recent priming have approximately additive effects on the asymptotes of the time-accuracy curves. The time to reach any given activation level shows a mild interaction, with priming having slightly more of an effect for unfamiliar than for familiar stimuli.

These results are consistent with the bulk of the findings concerning the effects of preexperimental familiarity and repetition in the recent series of experiments by Feustel, Shiffrin, and Salasoo (1983) and Salasoo et al. (1985). They found that preexperimental familiarity of an item (word vs. nonword) and prior exposure had this very kind of interactive effect on exposure time required for accurate identification of all the letters of a string, at least when words and nonwords were mixed together in the same lists of materials.

A further aspect of the results reported by Salasoo, Shiffrin, and Feustel is also consistent with our approach. In one of their experiments, they examined threshold for accurate identification as a function of number of prior presentations, for both words and pseudowords. Although thresholds were initially elevated for pseudowords,

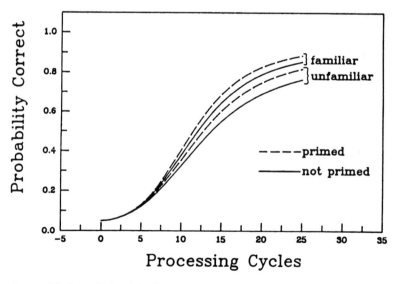

FIG. 9. Response to new distortions of primed, familiar patterns, unprimed, familiar patterns, primed, unfamiliar patterns, and unprimed, unfamiliar patterns.

relative to words, there was a rather rapid convergence of the thresholds over repeated presentations, with the point of convergence coming at about the same place on the curve for two different versions of their perceptual identification task. (Salasoo et al., 1985, Fig. 7.) Our model, likewise, shows this kind of convergence effect, as illustrated in Fig. 10.

The Feustel et al. (1983) and Salasoo et al. (1985) experiments provide very rich and detailed data that go beyond the points we have extracted from them here. We do not claim to have provided a detailed account of all aspects of their data. However, we simply wish to note that the general form of their basic findings is consistent with a model of the distributed type. In particular, we see no reason to assume that the process by which unfamiliar patterns become familiar involves the formation of an abstract, logogenlike unit separate from the episodic traces responsible for repetition priming effects.

There is one finding by Salasoo et al. (1985) that appears to support the view that there is some special process of unit formation that is distinct from the priming of old units. This is the fact that

after a year between training and testing, performance with pseudowords used during training is indistinguishable from performance with words, but performance with words used during training shows no residual benefit compared with words not previously used. The data certainly support the view that training experience made the pseudowords into lasting perceptual units, at the same time that is produced transitory priming of existing units. We have not attempted to account for this finding in detail, but we doubt that it is inconsistent with a distributed model. In support of this, we offer one reason why repetition effects might seem to persist longer for pseudowords rather than for words in the Salasoo et al. experiment. For pseudowords, a strong association would be built up between the item and the learning context during initial training. Such associations would be formed for words, but because these stimuli have been experienced many times before and have already been well learned, smaller increments in connection strength are formed for these stimuli during training, and thus the strength of the association between the item and the learning context would be less. If this view is correct,

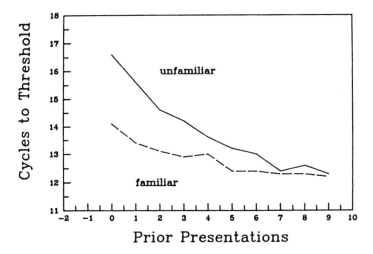

FIG. 10. Time to reach a fixed-accuracy criterion (60% correct) for previously familiar and unfamiliar patterns, as a function of repetitions.

we would expect to see a disadvantage for pseudo-words relative to words if the testing were carried out in a situation which did not reinstate the mental state associated with the original learning experience, because for these stimuli much of what was learned would be tied to the specific learning context: such a prediction would appear to differentiate our account from any view which postulated the formation of an abstract, context-independent logogen as the basis for the absence of a pseudoword decrement effect.

Representation of general and specific information

In the previous section, we cast our distributed model as an alternative to the view that familiar patterns are represented in memory either by separate detectors or by an enumeration of specific experiences. In this section, we show that the model provides alternatives to both abstraction and enumeration models of learning from exemplars of prototypes.

Abstraction models were originally motivated by the finding that subjects occasionally appeared to have learned better how to categorize the prototype of a set of distorted exemplars than the specific exemplars they experienced during learning (Posner & Keele, 1968). However, pure abstraction models have never fared very well, because there is nearly always evidence of some superiority of the particular training stimuli over other stimuli equally far removed from the prototype. A favored model, then, is one in which there is both abstraction and memory for particular training stimuli.

Recently, proponents of models involving only enumeration of specific experiences have noted that such models can account for the basic fact that abstraction models are primarily designed to account for — enhanced response to the prototype, relative to particular previously seen exemplars, under some conditions — as well as failures to obtain such effects under other conditions (Hintzman, 1983; Medin & Shaffer, 1978). In evaluating distributed models, it is important to see if they can do as well. Anderson (1977) has made important steps in this direction, and Knapp and Anderson (1984) have shown how their dis-

tributed model can account for many of the details of the Posner–Keele experiments. Recently, however, two sets of findings have been put forward which appear to strongly favor the enumeration of specific experiences view, at least relative to pure abstraction models. It is important, therefore, to see how well our distributed model can do in accounting for these kinds of effects.

The first set of findings comes from a set of studies by Whittlesea (1983). In a large number of studies, Whittlesea demonstrated a role for specific exemplars in guiding performance on a perceptual identification task. We wanted to see whether our model would demonstrate a similar sensitivity to specific exemplars. We also wanted to see whether our model would account for the conditions under which such effects are not obtained.

Whittlesea used letter strings as stimuli. The learning experiences subjects received involved simply looking at the stimuli one at a time on a visual display and writing down the sequence of letters presented. Subjects were subsequently tested for the effect of this training on their ability to identify letter strings bearing various relations to the training stimuli and to the prototypes from which the training stimuli were derived. The test was a perceptual identification task; the subject was simply required to try to identify the letters from a brief flash.

The stimuli Whittlesea used were all distortions of one of two prototype letter strings. Table 5 illustrates the essential properties of the sets of training and test stimuli he used. The stimuli in Set Ia were each one step away from the prototype. The Ib items were also one step from the prototype and one step from one of the Ia distortions. The Set IIa stimuli were each two steps from the prototype, and one step from a particular Ia distortion. The Set IIb items were also two steps from the prototype, and each was one step from one of the IIa distortions. The Set IIc distortions were two steps from the prototype also, and each was two steps from the closest IIa distortion. Over the set of five IIc distortions, the A and B subpatterns each occurred once in each position, as they did in the case of the IIa distortions. The distortions in Set III were three steps from the prototype, and one step from the closest

TABLE 5
Schematic Description of Stimulus Sets Used in Simulations of Whittlesea's Experiments

	Stimulus set						
Prototype	Ia	Ib	IIa	IIb	IIc	III	V
PPPPP	APPPP	BPPPP	ABPPP	ACPPP	APCPP	ABCPP	CCCCC
	PAPPP	PBPPP	PABPP	PACPP	PAPCP	PABCP	CBCBC
	PPAPP	PPBPP	PPABP	PPACP	PPAPC	PPABC	BCACB
	PPPAP	PPPBP	PPPAB	PPPAC	CPPAP	CPPAB	ABCBA
	PPPPA	PPPPB	BPPPA	CPPPA	PCPPA	BCPPA	CACAC

Note. The actual stimuli used can be filled in by replacing P with $+ - + -$; A with $+ + - -$; B with $+ - - +$; and C with $+ + + +$. The model is not sensitive to the fact the same subpattern was used in each of the five slots.

member of Set IIa. The distortions in Set V were each five steps from the prototype.

Whittlesea ran seven experiments using different combinations of training and test stimuli. We carried out simulation analogs of all of these experiments, plus one additional experiment that Whittlesea did not run. The main difference between the simulation experiments and Whittlesea's actual experiments was that he used two different prototypes in each experiment, whereas we only used one.

The simulation used a simple 20-unit module. The set of 20 units was divided into five submodules, one for each letter in Whittlesea's letter strings. The prototype pattern and the different distortions used can be derived from the information provided in Table 5.

Each simulation experiment began with null connections between the units. The training phase involved presenting the set or sets of training stimuli analogous to those Whittlesea used, for the same number of presentations. To avoid idiosyncratic effects of particular orders of training stimuli, each experiment was run six times, each with a different random order of training stimuli. On each trial, activations were allowed to settle down through 50 processing cycles, and then connection strengths were adjusted. There was no decay of the increments to the weights over the course of an experiment.

In the test phase, the model was tested with the sets of test items analogous to the sets Whittlesea used. As a precaution against effects of prior test

items on performance, we simply turned off the adjustment of weights during the test phase.

A summary of the training and test stimuli used in each of the experiments, of Whittlesea's findings, and of the simulation results are shown in Table 6. The numbers represent relative amounts of enhancement in performance as a result of the training experience, relative to a pretest baseline. For Whittlesea's data, this is the per letter increase in letter identification probability between a pre- and posttest. For the simulation, it is the increase in the size of the dot product for a pretest with null weights and a posttest after training. For comparability to the data, the dot product difference scores have been doubled. This is simply a scaling operation to facilitate qualitative comparison of experimental and simulation results.

A comparison of the experimental and simulation results shows that wherever there is a within-experiment difference in Whittlesea's data, the simulation produced a difference in the same direction. (Between experiment comparisons are not considered because of subject and material differences which renders such differences unreliable.) The next several paragraphs review some of the major findings in detail.

Some of the comparisons bring out the importance of congruity between particular test and training experiences. Experiments 1, 2, and 3 show that when distance of test stimuli from the prototype is controlled, similarity to particular training exemplars makes a difference both for the human subject and in the model. In Experiment 1, the

TABLE 6
Summary of Perceptual Identification Experiments With Experimental and Simulation Results

Whittlesea's experiment	Training stimulus set(s)	Test stimulus sets	Experimental results	Simulation results
1	Ia	Ia	.27	.24
		Ib	.16	.15
		V	.03	−.05
2	IIa	IIa	.30	.29
		IIc	.15	.12
		V	.03	−.08
3	IIa	IIa	.21	.29
		IIb	.16	.14
		IIc	.10	.12
4	IIa	P	—	.24
		Ia	.19	.21
		IIa	.23	.29
		III	.15	.15
4′	Ia	P	—	.28
		Ia	—	.24
		IIa	—	.12
5	IIa, b, c	P	—	.25
		Ia	.16	.21
		IIa	.16	.18
		III	.10	.09
6	III	Ia	.16	.14
		IIa	.16	.19
		III	.19	.30
7	IIa	IIa	.24	.29
		IIc	.13	.12
		III	.17	.15

relevant contrast was between Ia and Ib items. In Experiment 2, it was between IIa and IIc items. Experiment 3 shows that the subjects and the model both show a gradient in performance with increasing distance of the test items from the nearest old exemplar.

Experiments 4, 4′, and 5 examine the status of the prototype and other test stimuli closer to the prototype than any stimuli actually shown during training. In Experiment 4, the training stimuli were fairly far away from the prototype, and there were only five different training stimuli (the members of the IIa set). In this case, controlling for distance from the nearest training stimuli, test stimuli closer to the prototype showed more enhancement than those farther away (Ia vs. III comparison).

However, the actual training stimuli nevertheless had an advantage over both other sets of test stimuli, including those that were closer to the prototype than the training stimuli themselves (IIa vs. Ia comparison).

In Experiment 4′ (not run by Whittlesea) the same number of training stimuli were used as in Experiment 4, but these were closer to the prototype. The result is that the simulation shows an advantage for the prototype over the old exemplars. The specific training stimuli used even in this experiment do influence performance, however, as Whittlesea's first experiment (which used the same training set) shows (Ia–Ib contrast). This effect holds both for the subjects and for the simulation. The pattern of results is similar to the findings of Posner and Keele (1968), in the condition where subjects learned six exemplars which were rather close to the prototype. In this condition, their subjects' categorization performance was most accurate for the prototype, but more accurate for old than for new distortions, just as in this simulation experiment.

In Experiment 5, Whittlesea demonstrated that a slight advantage for stimuli closer to the prototype than the training stimuli would emerge, even with high-level distortions, when a large number of different distortions were used once each in training, instead of a smaller number of distortions presented three times each. The effect was rather small in Whittlesea's case (falling in the third decimal place in the per letter enhancement effect measure) but other experiments have produced similar results, and so does the simulation. In fact, because the prototype was tested in the simulation, we were able to demonstrate a monotonic drop in performance with distance from the prototype in this experiment.

Experiments 6 and 7 examine in different ways the relative influence of similarity to the prototype and similarity to the set of training exemplars, using small numbers of training exemplars rather far from the prototype. Both in the data and in the model, similarity to particular training stimuli is more important than similarity to the prototype, given the sets of training stimuli used in these experiments.

Taken together with other findings, Whittlesea's results show clearly that similarity of test items to particular stored exemplars is of paramount importance in predicting perceptual performance. Other experiments show the relevance of these same factors in other tasks, such as recognition memory, classification learning, and so forth. It is interesting to note that performance does not honor the specific exemplars so strongly when the training items are closer to the prototype. Under such conditions, performance is superior on the prototype or stimuli closer to the prototype than the training stimuli. Even when the training stimuli are rather distant from the prototype, they produce a benefit for stimuli closer to the prototype, if there are a large number of distinct training stimuli each shown only once. Thus, the dominance of

specific training experiences is honored only when the training experiences are few and far between. Otherwise, an apparent advantage for the prototype, though with some residual benefit for particular training stimuli, is the result.

The congruity of the results of these simulations with experimental findings underscores the applicability of distributed models to the question of the nature of the representation of general and specific information. In fact, we were somewhat surprised by the ability of the model to account for Whittlesea's results, given the fact that we did not rely on context-sensitive encoding of the letter string stimuli. That is, the distributed representation we assigned to each letter was independent of the other letters in the string. However, a context sensitive encoding would prove necessary to capture a larger ensemble of stimuli.

Whether a context-sensitive encoding would produce the same or slightly different results depends on the exact encoding. The exact degree of overlap of the patterns of activation produced by different distortions of the same prototype determines the extent to which the model will tend to favor the prototype relative to particular old exemplars. The degree of overlap, in turn, depends on the specific assumptions made about the encoding of the stimuli. However, the general form of the results of the simulation would be unchanged: When all the distortions are close to the prototype, or when there is a very large number of different distortions, the central tendency will produce the strongest response; but when the distortions are fewer, and farther from the prototype, the training exemplars themselves will produce the strongest activations. What the encoding would effect is the similarity metric.

In this regard, it is worth mentioning another finding that appears to challenge our distributed account of what is learned through repeated experiences with exemplars. This is the finding of Medin and Schwanenflugel (1981). Their experiment compared ease of learning of two different sets of stimuli in a categorization task. One set of stimuli could be categorized by a linear combination of weights assigned to particular values on each of four dimensions considered independently. The other set of stimuli could not be categorized in this way; and yet, the experiment clearly demonstrated that linear separability was not necessary for categorization learning. In one experiment, linearly separable stimuli were less easily learned than a set of stimuli that were not linearly separable but had a higher degree of intraexemplar similiarity within categories.

At first glance, it may seem that Medin and Schwanenflugel's experiment is devastating to our distributed approach, because our distributed model can only learn linear combinations of weights. However, whether a linear combination of weights can suffice in the Medin and Schwanenflugel experiments depends on how patterns of activation are assigned to stimuli. If each stimulus dimension is encoded separately in the representation of the stimulus, then the Medin and Schwanenflugel stimuli cannot be learned by our model. But if each stimulus dimension is encoded in a context sensitive way, then the patterns of activation associated with the different stimuli become linearly separable again.

One way of achieving context sensitivity is via separate enumeration of traces. But it is well known that there are other ways as well. Several different kinds of context-sensitive encodings which do not require separate enumeration of traces, or the allocation of separate nodes to individual experiences are considered in Hinton (1981a), Hinton, McClelland, and Rumelhart (1986), and Rumelhart and McClelland (1986).

It should be noted that the motivation for context-sensitive encoding in the use of distributed representations is captured by but by no means limited to the kinds of observations reported in the experiment by Medin and Schwanenflugel. The trouble is that the assignment of particular context-sensitive encodings to stimuli is at present rather ad hoc: There are too many different possible ways it can be done to know which way is right. What is needed is a principled way of assigning distributed representations to patterns of activation. The problem is a severe one, but really it is no different from the problem that all models face, concerning the assignment of representations to stimuli. What we can say for sure at this point is that context-sensitive encoding is necessary, for distributed models or for any other kind.

Discussion

Until very recently, the exploration of distributed models was restricted to a few workers, mostly coming from fields other than cognitive psychology. Although in some cases, particularly in the work of Anderson (1977; Anderson et al., 1977; Knapp & Anderson, 1984), some implications of these models for our understanding of memory and learning have been pointed out, they have only begun to be applied by researchers primarily concerned with understanding cognitive processes per se. The present article, along with those of Murdock (1982) and Eich (1982), represents what we hope will be the beginning of a more serious examination of these kinds of models by cognitive psychologists. For they provide, we believe, important alternatives to traditional conceptions of representation and memory.

We have tried to illustrate this point here by showing how the distributed approach circumvents the dilemma of specific trace models. Distributed memories abstract even while they preserve the details of recent, or frequently repeated, experiences. Abstraction and preservation of information about specific stimuli are simply different reflections of the operation of the same basic learning mechanism.

The basic points we have been making can of course be generalized in several different directions. Here we will mention two: The relation between episodic and semantic memory (Tulving, 1972) and the representations underlying the use of language.

With regard to episodic and semantic memory, our distributed model leads naturally to the suggestion that semantic memory may be just the residue of the superposition of episodic traces. Consider, for example, representation of a proposition encountered in several different contexts, and assume for the moment that the context and content are represented in separate parts of the same module. Over repeated experience with the same proposition in different contexts, the proposition will remain in the interconnections of the units in the proposition submodule, but the particular associations to particular contexts will wash out. However, material that is only encountered in one particular context will tend to be somewhat contextually bound. So we may not be able to retrieve what we learn in one context when we need it in other situations. Other authors (e.g. Anderson & Ross, 1980) have recently argued against a distinction between episodic and semantic memory, pointing out interactions between traditionally episodic and semantic memory tasks. Such findings are generally consistent with the view we have taken here.

Distributed models also influence our thinking about how human behavior might come to exhibit the kind of regularity that often leads linguists to postulate systems of rules. We have recently developed a distributed model of a system that can learn the past tense system of English, given as inputs pairs of patterns, corresponding to the phonological structure of the present and past tense forms of actual English verbs (Rumelhart & McClelland, 1986). Given plausible assumptions about the learning experiences to which a child is exposed, the model provides a fairly accurate account of the time course of acquisition of the past tense (Brown, 1973; Ervin, 1964; Kuczaj, 1977).

In general distributed models appear to provide alternatives to a variety of different kinds of models that postulate abstract, summary representations such as prototypes, logogens, semantic memory representations, or even linguistic rules.

Why prefer a distributed model?

The fact that distributed models provide alternatives to other sorts of accounts is important, but the fact that they are sometimes linked rather closely to the physiology often makes them seem irrelevant to the basic enterprise of cognitive psychology. It may be conceded that distributed models describe the *physiological substrate* of memory better than other models, but why should we assume that they help us to characterize human information processing at a more abstract level of description? There are two parts to the answer to this question. First, though distributed models may be approximated by other models, on close inspection they differ from them in ways that should have testable consequences. If tests of these consequences turn out to favor distributed models —

and there are indications that in certain cases they will – it would seem plausible to argue that distributed models provide an importantly different description of cognition, even if it does take the phenomena somewhat closer to the physiological level of analysis. Second, distributed models alter our thinking about a number of aspects of cognition at the same time. They give us a whole new constellation of assumptions about the structure of cognitive processes. They can change the way we think about the learning process, for example, and can even help shed some light on why and how human behavior comes to be as regular (as bound by rules and concepts) as it seems to be. In this section we consider these two points in turn.

A different level, or a different description?

Are distributed models at a different level of analysis than cognitive models, or do they provide a different description of cognition? We think the answer is some of both. Here we focus primarily on underscoring the differences between distributed and other models.

Consider, first, the class of models which state that concepts are represented by prototypes. Distributed models approximate prototype models, and under some conditions their predictions converge, but under other conditions their predictions diverge. In particular, distributed models account both for conditions under which the prototype dominates and conditions under which particular exemplars dominate performance. Thus, they clearly have an advantage over such models, and should be preferred as accounts of empirical phenomena.

Perhaps distributed models are to be preferred over some cognitive level models, but one might argue that they are not to be preferred to the correct cognitive level model. For example, in most of the simulations discussed in this article, the predictions of enumeration models are not different from the predictions of our distributed model. Perhaps we should see our distributed model as representing a physiologically plausible implementation of enumeration models.

Even here, there are differences, however. Though both models superimpose traces of different experiences, distributed models do so at the time of storage, while enumeration models do so at the time of retrieval. But there is no evidence to support the separate storage assumption of enumeration models. Indeed, most such models assume that performance is always based on a superimposition of the specific experiences. Now, our distributed model could be rejected if convincing evidence of separate storage could be provided, for example, by some kind of experiment in which a way was found to separate the effects of different memory experiences. But the trend in a number of recent approaches to memory has been to emphasize the ubiquity of interactions between memory traces. Distributed models are essentially constructed around the assumption that memory traces interact by virtue of the nature of the manner in which they are stored, and they provide an explanation for these interactions. Enumeration models, on the other hand, simply assume interactions occur and postulate separate storage without providing any evidence that storage is in fact separate.

There is another difference between our distributed model and the enumeration models, at least existing ones. Our distributed model assumes that learning is an *error-correcting* process, whereas enumeration models do not. This difference leads to empirical consequences which put great strain on existing enumeration models. In existing enumeration models, what is stored in memory is simply a copy of features of the stimulus event, independent of the prior knowledge already stored in the memory system. But there are a number of indications that what is learned depends on the current state of knowledge. For example, the fact that learning is better after distributed practice appears to suggest that more learning occurs on later learning trials, if subjects have had a chance to forget what they learned on the first trial. We would expect such effects to occur in an error-correcting model such as ours.

The main point of the foregoing discussion has been to emphasize that our distributed model is not simply a plausible physiological implementation of existing models of cognitive processes. Rather, the model is an alternative to most, if not all, existing models, as we have tried to emphasize by pointing out differences between our distrib-

uted model and other models which have been proposed. Of course this does not mean that our distributed model will not turn out to be an exact notational variant of some particular other model. What it does mean is that our distributed model must be treated as an alternative to — rather than simply an implementation of — existing models of learning and memory.

Interdependence of theoretical assumptions. There is another reason for taking distributed models seriously as psychological models. Even in cases where our distributed model may not be testably distinct from existing models, it does provide an entire constellation of assumptions which go together as a package. In this regard, it is interesting to contrast a distributed model with a model such as John Anderson's ACT* model (J. R. Anderson, 1983). One difference between the models is that in ACT* it is productions rather than connection strengths that serve as the basis of learning and memory. This difference leads to other differences: in our model, learning occurs through connection strength modulation, whereas in ACT* learning occurs through the creation, differentiation, and generalization of productions. At a process level the models look very different, whether or not they make different empirical predictions. Learning in our distributed model is an automatic consequence of processing based on information locally available to each unit whose connections are changing; in ACT*, learning requires an overseer that detects cases in which a production has been misapplied, or in which two productions with similar conditions both fit the same input, to trigger the differentiation and generalization processes as appropriate.

Similar contrasts exist between our distributed model and other models; in general, our model differs from most abstractive models (that is, those that postulate the formation of abstract rules or other abstract representations) in doing away with complex acquisition mechanisms in favor of a very simple connection strength modulation scheme. Indeed, to us, much of the appeal of distributed models is that they do not already have to be intelligent in order to learn, like some models do. Doubtless, sophisticated hypothesis testing models of learning such as those which have grown out of the early concept identification work of Bruner, Goodnow, and Austin (1956) or out of the artificial intelligence learning tradition established by Winston (1975) have their place, but for many phenomena, particularly those that do not seem to require explicit hypothesis formation and testing, the kind of learning mechanism incorporated in our distributed model may be more appropriate.

Two final reasons for preferring a distributed representation are that it leads us to understand some of the reasons why human behavior tends to exhibit such strong regularities. Some of the regularity is due to the structure of the world, of course, but much of it is a result of the way in which our cultures structure it; certainly the regularity of languages is a fact about the way humans communicate that psychological theory can be asked to explain. Distributed models provide some insight both into why it is beneficial for behavior to be regular, and how it comes to be that way.

It is beneficial for behavior to be regular, because regularity allows us to economize on the size of the networks that must be devoted to processing in a particular environment. If all experiences were completely random and unrelated to each other, a distributed model would buy us very little — in fact it would cost us a bit — relative to separate enumeration of experiences. An illuminating analysis of this situation is given by Willshaw (1981). Where a distributed model pays off, though, is in the fact that it can capture generalizations economically, given that there are generalizations. Enumeration models lack this feature. There are of course limits on how much can be stored in a distributed memory system, but the fact that it can abstract extends those limits far beyond the capacity of any system relying on the separate enumeration of experiences, whenever abstraction is warranted by the ensemble of inputs.

We have just explained how distributed models can help us understand why it is a good thing for behavior to exhibit regularity, but we have not yet indicated how they help us understand how it comes to be regular. But it is easy to see how distributed models tend to impose regularity. When a new pattern is presented, the model will impose regularity by dealing with it as it has learned to deal with similar patterns in the past; the model automatically generalizes. In our analysis of past tense learning (Rumelhart & McClelland, in press), it is just this property of distributed models which leads them to produce the kinds of over-regularizations we see in language development; the same property, operating in all of the members of a culture at the same time, will tend to produce regularizations in the entire language.

Conclusion

The distributed approach is in its infancy, and we do not wish to convey the impression that we have solved all the problems of learning and memory simply by invoking it. Considerable effort is needed on several fronts. We will mention four that seem of paramount importance: (a) Distributed models must be integrated with models of the overall organization of information processing, and their relation to models of extended retrieval processes and other temporally extended mental activities must be made clear. (b) Models must be formulated which adequately capture the structural relations of the components of complex stimuli. Existing models do not do this in a sufficiently flexible and open-ended way to capture arbitrarily complex propositional structures. (c) Ways must be found to take the assignment of patterns of activation to stimuli out of the hands of the modeler, and place them in the structure of the model itself. (d) Further analysis is required to determine which of the assumptions of our particular distributed model are essential and which are unimportant details. The second and third of these problems are under intensive study. Some developments along these lines are reported in a number of recent papers (Ackley, Hinton, & Sejnowski, 1985; McClelland, 1985; Rumelhart & Zipser, 1985).

Although much remains to be done, we hope we have demonstrated that distributed models provide distinct, conceptually attractive alternatives to models involving the explicit formation of abstractions or the enumeration of specific experiences. Just how far distributed models can take us toward an understanding of learning and memory remains to be seen.

References

Ackley, D., Hinton, G. E., & Sejnowski, T. J. (1985). Boltzmann machines: Constraint satisfaction networks that learn. *Cognitive Science, 9,* 147–169.

Anderson, J. A. (1977). Neural models with cognitive implications. In D. LaBerge & S. J. Samuels (Eds.), *Basic processes in reading: Perception and comprehension.* Hillsdale, NJ: Erlbaum.

Anderson, J. A. (1983). Cognitive and psychological computation with neural models. *IEEE Transactions on Systems, Man, and Cybernetics, SMC-13,* 799–815.

Anderson, J. A., & Hinton, G. E. (1981). Models of information processing in the brain. In G. E. Hinton & J. A. Anderson (Eds.), *Parallel models of associative memory.* Hillsdale, NJ: Erlbaum.

Anderson, J. A., Silverstein, J. W., Ritz, S. A., & Jones, R. S. (1977). Distinctive features, categorical perception, and probability learning: Some applications of a neural model. *Psychological Review, 84,* 413–451.

Anderson, J. R. (1983). *The architecture of cognition.* Cambridge, MA: Harvard.

Anderson, J. R., & Ross, B. H. (1980). Evidence against a semantic-episodic distinction. *Journal of Experimental Psychology: Human Learning and Memory, 6,* 441–465.

Brooks, L. R. (1978). Nonanalytic concept formation and memory for instances. In E. Rosch & B. B. Lloyd (Eds.), *Cognition and categorization.* Hillsdale, NJ: Erlbaum.

Brown, R. (1973). *A first language.* Cambridge, MA: Harvard University Press.

Bruner, J. S., Goodnow, J. J., & Austin, G. A. (1956). *A study of thinking.* New York: Wiley.

Eich, J. M. (1982). A composite holographic associative retrieval model. *Psychological Review, 89,* 627–661.

Ervin, S. (1964). Imitation and structural change in children's language. In E. Lenneberg (Ed.), *New directions in the study of language.* Cambridge, MA: MIT Press.

Feustel, T. C., Shiffrin, R. M., & Salasoo, A. (1983). Episodic and lexical contributions to the repetition effect in word identification. *Journal of Experimental Psychology: General, 112,* 309–346.

Glushko, R. J. (1979). The organization and activation of orthographic knowledge in reading aloud. *Journal of Experimental Psychology: Human Perception and Performance, 5,* 674–691.

Hinton, G. E. (1981a). Implementing semantic networks in parallel hardware. In G. E. Hinton & J. A. Anderson (Eds.), *Parallel models of associative memory.* Hillsdale, NJ: Erlbaum.

Hinton, G. E. (1981b). A parallel computation that assigns canonical object-based frames of reference. *Proceedings of the Seventh International Joint Conference in Artificial Intelligence* (pp.683–685). Vancouver, British Columbia, Canada.

Hinton, G. E., & Anderson, J. A. (Eds.) (1981). *Parallel models of associative memory.* Hillsdale, NJ: Erlbaum.

Hinton, G. E., McClelland, J. L., & Rumelhart, D. E. (1986). Distributed representations. In D. E. Rumelhart & J. L. McClelland (Eds.), *Parallel distributed processing: Explorations in the microstructure of cognition. Volume I: Foundations.* Cambridge, MA; MIT Press.

Hintzman, D. (1983). *Schema abstraction in a multiple trace memory model.* Paper presented at conference on "The priority of the specific." Elora, Ontario, Canada.

Jacoby, L. L. (1983a). Perceptual enhancement: Persistent effects of an experience. *Journal of Experimental Psychology: Learning, Memory, and Cognition, 9,* 21–38.

Jacoby, L. L. (1983b). Remembering the data: Analyzing interaction processes in reading. *Journal of Verbal Learning and Verbal Behavior, 22,* 485–508.

Knapp, A., & Anderson, J. A. (1984). A signal averaging model for concept formation. *Journal of Experimental Psychology: Learning, Memory, and Cognition, 10,* 616–637.

Kohonen, T. (1977). *Associative memory: A system-theoretical approach.* Berlin: Springer-Verlag.

Kohonen, T., Oja, E., & Lehtio, P. (1981). Storage and processing of information in distributed associative memory systems. In G. E. Hinton & J. A. Anderson (Eds.), *Parallel models of associative memory.* Hillsdale, NJ: Erlbaum.

Kuczaj, S. A., II. (1977). The acquisition of regular and irregular past tense forms. *Journal of Verbal Learning and Verbal Behavior, 16,* 589–600.

Lashley, K. S. (1950). In search of the engram. *Society for Experimental Biology Symposium No. 4: Physiological Mechanisms in Animal Behavior* (pp.478–505). London: Cambridge University Press.

Luce, R. D. (1963). Detection and recognition. In R. D. Luce, R. R. Bush, & E. Galanter (Eds.),

Handbook of Mathematical Psychology: Vol. I. New York: Wiley.

McClelland, J. L. (1979). On the time-relations of mental processes: An examination of systems of processes in cascade. *Psychological Review, 86,* 287–330.

McClelland, J. L. (1981). Retrieving general and specific information from stored knowledge of specifics. *Proceedings of the Third Annual Meeting of the Cognitive Science Society* (pp.170–172). Berkeley, CA.

McClelland, J. L. (1985). Putting knowledge in its place: A framework for programming parallel processing structures on the fly. *Cognitive Science, 9,* 113–146.

McClelland, J. L., & Rumelhart, D. E. (1981). An interactive activation model of the effect of context in perception, Part I. An account of basic findings. *Psychological Review, 88,* 375–407.

Medin, D., & Schwanenflugel, P. J. (1981). Linear separability in classification learning. *Journal of Experimental Psychology: Human Learning and Memory, 7,* 355–368.

Medin, D. L., & Shaffer, M. M. (1978). Context theory of classification learning. *Psychological Review, 85,* 207–238.

Morton, J. (1979). Facilitation in word recognition: Experiments causing change in the logogen model. In P. A. Kohlers, M. E. Wrolstal, & H. Bouma (Eds.), *Processing visible language I.* New York: Plenum.

Murdock, B. B. (1982). A theory for the storage and retrieval of item and associative information. *Psychological Review, 89,* 609–626.

Posner, M. I., & Keele, S. W. (1968). On the genesis of abstract ideas. *Journal of Experimental Psychology, 77,* 353–363.

Posner, M. I., & Keele, S. W. (1970). Retention of abstract ideas. *Journal of Experimental Psychology, 83,* 304–308.

Rosenblatt, F. (1962). *Principles of neurodynamics.* Washington, DC: Spartan.

Rumelhart, D. E., & McClelland, J. L. (1981). Interactive processing through spreading activation. In A. M. Lesgold & C. A. Perfetti (Eds.), *Interactive Processes in Reading.* Hillsdale, NJ: Erlbaum.

Rumelhart, D. E., & McClelland, J. L. (1982). An interactive activation model of the effect of context in perception Part II. The contextual enhancement effect and some tests and extensions of the model. *Psychological Review, 89,* 60–94.

Rumelhart, D. E., & McClelland, J. L. (1986). On learning the past tenses of English verbs. In J. L. McClelland & D. E. Rumelhart (Eds.), *Parallel distributed processing: Explorations in the microstructure of cognition. Volume II: Applications.* Cambridge, MA: MIT Press.

Rumelhart, D. E., & Zipser, D. (1985). Competitive learning. *Cognitive Science, 9,* 75–112.

Salasoo, A., Shiffrin, R. M., & Feustel, T. C. (1985). Building permanent memory codes: Codification and repetition effects in word identification. *Journal of Experimental Psychology: General, 114,* 50–77.

Stone, G. (1985). *An analysis of the delta rule.* Manuscript in preparation.

Sutton, R. S., & Barto, A. G. (1981). Toward a modern theory of adaptive networks: Expectation and prediction. *Psychological Review, 88,* 135–170.

Tulving, E. (1972). Episodic and semantic memory. In E. Tulving & W. Donaldson (Eds.), *Organization of Memory.* New York: Academic Press.

Whittlesea, B. W. A. (1983). *Representation and generalization of concepts: The abstractive and episodic perspectives evaluated.* Unpublished doctoral dissertation, MacMaster University.

Wickelgren, W. A. (1979). Chunking and consolidation: A theoretical synthesis of semantic networks, configuring in conditioning, S-R versus cognitive learning, normal forgetting, the amnesic syndrome, and the hippocampal arousal system. *Psychological Review, 86,* 44–60.

Willshaw, D. (1981). Holography, associative memory, and inductive generalization. In G. E. Hinton & J. A. Anderson (Eds.), *Parallel models of associative memory.* Hillsdale, NJ: Erlbaum.

Winston, P. H. (1975). Learning structural descriptions from examples. In P. H. Winston (Ed.), *The psychology of computer vision.* Cambridge, MA: Harvard.

Received May 22, 1984
Revision received October 2, 1984

ALCOVE: An exemplar-based connectionist model of category learning

John K. Kruschke

Indiana University, Bloomington

ALCOVE (attention learning covering map) is a connectionist model of category learning that incorporates an exemplar-based representation (Medin & Schaffer, 1978; Nosofsky, 1986) with error-driven learning (Gluck & Bower, 1988; Rumelhart, Hinton, & Williams, 1986). ALCOVE selectively attends to relevant stimulus dimensions, is sensitive to correlated dimensions, can account for a form of base-rate neglect, does not suffer catastrophic forgetting, and can exhibit 3-stage (U-shaped) learning of high-frequency exceptions to rules, whereas such effects are not easily accounted for by models using other combinations of representation and learning method.

This article describes a connectionist model of category learning called ALCOVE (attention learning covering map). Any model of category learning must address the two issues of what representation underlies category knowledge and how that representation is used in learning. ALCOVE combines the exemplar-based representational assumptions of Nosofsky's (1986) generalized context model (GCM) with the error-driven learning assumptions of Gluck and Bower's (1988a, 1988b) network models. ALCOVE extends the GCM by adding a learning mechanism and extends the network models of Gluck and Bower by allowing continuous dimensions and including explicit dimensional attention learning. ALCOVE can be construed as a combination of exemplar models (e.g. Medin & Schaffer, 1978; Nosofsky, 1986) with network models (Gluck & Bower, 1988a, 1988b), as suggested by Estes (1988; Estes, Campbell, Hatsopoulos, & Hurwitz, 1989; Hurwitz, 1990). Dimensional attention learning allows ALCOVE to capture human performance where other network models fail (Gluck & Bower, 1988a), and error-driven learning in ALCOVE generates interactions between exemplars that allow it to succeed where other exemplar-based models fail (e.g. Estes et al., 1989; Gluck & Bower, 1988b).

ALCOVE is also closely related to standard back-propagation networks (Rumelhart, Hinton, & Williams, 1986). Although ALCOVE is a feedforward network that learns by gradient descent on error, it is unlike standard back propagation in its architecture, its behavior, and its goals. Unlike the standard back-propagation network, which was motivated by generalizing neuronlike perceptrons, the architecture of ALCOVE was motivated by a molar-level psychological theory, Nosofsky's (1986) GCM. The psychologically constrained architecture results in behavior that captures the detailed course of human category learning in many situations where standard back propagation fares less well. Unlike many applications of standard back propagation, the goal of ALCOVE is not to discover new (hidden-layer) representations after lengthy training but rather to model the course of learning itself by determining which dimensions of the given representation are most relevant to the task and how strongly to associate exemplars with categories.

This article is based on a doctoral dissertation submitted to the University of California at Berkeley. The research was supported in part by Biomedical Research Support Grant RR 7031-25 from the National Institutes of Health.

I thank the members of my dissertation committee, Stuart Dreyfus, Jerry Feldman, Barbara Mellers, Rob Nosofsky, and Steve Palmer. I also thank Steve Palmer for his encouragement and helpfulness as my primary adviser. Rob Nosofsky gets special thanks for sharing with me (unpublished) data and many stimulating conversations and for commenting on earlier versions of this article. Roger Ratcliff and two anonymous reviewers of an earlier version of this article also provided very helpful comments.

Correspondence concerning this article should be addressed to John K. Kruschke, Department of Psychology, Indiana University, Bloomington, Indiana 47405. Electronic mail may be sent to kruschke@ucs.indiana.edu.

Psychological Review 1992, Vol. 99. No. 1, 22–44

The purposes of this article are to introduce the ALCOVE model, demonstrate its application across a variety of category learning tasks, and compare it with other models to highlight its mechanisms. The organization of the article is as follows: First, the ALCOVE model is described in detail; then, its ability to differentially attend to relevant or irrelevant dimensions is demonstrated by applying it to the classic category learning task of Shepard, Hovland, and Jenkins (1961) and to the correlated-dimensions situation studied by Medin, Altom, Edelson, and Freko (1982). Next, the interaction of exemplars during learning is demonstrated by showing that ALCOVE accounts for the apparent base-rate neglect observed by Gluck and Bower (1988a, 1988b) and by Estes et al. (1989) and by showing that ALCOVE learns Medin and Schwanenflugel's (1981) nonlinearly separable categories faster than the linearly separable ones. Afterward, the representation used in ALCOVE is contrasted with that used in standard back propagation, and it is shown that ALCOVE does not suffer the catastrophic retroactive interference seen in standard back propagation (McCloskey & Cohen, 1989; Ratcliff, 1990). Finally, I include a provocative demonstration of ALCOVE's ability to exhibit three-stage learning of rules and exceptions (cf. Rumelhart & McClelland, 1986) and speculate how ALCOVE might interact with a rule-hypothesizing system.

The model

ALCOVE is a feed-forward connectionist network with three layers of nodes. Its basic computations are a direct implementation of Nosofsky's (1986) GCM. Like the GCM, ALCOVE assumes that stimuli can be represented as points in a multi-dimensional psychological space, as determined by multidimensional scaling (MDS) algorithms (e.g. Shepard, 1957, 1962a, 1962b). Each input node encodes a single psychological dimension, with the activation of the node indicating the value of the stimulus on that dimension. For example, if the first node corresponds to perceived size, and the perceived size of the given stimulus is

some scale value v, then the activation of the first node is v. The activation of the ith input node is denoted a_i^{in}, and the complete stimulus is denoted by the column vector $a^{in} = (a_1^{in}, a_2^{in}, \dots)^T$. Figure 1 shows the basic architecture of ALCOVE, illustrating the case of just two input dimensions (in general the model can have any number of input dimensions).

Each input node is gated by a dimensional attention strength, α_i. The attention strength on a dimension reflects the relevance of that dimension for the particular categorization task at hand. Before training begins, the model is initialized with equal attention strengths on all dimensions, and as training proceeds, the model learns to allocate more attention to relevant dimensions and less to irrelevant dimensions. Attention Learning is an important aspect of the model and gives ALCOVE the first two letters of its name. The function of the attention strengths will be described in more detail after the hidden nodes are described.

Each hidden node corresponds to a position in the multidimensional stimulus space. In the simplest version of ALCOVE, there is a hidden node placed at the position of every training exemplar. For example, if the input dimensions are *perceived size* and *perceived brightness*, and one of the training stimuli has scale values of size = v and brightness = ξ, then there is a hidden node placed at the position (v, ξ). In a more complicated version,

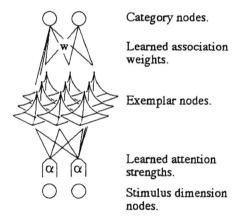

Category nodes.

Learned association weights.

Exemplar nodes.

Learned attention strengths.

Stimulus dimension nodes.

FIG. 1. The architecture of ALCOVE (attention learning covering map). (See The Model section.)

discussed at the end of the article, hidden nodes are scattered randomly across the space, forming a covering map of the input space. The covering map gives ALCOVE the last four letters of its name. Throughout the body of this article, however, the exemplar-based version is used.

For a given input stimulus, each hidden node is activated according to the psychological similarity of the stimulus to the exemplar at the position of the hidden node. The similarity function is the same as that used in the GCM, which in turn was motivated by Shepard's (1957, 1958, 1987) classic theories of similarity and generalization. Let the position of the jth hidden node be denoted as $(h_{j1}, h_{j2}, \ldots)$, and let the activation of the jth hidden node be denoted as a_j^{hid}. Then

$$a_j^{hid} = \exp[-c(\sum_i \alpha_i |h_{ji} - \alpha_i^{in}|^r)^{q/r}], \qquad (1)$$

where c is a positive constant called the *specificity* of the node, where the sum is taken over all input dimensions, and where r and q are constants determining the psychological-distance metric and similarity gradient, respectively. In the applications described in this article, separable psychological dimensions are assumed, so a city-block metric ($r = 1$) with exponential similarity gradient ($q = 1$) is used (Shepard, 1987). For integral dimensions, a Euclidean metric ($r = 2$) could be used (e.g. Nosofsky, 1987; Shepard, 1964).

The pyramids in the middle layer of Fig. 1 show the activation profiles of hidden nodes, as determined by Equation 1 with $r = q = 1$. Because the activation indicates the similarity of the input stimulus to the exemplar coded by the hidden node, the activation falls off exponentially with the distance between the hidden node and the input stimulus. The city-block metric implies that the iso-similarity contours are diamond shaped. The specificity constant, c, determines the overall width of the activation profile. Large specificities imply very rapid similarity decrease and hence a narrow activation profile, whereas small specificities correspond to wide profiles. Psychologically, the specificity of a hidden node indicates the overall cognitive discriminability or memorability of the corresponding exemplar. The region of stimulus space that significantly activates a hidden node

will be loosely referred to as that node's *receptive field*.

Equation 1 indicates the role of the dimensional attention strengths, α_i. They act as multipliers on the corresponding dimension in computing the distance between the stimulus and the hidden node (cf. Carroll & Chang, 1970). A closely related type of attentional weighting was introduced by Medin and Schaffer (1978) in their context model and generalized into the form shown in Equation 1 by Nosofsky (1984, 1986).

The attention strengths stretch and shrink dimensions of the input space so that stimuli in different categories are better separated and stimuli within categories are better concentrated. Consider a simple case of four stimuli that form the corners of a square in input space, as indicated in Fig. 2. If the two left stimuli are mapped to one category (indicated by dots), and the two right stimuli are mapped to another category (indicated by xs), then the separation of the categories can be increased by stretching the horizontal axis, and the proximity within categories can be increased by shrinking the vertical axis. Stretching a dimension can be achieved by increasing its attentional value; shrinking can be achieved by decreasing its attentional value. In ALCOVE, the dimensions most relevant to the category distinction learn larger attention strengths, and the less relevant dimensions learn smaller attention strengths.

Each hidden node is connected to output nodes that correspond to the possible response categories.

FIG. 2. Stretching the horizontal axis and shrinking the vertical axis causes exemplars of the two categories (denoted by dots and xs) to have greater between-categories dissimilarity and greater within-category similarity. (The attention strengths in the network perform this sort of stretching and shrinking function. From "Attention, Similarity, and the Identification–Categorization Relationship" by R. M. Nosofsky, 1986, *Journal of Experimental Psychology: General, 115*, p.42. Copyright 1986 by the American Psychological Association. Adapted by permission.)

The connection from the jth hidden node to the kth category node has a connection weight denoted w_{kj}. Because the hidden node is activated only by stimuli in a restricted region of input space near its corresponding exemplar, the connection weight is called the *association weight* between the exemplar and the category. The output (category) nodes are activated by the same linear rule used in the GCM and in the network models of Gluck and Bower (1988a, 1988b):

$$a_k^{out} = \sum_{\substack{hid \\ j}} w_{kj} a_j^{hid}. \tag{2}$$

In ALCOVE, unlike the GCM, the association weights are adjusted by an interactive, error-driven learning rule and can take on any real value, including negative values.

To compare model performance with human performance, the category activations must be mapped onto response probabilities. This is done in ALCOVE using the same choice rule as was used in the GCM and network models, which was motivated in those models by the classic works of Luce (1963) and Shepard (1957). Thus,

$$\Pr(K) = \exp(\phi a_K^{out}) / \sum_{\substack{out \\ k}} \exp(\phi a_k^{out}), \tag{3}$$

where ϕ is a real-valued mapping constant. In other words, the probability of classifying the given stimulus into category K is determined by the magnitude of category K's activation (exponentiated) relative to the sum of all category activations (exponentiated).

Here is a summary of how ALCOVE categorizes a given stimulus. Suppose, for example, that the model is applied to the situation illustrated in Fig. 2. In this case, there are two psychological dimensions, hence two input nodes; four training exemplars, hence four hidden nodes; and two categories, hence two output nodes. When an exemplar is presented to ALCOVE, the input nodes are activated according to the component dimensional values of the stimulus. Each hidden node is then activated according to the similarity of the stimulus to the exemplar represented by the hidden

node, using the attentionally weighted metric of Equation 1. Thus, hidden nodes near the input stimulus are strongly activated, and those farther away in psychological space are less strongly activated. Then the output (category) nodes are activated by summing across all the hidden (exemplar) nodes, weighted by the association weights between the exemplars and categories, as in Equation 2. Finally, response probabilities are computed using Equation 3.

It was stated that the dimensional attention strengths, α_i, and the association weights between exemplars and categories, w_{kj}, are learned. The learning procedure is gradient descent on sum-squared error, as used in standard back propagation (Rumelhart et al., 1986) and in the network models of Gluck and Bower (1988a, 1988b). In the learning situations addressed by ALCOVE, each presentation of a training exemplar is followed by feedback indicating the correct response. The feedback is coded in ALCOVE as *teacher* values, t_k, given to each category node. For a given training exemplar and feedback, the error generated by the model is defined as

$$E = \tfrac{1}{2} \sum_{\substack{out \\ k}} (t_k - a_k^{out})^2, \tag{4a}$$

with the teacher values defined as

$$t_k = \begin{cases} \max\,(+1, a_k^{out}) \text{ if the stimulus} \\ \quad \text{is in Category } K, \\ \min\,(-1, a_k^{out}) \text{ if the stimulus} \\ \quad \text{is not in Category } K. \end{cases} \tag{4b}$$

These teacher values are defined so that activations "better than necessary" are not counted as errors. Thus, if a given stimulus should be classified as a member of the kth category, then the kth output node should have an activation of at least +1. If the activation is greater than 1, then the difference between the actual activation and +1 is not counted as error. Because these teacher values do not mind being outshone by their students, I call them "humble teachers." The motivation for using humble teacher values is that the feedback given to subjects is nominal, indicating only which category the stimulus belongs to and not the degree of membership. Hence, the teacher used in the model should only require some minimal level of category-node activation and should not require all exemplars ultimately to produce the same activations. Humble teachers are discussed further at the conclusion of the article.

On presentation of a training exemplar to ALCOVE, the association strengths and dimensional attention strengths are changed by a small amount so that the error decreases. Following Rumelhart et al. (1986), they are adjusted proportionally to the (negative of the) error gradient, which leads to the following learning rules (derived in the Appendix):

$$\Delta w_{kj}^{out} = \lambda_w (t_k - a_k^{out}) a_j^{hid}, \tag{5}$$

$$\Delta \alpha_i = \lambda_\alpha \sum_{\substack{hid \\ j}} [\sum_{\substack{out \\ k}} (t_k - a_k^{out}) w_{kj}] a_j^{hid} c |h_{ji} - a_i^{in}|, \tag{6}$$

where the λs are constants of proportionality ($\lambda > 0$) called *learning rates*. The same learning rate, λ_w, applies to all the output weights. Likewise, there is only one learning rate, λ_α, for all the attentional strengths. The dimensional attention strengths are constrained to be nonnegative, as negative values have no psychologically meaningful interpretation. Thus, if Equation 6 were to drive an attention strength to a value less than zero, then the strength is set to zero.

Learning in ALCOVE proceeds as follows: For each presentation of a training exemplar, activation propagates to the category nodes as described previously. Then the teacher values are presented and compared with the actual category node activations. The association and attention strengths are then adjusted according to Equations 5 and 6. Several aspects of learning in ALCOVE deserve explicit mention.

First, learning is error driven. Both Equations 5 and 6 include the error term $(t_k - a_k^{out})$, so that changes are proportional to error. When there is no error, nothing changes. This is to be contrasted with learning rules that are based on accumulating constant increments on every trial, such as the array-exemplar model (Estes, 1986a, 1986b, 1988; Estes et al., 1989) and context model (Medin & Schaffer, 1978; Nosofsky, 1988b; Nosofsky, Kruschke, & McKinley, in press). In such models, the system changes independently of its actual performance.

Second, because of the similarity-based activations of the hidden nodes, the training exemplars interact during learning. For example, consider two training exemplars that are similar to each other. Because of their similarity, when either one is presented, both corresponding hidden nodes are activated (one just partially); and because learning is proportional to the hidden node activations (see Equation 5), the association strengths from both exemplars are adjusted (as long as there is error present). This interactive property is also to be contrasted with models such as the array-exemplar model, in which learning affects isolated exemplars one at a time (see also Matheus, 1988). The interactive character to learning in ALCOVE is comparable to the competitive nature of learning noted by Gluck and Bower (1988a, 1988b) in their network models and gives ALCOVE the ability to account for the base-rate neglect phenomena they observed, as is described later.

There are other notable implications of interactive learning in ALCOVE. It implies that similar exemplars from the same category should enhance each other's learning. Thus, it suggests that prototypical exemplars should be learned faster than peripheral exemplars, if it can be assumed that prototypical exemplars tend to be centrally located near several other exemplars from the same category. That is desirable insofar as it is also observed in human data (e.g. Rosch, Simpson, & Miller, 1976). Interactive learning also suggests that the shape of the category boundary will have no direct influence on the difficulty of learning the category distinction; rather, difficulty should be based on the clustering of exemplars (subject to the additional complication of attentional learning). In particular, it suggests that it is not necessary for linearly separable categories to be easier to learn than nonlinearly separable categories. Human data again make this a desirable property (Medin & Schwanenflugel, 1981).

A third property of learning in ALCOVE is that attention learning can only adjust the relative importance of the dimensions as given. ALCOVE cannot construct new dimensions to attend to. For example, consider the situation in Fig. 3, in which the four training exemplars form the corners of a diamond in the psychological space. Ideally, one might like to stretch the space along the right diagonal to better separate the two categories and shrink along the left diagonal to make within-category exemplars more similar, but ALCOVE cannot do that. Fortunately, it appears that people cannot do that either, as is described later. This anisotropy in attentional learning implies that when modeling human data with ALCOVE, one must be certain that the input dimensions used in the model match the psychological dimensions used by the human subjects.

In all the applications described in this article, the psychological dimensions are separable, not integral (Garner, 1974), but the model does not necessarily depend on that. ALCOVE might accommodate psychologically integral dimensions by using a Euclidean distance metric ($r = 2$) in Equation 1 (Nosofsky, 1987; Shepard, 1964). There is evidence to suggest that people can, with effort, differentially attend to psychologically integral dimensions when given opportunity to do so (e.g. Nosofsky, 1987).

In summary, ALCOVE incorporates the exemplar-based representation of Nosofsky's (1987) GCM with error-driven learning as in Gluck and Bower's (1988a, 1988b) network models. ALCOVE extends the GCM in several ways: For learning association weights, it uses an error-driven, inter-active rule, instead of a constant-increment rule, that allows association weights in ALCOVE to take on any positive or negative value. ALCOVE also provides a mechanism for attention-strength learning, whereas the GCM has none. ALCOVE extends Gluck and Bower's network models by allowing continuous input dimensions and by hav-

ing explicit dimensional attention learning. In fitting ALCOVE to human data, there are four free parameters: (a) the fixed specificity c in Equation 1, (b) the probability-mapping constant ϕ in Equation 3, (c) the association weight-learning rate λ_w in Equation 5, and (d) the attention-learning rate λ_α in Equation 6.

Applications

Learning to attend to relevant dimensions
In this section ALCOVE is applied to the category structures used in the classic research of Shepard, Hovland, and Jenkins (1961). There are three reasons for considering the work of Shepard et al.: First, the results of the study provide fundamental human data that any model of category learning should address, and in particular they have served as a benchmark for several recent models (e.g. Anderson, 1991; Gluck & Bower, 1988b; Nosofsky, 1984). Second, the structures described by Shepard et al. are well suited for demonstrating the capabilities of ALCOVE. Third, Shepard et al. argued explicitly that models of categorization based on reinforcement learning and graded generalization could not account for their data unless such models included some (un-specified) mechanism for selective attention. As ALCOVE does include such a mechanism, it faces a direct theoretical and empirical challenge.

The stimuli used by Shepard et al. (1961) varied on three binary dimensions. For example, figures could vary in shape (square vs. triangle), size (large vs. small), and color (filled vs. open). Each of the resulting eight training exemplars was assigned to one of two categories, such that both categories had four exemplars. It turns out that there are only six structurally distinct types of category assignments. Figure 4 shows the six types, with the eight exemplars indicated by the corners of a cube. The category assignment of an exemplar is indicated by either a filled or blank circle. For example, the top-left cube shows that for Category Type I, Exemplars 1 to 4 are assigned to the *blank* Category, and Exemplars 5 to 8 are assigned to the *filled* category. Any assignment

FIG. 3. Attentional learning in ALCOVE (attention learning covering map) cannot stretch or shrink diagonally. (Compare with Fig. 2.)

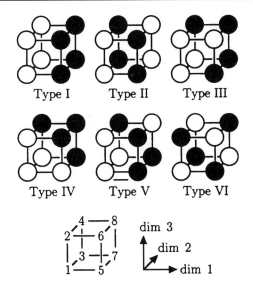

FIG. 4. The six category types used by Shepard, Hovland, and Jenkins (1961). (The three binary stimulus dimensions [labeled by the trident at lower right] yield eight training exemplars, numbered at the corners of the lower-left cube. Category assignments are indicated by the open or filled circles. From "Learning and Memorization of Classifications" by R. N. Shepard, C. L. Hovland, & H. M. Jenkins, 1961, *Psychological Monographs, 75*, 13, Whole No. 517, p.4. In the public domain.)

of exemplars to categories, with four exemplars in each category, can be rotated or reflected into one of the structures shown in Fig. 4.

A primary concern of Shepard et al. (1961) was to determine the relative difficulty of learning the six category types. Intuitively, Type I should be particularly easy to learn because only information about Dimension 1 is relevant to the categorization decision; variation on Dimensions 2 and 3 leads to no variation in category membership. However, Type II requires attention to both Dimensions 1 and 2 and therefore should be more difficult to learn. (Type II is the exclusive-or [XOR] problem in its two relevant dimensions.) Types III, IV, V, and VI require information about all three dimensions to make correct categorizations, but the dimensions are not equally informative in every type. For example, in Type V, six of eight exemplars can be correctly classified by considering only Dimension 1, with attention to Dimensions 2 and 3 needed only for the remain-

ing two exemplars. On the other hand, Type VI requires equal attention to all the dimensions, because exemplars of each category are symmetrically distributed on the dimensions. (Type VI is parity problem in three dimensions.) Thus, if it takes more cognitive effort or capacity to consider more dimensions, then Type I should be easiest to learn, followed by Types II, III, IV, V, and VI.

Shepard et al. (1961) found empirically that the order of difficulty was I < II < (III, IV, V) < VI. That is, Type I was easiest, followed by Type II, followed by Types III, IV, and V (they were very close) and Type VI. Difficulty of learning was measured by the total number of errors made until the subject correctly classified each of the eight exemplars four times in a row. Other measures, such as number of errors in recall, and response time, showed the same ordering.

How does one explain, in a formal quantitative theory, the observed difficulty of the types? Perhaps the most direct approach is a stimulus generalization hypothesis: Category structures that assign highly similar stimuli to the same category and highly dissimilar stimuli to different categories should be relatively easy to learn, whereas structures in which similar stimuli are mapped to different categories and dissimilar stimuli are assigned to the same category should be relatively difficult to learn. Shepard et al. (1961) formalized that hypothesis by measuring interstimulus similarities (inferred from separately obtained identification-confusion data) and by computing the difficulty of category types by considering similarities of all pairs of exemplars from different categories. They considered several variants of the generalization hypothesis, all of which failed to predict the observed order of learning. They argued that "the most serious shortcoming of the generalization theory is that it does not provide for a process of abstraction (or selective attention)." (Shepard et al., 1961, p.29). The idea was that by devoting attention to only relevant dimensions, confusability of stimuli that differed on those dimensions would be greatly reduced. In that way, Types I and II, especially, would be significantly easier to learn than predicated by a pure generalization theory.

The notion of selective attention was formalized by Nosofsky (1984, 1986) in his GCM. The

GCM added attention factors to each dimension of the input space. By using optimal attention weights, which maximized the average percentage correct, or by using attention weights freely estimated to best fit the data, the GCM was able to correctly predict the relative difficulties of the six category types, but the GCM has no attention learning mechanism.

Shepard et al. (1961) considered a variety of learning theories, to see if any provided the necessary attention-learning mechanism. Their answer, in brief, was no. *Cue conditioning* theories, in which associations between single cues (e.g. square) and categories are gradually reinforced, are unable to account for the ability to learn Types II, III, V, and VI, because no single cue is diagnostic of the category assignments. *Pattern conditioning* theories, in which associations between complete configurations of cues (e.g. large, white square) and categories are gradually reinforced, cannot account for the rapidity of learning Types I and II. They concluded

> Thus, although a theory based upon the notions of conditioning and, perhaps, the adaptation of cues at first showed promise of accounting both for stimulus generalization and abstraction, further investigation indicated that it does not, in any of the forms yet proposed, yield a prediction of the difficulty of each of our six types of classifications. (Shepard et al., 1961, p.32)

Gluck and Bower (1988a) combined cue and pattern conditioning into their "configural-cue model." The configural-cue model assumes that stimuli are represented by values on each single dimension, plus pairs of values on each pair of dimensions, plus triplets of values on each triplet of dimensions, and so on. Thus, for the stimuli from the Shepard et al. (1961) study, there are 6 one-value cues (two for each dimension), plus 12 two-value configural cues (four for each pair of dimensions), plus 8 three-value configural cues (the eight full stimuli themselves), yielding a total of 26 configural cues. Each configural cue is represented by an input node in a simple network, connected directly to category nodes. Presence of a configural cue is indicated by activating ($a = +1$) the corresponding input node, and absence is indicated by no activation. The model learns by gradient descent on sum-squared error. For the configural-cue model, Gluck and Bower made no explicit mapping from category-node activations to response probabilities, but in other network models they used the choice function of Equation 3 so that mapping is also assumed here. The configural-cue model has two parameters, the learning rate for the connection weights and the scaling constant ϕ in Equation 3. When applied to the six category types of Shepard et al., the result was that the configural-cue model failed to learn Type II fast enough (see Fig. 12 of Gluck & Bower, 1988a), as measured either by cumulative errors during learning or by time until criterion error level is reached. Thus Shepard et al.'s conclusion persists: Some mechanism for selective attention seems to be needed.[1]

ALCOVE was applied to the six category types by using three input nodes (one for each stimulus dimension), eight hidden nodes (one for each training exemplar), and two output nodes (one for each category). It was assumed that the three physical dimensions of the stimuli had corresponding psychological dimensions. In the Shepard et al. experiments, the three physical dimensions were counterbalanced with respect to the abstract dimensions shown in Fig. 4; therefore, the input encoding for the simulation gave each dimension equal scales (with alternative values on each dimension separated by one scale unit), and equal initial attentional strengths (set arbitrarily to 1/3). The association weights were initialized at zero, reflecting the notion that before training there should be no associations between any exemplars and particular categories.

In the Shepard et al. (1961) study, the difficulty of any given type was computed by averaging across subjects, each of whom saw a different random sequence of training exemplars. In the simulation, sequence effects were eliminated by executing changes in association weights and attention strengths only after complete epochs of all eight training exemplars. (In the connectionist literature, epoch updating is also referred to as *batch* updating.)

Figure 5 (A and B) show learning curves generated by ALCOVE when there was no attention learning and when there was moderate attention learning, respectively. Each datum shows the probability of selecting the correct category, averaged across the eight exemplars within an epoch. For both graphs, the response mapping constant was set to $\phi = 2.0$, the specificity was fixed at $c = 6.5$, and the learning rate for association weights was $\lambda_w = 0.03$. In Fig. 5A, there was no attention learning ($\lambda_\alpha = 0.0$), and it can be seen that Type II is learned much too slowly. In Fig. 5B, the attention-learning rate was raised to $\lambda_\alpha = 0.0033$, and consequently Type II was learned second fastest, as observed in human data. Indeed, it can be seen in Fig. 5B that the six types were learned in the same order as people, with Type I the fastest, followed by Type II, followed by Types III, IV, and V clustered together, followed by Type VI.

The dimensional attention strengths were redistributed as expected. For Category Type I, the attention strength on the relevant Dimension 1 increased, whereas attention to the two irrelevant Dimensions 2 and 3 dropped nearly to zero. For Type II, attention to the irrelevant Dimension 3 dropped to zero, whereas attention to the two relevant Dimensions 1 and 2 grew (equally for both

dimensions). For Types III to VI, all three dimensions retained large attention strengths. Type VI had all of its attention strengths grow, thereby better segregating all the exemplars. Such symmetrical growth of attention is functionally equivalent to increasing the specificities of all the hidden nodes (see Equation 1).

From a model-testing perspective, it is reassuring to note that the range of orderings illustrated in Fig. 5 (A and B) are the only orderings that ALCOVE is capable of generating (when $r = q = 1$). When the attention-learning rate is set to higher values, the same ordering as in Fig. 5B arises, but with Types I and II learned even faster. When the specificity is made larger (or smaller), the overall separation of the learning curves is lessened (or enlarged, respectively), but the same orderings persist. Adjusting the association-weight learning rate merely changes the overall number of epochs required to reach a certain probability correct.

ALCOVE accounts for the relative difficulty of Shepard et al.'s (1961) six category types by its ability to learn dimensional attention strengths. Such an attentional-learning mechanism is just the sort of thing Shepard et al. called for in their theoretical analyses. It is only fair to note, however, that Shepard et al. also concluded that in

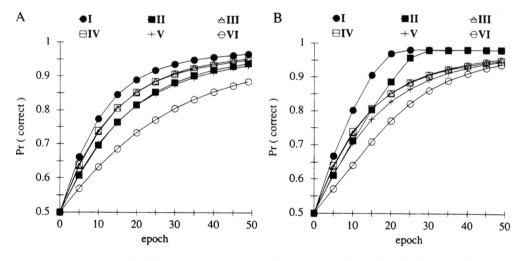

FIG. 5. A: Results of applying ALCOVE (attention learning covering map) to the Shepard, Hovland, and Jenkins (1961) category types, with zero attention learning. Here Type II is learned as slowly as Type V (the Type V curve is mostly obscured by the Type II curve). B: Results of applying ALCOVE to the Shepard et al. category types, with moderate attention learning. Note that Type II is now learned second fastest, as observed in human data. Pr = probability.

addition to abstracting the relevant dimensions, subjects formulated rules for specifying the categories. How ALCOVE might interact with a rule-generating system is discussed in a later section.

Learning to attend to correlated dimensions

Medin et al. (1982) have noted that prototype and other "independent cue" models are not sensitive to correlations between cues. In several experiments, they pitted single-cue diagnosticity against correlated cues to see which would be the better determinant of human categorization performance. They used a simulated medical diagnosis paradigm in which subjects were shown hypothetical patterns of four symptoms. Each of the four symptoms could take on one of two values; for example, watery eyes versus sunken eyes. Subjects were trained on four exemplars of the fictitious disease Terrigitis (T) and four exemplars of the fictitious disease Midosis (M). In this situation the four symptoms are the four dimensions of the stimulus space, and the two diseases are the two alternative categories. The abstract structure of the categories is shown in Table 1. One important aspect of the structure is that the first two symptoms are individually diagnostic, in that p (Terrigitis| Symptom 1 = "1") = .75 and p (Terrigitis|Symptom 2 = "1") = .75, whereas the third and fourth symptoms are not individually diagnostic, each being associated with each disease 50% of the time. Another important aspect of the structure is that the third and fourth symptoms are perfectly correlated in the training set, so that their combination forms a perfect predictor of the disease category. Thus, symptoms three and four are either both 1 or both 0 for cases of Terrigitis, but they are different values for cases of Midosis.

If subjects learn to attend to the correlated third and fourth symptoms to make their diagnoses, then when tested with novel symptom patterns, they should choose Terrigitis whenever the third and fourth symptoms agree. On the other hand, if subjects learn to use the first and second symptoms, then they should choose Terrigitis more often when those symptom values are 1.

Subjects were trained on the first eight exemplars of Table 1 using a free-inspection procedure. Unlike training paradigms in which stimuli are shown sequentially with a definite frequency, Medin et al. (1982) allowed their subjects to freely inspect the eight exemplars during a 10-min period (each exemplar was written on a separate card). After the 10-min training period, subjects were shown each of the possible 16 symptom combinations and asked to diagnose them as either Terrigitis or Midosis. The results are reproduced in Table 1. Three important trends are evident in the data. First, subjects were fairly accurate in classifying the patterns on which they had been trained (Exemplars T1–T4 and M1–M4), choosing the correct disease category 80% of the time. Second, subjects were sensitive to the diagnostic value of the first and second symptoms, in that Novel Patterns N3 and N4 were classified as Terrigitis more often than Patterns N1 and N2, and Patterns N5 and N6 were classified as Terrigitis more often than Patterns N7 and N8. Third, subjects were also apparently quite sensitive to the correlated features, because they classified Patterns N1 to N4, for which Symptoms 3 and 4 agree, as Terrigitis more than 50% of the time, and they classified patterns N5 to N8, for which Symptoms 3 and 4 differ, as Terrigitis less than 50% of the time.

The fourth column of Table 1 shows the results of applying ALCOVE. Eight hidden nodes were used, corresponding to the eight training exemplars. ALCOVE was trained for 50 sweeps, or epochs, on the eight patterns (T1 to T4 and M1 to M4). Association weights and attention strengths were updated after every complete sweep through the eight training patterns, because Medin et al. (1982) did not present subjects with a fixed sequence of stimuli. Best fitting parameter values were $\phi = 0.845$, $\lambda_w = 0.0260$, $c = 2.36$, and $\lambda_\alpha = 0.00965$, yielding a root-mean-squared deviation (RMSD) of 0.104 across the 16 patterns. (The number of epochs used was arbitrary and chosen only because it seemed like a reasonable number of exposures for a 10-min free-inspection period. The best fit for 25 epochs, for example, yielded an RMSD identical to three significant digits.)

All three of the main trends in the data are captured by ALCOVE. The trained exemplars were learned to 80% accuracy. The diagnosticities of the 1st two symptoms were picked up, because Patterns N3 and N4 were classified as Terrigitis

TABLE 1
Patterns Used by Medin, Altom, Edelson, and Freko (1982, Experiment 4) and Probabilities of Classifying as Terrigitis After Training

Exemplar	Symptoms	Observed	ALCOVE	Config cue
T1	1111	.88	.82	.76
T2	0111	.89	.78	.76
T3	1100	.73	.82	.76
T4	1000	.77	.78	.76
M1	1010	.12	.22	.25
M2	0010	.17	.18	.25
M3	0101	.25	.22	.25
M4	0001	.33	.18	.25
N1	0000	.53	.59	.44
N2	0011	.53	.59	.44
N3	0100	.75	.64	.46
N4	1011	.67	.64	.46
N5	1110	.45	.41	.58
N6	1101	.38	.41	.58
N7	0110	.36	.36	.55
N8	1001	.28	.36	.55

Note. Exemplar Labels T1–T4 refer to the four training exemplars for Terrigitis, and exemplar Labels M1–M4 refer to the four training exemplars for Midosis. Exemplar Labels N1–N8 refer to novel test patterns. Config cue = configural-cue model; ALCOVE = attention learning covering map. Data are from "Correlated Symptoms and Simulated Medical Classification" by D. L. Medin, M. W. Altom, S. M. Edelson, & D. Freko, 1982, *Journal of Experimental Psychology: Learning, Memory, and Cognition, 8*, p.47. Copyright 1982 by the American Psychological Association. Adapted by permission.

with higher probability than Patterns N1 and N2, whereas Patterns N5 and N6 were classified as Terrigitis more often than Patterns N7 and N8. It is important to note that the correlated symptoms were detected, because Patterns N1 to N4 were classiffied as Terrigitis with more than 50% probability, and Patterns N5 to N8, with less than 50% probability.

ALCOVE accounts for the influence of correlated dimensions by increasing attention to those dimensions. When the attention-learning rate is very large, then the correlated Symptoms 3 and 4 get all the attention, and Symptoms 1 and 2 are ignored. On the contrary, when attentional learning is zero, then the diagnosticities of the first two dimensions dominate the results. The results reported in Table 1 are for an intermediate attentional-learning rate, for which Symptoms 3 and 4 get more attention than Symptoms 1 and 2,

but some attention remains allocated to Symptoms 1 and 2.

The configural-cue model was also fitted to these data. For this situation, the configural-cue model requires 80 input nodes: 8 singlet nodes, 24 doublet nodes, 32 triplet nodes, and 16 quadruplet nodes. The model was trained for 50 epochs with epoch updating. The best-fitting parameter values were $\phi = 0.554$ and $\lambda_w = 0.0849$, yielding an RMSD of 0.217 across the 16 patterns, more than twice the RMSD of ALCOVE. As is clear from the results shown in Table 1, the configural-cue model is completely unable to detect the correlated symptoms, despite the presence of doublet nodes that are sensitive to pairwise combinations of dimensions. Contrary to human performance, the configural-cue model classifies Patterns N1 to N4 as Terrigitis with less than 50% probability and Patterns N5 to N8 with more than 50%

probability. That qualitative reversal is a necessary prediction of the configural-cue model and cannot be rectified by another choice of parameter values.

Gluck, Bower, and Hee (1989) showed that if only single symptoms and pairwise symptom combinations were used, with no three-way or four-way symptom combinations, then correlated symptoms could be properly accentuated (for Experiment 3 from Medin et al., 1982). However, by not including the higher order combinations, the model was told a priori that pairwise combinations would be relevant, which begs the fundamental question at issue here: namely, how it is that the relevance is learned.

The simulation results shown in Table 1 are to be construed qualitatively, despite the fact that they are quantitative best fits. That is because the free-inspection training procedure used by Medin et al. (1982) might very well have produced subtle effects caused by subjects exposing themselves to some stimuli more frequently than to others, or studying different exemplars later in training than early on. The simulations, on the other hand, assumed equal frequency of exposure and constant relative frequencies throughout training. Moreover, there is a disparity in the number of parameters in the two models: ALCOVE has four, whereas the configural-cue model has two. Nevertheless, the qualitative evidence is clear: Because of attention learning, ALCOVE can account for sensitivity to correlated dimensions, whereas the configural-cue model cannot.

Interactive exemplars and base-rate neglect

The previous sections emphasized the role of attention learning. This and the next section, instead, emphasize the learning of association weights and illustrate how hidden nodes (exemplars) interact during learning because of their similarity-based activations. In particular, it is shown that ALCOVE can quantitatively fit trial-by-trial learning curves and account for the apparent base-rate neglect observed by Gluck and Bower (1988b), Estes et al. (1989), Shanks (1990), and Nosofsky, Kruschke, and McKinley (in press).

Like the Medin et al. (1982) research, Gluck and Bower (1988b, Experiment 3) had subjects

learn to classify lists of four symptoms as one of two fictitious diseases. The base rates of the two diseases were unequal, with one disease occurring 75% of the time, and the other disease, 25% of the time. The diseases were referred to as either the *common* or *rare* disease, respectively (although subjects learned them using fictitious disease names). Symptoms were binary valued, and their alternative values were denoted s1 and s1*, s2 and s2*, and so on for each of the four symptoms. The correspondence of symptoms with diseases was probabilistic, so that on each trial a disease was selected according to the base rates, and then symptoms were selected according to the conditional probabilities in Table 2. The probabilities were designed so that the conditional probability of the rare disease, given only Symptom s1, was 50%. That is, according to Bayes' Theorem, when base rates are properly taken into account, Symptom s1 is completely undiagnostic by itself.

After considerable training, subjects estimated the probability of the diseases given each symptom alone. It turned out that when given Symptom s1 alone, subjects reliably overestimated the probability of the rare disease, apparently not taking full account of the base rates of the diseases.

To explain that apparent base-rate neglect, Gluck and Bower (1988a, 1988b) considered two candidate models of category learning. One was a simple exemplar-based model, in which all training instances were stored in memory along with

TABLE 2
Conditional Probabilities of Disease Symptoms in Four Experiments

	Disease	
Symptom	Rare	Common
s1 (s1*)	.6 (.4)	.2 (.8)
s2 (s2*)	.4 (.6)	.3 (.7)
s3 (s3*)	.3 (.7)	.4 (.6)
s4 (s4*)	.2 (.8)	.6 (.4)

Note. The table indicates, for example, that p (s1|rare) = .6. The base rate of the rare disease was .25, and the base rate of the common disease was .75. Parentheses indicate alternative symptom (*) values and corresponding probabilities.

their assigned categories. To predict categorization probabilities given a single symptom, the memory was scanned for all exemplars that matched on the given symptom, and the response probability for a category was taken as the frequency of matching exemplars assigned to that category, relative to the total frequency of matching exemplars. The simple exemplar-based model predicted that given Symptom s1 alone, the estimated probability of the rare disease should be .5, because exactly half of the training exemplars containing s1 were assigned to the rare disease. This is a special case of Medin and Schaffer's (1978) context model, in which the similarity of nonmatching features is taken to be zero. Nosofsky et al. (in press) described this in more detail, noting that if the context-model similarity parameters are taken to be nonzero, then the exemplar-based model does even worse.

Gluck and Bower (1988a, 1988b) also considered the "double-node" network model (so-called by Estes et al., 1989), illustrated in Fig. 6. In this model, each binary-valued stimulus dimension is represented by a pair of input nodes, one node for each of the alternative values on that dimension. When Symptom s1 was present, its node was activated, and the s1* node was deactivated. Each input node was directly connected to output nodes corresponding to the disease categories. The output nodes were linear, and response probabilities for complete (four-symptom) exemplars were computed as in Equation 3. The connection weights were adapted by gradient descent on error. When given just single symptoms, Gluck and Bower (1988b) used the corresponding connection weights to indicate ordinal estimates of disease probabilities. In subsequent work by Estes et al. (1989), quantitative predictions of choice probabilities, given single symptoms, were computed using Equation 3. The latter approach is also taken here.[2]

Unlike the simple exemplar-based model, the double-node model was able to account for the base-rate neglect. As explained by Gluck and Bower (1988b), the error-driven learning mechanism made individual symptom nodes "compete" for the right to activate the output nodes, and in the context of the other training patterns, symptom

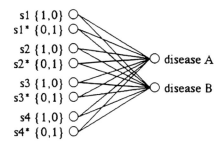

FIG. 6. The double node network model of Gluck and Bower (1988b). (Numbers after each symptom indicate the activation of the node pair when that symptom is present. From "From Conditioning to Category Learning: An Adaptive Network Model" by M. A. Gluck and G. H. Bower, 1988, *Journal of Experimental Psychology: General, 117,* p.239. Copyright 1988 by the American Psychological Association. Adapted by permission.)

s1 was a relatively better predictor of the rare disease than the common disease.

Estes et al. (1989) replicated and extended Gluck and Bower's (1988b) study. First, whereas Gluck and Bower were interested in asymptotic behavior after lengthy training, Estes et al. trained subjects on a single sequence of patterns so that trial-by-trial learning curves could be fitted by competing models. Second, whereas Gluck and Bower obtained explicit probability estimates after training, Estes et al. also obtained choice probabilities for each single symptom presented alone.

Estes et al. (1989) compared an exemplar-based model and (a single-node version of) the double-node model in their abilities to fit the trial-by-trial training data and fit the posttraining single-symptom transfer data. In fitting the training data, the Gluck and Bower network model was superior to the simple exemplar model. In fitting the transfer data, the exemplar model could sometimes give better overall fits, but in no case could it predict that p (rare|s1) > .50. In brief, the exemplar models tested by Gluck and Bower (1988b) and by Estes et al. failed to account for the apparent base-rate neglect. ALCOVE is an exemplar-based model, so it faces a direct challenge by these results.

Nosofsky et al. (in press) carried out partial replications and extensions of the experiments reported by Gluck and Bower (1988a, 1988b) and by Estes et al. (1989). The same sequence of training exemplars and feedback as used by Estes et al. was used in their experiment (hence the same probabilistic structure as shown in Table 2). Instead of using the present versus absent symptoms, as used by Estes et al., Nosofsky et al. (in press) used substitutive symptoms, for example, stuffy nose versus runny nose. One advantage of using substitutive symptoms is that there is no confusion on single-symptom test trials as to whether the unpresented symptoms are completely missing from the stimulus or have the informative value "absent" (Shanks, 1990). The Nosofsky et al. (in press) study also obtained data from a richer set of transfer stimuli, including not only single symptoms but also all pairs, triplets, and complete quadruplets of symptoms and the null pattern. The larger transfer data set is not considered here, as it is fully described in Nosofsky et al. (in press). Instead, only the eight single symptoms considered by Gluck and Bower and by Estes et al. are discussed.

In the Nosofsky et al. (in press) experiment, 84 subjects were trained on the same sequence of 240 exemplars, and then in the transfer stage were presented with patterns without feedback. (Details of the procedure can be found in Nosofsky et al., in press.) The proportion of subjects choosing each category was computed for every trial. The models were fitted to those data, using the sum of squared deviations as the measure of fit.

ALCOVE makes predictions on transfer trials by assuming that missing stimulus dimensions are collapsed. An equivalent method was used by Estes et al. (1989) to test their exemplar model. Functionally, that means that the sum in Equation 1 is taken only over the dimensions actually present in the stimulus. When all dimensions are missing, Equation 1 implies that every hidden node is maximally activated. That allows ALCOVE to predict base rates of the categories by integrating association weights across all the training exemplars.

The models were fitted simultaneously to the training and transfer data, minimizing the sum of the mean squared error on training trials plus the mean squared error on transfer trials. The resulting best fits are shown in Table 3. ALCOVE fits both training and transfer data slightly better than the double-node model. Figures 7 and 8 show the model's predictions for these best simultaneous fits. Figure 8 shows that both models predict that Symptom s1 (presented alone) should be classified as the rare disease more than 50% of the time and to about the same degree. (Although both models predict apparent base-rate neglect on Symptom s1, neither fits the transfer results in great detail. Extended versions of the models that address this problem are described in Nosofsky et al., in press.)

The configural-cue model was also fit to the data. Table 3 shows that it did noticeably worse than ALCOVE and the double-node models. In fact, the configural-cue model shows only slight base-rate neglect, with p (rare|s1) $= .531$. Because of those inadequacies, the configural-cue model is not shown in Figs. 7 and 8.

Some readers might object that these are unfair comparisons because ALCOVE has four free parameters, whereas the double-node (and configural-cue) model has only two. The purpose of the presentation here is to compare the basic versions of the models, and so the inequality in the number

TABLE 3
Fits of ALCOVE, the Double-Node, and Configural-Cue Models to Learning and Transfer Data

Model	RMSD			Parameter value			
	Total	Training	Transfer	ϕ	λ_w	c	λ_α
ALCOVE	.101	.106	.0955	1.06	.0393	2.55	0.0
Double node	.116	.109	.123	1.64	.0122	—	—
Configural cue	.151	.113	.181	2.07	.00312	—	—

Note. Dashes indicate nonapplicability. RMSD = root-mean-squared deviation; ALCOVE = attention learning covering map.

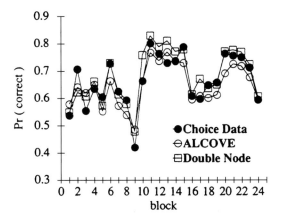

FIG. 7. Probability (Pr) of correct category choice during training. (Graph shows means for blocks of 10 trials, although data were fitted trial by trial. Because of averaging within blocks, it appears here that ALCOVE [attention learning covering map] has a worse fit than the double-node model, but the trial-by-trial fit is in fact slightly better. Results shown are for simultaneous fit to training and transfer data.)

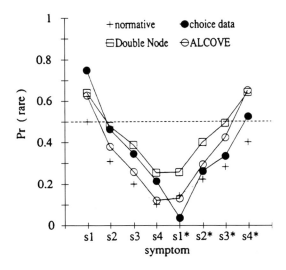

FIG. 8. Probability (Pr) of choosing the rare category given single symptoms after training. (Shown are results for simultaneous fit to training and transfer data. Points are connected by lines for visual appeal; no continuum of symptoms is meant to be implied. ALCOVE = attention learning covering map.)

of parameters is unavoidable. However, Nosofsky et al. (in press) used versions of the models with equal numbers of parameters. In one set of comparisons, each model was allowed three parameters. For ALCOVE, the attention-learning rate was set to zero, a priori, because the category structure used does not have a strongly asymmetrical distribution of exemplars over dimensions. The double-node model was given a third parameter by including a learning rate on an extra bias node. The bias node was necessary for the double-node model to make predictions about base rates on null patterns, that is, when all dimensions of the stimulus were missing. The results were that ALCOVE consistently did as well as the double-node model, even with equal numbers of parameters.

ALCOVE generates the apparent base-rate neglect on Symptom s1 because of interactions between exemplars during learning. For purposes of explanation, consider a simpler case with just two symptoms (two input dimensions). Figure 9 shows the frequencies of rare and common diseases for each combination of Symptoms a and b, out of a total of 104 cases. The top-left cell of Fig. 9 indicates that the symptom pair (a, b) occurred 11 times out of 104, with 10 rare cases and 1 common case. The frequencies were selected so

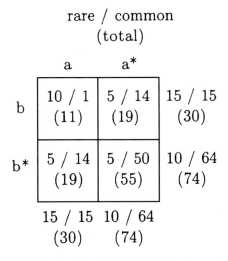

FIG. 9. A two-symptom situation to illustrate base-rate neglect in ALCOVE (attention learning covering map.) (Numbers in each cell indicate the frequency that the cell is assigned to the rare or common disease.)

that the conditional probability of the rare disease given Symptom a alone (or Symptom b alone) is $15/30 = .50$.

The table in Fig. 9 also acts as a geometric representation of the input space. The four cells are the four training exemplars. To model this situation in ALCOVE, there would be four hidden nodes with their receptive fields centered on the four cells of the table. Each hidden node has an association weight with the two disease (category) nodes (not shown).

The node centered on the symptom pair (a, b) should acquire a strong positive association weight with the rare disease node, because (a, b) is the rare disease 10 times as often as it is the common disease. By similar reasoning, one might suppose that the node centered on (a, b*) should acquire a strong negative association weight with the rare disease node, because it is the rare disease only about a third as often as it is the common disease. In fact, when ALCOVE is run on this situation, the magnitude of the negative association weight from (a, b*) is much less than the magnitude of the positive association weight from (a, b). That is because the (a, b*) node has a neighbor, (a*, b*), that gains a fairly strong negative association with the rare disease node. The three nodes, (a, b*), (a*, b), and (a*, b*), facilitate each other's learning because of their mutual similarity and because they all tend to be assigned to the common disease, and so their individual association weights remain relatively small. On the other hand, the association weight from (a, b) must become especially large to compensate for its competing neighbors.

When the single symptom (a, –) is presented, both the (a, b) and (a, b*) nodes are fully activated, whereas the (a*, b) and (a*, b*) nodes are both partially (and equally) activated. The net result is that the strong positive association weight from (a, b) to the rare disease node is sufficient to overcome the weaker negative associations from the other exemplars, and the rare disease node receives the greater activation. The model thereby displays apparent base-rate neglect when presented with single symptoms.

In summary, three points have been made in this section. First, the exemplar-based ALCOVE model has been shown to fit the learning and transfer data as well as the double-node model, whereas previously proposed exemplar-based models did not. In particular, ALCOVE accounts for apparent base-rate neglect as well as the double-node model. Second, there is no claim being made that ALCOVE is significantly better than the double-node model in this particular situation. Rather, ALCOVE has an advantage because it also fits several other situations where the double-node model fares less well or is inapplicable. Third, ALCOVE shows apparent base-rate neglect because the combination of error-driven learning and similarity-based hidden-node activations causes exemplars to interact during learning.

Interactive exemplars in linearly and nonlinearly separable categories

As suggested in the introduction, ALCOVE is only indirectly sensitive to the shape of category boundaries and is primarily affected by the clustering of exemplars and their distribution over stimulus dimensions. In particular, whether a category boundary is linear or nonlinear should have no direct influence, and it is possible that nonlinearly separable categories would be easier to learn than linearly separable ones.

A case in point comes from the work of Medin and Schwanenflugel (1981, Experiment 4). They compared two category structures, shown in Fig. 10. One structure was linearly separable, whereas the other was not. The two structures were equalized, however, in terms of mean city-block distance between exemplars within categories and between exemplars from different categories. For example, the mean city-block separation of exemplars within categories for the linearly separable structure is $(2 + 2 + 2 + 2 + 2 + 2)/6 = 2$, and the mean within-category separation for the nonlinearly separable category is the same, $(1 + 2 + 3 + 1 + 2 + 3)/6 = 2$. The mean separation between categories is $1^2/_3$ for both structures.

When human subjects were trained on the two structures, it was found that the linearly separable structure was no easier to learn than the nonlinearly separable structure. This result contradicts predictions of prototype models, such as the single- and double-node models of Gluck and

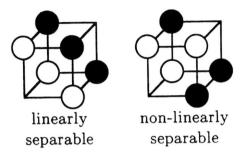

linearly
separable

non-linearly
separable

FIG. 10. Category structures used by Medin and Schwanenflugel (1981, Experiment 4). (The linearly separable structure is a subset of Type IV in the Shepard, Hovland, and Jenkins, 1961, studies [cf. Fig. 4], whereas the nonlinearly separable structure is the corresponding subset from Type III.)

Bower (1988a, 1988b; see Nosofsky, 1991, for a derivation that they are a type of prototype model), but is consistent with models that are sensitive to relational information, such as Medin and Schaffer's (1978) context model, and Nosofsky's GCM. In another experiment run by Medin and Schwanenflugel (1981, Experiment 3), a significant advantage for nonlinearly separable categories was observed.

The configural-cue model is able to show an advantage for the nonlinearly separable category, if the scaling constant ϕ is not too large. Gluck (1991; Gluck et al., 1989) has shown that if the triplet nodes are removed from the configural-cue representation, leaving only the singlet and doublet nodes, the advantage for the nonlinearly separable categories remains. Unfortunately, such a move requires an a priori knowledge of which combinations of dimensions will be useful for the task.

When ALCOVE is applied to these structures, the nonlinearly separable structure is indeed learned faster than the linearly separable structure. This result is true for every combination of parameter values I have tested (a wide range). In particular, attentional learning is not needed to obtain this result. Therefore, it is the interaction of the exemplars, due to similarity and error-driven learning, that is responsible for this performance in ALCOVE. Whereas the mean city-block separations of exemplars were equalized for the two category structures, the mean similarities of exemplars were not equal. ALCOVE exploits that difference in the learning rule for association weights (Equations 1 and 5). The flavor of this explanation is no different from that given for the context model (Medin & Schwanenflugel, 1981). The point is not that ALCOVE necessarily fits these data better than other models with exemplar-similarity-based representations like Medin and Schaffer's (1978) context model but that error-driven learning in ALCOVE does not impair its ability to account for these fundamental data.

Summary

The importance of dimensional attention learning was demonstrated by applying ALCOVE to the six category types from Shepard et al. (1961) and to the Medin et al. (1982) categories involving correlated dimensions. The importance of interaction between exemplars, produced by similarity-based activations and error-driven association-weight learning, was demonstrated in accounting for apparent base-rate neglect and the ability to learn nonlinearly separable categories faster than linearly separable categories. ALCOVE was shown to be quantitatively comparable or superior to the double-node and configural-cue models. Subsequent sections address domains that use continuous dimensions to which the double-node and configural-cue models, as presently formulated, are not applicable.

ALCOVE versus standard back propagation

As stated in the introduction, ALCOVE differs from standard back propagation in its architecture, behavior, and goals. A *standard back-propagation network* (later referred to as *backprop*) is a feedforward network with linear-sigmoid nodes in its hidden layer and with hidden weights and output weights that learn by gradient descent on error. Linear-sigmoid nodes have activation determined by

$$a_j^{hid} = 1/[1 + \exp(-\sum_{i}^{in} w_{ji}^{hid} a_i^{in})]. \tag{7}$$

The linear-sigmoid function was motivated as a generalized, or smoothed, version of the linear-threshold function in neuronlike perceptrons (Rumelhart et al., 1986). In contrast, the activation functions of ALCOVE were motivated by molar-level psychological theory. The activation profiles of hidden nodes in ALCOVE and in backprop, as determined by Equations 1 and 7, are shown in Fig. 11. Three important differences between the activation profiles are evident: First, the hidden node from ALCOVE has a limited receptive field, which means that the node is significantly activated only by inputs near its position. On the contrary, the hidden node from backprop is significantly activated by inputs from an entire half space of the input space. That difference in receptive field size has important consequences for how strongly hidden nodes interact during learning, as is demonstrated shortly. A second difference is that the level contours of the ALCOVE node are iso-distance contours (diamond shaped for a city-block metric), whereas the level contours of the backprop node are linear. (Examples of level contours are shown in Fig. 11 by the lines that mark horizontal cross sections through the activation profiles.) This implies that backprop will be especially sensitive to linear boundaries between categories. A third difference between the structure of ALCOVE and backprop is that the linear level contours of the backprop node can be oriented in any direction in input space, whereas attention learning in ALCOVE can only stretch or shrink along the given input dimensions (recall the discussion accompanying

Fig. 3). Those three differences result in short-comings of backprop that are now demonstrated with examples.

Insensitivity to boundary orientation

When backprop is applied to the six category types of Shepard et al. (1961; see Fig. 4), Type IV is learned almost as fast as Type I and much too fast compared to human performance. (Backprop does not learn Type IV quite as quickly as Type I because it is also sensitive to the clustering of exemplars near the boundary; e.g. see Ahmad, 1988.) This result holds over a wide range of learning rates for the two layers of weights, with or without momentum (Rumelhart et al., 1986), for different ranges of initial weight values and over a wide range in the number of hidden nodes. Type IV is learned so quickly by backprop because it can accentuate the diagonal axis through the prototypes of the two categories (Exemplars 1 and 8 in Fig. 4), unlike ALCOVE. In other words, the linear level contours of the backprop nodes align with the linear boundary between the categories in Type IV, despite the diagonal orientation of that boundary. ALCOVE cannot direct attention to diagonal axes (see discussion accompanying Fig. 3), so it does not learn Type IV so quickly.

Oversensitivity to linearity of boundary

When backprop is applied to the linearly or nonlinearly separable categories of Medin and Schwanenflugel (1981; see Fig. 10), the result is that the linearly separable structure is learned much faster than the nonlinearly separable one, contrary to human (and ALCOVE's) performance (e.g. Gluck, 1991). The reason is that the linear level contours of backprop's hidden nodes can align with the linear boundary between categories.

Catastrophic interference

McCloskey and Cohen (1989) and Ratcliff (1990) have shown that when a backprop network is initially trained on one set of associations, and subsequently trained on a different set of associations, memory for the first set is largely destroyed. Such catastrophic forgetting is not typical of normal humans and is a major shortcoming of backprop as a model of human learning and memory. As

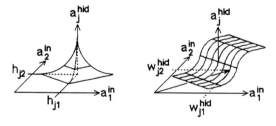

FIG. 11. Activation profile of a hidden node in ALCOVE (attention learning covering map) is shown on the left (Equation 1, with $r = q = 1$). (Activation profile of a hidden node in standard back propagation is shown on the right [Equation 7].)

ALCOVE is also a feed-forward network that learns by gradient descent on error, it is important to test it for catastrophic forgetting.

A simple demonstration of catastrophic forgetting in backprop is shown in Fig. 12 (a–c). The task is to learn the four exemplars in two phases: First learn that $(0, -1) \rightarrow$ "box" and $(-1, 0) \rightarrow$ "circle", then in a second phase learn that $(0, +1) \rightarrow$ "box" and $(+1, 0) \rightarrow$ "circle". The two graphs in panels b and c show typical results of applying backprop and ALCOVE, respectively. Each graph shows probability of correct categorization as a function of training epoch. Phase 1 consisted of Training Epochs 1 to 10, and Phase

2 began after the 10th epoch. Two trends are clear in the backprop results: In Phase 1, generalization performance on the untrained exemplars shifts dramatically to worse than chance, and in Phase 2 performance on the Phase 1 exemplars rapidly decays to worse than chance. On the contrary, ALCOVE shows virtually no interference between Phase 1 and Phase 2 exemplars (Fig. 12c).

For the results in Fig. 12b, the backprop network was made maximally comparable to ALCOVE. Thus, its input nodes were the same as in ALCOVE, and its output nodes were linear with weights initialized at zero, as in ALCOVE, with probability correct computed with Equation 3. There were 32

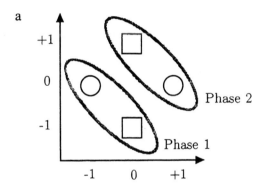

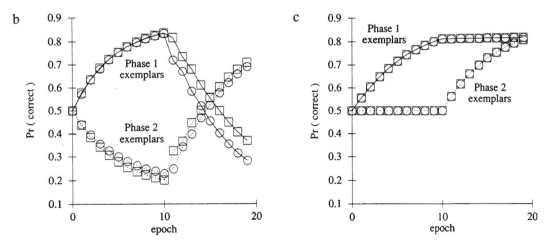

FIG. 12. a: Category structure for demonstrating catastrophic forgetting in back propagation and resistance to forgetting in ALCOVE (attention learning covering map.) b: Typical performance of back-propagation on the structure shown in Fig. 12a. c: Performance of ALCOVE on the structure shown in Fig. 12a. Pr = probability.

hidden nodes, with weights and thresholds initialized to random values between −2.5 and +2.5. Learning rates for output and hidden weights were both 0.06, with epoch updating. The same qualitative trends appear when using other parameter values and numbers of hidden nodes and for standard backprop using linear-sigmoid output nodes and output weights initialized to small random values. The results in Fig. 12c were obtained by running ALCOVE with four hidden nodes centered on the four exemplars, using $\phi = 1.0$, $\lambda_w = .15$, $c = 2.0$, and $\lambda_\alpha = .06$, with epoch updating.

Backprop shows such severe interference because the receptive fields of its hidden nodes cover such a huge portion of input space. When training on Phase 1, the hidden nodes shift so that their linear level contours tend to align with the right diagonal in Fig. 12a so that the two Phase 1 exemplars are accurately discriminated. In addition, nodes that happened to be initially placed in such an opportune orientation have their weights adjusted first and fastest. Unfortunately, those receptive fields cover the untrained Phase 2 exemplars in the same way, and the severe drop in generalization accuracy is the result. When subsequently trained on the Phase 2 exemplars, the same alignment of receptive fields occurs, but the category associations reverse, yielding the reversal of performance on the previously trained exemplars.

The receptive fields of hidden nodes in ALCOVE are much more localized, so that associations from exemplars to categories are not strongly affected by other exemplars, unless the exemplars are very similar. In general, the degree of interference generated in ALCOVE depends on two factors: the size of the receptive fields, as measured by the specificity parameter, c, and whether the exemplars from the two training phases have the same relevant or irrelevant dimensions.

The previous example was used because it was relatively easy to visualize the workings of the two models in terms of how receptive fields get distributed over the stimulus space. The relatively small interference in ALCOVE does not depend on using that particular configuration, however. Similar results also occur in a situation used by Ratcliff (1990) to demonstrate catastrophic

forgetting in backprop. Ratcliff used the "4–4 encoder" problem, in which a network with four input nodes and four output nodes must learn to reproduce isolated activity in each input node on the output nodes. That is, there are just four training patterns: $(+1, -1, -1, -1) \rightarrow (+1, -1, -1, -1)$, $(-1, +1, -1, -1) \rightarrow (-1, +1, -1, -1)$, etc. (These patterns use values of −1 instead of 0 merely to maintain symmetry. Similar qualitative conclusions apply when 0 is used.) The models are initially trained on just the first three training pairs; then, in the second phase of training, they are shown only the fourth pattern pair.

For this demonstration, the backprop network had three hidden nodes, the same number as used by Ratcliff (1990). To maximize comparison with ALCOVE, the four output nodes were linear, and response probabilities were computed with Equation 3, using $\phi = 1.0$. Hidden and output weights had learning rates of 0.2. Hidden weights and biases were initialized randomly in the interval (−2.5, +2.5). Similar qualitative trends obtain for other parameter values, numbers of hidden nodes, etc. (e.g. Ratcliff, 1990); 200 different randomly initialized runs were averaged.

ALCOVE used four hidden nodes, corresponding to the four training exemplars. Specificity of the hidden nodes was set to $c = 2.0$, with association-weight learning rate of 0.05 and attention-learning rate of 0.02. The response scaling constant was set as in the backprop model, $\phi = 1.0$. Similar qualitative trends obtain for other parameter values.

Both models were trained for 100 epochs on the 1st three pattern pairs, then 100 epochs on the fourth pattern pair. Response probabilities at the end of each phase are shown in Table 4. Backprop shows slightly more generalization error in Phase 1, classifying the untrained fourth pattern as one of the three trained patterns more than ALCOVE does. Backprop shows considerable retroactive interference from Phase 2 training: Correct response probabilities on the 1st three patterns drop from 70% to about 40%, and there is considerable bias for backprop to choose the fourth output category even when presented with one of the 1st three input patterns. By contrast, ALCOVE shows no such severe interference. Correct response

TABLE 4
Results of Applying Back Propagation or ALCOVE to the 4–4 Encoder Problem

Input	Back propagation	ALCOVE
	End of Phase 1	
+1 −1 −1 −1	.70 .10 .10 .10	.70 .10 .10 .10
−1 +1 −1 −1	.10 .70 .10 .10	.10 .70 .10 .10
−1 −1 +1 −1	.10 .10 .70 .10	.10 .10 .70 .10
−1 −1 −1 +1[a]	.28 .31 .29 .12	.27 .27 .27 .19
	End of Phase 2	
+1 −1 −1 −1[a]	.40 .07 .08 .45	.69 .09 .09 .13
−1 +1 −1 −1[a]	.08 .39 .07 .46	.09 .69 .09 .13
−1 −1 +1 −1[a]	.08 .07 .40 .45	.09 .09 .69 .13
−1 −1 −1 +1	.10 .10 .10 .70	.10 .10 .10 .70

Note. Data are the probabilities of choosing the corresponding output category. (For $\phi = 1.0$ and four output nodes, asymptotic correct performance in backprop is 0.71.) ALCOVE = attention learning covering map.
[a] Input patterns were not trained during that phase.

probabilities on the 1st three patterns decrease only slightly as a consequence of subsequent training on the fourth pattern. The exact amount of interference in ALCOVE is governed by the specificity and the attention-learning rate; the values used here were comparable to those that best fit human learning data in other studies.

In conclusion, the catastrophic forgetting that plagues backprop is not found in ALCOVE because of its localized receptive fields. ALCOVE is able to show significant interference only when the subsequently trained patterns are highly similar to the initially trained patterns or when the second phase of training has different relevant or irrelevant dimensions than the first phase.

Localized receptive fields versus local representations

Although the receptive fields of hidden nodes in ALCOVE are relatively localized, the hidden-layer representation is not strictly local, where *local* means that a single hidden node is activated by any one stimulus. In ALCOVE, an input can partially activate many hidden nodes whose receptive fields cover it, so that the representation of the input is indeed distributed over many hidden nodes. (This

is a form of continuous coarse coding; see Hinton, McClelland, & Rumelhart, 1986.) However, the character of that distributed representation is quite different from that in backprop because of the difference in receptive fields (Fig. 11). One might say that the representation in backprop is more distributed than the representation in ALCOVE and even that the representation in backprop is too distributed.

There are ways to bias the hidden nodes in backprop toward relatively localized representations, if the input patterns are restricted to a convex hypersurface in input space. For example, if the input patterns are normalized, they fall on a hypersphere in input space, in which case the linear level contours of the backprop hidden nodes can "carve off" small pieces of the sphere. For concreteness, consider a two-dimensional input space, so that the normalized input patterns fall on a circle. A given linear-sigmoid hidden node "looks down" on this space and makes a linear cut through it, so that all input points to one side of the line produce node activations greater than .5, and all points to the other side of the line produce node activations less than .5. If the linear cut is made near the edge of the circle, then only a small piece of the available input space causes node activations above .5. In particular, Scalettar and Zee (1988) demonstrated that such localized representations are a natural consequence of learning noisy input patterns (with weight decay). Unfortunately, a system that learns a localized representation might also unlearn it, and so it is not clear if the approach taken by Scalettar and Zee could solve the problem of catastrophic forgetting in backprop.

Goals of backprop versus goals of ALCOVE

I have tried to show that backprop and ALCOVE differ in their architecture and behavior. They are also different in their goals. A common goal of applications of backprop is to study the distributed representation discovered by the hidden nodes (e.g. Hanson & Burr, 1990; Lehky & Sejnowski, 1988; Rumelhart et al., 1986; Sejnowski & Rosenberg, 1987) but not to model the course of learning per se. The goals of ALCOVE are quite different. ALCOVE begins with a psychological representation derived from multidimensional scaling that is assumed to remain unchanged during learning. ALCOVE models the course of learning by adjusting attention strengths on the given dimensions and by adjusting association weights between exemplars and categories.

Learning rules and exceptions

So far the exemplar-similarity-based representation in ALCOVE has been compared with the featural- and configural-cue representations used in the network models of Gluck and Bower (1988a, 1988b) and with the "half-space receptor" representation in backprop. None of these representations directly addresses the fact that subjects in concept-learning tasks and many categorization tasks consciously generate another representation: rules (e.g. Bourne, 1970; Shepard et al., 1961). Ultimately, the relation of ALCOVE to rule generation must be determined. In this section I outline the beginnings of a theory of how ALCOVE might steer rule generation. The discussion is meant to be exploratory, suggestive, and perhaps provocative, but not conclusive.

One of the most widely known connectionist models of learning is the past-tense acquisition model of Rumelhart and McClelland (1986). That model learned to associate root forms of English verbs with their past-tense forms. The network consisted of input and output layers of nodes that represented *Wickel features*, which are triplets of phoneme features, one feature from each of three consecutive phonemes. The network had no hidden layer, and it learned the connection weights from the inputs to the outputs by using the perceptron convergence procedure, which can be considered to be a limiting case of backprop.

One of the main aspects of past-tense learning that Rumelhart and McClelland (1986) tried to model is the so-called three-stage or U-shaped learning of high-frequency irregular verbs. Children acquire these verbs, such as *go–went*, very early on, in Stage 1. Subsequently, they begin to acquire many regular verbs that form the past tense by adding *ed*. In this second stage, children apparently overgeneralize the rule and regularize

the previously well-learned irregular verbs. For example, they might occasionally produce forms like *goed* or *wented*. Finally, in Stage 3, the high-frequency irregular verbs are relearned. Three-stage learning has traditionally been used as evidence that people generate rules. The second stage is explained by suggesting that children literally learn the rule and overapply it. Rumelhart and McClelland's (1986) model had no mechanism for explicit rule generation, so if it could account for three-stage learning, it would pose a challenge to the necessity of rule-based accounts.

The Rumelhart and McClelland (1986) model was indeed able to show three-stage learning of irregular verbs, but that was accomplished only by changing the composition of the training patterns during learning. The network was initially exposed to eight high-frequency irregular verbs and only two regulars. After 10 epochs of training, the network achieved fairly good performance on those verbs. Then the training set was changed to include 334 additional regular verbs and only 76 more irregulars, so the proportion of regulars suddenly jumped from 20% to 80%. As might be expected (especially considering the results on catastrophic forgetting discussed in the previous section), when flooded with regular verbs, the network rapidly learned the regulars but suffered a decrement in performance on the previously learned irregulars. With continued training on the full set of verbs, the network was able to relearn the irregulars. Thus, the transition from Stage 1 to Stage 2 was accomplished only with the help of a deus ex machina, in the form of a radically altered training set. Rumelhart and McClelland defended the approach by saying, "It is generally observed that the early, rather limited vocabulary of young children undergoes an explosive growth at some point in development (Brown, 1973). Thus, the actual transition in a child's vocabulary of verbs would appear quite abrupt on a time-scale of years so that our assumptions about abruptness of onset may not be too far off the mark" (Rumelhart & McClelland, 1986, p.241). Several critics (e.g. Marcus et al., 1990; Pinker & Prince, 1988) were left unconvinced and argued that a cogent model would have the transition emerge from the learning mechanism, not exclusively from a discontinuity in the training corpus.

Connectionists are left with the challenge of how to model three-stage acquisition of high-frequency irregulars without changing the composition of the training set during learning.[3] It is now shown that ALCOVE can exhibit three-stage learning of high-frequency exceptions to rules in a highly simplified abstract analogue of the verb-acquisition situation. For this demonstration, the input stimuli are distributed over two continuously varying dimensions as shown in Fig. 13. Of the 14 training exemplars, the 12 marked with an *R* can be correctly classified by the simple rule, "If the value of the exemplar on Dimension 1 is greater than 4.5, then the exemplar is an instance of the box category; otherwise it is in the circle category." This type of rule is referred to as a *Type 1* rule by Shepard et al. (1961), because it segregates members of two categories on the basis of a single dimension. It is also called a *value-on-dimension* rule by Nosofsky, Clark, and Shin (1989), for obvious reasons. In Fig. 13 there are two exceptions to the rule, marked with an *E*. The exceptions are presented with higher relative frequency than individual rule exemplars. The analogy to the verb situation is that most of the exemplars are regular, in that they can be classified by the rule, but a few exemplars are irregular exceptions to the rule. The circle and box categories are not supposed to correspond to regular and irregular verbs; rather, they are arbitrary output values (+1 and −1) used only to establish distinct types of mappings on the rule-based and exceptional cases.

ALCOVE was applied to the structure in Fig. 13, using 14 hidden nodes and parameter values near the values used to fit the Medin et al. (1982) data: $\phi = 1.00$, $\lambda_\omega = 0.025$, $c = 3.50$, and $\lambda_\alpha = 0.010$. Epoch updating was used, with each rule exemplar occurring once per epoch and each exceptional case occurring four times per epoch, for a total of 20 patterns per epoch. (The same qualitative effects are produced with trial-by-trial updating, with superimposed trial-by-trial "sawteeth," what Plunkett and Marchman, 1991, called micro U-shaped learning.) The results are shown in Fig. 14. The learning curve for the exceptions (filled circles) shows a distinct nonmonotonicity so that near Epochs 10 to 15 there is a reversal of learning on the exceptions. (ALCOVE is always performing gradient descent on total error, even when performance on the exceptions drops, because performance on the rule cases improves so rapidly.) The other important feature of the results is that the learning curves for exceptional and rule cases cross over, so that early in training the high-frequency exceptions are learned more accurately, but later in learning the rule cases are learned better. Thus, we have a clear case of three-stage, U-shaped learning.

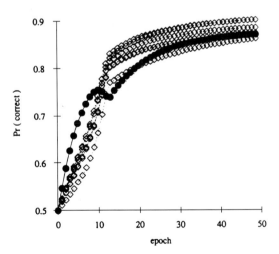

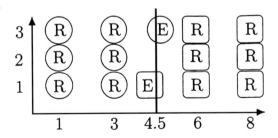

FIG. 13. Category structure used for demonstration of three-stage learning of rules and exceptions. (The exemplars marked with an *R* follow the rule, which separates the two categories by the dotted line. Exemplars marked with an *E* are exceptions to the rule. The *x* values of the exceptions were 4.4 and 4.6.)

FIG. 14. Results of applying ALCOVE (attention learning covering map) to the rules-and-exception structure of Fig. 13. (Filled circles show probability of correct classification for exceptions, whereas open diamonds indicate probability of correct classification for the various rule cases. Pr = probability.)

It should be emphasized that in this demonstration, all parameter values were fixed throughout training, and the composition of the training set was also fixed throughout training. Moreover, there were no order-of-presentation effects because epoch updating was used.

The results shown here should not be construed as a claim that ALCOVE is appropriate for modeling language acquisition. On the contrary, linguistic stimuli, in their natural context, might not be adequately represented by a multidimensional similarity space as demanded by ALCOVE (but cf. Elman, 1989, 1990). Moreover, the results in Fig. 14 should not be taken as a necessary prediction of ALCOVE, as some other combinations of parameter values do not show crossover or nonmonotonicities. Rather, the claim is that if such phenomena do occur in human learning, then ALCOVE might very well be able to model those effects.

How does three-stage learning happen in ALCOVE? In the initial epochs, the association weights between exemplars and categories are being established. The association weights from exceptions grow more quickly because the exceptions are presented more frequently. The attention strengths are not affected much in the early epochs because there is not much error propagated back to them by the weak association weights (see Equation 6). Thus, performance on the exceptions is initially better than on the rule cases entirely because of relative frequency.

The second stage begins as the association weights get big enough to back propagate error signals to the attention strengths. Then attention to the rule-irrelevant dimension rapidly decreases (in Fig. 13, the vertical dimension shrinks). That has two effects: The rule cases rapidly increase their within-category similarity, thereby improving performance, and the two exceptional cases rapidly increase their between-categories similarity, thereby decreasing accuracy. In other words, once the system learns a little about which exemplars belong in which category, it temporarily ignores the dimension that best distinguishes the exceptions, to benefit the ruly majority.

Such an account of three-stage learning does not prohibit the simultaneous existence of a distinct rule generating system. On the contrary, I believe that a more complete model of human category learning should also include a rule system that would simultaneously try to summarize and generalize the performance of ALCOVE by hypothesizing and testing rules. ALCOVE could help steer the rule-generating system and act as a fallback when adequate rules are not yet found. In such a scenario, the rule-generating system is neither epiphenomenal nor redundant; one major benefit is that rules abstract and unitize category knowledge so it can be transferred to other tasks and stimulus domains.

Perhaps the primary question for such a rule-generating system is which rules should be hypothesized and tested first? The behavior of ALCOVE suggests that one should generate and test rules using the dimensions that are most relevant, where relevance is measured by the dimensional attention strength learned in ALCOVE. This approach is akin to ideas of Bourne et al. (1976), but the notion of driving the rule system with an attention-learning system is new, as far as I know. Details of such an interaction are yet to be worked out; I (Kruschke, 1990a, 1990b) described applications of the idea to the results of Medin, Wattenmaker, and Michalski (1987) and to the learning of exemplars within the six types of Shepard et al. (1961).

In this section I have made two main points: First, ALCOVE is a connectionist network that can show three-stage learning of rules and exceptions without changing the composition of the training set during learning. Second, such a demonstration does not necessarily challenge rule-based accounts; rather, I should like to see future work incorporate ALCOVE-like mechanisms with rule-based systems to capture a wider range of human learning.

Discussion

I have tried to demonstrate that ALCOVE has significant advantages over some other models of category learning. ALCOVE combines an exemplar-based representation with error-driven learning.

The exemplar-based representation performs better than other models that also use error-driven learning but with different representations, such as the configural-cue model and backprop. Error-driven learning performs better than other models with exemplar-based representations but different learning rules, such as the array-exemplar model (Estes et al., 1989; Nosofsky et al., in press). In the remainder of the article I discuss variations, extensions, and limitations of ALCOVE.

Placement of hidden nodes

All the simulations reported here assumed that a hidden node was placed at the position of each training exemplar, and only at those positions, from the onset of training. That is a reasonable assumption in some circumstances; for example, when the subject previews all the training exemplars (without feedback) before training or when there are so few exemplars that the subject sees them all within a small number of trials. In general, however, the model cannot assume knowledge of the exemplars before it has been exposed to them. There are several ways to deal with that. One way is to recruit new exemplar nodes whenever a novel training exemplar is detected (Hurwitz, 1990). This requires some kind of novelty detection and decision device, which entails the introduction of new parameters, such as a threshold for novelty. An alternative method is to set some a priori bounds on the extent of the input space and randomly cover the space with hidden nodes (Kruschke, 1990a, 1990b). This also entails new parameters, such as the density of the nodes. A third possibility is to recruit a new node for every training trial, regardless of novelty. Careful comparison of these possibilities awaits future research, but I (Kruschke, 1990a, 1990b) reported some preliminary results that the covering map approach fit training data as well as the exemplar approach.

Humble versus strict teacher

The simulations reported here assumed the use of a humble teacher (Equation 4b). This was not an ad hoc assumption, but was motivated by the fact that feedback in category-learning experiments is nominal and does not specify the magnitude of category membership. The humble teachers tell the output nodes that their activation values should reach at least a certain level to indicate minimal membership, but there is no upper limit placed on their activations.

There are situations where a strict teacher is appropriate. Perhaps the most important use of a strict teacher has been the modeling of over-expectation error in animal learning (e.g. Kamin, 1969; Kremer, 1978; Rescorla & Wagner, 1972). Overexpectation occurs when an animal is first trained to associate Conditioned Stimulus (CS) 1 with an unconditioned stimulus (US), denoted $CS_1 \rightarrow US$, then trained on $CS_2 \rightarrow US$, and finally trained on the compound stimulus $(CS_1 + CS_2) \rightarrow US$. The result is that the final training on the compound stimulus actually reduces the individual association strengths from CS_1 and CS_2. A strict teacher with error-driven learning (the Rescorla-Wagner learning rule) can account for that, because at the beginning of training with the compound stimulus $(CS_1 + CS_2)$, the double-strength association overshoots the teacher and is counted as an overexpectation error, causing the individual associations to be reduced. In that situation, however, there is reason to believe that the feedback is encoded by the animal as having a certain magnitude, and not just nominally. For example, in many experiments the feedback was magnitude of electric shock or amount of food.

One difference between humble and strict teachers regards asymptotic performance. Strict teachers demand that all exemplars are equally good members of the category, in that they all activate the category nodes to the same degree. Humble teachers allow more typical exemplars to activate their category nodes more than peripheral exemplars, even after asymptotic training. That differences is robust when measured in terms of category node activations; however, when transformed into response probabilities by the choice rule (Equation 3), the difference is compressed by ceiling and floor effects and becomes very subtle. For the applications reported in this article, the difference in fits, using humble or strict teachers, is slight. Thus, although I believe the distinction between humble and strict teachers is conceptually well motivated, it remains for future research to decide conclusively which is best for modeling category learning.

Extensions of ALCOVE

Several reasonable extensions of ALCOVE that might allow it to fit a wider array of category learning phenomena, without violating the motivating principles of the model, are possible.

The choice rule in Equation 3 was used primarily because of historical precedents, but it is not a central feature of the model, and there might be better ways of mapping network behavior to human performance. For example, one might instead incorporate random noise into the activation values of the nodes and use a deterministic choice rule such as selecting the category with the largest activation (cf. McClelland, 1991). Also, the particular choice of teacher values in Equation 4b was arbitrary and motivated primarily by the precedent of Gluck and Bower (1988a, 1988b). It might be that a different choice of teacher values, for example, +1 for "in" and 0 (instead of −1) for "not in" would be more appropriate, especially in conjunction with different response rules.

Many researchers have suggested that training has local or regional attentional effects, rather than (or in addition to) global effects (e.g. Aha & Goldstone, 1990; Aha & McNulty, 1989; Medin & Edelson, 1988; Nosofsky, 1988a). ALCOVE is easily altered to incorporate local attention strengths by giving each hidden node j a full set of dimensional attention strengths α_{ji}. In this particular variation there are no new parameters added because there is still just one attention-learning rate. It remains to be seen if exemplar-specific attention strengths, or some combination of exemplar-specific and global attention strengths, can account for an even wider range of data.

A related approach to introducing local attentional effects is to adapt individual hidden node specificities. Specificity learning (by gradient descent on error) would adjust the receptive-field size of individual hidden nodes, so that nodes surrounded by exemplars assigned to the same category would enlarge their receptive fields to encompass those other exemplars, whereas nodes near exemplars assigned to other categories would

reduce their receptive fields to exclude those other exemplars. One implication is that asymmetric similarities (Rosch, 1975; Tversky, 1977) would evolve: Peripheral or boundary exemplars would be more similar to central or typical exemplars than vice versa, because the receptive field of the central exemplar would cover the peripheral exemplar, but the receptive field of the peripheral exemplar would not cover the central exemplar.

Another possible extension retains global dimensional attention strengths but changes the dynamics of attention learning. In this article it was assumed that the attention strengths α_i were primitives in the formalization, in that attention strengths were not themselves a function of some other underlying variables. If, however, each attention strength α_i is some nonlinear function of an underlying variable β_i, then gradient descent with respect to β_i will lead to different changes in α_i than gradient descent with respect to α_i itself. For example, suppose we let $\alpha_i = 1/(1 + e_i^{-\beta})$. This has three potentially desirable features: First, it automatically keeps the attention strengths α_i nonnegative, so that it is not necessary to clip them at zero. Second, it automatically keeps the attention strengths bounded above, so that there is a built-in "capacity" limit (cf. Nosofsky, 1986). Third, and perhaps most important, the gradient-descent learning rule for β_i is the same as the learning rule for α_i (Equation 6) except for the inclusion of a new factor, $\partial \alpha_i / \partial \beta_i = \alpha_i(1 - \alpha_i)$. This implies that the attention strength will not change very rapidly if it is near one of its extreme values of +1 or 0. In particular, if the system has learned that one dimension is highly relevant (α_1, nearly 1) and a second dimension is irrelevant (α_2, nearly 0), then it will be reluctant to change those attention strengths. Such an extension might allow ALCOVE to model the ease shown by adults to learn intradimensional feedback reversals relative to interdimensional relevance shifts (Kendler & Kendler 1962), which ALCOVE cannot capture in its present form (W. Maki, personal communication, October 1990).[4]

Limitations of ALCOVE

ALCOVE applies only to situations for which the stimuli can be appropriately represented as points in a multidimensional psychological similarity space. Moreover, ALCOVE assumes that the basis dimensions remain unchanged during category learning, and it does not apply to situations in which subjects generate new dimensions of representation, or otherwise recode the stimuli, during learning. Predictions made by ALCOVE are therefore based on two sets of premises: One set regards the representational assumptions just stated. The other set regards the exemplar-similarity-based architecture and error-driven learning rules of the model. If ALCOVE should fail to capture data from a given situation, either or both of the sets of premises might be wrong.

Another, perhaps more severe, limitation of ALCOVE is that it does not have a mechanism for hypothesizing and testing rules, whereas people clearly do. As suggested in a previous section, ALCOVE might subserve a rule-generating system, steering its selection of candidate rules. Until such a combination of systems is created, Holland, Holyoak, Nisbett, and Thagard's (1986) assessment of the Rescorla-Wagner learning rule might also apply to ALCOVE: "The limits of [Rescorla and Wagner's] approach can be characterized quite simply — their equation is generally able to account for phenomena that primarily depend on strength revision but is generally unable to account for phenomena that depend on rule generation" (p.167).

Notes

1. Recognizing the need to address the dimensional attention issue in the configural-cue model, Gluck and Chow (1989) modified it by making the learning rates on different modules of configural cues self-adaptive. In the case of the Shepard, Hovland, and Jenkins (1961) category types, there were seven different modules of configural cues: a module for each of the three dimensions (each module containing 2 one-value cues), a module for each of the three distinct pairs of dimensions (each module containing 4 two-value configural cues), and a module for the combination of three dimensions (containing 8 three-value configural cues). The learning rates for the seven modules were separately self-modifying

according to the heuristic described by Jacobs (1988), which says that if weights change consistently across patterns, then learning rates should increase. The modified configural-cue model was indeed able to capture the correct ordering of the six category types. Did the modified configural-cue model selectively attend to individual dimensions? That is a difficult question to answer. For example, in learning Type II, it seems likely (details were not provided in Gluck & Chow, 1989) that the modified configural-cue model increased its learning rates for the module that combined Dimensions 1 and 2, but decreased the learning rates of all other modules, in particular the modules that individually encode Dimensions 1 and 2. Thus, it increased attention to the combination of dimensions but decreased attention to the individual dimensions. Although this might or might not make sense psychologically, it is clear that further explication of the modified configural-cue model is needed. On the other hand, ALCOVE makes dimensional attention strengths an explicit part of the model and, unlike the modified configural-cue model, allows continuous-valued input dimensions.

2. Gluck and Bower (1988b) used a network with a single output node, with +1 indicating Disease A and −1 indicating Disease B. Two output nodes are used here because it is formally equivalent to the single node version when just two categories are used, but unlike the single node version it generalizes naturally to situations involving more than two categories. The formal equivalence is easy to demonstrate: Suppose there are two output nodes that always get equal- and opposite-teacher values, so that $a_1^{out} = -a_2^{out}$ at all times. Then Equation 3 can be rewritten as $\Pr(K) = 1/[1 + \exp(-2\phi a_k^{out})]$, the form used by Gluck and Bower. Compare with Footnote 2 of Gluck and Bower (1988b).

3. Plunkett and Marchman (1991) showed that a back-prop network trained on an unchanging set exhibited micro U-shaped learning, meaning that performance on individual patterns and pattern types fluctuated from epoch to epoch, but gradually improved overall. Their simulations did not exhibit macro U-shaped learning, in which there is a decrease in accuracy on all irregulars over several consecutive epochs, accompanied by an increase in accuracy on regulars, but they argued that such macro U-shaped learning does not occur in children either. Marcus et al. (1990) reported that some aspects of macro U-shaped learning do occur, although they are indeed subtle.

4. Hurwitz (1990; "hidden pattern unit model Version 2") independently developed a closely related

model that had hidden nodes with activation function determined by a multiplicative similarity rule (Medin & Schaffer, 1978). For direct comparison with ALCOVE's hidden nodes, Hurwitz's activation function can be formally reexpressed as follows:

$$a_j^{hid} = \prod_j (1/1 + e^{(\beta_i - k)})^{|h_{ji} - a_i^{in}|}$$

$$= \exp[-\sum_i \underbrace{\ln(1 + e^{(\beta_i - k)})}_{\alpha_i} |h_{ji} - a_i^{in}|],$$

where k is a constant. Thus, Hurwitz's model can be construed as a version of ALCOVE with $r = q = 1$ in Equation 1 and with $\alpha_i = \ln(1 + e^{(\beta_i - k)})$. Hurwitz's model therefore keeps the attention strengths α_i nonnegative but unbounded above. Gradient descent with respect to β_i results in the right-hand side of Equation 6 except for the absence of the specificity c and the inclusion of a new factor, $\partial \alpha_i / \partial \beta_i = (1 - e^{-\alpha_i})$. That causes attention strengths near zero to be reluctant to change, but causes large attention strengths to change rapidly.

References

Aha, D. W., & Goldstone, R. (1990). Learning attribute relevance in context in instance-based learning algorithms. *Proceedings of the Twelfth Annual Conference of the Cognitive Science Society* (pp.141–148). Hillsdale, NJ: Erlbaum.

Aha, D. W., & McNulty, D. M. (1989). Learning relative attribute weights for instance-based concept descriptions. *Proceedings of the Eleventh Annual Conference of the Cognitive Science Society* (pp.530–537). Hillsdale, NJ: Erlbaum.

Ahmad, S. (1988). *A study of scaling and generalization in neural networks* (Tech. Rep. No. UIUCDCS-R-88-1454). Urbana-Champaign: University of Illinois at Urbana-Champaign, Computer Science Department.

Anderson, J. R. (1991). The adaptive nature of human categorization. *Psychological Review, 98*, 409–429.

Bourne, L. E. (1970). Knowing and using concepts. *Psychological Review, 77*, 546–556.

Bourne, L. E., Ekstrand, B. R., Lovallo, W. R., Kellogg, R. T., Hiew, C. C., & Yaroush, R. A. (1976). Frequency analysis of attribute identification. *Journal of Experimental Psychology: General, 105*, 294–312.

Brown, R. (1973). *A first language*. Cambridge, MA: Harvard University Press.

Carroll, J. D., & Chang, J. J. (1970). Analysis of individual differences in multidimensional scaling via an n-way generalization of "Eckart-Young" decomposition. *Psychometrika, 35*, 283–319.

Elman, J. L. (1989). *Representation and structure in connectionist models* (Tech. Rep. No. 8903). San Diego: University of California at San Diego, Center for Research in Language.

Elman, J. L. (1990). Finding structure in time. *Cognitive Science, 14*, 179–211.

Estes, W. K. (1986a). Array models for category learning. *Cognitive Psychology, 18*, 500–549.

Estes, W. K. (1986b). Memory storage and retrieval processes in category learning. *Journal of Experimental Psychology: General, 115*, 155–174.

Estes, W. K. (1988). Toward a framework for combining connectionist and symbol-processing models. *Journal of Memory and Language, 27*, 196–212.

Estes, W. K., Campbell, J. A., Hatsopoulos, N., & Hurwitz, J. B. (1989). Base-rate effects in category learning: A comparison of parallel network and memory storage–retrieval models. *Journal of Experimental Psychology: Learning, Memory, and Cognition, 15*, 556–576.

Garner, W. R. (1974). *The processing of information and structure*. Hillsdale, NJ: Erlbaum.

Gluck, M. A. (1991). Stimulus generalization and representation in adaptive network models of category learning. *Psychological Science, 2*, 50–55.

Gluck, M. A., & Bower, G. H. (1988a). Evaluating an adaptive network model of human learning. *Journal of Memory and Language, 27*, 166–195.

Gluck, M. A., & Bower, G. H. (1988b). From conditioning to category learning: An adaptive network model. *Journal of Experimental Psychology: General, 117*, 227–247.

Gluck, M. A., Bower, G. H., & Hee, M. R. (1989). A configural-cue network model of animal and human associative learning. *Proceedings of the Eleventh Annual Conference of the Cognitive Science Society*. Hillsdale, NJ: Erlbaum.

Gluck, M. A., & Chow, W. (1989). *Dynamic stimulus-specific learning rates and the representation of dimensionalized stimulus structures*. Unpublished manuscript.

Hanson, S. J., & Burr, D. J. (1990). What connectionist models learn: Learning and representation in connectionist networks. *Behavioral and Brain Sciences, 13*, 471–489.

Hinton, G. E., McClelland, & Rumelhart, D. E. (1986). Distributed representations. In D. E. Rumelhart & J. L. McClelland (Eds.), *Parallel distributed processing* (chapter 3). Cambridge, MA: MIT Press.

Holland, J. H., Holyoak, K. J., Nisbett, R. E., & Thagard, P. R. (1986). *Induction.* Cambridge, MA: MIT Press.

Hurwitz, J. B. (1990). *A hidden-pattern unit network model of category learning.* Unpublished doctoral dissertation, Harvard University.

Jacobs, R. A. (1988). Increased rates of convergence through learning rate adaptation. *Neural Networks, 1*, 295–307.

Kamin, L. J. (1969). Predictability, surprise, attention, and conditioning. In B. A. Campbell & R. M. Church (Eds.), *Punishment.* New York: Appleton-Century-Crofts.

Kendler, H. H., & Kendler, T. S. (1962). Vertical and horizontal processes in problem solving. *Psychological Review, 69*, 1–16.

Kremer, E. F. (1978). The Rescorla-Wagner model: Losses in associative strength in compound conditioned stimuli. *Journal of Experimental Psychology: Animal Behavior Processes, 4*, 22–36.

Kruschke, J. K. (1990a). *A connectionist model of category learning.* Doctoral dissertation, University of California at Berkeley. University Microfilms International.

Kruschke, J. K. (1990b). *ALCOVE: A connectionist model of category learning* (Cognitive Science Research Rep. No. 19). Bloomington: Indiana University.

Lehky, S. R., & Sejnowski, T. J. (1988). Network model of shape-from-shading: Neural function arises from both receptive and projective fields. *Nature, 333*, 452–454.

Luce, R. D. (1963). Detection and recognition. In R. D. Luce, R. R. Bush, & E. Galanter (Eds.), *Handbook of mathematical psychology* (pp.103–189). New York: Wiley.

Marcus, G. F., Ullman, M., Pinker, S., Hollander, M., Rosen, T. J., & Xu, F. (1990). *Overregularization* (Occasional Paper No. 41). Cambridge, MA: MIT, Center for Cognitive Science.

Matheus, C. J. (1988). Exemplar versus prototype network models for concept representation (abstract). *Neural Networks, 1* (Suppl. 1), 199.

McClelland, J. L. (1991). Stochastic interactive processes and the effect of context on perception. *Cognitive Psychology, 23*, 1–44.

McCloskey, M., & Cohen, N. J. (1989). Catastrophic interference in connectionist networks: The sequential learning problem. In G. Bower (Ed.), *The psychology of learning and motivation* (Vol. 24, pp.109–165). San Diego, CA: Academic Press.

Medin, D. L., Altom, M. W., Edelson, S. M., & Freko, D. (1982). Correlated symptoms and simulated medical classification. *Journal of Experimental Psychology: Learning, Memory, and Cognition, 8*, 37–50.

Medin, D. L., & Edelson, S. M. (1988). Problem structure and the use of base-rate information from experience. *Journal of Experimental Psychology: General, 117*, 68–85.

Medin, D. L., & Schaffer, M. M. (1978). Context theory of classification learning. *Psychological Review, 85*, 207–238.

Medin, D. L., & Schwanenflugel, P. J. (1981). Linear separability in classification learning. *Journal of Experimental Psychology: Human Learning and Memory, 7*, 355–368.

Medin, D. L., Wattenmaker, W. D., & Michalski, R. S. (1987). Constraints and preferences in inductive learning: An experimental study of human and machine performance. *Cognitive Science, 11*, 299–339.

Nosofsky, R. M. (1984). Choice, similarity, and the context theory of classification. *Journal of Experimental Psychology: Learning, Memory, and Cognition, 10*, 104–114.

Nosofsky, R. M. (1986). Attention, similarity, and the identification–categorization relationship. *Journal of Experimental Psychology: General, 115*, 39–57.

Nosofsky, R. M. (1987). Attention and learning processes in the identification and categorization of integral stimuli. *Journal of Experimental Psychology: Learning, Memory, and Cognition, 13*, 87–108.

Nosofsky, R. M. (1988a). On exemplar-based exemplar representations: Reply to Ennis (1988). *Journal of Experimental Psychology: General, 117*, 412–414.

Nosofsky, R. M. (1988b). Similarity, frequency, and category representations. *Journal of Experimental Psychology: Learning, Memory, and Cognition, 14*, 54–65.

Nosofsky, R. M. (1991). Exemplars, prototypes, and similarity rules. In A. Healy, S. Kosslyn, & R. Shiffrin (Eds.), *Essays in honor of W. K. Estes.* Hillsdale, NJ: Erlbaum.

Nosofsky, R. M., Clark, S. E., & Shin, H. J. (1989). Rules and exemplars in categorization, identification, and recognition. *Journal of Experimental Psychology: Learning, Memory, and Cognition, 15*, 282–304.

Nosofsky, R. M., Kruschke, J. K., & McKinley, S. (in press). Combining exemplar-based category representations and connectionist learning rules. *Journal of Experimental Psychology: Learning, Memory, and Cognition.*

Pinker, S., & Prince, A. (1988). On language and connectionism: Analysis of a parallel, distributed processing model of language acquisition. *Cognition, 28*, 73–193.

Plunkett, K., & Marchman, V. (1991). U-shaped learning and frequency effects in a multi-layered perceptron: Implications for child language acquisition. *Cognition, 38*, 43–102.

Ratcliff, R. (1990). Connectionist models of recognition memory: Constraints imposed by learning and forgetting functions. *Psychological Review, 2*, 285–308.

Rescorla, R. A., & Wagner, A. R. (1972). A theory of Pavlovian conditioning: Variations in the effectiveness of reinforcement and nonreinforcement. In A. H. Black & W. F. Prokasy (Eds.), *Classical conditioning: II. Current research and theory*. New York: Appleton-Century-Crofts.

Robinson, A. J., Niranjan, M., & Fallside, F. (1988). *Generalising the nodes of the error propagation network* (Tech. Rep. No. CUED/F-IN-FENG/TR.25). Cambridge, England: Cambridge University Engineering Department.

Rosch, E. (1975). Cognitive reference points. *Cognitive Psychology, 7*, 532–547.

Rosch, E., Simpson, C., & Miller, R. S. (1976). Structural bases of typicality effects. *Journal of Experimental Psychology: Human Perception and Performance, 2*, 491–502.

Rumelhart, D. E., Hinton, G. E., & Williams, R. J. (1986). Learning internal representations by back-propagating errors. In D. E. Rumelhart & J. L. McClelland (Eds.), *Parallel distributed processing* (Vol. 1, chapter 8). Cambridge, MA: MIT Press.

Rumelhart, D. E., & McClelland, J. L. (1986). On learning the past tenses of English verbs. In J. L. McClelland & D. E. Rumelhart (Eds.), *Parallel distributed processing* (Vol. 2, chapter 18). Cambridge, MA: MIT Press.

Scalettar, R., & Zee, A. (1988). Emergence of grandmother memory in feed forward networks: Learning with noise and forgetfulness. In D. Waltz & J. A. Feldman (Eds.), *Connectionist models and their implications: Reading from cognitive science* (pp.309–327). Norwood, NJ: Ablex.

Sejnowski, T. J., & Rosenberg, C. R. (1987). Parallel networks that learn to pronounce English text. *Complex Systems, 1*, 145–168.

Shanks, D. R. (1990). Connectionism and the learning of probabilistic concepts. *Quarterly Journal of Experimental Psychology, 42A*, 209–237.

Shepard, R. N. (1957). Stimulus and response generalization: A stochastic model relating generalization to distance in psychological space. *Psychometrika, 22*, 325–345.

Shepard, R. N. (1958). Stimulus and response generalization: Deduction of the generalization gradient from a trace model. *Psychological Review, 65*, 242–256.

Shepard, R. N. (1962a). The analysis of proximities: Multidimensional scaling with an unknown distance function. I. *Psychometrika, 27*, 125–140.

Shepard, R. N. (1962b). The analysis of proximities: Multidimensional scaling with an unknown distance function. II. *Psychometrika, 27*, 219–246.

Shepard, R. N. (1964). Attention and the metric structure of the stimulus space. *Journal of Mathematical Psychology, 1*, 54–87.

Shepard, R. N. (1987). Toward a universal law of generalization for psychological science. *Science, 237*, 1317–1323.

Shepard, R. N., Hovland, C. L., & Jenkins, H. M. (1961). Learning and memorization of classifications. *Psychological Monographs, 75* (13, Whole No. 517).

Tversky, A. (1977). Features of similarity. *Psychological Review, 84*, 327–352.

Appendix
Derivation of learning rules

Here are derived the learning rules used in ALCOVE. Learning of any parameter in the model is done by gradient descent on a cost function such as sum-squared error. The purpose is to determine gradient-descent learning equations for the attention strengths, α_i, and the association weights, w_{kj}^{out}. All the derivations are simple insofar as they involve only the chain rule and algebra. On the other hand, they are complicated insofar as they involve several subscripts simultaneously, and care must be taken to keep them explicit and consistent. Subscripts denoting variables are in lowercase letters. Subscripts denoting constants are in uppercase letters. Vector notation is used throughout the derivations: Boldface variables denote vectors. For example, $\mathbf{a}^{out} = [\ldots a_k^{out} \ldots]^T$ is the column vector of output activation values for the current stimulus.

The general case

I first compute derivatives using an unspecified cost function C and then treat the specific case of sum-squared error. Suppose that C is some function of the output of the network and perhaps of some other constants (such as teacher values for the output nodes). In general, any parameter x is adjusted by gradient descent on C, which means that the change in x is proportional to the negative of the derivative: $\Delta x = -\lambda_x \partial C / \partial x$, where λ_x is a (nonnegative) constant of proportionality, called the learning rate of parameter x.

I begin by rewriting Equation 1 in two parts, introducing the notation net_j^{hid}:

$$\text{net}_j^{hid} = (\sum_i^{in} \alpha_i |h_{ji} - a_i^{in}|^r)^{1/r} \text{ and}$$

$$a_j^{hid} = \exp[-c(\text{net}_j^{hid})^q], \tag{A1}$$

where r and q are positive numbers. The special case of $r = 1$ (city-block metric) and $q = 1$ (exponential-similarity decay) are subsequently treated.

Because the output nodes are linear (Equation 2), the derivative of C with respect to the association weights between hidden and output nodes is

$$\frac{\partial C}{\partial w_{KJ}^{out}} = \frac{\partial C}{\partial a_K^{out}} \frac{\partial a_K^{out}}{\partial w_{KJ}^{out}} = \frac{\partial C}{\partial a_K^{out}} a_J^{hid}. \tag{A2}$$

The derivative $\partial C / \partial a_K^{out}$ must be computed directly from the definition of C, but it can presumably be evaluated locally in the Kth output node. Hence, the weight change resulting from gradient descent is locally computable.

In the applications reported in this article, there was never a need to alter the hidden node positions or specificities. Therefore, I do not compute the derivatives of the hidden node coordinates or specificities, although they certainly can be computed (e.g. Robinson, Niranjan, & Fallside, 1988). Now consider the attention strengths α_i. First note that

$$\frac{\partial C}{\partial \alpha_I} = \frac{\partial C}{\partial \mathbf{a}^{out}} \frac{\partial \mathbf{a}^{out}}{\partial \mathbf{a}^{hid}} \frac{\partial \mathbf{a}^{hid}}{\partial \alpha_I} = [\ldots \partial C / \partial a_{k^{out}} \ldots]$$

$$\times \begin{bmatrix} \vdots \\ \cdots w_{kj}^{out} \cdots \\ \vdots \end{bmatrix} \begin{bmatrix} \vdots \\ \partial a_j^{hid}/\partial \alpha_I \\ \vdots \end{bmatrix}. \tag{A3a}$$

Computation of $\partial a_j^{hid}/\partial \alpha_I$ requires a bit more work:

$$\frac{\partial a_j^{hid}}{\partial \alpha_I} = \frac{\partial a_j^{hid}}{\partial \text{net}_j^{hid}} \frac{\partial \text{net}_j^{hid}}{\partial \alpha_I} = -a_j^{hid} cq(\text{net}_j^{hid})^{(q-1)}$$

$$\times \frac{1}{r}(\sum_i^{in} \alpha_i |h_{ji} - a_i^{in}|^r)^{(1/r-1)} |h_{jI} - a_I^{in}|^r$$

$$= -a_j^{hid} c\frac{q}{r}(\text{net}_j^{hid})^{(q-r)} |h_{jI} - a_I^{in}|^r. \tag{A3b}$$

Substituting Equation A3b into Equation A3a yields

$$\frac{\partial C}{\partial \alpha_I} = \sum_j^{hid} \left(\sum_k^{out} \frac{\partial C}{\partial a_k^{out}} w_{kj}^{out} \right)$$

$$\times a_j^{hid} c\frac{q}{r}(\text{net}_j^{hid})^{(q-r)} |h_{jI} - a_I^{in}|^r. \tag{A4}$$

The factors of Equation A4 are all available to input node I if one permits backwards connections from hidden nodes to input nodes that have connection weight equal to the fixed value 1. (Usually in back propagation the backward links are conceived as having the same value as adaptive forward links.) The mechanism for computing the derivatives is the same, in spirit, as that used in "standard" back propagation (Rumelhart, Hinton, & Williams, 1986): The partial derivatives computed at each layer are propagated backwards through the network to previous layers.

Equation A4 reveals some interesting behavior for the adaptation of the attentional parameter α_I. The equation contains the factor

$$F_j = a_j^{hid}(\text{net}_j^{hid})^{(q-r)} |h_{jI} - a_{I^{in}}|^r.$$

All the other factors of Equation A4 can be considered constants in the present context, so that the change in attention α_I is proportional to F_j. The question now is when is the change large, that is, when is F_j significantly nonzero? The precise answer depends on the values of q and r, but a qualitative generalization can be made about the form of F_j. The graph of F_j (not shown) is a "hyper dumbbell" shape that is centered on the input stimulus, with its axis of symmetry along the Ith dimension. Hence, the attentional parameter is only affected by hidden nodes within the hyper dumbbell region.

Sum-squared error

Now consider a specific case for the objective function C, the sum-squared error, as in Equation 4a. Note first that

$$\frac{\partial E}{\partial a_K^{out}} = -(t_K - a_K^{out}). \tag{A5}$$

This derivative (Equation A5) is continuous and well behaved, even with the humble-teacher values. Then Equation A5 can be substituted into each of Equations A2 and A4.

Special Case of q = r = 1

In the special case when $q = r$ (and in particular when $q = r = 1$), the learning equation for attention strengths simplifies considerably. In this special case, the term $\frac{q}{r}(\text{net}_j^{hid})^{(q-r)}$ in Equation A4 reduces to 1. The initial computation of a_j^{hid} also simplifies (cf. Equation A1).

The learning rules reported in the text (Equations 5 and 6) are the result.

Received June 18, 1990
Revision received February 27, 1991
Accepted April 17, 1991

4

Perception

The processes involved in sensory analysis appear to be natural candidates for connectionist explanations. The rapid integration of vast amounts of data across a sensory surface such as the retina demands a highly parallel solution. Furthermore we will show in what follows that the parallel processes must cooperate to solve what would otherwise be intractable problems.

The perceptrons described in Chapter 2 were of course early connectionist models of visual pattern recognition. Compared with the more recent work we are to describe, they were naive. That is, the attempt to extract visual properties, suitable for object recognition, directly from an image on a retina was doomed to failure in all but the most trivial of cases. The reasons for the failure were two-fold. First it was not then recognised, as it now is, that any reasonably sophisticated visual system must involve a set of processes that extract a variety of types of information about the visual scene giving rise to the input image. This information is captured in a variety of internal intermediate-level representations which form the basis for higher-level recognition processes (Barrow & Tennenbaum, 1978; Bruce & Green, 1990; Marr, 1982; Mayhew & Frisby, 1984). In connectionist terms there is, in the case of vision, an obvious requirement for hidden units in order to map the input to output. Hinton (1989b, p.193) is persuasive:

The required mapping typically has a complicated structure that can only be expressed using multiple layers of hidden units. Consider, for example, the task of identifying an object when the input vector is an intensity array and the output vector has a separate component for each possible name. If a given type of object can be either black or white, the intensity of an individual pixel (which is what an input unit encodes) cannot provide any direct evidence for the presence or absence of an object of that type. So the object cannot be identified by using weights on direct connections from input to output units. Obviously, it is necessary to explicitly extract relationships among intensity values (such as edges) before trying to identify the object. Actually, extracting edges is just a small part of the problem, if recognition is to have the generative capacity to handle novel effects of variations in lighting and viewpoint, partial occlusion by other objects, and deformations of the object itself. There is a tremendous gap between these complex regularities and the regularities that can be captured by an associative net that lacks hidden units.

Second, of course, the perceptron convergence learning rule could not be applied to multilayer systems. So even where the need for intermediate-level representation had been recognised it could not be implemented in perceptron-like networks, except by a laborious hand-crafting of the connections.

Many of the current theories of visual processes are expressed in the language of von Neumann computation: they explain visual processes in terms of the derivation and operations on symbolic structures that represent visual information. This approach has contributed greatly to the appreciation of vision as a set of sub-processes or modules, each of which requires a theory. It is our view that this territory, which has been surveyed by these traditional computational approaches to vision, is likely to be colonised by connectionist models. To support this claim we show here how in a number of cases the sub-processes of vision are best understood as particular varieties of connectionist network.

Although our primary concern in this chapter will be vision, the implications for other sensory systems will be mentioned. The case of vision is meant to be an illustrative example. We begin by examining connectionist solutions to some of the problems of so-called low and intermediate-level vision.

4.1 LOW- AND INTERMEDIATE-LEVEL VISION

It is now common to categorise visual processes into low, intermediate, and high levels (for example see Ballard & Brown, 1982). The categorisation is rough and there is no agreed criteria for making it. What we mean here by low and intermediate level is all those processes that deliver information about the spatial and visual properties of visual scenes without necessary recourse to stored information. Low-level information is typically about the spatial relations among primitive, two-dimensional visual features such as edges and blobs. Intermediate information describes the properties that arise from forms of organisation of the low-level primitives, such as texture differences, and may include descriptions of the three-

dimensional spatial relationships among visual properties. The sense of these distinctions should become clearer as we describe examples.

Consider an image of a visual scene which is made up only of shades of grey as in a "black and white" photograph. The actual light intensity at any point in this grey-level image results from a number of factors. How then can information about the underlying structure be derived from values of intensity? One very influential theorist (Marr, 1982, p.41) expressed the problem thus:

> There are four main factors responsible for the intensity values in an image. They are (1) the geometry and (2) the reflectances of the visible surfaces, (3) the illumination of the scene, and (4) the viewpoint. In an image, all these factors are muddled up, some intensity changes being due to one cause, others to another, and some to a combination. The purpose of early visual processing is to sort out which changes are due to what factors and hence to create representations in which the four factors are separated.

This is clearly the same point as Hinton (1989b) makes in the quotation in the previous section, but now it is framed in the language of symbol manipulation. For Marr, and many others, the first step in these early processes is the identification of significant intensity changes; that is, those intensity changes that result from features of the visual scene such as the boundaries of objects. This turns out to be a surprisingly difficult thing to do! One immediate problem is that any real image contains a huge amount of data. To see this, consider how to represent a grey-level image as a set of numbers. If the image is divided into an array of square cells, called picture elements or pixels, the average intensity in each pixel may be represented by a number. Obviously the greater the number of pixels, and the greater the number of discrete levels of grey, the more faithful the digitised representation will be to the grey-level image. Merely adequate levels of resolution are obtained with a pixel array of 512 by 512 and 256 grey levels. This would require 262,114 eight-bit bytes of storage in a computer. The retina of the human eyes contain 250 million photoreceptive cells which signal the local light intensity with a resolution far greater than 256 grey levels!

There is a huge literature, indeed an industry, concerned with "edge detection" algorithms which are intended for application to digitised grey-level images (see Ballard & Brown, 1982, Charniak & McDermott, 1985, or Winston, 1975, for introductions to the problems of edge detection). In all cases the aim is to devise a computation on the set of numbers, which represent an image, that signals the presence of visual features such as edges at specified locations. All also involve the repetitive application of some calculation or set of calculations over all represented locations. As the resolution of the representation increases, so the computational requirements grow massively. The point to note here is that the problem very rapidly becomes one that a serial algorithm could never hope to solve in any reasonable timescale. It is simply a natural candidate for a parallel solution. Marr and Hildreth (1982) describe a theory of edge detection that illustrates the force of these comments. It is particularly useful to our purposes here because the authors pay regard to the neural implementation of the algorithm they propose. We therefore describe the theory next.

In any grey-level image of a real-world scene there will be variations of intensity at a variety of scales. If one gets close enough to a tiger both the stripes and the individual hairs may be seen.

This immediately creates a problem for any process that must, as edge detection must, measure variations in intensity in order to identify significant features. If both stripes and hairs are to be detected, measures of intensity change over a range of scales are needed. Marr and Hildreth's (1982) solution to this "range problem" is to make intensity measurements on a number of "smoothed" versions of the image. Smoothing, in the digital case, is simply the substitution of a pixel's actual intensity level by a value that is an average for the neighbourhood of that pixel. Marr and Hildreth (1982) use a mathematical function they describe as a Gaussian filter for the smoothing. This averages over a circular region around each pixel but weights the contribution of any intensity value according to a normal distribution centred on the pixel. That is, values close to the centre of the circle have greater weight than those at the edge. This process may be thought of as blurring the image, with the degree of blur determined by the standard deviation of the normal distribution. The greater the standard deviation, the greater is the degree of blur and the greater is the loss of high resolution or fine detail. The effects of Gaussian filters are illustrated in Fig. 4.1.

If a set of Gaussian filters of different standard deviations are applied to the input, a set of descriptions are obtained which carry information about intensity changes of different types at a range of scales. Marr and Hildreth (1982) proposed that

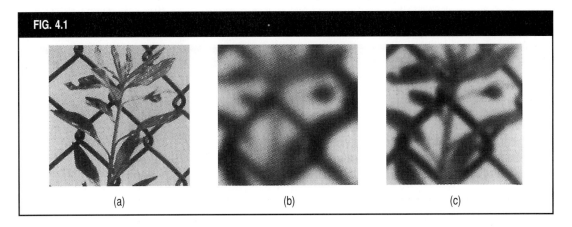

FIG. 4.1

(a)   (b)   (c)

(a), (b), and (c) show an image and the results of applying two Gaussian filters of different widths or variance respectively. Reprinted from Marr and Hildreth (1982).

these different changes may be discovered by examining the rate of changes of intensity in the different descriptions. In fact they suggest the rate of change of the rate of change is most informative. Examine Fig. 4.2. At a discontinuity, such as the edge of an object, intensity may vary as shown by the intensity profile in 4.2a. In such a case the rate of change in intensity, that is, its gradient, is shown by 4.2b. In turn the gradient of the function shown in 4.2b, the rate of change of the rate of change of intensity, can be seen in 4.2c. This latter function is the second derivative of the variation in intensity. As can be seen in 4.2c, the second derivative has the interesting property of passing through zero at locations of discontinuities in intensity. Thus, Marr and Hildreth (1982) reasoned, zero-crossings are good indicators of interesting or significant intensity changes. They proposed that zero-crossings were best measured by the Laplacian operator which effectively sums the rate of changes in intensity gradients around a point on the image. Adjacent zero crossings found by this operator may be grouped into zero-crossing segments on the basis of their shared orientation. As can be seen in Fig. 4.3, the application of the Laplacian operator to the filtered images ($\Delta^2 G$) results in descriptions of zero-crossings over a range of spatial scales: from fine to coarse resolution. Each description may be regarded as a channel of information. The detection of particular visual features depends on comparisons across these channels. For instance, edges that correspond to the boundaries of objects will be spatially localised and therefore elicit zero-crossing in all channels at the same locations. Comparisons of this sort effectively filter out intensity changes that do not arise from real-world features, such as a diffraction pattern. These techniques succeed in extracting a set of visual features from an image along with their relative locations.

How might this work be accommodated in a connectionist scheme? Marr and Hildreth (1982) presented the major part of their theory of edge detection at the level of algorithms and the representations that result from their application. However they also considered the neuronal implementation of their proposed algorithms. Consider, for example, the problem of detecting zero-crossings. The receptive field of centre-on retinal ganglion and lateral geniculate cells may be modelled by the difference of two Gaussian distributions: a narrow excitatory function superimposed on a broader inhibitory one, as in Fig. 4.4a. It turns out that this difference is a good approximation to $\Delta^2 G$. Moreover Marr and Ullman (1981) showed that the outputs of $\Delta^2 G$ applied to image features such as bars and edges are very similar to those found in the case of ganglion and lateral geniculate cells when stimulated by such features. Accordingly it is reasonable to suppose that the $\Delta^2 G$ function is computed by those cells in the biological case. Marr (1982) suggests that centre-on cells signal positive values of the function, centre-off cells signal negative values, and activity of both sorts must be summed to locate a zero-crossing, as shown in Fig. 4.4b. That is,

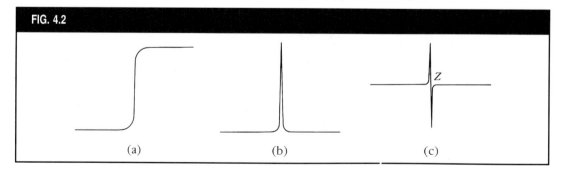

FIG. 4.2

(a)   (b)   (c)

(a) an intensity profile with edges marked by discontinuities, (b) the gradient of the intensity profile (the first derivative), (c) the gradient of the first derivative (the second derivative of intensity). Note the zero-crossings in the second derivative. From *Vision* by David Marr © 1982 by W.H. Freeman and Company. Used with permission.

FIG. 4.3

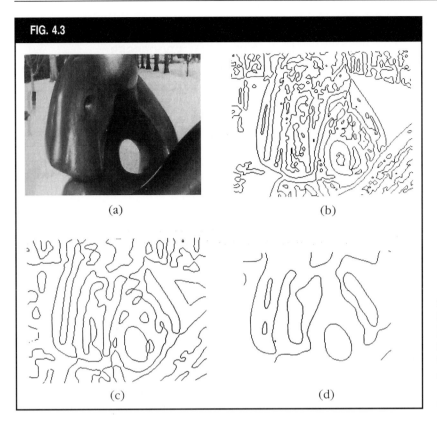

(a)   (b)

(c)   (d)

(b), (c), and (d) show the zero-crossings obtained by applying the Laplacian operator to the image filtered through three different width Gaussians. Reprinted from Marr and Hildreth (1982).

a zero-crossing is indicated if a centre-on and a centre-off, with adjacent receptive fields, are simultaneously active. Similar logic suggests that orientated zero-crossing segments may be indicated in the summed output of such cells arranged as shown in Fig. 4.4c.

It is clear enough that Marr's (1982) model of low-level vision may be readily conceived in the form of a feed-forward network as the following sketch shows. We will mention work later in which the receptive field properties of centre-on and centre-off cells can emerge in networks (Linsker, 1986). These units in turn can be combined in the manner indicated in the previous paragraph to find orientated zero-crossings at various scales of intensity change. Signals indicating zero-crossing in different channels may be summed by higher-level units so that an edge is indicated only when activity arrives from zero-crossing units in several channels. These latter units may therefore be thought of as representing an edge map of the visual field. Marr (1982) argued that descriptions of edge segments, and similar low-level visual features, which together constitute a representation he called a raw Primal Sketch, might be grouped together to form a full Primal Sketch. For example, adjacent, collinear edge segments in the raw Primal Sketch would be described as a single edge in the full Primal Sketch. The implementation of the grouping processes were not specified by Marr (1982), he simply described a number of plausible grouping principles. Other workers in computer vision have in fact used relaxation techniques to "grow" edges (Prager, 1980; Zucker, Hummel, & Rosenfeld, 1977). For instance if a weak or low-confidence edge segment (one that results in weak activity in the relevant neurons) is located between two strong collinear segments the confidence in the weak segment should be increased. One can conceive of lateral connections in the units representing the edge map implementing this sort of relaxation process.

FIG. 4.4

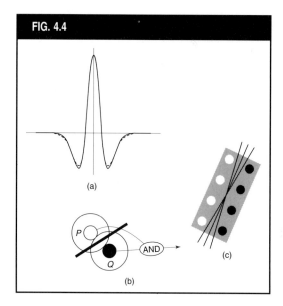

Here (a) the receptive fields of ganglion and lateral geniculate nuclei cells, in the mammalian visual pathway, are well modelled by the difference of two superimposed Gaussian distributions. In this example a circular receptive field results, with a central excitatory region, surrounded by an inhibitatory collar: a so-called centre-on receptive field. (b) demonstrates the pairing of centre-on and centre-off cells to signal the location of a zero-crossing, and (c) illustrates how the summed output of an assembly of such cells might signal orientated zero-crossing segments. Reprinted from Marr and Hildreth (1982).

Low-level visual processes deliver information about image features such as edges, intermediate-level visual processes may be best summarised as those processes that organise these features and which may even deliver information about surfaces in a visual scene. Marr (1982) has proposed that a number of independent modules serve to provide this latter type of information. Putative modules include: stereopsis, shape from shading, structure from motion, and surface orientation from optic flow. These too are very amenable to a connectionist approach and in Chapter 1 we described Marr and Poggio's (1976) relaxation model which succeeded in solving random dot stereograms. In the next section of this chapter we describe a network solution of the shape from shading problem — which has an interesting sting in its tail for our understanding of receptive field properties.

4.2 LEARNING LOW- AND INTERMEDIATE-LEVEL VISUAL PROCESSES

We have shown that the early stages of vision are often explained in terms of highly parallel and cooperative computations. This flavour predates the re-emergence of connectionism. Perhaps this is not surprising given the strong neurophysiological underpinnings of much of the work. We now turn to consider how some of the mechanisms may have arisen as a result of learning. Here the mark of the reborn connectionism is more obvious.

4.2.1 Learning receptive field properties

Linsker (1986) has shown how the receptive field properties found in mammalian visual pathways may arise from learning in networks given essentially random inputs! He simulated feedforward, multilayer networks in which each layer was arranged as a two-dimensional array. A unit in one layer projected to one at the same position in the higher layer and also some of the neighbours of the latter, so each unit in the higher layer had a receptive field of units in the lower level. The density of connectivity in this receptive field was weighted by a normal or Gaussian distribution: denser in the centre than the periphery. Learning was Hebbian in style so that the connections between units that were coactive tended to increase. In a simulation of a three-layer network, training produced three types of layer two unit: ones in which all connections from layer one were excitatory, ones in which they were all inhibitory, and ones in which they were mixed. The connectivity between layers two and three was more interesting. Depending on the precise nature of the learning rule, which depended on a pair of constants in the learning equation, layer three units were observed to develop centre-on/surround-off receptive fields or their converse.

Central nervous systems also appear to be tuned by their environment in a systematic way. That is, the mature physical structure is formed partly in response to the precise nature of the external conditions present during early periods in its development. Final structure does not appear to result from just the unfolding of genetic processes, or simply as a result of essentially random input as in Linsker's simulations. This can be shown experimentally: Hirsch and Spinelli (1970) demonstrated a link between the nature of an animal's early visual environment and the subsequent response preferences of cells in visual cortex. They raised kittens in darkness for three months, except for periods when the animals wore goggles, one lens of which was painted with three horizontal bars and the other with three vertical bars. Cortical neurons in these animals showed a marked orientation preference corresponding to the stimulus to which they were exposed. Also no cells having binocular receptive fields were found. It seems that the animals' visual system had tuned itself to its early environment.

How can such effects be accounted for? Clearly some sort of unsupervised learning appears to be possible given that the visual neurons have become sensitive to important features of their visual world, without being "told" what those features are. In Chapter 2 we described competitive learning rules which could extract or discover statistical regularities among a population of inputs. Such a learning rule has been used explicitly to account for some aspects of neuronal plasticity (von der Malsberg, 1973 and Grossberg, 1976a,b). For example Grossberg (1976b) demonstrated that feature-sensitive cells could develop in a network which combined competitive learning with activation rules that have some biological justification.

Consider the network shown in Fig. 4.5a, which Grossberg (1973) described as an on-centre/off-surround shunting competitive network, and which is consistent with the centre–surround receptive field organisation found in the visual pathway. Each unit feeds excitation back on itself and inhibition to its neighbours. If a sigmoid activation function is used it can be shown, mathematically, that such networks have desirable properties for spatial category learning. In particular they preserve the relative intensities of the input pattern. A system having layers of on-centre/off-surround competitive networks of this sort was shown by Grossberg (1976b) to be able to learn the weights needed for feature-detecting units to develop if a population of inputs containing the features were

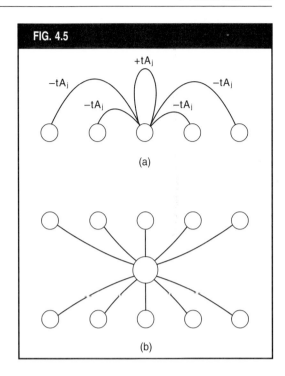

FIG. 4.5

(a)

(b)

(a) Grossberg's (1973) centre–surround shunting competitive network; (b) a simple network for the learning of invariant visual features in a fluctuating input pattern.

sampled. Figure 4.5b shows a three-layer network of this sort. The first two layers constitute a competitive network in which a spatial pattern over the input units will be trained to activate just one of the middle-layer units. Each middle-layer unit may also be trained to elicit a pattern of activity in the third layer of units. These sorts of connectivity, where a single unit influences, or is influenced by several others, is referred to, for obvious reasons, as out-star or in-star networks. In section 5.2 of the next chapter we detail the learning rule for networks of this type and apply them to motor behaviours. For our purposes here it is sufficient to note that the network sketched in Fig. 4.5b can learn to produce the same output for a number of different inputs: for instance signalling the presence of a visual feature despite fluctuations in intensity distributions to which it gives rise.

There is a proviso to this unsupervised feature learning: the number of features present in the population must be small compared to the populations of coding units. Grossberg (1976b) points out that these are precisely the circumstances that apply in neural systems, as indicated by studies like those of Hirsch and Spinelli (1970).

4.2.2 Kohonen nets

The foregoing indicates that competitive learning is capable of developing units or groups of units which signal the presence of particular features in an input. The work of Kohonen (1982a,b, 1984b and 1988; for a review see Kohonen, 1990) has extended these findings to cases in which feature-detecting units are arranged in spatial configurations in which nearby units represent similar inputs. He refers to such networks as self-organising maps and intends them to be taken as computational models of the cortical maps we mentioned earlier. We will describe this work in some detail as it illustrates interesting aspects of representation in networks, which we will return to after the description.

The network shown in Fig. 4.6 illustrates the basic elements of a self-organising map. Units arranged in a two-dimensional array each receive the same input vector. The units should be regarded as belonging to neighbourhoods with strong lateral interactions between close neighbours and weaker ones between distant neighbours. There are various ways of exploiting these local effects so as to arrange that, after learning, nearby units represent similar inputs, including the use of centre-on/surround-off interactions as described earlier. Perhaps the most efficient, however, is essentially a short-cut. Rather than calculate the relaxed activation levels of all the units in the network in response to a given input, one simply finds the unit whose weight vector is closest to the input vector and assumes that unit to be the

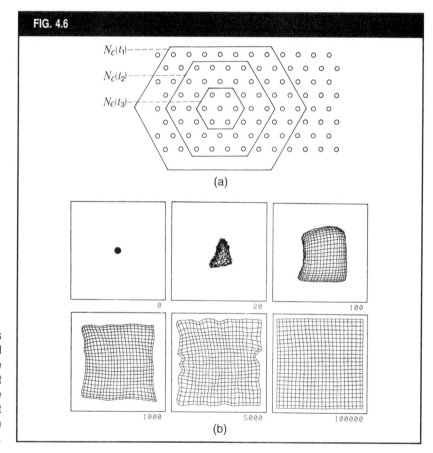

FIG. 4.6

(a)

(b)

(a) the array of units arranged in topological neighbourhoods; (b) the effects of learning, at various stages, on the weight vectors (see text for explanation). From Kohonen (1990).

winner. The learning rule is applied to all units within the neighbourhood of the winning unit and takes the form:

$$\Delta W_i = c(E_i - W_i) \qquad (1)$$

where ΔW_i is the change in weight on an input line to the ith unit, E_i is the external input to that unit and W_i is the current weight on that input line. The learning rate c may be adjusted so that it decreases with time and as one moves towards the periphery of a neighbourhood. It turns out that a good technique for forming well ordered maps is also to allow the area of the neighbourhoods to change as learning proceeds: start with large neighbourhoods and gradually decrease their area towards the limiting case of having just one unit to a neighbourhood.

The outcome of this simple technique is really quite startling and, we think, rather important! The weight vectors vary in value in an ordinal manner along the axes of the array. An example of the development of this ordering can be seen in Fig. 4.6b. In this example an artificial population of two-component input vectors was constructed so that they formed a uniform distribution over a bounded two-dimensional array. This population was sampled at random during learning, the progress of which is illustrated in Fig. 4.6b. The latter shows the weight vectors as points in the same coordinate space as the input vectors, with a line joining two weight vectors which correspond to units that are adjacent in the input space. In short, the competitive learning procedure is shown to be able to map the input space in a manner that preserves its spatial properties.

Any interesting input is unlikely to be expressible as a two-component vector. Self-organising networks can be shown to form interesting representations of higher-dimensional spaces however. Again a contrived example will illustrate this point. In Fig. 4.7a a set of items having arbitrary labels (A through to 6) is described by giving each a value (ranging from 0 to 6) on five attributes. As in the previous case, learning is accomplished by presenting a random set of the input population, after which the state of the network is represented by Fig. 4.7b where each unit is labelled according to which input it responds to. The remarkable fea-

ture of this organisation is that it approximates to the similarity relations among the input population, as can be seen by comparing it with the structure of Fig. 4.7c which is a minimal spanning tree linking the most similar pairs of items.

Self-organising maps can be utilised for perceptual classification problems, for instance Kohonen (1988) describes a phoneme recognition system for the Finnish language. The 21 phonemes of that language were presented to a self-organising network in the form of a 15-component vector. Each vector was constructed by the analysis of spectra from examples of spoken Finnish: the spectra were decomposed into 15 channels, with each channel dealing with a different range of temporal frequencies. The energy of each channel constituted one component of an input vector. Unsupervised learning, of the sort described for the previous contrived examples, was conducted, after which the units of the network were organised as shown in Fig. 4.8. In this illustration each cell has been labelled with the phoneme or, in some few cases, the pair of phonemes, to which each cell had come to respond. Remember the training set was unlabelled! This map may be tuned to individual speakers and has then been used in a system that functions as a "phonetic typewriter", which is able to convert spoken text into written text with an estimated accuracy, at the level of letter, of 92% to 97%.

A central theme of this book has been concerned with how connectionist models solve problems of representation. We will now dwell briefly on representation in competitive learning networks, such as the Kohonen network. In a basic winner-take-all competitive network only one unit can be active at a time — thus it is compelled to form orthogonal representations of its inputs (with one output unit representing each input pattern). This is good if the output of the network is to form the input to an associative layer (indeed, in the final chapter we consider the argument that, in the hippocampus of the brain, networks of these different types are used for the reasons we now consider). At several places we have pointed out that memory in simple associative networks is optimal for orthogonal inputs. Having a single unit represent an input has disadvantages however. As

FIG. 4.7

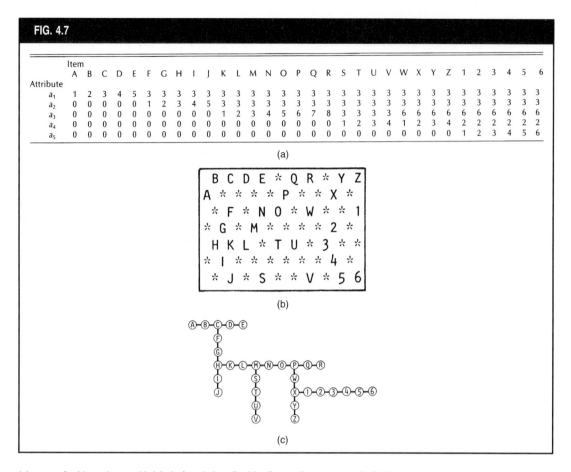

Item	A	B	C	D	E	F	G	H	I	J	K	L	M	N	O	P	Q	R	S	T	U	V	W	X	Y	Z	1	2	3	4	5	6
Attribute																																
a_1	1	2	3	4	5	3	3	3	3	3	3	3	3	3	3	3	3	3	3	3	3	3	3	3	3	3	3	3	3	3	3	3
a_2	0	0	0	0	0	1	2	3	4	5	3	3	3	3	3	3	3	3	3	3	3	3	3	3	3	3	3	3	3	3	3	3
a_3	0	0	0	0	0	0	0	0	0	0	1	2	3	4	5	6	7	8	3	3	3	3	6	6	6	6	6	6	6	6	6	6
a_4	0	0	0	0	0	0	0	0	0	0	0	0	0	0	0	0	0	0	1	2	3	4	1	2	3	4	2	2	2	2	2	2
a_5	0	0	0	0	0	0	0	0	0	0	0	0	0	0	0	0	0	0	0	0	0	0	0	0	0	0	1	2	3	4	5	6

(a)

```
B C D E * Q R * Y Z
A * * * * P * * X *
* F * N O * W * * 1
* G * M * * * * 2 *
H K L * T U * 3 * *
* I * * * * * * 4 *
* J * S * * V * 5 6
```

(b)

(c)

(a) a set of arbitrary items with labels A to 6 described by five attributes a1 to a5. (b) the representational state of a network after learning. (c) the similarity structure of the training set. From Kohonen (1990).

FIG. 4.8

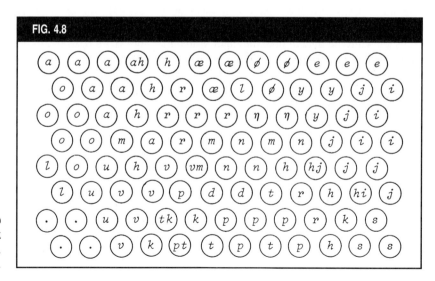

A phoneme map developed by a network trained on Finnish speech. From Kohonen (1990).

the representation is arbitrary and local it does not have those positive properties that come with the sorts of distributed representations discovered, for instance, by Hinton's (1989a) semantic memory network described in the previous chapter. In particular, generalisation or interpolation to novel inputs is not possible. Self-organising maps overcome this limitation to some extent in that the outputs vary more or less smoothly with the inputs, yet remain more orthogonal than those inputs. The transformation of a population of inputs into the map representation has been seen to preserve the topological relations among the members of the population; also the map will reflect, after adequate sampling, the density of the population, with a greater proportion of the map devoted to the vector space where most input items are found. Again we can compare this to the distributions found in cortical maps, which too are non-linear and can have more cells devoted important regions of the input space (such as the fovea rather than the visual periphery, for example). Given the ability of self-organising maps to develop useful representations of multi-dimensional inputs and their congruence with some aspects of coding in real brains, it seems they merit attention from cognitive scientists — perhaps even more than so far has been applied.

4.2.3 Learning shape from shading

The unsupervised networks we have described thus far in this section have features, such as the centre-on/surround-off lateral connections, which are consistent with known receptive field properties of real neurons. Such features underpin the abilities of the networks to code aspects of their inputs which may, in a very general sense, be the sort of features involved in low-level perceptual processes. The work that we will now describe shows how biologically plausible connectivity can arise as the result of supervised learning. Also the coding that develops is rather more explicitly linked to perceptual processing, in this case to do with solving problems in intermediate-level vision. Lehky and Sejnowski (1988) described a network that is designed to extract information about three-dimensional shape from shading patterns in an image. The network is illustrated in Fig. 4.9a.

An input layer of 122 units fed activation forward via a layer of 27 hidden units to an output layer of 24 units. The input units were arranged so as to have circular receptive fields of both centre-on and centre-off types, with the contribution of each sub-region of a unit's receptive field to its activation determined by the function shown in Fig. 4.9b. 61 input units were centre-on, 61 were centre-off, and all the units were arranged with overlapping receptive fields, as shown in Fig. 4.9c, with the two types superimposed. The response of each output unit, after learning, represented a combination of two measures of curvature which characterised the shape represented in the input image: the orientation and magnitude of the curvature of the shape's surface (see the response curve shown in Fig. 4.9d). As different values of these two variables can clearly produce the same output, their representation was distributed across the output units by having them tuned to different but overlapping response curves. The actual output required is in fact four values: the orientation and magnitude of the maximum and minimum curvature of the surface at the centre of the visual field. Together this information constitutes a useful local or partial description of input shapes like the simple elliptical paraboloid surface shown in Fig. 4.9e.

The question is: can such a network learn to produce the appropriate output response given a grey-level image of a shape as input? If so, the network may be said to be capable of solving a version of the shape from shading problem. Lehky and Sejnowski's (1988) results show that this is indeed the case. They generated a learning set of shapes similar to the example of Fig. 4.9e: each member had different curvatures, a different source of illumination, and was located at a different place in the input field. A set of input images was derived by calculating the light reflected from the shapes and forming the training set; an example is shown in Fig. 4.9f, together with the target network response to that example in Fig. 4.9g. Learning was by back-propagation. After 40,000 learning presentations performance stabilised and the network was able to respond correctly to novel inputs. Therefore, for at least local parts of an image, the system may be said to extract shape

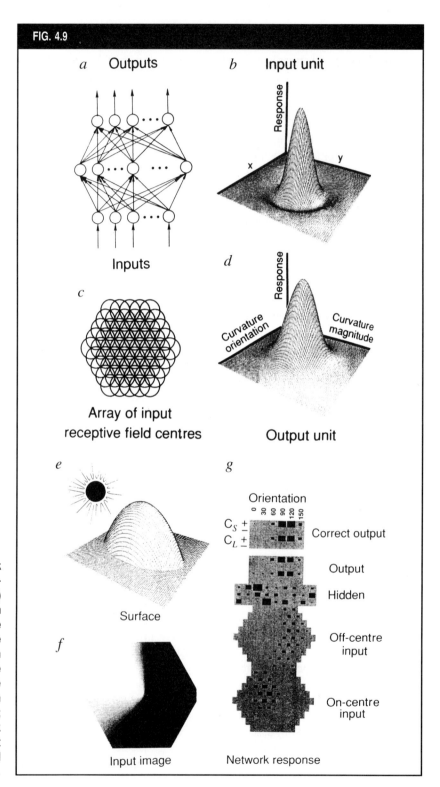

(a) the network architecture for the shape-from-shading problem; (b) the input units' activation function; (c) the receptive field organisation; (d) the output units' activation function; (e) an example of the shapes forming the basis of the inputs; (f) an example of an input array; (g) the target network response to that input. From Lehky and Sejnowski (1988).

FIG. 4.9

a Outputs

Inputs

b Input unit

Response

x   y

c

Array of input receptive field centres

d

Response

Curvature orientation   Curvature magnitude

Output unit

e

Surface

f

Input image

g

Orientation
0 30 60 90 120 150

C_S +/−
C_L +/−   Correct output

Output

Hidden

Off-centre input

On-centre input

Network response

information from shading. This is not a trivial achievement. As Marr (1982) has pointed out, how the visual system derives shape from shading is not at all clear. So how does the network do it?

One sort of answer to the latter question is to be found in the connectivity of the hidden units. Study the diagrams of Fig. 4.10 which show all the connections for each of the 27 hidden units that emerged after learning no matter where in weight space the network was started from. Connection strength is shown by the size of a square with white indicating excitatory and black inhibitory. Each of the pair of hexagons represent the receptive field of a single hidden unit. The spatial organisation is striking: many of the units show a clear orientation preference reminiscent of cells found in the primary visual pathway. Similarly the so-called "projective fields", the weights connecting the hidden units to the output units and

shown by the rectangular arrays in Fig. 4.10, have systematic spatial features. In fact there appear to be three types of projective field according to Lehky and Sejnowski (1988). Type 1 has vertical organisation, type 2 has a horizontal organisation with similar rows alternating, and type 3 has horizontal organisation also, but with adjacent rows being similar. The authors propose that type 1 units signal orientation of curvature, while type 3 signal its magnitude. Moreover by noting the responses of these two types of unit, after training, to the set of input images it was observed that they tended to take on intermediate values of activation. It may be reasoned that they indicate the values of the variables they represent directly by their level of activation. Type 2 units are different. Lehky and Sejnowski (1988) argued that they were feature detectors which signalled in a discrete manner whether a piece of surface was

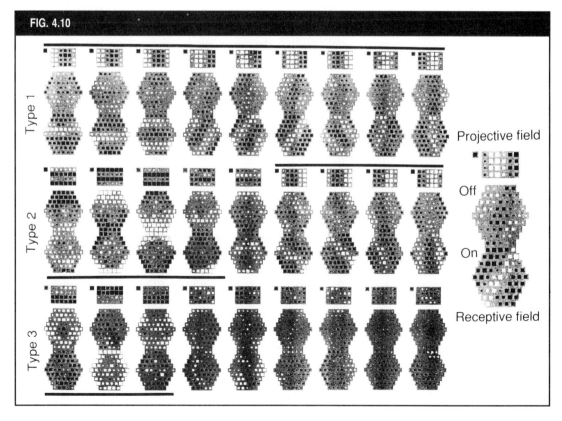

FIG. 4.10

Projective field

Off

On

Receptive field

Type 1

Type 2

Type 3

The weight structure of Lehky and Sejnowski's (1988) network, after learning, for the receptive and projective fields of the hidden units (see the text for explanation).

concave or convex (in effect the sign of the curvature). The responses of such units to the set of inputs was consistent with this argument, as they tended to be either fully active or inactive as if they were indeed signalling one of two states.

This work has a nice sting in its tail! Certainly its main result is to show that architectures that have similarity to brain structures can arise as a result of learning in connectionist networks. Indeed, early neurophysiological studies showed cells in the primary visual cortex that responded selectively to bars and edges at particular orientations (Hubel & Wiesel, 1959, 1968), and this evidence has been influential in leading theorists to propose that early stages of vision operate a form of "feature detection", with cells tuned to detect oriented edges at selective retinal locations (e.g. Marr, 1982; see earlier). But the function of the architecture in the artificial case was not that inferred of the biological case when its architecture was revealed by electrophysiology. No one suggested that simple cells in the visual pathway were involved in measuring curvature, yet the goal of the model is to do exactly this! Lehky and Sejnowski (1988, p.454) conclude that:

> Understanding the function of a neuron within a network appears to require not only knowledge of the pattern of input connections forming its receptive field, but also knowledge of the pattern of output connections, which forms its projective field. Indeed, the same neuron may have a number of different functions if it projects to several regions.

This model is illustrated in full in Lehky and Sejnowski's paper, included at the end of this chapter.

4.2.4 Learning to solve the stereopsis problem

Another source of information about the properties of surfaces is retinal disparity. We have discussed network models of stereopsis elsewhere, in particular Marr and Poggio's (1976) cooperative algorithm for solving random-dot stereograms (see section 1.4 of Chapter 1). Figure 1.6b should

remind the reader of the problem: the units represent possible matches between elements in the two random-dot images. Along a line of sight from one image there are a number of possible matches of which only one can be physically correct. Which match is correct depends on the distance, from the viewer, of the surface on which the elements lie. Marr and Poggio's (1976) solution to the problem of false matches depended on having inhibitory connections between units that shared a line of sight and excitatory connections between those that belong to the same depth plane. These relations were derived, the reader will recall, from two simple observations about the properties of surfaces which entailed constraints on stereo matching. First a element in visual space projects to only one point in each image, so each image element should be matched with only one element in the other image. This is the uniqueness constraint. Second the distance of surfaces varies smoothly in the main, so matching should be such that disparity varies smoothly in the main. This is the continuity constraint. This is a very elegant solution to the correspondence problem, but of course it is entirely contrived. The connections that implemented these constraints are "handcrafted". Qian and Sejnowski (1988) have shown that a version of back-propagation enables a network to learn the uniqueness and continuity constraints. So as to understand how this could be done, examine once again the network of Marr and Poggio (1976), shown in Fig. 1.6b. It should be apparent that there is no obvious way of applying the standard back-propagation procedure to this architecture as activity is not simply fedforward through a number of distinct layers. In fact the network is best regarded as recurrent with no distinction between input and output and hidden units. Given some initial state of the units, an input may be applied across them and the following activation rule used:

$$dA_i/dt = -A_i + \Sigma_j w_{ij} \cdot A_j + E_i \qquad (2)$$

where dA_i/dt is the rate of change of the activity of the ith unit, A_i is its current activation value, w_{ij} is the weight on the connection from the jth to the ith unit and E_i is the external input to the ith unit. Rather like the Hopfield network described in Chapter 2, the idea is that the network will relax to a stable state in time and this state may store information. How is the network to learn? Qian and Sejnowski (1988) adapted a version of back-propagation that had been devised to work in networks with arbitrary connectivity (Pineda, 1987). Given some difference between an actual stable state of the network and one that is desired, such as that representing a valid depth map, an error term akin to that derived in the standard back-propagation procedure can be calculated and used to determine weight changes that reduce the difference.

In order to test the procedure, 30×30 random-dot stereograms[1], in which three disparity planes were embedded, were generated and presented to networks composed of 2700 units. Each unit was connected to four neighbours in the same disparity plane and four neighbours along a line of sight. The weights started with random values. A learning trial involved clamping the external inputs to the units in what the authors termed the compatibility map. All possible matches received an external input of one, all others were set to zero. After relaxation the difference between the network state and the correct disparity map was used to calculate the weight changes in the manner we described earlier. The disparity map was simply the state of the network with only the correct matches active. After 250 such learning trials the network's performance on novel stereograms, with no clamping of the external inputs, was 99% accurate! Examination of the final weights showed them to be inhibitory along the line of sights and excitatory between units in the same depth plane. In short, the network had learned to implement Marr and Poggio's (1976) compatibility and continuity constraints.

In this section we have described several models, all of which illustrate connectionist implementations of low- and intermediate-level perceptual processes. We now wish to discuss some general implications of this work. One striking common feature is the relatively close relationship between the connectionist modelling and neurophysiological data. This is not unique to connectionist models

of perceptual processes of course. Theories of low-level vision have often cited work in the brain sciences as support for functional models, Marr (1982) being a particularly good example of this approach. We have seen, however, that inferences from neurophysiological data are not always straightforward. Connectionist models appear to provide the possibility of testing which architectures can support what functions. This appears to be a novel methodology and has been dubbed "computational neuroscience" by some (Sejnowski, Koch, & Churchland, 1988). Another feature of the work we have described is the emphasis on learning. This is really almost unique to the connectionist approach. We contend that adequate explanations of cognitive functions must not only deal with the computational, algorithmic, and implementational levels (Marr, 1982), but also account for the development of the function. We will have more to say on adequate explanation in the final chapter.

4.3 RECOGNITION AND HIGH-LEVEL PROCESSES

The products of low- and intermediate-level vision are not adequate for the purposes of deriving the identity and function of visual objects. The derivation and use of representations sufficient for object and scene recognition is generally regarded as defining of high-level visual processes. Here too there are problems for which connectionist solutions appear very appropriate.

4.3.1 Pandemonium

One characteristic feature of high-level perceptual processing is its heterarchical use of information. Or at least this is what many theorists assume to be the case. To understand what this means, consider an early example of a computational model having an heterarchical architecture which has some family resemblance to current connectionist models. Figure 4.11 illustrates a version of Pandemonium which is a model of pattern recognition very familiar to several generations of psychology undergraduates! In the model, processing demons

FIG. 4.11

A version of the Pandemonium model of pattern recognition with an heterarchical architecture and a blackboard communication channel. From Lindsay and Norman (1977) reproduced with permission.

each deal with some specialist task: letter recognition, syntactic analysis, semantic analysis and so forth. In fact each demon would deal with some sub-task of such tasks. A "blackboard" serves as a broad communication channel: the content of the blackboard provides the data for the demons, and their activity results in the content of the blackboard changing over time. In this manner a solution is arrived at by the concerted activity of the set of demons. Information passes from demon to demon according to need without any regard to their respective positions in any logical hierarchy. This latter feature is definitive of an heterarchical system.

Pandemonium was not intended to be a model of general object recognition. However it serves to show how problems in visual analysis can be conceived of as forms of multiple simultaneous constraint satisfaction: the identity of a particular letter both conditions and is conditioned by the syntactic and semantic context in which it is found. The theories of low- and intermediate-level vision described in the previous section were generally data driven: they did not use high-level stored knowledge to solve their problems. Recognition processes, by definition, require access to stored knowledge. The results of perceptual analysis, that is, some form of representation, must be compared with stored representations of categories in order to discover the identity of objects in the visual field. Just how representations access structures in long-term memory and to what degree the latter are involved in the actual derivation of representations of objects in the visual field are questions on which theories differ. What follows will focus on connectionist solutions to these two primary problems in high-level perceptual analysis: (1) the derivation of adequate representation and (2) the control of information flow.

4.3.2 Computing reference frames

The identity of a single object, for the human visual system, is constant despite enormous variations in such things as viewing angle, viewing distance, and location in the visual field. This observation leads to the conclusion that the visual system is able to form a representation that is independent of viewing conditions. Here is a typical conclusion about the, a priori, representational requirements for recognition (Marr, 1982, pp.295–296):

> The single most important point is that we must now abandon the luxury of a viewer-centred coordinate frame on which all representations discussed hitherto have been based because of their intimate connection with the imaging process. Object recognition demands a stable shape description that depends little, if at all, on the viewpoint. This, in turn, means that the pieces and articulation of a shape need to be described not relative to the viewer but relative to a frame of reference based on the shape itself. This has the fascinating implication

that a canonical coordinate frame must be set up within the object before its shape is described . . .

Expressed in this way, object recognition is paradoxical: recognition requires object-based representation, but how is the latter to be derived prior to the recognition of the object to be recognised? Hinton (1981b) devised a network that appears to solve the deep problem of deriving object-centred representation for simple two-dimensional patterns. The network is illustrated in Fig. 4.12 and has four types of unit. Image-based feature units respond to elements of the input image according to their viewed appearance. Thus an H rotated through ninety degrees would elicit responses in two horizontal line units and one vertical line unit. The image-based feature units connect to object-based feature units, which in the case of the rotated H should signal two vertical lines and one horizontal. This latter subset is connected to an H unit. There is one such object unit for each possible object. But how can it be arranged that the image-based feature units activate the correct object-based feature units? The problem is that a horizontal line, say, in the image may be part of almost any suitably rotated letter. The solution is provided by the fourth type of unit: the mapping

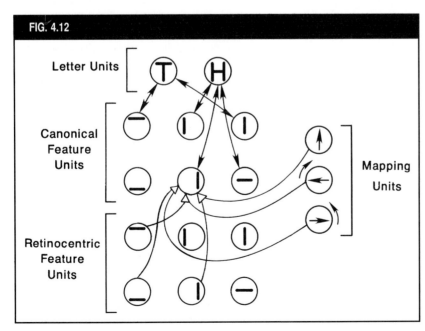

FIG. 4.12

Letter Units

Canonical Feature Units

Mapping Units

Retinocentric Feature Units

A sketch of Hinton's (1981) model of visual object constancy. See text for an explanation of the information flow within it. From Rumelhart and McClelland (1986).

units, each of which represents one possible transformation of image feature to object feature. A mapping unit is connected to the appropriate image- and object-based feature units. Activity in any one of the three units connected in this way tends to elicit activity in the other two. An input will initiate activity in a subset of image-based feature units which in turn will lead to simultaneous activity in several mapping units, which in turn will activate object-based feature units (see also Zemel, Mozer, & Hinton, 1988, for a different way of implementing the relationships between reference frames within a network). Some subsets of the latter will receive top-down support from units standing for specific objects. The network should relax to a state in which just one object and one mapping unit is active. This is a very nice idea! Notice that, in principle, it solves the twin problems of high-level vision: deriving an adequate representation and providing the appropriate flow of information. Indeed it solved the seemingly paradoxical problem of deriving object-based descriptions by adopting precisely the highly interactive architecture we speculated was required for access to the varieties of information involved in object recognition. It shows yet again the power of multiple simultaneous constraint satisfaction within a network.

Hinton's (1981b) model is only a sketch of the sort of solution connectionism may provide for the very deep problems in high-level vision. As a model it is inadequate in several respects. In an implementation of the scheme Hinton and Lang (1985) found that convergence to a unique activation pattern across the letter and mapping units did not always occur. Also the assumption that object recognition must involve object-based reference frames is often challenged. Connectionist models in which recognition depends on the storage of descriptions of multiple, canonical views of an object have also been developed (for an example of this approach see Pawlicki, 1988). The point is, as we suggested earlier, that connectionist models appear to have intrinsic properties that make them natural candidates in this area. In the next section we turn to a problem in vision which, in contrast, appears to raise particular difficulties for any connectionist model.

4.4 THE PROBLEM OF BINDING AND SOME SOLUTIONS

In the foregoing discussion of object recognition we have ignored a significant difficulty for connectionist schemes. How are multiple objects to be recognised? If active units represent the features present in an image of several objects, how does the system bind the right features to their objects? For example consider the simple case in which there are just two objects within the visual field: a green square and a red circle. Suppose further that these stimuli are represented by patterns of activation over units corresponding to red, green, circle, and square. However, how does the system "know" that a red circle and green square is present, rather than a green circle and a red square? The answer is that the system does not know the relations between the attributes (red, green, circle, and square), if the stimuli are represented simply by the activation values in the so-coded units. That is, the system does not know how the attributes are bound together. A possible solution to this conundrum is to bind by location: that is, have units representing the relevant feature for all locations in the visual field. The interactive activation model of word identification, discussed in Chapter 1 and considered in detail in Chapter 6, used this solution to encode the positions of features in letters and the positions of letters in words (McClelland & Rumelhart, 1981). Remember that, in that model, there were multiple representations for features and for letters for each letter position in a word. A problem here is that the number of units required to represent the features and the letters increases directly as a function of the lengths of the words, and indeed they would also have to be multiplied to represent words across all positions on the retina if the interactive activation system were to operate directly on input from a variety of retinal positions. Because of this problem of multiple units being required, several solutions to coding letter position for word recognition have been suggested in the later connectionist literature, and we will discuss these solutions in more detail in Chapter 6. As far as the more general case of visual object recognition is concerned, however, the binding problem is perhaps even more serious. For instance, the number of units required to represent all possible relations between the multiple components making up objects will increase exponentially as a function of the number of possible relations that occur.

A further real difficulty in dealing with higher-level visual processing is revealed in Fig. 4.13. In this case what determines which feature belongs to which object is independent of location. Binding in this type of case amounts to segmenting an image into objects. Hummel and Biederman (1992) have proposed a connectionist model of such a process. The binding mechanism they employ, which we describe in some detail later, depends on synchrony in the activation of units in a network. In crude terms, units whose activation varies together are bound together, therefore so are the features they represent. Similar notions have been formulated in theoretical models of brain activity (Crick, 1984; von der Malsburg, 1981). More recently there have been demonstrations that real neural networks show some of the properties suggested by these ideas (Eckhorn et al., 1988; Gray & Singer, 1989; and Gray, Konig, Engel, & Singer, 1989). In an intriguing set of experiments Gray et al. (1989) measured electrical activity in the visual cortex of a cat in response to various

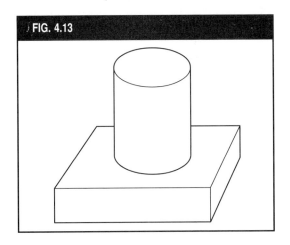

FIG. 4.13

A feature conjunction problem that cannot be solved by location. Why should the lower edge of the cylinder be bound with that object, rather than the object on which it rests?

visual stimuli. In one such experiment recordings were taken at separated sites while bar-shaped stimuli were presented in the respective receptive fields for the cells. If two separated but collinear bars were moved in opposite directions through the two visual fields, the correlation in activity between cells in the two sites was low but positive. If the bars moved in the same direction, the correlation increased. If the gap between the two bars was bridged so that effectively a single bar was swept through the visual fields, the cross correlation increased hugely. These data are consistent with the view that single stimuli are represented by groups of cells synchronised to fire at the same time, each of which represents some component of the object. Subsequently it has been shown that artificial neural networks of coupled oscillators can in principle support binding by synchrony (Baldi & Meir, 1990; Eckhorn, Reitbock, Arndt, & Dicke, 1990; Kammen, Koch, & Holmes, 1990; and Grossberg & Somers, 1991). Here we wish to dwell on Hummel and Biederman's (1992) work which elaborates on these general findings to produce a model of object recognition.

The model is illustrated in Fig. 4.14a. Each of the seven layers of units deals with a different class of visual or spatial feature. The first layer, L1, has a cluster of units for each region of an input array. Within a cluster there are some units that respond to the orientation of edges, some to their curvature, and some to the termination of an edge. Units in L1 feed units in L2, each of which responds to edge groupings defining vertices, axes of parallelism, axes of symmetry, and elongated blobs. Both L1 and L2 are retinotopic in the sense that adjacent clusters of cells deal with adjacent regions of the input array. Together sets of units in L1 and L2 represent geons, a set of representational, volumetric primitives, and units in L3 respond to properties of those geons such as their location, orientation, type of major axis and so forth. In L4 and L5 units code various spatial relations among geons ranging from location to "above". The units of L6 receive input from L3 and L5 and so code a geon and its relations with others. Finally L7 units integrate the geons signalled by L6 and so respond to whole objects constituted by geon assemblies.

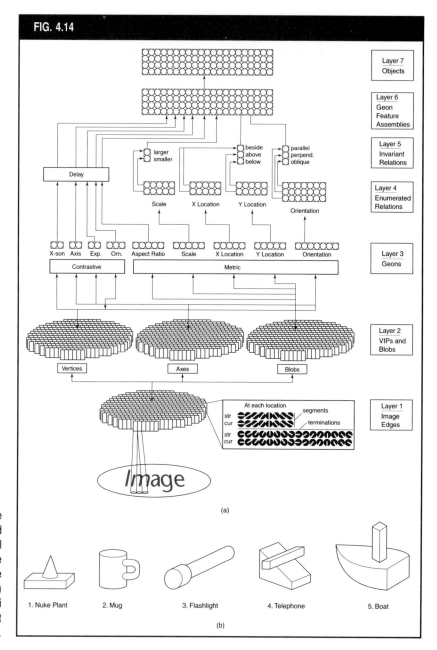

(a) the architecture of Hummel and Biederman's (1992) model of object recognition (the various terms are discussed in the text); (b) examples of the stimuli that it is able to segment and recognise.

The precise details of processing in this architecture are complex and will not be described fully here. However it should be clear that binding is necessary at several locations in the system and it is these processing details on which we shall focus. For example, geons are represented in the system by phased locked units in L1 and L2 which together represent an assembly of edges of particular spatial configurations. Hummel and Biederman proposed that the appropriate phase locking is brought about by the presence of a second type of connection among these units: so-called fast enabling links (FELs). A FEL affects a unit's activation in a different manner and on a different timescale to the connections we have so far described, as we will now explain. Each unit has associated with it a refractory state which varies with time. This variable enables time as well as activation values to be used to code inputs. Note that it also moves modelling one step closer to real neural networks, which have refractory periods after firing. In Hummel and Biederman's model, a unit, even if activated by input, will only generate an output, or fire, if its refractory state is less than its threshold. As refractory states are assumed to decline linearly with time, a unit's output will oscillate. Each time a unit fires, its activation is propagated along all its connections, including FELs. The effect on the unit that receives such a signal along a FEL is to instantly reset its refractory state below its threshold so that it fires if it is in an active state. It now returns a signal along the FEL to the first unit. As this signal and return of signal along the FEL linking two active units occurs an order of magnitude faster than the activation cycle, the refractory states of the two units are equalised and their activity will now vary in synchrony.

The problem of binding in this case has been reduced to arranging for FELs among units that could or should be bound together. The solution, again, depends on constraint analysis (see the model of stereopsis earlier in this chapter). Units that represent features which have a high probability of belonging together in the real world are linked by FELs. For example, units in L1 that represent adjacent, collinear edge segments are linked by FELs. Using this and similar constraints, implemented as FELs, units in L1 and L2 can be shown to segment the input image into an appropriate set of geon assemblies for the types of input illustrated by Fig. 4.14b. These assemblies project to appropriate units in L3, representing geon properties, causing the output of L3 units to oscillate in phase with the geon assemblies to which they are attached. For instance activation of units that together represent a cylinder will result in in-phase activation in L3 units standing for "straight axis", "curved cross section", and their like. Activity in these units, which code featural properties, projects directly to L6, while the remaining L3 units, which signal location, size, and orientation, feed to L4. Consider location. For each location specified by an L3 unit there are two L4 units which indicate whether that location is above or below a loca-

tion also occupied by a geon. In L5 there are two units: one signals the relationship "above", the other "below" and both are fed by corresponding L4 units. Active L3 and L4 units are bound together by FELs, so units signalling relative location come to oscillate in phase with the other properties of a geon. Units in L5 do not have FELs, so they fire with a lag of one time slice compared to the L4 units that feed them. The encoding of the size and orientation of parts takes a similar form. Units in L6 receive inputs directly from the units of L5 and also from L3 units describing a geon's axis, cross section, and so forth. The two sorts of input are synchronised by imposing a one-time slice delay on the L3 signals. Thus L6 receives inputs that describe a geon and its relationships with other geons in the image. Connections in L6 are modifiable, so that with exposure to objects each unit comes to signal a particular geon property list. The function of L7 is thus simply to integrate the sequence of firings in L6 which signal the components of an object and so, finally, signal the identity of a whole object.

In a series of simulation experiments Hummel and Biederman (1992) demonstrated the following properties of their model. During a training phase, single views of the five objects shown in Fig. 4.14b were repeatedly presented to the network, while connections to L6, within L6, and from L6 to L7 were modified. After 3000 training epochs, the activation of the target units in L7 approached 80% of their maximum value for each of the five objects. This was true whether the input was the same view as in the training phase, translated in the picture compared to the training set, or translated and rescaled compared to the training set. If shown scrambled objects in which geon features were switched, so for example the nuke plant was changed to a planar cone plus a cylinder base, activation fell to about 10% of maximum in the target L7 units.

There are at least three aspects of this model worth emphasising. First it implements a very efficient mechanism for binding. Just 44 units were needed to represent the geons and relations among them in two-geon objects. Had the binding problem been solved by brute enumeration with each possible feature combination represented by a unit then, Hummel and Biederman calculate,

1.985×10^{11} units would be needed! To represent three geon objects 2.084×10^{16} units would be required. As we have suggested earlier, combinatorial explosions can catch connectionist models out too. The second aspect of the model we wish to highlight is its achievement of invariant representation. In section 4.3 we argued that object-based representation seemed to be a logical requirement for object constancy and that the latter appears to be an achievement of the human visual system. We also discussed various connectionist schemes for deriving object-based representation. Here we note that the phase-locking solution to the binding problem in Hummel and Biederman's (1992) model is an additional way of obtaining object-based representation. As, in the model, features are not tied to location in the visual field but represented independently, the resulting descriptions can be said to be invariant in that regard. This is a most important feature. Third, and finally, yet again constraint analysis has been used with some success to solve a difficult problem. Although Hummel and Biederman (1992) contrived the network to implement the necessary constraints, it has also been shown that they can be learned. Mozer, Zemel and Behrmann (1991) report a model that learns constraints, such as coactive collinear edge segments tend to group, and represents them in phase relations.

There are other versions of the binding problem. Indeed we shall suggest that binding is one of the central issues in psychology, made manifest by connectionist modelling. It will arise again in our discussions of language in Chapters 6 and 7 and sequential behaviours in Chapter 5. It will also have implications for the discussion in section 4.8, which deals with the linking of perception to action.

4.5 ATTENTION IN VISION

Hummel and Biederman's model deals with the binding of parts into objects, and in so doing shows one way in which neural systems may cope with the processing problems produced when multiple stimuli are presented; multiple stimuli may be processed concurrently, without incurring any penalties on performance, if they can be encoded as parts of one object. In this case, of course, there is a level of representation at which a single stimulus is identified, so in a way the model finesses problems associated with the processing of objects that are independent of one another. Nevertheless, it may be possible for a model such as Hummel and Biederman's to cope with multiple independent objects to some degree, if each object is locked to a particular time interval in the synchronised firing pattern and if these intervals do not overlap or "leak" causing one to run into the other. Hummel and Biederman estimated that there may be a limit of 3–4 object representations that may be maintained this way. This is interesting in that there seems to be a limit of around the same order on the number of objects humans can assimilate at once, for instance if asked to count the number of objects present in the environment (e.g. Klar, 1973).

Other evidence with humans, however, demonstrates that we may have specific mechanisms for limiting the number of objects being processed simultaneously, presumably to avoid interference in identification. For example, when we are presented with several letters simultaneously and asked to identify just one, interference from the "distractor" letters can be eliminated if we are instructed to attend beforehand to the location of the target. This ability to select the target letter by attending to its location occurs even if we do not move our eyes to the cued position (see Eriksen, 1995, for a summary), and so reflects internal processes rather than changes in visual acuity. People are also able to select stimuli on the basis of other attributes, such as colour or size, in addition to position. For instance, interference between neighbouring stimuli can be eliminated if subjects can use colour consistently to select the target (Humphreys, 1981).

Single cell recording studies have revealed some of the underlying neural mechanisms for these effects. Moran and Desimone (1985) showed that the firing properties of visually tuned cells in the cortex was modulated if monkeys were instructed to attend to the location of a target stimulus. They presented two stimuli within the receptive field of a cell, having earlier found that the cell fired preferentially in response to one of the stimuli. Normally, presenting a non-preferred stimulus within the receptive field along with the preferred stimulus would reduce the firing rate of the cell. However, the firing rate of the cell was increased if the monkey was cued to attend to the location of the preferred stimulus. Moran and Desimone suggest that when the monkey attended to the location of a target, the receptive field of the cell was modified ("shrunk") so that only the preferred target fell within it. Mechanisms for the selection of non-spatial attributes have been studied by Chelazzi et al. (1993). They cued monkeys with the attributes of a forthcoming target (e.g. a blue square) and then had the animals make an eye movement to the cued stimulus when it was subsequently presented along with another distractor item. They found that cells responsive to the target attributes (blue & square) remained active during the cue interval, and this pre-activation boosted the activation of the cell when the target and distractor were presented afterwards. In this way, the target cell would "win" any competition with cells responsive to the distractor, enabling the target to be selected for the response. Such studies suggest that attentional operations can modify visual processing within biological systems so that relevant stimuli are processed selectively. As we shall see, these attentional processes may provide further solutions to the binding problem.

4.5.1 SLAM

SLAM (for SeLective Attention Model) was proposed by Phaf, van der Heijden, and Hudson (1990), and provides mechanisms for selection that are in some ways remarkably close to those subsequently found in the monkey. SLAM uses a processing architecture close to the interactive activation model of McClelland and Rumelhart (1981) (see Chapter 1; also Chapter 6). Input to the model was provided by units that stood for combinations of particular features — form and colour, colour and position, and form and position. These input units fed activation through to feature modules, in which the units responded only to colour, form, or position. Finally, the feature modules fed activation through to motor programme modules, used for verbal responses (e.g. red, blue, circle, square, left, and right). Units

within each higher-level module were inhibitory. Thus one colour (blue) inhibited another (red), one shape another (square to circle), and activation in one location another. This architecture is shown in Fig. 4.15. The organisation of the model, with higher-order units responsive to some features but not others, and with some of these higher-order features not being tightly bound to the visual field, is of interest because it mimics some of the properties of cells at higher levels of the visual pathways in the brain (Desimone & Ungerleider, 1989; Livingstone & Hubel, 1988). Note that, as these features are encoded independently of one another, there is a binding problem.

SLAM was used to model psychological data in which people are cued to report, say, the identity of a form when cued with its colour or position. Selection of the appropriate properties of the stimulus for response was enforced by activating the task-relevant attributes throughout a trial (e.g. the red unit in the colour module or the left unit in the position module). Due to the interactive nature of the model, activation from a stimulus, at level 1 (say, red square on the left), would be supported by activation of the task-attribute unit (e.g. red) to "win" the competition relative to other stimuli present without the task-relevant attribute (e.g. blue squares and circles), to enable to correct form then to be identified (square). This is very like the results reported by Chelazzi et al. (1993) for monkeys, in which the pre-activation of cells leads to selection of a target. Indeed, if a particular position unit is pre-activated, it will boost activation of all the attributes at its location in level 1, so that they can be selected together. Thus attributes of a single object, at a single position, will be selected together — a solution to the binding problem. In contrast, attributes belonging to different objects (at different positions) will compete and may only be selected in series, with the loser being selected after the winning stimuli. This matches human data. We are able to select together all the attributes of a single object, but are impaired at simultaneously selecting attributes belonging to different objects (Baylis & Driver, 1993; Duncan, 1984). Finally, this form of location-based selection in the model captures aspects of the results of Moran and Desimone

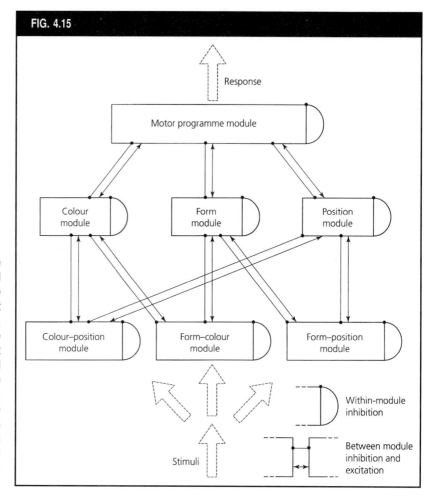

FIG. 4.15

The architecture of the SLAM model of visual selection. Units in the colour module represent different colours (red, green), in the form module they represent different forms (circle, square), and in the position module different locations (left, right). Input to these specialist modules is provided by modules where units respond to combinations of features. From Phaf et al. (1990).

(1985). For example, a cell in the colour module at level 2 of the model may be said to have a large receptive field, as it would normally respond to stimuli falling across the input field. However, when the target's position is pre-cued, the cell responds to stimuli primarily at that location — as if the receptive field is shrunk to that position. Also, a distractor stimulus of a different colour at another location would normally dampen the response of the colour cell, due to the inhibitory links within each module; however, pre-cueing the target's location lessens this competition so that the cell will fire almost as if the target were presented alone, as Moran and Desimone found.

SLAM uses two main procedures to select visual stimuli, within-module competition and pre-

cueing of behaviourally relevant attributes. These simple mechanisms appear similar to some of the mechanisms employed by biological visual systems to facilitate visual processing. However, SLAM also has some weaknesses. One is that, because of its simple architecture, the model fails to deal with the complexity of pattern-recognition processes. Units respond to complex attributes of shape, and the problem of how shape information is computed is by-passed. As models such as those of Hummel and Biederman (1992) have shown, the problem of computing shape information is far from trivial. Within SLAM, there would need to be many many cells, one for each shape, at each position on the retina (at level 1), and there would need to be many many connections from these units to the higher-order (position-independent) units at level 2. This is not realistic. Finally, selection in SLAM operates in an interactive fashion through input units that are position-coded. This means that objects that fall in the same location (e.g. if they overlap or partially occlude one another) would be selected together. In contrast, psychological evidence suggests that overlapping objects are selected serially (Duncan, 1984). Other connectionist models of visual attention overcome some of these difficulties.

4.5.2 Shifter circuits and SAIM

Models such as SLAM, and before it the interactive activation model of word recognition (Chapters 1 and 6), have multiple units for each position in space in order to solve the problem of translation-invariance — how we recognise objects irrespective of their lateral position in the visual field. One way that this problem may be overcome without replicating high-level units across the retina is to map input on the retina into a single set of units, with only these units being used to map activation into higher-level units; in effect, this set of mapping units act like a focus of attention that can be shifted across different locations on the retina. This is the idea of a shifter circuit, put forward in models of attention by Olshausen, Anderson, and Van Essen (1993) and by Humphreys and Heinke (Heinke & Humphreys, 1997; Humphreys & Heinke, 1997, 1998).

The architecture of the SAIM model (for Selective Attention for Identification Model) of Humphreys and Heinke is shown in Fig. 4.16. The model takes input from the retina and maps it through to a set of template units, which correspond to stored memories for objects. This mapping is funnelled through a "focus of attention" (FOA), into which activation can be passed from objects occurring at different retinal positions (stored memories for objects, then, are based on the weights connecting template units to units in the FOA). The excitation of units in the FOA is itself determined by two other sets of units, the contents and the selection networks. We describe this next.

The contents network utilises "sigma pi" units (Rumelhart, Hinton, & McClelland, 1986) which take activation from retinal units and multiply it with activation from units in the selection network, to create activation values for units in the FOA. Thus for every unit in the FOA there is one unit in the contents network.

The selection network is considerably larger and it determines which retinal locations have their activation values transmitted into the FOA (via the contents network). The selection network contains several "control layers" of units, with one unit in each control layer linked to one location on the retina; for each retinal location, there are also as many control layers in the network as there are FOA units (one layer for each mapping from a retinal location into a location in the FOA). The multiple control layers represent all the possible mappings between each retinal location and each location in the FOA.

To determine which retinal locations transmit their activation into the FOA (which retinal locations are "attended"), a process of mutual constraint satisfaction was used, reminiscent of the approach used in Marr and Poggio's (1976) model of stereopsis (Chapter 1; see also section 4.2.4). There were four main constraints:

1. There was competition between the units in one control layer so that only one location in each layer was allowed to be maximally active. The activation from the winning unit in a control layer was passed to the content unit determining access to one unit in the FOA, so that each unit in the FOA was determined by just one mapping from the retina.
2. There was competition between the units in separate control layers that projected to a common unit in the FOA. This ensured that each unit in the FOA was controlled by just one unit in one control layer.
3. There was inhibition across control layers between those units encoding the same retinal location.
4. Simple grouping between proximal elements was implemented by means of a Gaussian spread of activation from one unit in a control layer to units in other control layers representing neighbouring retinal locations.

Figure 4.17 illustrates the pattern of interconnectivity between the units in the selection

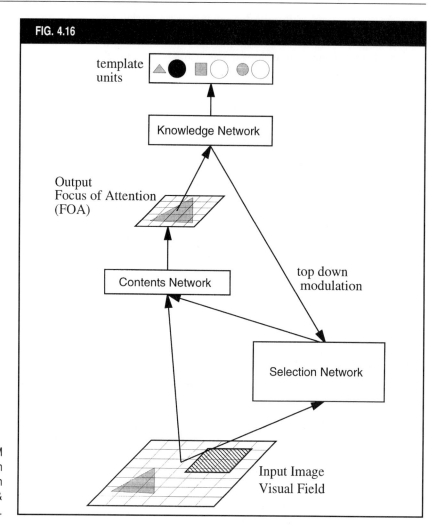

FIG. 4.16

template units

Knowledge Network

Output Focus of Attention (FOA)

Contents Network

top down modulation

Selection Network

Input Image Visual Field

Architecture of the SAIM model of visual attention and object recognition (from Humphreys & Heinke, 1998).

network, where the constraints are embodied. The diagram shows units in the selection network needed to map a one-dimensional input on the retina into one-dimension of the FOA. To cover the second dimension of the retina and of the FOA, more control layers must be added (not shown here).

Processing in SAIM operates across a time course based on the number of network iterations required to map first from the retina through to the FOA and then from the FOA to the object templates. Pixels that fall at the centre of gravity of objects tend to be mapped through to the centre of the FOA. Such pixels are strongly supported by occupied neighbouring locations on the

retina, and so are both maximally active and enjoy the greatest spread of activation — constraint 4 as described earlier. Object recognition (activation of object templates) is then based on where the parts of the object fall with respect to the centre of gravity of the shape, although these positions remain coded in retinal coordinates.

To achieve mapping from the retina into the FOA, SAIM instantiates a form of visual selection, determined by competition within the selection network when units from the same control layer, or from different control layers, try to "win" the same unit in the FOA. When two or more objects are present in the retina, the outcome of the competition is governed by the object that

FIG. 4.17

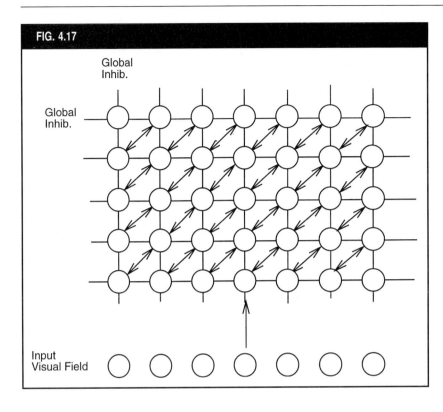

Global
Inhib.

Global
Inhib.

Input
Visual Field

The pattern of connectivity within the "selection network" of SAIM (Humphreys & Heinke, 1998). The network takes input from the retina, and there is competition to provide a mapping through to particular units in the "focus of attention".

receives the strongest activation in the selection network. For example, if objects differ in size, the largest object tends to win because it gains more mutual support through proximity grouping. In the selection network units activated by the larger object inhibit those activated by the smaller, so that units in the selection network represent the mapping from the area on the retina where the large object falls to the FOA. SAIM was also able to switch attention from one object to another. This was done by inhibiting the template units and units in the selection network associated with the object first identified, after identification had taken place. This enabled activation from the initial "losing" object to subsequently win the competition into the FOA; in this way the model would switch attention from a large object to a smaller one.

This model can mimic several of the properties of visual attention in humans. In SAIM, the number of iterations needed to map an input from the retina into the FOA is reduced if a brief cue is presented (for just a few iterations) at the location of the target prior to the target occurring.

Similarly, the time taken by people to detect a target is facilitated if they are given a visual pre-cue as to the target's location (e.g. Posner, 1980). The human results have typically been discussed in term of attention operating as a "mental spotlight", to enhance processing at the attended location. For the model, pre-cueing does not reflect movement of some internal spotlight but rather an initial bias within the selection network to give an early advantage to the location of the target over other locations in the field. Also, when two stimuli are presented there is competition within the network so that only one gets selected at a time; there is a limit on the number of objects that can be identified simultaneously. Interestingly, once an object wins the competition to be mapped into the FOA all of its parts are selected together, whereas the parts of separate objects must be selected serially (when processing is switched from the first to the second object). This mimics the results also found with SLAM (see section 4.5.1), and again captures human data on visual selection (Duncan, 1984).

SAIM does have limits as a general account of visual object identification and attention. One problem is that the selection network is computationally expensive, in that it uses one unit to represent each possible mapping between the retina and the FOA. For a large retina, very many units would be required. Olshausen et al. (1993) in their model of attention introduce the idea of multiscale representations, with coarser-scale representations covering the same retinal areas but with fewer units. This may enable models of this sort to "scale up" more successfully, and it may also enable networks to capture human data suggesting that spatial selection begins on a coarse scale before moving on to a fine scale (Navon, 1977). Another problem with SAIM is that, apart from simple coding of proximity, the model does not employ procedures for bottom-up grouping of information. The model thus does not simulate ways in which grouping can influence selection. For example, in humans, spatially separate elements can be selected together if they share some property of shape (e.g. by being identical or by being non-identical but collinear). Models need to incorporate such grouping mechanisms to provide a full account of human performance. A final model of visual attention that we will consider, SERR (for SEarch via Recursive Rejection), does this to some extent.

4.5.3 SERR

SERR (Humphreys & Müller, 1993) is a model that has been used to simulate effects of grouping on visual search for a pre-designated target amongst varying numbers of distractor stimuli (such as looking for a particular face in a crowd). Theories of visual search by humans have typically made a distinction between early "pre-attentive" stages of processing and a subsequent "attentive" stage, which is confined to one location at a time. Pre-attentive processing is thought to be spatially parallel (operating across the whole visual field), but to be based on the computation of primitive visual features (e.g. edges of a given orientation). Attentive processing is required when targets are defined not by some simple feature relative to the distractors but by a more complex combination of features. Attention may be necessary to "glue

together" the features encoded by early, parallel stages of human vision (see Treisman, 1988). Supportive evidence for this two-stage account comes through studies of human search. Search is usually fast and unaffected by the number of distractors when the target is defined by a simple feature difference relative to the display. In contrast search for a target defined by a conjunction of two or more features is slow and can be linearly related to the number of distractors. These two patterns of data, respectively flat and linear search functions, have been taken as evidence for spatially parallel and serial visual search processes. With linear search it is as if some form of internal "spotlight" of attention is moved across space, to bind together the features of each object — such binding is necessary to distinguish targets from distractors in conjunction search.

In contrast to such psychological theories, SERR used only spatially parallel grouping and search processes, but showed how the patterns of human search might arise in a system operating under conditions of noisy search and selection. The model used an hierarchical organisation. Input was provided on a retina. A first set of units coded the presence of horizontal or vertical edges on the retina. Activation from these units was transmitted through to units that coded combinations of the first sets of units (L-junctions, line terminators), and activation from these units was transmitted to further representations of T-junctions (formed by combining outputs from particular L- and line terminator units). In each case, a map of units was constructed to represent elements across the visual field. Activation from the T-junctions was then fed into template units, which acted to detect the targets and distractors in the experiments. The target might be a T in one orientation and the distractor Ts in other orientations.

What is of interest with such stimuli is that the targets and distractors contain the same local elements (horizontal and vertical edges), but are simply arranged in different ways. The detection of targets formed by combinations of features should be an attention-demanding process (Treisman, 1988). However, it turns out that this is dependent on the heterogeneity of the distractors. If the distractors are heterogeneous Ts in different orientations, search is indeed difficult and linearly related to the number of distractors. But, if the distractors are homogeneous Ts in one orientation, then search is much easier and can be unrelated to the number of distractors present (Duncan & Humphreys, 1989; Humphreys, Quinlan, & Riddoch, 1989). This result suggests that grouping does take place between complex stimuli. Search is easy if distractors group separately from targets (when distractors are identical); search is hard if distractors tend not to group between themselves while also grouping to some degree with the target (when the distractors are heterogeneous and share features with the target). SERR captures such grouping effects.

Grouping was implemented in the model by having excitatory connections between T units within the same map, and by having inhibitory connections between units standing for the same location but in different maps. Thus identical Ts supported one another in search, and heterogeneous Ts competed to form separate groups. At the template level, there was rapid accumulation of evidence for identical Ts, and slower accumulation of evidence for each type of T in a heterogeneous set. The template units themselves were also competitive, so that only one such unit was incremented on each iteration of the network. A particular target or distractor was said to be detected when its template unit reached threshold. If the first template to reach threshold was the target, search stopped. If it was a distractor, then (as in the SAIM model reviewed earlier) the template and associated T units were inhibited and search continued (reiteratively) over the remaining elements until either a target was present or all the items had been rejected.

One other point about SERR should be noted. This is that the model used a Boltzmann machine activation function, with units placed either into an "on" or "off" state subject to some degree of random noise (see section 2.6, Chapter 2 for a discussion of Boltzmann machine functions). This enabled the model to mimic some of the variance associated with human search data. However, it also had an unforeseen effect. At the level of the T maps in the model, under noisy conditions, units would sometimes be placed into an "on" state by

dint of support from other like-Ts in the field, even if no item fell at that location. Noisy grouping produced "ghosting" of elements. To prevent this, a further set of "location units" were added, which gated grouping between units in the T maps. Location units were only excited by activation from more than one early map, and tended not to come on unless there was something at that position in the field. Location units only allowed grouping at higher levels in the model if there was evidence for the grouped location being occupied. It turns out, however, that such location units can help SERR model aspects of human pathology, which we review in Chapter 8, as the coding of locations may be left intact even when grouping and recognition in the model is disrupted by lesioning the L- and T-junction units. The model can know "where" something is without knowing "what" it is. This distinction, between knowing "where" and "what" patterns are is matched by physiological data on the coding of these two properties in the brain. We discuss this last point further in Chapter 9 (section 9.3.2). The full architecture of SERR is shown in Fig. 4.18.

Even though SERR encoded shapes in a spatially parallel manner, it was able to simulate both patterns of search found in the human data with identical and heterogeneous distractors. With identical distractors, there was rapid grouping and rejection of the background items, enabling targets to be detected efficiently; search times (in terms of network iterations) were unrelated to the number of distractors present. In contrast, with heterogeneous distractors there was competition between the target and the separate groups of distractors. The time taken to detect the target was a function of the number of groups present, and linear search functions resulted (see Fig. 4.19).

These simulations provide an existence proof that linear search functions can be produced by spatially parallel search processes. Visual processes do not need to incorporate some form of serial, attentional spotlight to account for such search functions. However, such results also do not demonstrate that human vision actually does use parallel grouping processes to structure search. To test SERR's account of visual search, Müller, Humphreys, and Donnelly (1994) went on to run

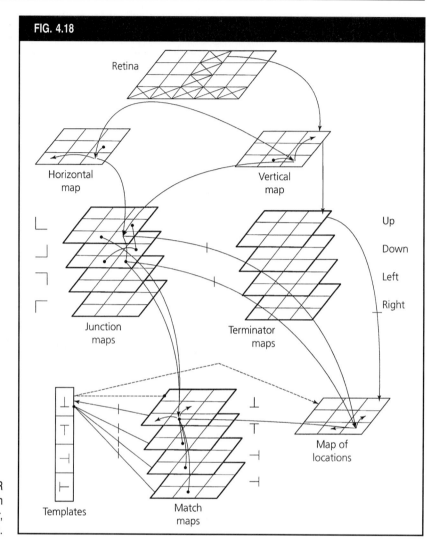

FIG. 4.18

Architecture of the SERR model of visual search (Humphreys & Müller, 1993).

psychological experiments where the model's predictions diverged from those given by theories assuming that a serial, attentional spotlight is applied during such searches. For example, consider what can happen when two or more T-type targets are presented among sets of heterogeneous Ts at different orientations. In serial search, there will be an increased chance of finding a target earlier in search, but detection times cannot become faster than the fastest time taken to find a single target (the fastest time is when the target is sampled first). In a model like SERR, with parallel search and grouping, identical targets

can group and so can be detected even faster than the fastest single targets. Müller et al. found evidence for this. Human reaction times when identical targets were present were faster than even the fastest times taken to detect a single target. This can only be accounted for if there is parallel processing of the T stimuli.

This last study shows how connectionist models can be used not only to simulate prior results but also predictively to advance our knowledge of psychological processes. Müller et al.'s work tests a qualitative property of SERR, its use of parallel grouping and search processes, which contradicts

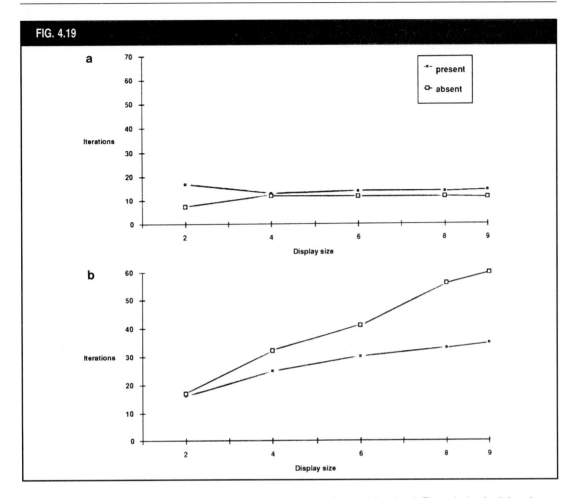

Visual search functions generated by SERR (measured in the number of network iterations). The tasks involved detecting an inverted T target. (a) shows performance with identical distractors (all upright Ts). (b) shows performance with heterogeneous T distractors (upright and rotated 90° left or right) (from Humphreys & Müller, 1993).

earlier psychological "spotlight" theories of visual attention. The evidence favours a model that uses parallel grouping and search, although of course the precise details of SERR are not confirmed. Indeed, like the other models of visual attention discussed here, SERR is limited in many ways. For example, although it allows grouping to take place between identical T-like stimuli, it does not incorporate more sophisticated forms of linkage between non-identical elements (e.g. between collinear edges); nevertheless grouping between similar but non-identical items occurs in human vision (see Donnelly, Humphreys, & Riddoch, 1991, for evidence using visual search). Also, the binding of elements into more complex shapes in SERR leads to an explosion of processing units, as there is one unit for each combination of elements at each location in the field (e.g. in a map of T units at a particular orientation). The model did not set out to simulate feature binding in the brain, but rather how both flat and linear search functions could be captured within a single, parallel architecture, and in this we suggest that it has had some success. However, overcoming the binding problem without increasing the size of such models unrealistically remains one of the serious challenges for future work in this area. At the close of this chapter, the Humphreys and

Müller paper on SERR is presented to illustrate both how connectionist models can be applied to the topic of attention, and how such models can be used productively, to generate further experiments.

The three models we have reviewed (SLAM, SAIM, and SERR) all have the characteristic of simulating human attentional operations without incorporating specialised attentional modules. All three models use competitive interactions between processing units to yield selective performance, but, for example, in SAIM and SERR visual selection is a by-product of the processes leading to translation-invariant pattern recognition and pattern grouping respectively. Attention may be an emergent property in such systems, rather than a separate mechanism operating independently of other perceptual and cognitive processes.

4.6 OBJECT IDENTIFICATION AND NAMING

So far we have covered the visual processes leading up to the activation of stored visual memories of objects, whether stored as geon-based structural descriptions (Hummel & Biederman, 1992) or as retinotopic templates (Humphreys & Heinke, 1997, 1998). However, we are not only able to recognise objects as having familiar visual structures, we can also retrieve other forms of stored knowledge about them — semantic information about their function or phonological information about their names. Although we have dealt with semantic memory to some degree in Chapter 3 (section 3.2), and although we will review aspects of speech production in Chapter 6 (section 6.15), there are particular ways in which visual processes impinge on the retrieval of these different forms of knowledge that bear separate consideration here. We now briefly consider visual constraints on access to semantic and name information about objects, before going on to discuss the retrieval of stored knowledge about a particular type of visual object, the face.

The time taken by people to make semantic decisions and to name objects can vary according to the category to which the objects belong. For example, semantic decisions (e.g. whether an object is living or non-living) are made rapidly to animate objects (e.g. animals) and more slowly to artefacts (e.g. clothing). In contrast, naming responses are often made more slowly to animate objects than to artefacts (Humphreys, Riddoch, & Quinlan, 1988; Lloyd-Jones & Humphreys, 1997; Riddoch & Humphreys, 1987a). How can these different patterns of performance emerge? There are grounds for arguing that object naming first requires access to semantic information concerned with our prior associations with objects. Naming errors made by normal subjects are typically semantically related to the target objects (Vitkovitch & Humphreys, 1991), and the evidence for patients being able to name objects without having associative knowledge is scanty (see Riddoch & Humphreys, 1987a, for one review, although see also Kremin, 1986). If semantic decisions and naming responses to objects were based on a series of discrete processing stages, it would be hard to understand why one class of stimuli might be faster at a first stage (e.g. accessing semantics) but slower at a second stage (name retrieval)[2]: any processing advantage at the first stage should be passed on to the second stage. However, the results are possible to understand if activation is passed on in cascade between the processing stages. Animate objects tend to share perceptual features with other items from the same category, whereas perceptual overlap within categories of artefacts tends to be less. Animate objects are "structurally similar" and artefacts "structurally dissimilar". Perceptual overlap will be beneficial for accessing general semantic information about the items, as it will correlate with the semantic decision: overlapping items will "gang up" to facilitate the decision for animate objects. In contrast, providing the consequences of perceptual overlap are passed on to stages of name retrieval (an important proviso), perceptual overlap will be detrimental for naming animate objects relative to artefacts, because animate objects will suffer greater competition when individual names are retrieved. The consequences of perceptual overlap may be passed on to post-perceptual stages of processing if activation is transmitted in cascade.

Humphreys, Lamote, and Lloyd-Jones (1995) simulated these results in an interactive activation and competition (IAC) model of object recognition and naming. The model contained pools of units corresponding to: stored structural descriptions of objects, semantic descriptions, and names and category labels (Fig. 4.20). Consistent with the idea that semantic knowledge mediates object naming, activation from the structural units was passed on first to semantic units before being transmitted to name representations. Units within each pool were mutually inhibitory; there were two-way excitatory connections between related units at each consecutive level of the model (from

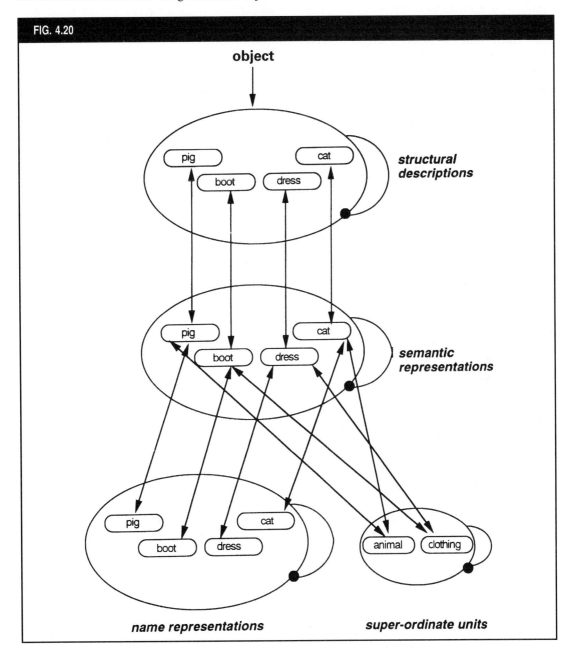

FIG. 4.20

The interactive activation and competition (IAC) model of object naming, implemented by Humphreys et al. (1995).

structural descriptions to semantic descriptions and back; from semantic descriptions to names and labels, and back), and two-way inhibitory connections between unrelated units. Within each pool, information was locally represented, so there was one structural description, one semantic description, and one name for each object. However, input to the model was distributed and based on the rated visual similarity between objects. Thus the input for "dog" activated the structural description *dog* most, but also the structural descriptions for *cat, fox, horse, donkey* (etc.) to some degree; in contrast, the input for *tie* (say) activated the structural description for *tie* most, but created little activation in the structural descriptions of other objects from the same category. This activation was transmitted continuously to the next processing stage (semantic descriptions) and from there to the name and category label representations, with activation at these later stages also feeding back to influence the earlier stages. Semantic decisions were based on units for the category labels, and naming responses on units for the name labels, reaching an arbitrary threshold of activation. Due to the facilitatory effect of perceptual overlap when accessing the category labels, semantic decisions were faster to animate than to artefactual objects; however, due to the interference from perceptual overlap when accessing individual name representations, simulated naming times were slower to animate objects than to artefacts (see Fig. 4.21).

Humphreys et al. also simulated the influence of the frequency of each name, by grading the weights from the semantic to name representations according to measures of name frequency. They found that the effects of frequency were greater on the naming of artefacts than on animate objects; with animate objects, the semantic and name competitors activated by the overlapping structural descriptions level damp-down any benefits to high-frequency names. Again this result is similar to data on human naming (Humphreys et al., 1988).

This model shows how a small set of simple principles can be used to account for the ways in which visual processes constrain the retrieval of semantic and name information from objects: perceptual overlap between category members,

continuous transmission of information between processing stages, gang effects when overlapping representations map onto the same (category) response, competition effects when overlapping representations map onto different (name) responses. As we show in the next section, quite similar results emerge from the study of face recognition and naming.

4.7 FACE RECOGNITION AND NAMING

Faces probably share more similar perceptual structures than any other individual stimuli that we are able to identify. For this reason, it may be that the brain has utilised special-purpose procedures for face recognition that are not shared with the visual processing of other objects (see Biederman & Kalocsai, 1997; Bruce & Humphreys, 1994, for recent reviews). It may also be argued that the separation of face processing from the processing of other objects extends even to the retrieval of name information (e.g. Semenza & Zettin, 1988, 1989, although see Bredart, Brennen, & Valentine, 1997). A connectionist model that attempts to account for psychological data on the retrieval of stored knowledge about faces has been presented by Burton, Bruce, and colleagues (Burton & Bruce, 1993; Burton et al., 1990). The architecture of this model was closely based on a psychological model of face processing proposed by Bruce and Young (1986). The Bruce and Young model maintained that face processing involves a number of separable stages, concerned with accessing stored visual memories for faces ("activating face recognition units", or FRUs), accessing associated semantic information ("activating semantic identification units", or SIUs, specifying information such as *is divorced, an actor, appeared controversially in a film* and so forth), and accessing name information ("activating lexical output units"). Access to these forms of stored knowledge would operate in parallel with visual processing of other forms of facial information, such as gender or expression. The forms of stored knowledge specified in this model, and the order

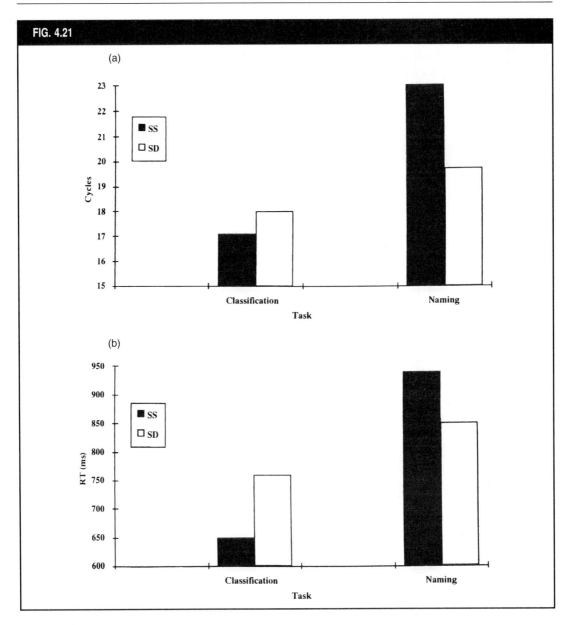

FIG. 4.21

(a)

(b)

The opposite effects of perceptual overlap on semantic classification and naming: (a) human data; (b) simulations by the IAC model of object naming (after Humphreys et al., 1995). SS = structurally similar objects, SD = structurally dissimilar objects.

of access to this knowledge, is similar to that assumed in the IAC model of object processing (see section 4.6). However, in addition, Bruce and Young proposed a further set of processing units, termed person identity nodes (PINs), that mediated access from the structural units (FRUs) to the semantic units (SIUs). PINs are activated not only by facial input but also by verbal input concerning people's names, and so serve as an interface between the visual and verbal processing systems, linking each to a common stored of semantic knowledge. As PINs respond to names as well as to faces, they can indicate the familiarity of a person, and not just a face.

Burton, Bruce, and colleagues implemented a version of this face-processing model using an IAC architecture (Fig. 4.22). In Burton and Bruce (1993), the SIUs were specified as containing information about a person's name as well as containing other forms of associated knowledge (although the name information at a semantic level would be separate from name information at a lexical or phonological level — see Fig. 4.22). This point is not crucial to the main simulations we

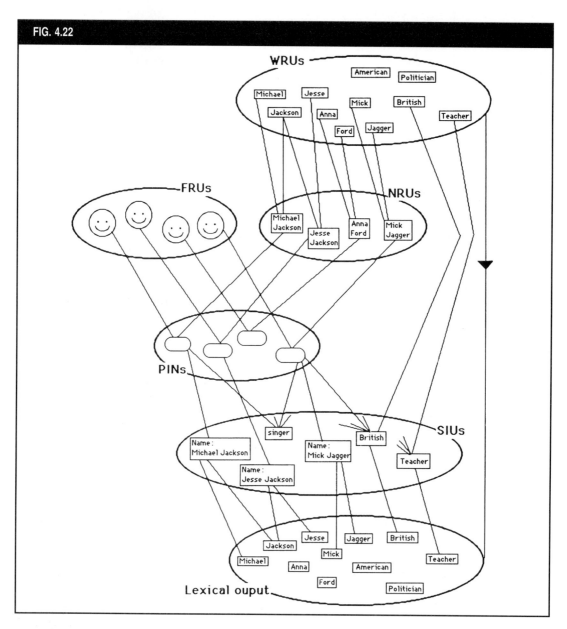

FIG. 4.22

The interactive activation and competition (IAC) model of face recognition and naming, simulated by Burton and Bruce (1993).

discuss, and it is controversial whether, in people, names are just another piece of semantic knowledge or whether they are represented independently (as are names in the IAC model of object identification, see section 4.6) (see papers in Cohen & Burke, 1993)[3].

The IAC model was able to account for a number of findings in the literature on human face processing. For example, associative priming occurs when responses to a second face are speeded by the immediately prior presentation of the face of an associated person. For example, a familiarity decision (is this person familiar?) to Hillary Clinton's face may be speeded by the earlier presentation of Bill Clinton's face (e.g. Bruce & Valentine, 1986). In the model, familiarity decisions can be simulated by monitoring activation in PIN units, to judge whether any rises above an arbitrary threshold level. A first face will activate SIUs, which, in the interactive architecture, feed back activation not only to the PIN of that face but also to the PINs of related faces. Familiarity decisions to a second, related face will then be facilitated, as activation of the PIN for this face is raised above its residual level. Now two further predictions can be made. One is that associative priming can operate across modalities, from names to faces; earlier presentation of the name Bill Clinton should facilitate familiarity decisions to the face of Hillary Clinton as much as the earlier presentation of his face. This prediction arises because the locus of associative priming is the activation states of PINs, and PINs receive input from faces and names alike (Fig. 4.22). The second prediction is that associative priming should be temporary; activation states in PINs are transitory and will be over-ridden by the subsequent presentation of other stimuli. Both predictions match with data on associative priming in people (e.g. Bruce & Valentine, 1986).

Most IAC models of human processing (such as the interactive activation model of word recognition, and the IAC model of object processing) are "steady-state", in the sense that weights between units are fixed and unaltered by learning. However, longer-term learning has been applied to the IAC model of face processing (Burton, 1994). Learning took the form of Hebbian updating of the weights between activated units. Thus presentation of a face would lead to activation of a FRU and of a particular PIN (given some initial variations in weights between these pools of units). Strengthening of the weights between these units would enable, over time, a given PIN to consistently signal the familiarity of a given face. This longer-term learning may not only play a part in forming new representations for faces, but also in repetition priming between known faces — when subsequent responses to a face are facilitated by its earlier presentation in an experiment. The effect of increasing a weight between a FRU and a PIN will be to facilitate activation of that PIN, for instance as measured in familiarity decisions. Now, as the updating will be between an input unit from one modality (e.g. an FRU) and a PIN, the effects of the earlier presentation will be confined to that modality; there will not be repetition priming across modalities. Also, as repetition priming reflects long-term changes in weight connections, it should be relatively long-lasting. Again this prediction is accurate (Ellis, Young, Flude, & Hay, 1987b).

Although the IAC models of face and object processing differ superficially, in that only the face-processing model has an explicit set of units (PINs) that respond to cross-modal input about particular stimuli, it might be argued that the semantic representations in the object-processing model serve a similar functional purpose, as a gateway to accessing super-ordinate information at another level in the model. The ways in which stored knowledge is accessed from objects and from faces may be functionally quite similar; further work is needed to examine any similarities and differences in detail, perhaps guided by models such as these. In Chapter 8 we return to the models, to evaluate how well they can account for disorders in object and face processing that are associated with a damage to brain structures.

4.8 LINKING PERCEPTION AND ACTION

In a famous critique of some aspects of the traditional, symbol-manipulation approach to cognitive processes, Neisser (1976) suggested that such theories often appear to be entirely concerned with the internal states of the perceiver and seeming to neglect behavioural acts. Certainly many influential models of vision treat the problem of vision as entirely to do with the derivation of internal representations whose role in action is woefully underspecified. In contrast Arbib and Hanson (1987, p.1) argue that:

> ...the job of the visual system is not to provide the animal with a representation of the world in abstract but to provide the animal with the information it needs to interact with the world about it...The spatial locations of objects, and the characteristics relevant to interaction with them, must be recognised and represented in the animal's brain in such forms that they can be used in the planning of actions. These representations must be responsive to the animal's goals and the context in which the animal finds itself.

As an illustration of how the relationship between representation and action might be achieved in a connectionist network we will describe Martinez, Ritter, and Schulten's (1990) model of the visuomotor coordination of a robot arm. The problem to be solved is shown in Fig. 4.23. The three-joint arm had to learn to use information provided by the two cameras in order to reach to objects in its three-dimensional work-space. From the two camera images, two retinal coordinate positions of an object in the work-space were calculated from which the system learned to derive the angles of the arm limbs needed to contact that object. Each pair of retinal coordinates were combined to form a four-component vector, i, which provided the input to a three-dimensional lattice of winner-take-all units. Each unit had a receptive field, in that it responded to only a range of inputs defined as a portion of the four-dimensional space representing all the possible input vectors. This portion was determined by a four-component vector, w, with each pair comprising the coordinates corresponding to some location on one of the two cameras' retina. The unit whose vector w was closest to input vector i won, and generated an output. This output was transformed into a specification of arm angles by having a vector V and a three by four matrix M associated with each unit. An output for unit i is then given by:

$$(\text{angle1}, \text{angle2}, \text{angle3})_i = V_i + M_i(u - w_i). \qquad (3)$$

Initially w, V, and M were assigned randomly. Learning consisted of adapting those values by the application of, essentially, the delta learning

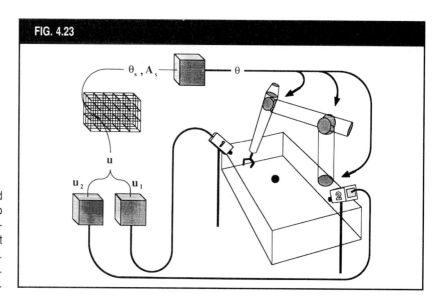

FIG. 4.23

A robot arm, provided with information by two cameras about a work-space, within which it must manipulate objects. From Martinez et al. (1990).

rule. The reader will recall that this learning procedure requires that the difference between an obtained output and some desired one be calculated. In this case the difference can be "seen" by the system. In a learning trial the position of an object was encoded in the vector u and in response to this input the network caused the arm to reach to a position that could similarly be represented by a four-component vector, say o. The cameras provided the information necessary for the calculation of (u − o), thus allowing error correction learning to be repeatedly applied for a large number of reaching trials.

The result of training was striking, and is illustrated in Fig. 4.24. In Fig. 4.24a the development of a topographic map of the work-space can be seen, while Fig. 4.24b shows the effect of this learning on reaching errors. After 30,000 iterations the lattice of neurons had developed a stable three-dimension map of the work-space and as a result reaching accuracy was high.

One notable feature of this model is the close coupling of visual representation and action. The neurons that code position as a result of visual input, also, as output, specify a reaching movement. There is some evidence for this type of close

FIG. 4.24

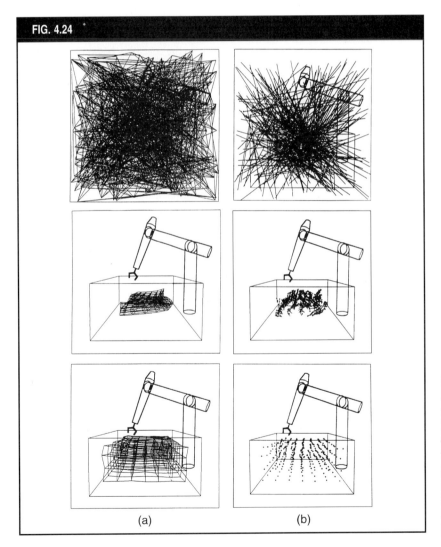

(a)   (b)

(a) the coding of retinal locations in the lattice of neurons during learning; (b) the errors in reaching during similar phases of training, with the end point marked by a cross and the deviation from the target by an appended line. From Martinez et al. (1990).

coupling of the representation of visual space and related behaviours in the biological case. Maunsell and Van Essen (1986) for example have found that in the macaque monkey cortex, a retinotopic representation of visual motion exists and within this the parts of the visual field in which hand–eye coordination occurs are very much over-represented relative to other parts.

Other psychological and neuropsychological data suggest that the visual information supporting action may be encoded somewhat independently of that supporting pattern recognition, requiring some separation between the routes for encoding visual information for recognition and visual information for action (see Jeannerod, 1996; Milner & Goodale, 1995). This distinction is also supported by a computational analysis. For instance, recognition processes need to be relatively indifferent to location and viewpoint variations, whereas actions such as reaching need to be exquisitely tied to such variations, making "vision for action" tap different processes from "vision for recognition" (see Marr, 1982). As we shall discuss in Chapter 9 (section 9.3.2), connectionist models are beginning to take such distinctions into account as they develop modular structures for different tasks. We expect models to account more fully for the details of human action as such networks develop.

4.9 CONCLUSIONS

The purpose of this chapter has been to illustrate the various ways in which connectionist models can provide solutions to some of the problems encountered in explaining visual processes. The development of connectionism in these regards, since the simple perceptron models of pattern recognition, should now be clear. No longer are single-network architectures seen as likely candidates for accounting for very broad visual abilities. More typical is the attempt to provide models for specific visual modules, which have often been identified by traditional, information-processing-style approaches. In this context connectionism has many attractive features. Two that have been dwelt

on here are elegant solutions to the problems of mapping between representational coordinate systems, and the ability to provide for highly interactive exchange of information within a multilayered system. Much work is still needed of course. For example, models that capture aspects of early visual processing (coding receptive field properties, stereopsis and so on) need to interface with the more abstract models of higher-order visual knowledge. Then we may begin to understand how early visual coding constrains access to stored knowledge — something only grasped at to date, using, for example, input that reflects ratings by observers (cf. Humphreys et al., 1995). In addition, models of attentional processes in vision need to relate to models that deal with object recognition (starting perhaps from models such as SAIM, section 4.5.2), so the interplay between attentional and recognition processes can be accounted for.

Connectionist networks also seem very well suited to allowing close and flexible relations between representations of the world and effector systems that act upon the world. This may be very important. There is an issue in the philosophy of mind to do with the nature of representation: how can any state of a nervous system be said to represent a state, event, or object in the world? There must be some relationship between the brain state and the world which legitimates or grounds the representation. This is sometimes referred to as the problem of symbol grounding. One possible relationship is that the representation potentiates appropriate action to the thing it represents. In the robot arm example, the units represent places in three-dimensional space precisely because they control, in principle, the reaching towards those places. We will return to the problem of symbol grounding and connectionism's role in its solution in the final chapter.

NOTES

1. As noted in Chapter 1 (section 1.4, Fig. 1.5), a random dot stereogram is created in the following way. A picture of random black and white squares is generated and replicated. One area in one of the

pictures (this can be a shape, such as a square) is cut and shifted so that its location differs slightly from one picture to another; the other parts of the two pictures are identical. One picture is then presented to the left eye and the other to the right. Now there is a disparity between parts of the pictures in the two eyes. The visual system uses this disparity to create the illusion of depth; for instance, the displaced shape may be perceived as floating in front of or behind the main picture (depending on the direction of the shift in the two eyes) (Julesz, 1971).

2. At least providing that the stimuli are matched for other variables, such as name frequency, that might affect the later stage.

3. One point here is how well these different conceptualisations account for very "pure" tip-of-the-tongue states, where people can retrieve detailed semantic knowledge but still cannot recall a name. Such "pure" dissociations between semantic and name information support the case for separate knowledge stores for semantic and name information.

Network model of shape-from-shading: Neural function arises from both receptive and projective fields

Sidney R. Lehky & Terrence J. Sejnowski

Department of Biophysics, Johns Hopkins University, Baltimore, Maryland 21218, USA

It is not known how the visual system is organized to extract information about shape from the continuous gradations of light and dark found on shaded surfaces of three-dimensional objects[1,2]. To investigate this question[3,4], we used a learning algorithm to construct a neural network model which determines surface curvatures from images of simple geometrical surfaces. The receptive fields developed by units in the network were surprisingly similar to the actual receptive fields of neurons observed in the visual cortex[5,6] which are commonly believed to be "edge" or "bar" detectors, but have never previously been associated with shading. Thus, our study illustrates the difficulty of trying to deduce neuronal function solely from determination of their receptive fields. It is also important to consider the connections a neuron makes with other neurons in subsequent stages of processing, which we call its "projective field".

The specific task we set for the network was to determine the magnitudes and orientations of the two principal surface curvatures at the centre of each input surface, and to do this independently both of lateral translations of the surface within a small patch of the visual field, and also independently of the direction of illumination. Surface curvature depends upon the direction of travel along a surface. The principle curvatures are the maximum and minimum curvatures for all trajectories through a particular point, which are always perpendicular to each other, and are good descriptors of local shape.

The network had three layers (Fig. 1a): an input layer (122 units), an output layer (24 units), and an intermediate hidden layer (27 units). The input layer consist of arrays of units with circular receptive fields (Fig. 1b, c), similar to neurons found in the retina and the lateral geniculate nucleus. Output units were selective for both the magnitude and orientation of curvature (Fig. 2d). Because of its non-monotonic, tuned response the activity of a single output unit represented the curvature parameters in a degenerate manner; that is, various input images could lead to the same response. To resolve this ambiguity, curvature parameters

were encoded by the pattern of activity in a population of output units having different, but overlapping tuning curves, analogous to the way that colour can be encoded by the pattern of activity in three broadly tuned channels. This network was intended to model processing for only a small patch of the visual field, about the size handled by a single cortical column. It would have to be replicated at different locations to cover the entire field, perhaps with all components feeding into a higher level network to integrate the local analyses.

Given this three-layer network architecture, the "back-propagation" learning algorithm[7] was used to organize the properties of the hidden units to provide a transform between the retinotopic space of the input units and the two-dimensional magnitude and orientation parameter space of the outputs. Images of elliptic paraboloid surfaces were used as inputs (Fig. 2a, b). Sharp edges were excluded from the images, and so the only cues available for computing curvatures were in the shading. The network was presented with many images, and, for each input, responses were propagated up to the output units. The actual output was then compared with the correct output for that image, and all connection strengths in the network were slightly modified to reduce error in the manner specified by the algorithm. Gradually, the initially random connection strengths became organized. The correlation between the correct and

Nature, Vol. 333, 2 June 1988, pp.452–454

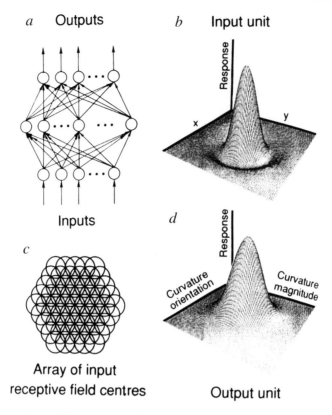

FIG. 1. Organization of neural network that extracts surface curvatures from images of shaded surfaces. *a*, Diagram of three-layer network. Each unit projects to all units in the subsequent layer. The responses of the units in the input layer are determined by the environment. The responses of each unit in the hidden and output layers are determined by summing the activities from all units in preceding layer, weighted by connection strengths which can be positive or negative, and then passed through a sigmoid nonlinearity. Unit activities can assume any value between 0.0–1.0. *b*, Input-unit receptive field, formed by the Laplacian of a two-dimensional gaussian. On-centre units have an excitatory centre and an inhibitory surround, while off-centre units have opposite centre/surround polarities. The on- and off-centre terminology does not imply any temporal properties for these units. *c*, Receptive field centres of input units overlapped in a hexagonal array. Images were sampled by both on-centre and off-centre arrays, which were spatially superimposed. *d*, Output-unit response curve, tuned to both curvature magnitude and orientation. The maximum response of each output unit was produced by a different combination of those two curvature parameters. The magnitude axis is on logarithmic scale. Multi-dimensional responses such as this are common in the visual cortex for various parameters, although units selective for surface curvature have not been reported.

the actual outputs reached a plateau of 0.88 after 40,000 presentations, and the network generalized well for images that were not part of the training set. Increasing the number of hidden units failed to improve the network performance, although it did deteriorate when there were too few hidden units. No biological significance is claimed for the algorithm by which the network developed but, rather, the focus of interest is on the resulting mature network.

An example of the network's response to an image is given in Fig. 2c and the network connection strengths underlying this response are shown in Fig. 3. Each of the 27 hourglass-shaped icons represents the connections associated with one hidden unit. The double hexagons in each icon show the connections from all input units to that hidden unit (that is, the receptive field), and the 4 × 6 array at the top shows the connections between that hidden unit and all output units (that is, the

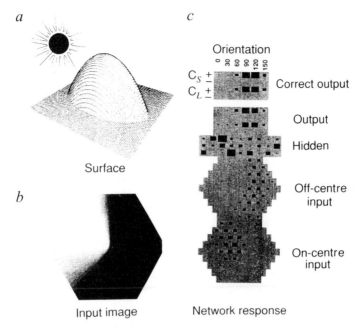

FIG. 2. Typical input image and resulting activity levels within a trained network. *a*, Example of an elliptical paraboloid surface. (The flat base did not fall within the input field of the network.) *b*, One of 2,000 images used to train the network, synthesized by calculating light reflected from the paraboloid surface. Each image differed in the magnitudes and orientation of the two principal curvatures, in the slant and tilt of illumination, and in the location of the surface centre within the input field. All image parameters were randomly selected from a uniform distribution. The curvature magnitude ranged from 2 deg^{-1} to 32 deg^{-1} and also −2 deg^{-1} to −32 deg^{-1}, and the curvature orientation from 0° to 180°. The centre of the paraboloid could fall anywhere within the central third of the input field, and the surface normal at the paraboloid centre was always perpendicular to the image plane. Surface reflection was Lambertian, or matte. Illumination came predominantly from one direction but was partially diffused to eliminate sharp shadow edges. The illumination slant fell between 0°–60°. The network was trained to interpret images assuming that illumination came from above (tilt between 0°–180°), and that the signs of both curvatures were the same (that is, the surface was convex or concave). *c*, The network response to an image. The area of a black square indicates a unit's activity. Double hexagons show the responses of 61 on-centre and 61 off-centre input units, calculated by convolving their receptive fields with the image. The responses were rectified, and so they only assumed positive values. These input units cause activity in the 27 hidden units, arranged in a 3 × 9 array above the hexagons. The hidden units in turn project to the output layer of 24 units, shown in a 4 × 6 array. This output should be compared with the other 4 × 6 at the very top, which shows a correct response to the image. Units within a 4 × 6 array are arranged as follows. The six columns correspond to different peaks in orientation tuning, at 0°, 30°, 60°, 90°, 120° and 150°. The rows correspond to different curvature magnitudes: the top two rows code for positive (tuning peak: +8 deg^{-1}) and negative (tuning peak: −8 deg^{-1}) magnitudes of the smaller of the two principal curvatures (C_S), while the bottom two rows code the same for the larger principal curvature (C_L) (same tuning peaks). Curvature orientation is unambiguously coded by the pattern of activity in six overlapping orientation-tuning curves. Representation of curvature magnitude, however, remains degenerate because output unit tuning curves in that domain do not overlap. An output can therefore correspond to two curvature magnitudes, which the network cannot distinguish. This remaining ambiguity could be resolved with a larger network containing units that are responsive at different spatial scales.

projective field). Repeating the learning procedure starting from completely different sets of random weights resulted in essentially the same pattern of connections.

The receptive fields in Fig. 3 are reminiscent of those in the visual cortex[5,6,8]. Excitatory and inhibitory connections are often organized in an orientation-specific and muti-lobed manner, although some are more or less circularly-symmetrical. Upon examining projective fields, however, three types become apparent: type 1 has a vertical pattern of organization to the 4×6 array of weights; type 2 has a horizontal organization with alternate rows being similar; and type 3 has a horizontal organization with adjacent rows being similar. These classes of hidden units appear to provide information to output units about, respectively, the orientation of the principal curvatures (type 1), their signs (convexity/concavity) (type 2), and their relative magnitudes (type 3). The units had different response distributions when presented with many stimuli. Type 1 and type 3 had unimodal distributions (Fig. 4a), whereas type 2 units had bimodal distributions (Fig. 4b). Based on these distributions, we interpret types 1 and 3 as being filters that indicate values for their respective

parameters, and type 2 units as being feature detectors that discriminate between discrete alternatives (convexity and concavity). A few hidden units were difficult to classify, and four failed to develop large weights.

We tried probing the units with simulated bars of light and found that the responses of the hidden units were easily predictable from the pattern of excitatory and inhibitory connections they received from the input units, and that most of these responses appear similar to those of simple cells in the visual cortex[5,8]. In contrast, it required extensive trial and error to find the optimal stimulus for the output units, but this was not surprising as each output unit received convergent inputs from all 27 hidden-unit receptive fields. Some output units had strong "end-stopped inhibition", similar to that of some complex cells in the cortex[6]. In

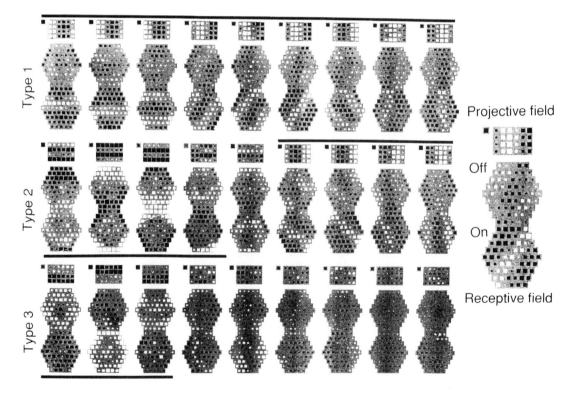

FIG. 3. Connection strength in a typical network. Excitatory weights are white and inhibitory ones are black, and the areas of the squares indicate the connection strengths. Each hidden unit is represented by one hourglass-shaped icon, showing its receptive field (double hexagons) and projective field (4×6 array at the top). The organization of units in the 4×6 array is as described in Fig. 2c. The isolated square at the left of each icon indicates the unit's bias (equivalent to a negative threshold). Black horizontal lines group units that have the same type of projective field organization.

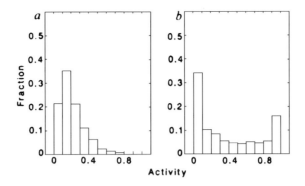

FIG. 4. Distribution of activity levels for two hidden units when the network was presented with the 2,000 images described in Fig. 2b. For each image, units gave responses between 0.0 and 1.0, which were grouped into ten bins. *a*, Histogram with a unimodal distribution typical of orientation-selective units (type 1) and of units selective for the relative magnitudes of the principal curvatures (type 3). These units tend to be activated over a range of intermediate levels when presented with many inputs, and appear to act as continuous, tuned filters indicating the values of their respective parameters. *b*, Histogram with typical bimodal distribution for a unit discriminating between positive and negative curvatures (type 2). These units are like feature detectors, tending to be either fully on or off to indicate whether a surface is convex or concave.

these units, responses dropped precipitously when the bar length was extended beyond a certain point.

Examination of the receptive fields of individual units does not make apparent what the network is doing, and interpretations other than that of extracting curvatures from shaded images are likely to spring to mind. While this model network obviously does not establish that receptive fields in the cortex which resemble those developed by the network are engaged in shading analysis, it does raise questions about conventional interpretations of the functions of receptive fields, not only in visual pathways, but in other sensory systems as well. Understanding the function of a neuron within a network appears to require not only knowledge of the pattern of input connections forming its receptive field, but also knowledge of the pattern of output connections, which forms its projective field. Indeed, the same neuron may have a number of different functions if it projects to several regions.

This work was supported by an NSF Presidential Young Investigator Award to TJS and a Sloan Foundation grant to TJS and Dr G. F. Poggio.

Notes

Received 7 March; accepted 25 April 1988.
1. Ramachandran, V. S. *Nature,* *331,* 163–166 (1988).
2. Mingolla, E. & Todd, J. T. *Biol. Cyber.,* *53,* 137–151 (1986).
3. Ikeuchi, K. & Horn, B. K. P. *Art. Intell.,* *17,* 141–184 (1981).
4. Pentland, A. P. *IE EE Transactions on Pattern Analysis and Machine Intelligence,* *6,* 170–187 (1984).
5. Hubel, D. H. & Wiesel, T. N. *J. Physiol, Lond.,* *160,* 106–154 (1962).
6. Hubel, D. H. & Wiesel, T. N. *J. Neurophysiol.,* *28,* 229–289 (1965).
7. Rumelhart, D. E., Hinton, G. E. & Williams, R. J. in *Parallel Distributed Processing: Explorations in the Microstructure of Cognition. Vol.* 1 (eds Rumelhart, D. E. & McClelland, J. L.) 318–362 (MIT Press, Cambridge, 1986).
8. Mullikan, W. H., Jones, J. P. & Palmet, L. A. *J. Neurophysiol.,* *52,* 372–387 (1984).

Search via Recursive Rejection (SERR):
A connectionist model of visual search

Glyn W. Humphreys

Cognitive Science Research Centre, School of Psychology, The University
of Birmingham, Birmingham, United Kingdom

Hermann J. Müller

University of London, London, United Kingdom

In studies of visual search, a general distinction is often made between the processes involved when detection of a target is unaffected by the number of distractors in the field and those involved when search time increases linearly as a function of the number of distractors present. In the former case, processes are said to be "pre-attentive" and to operate in parallel across the visual field; in the latter, processing is said to require focal attention and to be spatially serial. In this paper, we present a connectionist model which performs visual search in parallel across a window defining the model's functional field. Elements in the field are allowed to group, using simple principles of similarity and spatial proximity. Search operates via the recursive rejection of areas of field where stable and unambiguous grouping has been achieved. Performance of the model is unaffected by the number of distractors present when the distractors form a single group. As the number of competing distractor groups increases, there is an increased likelihood that targets are missed. Setting a response criterion to balance miss rates generates serial increases in search time as a function of the number of distractors. These results are shown to match the functions produced when human subjects search displays varying in the number of distractor groups. The implications of the model are discussed, and the results of five experiments are presented that test novel predictions derived from the model. © 1993 Academic Press, Inc.

Introduction

The distinction between spatially parallel, pre-attentive vision and spatially serial, focal attentional processes in vision has a long history in experimental psychology (e.g. James, 1890). Recently, stress has been placed on possible qualitative differences in the nature of these processes. For instance, workers such as Julesz, Treisman and their colleagues (e.g. Julesz, 1985; Julesz & Bergen, 1983; Treisman, 1988, 1991; Treisman & Gormican, 1988) have argued that spatially parallel,

pre-attentive processes perform computationally simple operations such as registering the presence of local visual features (edges of a particular orientation, color, size, or direction of movement) or signaling the difference in feature values between neighboring elements in the visual field. Serial processes are required in order to compute the relationships between local features (feature conjunctions).

Evidence supporting the relationship between spatially parallel and serial visual processes and feature and conjunction coding comes from studies of visual search. When targets contain a unique distinguishing feature relative to distractors (single-feature targets; e.g. Treisman & Gormican, 1988), the function for reaction times (RTs) relative to the number of distractors is nonlinear or even flat (typically, display size effects of 10 ms/item or less). In contrast, search times for targets defined by a combination of features (combined-feature

Address reprint requests to Professor Glyn W. Humphreys at Cognitive Science Centre, School of Psychology, The University of Birmingham, Edgbaston, Birmingham B15 2TT, UK.

Cognitive Psychology 25, 43–110 (1993)

targets) characteristically increase linearly as the number of distractors increases. In the prototypical case, the slope for target present decisions is also about half that for target absent decisions (Quinlan & Humphreys, 1987; Treisman & Gelade, 1980). This pattern of linear search functions and 1:2 present–absent slope ratios has been taken as indicative of a serial, self-terminating search process (Treisman & Gelade, 1980).

However, not all data on conjunction search fit with this pattern. At least four departures have recently been documented: (1) when one of the dimensions defining the conjunction is direction of movement, stereo depth, or Vernier displacement, search can be relatively little affected by the number of distractors present (e.g. McLeod, Driver, & Crisp, 1988; Nakayama & Silverman, 1986; Steinman, 1987); (2) when the values of the target are very different relative to those of the distractors along each of the dimensions defining the conjunction (e.g. Wolfe, Cave, & Franzel, 1989); (3) when targets and distractors have the same line orientations in 2D but differ in their 3D orientation (Enns, 1990; Enns & Rensink, 1991); and (4) when the target and distractors are composed of simple conjunctions of form elements, when the distractors are homogeneous and there is a relatively small ratio between the size of the stimuli and the size of the display area (Duncan & Humphreys, 1989; Humphreys, Quinlan, & Riddoch, 1989). Of primary concern to the present paper is the pattern of data under the last set of conditions.

In the studies of Duncan and Humphreys (1989) and Humphreys et al. (1989), subjects had to perform various search tasks including searching for an L among Γ's, ⊥ among T's, and ㅂ among ㅜ's. In all cases, search functions were relatively flat. Humphreys et al. further reported that absent responses can be faster than present responses (see also Humphreys, Riddoch, & Quinlan, 1985). Such fast absent responses argue against the possibility that parallel search was based on some local feature that "emerged" when the target was present (cf. Treisman & Paterson, 1984). A contrasting pattern of results occurred when heterogeneous distractors which shared some of the target features (e.g. L vs Γ's and ⌐'s; ⊥ vs T's and I's) were introduced. In this case RTs increased linearly as a function of the number of distractors present, and present responses were faster than absent responses. Various present: absent slope ratios were reported, with some approximating to the 1:2 ratio expected from a serial self-terminating search.

Humphreys et al. (1989) examined in some detail, and rejected, the possibility that efficient visual search with homogeneous form conjunctions was due to the presence of some differentiating local feature (e.g. the presence of an upward pointing terminator in ⊥ when presented among T distractors). Rather the data suggest that simple line conjunctions are computed in parallel, producing, under appropriate conditions, search functions that show only small effects of the number of distractors. Such flat search functions are produced when there is high distractor similarity; search for form conjunctions is difficult primarily when distractor similarity is decreased (see Duncan & Humphreys, 1989).

These effects of distractor similarity are indicative of the important role of stimulus grouping in conjunction search. With high distractor similarity (in the limit, when all distractors are identical), grouping between distractors is stronger than that between distractors and the target. This enables the target to be segmented from the distractors in a spatially parallel manner, producing flat search functions. With low distractor similarity (e.g. with heterogeneous distractors), grouping between distractors may be no stronger than target–distractor grouping. Distractors which are not part of a larger group may then compete for selection with each other and with the target since, by definition in conjunction search, distractors contain features that are part of the memory representation of the target (Duncan & Humphreys, 1992). In addition, the initial grouping in the display will not then respect the target–distractor distinction, but may involve grouping distractors with the target and segmentation between distractor types. Processing must then continue at a narrower spatial scale until distractors do segment from the target. When target–distractor similarity is greater than or equal to interdistractor similarity, the number of segmentations required to form separate target–distractor groups will be a function of the number of distractors present. Linearly increasing (serial) functions result.

This account of search stresses that: (i) search efficiency reflects the strength of grouping between distractors compared with that between the target and the distractors; (ii) grouping can be based on similarity between simple conjunctions of form elements; (iii) parallel search occurs when distractors and targets form separate groups (either when there is strong interdistractor grouping or when targets and distractors are very dissimilar); (iv) search becomes increasingly inefficient as target–distractor grouping becomes stronger than interdistractor grouping (see Duncan & Humphreys, 1989; Humphreys et al., 1989), at least when distractors compete for selection with targets (Duncan & Humphreys, 1992); (v) since absent responses can be faster than present responses with homogeneous displays (Humphreys et al., 1985, 1989), search can be based on the rapid rejection of distractor groups. Duncan and Humphreys (1989) termed this selection at the level of the whole display.

SEarch via Recursive Rejection (SERR)

The account of search we have developed suggests a continuum of search efficiency reflecting the relative strength of target–distractor and interdistractor grouping. The argument for a qualitative shift from parallel to serial search processes classically derives from the empirical distinction between flat or nonlinear search functions and search functions that increase linearly with the number of distractors present (see Neisser, 1967; Treisman & Gelade, 1980). Although it has long been known that, given appropriate assumptions, both linear and nonlinear search functions can be generated by both serial and parallel processing models (see Broadbent, 1988; Townsend, 1971, 1972; Townsend & Ashby, 1983), the association of linear and nonlinear search functions to serial and parallel search processes is still commonly made (e.g. Treisman & Souther, 1985). There are several reasons for this. One is that it is implaus-

ible that serial processing can be physiologically realized at a rate that would produce flat search functions or search rates of 10 ms or below (see Crick, 1984). A second is that the assumptions needed to make a parallel processing model generate linear search functions and 1:2 present: absent slope ratios depend on factors that are often poorly defined in processing terms. Linear search functions can be generated by capacity-limited parallel models or when there is internal noise such that the available capacity or degree of noise is proportional to the number of stimuli present. However, how capacity limitations or internal noise may be realized in processing terms remains a matter of controversy (see Allport, 1989). Confidence in a parallel processing model would be gained if it generates both serial and parallel search functions using a simple set of computationally explicit assumptions.

In this paper, we present the SERR model of visual search. SERR is based on the idea that visual processing of simple form conjunctions is spatially parallel, and that search can operate via recursive rejection of groups of those conjunctions. Nonlinear search functions occur when targets are detected following the selection of relatively few groups. Linear search functions occur when the number of rejected groups is proportional to the number of items in the display. Our main aim is to show how a computationally explicit parallel processing model can generate linear and nonlinear search functions under conditions where these two types of search function are generated by human observers. At this juncture, we do not aim to produce a complete account of visual search; rather, we introduce SERR as a general framework for search processes, which can be extended to model search across a wide variety of conditions.

The paper contains two main sections. In the first section, we present SERR and report on its ability to simulate data on search for simple conjunction targets with either homogeneous or heterogeneous distractors (Duncan & Humphreys, 1989; Humphreys et al., 1989). In the second section, we report five experiments testing predictions of the model.

Section 1: SERR

Architecture and activation function

SERR is a hierarchically organized network model, similar in many respects to other recent connectionist models of visual processing (see McClelland & Rumelhart, 1981, 1986; Rumelhart & McClelland, 1982, 1986; Kienker, Sejnowski, Hinton, & Schumacher, 1986). Within the network, visual processing is dependent on the activation of simple computational units corresponding to increasingly more complex aspects of visual form. At an initial level, units respond to simple line segments at a particular orientation. Units at this "single-feature" level feed into "combined-feature" units at a second level, corresponding to simple conjunctions of line segments (e.g. L-junctions). Thus, single features and feature conjunctions are coded hierarchically. Further, units are organized into separate topographic maps, enabling multiple items in the field to be encoded in parallel. At higher levels of representation, items in the field group by a process of facilitatory activation within a map. As we discuss below, there is evidence that, in human vision, grouping also operates between single-feature elements (Bacon & Egeth, 1991), and it is possible that grouping between single features and between combined features operates using different principles (Humphreys et al., 1989; Experiment 3 here). However, since our interest in this paper is with grouping between form conjunctions, grouping is implemented only at this level in the model.

The network uses a "Boltzmann machine" activation function (Hinton, Sejnowski, & Ackley, 1984; Hinton & Sejnowski, 1986), so that its operation is stochastic. Units within a network can be in one of two states, "on" or "off," and this varies probabilistically depending upon both the sum of the net input each unit receives and the "temperature" of the system. The temperature of the system modulates the degree to which units are placed in an on state by input or by random activation. At "high" temperature settings, there is a relatively strong probability that a unit will be switched into an on state even when its net input is below its threshold setting. As the temperature of the system decreases, so thresholds approximate to a binary function. The stochastic operation means that visual similarity between feature conjunctions can be captured in the model by the probability that one conjunction will switch into an on state a unit corresponding to another conjunction containing some of the same features. Since an incorrect conjunction unit receives some net activation from the features common to it and to the conjunction present in the field, there is a nonneglible probability that incorrect combined-feature units are pushed into an on state. The probability of this varies as a function of the number of features shared between stimuli.

Because the network operates stochastically, there are constraints on how grouping can be implemented. Since combined-feature units can come on incorrectly (due both to nonspecific random noise in the system and to the presence of other conjunctions sharing some features), grouping based on cross talk within a combined-feature map can be unstable. In early runs of the network we found that within-map cross talk caused many conjunctions to be "hallucinated" (due to their units being switched on incorrectly) once one or two units within a map were placed in an on state. This instability is not useful for visual selection. To remedy this, grouping between conjunctions is modulated by a set of "location" units. Location units gate cross talk within the combined-feature maps. Location units receive input from all combined-feature units at a particular spatial position; thus, they care whether conjunctions are present, but they are indifferent to their identity. Cross talk from unit n to unit $n + 1$ in a combined-feature map is enabled only if the location unit corresponding to $n + 1$ is activated. This corresponds to grouping being allowed once there is evidence for *something* at a given location. The gating function provided by the location units is implemented by replicating the combined-feature maps into a second set of maps, termed match maps. Match map units also draw different combinations together to form maps for the particular target and distractor stimuli in the experiment. These units are placed in an on state only when there is input from *both* the combined-feature and the location units. Note that the probability that a match map unit is placed in an on state by noise alone decreases multiplicatively as a function of the number of location units involved. Hence, the risk of "hallucinations" from grouping at the match map level is much reduced relative to that produced by grouping within the combined-feature maps. The location units also turn out to give the model several other interesting properties, such as the ability to know where something is without knowing precisely what it is (see Humphreys, Freeman, & Müller, 1992a).

Decisions on implementations

Grouping can be implemented either by excitatory connections between units representing like elements (as here) or by inhibitory connections between these units. With inhibitory connections, like elements would suppress one another. This would reduce the strength of grouping between distractors and targets and lead to strong suppression between like distractors, allowing targets to "pop out." Mechanisms of this sort are incorporated into several current accounts of visual search, such as Wolfe et al.'s (1989) Guided Search theory and Duncan and Humphreys's (1989) similarity-based account. Empirical evidence for suppression between like elements comes from the finding that RTs to detect a target can decrease as the number of like distractors increases (Bacon & Egeth, 1991; Sagi & Julesz, 1987). However, this mechanism alone would not give rise to "fast absent" responses. Absent responses could occur when all the elements in the field are suppressed, but it would be difficult to ensure that this is a genuine "absent" trial rather than one on which the target has been missed (due to suppression from distractors or to noise in target encoding). Hence absent responses may only be made by default, after ruling out a "present" response. Yet, fast absent responses do occur (Humphreys et al., 1985, 1989), and they are one of the phenomena we wish to capture. Fast absent responses may be accomplished more easily by grouping via facilitatory connections. By means of facilitatory interactions between like stimuli, new perceptual structures can be constructed that can be mapped onto a memory template, and so can be responded to directly on absent trials. The creation of new perceptual structures from local elements is likely to be important in form recognition in general, as evidenced by many Gestalt phenomena. Facilitatory interactions between higher order form elements (such as corner junctions, as implemented here) may thus be important in contexts beyond visual search.

The idea that SERR's coding scheme might be extended to account for more general phenomena in visual object processing lay behind its hierarchical organization. For instance, having single features represented explicitly prior to combined features allows the model to account for dissociations between the processing of single- and combined-form features in patients after brain damage (Humphreys, Riddoch, Quinlan, Price, & Donnelly, 1992b). Also, having L- but not T-junctions represented at the combined-feature level respects a computational distinction between these two types of junction. L-junctions signal convex areas within shapes; T-junctions are formed at the junction of separate objects and therefore act as cues for object segmentation (e.g. see Hummel & Biederman, 1992; Enns & Rensink, 1992). The separate representation of these two types of junction within SERR facilitates their separate use. The utility of facilitatory grouping for form perception is returned to under the General Discussion. Its psychological validity is tested in Experiment 3.

Operation of the model

Present and absent decisions can be made in either of two ways. Activation within the match maps is summed by template units, coded according to the targets and distractors being used in the experiment/simulation (see Duncan & Humphreys, 1989). Different templates may be employed for different search tasks. On each iteration of the model, there is competition between the templates, with only the winner being incremented. This ensures that selection is limited to one perceptual object at a time (cf. Duncan, 1984). Targets are selected as soon as their template reaches threshold level, when a "target present" response can be made. The second procedure for decision making comes via the recursive rejection of distractors. The template receiving the most activation on any iteration generally connects to the match map where grouping is strongest. Consider the case with homogeneous distractors. As there are more distractors than targets, the distractor template tends to reach threshold more quickly than the target template. This corresponds to a stable distractor group being formed. We suggested above that search can be based on the rapid rejection of distractor groups, as in the case of selection at the whole display level (Duncan & Humphreys, 1989; Humphreys et al., 1989). This implicates a second means of responding in search, this time dependent on the distractors present. However, note that responses cannot be contingent on the activation of distractor templates alone. A distractor template can be activated above threshold level both when a target is present and when it is absent. Instead, a process of recursive rejection is undertaken, where regions of field where stable groups have been established are rejected from further search. This is done by inhibiting the match map corresponding to the suprathreshold distractor template and by disabling the location units at positions supported by the inhibited match map. This removes the grouped distractors from the search, which then proceeds over a reduced set of items and a reduced region of field, provided some stimuli remain. This process operates recursively either until the target is detected (via activation of its template) or until no items are left. Absent responses are made when there are no items left and the target template has not been activated above threshold. Note that, when the distractors are homogeneous and there is no target present, responses can be made via the rejection of a single distractor group. There is selection at the whole display level.

The basic operation of the system is thus as follows. The network can be presented with targets and distractors composed of single conjunctions of line segments (e.g. T's at various orientations). These stimuli are encoded via the activation of combined-feature units, with this process being somewhat noisy due to the random "firing" of units in the system and due to activation from features shared between targets and distractors. In addition to stimulus-driven encoding, there is within-map grouping, in which identical stimuli in the field support (activate) one another. Evidence is accumulated (via template activation) for

the presence of particular targets and distractors. The stimuli which group most effectively (usually distractors) and selected (via the suprathreshold activation of their template) and then rejected from further search. Search proceeds either until all distractors are rejected (respond absent) or until the target's template reaches threshold (respond present). The network runs in real time, clocked in network iterations (the time taken to update all the units in the network). Search time is measured by the number of iterations required for the network to respond present or absent.

Details of the model
The basic architecture of SERR is shown in Fig. 1. In all reported simulations, weights and thresholds were set to produce stable performance in conjunction search with homogeneous distractors. The same settings were then used to model performance with heterogeneous distractors.

Retinal array
The retinal array is a map of $26 \times 26 = 676$ units (note that units in arrays are indexed r,c, where r denotes the row value and c the column value). The units on the margins of the map never receive any input. Presentation of a stimulus pattern clamps the retinal units that respond to the input into an on state. Permissible stimuli consist of lines 1 unit wide (directly adjacent lines are not permitted) and 3 or 5 units long.

Single-feature maps
Units in the vertical and horizontal feature maps compute the presence of critical single features (i.e. line segments) at given locations in the retinal array. The effective range of the vertical map is $25 \times 24 = 600$ units; the range of the horizontal map is $24 \times 25 = 600$ units.[1] A unit in a single feature map receives input from the retinal array through an orientation-sensitive filter of size 2×3 (vertical) or 3×2 units (horizontal). Orientation-sensitive filters comprise a middle bar and two flanking bars, with each bar "looking" at 2 adjacent retinal units. A single-feature unit receives positive input when the middle bar receives activation from 2 retinal units and the flanking bars

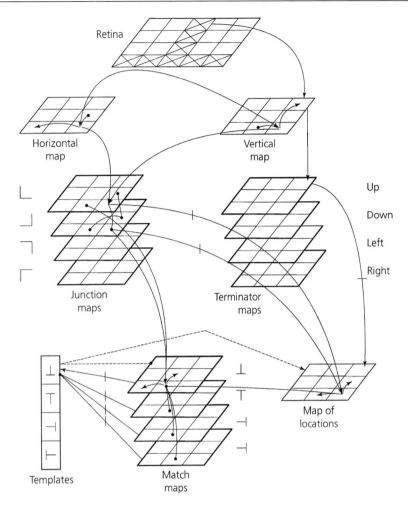

FIG. 1. SERR's basic architecture. Major connections are shown for units activated by an inverted T on the model's retina. → indicates an excitatory two-way connection; —• an inhibitory two-way connection; ↦ an excitatory one-way connection; -→ a fast excitatory connection used after a template's threshold is exceeded; -• a fast inhibitory connection used after a template's threshold is exceeded. See the text for details of other connections.

receive activation from less than 2 retinal units. This helps ensure that single-feature units respond to line segments of 1-unit width only.

Each single-feature unit is negatively connected with its immediate neighbors (weight, −36) that code a segment of a parallel line in the same direction. This helps to ensure that parallel lines are separated by at least 1 unit. Each unit is positively connected (weight, +16) with the two neighboring units which code a line segment extending the line of the reference unit. This helps

to ensure that line length is greater than 2 units. Single-feature units project upwards to compatible (weight, +24) and incompatible (weight, −24) combined-feature units: line-terminators and L-type junctions. The units' thresholds were set to 72.

Combined-feature maps

There are eight combined-feature maps; four for end-terminators (up, down, left and right) and four for each orientation of an L-junction. These maps integrate the output of at least two single-feature units either from the same or from different single-feature maps (for terminator and junction maps, respectively). The effective size of the terminator maps is 23×24 units for the up- and down-terminators, and 24×23 units for the left- and right-terminators. The size of each junction map is 23×23 units.

Terminators are positively connected (weight, +24) to neighboring single-feature units. For instance, an up-terminator at location r,c receives positive input from vertical feature unit r,c and negative input (weight, −24) from vertical-feature unit $r-1,c$. It thus receives overall positive input only when the positively linked unit is on and the negatively linked unit is off. When a line-terminator is in an on state, it inhibits the spread of activation between adjacent single-feature units in the line direction incompatible with its own direction, and it facilitates the spread of activation between units in the compatible line direction.

There are four L-type junction maps (for ∟, ⌐, ⌐, and Γ). Units are positively connected (weight, +24) to their supporting horizontal- and vertical-features. For example, L/unit r,c receives positive input when vertical-feature unit r,c and/ or horizontal-feature unit r,c are on. Thus, junction units respond on the basis of the number of features shared by the input and each stored representation. Combined-feature units inhibit (weight, −24) incompatible single-feature units that violate the "line width = 1 unit" constraint. Further, they inhibit (weight, −48) all their immediate neighbors, both within the same map and across the other combined-feature maps. This ensures that line length is at least 3 units and that parallel lines are separated by at least 1 unit. In addition, incompatible terminator and conjunction units at the same location (e.g. upper/vertical and lower/vertical terminator units) inhibit each other.

There are positive connections between combined-feature units in separate maps, which serve to implement the constraint that line length should be either 3 or 5 pixels and stimulus size be limited to a matrix (location) of 5×5 pixels (see above). There are three types of positive connections: between terminator units (weight, +16), between terminator and junction units (weight, +8), and between junction units (weight, +4). For example,

left/horizontal terminator r,c facilitates right/ horizontal terminators $r,c+2$ and $r,c+4$; also, it facilitates ⌐ and Γ units at r,c and ∟ and Γ units at $r,c+2$ and $r,c+4$. In addition to positive connections between terminator units in separate maps, there are inhibitory connections between terminator units within the same map, which constrain line length to 3 or 5 units. In particular, a terminator unit inhibits the same type of terminator 3 and 5 units distant on the same horizontal or vertical line (e.g. left/horizontal terminator r,c inhibits left/horizontal terminators $r,c-4$, $r,c-2$, $r,c+2$, and $r,c+4$) (weight, −24).

The threshold of terminator units was set to 24 and that of junction units to 54. The combined-feature units project upwards to the map of locations (via positive one-way connections only) and to the matching unit maps.

Match maps

Match map units mediate the mapping of information coded by the combined-feature units onto the decision units. Each match map unit samples an area of 5×5 units on the combined-feature maps for evidence for or against a particular target or distractor stimulus at this location. As the network is to simulate search through displays with T's at various orientations, match map units are tuned for T-conjunctions. There are four types of match unit for each 5×5 location, coding upright T, inverted T, left-pointing T, and right-pointing T, respectively. The effective size of the match maps is 20×20. Each matching unit receives facilitation (weight, +12) from all terminator and junction units compatible with its particular T-orientation. In addition, it receives inhibition (weight, −2) from all terminator and junction units incompatible with its T-orientation (i.e. from terminator and junction units compatible with other T-orientations).

Grouping is implemented in the match maps by within-map facilitatory links and between-map inhibitory links. Match map units inhibit (weight, −32) the units in other match maps that code competing T's at the same location. This implements the constraint of uniqueness: there should be only one match for a particular stimulus location. Match units also receive negative input (weight, −576) from their corresponding (5×5) location units. This ensures that only those match units not disabled by location units pass on activity to templates. Within-map cross talk is implemented by positive connections (weight, +16) between nearby units in the match maps. This facilitates the grouping of like conjunctions (range of facilitation: $r = r - 12, \ldots, r + 12; c = c - 12, \ldots, c + 12$). The thresholds of the match map units were set to 32.

Map of locations

The location units perform a gating function between the combined-feature and the matching maps. The effective size of the location map is 20×20. Units have a high threshold with reversed (i.e. negative) sign (-72), so that they are on in the absence of bottom-up input. Input from the combined-feature maps subtracts from the high threshold so that a location unit goes off when there is sufficient input. This removes the strong inhibition (-576) from the matching units. The weights on the connections between combined-feature (terminator and junction) and location units were set to -24.

Within the location map, each unit is positively reinforced (weight, +36) by its surrounding units (range: $r = r - 5, \ldots, r + 5; c = c - 5, \ldots, c + 5$) when they are in an off state. This implements an "inhibitory surround" mechanism (with reversed sign), ensuring that the unit stays on. This mechanism supports the constraint that there should not be two or more stimuli at overlapping (5×5) locations.

Template units

Four types of template unit were used, one for each type of match map unit. Template units compete with each other, as only one unit can be incremented on each network iteration. Template units sample evidence, over the whole visual array, in favor of compatible matches, corrected for evidence in favor of incompatible matches. The "count" on one iteration is most likely to be given to the template with the most net evidence in its favor. Templates accumulate evidence (counts) in favor of a particular match over

time (i.e. network iterations). If a template unit exceeds a threshold number of counts, there will be important consequences for the future behavior of the network.

Templates are positively connected with all the units in their corresponding match maps (weight, +1; one-way connections only), so that their input from the match maps is the sum of active matching units. That is, they summate the evidence in favor of a particular stimulus. Furthermore, templates are negatively connected with all the units in their incompatible match maps (weight, -1; one-way connections only). This effectively subtracts the evidence in favor of any other stimuli from the positive input to a template.

The template units are incremented once an iteration (but at a random point within the update sequence of all the other units), after the computation of the net input to each of the four templates in the simulation. The template order then is randomized and passed through an "update" loop. The count is given to the first template with a net input large enough to pass the probabilistic update test (i.e. the probability with which the template would come on given its net input must exceed a random number). Thus, a template may win the count even if there are other templates with a greater net input. It may also happen that no template takes the count (e.g. if the net inputs to the templates are negative). In this case, the net inputs divided by 2.0 (i.e. an arbitrarily chosen number >1.0), and the templates passed a second time through the update loop, but this time with an increased chance of being incremented. If no template takes the count, this sequence will be repeated up to a maximum number of eight passes.

Dividing the net input to a template by an arbitrary number (>1.0) relaxes the ("negative") contribution of each template's threshold, and so the probability increases that the template will be incremented in the new pass. If the original net input to the template is negative, successive divisions by a positive number will not change its sign. Rather the (negative) input to the template will only approach 0, where there is a .5 chance that the template will be incremented. The two advantages associated with this procedure are: (1) the probability that a template is incremented is always less than .5; (2) the gradual relaxation (in successive passes) ensures that the template with a (negative) net input closest to 0 has greatest chance of being incremented (i.e. even if it is not the first template passed through the update loop).

Templates differ from classical Boltzmann machine units in taking on an arbitrary number of different states (i.e. 0, . . . , 5 in the present simulations) instead of only two (off or on), although the way the templates are incremented follows the Boltzmann machine approach. The state of a template reflects the number of increments in its favor as the network samples the input. The "integer" counts of increments can be thought of as reflecting the probability with which decision units are in an off or on state. In the present simulations, there is no decay on the activation of template units (if increments occur on non-successive iterations). Each template has a threshold of 5. A template unit "fires" deterministically once that threshold is passed.

Recursive rejection is implemented via strong negative one-way connections between template and match map units (weight, −576) and strong positive one-way connections between template and location units (weight, +576). If a template fires, it inhibits all corresponding matching units. Furthermore, it excites all the location units for which there are no active match map units other than the one shut down. Thus, the firing of a template shuts down all the units in a particular match map, and disables location units (except for those that are supported by at least one remaining match map unit, signaling the remaining presence of other stimuli in the field). To ensure that location units are excluded from search when there are no corresponding active match map units, inhibition of the match map and location units occurs "instantaneously"; that is, within the same time slice as the updating of the relevant template unit. At present, "instant" inhibition is not implemented in connectionist terms (a C-routine disables match map units and then updates location units, using an IF. . . THEN . . . instruction). However, it is possible, in principle, to perform the same computations using a "pure" connectionist architecture: for instance, by means of "gap junction" synapses with delays that are essentially zero

(see Whitehead & Strong, 1989, p.388). Similar "fast" links have been hypothesized in Hummel and Biederman's (1992) recent connectionist account of object recognition.

Simulation of search for form conjunctions with homogeneous and heterogeneous distractors

SERR implements a spatially parallel visual pattern recognizer with internal noise. It also maintains that simple form conjunctions are encoded across its visual field. Hence, there should not be a necessary association between linear search functions and conjunction search. At the very least, the model should provide a reasonable fit to the nonlinear search functions exhibited by humans when they look for form conjunctions among homogeneous distractors (Duncan & Humphreys, 1989; Humphreys et al., 1989) — as homogeneous distractors should fully exploit SERR's ability to search via recursive grouping. We therefore report first a simulation of the homogeneous-distractor data of Duncan and Humphreys and Humphreys et al. However, to show generality, SERR must also be capable of producing linear search functions under conditions in which humans do so; specifically, when heterogeneous distractors are introduced which share features with the target. If the model can simulate both nonlinear and linear search functions under appropriate conditions, it would provide a working example of a computationally explicit parallel processing model giving rise to linear visual search functions (cf. Townsend, 1971, 1972).

The network's task was to find an inverted T target either among homogeneous (T, ⊣, or ⊢) or heterogeneous (T, ⊣, and ⊢) distractors (see Humphreys et al., 1989). In each condition, displays contained 2, 4, 6, 8, or 9 stimuli with a target being either present or absent. Thus, the simulation was equivalent to a three-factorial search experiment with the variables: (i) display (homogeneous vs heterogeneous), (ii) trial (absent vs present), and (iii) display size (2, 4, 6, 8, or 9). The simulations were run with a constant network temperature of .05 (pilot work showed that this yielded stable performance; see Humphreys et al., 1992a; Humphreys & Müller, 1989).

Preliminary results: The need for checking

In preliminary runs, we found that SERR could be set relatively easily to simulate human search with homogeneous form–conjunction distractors, producing flat search functions and faster absent than present responses (see Simulation 1 below). However, given the same network parameters, it did not simulate human search with heterogeneous distractors (e.g. ⊥ vs ⊤, ⊣, and ⊢). With heterogeneous distractors, search times were typically slower than those with homogeneous distractors and showed some trend to increase with increasing display size. Both of these properties are characteristic of human search for form conjunctions among heterogeneous distractors (Humphreys et al., 1989). However, unlike human subjects, present responses were typically slower than absent responses. Mean data from the initial runs, along with comparable data from human subjects on the same search tasks, are shown in Figs. 2 and 3.

SERR's response times are longer with heterogeneous than with homogeneous distractors for two main reasons. First, it takes longer for a dominant group to become established — because there is considerable competition between the incompatible T-type stimuli at the match map level. Second, there is typically recursive rejection of a number of distractor subgroups, as each in turn becomes dominant following the rejection of prior dominant groups from search. With homogeneous displays, only one distractor group is ever rejected. Further, since the number of distractor types on average increases across the display sizes in heterogeneous displays (see Simulation 2, Method), the recursive rejection of distractor groups introduces a linear component into the search functions.

With both homogeneous and heterogeneous displays, decision times are faster for target absent displays than for present displays. This is because distractor groups usually contain more members than the target group (limited to size 1). Since templates summate the evidence for targets and distractors across the field, they are sensitive to group size. The first template to have its threshold exceeded is typically that linked to the largest group. Hence distractors tend to be selected and rejected prior to targets, producing faster absent than present responses.

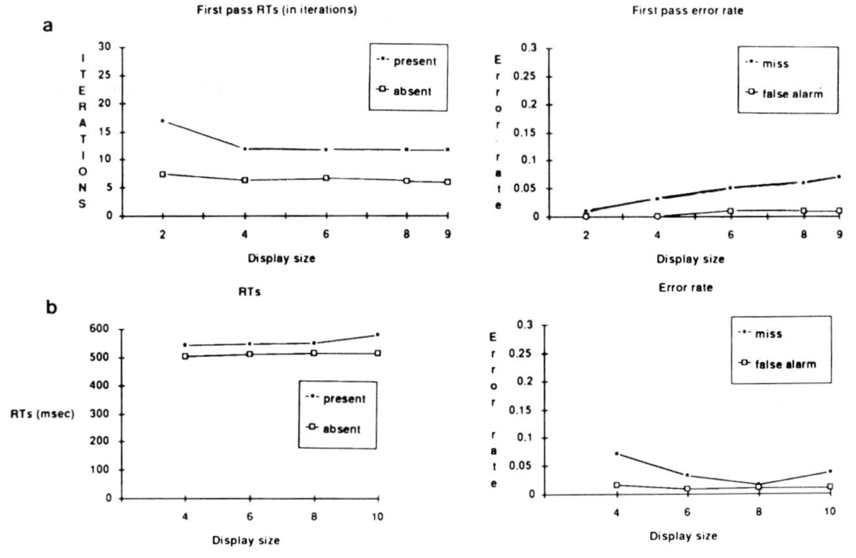

FIG. 2. Homogeneous displays. (a) SERR's first-pass (no-checking) absent and present RTs (in network iterations) and error rates as a function of display size. (b) Human absent and present RTs (in ms) and error rates (from Humphreys et al., 1989).

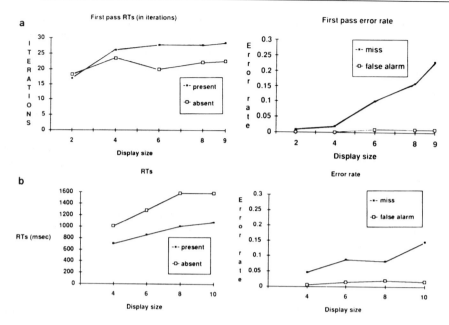

FIG. 3. Heterogeneous displays. (a) SERR's first-pass (no-check) absent and present RTs (in network iterations) and error rates as a function of display size. (b) Human absent and present RTs (in ms) and error rates as a function of display size.

However, these initial runs also indicated that SERR is relatively error-prone. Errors mainly consisted of misses, on target present trials. Misses tend to occur when two or more distractor types each attempt to "group" at the target's location (i.e. to place into an on state distractor units at the target's location). On such occasions, there is a strong likelihood that the unit corresponding to the target is inhibited below threshold. If, following the inhibition of the target unit, search runs quickly to completion, targets are "missed" (i.e. the target location is rejected from search).

There were also "partial location" (PL) errors. PL errors arise on trials when, by chance, the target produces grouping at locations occupied by distractors (i.e. other units within the target's match map are placed into an on state at those locations). If the threshold for the target template is then exceeded, SERR "knows" that the target is present but has only partial information about its location.

With heterogeneous displays, the miss rates can be quite serious. Figure 3a shows that, with heterogeneous displays, miss rates increase in a

nonlinear and positively accelerating fashion, and they are overall more than four times greater than those found with homogeneous displays. PL errors also increase with display size, but do not differ so greatly between the two display types (PL rates were: homogeneous displays, .00, .07, .12, .16, and .16; heterogeneous displays, .00, .04, .07, .09, and .08, across display sizes 2, 4, 6, 8, and 9, respectively).

The miss rates with heterogeneous displays far exceed those of human subjects when instructed to minimize errors. Human miss rates tend to increase under comparable conditions, but not by more than about .0017 per item (see Fig. 3b; Humphreys et al., 1989). One way to conceptualize this is as follows. The first run of SERR corresponds to a first glance at a visual display. Processing during this glance is relatively noisy and error-prone. Since subjects strive to minimize errors under normal viewing conditions, search may continue until the error rate reaches an acceptable level. This may be achieved by checking. In the network, this is analogous to rerunning the simulation. Since misses are stochastically independent of each other, rerunning the network following an absent decision will reduce the likelihood that a target has been missed. Note here that, since the miss rate increases with display size, the probability of reruns must also increase if error rates are to be reasonably equated across the display sizes.

The full simulations reported below are based on SERR's first-pass plus checking responses. Checking was carried out by modeling the effects of rerunning the network on a proportion of target absent decision runs — in order to equate the error rate across homogeneous and heterogeneous displays (around .01) and to have a growth in miss rates across the display sizes matched to that exhibited by human subjects (.001 per item). Modeling was based on linear fits of the miss rate data and used the following procedure:

Checking was optimized, to produce the minimal reruns necessary to achieve the required miss rate. More formally, let (i) a be the expected miss rate on each run (constant); (ii) b the probability of misses after run N; and (iii) c the intended probability of misses. Then the question is: What is the necessary rate of reruns after any given run N in order to achieve the intended probability of misses? This is equivalent to asking: What is the permissible rate of terminations after run N (without further runs $N + 1$)? Let (iv) d be the necessary rate of reruns after run N and (v) $1 - d$ the permissible rate of misses. The optimal rerun strategy then requires that

if $b <= c$, terminate search: $d = 0.0$;
if $a * b > c$, rerunning is obligatory: $d = 1.0$;
if $a * b <= c$, d is given by:
$d = [1 - (c/b)]/(1 - a)$.

The intended probability of misses c is the sum of the probabilities of misses incurred by rerunning (d) and by terminating ($1 - d$) the network after run N: $c = d * (a * b) + (1 - b) * b$. Solving for d gives $d = [1 - (c/b)]/(1 - a)$. In the modeling, d was rounded to the nearest .05 value. Note that it would be nonoptimal to allow a certain amount of "early" terminations if $a * b > c$. Such early

terminations would require a disproportionately high amount of "later" reruns to achieve the intended probability of misses.

Table 1 shows an example "rerun tree" for 9-item, heterogeneous displays. The miss rate after run 1 is .220 — that is, higher than the permissible rate of .018 for a 9-item, heterogeneous display. In order to bring the miss rate down, a run with a negative decision (correct rejection or miss) must always be repeated. This reduces the miss rate to $.220 * .220 = .048$. In order to reduce the miss rate further to .018, search can be terminated with $p = .200$, but must be repeated with $p = .800$. Thus, the (total) time needed to make an absent response is

$$A = .200 * (a + a) + .800 * (a + a + a),$$

where a is the time for an absent decision on run n (correct rejection or miss). The (total) time required to make a present response is

$$P = (.780 * p + .172 * (a + p) + .030 * \\ (a + a + p))/(.780 + .172 + .030),$$

where a is the time for absent decision, p is the time for a present decision, and .780, .172, and .030 are the probabilities of a hit or run 1, 2, and 3, respectively.

Simulation 1: Homogeneous displays

Method
The target was always an inverted T, and the distractors were either all upright T's, left-oriented T's, or right-oriented T's (see Fig. 4a for an example). All displays were presented within the nine center locations of SERR's retina, with the same spacing between adjacent stimuli. Under each display size condition, the network was presented with $2 \times 3 \times 50$ runs (i.e. 50 runs for each absent/present × distractor type [T, ⊣, or ⊢] combination). The performance scores were the means of the 150 runs per absent/present × display size condition. The performance measures correspond to the usual measures obtained in visual search experiments with human subjects, namely, RT, in network iterations, and error rates (after checking).

TABLE 1
Rerun Tree for a Nine-Item, Heterogeneous Display to Reduce Miss Rate from .220 to a Permissible Miss Rate of .018

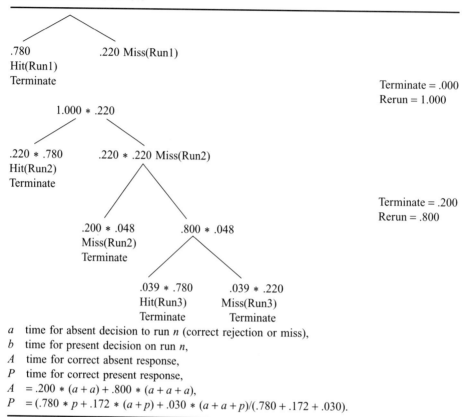

.780
Hit(Run1)
Terminate

.220 Miss(Run1)

Terminate = .000
Rerun = 1.000

1.000 * .220

.220 * .780
Hit(Run2)
Terminate

.220 * .220 Miss(Run2)

Terminate = .200
Rerun = .800

.200 * .048
Miss(Run2)
Terminate

.800 * .048

.039 * .780
Hit(Run3)
Terminate

.039 * .220
Miss(Run3)
Terminate

a time for absent decision to run n (correct rejection or miss),
b time for present decision on run n,
A time for correct absent response,
P time for correct present response,
A $= .200 * (a + a) + .800 * (a + a + a)$,
P $= (.780 * p + .172 * (a + p) + .030 * (a + a + p)/(.780 + .172 + .030)$.

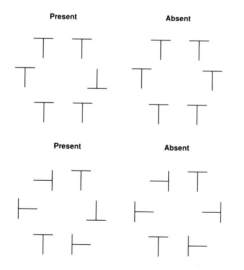

Present   Absent

Present   Absent

FIG. 4. Examples of homogeneous (a) and heterogeneous (b) displays.

Results and discussion

SERR's search RTs, in terms of network iterations, are shown in Fig. 5a. There was little effect of display size on either present or "absent" decision times; indeed, if anything, decision times tended to decrease on present trials as the display size increased from 2 to 4 items. In 2-item displays, present responses are relatively slow because there is no dominant group. Absent responses are overall faster than present responses, having an average advantage of about 2.7 iterations (10.22 iterations for absent vs 12.91 iterations for absent, averaged across the display sizes).

Simulation 2: Heterogeneous displays

Method

The target was always an inverted T; the distractors comprised at least 1 T, 1 ⊣, and 1 ⊢ (with display

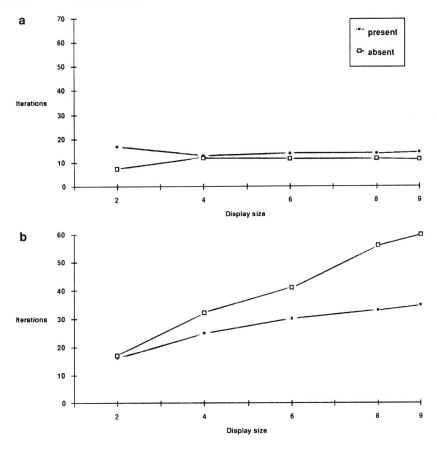

FIG. 5. SERR's absent and present RTs (in network iterations) after checking for both misses and partial location errors, for homogeneous (a) and heterogeneous (b) displays.

sizes greater than two; see Fig. 4b for an example). All possible permutations of heterogeneous display compositions were run. This was done because the display sizes used did not allow equal division between the three types of distractor. To use only one permutation would be to bias the simulation because the search times vary according to the particular targets and distractors used (see Experiment 2 here). The number of permutations for each display size is determined by a hypergeometrical distribution (see Table 2). Location of the target and distractors was disregarded because the network is not sensitive to the locations of target and distractor stimuli relative to each other.

Table 2 gives an example of the permutations that were run under one display size condition. This table lists all the permutations for 9-item displays and the (hypergeometric) probabilities for each subset of permutations, both for present and absent runs. For instance, on present runs, the most likely subset was

formed by displays that contained one target (T2), three distractors of one type (e.g. T1), three distractors of another type (e.g. T3), and two distractors of the remaining type (T4) ($p = .4995$). The least likely subset consisted of displays with one target (T2), six distractors of one type (e.g. T1), and each one distractor of the remaining two types (T3 and T4) ($p = .0001$).

Each permutation of distractors was presented to the network in 50 runs. The performance scores were averaged across all the runs within a subset of permutations; these (average) scores were then pooled across subsets, weighted by their hypergeometric probabilities.

Results and discussion

With checking, the search functions produced by SERR with heterogeneous displays (Fig. 5b) resemble those found with human subjects (Fig. 3b). In particular, both present and absent responses

TABLE 2
Nine-Item Displays: Numbers of Stimuli for Each Permutation and the Probability for Each Subset of Permutations

	Present						P	Absent						P
T	3	3	2				.4995	4	4	3	3	2	2	.5818
	1	1	1					0	0	0	0	0	0	
	3	2	3					3	2	4	2	4	3	
	2	3	3					2	3	2	4	3	4	
T	4	2	2				.2498	3	3	3				.1818
	1	1	1					0	0	0				
	2	4	2					3	3	3				
	2	2	4					3	3	3				
T	4	4	3	3	1	1	.1998	5	2	2				.0873
	1	1	1	1	1	1		0	0	0				
	3	1	4	1	4	3		2	5	2				
	1	3	1	4	3	4		2	2	5				
T	5	5	2	2	1	1	.0500	5	5	3	3	1	1	.0727
	1	1	1	1	1	1		0	0	0	0	0	0	
	2	1	5	1	5	2		3	1	5	1	5	3	
	1	2	1	5	2	5		1	3	1	5	3	5	
T	6	1	1				.0001	4	4	1				.0646
	1	1	1					0	0	0				
	1	6	1					4	1	4				
	1	1	6					1	4	4				
T								6	6	2	2	1	1	.0116
								0	0	0	0	0	0	
								2	1	6	1	6	2	
								1	2	1	6	2	6	
T								7	1	1				.0002
								0	0	0				
								1	7	1				
								1	1	7				

show a linear increase in iteration times with increasing display size. For present responses: $F(1,3) = 55.18$, $p < .005$, $r^2 = .92$. For absent responses: $F(1,3) = 565.88$, $p < .001$; $r^2 = .99$. The present:absent slope ratio was 2.7:6.1 iterations per item, which cannot, statistically, be distinguished from a 1:2 slope ratio.

Further simulation results and discussion

Absolute RTs
Using the error-checked simulation data, we can estimate the correspondence between iteration time and real time by comparing the slopes of the functions for SERR (in iterations) with that of humans (in ms). With data from Humphreys et al. (1989),

it turns out that an iteration in real time should correspond to about 15–20 ms [with heterogeneous displays, the slopes produced by SERR are 2.7 and 6.1 iterations/item for present and absent responses, respectively; in Humphreys et al. (1989), the mean slopes over subjects were 62 and 97 ms/item for present and absent responses]. Interestingly, in the version of the model run with error checking, the estimate of the overall advantage, with homogeneous displays, for absent over present responses is 45–60 ms (about 3 iterations), which compares well with the human data [around 45 ms; Humphreys et al. (1989), Experiments 1a and 2]. The pattern of intercepts produced by SERR (homogeneous present and absent and heterogeneous present and absent: 14, 11, 12, and 6 iterations) is also similar to the human data (homogeneous present and absent and heterogeneous present and absent: 503, 497, 499, and 400 ms). Thus, SERR provides a good account for the absolute RT differences between homogeneous and heterogeneous displays. Note, however, that SERR would not be refuted if RTs and iterations could not be related quantitatively. There need not be an exact correspondence between human RT and the model's iteration time; qualitative similarities are equally valid.

Variances

We also examined the variances associated with SERR's response times. A "blind" serial self-terminating search model predicts that the variances for present responses may both increase faster and be overall greater than those for absent responses (see Ward & McClelland, 1989). This is because search is terminated upon finding the target on present trials, while it proceeds exhaustively through all display items on absent trials.

Thus, the variability in the number of searches would be greatest under the present condition. Further, with absent displays, the variances should increase linearly with display size (see Schneider & Shiffrin, 1977); assuming that absent RTs reflect the sum of a number of comparison processes, one for each item, then the variance in the sum of comparison processes should be equal to the sum of the variances for each comparison process. Figure 6 presents the variances associated with SERR's search RTs after error checking (misses and partial location errors). With homogeneous displays (Fig. 6a), present variances showed no effect of display size; absent variances were greater than present and tended to increase linearly with display size (slope, .5 iteration/item, based on linear regression excluding 2-item displays). The variance for heterogeneous displays (Fig. 6b) was greater than that for homogeneous displays. With heterogeneous displays, both present and absent variances increased with display size, with present variances tending to increase

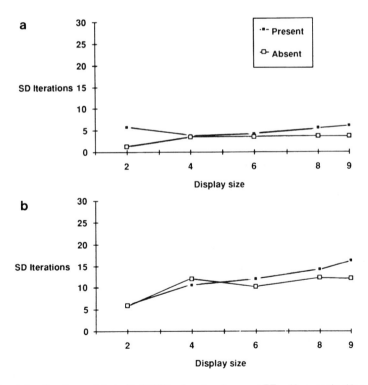

FIG. 6. *SD*s (in network iterations) associated with SERR's absent and present RTs with error checking (for misses and partial location errors) as a function of display size. (a) Homogeneous displays; (b) heterogeneous displays.

more steeply (present slope, 1.42 iteration/item; absent slope, 1.08 iteration/item). The linear components accounted for 70 and 93% of the present and absent variances, respectively.

Figure 7 presents the variances associated with human RTs (taken from Experiments 1a and 1b of Humphreys et al., 1989). With homogeneous displays, there was no effect of either target absent/present or display size (both F's < 1.0). With heterogeneous displays, there was no effect of target absent/present ($F < 1.0$), but there was a reliable effect of display size ($F(3,33) = 16.38$, $MS_e = 8773$, $p < .01$). The present variances tended to increase faster than the absent variances (the slopes of the functions were 36.8 and 21.7 ms^2/item, respectively), and the linear components accounted for most of the variance in both conditions (94.4 and 96.9%, respectively).

The patterns of variance produced by SERR and by human subjects are generally similar. The variances were greater with heterogeneous than with homogeneous distractors; and, in the former case, they tended to increase with display size. The variance was similar for present and absent trials although present variances tended to be greater and to increase more steeply with display size.

Note that the human data do not conform with the prediction of a serial self-terminating search model, that, with heterogeneous displays, present variances should increase more rapidly than absent variances, and that the present variance may overall be greater. Any tendency for a more rapid increase in present variances was weak, and there was no overall effect of response type — in accordance with SERR.

A serial self-terminating search model could assume that, in addition to variability in the number of searches required to find the target (present trials), there is also variability in the time to search each item. Since there should be more searches on absent than present trials, an overall difference between the variances on absent and present trials need not occur when single-item search times

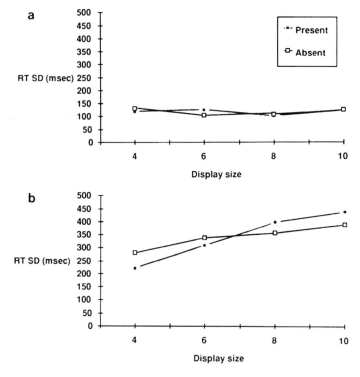

FIG. 7. *SD*s (in ms) associated with human absent and present RTs as a function of display size. (a) Homogeneous displays; (b) heterogeneous displays (data from Humphreys et al., 1989).

are highly variable. Ward and McClelland (1989) countered this argument by correlating the variance on present trials with the variance in the number of searches predicted by a serial search model. They found a strong correlation and so argued that their data reflected the variability in the number of searches required rather than variability in single-item search time. A linear regression comparing the variance in Experiment 1b of Humphreys et al. (1989) with that predicted by a serial search model gave an r^2 of .872. That is, the variability in the number of searches accounts for the variance on present trials. Hence, it is reasonable to expect a serial search model to predict that presence response variance should be greater than absent response variance.

To some extent, our data are inconsistent with those of Ward and McClelland (1989), who found greater absent than present variances in a conjunction search task with targets defined by color and form. We return to Ward and McClelland's finding under the General Discussion. Also, human performance is more variable than that of SERR, when network iterations are converted into time according to one iteration = 15–20 ms (see above). This may be attributed to additional variance contributed by the motor component (constant across display size conditions) in human responses.

Conclusions from simulations 1 and 2

With the growth in error rates equated to those found in human subjects, SERR generates an impressive fit to human data found in search for form conjunctions among both homogeneous and heterogeneous distractors. With homogeneous distractors, flat search functions are produced, with absent responses tending to be faster than present. With heterogeneous distractors, linear search functions are produced with present responses faster than absent, and present:absent slope ratios approximate 1:2. Thus, a computationally explicit parallel processing model, operating with some degree of stochastic "noise," can fit data traditionally taken to be indicative of serial, self-terminating search. SERR reiterates the arguments of Townsend (1972) that we should be cautious in directly allying search functions to process models.

The case for the psychological plausibility of SERR, however, remains to be made. Clearly, the model as currently implemented contains many simplifying assumptions, for instance, concerning how simple form conjunctions are coded and how grouping operates. Also, no justification has been given for the check process needed to match the model and the human data in errors and RTs. The psychological plausibility of SERR would be strengthened by showing that the model can be used to generate accurate predictions concerning human search. This turns out to be the case. The power of the model is in being able to account for a complete set of new results on human search. Although it may be possible to adapt other theories of search to explain single results, we suggest that it is difficult for other theories to accommodate the complete set.

Section 2: Predictions from, and tests of, SERR

SERR naturally gives rise to a number of predictions which are examined in Section 2 . The first prediction concerns the growth in miss rates on search through heterogeneous displays, when the check process is prevented. This was examined in Experiment 1. Experiment 2 examined the effects of stimulus similarity on search. Because of the way SERR maps features onto match map units, some features are more similar (and more likely to group) than others. The validity of SERR's coding of similarity was therefore tested. Experiment 3 tested a prediction arising from the implementation of grouping via facilitatory connections. SERR's grouping procedure leads to rapid rejection of stable distractor groups. Targets, being singletons, are usually detected after the rejection of such distractors. Detection may be slowed when the target is presented among homogeneous distractors relative to when it is presented alone (and thus detection is not delayed by the prior rejection of distractors). Experiment 3 contrasted search with single stimuli and search with targets presented among homogeneous distractors. Experiment 4 tested for PL errors. In particular, it examined whether subjects sometimes detect "that" a target is present without knowing "where" it is — even with form conjunction targets and heterogeneous distractors. Experiment 5 examined a prediction that arises from SERR's use of decision templates. Essentially, if SERR is prevented from coding templates for targets and distractors, it can only search via recursive rejection. This should be particularly harmful for present decisions, since in the model present responses are faster than absent responses only when the target's template reaches threshold prior to the recursive rejection of all distractors.

Experiment 1: Search with deadlines

SERR predicts that, in search for conjunction targets among heterogeneous distractors, there should be a nonlinearly accelerating increase in miss rates when checks are prevented. A test of this prediction is necessary to validate the check process in the simulations. An examination of conjunction search under deadline conditions is also of interest in its own right. There has been one previous study in which check processes in conjunction search may have been prevented. Klein and Farrell (1989) had subjects search for color–form conjunctions with displays presented for limited durations and pattern-masked. They found that miss rates increased substantially and, in their Experiment 2, nonlinearly with increasing display size. False alarm rates also showed some, relatively insignificant, increase (approximately 1% per item).

Klein and Farrell's results are interesting, since they contradict predictions of serial search models. For instance, consider what we might term the "plain vanilla" serial search model,[2] and let us assume that the deadline conditions are such as to allow subjects (on average) to search two locations. With a display size of 4, subjects search the two locations and respond correctly if the target is present at either one. If the target is not present at those locations, subjects make an unbiased guess. This produces a 50% miss rate at two locations and a 25% miss rate overall. With a display size of 6, subjects must guess whether the target is present at four locations, generating a 33% miss rate overall. The predicted miss rates are 37.5 and 40% for display sizes 8 and 10. Thus, there should

be an asymptotic increase in the miss rate up to a 50% level. If no guessing takes place, the miss rate should grow asymptotically up to a higher error plateau (100% in the limit).

Of course, subjects can adopt biased guessing strategies. For instance, in Experiment 1b of Humphreys et al. (1989), the relative probability of subjects making present to absent guesses was approximately 1:7.5 (averaged across display sizes of 4, 6, 8, and 10), making the likelihood of a target present guess 13.33%. Setting a miss rate of roughly 25% at display size 4 would then require that subjects search (on average) 3 items successfully and guess the fourth. If the number of items successfully searched is maintained at 3 for each display size, then miss rates of 21.7, 43.3, 54.2, and 60.7% would result for display sizes 4, 6, 8, and 10.

Thus, with both biased and unbiased guessing after inspection of a fixed number of locations, serial search predicts negatively accelerated quadratic miss rate functions (see Fig. 8). In contrast, SERR predicts nonlinear, positively accelerating miss rates when the check process is prevented (see Fig. 3b). The precise miss rate predicted can be estimated by running only sufficient checks to produce approximately 25% misses at display size 4. The predictions made by SERR are shown in Fig. 8, along with those derived from the unbiased and biased serial search models.

Experiment 1 examined these predictions by having subjects search for form conjunction targets among heterogeneous distractors under deadline conditions. We chose to impose a response deadline on subjects, rather than to limit exposure durations, to avoid response strategies introduced to deal with the rapid decay of the visual information (cf. Klein & Farrell, 1989).

Method

Subjects. There were eight subjects, six male and two female, aged between 22 and 35 years. All had either normal or corrected-to-normal vision.

Apparatus and stimuli. Stimulus presentation and timing was carried out using Enns, Ochs, and Rensink's (1990) VSearch package on an Apple MacIntosh IIcx computer. The target was an inverted T, and the distractors were T, ⊣, and ⊢. Under unlimited presentation conditions, search with such stimuli increases linearly with

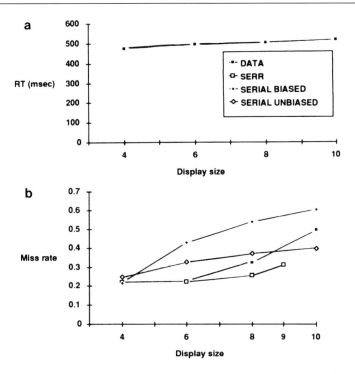

FIG. 8. Experiment 1. (a) Mean correct RTs with deadline (ms) and (b) observed miss rates as a function of display size, plus predictions from SERR and serial search models.

display size and there is roughly a 1:2 present:absent slope ratio (Humphreys et al., 1989). The stimuli were each .5 by .5 cm and were presented randomly in a display area of 24 by 16 cm, viewed from a distance of 50 cm. Responses were made by pressing the M key on the keyboard.

Design and procedures. Subjects performed a go–no go task. Pilot work showed that subjects found it difficult to adopt unbiased two-choice responding under deadline conditions, and the two-choice method also meant that their performance quickly reached chance levels. The go–no go procedure provided a more sensitive measure of performance.

At the onset of each trial, there was a fixation cross (for 500 ms), followed by a display (individual times set for each subject), and then feedback (+, –, or 0, according to whether subjects made a correct response, an error, or failed to meet the deadline). Subjects were instructed to respond as soon as they detected the presence of the target, but otherwise not to respond at all.

Each experimental session comprised two stages. In the first stage, deadlines were set for each subject. Subjects ran through blocks of 120 trials, with either display sizes 4, 6, 8; 4, 6, 10; or 4, 8, 10. If they achieved a 75% or above target detection rate on display size 4,

the deadline was decreased by 5 scans (75 ms), and a block of trials rerun. This procedure was repeated until subjects made about 75% correct detections at display size 4 over two consecutive blocks of trials. The deadline was signaled by the offset of the display. If subjects failed to respond before display offset, an error was recorded. The average deadline was 550 ms, with a range from 420 to 705 ms.

After setting the threshold, subjects received four blocks of 180 experimental trials. In each block of trials, a different combination of three of the four display sizes was presented. Overall subjects received 90 trials at each display size both with targets absent and present.

Results

Mean correct present RTs (in ms), and the miss rates, are given in Fig. 8, which also shows predictions from SERR and from a serial, self-terminating search model with either unbiased or biased guessing rates derived from Humphreys et al. (1989, Experiment 1b).

The effect of display size on RTs was not significant ($F < 1.0$). However, there was a significant main effect of display size on the target miss rate ($F(3,21) = 16.84$, $MS_e = 80.97$, $p < .001$). Misses tended to accelerate as a function of display size (Fig. 8). The data were best described by a second-order polynomial function: y = .403 − .085x + .01x², which accounted for 98% of the variance.

Relative to the human data, SERR tends to underestimate the increase in miss rate with increasing display size. Nevertheless, as with the human data, a second-order polynomial accounted for most (94%) of the variance: y = .357 − .056x + .006x². Both SERR and the human subjects generate positively accelerating miss rates as a function of display size.

The serial unbiased guessing model predicts that the data should be fit by a polynomial with a negative second-order factor, as does the serial biased guessing model: y = −.029 + .089x − .005x² and y = −.413 + .196x − .009x², respectively. That is, the miss rate would be negatively accelerating as a function of display size. This is countered by the human data.

Discussion

Under response deadline conditions, the target miss rate was positively accelerated as a function of display size. This fits the predictions of SERR and contradicts those made by serial, self-terminating search models (with both unbiased and empirically derived biased guessing). Also, RTs under the deadline condition were relatively unaffected by display size (the slope was only 6.7 ms/item). Both the RT and error functions resemble those produced when SERR is given a first "pass" at a visual display and checking is eliminated (cf. Fig. 3a). This finding gives some justification to the use of the check process in modeling linear RT functions in conjunction search under nondeadline conditions.

It is of course possible to derive variants of serial search other than the ones already considered. Two possibilities are as follows. (i) Although only a limited number of items may be serially scanned under the deadline conditions, subjects check information in feature maps to help support their decision. If this alternative strategy is effective at small but not large display sizes, the miss rate can be positively accelerated. (ii) Under the deadline conditions subjects adjust their per-

item scan time so as to check all the items in the time available. The per-item scan time may be related to the probability of target detection in such a way as to produce a positively accelerated miss function. However, account (i) suffers because, according to a serial search model such as feature integration theory (Treisman, 1988), serial search is necessary to detect conjunctions which are not represented in feature maps [see also Humphreys et al. (1989) for evidence against a role of emergent features in displays similar to those used here]. A check of activation in feature maps, even if possible, ought not to contribute to performance in the present task. Account (ii) is entirely post hoc. In addition, the time per scan would have to be adjusted on the basis of some form of initial, time-consuming subitization process. Hit rates at display size 4 in the experiment are consistent with either 2 or 3 items being detected via serial search (provided guessing is allowed); any time-demanding adjustment of the scan rate during search would be too late to beat the deadline. In contrast to these modified serial search accounts, SERR predicts the data in a straight-forward manner.

Experiment 2: Similarity effects

A second prediction of SERR concerns similarity between display members. In SERR, horizontal and vertical features are transformed onto higher-order conjunction units in a very direct way, essentially according to whether the features fall in optimal locations with in the "receptive field" of the conjunction units. When the features fall in optimal locations, activation is most pronounced. One effect of this is that target conjunctions containing horizontal and vertical line components activate distractor templates maximally when targets and distractors have features in the same relative locations. That is, similarity is coded not just in terms of the presence of features, but in terms of their spatial locations relative to the whole shape. For the stimuli used in Experiment 1, ⊥ and T (and ⊣ and ⊢) will be more similar than, for example, T and ⊣, or ⊥ and ⊢, since only the former shapes have features in matching locations. One consequence is that, in search for form conjunctions, the effects of heterogeneity should be most pronounced when one type of distractor is more similar to the target than it is to the other distractors. For instance, search for a ⊥ among T and ⊣ distractors should be more difficult than search for the same target among ⊣ and ⊢ distractors, since in the former case ⊥ and T are the more similar of the three stimuli; in the second case, ⊣ and ⊢ are more similar to each other than either is to the target. The tendency to group target and distractors together, hurting search, should be more pronounced in the first than in the second case.

A second prediction concerns search for form conjunctions among homogeneous distractors. Here flat search functions are expected for all target–distractor combinations (due to interdistractor grouping), while the advantage for absent over present responses should emerge most strongly with the most similar targets and distractors. This is because under conditions of high target–distractor similarity, there is a strong likelihood that distractor units are activated at the target location. This in turn slows the activation of the target template and retards present responses. However, this prediction is not particularly strong since the present–absent response difference may be influenced by a number of factors. In particular, when absent responses are fast (e.g. with homogeneous distractors), present responses may be made by default (e.g. the failure to respond absent after a certain time period; see Donnelly, Humphreys, & Riddoch, 1991). This may minimize variation in the absent response advantage, irrespective of target–distractor similarity.

Note that these predictions for search follow from the way in which form conjunctions are coded in SERR. Other accounts of form coding do not make similar predictions. For instance, feature integration theory (Treisman, 1988) and Duncan and Humphreys's (1989) similarity account, both presume that similarity is a function of the number of shared features in stimuli (e.g. the number of horizontal and vertical line components), rather than the arrangement of those features. Both accounts could, of course, be modified to account for similarity effects based on the arrangement of visual features; but neither at present does this. Note also that the idea of relative-position coding

runs counter to FIT's postulate that only the presence of simple features is coded in a spatially parallel manner, not their relative positions. Further, because the line components in the T's here were of equal length, elongation cannot determine the orientation of each stimulus. Approaches to form perception that stress the role of elongation in determining orientation do not predict differential similarity effects with the present stimuli (cf. Hummel & Biederman, 1992).

Method

Subjects. There were six subjects, three male and three female, all of whom had either normal or corrected-to-normal vision.

Apparatus and stimuli. The apparatus and stimuli was the same as those in Experiment 1, the only difference being that, because subjects responded absent as well as present, key presses were made on keys Z and M.

Design and procedure. Each subject took part in a single experimental session in which they received four sets of 180 trials. There were two sets of trials with homogeneous distractors, and two with heterogeneous distractors. For all conditions, the target was the same (⊥). In the homogeneous similar condition, the distractors were upright T's. In the homogeneous different condition, the distractors were ⊣'s (for half the subjects) or ⊢'s (for the other half). In the heterogeneous similar condition, the distractors were T and ⊣ (for half the subjects) or T and ⊢ (for the other half). In the heterogeneous different condition, the distractors were ⊣ and ⊢. The stimuli were constructed with identical horizontal and vertical line elements, so that items differed only in the arrangement of these elements.

At the start of each display, there was a fixation cross for 500 ms, followed by the display. The display remained on until the subject responded. Subjects then received a + or a − sign as feedback, according to whether they made the correct response or not. There were three display sizes, with 4, 6, or 8 items in the field, and 30 trials per display size for absent and present responses. Stimuli were presented at random locations in each display. Subjects received the four experimental conditions in random order.

Results

Homogeneous displays. The mean correct RTs (in ms) and errors in each condition are given in Fig. 9. Table 3 gives the summary statistics for each search function. Analysis of the RTs for the two homogeneous conditions revealed only a

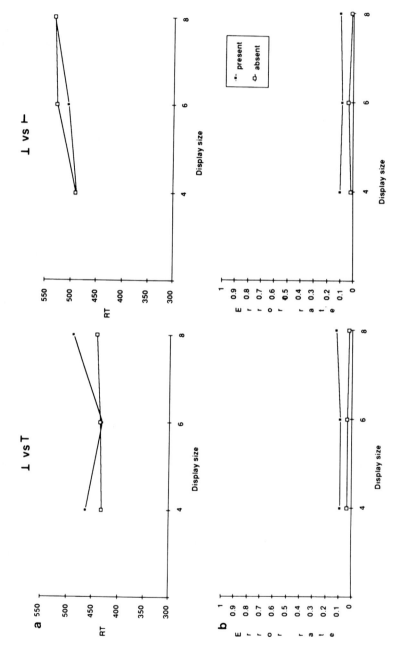

FIG. 9. Experiment 2. Homogeneous displays. (a) Mean correct RTs (ms) and (b) errors in each target–distractor condition.

TABLE 3
Summary Statistics for the Search Functions in Experiment 2 (Effects of Stimulus Similarity)

	Slope (ms/item)	*Intercept (ms)*	*Mean RT (ms)*	*% Variance*[a]
Homogeneous display				
Present	8.0	454	502	86.39
Absent	2.5	477	492	94.94
Present	9.0	459	513	90.67
Absent	1.2	453	517	83.59
Heterogeneous displays				
Present	28.0	464	634	94.55
Absent	50.5	504	806	99.90
Present	11.5	460	529	86.11
Absent	13.5	525	606	83.22

[a] Percentage variance attributable to the linear component.

significant main effect of display size ($F(2,10)$ = 16.90, MS_e = 336.8, $p < .01$). Neither the main effect of similarity nor that of target absent/present approached significance (both F's < 1.0). There were no reliable interactions.

The errors followed the same trends as the RTs, although in the analysis of the arcsine-transformed data there was a main effect of presence/absence ($F(1,9) = 50.61$, $MS_e = 0.001, p < .001$). More errors were made on present than on absent trials.

Although there was a main effect of display size with homogeneous displays, the slopes of the functions (particularly for absent responses) were very shallow (see Table 3). The functions cannot easily be attributed to serial search processes. Also, the trend for an absent advantage was only evident with similar distractors (there was a 10-ms absent advantage with similar distractors and a 4-ms present advantage with dissimilar distractors).

Heterogeneous displays. The mean correct RTs (in ms) and errors in each condition are shown in Fig. 10. There were significant main effects of distractor type ($F(1,7) = 118.38$, $MS_e = 3515$, $p < .001$), target presence/absence $F(1,9) = 40.40$, $MS_e = 6893$, $p < .001$), and display size ($F(2,10) = 9.47$, $MS_e = 64561$, $p < .01$). There were also significant interactions between distractor type and absence/presence ($F(1,10) = 19.81$, $MS_e = 10296$, $p < .001$), and distractor type and display size ($F(2,10) = 4.72$, $MS_e = 41030, p < .05$). The trend

for a three-way interaction between distractor type, absence/presence, and display size failed to reach significance ($F(2,10) = 2.78$, $MS_e = 901$, $p > .05$).

Analysis of the arcsine-transformed error scores showed a significant main effect of display size ($F(2,10) = 4.36$, $MS_e = 0.001$, $p < .05$). More errors occurred with larger display sizes. The search functions for the inverted T versus upright and left-oriented T discrimination were close to those expected from a serial self-terminating search process. There were substantial slopes and a present:absent slope ratio of 1:1.79. The inverted T versus left- and right-oriented T discrimination was considerably easier, with shallower slopes and a present:absent slope ratio of 1:1.17 (Table 3).

Simulations

Method. SERR was tested using similar stimuli to those employed with the human subjects. There were three display sizes (4, 6, and 8). The target was always ⊥. The distractors were either homogeneous or heterogeneous, and they were either similar (homogeneous T's or heterogeneous T's and ⊥'s) or dissimilar to the target (homogeneous ⊣'s or heterogeneous ⊣'s and ⊢'s). There were 50 trials for each condition. The target, when present, replaced a distractor. In the heterogeneous distractor conditions, it randomly replaced each type of distractor on 25 trials.

Results. Figure 11 shows the mean iteration time required by SERR, with the miss rate set at .01, .013, and .017 for display sizes 4, 6 and 8, in each condition.

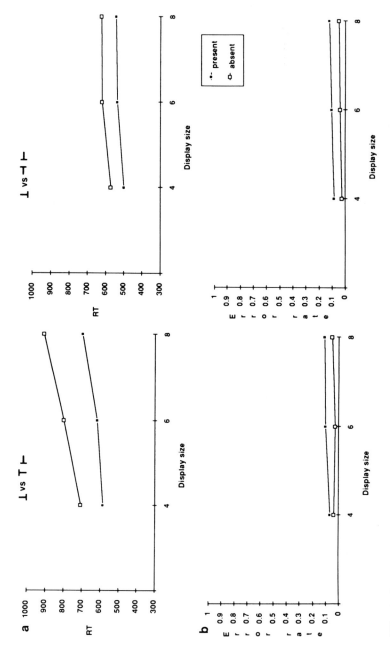

FIG. 10. Experiment 2. Heterogeneous displays. (a) Mean correct RTs (ms) and (b) errors in each target–distractor similarity condition.

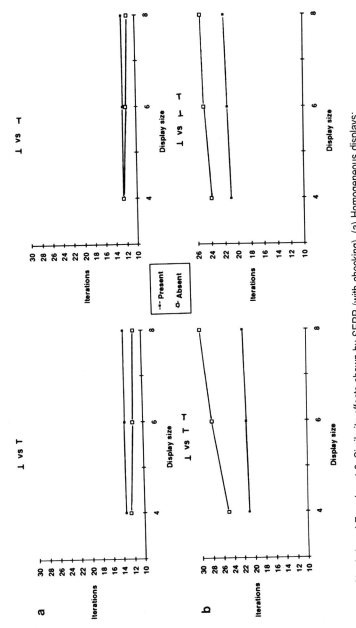

FIG. 11. Simulation of Experiment 2. Similarity effects shown by SERR (with checking). (a) Homogeneous displays; (b) heterogeneous displays.

The search functions are similar to those of the human observers. With homogeneous distractors, the advantage for absent over present trials was larger with similar distractors (an average 1.5 iteration advantage with similar distractors vs an average .5 iterations with dissimilar distractors). With both similar and dissimilar distractors, the search functions were either flat or decreasing. With heterogeneous distractors, performance was worse with similar than with dissimilar distractors. With similar distractors the slopes for present and absent responses were .25 and 1.25 iterations/item, and the linear component accounted for over 98% of the variance. With dissimilar distractors the slopes for present and absent responses were .125 and .375, respectively; the linear component accounted for 96% of the variance on absent trials, but only for 75% of the variance on present trials.[3]

Discussion

Both SERR and human observers show effects of similarity based on the relative locations of stroke features, not just on the presence of the features. Both also show stronger similarity effects with heterogeneous than with homogeneous distractors; with homogeneous distractors there is a larger "absent advantage" with similar distractors; with heterogeneous distractors there is a larger "present advantage" with similar distractors. These variations in human performance show that not all form conjunctions are perceived as equally similar because they contain the same features. Form conjunctions are perceived as more similar if their features fall in the same relative location, defined in terms of each form's orientation. This is captured in the way SERR encodes forms. The data also show that orientation does not necessarily depend on elongation (since the stimuli were not elongated), but they are not informative about alternative ways in which orientation might be coded. For instance, the axis of symmetry could be important (cf. Palmer, 1985), but this is not examined further.

Experiment 3: The cost of recursive rejection

In SERR, grouping is implemented in a particular way: through excitatory connections between like stimuli. As already noted (see Decisions on Implementations), grouping could also be implemented via inhibitory connections, so the choice

of excitatory connections needs justification. Experiment 3 tests this implementation choice. One consequence of using excitatory grouping mechanisms is that homogeneous distractors tend first to be rejected as a group before a singleton form conjunction target is detected. It is possible that this may delay RTs to the target, relative to when the target is presented alone. This was tested in Experiment 3, in which we examined performance with displays containing fewer items than hitherto examined.

Method

There were 10 subjects, 6 male and 4 female, all with either normal or corrected-to-normal vision. The subjects were presented with displays containing between one and five stimuli. The target was an inverted T and the distractors were upright T's. The stimuli were presented using an Apple II Europlus microcomputer, and they appeared at random, nonoverlapping positions within a virtual circle, diameter 4° 49″ in visual angle. Individual stimuli were .7 cm high by .5 cm wide. Subjects made button-press responses, responding present with their preferred hand. There were 280 trials, 40 at display sizes 1 and 5, 64 at display sizes 2 and 4, and 72 at display size 3. A target appeared on half the trials. There were 20 practice trials.

Results

Mean correct RTs are given in Fig. 12a. Error rates were low: .09, .07, .03, .01, and .01 on absent trials and .07, .04, .06, .09, and .09 on present trials, across display sizes 1–5. Descriptive statistics for the search functions are presented in Table 4. Analysis of both RTs and errors revealed a reliable display size × present/absent interaction, $F(4,36) = 4.37$ and 5.81, $MS_e = 610$ and $.055$, $p < .01$ and $.001$, respectively. On present responses, RTs and errors increased linearly as a function of the display size, $F(1,9) = 4.49$ and 7.56, $MS_e = 647$ and $.079$, $p = .06$ and $p < .025$, respectively, for the linear components. On absent responses, there was a reliable quadratic trend in the RT data, $F(1,9) = 9.40$, $MS_e = 254$, $p < .01$. Errors decreased linearly across the display sizes, $F(1,9) = 7.80$, $MS_e = .075$, $p < .025$.

Experiment 3 confirms that subjects can detect a form conjunction target among homogeneous distractors on the basis of a spatially parallel search.

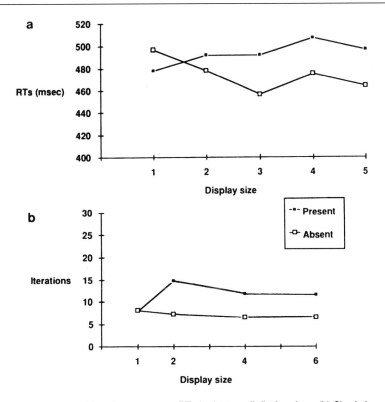

FIG. 12. (a) Homogeneous displays. Mean human correct RTs (ms) at small display sizes. (b) Simulation of Experiment 3. SERR's absent and present RTs (in network iterations).

TABLE 4
Summary Statistics for the Search Functions in Experiment 3 (the Cost of Recursive Rejection; Display Sizes One through Five)

	Slope (ms/item)	Intercept (ms)	Mean RT (ms)	% Variance[a]
Present	3	487	493	30.00
Absent	−7	495	474	49.08

[a] Percentage variance attributable to the linear component.

Search rates were in all cases less than 10 ms/item and absent RTs were faster than present. Even so, target detection was more efficient when it was presented alone than when it was presented among homogeneous distractors, and there was a reliable linear increase in both RTs and errors as the numbers of distractors increased from one to five. In contrast, absent responses were facilitated as the display size increased. The decreasing RT–display size function for absent responses is not due to the average interitem spacing being less at the larger display sizes. We have obtained essentially the same result using displays with items plotted so that interitem spacing is equated at the smaller and larger display sizes.

Simulation

Search was for an inverted T among upright T's, using display sizes of 1, 2, 4, and 6. There were 50 trials for each condition. Error rates were generally low and so checking was not implemented. Fig. 12b shows the resultant search functions.

On absent trials, RTs (in iterations) decreased as there were more distractors in the field. This speeding in RTs occurs because, with more distractors, grouping becomes established more quickly and the distractor's template is activated in fewer iterations. However, there is an opposite effect on present responses. This general pattern of performance — decreasing absent functions and increasing present functions (relative to display size 1) — fits with that observed with humans.

There is one discrepant aspect of SERR's performance: present responses are particularly slowed at display size 2. Present responses are then particularly slow because single targets and distractors are presented; consequently there is no dominant group. Selection is slowed because of the competition between targets and distractors to establish the dominant group.

Discussion

People can be faster at detecting a single target than at detecting a target among homogeneous distractors — even when performance seems based on spatially parallel search (e.g. when the slopes of the search functions are under 10 ms per item, there are fast absent responses). This same general pattern is shown by SERR. Mutual inhibition between distractors ought to lead to faster target detection as more distractors are presented. The data contradict this. Rather they are consistent with the early selection of grouped distractors prior to the selection of the target.

SERR produced one result that does not match the human data: for SERR, present RTs are particularly slowed at display size 2. Present responses are slowed under that condition because of competition between target and distractors to establish a dominant group. It is possible that something similar occurs in humans; however, the availability of other response strategies in humans may mask any effect. For instance, when there are decreasing Rt–display size functions on absent trials (as here), subjects may respond present by default — after an absent deadline has passed. The data suggest that this was not the only strategy adopted, since there were small but reliable increases in present RTs across the display sizes; however, if a deadline strategy was adopted on some trials, this could mask small perturbations in present RTs across the display sizes. Another possibility is that responses were based on a joint "target + distractor" template which would allow responses to be made without first resolving the competition for grouping. SERR does not have such additional strategies available.

Experiment 3 shows that, in search for a form conjunction target among homogeneous distractors, present responses can be slowed by distractors relative to when the target is presented alone. This suggests that grouped distractors are selected prior to targets, slowing present responses. Note also that this result differs from previous search results from tasks where targets and distractors differ in terms of a salient disjunctive feature, where decreasing RT–display size functions have been observed on present responses (Bacon & Egeth, 1991; Sagi & Julesz, 1987). We return to this under the General Discussion.

Experiment 4: Knowing "What" but not "Where"

We noted earlier that, in runs of SERR, the template for the target occasionally exceeded its threshold when the target produced grouping at distractor locations. On such occasions, the network had sufficient evidence to respond *that* a target was present, but not *where* it was. We termed this a PL error.

The prediction that PL errors occur in search for form conjunctions contradicts the prediction derived from serial search accounts. For instance, feature integration theory holds that arbitrary conjunctions between visual features are formed by subjects focally attending to the location where the features are registered (e.g. Treisman & Gelade, 1980; Treisman & Gormican, 1988). Hence, subjects should not know that a conjunction target is present without also knowing where it is. Support for this comes from studies requiring subjects to decide whether a color–form conjunction is present or absent in a display and, when present, where it is. There are, typically, few occasions when subjects know the target's identity but not its location; further, target mislocations fall within the vicinity of the target's actual location (e.g. Treisman & Gelade, 1980).

However, other data suggest that the location and identity of conjunction targets are not inextricably linked. Müller and Rabbitt (1989) had subjects match briefly presented targets with a previewed comparison stimulus. The distractors presented simultaneously with the target shared many target features (e.g. the target was a T and the distractors +'s). On some occasions, subjects could be at chance at same/different judgements but above chance at judging the target's location; conversely, on other occasions, they could be at chance in indicating the target's location but above chance at same/different judgements.

A problem with Müller and Rabbitt's experiment is that there was no converging evidence that targets and distractors were distinguished only by the conjunction of their features. For example, the presence or absence of a line intersection feature distinguish T's and +'s (Müller & Rabbitt, 1989). In that case, evidence for knowing what but not where a stimulus is would be consistent with features being detected without accurate localization, rather than this also being true of form conjunctions (although the converse finding, of knowing where but not what a stimulus is, cannot be accounted for in this way).

SERR accommodates both *what* and *where* errors in search for form conjunctions. *Where* errors occur on partial location trials. *What* errors can occur when there is inaccurate coding at the match map level along with accurate coding in the map of locations (this happens on both miss and false alarm trials; see also Humphreys et al., 1992a).

Experiment 4 tested whether identity and location judgments can be dissociated for form conjunctions. Subjects were presented with 8 items, two in each quadrant of the display, and they had to decide on the presence and location of a target. "Where" responses were required even on trials on which subjects responded absent; on such occasions, subjects were asked to guess which location a target might have occupied if it had been present. This allowed us to estimate the full contingency relations between presence/absence and location responses. The target was an inverted T, and the distractors were T's, ⊣'s, and ⊢'s. Humphreys et al. (1989) showed that, in visual

search, linear functions are found for such discriminations, with a present:absent slope ratio of about 1:2 (Fig. 3b). Thus, there is converging evidence that distractors contain the same features as the target.

There were two stimulus exposure durations. Joint presence/absence and localization responses may be impaired (relative to either judgement alone) because of the increased task and memory load. However, task and memory load constraints are constant across exposure durations. An interaction between exposure duration and mislocalization would rule out the possibility that mislocalizations are only produced by these constraints. SERR predicts such an interaction, with mislocalizations most likely at short exposure durations, when checking is minimized.

Method

Subjects. There were eight subjects, six female and two male, aged between 16 and 34 years. All had either normal or corrected-to-normal vision. They were paid £4.00 for each experimental session.

Apparatus and stimuli. Stimuli were presented on a Tektronix 608 X-Y display with P-31 phosphor. The CRT was controlled by a LSI-11/23 computer through a CED-502 interface; the display system used was EMDISP (Shepherd, 1984). The laboratory was illuminated by fluorescent overhead lighting to minimize the visible persistence of the P-31 phosphor. Subjects viewed the CRT from a distance of 50 cm with their heads resting on a chin rest.

Displays consisted of a central fixation mark and a circular arrangement of eight T-type stimuli which occupied the 1, 2, 4, 5, 7, 8, 10, and 11 o'clock positions (i.e. there were no stimuli on the vertical and horizontal axes). The eccentricity of the stimuli was 2.5° and their size 0.6°. On present trials, displays contained one inverted T-target at one position (in one of the four quadrants) and upright, left-, and right-oriented T-distractors (in random mixture) at the remaining locations; on absent trails, displays contained distractors at all locations.

Subjects responded by pressing designated keys on a hand-sized keypad in front of them, which was sampled by the CED 502 interface. For the detection response, subjects had to press one of four horizontally arranged keys (from left to right, 1 = yes/certain, 2 = yes/uncertain, 3 = no/uncertain, 4 = no/certain); for the localization response, they pressed two of four keys arranged in a square and representing the quadrants of the display

(3 = upper-right quadrant; 7 = lower-right quadrant 2; 6 = lower-left quadrant; 2 = upper-left quadrant).

Design and procedure. Trials started with the presentation of a fixation point. This was followed, after 500 ms by a display of T-type stimuli, with the individual exposure times set for each subject. Note that there were no postdisplay masks, which could have caused a specific decrement in localization accuracy (cf. Mewhort & Campbell, 1978; Mewhort, Campbell, Marchetti, & Campbell, 1981). Subjects responded by pressing the designated detection and localization keys. They were provided with feedback only after completed blocks of trials, when they were told their overall detection d' values. The intertrial interval was 500 ms. Subjects were instructed to respond as accurately as possible and avoid making erroneous key presses. They were told to monitor their responses visually and to use only one finger of one hand (to prevent response errors due to overlearned motor sequences).

There were two sessions. In the first, threshold exposure times were determined so as to allow individuals to achieve a performance level of about $D' = 2.0$. The average time thus estimated was 160 ms (with a range between 50 and 250 ms).

The second session consisted of two blocks of 240 trials, separated by an interval of 15 min. In one block, the exposure time was "long"; i.e. the same as that estimated in the practice session. In the other block, the time was "short"; i.e. 50 or, respectively, 25 ms shorter than the long time, depending upon whether a subject's long time was over or below 100 ms. Each block contained of 120 present and 120 absent trials, in random order. On present trials, the target was equally likely to appear in all quadrants of the display. Half the subjects were given the block with the long time first and that with the short time second; for the other half, the sequence was reversed. Further, half the subjects gave the detection response first and the localization response second; for the other half, the order was reversed.

By pressing two localization keys, subjects indicated the upper, lower, right, or left half of the display in which they had "seen" the target (diagonal responses were not permitted). The location response was counted as correct if the half-field containing the target had been correctly indicated. Therefore, effectively, the localization response involved a two-forced-choice decision, as did the detection (yes–no) response.

Results

The data were analyzed in two stages. In the first, Detection (D), responses were counted as correct if the detection (yes–no) responses were correct, irrespective of localization responses. In the second, Detection-plus-Localization ($D + L$), responses were counted as correct only if both the detection and localization responses were correct. d' scores were estimated from the Receiver Operating Characteristic (ROC) curves using Dorfman and Alf's (1969) maximum likelihood (ML) approach. Figure 13 presents the mean d' estimates, as a function of exposure duration (long or short) and analysis stage (D and $D + L$).

An ANOVA of d' with main terms for exposure duration and analysis stage revealed all effects

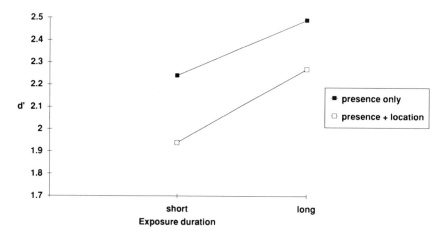

FIG. 13. Experiment 4: Knowing "where" and "what" — heterogeneous displays. Mean d' estimates as a function of exposure duration and type of decision (Detection and Detection-plus-Localization).

to be significant or marginally significant: (i) exposure duration: $F(1,7) = 4.31$, $MS_e = 0.1540$, $.075 > p > .05$; (ii) analysis stage: $F(1,7) = 6.77$, $MS_e = 0.0795$, $p < .035$; (iii) two-way interaction: $F(1,7) = 5.29$, $MS_e = .0023$, $p < .055$. Performance was worse with short than with long stimulus durations, and it was lower for joint $D + L$ than for D alone. Further, the performance loss between D and $D + L$ was greater with short than with long exposure times.

Discussion

Subjects' ability to detect the presence of a form conjunction can be superior to their ability to discern its location. This was particularly the case for the shorter of the two stimulus durations used here, even though response and memory load effects should be equated across the durations. The interaction between Detection/Localization performance and stimulus duration also rules out any argument that target localization was simply harder here, or that localization errors were produced by extraneous factors such as tending to respond with a key on the same side as the key used to make the detection response.[4] Instead, the data suggest that accurate localization is sometimes achieved only by a time-consuming checking process, which is limited under short exposure conditions.

Experiment 4 agrees with SERR's prediction that PL errors should occur in conjunction search. Previous findings, indicating that location errors with conjunction targets are clustered around a target's location (e.g. Treisman & Gelade, 1980), are also consistent with this. In SERR, PL errors are produced by grouping among display elements. To the extent that grouping is spatially limited (e.g. if within-map cross talk is only to near-neighbor locations), any uncertainty concerning the location of a conjunction target will be limited to the surrounding positions. It is nevertheless the case that detection can be significantly better than localization even in conjunction search, a finding contradictory to a serial search account.

Experiment 5: Search for singleton conjunctions

A fifth prediction from SERR concerns a contrast between two types of conjunction search.

Standardly, subjects search for a prespecified target. However, it is also possible to perform conjunction searches where subjects look for a single item of one (unspecified) type in a display. We term this search for a singleton conjunction, distinguishing it from the case where search is affected by the presence of an odd singleton feature in the display (cf. Pashler, 1988). In SERR, prespecified conjunction targets can be detected either by the target template reaching threshold or by the rejection of distractors. The target template can sometimes reach threshold before all the distractors have been rejected, making present responses faster than when they have to rely on recursive rejection of all the distractors. However, responding present by template activation is not possible in singleton search, since the target is not prespecified. In SERR, singleton search can only operate via the recursive rejection process. This should particularly disadvantage present responses relative to when the target is prespecified. Note that absent responses are based on recursive rejection in both cases. Indeed, absent responses may be faster than present responses even with heterogeneous distractors, as present responses will typically depend on detecting a target once all the distractors are rejected.

SERR provides an additional source of fast absent responses with heterogeneous distractors, when the display size is small. When like distractors form weak groups, containing, say, only two items, one of the items can be grouped with a dominant distractor group and inhibited — i.e. "missed." If this occurs, SERR can find two singleton targets, the real one and the leftover member of the weak group. The only way to make a decision in this circumstance is to rerun the search. Note that, when singleton distractors (i.e. leftover members of weak distractor groups) are incorrectly detected on absent trials, "false alarms" are made.

SERR's predictions again contrast with those of serial search models. In the general case, in serial search, singleton targets may be detected only once all the items in a display have been scanned. Search RTs should increase linearly with display size, with the slopes being equal for present and absent responses. Further, the slopes for present and absent functions should be equivalent and equal to those on absent trials in standard conjunction search with the same stimuli. A departure from this prediction may be made under particular circumstances. This is when a limited number of distractor types is used in an experiment. Then a target may be detected as soon as the scan finds the maximum number of stimulus types possible in the experiment, even without checking all the display members. This was possible in Experiment 5 because only two distractors types were used. With two distractor types, subjects could respond present as soon as a third, different type of item was encountered (e.g. on occasions as early as the third scan). This could render the slopes on present trials shallower than those on absent, but absent responses should not be faster than present.

In view of these contrasting predictions, the finding of fast absent responses with heterogeneous distractors would provide strong evidence in favor of SERR. Experiment 5 examined singleton search with both homogeneous and heterogeneous distractors.

Method

Subjects. There were six subjects, four female and two male, aged between 26 and 34 years. All had either normal or corrected-to-normal vision. They were paid £4.00 for each experimental session.

Apparatus and stimuli. The apparatus was the same as that in Experiment 4. The laboratory was dimly illuminated (to eliminate reflections on the CRT). Displays consisted of a central fixation mark and 6, 8, or 10 (or 5, 7, or 9) stimuli, arranged with equal spacing around the circumference of an imaginary circle. The eccentricity of the stimuli was 2.5° and their size 0.6°. Subjects responded by pressing designated (present or absent) keys on a hand-sized keypad in front of them, which was sampled by the laboratory interface system.

Design and procedures. Trials started with the presentation of a fixation point. This was followed, after 500 ms, by a display of T-type stimuli. The display stayed on until the subjects responded. Feedback was provided in the form of a brief "bleep" (of the bell of the computer terminal) which followed an incorrect response. The intertrial interval was 500 ms (tripled after an incorrect response). Subjects were instructed to respond as quickly as possible.

The experiment comprised six sessions. In the first, the subjects were familiarized with all the (four) display conditions. Experimental sessions two to five were devoted to one particular display condition: (i) homogeneous–blocked, (ii) homogeneous–random, (iii) heterogeneous–blocked, or (iv) heterogeneous–random. There was also a sixth session which presented heterogeneous–random displays with 5, 7, or 9 items (instead of the 6, 8, or 10 items presented in the previous sessions). This session was included because the data showed that an absent advantage did occur, but only at the smaller display size (display size 6). By including display sizes 5–9 we were able to sample a range of smaller display sizes in more detail.

Under the homogeneous display conditions, all the distractors were of the same type and the target was of a different type. There were six homogeneous subconditions: search for T vs inverted T's or I's; search for inverted T vs T's or I's; and search for I vs T's or inverted T's. Under the heterogeneous display conditions, the distractors were of two different types and the target of a third type. There were three heterogeneous subconditions: T vs inverted T's and I's; inverted T vs T's and I's; I vs T's and inverted T's. Performance was averaged across the different distractor types.

Homogeneous and heterogeneous displays were presented in blocked and random conditions. In the blocked conditions, subjects searched for a (constant) target that was prespecified at the beginning of a block of trials. In the random conditions, blocks of trials consisted of all subconditions in randomized order; that is, the target could vary from trial to trial. Thus, the blocked conditions required the standard type of search, while the random conditions required search for a singleton conjunction (see above). In the blocked conditions, there was varied mapping of target and distractors across trial blocks; in the random conditions, there was varied mapping across successive trials (cf. Schneider & Shiffrin, 1977; Shiffrin & Schneider, 1977).

Under the blocked conditions, the subjects were shown the target (T, inverted T, or I) in the center of the display at the beginning of each block of trials. Subjects were then given 10 practice trials (with the prespecified target), followed by 120 experimental trials. The latter consisted of 3 display sizes (6, 8, or 10 items) × 20 present and 20 absent trials, presented in randomized order. The order of the subconditions was randomized. In the random conditions, there were also 120 trials (3 display sizes × 20 present and 20 absent trials) per subcondition defined by a particular target. However, the subconditions were varied within each trial block. In both the blocked and random conditions, there were breaks after each 60 experimental trials. Each homogeneous and heterogeneous condition (blocked and random) consisted of 720 trials (6 subconditions × 120 trials for homogeneous displays; 3 subconditions presented twice × 120 trials for heterogeneous displays).

The order of the homogeneous–blocked, homogeneous–random, heterogeneous–blocked, and heterogeneous–random conditions was balanced across sessions and subjects. However, within the homogeneous and heterogeneous conditions, the order of blocked and random displays was completely balanced.

Results

Homogeneous displays. The search RT functions and error rates for the homogeneous–blocked and homogeneous–random conditions (averaged over all six subconditions) are shown in Fig. 14. Summary statistics of the search functions are given in Table 5.

RTs. Separate ANOVAs were carried out for the blocked and random condition RTs, with main terms for display subcondition, absent/present, and display size. These revealed the following significant effects.

Homogeneous blocked: (i) display condition: $F(5,25) = 5.72$, $MS_e = .0025$, $p < .005$; (ii) absent/present: $F(1,5) = 11.20$, $MS_e = .0025$, $p < .025$; (iii) display size: $F(2,10) = 16.80$, $MS_e = .0008$, $p < .001$;

(iv) display condition × absent/present interaction: $F(5,25) = 5.09$, $MS_e = .0005$, $p < .005$; (v) display condition × display size interaction: $F(10,50) = 2.18$, $MS_e = .0006$, $p < .05$.

Homogeneous random: (i) display condition: $F(5,25) = 4.29$, $MS_e = .0033$, $p < .01$; (ii) display size: $F(2,10) = 16.15$, $MS_e = .0009$, $p < .005$; (iii) display condition × absent/present interaction: $F(5,25) = 5.98$, $MS_e = .0025$, $p < .005$. Note that the main effect of absent/present was not significant: $F(1,5) = 0.09$, $MS_e = .0040$, ns.

In the homogeneous–blocked condition, present RTs were faster than absent (449 as compared to 472 ms). The search RTs showed an increase with increasing display size, but the slopes were shallow for both present and absent responses (4.3 and 9.0 ms per item, respectively; see Table 4).

Under the homogeneous–random condition, there was no overall difference between present and absent RTs (552 as compared to 550 ms). However, there was an absent advantage in four of the six subconditions (note the significant display condition × absent/present interaction). The search RTs showed again an increase with increasing display size, but the slopes were shallow for both present and absent responses (4.5 and 9.0 ms per item, respectively; see Table 4).

TABLE 5
Summary Statistics for the Search Functions in Experiment 5 (Singleton Search)

	Slope (msec/item)	*Intercept (msec)*	*Mean RT (msec)*	*% Variance*[a]
		Homogeneous–blocked		
Present	4.3	416	449	97.20
Absent	9.0	400	472	99.10
		Homogeneous–random		
Present	4.5	516	552	98.38
Absent	9.0	480	550	79.27
		Heterogeneous–blocked (6, 8, 10)		
Present	25.0	464	599	99.99
Absent	50.0	504	724	99.76
		Heterogeneous–random (6, 8, 10)		
Present	25.8	811	1017	94.02
Absent	73.5	440	998	99.65
		Heterogeneous–random (5, 7, 9)		
Present	38.5	647	916	99.99
Absent	58.3	461	863	99.87

[a] Percentage variance attributable to the linear component.

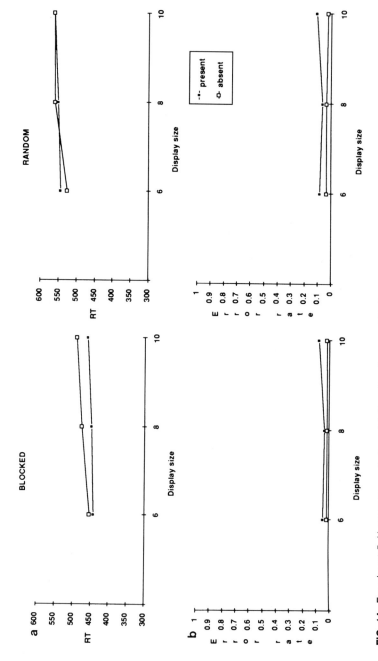

FIG. 14. Experiment 5. Homogeneous displays. (a) Absent and present RTs (in ms) and (b) error rates for the homogeneous–blocked and homogeneous–random conditions (averaged over six subconditions).

A combined ANOVA of the homogeneous–blocked and homogeneous–random conditions, with an additional main term for blocked/random, revealed the following effects: (i) blocked/random: $F(1,5) = 58.92$, $MS_e = .0150$, $p < .005$; (ii) blocked/random × absent/present interaction: $F(1,5) = 22.53$, $MS_e = .0008$, $p < .01$; (iii) blocked/random × absent/present × display condition interaction: $F(5,25) = 3.38$, $MS_e = .0012$, $p < .025$.

Overall, RTs were shorter in the blocked than the random condition. Further, although there was no (overall) absent advantage with either the blocked or the random condition, present responses were more disadvantaged by the random presentation of display subconditions (note the blocked/random × absent/present interaction and the blocked/random × absent/present × display condition interaction).

Errors. Error rates were low and there was no sign of a speed–accuracy trade-off. In summary, search in all the homogeneous conditions was relatively efficient (with slopes of less than 10 ms per item). Although there was no overall absent advantage in either the blocked or the random condition, present responses were selectively disadvantaged by the random condition.

Heterogeneous displays. The search RT functions for the heterogeneous–blocked and heterogeneous–random conditions (averaged over all three subconditions) are shown in Fig. 15. Summary statistics of the search functions are given in Table 5.

RTs. Separate ANOVAs of the blocked and random condition RTs with main terms for display subcondition, absent/present, and display size revealed the following significant effects. Heterogeneous–blocked: (i) display condition: $F(2,10) = 15.17$, $MS_e = .0177$, $p < .005$; (ii) absent/present: $F(1,5) = 10.76$, $MS_e = .0392$, $p < .025$; (iii) display size: $F(2,10) = 24.35$, $MS_e = .0088$, $p < .001$; (iv) display condition × display size interaction: $F(4,20) = 3.16$, $MS_e = .0017$, $p < .05$; (v) absent/present × display size interaction: $F(2,10) = 5.63$, $MS_e = .0049$, $p < .025$.

Heterogeneous–random (6/8/10): (i) display condition: $F(2,10) = 6.85$, $MS_e = .0215$, $p < .025$; (ii) display size: $F(2,10) = 66.62$, $MS_e = .0054$, $p < .001$; (iii) display condition × absent/present interaction: $F(2,10) = 4.76$, $MS_e = .0178$, $p < .05$;

(iv) absent/present × display size interaction: $F(2,10) = 27.65$, $MS_e = .0031$, $p < .001$. Note that the main effect of absent/present was not significant ($F(1,5) = .045$, $MS_e = .0217$, ns.).

Heterogeneous–random (5/7/9): (i) absent/present: $F(1,5) = 8.34$, $p < .05$; (ii) display size: $F(2,10) = 30.85$, $p < .001$; (iii) display condition × absent/present interaction: $F(2,10) = 5.41$, $p < .05$; (iv) absent/present × display size interaction: $F(2,10) = 6.54$, $p < .025$.

In the heterogeneous–blocked condition, present RTs were overall faster than absent (599 as compared to 724 ms). Search RTs showed a marked increase with increasing display size, with a present:absent slope ratio of 1:2.1. (Linear regressions: absent $F(1,1) = 179.88$, $p < .05$, $r^2 = .98$; present $F(1,1) = 20,981.83$, $p < .01$, $r^2 = 1.00$.) The overall search time, the magnitude of the present advantage, and the slope of the search functions depended on the display condition, with T vs inverted T's and I's showing the longest RTs and the greatest present advantage and slopes.

In the heterogeneous–random condition with 6, 8, or 10 display elements, there was no overall difference between present and absent RTs. Nevertheless, absent responses were 102 ms faster than present at display size 6 (Fig. 15). The search RTs showed a present:absent slope ratio of 1:2.8. (Linear regressions: absent $F(1,1) = 288.12$, $p < .05$, $r^2 = .99$; present $F(1,1) = 15.73$, ns, $r^2 = 0.83$.)

In the heterogeneous–random condition with five, seven, or nine display elements, there was an overall advantage for absent over present (863 ms as compared to 916 ms). The search RTs increased with increasing display size, with a present:absent slope ratio of 1:1.5. (Linear regressions: absent $F(1,1) = 368.75$, $p < .05$, $r^2 = .99$; present $F(1,1) = 18,775.77$, $p < .01$, $r^2 = 1.00$.) Absent RTs were faster than present with 5- and 7-item displays (see Fig. 15).

Taking the two heterogeneous–random conditions together, the present:absent slope ratio is about 1:2 (absent: 65.63 ms per item; present: 32.25 ms per item; averaged over the two display size conditions). At display sizes smaller than 8 or 9 items, there is an absent advantage; at greater display sizes, there is a present advantage.

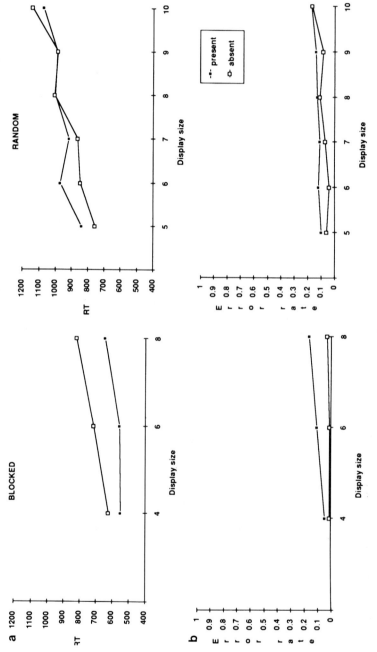

FIG. 15. Experiment 5. Heterogeneous displays. (a) Absent and present RTs (in ms) and (b) error rates for the heterogeneous–blocked and heterogeneous–random conditions (averaged over three subconditions).

Errors. The error rates were generally low and there was no sign of a speed–error trade-off. In summary, with both heterogeneous–blocked and heterogeneous–random displays, the search RT functions grew linearly with increasing display size, with a present:absent slope ratio of approximately 1:2. With heterogeneous–blocked displays, absent RTs were slower than present at all display sizes. However, with heterogeneous–random displays, absent RTs were faster than present at display sizes of less than 8 or 9 items. This absent advantage cannot be accounted for in terms of a bias towards responding absent. RTs were absolutely slower, and errors more frequent, with heterogeneous–random than with heterogeneous–blocked displays.

Simulation

To provide comparable data to that in Experiment 5, SERR was run with singleton target displays of 5, 6, 7, 8, and 9 items. Present displays consisted of one target ($\perp$) and two types of distractor ($\dashv$ or T). On absent trials, the target was replaced by one distractor. The numbers of each type of distractor were balanced as closely as possible (50 trials were run with each distractor type occurring one more time than the other). Figure 16 shows the decision times with the errors equated to those found in the human data. This meant running a check process to reduce misses, cases where the model records "two singletons" (due to incorrect inhibition of a distractor), and cases

where targets are coded at more than one location (PL errors).

SERR generates faster absent than present responses at the smaller display sizes (5 and 6), and faster present than absent responses at the larger display sizes (7–9). The present:absent slope ratio produced by SERR is about 1:8. This is markedly different from the 1:2 ratio produced by human subjects. Note however, that the present slope depends largely on the two singleton rate accepted after rechecking. If the accepted rate decreased with increasing display size, the present RTs would exhibit a correspondingly stronger increase (approximating the 1:2 present:absent slope ratio). Importantly, under this circumstance, the crossover interaction would remain.

Discussion

Experiment 5 shows that search for singleton conjunctions can produce an absent advantage even with heterogeneous displays, at least when the display size is small.[5] This finding, and the slope difference between absent and present responses, contradicts serial search models. A serial model could account for faster absent than present responses providing that, with present responses, subjects check the display to verify that a singleton target is present. Checking would be necessary if (for example) subjects kept a running count of the number of each stimulus type in the display, and there was some decay on the number count. However, if the absent advantage arises

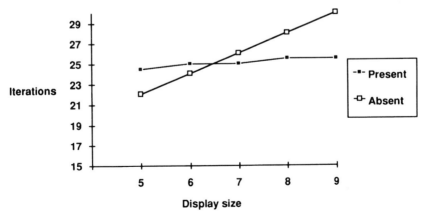

FIG. 16. Simulations of Experiment 5. SERR's absent and present RTs (in network iterations) after checking for misidentifications.

due to checking on present trials, then present responses should show a greater slope than absent responses (since more serial checks would be needed as the display size increased). In contrast, the slope for present responses was, on average, about half that for absent responses.

SERR correctly predicts both faster absent than present responses at smaller displays sizes and larger slopes on absent than present responses. The primary reason for the fast absent responses is that, at small display sizes, there is an increased likelihood that SERR will detect more than one singleton "target" and will need to be rerun in order to find the correct one.

In the human data there were longer RT intercepts in the blocked than in the random conditions (both with homogeneous and with heterogeneous displays; see also Treisman & Sato, 1990, Experiment 3). This can be accounted for by the following fact: in the random conditions there was varied mapping of target and distractors across successive trials, while in the blocked conditions there was consistent mapping within a block of trials (cf. Schneider & Shiffrin, 1977; Shiffrin & Schneider, 1977). There are various reasons why varied mapping across trials could produce an increase in human RTs. One is persistence of response inhibition from trial n to $n + 1$; that is, responding to the target on trial $n + 1$ might take longer because that target was distractor on trial n, whose activated representation had to be isolated from the control of action by inhibition of the response translation mechanism (cf. Tipper & Cranston, 1985; see also Allport, Tipper, & Chmiel, 1985). Note that SERR models only the detection part of a search system and is, thus, unaffected by the response-based effects of the mapping between target and distractors.

General discussion

We have demonstrated:

(1) A computational model of visual search which implements spatially parallel coding of simple form conjunctions and which generates both flat and linear search RT functions (the latter with present:absent slope ratios of approximately 1:2) under conditions in which humans produce similar functions.

(2) That the parallel search model gives rise to novel predictions which contradict those made by serial search models and are supported by human search experiments.

(3) From (1) and (2) it follows that linear search functions and 1:2 present:absent slope ratios on their own ought not to be taken to indicate serial search processes (see Townsend, 1971, 1972). The experiments here illustrate that, when human subjects are presented with displays that give rise to the above search functions, the predictions of serial search models can be refuted in tests which probe search processes in other ways.

The model we have proposed has several properties that we believe capture important aspects of pattern coding, grouping, and search in humans.

(1) There is parallel coding of at least simple-form conjunctions (in particular, corner junctions), and grouping operates on the basis of these junctions.

(2) Displays in which elements combine to form a single group can be selected as a single perceptual object; selection can operate at the level of the whole display (Duncan & Humphreys, 1989).

(3) Parallel pattern processing is noisy and error-prone, at least when there are a number of groups competing for selection. A check process is required to reduce errors.

(4) Although search is not spatially serial (at least within SERR's functional visual field), there are two kinds of seriality in processing: (i) overall search time is influenced by the number of competing groups present in the field (which are recursively selected and rejected from further search), and (ii) there can be reiterative checking, according to the speed–accuracy relations set in the task.

We discuss each of these points in turn and go on to consider SERR's relationship to other models of visual search.

Parallel coding and grouping of shape conjunctions

A number of workers have recently proposed that shape descriptions that are relatively invariant with respect to viewpoint can be derived by computing nonaccidental relations between image features (e.g. Biederman, 1987; Lowe, 1987). These relations can be based on relatively complex image properties, not just on simple geometric descriptors such as edges of a given orientation, contrast, or size. In particular, coding the relations between edge junctions can enable the computation of information about whether edges are concave, convex, or part of an object boundary (e.g. Clowes, 1971; Perkins, 1968; Mulder & Dawson, 1990). This information is sufficient to constrain interpretation of an object's orientation in 3D space (Perkins, 1968).

These proposals agree with a recent finding of Enns and Rensink (1990a,b); namely, that the detection of targets defined by differences in 3D orientation is little affected by the number of distractors in the field. Enns and Rensink also found that flat search functions in their task were crucially dependent on the presence of similar Y and arrow junctions in the shapes. Such findings strongly suggest that the visual system computes relationships between edge conjunctions in a spatially parallel manner in order to provide rapid "sketch" of 3D relationships between objects in the environment (see Enns, 1990). A necessary antecedent of such computations is that corner junctions are represented in a spatially parallel manner.

Donnelly et al. (1991) also recently showed that not all simple relationships between edge junctions can be used to generate flat search functions. They had subjects judge whether target corners faced in the wrong direction relative to others in the display. Performance was little affected by the number of junctions present provided the junctions had good continuation between their terminators and/or formed a closed shape (i.e. when the junctions were convex). Performance was strongly affected by the number of junctions present when the junctions were turned outwards (i.e. when they were concave). This occurred even though the displays were equally symmetrical with concave and convex junctions.

In SERR, grouping does not operate on the basis of the constraints that seem important for shape perception (continuation and closure), and further work is needed to implement such grouping procedures. Nevertheless, in the experiments modeled in this paper, relatively flat search functions were found when the homogeneous T distractors were randomly positioned in the visual field. With such displays, it is unlikely that grouping is based on either good continuation or closure. SERR produces flat search with such displays because it groups figures with junctions which fall in the same location relative to the main orientation of each shape (see Experiment 2 here). That is, it groups on the basis of forms having the same local structural identity. This type of grouping seems more akin to texture perception than to grouping fundamental to shape perception. Apparently, such texture-based coding processes operate in addition to the shape-based coding processes studied by Donnelly et al. (1991). Indeed, given that edge junctions are represented in a spatially parallel manner, it is plausible that they enter into both shape- and texture-based grouping procedures. SERR, as currently implemented, captures only the texture-based mechanism.

Whole-display selection

SERR is capable of selecting groups which subtend different regions of visual field. With homogeneous displays, the elements form a single group and strongly activate their template. When the template reaches threshold, the group is selected. Indeed, selection can even be facilitated when there are more elements present which produce stronger grouping (see the drop in the absent search function from display sizes 2 to 4 in Figs. 5 and 12b). This is in line with our own search data (Experiment 3) and with those of other researchers (e.g. Donderi & Zelnicker, 1969; Polich, 1986).

Since groups are selected, selection in SERR is object- rather than space-based (i.e. selection is not confined to one region on SERR's retina). This also meshes with a number of findings showing that the properties of perceptual groups are selected together (e.g. Driver & Baylis, 1989; Duncan, 1984). Selection does not operate within a limited spatial region, as suggested by the metaphor of attention as a spotlight with a fixed aperture (cf. Tsal, 1983).

Parallel processing is noisy

In its first pass at a display with a number of competing groups, SERR is inherently noisy. It is liable to miss individual items, it can make some false alarms, and it can mislocate items. Nevertheless, this noisy operation can serve a useful purpose, since it is via noisy interactions that item similarity influences performance. By operating with a nonneglible level of noise, early visual processing may rapidly code (at least some kinds of) item similarity, which can then guide further processing.

In addition to this, noise within a Boltzmann machine serves a particular purpose: it throws a network out of local minima in order to enable it to find the minimal global energy state (Hinton & Sejnowski, 1986). Noise may thus serve a useful computational purpose in vision, in not allowing the system to settle too early into a single (and possibly incorrect) interpretation of an image.

The view of noisy, but spatially parallel and rapid, early visual processing emphasizes that early vision's main purpose may not be to produce a veridical representation of the world. Rather, it provides a general sketch of certain similarity relationships, probably coded in 3D space (Enns, 1990). This sketch may be sufficient to guide certain behaviors such as locomotion over a terrain, for which the computation of 3D orientation (Enns & Rensink, 1990a,b) and texture (Gibson, 1979) may be particularly important. Subsequent checking processes may then be necessary to produce accurate metric representations.

Different kinds of seriality: Effects of the number of groups and reiterative checking

Psychological accounts have dichotomized visual search as either being spatially serial or parallel, with only one type of seriality — spatial seriality — being considered. SERR operates in a spatially parallel manner; nevertheless, two types of seriality are apparent: there are effects of the number of groups and there is reiterative checking in order to keep errors at acceptable levels.

Previous work on visual search has shown a direct relation between the number of groups pres-

ent and search time (e.g. Bundeson & Pedersen, 1983; Treisman, 1982). This is captured in a natural way in SERR, via its competitive group-based selection procedure. Interestingly, in addition to general increases in response time as the number of groups increase, there is a second consequence of having more groups; this is that, as the number of competing groups increases, so does the likelihood that single items are inhibited below threshold. The resulting increase in misses gives rise to increased checking, and slower response times.

A prediction that arises from the last point is that the amount of checking required should decrease when there are fewer groups present. In the limit, search can reduce to the case where there are either one or two groups present (the distractors or the distractors plus the target, as with homogeneous distractor displays). However, it also predicts that search rates should vary systematically with the number of distractor types in heterogeneous displays. This is verified by available data. Humphreys et al. (1989, Experiment 1b) used three distractors (T, ⊣, and ⊢) in search for an inverted T target, and reported a search rate of 56 ms/item on present trials (averaging across regularly and irregularly spaced displays). In Experiment 2 here we used two distractors (T and ⊣ or T and ⊢) in search for the same target. Search rates on target present trials were 28 ms/item (with the rates being even lower when only ⊣ and ⊢ distractors were used). Note that this contrast occurred even though, on grounds of linear search functions and 1:2 present:absent slope ratios, search in each instance may be characterized as spatially serial; also note that, in each case, targets and distractors shared local line segments and differed only in the arrangement of those segments. A serial model of search for such conjunction targets does not readily explain why search rates should differ so widely. SERR naturally predicts different search rates due to the increased rechecking required when more distractor groups are present.

The overriding point is that we need to distinguish between the different ways in which human performance can be serial. Proper understanding of processing mechanisms requires that these different forms of seriality be specified.

Relations to other models

Feature integration theory

SERR bears both similarities and dissimilarities to other recent accounts of visual search. Throughout the paper, we have contrasted SERR's emphasis on spatially parallel coding of simple form conjunctions with that of feature integration theory, with its stress on serial conjunction coding. However, feature integration theory has recently undergone several modifications, some of which enable conjunctions to be processed in parallel. In particular, when subjects search for conjunction targets in conditions of high feature discriminability, they are thought to eliminate particular locations from search by a process of selective inhibition from a feature map to a master map (of locations) that is subject to serial scrutiny. This special process can account for the finding of flat search functions for conjunction targets defined by highly discriminable features relative to distractors (Treisman & Sato, 1990; Wolfe, Cave, & Franzel, 1989). Within SERR, rapid rejection of distractors takes place naturally when distractors group separately from targets. The net effect will be the same as that posited by feature integration theory: distractors in rejected or inhibited locations will not be subject to further inspection.

A second similarity between the models is that, in its modified version, feature integration theory proposes a variable-size functional window, whose aperture varies according to the "signal-to-noise" ratio between targets and distractors (Treisman & Gormican, 1988). Within SERR, the size of functional window may be thought akin to the spatial area over which grouping and selection takes place. When distractors group separately from targets (i.e. when there is a high signal-to-noise ratio) selection operates across a broad area; when there is competition for grouping between different distractors and targets (i.e. when there is a low signal-to-noise ratio), selection operates across increasingly small perceptual groups. The models differ in that, within SERR, there is a natural temporal dynamic to selection; over time, selection is based on increasingly small groups of items.

However, despite these similarities, the models differ in important respects. Most crucial is the contrast between spatially serial and parallel coding of (simple form) conjunctions. The present data suggest that simple corner and T-junctions are encoded in parallel. The models also differ in that, in SERR, distractor locations are usually rejected from further processing prior to the target's template reaching threshold. This is not a special mechanism employed only under conditions of high feature discriminability. The area so rejected will simply vary according to the number of competing groups present.

One other difference between SERR and feature integration theory concerns their predictions concerning response variance. Feature integration theory predicts that, when search is serial, there should be linear increases in variance with display size, with, all other thing being equal, the increases being larger on present than on absent trials. In reanalyzing the data from Humphreys et al. (1989, Experiment 1b), where serial search apparently took place, we found the variance did increase with display size, but there were few differences between present and absent responses. This fits with the predictions of SERR (Fig. 6). Treisman (1991) has also reported quite similar findings when subjects search for color–form conjunctions. As noted earlier, Ward and McClelland found a contrasting result, namely that the variance on absent trials increased faster than that on present trials. Two reasons for their results are: (1) they used larger display sizes than here, which may have led to more checking on absent trials (although see Treisman, 1991); and (2) they alternated between search tasks (where targets were defined by one or two features being different, relative to distractors), which may again have led to variable rechecking on absent trials.

Guided search

According to Guided Search theory (Cave & Wolfe, 1990; Wolfe et al., 1989), parallel processes compute differences between neighboring stimuli along a number of dimensions (e.g. color and orientation). Activation values (enhanced by differences between neighboring items) are summed and passed on to a serial processing stage, in which items are inspected in an order corresponding to their activation values first computed. These are the main processes that operate in feature search. In conjunction search, top-down processes also operate to activate features for expected targets (this also operates in feature search, but it is more important in conjunction search). These top-down processes raise activation values for items with target features above those for items without such features, for each feature dimension. When activation values along each dimension are summed, to calculate the order of serial inspection, the target should be the first candidate. However, because of noise in the parallel processing stage, the target will not always be given the highest activation values. Consequently, some distractors will be inspected before conjunctions targets, producing effects of display size and visual search.

According to this account, the effects of display size on conjunction search will vary as a function of the similarity of target and distractor features. Essentially, the discriminability of the features will influence the similarity of the activation values for targets and distractors, and hence the likelihood that the target is not inspected first (when random noise is added). Thus Guided Search readily accounts for the flat search functions that occur in conjunction search under conditions of high feature discriminability (Wolfe et al., 1989).

SERR differs from Guided Search in that, in SERR, interactions within retinotopic (matching) maps are facilitatory; like elements support one another. In Guided Search, within-map interactions are inhibitory. The net effect of these different types of interaction is much the same; similar items are rapidly rejected from search. Experiment 3 tested one prediction arising from the way that grouping is implemented in SERR: when distractors form a homogeneous group, target detection can be slowed at larger display sizes relative to when targets are presented in isolation (due to the distractor group being selected first). This prediction was upheld. Target detection was slower when it was among homogeneous distractors relative to when it was presented alone. Such a result does not fit easily with grouping based on inhibitory interactions between like elements, where decreasing RT functions might be expected as more like distractors are presented in the field. The only way inhibitory interactions could produce the above effects would be if distractors inhibited targets, due to their shared features. However, as noted in the Introduction, it is then difficult to see how fast absent responses arise, since target absence may be genuine or due to distractors inhibiting the target. In SERR, fast absent responses arise when subjects respond to the presence of an emergent distractor group, constructed via facilitatory interactions between like conjunctions.

Although the present data on search for form conjunctions is consistent with grouping via facilitatory interactions, we do not wish to preclude the possibility of other types of grouping process. As we have already noted, decreasing RT–display size functions on present responses have been observed in disjunctive-feature search tasks (Bacon & Egeth, 1991; Sagi & Julesz, 1987). It is possible that grouping might operate in different ways at different levels of image processing; there may be inhibitory interactions at a single-feature level, but facilitatory interactions between representations of form conjunctions. These different types of interactions could also operate across different spatial regions — for instance, single-feature inhibition being the more local (though see Bacon & Egeth, 1991). Such different forms of interaction would serve different computational purposes. Single-feature inhibition would enhance the coding of regions of discontinuity. Combined-feature facilitation would serve the construction of new perceptual objects from local elements (e.g. descriptions of the 3D structure of objects can be constructed from the relations between 2D corner junctions, given the assumption that the corners are orthogonal; Perkins, 1968; Mulder & Dawson, 1989). Hummel and Biederman (1992) have also recently argued that representations coded at a combined-feature level (such as corner junctions) act in a top-down manner to constrain interactions between representations of their component features. Such top-down interactions may provide one way of resolving conflicts between groups formed at different levels of representation (as does having grouping operate across contrasting spatial areas at the different levels).

In addition, Guided Search, like feature integration theory, maintains that conjunctions are coded in a spatially serial manner. It thus fails to explain why search departs from that expected by a serial model under the conditions examined in Experiments 1, 4, and 5 here (with response deadlines, location vs detection responses, and singleton search). We conclude that models must allow that at least simple form conjunctions are represented in a spatially parallel manner.

Zoom lens accounts

Eriksen and colleagues (e.g. Eriksen & Yeh, 1985) have argued that visual attention can be likened to a zoom lens, in the sense that it can be focused to different degrees of resolution over different spatial areas. When given a broad setting, attention affects processing across a wide spatial area, but at relatively low levels of resolution. When given a narrow setting, processing is affected within a more narrow spatial area, but at a higher level of resolution (see Humphreys & Bruce, 1989, for a review of relevant evidence).

In SERR, there tends to be selection of larger groups prior to selection of smaller groups. In this sense, selection has a natural temporal dynamic: selection is initially based on wide areas of field (the larger group), and then, over time, on narrower areas (for smaller groups). However, SERR operates only at one spatial scale; thus selection operates across different apertures, but not at different levels of resolution.

Yet, there are aspects of the data that suggest that it may be useful to alter not only the aperture but also the resolution of selection in SERR. In particular, the positively accelerating miss rates found with heterogeneous displays should, in the limit, constrain SERR's functional field either in size or resolution. If the number of items within SERR's functional field becomes too large, misses will occur on almost every run. It would then be prohibitively expensive (in terms of processing time) or (ultimately) impossible to reduce the miss rate by rechecking. A solution is to limit SERR's functional field so that there is a balance between the first-pass miss rate and the time cost incurred by checking. This can be achieved either by limiting the region of field being sampled, or by limiting the number of items coded — when a larger area of field is sampled, coding must be coarser so that only the same number of items are processed. Recent work indicates that visual selection over broader spatial areas is based on lower spatial frequency components (Shulman & Wilson, 1987). Just this limitation could emerge naturally from SERR's noisy first-pass coding of complex multiple-group images.

Reconfiguring search

As currently implemented, SERR has a hard-wired set of weights that are not modifiable by learning or by task demands. Yet the general case of visual search requires that "templates" can be temporarily represented, with mappings to such representations being rapidly configurable, in accordance with the target and distractors used in the task. One way of doing this would be to reconfigure the match map units simply by changing the signs of the weights according to the target and distractor templates used in the search. However, SERR does not, as yet, embody any procedures that would enable it to achieve such a reconfiguration dynamically. The development of procedures for rapid dynamic reconfiguration awaits future research. However, answers to questions concerning the time required for learning (and unlearning of previous mappings) to occur, and the number of templates that can be represented at one time, naturally emerge once an explicit account has been developed. Similarly, questions concerning miss rates under deadline conditions, the relation between detection and localisation, and how singleton search operates have arisen via SERR's current implementation. We believe that the main utility of SERR is in forcing new issues and empirical tests to the fore. Developments are brought about through the reciprocal interaction of model and empirical data.

Acknowledgement

This work was supported by a grant from the Science and Engineering Research Council of Great Britain to both authors, by grants from the Human Science Frontier program and the Medical Research Council of Great Britain to the first author, and by a grant from the Deutsche Forschungsgemeinschaft, Germany, to the second author. We thank June Riddoch for help with the figures, and Jay McClelland and three anonymous referees for comments on an earlier version of the paper. Jane Riddoch and Philip Quinlan helped run some of the subjects for Experiment 3. Tom Freeman helped run the simulations for Experiments 2 and 3.

Notes

1. The size of single-feature maps is smaller than that of the retinal array because there is a reduced number of ways in which orientation-sensitive filters of size 2×3 and 3×2, respectively, can be placed within a 26×26 map. Similar arguments apply to the reduction in size of higher level maps.

2. We thank an anonymous referee for coining this phrase.

3. Note that the miss rates used in these simulations do not exactly match those produced by human subjects. For this reason, search rates and slope ratios cannot be directly compared. The emphasis here is on qualitative similarities.

4. The dissociation between Detection and Localization accuracy is also dependent on display size. In a control experiment with single-item displays, both participating subjects showed a reduced difference between Detection and Localization accuracy in comparison with eight-item displays (d' differences for the two subjects: .08 and .11 with one-item displays, .18 and .22 with eight-item displays). This pattern is predicted by SERR.

5. One important question is whether the finding of an absent advantage with small display sizes generalizes to search for conjunction targets defined across stimulus domains (e.g. form and color). Experiment 3 of Treisman and Sato (1990) is of interest here. They found that singleton search for an (unknown) cross-domain conjunction gave rise to linear RT functions, with an absent:present slope ratio of about 1:2. Further, the intercept for absent responses was 475 ms, as compared to 622 ms for present responses (see their Table 4). That is, there was an absent advantage at small display sizes. Note that no evidence of such an advantage was apparent in the blocked (target known) condition.

References

Allport, A. (1989). Visual attention. In M. I. Posner (Ed.), *Foundations of cognitive science* (pp.631–682). Cambridge, MA: The MIT Press.

Allport, D. A., Tipper, S. P., & Chmiel, N. R. J. (1985). Perceptual integration and post-categorical filtering. In M. I. Posner & O. S. M. Marin (Eds.), *Attention and performance XI* (pp.107–132), Hillsdale, NJ: Erlbaum.

Bacon, W. F., & Egeth, H. E. (1991). Local processes in preattentative feature detection. *Journal of Experimental Psychology: Human Perception and Performance*, *17*, 77–90.

Biederman, I. (1987). Recognition-by-components: A theory of human image understanding. *Psychological Review*, *94*, 115–147.

Broadbent, D. E. (1988). Simple models for experimentable situations. In P. E. Morris (Ed.), *Modelling Cognition* (pp.169–185). London: Wiley.

Bundeson, C., Pedersen, L. F. (1983). Color segregation and visual search. *Perception & Psychophysics*, *33*, 487–493.

Cave, K. R., & Wolfe, J. M. (1990). Modeling the role of parallel processing in visual search. *Cognitive Psychology*, *22*, 225–271.

Clowes, M. B. (1971). On seeing things. *Artificial Intelligence*, *2*, 79–116.

Cowey, A. (1985). Aspects of cortical organization related to selective attention and selective impairments of visual perception. In M. I. Posner & O. S. Marin (Eds.), *Attention & performance XI* (pp.41–62). Hillsdale, NJ: Erlbaum.

Crick, F. (1984). Function of the thalamic reticular complex: The search light hypothesis. *Proceedings of the National Academy of Sciences*, *81*, 4586–4590.

Donderi, D. C., & Zelnicker, D. (1969). Parallel processing in visual same–different decisions. *Perceptions & Psychophysics*, *5*, 197–200.

Donnelly, N., Humphreys, G. W., & Riddoch, M. J. (1991). Parallel computation of primitive shape descriptions. *Journal of Experimental Psychology: Human Perception and Performance*, *17*, 561–570.

Dorfman, D. D., & Alf, E. (1969). Maximum-likelihood estimation of parameters of signal detection theory and determination of confidence intervals: Rating method data. *Journal of Mathematical Psychology, 6,* 487–496.

Driver, J., & Baylis, G. C. (1989). Movement and visual attention: The spotlight metaphor breaks down. *Journal of Experimental Psychology: Human Perception and Performance, 15,* 448–456.

Duncan, J. (1984). Selective attention and the organization of visual information. *Journal of Experimental Psychology: General, 113,* 501–517.

Duncan, J., & Humphreys, G. W. (1989). Visual search and stimulus similarity. *Psychological Review, 96,* 433–458.

Duncan, J., & Humphreys, G. W. (1992). Beyond the search surface: Visual search and attentional engagement. *Journal of Experimental Psychology: Human Perception and Performance, 18,* 578–588.

Enns, J. T. (1990). Three-dimensional features that pop out in visual search. In D. Brogan (Ed.), *Visual Search I.* London: Taylor & Francis.

Enns, J. T., & Rensink, R. A. (1990a). Influence of scene-based properties on visual search. *Science, 247,* 721–723.

Enns, J. T., & Rensink, R. A. (1990b). Sensitivity to three-dimensional orientation in visual search. *Psychological Science, 1,* 323–326.

Enns, J. T., & Rensink, R. A. (1992). A model for the rapid interpretation of line drawings in early vision. In D. Brogan (Ed.), *Visual Search II.* London: Taylor & Francis.

Enns, J. T., Ochs, E., & Rensink, R. A. (1990). VSearch: Macintosh software for experiments in visual search. *Behavior Research Methods, Instruments, & Computers, 22,* 118–201.

Eriksen, C. W., & Yeh, Y.-Y. (1985). Allocation of attention in the visual field. *Journal of Experimental Psychology: Human Perception and Performance, 11,* 583–597.

Gibson, J. (1979). *The ecological approach to visual perception.* Boston: Houghton Mifflin.

Grossberg, S., & Mingolla, E. (1985). Natural dynamics of perceptual grouping: Texture boundaries and emergent segmentations. *Perception & Psychophysics, 38,* 141–161.

Hinton, G. E., & Sejnowski, T. J. (1986). Learning and relearning in Boltzmann machines. In D. E. Rumelhart & J. L. McClelland (Eds.), *Parallel distributed processing* (Vol. 1, pp.282–317). Cambridge, MA: The MIT Press.

Hinton, G. E., Sejnowski, T. J., & Ackley, D. H. (1984). *Boltzmann machines: Constraint satisfaction networks that learn* (Technical Report CMU-CS-84-119). Pittsburgh, PA: Carnegie-Mellon University.

Hummel, J. E., & Biederman, I. (1992). Dynamic binding in a neural network for shape recognition. *Psychological Review, 99,* 480–517.

Humphreys, G. W., & Bruce, V. (1989). *Visual cognition: computational, experimental and neuropsychological perspectives.* Hove, UK: Erlbaum.

Humphreys, G. W., Freeman, T. A. C., & Müller, H. J. (1992a). Lesioning a connectionist model of visual search: Selective effects on distractor grouping. *Canadian Journal of Psychology.*

Humphreys, G. W., & Müller, H. J. (1989). *A connectionist model of visual search: Parallel combined-feature coding and serial search* (Technical Report). London: Birkbeck College, Univ. of London.

Humphreys, G. W., Quinlan, P. T., & Riddoch, M. J. (1989). Grouping processes in visual search: Effects with single- and combined-feature targets. *Journal of Experimental Psychology: General, 118,* 258–279.

Humphreys, G. W., Riddoch, M. J., & Quinlan, P. T. (1985). Interactive processes in perceptual organization: Evidence from visual agnosia. In M. I. Posner and O. S. M. Marin (Eds.), *Attention and performance XI* (pp.301–318). Hillsdale, NJ: Erlbaum.

Humphreys, G. W., Riddoch, M. J., Quinlan, P. T., Price, C. J., & Donnelly, N. (1992b). Parallel pattern processing in visual agnosia. *Canadian Journal of Psychology.*

James, W. (1890). *The principles of psychology* (Vol. 1). New York: Dover.

Julesz, B. (1985, November). *Recent advances in the texton theory of preattentive vision.* Paper presented at the Third Workshop on Human and Machine Vision, Boston.

Julesz, B., & Bergen, J. R. (1983). Parallel versus serial processing in rapid pattern discrimination. *Nature, 303,* 696–698.

Kienker, P. K., Sejnowski, T. J., Hinton, G. E., & Schumacher, L. E. (1986). Separating figure from ground with a parallel network. *Perception, 15,* 197–216.

Klein, R., & Farrel, M. (1989). Search performance without eye movements. *Perception & Psychophysics, 46,* 476–482.

Koehler, W. (1920). *Die physischen Gestalten in Ruhe und im stationaeren Zustand.* Braunschweig.

Lowe, (1987). Three-dimensional object recognition from single two-dimensional images. *Artificial Intelligence, 31,* 355–395.

McClelland, J. L., & Rumelhart, D. E. (1981). An interactive model of context effects in letter perception. Part 1. An account of basic findings. *Psychological Review, 88,* 375–407.

McClelland, J. L., & Rumelhart, D. E. (1986). *Parallel distributed processing: Explorations in the microstructure of cognition* (Vol. 2). Cambridge, MA: The MIT Press.

McLeod, P., Driver, J., & Crisp, J. (1988). Visual search for a conjunction of movement and form is parallel. *Nature, 332,* 154–155.

Mewhort, D. J. K., & Campbell, A. J. (1978). Processing spatial information and the selective masking effect. *Perception & Psychophysics, 24,* 93–101.

Mewhort, D. J. K., Campbell, A. J., Marchetti, F. M., & Campbell, I. D. (1981). Identification, localization, and "iconic memory": An evaluation of the bar-probe task. *Memory & Cognition, 9,* 50–67.

Mulder, J. A., & Dawson, R. J. M. (1990). Reconstructing polyhedral scenes from single two-dimensional images: The orthogonality hypothesis. In P. K. Patel-Schneider (Ed.), *Proceedings of the 8th Bienniel Conference of the CSCSI* (pp.238–244). Palo Alto, CA: Morgan–Kaufman.

Müller, H. J., & Rabbitt, P. M. A. (1989). Spatial cueing and the relation between the accuracy of "where" and "what" decisions in visual search. *Quarterly Journal of Experimental Psychology, 41(A),* 747–773.

Nakayama, K., & Silverman, G. H. (1986). Serial and parallel processing of visual feature conjunctions. *Nature, 320,* 264–265.

Neisser, U. (1967). *Cognitive psychology.* Englewood Cliffs, NJ: Prentice–Hall.

Palmer, S. E. (1985). The role of symmetry in shape perception. *Acta Psychologica, 59,* 67–90.

Pashler, H. (1988). Cross-dimensional interaction and texture segregation. *Perception & Psychophysics, 43,* 307–318.

Perkins, D. N. (1968). Cubic corners. *MIT Research Laboratory of Electronics Quarterly Progress Report, 89,* 207–214.

Polich (1986). Hemispheric processing of multi-element displays. *Acta Psychologica, 61,* 137–151.

Quinlan, P. T., & Humphreys, G. W. (1987). Visual search for targets defined by combinations of color, form, shape, and size: An examination of the task constraints on feature and conjunction searches. *Perception & Psychophysics, 41,* 455–472.

Rumelhart, D. E., & McClelland, J. L. (1982). An interactive model of context effects in letter perception. Part 2. The contextual enhancement effect and some tests and extensions of the model. *Psychological Review, 89,* 60–94.

Rumelhart, D. E., & McClelland, J. L. (1986). *Parallel distributed processing: Explorations in the microstructure of cognition* (Vol. 1). Cambridge, MA: The MIT Press.

Sagi, D., & Julesz, B. (1987). Short-range limitation on detection of feature differences. *Spatial Vision, 2,* 39–49.

Schneider, W., & Shiffrin, R. M. (1977). Controlled and automatic human information processing. I. Detection, search, and attention. *Psychological Review, 84,* 1–66.

Shepherd, M. (1984). EMDISP: A visual display system with digital and analogue sampling. *Behavior Research Methods, Instruments, and Computers, 16,* 297–302.

Shriffin, R. M., & Schneider, W. (1977). Controlled and automatic human information processing. II. Perceptual learning, automatic attending, and a general theory. *Psychological Review, 84,* 127–190.

Shulman, G. L., & Wilson, J. (1987). Spatial frequency and selective attention to local and global information. *Perception, 16,* 89–101.

Steinman, S. B. (1987). Serial and parallel search in pattern vision? *Perception, 16,* 389–398.

Strong, G. W., & Whitehead, B. A. (1989). A solution to the tag-assignment problem for neural networks. *Behavioral and Brain Sciences, 12,* 381–433.

Tipper, S. P., & Cranston, M. (1985). Selective attention and priming: Inhibitory and facilitatory effects of ignored primes. *The Quarterly Journal of Experimental Psychology, 37(A),* 591–611.

Townsend, J. T. (1971). A note on the identifiability of parallel and serial processes. *Perception & Psychophysics, 10,* 161–163.

Townsend, J. T. (1972). Some results on the identifiability of parallel and serial processes. *British Journal of Mathematical and Statistical Psychology, 25,* 168–199.

Townsend. J. T., & Ashby, F. G. (1983). *Stochastic modelling of elementary psychological processes.* Cambridge, UK: Cambridge Univ. Press.

Treisman, A. (1982). Perceptual grouping and attention in visual search for features and objects. *Journal of Experimental Psychology: Human Perception and Performance, 8,* 194–214.

Treisman, A. (1988). Features and objects: The fourteenth Bartlett memorial lecture. *Quarterly Journal of Experimental Psychology, 40(A),* 201–237.

Treisman, A. (1991). Search, similarity, and the integration of features between and within dimensions.

Journal of Experimental Psychology: Human Perception and Performance, 17, 652–676.

Treisman, A., & Gelade, G. (1980). A feature integration theory of attention. *Cognitive Psychology, 12*, 97–136.

Treisman, A., & Gormican, S. (1988). Feature analysis in early vision: Evidence from search asymmetries. *Psychological Review, 95*, 15–48.

Treisman, A., & Paterson, R. (1984). Emergent features, attention, and object perception. *Journal of Experimental Psychology: Human Perception and Performance, 10*, 12–32.

Treisman, A., & Sato, S. (1990). Conjunction search revisited. *Journal of Experimental Psychology: Human Perception and Performance, 16*, 459–478.

Treisman, A., & Souther, J. (1985). Search asymmetry: A diagnostic for preattentive processing of separable features. *Journal of Experimental Psychology: General, 114*, 285–310.

Tsal, Y. (1983). Movements of attention across the visual field. *Journal of Experimental Psychology: Human Perception and Performance, 9*, 523–530.

Ward, R., & McClelland, J. L. (1989). Conjunctive search for one and two identical targets. *Journal of Experimental Psychology: Human Perception and Performance, 15*, 664–672.

Wolfe, J. M., Cave, K. R., & Franzel, S. L. (1989). Guided Search: An alternative to the Feature Integration Model for visual search. *Journal of Experimental Psychology: Human Perception and Performance, 15*, 419–433.

(Accepted May 11, 1992).

5

Sequential behaviours in networks

Some human behaviours are intrinsically serial. Consider a common situation in which we are faced with multiple tasks to perform. A guest at a cocktail party is given a telephone number to remember and, while holding a glass of wine in one hand and a plate in the other, is also offered a pistachio nut that lies in a bowl. As humans have only two hands, a response may not be made to the nut until the wine glass or the plate is put down, and a reach may not be initiated until (in some sense) the nut has been selected (and any empty shells rejected) as a target for action. To be successful, behavioural actions must be produced in the correct sequential order and the appropriate internal processes (such as selecting the pistachio as the target for action) need to instantiated first before any action is initiated. We cannot act on everything at once, hence forms of serial ordering are necessary. In addition, serial behaviour, once initiated, needs to be controlled (at least within certain limits). For example if, having picked up a pistachio nut, we are told that it had previously fallen on the floor, we may wish to change our action so that we discard the nut rather than eating it. How can serial acts not only be organised but also moderated in a way that is adaptive to new goals (don't eat the nut!)? And in particular, how can the serial ordering, organisation and control of behaviour be captured in connectionist models that are inherently parallel in their operation? In our example, even a single task, such as remembering the telephone number, depends on our maintaining serial order information and outputting the numbers in the correct sequence. How can order information be maintained and reproduced in a connectionist framework? This chapter is rather unusual in treating such behaviours together. Traditionally the problem of explaining how skilled limb movements are performed is seen as very different from the problem of recalling telephone numbers! However, viewed from a connectionist perspective such behaviours do present common problems, which a number of models have now attempted to address.

Like us, the physiological psychologist, Karl Lashley (1951, pp.114–115) thought that serial order (or, in his terms, the temporal integration of behavioural elements) was fundamental to understanding a wide range of behaviours. He wrote:

Temporal integration is not found exclusively in language; the coordination of leg movements in insects, the song of birds, the control of trotting and pacing in a gaited horse, the rat running the maze, the architect designing a house, and the carpenter sawing a board present a problem of sequences of action which cannot be explained in terms of successions of external stimuli . . . they [temporally integrated actions] are especially characteristic of human behaviour and contribute as much as does any single factor to the superiority of man's intelligence. A clearer formulation of the physiological problems which they raise should be of value, even though a solution of the problems is not yet in sight.

We hope to show how a number of different solutions have been offered to the problem of serial order, although in each case the work has revealed that serial behaviour is not an inherent problem for connectionist models. Indeed, an even wider point is that the sensitivity of learning in some models to regularities in serial order will play a fundamental role in other domains, such as the simulation of high-level cognitive problems in language understanding and reasoning. These last problems are dealt with in detail in Chapter 7; here we provide a foretaste to connectionist work in the field by illustrating how sequential dependencies can be learned in networks and how they can lead to the development of simple linguistic structures, such as the separate classification of nouns and verbs. As we will emphasise later, it is precisely the latter, so-called high-level, cases that are thought to be most resistant to connectionist accounts. We begin with a model of one form of sequential motor behaviour: typing.

5.1 TYPING

Typing is an activity in which serial order is clearly important: "teh" will not do! Yet observation of skilled typing quickly dispels the notion that the serial order of letters results from a corresponding

serial order in behaviours. Except in novice typists, typing "the" does not consist of three consecutive motor actions with the completion of one being required before the next can be initiated. Human typists can be very fast: the mean interval between keystrokes can approach 60ms in the most skilled. This alone suggests a highly parallel system, given the slow speed of information transmission in biological systems (see Chapter 1). Moreover Gentner, Grudin, and Conway (1980) investigated the microstructure of typing using high-speed photography. Rumelhart and Norman (1982, p.6) conclude the following from their data:

> The results of this study show the fingers of the hand in almost constant motion, with fingers starting to move toward their destination before the several preceding characters have been typed. A serial model of typing in which each finger in turn makes its stroke is incorrect. Rather, there seems to be a coordinated structure that allows the control of several fingers simultaneously.

Rumelhart and Norman described a model of the processes that control these motor actions which has a relaxation network as a central component. We will now describe the model and a simulation, and then discuss the degree to which the model accounts for the actual behaviour of skilled typists.

The model is illustrated in Fig. 5.1. There are two types of unit in the network: those standing for words and those standing for particular (letter) keypresses. Activation of a word unit will cause activation in the keypress units appropriate to that word. Each keypress unit specifies to the response system the target position of the key to be pressed relative to the keyboard. The response system uses this information to achieve an appropriate movement of hands and fingers. When the finger is within range of the target position a keypress is performed. Temporal order among keypresses is achieved by having each keypress schema inhibit all others, and an output is based on the most active schema. However, following each response the schema unit just output is inhibited. This leads to a release of inhibition of the

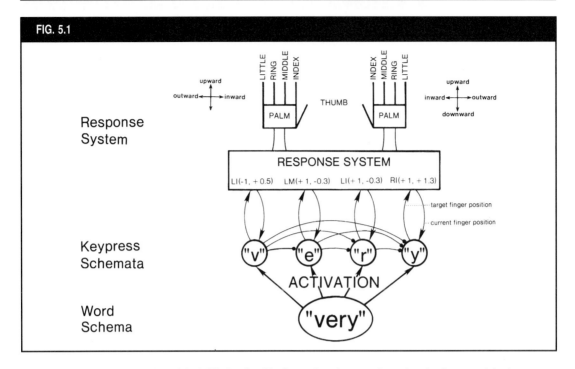

Rumelhart and Norman's (1982) model of skilled typing. The interactions between the various levels are explained in the text.

subsequent schema units, enabling the next most active to "win" the competition to be output next.

In the model there are units for each letter type rather than each letter token (each instance of a letter in a word). So typing "dead" involves the activation, deactivation, and reactivation of a single unit representing the "d" schema, rather than the activation of two units each of which represents a "d" schema. This assumption is motivated by observations of typing errors. In particular so-called doubling errors: for example typing "bokk" when "book" was intended. The authors propose a special unit for doubled letters to account for such errors: this must be the case, they argue, as the errors show that sometimes doubling can be applied or bound to the wrong letter schema. Moreover the need for such a special schema itself suggests that repeated tokens of each letter are not available and that the system has schemata for letter types only. A consequence of this view is that words containing repeated letters, such as "perception" must be parsed as "perc" and "eption",

with processing of the latter being delayed until the last repeated letter, that is, "e", has been typed.

According to the model, the control of hand and finger movements involves a relaxation process. Each active keypress schema specifies to the muscles the appropriate extension of hand and finger for its target location. The resultant or algebraic sum of the movements specified by all the active schemata causes a small movement. Repeated iterations of these processes results in an approach to the key whose schema is most active and consequently a keypress.

The model has been implemented, and we now describe various aspects of the simulation of the typing of a 2000-word text which are faithful to the observed properties of skilled typing. Figure 5.2 illustrates the simulation of typing "very well". For this, appropriate word schema units are activated, and then the activation states in the keypress schema units are monitored as a function of network iterations (the up-dating of activation values in each unit in the network). The model

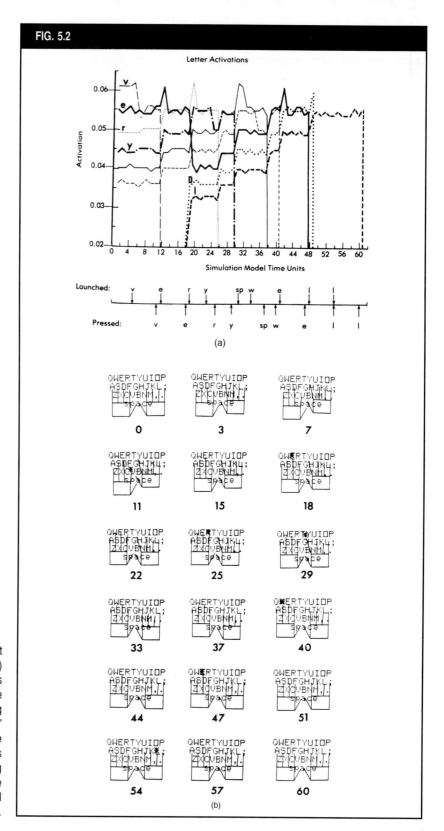

FIG. 5.2

Performance of Rumelhart and Norman's (1982) model of typing; (a) charts the progress of the activation states during the typing of "very well" and (b) shows the simulated movements on the keyboard during the same sequence (* indicates an actual keypress).

demonstrated the same highly parallel behaviour as observed in human typists. For example Fig. 5.2 shows that the keypress units corresponding to V, E, R, and Y are all initially active with V being the most active. This letter is then output, enabling E to become the most active unit and output next, and so on. Keypress units corresponding to V, R, and Y are all inhibited to the baseline level after the response, but activation values for E rise again, due to the influence of the word schema for "well". Like real typing, the model produces serial behaviour from a complex pattern of simultaneous activities. At a more microscopic level of analysis the model also appears valid in several respects. We now describe five of these.

1. The model used different sets of units in its response system for each hand (Fig. 5.1), with keys on the left of the keyboard linked to left hand responses, and keys on the right linked to right hand responses. One consequence of this was that the interval between consecutive keypresses performed by the same hand was *greater* than consecutive keypresses performed by different hands. In the model this emerges because within-hand (but not different-hand) keypresses will tend to move the hand away from the target for the next keypress.

2. The intervals between keypresses on the same hand were a simple function of the distance between keys. Taking the simulated timings for the 66 most common pairs of successive keypresses, the authors found a correlation of 0.86 with the average, comparable timings observed in six real typists. This correlation is as high as that between the six human typists.

3. The time between keypresses depended on their context: that is, the proceeding and preceding letters. Shaffer (1978), in a study of skilled human typists, reported (for example) that the interval between the "w" and "i" keypresses was greater when typing "wink" than when typing "wintry". In the model differences such as this arise because the letters proceeding and preceding any pair

are contributing components to the input to the motor system, and therefore influence the hand position. Essentially, differences in typing "i" here are influenced by the following letter contexts (e.g. in "wink", the "k" keypress [linked to the right hand] will tend to move the right hand response away from the "i", whereas in "wintry", the "t" keypress is associated with a left hand response, and so does not affect the right hand position).

4. There was a negative correlation between the intervals between successive keypresses. Shaffer (1978) found a similar relationship in skilled typists. In the model the negative correlation arises because of the overlapping of actions: a slow keypress entails more time for the finger to move to the target for the next keypress and therefore a shorter interval.

5. The model showed similar errors to those observed in human typing. These errors included: (i) transposition errors such as "whcih" instead of "which". These errors are not only very common in human typing, but also in the majority of cases occur across hands, as in our example. This pattern was also observed in the model, with three-quarters of the transposition errors coming from cross-hand pairs. In the model such errors would arise if there were some noise in the time-varying activation values, and errors are more common across rather than within hands because responses are affected by the finger linked to the activated keypress units being within striking distance of its target (this is more likely in the cross- than in the within-hand case); (ii) the doubling error, as already described. Double letters are produced by a special "doubling unit" being activated concurrently with a letter keypress unit. Doubling errors arise if the wrong letter keypress unit is activated along with the doubling unit. However, doubling errors motivated a fundamental feature of the model (the inclusion of doubling units) so it is perhaps not surprising that the simulation captures such effects; (iii) "adjacent"

errors, the striking of the wrong key adjacent to the actual target, for example "howeber" instead of "however". These arise if the time for the motor response is long, relative to the activation of the keypress schema. If the motor response is delayed (again perhaps because the system is inherently noisy), the keypress schema can be self-inhibited before the response is completed, causing the hand to be moved away from the correct key, perhaps to an adjacent location by the time the response is activated.

There are many aspects of skilled typing that the model does not simulate, however. For example, although context effects were observed in the simulation (point 2) the relative times for keypresses within words were different between the real and simulated cases: in the model the time to type "i" and "n" in "wink" was about the same, whereas in Shaffer's (1978) data from humans, such keypress times can differ greatly. According to Rumelhart and Norman (1982), this sort of difference may arise because in the simulation the fingers were assumed to start from a fixed position at the beginning of each word (the so-called home keys), whereas in actual typing the positions of the fingers at any time depend on the preceding letter string typed. The model also did not lead to some types of error observed in humans; an example here would be "capture errors" in which the intended sequence appears to be captured by a word having the same beginning: "connectionism" becomes "connectionist", say. The authors speculate that the origin of capture errors is in an earlier perceptual or encoding stage, prior to the activation of word schema. Such errors are simply outside the scope of the model. Finally, the model did not learn any representations or mappings from the word schema to the responses, and so it illustrates only a static "snapshot" at a particular level of typing skill.

Despite these limitations the model serves to illustrate a possible answer as to how serial order arises in massively parallel mechanisms like the brain. The model has also helped to inspire subsequent attempts to simulate serial behaviour in networks, particularly in the field of short-term

verbal memory, writing, and speech production, where some factors related to the learning of sequential behaviour have been explored. We cover writing and speech production in Chapter 6, where models of language processing are reviewed. By way of introduction, however, we outline in the next section a simulation of immediate verbal memory that incorporates Rumelhart and Norman's notion that sequential behaviours are a consequence of both competitive interactions between units and activation-suppression cycles of "winning" units.

5.2 IMMEDIATE VERBAL MEMORY

Consider a situation discussed in our initial example, in which you hear a new phone number for the first time and then try to recall it. Typically people report that this is done by saying the numbers silently to themselves and trying to "run off" the numbers in the correct order. Clearly maintenance of the correct temporal order of the numbers is of the essence; we will fail to ring the correct number if we transpose the order of the numbers in recall. Tasks such as this are thought to depend on a temporary verbal memory, which psychological research has indicated is closely linked to the speech system. For instance: (i) recall is affected by phonemic similarity between items and by their length; letters are more difficult to recall if they sound alike and long words are more difficult to recall then short words (Baddeley et al., 1975); and (ii) performance is disrupted when subjects carry out secondary tasks that prevent them from performing articulatory rehearsal during list presentations (Murray, 1968). Other properties of this memory system are that (iii) there is a decline in the number of items that can be immediately recalled from lists as the length of the lists increases, with often the limit of the number of items correct being around seven (Miller, 1956); and (iv) particular types of error are made, with "order" errors (where the correct items are recalled but in the incorrect order) more likely than "item" errors (where items are not recalled at all) (Aaronson, 1968).

The evidence indicating that word length and articulatory suppression impair immediate verbal recall has been taken as indicating that immediate verbal memory depends heavily on an articulatory rehearsal system. One analogy is that this rehearsal system operates like a closed tape loop that stores a sequence in "inner speech" over a set time period (e.g. Baddeley, 1986). However, this model has little to say about why order errors tend to occur and, at a more detailed level, about why (for instance) such errors are most likely with phonologically similar items (e.g. Conrad, 1964, reported that phonemically similar letters tend to be involved in paired transpositions — *b g* becoming *g b*). Other attempts to explain serial behaviour in immediate memory tasks have used the idea of "associative chaining", in which a sequence is learned by forming associations between representations of successive items. Recall can then proceed through a process of "chaining"; in this a sequence such as B G is recalled by using the response of B as a cue for its associate G and so on through a list (e.g. Jordan, 1986; Wickelgren, 1965). However, chaining models have several problems. For example, how are items recalled when they are repeated in a list and so serve as cues for more than one item — in the sequence *a x a y*, does *a* cue *x* or *y*? Also, experiments on interpolated confusable and non-confusable items make a chaining account implausible. Baddeley (1968) and Henson, Norris, Page, and Baddeley (1996) presented phonemically confusable items (B G P T etc.) interleaved with non-confusable items (F M R W etc.). On a chaining account, recall of the non-confusable items should be disrupted by the interleaved confusable items, because the confusable items should serve as poor cues to the associated non-confusable items in the list. In contrast to this, the data show that confusable items can have minimal effect on recall of the non-confusable stimuli (although the confusable items are poorly recalled). Simple associative chaining will not do.

A connectionist model of immediate verbal memory that successfully accommodates many of these results with humans was developed by Burgess and Hitch (Burgess, 1995; Burgess & Hitch, 1992; Hitch, Burgess, Towse, & Culpin,

1996). Fig. 5.3 shows the architecture of the model. There were two sets of units providing input into the model: one representing input phonemes (e.g. /s/ and /ea/ for the letter C) and one representing context units. The context units help to differentiate between the input phonemes and to separate, for example, repeated letters (which will be associated with different context representations). Activation values passed sequentially along the context units as a function of the order of the letters given to the model, with some of the units shared between neighbouring letters (Fig. 5.4a). This meant that neighbouring items tended to have more similar representations than non-neighbouring items and so were more likely to be confused; in addition, items at the beginning and end of the list tended to have less overlap with their neighbours than other items in the list as at least one context unit will differ (respectively at the beginning and end of the list; see Fig. 5.4a), leading to less confusion for these positions. In human immediate recall, performance also tends to be better for the beginning and end items, producing a "bow-shaped" curve for recall as a function of serial position (Baddeley, 1986).

The context and input phoneme units activated a further set of units corresponding to the letter items for recall (the Word Layer, in Figure 5.3). Note that letter units will be activated by more than one input phoneme unit, and input phoneme units will activate more than one letter unit; thus the activation within the letter units will vary as a function of the phonemic similarity between items. There were 26 letter units, 1 for each letter. Each letter was also connected to a node in a competitive filter, which initially reproduced the pattern of activation in the letter layer. However, the competitive filter also included strong lateral inhibitory links between units so that, after a few iterations of the model, the most active mode would suppress the others in a "winner-take-all" style. The winning node then activated a set of output phoneme units. Once this takes place, the linked node in the letter layer is suppressed by the winning unit in the competitive filter, enabling the next letter to be encoded into the output units. This competitive filter incorporates a process that has come to be known as "competitive

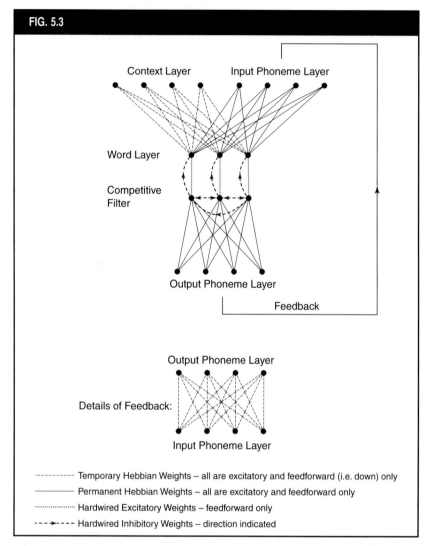

FIG. 5.3

Context Layer   Input Phoneme Layer

Word Layer

Competitive
Filter

Output Phoneme Layer

Feedback

Output Phoneme Layer

Details of Feedback:

Input Phoneme Layer

---------- Temporary Hebbian Weights – all are excitatory and feedforward (i.e. down) only

————— Permanent Hebbian Weights – all are excitatory and feedforward only

·················· Hardwired Excitatory Weights – feedforward only

- - -►- - - - Hardwired Inhibitory Weights – direction indicated

Architecture of the model of immediate verbal memory proposed by Burgess, Hitch, and colleagues, including a "competitive filter" mechanism; see the text for details (Burgess & Hitch, 1992; Hitch et al., 1996). From Burgess and Hitch (1992).

queuing" (Houghton, 1990), which is also used in models of spelling and speech production (see Chapter 6). The idea is close to that used originally by Rumelhart and Norman (1982), when they used lateral inhibition between keypress units to produce serial order (Fig. 5.1). Due to the sequential coding of the context units, the initial item in the competitive queue will be the first letter in the list (as there is strongest contextual activation associated with this letter), and next the second letter and so forth. Once output phoneme units are excited, their activation is cycled round to provide new input; this cycle is equivalent to

the articulatory loop in psychological models of immediate verbal memory (Baddeley, 1986).

Prior to simulating immediate verbal recall, the model was trained to associate input and output phonemes with letter units (essentially the association between speech sounds and letter names was part of a pre-formed long-term memory). Then, during the encoding of items for subsequent recall, Hebbian learning was used to learn the association between the appropriate representation over the context units and the letter unit, and associations between the output phoneme units of one word and the input phoneme units of the next.

FIG. 5.4

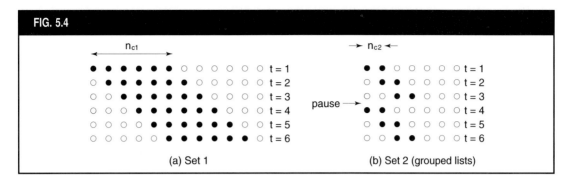

(a) Set 1   (b) Set 2 (grouped lists)

The context timing signal used by Hitch et al. (1996). Filled circles are active units and unfilled circles are inactive units. The index t represents the serial position of each item in a list. (a) gives the representation for ungrouped items in a list. A moving window of n_{c1} temporal oscillators are reset at the start of recall. (b) gives the second set of context nodes, supported by a set of n_{c2} oscillators. These last oscillators are reset after each pause in the presentation of a list — here between $t = 3$ and $t = 4$.

These associative weights decayed over time, if not refreshed by cycling activation from the output to the input units ("rehearsal"). The connections between the letters and the context units provided a form of learning for the positions of the items in the list, and the connections from the output to the input units provided a form of inter-item chaining. To produce some errors in recall, noise was also added to activation values of the units. If the decay rate of the units was sufficiently fast, performance was affected by noise. The noise and decay rate parameters were set to give a span of about seven, matching average human performance (Miller, 1956).

The model was able to simulate several of the properties of immediate verbal recall in humans. For instance, like humans, the probability of correct recall declined as a function of the length of the list given to recall and this drop was more severe if the lists contained phonemically similar letters than if they contained phonemically dissimilar letters (see Fig. 5.5). Phonemic similarity affects the performance of the model because there is a distributed spread of activation across letter units according to whether the letters share phonemes. Under noisy conditions, and with decay on the temporary weights between the context units and the letter units, phonemically similar letters

FIG. 5.5

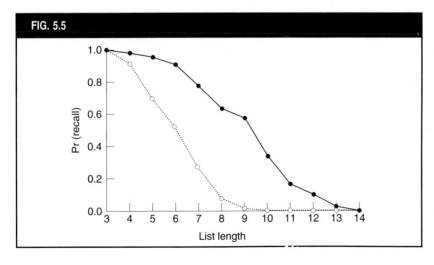

Effects of list length and phonemic similarity on the probability of correct recall. Lists were selected either from the phonemically dissimilar letters b f j i o u r t n h y q v s (solid line) or the phonemically similar letters b c d g p v t f l m n s x z (dashed line). From Burgess and Hitch (1992).

can become confused and are output in the incorrect order. Transpositions tended to be between adjacent items in the list because these items have the most similar context units. This is in close agreement with the human data, where transpositions are particularly likely between phonemically similar items (Conrad, 1964). To test the effects of word length on recall, the model was given letters made up of different numbers of phonemes. Performance declined on the items with more phonemes. This reflects the delay in establishing the competitive queue for longer items, with a subsequent delay in any "articulatory refresh" process and more time for decay to occur. Articulatory suppression was simulated by preventing output phonemes from recycling activation to input phonemes. Under this condition there was a sharp drop in recall, the advantages for phonemically dissimilar letters over phonemically similar letters were considerably reduced, and there was also a reduction in the effects of item length on performance. Both results resemble those found in humans (Baddeley et al., 1975; Murray, 1968), although in humans articulatory suppression eliminates rather than reduces the effects of word length on immediate recall.

By adding in a second set of context units (Fig. 5.4b), Hitch et al. (1996) were also able to accommodate data on the effects of temporal grouping on immediate recall. In studies of human recall, performance is improved if a temporal gap is introduced within lists; also, within each set of items separated by the gap, there is mimicking of the effects of position found across the whole list when no gap is present. For example, for a list of nine items there is typically relatively good recall for the first and last items and worse report for items in the middle. When the nine items are separated by temporal breaks after three and six items, a different pattern of performance is observed with recall being relatively good on items three and six (the last items before the breaks) and somewhat poorer on items two and five; that is, there are small bow-shaped serial position effects within each temporal group (Ryan, 1969). In addition to this, errors can occur in which there are order switches between items in the same relative positions in each group (1 & 4, 3 & 6 etc.). These

position-specific switches are difficult to explain in terms of associative chaining. Hitch et al. proposed that temporal grouping may affect performance by resetting contextual signals concerning the positions of items in a list. They suggest that context units in their model may actually provide timing signals, with each unit acting as an oscillator that is active and then inactive according to a particular rhythm. To account for effects of temporal grouping, the second set of context units contains oscillators that are reset by every pause within a list. The contextual timing signal, used to activate letter representations (Fig. 5.3), is then a product of the first set of context signals (changing across the whole list) and the second set, which change within each group. With the introduction of this second set of context units, Hitch et al. were able to simulate effects of temporal grouping, with bow-like serial position effects within each subgroup. These serial position effects occurred because items in the middle of each subgroup have fewer discriminable contextual signals (overlapping with those of neighbours) than items on the extreme of each subgroup. In addition, errors typically involved items switching between groups but maintaining the same relative position within each group. Position-specific switches occurred because, in the second set of contextual signals, similarity was based on the position of the items within each subgroup.

The model of Burgess and Hitch, like that of Rumelhart and Norman (1982) on typing, illustrates how serial behaviour can be generated within a connectionist framework. In addition, by using a contextual signal linking to the time of presentation of items, it shows how serial order can be encoded. The model has some limitations, however. One is that it fails to capture human performance when phonemically similar (confusable) and phonemically dissimilar (non-confusable) items are interleaved in a list presentation (Baddeley, 1968; Henson et al., 1996): for the model (but not for humans) report of the non-confusable items is worse when they accompany confusable items. Even when the context units cue the non-confusable item, shared overlap at the phonological level leads to the confusable items providing more competition than other non-confusable items;

this is because activation from context units is multiplied along with that from the input phonological units to provide ordering information. In addition to this, studies of human memory show that there is a stronger "bow" in the recall serial position curve when stimuli are presented auditorily rather than visually (i.e. there is a bigger "recency" effect for auditory stimuli; Baddeley, 1986), which is not captured by the model. It may be that, for humans, there is some additional auditory memory store that provides extra support in immediate memory tasks; this is outside the scope of the model.

The Burgess and Hitch model provides one example of how a model employing "competitive queuing" can produce serial behaviour; it also illustrates how connectionist models can be linked to psychological data. For this reason it is included at the end of this chapter.

A related but slightly different approach to that of Burgess and Hitch has been proposed by Henson et al. (1996). They suggest that, instead of there being context units sensitive to the temporal order of items, there are units whose values themselves directly correspond to temporal order (Grossberg, 1978, first formulated this proposal). Thus units representing the items in a list will be activated most if they are the first to occur, somewhat less if they are next and so forth. Items are selected for response on the basis of their being the most active and, following their selection, their representations are suppressed. As activation values become more similar as recall through the list progresses, so the chances increase of order errors occurring; this is so until the last item in the list, which faces little competition because other items have been suppressed. The net result is a characteristic bowed serial position curve. According to Henson et al., effects of phonemic similarity arise after the selection of items for response, due to overlap in their phonological output representations. Because confusability effects between phonemically similar items arise after selection, confusable items do not affect the recall of non-confusable (phonemically dissimilar) items when interleaved on a trial. This work suggests that, using variations on the idea of a time-varying signal for position coding, connectionist models may successfully account for the coding of serial order in behaviour.

5.3 SELECTIVE ATTENTION

Now, in our original problem of the cocktail party, the guest had not only to remember a telephone number but also had to select a particular pistachio nut, reach for it, and then discard it when a new task-goal is set ("do not eat the nut!"). This additional behaviour involves at least three operations — the internal "visual selection" of a target pistachio, the sequential reach, and the internal operation involved in preventing one overlearned action (taking the hand to the mouth) from happening. We deal with each in turn.

Our ability to select more than one object for action is limited. When asked to select together the properties of two stimuli (for a verbal report), our performance is disrupted when the stimuli are presented simultaneously relative to when they occur sequentially (Duncan, 1984). Apparently the act of selecting the target involves (necessarily) the rejection of other items as targets for action, so these rejected items cannot simultaneously be selected as targets. On the other hand, when items are presented sequentially they can be selected in series, with few costs. Connectionist models of visual selection (SLAM, SAIM, and SERR) were reviewed in Chapter 4 (section 4.5), and we will not consider them in detail again. Nevertheless, some points about the underlying processes in these models should be highlighted, so that we can understand the relations between these models and the models of typing and immediate memory, which may seem at first sight to be very different creatures.

Models such as SAIM and SERR each have, as the process of selection, a procedure in which items are matched against templates. This matching is competitive, so that activation favouring one item leads to the inhibition of other items. This is similar to the competitive filter employed in the models of typing and immediate verbal memory that we have just reviewed. In general terms, this is a form of "lateral inhibition". In addition, after a template reaches threshold, when its activation state is made available to other processes (e.g. to make a response), both the template and its associated input units are inhibited. This enables other inputs to be selected and "attention" to be switched. Again this is similar to the procedure used to select a response in the models of typing and immediate memory. The main difference between these last models and models of visual selection is that, in the models of selection, the order of selection (which object is selected after which) is determined primarily by the input. In the models of typing and immediate memory, where the order of output is important (and even learned), the means by which outputs are selected is determined by an externally applied gradient of activation (from context units or oscillators). It is possible to consider similar mechanisms within theories of visual selection, for instance to enable some form of top-down structuring of search to operate. Such top-down strategies have not yet been applied, although it represents one interesting direction for future research.

5.4 REACHING

Now let us consider the behaviour that may follow once a target has been selected, such as reaching to pick the target up ("grasp the pistachio"). Reaching itself, although apparently a simple behaviour, involves a sequence of processes, and this sequence must be generated in the appropriate way to enable the action to be successful. Reaching, like the other processes we have considered in this chapter, involves accessing responses in a necessary serial order and so requires a solution to the problem of computing serial behaviour.

Consider the problem of specifying an arm movement towards a target object. The underlying mechanisms that control the movements can be analysed as a sequence of computations which control the resultant actions (for example see Hollerbach, 1982). A plausible sequence of five stages is as follows. First the location of the object in space must be determined. Second the route or trajectory of the hand to that object has to be computed. Third the combination of joint movements needed to achieve the desired trajectory has to be found. Fourth the joint torques required for the set of joint movements must be derived. Fifth the pattern of muscular extensions and contractions that result in those torques has to be calculated. Each of these stages involves considerable computational problems. For example calculating the torques involves fearsome difficulties. The torque required to deliver a certain angular velocity or acceleration at one joint will almost certainly depend on what is happening at the other joints. To illustrate: movements around the shoulder joints produce centripetal forces at the lower arm joints that must be taken into account in calculating their torques, and what happens at the wrist joint influences what must happen at the elbow, because applying force at the wrist produces equal and opposite forces in the lower arm.

Typical solutions to these problems in robotics have involved a great deal of precise, numerical, and sequential computation. Hinton (1984), however, has reported work which suggests that a sequential computation would be too cumbersome to model biological reaching movements and even a single parallel computation is not optimal. In fact cooperation between parallel processes is required. Hinton (1984) developed a simulation of a particular case of reaching which is illustrated in Fig. 5.6. The stick figure shown has to reach to touch a target without overbalancing. Finding a trajectory in this case is difficult because several goals must be satisfied by the one solution and because of the large number of degrees of freedom provided by articulations of the limbs.

Consider first the derivation of a trajectory for the stick figure shown in Fig. 5.6. If balance is ignored, the problem becomes one of surplus degrees of freedom: the stick figure body has five degrees of freedom (altering the angle of the body at the ankle, the knee, the hip, the shoulder, and the elbow), but only two degrees of constraint are provided by the target position (its x,y location, in this two-dimensional example). There is no single solution to this problem. Imagine, however, connecting the tip of the arm to the target by a rubber band which pulls the tip to the target. In such circumstances the solution results

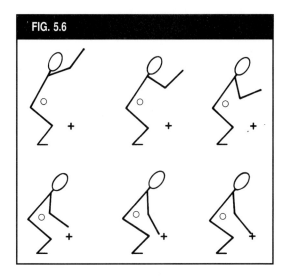

FIG. 5.6

A sequence of postures adopted by Hinton's (1984) simulation of a stick figure reaching for the target marked + (the o represents the figure's centre of gravity).

from the set of forces exerted by the rubber band, and Hinton's model of reaching in effect simulates those forces. In an iterative computation, the position of each joint angle was incremented at each time interval by an amount that was proportional to the notional torque exerted at that joint by the imaginary rubber band. Calculation of these quantities required knowledge of the vector that specifies the difference between the tip and target, and the position of each joint in space. In the model this information is stored in a "motion blackboard". This data structure may be used in parallel by a set of autonomous processes, one for each joint, to calculate the new joint angles at each iteration, which leads to the appropriate amendment of the contents of the blackboard. One further function of the blackboard is to maintain consistency among its internal representations of joint positions by parallel constraint satisfaction.

Consider now the goal of maintaining balance. The combination of joint angles must be such that the figure's centre of gravity remains over the foot. One way to achieve this is to seek a set of joint angles that minimise the distance between the centre of gravity and a perpendicular through the foot. In effect each joint angle must be changed so as to reduce this distance. Not all joints con-

tribute equally to its reduction: the nearer the foot the greater the effect a change of joint angle has on the position of the centre of gravity. The joint increments should therefore be proportional to their effect on the centre of gravity. When combined with the reaching task, the joint angles required for balance could conflict, of course, with the changes required for movement towards the target. In the simulation this was resolved in the following manner. The joint angles required for a small increment towards the target were calculated. If their combined effect was to disturb the balance, angular increments to move the figure back towards balance were calculated, as outlined in the previous paragraph. The actual movement, on any iteration, was a sum of the two sets of increments.

In summary, in the simulation, each of the figure's joints had a processor that received information, from the blackboard, about how far the hand was from its target and the position of the figure's centre of gravity relative to its foot. The joints were adjusted iteratively and independently of each other. This method worked but required a large number of iterations. The reason for this is simple: the angles were changed without regard to each other, but in fact their effects on the movements towards the target are not independent. Their effects can be made approximately independent by having very small increments and thus a large number of iterations to a solution. In an elaboration of the model the dependencies between joints were resolved by having additional processors that coordinated activity at groups of joints. For instance one such group was the hip, knee, and ankle joints. In these circumstances not only did the number of iterations to a solution decrease but the actual path arrived at looked more like a human reaching movement. Figure 5.6 actually illustrates such a solution.

Hinton's (1984) model was not implemented as a simulation of a connectionist network. It is the logic of this model rather than the implementational details that is at issue here, however. The style of computation, involving interactions operating in parallel between several processes, each concerned with a local task, is closely linked to connectionist approaches to modelling. Having described reaching in terms that appeared to emphasise its intrinsic sequential character, we have again found that a model which applies multiple, simultaneous, constraint satisfaction is a promising explanation of how the sequential behaviours are produced.

5.5 CONTROLLING ACTIONS

To some degree, actions can be controlled. A reach, once started, can usually be stopped (although admittedly this is more difficult if the reach has a high velocity, as time is needed to counteract one physical force with another in order to stop an action). However, how can one goal be overridden and a new one imposed ("do not eat the nut!")? Also, what if the goal that must be overridden involves a very overlearned response, and the goal that must be imposed is much less well learned? How are we able to stop the overlearned response from being made, if it is inappropriate to the task at hand?

Connectionist modellers have encountered this problem when trying to simulate an experimental phenomenon termed the Stroop effect. The Stroop effect is as follows. The subject is presented with a colour name (e.g. green) written in ink of a particular hue (say red). The task is to name the colour of the ink ("red"). This turns out to be difficult, and response times can be very protracted and certainly much longer than when the task is to name the colour of a row of Xs (a control condition). When the colour word and ink are congruent (red written in red), responses can be a little faster than the neutral condition, but this benefit typically is not equal to the cost when the colour word and ink are incongruent (MacLeod, 1992, 1993; Stroop, 1935). The Stroop effect is typically attributed to one response (identify the colour word — green) being considerably more practised than the other (name the colour — red). The overlearned colour word response is "automatically" activated, and so interferes with the response to the colour when the two are incongruent. Why the effect tends to emerge in response times rather than accuracy (e.g. where subjects

produce the colour word rather than the name of the colour) is often left unexplained — although it is by no means obvious how this can be accounted for without there being some additional monitoring process (and then how would this know whether a name belonged to the word or the ink colour, without rechecking the input?). It is also unclear why interference, when the colour word and ink are incongruent, is greater than facilitation, when the colour word and ink are congruent (measured relative to the control condition).

Within a connectionist framework, automaticity may be a matter of degree rather than some all-or-none property of the processing system. All stimuli activate their associated representations to some degree, with the degree of activation determined by the strength of the connections. Connection strength will be a matter of practice or learning; with more practice, connection strengths increase and a behaviour becomes more automatic. So, in the case of the Stroop effect, we may presume that connections from a colour word to a name are stronger than those from the ink colour to a colour name, due to word naming being the more practised task. In addition, however, activation may be moderated by other inputs — for instance, by a top-down process that reflects the task goals (name the ink colour not the colour word). This top-down influence may control performance, so that responses are not necessarily made to the more practised response, although responses may be faster when the practised response is congruent rather than incongruent with the required response.

A simple model that illustrates these ideas was proposed by Cohen, Dunbar, and McClelland (1990). Input units for the model corresponded either to colour words (one unit for red, another for green) or to ink colours (one for red and one for green again); output units represented colour names (red and green). Activation from the input units to the response units was transmitted through a set of hidden units, divided for each task (i.e. one set for word naming and one for colour naming). Using back-propagation (see Chapter 2), the model was trained to assign the appropriate name output to either the word input or the ink colour input, with unambiguous word and ink colour inputs being given on separate learning trials. Within a training set there were more word naming than ink colour naming trials, so word naming was the more practised task, and the weights on the connections from word inputs were correspondingly larger than the weights on the connections from the ink colour inputs. So much is straightforward. However, in addition to this, Cohen et al. introduced task-demand units that were activated according to the task being assessed (one unit for word naming, one for naming the ink colour). These task-demand units connected directly to the intermediate, hidden units and modified their activation. Units had a sigmoid activation function according to the net input they received, which could vary from –5 to +5 (see Fig. 5.7). At the hidden layer, units were set to start with a negative value. Input from a task-demand unit was sufficient to offset this negative bias in the hidden layer (to zero), selectively pushing task-relevant units into the most sensitive portion of the activation function (Fig. 5.7). The weights from the task-demand units to the hidden units were not modifiable during learning. The model is shown in Fig. 5.8.

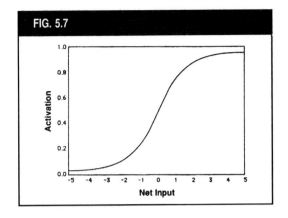

FIG. 5.7

The logistic activation function used by Cohen et al. (1990) in their model of Stroop interference effects. Note that the slope of the function is largest when the net input is zero and decreases when the input is larger or smaller than that. In the model, "task-demand" units acted to modulate the activation functions of units in the colour and word naming pathways, pushing the units into the most sensitive part of their activation function (around zero). See the text for details.

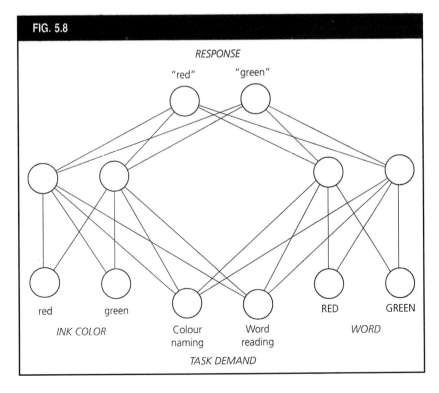

FIG. 5.8

Architecture of the Cohen et al. (1990) model of colour and word naming. Weights from the task-demand units to the intermediate (hidden) units were fixed.

After training using unambiguous input, a test phase was carried out (during which the weights were no longer modified). Stroop conditions were simulated by presenting the model with ambiguous input, corresponding to both a word and an ink colour. In the congruent condition the word and ink colour inputs related to the same output; in the incongruent condition they related to incompatible responses (the word green written in red ink). In a control condition the model received only colour ink input (for the task of naming the ink colour) or only the word input (for the task of naming the word). Response latencies were simulated by having response accumulators, which took activation values from the output units. On each trial, the task-demand units were first activated, which placed the task-relevant hidden units into a primed state and left the task-irrelevant hidden units in an inactive state. Word and ink colour inputs were then provided and activation cycled around until one response accumulator reached threshold; latencies were based on the time to reach threshold.

Empirical data from humans, along with the results of the simulations, are depicted in Fig. 5.9. For this figure, response times in msec for the network were derived by matching network iterations to the response latencies produced by human subjects (msec times for humans related to 12 × each network iteration plus 206!). The results show a close match between the human data and those derived from the model, both in terms of the pattern and magnitudes of the effects. The fit

to the magnitudes of the effects may be somewhat arbitrary, and depend on how network activation is mapped onto the accumulator units and how thresholds are set in the latter units. Perhaps more important are the qualitative similarities in performance: (i) for the word reading task there is minimal effect of colour congruency whereas word congruency influences colour naming; (ii) the effect of word congruency is on response time rather than accuracy; (iii) the congruency effect is asymmetrical, with interference (on incongruent trials) being greater than facilitation (on congruent trials)(relative to the control condition). How does the model produce these effects?

Performance in the model is determined both by the strength of the connections from the input units to the output units (via the hidden units), and by the task-demand units. Colour congruency has little effect on word naming because word naming benefits both from strong input–output connections (given the greater number of training trials for this task) and from activation from the appropriate task-demand unit. In contrast, colour naming is affected by word congruency because word input units have stronger input–output connections than colour input units. Even though input activation from the word units is insufficient to overcome the task-demand activation for naming the ink, it remains enough to affect the speed of naming the ink colour. The asymmetry of the effects on naming the ink colour (more interference than facilitation) results primarily from the sigmoid activation functions used in the model. Essentially

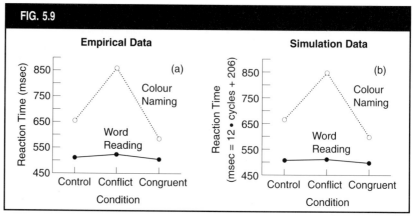
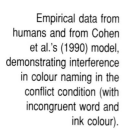

FIG. 5.9

Empirical data from humans and from Cohen et al.'s (1990) model, demonstrating interference in colour naming in the conflict condition (with incongruent word and ink colour).

there is a ceiling on activation at the high end of the function, making it increasingly difficult to generate further activation in a unit as the input values increase. A congruent word input consequently has little effect relative to the control condition, where only colour input is given to the model and where the model is quite strongly activated in any case. On the other hand, incongruent word input has a large effect, as it can shift the activation function downwards in the range of the activation function that is most linear (e.g. where net input varies between −2 and +2).

Cohen et al.'s (1990) model shows how overlearned responses may be moderated within connectionist networks, given the operation of top-down as well as bottom-up influences on performance. Providing response thresholds are set appropriately, and depending on the relative strengths of learning between stimuli and responses, overlearned responses can be overcome — although there can be time costs on performance. The model predicts that the more overlearned the response, the greater will be the need for goal-based activation to be maintained and the stronger will be the likelihood that the overlearned response is generated if this activation wanes. This fits with a good deal of the human data on so-called "slips of action", when we may perform an overlearned rather than a goal-specific behaviour when vigilance on a task momentarily decreases (e.g. taking a familiar turning instead of following a novel route; Reason, 1984). The notion that "automaticity" is a continuous variable, moderated by both bottom-up and top-down constraints, appears to be a useful way of capturing psychological data on the effects of practice on human performance. It also suggests another way in which we can conceptualise how selection takes place in human behaviour. In this case, we may speak of task- or goal-based selection, which can help over-ride learned behaviours when responses are retrieved.

We should add a caveat, which is that it is unlikely that the Cohen et al. model of the Stroop effect is psychologically plausible in all its details. For instance, the response latencies generated by the model have been criticised for not following the same distribution as found with human observers (Heathcote, Popiel, & Mewhort, 1991).

Also, within the time course of a trial the initial activation of output units will be strongly affected by task-based activation (which sets the states of the hidden units prior to ink colour and word inputs being given). In the incongruent Stroop condition, word information will only affect performance later on, as activation is accumulated at the output level. However, when people perform under deadline conditions they make many erroneous word-naming errors (Starreveld & la Heij, in press), suggesting that word information is available early on in processing. The details of the model may need to be changed to capture the full details of human performance (e.g. task-based activation may need to come into play over time rather than before stimuli are presented). It is also unclear how far the approach may be extended, to cover other aspects of behaviour (such as carrying out tasks with several stages). In the Cohen et al. model, task-based modulation works because it can be imposed on separated sets of hidden units — it is as if there are separate modules for processing the word and the ink colour. Can similar constraints be imposed within non-modular systems? Also, is there psychological evidence for control being easier when the attributes of stimuli are processed along separate neural pathways (see Humphreys & Boucart, 1997, for some evidence on this)?

In the light of this last point, it is of some interest to note psychological evidence on the effects of practice on human performance. It is a common experience that, with practice, we are able to perform more than one task at a time; practice makes a behaviour more "automatic". This has been shown by studies of skilled typists, linking to our example at the start of this chapter. Skilled typists are able to carry out some demanding tasks simultaneously with little apparent loss while they are copy typing from a written text (e.g. Shaffer, 1975, found little disruption to copy typing when typists had simultaneously to repeat back [or shadow] an auditory message). But there are limits to this. If the typing and shadowing tasks are switched (to audio-typing and shadowing a written message), skilled typists perform less well. Why should this be? One reason is that, in connectionist terms, skilled typists develop new mappings between inputs (letters) and outputs (finger movements) during copy typing, so that with practice they no longer use word recognition processes to guide typing. Hence copy typing can be conducted in conjunction with a task demanding word recognition, verbal shadowing, as the two tasks demand different processing routes. However, mapping from letters to finger movements cannot be learned for audio-typing in English; first because the perceptual units from speech are phonemes rather than letters, and second because there are not systematic relations between phonemes and English letters (e.g. the phoneme /f/ can be expressed as "F" or "PH"). Audio-typing may therefore demand word recognition processes, even when practised. On this view, one way in which automaticity develops in humans is via the setting up of new "routes" for mapping inputs to outputs. Once established, such routes may need to be modulated in the manner suggested by Cohen et al. Whatever the case, this modelling work demonstrates the importance of task-based constraints as an additional source of input in connectionist models, to enable behaviour to be controlled and not simply based on prior associations.

5.6 LEARNING TEMPORAL ORDER

5.6.1 Time as space

Having considered how serial processes can be simulated and controlled in connectionist networks, in the final section of this chapter we review attempts to train such models to produce or respond to temporally ordered events. The problem of learning and maintaining temporal order information over the short term was covered in section 5.2, where we summarised models of verbal immediate memory. Here we consider long-term learning. As we shall see, the topic is of general as well as particular interest because it turns out that long-term learning of sequential information may also help connectionist models to address other problems in high-level cognition, such as learning linguistic categories.

Grossberg (1969, 1970a,b, 1978, 1982) has investigated the properties of several classes of

network, of which one is highly relevant to the problem of long-term learning of serial order. The so-called *outstar network* is illustrated in Fig. 5.10.

This form of network can be trained so that a single unit can elicit, when active, a particular pattern of activity, expressed in a vector A_1 to A_n, in a set of other units in the following manner. The network is trained on a set of vectors which are normal variations on the vector A_1 to A_n, using the learning rule:

$$W_i(t + 1) = W_i(t) + R(A_i - W_i(t)) \qquad (1)$$

where $W_i(t)$ is the ith weight connecting out from a processing unit at time t, A_i is the ith activation value given out and R is a value that determines the rate of learning. If the latter is set at 1 initially and gradually reduced to 0 during the learning phase, it can be shown that the network is able to develop a set of weights that encode the required output vector, A_1 to A_n. In effect the network has learned to output a spatial pattern (A_1 to A_n) whenever the key node is at an appropriate level of activity. It is therefore a type of associative memory. The pattern to be learned can be extracted, during learning, from fluctuating inputs provided the elements of the input have a fixed relative size. The network can thus be said to factorise out the pattern from the fluctuating inputs. This ability to learn patterns is general: the network could be encoding visual information or, more appropriate to our interests in this chapter, a set of motor

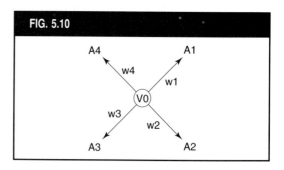

FIG. 5.10

An outstar network made up of a node unit V0 which can be trained, by adaption of the weights W1 to W4, to elicit the pattern A1 to A4 (after Grossberg, 1982).

commands. Suppose for instance that each component (A_i) of the activity vector innervated a set of muscles, and the activity levels were proportional to the rate of contraction of those muscles. Such a network would be capable of representing a motor synergy in which absolute contraction rates may vary but the relative rates remain constant. For example playing a chord on a piano or uttering a speech sound that depends on a particular configuration of tongue and lips.

Grossberg (1969, 1970a,b) has applied outstar learning to serial behaviours in a network architecture he refers to as an *avalanche*, which is illustrated in Fig. 5.11. A single unit is connected to a set of outstar networks arranged serially along its axon. Such a network can learn, and subsequently generate, any space–time pattern including sequences of actions. During the learning phase each outstar learns a single spatial pattern in the manner described in the last paragraph. After learning, a single pulse along the axon activates the outstars in sequence producing a series of speech sounds or a sequence of motor actions, for example.

5.6.2 Recurrent networks

Grossberg's work, just described, reduces the problem of producing or detecting serial order to one of learning a spatial pattern. The temporal properties of the behaviour are explicitly represented by the spatial properties of a vector. A different approach, suggested by Elman (1990), is to represent time implicitly in the effect it has on processing.

Elman considered the behaviour of the seemingly simple recurrent network shown in Fig. 5.12 (see also Jordan, 1986). The network is recurrent in that activity in the middle, hidden layer is fed back to the lower-level "state" units via a set of fixed weights (each set at one; see section 2.8). Hidden unit activity from the immediately preceding event is thereby replicated as part of the input associated with the next event, on the state units. Given an input at time t, the hidden unit activity will feed forward to the output units, but also back to the state units. At time $t + 1$ therefore the input to the hidden units will be the new input unit values plus the previous activity pattern on the hidden units. In effect the state units serve as a memory, which provides the possibility of the network learning temporal relations among inputs. In fact Elman (1990) shows that for a variety of contrived but intriguing input sequences, the network develops representations that are sensitive to temporal relations in the input stream. We will now describe the simulations of some of those cases.

An input stream of consonants and vowels was created in the following manner. The consonants b, d, and g were arranged in a random sequence of 1000 letters. Each consonant was replaced thus: b became ba, d become dii, and g became guuu. For instance, the sequence dbg would become diibaguuu. The resulting sequence had structure in that although the position of the consonants was random, what followed each occurrence was

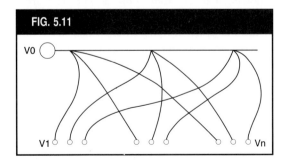

FIG. 5.11

An avalanche network in which the node unit V0 elicits a space–time pattern by serially exciting the nests of units V1 to Vn, to which it is connected (after Grossberg, 1982).

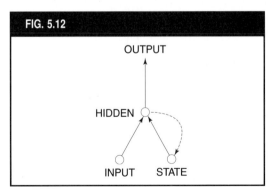

FIG. 5.12

Adapted from a simple recurrent network of the sort used by Elman (1990) to learn structured representations of sequences.

TABLE 2.1

Vector definitions of vowel and consonants

	Consonant	Vowel	Interrupted	High	Back	Voiced
b	1	0	1	0	0	1
d	1	0	1	1	0	1
g	1	0	1	0	1	1
a	0	1	0	0	1	1
i	0	1	0	1	0	1
u	0	1	0	1	1	1

fixed. Could a network discover this structure so that it could generate the next member of the series as an output, given its predecessor as input? Each letter was represented to the network as a six-bit vector defined as shown in Table 5.1. The simulated network had six input units, twenty hidden units, twenty context units, and six output units. For a given letter input, the output expected was the next letter in the sequence. During a training phase the input letter sequence was presented 200 times, and weight changes were calculated using the back-propagation procedure (see Chapter 2). The abilities of the network were then assessed with a new letter series and Fig. 5.13

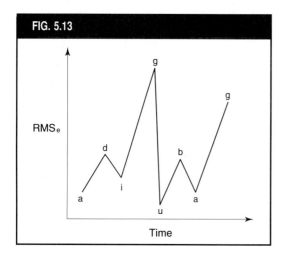

FIG. 5.13

RMS$_e$ values similar to those for Elman's (1990) recurrent network when predicting letters in a vowel–consonant sequence, with the correct response labelled.

shows the RMS$_{error}$ over the output vector for particular letters in a test sequence (the root of the mean squared differences between the expected and observed outputs). It is clear that the network has learned that a particular sequence of vowels follows each consonant. Its error for vowels is therefore low, but as the order of consonants is random, the error for predicting these is high. However the network did learn to expect some consonant or other following completion of each vowel sequence, as demonstrated by a low error on the first bit of the output vector which, as indicated in Fig. 5.13, effectively labels the output as a consonant.

Given that the simple recurrent network has developed a coding that is sensitive to regularities in contrived letter strings, it is reasonable to ask whether it can learn something useful from word sequences. The next simulation investigated this possibility. A training set was created in the following manner. From a population of 15 words, 200 sentences were generated and concatenated to form a string of 4963 letters. Each letter was represented on the input units as a five-bit vector, for example 01101 represented the letter "m". A network of five input units, twenty hidden units, twenty context units, and five output units was used, and training again involved the production of an output corresponding to the next letter in the sequence following a given letter input. The model was trained on 10 passes through the letter sequence, at which point the RMS$_{error}$ values on the output units were as indicated in Fig. 5.14. The pattern of errors is striking: it is high at the

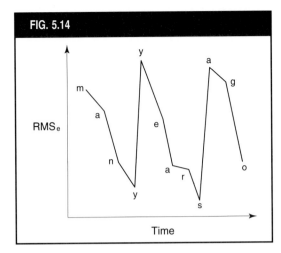

FIG. 5.14

RMS$_e$ values similar to those found in Elman's (1990) network when predicting letters learned from a sequence of words. Again the correct responses are labelled (for the input sentence: "many years ago a boy and girl lived by the sea they played happily m. . . .)".

beginning of a word and decreases with each subsequent letter within that word. The network has learned something about the orthographic regularities found in words from the co-occurrence statistics between the letters in the words in the training set.

Elman's work demonstrates how temporal sequences can be learned and reproduced by recurrent networks, and it provides one solution to the problem of how long-term representations of serial order can be incorporated in connectionist models. It also goes beyond this, because it shows that, in learning temporal sequences, models can develop sensitivities to high-order regularities in the training environment (orthographic regularities, with letter strings). In Chapter 7 we elaborate this point using one further example from Elman's work, which indicates that the syntactic categories of words may be derived in recurrent networks responsive to temporal order in sentences. Such networks suggest that connectionist models may be capable of representing and expressing syntactic operations. Due to the contribution of Elman's paper to understanding both sequential and language processes, it is reprinted at the close of this chapter.

5.7 CONCLUSIONS

Revolutions change things! They especially change ways of viewing the world, including ways of categorising phenomena. One aim of this chapter has been to suggest the radical effect connectionism may have on dividing up mental phenomena. Within a connectionist perspective some sorts of memory, attention, and action are similar problems. They all require an account of how serial order can arise and be controlled in parallel computing architectures. The models described have often required solutions to deep problems in representation which are of direct relevance to other aspects of mental life, most notably language. Is it surprising that so much in psychology seems to pivot on serial order? From the connectionist perspective, perhaps not; forms of language involving the sequential comprehension and generation of words in sentences may well depend intimately on some general computational machinery required for encoding and producing serial behaviour. The work suggests that connectionist models have much to offer here and can provide a new perspective on some old and knotty problems. For instance, the work on task-based control of learned responses suggests one solution to the venerable question of what makes a process automatic. For such models there is no strict dichotomy between a process that is automatic and one that is not, it is simply that an automatic process can operate even in the absence of top-down goal-based activation and that it is less easy to override (although this is still possible). Further, the development of automatic processes involves establishing special-purpose processing routes, so that other tasks no longer impinge and interfere. The move is towards a finer-grained account of human performance in which differences between tasks are emergent properties of the general characteristics of networks (e.g. in this case bottom-up learning vs. top-down modulation of responses). In the future, similar emergent properties of networks may help to explain other aspects of cognition such as language behaviour, reasoning, and planning.

Toward a network model of the articulatory loop

Neil Burgess and Graham J. Hitch

The University of Manchester, Manchester, United Kingdom

The basic features of verbal short-term memory for serially ordered lists are reviewed. A feed-forward network model based on Baddeley's concept of an "articulatory loop" is presented. One of its aims was to explore mechanisms for the storage of serial order information in the articulatory loop. Information is represented locally, learning is by "one-shot" Hebbian adjustment of weighted connections, corresponding to item–item and item–context associations, which decay with time. Items are modeled at the level of phonemes and phonemic output is fed back to the next phonemic input. At recall, items are selected serially by "competitive queuing." Noisy activation values are used, resulting in errors during recall. Simulations of recall showed good agreement with human performance with respect to memory span, phonemic similarity, word length, and patterns of error. There was good but incomplete agreement on the shape of the serial position curve and on the effects of articulatory suppression. A simple modification is shown to produce the correct serial position curve. However, the model was unable to simulate human memory for sequences containing mixtures of phonemically similar and dissimilar items. A suggested modification which retains the central idea of using competitive queuing to select among noisy activation values is described. © 1992 Academic Press, Inc.

A considerable amount of empirical evidence suggests that human short-term memory is mediated by a relatively simple system with a highly restricted storage capacity. For example, immediate recall of random sequences of verbal stimuli such as words, letters, or digits is inaccurate if the sequences are more than only a few items long (Miller, 1956). This limited span of short-term memory contrasts with the very much larger storage capacity of long-term memory. The limited capacity system responsible for span appears to be involved in a wide range of more general cognitive tasks. This assumption is implicit in the inclusion of memory span in many tests of general intelligence (see, e.g. Terman & Merrill, 1961; Wechsler, 1955). It is explicit in a number of functional models which identify short-term memory with a general-purpose working memory (see, e.g. Atkinson & Shiffrin, 1971; Baddeley & Hitch, 1974; Broadbent, 1984).

Psychological studies of short-term memory have established that it involves multiple subsystems (see, e.g. Baddeley, 1986). The most important storage system in short-term memory for verbal stimuli appears to be a phonological system which holds information about serial order. Baddeley (1986) has presented a simplified model of this component which describes it as an *articulatory loop*. The main purpose of the present investigation was to construct and evaluate a network model of the articulatory loop. We begin by describing the concept of the articulatory loop and summarizing some of the behavioral evidence supporting it. Having done this, we go on to consider the rationale for modeling and the particular approach we adopted.

This work was done while Neil Burgess was supported by an S.E.R.C. Ph.D. studentship and, subsequently, by the European Scientific Exchange Programme of the Royal Society and the hospitality of the Institute of Psychology of the C.N.R., Rome. We acknowledge many useful discussions we have had with M. A. Moore and J. L. Shapiro. We also thank G. Houghton for helpful private communications, D. Hintzman for trenchant comments on our original manuscript, and D. Bowie for help in preparing the manuscript. Requests for reprints should be addressed to Graham Hitch, Department of Psychology, Lancaster University, Lancaster LA1 4YF, UK or Neil Burgess, Department of Anatomy, University College, London WC1E 6BT, UK.

Journal of Memory and Language 31, 429–460 (1992)

The articulatory loop

Following Miller's (1956) paper it became standard to assume that memory span reflects the limited capacity of a single system for attention and short-term memory. However, it has gradually become apparent that more than one system is involved (see, e.g. Baddeley & Hitch, 1974) and that an important limitation on span arises from the contribution of a specifically speech-based subsystem. Early evidence was the observation that substitution errors in recall of visually presented sequences of letters tend to share phonemes in common with the correct items (Conrad, 1964). Phonemically similar items are also particularly difficult to recall (Baddeley, 1966) and Murray (1968) found that this effect could be abolished by requiring subjects to perform articulatory suppression, the repetition of redundant words such as "the–the–the," during the memory task. Suppression therefore appears to disrupt phonological short-term memory. However, suppression does not reduce recall to chance levels (Estes, 1973; Peterson & Johnson, 1971), confirming that a second, non-phonological component contributes to performance. In the working memory model of Baddeley and Hitch (1974), this second component was seen as a limited capacity central executive, which could control the operation of the articulatory loop.

The articulatory loop is thought to be particularly concerned with retaining information about serial order. In the most recent account (Baddeley, 1986) it is described as a limited capacity phonological store coupled with a control process of subvocal rehearsal. Memory traces in the phonological store are assumed to decay in 1 or 2 s unless refreshed serially by rehearsal. This simple model can give a coherent account of the effects of word length, phonemic similarity and articulatory suppression on short-term recall, as follows.

The word length effect is the tendency for short-term recall to be poorer for longer than shorter words. Baddeley, Thompson, and Buchanan (1975) observed a linear relationship between the number of words recalled and the time taken to articulate them such that the amount subjects could recall equalled the number of words they could say in about 1 or 2 s, plus a constant. This relationship was interpreted in terms of the longer time taken in subvocal rehearsal of longer words allowing more trace decay. A simple metaphor is that of a closed tape loop which can store a 1 or 2 s sequence of "inner speech." Baddeley et al. (1975) confirmed this interpretation in subsequent experiments in which they demonstrated that the word length effect could be abolished by articulatory suppression. The phonemic similarity effect and its sensitivity to articulatory suppression can also be explained in terms of the loop by assuming that it reflects confusions among similarly coded items.

The empirical evidence about the loop is not, however, quite as straightforward as has been described. In particular, it was discovered that whereas suppression removed the word length effect for spoken or visual stimuli, it removed the phonemic similarity effect only when stimuli were presented visually and not when they were spoken (Baddeley, Lewis, & Vallar, 1984). These findings suggested that although the phonemic similarity and word length effects are closely related, they must be carefully distinguished from one another. The model of the articulatory loop has been refined to accommodate these effects of presentation modality. It does so by maintaining that whereas the word length effect is due to rehearsal processes, the phonemic similarity effect arises within the phonological store. The modality-specific effect of articulatory suppression can then be explained by assuming that visual stimuli, but not auditory stimuli, have first to be recoded in order to enter the phonological store, and that this extra process involves subvocalization. Further evidence for the complementarity of word length and phonemic similarity effects has come from analysis of the temporal limit associated with memory span (Schweickert, Guentert, & Hersberger, 1990).

The articulatory loop is still a relatively simple theoretical concept even when it is modified to account for the role of presentation modality and differences between the phonemic similarity and word length effects. However, despite its simplicity, it has been shown to be a remarkably robust concept with considerable generality and applicability. The basic empirical effects on which it is based have been replicated several times. Furthermore, the model has been shown to account for a number of new findings. Foremost among these is the tendency for short-term recall to be disrupted by exposing subjects to unattended speech (Salamé & Baddeley, 1982). This effect is explained by the assumption that unattended speech gains obligatory access to the phonological store, where it competes with traces of the memory items. The articulatory loop has also been surprisingly successful in accounting for cross-linguistic differences in digit span. When the rate at which digits can be spoken in different languages is taken into account and the underlying temporal capacity of the loop is calculated, such differences largely disappear (Ellis & Hennelly, 1980; Naveh-Benjamin & Ayers, 1986). The developmental increase in the memory span of children has also been analyzed in terms of the articulatory loop. For example, it has been found that the temporal capacity of the loop remains constant during development and that the improvement in span is predictable from an increase in speech rate as children grow older (Hulme, Thompson, Muir, & Lawrence, 1984; Hitch, Halliday, & Littler, 1989). There have also been applications to routine cognitive skills such as reading and to the analysis of neuropsychological impairments (see, e.g. Baddeley, 1986). To sum up, the properties of simplicity, robustness, generality, and applicability underpin the usefulness of the articulatory loop as a theoretical concept.

Limitations of the articulatory loop model: The problem of serial order

Although the articulatory loop is clearly a useful concept, it has some important limitations as an explanatory account. For example, given that one of its major functions is the preservation of order information, surprisingly little is said about how this is achieved, and some of what is said is clearly incorrect. As has been seen, the model accounts for the phonemic similarity effect in terms of increased difficulty in discriminating among the memory traces of similar items. This explanation is consistent with the well established finding that

phonemic similarity tends to disrupt memory for the serial order of the items rather than memory for the items themselves (Wickelgren, 1965a). However, there is only a hint of a mechanism here, and the model fails to explain important observations such as the tendency for phonemically similar items to be involved in paired transpositions — where one item is interchanged with another in recall (Conrad, 1964). More generally, the model does not attempt to explain other aspects of order errors such as the tendency for paired transpositions to involve adjacent items (Conrad, 1964), nor the characteristic bowed shape of the curve relating probability of error to serial position (Murray, 1966). Where the model is explicit about a mechanism for storing order, as in the tape loop metaphor, it is clearly unable to explain any of the above effects without additional elaboration. However, it remains an open issue whether the model can be extended to give an account of order errors.

The problem of how serial order is retained in short-term memory is one aspect of the general problem of how serial order is remembered at all. This problem has a long history which includes Hull's ideas about interitem associations, Lashley's (1951) powerful critique of associative "chaining," the idea of position–item or contextual associations, and various more complex proposals (see, e.g. Young, 1968). There have been numerous models which attempt to deal with serial order in short-term memory (see, e.g. Lee & Estes, 1981; Lewandowsky & Murdock, 1989; Shiffrin & Cook, 1978), by making different assumptions about the associations which encode serial order, but they fail to deal fully with the pattern of phonemic similarity, word length, and articulatory suppression effects that are so well explained by the articulatory loop account.

There is some evidence for interitem chaining from observations of "associative intrusions" in recall (Wickelgren, 1965b). These are errors involving switching the elements following repeats, as in the sequence a x b a y being recalled as a y b a x. However, simple chaining (that is, the recall of an item being prompted only by the recall of the previous item) would predict that sequences containing repeated items would be extremely difficult to recall and this is evidently not so (Jahnke, 1969). The existence of position–item associations is indicated by the observation of "serial order intrusions" in recall (Conrad, 1960). These are intrusions where the error is the item that was correct (at that position) in the immediately preceding list. However, any purely positional account would of course have difficulty explaining associative intrusions. It seems probable therefore that an extended model of the articulatory loop will have to incorporate some mechanism for storing both interitem and position–item associations if it is to account for behavioral data on the storage of order information in short-term memory.

Rationale for modeling

We have argued that the Baddeley (1986) model of the articulatory loop captures some important regularities about short-term recall but fails to give a realistic account of the problem of serial order. The simplicity of the model holds the attraction of making it easy to understand and apply, but it has the disadvantage of restricting its explanatory value. The primary motivation for constructing a network model of the articulatory loop was to specify a system which would retain the advantages of the present simplistic model, in accounting for the word length, phonemic similarity, and articulatory suppression effects, but which would deal more effectively with the problem of serial order and with patterns of error in recall. A successful model might also be expected to make some novel predictions and to generate insights into other related phenomena.

Approach to modeling

Any attempt to build a network model of the articulatory loop must adopt an approach falling somewhere between two extremes. At one end is a top-down approach which attempts to implement the current concept of the articulatory loop. At the other is a bottom-up approach which attempts to identify the computational problem that is solved by phonological short-term memory. We rapidly rejected an entirely top-down approach on the grounds that it would be impractical given the underspecification of the articulatory loop as

described by Baddeley (1986). In any case, our network model was intended not merely as an implementation of the articulatory loop, but as a development from it which would include a solution to the problem of serial order. To satisfy this goal a bottom-up approach seemed more appropriate. This takes the computational problem of storing information about the serial order of an unpredictable series of verbal stimuli during a single presentation as its starting point. It then goes on to ask if the solution to this computational problem is a system which behaves similarly to what is already known about the articulatory loop. However, it is important to appreciate the practical reality that no bottom-up approach to modeling can proceed without the intrusion of insights from known human data and without influence from previous thinking. This was certainly the case here, as will be clear in the selection of constraints to guide model building and, in particular, in an early decision to include item–item and context–item associations.

Empirical constraints on modeling

In the following section, we describe the empirical constraints from human data which were considered important in determining the architecture of the model. These include effects that are currently attributed to the articulatory loop and, in addition, others we judged basic to people's ability to remember the order of series of items immediately after a single presentation.

a. Decline in immediate recall with increasing list length. Although any model ought to predict the limit on the span of short-term memory to about seven items, this is only a relatively crude index of performance. The mechanism for storing serial order has an even more limited capacity than is implied by span, as shown by the function relating the probability of correct recall to sequence length. Figure 1 illustrates this function for sequences of auditorily presented digits using data reported by Guildford and Dallenbach

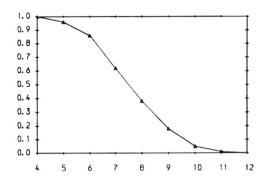

FIG. 1. The fraction of lists of digits that were correctly recalled versus list length, adapted from Guildford and Dallenbach (1925).

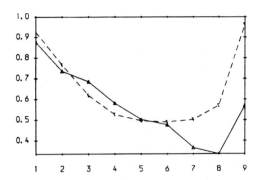

FIG. 2. The fraction of digits correctly recalled at each serial position in lists of nine digits. Visual presentation: full line, simultaneous visual and oral presentation: dashed line, adapted from Crowder (1972).

(1925). It is clear that recall is virtually perfect up to about five digits and that the proportion correct drops dramatically thereafter to reach zero by sequence length 10. One of the targets for modeling was to reproduce the general form of this function.

b. Phonemic similarity, word length, and articulatory suppression. One of the successes of the current articulatory loop model is its ability to account for the disruption to short-term recall arising from increasing phonemic similarity of the items (Baddeley, 1966) and from increasing word length (Baddeley et al., 1975), and the sensitivity of these effects to articulatory suppression. It was considered fundamental that the network should show these effects.

c. Shape of the serial position curve. The serial position curve is one of the best known aspects of short-term recall. It characterizes performance for sequences of intermediate length, where performance is breaking down for part but not all of the list. An important determinant of the shape of the serial position curve is whether items are presented visually or auditorily (Crowder, 1972). As can be seen in Fig. 2, there is a clear primacy effect for both methods of presentation, corresponding to a decline in accuracy from the start of the sequence onwards. However, superimposed on this tendency is a recency effect which is markedly greater for auditorily presented items, and which is restricted

to the final item. The present account of the articulatory loop has very little to say about this phenomenon (Baddeley, 1986). Therefore, an immediate problem is whether to attempt to simulate both forms of presentation or just one, and if the latter, which.

Conventional accounts of the influence of presentation modality on the shape of the serial position curve have maintained that it reflects the operation of a speech-specific auditory input store (Crowder, 1972). However, this explanation has been seriously challenged by more recent data (Gardiner, 1983) and there is at present no generally accepted account. Given that the articulatory loop is assumed to be a mechanism that is fed by visual or auditory input, the obvious choice here was to model features of performance common to both presentation modalities. Therefore, the initial target for simulation was the serial position curve for visual presentation. Since the recall data suggest that whatever is responsible for auditory recency is additive to this common system, it seemed reasonable to regard extension of the model to account for the modality effect as a longer-term goal.

d. Types of recall error. An error in recalling an individual item from a sequence must be either an order error, where an item drawn from elsewhere in the presented sequence is reported, or an item error, where an item from outside the presented sequence is reported, or an omission. By far the greater proportion of errors are order errors (see, e.g. Aaronson, 1968; Bjork & Healey, 1974), and these often involve paired transpositions where the positions of two items from the sequence have been interchanged. Conrad (1964) presented data showing that the majority of paired transpositions involve adjacent items, e.g. the sequence a b c d e f recalled as a b d c e f. He found that the frequency of paired transpositions declines with the number of intervening items. Paired transposition errors are impossible to explain in terms of a simple chain of inter-item associations, and so accounting for their occurrence was a key target for the present simulation.

e. Phonemic confusion and order errors. It has already been noted that errors where one item is substituted for another tend to share phonemes in common. Conrad (1964) published a confusion matrix showing that, for example, f is more likely to be substituted by s than t. It has also been noted that short-term recall is disrupted when the presented items are phonemically similar and that this effect is associated with an increase in order errors (Wickelgren, 1965c). It was considered fundamental that the simulation should have these properties.

Note that constraints c and d refer to empirical data outside the scope of the simple concept of the articulatory loop, while the others refer to effects for which the loop does provide some form of explanation. The goal of simulation was to build a model satisfying the above constraints and to explore its ability to account for other aspects of short-term recall.

A network model of the articulatory loop

Connectionist modeling background
Part of the problem of modeling short-term memory is that it requires a network with unusual characteristics. The net must be able to encode a novel sequence of stimuli in a single presentation and then recall the stimuli immediately in the correct order. Most network models of memory attempt to solve the problem of storing large numbers of patterns without regard to their order, and the application of network modeling techniques to problems involving temporally ordered behavior is relatively new (see, e.g. Jordan, 1986).

Most of the work on creating explicit "neural network" models can be divided into two areas:

1. Networks in which units are arranged in layers; activity in the units of one layer feeding forward to the next layer. The input and output information is often (but not necessarily) represented locally, i.e. each item is represented by the activity of a single unit.

2. Networks in which each unit is connected homogeneously to a fraction of all the other units. Information is distributed throughout the pattern of activity of all the units. The archetypal example of this kind of network is the Hopfield model (Hopfield, 1982).

There have been some models of short-term memory based on modified Hopfield models (Hopfield, 1982). The Hopfield model can be changed in a variety of ways so that a limited number of the most recent patterns of activity can always be stored (Parisi, 1986; Nadal, Toulouse, Changeux, & Dehaene, 1986; Mezard, Nadal, & Toulouse, 1986). Of these only a few have been compared with psychological phenomena (e.g. Nadal, 1987; Virasoro, 1989) or with human data (e.g. Burgess, Moore, & Shapiro, 1989; Burgess, Shapiro, & Moore, 1991). However, actual models of recall within the Hopfield paradigm are very scarce (see Amit, Sagi, & Usher, 1990, for a model of Sternberg fast scanning) and none model the serially ordered recall of whole lists.

A temporal sequence of patterns can be stored in a Hopfield network by using Hebbian learning (see below) that partly stores each pattern and partly stores the association between previous patterns and subsequent patterns. The network can be made to cycle through the various stored patterns in order. This has been done in many slightly different ways (see, e.g. Kleinfeld, 1986; Buhmann & Schulten, 1987; Amit et al., 1990). However, although order information can be stored as a temporal sequence of patterns of activity, the kinds of errors typically made by humans denies this type of system. It is hard to see how such a system would make order errors on recall such as paired transpositions. If errors were made in the temporal sequence of patterns of activity it is unlikely that each pattern would still be visited once or that the temporal positions of a pair of patterns could be transposed. The same difficulty applies to models which involve error back-propagation through time (Rumelhart, Hinton, & Williams, 1986) and back-propagation with feedback (Jordan, 1986; Elman, 1990), added to the necessity of repetitive learning with such models.

There is a longer history of memory modeling using layered networks and local representations, particularly with "on-center off-surround" models in which connections are excitatory between nearby units and inhibitory between distant units. There are many interesting properties shown by networks with this type of architecture (see, for example, Kohonen, 1984; Grossberg, 1987). Given the speech-like nature of the articulatory loop one of these, Houghton's (1990) "competitive queuing" model of speech production, is particularly interesting. In his model of the production of a serially ordered string of sounds, each phoneme is represented by a single node. The main feature of the model is that nodes can be active before their articulation, the most active node being selected by a "competitive filter" (see below). This, together with the way that nodes are temporally cued, results in the coarticulation effects necessary in a realistic model of speech production. Although the model does not use "one shot" learning, this is mainly to prevent order errors. The pronunciations of words are learned gradually and are stored in long-term memory. It is Houghton's method of temporal cuing that necessitates repetitive learning and does not seem appropriate here. However, the selection and subsequent suppression of each item by a competitive filter seems a natural choice for our model of the articulatory loop.

Brief outline of the model

We use a layered architecture (see Fig. 3) in which information is locally represented by nodes taking activation values between ±1. Positive activation values represent activity above background or resting levels, and only positive activation values are propagated forward between layers via weighted connections. The activation value of each node depends on the weighted sum of the activations of nodes to which it is connected. The activation values of nodes are "noisy": they do not respond perfectly but include a small random element. Learning takes place by "one-shot" Hebbian adjustment of the weighted connections.

Presentation and articulation of items is modeled at the level of phonemes. The presentation of an item excites a layer of "input phoneme" nodes, and the articulation of an item involves exciting a separate layer of "output phoneme" nodes. The phonemic output for one item is fed back to excite the phonemic input for the next. That is, there is a set of feedback weights which store item–item associations or links. It is by this feedback that the model forms a basic "articulatory loop." A second set of weights stores context–item associations; the relative influence of these two mechanisms can be varied and is an important free parameter of the model. The "context" for each item is represented by a random pattern of activation which alters progressively with the passage of time. These two sets of "temporary" wights are

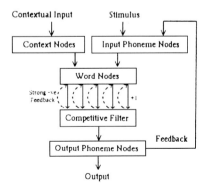

FIG. 3. An outline of the architecture of the model.

"learned" during a single presentation of a series of stimuli. They also decay with time.

The associations between a word or letter and its constituent phonemes necessary for its recognition and articulation are stored in "permanent" weighted connections. Presenting the "input phoneme" and "context" states of a word excites the node corresponding to that word which, if selected, excites the relevant "output phoneme" nodes. The articulation of each word in the list is achieved by "competitive queuing": a "competitive filter" (in which there is strong lateral inhibition) selects the most active word node and then suppresses it before recall of the next word.

The model can perform rehearsal in this way: the temporary weights that store associations for a particular item are automatically refreshed (by Hebbian adjustment) each time an item is rehearsed. Thus temporary weights do not decay to zero and the associations that they store may change. Thus "recall" of the list can be triggered many times. Errors in recall (that is, selecting the wrong item nodes, or selecting the right nodes in the wrong order) occur according to the amount of noise that is introduced into the activation levels.

It should be noted that the use of permanent connections to store associations between words or letters and their constituent phonemes is an obvious simplification since unfamiliar nonsense words can also be stored in phonological short-term memory (see, e.g. Gathercole & Baddeley, 1989; Hintzman, 1967). However, this simplification was regarded as a reasonable starting point given that most data on human behavior are concerned with familiar stimuli and given that the model could be simply modified to allow weights connecting the phoneme and word layers to be learned at presentation.

Description of the model

Four layers of nodes feed directly from one to the next: a layer representing input or presented phonemes, a layer representing each word, a related "competitive filter" layer that selects which word to articulate and a layer representing output or articulated phonemes.

Feedback occurs in two places. There is strong inhibitory feedback from the competitive filter to the word nodes (to suppress a word node after the word has been articulated) and excitatory feedback from the output phoneme nodes to the input phoneme nodes. Excitatory feedback allows the articulation of a word to excite the input phoneme nodes corresponding to the next word in the sequence during rehearsal or recall (we refer to this as "chaining"). For simplicity the model does not distinguish between subvocal rehearsal of a list and actual vocal recall of a list.

The "context" layer

The context layer feeds forward to the word nodes and is used to represent all the nonphonological information in the input, including temporal information. As far as possible, the context and the input phoneme layer (see below) were made to have similar characteristics. There were thus 50 context nodes. During the presentation of each word a random two-thirds of these are updated and the remainder are left unaltered. Of the updated nodes, a randomly chosen subset of six are given a nonzero activation comparable to the average activation in the phoneme layers. The remainder are given an activation of zero. In this way, an average of only nine context nodes are active during the presentation of any item. Importantly, the fact that some context nodes are not updated when a new word is presented gives some time correlation to the patterns of activation for successive inputs. Thus the similarity of the activation patterns for two words will on average vary monotonically with their temporal separation in the input sequence.

How activations propagate

The activity of all other (i.e. noncontext) nodes is determined by the activities of the nodes to which they are connected. The activity $a_j(t)$ of a node onto which arrive connections (of "weight" W_{ij}) from c nodes each of positive activity $\{a_i(t) > 0, i = 1$ to $c\}$ is updated at time t according to the weighted sum of activities,

$$a_j(t+1) = f\left(\sum_{i=1}^{c} W_{ij}a_i(t)\right), \tag{1}$$

where f is a squashing function which keeps the value of a_j between -1 and $+1$. Note that only positive activation values are propagated and updating is done in parallel (i.e. synchronously).

This equation shows the activity of an immediately reactive node, i.e. one which responds to the signals it receives as soon as it is updated. If a node has been suppressed to a very inactive state (denoted by a negative activation level), or if it is in the competitive filter (which is updated on a much shorter time scale than other layers) its activity does not change so immediately — but depends partly on its previous value according to:

$$a_j(t+1) = f(a_j(t) + \sum_{i=1}^{c} W_{ij}a_i(t)). \tag{2}$$

Selecting a word in recall

The output of each word involves a cycle in which the most active word node is selected, exciting its corresponding output phoneme nodes, and it is then suppressed. This is done by "competitive queuing" (Houghton, 1990), as follows. Each word node connects to a competitive filter node with an excitatory connection. Thus the competitive filter initially reproduces the pattern of activation of the word layer. However, there is strong lateral inhibition between nodes in the competitive filter (cf) which, after relatively few iterations of the activations in this layer, results in the cf node connected to the most active word node suppressing all the other cf nodes to negative activation levels. The winning cf node then excites the output phoneme nodes corresponding to the selected word node.

There are also strongly inhibitory connections from each competitive filter node back to the corresponding word node. Thus the next time the word layer is updated the selected word node is suppressed by the winning competitive filter node (see Fig. 4).

Connections, weights and learning

There are three types of connections between nodes: "hard wired" connections, prelearned permanent connections, and temporary connections

which are learned, and decay, during an experiment (see Fig. 4).

The lateral inhibition in the competitive filter layer, the one-to-one excitatory connections from word nodes to competitive filter nodes and the one-to-one inhibitory feedback to the word nodes are hard wired. The values of the connection weights do not change and are the same for all connections involved in the same task.

Learning (i.e. weight modification) only occurs in excitatory connections and is achieved by "one-shot" Hebbian increment of connections between two nodes with positive activation.

Permanent connections store the associations enabling the "recognition" and "articulation" of individual words. These are the connections which excite the relevant word node when the corresponding input phoneme nodes are active or excite the relevant output phoneme nodes when a particular word has been selected by the competitive filter. The weights for these connections are prelearned before the model is presented with immediate recall tasks.

Temporary weighted connections are used to learn (i) the association between the state of the context nodes when a word is presented and the corresponding word node, and (ii) the association between the output phonemes of a word and the input phonemes of the next word.

If a connection of weight W_{ij} connects two nodes of activity a_i and a_j then learning implies

if $a_i > 0$ and $a_j > 0$
$$\text{then } W_{ij} = \varepsilon a_i a_j, \tag{3}$$

where ε is a parameter governing the size of the weights (see implementation).

The temporary weights decay with elapsed time. We (crudely) take the amount of time that elapses during the presentation or rehearsal of a word to be proportional to the total number of phonemes output. Thus the decay of a temporary weight during the presentation or rehearsal of a word containing n phonemes is

$$W_{ij} \mapsto \Delta^n W_{ij},$$

where Δ is the decay factor per (phonemic) time step.

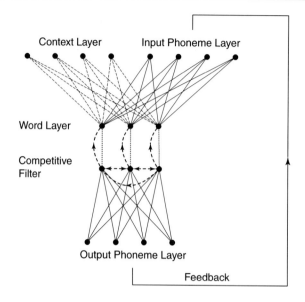

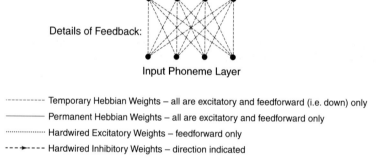

--------- Temporary Hebbian Weights – all are excitatory and feedforward (i.e. down) only
————— Permanent Hebbian Weights – all are excitatory and feedforward only
················ Hardwired Excitatory Weights – feedforward only
---➤--- Hardwired Inhibitory Weights – direction indicated

FIG. 4. A schematic representation of the model of the articulatory loop — in reality there are more nodes.

The word layer

For most of our simulations we use the letters of the alphabet as the vocabulary of the system. Accordingly there are 26 "word" nodes, one for each letter. To investigate the word length effect systematically we sometimes use a vocabulary of "random words," i.e. "words" made from random selections of phonemes, with different numbers of phonemes per word.

As described above, the weighted connections between the input phoneme layer and the word layer for the recognition of all the words in the vocabulary are prelearned, and are permanent.

For example, to learn to recognize the letter c the input phoneme nodes for "s" and "ee" and the word node for c are activated and connection weights are incremented according to Eq. (3).

Thus activation of input phoneme nodes "s" and "ee" will cause activation of the word node c; it will also cause lesser activation of the word nodes b d e g p t v s x which will also have excitatory connections to either "s" or "ee." We opted to see how much could be achieved by making the simplest possible choice of phonological coding. Thus, the phoneme nodes were not ordered in any way, and so the system would treat "s-ee" and "ee-s" as equivalent. For most stimuli and in particular those used in testing the model, this simplification does not lead to any errors of recognition.

There are also excitatory connections from the context layer to the word layer. These learn the association between each word and the context state for each word. Thus, if at recall the nodes in the context layer have the pattern of activation that coincided with presentation of the first word, the corresponding word node will be activated. As with the input phoneme nodes, there will be nodes that are active in the context state for more than one word. Because of the way context is assumed to vary, the overlap will be greatest for words that are adjacent in the list. Thus, if the context nodes are in the pattern of activation for the first word, the corresponding word node will be the most active, but others will also be active (particularly the second word node)–but to a lesser degree.

The connection weights from the context layer are learned on the presentation of each word and decay with time (see above). Each time a word node is selected during rehearsal the temporary weights between the current context state and that word node are relearned.

A fraction F_{ph} of the activation of a word node is determined by the input phoneme layers and $1 - F_{ph}$ by the context layer (see "Setting Correct Weight Strengths"). During rehearsal or recall some word nodes will be active before their time of recall, irrespective of which layer is driving the word layer. The competitive queuing (see above) serves to select the most active node each time a word should be recalled and then to suppress it in time for the next word to be recalled.

The phoneme layers

There are 53 input and output phoneme nodes, one for each possible phoneme. For simplicity, no attempt is made to represent the similarity space of phonemes. Most of the phoneme nodes are not used in lists of letters of the alphabet, although they are all used to make up "random words." Output phoneme nodes are excited by activation in a competitive filter node. The excitatory connections required to articulate a word are prelearned. For

example, to learn to articulate c, the competitive filter node corresponding to word node c and the output phoneme nodes "s" and "ee" are activated, and the connection weights are updated according to Eq. (3).

The input phoneme nodes are excited by temporary connections from the output phoneme layer. These connection weights store item–item associations, referred to here as chaining weights. They are learned during presentation and decay with time. During the presentation of a word, the corresponding input phoneme nodes are activated while output phoneme nodes corresponding to the phonemes in the preceding word are still active. The chaining weights are incremented according to Eq. (3). Thus, during recall or rehearsal, the "saying" of each word will excite the input phoneme nodes for the next word.

There is opportunity for erroneous activation of input phoneme nodes (as there is for word nodes) if words in a list share phonemes. For example in the list a b f c q, excitatory weights will be learned from output phoneme node "ee" to input phoneme nodes "e," "f," "kh," and "uu" (in the associations b $\mapsto$ f and c $\mapsto$ q). Thus when letter b is output the input phoneme nodes for f will be excited, but so will (to a lesser extent) the input phoneme nodes for q. During recall/rehearsal the chaining weights are relearned each time a word is articulated.

These decaying chaining weights which store phonemic item–item associations and must be relearned during rehearsal are our interpretation of a decaying phonological store. For example, we interpret articulatory suppression as putting these weights out of action (i.e. preventing them propagating activations).

There are two immediate constraints on the size of connection weights in the phonological store:

(i) When a word is presented (i.e. its input phoneme nodes are excited) the corresponding word node should become equally excited whether the word contains many or few phonemes.

(ii) Nodes corresponding to words that share phonemes with an input word should be less activated by the input phoneme nodes than the node for the inputted word itself.

These are made harder to satisfy by the fact that words within a list may be of different lengths and may have phonemes in common.

The prescription we have used is to ensure that the phoneme nodes corresponding to the input or output of a word of n phonemes have activity proportional to $1/\sqrt{n}$. The two most obvious choices of having activity independent of n or proportional to $1/n$ (so that the total phonemic activity for a word is independent of n) will not satisfy (i) and (ii), whatever the choice of strengths for the other weights in the model.

Noise

Up to this point we would have a system which could recall perfectly. However, the occurrence of errors in humans is both fundamental and instructive: a realistic model must also show this type of unreliability. The behavior of microscopic biological systems tends to be probabilistic, i.e. while behavior averaged over time or over many systems depends on an external influence, the behavior of, say, an individual neuron at a particular time is erratic. So a natural choice for our model is to put noise equally into the rule determining the activation level of nodes. The success of this choice should be judged by how humanlike the resulting errors are. Accordingly we adapted Eq. (1) to become

$$a_j(t+1) = f\left(\sum_{i=1}^{c} W_{ij}\, a_i(t)\right) + \eta, \qquad (4)$$

where η is a random variable taking values uniformly between $\pm\sigma$. Equation (2) changes similarly. The strength of the noise is determined by σ. This also introduces noise into the connection weights through Eq. (3). Note that the bounds ±1 on the activity of a node are not rigid. If a node has an activation level of very nearly 1 in Eq. (1), the addition of noise as in Eq. (4) could make its activation greater than 1.

The introduction of noise ensures that the decay of the temporary weights has an effect. Without noise, decay would result in the typical levels of

activation in the system continually decreasing, but not necessarily in any change of behavior. With noise the level of activation of the nodes in a layer must be large in comparison to the level of noise or the information held by the layer will be lost.

If the system is not making mistakes then a temporary weight will decay by Δ^M between each relearning, where M is the total number of phonemes in the list. The activation levels of nodes in the word layer will decrease by the same factor. Errors will occur when the activation level of word nodes is low enough for the noise term in Eq. (4) to be significant in determining which one is the most active. Thus the length of a list that the model can recall without error should be determined by M, i.e. by the time taken to articulate a list (within our approximation that all phonemes take the same length of time to articulate).

Rehearsal and relearning

During recall or rehearsal the temporary weights are relearned to prevent them from decaying to zero. With the output of each word there occurs Hebbian relearning of both sets of temporary weights. The temporary weights storing the (context–word or output phoneme–input phoneme) associations for a particular word are only incremented if that word is selected in rehearsal. For the chaining weights between output and input phoneme layers this cannot be otherwise; the only output phoneme nodes that are excited at any one time are those corresponding to the most recently selected word. In the context–word weights, relearning occurs only in those weights connected to the word node corresponding to an active competitive filter node (i.e. the most recently selected word node). Note that if a word is omitted in recall its temporary weights will continue to decay, and when an error occurs the erroneous context–word and phonemic associations will be learned.

We want temporary weights only to decrease by means of decay, so if the connection weight W_{ij} is already greater than $\varepsilon a_i a_j$ before learning, no change should take place. Hence Eq. (3) becomes

$$W_{ij}(t+1) = \begin{cases} \varepsilon a_i(t)a_j(t) & \text{if } W_{ij}(t) < \varepsilon a_i(t)a_j(t), \\ W_{ij}(t) & \text{otherwise.} \end{cases} \qquad (5)$$

Thus temporary weights can only be increased by relearning; they are only decreased by decaying. This change only affects the temporary weights; permanent weights are incremented once each from zero so that, for them, Eqs. (3) and (5) are equivalent. In this paper we only consider immediate recall, involving a single rehearsal, in any detail.

Setting correct weight strengths

The size of the connection weights will determine the typical activation values of excited nodes in the various layers. The size of a weight is set by the value of ε during learning in Eq. (3). We can calculate the values of ε that will result in the desired activation values. If the desired running activation levels for word, input phoneme, output phoneme, and context nodes are A_{wd}, $1/\sqrt{n}$, $1/\sqrt{n}$, and A_{ct} respectively, then the correct learning strength ε for weights can be calculated from Eq. (1). For example, the learning strength for weights from the context to word layers is: $\varepsilon = (1 - F_{ph})f^{-1}(A_{wd})/A_{wd}A_{ct}^2 N_{act}$. Thus weights learned according to Eq. (3) when context and word nodes have activation A_{ct} and A_{wd} will be of the correct strength to ensure that these nodes will have activations A_{ct} and A_{wd} when they are excited during rehearsal/recall.

For the hard wired connections all weights sharing the same function have the same value; e.g. weights from the word layer to the competitive filter are all +1.0.

The decay of temporary weights means that the activation values of word nodes will also be lower by a factor of Δ^M after each rehearsal. Thus during Hebbian relearning the learning factor ε must be increased to ε/Δ^M if relearned weights are to have the same magnitude as before decay (otherwise all activation values will decay by Δ^M for each rehearsal until they are lost in the noise).

Parameter values

To determine the weight strengths we use in the model we must decide on the activation values we want for excited nodes in layers other than the phoneme layers. These are as follows:

$A_{ct} = 0.50$ so that the context layer is as comparable to the input phoneme layer as possible.

$A_{cf} = 0.50$ for convenience — this value is not important.

$A_{wd} = 0.25$ — any small value will do, so that weight strengths to the word layer are relatively low and previously suppressed word nodes will not often become reexcited and get repeated (repetition errors are rare in the human data).

$\Delta = 0.95$ — this cannot be much smaller than 1 or else at the beginning of recall the temporary weights for early items in the list will be very much smaller than those for later items. If this happens later items will be recalled in place of earlier ones, but not because of either of the confusion mechanisms intentionally in the model (confusion in the context or phoneme layers).

It is hard to see what the remaining two parameters in the model should be without reference to the human data; these are:

F_{ph} — the fraction of input to the word nodes from the phonological store rather than from the context nodes; this will determine the strength of effects dependent on phonemic similarity and item–item association (i.e. "chaining").

σ — the amount of noise in the activation levels of nodes; this will determine the capacity of the model.

Thus we left only two independent parameters to vary during simulations of the model.

Simulation procedure

The procedure to model presentation and rehearsal/recall is as follows (see also Figs. 3 and 4):

- All nodes and connection weights are set to zero (excluding the "hard wired" connections which are fixed).
- Prelearning. The association between the input phoneme nodes corresponding to a word and the relevant word node is learned. Similarly the association between a competitive filter node (corresponding to a selected word) and the relevant output phoneme nodes is learned.
- Presentation. 1. Initialization. A sequence of words to be learned is chosen. The context nodes are set to a random initial state.
  2. Presentation and learning of the ith word.
     i. The input phoneme nodes are set to the phonemic activity of the i_{th} word. Two-thirds of the context nodes are updated.

ii. The "chaining" weights from the output phoneme layer to the input phoneme layer are learned using Hebbian learning as in Eq. (5); the output phoneme nodes are still active from the articulation of the last word. Note that for the first word in a sequence the output phoneme nodes are zero and no weights are changed.

iii. The word nodes (particularly the ith word node) are excited by the input phoneme nodes and suppressed by the competitive filter nodes (generally only the $(i-1)^{th}$ word node is suppressed). The weights from the context layer to the ith word node are learned as in Eq. (5). See Eqs. (1) and (2) for how activation levels are updated. Note that for the first word in a sequence this is the only learning that takes place.

iv. The competitive filter nodes are updated several times. The hard wired connections from the word nodes and strong lateral competition result in the node connected to the most active word node (the ith) dominating and suppressing all the others.

3. The output phoneme nodes are excited by the winning competitive filter node (i.e. the only active competitive filter node) to show the phonemic activity of the ith word.

4. Decay. The temporary weights (between the output and input phoneme layers and the context and word layers) decay by factor Δ for each output phoneme excited in stage 3.

5. Return to 2(i) for the next word.

• Recall/rehearsal (deliberately similar to presentation):

1. Initialization. The word nodes are reset to zero, the context nodes are reset to the initial state they had in step (1) of the presentation.

2. Recall/rehearsal of the ith word:

i. The input phoneme nodes are excited by the chaining weights from the output phoneme nodes. There is "cuing"

for the first word in the list; i.e. the input phoneme nodes are set to the phonemic activity of the first word. The context nodes replicate the state of activity they had in step 2(i) of the presentation. (The rationale for cuing the first word and the context states is that these processes occur outside the articulatory loop and without significant error. That is, we assume the phenomena we are trying to explain are not due to errors in cuing the loop at recall, but in the temporary associations and in the mechanism we have chosen for the selection of each item within the loop itself).

ii. The "chaining" weights from the output phoneme layer to the input phoneme layer are relearned. The output phoneme nodes are still active from the output of the $(i-1)^{th}$ word. (For the first word the output phoneme nodes are still active from the last word in the presented list).

iii. The word nodes are excited by the input phoneme nodes and context nodes and suppressed by the competitive filter nodes (generally only the $(i-1)^{th}$ word node is suppressed).

iv. The competitive filter nodes are updated several times.

3. The output phoneme nodes are excited by the winning competitive filter node (i.e. the only active competitive filter node) to show the phonemic activity of the ith word.

4. Decay. The temporary weights (between the output and input phoneme layers and the context and word layers) decay by a factor Δ for each phoneme outputted in stage 3.

5. Return to 2(i) for the next word.

6. Return to 1 for the next rehearsal.

Performance and evaluation

In this section we compare the performance of the model with the main features of human performance outlined earlier. Note that the simulations repeated in this section are examples of the behavior of the model for certain values of F_{ph}, Δ, etc. We have a more general understanding of the dependence of its behavior on these and other parameters than is shown in these few examples. Thus we have derived approximate mathematical expressions for the probability of an error between two items and for span as a function of the parameters. Extensive simulations showed good agreement with these mathematical expressions (see Burgess, 1990, for a full description).

The most basic property of a model of short-term memory is its capacity. We begin by examining the word span of the model (how long a list can be correctly recalled), giving regard also to the length and similarity of the words used. We then consider the frequencies of errors made at the different serial positions in the list. This also depends on the phonemic similarity of the words. We also examine the types and relative proportions of errors made by the model. We consider chiefly only the errors made in the first rehearsal, i.e. in "immediate recall." The occurrence of errors during further rehearsals is briefly discussed at the end of this section.

The decay of temporary weights in the model depends on the total number of phonemes in the list (M). We expected this to determine the model's span, in accordance with evidence that the span for human short-term memory is determined by the time taken to articulate the list (given our approximation that all phonemes take the same time to articulate). Forgetting will occur when the difference in activation between the correct word node and competing word nodes is of the same order of magnitude as the noise.

In the simulations that are reported, the noise parameter, σ, was adjusted to give a span of seven letters (of length two phonemes) so as to establish a point of correspondence with the general level of human performance. This was done for $F_{ph} = 0.5$, i.e. equal influence of chaining and contextual associations to the word layer. As a result, the noise parameter was set at $\sigma = 0.03$. Thereafter, simulations were run across the whole range of values of F_{ph} to explore the influence of chaining on the performance of the model. In the fol-

lowing sections, data are in general presented for simulations with $F_{ph} = 0.5$, with additional data for simulations with $F_{ph} = 0.02$ (i.e. almost no chaining) and $F_{ph} = 0.98$ (almost "pure" chaining), where the differences in performance are considered important.

Capacity: Effects of list length, word length, and item similarity

Figure 5 shows the probability of a whole list being correctly recalled (on the first rehearsal) as a function of list length. Lists were random selections from a set of "dissimilar" letters (b f j i o u r t n h y q v s), or "similar" letters (b c d g p v t f l m n s x z). The prelearned vocabulary was the set of all the letters of the alphabet. The curves were calculated from 200 trials of each list length; parameter values were $F_{ph} = 0.5$ and $\sigma = 0.03$.

We see that the "span" of the model (the list length at which half of the lists are correctly recalled) is greater for dissimilar letters than for similar letters. The reduction due to similarity is 33% which appears to be slightly greater than in humans. For example, in a similar but not identical comparison, Schweickert et al. (1990) reported a difference of 20%. Note also that the dissimilar letters are "shorter" than the similar letters. The 14 dissimilar letters contained a total of 24 phonemes, whereas the similar letters contained 30. However, this small difference in word length is too

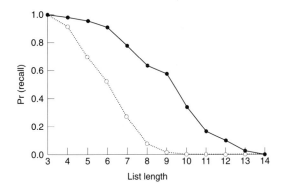

FIG. 5. The probability of correctly recalling (on the first rehearsal) a list of N letters versus list length N. Lists were selected from the letters b f j i o u r t n h y q v s (full line) and b c d g p v t f l m n s x z (dashed line). There were 200 trials of each list length, $F_{ph} = 0.5$ and $\sigma = 0.03$.

slight to provide an adequate explanation of the phonemic similarity effect (cf. also Schweickert et al., 1990).

The span for dissimilar words of exactly two phonemes is best shown in Fig. 6. Because we are approximating the time taken to articulate a word by the number of phonemes it contains, the phonemic word length is important in terms of model span. Figure 6 shows that word span does have this type of dependence on phonemic word length. It shows the probability of correctly recalling an item from a list of words as a function of word length. Each list was comprised of "words" made from *n* randomly selected phonemes. Lists were chosen from a pool of 14 of these "random words," the prelearned vocabulary consisted of 26 "random words" (including the 14 used in lists). The number of phonemes per word was varied between two and five. Performance declines noticeably with word length in a way that looks remarkably similar to human data (Baddeley et al., 1975, Fig. 1).

The data in Fig. 6 could be interpreted in terms of articulation rate: simulations involving five-phoneme words correspond to an articulation rate 2.5 times slower than those involving two-phoneme words. Figure 7 shows the relationship between span, defined as the list length at which 50% of recalls are correct, and articulation rate using the data in Fig. 6. The linearity of this relationship corresponds well with equivalent

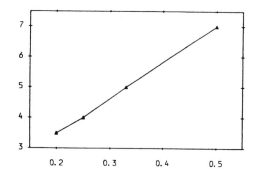

FIG. 7. Item span (ordinate) versus articulation rate. The data for random words in Fig. 6 are replotted to show the effect on span of the number of words that can be articulated per time step (= 1/the number of phonemes per word).

plots of psychological data (Baddeley et al., 1975; Hulme et al., 1984; Hitch et al., 1989). Figure 7 shows that the model's span *s* increases proportional to the speech rate *r*. Assuming a speech rate of about 12 phonemes per second as a rough estimate, the constant of proportionality is approximately 1, which compares well with values of between 1 and 2 from the psychological studies. In fact the simulations show $s \approx r + 1$, in close agreement with the equation reported by Hitch et al. (1991).

Note that the total number of phonemes in the list is not the sole factor that determines span. Figure 8 shows the same curves as Fig. 6 plotted

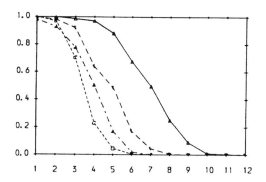

FIG. 6. The probability of correctly recalling a list of *N* "random words" versus list length *N*. A "random word" is a random selection of *n* phonemes. The phonemic word lengths *n* are 2 (full line), 3 (dashed line), 4 (dash-dot-dash line), and 5 (dotted line). There are 200 trials for each word length, $F_{ph} = 0.5$ and $\sigma = 0.03$.

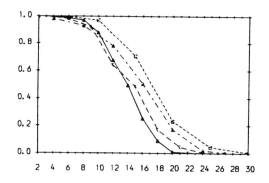

FIG. 8. The probability of correctly recalling a list of *N* "random words" (each of *n* phonemes) versus the total number of phonemes in the list $N \times n$. The data are the same as in Fig. 6: full line, *n* = 2; dashed line, *n* = 3; dash-dot-dash line, *n* = 4; dotted line, *n* = 5.

as a function of the total number of phonemes in the list. The performance on long lists of short words is a little worse than that on short lists of long words even where both lists contain the same total number of phonemes. This is because more words means a greater number of excited word nodes, which increases the possibility of a noise-induced error.

Interestingly, there may be a parallel for such effects in human data. Zhang and Simon (1985) found that while span was related to the time to articulate individual items, there was a second factor (which they interpreted as the time taken to access each "chunk"). The direction of this effect was the same as in Fig. 7. However, our model suggests an alternative interpretation of the mechanism responsible.

In summary the model reproduces the psychological data on memory span and its susceptibility to the effects of phonemic similarity and word length. In all three cases the model shows effects of the right type with the same order of magnitude as the human data. Note that the span of the model is arbitrary and is determined by choosing a suitable level of noise (i.e. σ). However, once this parameter has been set, the phonemic similarity and word length effects, particularly the encouraging dependence of recall on speech rate, are emergent features of the model.

Serial position and item similarity

Figure 9 shows the probability of correct recall (on the first rehearsal) as a function of serial position. The letters b f j i o u r t n h y q v s were used, and the data are from the simulation shown in Fig. 5. The serial position curves clearly show primacy and no recency.

The model also shows primacy when it is running with $F_{ph} = 0.02$ (i.e. the word nodes are driven almost entirely by the context layer) or with $F_{ph} = 0.98$ (i.e. the word nodes are driven almost entirely by the phoneme layers). This is because an error near the beginning of a list (i.e. a later item being recalled too soon) tends to increase the chance of subsequent errors. Thus even if spontaneous errors occurred uniformly throughout the list the increased chance of "knock on" errors would ensure primacy. This effect is very robust

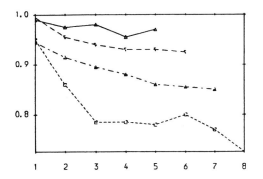

FIG. 9. The probability of correctly recalling an item from a list of N of the letters: b f j i o u r t n h y q v s, versus the serial position of the item. The values of N are 5 (full line), 6 (dashed line), 7 (dash-dot-dash line), and 8 (dotted line). The data are the same as in Fig. 5.

when the word nodes are driven purely by the phoneme layers ($F_{ph} = 0.98$). The chaining of the phoneme layers results in serial position curves that decrease progressively in nearly all trials. This is a fundamental problem with excessive chaining since an error anywhere in the sequence will throw out everything that follows. When $F_{ph} = 0.02$ there is much greater individual variation in serial position curves, although the averaged curve also shows primacy of similar downward slope. In a later section we show how a simple alteration of the way contextual information is encoded can result in recency when the model is run without chaining.

We also ran the model with the same parameters as in Fig. 9, but with lists chosen from the letters b c d g p t v f l m n s x z. Half of these letters share the phoneme "ee," and half the phoneme "e," but there are also other shared phonemes. Thus the phonemic similarity encountered by the model was much greater than in Fig. 9. Consistent with the span data (see Fig. 5), performance is much decreased, as shown in Fig. 10. The reduction is about 14% for five-item lists, 24% for six items, and somewhat more for longer lists. Typical human data show reductions of the order of 22% for five-item lists (Peterson & Johnson, 1971, Experiment 1) and 37% for six items (Baddeley, 1968, Experiment 5). The agreement is therefore quite close here, bearing in mind that the model was run with a slightly lower degree

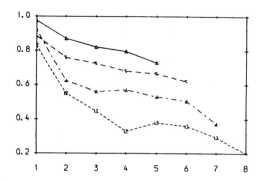

FIG. 10. The probability of correctly recalling an item from a list of N of the letters: b c d g p t v f l m n s x z versus the serial position of the item. Note the phonemic similarity of these items. The list length N is 5 (full line), 6 (dashed line), 7 (dot-dash-dot line), and 8 (dotted line). There were 200 trials for each list length, $F_{ph} = 0.5$ and $\sigma = 0.03$.

similar items tend to be confused with each other. Note that c shares phoneme "s" with s and x, also d shares phoneme "d" with z. The letter e occurred as an intrusion error almost as frequently as letters from the list, accounting for the greater difference in proportions of "similar" and "different" errors shown by the letters containing phoneme "ee" (b c d g p t v) than those containing "e" (f l m n s x z).

The similarity effect is clearly shown. However, the effect of chaining is that the similarity of two items has as much effect on their immediate successors in the list as on themselves. This partially obscures the similarity effect in the confusion matrix (Table 1). It also prevents the modeling of experiments involving alternating similar and different items (see below).

of phonemic similarity than was experienced by the human subjects. It is interesting to note the similarity in the shape of serial position curves for lists of similar and dissimilar letters. This is also a feature of human performance (Baddeley, 1968).

Table 1 shows an analysis of substitution errors and indicates the proportion of times the substitutions shared a phoneme with the correct letter. This was done for the simulations shown in Fig. 10. The expected proportions of errors if substitution occurs at chance are also shown (i.e. assuming that errors are independent of phonemic similarity). It can be seen that, when errors are made,

Types and proportions of errors made

We counted the number of various types of errors made by the model in simulations with $F_{ph} = 0.02$, 0.5, and 0.98 to illustrate the different effects of the context and phoneme layers on the word layer. The results for lists of phonemically similar and dissimilar items are shown in Table 2. Apart from a very small number of repetition errors all the errors made were order errors or extra-list intrusion errors. There were no "don't knows" since the competitive filter always selected an item for output.

Note first that performance for $F_{ph} = 0.5$ is much better than for either $F_{ph} = 0.02$ or $F_{ph} = 0.98$.

TABLE 1
The Proportion of Times a Letter Was Substituted by a Similar Letter (One with a Phoneme or Phonemes in Common) in the Errors Made in the Recall of Lists of 5 to 8 of the Letters: b c d g p t v f l m n s x z

Types of error	Input letter													
	b	c	d	g	p	t	v	f	l	m	n	s	x	z
Similar	.59	.73	.73	.65	.63	.61	.55	.55	.53	.53	.59	.71	.63	.62
Different	.41	.27	.27	.35	.37	.39	.45	.45	.47	.47	.41	.29	.37	.38
Chance														
Similar	.46	.62	.54	.46	.46	.46	.46	.46	.46	.46	.46	.54	.54	.54
Different	.54	.38	.46	.54	.54	.54	.54	.54	.54	.54	.54	.46	.46	.46

Note. Also shown are the proportions expected if substitution occurred by chance. The data are from the simulations in Fig. 10, $F_{ph} = 0.50$, $\sigma = 0.03$.

TABLE 2
The Different Types and Proportions of Errors Produced by the Model as a Function of List Length, Item Similarity, and F_{ph}

F_{ph}	Error type	Phonemically dissimilar letters list length					Phonemically similar letters list length				
		5	6	7	8	Mean	5	6	7	8	Mean
0.02	Item	1.2	3.0	5.9	9.4	4.9	4.6	9.8	11.7	15.6	10.4
	Order	60.8	71.3	95.5	107.7	83.8	85.6	101.5	108.9	117.7	103.4
0.50	Item	0.6	2.7	6.0	10.1	4.9	4.8	12.5	17.3	21.7	14.1
	Order	4.6	8.1	16.9	28.5	14.5	27.6	43.0	66.0	93.6	57.6
0.98	Item	7.6	11.0	18.0	23.9	15.1	19.6	26.0	27.0	25.0	24.4
	Order	8.0	20.8	33.0	50.7	28.1	38.8	66.3	99.0	118.3	80.6

Note. The values shown are the number of errors/list length during 200 trials, i.e. the number of times that an item is incorrectly recalled averaged over serial position, $\sigma = 0.03$.

This is interesting in that it demonstrates a natural advantage of having two different mechanisms controlling recall. An error in either system alone may be tolerated; the incidence of two different types of error occurring coincidentally for the same item is lower than for either error alone. Table 2 also shows that errors increase with both list length and phonemic similarity for all values of F_{ph}. Furthermore, order errors consistently form the majority of errors, ranging between 74% and 88% for $F_{ph} = 0.5$. This is in agreement with estimates of around 75% for human recall under similar conditions (Aaronson, 1968; Bjork & Healy, 1974). The main effect of phonemic similarity is to increase order errors, again in good agreement with the psychological data (Wickelgren, 1965c). However, there is also a slight increase in item errors, which is unlike the data from human subjects. As is to be expected the effect of phonemic similarity increases as the amount of chaining, given by the parameter F_{ph}, increases. However, phonemic similarity has a slight effect even for $F_{ph} = 0.2$ because the effect of the phoneme layer on the word layer is of the same order of magnitude as (although smaller than) the noise.

The absence of "don't know" responses (omissions) is not characteristic of human behavior, it is a consequence of the fact that when the competitive filter has reached a steady state, it has always chosen a word node (the most strongly activated). A simple way of producing omissions is to apply a threshold to the output from the competitive filter such that the response is "don't know" if the activation of the winning word node is below the threshold. Further simulations illustrate the effects of this modification for different thresholds (see Table 3). Interestingly, while omissions tend to increase towards later serial positions, commission errors (which are mainly order errors) show some evidence of recency. This suggests that the model is capable of producing recency given suitable modification (see below). Note that for very high thresholds the overall accuracy of recall drops sharply because the activation of correct winners sometimes falls below threshold.

We can also investigate the difference in serial position of items that are confused in recall. In human data the majority of order errors involve an item being substituted by an adjacent or very near item (Healy, 1974). In Fig. 11 we show the distribution of the separations between pairs of items whose positions are transposed in simulations with $F_{ph} = 0.02$, 0.5, and 0.98. For example, recall of the sequence a b c d e f g h as a b c f e d g h would correspond to a separation of two positions. Figure 11 gives us an indication of the range in serial position over which paired transposition errors occur.

When the context layer alone is driving the word layer ($F_{ph} = 0.02$), paired transpositions tend

TABLE 3
Effect of Applying Different Thresholds to the Output of the Competitive Filter to Produce Omission Errors

Threshold		Serial position							Proportion of lists correct
		1	2	3	4	5	6	7	
0.38	Omissions	—	—	—	.01	.01	.01	.03	
	Commissions	.03	.10	.18	.17	.16	.17	.16	.81
0.40	Omissions	—	—	—	.02	.02	.04	.06	
	Commissions	.03	.10	.18	.16	.16	.15	.13	.81
0.42	Omissions	.02	.01	.01	.05	.05	.07	.12	
	Commissions	.03	.11	.18	.14	.14	.13	.08	.76
0.44	Omissions	.24	.09	.08	.10	.14	.17	.22	
	Commissions	.01	.09	.17	.13	.09	.11	.03	.46

Note. The values shown are mean probability correct from 200 trials ($F_{ph} = 0.05$, $\sigma = 0.03$).

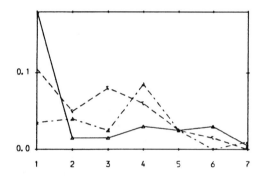

FIG. 11. The distribution of the separation of items involved in paired transpositions. The data are from the same simulation as Table 2. Lists were of eight dissimilar letters, $F_{ph} = 0.02$ (full line), $F_{ph} = 0.50$ (dashed line), and $F_{ph} = 0.98$ (dot-dash line).

to be between adjacent items because of the temporal correlation in the context layer. However, when the input phoneme layer alone is driving the word layer ($F_{ph} = 0.98$) there is no such bias towards nearby items. The model running with both types of input to the word layer ($F_{ph} = 0.50$) shows only a slight increase in the incidence of paired transpositions between adjacent items.

The root cause of the large proportion of well separated paired transposition errors and the higher incidence in omissions towards later serial positions is decay. If there are decaying weights or activities in the phoneme or context layers then there will be a tendency for a word wd_{err} late in the list to be substituted for a word wd_{cor} early in the list. At the time of recall for wd_{cor} the temporary weights that store the associations necessary for its excitation will have decayed by much more than those for wd_{err}. Thus if any of the context or phoneme nodes that excite wd_{cor} also excite wd_{err} (because of correlations in the states of the context layer or item similarity) they will do so via much stronger weights. In fact for very strong decay ($\Delta = 0.5$, say) this effect is so strong that lists can be recalled in reverse order! Clearly decay must be in the model, as the information stored is temporary. Furthermore, it is interesting to note that in free recall of very long lists the subject can often remember only the last few items (see, e.g. Murdock, 1962). However, some modification of the model is indicated, as described later.

In summary, the model is capable of producing the same types of errors as humans. It does well in that there are typically more order errors than item errors and in that phonemic similarity has its effect chiefly on order errors. Both of these are robust features of the model. Paired transpositions are also relatively common, but they tend to involve adjacent items only when the amount of chaining is minimal. A major problem is the unnaturally large separation of items involved in some paired transpositions even when there is little chaining.

Articulatory suppression. We interpret interference with subvocal rehearsal as preventing the use of the chaining weights. Thus only the context layer will affect the word layer, as input phoneme nodes will no longer be excited. We simulated suppression by running the model with the excitation from context as if $F_{ph} = 0.5$, but with $F_{ph} = 0.02$. Figure 12 shows the probability of correctly recalling lists of either phonemically similar or dissimilar letters as a function of list length. In this simulation the parameters of the model were the same as for the equivalent "no suppression" simulations illustrated in Fig. 5. Span is reduced to less than half its normal value because excited word nodes are typically at half their normal activation and because the effect of using only the context to drive the word layer also leads to lower performance (as illustrated in Table 2). The phonemic similarity effect largely disappears and this is because of the virtual inactivity of the input phoneme layer. These results closely resemble human data for the recall of visually presented sequences under suppression (Estes, 1973; Murray, 1968; Peterson & Johnson, 1971).

Figure 13 shows the probability of correct recall versus list length for lists of items of different word lengths. These "suppression" results can be directly compared with the equivalent "no suppression" simulations shown in Fig. 6. The word length effect is reduced under suppression but

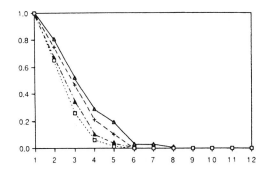

FIG. 13. The probability of correctly recalling a list of *N* random words under articulatory suppression as a function of word length. The phonemic word lengths are 2 (full line), 3 (dashed line), 4 (dash-dot-dash line), and 5 (dotted line). There were 200 trials for each list length, $\sigma = 0.03$. For other parameters see text.

persists because weights from the context layer decay according to the time taken to articulate the list. Human data show that suppression eliminates the word length effect for visually presented stimuli (Baddeley et al., 1975).

The model is therefore partially, but not completely, successful in accounting for the effects of articulatory suppression on recall. As in humans, performance is disrupted, the phonemic similarity effect almost disappears, and the word length effect is markedly reduced. However, unlike in humans, a residual word length effect remains. It would be a simple matter to improve the performance of the model by altering the way that weights from the context layer decay. However, more realistic behavior under articulatory suppression can be expected from changing the architecture of the model as part of a set of general improvements, as described later in this paper.

Further properties of the model

In this section we briefly examine the performance of the model in tasks beyond those set out as its primary objectives.

More subtle similarity experiments. There is an interesting experiment by Baddeley (1968) in which subjects were tested on lists of alternating phonemically similar and dissimilar items (e.g. a b f c q d). Performance was worse only for the similar items in the list giving a serial position curve that zigzags between the serial position

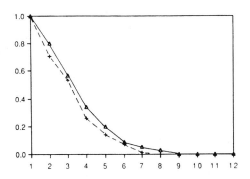

FIG. 12. The probability of correctly recalling a list of *N* phonemically similar letters (dashed line) or dissimilar letters (full line) under articulatory suppression. (Letters as in Fig. 5.) There were 200 trials at each list length, $\sigma = 0.03$. For other parameters see text.

curves for all similar or all dissimilar items (see Fig. 14). We performed the equivalent simulation for 500 trials of lists of six dissimilar, similar, and alternating items (see Fig. 15). The effect seen in Baddeley's experiment was not shown; the serial position curve for alternating similar and dissimilar items lies between those for all similar or all dissimilar items but does not zigzag.

The reason for this limitation of the model is that when two items are phonemically similar there is as much chance of error between the two items following them in the list as between themselves (see Burgess, 1990). For example, with the list a b f c q, the similarity of b and c results in the same increased chance of error in recalling f and q as in recalling b and c. This happens because all phonemic information is stored in the phoneme layers which are a self-contained *chaining* system — there is no contextual input into the phoneme layers, only to the word layer.

In the above example, at the recall of b the word node b is fully activated (to activation A_{wd}) by the input phoneme nodes "b" and "ee" but word node c is also activated (to $A_{wd}/2$) by "ee." At the recall of f the input phoneme nodes "e" and "f" will be fully activated (to A_{ph}) by the chaining weights from output phoneme nodes "b" and "ee." However, input phoneme nodes "kh" and "yu" will also be excited (to $A_{ph}/2$) by output phoneme node "ee." Thus word node f is fully activated (to A_{wd}) and word node q is activated to

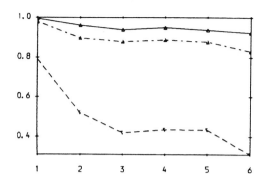

FIG. 15. Serial position curves for six similar (full line), dissimilar (dashed line), or alternately similar and dissimilar items (dot-dash line). There were 500 trials, $F_{ph} = 0.5$ and $\sigma = 0.03$.

$A_{wd}/2$. Hence the presence of noise will be as likely to produce errors where q is substituted for f as errors where c is substituted for b.

This view is supported by the separations of items in paired transposition errors. A large proportion of errors in the simulations with alternating phonemically similar and dissimilar items were transpositions of items 2 or 4 positions away from each other, i.e. transpositions between similar items or between dissimilar items. For the simulation of 200 lists of six letters there were 67 paired transpositions in total, 49 of which were between items of separation two. In a similar simulation of 200 lists of eight letters, 165 out of 194 paired transpositions were between items of separation two or four.

Rehearsal. We did not systematically investigate the behavior of the model after many rehearsals in this work. Suffice it to say that to a first approximation we expect errors to occur in each rehearsal with approximately the same frequency as in the first rehearsal. After enough rehearsals have been made for several errors to have occurred, performance will probably decline more quickly. Table 4 shows 10 rehearsals of lists of five and eight letters.

To be more compatible with human rehearsal we would like to make the occurrence of errors decrease after the first rehearsal (e.g. see Heffernan, 1991) and curb the tendency of w to appear as an intrusion error. The letters e and w are the most frequent extra-list intrusions because they so often

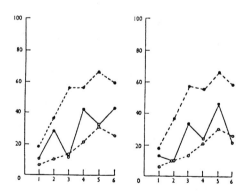

FIG. 14. Mean (percent) errors as a function of serial position. Filled circles represent acoustically similar letters, open circles dissimilar letters. Presentation was visual, taken from Baddeley (1968).

TABLE 4
An Example of 10 Rehearsals of the Lists of 5 and 8 Letters

o	s	b	n	r	o	s	b	n	r	f	h	t
o	s	b	n	r	o	s	b	n	r	f	h	t
o	s	b	n	r	o	s	b	n	r	f	h	t
o	s	r	n	b	o	s	b	n	r	f	h	t
o	s	b	n	r	h	t	o	r	f	b	n	c
o	s	b	n	r	h	t	o	c	n	b	f	w
o	s	b	n	r	h	t	n	b	w	x	f	c
o	s	b	n	w	b	w	h	c	x	n	l	f
o	s	w	n	g	b	w	h	n	x	c	t	w
o	s	w	n	g	w	t	x	p	k	c	w	n
o	s	w	n	b	w	t	x	k	z	c	w	n

Note. $F_{ph} = 0.5$, $\sigma = 0.03$.

share a phoneme with other letters (see Table 1). Furthermore, we know that rehearsal in short-term memory tasks can involve complex strategies such as grouping and cumulative repetition. In its present form the model can only rehearse an entire list an integer number of times.

Conclusions

In this section we evaluate the performance of our model with respect to the aims we had when starting. Successes and limitations are noted; simple modifications are suggested to address each limitation individually. Finally we identify and discuss two or three major flaws in our model, some of which necessarily arise from deficiencies in the articulatory loop idea. Further changes in the model are proposed to allow these limitations to be addressed simultaneously.

Successes
Points 1–4 are robust features of the model, found regardless of the amount of chaining.

1. Span. The probability of successfully recalling a list shows the right dependence on list length showing a dramatic fall-off around span (cf. Guildford et al., 1925).

2. Phonemic similarity effect. The use of similar items reduces performance as in humans (see, e.g. Baddeley, 1968; Peterson & Johnson, 1971; Schweickert et al., 1990). Further, when an error occurs, there is a tendency for the erroneous item to be phonemically similar to the (correct) item it replaces. This is also a characteristic of human performance (Conrad, 1964).

3. Word length. We made the approximation that the time taken to articulate a word is proportional to the number of phonemes it contains. Within this approximation the model shows performance decreasing with increasing word length. It is interesting to note that the simulations show a linear dependence of span on articulation rate (as determined by the number of phonemes per letter) with a slope of about 1, thus modeling the human data quite closely (Baddeley et al., 1975; Hulme et al., 1984; Hitch et al., 1989). It was noted that capacity is not entirely determined by the total articulation time of a list. However, this unanticipated effect is also found in psychological data (Zhang & Simon, 1985).

4. Serial position curve. The model shows a strong primacy effect. This is a common feature of the serial position curves for visual and auditory presentation (Crowder, 1972).

5. Types of error. The model produces the same categories of error as humans (i.e. order errors, item errors and, with a simple modification, omissions). Most of the errors are order errors (Aaronson, 1968; Bjork & Healy, 1974), and the effect of phonemic similarity is chiefly on order errors, as in human data (Wickelgren, 1965c). The model produces paired transpositions in recall and, provided there is not too much chaining, these tend to involve adjacent items, as in human subjects (Conrad, 1964).

6. Articulatory suppression. We interpret the prevention of subvocal rehearsal as preventing the use of the chaining weights. As with human data (at least for visual presentation) the effect of suppression is that span is reduced and the phonemic similarity effect

disappears. However, the word length effect is not completely lost when there is articulatory suppression because the weights from the context layer decay per phoneme, and not, for example, per word.

We take these successes as suggesting that, despite its many simplifying assumptions, our network model of phonological short-term memory is a reasonable first approximation. We interpret these successes as confirming the utility of competitive queuing as a mechanism for serial output, and our assumption that short-term memory phenomena can be captured in terms of the effects of noise on a system of rapidly decaying temporary associations.

Limitations of the model

1. Absence of recency. Human data show a small recency effect for visual presentation (Crowder, 1972), but our model shows none at all.
2. Articulatory suppression. The model does not fully simulate the effects of suppression on memory for visually presented sequences. Furthermore, since there is no difference between oral and vocal presentation in the model the effects of articulatory suppression are necessarily the same for both modes of presentation. As described in the introduction, articulatory suppression effects depend on presentation modality. To model these differences we must explicitly model the two modes of presentation.
3. Lists of alternating similar and dissimilar words. Our model cannot show the zigzag in levels of recall observed by Baddeley (1968). This is because the chaining nature of the phoneme nodes means that the acoustic similarity of two items is as likely to cause an error in the recall of words immediately after them as in their own recall.
4. The separation of items involved in order errors. Because of the decaying nature of the temporary weights there is a tendency for items late in the list to replace items early in the list. If there is any correlation in the state of the context layer for early and late

items (or if the items preceding them share phonemes) then, even early on in recall, later word nodes may be more excited than early ones purely because their temporary weights have decayed less.

5. Order errors in structured lists. In experiments using lists of items that are grouped in some way there is a tendency for paired transpositions to be between items at similar positions within each group (see, e.g. Estes, 1985). Also, where subjects have had to learn many lists, extra-list intrusions tend to be an item from the same serial position in a previous list (Conrad, 1960). In our model all lists are homogeneous and all temporary information decays to zero between list presentations.

Suggested modifications

The main lessons that we draw from the limitations of this first attempt to model the articulatory loop are as follows:

1. We have stored the short-term associations necessary for the serial recall of a list in connections whose strength decays with time. (These temporary associations were between the context and item layers and the output and input phoneme layers.) Because of this, any correlation between temporally well separated states in the context or output phoneme layers can lead to items from the end of the list replacing those at the beginning, purely because they are excited via connection weights that have decayed less. This defect shows itself in the unusually wide separation of items involved in order errors. This in turn makes it unlikely that the model could ever show recency; if errors tend to be long-range then there is little chance that recall of the last item could remain undisturbed by errors earlier in the list.

   To remedy this behavior we can use context states in which there is zero correlation between temporally well separated states. Further, because correlations in the output phoneme layer (determined solely by items' phonemic similarity) are independent of item separation, this layer should not be used to excite the next item in the list (as occurs through the phonemic chaining mechanism we used).

We can test the effect of these changes using the present model by putting $F_{ph} = 0.02$ and using activation states in the context layer with nonzero correlation only for temporally adjacent or very nearby states. A simple set of states with these properties is shown in Table 5.

For the context states shown in Table 5, four context nodes out of six remain active at successive times. Thus the correlation with the state at time 1 is 0.66 for the state at time 2, 0.33 for the state at time 3, and 0.0 for states at all other times. Note that (similarly to the context states used before) the context states for the first and last items have nonzero correlation with half as many other states as do the context states for the items in between; i.e. they are twice as "distinctive." Murdock (1960) demonstrated how the distinctiveness of different serial positions could contribute to serial position effects in recall.[1]

The serial position curves (for $F_{ph} = 0.02$ and the context states described above and the set of "dissimilar" letters: b f j i o u r t n h y q v s) show modest recency for the last item (see Fig. 16) reminiscent of psychological data for visual presentation (see Fig. 2). The recency effect is caused by

the extra discriminability of the context state of the last item, the effect of which is not swamped by long-range disturbance from errors earlier in the list. The majority of order errors occur between adjacent items (see Fig. 17).

Simulations with $F_{ph} = 0.5$ also show slight recency for the last item (i.e. less than in Fig. 16) and a majority of order errors between adjacent items (see Fig. 17). When $F_{ph} = 0.5$ and the set of "similar" letters: b c d g p v t f l m n s x z are used, recency is no longer shown — the number

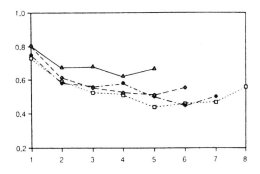

FIG. 16. The probability of correctly recalling an item from a list of N of the letters: b f j i o u r t n h y q v s, versus the serial position of the item. The context states shown in Table 5 were used. The values of N are 5 (full line), 6 (dashed line), 7 (dash-dot-dash line), and 8 (dotted line). There were 200 trials for each list length, $F_{ph} = 0.02$ and $\sigma = 0.03$.

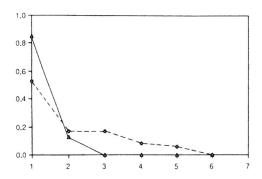

FIG. 17. The distribution of the separation of items involved in order errors. The context states as shown in Table 5 were used, $F_{ph} = 0.02$ (full line), $F_{ph} = 0.50$ (dashed line).

TABLE 5
A Set of Context States with Nonzero Correlation Only for States at Similar Times

Time	Activation of context nodes
1	* * * * * * 0 0 0 0 0 0 0 0 0 0 ...
2	0 0 * * * * * * 0 0 0 0 0 0 0 0 ...
3	0 0 0 0 * * * * * * 0 0 0 0 0 0 ...
4	0 0 0 0 0 0 * * * * * * 0 0 0 0 ...
.	.
.	.
.	.
.	.

Note. *indicates an activation of Act = 0.5.

of errors due to phonemic similarity swamps the effect of the extra discriminability of the last item.

2. The experiments involving alternating similar and dissimilar words provide evidence that the phonemic component of an item should not be used to cue the recall of the next item. While it seems natural to use the output of one item to trigger the recall of the next, this should be independent of (a) the acoustic properties of the outputted item and (b) whether it was the correct item or a mistake. Acoustic similarity effects indicate that we must retain a phonemic component to the model, and the excitation of item nodes by the corresponding input phoneme nodes still seems natural.

Thus the architecture we propose for future modeling would have a "loop" in which activation spreads from context layer to input phoneme layer to item layer to competitive filter which then triggers the activation of the next context state, see Fig. 18. Note that we would take the output phoneme layer out of the loop and put the context layer in (removing explicit item–item chaining). The output phoneme layer would be concerned only with the articulatory details of output, either vocal or subvocal. Note also that the only temporary associations learned would be those between the context and input phoneme layers.

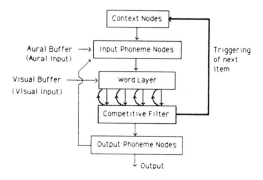

FIG. 18. The modified architecture proposed for an improved model of the articulatory loop.

3. Our first step towards modeling aural and visual presentation separately would be to include an aural input buffer that serves to excite the input phoneme layer and a visual input buffer that serves to excite the item layer directly (see Fig. 18). The motivation for this is for aural input to be "heard" by the input phoneme layer and visual input to be "recognized" by the item layer without being heard.

Visually input items must excite the input phoneme layer for the temporary weighted connections from the context layer to be learned (so that the sequence can be recalled by the loop). This could occur by one-to-one excitatory connections from output phoneme nodes to input phoneme nodes (i.e. output is also "heard" by the input phoneme layer). Thus, by exciting an item node and, in turn, the corresponding competitive filter node, input phoneme nodes corresponding to a visually presented item can be excited. We would then interpret the effect of articulatory suppression as occupying the output phoneme layer with a redundant articulatory task — preventing visually presented items from entering the loop at all and lessening the activation input phoneme nodes (and, hence, connection weights from the context layer) for aurally presented items.

The effect of connections from output to input phoneme layers during recall and rehearsal will need investigating. It may be that we would have to assume that input from the context layer has preferential access to the input phoneme layer for the occurrence of an error not to affect the recall of the next item.

Relationship to other models

Our present simulation differs in interesting ways from other models of memory span and related tasks. Some of these models share the assumption that both chaining associations between successive items and associations between items and their contexts are stored (see, e.g. Shiffrin & Cook, 1978). However, models of a chaining nature have been proposed (e.g. Lewandowsky & Murdock,

1989) as have models which reject chaining and rely entirely on some equivalent of context–item associations (e.g. Lee & Estes, 1981). We consider pure chaining of items to be implausible. Our simulations provide good evidence that if a model contains chaining, the occurrence of errors must rely on some other mechanism, i.e. the way a chained activation vector is used to determine which item is actually output. We also know that chaining models ought to have great difficulty recalling sequences containing repeated items, whereas repetitions lead to only a slight disruption in human performance (Jahnke, 1969; Baddeley, 1990, personal communication).

An important feature of the present model is that the relative contributions of chaining and contextual associations can be varied. This has made it clear that simulations with little or no chaining come closest to reproducing human behavior, particularly in relation to order errors and the shape of the serial position curve. This outcome is of course fully consistent with Lashley's (1951) original arguments against chaining.

Our simulation differs from other models in a number of other ways. Most notably it attempts to model only short-term memory and is therefore of more restricted scope than, for example, TODAM (Lewandowsky & Murdock, 1989), which attempts to explain serial order phenomena in both short-term and long-term memory. Unlike TODAM, our model uses local, as opposed to distributed, representations of information. Of course the local units in our model would not necessarily represent local objects at a more detailed level of implementation.

Finally, it is interesting to note that our model has a certain similarity with that of Lee and Estes (1981). For example, errors in both models occur because of the effects of noise or perturbation. However, Lee and Estes (1981) use reverberatory loops to preserve order information and introduce noise into the timing of these loops, whereas in our model noise is introduced into activation levels. It seems that Lee and Estes favored noisy timing in order that the characteristic errors of their model would be order errors. The present simulation shows that this is not a necessary assumption.

The recent explosion of interest in parallel distributed processing and neural network modeling has led to much work in related fields, inspired by the discovery of the error back-propagation algorithm (see, e.g. Rumelhart, Hinton, & Williams, 1986) and the Hopfield model (Hopfield, 1982). While there is not room to review more of this vast and growing area of research than those bits we have already mentioned, the present approach (and that of some of the above models) holds a relevant lesson.

There are many possible ways to incorporate serial order into standard connectionist models (see, e.g. Jordan, 1986; Elman, 1990) using multilayer perceptrons and error back-propagation, or using Hopfield type networks (e.g. Kleinfeld, 1986). However, a model whose architecture is chosen, ad hoc, simply because it can address the problem of serial order is most unlikely to solve this problem in a human-like way. In the present paper we have a connectionist model whose architecture (i.e. its structure and dynamics) is inspired by psychological thinking — representing full consideration of the lessons to be drawn from experimental constraints. The successes of the model so far reflect the validity of these psychological ideas; its limitations indicate the need for further development of the architecture used to implement them.

Discussion

In the section "Rationale for Modeling" we said that a successful model should reproduce both the detailed pattern of errors observed in short-term recall, which the Baddeley (1986) model of the "articulatory loop" cannot explain, and the more global effects of word length and similarity and articulatory suppression, which it can explain. To a first approximation then, our model is successful in that it shows word length, similarity, and suppression effects as well as the correct types of error. In light of this it might be fruitful to apply the model to some of the other phenomena for which the concept of the articulatory loop has proved valuable, e.g. developmental increases in memory span in children and cross-linguistic differences in digit span. It may also be informative to try to simulate neuropsychological disorders of short-term memory that have been attributed to impairment of the articulatory loop (e.g. Vallar & Baddeley, 1984). Progress in any of these areas can be regarded as testing the generality and applicability of the model.

However, the major motivation for our present work is that it should go some way toward providing an *explanatory* account of the core phenomena associated with the articulatory loop. The simple concept of the loop (Baddeley, 1986) is a useful model of many of the behavioral effects observed in short-term memory experiments but does not specify exactly how it could operate. In this paper we have provided a relatively simple candidate mechanism for the articulatory loop at a much more detailed level than the current conceptual account.

We also noted that a successful model might be expected to make some novel predictions and to generate insights into other activities involving the temporary storage of phonemes. The model does show behavior beyond the basics that we set out to reproduce. However, unsurprisingly in a first attempt, the further behavior of the model that we can explore has tended to correspond to more complex experiments that have already been done, rather than to novel predictions. In some cases the model shows the right behavior and in others it does not. Where the model does not match human data we suggest the modifications we would make for a second attempt. Clearly we will not really be at the stage of making novel predictions to test until we have a model that reflects the considerable amount that is already known about human behavior in short-term memory tasks.

Finally, we consider whether we have generated any insight into activities involving the temporary storage of phonological information. First, the articulatory loop should not be thought of as a chain of item–item associations, because the types of errors observed (particularly order errors) would not be natural to such a system. If we use the loop metaphor (or any chaining mechanism) it should perhaps be in terms of a loop of labels or contexts with associated items which are selected

for recall by a mechanism, such as competitive queuing, in which item selection is prone to error.

Second, the limited capacity of short-term memory should not be thought of in terms of a box with a limited number of slots, or a loop of tape of finite length. It would seem to be more useful to think of it as a noisy system in which the opportunity for confusion increases with the number of items until the system cannot reliably select the correct one.

Third, if short-term associations (e.g. context–item associations) are stored in connections of decaying strength then the cues that excite temporally well separated items for recall via such connections must have no significant correlation.

Fourth, it seems to be useful to distinguish between input and output phoneme layers in the "phonological store." However, the Baddeley (1968) experiments indicate that triggering of the next item only requires that the recall of the previous item is finished — it should not depend on the phonemic composition of the recalled item.

The final point we note is the natural way in which the idea of competitive queuing solves the problem of choosing items in order. The way in which item nodes are active before they are recalled, but are suppressed after recall is naturally prone to order errors and also accounts for the relative lack of repetition errors. We believe that experiments involving repeated items (in which omission of the repeated item tends to be a common error) will also be relatively easy to model using competitive queuing. The activation of items before recall is mentioned by Houghton (1990) as natural in the context of modeling speech production. It is surely no coincidence that the same mechanism seems natural in the articulatory loop, given that it is based on the idea of using "inner speech" or "subvocal rehearsal" to prolong the life of items in a short-term phonological store.

Note

1. We are grateful to D. Hintzman for bringing this to our attention.

References

Aaronson, D. (1968). Temporal course of perception in an immediate recall task. *Journal of Experimental Psychology*, *76*, 129–140.

Amit, D. J., Sagi, D., & Usher, M. (1990). Architecture of attractor neural networks performing cognitive fast scanning. *Network*, *14*, 189–216.

Atkinson, R. C., & Shiffrin, R. M. (1971). The control of short-term memory. *Scientific American*, *225*, 82–90.

Baddeley, A. D. (1966). Short-term memory for word sequences as a function of acoustic, semantic and formal similarity. *Quarterly Journal of Experimental Psychology*, *18*, 362–365.

Baddeley, A. D. (1968). How does acoustic similarity influence short-term memory. *Quarterly Journal of Experimental Psychology*, *20*, 249–264.

Baddeley, A. D. (1986). *Working memory*. Oxford: Clarendon Press.

Baddeley, A. D., & Hitch, G. J. (1974). Working memory. In G. H. Bower (Ed.), *Recent advances in the psychology of learning and motivation* (Vol. VIII, pp.47–90). New York: Academic Press.

Baddeley, A. D., Lewis, V. J., & Vallar, G. (1984). Exploring the articulatory loop. *Quarterly Journal of Experimental Psychology*, *36*, 233–252.

Baddeley, A. D., Thomson, N., & Buchanan, M. (1975). Word length and the structure of short-term memory. *Journal of Verbal Learning and Verbal Behavior*, *14*, 575–589.

Bjork, E. L., & Healy, A. F. (1974). Short-term order and item retention. *Journal of Verbal Learning and Verbal Behavior*, *13*, 80–97.

Broadbent, D. E. (1984). The Maltese cross: A new simplistic model for memory. *Behavioral and Brain Sciences*, *7*, 55–94.

Buhmann, J., & Schulten, K. (1987). Noise-driven temporal association in neural networks. *Europhysics Letters*, *4*, 1205–1209.

Burgess, N. (1990). *Neural networks, human memory and optimisation*. Ph.D. thesis, Faculty of Science, Manchester University.

Burgess, N., Moore, M. A., & Shapiro, J. L. (1989). Human-like forgetting in neural network models of memory. In W. K. Theumann & R. Koeberle (Eds.), *Neural networks and spin glasses, proceedings, Porto Alegre, 1989*. Singapore: World Scientific, 1990.

Burgess, N., Shapiro, J. L., & Moore, M. A. (1991). Neural network models of list learning. *Network*, *2*, 399–422.

Conrad, R. (1960). Serial order intrusions in immediate memory. *British Journal of Psychology*, *51*, 45–48.

Conrad, R. (1964). Acoustic confusions in immediate memory. *British Journal of Psychology*, *55*, 75–84.

Conrad, R., & Hull, A. J. (1964). Information, acoustic confusion and memory span. *British Journal of Psychology*, *55*, 429–432.

Crowder, R. G. (1972). Visual and auditory memory. In J. F. Kavanagh & I. G. Mattingly (Eds.), *Language by ear and by eye* (pp.251–276). Cambridge, MA: MIT Press.

Ellis, N. C., & Hennelly, R. A. (1980). A bilingual word length effect: Implications for intelligence testing and the ease of mental calculation in Welsh and English. *British Journal of Psychology*, *71*, 43–51.

Elman, J. L. (1990). Finding structure in time. *Cognitive Science*, *14*, 179–211.

Estes, W. K. (1973). Phonemic coding and rehearsal in short-term memory for letter strings. *Journal of Verbal Learning and Verbal Behavior*, *12*, 360–372.

Estes, W. K. (1985). Memory for temporal information. In J. A. Michon & J. L. Jackson (Eds.), *Time, mind and behaviour*. Heidelberg: Springer-Verlag.

Gardiner, J. (1983). On recency and echoic memory. *Philosophical Transactions of the Royal Society London, Series B*, *302*, 267–282.

Grossberg, S. (1987). Competitive learning: From interactive activation to adaptive resonance. *Cognitive Science*, *11*, 23–63.

Guildford, J. P., & Dallenbach, K. M. (1925). The determination of memory span by the method of constant stimuli. *American Journal of Psychology*, *36*, 621–628.

Healy, A. F. (1974). Separating item from order information in short-term memory. *Journal of Verbal Learning and Verbal Behavior*, *13*, 644–655.

Hebb. D. O. (1961). Distinctive features of learning in the higher animal. In J. F. Delafresnaye (Ed.), *Brain mechanisms and learning*. Oxford: Blackwell.

Heffernan, T. (1991). Ph.D. thesis, Manchester University.

Hintzman, D. L. (1967). Articulatory coding in short-term memory. *Journal of Verbal Learning and Verbal Behavior*, *6*, 312–316.

Hitch, G. J., Halliday, M. S., & Littler, J. E. (1989). Item identification time and rehearsal rate as predictors of memory span in children. *Quarterly Journal of Experimental Psychology, Series A*, *41*, 321–338.

Hopfield, J. J. (1982). Networks and physical systems with emergent collective computational abilities. *Proceedings of the National Academy of Science USA*, *79*, 2554–2558.

Houghton, G. (1990). The problem of serial order: A neural network model of sequence learning and recall. In R. Dale, C. Mellish, & M. Zock (Eds.), *Current research in natural language generation* (pp.287–319). London: Academic Press.

Hulme, C., Thomson, N., Muir, C., & Lawrence, A. L. (1984). Speech rate and the development of short-term memory. *Journal of Experimental Child Psychology, 38*, 241–253.

Jahnke, J. C. (1969). The Ranschburg effect. *Psychological Review, 76*, 592–605.

Jordan, M. I. (1986). *Serial order: A parallel distributed approach.* ICI Report 8604, Institute for Cognitive Science, University of California, San Diego, La Jolla, CA.

Kleinfeld, D. (1986). Sequential state generation by model neural networks. *Proceedings of the National Academy of Science USA, 83*, 9469–9473.

Kohonen, T. (1984). *Self-organisation and associative memory.* Berlin: Springer-Verlag.

Lashley, K. S. (1951). The problem of serial order in behaviour. In L. A. Jeffress (Ed.), *Cerebral mechanisms in behaviour* (pp.112–136). New York: Wiley.

Lee, C. L., & Estes, W. K. (1981). Item and order information in short-term memory: Evidence for a multilevel perturbation process. *Journal of Experimental Psychology: Human Learning and Memory, 7*, 149–169.

Lewandowsky, S., & Murdock, B. B., Jr. (1989). Memory for serial order. *Psychological Review, 96*, 25–57.

Mezard, M., Nadal, J. P., & Toulouse, G. (1986). Solvable models of working memories. *J. Physique, 47*, 1457–1462.

Miller, G. A. (1956). The magical number seven, plus or minus two: Some limits on our capacity for processing information. *Psychological Review, 63*, 81–97.

Murdock, B. B. (1960). The distinctiveness of stimuli. *Psychological Review, 67*, 16–31.

Murdock, B. B. (1962). The serial position effect in free recall. *Journal of Experimental Psychology, 64*, 482–488.

Murray, D. J. (1966). Vocalization-at-presentation and immediate recall with varying recall methods. *Quarterly Journal of Experimental Psychology, 18*, 9–18.

Murray, D. J. (1968). Articulation and acoustic confusability in short-term memory. *Journal of Experimental Psychology, 78*, 679–684.

Nadal, J. P. (1987). *Neural networks: A path from neurobiology to psychology?* Paper presented at the proceedings of "Chaos and Complexity," Turin, Italy.

Nadal, J. P., Toulouse, G., Changeux, J. P., & Dehaene, S. (1986). Networks of formal neurons and memory palimpsests. *Europhysics Letters, 1*, 535.

Naveh-Benjamin, M., & Ayres, T. J. (1986). Digit span, reading rate, and linguistic relativity. *Quarterly Journal of Experimental Psychology, Series A, 38*, 739–752.

Parisi, G. (1986). A memory which forgets. *Journal of Physics A, 19*, L617.

Peterson, L. R., & Johnson, S. T. (1971). Some effects of minimizing articulation on short-term retention. *Journal of Verbal Learning and Verbal Behavior, 10*, 346–354.

Rumelhart, D. E., Hinton, G. E., & Williams, R. J. (1986). Learning internal representations by error propagation. In D. E. Rumelhart, J. L. McClelland, and the PDP Research Group (Eds.), *Parallel Distributed Processing: Explorations in the Microstructure of Cognition. Vol. I. Foundations.* Cambridge, MA: MIT Press.

Salamé, P., & Baddeley, A. D. (1982). Disruption of short-term memory by unattended speech: Implications for the structure of working memory. *Journal of Verbal Learning and Verbal Behavior, 21*, 150–164.

Schweickert, R., Guentert, L., & Hersberger, L. (1990). Phonological similarity, pronunciation rate, and memory span. *Psychological Science, 1*, 74–77.

Shiffrin, R. M., & Cook, J. R. (1978). A model for short-term item and order retention. *Journal of Verbal Learning and Verbal Behavior, 17*, 189–218.

Terman, L. M., & Merrill, M. A. (1961). *Stanford-Binet intelligence scale — Manual for the third revision form L-M.* London: Harrap.

Vallar, G., & Baddeley, A. D. (1984). Fractionation of working memory: Neuropsychological evidence for a phonological short-term store. *Journal of Verbal Learning and Verbal Behavior, 23*, 151–161.

Finding structure in time

Jeffrey L. Elman

University of California, San Diego

Time underlies many interesting human behaviors. Thus, the question of how to represent time in connectionist models is very important. One approach is to represent time implicitly by its effects on processing rather than explicitly (as in a spatial representation). The current report develops a proposal along these lines first described by Jordan (1986) which involves the use of recurrent links in order to provide networks with a dynamic memory. In this approach, hidden unit patterns are fed back to themselves; the internal representations which develop thus reflect task demands in the context of prior internal states. A set of simulations is reported which range from relatively simple problems (temporal version of XOR) to discovering syntactic/semantic features for words. The networks are able to learn interesting internal representations which incorporate task demands with memory demands; indeed, in this approach the notion of memory is inextricably bound up with task processing. These representations reveal a rich structure, which allows them to be highly context-dependent, while also expressing generalizations across classes of items. These representations suggest a method for representing lexical categories and the type/token distinction.

Introduction

Time is clearly important in cognition. It is inextricably bound up with many behaviors (such as language) which express themselves as temporal sequences. Indeed, it is difficult to know how one might deal with such basic problems as goal-directed behavior, planning, or causation without some way of representing time.

The question of how to represent time might seem to arise as a special problem unique to parallel-processing models, if only because the parallel nature of computation appears to be at odds with the serial nature of temporal events. However, even within traditional (serial) frameworks, the representation of serial order and the interaction of a serial input or output with higher levels of representation presents challenges. For example, in models of motor activity, an important issue is whether the action plan is a literal specification of the output sequence, or whether the plan represents serial order in a more abstract manner (e.g. Fowler, 1977, 1980; Jordan & Rosenbaum, 1988; Kelso, Saltzman, & Tuller, 1986; Lashley, 1951; MacNeilage, 1970; Saltzman & Kelso, 1987). Linguistic theoreticians have perhaps tended to be less concerned with the representation and processing of the temporal aspects to utterances (assuming, for instance, that all the information in an utterance is somehow made available simultaneously in a syntactic tree); but the research in natural language parsing suggests that the problem is not trivially solved (e.g. Frazier & Fodor, 1978; Marcus, 1980). Thus, what is one of the most elementary facts about much of human activity — that it has temporal extend — is sometimes ignored and is often problematic.

In parallel distributed processing models, the processing of sequential inputs has been accomplished in several ways. The most common solution is to attempt to "parallelize time" by giving it a spatial representation. However, there are problems with this approach, and it is ultimately not

I would like to thank Jay McClelland, Mike Jordan, Mary Hare, Dave Rumelhart, Mike Mozer, Steve Poteet, David Zipser, and Mark Dolson for many stimulating discussions. I thank McClelland, Jordan, and two anonymous reviewers for helpful critical comments on an earlier draft of this article.

This work was supported by contract N000114-85-K-0076 from the Office of Naval Research and contract DAAB-07-87-C-H027 from Army Avionics, Ft. Monmouth.

Correspondence and requests for reprints should be sent to Jeffrey L. Elman, Center for Research in Language, C-008, University of California, La Jolla, CA 92093.

Cognitive Science 14, 179–211 (1990)

a good solution. A better approach would be to represent time implicitly rather than explicitly. That is, we represent time by the effect it has on processing and not as an additional dimension of the input.

This article describes the results of pursuing this approach, with particular emphasis on problems that are relevant to natural language processing. The approach taken is rather simple, but the results are sometimes complex and unexpected. Indeed, it seems that the solution to the problem of time may interact with other problems for connectionist architectures, including the problem of symbolic representation and how connectionist representations encode structure. The current approach supports the notion outlined by Van Gelder (1990) (see also, Elman, 1989; Smolensky, 1987, 1988), that connectionist representations may have a functional compositionality without being syntactically compositional.

The first section briefly describes some of the problems that arise when time is represented externally as a spatial dimension. The second section describes the approach used in this work. The major portion of this article presents the results of applying this new architecture to a diverse set of problems. These problems range in complexity from a temporal version of the Exclusive-OR function to the discovery of syntactic/semantic categories in natural language data.

The problem with time

One obvious way of dealing with patterns that have a temporal extent is to represent time explicitly by associating the serial order of the pattern with the dimensionality of the pattern vector. The first temporal event is represented by the first element in the pattern vector, the second temporal event is represented by the second position in the pattern vector, and so on. The entire pattern vector is processed in parallel by the model. This approach has been used in a variety of models (e.g. Cottrell, Munro, & Zipser, 1987; Elman & Zipser, 1988; Hanson & Kegl, 1987).

There are several drawbacks to this approach, which basically uses a spatial metaphor for time. First, it requires that there be some interface with the world, which buffers the input, so that it can be presented all at once. It is not clear that biological systems make use of such shift registers. There are also logical problems: How should a system know when a buffer's contents should be examined?

Second, the shift register imposes a rigid limit on the duration of patterns (since the input layer must provide for the longest possible pattern), and furthermore, suggests that all input vectors be the same length. These problems are particularly troublesome in domains such as language, where one would like comparable representations for patterns that are of variable length. This is as true of the basic units of speech (phonetic segments) as it is of sentences.

Finally, and most seriously, such an approach does not easily distinguish relative temporal position from absolute temporal position. For example, consider the following two vectors.

[0 1 1 1 0 0 0 0]
[0 0 0 1 1 1 0 0]

These two vectors appear to be instances of the same basic pattern, but displaced in space (or time, if these are given a temporal interpretation). However, as the geometric interpretation of these vectors makes clear, the two patterns are in fact quite dissimilar and spatially distant.[1] PDP models can, of course, be trained to treat these two patterns as similar. But the similarity is a consequence of an external teacher and not of the similarity structure of the patterns themselves, and the desired similarity does not generalize to novel patterns. This shortcoming is serious if one is interested in patterns in which the relative temporal structure is preserved in the face of absolute temporal displacements.

What one would like is a representation of time that is richer and does not have these problems. In what follows here, a simple architecture is described, which has a number of desirable temporal properties, and has yielded interesting results.

Networks with memory

The spatial representation of time described above treats time as an explicit part of the input. There is another, very different possibility: Allow time to be represented by the effect it has on processing. This means giving the processing system dynamic properties that are responsive to temporal sequences. In short, the network must be given memory.

There are many ways in which this can be accomplished, and a number of interesting proposals have appeared in the literature (e.g. Jordan, 1986; Pineda, 1988; Stornetta, Hogg, & Huberman, 1987; Tank & Hopfield, 1987; Waibel, Hanazawa, Hinton, Shikano, & Lang, 1987; Watrous & Shastri, 1987; Williams & Zipser, 1988). One of the most promising was suggested by Jordan (1986). Jordan described a network (shown in Fig. 1) containing recurrent connections that were used to associate a static pattern (a "Plan") with a serially ordered output pattern (a sequence of "Actions"). The recurrent connections allow the network's hidden units to see its own previous output, so that the subsequent behavior can be shaped by previous responses. These recurrent connections are what give the network memory.

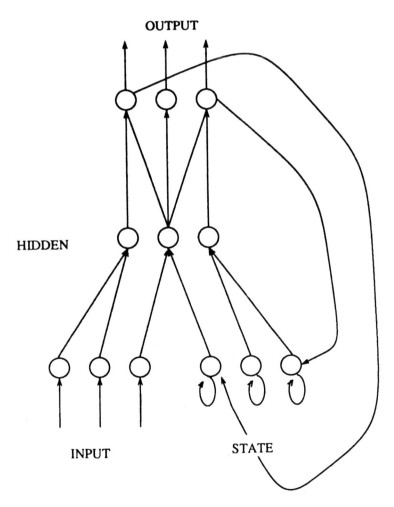

FIG. 1. Architecture used by Jordan (1986). Connections from output to state units are one-for-one, with a fixed weight of 1.0 Not all connections are shown.

This approach can be modified in the following way. Suppose a network (shown in Fig. 2) is augmented at the input level by additional units; call these *Context Units*. These units are also "hidden" in the sense that they interact exclusively with other nodes internal to the network, and not the outside world.

Imagine that there is a sequential input to be processed, and some clock which regulates presentation of the input to the network. Processing would then consist of the following sequence of events. At time *t*, the input units receive the first input in the sequence. Each unit might be a single scalar value or a vector, depending upon the nature of the problem. The context units are initially set to 0.5.[2] Both the input units and context units activate the hidden units; the hidden units then feed forward to activate the output units. The hidden units also feed back to activate the context units. This constitutes the forward activation. Depending upon the task, there may or may not be a learning phase in this time cycle. If so, the output is compared with a teacher input, and back propagation of error (Rumelhart, Hinton, & Williams, 1986) is used to adjust connection strengths incrementally. Recurrent connections are fixed at 1.0 and are not subject to adjustment.[3] At the next time step, *t* + 1, the above sequence is repeated. This time the context units contain values which are exactly the hidden unit values at time *t*. These context units thus provide the network with memory.

Internal Representation of Time. In feed forward networks employing hidden units and a learning algorithm, the hidden units develop internal representations for the input patterns that recode those patterns in a way which enables the network to

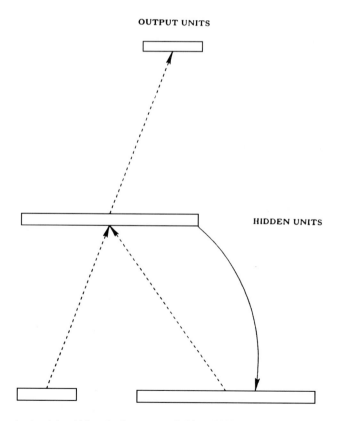

OUTPUT UNITS

HIDDEN UNITS

FIG. 2. A simple recurrent network in which activations are copied from hidden layer to context layer on a one-for-one basis, with fixed weight of 1.0. Dotted lines represent trainable connections.

produce the correct output for a given input. In the present architecture, the context units remember the previous internal state. Thus, the hidden units have the task of mapping both an external input, and also the previous internal state of some desired output. Because the patterns on the hidden units are saved as context, the hidden units must accomplish this mapping and at the same time develop representations which are useful encodings of the temporal properties of the sequential input. Thus, the internal representations that develop are sensitive to temporal context; the effect of time is implicit in these internal states. Note, however, that these representations of temporal context need not be literal. They represent a memory which is highly task- and stimulus-dependent.

Consider now the results of applying this architecture to a number of problems that involve processing of inputs which are naturally presented in sequence.

Exclusive-Or

The Exclusive-Or (XOR) function has been of interest because it cannot be learned by a simple two-layer network. Instead, it requires at least three layers. The XOR is usually presented as a problem involving 2-bit input vectors (00, 11, 01, 10) yielding 1-bit output vectors (0, 0, 1, 1, respectively).

This problem can be translated into a temporal domain in several ways. One version involves constructing a sequence of 1-bit inputs by presenting the 2-bit inputs one bit at a time (i.e. in 2 time steps), followed by the 1-bit output; then continuing with another input/output pair chosen at random. A sample input might be:

1 0 1 0 0 0 0 1 1 1 1 0 1 0 1 . . .

Here, the first and second bits are XOR-ed to produce the third; the fourth and fifth are XOR-ed to give the sixth; and so on. The inputs are concatenated and presented as an unbroken sequence.

In the current version of the XOR problem, the input consisted of a sequence of 3,000 bits constructed in this manner. This input stream was presented to the network shown in Fig. 2 (with 1

input unit, 2 hidden units, 1 output unit, and 2 context units), one bit at a time. The task of the network was, at each point in time, to predict the next bit in the sequence. That is, given the input sequence shown, where one bit at a time is presented, the correct output at corresponding points in time is shown below.

input: **1 0 1 0 0 0 0 1 1 1 1 0 1 0 1 . . .**
output: **0 1 0 0 0 0 1 1 1 1 0 1 0 1 ? . . .**

Recall that the actual input to the hidden layer consists of the input shown above, as well as a copy of the hidden unit activations from the previous cycle. The prediction is thus based not just on input from the world, but also on the network's previous state (which is continuously passed back to itself on each cycle).

Notice that, given the temporal structure of this sequence, it is only sometimes possible to predict the next item correctly. When the network has received the first bit — **1** in the example above — there is a 50% chance that the next bit will be a **1** (or a **0**). When the network receives the second bit (**0**), however, it should then be possible to predict that the third will be the XOR, **1**. When the fourth bit is presented, the fifth is not predictable. But from the fifth bit, the sixth can be predicted, and so on.

In fact, after 600 passes through a 3,000-bit sequence constructed in this way, the network's ability to predict the sequential input closely follows the above schedule. This can be seen by looking at the sum squared error in the output prediction at successive points in the input. The error signal provides a useful guide as to when the network recognized a temporal sequence, because at such moments its outputs exhibit low error. Figure 3 contains a plot of the sum squared error over 12 time steps (averaged over 1,200 cycles). The error drops at those points in the sequence where a correct prediction is possible; at other points, the error is high. This is an indication that the network has learned something about the temporal structure of the input, and is able to use previous context and current input to make predictions about future input. The network, in fact, attempts to use the XOR rule at all points in time; this fact is obscured by the averaging of

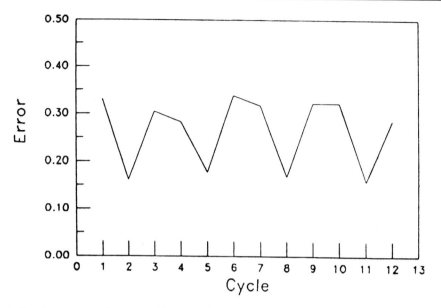

FIG. 3. Graph of root mean squared error over 12 consecutive inputs in sequential XOR task. Data points are averaged over 1200 trials.

error, which is done for Fig. 3. If one looks at the output activations, it is apparent from the nature of the errors that the network predicts successive inputs to be the XOR of the previous two. This is guaranteed to be successful every third bit, and will sometimes, fortuitously, also result in correct predictions at other times.

It is interesting that the solution to the temporal version of XOR is somewhat different than the static version of the same problem. In a network with two hidden units, one unit is highly activated when the input sequence is a series of identical elements (all 1s or 0s), whereas the other unit is highly activated when the input elements alternate. Another way of viewing this is that the network develops units which are sensitive to high- and low-frequency inputs. This is a different solution than is found with feed-forward networks and simultaneously presented inputs. This suggests that problems may change their nature when cast in a temporal form. It is not clear that the solution will be easier or more difficult in this form, but it is an important lesson to realize that the solution may be different.

In this simulation, the prediction task has been used in a way that is somewhat analogous to auto-association. Auto-association is a useful technique for discovering the intrinsic structure possessed by a set of patterns. This occurs because the network must transform the patterns into more compact representations; it generally does so by exploiting redundancies in the patterns. Finding these redundancies can be of interest because of what they reveal about the similarity structure of the data set (cf. Cottrell et al. 1987; Elman & Zipser, 1988).

In this simulation, the goal is to find the temporal structure of the XOR sequence. Simple auto-association would not work, since the task of simply reproducing the input at all points in time is trivially solvable and does not require sensitivity to sequential patterns. The prediction task is useful because its solution requires that the network be sensitive to temporal structure.

Structure in letter sequences

One question which might be asked is whether the memory capacity of the network architecture employed here is sufficient to detect more complex sequential patterns than the XOR. The XOR pattern is simple in several respects. It involves single-bit inputs, requires a memory which extends only one bit back in time, and has only four different input patterns. More challenging inputs would require multi-bit inputs of greater temporal extent, and a larger inventory of possible sequences. Variability in the duration of a pattern might also complicate the problem.

An input sequence was devised which was intended to provide just these sorts of complications. The sequence was composed of six different 6-bit binary vectors. Although the vectors were not derived from real speech, one might think of them as representing speech sounds, with the six dimensions of the vector corresponding to articulatory features. Table 1 shows the vector for each of the six letters.

The sequence was formed in two steps. First, the three consonants (b, d, g) were combined in random order to obtain a 1,000-letter sequence. Then, each consonant was replaced using the rules

b → ba
d → dii
g → guuu

Thus, an initial sequence of the form **dbgbddg** . . . gave rise to the final sequence **diibaguuuba-diidiiguuu** . . . (each letter being represented by one of the above 6-bit vectors). The sequence was semi-random; consonants occurred randomly, but following a given consonant, the identity and number of following vowels was regular.

The basic network used in the XOR simulation was expanded to provide for the 6-bit input vectors; there were 6 input units, 20 hidden units, 6 output units, and 20 context units.

The training regimen involved presenting each 6-bit input vector, one at a time, in sequence. The task for the network was to predict the next input. (The sequence wrapped around, that the first pattern was presented after the last.) The network was trained on 200 passes through the sequence. It was then tested on another sequence that obeyed the same regularities, but created from a different initial randomization.

The error signal for part of this testing phase is shown in Fig. 4. Target outputs are shown in parenthesis, and the graph plots the corresponding error for each prediction. It is obvious that the error oscillates markedly; at some points in time, the prediction is correct (and error is low), while at other points in time, the ability to predict correctly is quite poor. More precisely, error tends to be high when predicting consonants, and low when predicting vowels.

Given the nature of the sequence, this behavior is sensible. The consonants were ordered randomly, but the vowels were not. Once the network has received a consonant as input, it can predict the identity of the following vowel. Indeed, it can do more; it knows how many tokens of the vowel to expect. At the end of the vowel sequence it has no way to predict the next consonant; at these points in time, the error is high.

This global error pattern does not tell the whole story, however. Remember that the input patterns (which are also the patterns the network

TABLE 1
Vector Definitions of Alphabet

	Consonant	Vowel	Interrupted	High	Back	Voiced
b	[1	0	1	0	0	1]
d	[1	0	1	1	0	1]
g	[1	0	1	0	1	1]
a	[0	1	0	0	1	1]
i	[0	1	0	1	0	1]
u	[0	1	0	1	1	1]

is trying to predict) are bit vectors. The error shown in Fig. 4 is the sum squared error over all 6 bits. Examine the error on a bit-by-bit basis; a graph of the error for bits [1] and [4] (over 20 time steps) is shown is Fig. 5. There is a striking difference in the error patterns. Error on predicting the first bit is consistently lower than error for the fourth bit, and at all points in time. Why should this be so?

The first bit corresponds to the features **Consonant**; the fourth bit corresponds to the feature **High**. It happens that while all consonants have the same value for the feature **Consonant**, they differ for **High**. The network has learned which vowels follow which consonants; this is why error on vowels is low. It has also learned how many vowels follow each consonant. An interesting corollary is that the network also knows how soon to expect the next consonant. The network cannot know *which* consonant, but it can predict correctly that a consonant follows. This is why the

bit patterns for **Consonant** show low error, and the bit patterns for **High** show high error. (It is this behavior which requires the use of context units; a simple feed-forward network could learn the transitional probabilities from one input to the next, but could not learn patterns that span more than two inputs.)

This simulation demonstrates an interesting point. This input sequence was in some ways more complex than the XOR input. The serial patterns are longer in duration; they are of variable length so that a prediction depends upon a variable amount of temporal context; and each input consists of a 6-bit rather than a 1-bit vector. One might have reasonably thought that the more extended sequential dependencies of these patterns would exceed the temporal processing capacity of the network. But almost the opposite is true. The fact that there are subregularities (at the level of individual bit patterns) enables the network to make partial predictions, even in cases where the

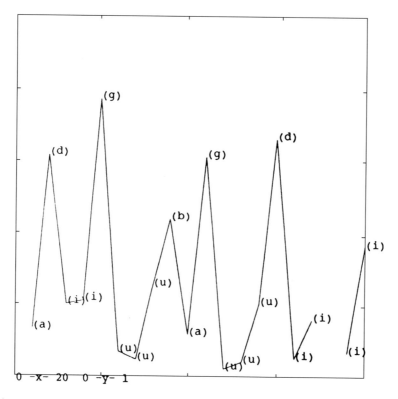

FIG. 4. Graph of root mean squared error in letter prediction task. Labels indicate the correct output prediction at each point in time. Error is computed over the entire output vector.

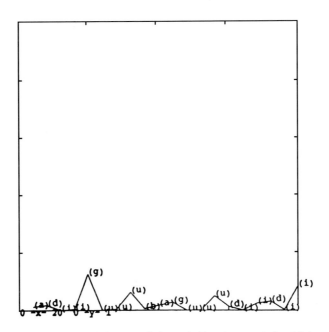

FIG. 5(a). Graph of root mean squared error in letter prediction task. Error is computed on bit 1, representing the feature CONSONANTAL.

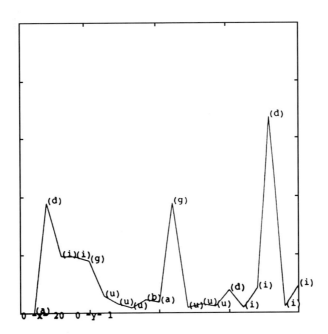

FIG. 5(b). Graph of root mean squared error in letter prediction task. Error is computed on bit 4, representing the feature HIGH.

complete prediction is not possible. All of this is dependent upon the fact that the input is structured, of course. The lesson seems to be that more extended sequential dependencies may not necessarily be more difficult to learn. If the dependencies are structured, that structure may make learning easier and not harder.

Discovering the notion "word"

It is taken for granted that learning a language involves (among many other things) learning the sounds of that language, as well as the morphemes and words. Many theories of acquisition depend crucially upon such primitive types as word, or morpheme, or more abstract categories as noun, verb, or phrase (e.g. Berwick & Weinberg, 1984; Pinker, 1984). Rarely is it asked how a language learner knows when to begin or why these entities exist. These notions are often assumed to be innate.

Yet, in fact, there is considerable debate among linguists and psycholinguists about what representations are used in language. Although it is commonplace to speak of basic units such as "phoneme," "morpheme," and "word," these constructs have no clear and uncontroversial definition. Moreover, the commitment to such distinct levels of representation leaves a troubling residue of entities that appear to lie between the levels. For instance, in many languages, there are sound/meaning correspondences which lie between the phoneme and the morpheme (i.e. sound symbolism). Even the concept "word" is not as straightforward as one might think (cf. Greenberg, 1963; Lehman, 1962). In English, for instance, there is no consistently definable distinction among words (e.g. "apple"), compounds ("apple pie") and phrases ("Library of Congress' or "man in the street"). Furthermore, languages differ dramatically in what they treat as words. In polysynthetic languages (e.g. Eskimo), what would be called words more nearly resemble what the English speaker would call phrases or entire sentences.

Thus, the most fundamental concepts of linguistic analysis have a fluidity, which at the very least, suggests an important role for learning; and the exact form of the those concepts remains an open and important question.

In PDP networks, representational form and representational content often can be learned simultaneously. Moreover, the representations which result have many of the flexible and graded characteristics noted above. Therefore, one can ask whether the notion "word" (or something which maps on to this concept) could emerge as a consequence of learning the sequential structure of letter sequences that form words and sentences (but in which word boundaries are not marked).

Imagine then, another version of the previous task, in which the latter sequences form real words, and the words form sentences. The input will consist of the individual letters (imagine these as analogous to speech sounds, while recognizing that the orthographic input is vastly simpler than acoustic input would be). The letters will be presented in sequence, one at a time, with no breaks between the letters in a word, and no breaks between the words of different sentences.

Such a sequence was created using a sentence-generating program and a lexicon of 15 words.[4] The program generated 200 sentences of varying length, from four to nine words. The sentences were concatenated, forming a stream of 1,270 words. Next, the words were broken into their letter parts, yielding 4,963 letters. Finally, each letter in each word was converted into a 5-bit random vector.

The result was a stream of 4,963 separate 5-bit vectors, one for each letter. These vectors were the input and were presented one at a time. The task at each point in time was to predict the next letter. A fragment of the input and desired output is shown in Table 2.

A network with 5 input units, 20 hidden units, 5 output units, and 20 context units was trained on 10 complete presentations of the sequence. The error was relatively high at this point; the sequence was sufficiently random that it would be difficult to obtain very low error without memorizing the entire sequence (which would have required far more than 10 presentations).

Nonetheless, a graph of error over time reveals an interesting pattern. A portion of the error is

TABLE 2
Fragment of Training Sequence for Letters-in-Words Simulation

Input		Output	
01101	(*m*)	00001	(*a*)
00001	(*a*)	01110	(*n*)
01110	(*n*)	11001	(*y*)
11001	(*y*)	11001	(*y*)
11001	(*y*)	00101	(*e*)
00101	(*e*)	00001	(*a*)
00001	(*a*)	10010	(*r*)
10010	(*r*)	10011	(*s*)
10011	(*s*)	00001	(*a*)
00001	(*a*)	00111	(*g*)
00111	(*g*)	01111	(*o*)
01111	(*o*)	00001	(*a*)
00001	(*a*)	00010	(*b*)
00010	(*b*)	01111	(*o*)
01111	(*o*)	11001	(*y*)
11001	(*y*)	00001	(*a*)
00001	(*a*)	01110	(*n*)
01110	(*n*)	00100	(*d*)
00100	(*d*)	00111	(*g*)
00111	(*g*)	01001	(*i*)
01001	(*i*)	10010	(*r*)
10010	(*r*)	01100	(*l*)
01100	(*l*)	01100	(*i*)
11001	(*i*)		

plotted in Fig. 6; each data point is marked with the letter that should be predicted at that point in time. Notice that at the onset of each new word, the error is high. As more of the word is received the error declines, since the sequence is increasingly predictable.

The error provides a good clue as to what the recurring sequences in the input are, and these correlate highly with words. The information is not categorical, however. The error reflects statistics of co-occurrence, and these are graded. Thus, while it is possible to determine, more or less, what sequences constitute words (those sequences bounded by high error), the criteria for boundaries are relative. This leads to ambiguities, as in the case of the *y* in *they* (see Fig. 6); it could also lead to the misidentification of common sequences that incorporate more than one word, but which co-occur frequently enough to be treated as a

quasi-unit. This is the sort of behavior observed in children, who at early stages of language acquisition may treat idioms and other formulaic phrases as fixed lexical items (MacWhinney, 1978).

This simulation should not be taken as a model of word acquisition. While listeners are clearly able to make predictions based upon partial input (Grosjean, 1980; Marslen-Wilson & Tyler, 1980; Salasoo & Pisoni, 1985), prediction is not the major goal of the language learner. Furthermore, the co-occurrence of sounds is only part of what identifies a word as such. The environment in which those sounds are uttered, and the linguistic context, are equally critical in establishing the coherence of the sound sequence and associating it with meaning. This simulation focuses only on a limited part of the information available to the language learner. The simulation makes the simple point that there is information in the signal that could serve as a cue to the boundaries of linguistic units which must be learned, and it demonstrates the ability of simple recurrent networks to extract this information.

Discovering lexical classes from word order

Consider now another problem which arises in the context of word sequences. The order of words in sentences reflects a number of constraints. In languages such as English (so-called "fixed word-order" languages), the order is tightly constrained. In many other languages (the "free word-order" languages), there are more options as to word order (but even here the order is not free in the sense of random). Syntactic structure, selective restrictions, subcategorization, and discourse considerations are among the many factors which join together to fix the order in which words occur. Thus, the sequential order of words in sentences is neither simple, nor is it determined by a single cause. In addition, it has been argued that generalizations about word order cannot be accounted for solely in terms of linear order (Chomsky, 1957, 1965). Rather, there is an abstract structure which underlies the surface strings and it is this structure

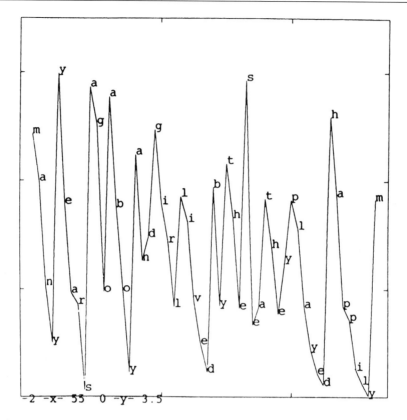

FIG. 6. Graph of root mean squared error in letter-in-word prediction task.

which provides a more insightful basis for understanding the constraints on word order.

While it is undoubtedly true that the surface order of words does not provide the most insightful basis for generalizations about word order, it is also true that from the point of view of the listener, the surface order is the only visible (or audible) part. Whatever the abstract underlying structure be, it is cued by the surface forms, and therefore, that structure is implicit in them.

In the previous simulation, it was demonstrated that a network was able to learn the temporal structure of letter sequences. The order of letters in that simulation, however, can be given with a small set of relatively simple rules.[5] The rules for determining word order in English, on the other hand, will be complex and numerous. Traditional accounts of word order generally invoke symbolic processing systems to express abstract structural relationships. One might, therefore, easily believe

that there is a qualitative difference in the nature of the computation needed for the last simulation, which is required to predict the word order of English sentences. Knowledge of word order might require symbolic representations that are beyond the capacity of (apparently) nonsymbolic PDP systems. Furthermore, while it is true, as pointed out above, that the surface strings may be cues to abstract structure, considerable innate knowledge may be required in order to reconstruct the abstract structure from the surface strings. It is, therefore, an interesting question to ask whether a network can learn any aspects of that underlying abstract structure.

Simple sentences

As a first step, a somewhat modest experiment was undertaken. A sentence generator program was used to construct a set of short (two- and three-word) utterances. Thirteen classes of nouns and verbs were chosen; these are listed in Table 3. Examples of each category are given; it will be noticed that instances of some categories (e.g. VERB-DESTROY) may be included in others (e.g. VERB-TRAN). There were 29 different lexical items.

The generator program used these categories and the 15 sentence templates given in Table 4 to create 10,000 random two- and three-word sentence frames. Each sentence frame was then filled in by randomly selecting one of the possible words appropriate to each category. Each word was replaced by a randomly assigned 31-bit vector in which each word was represented by a different bit. Whenever the word was present, that bit was flipped on. Two extra bits were reserved for later simulations. This encoding scheme guaranteed that each vector was orthogonal to every other vector and reflected nothing about the form class or meaning of the words. Finally, the 27,534 word vectors in the 10,000 sentences were concatenated, so that an input stream of 27,534 31-bit vectors was created. Each word vector was distinct, but there were no breaks between successive sentences. A fragment of the input stream is shown in Column 1 of Table 5, with the English gloss for each vector in parentheses. The desired output is given in Column 2.

For this simulation a network similar to that in the first simulation was used, except that the input layer and output layers contained 31 nodes each, and the hidden and context layers contained 150 nodes each.

The task given to the network was to learn to predict the order of successive words. The training strategy was as follows. The sequence of 27,354

TABLE 3
Categories of Lexical Items Used in Sentence Simulation

Category	Examples
NOUN-HUM	man, woman
NOUN-ANIM	cat, mouse
NOUN-INANIM	book, rock
NOUN-AGRESS	dragon, monster
NOUN-FRAG	glass, plate
NOUN-FOOD	cookie, break
VERB-INTRAN	think, sleep
VERB-TRAN	see, chase
VERB-AGPAT	move, break
VERB-PERCEPT	smell, see
VERB-DESTROY	break, smash
VERB-EAT	eat

TABLE 4
Templates for Sentence Generator

WORD 1	WORD 2	WORD 3
NOUN-HUM	VERB-EAT	NOUN-FOOD
NOUN-HUM	VERB-PERCEPT	NOUN-INANIM
NOUN-HUM	VERB-DESTROY	NOUN-FRAG
NOUN-HUM	VERB-INTRAN	
NOUN-HUM	VERB-TRAN	NOUN-HUM
NOUN-HUM	VERB-AGPAT	NOUN-INANIM
NOUN-HUM	VERB-AGPAT	
NOUN-ANIM	VERB-EAT	NOUN-FOOD
NOUN-ANIM	VERB-TRAN	NOUN-ANIM
NOUN-ANIM	VERB-AGPAT	NOUN-INANIM
NOUN-ANIM	VERB-AGPAT	
NOUN-INANIM	VERB-AGPAT	
NOUN-AGRESS	VERB-DESTROY	NOUN-FRAG
NOUN-AGRESS	VERB-EAT	NOUN-HUM
NOUN-AGRESS	VERB-EAT	NOUN-ANIM
NOUN-AGRESS	VERB-EAT	NOUN-FOOD

TABLE 5
Fragment of Training Sequences for Sentence Simulation

Input	Output
0000000000000000000000000000010 (woman)	0000000000000000000000000010000 (smash)
0000000000000000000000000010000 (smash)	0000000000000000000001000000000 (plate)
0000000000000000000001000000000 (plate)	0000010000000000000000000000000 (cat)
0000010000000000000000000000000 (cat)	0000000000000000000100000000000 (move)
0000000000000000000100000000000 (move)	0000000000000001000000000000000 (man)
0000000000000001000000000000000 (man)	0001000000000000000000000000000 (break)
0001000000000000000000000000000 (break)	0000100000000000000000000000000 (car)
0000100000000000000000000000000 (car)	0100000000000000000000000000000 (boy)
0100000000000000000000000000000 (boy)	0000000000000000000100000000000 (move)
0000000000000000000100000000000 (move)	0000000000000100000000000000000 (girl)
0000000000000100000000000000000 (girl)	0000000000010000000000000000000 (eat)
0000000000010000000000000000000 (eat)	0010000000000000000000000000000 (bread)
0010000000000000000000000000000 (bread)	0000000010000000000000000000000 (dog)
0000000010000000000000000000000 (dog)	0000000000000000000100000000000 (move)
0000000000000000000100000000000 (move)	0000000000000000001000000000000 (mouse)
0000000000000000001000000000000 (mouse)	0000000000000000001000000000000 (mouse)
0000000000000000001000000000000 (mouse)	0000000000000000000100000000000 (move)
0000000000000000000100000000000 (move)	1000000000000000000000000000000 (book)
1000000000000000000000000000000 (book)	0000000000000001000000000000000 (lion)

31-bit vectors formed an input sequence. Each word in the sequence was input, one at a time, in order. The task on each input cycle was to predict the 31-bit vector corresponding to the next word in the sequence. At the end of the 27,534 word sequence, the process began again, without a break, starting with the first word. The training continued in this manner until the network had experienced six complete passes through the sequence.

Measuring the performance of the network in this simulation is not straightforward. RMS error after training dropped to 0.88. When output vectors are as sparse as those used in this simulation (only 1 out of 31 bits turned on), the network quickly learns to turn off all the output units, which drops error from the initial random value of ~15.5 to 1.0. In this light, a final error of 0.88 does not seem impressive.

Recall that the prediction task is nondeterministic. Successors cannot be predicted with absolute certainty; there is a built-in error which is inevitable. Nevertheless, although the prediction cannot be error-free, it is also true that word order is not random. For any given sequence of words there are a limited number of possible successors.

Under these circumstances, the network should learn the expected frequency of occurrence of each of the possible successor words; it should then activate the output nodes proportional to these expected frequencies.

This suggests that rather than testing network performance with the RMS error calculated on the actual successors, the output should be compared with the expected frequencies of occurrence of possible successors. These expected latter values can be determined empirically from the training corpus. Every word in a sentence is compared against all other sentences that are, up to that point, identical. These constitute the comparison set. The probability of occurrence for all possible successors is then determined from this set. This yields a vector for each word in the training set. The vector is of the same dimensionality as the output vector, but rather than representing a distinct word (by turning on a single bit), it represents the likelihood of each possible word occurring next (where each bit position is a fractional number equal to the probability). For testing purposes, this likelihood vector can be used in place of the actual teacher and a RMS error computed based on the comparison with the network output. (Note that it is appropriate to use these likelihood vectors only for the testing phase. Training must be done on actual successors, because the point is to force the network to learn the probabilities.)

When performance is evaluated in this manner, RMS error on the training set is 0.053 (SD = 0.100). One remaining minor problem with this error measure is that although the elements in the likelihood vectors must sum to 1.0 (since they represent probabilities), the activations of the network need not sum to 1.0. It is conceivable that the network output learns the relative frequency of occurrence of successor words more readily than it approximates exact probabilities. In this case the shape of the two vectors might be similar, but their length different. An alternative measure which normalizes for length differences and captures the degree to which the shape of the vectors is similar is the cosine of the angle between them. Two vectors might be parallel (cosine of 1.0) but still yield an RMS error, and in this case it might be felt that the network has extracted the crucial information. The mean cosine of the angle between network output on training items and likelihood vectors is 0.916 (SD = 0.123). By either measure, RMS or cosine, the network seems to have learned to approximate the likelihood ratios of potential successors.

How has this been accomplished? The input representations give no information (such as form class) that could be used for prediction. The word vectors are orthogonal to each other. Whatever generalizations are true of classes of words must be learned from the co-occurrence statistics, and the composition of those classes must itself be learned.

If indeed the network has extracted such generalizations, as opposed simply to memorizing the sequence, one might expect to see these patterns emerge in the internal representations which the network develops in the course of learning the task. These internal representations are captured by the pattern of hidden unit activations which are evoked in response to each word and its context. (Recall that hidden units are activated by both input units and context units. There are no representations of words in isolation.)

The nature of these internal representations was studied in the following way. After the learning

phase of six complete passes through the corpus, the connection strengths in the network were frozen. The input stream was passed through the network one final time, with no learning taking place. During this testing, the network produced predictions of future inputs on the output layer. These were ignored. Instead, the hidden unit activations for each word + context input were saved, resulting in 27,354 150-bit vectors. Each word occurs many times, in different contexts. As a first approximation of a word's prototypical or composite representation, all hidden unit activation patterns produced by a given word (in all its contexts) were averaged to yield a single 150-bit vector for each of the 29 unique words in the input stream.[6] (In the next section it will be shown how it is possible to study the internal representations of words in context.) These internal representations were then subject to a hierarchical clustering analysis. Figure 7 shows the resulting tree; this tree reflects the similarity structure of the internal representations these lexical items. Lexical items which have similar properties are grouped together lower in the tree, and clusters of similar words which resemble other clusters are connected higher in the tree.

The network has discovered that there are several major categories of words. One large category corresponds to *verbs*; another category corresponds to *nouns*. The verb category is broken down into groups that *require a direct object*, or are *intransitive*, or where a *direct object is optional*. The noun category is broken into two major groups: *inanimates*, and *animates*. Animates are divided into *human* and *nonhuman*; the nonhuman are divided into *large animals* and *small animals*. Inanimates are broken into *breakable*, *edibles*, and nouns which appeared as subjects of agentless active verbs.

The network has developed internal representations for the input vectors which reflect facts about the possible sequential ordering of the inputs. The network is not able to predict the precise order of words, but it recognizes that (in this corpus) there is a class of inputs (namely, verbs) that typically follow other inputs (namely, nouns). This knowledge of class behavior is quite detailed; from the fact that there is a class of items which always precedes "chase," "break," "smash," it infers that the large animals form a class.

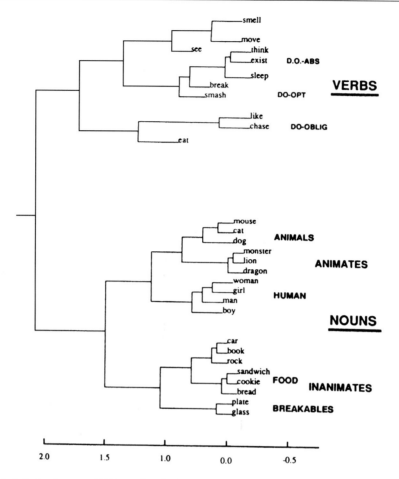

FIG. 7. Hierarchical cluster diagram of hidden unit activation vectors in simple sentence prediction task. Labels indicate the inputs which produced the hidden unit vectors; inputs were presented in context, and the hidden unit vectors averaged across multiples contexts.

Several points should be emphasized. First, the category structure appears to be hierarchical. Thus, "dragons" are large animals, but also members of the class of [– human, + animate] nouns. The hierarchical interpretation is achieved through the way in which the spatial relations (of the representations) are organized. Representations that are near one another in the representational space form classes, while higher level categories correspond to larger and more general regions of this space.

Second, it is also true that the hierarchy is "soft" and implicit. While some categories may be qualitatively distinct (i.e. very far from each other in space), there may also be other categories that share properties and have less distinct boundaries. Category membership in some cases may be marginal of unambiguous.

Finally, the content of the categories is not known to the network. The network has no information available which would "ground" the structural information in the real world. In this respect, the network has much less information to work with than is available to real language learners.[7] In a more realistic model of acquisition, one might imagine that the utterance provides one source of information about the nature of lexical categories; the world itself provides another source. One might model this by embedding the "linguistic" task in an environment; the network would have the dual task of extracting structural information contained in the utterance, and structural information about the environment. Lexical meaning would grow out of the associations of these two types of input.

In this simulation, an important component of meaning is context. The representation of a word is closely tied up with the sequence in which it is embedded. Indeed, it is incorrect to speak of the hidden unit patterns as word representations in the conventional sense, since these patterns also reflect the prior context. This view of word meaning, that is, its dependence upon context, can be demonstrated in the following way.

Freeze the connections in the network that has just been trained, so that no further learning occurs. Imagine a novel word, *zog*, which the network has never seen before, and assign to this word a bit pattern which is different from those it was trained on. This word will be used in place of the word *man*; everywhere that *man* could occur, *zog* will occur instead. A new sequence of 10,000 sentences is created, and presented once to the trained network. The hidden unit activations are saved, and subjected to a hierarchical clustering analysis of the same sort used with the training data.

The resulting tree is shown in Fig. 8. The internal representation for the word *zog* bears

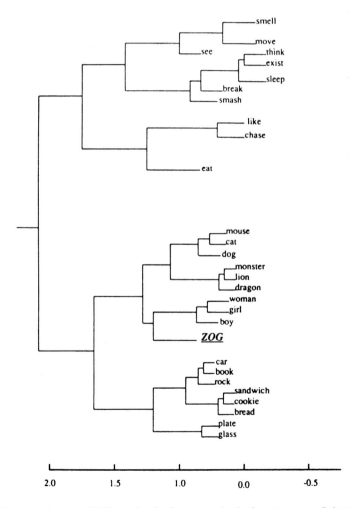

FIG. 8. Hierarchical clustering diagram of hidden unit activation vectors in simple sentence prediction task, with the addition of the novel input ZOG.

the same relationship to the other words as did the word *man* in the original training set. This new word has been assigned an internal representation that is consistent with what the network has already learned (no learning occurs in this simulation) and the new word's behavior. Another way of looking at this is in certain contexts, the network expects *man*, or something very much like it. In just such a way, one can imagine real language learners making use of the cues provided by word order to make intelligent guesses about the meaning of novel words.

Although this simulation was not designed to provide a model of context effects in word recognition, its behavior is consistent with findings that have been described in the experimental literature. A number of investigators have studied the effects of sentential context on word recognition. Although some researchers have claimed that lexical access is insensitive to context (Swinney, 1979), there are other results which suggest that when context is sufficiently strong, it does indeed selectively facilitate access to related words (Tabossi, Colombo, & Job, 1987). Furthermore, individual items are typically not very predictable but classes of words are (Schwanenflugel & Shoben, 1985; Tabossi, 1988). This is precisely the pattern found here, in which the error in predicting the actual next word in a given context remains high, but the network is able to predict the approximate likelihood of occurrence of classes of words.

Types, tokens, and structured representations

There has been considerable discussion about the ways in which PDP networks differ from traditional computational models. One apparent difference is that traditional models involve symbolic representations, whereas PDP nets seem, to many people, to be non- or perhaps subsymbolic (Fodor & Pylyshyn, 1988; Smolensky, 1987, 1988). This is a difficult and complex issue, in part because the definition of symbol is problematic. Symbols do many things, and it might be more useful to contrast PDP versus traditional models with regard to the various functions that symbols can serve.

Both traditional and PDP networks involve representations which are symbolic in the specific sense that the representations refer to other things. In traditional systems, the symbols have names such as A, or x, or β. In PDP nets, the internal representations are generally activation patterns across a set of hidden units. Although both kinds of representations do the task of referring, there are important differences. Classical symbols typically refer to classes or categories, but in PDP nets the representations may be highly context-dependent. This does not mean that the representations do not capture information about category or class (this should be clear from the previous simulation); it does mean that there is also room in the representation scheme to pick out individuals.

This property of PDP representations might seem to be a serious drawback to some. In the extreme, it suggests that there could be separate representations for the entity *John* in every different context in which that entity can occur, leading to an infinite number of $John_i$. But rather than being a drawback, I suggest this aspect of PDP networks significantly extends their representational power. The use of distributed representations, together with the use of context in representing words (which is a consequence of simple recurrent networks) provides one solution to a thorny problem — the question of how to represent type/token differences — and sheds insight on the ways in which distributed representations can represent structure.

In order to justify this claim, let me begin by commenting on the representational richness provided by the distributed representations developed across the hidden units. In localist schemes, each node stands for a separate concept. Acquiring new concepts usually requires adding new nodes. In contrast, the hidden unit patterns in the simulations reported here have tended to develop distributed representations. In this scheme, concepts are expressed as activation patterns over a fixed number of nodes. A given node participates in representing multiple concepts. It is the activation pattern in its entirety that is meaningful. The activation of an individual node may be uninterpretable in isolation (i.e. it may not even refer to a feature or microfeature).

Distributed representations have a number of advantages over localist representations (although the latter are not without their own benefits).[8] If the units are analog (i.e. capable of assuming activation states in a continuous range between some minimum and maximum values), then, in principle, there is no limit to the number of concepts which can be represented with a finite set of units. In the simulations here, the hidden unit patterns do double duty. They are required not only to represent inputs, but to develop representations which will serve as useful encodings of temporal context that can be used when processing subsequent inputs. Thus, in theory, analog hidden units would also be capable of providing infinite memory.

Of course, there are many reasons why in practice the memory is bounded, and why the number of concepts that can be stored is finite. There is limited numeric precision in the machines on which these simulations are run; the activation function is repetitively applied to the memory and results in exponential decay; and the training regimen may not be optimal for exploiting the full capacity of the networks. For instance, many of the simulations reported here involve the prediction task. This task incorporates feedback on every training cycle. In other pilot work, it was found that there was poorer performance in tasks in which there was a delay in injecting error into the network. Still, just what the representational capacity is of these simple recurrent networks remains an open question (but, see Servan-Schreiber, Cleeremans, & McClelland, 1988).

Having made these preliminary observations, the question of the context-sensitivity of the representations developed in the simulations reported here will be addressed. Consider the sentence-processing simulation. It was found that after learning to predict words in sentence sequences, the network developed representations that reflected aspects of the words' meaning as well as their grammatical category. This was apparent in the similarity structure of the internal representation of each word; this structure was presented graphically as a tree in Fig. 7.

In what sense are the representations, which have been clustered in Fig. 7, context sensitive? In fact, they are not; recall that these representations are composites of the hidden unit activation patterns in response to each word averaged across many different contexts. So the hidden unit activation pattern used to represent *boy*, for instance, was really the mean vector of activation patterns in response to *boy* as it occurs in many different contexts.

The reason for using the mean vector in the previous analysis was in large part practical. It is difficult to do a hierarchical clustering of 27,454 patterns, and even more difficult to display the resulting tree graphically. However, one might want to know whether the patterns displayed in the tree in Fig. 7 are in any way artifactual. Thus, a second analysis was carried out, in which all 27,454 patterns were clustered. The tree cannot be displayed here, but the numerical results indicate that the tree would be identical to the tree shown in Fig. 7; except that instead of ending with the terminals that stand for the different lexical items, the branches would continue with further arborization containing the specific instances of each lexical item in its context. No instance of any lexical item appears inappropriately in a branch belonging to another.

It would be correct to think of the tree in Fig. 7 as showing that the network has discovered that there are 29 *types* (among the sequence of 27,454 inputs). These types are the different lexical items shown in that figure. A finer grained analysis reveals that the network also distinguishes between the specific occurrences of each lexical item, that is, the *tokens*. The internal representations of the various tokens of a lexical type are very similar. Hence, they are all gathered under a single branch in the tree. However, the internal representations also make subtle distinctions between (for example), *boy* in one context and *boy* in another. Indeed, as similar as the representations of the various tokens are, no two tokens of a type are exactly identical.

Even more interesting is that there is a substructure of the representations of the various types of a token. This can be seen by looking at Fig. 9, which shows the subtrees corresponding to the

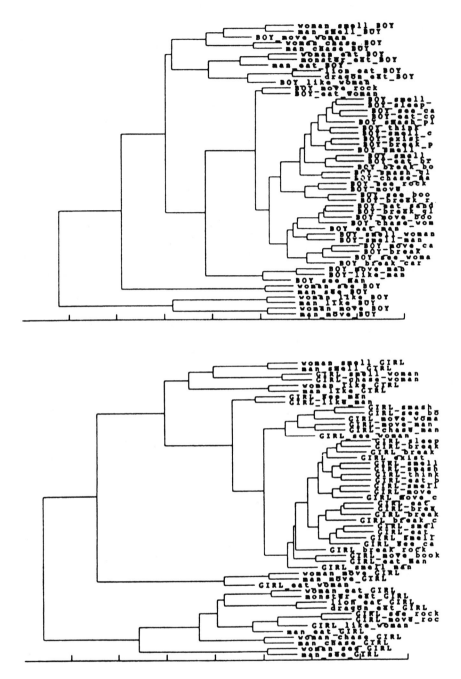

FIG. 9. Hierarchical cluster diagram of hidden unit activation vectors in response to some occurrences of the inputs BOY and GIRL. Upper-case labels indicate the actual input; lower-case labels indicate the context for each input.

tokens of *boy* and *girl*. (Think of these as expansions of the terminal leaves for *boy* and *girl* in Fig. 8.) The individual tokens are distinguished by labels which indicate their original context.

One thing that is apparent is that subtrees of both types (*boy* and *girl*) are similar to one another. On closer scrutiny, it is seen that there is some organization here; (with some exceptions) tokens of *boy* that occur in sentence-initial position are clustered together, and tokens of *boy* in sentence-final position are clustered together. Furthermore, this same pattern occurs among the patterns representing *girl*. Sentence-final words are clustered together on the basis of similarities in the preceding words. The basis for clustering of sentence-initial inputs is simply that they are all preceded by what is effectively noise (prior sentences). This is because there are no useful expectations about the sentence-initial noun (other than that it will be a noun) based upon the prior sentences. On the other hand, one can imagine that if there were some discourse structure relating sentences to each other, then there might be useful information from one sentence which would affect the representation of sentence-initial words. For example, such information might disambiguate (i.e. give referential content to) sentence-initial pronouns.

Once again, it is useful to try to understand these results in geometric terms. The hidden unit activation patterns pick out points in a high (but fixed) dimensional space. This is the space available to the network for its internal representations. The network structures that space in such a way that important relations between entities is translated into spatial relationships. Entities which are nouns are located in one region of space and verbs in another. In a similar manner, different types (here, lexical items) are distinguished from one another by occupying different regions of space; but also, tokens of a same type are differentiated. The differentiation is nonrandom, and the way in which tokens of one type are elaborated is similar to elaboration of another type. That is, *John*$_1$ bears the same spatial relationtionship to *John*$_2$ as *Mary*$_1$ bears to *Mary*$_2$.

This use of context is appealing, because it provides the basis both for establishing generalizations about classes of items and also allows for the tagging of individual items by their context. The result is that types can be identified at the same time as tokens. In symbolic systems, type/token distinctions are often made by indexing or binding operations; the networks here provide an alternative account of how such distinctions can be made without indexing or binding.

Conclusions

There are many human behaviors which unfold over time. It would be folly to try to understand those behaviors without taking into account their temporal nature. The current set of simulations explores the consequences of attempting to develop representations of time that are distributed, task-dependent, and in which time is represented implicitly in the network dynamics.

The approach described here employs a simple architecture, but is surprisingly powerful. There are several points worth highlighting.

- *Some problems change their nature when expressed as temporal events.* In the first simulation, a sequential version of the XOR was learned. The solution to this problem involved detection of state changes, and the development of frequency-sensitive hidden units. Casting the XOR problem in temporal terms led to a different solution than is typically obtained in feed-forward (simultaneous input) networks.
- *The time-varying error signal can be used as a clue to temporal structure.* Temporal sequences are not always uniformly structured, nor uniformly predictable. Even when the network has successfully learned about the structure of a temporal sequence, the error may vary. The error signal is a good metric of where structure exists; it thus provides a potentially very useful form of feedback to the system.
- *Increasing the sequential dependencies in a task does not necessarily result in worse performance.* In the second simulation, the task was complicated by increasing the dimensionality of the input vector, by extending the

duration of the sequence, and by making the duration of the sequence variable. Performance remained good, because these complications were accompanied by redundancy, which provided additional cues for the task. The network was also able to discover which parts of the complex input were predictable, making it possible to maximize performance in the face of partial unpredictability.

- *The representation of time — and memory — is highly task-dependent.* The networks here depend upon internal representations which have available, as part of their input, their own previous state. In this way the internal representations intermix the demands of the task with the demands imposed by carrying out that task over time. There is no separate "representation of time." There is simply the representation of input patterns in the context of a given output function; it just happens that those input patterns are sequential. That representation, and thus the representation of time, varies from task to task. This presents a somewhat novel view of memory. In this account, memory is neither passive nor a separate subsystem. One cannot properly speak of a memory for sequences; that memory is inextricably bound up with the rest of the processing mechanism.

- *The representations need not be "flat," atomistic, or unstructured.* The sentence task demonstrated that sequential inputs may give rise to internal representations which are hierarchical in nature. The hierarchy is implicit in the similarity structure of the hidden unit activations and does not require an a priori architectural commitment to the depth or form of the hierarchy. Importantly, distributed representations make available a space which can be richly structured. Categorical relationships as well as type/token distinctions are readily apparent. Every item may have its own representation, but because the representations are structured, relations between representations are preserved.

The results described here are preliminary in nature. They are highly suggestive, and often raise more questions than they answer. These networks are properly thought of as dynamical systems, and one would like to know more about their properties as such. For instance, the analyses reported here made frequent use of hierarchical clustering techniques in order to examine the similarity structure of the internal representations. These representations are snapshots of the internal states during the course of processing a sequential input. Hierarchical clustering of these snapshots gives useful information about the ways in which the internal states of the network at different points in time are similar or dissimilar. But the temporal relationship between states is lost. One would like to know what the trajectories between states (i.e. the vector field) look like. What sort of attractors develop in these systems? It is a problem, of course, that the networks studied here are high-dimensional systems, and consequently difficult to study using traditional techniques. One promising approach, which is currently being studied, is to carry out a principal components analysis of the hidden unit activation pattern time series, and then to construct phase state portraits of the most significant principal components (Elman, 1989).

Another question of interest is what is the memory capacity of such networks. The results reported here suggest that these networks have considerable representational power; but more systematic analysis using better defined tasks is clearly desirable. Experiments are currently underway using sequences generated by finite state automata of various types; these devices are relatively well understood, and their memory requirements may be precisely controlled (Servan-Schreiber et al., 1988).

One of the things which feedforward PDP models have shown is that simple networks are capable of discovering useful and interesting internal representations of many static tasks. Or put the other way around: Rich representations are implicit in many tasks. However, many of the most interesting human behaviors have a serial component. What is exciting about the present results is that they suggest that the inductive power of the PDP approach can be used to discover structure and representations in tasks which unfold over time.

Notes

1. The reader may more easily be convinced of this by comparing the locations of the vectors **[1 0 0]**, **[0 1 0]**, and **[0 0 1]** in 3-space. Although these patterns might be considered "temporally displaced" versions of the same basic pattern, the vectors are very different.

2. The activation function used here bounds values between 0.0 and 1.0.

3. A little more detail is in order about the connections between the context units and hidden units. In the networks used here, there were one-for-one connections between each hidden unit and each context unit. This implies that there are an equal number of context and hidden units. The upward connections between the context units and the hidden units were fully distributed, such that each context unit activates all the hidden units.

4. The program used was a simplified version of the program described in greater detail in the next simulation.

5. In the worst case, each word constitutes a rule. Hopefully, networks will learn that recurring orthographic regularities provide additional and more general constraints (cf. Sejnowski & Rosenberg, 1987).

6. Tony Plate (personal communication) has pointed out that this technique is dangerous, inasmuch as it may introduce a statistical artifact. The hidden unit activation patterns are highly dependent upon preceding inputs. Because the preceding inputs are not uniformly distributed (they follow precisely the co-occurrence conditions which are appropriate for the different categories), this means that the mean hidden unit pattern across all contexts of a specific item will closely resemble the mean hidden unit pattern for other items in the same category. This could occur even without learning, and is a consequence of the averaging of vectors which occurs prior to cluster analysis. Thus the results of the averaging technique should be verified by clustering individual tokens; tokens should always be closer to other members of the same type than to tokens of other types.

7. Jay McClelland has suggested a humorous — but entirely accurate — metaphor for this task: It is like trying to learn a language by listening to the radio.

8. These advantages are discussed at length in Hinton, McClelland, and Rumelhart (1986).

References

Berwick, R. C., & Weinberg, A. S. (1984). *The grammatical basis of linguistic performance*. Cambridge, MA: MIT Press.

Chomsky, N. (1957). *Syntactic structures*. The Hague: Moutin.

Chomsky, N. (1965). *Aspects of the theory of syntax*. Cambridge, MA: MIT Press.

Cottrell, G. W., Munro, P. W., & Zipser, D. (1987). Image compression by back propagation: A demonstration of extensional programming. In N. E. Sharkey (Ed.), *Advances in cognitive science* (Vol. 2). Chichester, England: Ellis Horwood.

Elman, J. L. (1989). *Structured representations and connectionist models*. (CRL Tech. Rep. No. 8901). San Diego: University of California, Center for Research in Language.

Elman, J. L., & Zipser, D. (1988). Discovering the hidden structure of speech. *Journal of the Acoustical Society of America, 83*, 1615–1626.

Fodor, J., & Pylyshyn, Z. (1988). Connectionism and cognitive architecture: A critical analysis. In S. Pinker & J. Mehler (Eds.), *Connections and symbols* (pp.3–71). Cambridge, MA: MIT Press.

Fowler, C. (1977). *Timing control in speech production*. Bloomington, IN: Indiana University Linguistics Club.

Fowler, C. (1980). Coarticulation and theories of extrinsic timing control. *Journal of Phonetics, 8*, 113–133.

Frazier, L., & Fodor, J. D. (1978). The sausage machine: A new two-stage parsing model. *Cognition, 6*, 291–325.

Greenberg, J. H. (1963). *Universals of language*. Cambridge, MA: MIT Press.

Grosjean, F. (1980). Spoken word recognition processes and the gating paradigm. *Perception & Psychophysics, 28*, 267–283.

Hanson, S. J., & Kegl, J. (1987). Parsnip: A connectionist network that learns natural language grammar from exposure to natural language sentences. *Ninth Annual Conference of the Cognitive Science Society*, Seattle, Washington. Hillsdale, NJ: Erlbaum.

Hinton, G. E., McClelland, J. L., & Rumelhart, D. E. (1986). Distributed representations. In D. E. Rumelhart & J. L. McClelland (Eds.), *Parallel distributed processing: Explorations in the microstructure of cognition* (Vol. 1, pp.77–109). Cambridge, MA: MIT Press.

Jordan, M. I. (1986). *Serial order: A parallel distributed processing approach* (Tech. Rep. No. 8604). San Diego: University of California, Institute for Cognitive Science.

Jordan, M. I., & Rosenbaum, D. A. (1988). *Action* (Tech. Rep. No. 88–26). Amherst: University of Massachusetts, Department of Computer Science.

Kelso, J. A. S., Saltzman, E., & Tuller, B. (1986). The dynamical theory of speech production: Data and theory. *Journal of Phonetics, 14,* 29–60.

Lashley, K. S. (1951). The problem of serial order in behavior. In L. A. Jeffress (Ed.), *Cerebral mechanisms in behavior.* New York: Wiley.

Lehman, W. P. (1962). *Historical linguistics: An introduction.* New York: Holt, Rinehart, and Winston.

MacNeilage, P. F. (1970). Motor control of serial ordering of speech. *Psychological Review, 77,* 182–196.

MacWhinney, B. (1978). The acquisition of morphophonology. *Monographs of the Society for Research in Child Development, 43,* (Serial No. 1).

Marcus, M. (1980). *A theory of syntactic recognition for natural language.* Cambridge, MA: MIT Press.

Marslen-Wilson, W., & Tyler, L. K. (1980). The temporal structure of spoken language understanding. *Cognition, 8,* 1–71.

Pineda, F. J. (1988). Generalization of back propagation to recurrent and higher order neural networks. In D. Z. Anderson (Ed.), *Neural information processing systems.* New York: American Institute of Physics.

Pinker, S. (1984). *Language learnability and language development.* Cambridge, MA: Harvard University Press.

Rumelhart, D. E., Hinton, G. E., & Williams, R. J. (1986). Learning internal representations by error propagation. In D. E. Rumelhart & J. L. McClelland (Eds.), *Parallel distributed processing: Explorations in the microstructure of cognition* (Vol. 1, pp.318–362). Cambridge, MA: MIT Press.

Salasoo, A., & Pisoni, D. B. (1985). Interaction of knowledge sources in spoken word identification. *Journal of Memory and Language, 24,* 210–231.

Saltzman, E., & Kelso, J. A. S. (1987). Skilled actions: A task dynamic approach. *Psychological Review, 94,* 84–106.

Schwanenflugel, P. J., & Shoben, E. J. (1985). The influence of sentence constraint on the scope of facilitation for upcoming words. *Journal of Memory and Language, 24,* 232–252.

Sejnowski, T. J., & Rosenberg, C. R. (1987). Parallel networks that learn to pronounce English text. *Complex Systems, 1,* 145–168.

Servan-Schreiber, D., Cleeremans, A., & McClelland, J. L. (1988). *Encoding sequential structure in simple recurrent networks* (CMU Tech. Rep. No. CMU–CS–88–183). Pittsburgh, PA: Carnegie-Mellon University, Computer Science Department.

Smolensky, P. (1987). *On variable binding and the representation of symbolic structures in connectionist systems* (Tech. Rep. No. CU–CS–355–87). Boulder, CO: University of Colorado, Department of Computer Science.

Smolensky, P. (1988). On the proper treatment of connectionism. *The Behavioral and Brain Sciences, 11.*

Stornetta, W. S., Hogg, T., & Huberman, B. A. (1987). A dynamical approach to temporal pattern processing. *Proceedings of the IEEE Conference on Neural Information Processing Systems.* Denver, CO.

Swinney, D. (1979). Lexical access during sentence comprehension: (Re)consideration of context effects. *Journal of Verbal Learning and Verbal Behavior, 6,* 645–659.

Tabossi, P. (1988). Effects of context on the immediate interpretation of unambiguous nouns. *Journal of Experimental Psychology: Learning, Memory, and Cognition, 14,* 153–162.

Tabossi, P., Colombo, L., & Job, R. (1987). Accessing lexical ambiguity: Effects of context and dominance. *Psychological Research, 49,* 161–167.

Tank, D. W., & Hopfield, J. J. (1987, June). Neural computation by concentrating information in time. *Proceedings of the IEEE International Conference on Neural Networks.* San Diego, CA.

Van Gelder, T. J. (1990). Compositionality: Variations on a classical theme. *Cognitive Science, 14,* 355–384.

Waibel, A., Hanazawa, T., Hinton, G., Shikano, K., & Lang, K. (1987). *Phoneme recognition using time-delay neural networks* (ATR Tech. Rep. TR–I–0006). Japan: ATR Interpreting Telephony Research Laboratories.

Watrous, R. L., & Shastri, L. (1987). Learning phonetic features using connectionist networks: An experiment in speech recognition. *Proceedings of the IEEE International Conference on Neural Networks.* San Diego, CA.

Williams, R. J., & Zipser, D. (1988). *A learning algorithm for continually running fully recurrent neural networks* (Tech. Rep. No. 8805). San Diego: University of California, Institute for Cognitive Science.

6

Word recognition and production

6.1 MULTIPLE CONSTRAINTS IN LANGUAGE PROCESSING

One of the basic features of human life is our ability to communicate with other people through language, that is, through a series of spoken or written words that convey meaning and that link together in a non-arbitrary fashion determined by what is known as syntax (loosely, the rules of grammar). Although having no meaning in their own right, words act to represent objects in the world and to represent concepts that can be generated both about concrete objects and also about more abstract ideas — plans, future intentions and so forth. Further, although the ways in which different words are linked together vary across languages (compare English, where verbs have high degrees of freedom over where they can appear within a sentence, with German, where in subordinate clauses verbs are assigned to a specific position), all can be described by a set of syntactic rules that link the surface structure of the sentence (as the sentence is expressed within a given language) to a common underlying meaning or deep structure. For instance, these rules may "parse" a sentence into distinct noun and verb phrases, each with their own constituent structure. Sentences with the same surface structure can then be assigned different deep structures if one of the words is ambiguous, allowing it to be coded as either part of a noun or a verb phrase, depending on its reading. Take the sentence:

The boys liked cooking apples.

This can be parsed in either of two ways, depending on whether the word *cooking* is coded as part of the verb phrase (*like cooking*) or the final noun phrase in the sentence (*cooking apples*). On one reading, we may infer that the boys like to eat cooking apples; in another, however, we may infer that the boys like to cook apples.

Such examples demonstrate that language understanding is not based on the surface structure of sentences, rather it involves syntactic operations that parse sentences into their underlying constituents (nouns, verb phrases etc.). The linguist Chomsky noted that syntactic relations can be used to convey the feeling that a sentence is correct even when the words involved have no meaning with respect to one another, as illustrated by his famous example "sentence": colourless green ideas sleep furiously (Chomsky, 1957). Apparently syntactic operations can function in a way that is relatively independent of the meaning of the words. Nevertheless our interpretation of sentences is not based solely on the syntactic properties of language, but also on additional factors such as the meaning of the words and the more general context in which the sentence occurs. For example, Bransford and Johnson (1973, p.40) gave readers a passage of which the following is an extract:

the procedure is actually quite simple. First you arrange things into different groups. Of course, one pile may be sufficient depending on how much there is to do. If you have to go somewhere else due to a lack of facilities that is the next step, otherwise you are pretty well set. It is important not to overdo things. That is, it is better to do too few things at once than too many.

Readers given the passage without a title found the text both difficult to comprehend and to recall. In contrast, readers given the same passage but with the title "washing clothes" found the material easy to understand and to recall. They could assign specific meanings to words such as *pile* and *facilities* and recognise how the statements inter-related. Here the general context provided by the title's passage was required to make sense of the paragraph; the meanings of the individual words taken in isolation were insufficient. The semantic properties of words also can impinge on our interpretation of perceived events. In studies of eye witness testimony, Loftus and Palmer (1974) had subjects watch a film of a car crash and then had them estimate the speed of the vehicles involved. Estimates of the speed were higher when subjects were asked: "how fast were the cars going when they *smashed* into one another", relative to when they were asked: "how fast were the cars going when they *contacted* one another". Subjects prompted with the word *smash* were also twice as likely to agree (incorrectly) that they saw broken glass at the incident. Here the semantics of the words seems to distort people's memory

for events (see Fruzzetti, Toland, Teller, & Loftus, 1992, for a review).

The syntactic and semantic properties of sentences also directly affect word perception in a "top-down" manner, but with the effects weighted by bottom-up perceptual information. For example, in tasks requiring subjects to repeat back heard sentences ("shadowing"), people frequently "restore" words that have been changed into nonwords in the input signal. These restorations are reduced when the semantic or syntactic characteristics of the sentences are changed, indicating that the perceptual input is over-ridden (to produce the restoration) only when words are within the appropriate sentence contexts. Also, even within the appropriate sentential contexts, restorations occur more frequently for changes made at the end rather than the beginning of words (see Marslen-Wilson, 1984). This suggests that top-down influences are ineffective when the stimulus information (in this case, at the beginning of words) is sufficient to counter them, but top-down information can over-ride bottom-up signals when enough bottom-up information is consistent with the top-down "hypothesis" (in this case, when the beginning of the word is consistent with the sentential context, changes at the end of the word are over-ridden).

From these simple examples, it is clear that our ability to process and to understand language depends on multiple factors, including the quality of the perceptual input, syntactic properties of the language, the meaning of the words, and the more general context. Similar factors also operate when we produce language — although rather than the quality of the perceptual input we may speak then about our strength of knowledge of spellings (e.g. for writing) or our familiarity with particular words (e.g. for speech). Viewed within a connectionist light, these multiple factors may be considered as constraints that can interact to generate ongoing language comprehension and production. Language comprehension and production, like many other human abilities, can be considered as processes of multiple constraint satisfaction. In this chapter, we deal with connectionist models that have attempted to simulate the recognition and production of single words.

In Chapter 7, we introduce connectionist simulations of language acquisition and of syntactic operations in language processing.

6.2 THE INTERACTIVE ACTIVATION MODEL: A PARADIGM EXAMPLE

One of the earliest attempts to model human language processing in connectionist terms was the interactive activation model proposed by McClelland and Rumelhart (1981; Rumelhart & McClelland, 1982), and first discussed in Chapter 1 (section 1.4). This was a model of human visual word recognition which incorporated the idea that performance was based on parallel, mutual constraint satisfaction between processing units representing knowledge coded at different levels of written words: their visual features (lines at particular positions and orientations), their letters, and knowledge of the whole word. McClelland and Rumelhart suggested that the representations of features, letters, and words were organised in an hierarchical fashion, features feeding into letters and letters into words. Processing constraints were built into the model in terms of the way in which connections were established between the units (see Fig. 6.1). Features that are part of particular letters had excitatory connections with those letter representations, and letters that are

part of particular words had excitatory connections with those word representations. In addition there were top-down connections so that words "supported" (by excitatory connections) the letters they contained. Matching these excitatory connections were inhibitory connections set both between the different levels of representation and within a given level. Features had inhibitory connections to letters that they were not a part of, and letters had inhibitory connections to words they were not a part of; top-down inhibitory connections went from words to letters not present in the words. All connection strengths between the units in the model were preset, and there was no attempt to simulate word learning. The mutual inhibition built into each layer of the model ("within-layer" inhibition) implements a type of "winner-take-all" process, in which the network in effect makes local decisions about the best alternative for the input at each level of representation. Networks that use similar winner-take-all and similar activation functions had also been previously explored by Grossberg (1978), but not applied directly to psychological data on human word recognition.

These different patterns of connectivity within the model can be thought of as expressing our stored knowledge of the relations between features, letters, and words. McClelland and Rumelhart (1981; Rumelhart & McClelland, 1982) proposed that visual word recognition involved a process of mutual constraint satisfaction between the bottom-up information gained about the features in the words and the top-down knowledge about word and letter identities. This top-down knowledge can help the model recognise letters in words even when bottom-up perceptual signals are degraded.

The interactive activation model has been applied to account for a large body of evidence on human reading performance. Cattell in 1886 first showed what at first sight appears to be a contradictory finding concerning word recognition. When stimuli are briefly presented, skilled readers can recognise words better than they can recognise the constituent letters; letter recognition here might be tested by presenting the letters in an unfamiliar order (i.e. to make a nonword), or by presenting them in isolation. This phenomenon, of apparently superior identification of

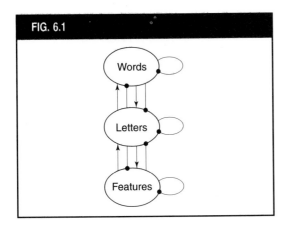

FIG. 6.1

The interactive activation model of visual word recognition.

letters in words relative to letters in nonwords and letters presented alone, is known as the *word superiority effect (WSE)*. Words may be better identified than nonwords and even isolated letters for a number of reasons. For instance, under brief presentation conditions, readers may only derive partial visual information from the stimulus. From this partial information they may be better able to guess the identity of the letters in words because they can deduce the identity of the words from the partial information about each of the letters. The ability to guess the identities of letters in nonwords will be much poorer of course, as the possible letters that can be present in the nonwords is not so constrained. In more recent times, experimenters have gone to considerable pains to try and rule out the possibility that the WSE is simply due to guessing. One procedure used to do this involves "probed recognition" of letters when subjects are given a forced-choice between two alternatives as to what the target letter is. In this procedure, adopted initially by Reicher (1969) and Wheeler (1970), words, nonwords, or isolated letters are briefly presented and typically followed by some form of pattern mask. This mask can contain features that are present in the letters and makes it relatively difficult to identify the stimuli, at least in part by destroying any after-image that might otherwise be present (see Breitmeyer, 1988; Humphreys & Bruce, 1989, for reviews of how masking occurs). Following the presentation of the stimulus, subjects are "probed" concerning the identity of a letter in a particular position, for instance by a bar being presented at that position. They are then given two choices as to what the identity of the letter was. The important point about this procedure is that by limiting the choice to two alternatives, differences in guessing between words, nonwords, and letters can be reduced. This is done by choosing as alternatives letters that would both make a word, for a word stimulus. For instance, if the target was the word WORK, and the fourth letter position was probed, then subjects may be asked to choose between a K and a D. As both of the alternatives make a word, subjects cannot gain an advantage with a word relative to either a nonword or an isolated letter by guessing the probed letter using information

derived from the other letters. However, even when these so-called "forced-choice" procedures are used to minimise guessing effects, there remain reliable advantages for identifying letters in words over letters in nonwords (on average there is about a 15% advantage in identification accuracy for words) and over isolated letters (on average there is about a 10% advantage for letters in words; see McClelland & Rumelhart, 1981, for a review).

The WSE can be simulated within the interactive activation model in the following way. The model can be presented with a vector corresponding to the features present in the letters in the word. When this input is given to the system, the feature representations are activated and these in turn activate the letters they are a part of (stored representations becoming active when the sum of their positive [excitatory] input, relative to their negative [inhibitory] input, is greater than a threshold level). Now, as any particular feature will be a part of a number of letters, several "competitor" letter representations can become active simultaneously. On a second iteration of the model, all the units are again updated according to both their current activation values and their connections to other units in the system. Thus the active letter units will excite the words of which they are members, and, in a top-down fashion, the words will activate further the letters they contain. For the initial iterations of the model, then, a substantial number of units at the letter and word levels can be activated (indeed see Fig. 1.4, Chapter 1). However, as the model continues to be updated, the units that gain greatest support begin to inhibit their competitors so that, over time, the model converges on a solution as to the features, letters, and words presented — ideally, only the features, letters, and word units corresponding to the stimulus will remain active and other units will be inhibited to resting level. Factors such as the frequency of occurrence of the word can affect the setting of the thresholds in the word units.

The WSE can be captured by assuming that, when a pattern mask is presented to the system, the features present in the mask activate matching feature units, and they in turn activate and inhibit letter representations. The features activated by the mask act as competitors with the features from the letters, impairing letter identification. The effect of competition from the mask can be particularly serious for single letters and letters in nonwords, as these items will enjoy little top-down support from word representations. On the other hand letters in words can be spared the most harmful effects of feature-competition from the mask because such letters enjoy top-down support from word representations. Figure 6.2 illustrates activation at the letter and word levels in the model when a degraded word is presented. Here, although

the features present in the final K of the word *work* are insufficient to identify the letter in isolation, there is still strong activation of the representation for K due to top-down feed-back from the representation for *work*.

McClelland and Rumelhart (1981; Rumelhart & McClelland, 1982) also report some emergent properties of the simulations. For example, they noted that letter groups that occur in many words tended to have their letter representations strongly supported, because the letters activate a number of word representations, all of which can offer

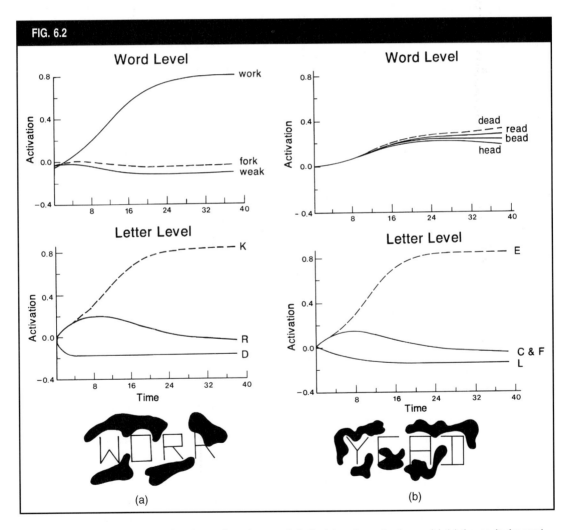

FIG. 6.2

Activation of letter-level representations by words and nonwords in the interactive activation model; (a) the results for word presentations; (b) the results for nonword presentations. From McClelland and Rumelhart (1981).

top-down activation — the "gang" effect. Interestingly, this suggested that letter recognition might also vary in different nonwords, according to whether the letters in the nonwords activate word representations. Consistent with this, Rumelhart and McClelland (1982) found that skilled readers show a benefit for letter identification in a nonword such as SPNT, with a letter pattern matching that in many words, relative to a nonword such as PTSN, whose letter pattern does not conform to that in many words. Previous experimenters had found that letter report was better in "regular" nonwords that have a similar spelling pattern (orthography) to English words (e.g. SPINT vs. PTISN), but, as such nonwords are also typically pronounceable (whereas irregular nonwords tend to be unpronounceable), this effect has been attributed to effects of pronounceability on letter identification (e.g. Hawkins, Reicher, Rogers, & Peterson, 1976). Rumelhart and McClelland, guided by their model, advanced such work by showing that there can be a benefit which seems purely orthographic, found even with regular but unpronounceable nonwords.

6.2.1 Constraints on the model

Although the interactive activation model simulates the word superiority effect, there are undoubted constraints on the model's operation. Here we mention two: the use of local representations of visual features and letters, and the simulation of just four-letter words. In performing almost any simulation, modellers are forced into making certain assumptions or simplifications. From a psychological perspective, what may be important to judge is, first, whether the assumptions are critical to the way the model operates or whether they are simply implementational details, and second, whether the assumptions are psychologically valid (see Humphreys, 1993). We illustrate these points with respect to the interactive activation model.

One major constraint on the interactive activation model concerns the nature of its representations of features and letters. The representations used by the model are local; each unit represents a psychologically identifiable object (a feature, a letter, a word), and each unit is tied to the position

of the stimulus in the visual field (i.e. there is local coding of both stimulus identity and location). Local coding of location information was used for the following reason. The model incorporates sets of inhibitory connections within its letter and word representations to better ensure that there is a "winner" in the competition that takes place to form a dominant representation at each level. However, words contain multiple letters, and word identification in the model depends on activation from all of the letters: letters within a word should not compete with one another. To ensure that such competition was minimised, the model used position-specific letter representations, so that "within-layer" competition acted only within each "pool" of position-specific letter representations. Activation from each letter position could then be fed forward to activate word representations. The position-specific letter representations were in turn activated by position-specific feature units (see Fig. 6.3).

There are several problems with such position-specific letter representations. From a computational viewpoint, a system incorporating such representations is expensive in hardware terms; very many position-specific detectors would need to exist to enable word recognition to operate when words are presented at varying locations on the retina. In addition, psychological evidence indicates that letter codes are tied more to the relative than to the absolute positions of letters in words. For example, consider the following stimuli:

PSYCHMENT
DEPARTOLOGY

When seen briefly, these letter strings are likely to be misread as PSYCHOLOGY DEPARTMENT. This is not simply because people tend to guess words from nonwords. Similar errors, in which the letters from one string seem to "migrate" to another, can occur with briefly presented words (e.g. MINE and LINK might be misread as MINK and LINE; Mozer, 1983; McClelland & Mozer, 1986). One interesting aspect of such migration errors is that the letters that migrate typically preserve their relative positions within the string: beginning letters remain at the beginning of the

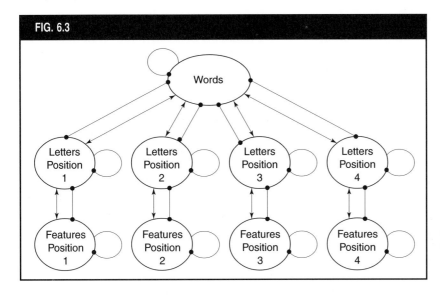

FIG. 6.3

Illustration of the position-specific feature and letter-detection pools, in the interactive activation model of word recognition.

string, end letters remain at the end. This suggests that the letters are represented in terms of their relative positions within the string, even when absolute position information is lost (e.g. due to the brief presentation conditions).

Other evidence for relative-position coding of letters in words comes from studies of priming. Studies of priming examine the effects of a first stimulus (the prime) on responses to a second, target stimulus. Evett and Humphreys (1981) examined the effects of priming from briefly presented letter strings on the accuracy of identification responses to a target word, and found that target identification was more accurate when the strings had letters in common than when their letters were different (e.g. minp → MINT vs. ronp → MINT). They proposed that the prime string activated the orthographic representations mediating visual identification of target words. Hence performance benefited when the orthographic representations of words matched relative to when they mismatched. Humphreys, Evett, and Quinlan (1990) went on to show that this "orthographic priming" effect was maintained even when the letters in primes and targets were in different locations in the visual field, providing letters were in the same relative positions in the strings (e.g. blck was an effective prime for the target word BLACK). Again, such a result is consistent with

letters being coded for their relative positions within words but not for their absolute positions in the visual field.

The psychological evidence suggests that letters are not coded for their absolute positions in the visual field, and thus we may question the psychological validity of the letter representations used in the model. However, is the assumption of position-specific letter coding critical or is it merely an implementational detail? We suggest that the assumption is critical, in the sense that the nature of stimulus coding in the interactive activation model would change dramatically if the assumption of position-specific letter representations were dropped. As we will review later, other simulations of visual word processing have gone on to incorporate the idea of relative position coding for letters. From a computational perspective, relative position coding may also be more economic, as fewer units will be required to code letters occurring in different positions in the visual field. For example, let us assume that representations take the form of letter triplets. A word such as MINT might then be represented by the activity pattern across units corresponding to: *MI, MIN, INT, and NT* (where * is a space). Although four units are used here to represent the word, just as four letter units would also be involved in the interactive activation model, the same cluster units could be used irrespective of the absolute positions of the letters in the visual field; this would not be the case for letter representations tied to the absolute positions of the letters in the visual field. Mozer (1991) estimated that with only 1000 or so cluster units, over 50% of the clusters that occur in English words can be accounted for. With 6000 or so units, 95% of all English words can be accommodated, when the frequency of occurrence of the words is taken into consideration. On such estimates, hardware requirements concerning the number of cluster units needed by a real brain are not unreasonable.

One other constraint on the interactive activation model was that it only contained representations for four-letter words in its internal lexicon. This restriction can be seen as a compromise forced on the modeller by the use of local letter and feature representations: the number of feature and letter representations would need to double to simulate the reading of eight-letter words. However, we suggest that, unlike the assumption of position-specific letter representations, the limitation of using just four-letter words is not critical to the model. The number of "slots" for position-specific feature and letter representations could be increased without changing the basic architecture of the model. Nevertheless, it does raise the interesting question of whether visual word processing in human observers can deal effectively with only a limited number of letters at a time. Here human evidence accords with the model. In visual lexical decision tasks, subjects are asked to decide whether a printed letter string is a real word or a nonword. Such tasks are frequently taken as measures of the time to access the visual lexicon for words. Frederiksen and Kroll (1976) showed that there were relatively minor effects on lexical decision latencies of the number of letters in words until words were about six letters long, but after that there were reaction time (RT) increases. Similarly, whereas short words (six letters or less) may typically be read within a single fixation, longer words frequently require more than one fixation to be read (O'Regan & Levy-Schoen, 1987). Word processing may well be limited to about six letters at a time (see also Carr & Pollatsek, 1985).

6.2.2 Extensions to the interactive activation model

Extensions to the interactive activation model to enable it to simulate data from studies of word recognition measuring reading latencies rather than accuracy were made by Jacobs and Grainger (1992). They added a variable response threshold (with a normal distribution) to units at the word level in the model, so that responses were made as soon as activation at the word level reached this threshold. The number of iterations to reach the threshold was taken as the measure of response speed, and predictions were made concerning mean response latencies, and response latency distributions based on the activation of word-level representations. Activation of word-level representations might be used in tasks commonly used to explore word recognition — such as lexical decision, where subjects have to decide whether a letter string is a word or a nonword. Jacobs and Grainger found that response distributions in the model approximated those found for lexical decisions with human subjects. Further, they were able to simulate effects on lexical decision of the relative word frequency between words sharing letter patterns. Grainger and Segui (1990) (see also Grainger, 1990) found that lexical decision times were slowed when words were similar in spelling to another word of higher frequency, relative to when there was no such higher-frequency word; for example, lexical decision times to a low-frequency word such as BLUR, which has a higher-frequency neighbour, BLUE, were slowed relative to control words of similar (low) frequency. This result is captured by the extended interactive activation model because the high-frequency neighbour can be activated by the letters shared with the lower-frequency target. As high-frequency words have a lower activation threshold than low-frequency words, high-frequency words can be activated more strongly and inhibit the lower-frequency target. McClelland (1991, 1993) has also extended the interactive activation model to incorporate variable (stochastic) processes. In a stochastic approach, activation values of units are set probabilistically according to their inputs (e.g. the probability that a unit is "on" rather than "off" will increase when there is stronger input); this contrasts with a "deterministic" approach, in which the activation values of units are completely determined by their inputs. In a stochastic model, the same input will generate variable outputs on different trials, rather as people do. Hence a stochastic model can be used to simulate the response distributions people generate across trials in an experiment. We delay a fuller discussion of McClelland's extension until we deal with the TRACE model of speech perception (Elman & McClelland, 1986; McClelland & Elman, 1986).

Extensions such as those of Jacobs and Grainger show the power of the interactive activation approach for accounting for a variety of phenomena on word processing, ranging from studies of letter identification to studies of word recognition. The idea of there being competition between stimulus representations during the recognition process, and of knowledge retrieval based on mutual constraint satisfaction, captures important aspects of human performance. However, these extensions do not overcome some of the fundamental limitations in the model, which concern the nature of its representations. Attempts to overcome the limitations have been made in other models, where a rather different approach to letter and word representations has been taken. In the next two sections we consider two such attempts: PABLO (for Programmable Blackboard model; McClelland, 1986) and BLIRNET (Mozer, 1987, 1991). Readers interested less in how visual word recognition takes place, and more in how written words access other types of knowledge (such as their pronunciation), may wish to move directly to section 6.5.

6.3 PABLO

PABLO was derived from the interactive activation model, and clearly bears a family resemblance to that model. PABLO uses a mechanism suggested by McClelland (1985) to overcome the problem of position-specific coding; he termed this mechanism the *connection information distributor (CID)*. The basic notion of a CID is that

there can be position-specific input and output units, a central knowledge store — abstracted from position — and a set of programmable connections between the central knowledge store and the position-specific input–output units. Input from the position-specific units is used to activate the central knowledge store, and output from the central knowledge store is used to "program" the connections between the position-specific input and output units. Applied to the problem of visual word recognition, the model has an advantage over the interactive activation model because connection strengths between each position-specific input unit (e.g. for a letter) and each position-specific output unit (e.g. for a word) do not have to be "hardwired" into the system; rather connection strengths can be programmed on-line. This may simplify the problem of learning, as connection strengths between every position-specific letter and word detector do not need to be trained; training could be reduced to the connections between the "abstracted" letter and word detectors in the central knowledge store. Let us now consider how the CID might work in practice.

In Fig. 6.4, a set of position-specific letter detectors are shown (for just two positions in the visual field), along with a set of connections between these position-specific letters and a set of word detectors. The model has the same basic architecture (from the letter to the word level) as the interactive activation model, although connections between the letters and words are shown in a different way. This is done in order to illustrate that there are potential connections (in white) between each letter and each word; we may note however that in a hardwired version of this model (such as the interactive activation model), only certain connections would have weights (shown in black — these weights represent the stored knowledge that a letter in a particular position is part of a particular word). The idea of the CID is that the connections between the position-specific letter detectors and the position-specific word detectors can be set by top-down knowledge (from the central knowledge store), and do not have to be pre-specified for each position in the field (nevertheless there would still need to be some additional process that enables letters to

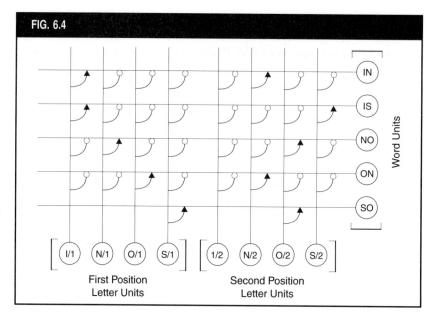

Letter coding in PABLO, with units corresponding to letters feeding into units corresponding to letter positions in words. This model can only respond to the letters I, N, O, and S, and it only knows the words IN, IS, NO, ON, and SO. Adapted from McClelland and Rumelhart (1986).

be lined up precisely with their position-specific slots; e.g. for I in position 1 and N in position 2, for the word IN.

The way in which top-down knowledge is used to program connections is illustrated in Fig. 6.5. This figure shows two sets of position-specific input (letter) and output units (words) on the bottom left and right of the figure (letters come in at the bottom and pass activation onto word representations on the sides). These are termed *programmable modules*, because the connections between the input and output units within each module are not hardwired but rather programmed by top-down knowledge (note that the connections

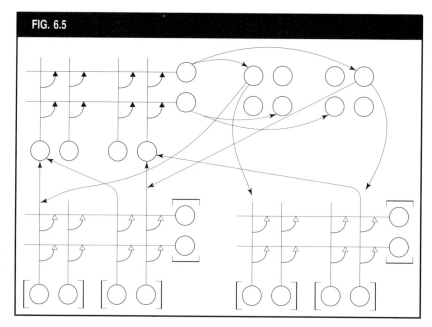

The operation of the *connection activation system* in PABLO (see the text for details). Adapted from McClelland (1985).

between the position-specific letter and word representations are shown in white). Two sets of these programmable units would be activated if there were two words present in the field. Activation from the position-specific input units (e.g. for a given letter in a given retinal position) is fed through to a *central module* in which there are hardwired connections between letters in particular positions and words (the top left part of the model, where the hardwired connections are shown in black). This hardwired central module can be thought of as equivalent to the interactive activation model. Activation of word knowledge in the central module is then used to set the connection weights between position-specific input and output units. This is done by activating a further set of units within a *connection activation system* (the top right matrix, shown in Fig. 6.5). There is one connection activation unit for each connection between a position-specific input and output unit, although the same connection activation unit will also instantiate the connection between the same position-specific input and output units in other programmable modules.

As activation from more than one set of programmable units can be fed through to the same central word recognition module, the model also has a second advantage over the interactive activation model, which is that more than one word can be processed at a time. However, there are constraints on the way in which the model can operate with two simultaneously present words. When two words are presented, the activation from each set of position-specific letter detectors is mapped through to the central word recognition module. Units for more than one word can then be activated, and connections for *both* words can be set in each programmable module. Activation of the position-specific word units within each programmable module is based on the product of activation from the input letters and the connections set by the connection activation system. This means that, generally, position-specific word units appropriate to the input letters will be activated and the appropriate words can be detected within each set of position-specific word units: both words can be identified. However, there is also an increased probability that letters from the second word

become incorporated into the response to the first word, as connections in the first programmable module are set to the letters in the second word as well as to the first. This problem is exacerbated if the two words have other letters in common, so that there is bottom-up support for the "migration" of the letter from the second word to the first. Figure 6.6 shows activation curves for units in the programmable, position-specific word units following the presentation of the target word SAND in the company of the word LANE (in a second programmable module). This figure illustrates that activation in units for words created by migrations of letters from word 2 to word 1 are raised above their baseline level (e.g. for LAND and SANE). Activation in the units of words that are one letter different from the target word, but where the different letter is not present in the display (e.g. BAND), remains at a baseline level. Migration errors are more likely than other types of errors.

As we have already noted, humans readers can make migration errors in which letters from one of two simultaneously presented words migrate into the response to a first word. McClelland and Mozer (1986) further report that (1) such migration errors are increased when the words have a number of letters in common, as found with CID mechanisms, and (2) the migrating errors, when present, tend to preserve their relative position within the word. This last result is achieved by the CID mechanism because the connections set within the position-specific programmable modules are specific to the relative locations of the stimuli in the field (e.g. with the stimuli SAND and LANE, connections for the first letter positions in each programmable module are both set for S and L for both words). It is interesting that the CID mechanism achieves this effect of relative-position migrations even though relative position is only implicit within the model; connections within the programmable modules are specific to the retinal positions of the letters.

There remain several clear problems with the CID approach to visual word recognition. One is that there needs to be a process outside the model that aligns letters with the position-specific letter units for each programmable module. A way

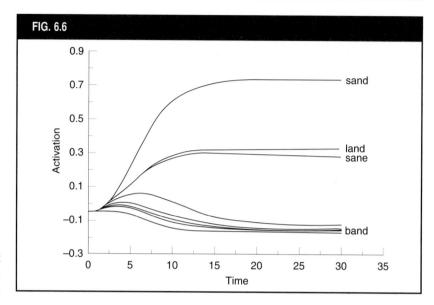

FIG. 6.6

Activation of the word unit for SAND in PABLO. From McClelland (1985).

around this is to use a scheme in which inputs do not correspond to letters in exact positions but to letters in roughly indicated positions in strings. This approach was employed in PABLO (McClelland, 1986), which extended the CID approach to position-invariant word processing. PABLO employed a coarse coding scheme in which units no longer correspond to a single word but to letter clusters in words, and each word is represented by the pattern of activation across a number of units. In PABLO, cluster units were activated by letters in the context of their nearest neighbours. For example, EVE was coded as: [(_E Ex) (xV Vx) (xE E_)], where (_E Ex) corresponds to E preceded by a space and followed by some other letter (to its right). This form of coarse coding also means that processing, and programming modules, are not restricted to words of a set length.

In addition to this, the model approximated the reading of text along a line of a page by assuming that words at fixation and to the right of fixation are mapped into successive programmable modules. McClelland assumed that connections would be set up in each module in parallel and, once established, the connections remained for some limited period of time; that is, the connections are "sticky". Because the connections are sticky, words that reach fixation having earlier

been processed at more peripheral retinal regions will have their connections already established to some degree within the programmable module at fixation, as connections are set by the central word module across all the programmable modules in the field. The use of "sticky" connections seems motivated less by computational needs than by the attempt to simulate psychological data on the reading of texts. For example, numerous studies have shown that fixation times on words are decreased if the words have previously been presented to the right of fixation (e.g. see Rayner & Pollatsek, 1987, for a review). This suggests both that processing can operate on more than one word at a time during reading, and that there is carry-over of peripheral information to help assimilate words that are subsequently fixated. In PABLO such carry-over effects emerge because connections for words subsequently fixated can be preset by the words when they appear peripherally.

6.4 BLIRNET AND MORSEL

PABLO deals with the problem of position in-variance by wiring up "on the fly" the relations between letter inputs and word outputs at each (coarsely coded) retinal location. Even so, replication of hardware is needed in the model. Each module requires dedicated hardware, and a programmable module is needed for every possible location where a word might appear. Also, the number of connections required is very large, when all possible letter positions are taken into account, and connectivity requirements are precise. There need to be one-to-one mappings between units in each of the programmable modules, the central (lexical) module, and the connection activation system. The model remains unwieldy.

A rather different approach to modelling visual word processing was proposed by Mozer (1987, 1991) in his BLIRNET model. BLIRNET used a hierarchical coding scheme, progressing from position-coded units that were activated by simple visual features (lines at particular orientations) to units that were activated by more complex features (combinations of the earlier features) but were less tied to retinal locations (this abstracting across retinal position was produced by summing activity from similar, lower-level detectors at more than one retinal position; see Fig. 6.7). There were

five layers of units that encoded such features, with outputs from the final layer being relatively position-invariant. In a sixth layer, units were set to code letter clusters. This was done by training the abstract feature units, in layer 5 of the model, to map onto appropriate units corresponding to letter clusters in level 6, using a simple delta-rule form of supervised learning. Word recognition is based on the activation of the letter clusters conforming to a particular word. In other simulations (Mozer, 1991), the cluster units have themselves been trained to associate with a further set of "lexical–semantic" units, which help to "pull out" words from activated letter clusters by means of top-down activation (see Fig. 6.8). In this "pull-out" network, the model uses top-down activation to converge on a set of letter cluster units, even though a broader range of letter cluster units may initially be activated by the input. This form of top-down convergence is similar to that used in the interactive activation model of word recognition, with one difference being that, in BLIRNET, knowledge about an individual word is distributed across a number of lexical–semantic units, whereas

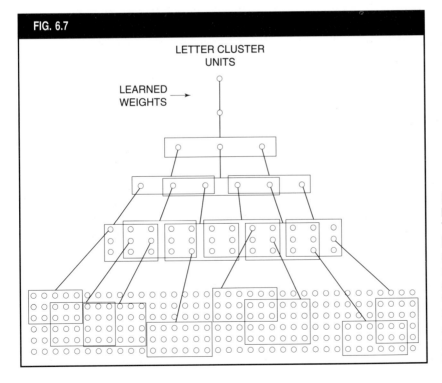

FIG. 6.7

LETTER CLUSTER UNITS

LEARNED WEIGHTS →

Input coding of letters and letter clusters in BLIRNET. The network contains six layers of units which are arranged in retinotopic maps of decreasing dimensions. The "receptive" field of a unit is depicted by a box around its set of input units. Adapted from Mozer (1987).

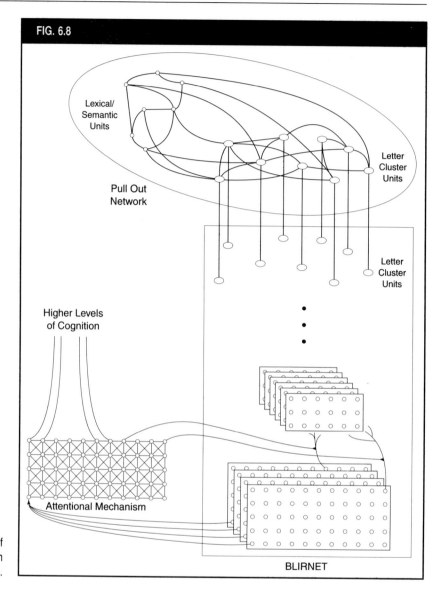

FIG. 6.8

Lexical/
Semantic
Units

Letter
Cluster
Units

Pull Out
Network

Letter
Cluster
Units

Higher Levels
of Cognition

Attentional Mechanism

BLIRNET

The MORSEL model of word recognition. From Behrman et al. (1991).

in the interactive activation model each word had a separate, local representation. Word-knowledge is instantiated in the weights on the connections between the lexical–semantic units and the letter cluster units, so that activation is reinforced in cluster units which, when combined, form words.

BLIRNET provides a relatively straightforward approach to position-invariant letter coding, by essentially "throwing away" spatial position information at higher levels of the model. Letter cluster units can thus be activated by appropriate

input presented at different positions on BLIRNET's retina. More than one word at a time can also be presented to the model. At the cluster level, differences between the words are not preserved, so that clusters for all the words present would be activated. Nevertheless different words can be distinguished if they activate non-overlapping letter clusters, as then distinct lexical–semantic units will be activated. Like PABLO, the model encounters problems in separating activation from two or more words if the words contain similar letters (as there is then no way for the model to "know" which words the clusters belong to). This aspect of the model has psychological validity, as it predicts that migration errors should occur when humans are briefly presented with more than one word at a time, and that these errors should increase when the words have more letters in common. As we have already noted, psychological evidence supports this (McClelland & Mozer, 1986).

Of course, with unlimited presentation times, normal readers do not make migration errors, otherwise it would be impossible to read text. Mozer (1991) produced an extension of BLIRNET (the model was relabelled MORSEL) in which a separate "attentional" module was added (see Fig. 6.8). The goal of the attention module was to raise activation levels for stimuli in attended parts of the visual field over activation levels for stimuli in unattended parts of the field. This biasing of activation was done by reciprocally linking each unit in the attention module (on the left of Fig. 6.8) to the retinal locations that provide input into BLIRNET; activation of an attentional unit led to increased activation at the associated retinal location. Within the attentional module, there were excitatory cross-links between neighbouring units, so that activated units tended to support one another, but units also shut-off if their activation was below a threshold level. This use of top-down activation to bias processing at particular spatial regions has been adopted in other simulations of visual attention, reviewed in Chapter 8 (Cohen, Farah, Romero, & Servan-Schreiber, 1994; section 8.8). By boosting the activation for words at attended regions relative to those at unattended regions, MORSEL was able to prevent migration errors; now letter clusters for the attended word would be activated more strongly than those for the unattended word, and so the two sets of clusters would no longer be confused. Human migration errors can still be simulated, however, if it is assumed that the effect of short exposure durations (as used in the human studies) is to prevent readers from attending to the location of a target word.

BLIRNET has several advantages over PABLO. Perhaps most important, BLIRNET uses fewer representations, as position-specific letter and word detectors are not required; indeed high-level letter

and word representations within the model are relatively abstracted for position. BLIRNET's architecture also makes it feasible to implement learning in a relatively straightforward way (although learning was only carried out at the higher levels in the model in the simulations reported by Mozer, 1987, 1991). In addition, in the extension of BLIRNET into MORSEL, the model begins to address important issues concerned with the interactions between visual attention and word recognition, which are important not only for explaining normal, skilled reading (see section 6.4.1) but also for explaining some neuropsychological disorders of reading (Chapter 8).

6.4.1 Simulating normal word recognition in MORSEL

We have already noted that BLIRNET gives a ready account of the types of migration error that arise when people have to read multiple, briefly presented words. When an attentional mechanism is added, to effect control over bottom-up activation (in MORSEL), the model can also be applied to other results in the normal reading literature. Behrmann, Moscovitch, and Mozer (1991) had readers carry out lexical decisions to the underlined sections of letter strings. This underlined, *target* section could be a word or a nonword, and it could be embedded in a non-underlined *context* section which, when combined with the target section, could make a word or a nonword. For example, the stimuli could include F<u>ARM</u> (word target in word context), G<u>ARM</u> (word target in nonword context), E<u>AST</u> (nonword target in word context), and W<u>AST</u> (nonword target in nonword context). Behrmann et al. found that human performance was affected by the contexts, and in particular that word contexts slowed performance. Within MORSEL, Behrmann et al.'s task can be simulated by setting the attentional module to the underlined portion of each stimulus and by reading-out activation values in the letter cluster units (for lexical decision, word responses can be made if the activated units correspond to a known word, otherwise respond nonword[1]). In the model the attentional module boosts activation at attended locations but it does not completely suppress activation at unattended locations. As a consequence, "unattended" (i.e. non-underlined) context letters can partially activate stored representations. This can create noise in the process of selecting the target, especially when the context units activate clusters that receive top-down, semantic support (i.e. for word rather than nonword contexts). Thus, even though targets may eventually be selected correctly, unattended stimuli still affect performance, and the magnitude of any effect is larger if the unattended stimulus is known to the model. In this respect MORSEL produces results that are similar to other simulations of "automatic" processing of unattended stimuli in connectionist models (see Chapter 5 for discussion of simulations of the Stroop effect).

Mozer (1991) also simulated the WSE. The brief presentation and masking conditions typically used to elicit the WSE using forced-choice procedures in humans (Reicher, 1969; Wheeler, 1970), were modelled by initially activating the retina of MORSEL with the letters in the strings and then giving the model random noise input. Activation in letter cluster units was measured. Mozer found that the correct letter cluster units were more likely to be activated for words than for nonwords, even when top-down feedback from the "pull out" network was not used. The advantage for clusters in words over nonwords reflects the training on words given to the connections between abstract feature units and letter cluster units. It is of some interest that a WSE was found even in the absence of top-down feedback within the model. The question of whether top-down processes are necessary to account for human data is one that has vexed connectionist modelling on other occasions, as we review in more detail in section 6.10. The simulations with MORSEL show that top-down activation is not *necessary* to produce context effects in processing, providing high-level activation can be used for responding to known and unknown stimuli alike (in this case, activation in distributed letter cluster units can be used both for words and nonwords).

In studies with skilled readers, Johnston and McClelland (1974) found that the WSE could be eliminated if pre-cues were given indicating the location of a target letter. The pre-cue presumably enables readers to focus attention on the letter

and to ignore the word. In MORSEL, the pre-cue may enable the attention module to selectively pre-activate the location of the target letter over those of other letters in the words and nonwords. Mozer (1991) demonstrated that such selective pre-activations were sufficient to minimise the WSE.[2]

6.5 FROM SPELLING TO SOUND: A TEST OF RULE-BASED OPERATIONS

The interactive activation model, PABLO, BLIRNET, and MORSEL all deal with the processes involved in visual word recognition, that is, in accessing stored representations of words from print. Of course, skilled readers are able to do more than recognise words as familiar orthographic forms, they are also able to derive meaning from the words and they are able to pronounce them. Indeed, psychological studies demonstrate that readers sometimes derive the meaning of words from their sounds rather than directly from print (e.g. Van Orden, 1987), indicating the importance of understanding how sound is derived from print for understanding reading. For connectionist modellers the issue of deriving spelling from print is also of broader theoretical interest, as many psychologists have thought that word pronunciation depends on rule-based operations rather than stimulus–response learning of the type frequently employed in connectionist modelling. We now make a brief aside to consider why this issue might be important.

Learning in connectionist models is essentially based on processes of association (see Chapter 3). Unsupervised learning algorithms, such as the Hebb rule, typically involve stimulus–stimulus associations (weights are altered as a function of the co-occurrence of activation in linked processing units). Supervised learning algorithms, such as back-propagation, involve stimulus–response associations (weights are altered according to whether a given stimulus elicits an expected response). In contrast to this, as we shall illustrate in several places in this chapter, it has often been argued that human language is determined by rule-based, symbolic operations. As far as English is concerned, the rule-based operations may involve going directly from letters or groups of letters to sounds (or at least to phonological representations of letters and letter groups). The operations can be thought of as rule-based because they are not mediated by memories of individual instances (individual words, in this case), but by condition–action rules abstracted across instances. For example, readers of English may incorporate rules such as: the spelling a is assigned the phonology /a/; the spelling ph is assigned the phonology /f/, and so forth. These rules will work for the great majority of English words, and they can be applied across known and unknown examples alike (i.e. they do not require access to memories of individual instances of words). Connectionist models, learning by association between individual stimulus or response instances, provide a challenge to simple rule-based accounts of language processing.

So-called "dual-route" models of reading assume that readers of English employ both rule-based procedures and procedures based on the recognition of individual instances in order to pronounce printed words: readers employ both "non-lexical" and "lexical" procedures (here we define lexical procedures as those requiring access to memory representations of individual word instances). The involvement of independent lexical and non-lexical reading processes may also be determined by the regularity of the relations between spelling and sound in the language. English has mixed regularity in this respect. The majority of words have "regular" pronunciations that would be produced by the application of a set of non-lexical rules operating at the level of letters or letter clusters (in one view, the orthographic units mediating non-lexical reading in English are *graphemes* — letters or letter clusters that conform to a single phoneme). However, there are also a set of irregular words, whose pronunciations cannot be derived by the application of rules to letter groups smaller than the word (e.g. words such as "have", "pint" and "yacht", which are pronounced differently from other words having the same spelling patterns). A lexical as well as a non-lexical route may be required in order for irregular as well as regular words to be pronounced correctly. Other languages have relationships between spelling and

sound that are either more regular (e.g. Italian; the Japanese script kana) or less regular than English (e.g. Hebrew; the Japanese script kanji). For such languages, it is possible that either a purely non-lexical or a purely lexical (instance-based) system is utilised (although see Seidenberg, 1992).

Figure 6.9 illustrates a simple dual-route model for pronouncing English words, in which there are separate routes for lexical reading and for non-lexical, grapheme–phoneme translation processes (see Coltheart, 1987). Psychological evidence for the operation of dual routes comes from several sources, involving both normal readers and readers with acquired reading disorders. We cover the modelling of reading disorders in Chapter 8, and deal only with skilled reading here. One piece of evidence for non-lexical reading in English is that skilled readers are able to pronounce nonwords (letter strings that they have never seen before); further, these pronunciations tend to follow standard spelling–sound rules even when the word with the closest spelling pattern is pronounced irregularly. For example, a nonword such as nacht will tend to be pronounced /næʧt/ (to rhyme with thatched) rather than /nɒt/ (to rhyme with yacht). If nonwords were pronounced by some form of analogy with similarly spelled words, then such nonwords ought to be pronounced similarly to their nearest word "neighbour". That they are not suggests that nonwords are pronounced using an abstracted set of rules. In addition to this, regular words are named more quickly than irregular words, at least when the words have low frequencies of occurrence in English (Seidenberg, Waters, Barnes, & Tanenhaus, 1984). High-frequency words may be read more quickly lexically than non-lexically. For low-frequency regular words, however, the non-lexical route may offer a pronunciation prior to the lexical route, facilitating their naming relative to when the stimuli can only be read lexically (with low-frequency irregular words). A third piece of evidence, this time suggesting the existence of the lexical route, is that words are named more quickly than nonwords, even when the nonwords have similar spellings (e.g. when comparisons are made between matched words and nonwords, such as nail and naid) and even when they have the same pronunciation

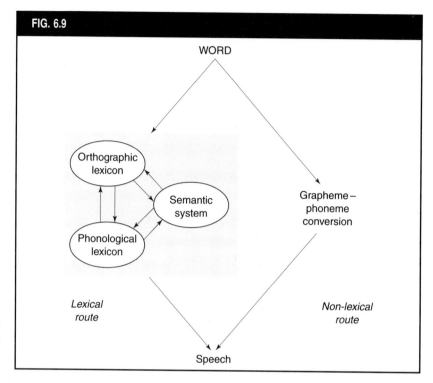

FIG. 6.9

The standard dual route theory of visual word naming (from Humphreys & Evett, 1985).

(with so-called pseudohomophones, such as nale; McCann & Besner, 1987). Thus word pronunciation seems to benefit relative to nonword pronunciation from the existence of a second (lexical) reading route.

However, there are other data that indicate that the situation is not so clear-cut. For example, if nonword pronunciation were completely independent of lexical pronunciation processes, then the names assigned to nonwords should show no effect of the pronunciations assigned earlier to words. Psychological evidence indicates otherwise. The pronunciation of a nonword such as raste can be biased by a prior preceding irregular word such as caste (caste increases the likelihood that irregular rather than regular phonology is assigned to the nonword; in this case, raste would be pronounced /rɑːst/, to rhyme with mast rather than taste, see Kay & Marcel, 1981). Similarly, a nonword such as louch is more likely to be pronounced /laʊtʃ/, to rhyme with couch, when this pronunciation has been semantically biased by the preceding word sofa (Rosson, 1983). Such results suggest that the non-lexical route may not operate independently of lexical processing.

Connectionist modellers have attempted to train networks to learn the spelling-to-sound relationships for English by teaching them to associate phonological "output" with orthographic "input". In this modelling, words with both regular and irregular spelling–sound relationships can be presented to the model, and no *a priori* distinction is made between separate lexical and non-lexical routes to phonology. Nevertheless, if there is generalisation of the learning, the model should be able to pronounce nonwords whose spelling–sound relationships overlap with those of trained words. Thus the models test whether a single route, based on learning by association, is able to perform the jobs typically assigned to separate instance-based and rule-based procedures.

6.6 NETtalk

A first attempt to learn spelling–sound relationships in English in a connectionist system was made by Sejnowski and Rosenberg (1987) in their NETtalk model. They used a three-layer network, trained to associate single phonemes as output to input graphemes. Graphemes were fed into the model by means of a "moving window", so that on each learning trial a central grapheme was presented along with a context of three graphemes to either side (including units representing spaces). The window was moved from left to right along the word on sequential learning trials, so that the model was trained to associate phonemes with particular graphemic contexts. The moving window scheme is illustrated in Fig. 6.10. Using this scheme, Sejnowski and Rosenberg trained the model to learn grapheme–phoneme associations on a set of 1000 words (of mixed spelling–sound regularity), achieving a 95% success criterion after 50,000 learning trials (where success was judged on the model making a "best guess" to associate its output vector with the nearest output vector for a phoneme). The model also generalised relatively well, giving about 77% best guess responses when applied to a large dictionary of 20,000 words (although the majority of these would be "nonwords" as far as the model is concerned of course).

Sejnowski and Rosenberg also performed a cluster analysis on the hidden unit activations produced by each grapheme, averaged across the different contexts in which the grapheme had appeared. As we noted when we dealt with Elman's (1990) work on recurrent networks (Chapter 5, section 5.2), clustering provides a way of grouping together activation values that are similar (these are shown located within a single cluster) and separating those that differ from this cluster (these are shown located within a separate cluster).

Clustering is typically hierarchical, so that the first clusters represent the coarsest distinction within the set of activations analysed, with progressively finer distinctions made as activation values are clustered into smaller groups. Cluster analysis provides one way of trying to analyse the form of internal representation settled on by a network when it learns a task. The results found by Sejnowski and Rosenberg are given in Fig. 6.11. As can be seen from the figure, the hidden unit values separated according to whether vowels or consonants were the input to the model; hidden unit values for consonants were more similar to each other than they were to the hidden unit values of vowels, and vice versa. This suggests that, in learning, the model found it useful to distinguish consonants and vowels, possibly because, in English, spelling–sound correlations across different words are much more consistent for consonants than they are for vowels. Interestingly, there is psychological evidence that spelling–sound relationships are realised more rapidly for consonants than for vowels in English readers (Berent & Perfetti, 1995), a result that might follow from the separate representations of these spelling–sound relationships within a model of the type explored by Sejnowski and Rosenberg.

However, despite the impressive learning of spelling–sound relationships for both regular and irregular words, and despite the model's ability to generalise its learning, NETtalk was not closely tied to psychological data on reading. For instance NETtalk depends on serial processing as a spatial

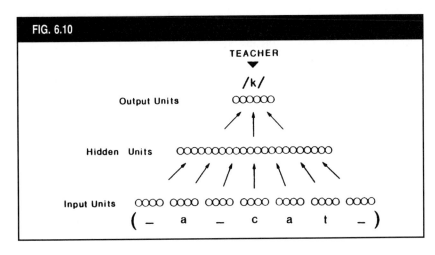

FIG. 6.10

The NETtalk architecture. From Sejnowski and Rosenberg (1987).

FIG. 6.11

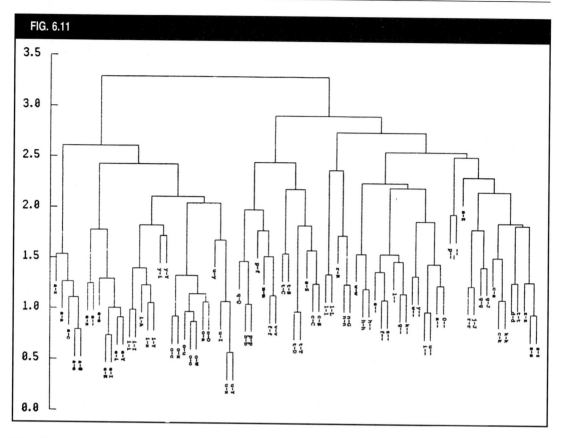

Hierarchical clustering of hidden unit activation functions in NETtalk, showing a separation between the model's representation of vowels and consonants. From Sejnowski and Rosenberg (1987).

window is passed across each word or nonword; it also requires that letters are aligned accurately within the spatial window. However, there is little evidence indicating that (at least short) English words are read in a serial fashion from left-to-right (section 6.2.1). To capture human reading processes, models need to deal with information presented in parallel across words. Also, the model was applied to a relatively small training set, which took no account of factors such as the frequency of occurrence of the words in English.

6.7 SEIDENBERG AND MCCLELLAND'S (1989) MODEL OF WORD NAMING

A connectionist model designed to capture psychological data on reading was proposed by Seidenberg

and McClelland (1989). Like Sejnowski and Rosenberg (1987), Seidenberg and McClelland also trained a three-layer network using back-propagation (see Fig. 6.12 for the architecture of the model). However, instead of presenting input sequentially, from left to right across each word (as did Sejnowski & Rosenberg), they presented the full spelling of each word simultaneously to the model — a procedure that seems more analogous to skilled reading of English (at least for words up to six letters long, Carr & Pollatsek, 1985).

Spellings were coded in terms of activation patterns across units which represented letter triplets (and word boundaries) (see also sections 6.3 and 6.4). On average, any three consecutive characters in a word activated about 20 different orthographic units, so that the probability that two different input strings activated exactly the same set of

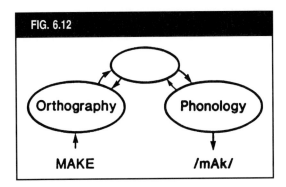

FIG. 6.12

Processing architecture of the Seidenberg and McClelland (1989) model of word naming.

phonemes in a word. For instance, in the word MAKE, one unit would correspond to /#Ma/ (the phoneme /M/ in the context of a word boundary and a following phoneme /a/), another to /mAk/, another to /aKe/, another to /kE#/. However, rather than using coarsely coded *phonemic* representations, Seidenberg and McClelland used the same adaptation of this scheme as had been used earlier by Rumelhart and McClelland (1986) in their model of learning the past tense of English verbs (see Chapter 7): Wickelfeature rather than Wickelphone representations were used. In Wickelfeature representations, each unit represents a triple of the phonetic features comprising phonemes (e.g. such features correspond to properties such as vowel, fricative, stop). For the Seidenberg and McClelland simulation, each Wickelfeature representation was encoded as a distributed pattern of activation across a set of output units. When we discuss the outputs of the Seidenberg and McClelland model we, following the authors, will refer to phonological output representations (as labelled in Fig. 6.12), although it should be remembered that the output units corresponded to phonetic features rather than phonemes.

Using this coding scheme, Seidenberg and McClelland trained a network with 400 orthographic units, 200 hidden units, and 460 output

orthographic units was effectively zero. As a consequence, all input strings derived from English words should be discriminable at the input level (even anagrams and strings with repeated letters, as the local contexts around the letters will differ).

Output phonological representations were similar in spirit to the coarse input representations of letter triplets, and were derived from the concept of the "Wickelphone" (this term stems from the notion of using a coarse coding scheme of this type, which was first suggested by Wickelgren, 1969). A Wickelphone representation is one in which each unit corresponds to three consecutive

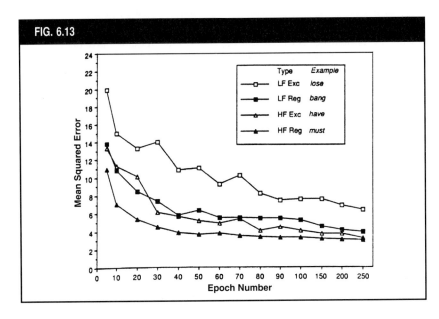

FIG. 6.13

Learning functions for words varying in regularity and frequency of occurrence in Seidenberg and McClelland (1989).

units to produce output phonological representations for all the monosyllabic words in the Kuçera and Francis (1967) word count (a large count of word occurrences in printed American English). Stimuli were represented in the training set as a function of their frequency of occurrence in the language (thus high-frequency words appeared more often than low-frequency words in each run through the training set, or "epoch"). As an indication of the ease of pronunciation, Seidenberg and McClelland used a measure of how far away was the phonological representation produced by the model from the phonological representation expected. This measure was the root mean square of the error score (the RMS_{error}) for the output phonological representation of the word (i.e. a measure of the difference between the output the model actually produced and the output it should have produced, given the input). They proposed that the smaller the error score, the easier it would be for the model to pronounce the word; for human subjects, this may be reflected in the time taken to name the word.

As we have already noted, Seidenberg et al. (1984) found that, for skilled human readers, there is an interaction between the spelling-to-sound regularity of the word and its frequency of occurrence; the effects of regularity are larger on low-frequency than on high-frequency words. The performance of the model, in terms of the RMS_{error}, as learning took place with high- and low-frequency words varying in regularity, is shown in Fig. 6.13. Not surprisingly, for all word types, the RMS_{error} scores decreased with training, but across trials, the error scores for low-frequency, irregular words remained higher than for the other word types. This mimics the pattern of data for human readers, who are particularly slow to name low-frequency irregular words. For the model, an interaction emerges because regularity and frequency are tightly coupled. The frequency of occurrence of individual words is a measure of the number of *tokens* of those stimuli in the language. The regularity of the spelling–sound correspondence for words reflects the number of *types* there are of particular spelling–sound patterns. Regular words are regular simply because they share the same spelling–sound patterns with the majority

of other words in the language. In the model, stimuli are represented by activation patterns across units corresponding to sub-word segments. During training, the mappings from the sub-word orthographic units to the sub-word phonological units are strongly reinforced for regular words, as the same sub-word mappings occur across many words in the training set. In addition, the mappings between orthography and phonology for high-frequency irregular words are strongly reinforced, as these particular stimuli occur many times in the training set. In contrast, the mappings for low-frequency irregular words are given less reinforcement. Hence, RMS_{error} scores remain high for such words.

The network of Seidenberg and McClelland not only gives phonological outputs for words (i.e. for items in its training set), it also gives outputs for nonwords (i.e. for items not present in its training set). For example, an RMS_{error} value for a nonword can be calculated by presenting a nonword as input to the model and assessing the distance between the output values given and the output values expected if the pronunciation were correct. The RMS_{error} values for nonwords can be affected by the preceding word context. To mimic context effects in human reading, Seidenberg and McClelland ran a blocked set of training trials in which the model was trained on just one word. Immediately after this training, a nonword was presented to the model and the RMS_{error} values measured, using the "regular" pronunciation of the nonword as the target output for calculating the RMS_{error}. Seidenberg and McClelland reasoned that the blocked training would alter the weights on the connections within the model, temporarily biasing pronunciations. Consistent with this, they found that the RMS_{error} decreased when the nonword pronunciation had been biased by a regular word (e.g. using our earlier example from the psychology literature, if gaste had been preceded by waste), whereas the RMS_{error} increased when the nonword pronunciation had been biased by an irregular word (gaste preceded by caste). Within the model, these biasing effects arise as a natural consequence of regular words, irregular words, and nonwords all using the same "route" for pronunciation. The results simulate the biasing effects on nonword pronunciation reported with human readers by Kay and Marcel (1981).

Seidenberg and McClelland also note how lexical decision responses could be made on the basis of the outputs from the model. They suggest that lexical decisions could be performed by checking the familiarity of the orthographic input (the stimulus) given to the model. An "orthographic check" could involve a comparison between (i) the original input activation values for a letter string and (ii) the activation values generated by passing the input through the hidden units and then back down to the input units after the model had been trained. In effect this uses an RMS_{error} score on the orthography of the stimulus as a measure of the familiarity of the word form. A similar notion of lexical decisions being based on an orthographic check has also been proposed to explain lexical decision performance in human readers. For instance, Besner and McCann (1987) suggested that, for human readers, a check could be made on the familiarity of the visual form of words and nonwords. This would help explain why the effect of altering the familiarity of the form, for instance by mixing the case of the letters within the letter strings, affects lexical decision more strongly than naming (as naming need not involve a check of orthographic familiarity; see also Mayall & Humphreys, 1996a, and Chapter 8 for attempts to simulate lexical decision performance in neuropsychological patients).

For the model, the orthographic check process will be effective for lexical decision providing that words and nonwords have discriminably different orthographic RMS_{error} scores (i.e. if the distributions of these scores over the population of words and nonwords have little overlap). It will not be effective when orthographic RMS_{error} scores overlap for words and nonwords. Seidenberg and McClelland speculated that, when there is overlap in the orthographic RMS_{error} scores, some further source of knowledge would need to be called upon, such as the RMS_{error} scores for phonological outputs, to discriminate words from nonwords. Thus lexical decisions may be based on different sources of information, depending on the exact composition of words and nonwords used in an experiment. Again there is some fit with the

psychological literature here. For example, effects of the semantic and phonological relations between words in lexical decision are larger when nonwords are orthographically legal relative to when they are orthographically illegal (Shulman, Hornak, & Sanders, 1978). Apparently, semantic and phonological information may be brought to bear on lexical decisions by human subjects, in addition to pure orthographic check processes, when words and nonwords are orthographically similar.

The Seidenberg and McClelland model simulates results such as regularity effects on word naming times, which had traditionally been taken as evidence for separate lexical and non-lexical processes, and it does this using a single processing route that operates for regular words, exception words, and nonwords alike. The model thus does away with the contrast between instance-based "lexical" knowledge and rule-based "non-lexical" knowledge for associating spelling with sound. It also contrasts with traditional dual-route models of reading in terms of its processing architecture. The Seidenberg and McClelland model uses distributed representations, in which words are represented by patterns of activity over groups of units, and each unit can participate in the representation of many items. Dual-route models, in contrast, typically assume that there exists local "lexical" knowledge, independently represented for each word in the reader's vocabulary.

6.7.1 Dual route accounts revisited

Seidenberg and McClelland's (1989) model provides a detailed account of several of the psychological phenomena concerned with the reading of printed English words. However, it has also been subject to criticisms relating to its success as a psychological model; these criticisms have again raised the question of whether separate lexical and non-lexical (rule-based) procedures are used by readers of English.

To begin with, note that Seidenberg and McClelland's model does not actually "name" words in any direct sense; successful naming is judged on the basis of RMS_{error} scores. There are two problems here. One is that it is by no means obvious that differences in RMS_{error} scores translate into differences in response latencies, although the majority of studies on the relations between lexical and non-lexical reading processes in humans measure response latencies. Kawamoto and Kitzis (1991) derived latency measures in a similar model by using cascade activation values to test the model after it has been trained using the standard back-propagation algorithm. In the cascade version of the activation function, the net input to a unit gradually accumulates over time instead of being calculated in full on a single "pass" of activation through the model as is usual in feed-forward networks[3]. However, having done this they noted some problems in fitting the model to human data. In particular, when people make naming errors to irregular words by giving the "regularised" form, the latencies for the errors can be shorter than the latencies for the correct irregular pronunciations. The error /pɪnt/, to rhyme with mint, is produced more quickly than the correct pronunciation /paɪnt/. Contrary to this, even in the cascade version of the Seidenberg and McClelland model, naming latencies tended to be faster for the correct over any incorrect pronunciations. Kawamoto and Kitzis suggest that, to account for the human data, there may need to be separate constraints on word pronunciation, operating over different time courses; a regularity constraint (favouring regular pronunciations, with a fast time course), and a word-specific constraint (for known words, and necessary for irregular pronunciations). That is, there may need to be separate routes to word pronunciation. Subsequently, Plaut, McClelland, Seidenberg, and Patterson (1996) developed a further version of the original Seidenberg and McClelland model that also simulated reaction time (RT) data directly, although they did not consider the issue of the speed of incorrect responses. We consider the Plaut et al. model in more detail in section 6.8.

A second problem is that a low RMS_{error} score does not necessarily guarantee that the model will pronounce a given letter string correctly; in particular, it does not even guarantee that the expected pronunciation is the one that is most likely to be given by the model. This problem arises because pronunciation by the model should be based on both absolute and relative measures of output activations. For correct pronunciation,

activations should be close to those expected (units expected to be "on" should have activation values close to 1, units expected to be "off" should have activation values close to 0: the absolute measure). In addition, RMS_{error} scores should be lower for the target than for any other possible pronunciations: the relative measure. To provide a relative measure of pronunciation accuracy, Seidenberg and McClelland generated something they termed a BEATENBY criterion. They calculated the RMS_{error} scores not only for the target pronunciation but also for all other outputs that would be one phoneme away from the target (this involved calculating the difference scores between the actual output and these other outputs). Using the BEATENBY criterion, a response was judged as correct if the RMS_{error} score for the target pronunciation was less than for any of the "one phoneme different pronunciations". The BEATENBY criterion puts a lower bound on pronunciation errors (it shows that the target pronunciation is more likely than these other possible pronunciations), but it does not guarantee correct pronunciation (note that RMS_{error} scores could in theory be lower for outputs that are two or more phonemes away from the target).

Seidenberg and McClelland employed the BEATENBY criterion to evaluate their model's ability to name irregular words correctly. They report that, after training, errors were only made on 2.7% of these items; a result that is quantitatively close to human data. However, using the same criterion, the model's performance with nonwords was less impressive. Besner, Twilley, McCann, and Seergobin (1990) analysed the performance of the model on a set of nonwords used by Glushko (1979) in a study of human reading. They found that the model was correct between 51 and 65% of the times (depending on the nonword set used in the particular experiments of Glushko), yet human "accuracy" (the proportion of trials on which the regular pronunciation was given to the nonwords) was 89% or above. Here the model does not provide a good quantitative fit to human data.

Seidenberg and McClelland (1990) suggest that the model's naming accuracy on nonwords would be improved by training the model on a larger set of words (they used only 2897 words in their training set, as opposed to over 30,000 or so words in most people's vocabulary). This may well be the case. However, Coltheart, Curtis, Atkins, and Haller (1993) have shown that it is possible to learn spelling–sound correspondences sufficiently well to pronounce nonwords correctly using just the same size training set as Seidenberg and McClelland. Coltheart et al. used an algorithm for learning grapheme–phoneme conversion (GPC) rules. The spelling of a word was presented along with its phonetic transcription. The model then inferred all possible letter–phoneme relations, adding to its data base any rules not present in the current set and incrementing a frequency count on the rules already present (to determine the regular rules). Double letter–phoneme rules were inferred when the letter–phoneme assignments left some letters unassigned when compared to the correct phonetic transcription for the word, and a similar operation was applied to create further higher-order letter–phoneme assignments (when lower-order assignments failed to match the number of letters present). Having built a data base of GPC rules, the model applied the rules to input strings in the order "largest rule first", with there being a minimal frequency of occurrence for the rule before it could be applied. Coltheart et al. showed that, when trained on the Kucera and Francis word set, the GPC procedure was able to produce about 78% correct pronunciations for nonwords taken from Glushko (1979); this is considerably more successful than the Seidenberg and McClelland model when trained on the same word set (although it is also true that the rules built into the GPC model incorporated considerable knowledge from the experimenters of the contexts over which particular rules are applied, whereas the Seidenberg and McClelland model had to derive such knowledge through learning). Coltheart et al. suggest that human word processing is best understood in terms of independent lexical and non-lexical routes, with the non-lexical route taking the form of GPC rules.

In addition to pointing out the problems of Seidenberg and McClelland's model with nonword naming, Besner et al. (1990) also analysed the accuracy of lexical decision responses by the model. Remember that the basic mechanism for lexical decision in the model is a measure of orthographic familiarity based on an orthographic RMS_{error} score. Besner et al. took words and nonwords from a study of human reading (Waters & Seidenberg, 1985), and set a criterion for the orthographic RMS_{error} score so that the model would make about the same number of misclassifications of words as did human readers. When this was done, they found that the model made around 80% misclassifications of the nonwords; this far exceeds nonword misclassifications made by human readers.

Other evidence that is difficult for the Seidenberg and McClelland model to accommodate concerns the effects of dual tasks on reading and differences in naming times by humans to different types of nonwords. Paap and Noel (1991) had subjects read regular and irregular words while concurrently having to remember a set of numbers. Under these memory load conditions, they found the rather counterintuitive result that naming times to low-frequency exception words were speeded (see also Herdman & Beckett, 1996). Paap and Noel interpreted their result in terms of a dual-route account of reading. They proposed that the non-lexical route required attentional resources, which were depleted under the memory load conditions, slowing the non-lexical route. This slowing of the non-lexical route prevented it from competing with outputs from the lexical route for low-frequency exception words. Hence these words were (surprisingly) named more quickly.

McCann and Besner (1987) reported that people name nonwords that have the same pronunciations as words ("pseudohomophones") faster than nonwords that are similar in spelling but not pronounced as words (compare "brane" and "frane"). In the Seidenberg and McClelland model this benefit for the naming of pseudohomophones is difficult to explain. The model does not have a specific representation for the spelling or pronunciation "brane", so it is unclear why sharing its pronunciation with a word should affect nonword naming latency. For a dual-route account, however, this result is relatively straightforward. If the non-lexical route activates a common phonological representation with the lexical route, then the phonological entry for "brain" in the lexicon can contribute to the naming of its pseudohomophone. Besner (1996) provides a thorough review of these and other arguments favouring a dual-route approach.

6.8 EXTENDING SEIDENBERG AND MCCLELLAND (1989): THE "ATTRACTOR" MODEL OF PLAUT ET AL. (1996)

There may be several ways in which models of the type constructed by Seidenberg and McClelland (1989) could be adapted to overcome some of the difficulties noted by Besner et al. (1990), and Coltheart et al. (1993) without having to resort to rule- as opposed to instance-based learning algorithms. Two extensions to the model were reported by Plaut et al. (1996). The first extension used a similar approach to Seidenberg and McClelland, but adapted the representations involved. They suggested that, in conjunction with the size of the training vocabulary, a primary limitation in the accuracy of nonword pronunciation in the Seidenberg and McClelland model was the nature of its representations, which do not serve as an ideal basis for generalising the (word) pronunciations that the model learns. To explain this point, we need to consider the nature of learning and generalisation in connectionist models.

One limit with models such as the interactive activation model (section 6.2) is that it would not lead to a good transfer of learning (if learning had been implemented). The interactive activation model used local representations in which letters were coded for their positions within words. This means that the ls in two words such as "lip" and "slam" have no common representation (in lip, the "l" activates the "l" unit for position 1; in "slam" it activates the "l" unit for position 2). If such a representation was used when the model was trained to pronounce both words, any learning for the written "l" to the spoken /l/ for "lip" would not affect the learning of a similar relationship in "l" in "slam". The distributed representation scheme used by Seidenberg and McClelland overcomes this problem to some degree, because some "triplet" units would be shared by common

letters in words of different length and spelling. Nevertheless, there would still be no common units for instances such as the ls in "lip" and "slam" (which would be represented by units responding to %li, lip and by sal, lam respectively). Nonword pronunciation may be limited by this lack of overlap and subsequent generalisation of learning. The NETtalk model of Sejnowski and Rosenberg (1987) overcomes this problem by using a moving window to ensure that the same input units are used irrespective of the positions of letters in words, but this then introduces other problems concerned with left-to-right scanning in reading.

Plaut et al. increased the overlap between the crucial representations involved in spelling–sound relationships. They had input units correspond to graphemes, with separate sets of units for the initial consonant cluster, the medial vowel, and the final consonant cluster in monosyllabic words. Output units corresponded to single phonemes plus a few instances where a unit corresponded to double phonemes (e.g. for consonants such as ps and sp). They noted that, in English there are strong "phonotactic" constraints on pronunciation, which force multiple phonemes into a limited number of positions respectively within an initial or final consonant cluster (as some phoneme combinations cannot be pronounced). By separating representations of consonants according to their position at the beginning or end of the string, and by adding units for the few instances in which consonants can swop positions (as in the sp and ps examples just given), the order of phonemes can be determined by the phonotactic constraints without having to specify additional units. Table 6.1 shows the representations used by Plaut et al. To illustrate how these phonotactic constraints can be used in pronunciation let us take a concrete example. A word such as "slam" would activate grapheme units for S and L in the initial consonant position, A in the vowel position and M in the final consonant position. The graphemes S and L can only be pronounced in the order SL but not in the order LS in English (a phonotactic constraint). Hence, given activation of the phonemes /s/ and /l/ at the output level (associated to the inputs S and L), the outputs can be ordered on the basis of phonotactic constraints.

TABLE 6.1

Phonological units used by Plaut et al. (1992)

Phonology

onset	s S C z Z j f v T D p b t d k g m n h l r w y
vowel	a e i o u @ ʌ A E I O U W Y
coda	r l m n N b g d ps ks ts s z f v p k t S Z T D C j

Orthography

onset	Y S P T K Q C B D G F V J Z L M N R W H CH GH GN PH PS RH SH TH TS WH
vowel	E I O U A Y AI AU AW AY EA EE EI EU EW EY IE OA OE OI OO OU OW OY UE UI UY
coda	H R L M N B D G C X F V J S Z P T K Q BB CH CK DD DG FF GG GH GN KS LL NG NN PH PP PS RR SH SL SS TCH TH TS TT ZZ U E ES ED

Orthographic and phonological units are coded according to their position in a syllable, as onset, vowel, or coda.

The full pronunciation of the word can then be derived by reading out the phonemes sequentially from the initial consonant cluster, the vowel, and the final consonant cluster.

Note that, using this representation scheme, the model has the basis for generalising its learning for l → /l/ from a word like "slam" to another word such as "lip", even though the ls are in different positions and surrounded by different neighbouring letters in the words; in this case, the orthographic and phonological representations for the ls would both be coded for their position as onset consonants, and so would be utilised for both words. Generalisation of knowledge about spelling-to-sound relationships from trained instances to new exemplars should consequently be improved.

Plaut et al. trained a network with 105 orthographic input units, 100 hidden units, and 61 phonological output units on the 2897 monosyllabic words used by Seidenberg and McClelland (1989), using back-propagation. To evaluate the success of pronunciation, a measure termed the "cross-entropy" function was used[4]. Using this measure, the model was shown to replicate the crucial interaction between spelling-to-sound regularity and word frequency after 300 epochs of training, similarly to the model of Seidenberg and McClelland (1989). In addition, the model was found to name nonwords relatively well. To measure the responses

to nonwords, output units with activation values greater than 0.5 were judged to be "on", except for the vowel units, for which the response was taken as the most active unit in its set. Plaut et al. found that on "regular" nonwords from the Glushko (1979) set (i.e. nonwords derived from words that only have regular spelling–sound correspondences, such as HEAN derived from DEAN), the model scored 98% correct (where correct means that the regular spelling–sound correspondence was applied); on "irregular" nonwords (derived from words with irregular spelling–sound correspondences, such as HEAF from DEAF), the model scored 72% correct. These scores are close to those reported for human readers by Glushko (94 and 78% correct respectively, for the two types of nonword). The model provides a good quantitative fit to the data on nonword reading by human readers (and note that this was done using the relatively small word set of Seidenberg & McClelland, 1989).

It is always possible that, in a network trained in this way, there has been partitioning of the net into two routes, one (lexical route) that operates for irregular words and one (non-lexical route) that operates on the basis of GPC rules extracted from the learning set. If this held, then the model might in effect have developed a dual-route architecture, even though this has been driven by instance-based learning. Plaut et al. assessed this possibility by measuring the hidden units activated by irregular words, regular words, and nonwords. There was a positive correlation between the hidden units activated by irregular words and nonwords, which is not consistent with the operation of separate lexical and non-lexical reading routes.

In a further extension Plaut et al. examined the effects of learning orthographic to phonological associations in a so-called "attractor" network (we will consider networks of this type further in Chapter 8, where their application to patients with neuropsychological disorders will be covered). The architecture of the model is shown in Fig. 6.14. The network used a standard feed-forward design, in which activation in input units corresponding to graphemes (separated for initial consonant, vowel, and final consonant position) was passed through a set of hidden units to activate a set of phoneme units (again separated for initial consonant, vowel, and final consonant positions). The difference relative to their earlier simulations was that a further set of recurrent connections were added at the phonological level. The operation of the network can be thought of in the following way. In its first pass, activation is fed-forward from the grapheme input units to excite phoneme output units. This activation pattern on the output units is then circulated around a further set of weights and fed-back to alter the states of the phonological representation until activation arrives at a stable point (the *attractor*) corresponding to the network's phonological interpretation of the word. The initial phonological states that settle into the same end state can be thought of as a *basin* surrounding the attractor; activations that

fall within a given "basin of attraction" are pushed into the same end state. One advantage of using an "attractor" model of this type is that the time taken for the network to converge on a stable pattern of activation can be taken as an analogue of reaction time. Such a model can also be trained using variants of standard learning algorithms (such as back-propagation), except that units are not updated in a straightforward feed-forward manner (first hidden and then output etc.), but rather any unit can be affected by any other one to which it is connected. In training, the error term for an output unit is then both the discrepancy between its own state and its target state *plus* the error back-propagated to it from other units (one such learning algorithm is termed back-propagation through time; Pearlmutter, 1989). Plaut et al. trained their model on the Seidenberg and McClelland (1989) training set and then tested it on regular and irregular words varying in frequency. They again showed an interaction between frequency and regularity, with the effects of regularity being stronger on low-frequency words, with the effects now revealed in terms of the time for the network to reach a stable state.

Plaut et al.'s study indicates that instance-based learning can lead to a development of a single spelling–sound route that operates for regular and irregular words alike, and that provides at least reasonable generalisation (to the same degree as human subjects) when presented with nonwords. This suggests that at least some of the problems with nonword naming in the Seidenberg and McClelland (1989) simulation are due to the nature of the representations employed rather than some inherent difficulty in the approach taken. Whether all aspects of Plaut et al.'s model are psychologically valid, however, might be questioned. For instance, evidence suggests that at least short words can be named without recourse to sequential letter processing (Frederiksen & Kroll, 1976), so the validity of the sequential read-out mechanism might be questioned. In addition to this there remain difficulties in the account offered by Seidenberg and McClelland (1989) for human lexical decision performance. Seidenberg and McClelland suggest that lexical decisions utilise an orthographic check procedure, based on an

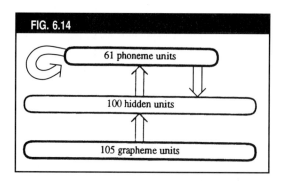

FIG. 6.14

Plaut et al.'s (1996) attractor model of word naming.

orthographic RMS_error score, with this procedure being augmented by information derived from the phonological output units when there is overlap in the distributions of the orthographic error scores for words and nonwords. Whether an additional phonological check process would facilitate the discrimination between words and nonwords that overlap at the orthographic level is of course an empirical question (see Coltheart et al., 1993, for this point), but it is by no means certain that phonological RMS_error scores will help in such a case (note that it is likely that words and nonwords would have overlapping phonological error scores too). In addition, the model would face extreme difficulty in making correct positive (word) responses when presented with sets of orthographically irregular words (yacht, aisle) and nonwords that are not only orthographically regular but also phonologically equivalent to words (with pseudo-homophones such as nale, phare) (Coltheart et al., 1993).

To deal with these problems in lexical decision, at least two further options might be considered. One would be to implement a more complete model of reading which incorporates an additional route, this time from orthography to meaning (added to the single direct route from orthography to sound, by-passing meaning)[5]. There is good neuropsychological evidence for such a route. For example, in the syndrome *deep dyslexia*, patients make a characteristic reading error in which they misname a word as another word from the same semantic category (e.g. sword → dagger; Coltheart, Patterson, & Marshall, 1980). Such an error is unlikely to be due to a breakdown in a direct route from orthography to phonology, as it is neither orthographically (or visually) or phonologically related to the target word. Instead, the patient seems to have accessed part of the meaning of the word based on its spelling without any access to the word's phonology (see also Strain, Patterson, & Seidenberg, 1995, for evidence from normal readers). If a route from orthography to meaning were added to the model, it would be possible to use the meaning from words to help discriminate words from nonwords in lexical decision. Discrimination based on units representing word meanings is more likely to "pull apart" activation from

words and nonwords than activation based on phonology, as only words have associated meaning but both words and nonwords can have associated phonology (from sub-word segments). We have already pointed to psychological evidence consistent with the idea that word meanings are activated when lexical decisions require discrimination between words and orthographically familiar nonwords, based on evidence from semantic priming (Shulman et al., 1978). Note also that Kawamoto and Kitzis's (1991) suggestion, for separate constraints based on regularity and on word-specific mappings could be instantiated this way (see earlier). An attempt by Plaut et al. (1996) to instantiate a semantic route to word naming, in addition to a direct phonological route, will be reviewed in Chapter 8 in the context of the application of the model to the neuropsychological syndrome *surface dyslexia*.

A second possibility would be to use a different representation scheme, in which units at at least one level of the model correspond to words rather than sub-word segments; that is, if some form of lexical representation was incorporated into the model (and see Norris, 1994a, for a similar approach). For instance, an orthographic lexicon could take the form of the word-level representations used in the interactive active model of word recognition (McClelland & Rumelhart, 1981). Learning to pronounce words would then involve the development of appropriate correspondences between orthographic representations of the words and sub-word phonological units (e.g. single phonemes, of the type used by Plaut et al., 1996)[6]. Lexical decisions could determined by activation values at the orthographic level, as only words will activate these units at a level close to asymptote (Jacobs & Grainger, 1992). Alternatively, sub-word orthographic segments could still be used for lexical decision but these would map onto word-level phonological representations. Lexical decisions could be based on activation of the phonological lexicon, when words and nonwords overlap in their orthographic RMS_error scores. As words and nonwords should differentially activate word-level phonological representations, phonological information may then play a useful part in discriminating between the two types of stimulus. In addition to improving lexical decision perform-ance, a lexicon may be beneficial for broader lin-guistic purposes, which we cover in more detail in Chapter 7. Clearly, for these proposals to be tested in practice there would need to be con-siderable detailed research; our aim is simply to illustrate how an instance-based approach to word naming might be maintained. Such an approach, if successful, would represent a challenge to tradi-tional rule-based accounts of the naming of regu-lar orthographies. Plaut et al.'s (1996) model builds on the earlier work of Seidenberg and McClelland (1989) and extends it by showing how learning can be affected by modularity within networks. The model also serves as a useful framework for understanding neuropsychological disorders of cognition. The full paper on the model is pre-sented after this chapter.

6.9 SEMANTIC PRIMING BETWEEN WORDS

One standard procedure used to examine the word recognition system in humans is priming, in which experimenters assess the effects of one stimulus (the prime) on responses to another (the target). We have already considered one example of prim-ing, when the pronunciation of nonword targets was shown to be affected by the pronunciation of earlier word primes (Kay & Marcel, 1981). This was simulated in the Seidenberg and McClelland (1989) model by temporarily training the model (presetting the weights to favour) on prime stimuli before target stimuli were presented. A rather dif-ferent approach to priming between words was taken by Masson (1991). Masson was concerned with semantic priming between words, whereby lexical decision responses to a target word are facilitated if the target is preceded by a semantic-ally related prime (Meyer & Schvaneveldt, 1971). This well documented result has been used to argue for the existence either of a semantically coded lexicon, or for the operation of a semantic-ally coded network that interacts with a lexicon in word recognition (see Neely, 1991, for a review).

Masson simulated semantic priming using a Hopfield net (see Chapter 2 for an example of this type of network). Unlike standard Hopfield networks, the units were divided into two sets, one set corresponding to perceptual input units, the other to conceptual output units. The concep-tual units were fully interconnected so that they received inputs from both the perceptual input units and from the other conceptual units (see Fig. 6.15). The model was trained using Hebbian learning to establish representations for a small set of words (increasing the weights between units that were both activated, decreasing the weights if one unit was active and the connecting unit inactive). Priming experiments were simulated in the following way. The perceptual input units were set to the values corresponding to one of the trained words, and the conceptual units were set to random values. Activation values were then cycled around the conceptual units while the values in the perceptual units remained clamped. This recycling operated until a stable state was achieved, typically involving retrieval of the appro-priate conceptual unit values for the trained word. The number of cycles the model took to reach this stable state was taken as a measure of reaction time. On priming trials, a "prime" would be pre-sented as the perceptual input to the model, and activation values left to cycle. After varying num-bers of cycles, however, the prime was replaced by a new target word (i.e. there was a new per-ceptual input, corresponding to another word in the original training set). Primes and targets could either be semantically related or unrelated to one

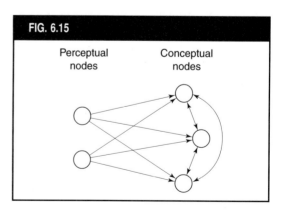

FIG. 6.15

Perceptual nodes   Conceptual nodes

The modified Hopfield net used by Masson (1991) to simulate semantic priming effects on word recognition.

another, captured in terms of the number of shared states in the conceptual units (i.e. semantically related words tended to have conceptual units in the same state). Masson found that the time taken for the target's conceptual representation to be recovered was reduced by priming with a semantically related prime. If the time taken to recover the conceptual representation is taken as a measure of word identification, the result fits with demonstrations of semantic priming on human reading. Within the model, semantic priming occurs because the related prime moves activation states in the model towards the stable state associated with the target stimulus. In contrast, an unrelated prime can move the activation states away from those associated with the target, disrupting target recognition. Indeed, Masson found that the presence of an intervening unrelated word, between related primes and targets, was sufficient to abolish the semantic priming effect, a result he replicated with human subjects.

The Hopfield net simulation conducted by Masson (1991) is in many respects very simplistic, and fails to provide any analysis of the different tasks used by psychologists to explore word processing; similarly it fails to account for how human performance varies across the tasks (see Neely, 1991, for a detailed account of semantic priming effects across different tasks). Nevertheless, it does provide another example of how the process of moving into a stable activation state can be used to simulate dynamic aspects of human performance.

Another attempt to capture priming effects within a connectionist framework was made by Grossberg and Stone (1986). They suggested how an ART (Adaptive Resonance Theory) network could accommodate psychological data distinguishing between "automatic" and "expectation-dependent" forms of semantic priming. For instance, with short durations between stimuli, priming seems to be determined (automatically) by learned relations between words; however, with longer intervals, priming can be based on task-specific expectations for targets which may be formed only in the experiment (see Neely, 1977, for an example). ART networks have a purely bottom-up mechanism for activating stored knowledge, from the input units to the stored templates, and this may mediate so-called automatic priming — in this case, due to top-down feedback from the templates to the associated input units. In addition, however, there is an arousal mechanism, which needs to be active in order to allow input activation to be sustained when it does not fit with stored template representations. When primes do not have a learned relationship with targets, inputs for targets may only be weakly supported by top-down feedback from the templates. However, activation of arousal units then enables other templates to be recruited, to support target recognition. Only under this circumstance may performance be affected by templates that are weakly related to the target (when task-specific rather than learned relationships are involved). Also within ART networks, arousal units are only activated when input units fail to find strong top-down support from templates, and so arousal units are activated relatively slowly (following the failure of top-down support). Priming of this form should thus occur relatively slowly when compared to priming dependent on learned relationships between stimuli (and indeed it may require that activity in templates decays away prior to targets appearing, so that the arousal units can bring new templates into play). This accords with psychological data on the time course of automatic and expectation-dependent priming.

For such an account to be sustained, the connections between the input and template units would need to be sensitive to semantic relations between words, rather than being sensitive only to form information within words. Such sensitivity is captured in other models that deal with the procedures involved in accessing meaning from print (e.g. Hinton & Shallice, 1991; Plaut & Shallice, 1993a). We cover these models in Chapter 8, when we review their application to neuropsychological disorders such as deep dyslexia.

6.10 SPOKEN WORD RECOGNITION: TRACE

Visual word recognition (at least for short words) is based on stimuli whose components are present simultaneously. In contrast to this, speech signals emerge over time. This difference in the nature of visual and spoken signals undoubtedly has a profound effect on word recognition in the two modalities. Visual word processing can operate in parallel across the words. This is less likely for speech, where the processing of the first components (the first phonemes) of the words can begin prior to that of the final components. Indeed, one of the most influential psychological models of spoken word recognition, the Cohort model (Marslen-Wilson, 1984), holds that recognition operates in a left-to-right manner across words, and that words are recognised as soon as sufficient phonemes are processed for a word to be identified uniquely. For instance, consider the word TREASURE. The first components of the speech signal will activate representations for consistent lexical representations: treble, treasure, trek, tremble etc. However, as more of the speech signal is processed, so the membership of this "cohort" is reduced, so that by the time the signal covers TREAS, the cohort has reduced to one: the target word. This is the "recognition point" for the word.

Elman and McClelland (1986; McClelland & Elman, 1986) implemented a connectionist model of spoken word recognition that accounts for psychological data on the recognition points for words. This model, TRACE, can be thought of as a sister to the interactive activation model of visual word recognition (McClelland & Rumelhart, 1981; see section 6.2). Like the interactive activation model, TRACE uses hierarchically arranged local representations standing for (in this case) acoustic signals, phonemes, and words (cf. visual features, letters, and words in the interactive activation model). Units at a lower level in the network have excitatory connections to higher-order units that they are part of and inhibitory connections to units that they are not part of. There are also within-level inhibitory links (from features to other features, phonemes to other phonemes etc.) and top-down connections from higher levels to influence activation at lower levels in the hierarchy. Spoken word recognition emerges when a stable pattern of activation occurs across the net-

work, enforced by the interactions across the different levels of representation in the model. The main difference relative to the interactive activation model is that, in TRACE, units are represented independently for different time slots (remember that, in the interactive activation model units are represented separately for different letters' positions in space). The time slots over which features are coded are shorter than those over which phonemes are coded (as more than one feature can make up a phoneme), and those over which phonemes are coded are shorter than those for words. Excitatory and inhibitory connections are maintained only within appropriate time slots.

As we have noted, the interactive activation model runs into some problems with its local representation scheme because it cannot encode letters across different spatial positions without replicating feature and letter representations (and their connections to other levels of representation). Spatial invariance is achieved by hardware duplication. A similar problem exists with TRACE, but it concerns time rather than space. A word occurring at one moment would be recognised by its representation at the appropriate time slot being strongly activated. If the word had occurred at another time, a different word unit would be activated, and so forth. Figure 6.16 illustrates the architecture of TRACE, suggested by Elman and McClelland.

TRACE provides a natural account of left-to-right effects in spoken word recognition. A word is presented to the model sequentially, with the initial features occurring first. Activation from these features is fed through to the higher levels of representation within the model as the next features are given as input. At the higher levels of representation, many units may be activated at first, but as the speech signal unfolds over time, so word and phoneme representations supported by the input come to inhibit those for which there is disconfirmatory evidence. "Recognition" can take place as soon as there is strong activation for one word over other competitors: this will represent the recognition point for the word, and for some words the recognition point will occur even before all the speech signal has been received.

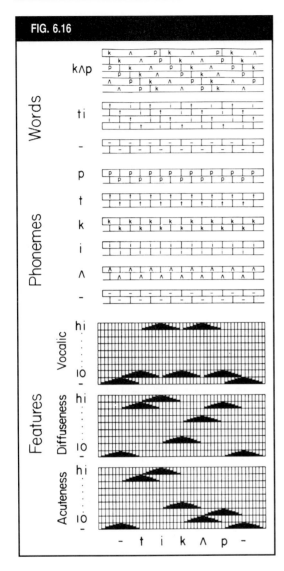

FIG. 6.16

Architecture of the TRACE model of speech recognition. Each rectangle represents one unit. Units at different levels span different portions of the speech trace. In this example, the phrase "tea cup" has been presented to the model, and its input features on three dimensions are illustrated by the blackened histograms. From McClelland and Rumelhart (1986).

An example of left-to-right processing effects in TRACE is given in Fig. 6.17.

In addition to accounting for left-to-right effects in speech recognition, TRACE can also simulate several other results from the psychological literature. We mention three: categorical phoneme perception; lexical effects on phoneme discrimination; and the resolution of ambiguous phonemes.

Categorical speech perception

The term categorical perception is used to refer to instances when human perceptual abilities discriminate sharply at the boundary between two classes of stimulus, when the physical signal separating the stimuli varies continuously. Categorical speech perception refers to the fact that, although speech signals can vary continuously between two phonemes, humans tend to classify stimuli as being either one or the other phoneme, producing a discrimination boundary that is much sharper than the boundary between the physical signals (e.g. see Miller & Eimas, 1995, for a recent review). In TRACE, categorical perception of phonemes arises out of the inhibitory interactions between phoneme units. Figure 6.18 illustrates this. Elman and McClelland presented stimuli that were closer in their coding to either the phoneme /g/ or the phoneme /k/ (varying one feature of the input coding, the voice onset time). At the feature level, stimulus 3 was /g/ and stimulus 9 was /k/; they presented a set of 13 stimuli (0–12), with 0 being further away from /k/ into the /g/ category than the prototypical /g/ itself, and 12 being further away from the /g/ category into the /k/ category than the prototypical /k/. The initial activation values at the feature level reflected this continuous variation, as did activation at the phoneme unit level. However, as activation was left to cycle, so mutual inhibition between phoneme units led to a sharpening of the discrimination boundary at the phoneme level (Fig. 6.18). Forced-choice decisions made on these last activation values produce discrimination functions which cross at the categorical boundary between phonemes and vary little as the physical stimulus changes to approach the prototypical phoneme; that is, there is categorical phoneme perception.

Context effects in phoneme discrimination

The WSE in reading denotes the better identification of letters in words than in nonwords, and this effect has been used to argue that the recognition

FIG. 6.17

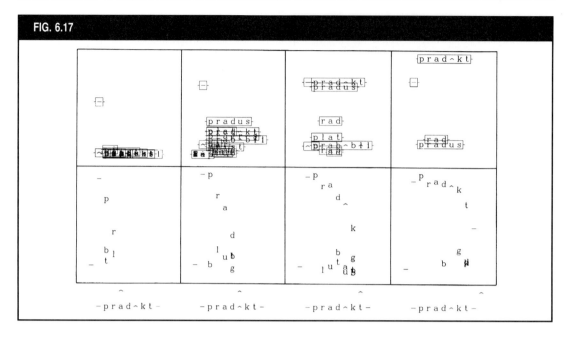

Simulating recognition point effects in TRACE. The figure represents activation in the phoneme (bottom sections) and word units (top sections) in terms of the positions of items within each section (higher positions = more activation). Each section, moving from left to right, represents a subsequent time slot. Initially a number of word competitors are activated, but one representation comes to dominate as further information is accumulated over time. From McClelland and Rumelhart (1986).

of printed words involves top-down as well as bottom-up processes (McClelland & Rumelhart, 1981). The interactive activation model of word recognition was developed at least in part to demonstrate how top-down effects might be realised in human word processing. In speech perception, a rather similar phenomenon occurs, in which the perception of phonemes is found to be better when they are in words than when they are in nonwords. In the task of phoneme monitoring, listeners are asked to respond as soon as they detect the occurrence of a target phoneme. Response latencies in phoneme monitoring are reduced when phonemes are in words than when they are in nonwords (Cutler, Mehler, Norris, & Segui, 1987), and this effect tends to increase the later the target phoneme appears in the stimulus (Marslen-Wilson & Tyler, 1980). Such effects emerge naturally in TRACE due to top-down lexical feedback from word to phoneme representations, with this feedback being stronger on late-occurring phonemes, due to lexical activation itself then having longer to be effected.

Ambiguous phonemes

Speech perception can often operate in noisy circumstances, so that the speech signal received by the ears is distorted; the acoustic features present may fail to differentiate between phonemes. Ganong (1980) showed that the interpretation of an ambiguous phoneme in a word was affected by whether disambiguation of the phoneme created a word or a nonword. Subjects heard a sequence of phonemes beginning with a phoneme that, in terms of its acoustic features, could vary on a continuum between /t/ and /d/. At one end of the continuum, a word was created, at the other a nonword. When the signal was about midway between /t/ and /d/, listeners were more likely to identify the ambiguous phoneme as being consistent with the word rather than the nonword interpretation. This result can be accommodated by TRACE, as top-down feedback from word-level representations (partially activated by the other phonemes present) biases activation at the phoneme-level to favour the "word" interpretation. The fact that the contextual effect can operate from later phonemes

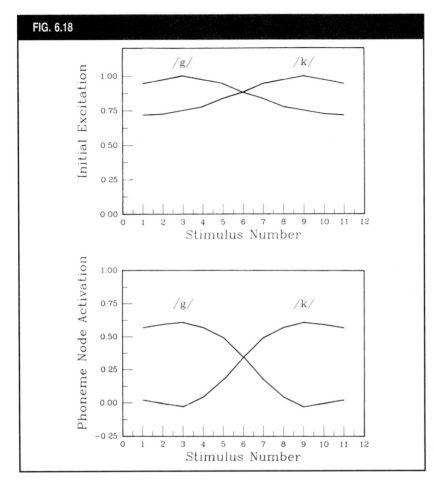

Categorical phoneme perception in TRACE. The top panel shows the level of bottom-up activation to the phoneme units /g/ and /k/, for each of 12 stimuli (shown on the x-axis). The lower panel shows the activation for the same phoneme units after cycle 60. Stimuli 3 and 9 correspond to canonical /g/ and /k/ respectively. At cycle 60, the boundary between the phonemes is much sharper. From McClelland and Rumelhart (1986).

onto earlier phonemes is also simulated. Due to the input signal being ambiguous, the first phoneme may not be resolved (the activation for any one phoneme unit does not reach asymptotic levels) until the later phonemes are processed (Elman & McClelland, 1988). This effect on the processing of the first phoneme is difficult to account for if speech processing in a strictly left-to-right fashion (cf. Marslen-Wilson, 1984).

6.11 PROBLEMS FOR TRACE IN FITTING PSYCHOLOGICAL DATA

Despite the success of TRACE in accounting for a relatively wide set of results from human speech recognition, the psychological validity of some its claims have been queried. We again present three examples. First, with unambiguous phonemes there are advantages in the latencies of phoneme monitoring for initial phonemes in words relative to nonwords (Cutler et al., 1987). However, lexical effects should take some time to build up in TRACE, as lexical activation is itself contingent on activation at the phoneme level in the model, and the unambiguous phonemes are input sequentially.

Second, Frauenfelder, Segui, and Dijkstra (1990) investigated whether there is inhibition of phonemes in stimuli, as would be predicted by TRACE (because representations inconsistent with the input are inhibited by representations consistent with the input). Listeners performed a phoneme monitoring task in which phonemes could occur after the recognition point in stimuli. The phonemes present on such occasions created nonwords, and performance on phonemes in these stimuli was compared with that on phonemes in control nonwords, which should not initially activate word representations. For example, a critical nonword *vocabutaire* could be created from the word *vocabulaire* (here the new phoneme /t/ occurs after the recognition point for the word), and RTs to monitor this phoneme were compared with RTs to a control nonword *socabutaire*, which should create minimal lexical activation. TRACE predicts that the phoneme /t/ in *vocabutaire* should be subject to top-down inhibition once the lexical representation for *vocabulaire* is accessed, slowing phoneme monitoring relative to the nonword control condition. However, Frauenfelder found no evidence for such inhibition.

Third, evidence for effects of top-down feedback on the interpretation of ambiguous phonemes seems critically dependent on stimulus degradation (see Norris, 1994b; Pitt & Samuel, 1993). For example, McQueen (1991) conducted a study similar to that of Ganong (1980) in which listeners received an ambiguous phoneme at the end of the stimulus, which they then had to categorise as being one of two phonemes. McQueen found a lexical bias in interpretation (for the phoneme that would create a word with the other phonemes present) only when the input was degraded. Although interactive activation approaches to perception (of which TRACE is an example) hold that effects of context should increase as stimulus quality decreases (see McClelland, 1987), effects should still be apparent on the interpretation of ambiguous phonemes when the input is not degraded.

A related point to the last one concerns the ability of TRACE to accommodate context effects on phoneme perception from other phonemes present. In particular, the original TRACE model failed to make correct detailed predictions about the relations between local context and stimulus discriminability. For human subjects, the effects of context and stimulus discriminability combine in an additive way. Massaro (1989) had listeners make a two-choice discrimination between two phonemes, /r/ and /l/, when the speech signal varied continuously between the two phonemes. The phonemes occurred in the contexts /s_i/, /p_i/, or /t_i/. The

first context favours /l/ as there are English words that begin /sli/ but not /sri/. The third context favours /r/ (as there are words beginning /tri/ but not /tli/). The second context lies between the first two, as there are words beginning both /pli/ and /pri/. Massaro found that the different contexts affected performance (listeners were more likely to discriminate an /r/ relative to an /l/ when in the context of /t_i/ than when in the context of /s_i/, and vice versa for an /l/; performance with the /p_i/ context fell in between). Also, the ambiguity of the speech signal affected performance (an /l/ being more likely to be reported, as the features favoured this phoneme). However, the differences in discrimination between the contexts were constant as the speech signal varied. In the original TRACE model, the effects of context were largest when the speech signal was most ambiguous, and effects reduced as the signal became less ambiguous. Massaro (1989) used this result to argue against the assumption of top-down processing in speech perception (indeed, in perception in general).

Other researchers, notably Cutler and Norris (1979), have similarly proposed non-interactive accounts of human speech perception, which hold that lexical knowledge does not directly influence phoneme perception (as maintained by TRACE). Non-interactive models accommodate data on faster phoneme monitoring in words than in nonwords as being due to information being made available for responses independently from phoneme and word levels. Phoneme monitoring will be determined by whichever level is able to make its output first. For words, responses can be based on both the phoneme and the word levels. However, for nonwords, responses can only be based on the phoneme level. Providing there is at least some overlap in the distribution of times over which responses are made available by the phoneme and word levels (so that the word level "wins" on some occasions), phonemes will be detected more quickly in words than in nonwords.

6.12 COMPUTATIONAL PROBLEMS WITH TRACE

Speech recognition needs to be time-invariant; a given word needs to be recognised irrespective of when it occurs in a speech signal. TRACE deals with the computational problem of time invariance by replicating acoustic feature, phoneme, and word representations across different time slots. As we have noted, this particular stance is similar to that taken in the interactive activation model of visual word recognition when it attempted to deal with the problem of spatial position invariance in reading. In reading, however, it might be possible to align features with the position slots beginning at position 1 in words, as there are reliable cues to where words begin and end: white spaces. This may reduce the number of units that need to be replicated. Unfortunately, in continuous speech there are typically no reliable cues to word onsets; words run into one another without pauses. Hence the need remains to replicate units across time in a model such as TRACE. The problem with this of course is that it requires massive numbers of units, and of connections between units, if the model is to deal with speech spanning any reasonable length of time. Even if there is a limit to the duration over which temporal units are coded (e.g. it might be equivalent to human auditory memory span), the hardware requirements are formidable.

A further computational problem concerns the variations in speech rate that occur across speakers or even with the same speaker across contexts. Listeners can generally deal well with both fast and slow speech (although clearly there are bounds on this ability). However, TRACE has local units that are set to a given time slot. There is no guarantee that the speech signal will match the time slots set in the model. As a consequence, the model may fail to generalise its recognition across different speech rates.

6.13 RESPONSES TO THE PROBLEMS: STOCHASTIC PROCESSING, RECURRENT NETWORKS, COMBINED NETWORKS

There are several ways in which TRACE can (and indeed has) been modified to meet some of these criticisms. First, TRACE (and the interactive activation model before it), used *deterministic* activation functions. Thus, given the same input to the model on two or more occasions, the model

was guaranteed to produce the same response with the same response latency. However, there is no need for such functions to be used. McClelland (1991) investigated performance of the model when *stochastic* activation functions were employed. To do this, McClelland added a small amount of normally distributed random noise to the activation function determining the net input activation coming into each unit in the model, at each time step in processing. This has some psychological validity, because human processing undoubtedly varies in efficiency on different occasions, and stochastic activation functions lead to variations in response times as found with human observers. In addition to this, McClelland found that TRACE was able to give a better detailed account of the effects of local phoneme contexts on phoneme discrimination, and in particular that TRACE now produced the additive effects of context and signal discriminability given by human listeners (see Fig. 6.21). To understand why this should be the case, it is important to realise that the effects of top-down feedback in the model are to amplify any differences that are present in the inputs coming into units at lower levels of the processing system. For example, any differences in the activation strengths of the feature units corresponding to /l/ and /r/, due to signal variation, will be increased by appropriate top-down feedback. In a deterministic system, this feedback has the greatest effects when the differences between the signals are smallest. In a stochastic system, however, differences in the activation values for input units are sometimes due to noise, particularly when differences between signals are smallest. Beneficial effects of top-down feedback will be reduced on such occasions, evening out the effects of feedback when signal differences are large relative to when they are small.

It should also be noted that any arguments against top-down effects in perception do not necessarily apply to all classes of connectionist model, but only to those in which top-down feedback is intrinsic, such as the interactive activation model and TRACE.

The problem with generalising recognition across speech rates is more difficult for the fixed TRACE architecture to deal with, as the model employs fixed time-based units. Norris (1990,

1993b) suggested an alternative approach using simple recurrent networks of the type explored by Elman (1990, see Chapter 5). Norris had a set of input units corresponding to a featural description of phonemes, and a set of local output representations, with one unit for each word in the model's vocabulary. The hidden units were fed around (using connections with weights of 1) to provide extra inputs sensitive to the mappings between the input and output units on the preceding trial. Thus, as in the study of Elman (1990), the delayed (recurrent) connections provide a memory for the network's prior mappings and facilitate the integration of information across time. As a result of this property, Norris proposed that the network could construct the same internal representation of words irrespective of when in time the word began.

As also holds for TRACE, Norris's recurrent network was able to identify words at the earliest point at which they become unique (at their recognition point), as output units ceased to be active once inconsistent information was revealed by the phonemes being presented sequentially to the model. Furthermore, the model was able to recognise patterns presented at different rates. Norris (1990) trained the network using two different speech rates, and then tested the model's ability to recognise words presented at a third, new rate. Relatively good generalisation to the new rate was found. Hence the problem of temporal invariance in speech recognition may be solvable using networks that are sensitive to, and generalise, the recognition of patterns across time.

Norris (1994b), however, noted one problem with his recurrent network that was not present in TRACE. This is that the recurrent net has no way of undoing early decisions concerned with identification of parts of words. Take a word such as CATALOG. When the input reaches the phoneme /t/, the output unit for /cat/ should be strongly activated; all other output units will be (at the most) weakly activated (even the unit for /catalog/, as the input /cat/ mismatches the expected input for /catalog/ by a substantial margin). If the input is continued, so that all the word is presented, then the input will then match /catalog/ rather than /cat/, and the output unit for /catalog/ alone will

be activated. However, if the input had been two separate words, CAT LOG, again the output unit for /cat/ would initially be activated and then it would be replaced by activation of the output unit for /log/ (the last input into the model). The network has no way of knowing that the output /cat/ should be identified as the first of two words presented in the last instance, but that it should not be identified in the first instance, when it is merely a part of a longer word. In TRACE, problems of this sort were overcome because word-level representations compete against one another (providing they demand overlapping time slots). Thus representations for /cat/ and /catalog/ will compete in this instance, so that only one is dominant; in contrast, the representations for /cat/ and /log/ will not compete (being in different time slots), so that both may be identified when separate words are presented. Lexical competition provides a mechanism by which to select *catalog* when that word is presented, but *cat* and *log*, when *cat log* is presented.

Norris (1994b) attempted to combine the useful attributes of TRACE (lexical competition) and the recurrent speech recognition network (temporal invariance) in his SHORTLIST model. This model provides a kind of hybrid architecture, in which a recurrent network provides an input to a second, interactive activation type network, in which there are inhibitory links between units that would represent the same part of the speech signal (Fig. 6.19). Although these interlinked networks were not fully implemented in connectionist terms, Norris showed that when input was provided to the lexical competition network to simulate output from a recurrent net, the model responded appropriately, recovering words from degraded input, showing effects of the cohort size and resolving ambiguity with embedded words.

These results indicate that connectionist models can capture the major aspects of auditory word recognition in humans, and that factors such as temporal invariance may be simulated within recurrent networks. The attempt to construct larger networks from more modular nets is also of general interest for modelling more complex human abilities. Certainly, as we shall review in Chapter 8, there is plenty of neuropsychological

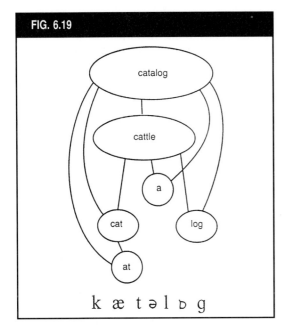

FIG. 6.19

catalog

cattle

a

cat   log

at

k æ t ə l ɒ g

The pattern of inhibitory connections between candidate words in the SHORTLIST model (Norris, 1994b). Only the subset of candidates that completely match the input are shown.

evidence indicating that cognition can break down in a relatively modular way leaving some abilities spared and others affected, and such effects can be understood in terms of damage affecting processing networks selectively. We also return to this point in the final chapter. Of course there remain many challenges for connectionist models of speech perception to surmount. For example, exactly how an interactive activation network could be set up "on the fly", to resolve the competition for lexical selection, is a major question that is not resolved in SHORTLIST.

6.14 SPELLING

Visual and auditory word recognition are both essentially receptive abilities. Of course, single words can also be produced as output, either in writing or in speech. Do connectionist models provide accurate accounts of our ability to pro-

duce (in writing and speech) as well as to receive language?

One connectionist model of spelling was proposed by Olson and Caramazza (1994), using a similar approach to Sejnowski and Rosenberg (1987) in their NETtalk model of reading. In Olson and Caramazza's model, NETspell, the input took the form of a seven-phoneme window, which was moved from left-to-right across a word during training (for one central phoneme and three contextual phonemes). The output units were locally coded and represented each grapheme in the word's dictionary; one unit alone came on for each grapheme. The network was trained on dictionaries of 1000 and 1628 words (including regular as well as irregular words), sampled according to their frequency of occurrence in English. Performance was considered as correct if the appropriate output unit was activated above a .3 level. NETspell learned to spell about 94% of the words correctly, and of the errors made (i.e. when the wrong output units were activated above .3), the majority involved phonologically plausible renditions (e.g. syntax → sintax; deficient → dificient). NETspell also generalised its outputs reasonably well, when tested on a set of nonwords, generating phonologically plausible spellings to about 87% of the nonword set.

Brown, Loosemore, and Watson (1994) also trained a three-layer model using back-propagation to associate simultaneously presented phonemes to orthographic forms. This model resembled that of Seidenberg and McClelland (1989), using a distributed representation of phonological and orthographic forms, coded at a sub-word level. The model was trained on a relatively small word set (227 words), chosen so that words fell into one of three classes: either they had "enemies" but no "friends" (i.e. all other words with similar phonologies had different spellings); or they had neither friends nor enemies; or they had many friends and no enemies (i.e. all other words with similar phonologies also had similar spellings). During training, correct associations between phonology and orthography were formed most rapidly for the stimuli with friends but no enemies, then for the items with neither friends nor enemies, then for the stimuli with enemies but no friends.

Figure 6.20 demonstrates differences in the numbers of words correctly spelled for the three types of word, where a correct spelling is accepted if the output value is closer to the target word than to any other word. Brown et al. compared the performance of the model with that of children learning to spell English words from these three classes. The children were divided according to their ability to spell words, and their performance with the three classes of words is shown in Fig. 6.21. Words with enemies and no friends were learned most slowly by the children, those with neither enemies nor friends were learned next, and learning was most rapid for words with friends but no enemies. The comprehension of the words in each class did not differ, so the results cannot be attributed to variations in the knowledge of the word meanings, but rather specifically to variations in the ease with which spellings could be learned for the known words. The model captures these differences in the ease with which spellings can be learned for known words. For the model, the differences emerge due to variations in the statistical properties of the different word sets; sub-word mappings for words with friends but no enemies receive more reinforcement during learning than the mappings for words with only enemies and no friends. Note that the results also show separate effects of the number of friends and enemies on performance. Relative to the "baseline" condition, where words have neither friends nor enemies, performance is improved by the presence of friends (for stimuli with friends but no enemies), and it is impaired by the presence of enemies (for the stimuli with enemies but no friends). The two effects, of the number of friends and the number of enemies, cut across the strict distinction between regular and irregular words in English, as both regular and irregular items can have both friends and enemies, although regular words tend to have more friends than enemies. Brown et al.'s model suggests that this factor, the ratio of friends to

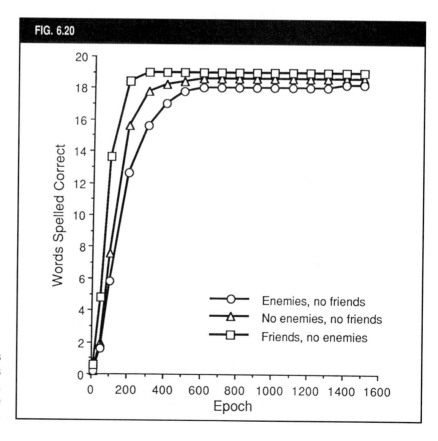

FIG. 6.20

Words Spelled Correct

Epoch

— ○ — Enemies, no friends
— △ — No enemies, no friends
— □ — Friends, no enemies

The accuracy of spellings produced by Brown et al.'s (1994) model of spelling, as a function of the degree of training.

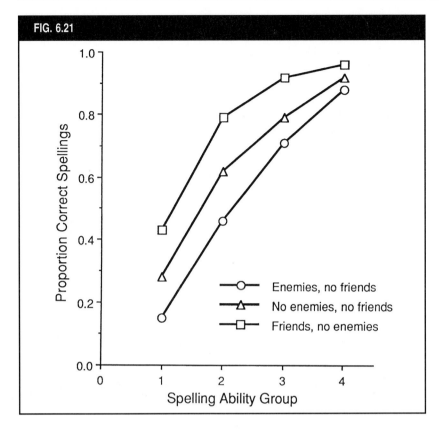

FIG. 6.21

Accuracy of spelling, in children of different spelling ability (from Brown et al., 1994).

enemies, is more important than the rule-based regularity of phonology to orthography, and so provides a new focus for research on children's spelling.

Spelling and writing, like many production tasks, require that behaviour is produced in a specific (learned) serial order. In Brown et al.'s model the problem of serial order is by-passed, as spellings are retrieved in parallel, for all the letters in words together. In Olson and Caramazza, serial order is generated by moving a window across a phonological representation of a word, with this representation being in a form that enables such left-to-right encoding to take place (e.g. being held in some form of phonological buffer?). Other approaches to modelling spelling have used ideas similar to those we encountered in Chapter 5, when we considered the production of serial behaviour in tasks such as typing and serial recall. Houghton, Glasspool, and Shallice (1994), for example, used the notion of "competitive queuing" to model

serial letter production in spelling. The model comprised three layers of processing units, as shown in Fig. 6.22. The first layer contained "control units", to which we will return. The second layer contained units representing letters. The third had units that formed a "competitive filter". The competitive filter was of the same type as that proposed by Houghton (1990) to account for serial behaviour (see Chapter 5). The competitive filter contained one unit for each letter unit at layer 2, and units within the filter were inhibitory with each other. The mutual inhibition between the units in the filter produces competition, with only the most active unit at any time being made available for output (after exceeding a threshold). Importantly, once a unit in the competitive filter "fires", it passes inhibition back to the connected letter unit so that, temporarily, it is no longer a strong competitor with other letters. This pattern, of units firing and then being suppressed, enables the model to produce serial output for spelling. The order in

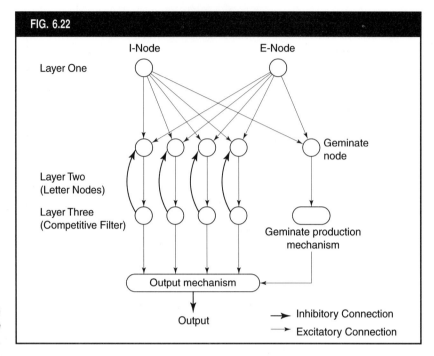

FIG. 6.22

I-Node   E-Node

Layer One

Geminate node

Layer Two (Letter Nodes)

Layer Three (Competitive Filter)

Geminate production mechanism

Output mechanism

Output

→ Inhibitory Connection

→ Excitatory Connection

Houghton et al.'s (1994) model of spelling. See the text for details.

which letters are produced is determined by the control units. In Houghton et al.'s model, there are two control units, one representing the start of the word (the I unit, for initiate) and one the end of the word (the E unit). Letters that start particular words have strong connections with the I control unit, and the strength of the connections for later letters in the word to the I unit tends to decrease as a function of the position of the letters in the word. Letters that end particular words have strong connections with the E control unit, and the strength of these connections again varies as a function of the positions of the letters in the word. The strength of these connections was learned through a mixture of Hebbian and supervised learning. In the Hebbian learning phase, the I node was given its maximum activation and allowed to decay; the E node remained at zero. The model was presented with one grapheme from a word at a time, and an association formed between the active units in the letter and the control layers. This produces strong connections between the first letters in words and the I node. After activation in the I node has decayed, the E node is then activated, enabling letters at the ends

of words to build up weights to this node. This simple Hebbian learning is sufficient to learn the spellings of short words, but due to the involvement of only two control nodes, it is not necessarily sufficient to enable the spellings of longer words to be learned correctly. Subsequently, a form of supervised learning was added in which the recall of each word (following Hebbian learning) was compared with the correct response at each time step. If the incorrect grapheme was produced at a time step, the connections to the control nodes were lowered and the weights from the letter to the correct node were increased. For each new word that was learned, a new set of control nodes was added. Having learned connections from the letter units to the control nodes, the retrieval of a word's spelling is effected by having the activation of the I and E nodes vary over time. Initially the I node is strongly activated, but its activation decays; the E node is initially not activated but its activation builds up over time (see Fig. 6.23). As the I node starts in a highly active state, the letter unit most strongly associated with it "wins" the initial competition and is output first; this is then suppressed allowing the next-most letter to be

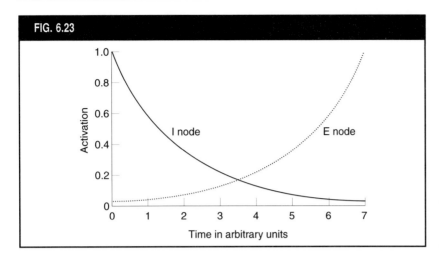

FIG. 6.23

Activation of the I and E nodes over time, in Houghton et al.'s model of spelling (1994).

retrieved and so forth. The retrieval of letters at the end of the word are supported by the later activation of the E node, allowing them too to be reported in time.

As there are two control nodes, the model is able to recall spellings even when letters are repeated in words (with one exception, see later). For example, a letter node can have connections to both the I and the E nodes, so that the letter is first recalled at the start of a word (when the I node is active) and also at the end of the word (when the E node is active). The model does have difficulty, however, when letters are repeated in adjacent positions, because a letter unit will temporarily be suppressed after it has won the competition in the competitive filter. The problem in producing double responses in models of this sort was first encountered in Chapter 5, when we discussed Rumelhart and Norman's (1982) model of typing. Rumelhart and Norman solved the problem by having a "doubling" schema (see Chapter 5 for details). Houghton et al. (1994) solved the problem by having a so-called "geminate" node alongside the letter units in layer 2 of their model (see Fig. 6.22). The geminate node serves to double the grapheme that is currently being output. In training, the geminate node is activated along with the appropriate letter, enabling appropriate weights to be learned between the geminate node and the control nodes. The geminate node (unlike the letter nodes) also does not connect

into the competitive filter, and so does not compete for output with letter units. A "doubling" response is made whenever, at a given time step, the geminate node is more active than any of the current letter units (this signals for the current output to be repeated). Subsequently the geminate node is inhibited to prevent any further immediate repetitions.

The Houghton et al. model may seem to be relatively rococo in its design, having processes that produce the correct letter order (based on the weights between the control nodes and the letter units) and others that output that order in the correct sequence (the competitive filter). However, in its favour is that the model follows the architecture suggested for other forms of serial behaviour in connectionist models (Chapter 5), and it is possible that such an architecture serves as a general blueprint for serial behaviour, perhaps replicated for different production tasks. Indeed, in section 6.15 we show how this approach can be applied to the topic of speech production. In addition, Houghton et al.'s model is able to capture some of the errors found in writing and spelling, in both non-brain-damaged and brain-damaged populations (see Chapter 8 for discussion of the latter). For example, in an analysis of spelling errors made by university students, Wing and Baddeley (1980) reported that a majority of errors involved the middle letters in words. They note that the result was somewhat unexpected; if errors occurred because spellings were held in some form of memory buffer that decayed over time, then errors should tend to occur at the end rather than in the middle of words. However, Houghton et al.'s model too makes a majority of errors in the middle of words (and particularly if noise is added to the activation functions), as letters in the middle tend to be less supported by the control nodes than those at either the beginning or end of words. The model also makes errors in which there is doubling of the wrong letter in a word (e.g. producing *laater* rather than *latter*), when the geminate node is activated out of sequence; the same error can also be found in human error corpuses.

Houghton et al.'s model of spelling also has limitations. Long words, with multiple repeats of letters (e.g. banana), are difficult to learn (note that here the letter unit for "a" would have to "win" the competition for selection three times, which is difficult to achieve with a relatively simple control structure, e.g. using just two control nodes). Also phonological spelling errors are never made (e.g. deficient → dificient), as outputs are determined purely by orthographic (letter-order) constraints. However, the spelling processes simulated by this model may represent only one procedure used by humans; namely an orthographic procedure in which learned graphemes are assembled for output. It is possible that, in addition to this, humans use phonological processes to guide spelling, with one phoneme at a time being fed through to activate associated graphemes; that is, humans may additionally use a sound-based spelling procedure perhaps akin to that modelled by Olson and Caramazza (1994). Neuropsychological evidence, which we cover in Chapter 8, is consistent with this proposal. Future models may seek to integrate the different spelling procedures to provide a more complete account of the spelling process.

6.15 SPEAKING

6.15.1 Models with local representations

Traditional models of speech production make a distinction between the linguistic structure of sentences and words and the content of particular sentences and words (e.g. Garrett, 1975). Initially a semantic representation is generated, specifying the meaning that the speaker wishes to convey. Following this, syntactic and phonological representations are constructed, with the phonological representation ultimately being used to direct the generation of a motor program for articulation. The syntactic and phonological representations are built using a "frame-and-slot" mechanism; a linguistic frame is first generated, and the words and phonemes to be used are inserted into the slots in the frame. For example, according to the meaning to be communicated, a syntactic frame will be generated specifying the noun and verb-phrase structure of the sentence. This frame contains grammatically labelled slots for words. Words are retrieved from the mental lexicon and inserted into the slots (the content for the linguistic structure, at the syntactic level). Similarly, a phonological frame may be constructed for each word to be spoken. This phonological frame will specify the syllabic structure for the word, and subsequently phonological segments are inserted into the slots in the phonological frame (here the phonological segments are the content for the linguistic structure at the phonological level). The articulatory program for speech can be "read off" from left to right across the phonological slots (see Garrett, 1980; Levelt, 1989, for examples of this approach to speech production).

These two-stage models of speech production, with a formal separation between linguistic structure and content, are able to account for some of the types of errors that are made in everyday speech. Freud (1901/1958) was among the first to note that errors in everyday speech were not random but occurred in a relatively systematic fashion. Freud proposed that the errors reflected unconscious motivations on the part of speakers, although there is scanty psychological evidence for this (Ellis, 1980). However, there is good evidence to suggest that systematic speech errors reflect linguistic constraints on speech production. According to two-stage theories, speech errors can arise at each level of linguistic representation. Also, as each level of representation is sensitive to different linguistic variables (e.g. syntactic properties of the words, at the syntactic level; the position and consonant–vowel specification of phonemes, at the phonological level), the errors at each level can be identified. At the syntactic level, speech errors might reflect the exchange of whole words between their positions in a sentence, as in the example: "*he eats yoga and does yoghurt*" (instead of "*he eats yoghurt and does yoga*"; Dell, 1990). As the words undergoing such exchanges should be specified for their syntactic role (e.g. as a noun or verb), word exchanges should only be made between words from the same syntactic category. Psychological evidence supports this assertion (Fay & Cutler, 1977; Garrett, 1975). Other forms of relatively common speech errors involve the exchange of phonemes between words, as in the example: "*a barn door → a darn bore*" (Dell, 1989). Such phoneme exchanges typically preserve both the position of the phoneme within the word and whether the phoneme is a vowel or a consonant (consonants slip with consonants, vowels with vowels; Mackay, 1970; Stemberger, 1984). Again, the systematic effects of position and consonant–vowel structure are predicted if exchanges operate between phonemes in equivalent slots in the phonological frames for consecutive words.

This traditional approach to speaking emphasises that each process in sentence production takes place sequentially, as a series of discrete stages. Hence errors originating at one level of the model should be independent of those occurring at other levels. However, in many examples (such as the *yoga–yoghurt* word exchange just given), the items undergoing transition can be related in several ways. For example, in corpora of speech errors there are more word-level substitutions where there is semantic and phonological similarity between the words than would be expected by chance (Dell & Reich, 1981; Harley, 1984). In a model where there is a strict ordering of discrete processing stages, multiple relations between stimuli, at different levels of representation, should not impinge on performance.

In contrast to the traditional approach, the connectionist models of speaking put forward by Dell (1985, 1986, 1988) and by Harley and MacAndrew (1992, 1995) emphasise interactions between the different levels of representation in speech production. Both models use interactive activation approaches to production, in which activation values are fed continuously between processing levels. Dell's model is in some respects closer to the traditional approach to speech production, because it maintains a frame-and-slot approach to production, although in this case the frame is essentially an interconnected set of processing units, each representing some structural category property of the language (e.g. a particular consonant in an onset position). Dell (1986) proposed that processing units exist at different levels of representation, specifying the syntactic, morphological, and phonological properties of words[7] (see Fig. 6.24). Activation begins at the highest level in the model (from a sentence representation in which words are coded by their syntactic properties) and propagates down to units at lower levels of representation (to morphemes and to phonological representations). Units at each level are locally represented. Thus, at the syntactic level there would be separate units representing a word such as *sink* according to whether it is a verb or a noun; at the phonological level there would be separate representations for consonants that are in the onset or coda (ending) of a word, etc. At the morphological level, there is separate representation of the root morpheme of a word and its affix (as in the swimmer example, in Fig. 6.24). Activation is transmitted to the morphological level of representation in a time-based fashion, so that (for instance) representations corresponding to the first noun in a phrase become activated prior to representations for a second noun. Units at the morphological level are selected on the basis of being the most strongly activated. When selected, the unit receives an extra boost of activation, enabling the appropriate phonological units to become significantly activated and selected in turn. All units are positively connected, but there is inhibition of each unit after it has been selected, with the unit's activation level then being set to zero. In addition to this, after selection units at each level are "flagged" — that is, they are given a tag specifying the order in time at which the unit was selected — outputs can be given on the basis of these time tags.

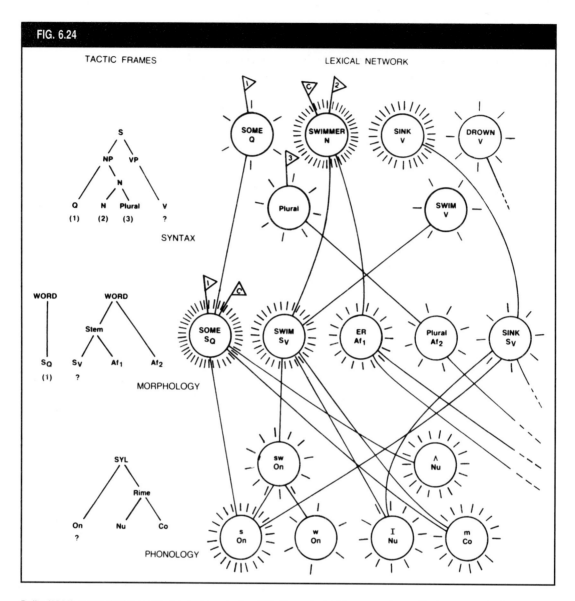

FIG. 6.24

Dell's (1986) connectionist model of speech production. This figure depicts the momentary activation present in the production of the sentence "some swimmers sink". On the left there are tree structures analogous to the representation at each level of the model. The numbered slots have already been filled in and the "flag" indicates each node in the network that stands for an item filling a slot (the number indicates the order and the c flag indicates the current node on each level). The ? indicates the slot in each linguistic frame that is currently being filled. The highlighting on each unit indicates the current activation level. Each node is labelled for membership of some category. Syntactic categories are: Q for quantifier; N for noun; V for verb, plural marker. Morphological categories are S for stem; Af for affix. Phonological categories are: On for onset; Nu for nucleus and Co for coda.

Dell's model is able to give a good account of many of the speech errors that occur in everyday life. For instance, because several units can be activated simultaneously at each level of representation, substitution errors emerge when units for a second word receive higher activation levels than those present in a first word, when random noise is added to activation values. As units are coded for their syntactic roles (at the syntactic level) and for their position in a word (at the phonological level), then word-level substitutions tend to maintain their word class and phonological substitutions tend to maintain their position in the word. In addition, because processing is interactive (so that activation at a phonological level feeds-back and activates morphological representations, for instance), the model can account for the effects of multiple constraints on speech errors (e.g. with substitution errors tending to be both semantically and phonologically related). The model also explains why some substitutions tend to be more frequent than others. In particular, the likelihood of phonological substitutions is increased if the transitions create words than if they create nonwords (e.g. a substitution such as *dean bad* → *bean dad* is more likely than one such as *deal back* → *beal dack*) (see Baars, Motley, & Mackay, 1975, for experimental evidence). This "lexical bias" occurs in the model because feedback from the phonological level will activate morpheme representations, sometimes leading to the incorrect morpheme representations being selected, to produce the substitution error. When phoneme substitutions may produce nonwords, activation at the morpheme level is reduced, as the phonemes present will not uniquely favour one morpheme representation; fewer substitution errors result.

Hartley and Houghton (1996) have recently extended Dell's model to incorporate procedures for producing phonemes in the correct order in speech, rather than having the output process rely on explicit "flags" which specify when a unit was selected. Their model uses a competitive queuing procedure (cf. Houghton, 1990; Rumelhart & Norman, 1982; see Chapter 5), in which units representing "syllabic templates" control the output order for phonemes. This model had units at three levels, corresponding to syllables, syllable templates (to control temporal order of output), and phonemes. The syllable units themselves comprised pairs of nodes, one corresponding to the onset of the syllable and the other to its rhyme. The syllable templates contained five units that were activated in a cyclical fashion; the first two nodes were linked to phonemes occurring at the onsets of words, the third node was connected to phonemes for vowels, and the final two nodes were connected to phonemes occurring at the offsets for words. The weights between the template units and the phoneme units were fixed. Other connections, between the phoneme and the syllable units and between the syllable units and the templates, were learned using a Hebbian procedure, in which the template nodes were activated at consecutive time slices as consecutive phonemes were activated. In this way, connections were established between the template unit and the syllable unit active concurrently, and between the syllable unit and the phoneme unit active concurrently. This architecture is illustrated in Fig. 6.25. During learning, the onset part of the syllable unit was active when the first two template nodes were active, and the rhyme part of the syllable unit was active when the other three template units were active. Following one cycle of the template units during training, the next syllable unit was activated. A training cycle is shown in Fig. 6.26.

Following learning, the model could be tested for speech production. The production process was initiated by activating the syllable template, again in a cyclical fashion (from the first unit through to the fifth), along with the syllable units corresponding to the syllables present in the speech segment. These syllable units were activated in parallel, with the order of output being based on a competitive queuing procedure. The response was based on the unit that was most active, and this unit was then suppressed to enable consecutive parts of syllables (rhymes after onsets) and consecutive syllables, to be output. In a larger model of the whole speech production system, the syllable units would be activated by the intended meaning of the speaker and by connected lexical units (as in both traditional models of speech production and in Dell's earlier model; Fig. 6.24).

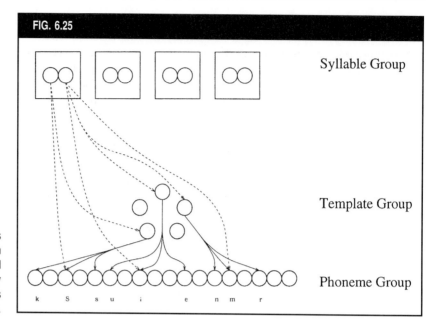

FIG. 6.25

Syllable Group

Template Group

Phoneme Group

k   S   s   u   i   e   n   m   r

Hartley and Houghton's (1996) model of speech production. The dashed lines represent temporary weights, the solid lines permanent connections.

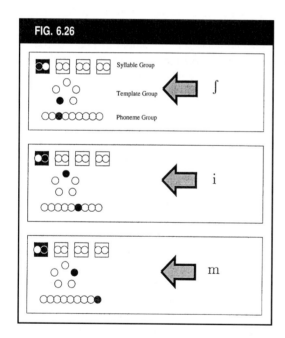

FIG. 6.26

Syllable Group

Template Group

Phoneme Group

ʃ

i

m

Example of a training cycle from Hartley and Houghton (1996), for the monosyllabic nonword /ʃim/. The activation of each node is shown by its shading (the darker the more active). Successive frames (from top to bottom) show the state of the network as each phoneme appears in the stream.

By and large, the combination of activation in the syllable units, and cyclical activation of the template units, is sufficient to generate correct selection of the target syllable and activation of associated phonemes. However, because more than one syllable will be active at one time, the model is prone to some errors in which phonemes within the same parts of consecutive syllables can be interchanged. Note that the first units in the syllable templates will be linked to the onsets of consecutive syllables, and the final template units will be linked to syllable rhymes; thus activation driven by the templates will lead to phoneme exchanges that preserve the positions of phonemes in the syllables. This matches data on human speech production (Treiman & Danis, 1988). Hartley and Houghton's model shows how the correct serial order between phonemes can be learned in speech production, going beyond models such as Dell (1986), in which hard-wired connections were used.

Effects of higher-order variables, such as the imageability of words, on speech production has been examined by Harley and MacAndrew (1992, 1995). Like Dell's model, Harley and MacAndrew also employed units at three levels of representation, corresponding in this case to semantic, lexical (word-specific phonological), and phoneme units. Units at the lexical and phoneme levels were locally represented, semantic representations were distributed. Phonemes were coded according to their positions in words, and they were output as a function of their serial position in words. Unlike Dell's model, however, Harley and MacAndrew incorporated within-level inhibitory connections, which allow competition at each level in the model to be resolved more quickly (see Fig. 6.27). Imageability was manipulated by varying the number of semantic units that were activated for a given stimulus; highly imageable stimuli had more "on" semantic units than stimuli low in imageability (see also Hinton & Shallice, 1991; Plaut & Shallice, 1993a for a similar approach; see Chapter 8). Harley and MacAndrew (1992) found that errors were less likely for highly imageable words, both in their model and in a corpus of human speech errors. Also by incorporating within-level inhibitory links into their model, Harley and MacAndrew claimed to account for inhibitory

effects in human speech production. For example, Wheeldon and Monsell (1994) found that picture naming was slowed when subjects had recently produced a definition to a semantically related word (e.g. for a definition such as "an . . . a day keeps the doctor away" followed by the picture of an orange). This inhibition might occur because there is suppression of the semantic representations of related items when the semantic representation of a target word is selected for the naming response. Similarly name retrieval can be blocked when subjects are cued with a phonological neighbour of a target word when they are in a "tip of the tongue" state (Jones, 1989). Phonological blocking could reflect the suppression of phonological competitors to the cued word.

6.15.2 Discrete vs. cascade processing in naming

One strong contrast between connectionist accounts of naming such as those of Dell, Harley, and MacAndrew (and see also Humphreys et al., 1995; see Chapter 4, section 4.6) and traditional discrete stage accounts concerns whether information is passed from one level of representation to others only after processing has been completed at the earlier stage. These connectionist models use an interactive activation and competition framework, and so hold that partial activation can be transmitted between processing stages. The transmission of partial activation in the models is used to account for multiple-level constraints on errors in speech production (and particularly for joint semantic and phonological errors). In studies of object naming, evidence for errors that tend to be both visually and semantically related to targets also suggests that visual information is transmitted to semantic representations in cascade (Vitkovitch et al., 1993; see Chapter 4). One attempt to examine the issue of discrete vs. continuous processing in naming has come from studies investigating the time course of picture name retrieval. For instance, Levelt et al. (1991) had subjects name a series of pictures, each of which could be followed (at various time intervals) by an auditory stimulus. When the auditory stimulus occurred, subjects had to make a lexical decision response to the item. In the crucial conditions, a target word

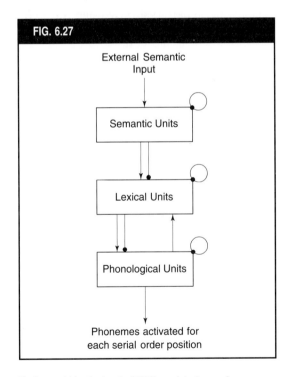

FIG. 6.27

External Semantic Input

Semantic Units

Lexical Units

Phonological Units

Phonemes activated for each serial order position

Harley and MacAndrew's (1992) model of speech production.

in the lexical decision task was (a) semantically related to the picture (picture of *sheep*, target word *goat*), (b) phonologically related to the picture name (*sheep → sheet*), (c) phonologically related to another word that was itself semantically related to the picture (*sheep → goal*; the mediated condition). Levelt et al. found reliable priming (relative to a baseline condition) in the semantically related and in the phonologically related conditions, but not in the mediated condition. They used this result to argue against cascade accounts of phonological activation in naming. They proposed that, according to a cascade account, activation in the semantic system (for the concept *goat*, following the picture *sheep*) should be transmitted through to the phonological level, priming lexical decision to phonologically related words (e.g. *goal*).

However, the strength of this test can be questioned. For example, within-level semantic inhibition (as in Harley and MacAndrew's model) should result in the representations for semantic competitors to pictures being considerably less activated than the semantic representations of the pictures themselves (and see Harley, 1993, for a simulation of the results within his model). Also in more recent studies several investigators have found evidence consistent with cascade processing in mediated priming conditions with synonyms (e.g. there is activation of the phonology for both hen and chicken, in picture naming; see Peterson & Savoy, in press; Schriefers, 1996)[8]. This recent evidence suggests that, at least for synonyms, several phonological representations can be partially activated in naming, consistent with the connectionist accounts. These experiments also illustrate how connectionist models can serve to direct new research (in this case to test whether processing is discrete or operates in cascade).

6.15.3 Merging structure and content

Traditional models of speech production distinguish between the linguistic structures involved in planning sentences and the content that "fills" the slots in linguistic structures. This distinction is also preserved in connectionist models such as those of Dell (1986, 1988) and Hartley and Houghton (1996). In contrast, Dell, Juliano, and Govindjee (1995) present a connectionist model

of language production in which some of the evidence favouring the structure–content distinction is shown to emerge from the phonological structure of the language in the absence of a separate set of linguistic rules or frames. The Dell et al. (1995) model was trained to develop representations that mapped between word-level input representations and phonological output representations (in the other models connection weights have been pre-set, and no learning has been involved). The model used a recurrent architecture similar to that explored by Elman (1990; see Chapter 5), but with there being two forms of feedback from higher levels in the model to the input level. One set of recurrent connections fed-back activation values from the hidden units on learning trial N as input on trial N+1 (Dell et al. term these the *internal feedback* units; this set of connections is the same as that used by Elman, 1990). A second set of connections fed-back activation from the output phonological representations on trial N as input on trial N+1 (Dell et al. term these the *external feedback* units; connections of this sort were first explored by Jordan, 1986). By using two forms of feedback, Dell et al. aimed to build a model that was more sensitive to the most recently output segment of speech than a model with internal feedback alone; such sensitivity may help in the development of rule-like behaviour[9]. The architecture of the model is shown in Fig. 6.28.

The lexical input into the model consisted of sets of unique distributed representations, one for each word. The output representations conformed to single phonemes, with consecutive phonemes being trained across consecutive learning trials over which the lexical input was maintained but the input provided by the recurrent connections changed. In this sense, the recurrent units kept track of where the model was through each word during training. After the presentation of each word, and prior to the presentation of the next word in the training sequence, the model was trained to "stop", that is, to generate neutral activation values of .5 for all output units. On the first presentation of a word the external feedback units were initialised to the "stop" value (.5), and the internal feedback units were set to zero. The model was trained on a set of 50 three-letter words

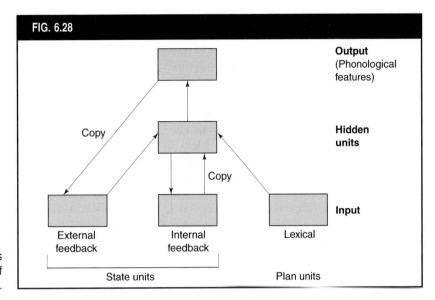

FIG. 6.28

Output (Phonological features)

Hidden units

Copy

Copy

External feedback

Internal feedback

Lexical

Input

State units

Plan units

Architecture of Dell et al.'s (1995) recurrent model of speech production.

to achieve 90% correct report (an output was considered correct if closer in Euclidean distance to the target output than to any other known output representation).

Inspection of the errors made by the model after training revealed patterns of performance consistent with human speech production. For instance, very few errors violated the so-called "phonotactic" constraints of English; such violations would occur if phoneme substitutions created sound sequences that do not occur in the language. Humans too make few errors that are phonotactically inappropriate (Meyer & Dell, 1993). Also, the consonant or vowel class of the stimulus was maintained in about 98% of the errors, similar to the human data. Note that these regularities emerged even though the model had no explicit representations of either the phonotactic constraints of English or of the consonant–vowel category of phonemes; rather the effects were generated as a function of the regularities across the vocabulary set in mapping from lexical to phonological representations. The simulations suggest that it may not be necessary for models to incorporate explicit representations of linguistic structures to account for some of the regularities present in human speech production.

The Dell et al. model, although promising, is also limited in important ways. For example,

the model dealt only with single word utterances, and so did not deal with the types of phoneme exchange errors that can occur in human speech production (e.g. the *darn bore* example given in section 6.15.1). This could be amended by having output units influenced by more than one word at a time, which itself might arise if the input lexical representations were generated by consecutive words. However, there would be no guarantee that phoneme exchanges would maintain their positions. As we have noted, phoneme exchanges do tend to maintain their positions in human speech errors, and this is one reason why other theories of speech production (connectionist and non-connectionist alike) maintained the existence of phonological frames with position-marked representations. Future work needs to address the issue of how position-based regularities may emerge in learning models of the sort examined by Dell et al. (1995).

6.16 SOME SUMMARY POINTS

The connectionist models of single word processing we have reviewed have achieved significant successes in simulating many pieces of psychological data. The simulations of word naming, by Seidenberg and McClelland (1989) and by Plaut et al. (1996), and of word production, by Dell et al. (1995), also illustrate how apparent rule-governed behaviour can emerge from models that have essentially internalised the statistical regularities in their learning environments. This last point will be returned to in Chapter 7, when we review attempts to capture higher-level aspects of language processing in connectionist models. A further strength of the models is that they can be applied to simulate the large body of data on neuropsychological disorders of word processing, which we cover in Chapter 8.

Of course, many issues remain. We mention just three. One question concerns how well the models will "scale up" when extended to deal with large vocabularies and bodies of data. This point about scaling applies even if networks continue to deal with only one aspect of language processing, such as speech production or comprehension. A second question concerns how separate networks may be linked together to create broader models of language performance, for instance incorporating both phonological and orthographic procedures for spelling (section 6.14) and networks for both memory retrieval and lexical selection in speech comprehension (section 6.13). In Chapter 8 we review the Plaut et al. (1996) model of reading again, as a framework for understanding neuropsychological disorders; however, foreshadowing this, we note that this model suggests one means by which a form of modular structure can be developed in connectionist networks. Other approaches to the development of modular structure within networks are taken up in Chapter 9. A third question concerns how broader models of language, if developed, can reconcile psychological data showing apparently opposite effects of variables on different tasks. One such variable is semantic priming. In this chapter we have reviewed evidence showing that semantic priming can exert positive effects on word recognition (measured using lexical decision tasks; e.g. Meyer & Schvaneveldt, 1971; section 6.9). However, we have also noted evidence indicating that semantic primes can interfere with name retrieval in speech production tasks (Wheeldon & Monsell, 1994; section 6.15.1). In each case models have been

developed to account for these effects and these models have been internally consistent, but it will be a challenge to show how, when linked to form different parts of the language system, the models can generate opposite effects of a common variable. In fact, opposite effects may emerge if the same variable exerts different influences at different stages of performance. For example, access to semantics may be facilitated by activating common parts of a distributed representation; in contrast, name retrieval may be inhibited (by semantic priming), as overlapping prime and target representations may then be strong competitors in the selection of a unique representation for name output. Whether such results emerge naturally from models is a question that must be addressed by future research. Overall, however, and despite these caveats, we conclude that connectionist accounts are not inherently limited as viable psychological models at a single word level. We next consider whether inherent limitations do emerge when more complex aspects of language are considered.

NOTES

1. In fact the decision rule was more complex than this because the model would sometimes respond "word" to a stimulus such as E<u>AST</u>, due to partial activation of letter cluster units from the unattended (non-underlined) letters. To prevent this occurring, Behrmann et al. (1991) also conducted a verification process in which the first underlined letter was matched against the first letter read out of the "pull out" network. If there was a mismatch (e.g. for E<u>AST</u>), the model re-processed the input.

2. One difference relative to the simulations of the lexical decision study of Behrmann et al. (1991) should be noted here. In Behrmann et al., readers were not pre-cued to focus attention on the critical letters but had to focus attention on presentation of the stimuli. If the spread of activation from the attentional module in MORSEL is narrowed over time, attentional effects will be more powerful under pre-cue conditions relative to when focusing takes place "on-line" to stimuli.

3. The specific form of this function was as follows:

$$\text{net}^i(t) = k\sum w_{ij}a_{js}(t) + (1-k)\text{net}_i(t-1)$$

where w_{ij} is the connection strength from unit j to unit i, a_{js} is the stimulus-driven activation value of unit j, $net_i(t-1)$ is the net activation of unit i on iteration $t-1$, and $net^i(t)$ is the net activation of unit i on iteration t. k is a constant, which in the cascade version is <1, whereas in the non-cascade version it is 1.

4. This measure is useful for cases in which many of the output units are "off" for a given input. The problem in such cases is that a model may quickly learn to reduce an RMS_{error} score by turning off all the output units. To change the states of units then requires large alterations in the weight values. When the state of a unit diverges from its expected target, the change in the cross-entropy measure takes place much more rapidly than the change in the RMS_{error} measure, so that the cross-entropy measure can lead to large weight changes and better learning. The specific measure used by Plaut et al. (1996) was:

$$C = -t_i \log_2(s_i) + (1 - t_i)\log_2(1 - s_i)$$

where C is the cross-entropy measure, s_i is the state of the phoneme unit i and t_i is its correct (target) value.

5. In a traditional dual-route model of reading, this additional route would lead to the existence of three routes: one from orthography to meaning; one lexical route from orthography to phonology, and one non-lexical route from orthography to phonology (see Humphreys & Evett, 1985, for discussion).

6. We suggest that at least one level of representation be maintained at a sub-word level, in order that there be some degree of generalisation to new stimuli (nonwords) after learning.

7. A morpheme is the term used to describe the smallest unit of meaning in a language. Thus a word such as swimmer would be composed of a root morpheme (swim), along with a suffix (er) (see Fig. 6.24 for an example).

8. Importantly, here the semantic representations activated will be consistent with both names.

9. Note that recurrent networks with external feedback alone can have difficulty in learning sequential outputs with repeated items in a sequence. For example, consider a stimulus such as *gig*. After training on the first /g/, the output representation is fed-back as input. However, from the feedback the model cannot tell whether next to produce an /I/ or to stop, as the external feedback will be the same for the first and second /g/s. In contrast, internal feedback can differ for the first and second /g/s, as hidden unit activation is not constrained to have identical states for each /g/. Hence models with internal feedback are better able to deal with repeated stimuli.

Understanding normal and impaired word reading: Computational principles in quasi-regular domains

David C. Plaut and James L. McClelland
Carnegie Mellon University and the Center for the Neural Basis of Cognition

Mark S. Seidenberg
University of Southern California

Karalyn Patterson
Medical Research Council Applied Psychology Unit

A connectionist approach to processing in quasi-regular domains, as exemplified by English word reading, is developed. Networks using appropriately structured orthographic and phonological representations were trained to read both regular and exception words, and yet were also able to read pronounceable nonwords as well as skilled readers. A mathematical analysis of a simplified system clarifies the close relationship of word frequency and spelling–sound consistency in influencing naming latencies. These insights were verified in subsequent simulations, including an attractor network that accounted for latency data directly in its time to settle on a response. Further analyses of the ability of networks to reproduce data on acquired surface dyslexia support a view of the reading system that incorporates a graded division of labor between semantic and phonological processes, and contrasts in important ways with the standard dual-route account.

Many aspects of language can be characterized as *quasi-regular* — the relationship between inputs and outputs is systematic but admits many excep-

David C. Plaut and James L. McClelland, Department of Psychology, Carnegie Mellon University, and the Center for the Neural Basis of Cognition; Mark S. Seidenberg, Neuroscience Program, University of Southern California; Karalyn Patterson, Medical Research Council Applied Psychology Unit, Cambridge, England.

This research was supported financially by National Institute of Mental Health Grants MH47566, MH01188, and MH00385, National Institute on Aging Grant Ag10109, National Science Foundation Grant ASC-9109215, and McDonnell-Pew Program in Cognitive Neuroscience Grant T89-01245-016.

We thank Marlene Behrmann, Derek Besner, Max Coltheart, Joe Devlin, Geoff Hinton, and Eamon Strain for helpful discussions and comments. We also acknowledge Derek Besner, Max Coltheart, and Michael McCloskey for directing attention to many of the issues addressed in this article.

Correspondence concerning this article should be addressed to David C. Plaut, Department of Psychology, Carnegie Mellon University, Pittsburgh, Pennsylvania 15213-3890. Electronic mail may be sent via Internet to plaut@cmu.edu.

Psychological Review 1996, Vol. 103, No. 1, 56–115

tions. One such task is the mapping between the written and spoken forms of English words. Most words are *regular* (e.g. GAVE, MINT) in that their pronunciations adhere to standard spelling–sound correspondences. There are, however, many irregular or *exception* words (e.g. HAVE, PINT) whose pronunciations violate the standard correspondences. To make matters worse, some spelling patterns have a range of pronunciations with none clearly predominating (e.g. _OWN in DOWN, TOWN, BROWN, CROWN vs. KNOWN, SHOWN, GROWN, THROWN, or _OUGH in COUGH, ROUGH, BOUGH, THOUGH, THROUGH). Nonetheless, in the face of this complexity, skilled readers pronounce written words quickly and accurately and can also use their knowledge of spelling–sound correspondences to read pronounceable nonwords (e.g. MAVE, RINT).

An important debate within cognitive psychology is how best to characterize knowledge and processing in quasi-regular domains in order to account for human language performance. One view (e.g. Pinker, 1984, 1991) is that the systematic aspects of language are represented and processed in the form of an explicit set of rules. A rule-based approach has considerable intuitive appeal because much of human language behavior can be characterized at a broad scale in terms of rules. It also provides a straightforward account of how language knowledge can be applied productively to novel items (Fodor & Pylyshyn, 1988). However, as illustrated above, most domains are only partially systematic; accordingly, a separate mechanism is required to handle the exceptions. This distinction between a rule-based mechanism and an exception mechanism, each operating according to fundamentally different principles, forms the central tenet of so-called "dual-route" theories of language.

An alternative view comes out of research on connectionist or parallel distributed processing networks, in which computation takes the form of cooperative and competitive interactions among large numbers of simple, neuron-like processing units (McClelland, Rumelhart, & the PDP Research Group, 1986; Rumelhart, McClelland, & the PDP Research Group, 1986). Such systems learn by adjusting weights on connections between units in a way that is sensitive to how the statistical structure of the environment influences the behavior of the network. As a result, there is no sharp dichotomy between the items that obey the rules and the items that do not. Rather, all items coexist within a single system whose representations and processing reflect the relative degree of *consistency* in the mappings for different items. The connectionist approach is particularly appropriate for capturing the rapid, on-line nature of language use as well as for specifying how such processes might be learned and implemented in the brain (although still at a somewhat abstract level; see Sejnowski, Koch, & Churchland, 1989, for discussion). Perhaps more fundamentally, connectionist modeling provides a rich-set of general computational principles that can lead to new and useful ways of thinking about human performance in quasi-regular domains.

Much of the initial debate between these two views of the language system focused on the relatively constrained domain of English inflectional morphology — specifically, forming the past tense of verbs. Past-tense formation is a rather simple quasi-regular task: There is a single regular "rule" (add -ed; e.g. WALK ⇒ "walked")

and only about 100 exceptions, grouped into several clusters of similar items that undergo a similar change (e.g. SING ⇒ "sang," DRINK ⇒ "drank") along with a very small number of very high-frequency, arbitrary forms (e.g. GO ⇒ "went"; Bybee & Slobin, 1982). Rumelhart and McClelland (1986) attempted to reformulate the issue away from a sharp dichotomy between explicit rules and exceptions toward a view that emphasizes the graded structure relating verbs and their inflections. They developed a connectionist model that learned a direct association between the phonology of all types of verb stems and the phonology of their past-tense forms. Pinker and Prince (1988) and Lachter and Bever (1988), however, pointed out numerous deficiencies in the model's actual performance and in some of its specific assumptions, and they argued more generally that the applicability of connectionist mechanisms in language is fundamentally limited (also see Fodor & Pylyshyn, 1988). However, many of the specific limitations of the Rumelhart and McClelland model have been addressed in subsequent simulation work (Cottrell & Plunkett, 1991; Daugherty & Seidenberg, 1992; Hoeffner, 1992; MacWhinney & Leinbach, 1991; Marchman, 1993; Plunkett & Marchman, 1991, 1993). Thus, the possibility remains strong that a connectionist model could provide a full account of past-tense inflection. Furthermore, some recent applications to aspects of language disorders (Hoeffner & McClelland, 1993; Marchman, 1993) and language change (Hare & Elman, 1992, 1995) demonstrate the ongoing extension of the approach to account for a wider range of language phenomena.

Very similar issues arise in the domain of oral reading, where there is a much richer empirical database with which to make contact. As in the domain of inflectional morphology, many researchers assume that accounting for the wealth of existing data on both normal and impaired word reading requires postulating multiple mechanisms. In particular, dual-route theorists (e.g. Besner & Smith, 1992; Coltheart, 1978, 1985; Coltheart, Curtis, Atkins, & Haller, 1993; Coltheart & Rastle, 1994; Marshall & Newcombe, 1973; Meyer, Schvaneveldt, & Ruddy, 1974; Morton & Patterson, 1980; Paap & Noel, 1991) have claimed that pronouncing exception words requires a lexical lookup mechanism that is separate from the sublexical spelling–sound correspondence rules that apply to regular words and nonwords (also see Humphreys & Evett, 1985, and the accompanying commentaries for discussion of the properties of dual-route theories). The separation of lexical and sublexical procedures is motivated primarily by evidence that they can be independently impaired, either by abnormal reading acquisition (developmental dyslexia) or by brain damage in a previously literate adult (acquired dyslexia). Thus, *phonological* dyslexics, who can read words but not nonwords, appear to have a selective impairment of the sublexical procedure, whereas *surface* dyslexics, who can read nonwords but who "regularize" exception words (e.g. SEW ⇒ "sue"), appear to have a selective impairment of the lexical procedure.

Seidenberg and McClelland (1989), hereafter SM89, challenged the central claim of dual-route theories by developing a connectionist simulation that learned to map representations of the written forms of words (orthography) to representations of their spoken forms (phonology). The network successfully pronounces both regular and exception words and yet is not an implementation of two separate mechanisms (see Seidenberg & McClelland, 1992, for a demonstration of this last point). The simulation was put forward in support of a more general framework for lexical processing in which orthographic, phonological, and semantic information interact in gradually settling on the best representations for a given input (see Stone & Van Orden, 1989, 1994; Van Orden & Goldinger, 1994; Van Orden, Pennington, & Stone, 1990, for a similar perspective on word reading). A major strength of the approach is that it provides a natural account of the graded effects of spelling–sound consistency among words (Glushko, 1979; Jared, McRae, & Seidenberg, 1990) and how this consistency interacts with word frequency (Andrews, 1982; Seidenberg, 1985; Seidenberg, Waters, Barnes, & Tanenhaus, 1984; Taraban & McClelland, 1987; Waters & Seidenberg, 1985).[1] Furthermore, SM89 demonstrated that undertrained versions of the model exhibit some aspects of developmental surface dyslexia, and Patterson (1990; Patterson, Seidenberg, & McClelland, 1989) showed how damaging the normal model can reproduce some aspects of acquired surface dyslexia. The SM89 model also contributes to the broader enterprise of connectionist modeling of cognitive processes in which a common set of general computational principles are being applied successfully across a wide range of cognitive domains.

However, the SM89 work has a serious empirical limitation that undermines its role in establishing a viable connectionist alternative to dual-route theories of word reading in particular and in providing a satisfactory formulation of the nature of knowledge and processing in quasi-regular domains more generally. Specifically, the implemented model is significantly worse than skilled readers at pronouncing nonwords (Besner, Twilley, McCann, & Seergobin, 1990). This limitation has broad implications for the range of empirical phenomena that can be accounted for by the model (Coltheart et al., 1993). Poor nonword reading is exactly what would be predicted from the dual-route claim that no single system — connectionist or otherwise — can read both exception words and pronounceable nonwords adequately. Under this interpretation, the model had simply approximated a lexical lookup procedure: It could read both regular and exception words but had not separately mastered the sublexical rules necessary to read nonwords. An alternative interpretation, however, is that the empirical shortcomings of the SM89 simulation stem from specific aspects of its design and not from inherent limitations on the abilities of connectionist networks in quasi-regular domains. In particular, Seidenberg and McClelland (1990) suggested that the model's nonword reading might be improved — without adversely affecting its other properties — by using either a larger training corpus or different orthographic and phonological representations.

A second limitation of the SM89 work is that it did not provide a very extensive examination of underlying theoretical issues. The main emphasis was on demonstrating that a network that operated according to fairly general connectionist principles could account for a wide range of empirical findings on normal and developmentally impaired reading. Relatively little attention was paid in that article to articulating the general principles them-selves or to evaluating their relative importance. Thus, much of the underlying theoretical founda-tion of the work remained implicit. Despite sub-sequent efforts at explicating these principles (Seidenberg, 1993), considerable confusion re-mains with regard to the role of connectionist modeling in contributing to a theory of word read-ing (or of any other cognitive process). Thus, some researchers (e.g. Forster, 1994; McCloskey, 1991) have claimed that the SM89 demonstration, while impressive in its own right, has not extended our understanding of word reading because the opera-tion of the model itself — and of connectionist networks more generally — is too complex to understand. Consequently, "connectionist networks should not be viewed as theories of human cognit-ive functions, or as simulations of theories, or even as demonstrations of specific theoretical points" (McCloskey, 1991, p. 387; also see Massaro, 1988; Olsen & Caramazza, 1991). Although we reject the claim that connectionist modeling is atheor-etical (see Seidenberg, 1993) and that there are no bases for analyzing and understanding networks (see, e.g. Hanson & Burr, 1990), we agree that the theoretical principles and constructs for developing connectionist explanations of empirical phenom-ena are in need of further elaboration.

In this article we develop a connectionist account of knowledge representation and cognit-ive processing in quasi-regular domains in the specific context of normal and impaired word read-ing. We draw on an analysis of the strengths and weaknesses of the SM89 work, with the dual aim of providing a more adequate account of the relev-ant empirical phenomena and of articulating in a more explicit and formal manner the theoretical principles that underlie the approach. We explore the use of alternative representations that make the regularities between written and spoken words more explicit. In the first simulation experiment, a network using the new representations learned to read both regular and exception words, includ-ing low-frequency exception words, and yet was still able to read pronounceable nonwords as well as skilled readers. The results open up the range of possible architectures that might plausibly under-lie human word reading. A mathematical analysis

of the effects of word frequency and spelling–sound consistency in a simpler but related system serves to clarify the close relationship of these factors in influencing naming latencies. These insights were verified in a second simulation. In a third simulation we developed an attractor network that reproduces the naming latency data directly in its time to settle on a response and thus obvi-ates the need to use error as a proxy for reaction time. The implication of the semantic contribution to reading was considered in our fourth and final simulation in the context of accounting for the impaired reading behavior of acquired surface dys-lexic patients with brain damage. Damage to the attractor network provides only a limited account of the relevant phenomena; a better account is provided by the performance of a network that learns to map orthography to phonology in the context of support from semantics. Our findings lead to a view of the reading system that incorpor-ates a graded division of labor between semantic and phonological processes. Such a view is con-sistent with the more general SM89 framework and has some similarities with — but also import-ant differences from — the standard dual-route account. In the General Discussion we articulate these differences and clarify the implications of the current work for a broader range of empirical findings, including those raised by Coltheart et al. (1993) as challenges to the connectionist approach.

We begin with a brief critique of the SM89 model in which we try to distinguish its central computational properties from less central aspects of its design. An analysis of its representations led to the design of new representations that we used in a series of simulations analogous to the SM89 simulation.

The Seidenberg and McClelland model

The general framework

Seidenberg and McClelland's (1989) general frame-work for lexical processing is shown in Fig. 1. Orthographic, phonological, and semantic informa-tion is represented in terms of distributed pat-terns of activity over separate groups of simple

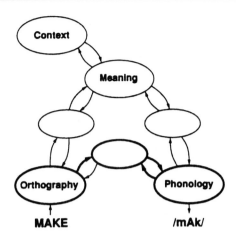

FIG. 1. Seidenberg and McClelland's (1989) general framework for lexical processing. Each oval represents a group of units, and each arrow represents a group of connections. The implemented model is shown in bold. From "A Distributed, Developmental Model of Word Recognition and Naming," by M. S. Seidenberg and J. L. McClelland, 1989, *Psychological Review, 96*, p.526. Copyright 1989 by the American Psychological Association. Adapted with permission.

neuron-like processing units. Within each domain, similar words are represented by similar patterns of activity. Lexical tasks involve transformations among these representations — for example, oral reading requires the orthographic pattern for a word to generate the appropriate phonological pattern. Such transformations are accomplished via the cooperative and competitive interactions among units, including additional *hidden units* that mediate among the orthographic, phonological, and semantic units. Unit interactions are governed by weighted connections between them, which collectively encode the system's knowledge about how the different types of information are related. The specific values of the weights are derived by an automatic learning procedure on the basis of the system's exposure to written words, spoken words, and their meanings.

The SM89 framework is broadly consistent with a more general view of information processing that has been articulated by McClelland (1991, 1993) in the context of GRAIN networks. These networks embody the following general computational principles:

Graded: Propagation of activation is not all-or-none but rather builds up gradually over time.

Random: Unit activations are subject to intrinsic stochastic variability.

Adaptive: The system gradually improves its performance by adjusting weights on connections between units.

Interactive: Information flows in a bidirectional manner between groups of units, allowing their activity levels to constrain each other and to be mutually consistent.

Nonlinear: Unit outputs are smooth, nonlinear functions of their total inputs, significantly extending the computational power of the entire network beyond that of purely linear networks.

The acronym GRAIN is also intended to convey the notion that cognitive processes are expressed at a finer grain of analysis, in terms of interacting groups of neuronlike units, than is typical of most "box-and-arrow" information-processing models. Additional computational principles that are central to the SM89 framework but not captured by the acronym are the following:

Distributed Representations: Items in the domain are represented by patterns of activity over groups of units that participate in representing many other items.

Distributed Knowledge: Knowledge about the relationship between items is encoded across large numbers of connection weights that also encode many other mappings.

Much of the controversy surrounding the SM89 framework, and the associated implementation, stems from the fact that it breaks with traditional accounts of lexical processing (e.g. Coltheart, 1985; Morton & Patterson, 1980) in two fundamental ways. The first is in the representational status of words. Traditional accounts assume that words are represented in the structure of the reading system — in its *architecture*. Morton's (1969) "logogens" are well-known instances of this type of word representation. By contrast, within the SM89 framework the lexical status of a string of letters or phonemes is not reflected in the structure of the reading system. Rather, words are distinguished from nonwords only by *functional* properties of the system — the way in which particular orthographic, phonological, and semantic patterns of activity interact (also see Van Orden et al., 1990).

The SM89 framework's second major break with tradition concerns the degree of uniformity in the mechanism(s) by which orthographic, phonological, and semantic representations interact. Traditional accounts assume that pronouncing exception words and pronouncing nonwords require separate lexical and sublexical mechanisms, respectively. By contrast, the SM89 framework employs far more homogeneous processes in oral reading. In particular, it eschews separate mechanisms for pronouncing nonwords and exception words. Rather, all of the system's knowledge of spelling–sound correspondences is brought to bear in pronouncing all types of letter strings. Conflicts among possible alternative pronunciations of a letter string are resolved not by structurally distinct mechanisms, but by cooperative and competitive interactions based on how the letter string relates to all known words and their pronunciations. Furthermore, the semantic representation of a word participates in oral reading in exactly the same manner as do its orthographic and phonological representations, although the framework leaves open the issue of how important these semantic influences are in skilled oral reading.

Regularity versus consistency. An issue that is intimately related to the tension between the SM89 framework and traditional dual-route theories concerns the distinction between regularity and consistency. Broadly speaking, a word is *regular* if its pronunciation can be generated "by rule," and it is *consistent* if its pronunciation agrees with those of similarly spelled words. Of course, to be useful these definitions must be operationalized in more specific terms. The most commonly proposed pronunciation rules are based on the most frequent

grapheme–phoneme correspondences (GPCs) in the language, although such GPC rules must be augmented with considerable context-sensitivity to operate adequately (see Coltheart et al., 1993; Seidenberg, Plaut, Petersen, McClelland, & McRae, 1994, for discussion). Consistency, on the other hand, has typically been defined with respect to the orthographic body and the phonological rime (i.e. the vowel plus any following consonants). This choice can be partly justified on the grounds of empirical data: For example, Treiman, Mullennix, Bijeljac-Babic, and Richmond-Welty (1995) have recently demonstrated that, in naming data for all 1,329 monosyllabic words in English with a consonant-vowel-consonant (CVC) pronunciation, the consistency of the body (VC) accounts for significantly more variance in naming latency than the consistency of the onset plus vowel (CV). There are also pragmatic reasons for restricting consideration to body-level consistency — bodies constitute a manageable manipulation in the design of experimental lists. If experimenters had to consider consistency across orthographic neighborhoods at all possible levels, from individual graphemes up to the largest subword-sized chunks, their selection of stimulus words would be an even more agonizing process than it already is. Nonetheless, the general notion of consistency is broader than a specific instantiation in terms of body consistency, just as the general notion of regularity is broader than that defined by any particular set of spelling–sound correspondence rules.

On the basis of the frequent observation (e.g. Coltheart, 1978; Parkin, 1982; Waters & Seidenberg, 1985) that words with regular or typical spelling–sound correspondences (such as MINT) produce shorter naming latencies and lower error rates than words with exceptional correspondences (such as PINT), regularity was originally considered to be the critical variable. In 1979, however, Glushko argued that consistency provided a better account of empirical results. Although MINT may be a regular word according to GPC rules, its spelling–sound relationship is inconsistent with that of its orthographic neighbor, PINT. To the extent that the process of computing phonology from orthography is sensitive to the characteristics of the neighborhood, performance on a regular but inconsistent word like MINT may also be adversely affected. Glushko (1979) did indeed demonstrate longer naming latencies for regular inconsistent words than for regular words from consistent body neighborhoods, though this result was not always obtained in subsequent experiments (e.g. Stanhope & Parkin, 1987).

In 1990, Jared, McRae, and Seidenberg offered a more sophisticated hypothesis that captures aspects of results not handled by previous accounts referring solely to either regularity or consistency. According to Jared and colleagues, the magnitude of the consistency effect for a given word depends on the summed frequency of that word's *friends* (words with a similar spelling pattern and similar pronunciation) and of its *enemies* (words with a similar spelling pattern but a discrepant pronunciation). For example, an inconsistent word like MINT has a number of friends (e.g. LINT, TINT, PRINT) and just a single enemy, PINT. Against the strength of friends, the single enemy cannot exert a marked influence (especially when, as is true of PINT, the enemy is of relatively low frequency); its negative impact on the computation of the pronunciation of MINT will thus be small and perhaps undetectable. By contrast, an inconsistent word like GOWN, with many enemies (e.g. BLOWN, SHOWN, GROWN) as well as friends (e.g. DOWN, BROWN, TOWN), gives rise to a more substantial effect. Such words, with roughly balanced support from friends and enemies, have been termed *ambiguous* (with respect to the pronunciation of their body; Backman, Bruck, Hébert, & Seidenberg, 1984; Seidenberg et al., 1984).

The commonly observed effect of regularity also finds a natural explanation within Jared et al.'s (1990) account, because most regular words (as defined by GPC rules) have many friends and few if any enemies, whereas words with irregular spelling–sound correspondences (such as PINT or SEW) typically have many enemies and few if any friends. Given this correspondence, and following Glushko (1979) and Taraban and McClelland (1987), we will refer to words with many enemies and few if any friends as *exception* words, acknowledging that this definition excludes many words that would be considered exceptional according to GPC rules (e.g. many ambiguous words).

Jared et al.'s hypothesis and supporting data also mesh well with other results demonstrating the inadequacy of a simple regular–irregular dichotomy, such as the "degrees of regularity" effect observed in acquired surface dyslexia (Shallice, Warrington, & McCarthy, 1983, also see Patterson & Behrmann, 1995; Plaut, Behrmann, Patterson, & McClelland, 1993, for more direct evidence of consistency effects in surface dyslexia).

It must be kept in mind, however, that a definition of consistency based solely on body neighborhoods, even if frequency-weighted, can provide only a partial account of the consistency effects that would be expected to operate over the full range of spelling–sound correspondences. Thus, for example, the word CHEF could not be considered inconsistent on a body-level analysis because all of the words in English with the body _EF (i.e. CLEF, REF) agree with its pronunciation. On a broader definition of consistency, however, CHEF is certainly inconsistent, because the overwhelmingly most common pronunciation of CH in English is the one appropriate to CHIEF, not CHEF. This broad view of consistency is also important when considering what might be called irregular consistent words — that is, words such as KIND, BOLD, and TOOK that have highly consistent body neighborhoods but that are nonetheless irregular according to GPC rules such as those of Coltheart et al. (1993). The processing of such items would be expected to be sensitive to the conflict between consistency at the body–rime level and inconsistency at the grapheme–phoneme level. In all of what follows, therefore, although we adopt the standard practice of using body-level manipulations for empirical tests, this should be interpreted as providing only an approximation of the true range of consistency effects.

Relationship to other approaches. A cursory inspection of Fig. 1 might suggest that the SM89 framework is, in fact, a dual-route system: Orthography can influence phonology either directly or via semantics. To clarify this possible source of confusion, we must be more explicit about typical assumptions in dual-route theories concerning the structure and operation of the different procedures. As described earlier, the central distinction in such theories is between lexical and sublexical procedures. The sublexical procedure applies GPC rules to produce correct pronunciations for regular words, reasonable pronunciations for nonwords, and incorrect, "regularized" pronunciations for exception words. The lexical procedure produces correct pronunciations for all words and no response for nonwords. When the outputs of the two procedures conflict, as they do for exception words, some models (e.g. Paap & Noel, 1991) assume a "horse race," with the faster (typically lexical) procedure generating the actual response. Others (e.g. Monsell, Patterson, Graham, Hughes, & Milroy, 1992) suggest that output from the two procedures is pooled until a phonological representation sufficient to drive articulation is achieved (although the specific means by which this pooling occurs is rarely made explicit). The lexical procedure is often subdivided into a *direct* route that maps orthographic word representations directly onto phonological word representations, and an *indirect* route that maps via semantics. In these formulations, the "dual-route" model is in a sense a three-route model, although researchers typically assume that the indirect, semantic route would be too slow to influence skilled word pronunciation (Coltheart, 1985; Patterson & Morton, 1985).

By contrast, the nonsemantic portion of the SM89 framework does not operate by applying GPC rules, but by the simultaneous interaction of units. It is also capable of pronouncing all types of input, including exception words, although the time it takes to do so depends on the type of input. Furthermore, the semantic portion of the framework does not operate in terms of whole-word representations, but rather in terms of interacting units, each of which participates in the processing of many words. In addition, nonwords may engage semantics to some degree, although the extent to which this occurs is likely to be minimal (see the discussion of lexical decision in the General Discussion). Thus, the structure and operation of the SM89 framework is fundamentally different from existing dual-route theories.

It may also help to clarify the relationship between the SM89 framework and approaches to word reading other than dual-route theories. The two main alternatives are lexical-analogy theories and multiple-levels theories. Lexical-analogy theories (Henderson, 1982; Marcel, 1980) dispense with the sublexical procedure and propose that the lexical procedure can pronounce nonwords by synthesizing the pronunciations of orthographically similar words. Unfortunately, the way in which these pronunciations are generated and synthesized is rarely fully specified. Multiple-levels theories (Shallice & McCarthy, 1985; Shallice et al., 1983) dispense with the (direct) lexical route (or rather, incorporate it into the sublexical route) by assuming that spelling–sound correspondences are represented for segments of all sizes, ranging from single graphemes and phonemes to word bodies and entire morphemes.

In a way, the SM89 framework can be thought of as an integration and more detailed specification of lexical-analogy and multiple-level theories (also see Norris, 1994, for a connectionist implementation of the latter). The pronunciations of nonwords are generated on the basis of the combined influence of all known word pronunciations, with those most similar to the nonword having the strongest effect. In order for the system to pronounce exception words as well as nonwords, the hidden units must learn to be sensitive to spelling–sound correspondences of a range of sizes. The framework is also broadly consistent with Van Orden et al.'s (1990) proposal that orthography and phonology are strongly associated via covariant learning, although the SM89 framework incorporates direct interaction between orthography and semantics, which Van Orden and colleagues dispute.

The implemented model

The SM89 framework clearly represents a radical departure from widely held assumptions about lexical processing, but is it plausible as an account of human word reading? In the service of establishing the framework's plausibility, SM89 implemented a specific connectionist network that, they implicitly claimed, embodies the central theoretical tenets of the framework.

The network, highlighted in bold in Fig. 1, contains three groups of units: 400 orthographic units, 200 hidden units, and 460 phonological units. The hidden units receive connections from all of the orthographic units and, in turn, send connections to all of the phonological units as well as back to all of the orthographic units. The network contains no semantic or context information.

Orthographic and phonological forms are represented as patterns of activity over the orthographic and phonological units, respectively. These patterns are defined in terms of context-sensitive triples of letters and phonemes (Wickelgren, 1969). It was computationally infeasible for SM89 to include a unit for each possible triple, so they used representations that require fewer units but preserve the relative similarities among patterns. In orthography, the letter triples to which each unit responds are defined by a table of 10 randomly selected letters (or a blank) in each of three positions. In the representation of a letter string, an orthographic unit is active if the string contains one of the letter triples than can be generated by sampling from each of the three positions of that unit's table. For example, GAVE would activate all orthographic units capable of generating _GA, GAV, AVE, or VE_.

Phonological representations are derived in an analogous fashion, except that a phonological unit's table entries at each position are not randomly selected phonemes, but rather all phonemes containing a particular phonemic feature (as defined by Rumelhart & McClelland, 1986). A further constraint is that the features for the first and third positions must come from the same phonetic dimension (e.g. place of articulation). Thus, each unit in phonology represents a particular ordered triple of phonemic features, termed a *Wickelfeature*. For example, the pronunciation /gAv/ would activate phonological units representing the Wickelfeatures [*back, vowel, front*], [*stop, long, fricative*], and many others (given that /g/ has *back* and *stop* among its features, /A/ has *vowel* and *long*, and /v/ has *front* and *fricative*). On average, a word activates 81 (20.3%) of the 400 orthographic units, and 54 (11.7%) of the 460 phonological units. We will return to an analysis of the properties of these representations after summarizing the SM89 simulation results.

The weights on connections between units were initialized to small random values. The network then was repeatedly presented with the orthography of each of 2,897 monosyllabic words and trained both to generate the phonology of the word and to regenerate its orthography (see Seidenberg & McClelland, 1989, for details). During each sweep through the training set, the probability that a word was presented to the network was proportional to a logarithmic function of its frequency (Kuçera & Francis, 1967). Processing a word involved setting the states of the orthographic units (as defined above), computing hidden unit states based on states of the orthographic units and the weights on connections from them, and then computing states of the phonological and orthographic units based on those of the hidden units. Back-propagation (Rumelhart, Hinton, & Williams, 1986a, 1986b) was used to calculate how to adjust the weights to reduce the differences between the correct phonological and orthographic representations of the word and those generated by the network. These weight changes were accumulated during each sweep through the training set; at the end, the changes were carried out and the process was repeated.

The network was considered to have named a word correctly when the generated phonological activity was closer to the representation of the correct pronunciation of the word than to than of any pronunciation which differed from the correct one by a single phoneme. For the example GAVE ⇒ /gAv/, the competing pronunciations are all those among /*Av/, /g*v/, or /gA*/, where /*/ is any phoneme. After 250 training sweeps through the corpus, amounting to about 150,000 word presentations, the network correctly named all but 77 words (97.3% correct), most of which were low-frequency exception words.

A considerable amount of empirical data on oral reading concerns the time it takes to name words of various types. A natural analogue in a model to naming latency in human readers would be the amount of computing time required to produce an output. SM89 could not use this measure because their network takes exactly the same amount of time — one update of each unit — to compute phonological output for any letter string. Instead, they approximated naming latency with a measure of the accuracy of the phonological activity produced by the network — the *phonological error score*. SM89 showed that the network's distribution of phonological error scores for various words reproduces the effects of frequency and consistency in naming latencies found in a wide variety of empirical studies that used the same words. Figure 2 presents particularly illustrative results in this regard, using high- and low-frequency words at four levels of consistency (listed in Appendix A and used in the current simulations):

Exception words from Experiments 1 and 2 of Taraban and McClelland (1987): They have an average of 0.73 friends in the SM89 corpus (not counting the word itself) and 9.2 enemies.

Ambiguous words generated by SM89 to be matched in Kuçera and Francis (1967) frequency with the exception words: They average 8.6 friends and 8.0 enemies.

Regular inconsistent words, also from Taraban and McClelland (1987): These average 7.8 friends and only 2.1 enemies.

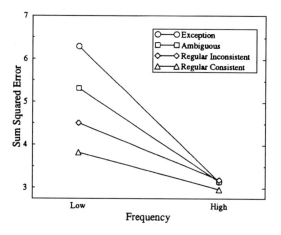

FIG. 2. Mean phonological error scores produced by the Seidenberg and McClelland (1989) network for words with various degrees of spelling–sound consistency (listed in Appendix A) as a function of frequency. Regenerated from Fig. 16 of "A Distributed, Developmental Model of Word Recognition and Naming," by M. S. Seidenberg and J. L. McClelland, 1989, *Psychological Review, 96,* p.542. Copyright 1989 by the American Psychological Association. Adapted with permission.

Regular consistent words that were the control items for the exception words in the Taraban and McClelland (1987) study: They have an average of 10.7 friends and 0.04 enemies (the foreign word COUP for the item GROUP, and one of the pronunciations of BASS for the item CLASS).

The relevant empirical effects in naming latency exhibited by the SM89 model are, specifically, as follows:

1. High-frequency words are named faster than low-frequency words (e.g. Forster & Chambers, 1973; Frederiksen & Kroll, 1976).
2. Consistent words are named faster than inconsistent words (Glushko, 1979), and latencies increase monotonically with increasing spelling–sound inconsistency (as approximated by the relative proportion of friends vs. enemies; Jared et al., 1990). Thus, regular inconsistent words like MOTH (cf. BOTH) are slower to be named than regular consistent words like MUST (Glushko, 1979), and exception words like PINT and SEW are the slowest to be named (Seidenberg et al., 1984). Performance on ambiguous words like GOWN (cf. GROWN) falls between that on regular inconsistent words and that on exception words, although this has been investigated directly only with respect to reading acquisition (Backman et al., 1984).
3. Frequency interacts with consistency (Seidenberg, 1985; Seidenberg et al., 1984; Waters & Seidenberg, 1985) such that the consistency effect is much greater among low-frequency words than among high-frequency words (where it may even be absent; see, e.g. Seidenberg, 1985), or equivalently, the frequency effect decreases with increasing consistency (perhaps being absent among regular words; see, e.g. Waters & Seidenberg, 1985).

In considering these empirical and simulation results, it is important to keep in mind that the use of a four-way classification of consistency is not in any way intended to imply the existence of four distinct subtypes of words; rather, it is intended to help illustrate the effects of what is actually an underlying continuum of consistency (Jared et al., 1990).[2]

The model also shows analogous effects of consistency in nonword naming latency. In particular, nonwords derived from regular consistent words (e.g. NUST from MUST) are faster to name than nonwords derived from exception words (e.g. MAVE from HAVE; Glushko, 1979; Taraban & McClelland, 1987). As mentioned in the Introduction, however, the model's nonword naming accuracy is much worse than that of skilled readers. Besner et al. (1990) reported that, on nonword lists from Glushko (1979) and McCann and Besner (1987), the model is only 59% and 51% correct, whereas skilled readers are 94% and 89% correct, respectively. Seidenberg and McClelland (1990) pointed out that the scoring criterion used for the network was more strict than that used for the human readers. We will return to the issue of scoring nonword reading performance — for the present purposes, it suffices to acknowledge that, even taking differences in scoring into account, the performance of the SM89 model on nonwords is inadequate.

The SM89 model replicates the effects of frequency and consistency in lexical decision (Waters & Seidenberg, 1985) when responses are based on *orthographic error scores*, which measure the degree to which the network succeeds at recreating the orthography of each input string. Again, however, the model is not as accurate at lexical decision under some conditions as are human readers (Besner et al., 1990; Fera & Besner, 1992).

Consistency also influences the ease with which word naming skills are acquired. Thus, less skilled readers — whether younger or developmentally dyslexic — show larger consistency effects than do more skilled readers (Backman et al., 1984; Vellutino, 1979). The model shows similar effects both early in the course of learning and when trained with limited resources (e.g. too few hidden units).

Finally, damaging the model by removing units or connections results in a pattern of errors that is somewhat similar to that of brain-injured patients with one form of surface dyslexia (Patterson, 1990; Patterson et al., 1989). Specifically, low-frequency exception words become particularly prone to being regularized (see Patterson, Coltheart, & Marshall, 1985). Overall, however, attempts to model surface dyslexia by "lesioning" the SM89 model have been less than satisfactory (see Behrmann & Bub, 1992; Coltheart et al., 1993, for criticism). We consider this and other types of developmental and acquired dyslexia in more detail after presenting new simulation results on normal skilled reading.

Evaluation of the model

In evaluating the SM89 results, it is important to bear in mind the relationship between the implemented model and the more general framework for lexical processing from which it was derived. In many ways, the implemented network is a poor approximation to the general framework: It contains no semantic representations or knowledge, it was trained on a limited vocabulary, and its feedforward architecture severely restricts the way in which information can interact within the system. In addition, as a working implementation, the network inevitably embodies specific representational and processing details that are not central to the overall theoretical framework. Such details include the specific orthographic and phonological representation schemes, the logarithmic frequency compression used in training, the use of error scores to model naming latencies, and the use of a supervised, error-correcting training procedure (but see Jordan & Rumelhart, 1992). Nonetheless, the implemented network is faithful to most of the central theoretical tenets of the general framework (see also Seidenberg, 1993): (a) The network uses distributed orthographic and phonological representations that reflect the similarities of words within each domain, (b) the computation of orthography and phonology involves nonlinear cooperative and competitive influences governed by weighted connections between units, (c) these weights encode all of the network's knowledge about how orthography and phonology are related, and (d) this knowledge is acquired gradually on the basis of the network's exposure to written words and their pronunciations. It is important to note that two central principles are lacking in the implemented network: interactivity and intrinsic variability. We consider the implications of these principles later.

Before we focus on the limitations of SM89's work, it is important to be clear about its strengths. First and foremost, the general framework is supported by an explicit computational model that actually implements the mapping from orthography to phonology. Of course, implementing a model does not make it any more correct, but it does, among other things, allow it to be more thoroughly and adequately evaluated (Seidenberg, 1993). Many models of reading are no more explicit than "box-and-arrow" diagrams accompanied by descriptive text on how processing would occur in each component (a notable recent exception to this is the implementation of Coltheart et al. [1993; Coltheart & Rastle, 1994], which is compared in detail with the current approach by Seidenberg et al., 1994). In fact, the SM89 general framework amounts to such a description. By taking the further step of implementing a portion of the framework and testing it on the identical stimuli used in empirical studies, SM89 enabled the entire approach to be evaluated in much greater detail than has been possible with previous, less explicit models.

Furthermore, it should not be overlooked that the implemented model succeeds in accounting for a considerable amount of data on normal and impaired word reading. The model reproduces the quantitative effects found in over 20 empirical studies on normal reading, as well as some basic findings on developmental and acquired dyslexia. No other existing implementation covers anything close to the same range of results.

Finally, it is important to bear in mind that the basic computational properties of the SM89 framework and implementation were not developed specifically for word reading. Rather, they derive from the much broader enterprise of connectionist modeling in cognitive domains. The same principles of distributed representations, interactivity, distributed knowledge, and gradient-descent learning are also being applied successfully to problems in high-level vision, learning and memory, speech and language, reasoning and problem solving, and motor planning and control (see Hinton, 1991; McClelland et al., 1986; Quinlan, 1991, for examples). Two distinctive aspects of the connectionist approach are its strong emphasis on general learning principles and its attempt to make contact with neurobiological as well as cognitive phenomena. Neurally plausible learning is particularly critical to understanding reading because it is unlikely that the brain has developed innate, dedicated circuitry for such an evolutionarily recent skill. Thus, the SM89 work not only makes specific contributions to the study of reading but also fits within a general computational approach for understanding how cognitive processes are learned and implemented in the brain.

The SM89 implementation does, however, have serious limitations in accounting for some empirical data. Some of these limitations no doubt stem from the lack of unimplemented portions of the framework — most important, the involvement of semantic representations, but also perhaps visual and articulatory procedures. A full consideration of the range of relevant empirical findings will be better undertaken in the General Discussion in the context of the new simulation results. Consideration of the poor nonword reading performance of the SM89 network, however, cannot be postponed. This limitation is fundamental because nonword reading is unlikely to be improved by the addition of semantics. Furthermore, Coltheart et al. (1993) have argued that, primarily as a result of its poor processing of nonwords, the model is incapable of accounting for five of six central issues in normal and impaired word reading. More fundamental, by not reading nonwords adequately, the model fails to refute the claim of dual-route theorists that reading nonwords and reading exception words require separate mechanisms.

Seidenberg and McClelland (1990) argued that the model's poor nonword reading was not an inherent problem with the general framework, but rather was the result of two specific limitations in the implementation. The first is the limited size of the training corpus. The model was exposed to only about 3,000 words, whereas the skilled readers with whom it is compared know approximately 10 times that number. Given that the only knowledge that the model has available for reading nonwords is what it has derived from words, a limited training corpus is a serious handicap.

Coltheart et al. (1993) have argued that limitations of the SM89 training corpus cannot explain the model's poor nonword reading because a system that learns GPC rules using the same corpus performs much better. This argument is fallacious, however, because the effectiveness of a training corpus depends critically on other assumptions built into the training procedure. In fact, Coltheart and colleagues' procedure for learning GPC rules has built into it a considerable amount of knowledge that is specific to reading, concerning the possible relationships between graphemes and phonemes in various contexts. In contrast, SM89 applied a general learning procedure to representations that encode only ordered triples of letters and phonemic features but nothing of their correspondences. A demonstration that the SM89 training corpus is sufficient to support good nonword reading in the context of strong, domain-specific assumptions does not invalidate the claim that the corpus may be insufficient in the context of much weaker assumptions.

The second aspect of the SM89 simulation that contributed to its poor nonword reading was the use of Wickelfeatures to represent phonology. This representational scheme has known limitations, many of which are related to how well the scheme can be extended to more realistic vocabularies (see Lachter & Bever, 1988; Pinker & Prince, 1988, for detailed criticism). In the current context, Seidenberg and McClelland (1990) pointed out that the representations do not adequately capture phonemic structure. Specifically, the features of a phoneme are not bound with each other, but only with features of neighboring phonemes. As a result, the surrounding context can too easily introduce inappropriate features, producing many single-feature errors in nonword pronunciations (e.g. TIFE $\Rightarrow$ /tIv/).

Neither the specific training corpus nor the Wickelfeature representation are central to the SM89 general framework for lexical processing. If Seidenberg and McClelland (1990) are correct in suggesting that it is these aspects of the simulation that are responsible for its poor nonword reading, their more general framework remains viable. On the other hand, the actual performance of an implementation is the main source of evidence that SM89 put forward in support of their view of the reading system. As McCloskey (1991) has recently pointed out, it is notoriously difficult both to determine whether an implementation's failings are due to fundamental or incidental properties of its design, and to predict how changes to its design would affect its behavior. Thus, to support the SM89 connectionist framework as a viable alternative to rule-based, dual-route accounts, it is critical that we develop further simulations that account for the same range of findings as the original implementation and yet also pronounce nonwords as well as skilled readers do. In this article we present such simulations.

Orthographic and phonological representations

Wickelfeatures and the dispersion problem

For the purposes of supporting good nonword reading, the Wickelfeature phonological representation has a more fundamental drawback. The problem stems from the general issue of how to represent structured objects, such as words composed of ordered strings of letters and phonemes, in connectionist networks. Connectionist researchers would like their networks to have three properties (Hinton, 1990):

1. All the knowledge in a network should be in connection weights between units.
2. To support good generalization, the network's knowledge should capture the important regularities in the domain.
3. For processing to be fast, the major constituents of an item should be processed in parallel.

The problem is that these three properties are difficult to reconcile with each other.

Consider first the standard technique of using position-specific units, sometimes called a *slot-based* representation (e.g. McClelland & Rumelhart, 1981). The first letter goes in the first slot, the second letter in the second slot, and so forth. Similarly for the output, the first phoneme goes in the first slot, and so on. With enough slots, words up to any desired length can be represented.

This scheme satisfies Properties 1 and 3 above but at a cost to Property 2. That is, processing can be done in parallel across letters and phonemes using weighted connections, but at the cost of dispersing the regularities of how letters and phonemes are related. The reason is that there must be a separate copy of each letter (and phoneme) for each slot, and because the relevant knowledge is embedded in connections that are specific to these units, this knowledge must be replicated in the connections to and from each slot. To some extent this is useful in the domain of oral reading because the pronunciation of a letter may depend on whether it occurs at the beginning, middle, or end of a word. However, the slot-based approach carries this to an extreme, with unfortunate consequences. Consider the words LOG, GLAD, and SPLIT. The fact that the letter L corresponds to the phoneme /l/ in these words must be learned and stored three separate times in the system. There is no generalization of what is learned about letters in one position to the same letter in other positions. The problem can be alleviated to some degree by aligning the slots in various ways (e.g. centered around the vowel; Daugherty & Seidenberg, 1992), but it is not eliminated completely (see Table 1). Adequate generalization still requires learning the regularities separately across several slots.

An alternative scheme is to apply the network to a single letter at a time, as in Sejnowski and Rosenberg's (1987) NETtalk model.[3] Here, the same knowledge is applied to pronouncing a letter regardless of where it occurs in a word,

and words of arbitrary length can be processed. Unfortunately, Properties 1 and 2 are now being traded off against Property 3. Processing becomes slow and sequential, which may be satisfactory in many domains but not in word reading. Note that the common finding of small but significant effects of word length on naming latency (e.g. Butler & Hains, 1979; Frederiksen & Kroll, 1976; Richardson, 1976) does not imply that the computation from orthography to phonology operates sequentially over letters; a parallel implementation of this mapping may also exhibit small length effects (as will be demonstrated in Simulation 3 of this article).

The representations used by SM89 were an attempt to avoid the specific limitations of the slot-based approach, but in the end they turn out to have a version of the same problem. Elements such as letters and phonemes are represented, not in terms of their absolute spatial position, or relative position within the word, but in terms of the adjacent elements to the left and right. This approach, which originated with Wickelgren (1969), makes the representation of each element context sensitive without being rigidly tied to position. Unfortunately, however, the knowledge of spelling–sound correspondences is still dispersed across a large number of different contexts, and adequate generalization still requires that the training effectively cover them all. Returning to Table 1, one can see that although the words LOG, GLAD, and SPLIT share the correspondence L ⇒ /l/, they have no triples of letters in common. A similar property holds in phonology among triples of phonemes or phonemic features. Thus, as in the

TABLE 1
The Dispersion Problem

Slot-based representations														
Left-justified					*Vowel-centered*									
1	*2*	*3*	*4*	*5*	*–3*	*–2*	*–1*	*0*	*1*	*Context-sensitive triples ("Wickelgraphs")*				
L	O	G				S	U	N		LOG:			_LO	LOG	OG_
G	L	A	D			S	W	A	M	GLAD:		_GL	GLA	LAD	AD_
S	P	L	I	T	S	P	L	I	M	SPLIT:	_SP	SPL	PLI	LIT	IT_

slot-based approach, although the same correspondence is present in these three cases, different units are activated. As a result, the knowledge that is learned in one context — encoded as connection weights — does not apply in other contexts, which thus hinders generalization.

Notice that the effect of dispersing regularities is much like the effect of limiting the size of the training corpus. The contribution that an element makes to the representation of the word is specific to the context in which it occurs. As a result, the knowledge learned from one item is beneficial only to other items which share that specific context. When representations disperse the regularities in the domain, the number of trained mappings that support a given pronunciation is effectively reduced. As a result, generalization to novel stimuli, as in the pronunciation of nonwords, is based on less knowledge and suffers accordingly. In a way, Seidenberg and McClelland's (1990) two suggestions for improving their model's nonword reading performance — enlarge the training corpus and improve the representations — amount to the same thing. Using improved representations that minimize the dispersion problem increases the effective size of the training corpus for a given pronunciation.

Condensing spelling–sound regularities

The hypothesis guiding the current work was the idea that the dispersion problem prevented the SM89 network from exploiting the structure of the English spelling-to-sound system as fully as human readers do. We set out, therefore, to design representations that minimize this dispersion.

The limiting case of our approach would be to have a single set of letter units, one for each letter in the alphabet, and a single set of phoneme units, one for each phoneme. Such a scheme satisfies all three of Hinton's (1990) desired properties: All of the letters in a word map to all of its phonemes simultaneously via weighted connections (and presumably hidden units), and the spelling–sound regularities are condensed because the same units and connections are involved whenever a particular letter or phoneme is present. Unfortunately, this approach has a fatal flaw: It does not preserve the relative order of letters and phonemes.

Thus, it cannot distinguish TOP from POT or SALT from SLAT.

It turns out, however, that a scheme involving only a small amount of replication is sufficient to provide a unique representation of virtually every uninflected monosyllabic word. By definition, a monosyllable contains only a single vowel, so only one set of vowel units is needed. A monosyllable may contain both an initial and a final consonant cluster, and almost every consonant can occur in either cluster, so separate sets of consonant units are required for each of these clusters. The remarkable thing is that this is nearly all that is necessary. The reason is that within an initial or final consonant cluster, there are strong phonotactic constraints that arise in large part from the structure of the articulatory system. At both ends of the syllable, each phoneme can occur only once, and the order of phonemes is strongly constrained. For example, if the phonemes /s/, /t/, and /r/ all occur in the onset cluster, they must be in that order, /str/. Given this, all that is required to specify a pronunciation is which phonemes are present in each cluster — the phonotactic constraints uniquely determine the order in which these phonemes occur.

The necessary phonotactic constraints can be expressed simply by grouping phonemes into mutually exclusive sets and ordering these sets from left to right in accordance with the left-to-right ordering constraints within consonant clusters. Once this is done, reading out a pronunciation involves simply concatenating the phonemes that are active in sequence from left to right, including at most one phoneme per mutually exclusive set (see Table 2).

There are a few cases in which two phonemes can occur in either order within a consonant cluster (e.g. /p/ and /s/ in CLASP and LAPSE). To handle such cases, it is necessary to add units to disambiguate the order (e.g. /ps/). The convention is that if /s/ and /p/ are both active, they are taken in that order unless the /ps/ unit is active, in which case the order is reversed. To cover the pronunciations in the SM89 corpus, only three such units are required: /ps/, /ks/, and /ts/. Interestingly, these combinations are sometimes written with single letters (e.g. English x, German z)

TABLE 2
Phonological and Orthographic Representations Used in the Simulations

	Phonology[a]
onset	s S C z Z j f v T D p b t d k g m n h l r w y
vowel	a e i o u @ ʌ A E I O U W Y
coda	r l m n N b g d ps ks ts s z f v p k t S Z T D C j

	Orthography
onset	Y S P T K Q C B D G F V J Z L M N R W H CH GH GN PH PS RH SH TH TS WH
vowel	E I O U A Y AI AU AW AY EA EE EI EU EW EY IE OA OE OI OO OU OW OY UE UI UY
coda	H R L M N B D G C X F V J S Z P T K Q BB CH CK DD DG FF GG GH GN KS LL NG
	NN PH PP PS RR SH SL SS TCH TH TS TT ZZ U E ES ED

Note. The notation for vowels is slightly different from that used by Seidenberg and McClelland (1989). Also, the representations differ slightly from those used by Plaut and McClelland (1993; Seidenberg, Plaut, Petersen, McClelland, & McRae, 1994). In particular, /C/ and /j/ have been added for /tS/ and /dZ/, the ordering of phonemes is somewhat different, the mutually exclusive phoneme sets have been added, and the consonantal graphemes U, GU, and QU have been eliminated. These changes capture the relevant phonotactic constraints better and simplify the encoding procedure for converting letter strings into activity patterns over grapheme units.

[a] /a/ in POT, /@/ in CAT, /e/ in BED, /i/ in HIT, /o/ in DOG, /u/ in GOOD, /A/ in MAKE, /E/ in KEEP, /I/ in BIKE, /O/ in HOPE, /U/ in BOOT, /W/ in NOW, /Y/ in BOY, /ʌ/ in CUP, /N/ in RING, /S/ in SHE, /C/ in CHIN /Z/ in BEIGE, /T/ in THIN, /D/ in THIS. All other phonemes are represented in the conventional way (e.g. /b/ in BAT). The groupings indicate sets of mutually exclusive phonemes.

and are closely related to other stop-fricative combinations, such as /C/ (/tS/) and /j/ (/dZ/), that are typically considered to be single phonemes called *affricates*. In fact, /ts/ is often treated as an affricate and, across languages, is among the most common (see Maddieson, 1984), and postvocalic /ps/ and /ks/ behave similarly to affricates (Lass, 1984).

This representational scheme applies almost as well to orthography as it does to phonology because English is an alphabetic language (i.e. parts of the written form of a word correspond to parts of its spoken form). However, the spelling units that correspond to phonemes are not necessarily single letters. Rather, they are what Venezky (1970) termed *relational units*, sometimes called graphemes, that can consist of from one to four letters (e.g. L, TH, TCH, EIGH). Because the spelling–sound regularities of English are primarily grapheme–phoneme correspondences, the regularities in the system are captured most elegantly if the orthographic units represent the graphemes present in the string rather than simply the letters that make up the word.

Unfortunately, it is not always clear what graphemes are present in a word. Consider the word SHEPHERD. In this case, there is a P next to an H,

so we might suppose that the word contains a PH grapheme, but in fact it does not; if it did it would be pronounced "she-ferd." It is apparent that the input is ambiguous in such cases. Because of this, there is no simple procedure for translating letter strings into the correct sequence of graphemes. It is, however, completely straightforward to translate a letter sequence into a pattern of activity representing all possible graphemes in the string. Thus, whenever a multiletter grapheme is present, its components are also activated. This procedure is also consistent with the treatment of /ps/, /ks/, and /ts/ in phonology.

To this point, the orthographic and phonological representations have been motivated purely by computational considerations: to condense spelling–sound regularities in order to improve generalization. Before turning to the simulations, however, it is important to be clear about the empirical assumptions that are implicit in the use of these representations. Certainly, a full account of reading behavior would have to include a specification of how the representations themselves develop prior to and during the course of reading acquisition. Such a demonstration is beyond the scope of the current work. In fact, unless we are to model everything from the eye to the mouth, we cannot avoid making assumptions about the reading system's inputs and outputs, even though, in actuality, these are learned, internal representations. The best we can do is ensure that these representations are at least broadly consistent with the relevant developmental and behavioral data.

The relevant assumptions about the phonological representations are that they are segmental (i.e. they are composed of phonemes) and that they are strongly constrained by phonotactics. We presume that this phonological structure is learned, for the most part, prior to reading acquisition, on the basis of speech comprehension and production. This is not to deny that phonological representations may become further refined over the course of reading acquisition, particularly under the influence of explicit phoneme-based instruction (see, e.g. Morais, Bertelson, Cary, & Alegria, 1986; Morais, Cary, Alegria, & Bertelson, 1979). For simplicity, however, our modeling work uses fully developed phonological representations from the outset of training.

Analogous assumptions apply with regard to the orthographic representations. We assume that they are based on letters and letter combinations and that the ordering of these obeys graphotactic constraints (although in English such constraints are generally weaker than those in phonology). Although these properties are not particularly controversial per se, orthographic representations must develop concurrently with reading acquisition. Thus, the use of fully articulated orthographic representations from the outset of reading acquisition is certainly suspect.

Again, a complete account of how orthographic representations develop from more primitive visual representations is beyond the scope of the current work. Here we provide only a general characterization of such an account. We suppose that children first learn visual representations for individual letters, perhaps much like those of other visual objects. In learning to read, they are exposed to words that consist of these familiar letters in various combinations. Explicit representations gradually develop for letter combinations that occur often or have unusual consequences (see Mozer, 1990). In the context of oral reading, many of these combinations are precisely those whose pronunciations

are not predicted by their components (e.g. TH, PH), corresponding to Venezky's (1970) relational units. Of course, explicit representations may develop for other, regularly pronounced letter combinations. In the limit, the orthographic representation might contain all the letter combinations that occur in the language. Expanding our orthographic representation with multiletter units for all of these additional combinations would have little consequence because there would be little pressure for the network to learn anything about them, given that the correspondences of their components are already learned. In this way, the particular set of multiletter graphemes we use can be viewed as an efficient simplification of a more general orthographic representation that would be expected to develop through exposure to letter combinations in words.

To be clear, we do not claim that the orthographic and phonological representations we use are fully general. Some of their idiosyncrasies stem from the fact that their design took into account specific aspects of the SM89 corpus. Nonetheless, we do claim that the principles on which the representations were derived — in particular, the use of phonotactic and graphotactic constraints to condense spelling–sound regularities — are general.

Simulation 1: Feedforward network

The first simulation was intended to test the hypothesis that the use of representations that condensed the regularities between orthography and phonology would improve the nonword reading performance of a network trained on the SM89 corpus of monosyllabic words. Specifically, the issue is whether a single mechanism, in the form of a connectionist network, can learn to read a reasonably large corpus of words, including many exception words, and yet also read pronounceable nonwords as well as skilled readers. If such a network can be developed, it would undermine the claims of dual-route theorists that skilled word reading requires the separation of lexical and sublexical procedures for mapping print to sound.

Method

Network architecture. The architecture of the network, shown in Fig. 3, consisted of three layers of units. The input layer of the network contained 105 *grapheme* units, one for each grapheme in Table 2. Similarly, the output layer contained 61 *phoneme* units. Between these two layers was an intermediate layer of 100 *hidden* units. Each unit j had a real-valued activity level or state, s_j, that ranged between 0 and 1 and was a smooth, non-linear (logistic) function, $\sigma(\cdot)$, of the unit's total input, x_j.

$$x_j = \sum_i s_i w_{ij} + b_j \qquad (1)$$

and

$$s_j = \sigma(x_j) = \frac{1}{1 + \exp(-x_j)}, \qquad (2)$$

where w_{ij} is the weight from unit i to unit j, b_j is the real-valued *bias* of unit j, and $\exp(\cdot)$ is the exponential function.

Each hidden unit received a connection from each grapheme unit and in turn sent a connection to each phoneme unit. In contrast to the Seidenberg and McClelland (1989) network, the grapheme units did not receive connections back from the hidden units. Thus, the network mapped only from orthography to phonology, not also from orthography to orthography (also see Phillips, Hay, & Smith, 1993). Weights on connections were initialized to small, random values, uniformly distributed between ±0.1. The bias terms for the hidden and phoneme units can be thought of as the weight on an additional connection from a unit whose state was always 1.0 (and so could be learned in the same way as other connection weights). Including biases, the network had a total of 17,061 connections.

Training procedure. The training corpus consisted of the 2,897 monosyllabic words in the SM89 corpus, augmented by 101 monosyllabic words missing from that corpus but used as word stimuli in various empirical studies, for a total of 2,998 words.[4] Among these were 13 sets of homographs (e.g. READ ⇒ /rEd/ and READ ⇒ /red/) — for these, both pronunciations were included in the corpus. Most of the words were uninflected, although there were a few inflected forms that had been used in some empirical studies (e.g. ROLLED, DAYS). Although the orthographic and phonological representations are not intended to handle inflected monosyllables, they happen to be capable of representing those in the training corpus, and so these were left in. It should be kept in mind, however, that

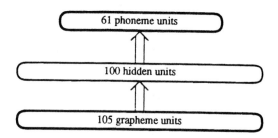

FIG. 3. The architecture of the feedforward network. Ovals represent groups of units, and arrows represent complete connectivity from one group to another.

the network's exposure to inflected forms was extremely impoverished relative to that of skilled readers.

A letter string was presented to the network by clamping the states of the grapheme units representing graphemes contained in the string to 1, and the states of all other grapheme units to 0. In processing the input, hidden units computed their states based on those of the grapheme units and the weights on connections from them (according to Equations 1 and 2), and then phoneme units computed their states based on those of the hidden units. The resulting pattern of activity over the phoneme units represented the network's pronunciation of the input letter string.

After each word was processed by the network during training, back-propagation (Rumelhart et al., 1986a, 1986b) was used to calculate how to change the connection weights so as to reduce the discrepancy between the pattern of phoneme activity generated by the network and the correct pattern for the word (i.e. the derivative of the error with respect to each weight). A standard measure of this discrepancy, and the one used by SM89, is the summed squared error, E, between generated and correct output (phoneme) states:

$$E = \sum_i (s_i - t_i)^2, \qquad (3)$$

where s_i is the state of phoneme unit i and t_i is its correct (target) value. However, in the new representation of phonology, each unit can be interpreted as an independent hypothesis that a particular phoneme is present in the output pronunciation.[5] In this case, a more appropriate error measure is the *cross-entropy, C,* between the generated and correct activity patterns (see Hinton, 1989; Rumelhart, Durbin, Golden, & Chauvin, 1995), which is also termed in *asymmetric divergence* or the *Kullback–Leibler distance* (Kullback & Leibler, 1951):

$$C = -\sum_i t_i \log_2(s_i) + (1 - t_i)\log_2(1 - s_i). \qquad (4)$$

Notice that the contribution to cross-entropy of a given unit i is simply $-\log_2(s_i)$ if its target is 1 and $-\log_2(1 - s_i)$ if its target is 0. From a practical point of view, cross-entropy has an advantage over summed squared error when it comes to correcting output units that are completely incorrect (i.e. on the opposite flat portion of the logistic function). This is a particular concern in tasks in which output units are off for most inputs — the network can eliminate almost all of its error on the task by turning all of the output units off regardless of the input, including those few that should be on for this input. The problem is that when a unit's state falls on a flat portion of the logistic function, very large weight changes are required to change its state substantially. As a unit's state diverges from its target, the change in cross-entropy increases much faster than the change in summed squared error (exponentially vs. linearly) so that cross-entropy is better able to generate sufficiently large weight changes.[6]

During training, we also gave weights a slight tendency to decay toward zero by augmenting the cross-entropy error function with a term proportional (with a constant of 0.0001 in the current simulation) to the sum of the squares of each weight, $\sum_{i<j} w_{ij}^2$. Although not critical, weight decay tends to aid generalization by constraining weights to grow only to the extent that they are needed to reduce the error on the task (Hinton, 1989).

In the SM89 simulation, the probability that a word was presented to the network for training during an epoch was a logarithmic function of its written frequency (Kuçera & Francis, 1967). In the current simulation, we used the same compressed frequency values instead to scale the error derivatives calculated by back-propagation. This manipulation had essentially the same effect: More frequent words had a stronger impact than less frequent words on the knowledge learned by the system. In fact, using frequencies in this manner is exactly equivalent to updating the weights after each sweep through an expanded training corpus in which the number of times a word is presented is proportional to its (compressed) frequency. The new procedure was adopted for two reasons. First, by presenting the entire training corpus every epoch, learning rates on each connection could be adapted independently (Jacobs, 1988; but see Sutton, 1992, for a recently developed on-line version).[7] Second, by implementing frequencies with multiplication rather than sampling, we could use any range of frequencies; later we will investigate the effects of using the actual Kuçera and

Francis (1967) frequencies in simulations. SM89 was constrained to use a logarithmic compression because less severe compressions would have meant that the lowest frequency words might never have been presented to their network.

The actual weight changes administered at the end of an epoch were a combination of the accumulated frequency-weighted error derivatives and a proportion of the previous weight changes:

$$\Delta w_{ij}^{[t]} = \varepsilon\, \varepsilon_{ij}\left(\frac{\partial C}{\partial w_{ij}} + \alpha \Delta w_{ij}^{[t-1]}\right), \qquad (5)$$

where t is the epoch number, ε is the global learning rate (0.001 in the current simulation), ε_{ij} is the connection-specific learning rate, C is the cross-entropy error function with weight decay, and α is the contribution of past weight changes, sometimes termed *momentum* (0.9 after the first 10 epochs in the current simulation). We introduced momentum only after the first few initial epochs to avoid magnifying the effects of the initial weight gradients, which were very large because, for each word, any activity of all but a few phoneme units — those that should be active — produced a large amount of error (Plaut & Hinton, 1987).

Testing procedure. The network, as described above, learned to take activity patterns over the grapheme units and produce corresponding activity patterns over the phoneme units. The behavior of human readers, however, is better described in terms of producing phoneme strings in response to letter strings. Accordingly, for a direct comparison of the network's behavior with that of human readers, we needed one procedure for encoding letter strings as activity patterns over the grapheme units and another procedure for decoding activity patterns over the phoneme units into phoneme strings.

The encoding procedure we used was the same one that generated the input to the network for each word in the training corpus. To convert a letter string into an activity pattern over the grapheme units, the string is parsed into onset consonant cluster, vowel, and final (coda) consonant cluster. This involved simply locating in the string the leftmost contiguous block composed of the letters A, E, I, O, U, or (non-initial) Y. This block of letters was encoded using vowel graphemes listed in Table 2 — any grapheme contained in the vowel substrings was activated; all others were left inactive. The substrings to the right and left of the vowel substring were encoded similarly using the onset and coda consonant graphemes, respectively. For example, the word

SCHOOL activated the onset units S, C, H, and CH, the vowel units O and OO, and the coda unit L. Notice that in words like GUEST, QUEEN, and SUEDE, the U is parsed as a vowel although it functions as a consonant (cf. GUST, QUEUE, and SUE; Venezky, 1970). This is much like the issue with PH in SHEPHERD — such ambiguity was left for the network to cope with. The analogous encoding procedure for phonemes used to generate the training patterns for words was even simpler because monosyllabic pronunciations must contain exactly one vowel.

The decoding procedure for producing pronunciations from phoneme activities generated by the network was likewise straightforward. As shown in Table 2, phonemes are grouped into mutually exclusive sets, and these sets are ordered left to right (and top to bottom in the table). This grouping and ordering encode the phonotactic constraints that are necessary to disambiguate pronunciations. The response of the network was simply the ordered concatenation of all active phonemes (i.e. with state above 0.5) that were the most active in their set. There were only two exceptions to this rule. The first was that, because monosyllabic pronunciations must contain a vowel, the most active vowel was included in the network's response regardless of its activity level. The second exception relates to the affricate-like units /ps/, /ks/, and /ts/. As described earlier, if one of these units was active along with its components, the order of those components in the response was reversed.

The simplicity of these encoding and decoding procedures is a significant advantage of the current representations over those used by SM89. In the latter case, reconstructing a unique string of phonemes corresponding to a pattern of activity over triples of phonemic features is exceedingly difficult, and sometimes impossible (also see Mozer, 1991; Rumelhart & McClelland, 1986). In fact, SM89 did not confront this problem — rather, they simply selected the best among a set of alternative pronunciations on the basis of their error scores. In a sense, the SM89 model does not produce explicit pronunciations; it enables another procedure to select among alternatives. In contrast, the current decoding procedure does not require externally generated alternatives; every possible pattern of activity over the phoneme units corresponds directly and unambiguously to a particular string of phonemes. Nonetheless, it should be kept in mind that the encoding and decoding procedures are external to the network and, hence, constitute additional assumptions about the nature of the knowledge and processing involved in skilled reading, as discussed earlier.

Results

Word reading. After 300 epochs of training, the network correctly pronounced all of the 2,972 nonhomographic words in the training corpus. For each of the 13 homographs, the network produced one of the correct pronunciations, although typically the competing phonemes for the alternatives were about equally active. For example, the network pronounced LEAD as /lEd/; the activation of the /E/ was 0.56, whereas the activation of /e/ was 0.44. These differences reflect the relative consistency of the alternatives with the pronunciations of other words.

Given the nature of the network, this level of performance on the training corpus is optimal. Because the network is deterministic, it always produces the same output for a given input. Thus, in fact, it is impossible for the network to learn to produce both pronunciations of any of the homographs. Note that this determinacy is not an intrinsic limitation of connectionist networks (see, e.g. Movellan & McClelland, 1993). It merely reflects the fact that the general principle of intrinsic variability was not included in the present simulation for practical reasons — to keep the computational demands of the simulation reasonable.

For the present purposes, the important finding is that the trained network reads both regular and exception words correctly. We were also interested in how well the network replicates the effects of frequency and consistency on naming latency. However, we will return to this issue after we consider the more pressing issue of the network's performance in reading nonwords.

Nonword reading. We tested the network on three lists of nonwords from two empirical studies. The first two lists came from an experiment by Glushko (1979), in which he compared subjects, reading of 43 nonwords derived from regular words (e.g. HEAN from DEAN) with their reading of 43 nonwords derived from exception words (e.g. HEAF from DEAF). Although Glushko originally termed these *regular* nonwords and *exception* nonwords, respectively, they are more appropriately characterized in terms of whether their body neighborhood is consistent or not, and hence we will refer to them as *consistent* or *inconsistent* nonwords. The third nonword list came from a study by McCann and Besner (1987) in which they compared performance on a set of 80 pseudohomophones (e.g. BRANE) with a set of 80 control nonwords (e.g. FRANE). We used only their control nonwords in the present investigation because we believe pseudohomophone effects are mediated by aspects of the reading system, such as semantics and the articulatory system, that were not implemented in our simulation (see the General Discussion).

As nonwords are, by definition, novel stimuli, exactly what constitutes the "correct" pronunciation of a nonword is a matter of considerable debate (see, e.g. Masterson, 1985; Seidenberg et al., 1994). The complexity of this issue will become apparent momentarily. For the purposes of an initial comparison, we considered the pronunciation of a nonword to be correct if it was regular, as defined by adhering to the GPC rules outlined by Venezky (1970).

Table 3 presents the correct performance of skilled readers reported by Glushko (1979) and by McCann and Besner (1987) on their nonword lists and the corresponding performance of the network. Table 4 lists the errors made by the network on these lists.

First consider Glushko's (1979) consistent nonwords. The network made only a single minor mistake on these items, just failing to introduce the transitional /y/ in MUNE. In fact, this inclusion varies across dialects of English (e.g. DUNE ⇒ /dUn/ vs. /dyUn/). In the training corpus, the four words ending in _UNE (DUNE, JUNE, PRUNE, TUNE) are all coded without the /y/. In any case, overall both the network and human readers have no difficulty on these relatively easy nonwords.

The situation is rather different for the inconsistent nonwords. Both the network and the human

readers produced non-regular pronunciations for a significant subset of these items, with the network being slightly more prone to do so. However, a closer examination of the responses in these cases reveals why. Consider the nonword GROOK. The grapheme OO most frequently corresponds to /U/, as in BOOT, and so the correct (regular) pronunciation of GROOK is /grUk/. However, the body _OOK is almost always pronounced /u/, as in TOOK. The only exception to this among the 12 words ending in _OOK in the training corpus is SPOOK ⇒ /spUk/. This suggests that /gruk/ should be the correct pronunciation.

Actually, the issue of whether the network's pronunciation is correct or not is less relevant than the issue of whether the network behaves similarly to human readers. In fact, both the human readers and the network were sensitive to the context in which vowels occur, as is evidenced by their much greater tendency to produce irregular pronunciations for inconsistent nonwords compared with consistent nonwords. Glushko (1979) found that 80% of readers' irregular responses to inconsistent nonwords were consistent with some other pronunciation of the nonword's body in the Kuçera and Francis (1967) corpus, which left only 4.1% of all responses as actual errors. In the network, all of the irregular responses to inconsistent nonwords matched some other pronunciation in the training corpus for the same body, with half of these being the most frequent pronunciation of the body. None of the network's responses to inconsistent nonwords were actual errors. Overall, the network performed as well if not slightly better than skilled readers on the Glushko nonword lists. Appendix B lists all of the pronunciations accepted as correct for each of the Glushko nonwords.

TABLE 3
Percentages of Regular Pronunciations of Nonwords

| Reader | Glushko (1979) | | McCann and Besner (1987) |
	Consistent nonwords	Inconsistent nonwords	Control nonwords
Humans	93.8	78.3	88.6
Network	97.7	72.1	85.0

TABLE 4
Errors by the Feedforward Network in Pronouncing Nonwords

Glushko (1979)			McCann and Besner (1987)		
Nonword	*Correct*	*Response*	*Nonword*	*Correct*	*Response*
Consistent Nonwords			Control Nonwords		
(1/43)			(12/80)		
MUNE	/myUn/	/m(y 0.43)Un/	*PHOYCE	/fYs/	/(f 0.42)Y(s 0.00)/
Inconsistent Nonwords			*TOLPH	/tolf/	/tOl(f 0.12)/
(12/43)					
BILD	/bild/	/bIld/	*ZUPE	/zUp/	/zyUp/
BOST	/bost/	/bOst/	SNOCKS	/snaks/	/snask(ks 0.31)/
COSE	/kOz/	/kOs/	*LOKES	/lOks/	/lOsk(ks 0.02)/
GROOK	/grUk/	/gruk/	*YOWND	/yWnd/	/(y 0.47)and/
LOME	/lOm/	/lʌm/	KOWT	/kWt/	/kOt/
MONE	/mOn/	/mʌn/	FAIJE	/fAj/	/fA(j 0.00)/
PILD	/pild/	/pIld/	*ZUTE	/zUt/	/zyUt/
PLOVE	/plOv/	/plʌv/	*VEEZE	/vEz/	/(v 0.40)Ez/
POOT	/pUt/	/put/	*PRAX	/pr@ks/	/pr@sk(ks 0.33)/
SOOD	/sUd/	/sud/	JINJE	/jinj/	/jIn(j 0.00)/
SOST	/sost/	/sʌst/			
WEAD	/wEd/	/wed/			

Note. /a/ in POT, /@/ in CAT, /e/ in BED, /i/ in HIT, /o/ in DOG, /u/ in GOOD, /A/ in MAKE, /E/ in KEEP, /I/ in BIKE, /O/ in HOPE, /U/ in BOOT, /W/ in NOW, /Y/ in BOY, /ʌ/ in CUP, /N/ in RING, /S/ in SHE, /C/ in CHIN, /Z/ in BEIGE, /T/ in THIN, /D/ in THIS. The activity levels of correct but missing phonemes are listed in parentheses. In these cases, the actual response is what falls outside the parentheses. Words marked with "*" remain errors after properties of the training corpus are considered (as explained in the text).

Both the human readers and the network found McCann and Besner's (1987) control nonwords more difficult to pronounce, which is not surprising because the list contains a number of orthographically unusual nonwords (e.g. JINJE, VAWX). Overall, the network's performance was slightly worse than that of the human readers. However, many of the network's errors can be understood in terms of specific properties of the training corpus and network design. First, although there is no word in the training corpus with the body _OWT, medial ow is often pronounced /O/ (e.g. BOWL ⇒ /bOl/) and so KOWT ⇒ /kOt/ should be considered a reasonable response. Second, two of the errors were on inflected forms, SNOCKS and LOKES, and as previously acknowledged, the network had minimal experience with inflections and was not designed to apply to them. Finally, there are no instances in the training corpus of words containing the grapheme J in the coda, and so the network could not possibly have learned to map it

to /j/ in phonology. In a way, for a nonword like JINJE, the effective input to the network is JINE, to which the network's response /jIn/ is correct. This also applies to the nonword FAIJE. Excluding these and the inflected forms from the scoring, and considering KOWT ⇒ /kOt/ correct, the network performed correctly on 69/76 (90.8%) of the remaining control nonwords, which is slightly better than the human readers. Most of the remaining errors of the network involved correspondences that were infrequent or variable in the training corpus (e.g. PH ⇒ /f/, U ⇒ /yU/).

It must be acknowledged that the failure of the model on inflected forms and on those with J in the coda are real shortcomings that would have to be addressed in a completely adequate account of word reading. Our purpose in separating out these items in the above analysis simply acknowledges that the model's limitations are easily understood in terms of specific properties of the training corpus.

Is it a dual-route model? One possibility, consistent with dual-route theories, is that, over the course of learning the network partitioned itself into two subnetworks, one that reads regular words and another that reads exception words. If this were the case, some hidden units would contribute to exception words but not to nonwords, whereas others would contribute to nonwords but not to exception words. To test this possibility, we measured the contribution a hidden unit makes to pronouncing a letter string by the amount of increase in cross-entropy error when the unit is removed from the network. If the network had partitioned itself, there would be a negative correlation across hidden units between the number of exception words and the number of nonwords to which each hidden unit makes a substantial contribution (defined as greater than 0.2). In fact, for the Taraban and McClelland (1987) exception words and a set of orthographically matched nonwords (listed in Appendix A), there was a moderate positive correlation between the numbers of exception words and nonwords to which hidden units contributed, $r = .25$, $t(98) = 2.59$, $p = .011$ (see Fig. 4). Thus, some units were more important for the overall task and some were less important, but the network had not partitioned itself into one system that learned the rules and another system that learned the exceptions.

Frequency and consistency effects. It is important to verify that in addition to producing good nonword reading, the new model replicates the basic effects of frequency and consistency in naming latency. Like the SM89 network, the current network takes the same amount of time to compute the pronunciation of any letter string. Hence, we must also resort to using an error score as an analogue of naming latency. In particular, we used the cross-entropy between the network's generated pronunciation of a word and its correct pronunciation, because this is the measure that the network was trained to minimize. Later we examine the effects of frequency and consistency directly in the settling time of an equivalently trained recurrent network when pronouncing various types of words.

Figure 5 shows the mean cross-entropy error of the network in pronouncing words of varying

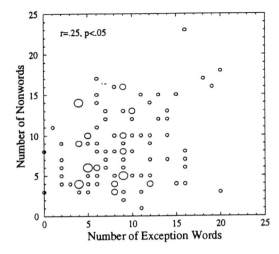

FIG. 4. The numbers of exception words and nonwords ($n = 48$ for each, listed in Appendix A) to which each hidden unit makes a significant contribution, as indicated by an increase in cross-entropy error of at least 0.2 when the unit is removed from the network. Each circle represents one or more hidden units, and the size of the circle is proportional to the number of hidden units making significant contributions to the indicated numbers of exception words and nonwords.

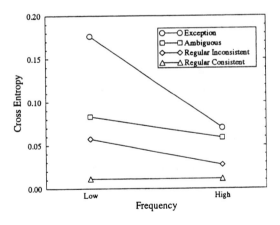

FIG. 5. Mean cross-entropy error produced by the feedforward network for words with various degrees of spelling–sound consistency (listed in Appendix A) as a function of frequency.

degrees of spelling–sound consistency as a function of frequency. Overall, high-frequency words produced less error than low-frequency words, $F(1, 184) = 17.1$, $p < .001$. However, frequency interacted significantly with consistency,

$F(3, 184) = 5.65$, $p = .001$. Post hoc comparisons within each word type separately revealed that the effect of frequency reached significance at the .05 level only for exception words (although the effect for regular inconsistent words was significant at .053). The effect of frequency among all regular words (consistent and inconsistent) just failed to reach significance, $F(1, 94) = 3.14$, $p = .08$.

There was also a main effect of consistency in the error made by the network in pronouncing words, $F(3, 184) = 24.1$, $p < .001$. Furthermore, collapsed across frequency, all post hoc pairwise comparisons of word types were significant. Specifically, regular consistent words produced less error than regular inconsistent words, which in turn produced less error than ambiguous words, which in turn produced less error than exception words. Interestingly, the effect of consistency was significant when only high-frequency words are considered, $F(3, 92) = 12.3$, $p < .001$. All pairwise comparisons were also significant except between exception words and ambiguous words. This contrasts with the performance of normal human readers, who typically show little or no effect of consistency among high-frequency words (e.g. Seidenberg, 1985; Seidenberg et al., 1984).

Summary

A feedforward connectionist network, which used orthographic and phonological representations that condense the regularities between these domains, was trained on an extended version of the SM89 corpus of monosyllabic words. After training, the network read regular and exception words flawlessly and yet also read pronounceable nonwords (Glushko, 1979; McCann & Besner, 1987) essentially as well as skilled readers. Minor discrepancies in performance could be ascribed to nonessential aspects of the simulation. Critically, the network did not segregate itself over the course of training into separate mechanisms for pronouncing exception words and nonwords. Thus, the performance of the network directly refutes the claims of dual-route theorists that skilled word reading requires the separation of lexical and sublexical procedures for mapping print to sound.

Furthermore, the error produced by the network on various types of words, as measured by the cross-entropy between the generated and correct pronunciations, replicates the standard findings of frequency, consistency, and their interaction in the naming latencies of human readers (Andrews, 1982; Seidenberg, 1985; Seidenberg et al., 1984; Taraban & McClelland, 1987; Waters & Seidenberg, 1985). A notable exception, however, is that, unlike human readers and the SM89 network, the current network exhibited a significant effect of consistency among high-frequency words.

Analytic account of frequency and consistency effects

The empirical finding that naming latencies for exception words are slower and far more sensitive to frequency than those for regular words has often been interpreted as requiring explicit lexical representations and grapheme-phoneme correspondence rules. By recasting regularity effects in terms of spelling–sound consistency (Glushko, 1979; Jared et al., 1990), the SM89 network and the one presented in the previous section reproduce the empirical phenomena without these properties. What, then, are the properties of these networks (and of the human language system, by our account) that give rise to the observed pattern of frequency and consistency effects?

The relevant empirical pattern of results can be described in the following way. In general, high-frequency words are named faster than low-frequency words, and words with greater spelling–sound consistency are named faster than words with less consistency. However, the effect of frequency diminishes as consistency is increased, and the effect of consistency diminishes as frequency is increased. A natural interpretation of this pattern is that frequency and consistency contribute independently to naming latency but that the system as a whole is subject to what might be termed a gradual ceiling effect: The magnitude of increments in performance decreases as performance improves. Thus, if either the frequency or the consistency of a set of words is sufficiently high on its own to produce fast naming latencies, increasing the other factor will yield little further improvement.

A close analysis of the operation of connectionist networks reveals that these effects are a direct consequence of properties of the processing and learning in these networks — specifically, the principles of nonlinearity, adaptivity, and distributed representations and knowledge referred to earlier. In a connectionist network, the weight changes induced by a word during training serve to reduce the error on that word (and hence, by definition, its naming latency). The frequency of a word is reflected in how often it is presented to the network (or, as in the previous simulation, in the explicit scaling of the weight changes it induces). Thus, word frequency directly amplifies weight changes that are helpful to the word itself.

The consistency of the spelling–sound correspondences of two words is reflected in the similarity of the orthographic and phonological units that they activate. Furthermore, two words will induce similar weight changes to the extent that they activate similar units. Given that the weight changes induced by a word are superimposed on the weight changes for all other words, a word will tend to be helped by the weight changes for words whose spelling–sound correspondences are consistent with its own (and, conversely, hindered by the weight changes for inconsistent words). Thus, frequency and consistency effects contribute independently to naming latency because they both arise from similar weight changes that are simply added together during training.

Over the course of training, the magnitudes of the weights in the network increase in proportion to the accumulated weight changes. These weight changes result in corresponding increases in the summed input to output units that should be active, and decreases in the summed input to units that should be inactive. However, because of the nonlinearity of the input–output function of units, these changes do not translate directly into proportional reductions in error. Rather, as the magnitude of the summed inputs to output units increases, their states gradually asymptote toward 0 or 1. As a result, a given increase in the summed input to a unit yields progressively smaller decrements in error over the course of training. Thus, although frequency and consistency each contribute to the weights, and hence to the summed input to units, their effect on error is subjected to a gradual ceiling effect as unit states are driven toward extremal values.

The frequency–consistency equation

To see the effects of frequency and consistency in connectionist networks more directly, it will help to consider a network that embodies some of the same general priniciples as the SM89 and feedforward networks but that is simple enough to permit a closed-form analysis (following Anderson, Silverstein, Ritz, & Jones, 1977; also see Stone, 1986). In particular, consider a nonlinear network without hidden units and trained with a correlational (Hebbian) rather than an error-correcting learning rule (see Fig. 6). Such a network is a specific instantiation of Van Orden et al.'s (1990) *covariant learning hypothesis*. To simplify the presentation, we will assume that input patterns are composed of 1s and 0s, output patterns are specified in terms of +1s and −1s, connection weights are all initialized to zero, and units have no bias terms. We will derive an equation that expresses in concise form the effects of frequency and consistency on the response of this network to any given input.

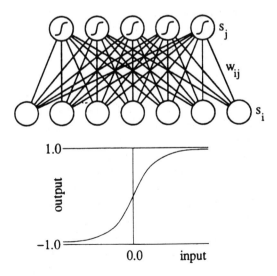

FIG. 6. A simple network for analyzing frequency and consistency effects and the sigmoidal input–output function of its units.

A learning trial involves setting the states of the input units to the input pattern (e.g. orthography) for a word, setting the output units to the desired output pattern (e.g. phonology) for the word, and adjusting the weight from each input unit to each output unit according to

$$\Delta w_{ij} = \varepsilon s_i s_j, \tag{6}$$

where ε is a learning rate constant, s_i is the state of input unit i, s_j is the state of output unit j, and w_{ij} is the weight on the connection between them. After each input–output training pattern is presented once in this manner, the value of each connection weight is simply the sum of the weight changes for each individual pattern:

$$w_{ij} = \varepsilon \sum_p s_i^{[p]} s_j^{[p]}, \tag{7}$$

where p indexes individual training patterns.

After training, the network's performance on a given test pattern is determined by setting the states of the input units to the appropriate input pattern and having the network compute the states of the output units. In this computation, the state of each output unit is assumed to be a nonlinear, monotonically increasing function of the sum, over input units, of the state of the input unit times the weight on the connection from it:

$$s_j^{[t]} = \sigma(\sum_i s_i^{[t]} w_{ij}), \tag{8}$$

where t is the test pattern and $\sigma(\cdot)$ is the nonlinear input–unit function. An example of such a function, the standard logistic function commonly used in connectionist networks, is shown in Fig. 6. The input–output function of the output units need not be this particular function, but it must have certain of its properties: It must vary monotonically with input, and it must approach its extreme values (here, ± 1) at a diminishing rate as the magnitude of the summed input increases (positively or negatively). We call such functions *sigmoid* functions.

We can substitute the derived expression for each weight w_{ij} from Equation 7 into Equation 8, and pull the constant term ε out of the summation over i to obtain

$$s_j^{[t]} = \sigma(\varepsilon \sum_i s_i^{[t]} \sum_p s_i^{[p]} s_j^{[p]}). \tag{9}$$

This equation indicates that the activation of each output unit reflects a sigmoid function of the learning rate constant ε times a sum of terms, each consisting of the activation of one of the input units in the test pattern times the sum, over all training patterns, of the activation of the input unit times the activation of the output unit. In our present formulation, where the input unit's activation is 0 or 1, this sum reflects the extent to which the output unit's activation tends to be equal to 1 when the input unit's activation is equal to 1. Specifically, it will be exactly equal to the number of times the output unit is equal to 1 when the input unit is equal to 1, minus the number of times the output unit is equal to -1 when the input unit is equal to 1. We can see from Equation 9 that if, over an entire ensemble of training patterns, there is a consistent value of the activation of an output unit when an input unit is active, then the connection weights between them will come to reflect this. If the training patterns come from a completely regular environment, such that each output's activation depends on only one input unit and is completely uncorrelated with the activation of every other input unit, then all the weights to each output unit will equal 0 except the weight from the particular input unit on which it depends. (If the training patterns are sampled randomly from a larger space of patterns, the sample will not reflect the true correlations exactly but will be scattered approximately normally around the true value.) Thus, the learning procedure discovers which output units depend on which input units and sets the weights accordingly. For our purposes in understanding quasi-regular domains, in which the dependencies are not so discrete in character, the weights will come to reflect the degree of consistency between each input unit and each output unit over the entire ensemble of training patterns.

Equation 9 can be written a different way to reflect a relationship that is particularly relevant to the word reading literature, in which the frequency of a particular word and the consistency of its pronunciation with the pronunciations of other, similar words are known to influence the accuracy and latency of pronunciation. The rearrangement expresses a very revealing relationship between the output at test and the similarity of the test pattern to each input pattern:

$$s_j^{[t]} = \sigma(\varepsilon \sum_p s_j^{[p]} \sum_i s_i^{[p]} s_i^{[t]}). \tag{10}$$

This expression shows the relationship between the state of an output unit at test as a function of its states during training and the *similarity* between the test input pattern and each training input pattern, measured in terms of their dot product, $\sum_i s_i^{[p]} s_i^{[t]}$. For input patterns consisting of 1s and 0s, this measure amounts to the number of 1s the two patterns have in common, which we refer to as the *overlap* of training pattern p and test pattern t and designate $\mathcal{O}^{[pt]}$. Substituting into the previous expression, we find that the state of an output unit at test reflects the sum over all training patterns of the unit's output for that pattern times the overlap of the pattern with the test pattern:

$$s_j^{[t]} = \sigma(\varepsilon \sum_p s_j^{[p]} \mathcal{O}^{[pt]}). \tag{11}$$

Notice that the product $s_j^{[p]} \mathcal{O}^{[pt]}$ is a measure of the input–output consistency of the training and test patterns. To see this, suppose that the inputs for the training and testing patterns have considerable overlap. Then the contribution of the training pattern depends on the sign of the output unit's state for that pattern. If this sign agrees with that of the appropriate state for the test pattern (i.e. the two patterns are consistent), the training pattern will help to move the state of the output unit toward the appropriate extreme value for the test pattern. However, if the signs of the states for the training and test patterns disagree (i.e. the patterns are inconsistent), performance on the test pattern will be worse for having learned the training pattern. As the input for the training pattern becomes less similar to that of the test pattern, reducing $\mathcal{O}^{[pt]}$, the impact of their consistency on test performance diminishes.

To clarify the implications of Equation 11, it will help if we consider some simple cases. First, suppose that the network is trained on only one pattern and tested with a variety of patterns. Then the state of each output unit during testing will be a monotonic function of its value in the training pattern times the overlap of the training and test input patterns. As long as there is any overlap in these patterns, the test output will have the same sign as the training output, and its magnitude will increase with the overlap between the test pattern and training pattern. Thus, the response of each output unit varies with the similarity of the test pattern to the pattern used in training.

As a second example, suppose we test only on the training pattern itself but vary the number of training trials on the pattern. In this case, the summation over the p training patterns in Equation 11 reduces to a count of the number of training presentations of the pattern. Thus, the state of the output unit on this pattern will approach its correct asymptotic value of ±1 as the number of training presentations increases.

Finally, consider the more general case in which several different input–output patterns are presented during training, with each one presented some number of times. Then, elaborating on Equation 11, we can write the state of an output unit at test as

$$s_j^{[t]} = \sigma(\varepsilon \sum_p F^{[p]} s_j^{[p]} \mathcal{O}^{[pt]}). \tag{12}$$

where $F^{[p]}$ is the number (frequency) of training presentations of pattern p.

We will refer to Equation 12 as the *frequency–consistency equation*. Relating this equation to word and nonword reading simply involves identifying the input to the network with a representation of the spelling of a word, and the output of the network with a representation of its pronunciation. Given the assumption that stronger activations correspond to faster naming latencies, we can use the frequency–consistency equation to derive predictions about the relative naming latencies of different types of words. In particular, the equation provides a basis for understanding why naming latency depends on the frequency of a word, $F^{[p]}$, and the consistency of its spelling–sound correspondences with those of other words, $s_j^{[p]} \mathcal{O}^{[pt]}$. It also accounts for the fact that the effect of consistency diminishes as the frequency of the word increases (and vice versa), because high-frequency words push the value of the sum out into the tail of the input–output function, where influences of other factors are reduced (see Fig. 7).

Quantitative results with a simple corpus

To make the implications of the frequency–consistency equation more concrete, suppose a given output unit should have a value of +1 if a word's pronunciation contains the vowel /I/ (as in DIVE) and −1 if it contains the vowel /i/ (as in GIVE). Suppose further that we have trained the network on a set of words ending in _IVE which all contain either /I/ or /i/ as the vowel. Then the frequency–consistency equation tells us immediately that the response to a given test input should reflect the influence of every one of these words to some degree. If all else is held constant, the higher the frequency of the word, the more closely the output will approach the desired value. If the frequency of the word itself is held constant, the more other similar words agree with its pronunciation (and the higher their frequency), the more closely the output will approach the correct extreme value. The distance from the desired value

will vary continuously with the difference between the total influence of the neighbors that agree with the word and the neighbors that disagree, with the contribution of each neighbor being weighted by its similarity to the word and its frequency. When the word itself has a high frequency, it will tend to push the activation close to the correct extreme. Near the extremes, the slope of the function relating the summed input to the state of the output unit becomes relatively shallow, so the influence of the neighbors is diminished.

To illustrate these effects, Fig. 8 shows the cross-entropy error for a particular output unit as we vary the frequency of the word being tested and its consistency with 10 other, overlapping words (also see Van Orden, 1987). For simplicity, we assume that all 10 words have a frequency of 1.0 and an overlap of 0.75 with the test word — this would be true, for example, if input units represented letters and words differed in a single letter out of four. Four degrees of consistency are examined: (a) exception words (e.g. GIVE), for which all but one of the 10 neighbors disagree with the test word on the value of the output unit; (b) ambiguous words (e.g. PLOW), for which the neighbors are split evenly between those that agree and those that disagree; (c) regular inconsistent words (e.g. DIVE), for which most neighbors agree but two disagree (namely GIVE and LIVE); and (d) regular consistent words (e.g. DUST), for which

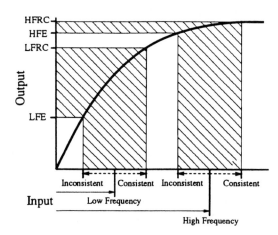

FIG. 7. A frequency by consistency interaction arising out of applying an asymptotic output activation function to the additive input contributions of frequency (solid arrows) and consistency (dashed arrows). Notice in particular that the identical contribution from consistency has a much weaker effect on high-frequency words than on low-frequency words. Only the top half of the logistic activation function is shown. HF = high frequency; LF = low frequency; RC = regular consistent; E = exception.

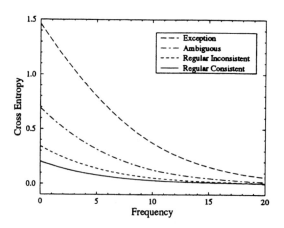

FIG. 8. The effects of frequency and consistency in a network without hidden units trained with correlational (Hebbian) learning ($\varepsilon = 0.2$ in Equation 12).

all neighbors agree on value of the output unit. In the present analysis, these different cases are completely characterized in terms of a single variable: the consistency of the pronunciation of the vowel in the test word with its pronunciation in other words with overlapping spellings. The analysis clearly reveals a graded effect of consistency that diminishes with increasing frequency.

Error correction and hidden units

It should be noted that the Hebbian approach described here does not, in fact, provide an adequate mechanism for learning the spelling–sound correspondences in English. For this, we require networks with hidden units trained using an error-correcting learning rule such as back-propagation. In this section we take some steps in the direction of extending the analyses to these more complex cases.

First we consider the implications of using an error-correcting learning rule rather than Hebbian learning, still within a network with no hidden units. Back-propagation is a generalization of one such rule, known as the *delta rule* (Widrow & Hoff, 1960). The first observation is that, when the delta rule is used, the change in weight w_{ij} that is due to training on pattern p is proportional to the state of the input unit, $s_i^{[p]}$, times the partial derivative to the error on pattern p with respect to the summed input of the output unit j, $\delta_j^{[p]}$, rather than simply times the correct state of unit j, $s_j^{[p]}$ (cf. Equation 6). As a result, Equation 12 becomes

$$s_j^{[t]} = \sigma(\varepsilon \sum_p F^{[p]} \delta_j^{[p]} \mathcal{O}^{[pt]}).\tag{13}$$

Matters are more complex here because $\delta_j^{[p]}$ depends on the actual performance of the network on each trial. However, $\delta_j^{[p]}$ will always have the same sign as $s_j^{[p]}$, because an output unit's error always has the same sign as its target as long as the target is an extreme value of the activation function (± 1 here), and because only unit j is affected by a change to its input. Thus, as in the Hebbian case, training on a word that is consistent with the test word will always help unit i to be correct, and training on an inconsistent word will always hurt, thereby giving rise to the consistency effect.

The main difference between the Hebb rule and the delta rule is that, with the latter, if a set of weights exists that allows the network to produce the correct output for each training pattern, the learning procedure will eventually converge to it.[8] This is generally not the case with Hebbian learning, which often results in responses for some cases that are incorrect. To illustrate this, we consider applying the two learning rules to a training set for which a solution does exist. The solution is found by the delta rule and not by the Hebb rule.

The problem is posed within the framework we have already been examining. The specific network consists of 11 input units (with values of 0 and 1) representing letters of a word. The input units send direct connections to a single output unit that should be +1 if the pronunciation of the word contains the vowel /I/ but −1 if it contains the vowel /i/. Table 5 shows the input patterns and the target output for each case, as well as the net inputs and activations that result from training with each learning rule. There are 10 items in the training set, six with the body _INT and four with the body _INE. The _INE words all take the vowel /I/, so for these the vowel has a target activation of +1; five of the _INT words take /i/, so the vowel has a target of −1. The _INT words also include the exception word PINT that takes the vowel /I/. For this analysis, each word is given an equal frequency of 1.

Table 6 lists the weights from each input unit to the output unit that are acquired after training with each learning rule. For the Hebb rule, this involved five epochs of training using a learning rate $\varepsilon = 0.1$. The resulting weights are equal to 0.5 (the number of epochs times the learning rate) times the number of training items in which the letter is present and the vowel is /I/, minus the number of items in which the letter is present and the vowel is /i/. Specifically, the letters L and M occur once with /I/ and once with /i/, so their weights are 0; the letters I and N occur five times with /I/ and five times with /i/, so their weights are also 0. Final E and final T have the largest magnitude weights; E is strongly positive because it occurs four times with /I/ and never with /i/, and T is strongly negative because it occurs five

TABLE 5
Input Patterns, Targets, and Activations After Training With the Hebb Rule and the Delta Rule

	Letter inputs												Hebb rule		Delta rule	
Word	D	F	H	L	M	P	T	I	N	E	T	Target	Net	Act	Net	Act
DINT	1	0	0	0	0	0	0	1	1	0	1	−1	−2.5	−0.85	−2.35	−0.82
HINT	0	0	1	0	0	0	0	1	1	0	1	−1	−2.5	−0.85	−2.29	−0.82
LINT	0	0	0	1	0	0	0	1	1	0	1	−1	−2.0	−0.76	−1.70	−0.69
MINT	0	0	0	0	1	0	0	1	1	0	1	−1	−2.0	−0.76	−1.70	−0.69
PINT	0	0	0	0	0	1	0	1	1	0	1	+1	−1.0	−0.46	0.86	0.41
TINT	0	0	0	0	0	0	1	1	1	0	1	−1	−2.5	−0.85	−2.25	−0.81
FINE	0	1	0	0	0	0	0	1	1	1	0	+1	2.5	0.85	3.31	0.93
LINE	0	0	0	1	0	0	0	1	1	1	0	+1	2.0	0.76	2.52	0.85
MINE	0	0	0	0	1	0	0	1	1	1	0	+1	2.0	0.76	2.52	0.85
PINE	0	0	0	0	0	1	0	1	1	1	0	+1	3.0	0.91	5.09	0.98

Note. "Net" is the net input of the output unit; "Act" is its activation.

TABLE 6
Weights From Letter Units to Output Unit After Training With the Hebb Rule and the Delta Rule

	Letter units										
Rule	D	F	H	L	M	P	T	I	N	E	T
Hebb	−0.50	0.50	−0.50	0.00	0.00	1.00	−0.50	0.00	0.00	2.00	−2.00
Delta	−0.84	0.59	−0.77	−0.19	−0.18	2.37	−0.73	0.24	0.24	2.23	−1.99

times with /i/ and only once with /I/. F is weakly positive because it occurs once with /I/, and D, H, and onset T are weakly negative because each occurs once with /i/. P is moderately positive, because it occurs twice with /I/ — once in PINE and once in PINT. Thus, these weights directly reflect the co-occurrences of letters and phonemes.

The outputs of the network when the weights produced by the Hebb rule are used, shown in Table 5, illustrate the consistency effect, both in net inputs and in activations. For example, the net input for FINE is stronger than for LINE because LINE is more similar to the inconsistent LINT; and the net input for PINE is stronger than for LINE because PINE benefits from its similarity with PINT, which has the same correspondence. However, the weights do not completely solve the task: For the word PINT, the net input is −1.0 (1.0 from the P minus 2.0 from the T), and passing this

through the logistic function results in an activation of −0.46, which is quite different from the target value of +1. What has happened is that PINT's neighbors have cast slightly more votes for /i/ than for /I/.

Now consider the results obtained using the delta rule. In this case, we trained the network for 20 epochs, again with a learning rate of 0.1. The overall magnitude of the weights is comparable to the Hebb rule case with only 5 epochs because, with the delta rule, the weight changes get smaller as the error gets smaller, and so the cumulative effect generally tends to be less. More important, though, when the delta rule is used, the same general effects of consistency are observed, but now the response to PINT, though weaker than other responses, has the right sign. The reason for this is that the cumulative weight changes caused by PINT are actually larger than those caused by other items, because after the first epoch, the error is larger for PINT than for other items. Error-correcting learning eventually compensates for this but, before learning has completely converged, the effects of consistency are still apparent.

The error-correcting learning process causes an alteration in the relative weighting of the effects of neighbors by assigning greater relative weight to those aspects of each input pattern that differentiate it from inconsistent patterns (see Table 6). This is why the weight tends to accumulate on P, which distinguishes PINT from the inconsistent neighbors DINT, HINT, LINT, MINT, and TINT. Correspondingly, the weights for D, H, and T are slightly more negative (relative to the Hebb weights) to accentuate the differentiation of DINT, HINT, and TINT from PINT. The effect of consistency, then, is still present when the delta rule is used but, precisely because it makes the biggest changes where the errors are greatest, the delta rule tends to counteract the consistency effect.

A related implication of using error-correcting learning concerns the degree to which an output unit comes to depend on different parts of the input. If a particular input–output correspondence is perfectly consistent (e.g. onset B $\Rightarrow$ /b/), so that the state of a given output unit is predicted perfectly by the states of particular input units, the delta rule will set the weights from all other input units to 0, even if they are partially correlated with the output unit. By contrast, when a correspondence is variable (e.g. vowel I $\Rightarrow$ /i/vs. /I/), so that no input unit on its own can predict the sate of the output unit, the delta rule will develop significant weights from the other parts of the input (e.g. consonants) that disambiguate the correspondence. Thus, if there is a componential correspondence, as for most consonants, other partial correspondences will not be exploited; however, when componentiality breaks down, as it often does with vowels, there will be a greater reliance on context and therefore a greater consistency effect.

For some tasks, including English word reading, no set of weights in a two-layer network that maps letters to phonemes will work for all of the training patterns (see Minsky & Papert, 1969). In such cases, hidden units that mediate between the input and output units are needed to achieve adequate performance.[9] Things are considerably more complex in networks with hidden units, but Equation 13 still provides some guidance. The complexity comes from the fact that, for an output unit, $O^{[pt]}$ reflects the similarities of the patterns of activation for training pattern p and test pattern t over the hidden units rather than over the input units. Even so, hidden units have the same tendency as output units to give similar output to similar inputs, because they use the same activation function. In fact, Equation 13 applies to them as well if $\delta_j^{[p]}$ is interpreted as the partial derivative of the error over all output units with respect to the summed input to the hidden unit j. The values of particular weights and the non-linearity of the activation function can make hidden units relatively sensitive to some dimensions of similarity and relatively insensitive to others and can even allow hidden units to respond to particular combinations of inputs and not to other, similar combinations. Thus, from the perspective of the output units, hidden units *re-represent* the input patterns so as to alter their relative similarities. This is critical for learning complex mappings like those in the English spelling-to-sound system. Phoneme units respond on the basis of hidden-layer similarity, and they must respond quite differently to exception words than to their inconsistent neighbors in order for all of them to be pronounced correctly. Thus, by altering the effective similarities among input patterns, a network with hidden units can overcome the limitations of one with only input and output units. The process of learning to be sensitive to relevant input combinations occurs relatively slowly, however, because it goes against the network's inherent tendency toward making similar responses to similar inputs.

The fact that hidden units can be sensitive to higher order combinations of input units has important implications for understanding body-level consistency effects. In a one-layer network without hidden units, the contribution of an input unit to the total signal received by an output unit summed over all its input is unconditional; that is, the contribution of each input unit is independent of the state of the other input units. As mentioned earlier, however, the pronunciations of vowels cannot typically be predicted from individual letters or graphemes. Rather, the correlations between vowel graphemes and phonemes are highly conditional on the presence of particular consonant graphemes. For example, the mapping from I to /i/ is inconsistent, but the mapping from I to /i/ is perfectly reliable in the context of a coda consisting only of the letter N (e.g. PIN, WIN, THIN). In English, the predictiveness of vowels conditional on codas is generally greater than that of vowels conditional on onsets (Treiman et al., 1995). Consequently, a multilayer network will be aided in generating appropriate vowel pronunciations by developing hidden units that respond to particular combinations of orthographic vowels and codas (i.e. word bodies). Even when the coda is taken into account, however, its correlation with the vowel pronunciation may be less than perfect (e.g. I in the context of NT in MINT vs. PINT). In this case, the choice of vowel must be conditioned by both the onset and coda for the correspondence to be reliable. Because of the fact that hidden units tend to make similar responses to similar inputs, hidden units that respond to an entire input pattern and contribute to a nonstandard vowel pronunciation (e.g. I ⇒ /I/ in the context of P_NT) will tend to be partially active when similar words are presented (e.g. MINT). These will tend to produce interference at the phoneme level, giving rise to a consistency effect. It is important to note, however, that a multilayer network will exhibit consistency effects only when trained on tasks that are at least partially inconsistent — that is, quasi-regular; as in one-layer networks that use the delta rule, if the training environment involves only componential correspondences, hidden units will learn to ignore irrelevant aspects of the input.

In summary, a broad range of connectionist networks, when trained in a quasi-regular environment, exhibit the general trends that have been observed in human experimental data: robust consistency effects that tend to diminish with experience, both with specific items (i.e. frequency) and with the entire ensemble of patterns (i.e. practice). These factors are among the most important determinants of the speed and accuracy with which people read words aloud.

Balancing frequency and consistency

The results of these analyses concur with the findings in empirical studies and in the SM89 and feedforward network simulations: There is an effect of consistency that diminishes with increasing frequency. Furthermore, details of the analytic results are also revealing. In particular, the extent to which the effect of consistency is eliminated in high-frequency words depends on just how frequent they are relative to words of lower frequency. In fact, this effect may help to explain the discrepancy between the findings in the feedforward network and those in the SM89 network — namely, the existence of consistency effects among high-frequency words in the former but not in the latter (and not generally in empirical studies). At first glance, it would appear that the pattern observed in the feedforward network matches one in which the high-frequency words are of lower frequency relative to the low-frequency words (e.g. a frequency of 10 in Fig. 8) than in the SM89 network (e.g. a frequency of 20). This is not literally true, of course, because the same (logarithmically compressed) word frequencies were used in the two simulations.

A better interpretation is that, in the feedforward network, the effect of consistency is stronger than in the SM89 network and, relative to this, the effect of frequency appears weaker. As described earlier, the orthographic and phonological representations used by SM89, based on context-sensitive triples of letters and phonemes, disperse the regularities between the written and spoken forms of words. This has two relevant effects in the current context. The first is to reduce the extent to which the training on a given word improves performance on other words that share the same spelling–sound correspondences and impairs performance on words that violate those correspondences. As illustrated earlier with the words LOG, GLAD, and SPLIT, even though a correspondence may be the same in a set of words, it may activate different orthographic and phonological units for each of them. As mentioned above, the weight changes induced by one word will help another only to the extent that they activate similar units (i.e. as a function of their overlap $O^{[pn]}$). This effect is particularly important for low-frequency regular words, for which perform-ance depends primarily on support from higher frequency words rather than from training on the word itself. In contrast, the new representations condense the regularities between orthography and phonology, so that weight changes for high-frequency words also improve performance on low-frequency words with the same spelling–sound correspondences to a greater extent. Thus, there is an effect of frequency among regular words in the SM89 network but not in the feedforward network. For the same reason, in the SM89 net-work, performance on an exception word is less hindered by training on regular words that are inconsistent with it. It is almost as if regular words in the SM89 network behave like regular incon-sistent words in the feedforward network, and exception words behave like ambiguous words: The support or interference they receive from similar words is somewhat reduced (see Fig. 9).

The SM89 representations also reduce the effect of consistency in an indirect manner by improving performance on exception words. This arises because the orthographic representations contain units that explicitly indicate the presence of context-sensitive triples of letters. Some of these triples correspond to onset–vowel combinations and to word bodies (e.g. PIN, INT) that can dir-ectly contribute to the pronunciation of excep-tion words (PINT). In contrast, although the new orthographic representations contain multiletter graphemes, none of them include both consonants and vowels or consonants from both the onset and coda. Thus, for example, the orthographic units for P, I, N, and T contribute independently to the hidden representations. It is only at the hid-den layer that the network can develop context-sensitive representations in order to pronounce exception words correctly, and it must learn to do this only on the basis of its exposure to words of varying frequency.

Nonetheless, it remains true that the pattern of frequency and consistency effects in the SM89 network reproduces the findings in empirical stud-ies better than does the pattern in the feedforward network. Yet the same skilled readers exhibit a high level of proficiency at reading nonwords that is not matched in the SM89 network, but only in

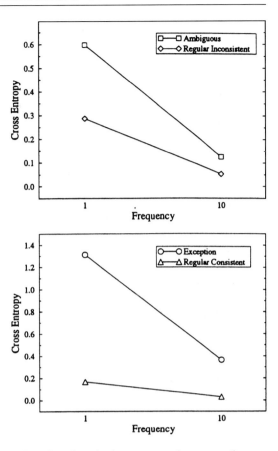

FIG. 9. Data from the frequency–consistency equation (Equation 12 and Fig. 8) for test words of frequencies 1 and 10, plotted separately for regular inconsistent and ambiguous words (upper graph) and regular consistent and exception words (lower graph). The upper pattern is similar to that found for regular and exception words in the Seidenberg and McClelland (1989) network (see Fig. 2), whereas the lower one is similar to the pattern for the feedforward network (see Fig. 5). The correspondences are only approximate because of the simplifying assumptions of the frequency–consistency equation.

a network that uses alternative representations that better capture the spelling–sound regularities. How can the effect of frequency and consistency be reconciled with good nonword reading?

The answer may lie in the fact that both the SM89 and the feedforward networks were trained using word frequency values that are logarith-mically compressed from their true frequencies of occurrence in the language. Thus, the SM89 network replicates the empirical naming latency pattern because it achieves the appropriate balance between the influence of frequency and that of consistency, although both factors are suppressed relative to the effects in human readers. This suppression is revealed when nonword reading is examined, because on this task it is primarily the network's sensitivity to consistency that dictates performance. In contrast, by virtue of the new representations, the feedforward network exhibits a sensitivity to consistency that is comparable to that of human readers, as evidenced by its good nonword reading. But now, with logarithmic frequencies, the effects of frequency and consistency are unbalanced in the network and it fails to replicate the precise pattern of naming latencies of human readers.

This interpretation leads to the prediction that the feedforward network should exhibit both good nonword reading and the appropriate frequency and consistency effects if it is trained on words according to their actual frequencies of occurrence. In the next simulation we tested this prediction.

Simulation 2: Feedforward network with actual frequencies

The most frequent word in the Kuçera and Francis (1967) list, THE, has a frequency of 69,971 per million, whereas the least frequent words have a frequency of 1 per million. In the training procedure used by SM89 the probability that a word was presented to the network for training was proportional to the logarithm of its frequency rather than its actual frequency. This compresses the effective frequency range from about 70,000:1 to about 16:1. Thus, the network experienced much less variation in the frequency of occurrence of words than do normal readers.

SM89 put forward a number of arguments in favor of using logarithmically compressed frequencies rather than actual frequencies in training their network. Beginning readers have yet to experience enough words to approximate the actual frequency range in the language. Also, low-frequency words disproportionately suffer from the lack of inflectional and derivational forms in the training corpus. However, the main reason

for compressing the frequency range was a practical consideration based on limitations of the available computational resources. If the highest frequency word was presented every epoch, the lowest frequency words would be presented on average only about once every 70,000 epochs. Thus, if actual frequencies had been used, SM89 could not have trained their network long enough for it to have had sufficient exposure on low-frequency words.

To compound matters, as SM89 pointed out, basic properties of the network and training procedure already serve to progressively weaken the impact of frequency over the course of training. In an error-correcting training procedure like back-propagation, weights are changed only to the extent that doing so reduces the mismatch between the generated and correct output. As high-frequency words become mastered, they produce less mismatch and so induce progressively smaller weight changes. This effect is magnified by the fact that, because of the asymptotic nature of the unit input–output function, weight changes have smaller and smaller impact as units approach their correct extreme values. As a result, learning becomes dominated mostly by lower frequency words that are still inaccurate, effectively compressing the range of frequency that is driving learning in the network.

Thus, SM89 considered it important to verify that their results did not depend critically on the use of such a severe frequency compression. They trained a version of the network in which the probability that a word was presented during an epoch was based on the square root of its frequency rather than on the logarithm (resulting in a frequency range of about 265:1 rather than 16:1). They found the same basic pattern of frequency and consistency effects in naming latency for the Taraban and McClelland (1987) words, although there was a larger effect of frequency among regular words and virtually no effect of consistency among high-frequency words even early in training. This shift corresponds predictably to a pattern in which the influence of frequency is stronger relative to the influence of consistency. However, SM89 presented no data on the network's accuracy in reading words or nonwords.

In the current simulation, we trained a version of the feedforward network (with the new representations) using the actual frequencies of occurrence of words. The training procedure in the current work avoids the problem of sampling low-frequency words by using frequency directly to scale the magnitude of the weight changes induced by a word — this is equivalent to sampling in the limit of a small learning rate, and it allows any range of frequencies to be used. The goal is to test the hypothesis that by balancing the strong influence of consistency that arises from the use of representations that better capture spelling–sound regularities with a realistically strong influence of frequency, the network should exhibit the appropriate pattern of frequency and consistency effects in naming latency while also producing accurate performance on word and nonword pronunciation.

Method

Network architecture. The architecture of the network was the same as in Simulation 1 (see Fig. 3).

Training procedure. The only major change in the training procedure from Simulation 1 was that, as described above, the values used to scale the error derivatives computed by back-propagation were proportional to the actual frequencies of occurrence of the words (Kuçera & Francis, 1967) rather than to a logarithmic compression of their frequencies. Following SM89 we assigned the 82 words in the training corpus that are not listed in Kuçera and Francis (1967) a frequency of 2, and all others, their listed frequency plus 2. We then divided these values by the highest value in the corpus (69,973 for THE) to generate the scaling values used during training. Thus, the weight changes produced by the word THE were unscaled (i.e. scaling value of 1.0). For comparison, AND, the word with the next highest frequency (28,860 occurrences per million), had a value of 0.412. By contrast, the relative frequencies of most other words were extremely low. The mean scaling value across the entire training corpus was 0.0020 and the median value was 0.00015. Taraban and McClelland's (1987) high-frequency exception words had an average value of 0.014, and their low-frequency exception words averaged 0.00036. Words not in the Kuçera and Francis (1967) list had a value just under 0.00003.

In addition, we modified two parameters of the training procedure to compensate for the changes in word frequencies. First , the global learning rate, ε in Equation 5, was increased from 0.001 to 0.05 to compensate for the fact that the summed frequency for the entire training corpus was reduced from 683.4 to 6.05 because actual rather than logarithmic frequencies were used. Second, we removed the slight tendency for weights to decay toward zero to prevent the very small weight changes induced by low-frequency words (due to their very small scaling factors) from being overcome by the tendency of weights to shrink toward zero.

Other than for these modifications, the network was trained in the same way it was in Simulation 1.

Testing procedure. The procedure for testing the network's procedure on words and nonwords was the same as in Simulation 1.

Results

Word reading. Because the weight changes caused by low-frequency words are so small, considerably more training is required to reach approximately the same level of performance as when logarithmically compressed frequencies are used. After 1,300 epochs of training, the network mispronounced only seven words in the corpus: BAS, BEAU, CACHE, CYST, GENT, TSAR, and YEAH (99.8% correct, where homographs were considered correct if they elicited either correct pronunciation). These words have rather inconsistent spelling–sound correspondences and have very low frequencies (i.e. and average scaling value of 0.00009). Thus, the network mastered all of the exception words except a few of the very lowest in frequency.

Nonword reading. Table 7 lists the errors made by the network in pronouncing the lists of nonwords from Glushko (1979) and from McCann and Besner (1987). The network produced "regular" responses to 42/43 (97.7%) of Glushko's consistent nonwords, 29/43 (67.4%) of the inconsistent nonwords, and 66/80 (82.5%) of McCann and Besner's control nonwords. Using a criterion that more closely corresponds to that used with human readers — considering a response correct if it is consistent with the pronunciation of a word in the training corpus (and not considering inflected nonwords or those with J in the coda) — the network achieved 42/43 (97.7%) correct on both the consistent and inconsistent nonwords and 68/76 (89.5%) correct on the control nonwords. Thus, the network's performance on these sets of

TABLE 7
Errors by the Feedforward Network Trained With Actual Frequencies in Pronouncing Nonwords

Glushko (1979)			McCann and Besner (1987)		
Nonword	Correct	Response	Nonword	Correct	Response
Consistent Nonwords (1/43)			Control Nonwords (14/80)		
*WOSH	/waS/	/woS/	TUNCE	/tʌns/	/tUns/
Inconsistent Nonwords (14/43)			*TOLPH	/tolf/	/tOl(f0.13)/
BLEAD	/blEd/	/bled/	*ZUPE	/zUp/	/(z 0.09)yUp/
BOST	/bost/	/bOst/	SNOCKS	/snaks/	/snask(ks 0.31)/
COSE	/kOz/	/kOs/	*GOPH	/gaf/	/gaT/
GROOK	/grUk/	/gruk/	*VIRCK	/vurk/	/(v 0.13)urk/
*HEAF	/hEf/	/h@f/	LOKES	/lOks/	/lOsk(ks 0.00)/
HOVE	/hOv/	/hʌv/	*YOWND	/yWnd/	/(y 0.04)and/
LOME	/lOm/	/lʌm/	KOWT	/kWt/	/kOt/
PILD	/pild/	/pIld/	*FUES	/fyUz/	/fyU(z 0.45)/
PLOVE	/plOv/	/plʌv/	*HANE	/hAn/	/h@n/
POOT	/pUt/	/put/	FAIJE	/fAj/	/fA(j 0.00)/
POVE	/pOv/	/pʌv/	*ZUTE	/zUt/	/(z 0.01)yUt/
SOOD	/sUd/	/sud/	JINJE	/jinj/	/jIn(j 0.00)/
WEAD	/wEd/	/wed/			
WONE	/wOn/	/wʌn/			

Note. /a/ in POT, /@/ in CAT, /e/ in BED, /i/ in HIT, /o/ in DOG, /u/ in GOOD, /A/ in MAKE, /E/ in KEEP, /I/ in BIKE, /O/ in HOPE, /U/ in BOOT, /W/ in NOW, /Y/ in BOY, /ʌ/ in CUP, /N/ in RING, /S/ in SHE, /C/ in CHIN, /Z/ in BEIGE, /T/ in THIN, /D/ in THIS. The activity levels of correct but missing phonemes are listed in parentheses. In these cases, the actual response is what falls outside the parentheses. Words marked with "*" remain errors after properties of the training corpus are considered (as explained in the text).

nonwords is comparable to that of skilled readers and to that of the network trained on logarithmic frequencies.

Frequency and consistency effects. Figure 10 shows the mean cross-entropy error of the network in pronouncing words of varying degrees of spelling–sound consistency as a function of frequency. There was a main effect of frequency, $F(1, 184) = 22.1, p < .001$, a main effect of consistency, $F(3, 184) = 6.49, p < .001$, and an interaction of frequency and consistency, $F(1, 184) = 5.99$, $p < .001$. Post hoc comparisons showed that the effect of frequency was significant at the .05 level among words of each level of consistency when considered separately.

The effect of consistency was significant among low-frequency words, $F(3, 92) = 6.25, p = .001$, but not among high-frequency words, $F(3, 92) = 2.48, p = .066$. Post hoc comparisons among low-frequency words revealed that the difference in error between exception words and ambiguous

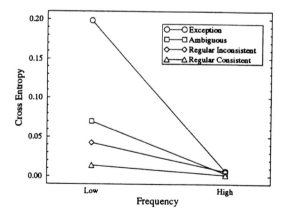

FIG. 10. Mean cross-entropy error produced by the feedforward network trained on actual frequencies for words with various degrees of spelling–sound consistency (listed in Appendix A) as a function of frequency.

words was significant, $F(1, 46) = 4.09, p = .049$, the difference between regular consistent and inconsistent words was marginally significant, $F(1, 46) = 3.73, p = .060$, but the difference between ambiguous words and regular inconsistent words failed to reach significance, $F(1, 46) = 2.31, p = .135$.

Overall, this pattern of results matches the one found in empirical studies fairly well. Thus, with a training regime that balances the influence of frequency and consistency, the network replicates the pattern of interaction of these variables on naming latency while also reading words and nonwords as accurately as skilled readers.

Training with a moderate frequency compression

As SM89 argued, training with the actual frequencies of monosyllabic words might not provide the best approximation to the experience of readers. For example, because many multisyllabic words have consistent spelling–sound correspondences — both in their base forms and with their various inflections and derivations — training with only monosyllabic words will underestimate a reader's exposure to spelling–sound regularities. Training with a compressed frequency range compensates for this bias because exception words tend to be of higher frequency than regular words and, thus, are disproportionately affected by the compression.

We have seen that a very severe (logarithmic) compression reduces the effects of frequency to such an extent that a network using representations that amplify consistency effect fails to exhibit the exact pattern of naming latencies found in empirical studies. Nonetheless, it would seem appropriate to test whether a less severe compression results in a better match to the empirical findings. As mentioned earlier, SM89 found that presenting words during training with a probability proportional to the square root of their frequency replicated the basic frequency and consistency effects in their network, but they presented no data on the accuracy of the network's performance. Accordingly, it seemed worthwhile for comparison purposes for us to train a network with the new representations also using a square-root compression of word frequencies.

Analogous to the use of actual frequencies, the scaling value for each word was the square root of its Kučera and Francis (1967) frequency plus 2, divided by the square root of the frequency of THE plus 2 (264.5). The value for AND was 0.642. The mean for the corpus was 0.023 and the median was 0.012. Taraban and McClelland's (1987) high-frequency exception words averaged 0.097, whereas the low-frequency exception words averaged 0.017. Words not in the Kučera and Francis (1967) list had a value of 0.0053. Thus, the compression of frequency was much less severe than when logarithms were used, but it was still substantial.

The summed frequency of the training corpus was 69.8; accordingly, the global learning rate, ε, was adjusted to 0.01. The training procedure was otherwise identical to that used when training on the actual word frequencies.

Word reading. After 400 epochs, the network pronounced correctly all words in the training corpus except for the homograph HOUSE, for which the states of both the final /s/ and the final /z/ just failed to be active (/s/: 0.48, /z/:0.47). Thus, the network's word reading was essentially perfect.

Nonword reading. The network made no errors on Glushko's (1979) consistent nonwords. On the inconsistent nonwords, 14 of the network's responses were irregular, but all but one of these (POVE $\Rightarrow$ /pav/) were consistent with some word in the training corpus (97.7% correct). The network mispronounced 13 of McCann and Besner's (1987) control nonwords. However, only 7 of these remained as errors when the same scoring criterion as was used with human readers was used and when inflected forms and those with ɹ in the coda (90.8% correct) were ignored. Thus, the network trained with square-root frequencies pronounced nonwords as well, if not slightly better, than the network trained with actual frequencies.

Frequency and consistency effects. Figure 11 shows the mean cross-entropy error of the network in pronouncing words of varying degrees of spelling–sound consistency as a function of frequency. Overall, there was a significant effect of frequency, $F(1, 184) = 47.7, p < .001$, and consistency, $F(1, 184) = 14.9, p < .001$, and an interaction of frequency and consistency, $F(3, 184) = 8.409$,

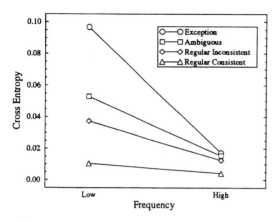

FIG. 11. Mean cross-entropy error produced by the feedforward network trained on square-root frequencies for words with various degrees of spelling–sound consistency (listed in Appendix A) as a function of frequency.

$p < .001$. The effect of frequency was also significant at the .05 level among words of each level of consistency when considered separately. Among high-frequency words, regular inconsistent, ambiguous, and exception words were significantly different from regular consistent words but not from each other. Among low-frequency words, the difference between regular inconsistent words and ambiguous words was not significant, $F(1, 46) = 1.18$, $p = .283$, but all other pairwise comparisons were. Thus, this network also replicated the basic empirical findings of the effects of frequency and consistency on naming latency.

Summary

The SM89 simulation replicated the empirical pattern of frequency and consistency effects by appropriately balancing the relative influences of these two factors. Unfortunately, both were reduced relative to their strength in skilled readers. The fact that the orthographic and phonological representations disperse the regularities between spelling and sound served to diminish the relative impact of consistency. Likewise, the use of a logarithmic compression of the probability of word presentations served to diminish the impact of frequency. As a result of the reduced effectiveness of consistency, nonword reading suffered.

The current work uses representations that better capture spelling–sound regularities, thereby increasing the relative influence of consistency. One effect of this is to improve nonword reading to a level comparable to that of skilled readers. However, if a logarithmic frequency compression continues to be used, the relative impact of frequency is too weak and the network exhibits consistency effects among high-frequency words not found in empirical studies.

The appropriate relative balance of frequency and consistency can be restored, while maintaining good nonword reading, by using the actual frequencies of words during training. In fact, a square-root frequency compression that is much more moderate than a logarithmic one also reproduced the empirical naming latency pattern, although a consistency effect among high-frequency words began to emerge. In this way, the three networks presented thus far — trained on logarithmic frequencies, square-root frequencies, or actual frequencies — provide clear points of comparison of the relative influences of word frequency and spelling–sound consistency on naming latency. Together with the analytical results from the previous section, these findings suggest that the central empirical phenomena in word and nonword reading can be interpreted naturally in terms of the basic principles of operation of connectionist networks that are exposed to an appropriately structured training corpus.

Simulation 3: Interactivity, componential attractors, and generalization

As outlined earlier, the current approach to lexical processing is based on a number of general principles of information processing, loosely expressed by the acronym GRAIN (for Graded, Random, Adaptive, Interactive, and Nonlinear). Together with the principles of distributed representations and knowledge, the approach constitutes a substantial departure from traditional assumptions about the nature of language knowledge and processing (e.g. Pinker, 1991). It must be noted, however, that the simulations presented so far involve only deterministic, feedforward networks and thus fail to incorporate two important principles: inter-activity and randomness (intrinsic variability). In part, this simplification has been necessary for practical reasons; interactive, stochastic simula-tions are far more demanding of computational resources. More important, including only some of the relevant principles in a given simulation enables more detailed analysis of the specific con-tribution that each makes to the overall behavior of the system. This has been illustrated most clearly in the current work with regard to the nature of the distributed representations used for ortho-graphy and phonology and the relative influences of frequency and consistency on network learn-ing (adaptivity). Nonetheless, each such network constitutes only an approximation or abstraction of a more complete simulation that would incor-porate all of the principles. The methodology of considering sets of principles separately relies on the assumption that there are no unforeseen, prob-lematic interactions among the principles such that the findings with simplified simulations would not generalize to more comprehensive ones.

The current simulation investigates the implica-tions of interactivity for the process of pronoun-cing written words and nonwords. Interactivity plays an important role in connectionist explanations of a number of cognitive phenomena (McClelland, 1987; McClelland & Elman, 1986; McClelland & Rumelhart, 1981) and constitutes a major point of contention with alternative theoretical formu-lations (Massaro, 1988, 1989). Processing in a network is interactive when units can mutually constrain each other in settling on the most con-sistent interpretation of the input. For this to be possible, the architecture of the network must be generalized to allow feedback or *recurrent* connec-tions among units. For example, in the interactive activation model of letter and word perception (McClelland & Rumelhart, 1981; Rumelhart & McClelland, 1982), letter units and word units are bidirectionally connected so that the partial activa-tion of a word unit can feed back to support the activation of letter units with which it is consistent.

A common way in which interactivity has been used in networks is in making particular patterns of activity into stable *attractors*. In an attractor network, units interact and update their states

repeatedly in such a way that the initial pattern of activity generated by an input gradually settles to the nearest attractor pattern. A useful way of con-ceptualizing this process is in terms of a multi-dimensional *state space* in which the activity of each unit is plotted along a separate dimension. At any instant in time, the pattern of activity over all of the units corresponds to a single point in this space. As units change their states in response to a given input, this point moves in state space, eventually arriving at the point (attractor) corres-ponding to the network's interpretation. The set of initial patterns that settle to this same final pat-tern corresponds to a region around the attractor, called its *basin* of attraction. To solve a task, the network must learn connection weights that cause units to interact in such a way that the appropriate interpretation of each input is an attractor whose basin contains the initial pattern of activity for that input.

In the domain of word reading, attractors have played a critical role in connectionist accounts of the nature of normal and impaired reading via meaning (Hinton & Sejnowski, 1986; Hinton & Shallice, 1991; Plaut & Shallice, 1993). Accord-ing to these accounts, the meanings of words are represented in terms of patterns of activity over a large number of semantic features. These fea-tures can support structured, frame-like repres-entations (e.g. Minsky, 1975) if units represent conjunctions of roles and properties of role fillers (Derthick, 1990; Hinton, 1981). Because only a small fraction of the possible combinations of fea-tures correspond to the meanings of actual words, it is natural for a network to learn to make these semantic patterns into attractors. Then, in deriv-ing the meaning of a word from its orthograph, the network need only generate an initial pat-tern of activity that falls somewhere within the appropriate semantic attractor basin; the settling process will clean up this pattern into the exact meaning of the word.[10] If, however, the system is damaged, the initial activity for a word may fall within a neighboring attractor basin, typically corresponding to a semantically related word. The damaged network will then settle to the exact meaning of that word, resulting in a semantic error (e.g. CAT read as "dog"). In fact, the occurrence of such errors is the hallmark symptom of a type of acquired reading disorder known as *deep dyslexia* (see Coltheart, Patterson, & Marshall, 1980, for more details on the full range of symptoms of deep dyslexia, and Plaut & Shallice, 1993, for connectionist simulations replicating these symptoms). In this way, attractors obviate the need for word-specific units in mediating between orthography and semantics (see Hinton, McClelland, & Rumelhart, 1986, for discussion).

When applied to the mapping from orthography to phonology, however, the use of interactivity to form attractors appears problematic. In particular, the correct pronunciation of a nonword typically does not correspond to the pronunciation of some word. If the network develops attractors for word pronunciations, one might expect that the input for a nonword would often be captured within the attractor basin for a similar word, resulting in many incorrect *lexicalizations*. More generally, attractors seem to be appropriate only for tasks, such as semantic categorization or object recognition, in which the correct response to a novel input is a familiar output. By contrast, in oral reading, the correct response to a novel input is typically a novel output. If it is true that attractors cannot support this latter sort of generalization, their applicability in reading specifically, and cognitive science more generally, would be fundamentally limited.

The current simulation demonstrates that these concerns are ill-founded and that, with appropriately structured representations, the principle of interactivity can operate effectively in the phonological pathway as well as in the semantic pathway (see Fig. 1). The reason is that, in learning to map orthography to phonology, the network develops attractors that are *componential* — they have substructure that reflects common sublexical correspondences between orthography and phonology. This substructure applies not only to most words but also to nonwords, enabling them to be pronounced correctly. At the same time, the network develops attractors for exception words that are far less componential. Thus, rather than being a hindrance, attractors are a particularly effective style of computation for quasi-regular tasks such as word reading.

A further advantage of an attractor network over a feedforward network in modeling word reading is that the former provides a more direct analogue of naming latency. Thus far, we have followed SM89 in using an error measure in a feedforward network to account for naming latency data from skilled readers. SM89 offered two justifications for this approach. The first is based on the assumption that the accuracy of the phonological representation of a word would directly influence the execution speed of the corresponding articulatory motor program (see Lacouture, 1989, and Zorzi, Houghton, & Butterworth, 1995, for simulations embodying this assumption). This assumption is consistent with the view that the time required by the orthography-to-phonology computation itself does not vary systematically with word frequency or spelling–sound consistency. If this were the case, a feedforward network of the sort SM89 and we have used, which takes the same amount of time to process any input, would be a reasonable rendition of the nature of the phonological pathway in skilled readers.

An alternative justification for the use of error scores to model naming latencies, mentioned only briefly by SM89, is based on the view that the actual computation from orthography to phonology involves interactive processing such that the time to settle on an appropriate phonological representation does vary systematically with word type. The naming latencies exhibited by skilled readers are a function of this settling time, perhaps in conjunction with articulatory effects. Accordingly, a feedforward implementation of the mapping from orthography to phonology should be viewed as an abstraction of a recurrent implementation that would more accurately approximate the actual word reading system. Studying the feedforward implementation is still informative because many of its properties, including its sensitivity to frequency and consistency, depend on computational principles of operation that would also apply to a recurrent implementation — namely, adaptivity, distributed representations and knowledge, and nonlinearity. These principles merely manifest themselves differently: Influences that reduce error in a feedforward network serve to accelerate settling in a recurrent network. Thus, error in a feedforward network is a valid approximation of settling time in a recurrent network because they both arise from the same underlying causes: additive frequency and consistency effects in the context of a nonlinear gradual ceiling effect. Nonetheless, even given these arguments, it is important to verify that a recurrent implementation that reads words and nonwords as accurately as skilled readers also reproduces the relevant empirical pattern of naming latencies directly in the time it takes to settle in pronouncing words.

Method

Network architecture. The architecture of the attractor network is shown in Fig. 12. The numbers of grapheme, hidden, and phoneme units were the same as in the feedforward networks, but the attractor network had some additional sets of connections. Each input unit was still connected to each hidden unit, which, in turn, was connected to each phoneme unit. In addition, each phoneme unit was connected to each other phoneme unit (including itself), and each phoneme unit sent a connection back to each hidden unit. The weights on the two connections between a pair of units (e.g. a hidden unit and a phoneme unit) were trained separately and did not have to have identical values. Including the biases of the hidden and phoneme units, the network had a total of 26,582 connections.

The states of units in the network change smoothly over time in response to influences from other units. In particular, the instantaneous change over time t of the input x_j to unit j is proportional to the difference between its current input and the summed contribution from other units:

$$\frac{dx_j}{dt} = \sum_i s_i w_{ij} + b_j - x_j . \quad (14)$$

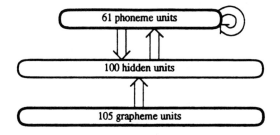

FIG. 12. The architecture of the attractor network. Ovals represent groups of units, and arrows represent complete connectivity from one group to another.

The state s_j of unit j is $\sigma(x_j)$, the standard logistic function of its integrated input, which ranges between 0 and 1 (see Equation 2). For clarity, we will call the summed input from other units i (plus the bias) the *external* input to each unit, to distinguish it from the *integrated* input x, that governs the unit's state.

According to Equation 14, when a unit's integrated input is perfectly consistent with its external input (i.e. $x_j = \sum_i s_i w_{ij} + b_j$), the derivative is zero and the unit's integrated input, and hence its state, ceases to change. Notice that its activity at this point, $\sigma(\sum_i s_i w_{ij} + b_j)$, is the same as it would be if it were a standard unit that computes its state from the external input instantaneously (as in a feedforward network; see Equations 1 and 2). To illustrate this, and to provide some sense of the temporal dynamics of units in the network, Fig. 13 shows the activity over time of a single unit, initialized to 0.5 and governed by Equation 14, in response to external input of various magnitudes. Notice that, over time, the unit state gradually approaches an asymptotic value equal to the logistic function applied to its external input.

For the purposes of simulation on a digital computer, it is convenient to approximate continuous units with finite difference equations in which time is discretized into *ticks* of some duration τ:

$$\Delta x_j = \tau(\sum_i s_i w_{ij} + b_j - x_j),$$

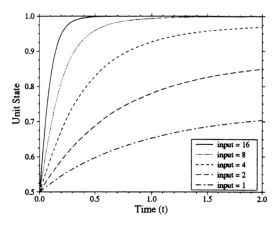

FIG. 13. The state over time of a continuous unit, initialized to 0.5 and governed by Equation 14, when presented with fixed external input from other units of various magnitudes. The curves of state values for negative external input are the exact mirror images of these curves, approaching 0 instead of 1.

where $\Delta x_j = x_j^{[t]} - x_j^{[t-\tau]}$. Using explicit superscripts for discrete time, we can rewrite this as

$$x_j^{[t]} = \tau(\sum_i s_i^{[t-\tau]} w_{ij} + b_j) + (1 - \tau)x_j^{[t-\tau]}. \qquad (15)$$

According to this equation, a unit's input at each time tick is a weighted average of its current input and that dictated by other units, where τ is the weighting proportion.[11] Notice that, in the limit (as $\tau \to 0$), this discrete computation becomes identical to the continuous one. Thus, adjustments to τ affect the accuracy with which the discrete system approximates the continuous one but do not alter the underlying computation being performed. This is of considerable practical importance, because the computational time required to simulate the system is inversely proportional to τ. A relatively larger τ can be used during the extensive training period (0.2 in the current simulation), when minimizing computation time is critical, whereas a much smaller τ can be used during testing (e.g. 0.01), when a very accurate approximation is desired. As long as τ remains sufficiently small for the approximations to be adequate, these manipulations do not fundamentally alter the behavior of the system.

Training procedure. The training corpus for the network was the same as that used with the feedforward network trained on actual word frequencies. As in that simulation, the frequency value of each word was used to scale the weight changes induced by the word.

The network was trained with a version of back-propagation designed for recurrent networks, known as *back-propagation through time* (Rumelhart et al., 1986a, 1986b; Williams & Peng, 1990), and further adapted for continuous units (B. Pearlmutter, 1989). In understanding back-propagation through time, it may help to think of the computation in standard back-propagation in a three-layer feedforward network as occurring over time. In the forward pass, the states of input units are clamped at time $t = 0$. Hidden unit states are computed at $t = 1$ from these input unit states, and then output unit states are computed at $t = 2$ from the hidden unit states. In the backward pass, error is calculated for the output units based on their states ($t = 2$). Error for the hidden units and weight changes for the hidden-to-output connections are calculated based on the error of the output units ($t = 2$) and the states of hidden units ($t = 1$). Finally, the weight changes for the input-to-hidden connections are calculated based on the hidden unit error ($t = 1$) and the input unit states ($t = 0$). Thus, feedforward back-propagation can be interpreted as involving a pass forward in time to compute unit states,

followed by a pass backward in time to compute unit error and weight changes.

Back-propagation through time has exactly the same form, except that, because a recurrent network can have arbitrary connectivity, each unit can receive contributions from any unit at any time, not just from those in earlier layers (for the forward pass) or later layers (for the backward pass). This means that each unit must store its state and error at each time tick so that these values are available to other units when needed. In addition, the states of noninput units affect those of other units immediately, so they need to be initialized to some neutral value (0.5 in the current simulation). In all other respects, back-propagation through time is computationally equivalent to feedforward back-propagation. In fact, back-propagation through time can be interpreted as "unfolding" a recurrent network into a much larger feedforward network with a layer for each time tick composed of a separate copy of all the units in the recurrent network (see Minsky & Papert, 1969; Rumelhart et al., 1986a, 1986b).

In order to apply back-propagation through time to continuous units, one must make the propagation of error in the backward pass continuous as well (B. Pearlmutter, 1989). If we use δ_j to designate the derivative of the error with respect to the input of unit j, then, in feedforward back-propagation

$$\delta_j = \frac{\partial C}{\partial s_j} \sigma'(x_j),$$

where C is the cross-entropy error function and $\sigma'(\cdot)$ is the derivative of the logistic function. In the discrete approximation to back-propagation through time with continuous units, this becomes

$$\delta_j^{[t]} = \tau \frac{\partial C}{\partial s_j^{[t+\tau]}} \sigma'(x_j^{[t+\tau]}) + (1 - \tau)\delta_j^{[t+\tau]}.$$

Thus, δ_j is a weighted average backward in time of its current value and the contribution from the current error of the unit. In this way, as in standard back-propagation, δ_j in the backward pass is analogous to x_j in the forward pass (cf. Equation 15).

Because output units can interact with other units over the course of processing a stimulus, they can indirectly affect the error for other output units. As a result, the error for an output unit becomes the sum of two terms: the error that is due to the discrepancy between its own state and its target and the error back-propagated to it from other units. The first term is often referred to as error that is *injected* into the network by the training environment, whereas the second term might be thought of as error that is *internal* to the network.

Given that the states of output units vary over time, they can have targets that specify what states they should be in at particular points in time. Thus, in back-propagation through time, error can be injected at any or all time ticks, not just at the last one as in feedforward back-propagation. Targets that vary over time define a trajectory that the output states will attempt to follow (see B. Pearlmutter, 1989, for a demonstration of this type of learning). If the targets remain constant over time, however, the output units will attempt to reach their targets as quickly as possible and remain there. In the current simulation, we used this technique to train the network to form stable attractors for the pronunciations of words in the training corpus.

It is possible for the states of units to change quickly if they receive a very large summed input from other units (see Fig. 13). However, even for rather large summed input, units typically require some amount of time to approach an extreme value, and they may never reach it completely. As a result, it is practically impossible for units to achieve targets of 0 or 1 immediately after a stimulus has been presented. For this reason, in the current simulation, a less stringent training regime was adopted. Although the network was run for 2.0 units of time, error was injected only for the second unit of time; units received no direct pressure to be correct for the first unit of time (although back-propagated internal error caused weight changes that encouraged units to move toward the appropriate states as early as possible). In addition, output units were trained to targets of 0.1 and 0.9 rather than 0 and 1, although no error was injected if a unit exceeded its target (e.g. reached a state of 0.95 for a target of 0.9). This training criterion can be achieved by units with only moderately large summed input (see the curve for input = 4 in Fig. 13).

As with the feedforward network using actual frequencies, the attractor network was trained with a global learning rate $\varepsilon = 0.05$ (with adaptive connection-specific rates) and momentum $\alpha = 0.9$. Furthermore, as mentioned above, the network was trained using a discretization $\tau = 0.2$. Thus, units updated their states 10 times (2.0/0.2) in the forward pass, and they back-propagated error 10 times in the backward pass. As a result, the computational demands of the simulation were about 10 times that of one of the feedforward simulations. In an attempt to reduce the training time, we increased momentum to 0.98 after 200 epochs. To improve the accuracy of the network's approximation to a continuous system near the end of training, we reduced τ from 0.2 to 0.05 at Epoch 1,800, and

reduced it further to 0.01 at Epoch 1,850 for an additional 50 epochs of training. During this final stage of training, each unit updated its state 200 times over the course of processing each input.

Testing procedure. A fully adequate characterization of response generation in distributed connectionist networks would involve stochastic processing (see McClelland, 1991) and thus is beyond the scope of the present work. As an approximation in a deterministic attractor network, we used a measure of the time it takes the network to compute a stable output in response to a given input. Specifically, the network responds when the average change in the states of the phoneme units falls below some criterion (0.00005 with $\tau = 0.01$ for the results below).[12] At this point, the network's naming latency is the amount of continuous time that has passed in processing the input, and its naming response is generated on the basis of the current phoneme states using the same procedure as for the feedforward networks.

Results

Word reading. After 1,900 epochs of training, the network pronounced correctly all but 25 of the 2,998 words in the training corpus (99.2% correct). About half of these errors were regularizations of low-frequency exception words (e.g. SIEVE $\Rightarrow$ /sEv/, SUEDE $\Rightarrow$ /swEd/, and TOW $\Rightarrow$ /tW/). Most of the remaining errors would be classified as visual errors (e.g. FALL $\Rightarrow$ /folt/, GORGE $\Rightarrow$ /grOrj/, and HASP $\Rightarrow$ /h@ps/), although four merely had consonants that failed to reach threshold (ACHE $\Rightarrow$ /A/, BEIGE $\Rightarrow$ /bA/, TZAR $\Rightarrow$ /ar/, and WOUND $\Rightarrow$ /Und/). All in all, the network came close to mastering the training corpus, although its performance was slightly worse than that of the equivalent feedforward network.

Even though the network settles to a representation of the phonemes of a word in parallel, the time it takes to do so increases with the length of the word. To demonstrate this, we entered the naming latencies of the network for the 2,973 words it pronounces correctly into a multiple linear regression, using as predictors (a) orthographic length (i.e. number of letters), (b) phonological length (i.e. number of phonemes), (c) logarithmic word frequency, and (d) a measure of spelling-sound consistency equal to the number of friends (including the word itself) divided by the total number of friends and enemies; thus, highly consistent words have values near 1 and exception words have values near 0. Collectively, the four factors accounted for 15.9% of the variance in the latency values, $F(4, 2,968) = 139.92$, $p < .001$. More important, all four factors accounted for significant unique variance after we factored out the other three (9.9%, 5.6%, 0.8%, and 0.1% for consistency, log-frequency, orthographic length, and phonological length, respectively, $p < .05$ for each). In particular, orthographic length was positively correlated with naming latency semipartial $r = .089$) and accounted uniquely for 0.8% of its variance, $F(1, 2,968) = 40.0$, $p < .001$. To convert this correlation into an increase in reaction time (RT) per letter, we regressed the network's mean RTs for the Taraban and McClelland (1987) high- and low-frequency exception words and their regular

consistent controls against the means for skilled readers reported by Taraban and McClelland; this resulted in a scaling of 188.5 ms per unit of simulation time (with an intercept of 257 ms). Given this scaling, the effect of orthographic length in the network is 4.56 ms/letter based on its semipartial correlation with RT (after factoring out the other predictors) and 7.67 ms/letter based on its direct correlation with RT ($r = .139$). Length effects of this magnitude are at the low end of the range found in empirical studies, although such effects can vary greatly with reading skill (Butler & Hains, 1979) and with the specific stimuli and testing conditions used (see Henderson, 1982).

Nonword reading. Table 8 lists the errors made by the network in pronouncing the lists of nonwords from Glushko (1979) and from McCann and

TABLE 8
Errors by the Attractor Network in Pronouncing Nonwords

Glushko (1979)			McCann and Besner (1987)		
Nonword	*Correct*	*Response*	*Nonword*	*Correct*	*Response*
Consistent Nonwords (3/43)			Control Nonwords (11/80)		
*HODE	/hOd/	/hOdz/	*KAIZE	/kAz/	/skwAz/
*SWEAL	/swEl/	/swel/	*ZUPE	/zUp/	/zyUp/
*WOSH	/waS/	/wuS/	*JAUL	/jol/	/jOl/
Inconsistent Nonwords (16/43)			*VOLE	/vOl/	/vOln/
BLEAD	/blEd/	/bled/	*YOWND	/yWnd/	/(y 0.04)Ond/
BOST	/bost/	/bOst/	KOWT	/kWt/	/kOt/
COSE	/kOz/	/kOs/	*VAWX	/voks/	/voNks/
COTH	/koT/	/kOT/	FAIJE	/fAj/	/fA(j 0.00)/
GROOK	/grUk/	/gruk/	*ZUTE	/zUt/	/zyUt/
LOME	/lOm/	/lʌm/	*YOME	/yOm/	/yam/
MONE	/mone/	/mʌn/	JINJE	/jinj/	/jIn(j 0.00)/
PLOVE	/plOv/	/plUv/			
POOT	/pUt/	/put/			
*POVE	/pOv/	/pav/			
SOOD	/sUd/	/sud/			
SOST	/sost/	/sOst/			
SULL	/sʌl/	/sul/			
WEAD	/wEd/	/wed/			
WONE	/wOn/	/wʌn/			
WUSH	/wʌS/	/wuS/			

Note. /a/ in POT, /@/ in CAT, /e/ in BED, /i/ in HIT, /o/ in DOG, /u/ in GOOD, /A/ in MAKE, /E/ in KEEP, /I/ in BIKE, /O/ in HOPE, /U/ in BOOT, /W/ in NOW, /Y/ in BOY, /ʌ/ in CUP, /N/ in RING, /S/ in SHE, /C/ in CHIN, /Z/ in BEIGE, /T/ in THIN, /D/ in THIS. The activity levels of correct but missing phonemes are listed in parentheses. In these cases, the actual response is what falls outside the parentheses. Words marked with "*" remain errors after properties of the training corpus are considered (as explained in the text).

Besner (1987). The network produced "regular" pronunciations to 40/43 (93.0%) of Glushko's consistent nonwords, 27/43 (62.8%) of the inconsistent nonwords, and 69/80 (86.3%) of McCann and Besner's control nonwords. If we accept as correct any pronunciation that is consistent with that of a word in the training corpus with the same body (and ignore inflected words and those with J in the coda), the network pronounced correctly 42/43 (97.7%) of the inconsistent nonwords and 68/76 (89.5%) of the control nonwords. Although the performance of the network on the consistent nonwords was somewhat worse than that of the feedforward networks, it is about equal to the level of performance Glushko (1979) reported for subjects (93.8%; see Table 3). Thus, overall, the ability of the attractor network to pronounce nonwords is comparable to that of skilled readers.

Frequency and consistency effects. Figure 14 shows the mean latencies of the network in pronouncing words of various degrees of spelling-sound consistency as a function of frequency. One of the low-frequency exception words from the Taraban and McClelland (1987) list was withheld from this analysis because it was pronounced incorrectly by the network (SPOOK $\Rightarrow$ /spuk/). Among the remaining words, there were significant main effects of frequency, $F(3, 183) = 25.0$, $p < .001$, and consistency, $F(3, 183) = 8.21$, $p < .001$, and a

significant interaction of frequency and consistency, $F(3, 183) = 3.49$, $p = .017$. These effects also obtained in a comparison of only regular and exception words: frequency, $F(1, 91) = 10.2$, $p = .002$; consistency, $F(1, 91) = 22.0$, $p < .001$; frequency by consistency, $F(1, 91) = 9.31$, $p = .003$. Considering each level of consistency separately, the effect of frequency was significant for exception words, $F(1, 45) = 11.9$, $p = .001$, and for ambiguous words, $F(1, 46) = 19.8$, $p = .001$, and was marginally significant for regular inconsistent words, $F(1, 46) = 3.51$, $p = .067$. There was no effect of frequency among regular words ($F < 1$).

The naming latencies of the network showed a significant effect of consistency for low-frequency words, $F(3, 91) = 6.65$, $p < .001$, but not for high-frequency words, $F(3, 91) = 1.71$, $p = .170$. Among low-frequency words, regular consistent words were significantly different from each of the other three types (at $p < .05$), but regular inconsistent, ambiguous, and exception words were not significantly different from each other (although the comparison between regular inconsistent and exception words was significant at $p = .075$). Among high-frequency words, none of the pairwise comparisons was significant except between regular and exception words, $F(1, 46) = 4.87$, $p = .032$. Thus, overall, the naming latencies of the network replicate the standard effects of frequency and consistency found in empirical studies.

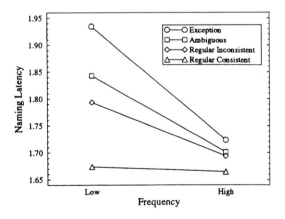

FIG. 14. Naming latency of the attractor network trained on actual frequencies for words with various degrees of spelling–sound consistency (listed in Appendix A) as a function of frequency.

Network analyses

The network's success at word reading demonstrates that, through training, it developed attractors for the pronunciations of words. How then is it capable of reading nonwords with novel pronunciations? Why isn't the input for a nonword (e.g. MAVE) captured by the attractor for an orthographically similar word (e.g. GAVE, MOVE, MAKE)? We carried out a number of analyses of the network to gain a better understanding of its ability to read nonwords. Because nonword reading involves recombining knowledge derived from word pronunciation, we were primarily concerned with how separate parts of the input contribute to (a) the correctness of parts of the output and (b) the hidden representation for the input. As with naming latency, the item SPOOK was withheld from these analyses because it was mispronounced by the network.

Componential attractors. In the first analysis we measured the extent to which each phonological cluster (onset, vowel, coda) depends on the input from each orthographic cluster. Specifically, for each word, we gradually reduced the activity of the active grapheme units in a particular orthographic cluster until, when the network was re-run, the phonemes in a particular phonological cluster were no longer correct.[13] This *boundary* activity level measures the importance of input from a particular orthographic cluster for the correctness of a particular phonological cluster; a value of 1 means that the graphemes in that cluster must be completely active; a value of 0 means that the phonemes are completely insensitive to the graphemes in that cluster. In state space, the boundary level corresponds to the radius of the word's attractor basin along a particular direction (assuming state space includes dimensions for the grapheme units).

This procedure was applied to the Taraban and McClelland (1987) regular consistent, regular inconsistent, and exception words, as well as to the corresponding set of ambiguous words (see Appendix A). Words were excluded from the analysis if they lacked an orthographic onset or coda (e.g. ARE, DO). The resulting boundary values for each combination of orthographic and phonological clusters were subjected to an analysis of variance (ANOVA) with frequency and consistency as between-items factors and orthographic cluster and phonological cluster as within-item factors.

With regard to frequency, high-frequency words had lower boundary values than low-frequency words (0.188 vs. 0.201, respectively), $F(1, 162) = 6.48$, $p = .012$. However, frequency did not interact with consistency, $F(3, 162) = 2.10$, $p = .102$, nor did it interact with orthographic or phonological cluster, $F(2, 324) = 1.49$, $p = .227$, and $F(2, 324) = 2.46$, $p = .087$, respectively. Thus, we will consider high- and low-frequency words together in the remainder of the analysis.

There was a strong effect of consistency on the boundary values, $F(3, 162) = 14.5$, $p < .001$, and this effect interacted both with orthographic cluster, $F(6, 324) = 16.1$, $p < .001$, and with phonolo-

gical cluster, $F(6, 324) = 20.3$, $p < .001$. Figure 15 presents the average boundary values of each orthographic cluster as a function of phonological cluster, separately for words of each level of consistency. Thus, for each type of word, the set of bars for each phonological cluster indicates how sensitive that cluster is to input from each orthographic cluster. If we consider regular consistent words first, the figure shows that each phonological cluster depends almost entirely on the corresponding orthographic cluster and little, if at

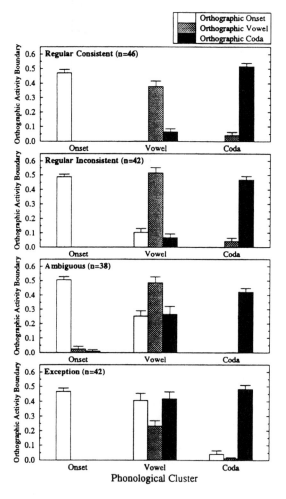

FIG. 15. The degree of activity in each orthographic cluster required to activate each phonological cluster correctly, for words of various spelling–sound consistency (listed in Appendix A). Words lacking either an onset or coda consonant cluster in orthography were excluded from the analysis.

all, on the other clusters. For instance, the vowel and coda graphemes can be completely removed without affecting the network's pronunciation of the onset. There is a slight interdependence among the vowel and coda, consistent with the fact that word bodies capture important information in pronunciation (see, e.g. Treiman & Chafetz, 1987; Treiman et al., 1995). Nonetheless, neither the phonological vowel nor the coda cluster depends on the orthographic onset cluster. Thus, for a regular word like MUST, an alternative onset (e.g. N) can be substituted and pronounced without depending on or affecting the pronunciation of the body (producing the correct pronunciation of the nonword NUST).

Similarly, for regular inconsistent, ambiguous, and exception words, the correctness of the phonological onset and coda was relatively independent of noncorresponding parts of the orthographic input. The pronunciation of the vowel, by contrast, was increasingly dependent on the orthographic consonants as consistency decreased: $F(3, 166) = 47.7$, $p < .001$ for the main effect of consistency; $p < .05$ for all pairwise comparisons. In fact, most spelling–sound inconsistency in English involves unusual vowel pronunciations. Interestingly, for exception words, the vowel pronunciation was less sensitive to the orthographic vowel itself than it was to the surrounding (consonant) context: $F(1, 41) = 8.39$, $p = .006$ for orthographic onset versus vowel; $F(1, 41) = 6.97$, $p = .012$ for coda versus vowel. This makes sense, because the orthographic vowel in an exception word is a misleading indicator of the phonological vowel. Thus, in contrast to regular consistent words, words with ambiguous or exceptional vowel pronunciations depend on the entire orthographic input to be pronounced correctly.

These effects can be understood in terms of the nature of the attractors that develop when training on different types of words. The relative independence of the onset, vowel, and coda correspondences indicates that the attractor basins for regular words consist of three separate, orthogonal sub-basins (one for each cluster). When a word is presented, the network settles into the region in state space where these three sub-basins overlap, which corresponds to the word's pro-

nunciation. However, each sub-basin can apply independently, so that "spurious" attractor basins exist where the sub-basins for parts of words overlap (see Fig. 16). Each of these combinations corresponds to a pronounceable nonword that the network will pronounce correctly if presented with the appropriate orthographic input. This componentiality arises directly out of the degree to which the network's representations make explicit the structure of the task. By minimizing the extent to which information is replicated, the representations condense the regularities between orthography and phonology. Only small portions of the input and output are relevant to a particular regularity, which allows it to operate independently of other regularities.

The attractor basins for exception words, by contrast, are far less componential than those for regular words (unfortunately, this cannot be depicted adequately in a two-dimensional diagram such as Fig. 16). In this way, the network can pronounce exception words and yet still generalize well to nonwords. It is important to note, however, that the attractors for exception words are non-componential only in their exceptional aspects — not in a monolithic way. In particular, whereas the consonant clusters in (most) exception words combine componentially, the correct vowel phoneme depends on the entire orthographic input. Thus, a word like PINT is in some sense three-quarters regular in that its consonant correspondences contribute to the pronunciations of regular words and nonwords just like those of other items. The traditional dual-route characterization of a lexical "lookup" procedure for exception words fails to do justice to this distinction.

The development of componentiality in learning. We can gain insight into the development of this componentiality by returning to the simple, two-layer Hebbian network that formed the basis for the frequency-consistency equation (see Fig. 6; also see Van Orden et al., 1990, for related discussion). As expressed by Equation 7, the value of each weight w_{ij} in the network is equal to the sum over training patterns, weighted by the learning rate, of the product of the state of input unit i and the state of output unit j. Patterns for which the input state is 0 do not contribute to the sum, and

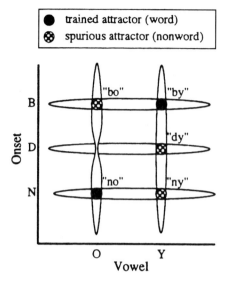

FIG. 16. A depiction of how componential attractors for words can recombine to support pronunciations of nonwords. The attractor basins for words consist of orthogonal sub-basins for each of its clusters (only two are depicted here). Spurious attractors for nonwords exist where the sub-basins for parts of words overlap. To support the noncomponential aspects of attractors for exception words (e.g. DO), the sub-basins for vowels in the region of the relevant consonant clusters must be distorted somewhat (into dimensions in state space other than the ones depicted).

those for which it is 1 contribute the value of the output state, which is either +1 or −1 in this formulation. Thus, the value of the weight can be re-expressed in terms of two counts: the number of consistent patterns, $N^{[C_{ij}]}$, in which the states of units i and j are both positive, and the number of inconsistent patterns, $N^{[I_{ij}]}$, in which i is positive but j is negative:

$$w_{ij} = \varepsilon(N^{[C_{ij}]} - N^{[I_{ij}]}).$$

If patterns differ in their frequency of occurrence, these counts simply become cumulative frequencies (see Equation 12); for clarity of presentation, we leave this out here (see Reggia, Marsland, & Berndt, 1988, for a simulation based directly on these frequencies).

Now consider a word like PINT ⇒ /pInt/. Over the entire set of words, the onset P and /p/ typic-

ally co-occur (but not always; cf. PHONE), so that $N^{[C_{ij}]}$ is large and $N^{[I_{ij}]}$ is small, and the weight between these two units becomes strongly positive. By contrast, /p/ never co-occurs with, for example, an onset K (i.e. $N^{[C_{ij}]} = 0$ and $N^{[I_{ij}]}$ is large), which leads to a strongly negative weight between them. For onset letters that can co-occur with /p/ and P, such as L, $NN^{[C_{ij}]}$ is positive and the resulting weight is therefore less negative. Going a step further, onset /p/ can co-occur with virtually any orthographic vowel and coda, so $NN^{[C_{ij}]}$ for each relevant connections is larger and the weight is closer to zero. Actually, given that each phoneme is inactive for most words, its weights from graphemes in noncorresponding clusters will tend to become moderately negative when Hebbian learning is used. With error-correcting learning, however, these weights remain near zero because the weights between corresponding clusters are sufficient — and more effective, because of the higher unit correlations — for eliminating the error. These same properties hold for /n/ and /t/ in the coda. Thus, the unit correlations across the entire corpus give rise to a componential pattern of weights for consonant phonemes, with significant values only on connections from units in the corresponding orthographic cluster (see Brousse & Smolensky, 1989, for additional relevant simulations).

The situation is a bit more complicated for vowels. First, there is far more variability across words in the pronunciation of vowels compared with consonants (see Venezky, 1970). Consequently, generally $N^{[C_{ij}]}$ is smaller and $N^{[I_{ij}]}$ is larger for connections between vowel graphemes and phonemes than for the corresponding onset and coda connections. The more critical issue concerns exceptional vowel pronunciations in words like PINT. Here, for the I–/I/ correspondence, the small $N^{[C_{ij}]}$ is overwhelmed by the large $N^{[I_{ij}]}$ that comes from the much more common I–/i/ correspondence (in which /I/ has a state of −1). Furthermore, with Hebbian learning, the correlations of /i/ with the consonants P, N, and T are too weak to help. Errorcorrecting learning can compensate to some degree by allowing the weights from these consonant units to grow larger than dictated by correlation under the pressure to eliminate error. Note that this reduces the componentiality of the vowel phoneme weights. Such cross-cluster weights cannot provide a general solution to pronouncing exception words, however, because, in a diverse corpus, the consonants must be able to co-exist with many other vowel pronunciations (e.g. PUNT, PANT). In order for a network to achieve correct pronunciations of exception words while still maintaining the componentiality for regular words (and nonwords), error correction must be combined with the use of hidden units in order to re-represent the similarities among the words in a way that reduces the interference from inconsistent neighbors (as discussed earlier).

Internal representations. In the first analysis we established the componentiality of the attractors for regular words behaviorally, and in the second we showed how it arises from the nature of learning in a simpler, related system. We know that simultaneously supporting the less componential aspects of word reading in the same system requires hidden units and error correction, but we have yet to characterize how this is accomplished. The most obvious possibility would be the one raised for the feedforward networks — that the network had partitioned itself into two subnetworks: a fully componential one for regular words (and nonwords), and a much less componential one for exception words. As before, however, this does not seem to be the case. If we apply the criterion that a hidden unit is important for pronouncing an item if its removal increases the total error on the item by more than 0.1, then there is a significant positive correlation between the numbers of exception words and the numbers of orthographically matched nonwords (listed in Appendix A) for which hidden units are important, $r = .71$ and $t(98) = 9.98, p < .001$. Thus, the hidden units have not become specialized for processing particular types of items.

The questions remains, then, as to how the attractor network — as a single mechanism — implements componential attractors for regular words (and nonwords) and less componential attractors for exception words. In a third analysis we attempted to characterize the degree to which hidden representations for regular versus exception words reflect the differences in the componentiality of their attractors. Specifically, we attempted to determine the extent to which the contribution that an orthographic cluster makes to the hidden representation depends on the context in which it occurs — this should be less for words with more componential representations. For example, consider the onset P in an exception word like PINT. When presented by itself, the onset need only generate its own pronunciation. When presented in the context of _INT, the P must also contribute to altering the vowel from /i/ to /I/. By contrast, in a regular word like PINE, the onset P plays the same role in the context of _INE as when presented in isolation. Thus, if the hidden representations of regular words are more componential than those of exception words, the contribution of an onset (P) should be affected more greatly by the presence of an exception context (_INT) than by a regular context (_INE).

We measured the contribution of an orthographic cluster in a particular context by first computing the hidden representation generated by the cluster with the context (e.g. PINT), and subtracting from this (unit by unit) as a baseline condition the hidden representation generated by the context alone (e.g. _INT). The contribution of a cluster in isolation was computed similarly, except that the baseline condition in this case was the representation generated by the network when presented with no input (i.e. with all grapheme units set to 0). The correlation between these two vector differences was used as a measure of the similarity of the contribution of the cluster in the two conditions. A high correlation indicates that the contribution of a cluster to the hidden representation is independent of the presence of other clusters, and hence reflects a high degree of componentiality.

These contribution correlations were computed separately for the onset, vowel, and coda clusters of the Taraban and McClelland (1987) exception words and their frequency-matched regular consistent control words. Words lacking either an onset or a coda were withheld from the analysis. The correlations for the remaining words were subjected to an ANOVA with frequency and consistency as between-items factors and orthographic cluster as a within-item factor. There was no main effect of frequency, $F(1, 85) = 2.19$, $p = .143$, nor was there any significant interaction of frequency with consistency or orthographic cluster ($F < 1$ for both) so this factor was not considered further. Figure 17 shows the average correlations for regular and exception words as a function of orthographic cluster.

There was no significant interaction of consistency with orthographic cluster ($F < 1$). There was, however, a significant main effect of cluster, $F(2, 170) = 16.1, p < .001$, with the vowel cluster producing lower correlations than either consonant cluster: $F(1, 88) = 26.8, p < .001$ for vowel versus onset; $F(1, 88) = 21.0, p < .001$ for vowel versus coda. More important, regular words ($M = .828$, $SD = .0506$) had higher correlations than exception words ($M = .795$, $SD = .0507$), $F(1, 85) = 20.7$, $p < .001$. Thus, the contributions of orthographic clusters to the hidden representations were more independent of context in regular words than in exception words. In this sense, the representations of regular words were more componential. What is surprising, however, is that the average correlations for exception words, though lower than those of regular words, were still quite high, and there was considerable overlap between the distributions. Furthermore, the representations for regular words were not completely componential in that their correlations were significantly less than 1.0.

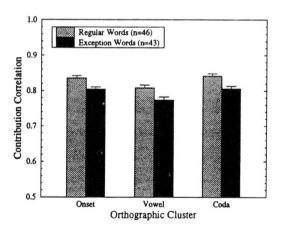

FIG. 17. The similarity (correlations) of the contribution that each orthographic cluster makes to the hidden representation in the context of the remaining clusters versus in isolation, for the Taraban and McClelland (1987) exception words and their regular consistent control words.

Apparently, the hidden representations of words reflect their spelling–sound consistency only slightly. An alternative possibility is that these representations capture predominantly orthographic information across a range of levels of structure (from individual graphemes to combinations of clusters; cf. Shallice & McCarthy, 1985). If this were the case, the low-order orthographic structure about individual graphemes and clusters could support componential attractors for regular words. The presence of higher order structure would make the representation of clusters in both regular and exception words somewhat sensitive to the context in which they occur. More important, this higher order structure would be particularly useful for pronouncing exception words by overriding at the phonological layer the standard spelling–sound correspondences of individual clusters. In this way, noncomponential aspects of the attractors for exception words could co-exist with componential attractors for regular words.

To provide evidence bearing on this explanation, we carried out a final analysis to determine the extent to which the hidden representations are organized on the basis of orthographic (as opposed to phonological) similarity. The hidden representations for a set of items are organized orthographically (or phonologically) to the extent that pairs of items with similar hidden representations have similar orthographic (or phonological) representations. Put more generally, the sets' representations over two groups of units have the same structure to the extent that they induce the same relative similarities among items.

To control for the contribution of orthography as much as possible, the analysis involved 48 triples, each consisting of a nonword, a regular inconsistent word, and an exception word that all shared the same body (e.g. PHINT, MINT, PINT; listed in Appendix A). For each item in a triple, we computed the similarity of its hidden representation with the hidden representations of all of the other items of the same type (measuring similarity by the correlation of unit activities). The similarities among orthographic representations and among phonological representations were computed analogously. The orthographic, hidden, and phonological similarity values for each item were then correlated in a pairwise fashion (i.e. ortho-graphic-phonological, hidden-orthographic, and hidden-phonological). Figure 18 presents the means of these correlation values for nonwords, regular words, and exception words, as a function of each pair of representation types.

First consider the correlation between the orthographic and phonological similarities. These values reflect the relative amounts of structure in the spelling–sound mappings for different types of items. All of the values were relatively high because of the systematicity of English word pro-nunciations; even within exception words, the consonant clusters tended to map consistently. Nonetheless, the mappings for exception words were less structured than those for nonwords or regular words: paired $t(47) = 5.48$, $p < .001$; and $t(47) = 5.77$, $p < .001$, respectively. In other words, orthographic similarity is less related to phono-logical similarity for exception words than for the other items. In a sense, this is the defining char-acteristic of exception words, and thus this find-ing simply verifies that the representations used in the simulations have the appropriate similarity structure.

The more interesting comparisons are those that involve the hidden representations. As Fig. 18

shows, the similarities among the hidden rep-resentations of all types of items were much more highly correlated with their orthographic similarities than with their phonological similar-ities ($p < .001$ for all pairwise comparisons). The representations of nonwords and regular words behave equivalently in this regard. The representa-tions of exception words showed the effect even more strongly, having significantly less phono-logical structure than the other two item types: paired $t(47) = 2.81$, $p = .007$ for exception ver-sus nonword; paired $t(47) = 3.22$, $p = .002$ for exception versus regular. This may be due to the reliance of these words on higher-order ortho-graphic structure to override standard spelling–sound correspondences. Overall, consistent with the explanation offered above, the hidden repres-entations are organized more orthographically than phonologically.

Summary

Interactivity, and its use in implementing attractors, is an important computational principle in con-nectionist accounts of a wide range of cognitive phenomena. Although the tendency of attractors to capture similar patterns might appear to make them inappropriate for tasks in which novel inputs require novel responses, such as pronouncing nonwords in oral reading, the current simulation showed that using appropriately structured repre-sentations led to the development of attractors with componential structure that supported effect-ive generalization to nonwords. At the same time, the network also developed less componential attractors for exception words that violate the regu-larities in the task. A series of analyses suggested that both the componential and noncomponential aspects of attractors were supported by hidden representations that reflect orthographic informa-tion at a range of levels of structure. In this way, attractors provide an effective means of capturing both the regularities and the exceptions in a quasi-regular task.

A further advantage of an attractor network in this domain is that its temporal dynamics in set-tling to a response provide a more direct analogue of readers' naming latencies than does error in a

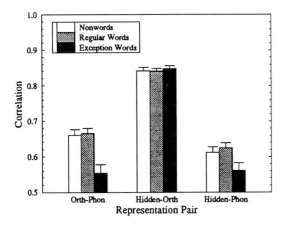

FIG. 18. The correlations among orthographic (Orth), hidden, and phonological (Phon) similarities for body-matched nonwords, regular inconsistent words, and exception words (listed in Appendix A).

feedforward network. In fact, the time it took the network to settle to a stable pronunciation in response to words of varying frequency and consistency reproduced the standard pattern found in empirical studies.

Simulation 4: Surface dyslexia and the division of labor between the phonological and semantic pathways

A central theme of the current work is that the processing of words and nonwords can coexist within connectionist networks that use appropriately structured orthographic and phonological representations and that operate according to certain computational principles. It must be kept in mind, however, that the SM89 general lexical framework — on which the current work is based — contains two pathways by which orthographic information can influence phonological information: a *phonological* pathway and a *semantic* pathway (see Fig. 1). Thus far, we have ignored the semantic pathway in order to focus on the principles that govern the operation of the phonological pathway. However, in our view, the phonological and semantic pathways must work together to support normal skilled reading. For example, semantic involvement is clearly necessary for correct pronunciation of homographs like WIND and READ. Furthermore, a semantic variable — imageability — influences the strength of the frequency by consistency interaction in the naming latencies and errors of skilled readers (Strain, Patterson, & Seidenberg, 1995). Even in traditional dual-route theories (see, e.g. Coltheart et al., 1993; Coltheart & Rastle, 1994), the lexical procedure must influence the output of the sublexical procedure to account for consistency effects among regular words and nonwords (Glushko, 1979).

The SM89 framework (and the implied computational principles) provides a natural formulation of how contributions from both the semantic and phonological pathways might be integrated in determining the pronunciation of a written word. Critically, when formulated in connectionist terms, this integration also has important implications for the nature of learning in the two pathways. In most connectionist systems, learning is driven by some measure of the discrepancy or error between the correct response and the one generated by the system. To the extent that the contribution of one pathway reduces the overall error, the other pathway will experience less pressure to learn. As a result, on its own, it may master only those items it finds easiest to learn. Specifically, if the semantic pathway contributes significantly to the pronunciation of words, then the phonological pathway need not master all of the words by itself. Rather, it will tend to learn best those words high in frequency, consistency, or both; low-frequency exception words may never be learned completely. This is especially true if there is some intrinsic pressure within the network to prevent overlearning — for example, if weights have a slight bias toward staying small. Of course, the combination of the semantic and phonological pathways will be fully competent. But readers of equivalent overt skill may differ in their division of labor between the two pathways (see, e.g. Baron & Strawson, 1976). In fact, if the semantic pathway continues to improve with additional reading experience, the phonological pathway would become increasingly specialized for consistent spelling–sound mappings at the expense of higher frequency exception words. At any point, brain damage that impaired or eliminated the semantic pathway would lay bare the latent inadequacies of the phonological pathway. In this way, a detailed consideration of the division of labor between the phonological and semantic pathways is critical to understanding the specific patterns of impaired and preserved abilities of brain-damaged patients with acquired dyslexia.

Of particular relevance in this context is the finding that brain damage can selectively impair either nonword reading or exception word reading while leaving the other (relatively) intact. Thus, phonological dyslexic patients (Beauvois & Derouesné, 1979) read words (both regular and exception) much better than nonwords, whereas surface dyslexic patients (Marshall & Newcombe, 1973; Patterson et al., 1985) read nonwords much better than (exception) words.

Phonological dyslexia has a natural interpretation within the SM89 framework in terms of selective damage to the phonological pathway (or perhaps within phonology itself; see Patterson & Marcel, 1992), so that reading is accomplished primarily (perhaps even exclusively in some patients) by the semantic pathway. This pathway can pronounce words but is unlikely to provide much useful support in pronouncing nonwords because, by definition, these items have no semantics. Along these lines, as mentioned in the previous section, Plaut and Shallice (1993; also see Hinton & Shallice, 1991) used a series of implementations of the semantic route to provide a comprehensive account of deep dyslexia (Coltheart et al., 1980; Marshall & Newcombe, 1966), a form of acquired dyslexia similar to phonological dyslexia but also involving the production of semantic errors (see Friedman, 1996; Glosser & Friedman, 1990, for arguments that deep dyslexia is simply the most severe form of phonological dyslexia). The question of the exact nature of the impairment that gives rise to reading via semantics in phonological dyslexia, and whether this interpretation can account for all of the relevant findings, is taken up in the General Discussion.

Surface dyslexia, on the other hand, seems to involve reading primarily via the phonological pathway because of an impairment of the semantic pathway. In its purest, *fluent* form (e.g. Patient MP, Behrmann & Bub, 1992; Bub, Cancelliere, & Kertesz, 1985; Patient KT, McCarthy & Warrington, 1986; Patient HTR, Shallice et al., 1983), patients exhibit normal accuracy and latency in reading words with consistent spelling–sound correspondences and in reading nonwords but often misread exception words, particularly those of low frequency, by giving a pronunciation consistent with more standard correspondences (e.g. SEW ⇒ "sue"). Although we ascribe such errors to influences of consistency, they are conventionally termed *regularizations* (Coltheart, 1981), and we have retained this terminology. Thus, there is a frequency by consistency interaction in accuracy that mirrors the interaction in latency exhibited by normal skilled readers (Andrews, 1982; Seidenberg, 1985; Seidenberg et al., 1984; Taraban & McClelland, 1987; Waters & Seidenberg, 1985).

The relevance of the semantic impairment in surface dyslexia is supported by the finding that, in some cases of semantic dementia (Graham, Hodges, & Patterson, 1994; Patterson & Hodges, 1992; Schwartz, Marin, & Saffran, 1979) and of Alzheimer's type dementia (Patterson, Graham, & Hodges, 1994), the surface dyslexic reading pattern emerges as lexical semantic knowledge progressively deteriorates.

The previous simulations of the phonological pathway, along with that of SM89, are similar to surface dyslexic patients in that they read without the aid of semantics. The simulations do not provide a direct account of surface dyslexia, however, because they all read exception words as well as skilled readers. One possibility is that surface dyslexia arises from partial impairment of the phonological pathway in addition to severe impairment of the semantic pathway. A more interesting possibility, based on the division-of-labor ideas mentioned above, is that the development and operation of the phonological pathway are shaped in an important way by the concurrent development of the semantic pathway and that surface dyslexia arises when the intact phonological pathway operates in isolation because of an impairment of the semantic pathway.

We used two sets of simulations to test the adequacy of these two accounts of surface dyslexia. The first set investigated the effects of damage to the attractor network developed in the previous simulation. The second involved a new network trained in the context of support from semantics.

Phonological pathway lesions

Patterson et al. (1989) investigated the possibility that surface dyslexia might arise from damage to an isolated phonological pathway. They lesioned the SM89 model by removing different proportions of units or connections, and they measured its performance on regular and exception words of various frequencies. The damaged network's pronunciation of a given word was compared with the correct pronunciation and with a plausible alternative — for exception words, this was the regularized pronunciation. Patterson and colleagues found that, after damage, regular and exception words produced about equal amounts of error, and there was no effect of frequency in reading exception words. Exception words were much more likely than regular words to produce the alternative pronunciation, but a comparison of the phonemic features in errors revealed that the network showed no greater tendency to produce regularizations than other errors that differ from the correct pronunciation by the same number of features. Thus, the damaged network failed to show the frequency by consistency interaction and the high proportion of regularization errors on exception words characteristic of surface dyslexia.

Using a more detailed procedure for analyzing responses, Patterson (1990) found that removing 20% of the hidden units produced better performance on regular versus exception words and a (nonsignificant) trend toward a frequency by consistency interaction. Figure 19 shows analogous data from 100 instances of lesions to a replication of the SM89 network, in which each hidden unit had a probability of either .2 or .4 of being

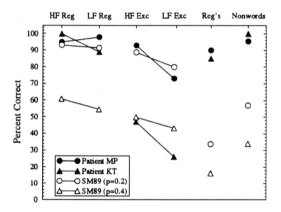

FIG. 19. Performance of two surface dyslexic patients, MP (Behrmann & Bub, 1992; Bub, Cancelliere, & Kertesz, 1985) and KT (McCarthy & Warrington, 1986), and of a replication of the Seidenberg and McClelland (1989) model (SM89) when lesioned by removing each hidden unit with probability $p = .2$ or .4 (results are averaged over 100 such lesions). Correct performance is given for Taraban and McClelland's (1987) high-frequency (HF) and low-frequency (LF) regular consistent words (Reg) and exception words (Exc) and for Glushko's (1979) nonwords. "Reg's" is the approximate percentage of errors on the exception words that were regularizations.

removed. Plotted for each severity of damage are the network's percentage correct on Taraban and McClelland's (1987) high- and low-frequency exception words and their regular consistent control words, percentage of errors on the exception words that are regularizations, and percentage correct on Glushko's (1979) nonwords; any pronunciation consistent with that of some word with the same body in the training corpus was counted as correct. Also shown in the figure are the corresponding data for two surface dyslexic patients, MP (Behrmann & Bub, 1992; Bub et al., 1985) and KT (McCarthy & Warrington, 1986).

The milder lesions ($p = .2$) produced a good match to MP's performance on the Taraban and McClelland (1987) words. However, the more severe lesions ($p = .4$) failed to simulate the more dramatic effects shown by KT. Instead, while the damaged network and KT performed about equally well on the high-frequency exception words, the network was not as impaired on the low-frequency exception words and was much more impaired on both high- and low-frequency regular words. In addition, with the less severe damage, only about a third of the network's errors to exception words were regularizations, and only just above half of the nonwords were pronounced correctly; for more severe damage, these figures were even lower. By contrast, both MP and KT produced regularization rates around 85–90% and were near perfect at nonword reading. Overall, the attempts to account for surface dyslexia by damaging the SM89 model have been less than satisfactory (see Behrmann & Bub, 1992; Coltheart et al., 1993, for further criticisms).

One possible explanation of this failing parallels our explanation of the SM89 model's poor nonword reading: It is due to the use of representations that do not make the relevant structure between orthography and phonology sufficiently explicit. In essence, the influence of spelling–sound consistency in the model is too weak. This weakness also seems to be contributing to its inability to simulate surface dyslexia after severe damage: Regular word reading, nonword reading, and regularization rates were all too low. This interpretation leads to the possibility that a network trained with more appropriately structured representations would, when damaged, successfully reproduce the surface dyslexic reading pattern.

Method. We lesioned the attractor network either by removing each hidden unit or each connection between two groups of units with some probability p, or by adding normally distributed noise to the weights on connections between two groups of units. In the latter case, the severity of the damage depends on the standard deviation of the noise — a higher standard deviation constitutes a more severe impairment. This form of damage has the advantage over the permanent removal of units or connections of reducing the possibility of idiosyncratic effects from lesions to particular units or connections. As Shallice (1988) has pointed out, such effects in a network simulation are of little interest to the study of the cognitive effects of damage to the brain given the vast difference in scale between the two systems (also see Plaut, 1995). In general, simulation studies comparing the effects of adding noise to weights with the effects of removing units or connections (e.g. Hinton & Shallice, 1991) have found that the two procedures yield qualitatively equivalent results.[14]

Fifty instances of each type of lesion of a range of severities were administered to each of the main sets of connections in the attractor network (graphemes-to-hidden, hidden-to-phonemes, phonemes-to-hidden, and phonemes-to-phonemes connections) and to the hidden units. After a given lesion, the operation of the network when presented with an input and the procedure for determining its response were the same as those in Simulation 3.

To evaluate the effects of lesions, we tested the network on Taraban and McClelland's (1987) high- and low-frequency regular consistent words and exception words and on Glushko's (1979) nonwords. For the words, in addition to measuring correct performance, we calculated the percentage of errors on the exception words that corresponded to a regularized pronunciation. The full list of responses that were accepted as regularizations is given in Appendix C. Because the undamaged network mispronounces the word SPOOK, this item was not included in the calculation of regularization rates. For the nonwords, a pronunciation was accepted as correct if it was consistent with the pronunciation of some word in the training corpus with the same body (see Appendix B).

Results and discussion. Figure 20 shows the data from the attractor network after the weights of each of the four main sets of connections were corrupted by noise of varying severities. The milder lesions to the graphemes-to-hidden connections

(on the top left of the figure) produce clear interactions of frequency and consistency in correct performance on word reading. For instance, after noise with a standard deviation of 0.4 was added, the network pronounced correctly over 96% of regular words and 93% of high-frequency exception words but only 77% of low-frequency exception words. In addition, for these lesions, 68% of errors on exception words were regularizations, and 89% of the nonwords were pronounced correctly. Compared with the results from lesions to 20% of the hidden units in the SM89 network, these showed a stronger effect of consistency and were a better match to the performance of MP (although the regularization rate was somewhat low; see Fig. 19). Thus, as predicted, the use of representations that better capture spelling–sound structure produces a stronger frequency by consistency interaction, more regularizations, and better nonword reading.

As found for the SM89 network, however, more severe lesions did not reproduce the pattern shown by KT. Lesions that reduced correct performance on high-frequency exception words to equivalent levels ($SD = 1.0$; network, 46%; KT, 47%) did not impair performance on low-frequency exception words sufficiently (network, 38%; KT, 26%) and, unlike KT, showed impaired performance on both high- and low-frequency regular words (network, 65% and 60%; KT, 100% and 89%, respectively). Furthermore, and even more unlike KT's performance, there was a substantial drop in both the regularization rate (network, 32%; KT, 85%) and in performance on nonwords (network, 60%; KT, 100%).

Lesions to the other sets of connections produced broadly similar but even weaker results: The frequency by consistency interactions were weaker (especially for severe lesions), the impairment of regular words was more severe (except for phoneme-to-hidden lesions), and the regularization rates were much lower (note that a different range of lesion severities was used for the hidden-to-phonemes connections because they are much more sensitive to noise). Thus, in summary, mild grapheme-to-hidden lesions in the attractor network could account for MP's behavior, but more severe lesions could not reproduce KT's behavior.

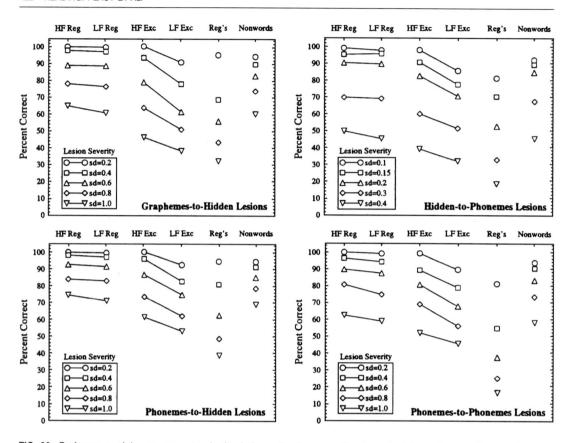

FIG. 20. Performance of the attractor network after lesions of various severities to each of the main sets of connections, in which weights are corrupted by noise with $M = 0$ and SDs as indicated. Correct performance is given for Taraban and McClelland's (1987) high-frequency (HF) and low-frequency (LF) regular consistent words (Reg) and exception words (Exc), and for Glushko's (1979) nonwords. "Reg's" is the percentage of errors on the exception words that were regularizations.

These negative findings are not specific to the use of noise in lesioning the network; removing units or connections produced qualitatively equivalent results, except that the regularization rates were even lower. To illustrate this, Table 9 presents data for the two patients and for the attractor network after either mild or severe lesions of the graphemes-to-hidden connections, the hidden units, or the hidden-to-phonemes connections. The levels of severity were chosen to approximate the performance of MP and KT on low-frequency exception words.

In summary, some types of lesion to a network implementation of the phonological pathway were able to approximate the less impaired pattern of performance shown by MP but were unable to account for the more dramatic pattern of results

shown by KT. These findings suggest that impairment to the phonological pathway may play a role in the behavior of some surface dyslexic patients, but they seem unlikely to provide a complete explanation of some patients — particularly those with normal nonword reading and severely impaired exception word reading.

Phonological and semantic division of labor

We now consider an alternative view of surface dyslexia: that it reflects the behavior of an undamaged but isolated phonological pathway that had learned to depend on support from semantics in normal reading. All of the previous simulations of the phonological pathway were trained to be fully competent on their own. Thus, if this explanation for surface dyslexia holds, it entails

TABLE 9
Performance of Two Patients and of the Attractor Network After Lesions of Units or Connections

Reader	Correct performance					
	HF reg	LF reg	HF exc	LF exc	Reg's	Nonwords
Patient MP[a]	95	98	93	73	90[c]	95.5
Patient KT[b]	100	89	47	26	85[c]	100
Attractor network after lesions to:						
Graphemes-to-hidden connections						
$p = .05$	95.8	94.4	88.9	75.8	65.6	89.6
$p = .3$	49.0	42.8	37.8	27.9	26.0	45.3
Hidden units						
$p = .075$	93.9	93.5	85.6	75.8	51.4	85.6
$p = .3$	54.5	49.4	45.3	31.7	18.0	48.4
Hidden-to-phonemes connections						
$p = .02$	89.0	89.2	81.0	70.0	48.3	82.4
$p = .1$	36.3	31.8	26.4	24.8	13.3	35.5

Note. p is the probability that each of the specified units or connections is removed from the network for a lesion; results are averaged over 50 instances of such lesions. Correct performance is given for Taraban and McClelland's (1987) high-frequency (HF) and low-frequency (LF) regular consistent words (reg) and exception words (exc), and for Glushko's (1979) nonwords. "Reg's" is the percentage of errors on the exception words that are regularizations.
[a] From Bub, Cancelliere, and Kertesz (1985; also see Behrmann & Bub, 1992).   [b] From Patterson (1990, based on McCarthy & Warrington, 1986).   [c] Approximate (from Patterson, 1990).

a reappraisal of the relationship between those simulations and the word reading system of normal skilled readers.

The current simulation involved training a new network in the context of an approximation to the contribution of semantics. Including a full implementation of the semantic pathway is, of course, beyond the scope of the present work. Rather, we will characterize the operation of this pathway solely in terms of its influence on the phoneme units within the phonological pathway. Specifically, to the extent that the semantic pathway has learned to derive the meaning and pronunciation of a word, it provides additional input to the phoneme units, pushing them toward their correct activations. Accordingly, we can approximate the influence of the semantic pathway on the development of the phonological pathway by training the latter in the presence of some amount of appropriate external input to the phoneme units.

A difficult issue arises immediately in the context of this approach, concerning the time-course of development of the semantic contribution during the training of the phonological pathway.

Presumably, the mapping between semantics and phonology develops, in large part, prior to reading acquisition, as part of speech comprehension and production. By contrast, the orthography-to-semantics mapping, like orthography-to-phonology mapping, obviously can develop only while learning to read. In fact, it is likely that the semantic pathway makes a substantial contribution to oral reading only once the phonological pathway has developed to some degree — in part because of the phonological nature of typical reading instruction and in part because, in English, the orthography-to-phonology mapping is far more structured than the orthography-to-semantics mapping. The degree of learning within the semantic pathway is also likely to be sensitive to the frequency with which words are encountered. Accordingly, as a coarse approximation, we will assume that the strength of the semantic contribution to phonology in reading increases gradually over time and is stronger for high-frequency words.

It must be acknowledged that this characterization of semantics fails to capture a number of properties of the actual word reading system that are certainly important in some contexts: other lexical factors, such as imageability, that influence the contribution of semantics to phonology, interactivity between phonology and semantics, and the relative time-course of processing in the semantic and phonological pathways. Nonetheless, the manipulation of external input to the phoneme units allows us to investigate the central claim in the proposed explanation of surface dyslexia: that partial semantic support for word pronunciations alleviates the need for the phonological pathway to master all words such that, when the support is eliminated by brain damage, the surface dyslexic reading pattern emerges.

Method. As will become apparent below, the necessary simulation requires from four to five times more training epochs than the corresponding previous simulation. Thus, an attractor network trained on actual word frequencies could not be developed because of the limitations of available computational resources. Rather, the simulation involved training a feedforward network using a square-root compression of word frequencies. Such a network produces a pattern of results in word and nonword reading that is quite similar to the attractor network (see Simulation 2). More important, there is nothing specific about the feedforward nature of the network that is necessary to produce the results we report below; an attractor network trained under analogous conditions would be expected to produce qualitatively equivalent results.

The network was trained with the same learning parameters as the corresponding network from Simulation 2 except for one change: A small amount of *weight decay* was reintroduced, such that each weight experienced a slight pressure to decay toward zero, proportional (with constant 0.001) to its current magnitude. As mentioned in the context of Simulation 1, this provides a bias toward small weights that prevents the network from overlearning and thereby encourages good generalization (see Hinton, 1989). As is demonstrated below, the introduction of weight decay does not alter the ability of the network to replicate the patterns of normal skilled performance on words and nonwords.

Over the course of training, the magnitude S of the input to phoneme units from the (putative) semantic pathway for a given word was set to be

$$S = g \frac{\log(f+2)t}{\log(f+2)t+k} \qquad (16)$$

where f is the Kuçera and Francis (1967) frequency of the word and t is the training epoch. The parameters g

and k determine the asymptotic level of input and the time to asymptote, respectively. Their values ($g = 5$, $k = 2,000$ in the current simulation) and, more generally, the specific analytic function used to approximate the development of the semantic pathway affect the quantitative but not the qualitative aspects of the results reported below. Figure 21 shows the mean values of this function over training epochs for the Taraban and McClelland (1987) high- and low-frequency words. If, for a given word, the correct state of a phoneme unit was 1.0, then its external input was positive; otherwise it was the same magnitude but negative.

For the purposes of comparison, we trained a second version of the network without semantics, using the same learning parameters and initial random weights.

Results and discussion. Learning in the network trained without semantics reached asymptote by Epoch 500, at which point it pronounced correctly all but 9 of the 2,998 words in the training corpus (99.7% correct). Figure 22 shows the performance of the network on Taraban and McClelland's (1987) high- and low-frequency exception words and their regular consistent control words and on Glushko's (1979) nonwords over the course of training. Performance on regular words and on nonwords improved quite rapidly over the first 100 epochs, reaching 97.9% for the words and 96.5% for the nonwords at this point. Performance on high-frequency exception words improved somewhat more slowly. By contrast, performance on the low-frequency exception words improved far more slowly, only becoming perfect

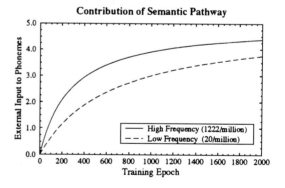

FIG. 21. The magnitude of the additional external input supplied to phoneme units by the putative semantic pathway, as a function of training epoch, for the Taraban and McClelland (1987) high- and low-frequency words.

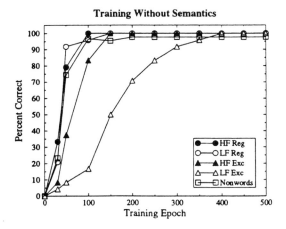

FIG. 22. Correct performance of the network trained without semantics, as a function of training epoch, on Taraban and McClelland's (1987) high-frequency (HF) and low-frequency (LF) regular consistent words (Reg) and exception words (Exc), and on Glushko's (1979) nonwords.

at Epoch 400. At this point, all of the words were read correctly. Even so, there were significant main effects of frequency, $F(1, 92) = 35.9, p < .001$, and consistency, $F(1, 92) = 64.3, p < .001$, and a significant interaction of frequency and consistency, $F(1, 92) = 26.4, p < .001$, in the cross-entropy error produced by the words: The means were 0.031 for the high-frequency regular (HFR) words, 0.057 for the low-frequency regular (LFR) words, 0.120 for the high-frequency exception (HFE) words, and 0.465 for the low-frequency exception (LFE) words. Thus, the network exhibited the standard pattern of normal skilled readers; the use of weight decay during training did not substantially alter the basic influences of frequency and consistency in the network.

In the current context, the network that was trained with a concurrently increasing contribution from semantics (as shown in Fig. 21) is the more direct analogue of a normal reader. Not surprisingly, overall performance improved more rapidly in this case. All of the regular words and the high-frequency exception words were pronounced correctly by Epoch 110, and the low-frequency exception words were 70.8% correct. By Epoch 200, all of the low-frequency exception words were correct, and nonword reading was 95.4% correct (where we assume nonwords receive no contribu-

tion from semantics). At this point, the network with semantics exhibited the standard effects of frequency and consistency in cross-entropy error (means: HFR = 0.021, LFR = 0.025, HFE = 0.102, LFE = 0.382): for frequency, $F(1, 92) = 19.0, p < .001$; for consistency, $F(1, 92) = 45.0, p < .001$; and for the frequency by consistency interaction, $F(1, 92) = 17.8, p < .001$. Even after a considerable amount of additional training (Epoch 2,000), during which the division of labor between the semantic and phonological pathways changed considerably (as shown below), the overt behavior of the normal "combined" network showed the same pattern of effects (nonword reading: 97.7% correct; word cross-entropy error means: HFR = 0.013, LFR = 0.014, HFE = 0.034, LFE = 0.053): for frequency, $F(1, 92) = 13.6, p < .001$; for consistency, $F(1, 92) = 125.1, p < .001$; and for the frequency by consistency interaction, $F(1, 92) = 9.66, p = .003$.

This last finding may help explain why, as in previous simulations, networks that are trained to be fully competent on their own replicate the effects of frequency and consistency in naming latency, even though, from the current perspective, such simulations are not fully adequate characterizations of the isolated phonological pathway in skilled readers. The reason is that when performance is near asymptote — because of either extended training or semantic support — word frequency and spelling–sound consistency affect the relative effectiveness of processing different words in the same way. This asymptotic behavior follows from the frequency–consistency equation (see Equation 12 and Fig. 8). Increasing training (by increasing each $F^{[p]}$ in the equation) or adding an additional semantic term to the sum serves equally to drive units further toward their extreme values (also see the General Discussion).

Figure 23 shows the performance of the network at each point in training when the contribution from semantics was eliminated — that is, after a complete semantic "lesion." These data reflect the underlying competence of the phonological pathway when trained in the context of a concurrently developing semantic pathway. First notice that the simulation involves training for 2,000 epochs, even though the bulk of "overt"

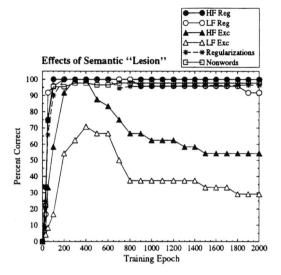

FIG. 23. Performance of the network trained with semantics after a semantic "lesion," as a function of the training epoch at which semantics was eliminated, for Taraban and McClelland's (1987) high-frequency (HF) and low-frequency (LF) regular consistent words (Reg) and exception words (Exc), and for Glushko's (1979) nonwords, and the approximate percentage of errors on the exception words that were regularizations.

reading acquisition occurs in the first 100 epochs. Thus, the effects in the network should be thought of as reflecting the gradual improvement of skill from reading experience that, in the human system, spans perhaps many decades.

Initially, performance on nonwords and all types of words improved as the phonological pathway gained competence in the task, much as when the network was trained without semantics (see Fig. 22). But as the semantic pathway increased in strength (as characterized by the curves in Fig. 21), the accuracy of the combined network's pronunciations of words improved even faster (recall that the combined network was perfect on the Taraban and McClelland, 1987, words by Epoch 200). The pressure to continue to learn in the phonological pathway was thereby diminished. Eventually, at about Epoch 400, this pressure was balanced by the bias for weights to remain small. At this point, most of the error that remained came from low-frequency exception words. This error was reduced as the semantic pathway continued to increase its

contribution to the pronunciation of these (and other) words. As a result, the pressure for weights to decay was no longer balanced by the error, and the weights became smaller. This caused a deterioration in the ability of the phonological pathway to pronounce low-frequency exception words by itself. With further semantic improvement, the processing of high-frequency exception words in the phonological pathway also began to suffer. Virtually all of the errors on exception words that resulted from this process were regularizations (plotted as asterisks in Fig. 23). Larger weights were particularly important for exception words because they had to override the standard spelling–sound correspondences that were implemented by many smaller weights. Furthermore, high-frequency words were less susceptible to degradation because any decrement in overt performance induced much larger weight changes to compensate. By contrast, the processing of regular words and nonwords was relatively unaffected by the gradual reduction in weight magnitudes. Low-frequency regular words just began to be affected at Epoch 1,900.

Thus, with extended reading experience, there was a redistribution of labor within the model between the semantic and phonological pathways. As the semantic pathway gained in competence, the phonological pathway increasingly specialized for consistent spelling–sound correspondences at the expense of exception words. Notice, however, that even with extended training, the phonological pathway continued to be able to read some exception words — particularly those of high frequency. In this way it is quite unlike the sublexical procedure in a traditional dual-route theory, which can read only regular words and no exception words. It is also important to keep in mind that normal overt performance — as supported by the combination of the phonological and semantic pathways — became fully accurate very early on and continued to improve in naming latency (as reflected indirectly by error). Finally, we should emphasize that, although the only factor we manipulated in the current simulation was extent of reading experience, we envision that a wide variety of factors may influence the division of labor and overall competence of an individual's reading system, including the nature of reading instruction, the sophistication of preliterate phonological representations, relative experience in reading aloud versus silently, the computational resources devoted to each pathway, and the reader's more general skill levels in visual pattern recognition and in spoken word comprehension and production.

According to this interpretation of surface dyslexia, differences among patients in their ability to read exception words may not reflect differences in the severities of their brain damage. Rather, they may reflect differences in their premorbid division of labor between pathways, with the patients exhibiting the more severe impairment being those who had relied to a greater extent on semantic support. To illustrate this more directly, Fig. 24 presents data from MP and KT as well as data from the network at two different points in training, when semantics was eliminated. Overall, the network at Epoch 400 provided a close match to MP's performance, whereas the network at Epoch 2,000 matched KT's performance. The only substantial discrepancy was that, in both conditions, the network's rate of regularizations was higher than that of the corresponding

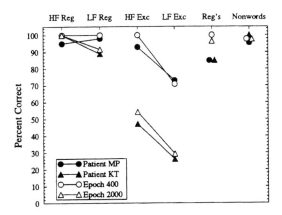

FIG. 24. Performance of two surface dyslexic patients, MP (Behrmann & Bub, 1992; Bub, Cancelliere, & Kertesz, 1985) and KT (McCarthy & Warrington, 1986), and of the network at different points in training when semantics was eliminated. Correct performance is given for Taraban and McClelland's (1987) high-frequency (HF) and low-frequency (LF) regular consistent words (Reg) and exception words (Exc), and for Glushko's (1979) nonwords. "Reg's" is the approximate percentage of errors on the exception words that were regularizations.

patient (although the patient data are only approximate; see Patterson, 1990).

Thus far, we have assumed that surface dyslexic patients, at least those of the fluent type, have a lesion that completely eliminates any contribution of the semantic pathway in reading. This assumption may be reasonable for MP and KT because both patients had very severe impairments in written word comprehension. MP was at chance at selecting which of four written words was semantically related to a given word or picture (Bub et al., 1985; also see Bub, Black, Hampson, & Kertesz, 1988). KT's severe word comprehension deficit prevented him from scoring on either the Vocabulary or Similarities subtests of the Wechsler Adult Intelligence Scale (WAIS; e.g. "Bed, bed, I do not know what a bed is"; McCarthy & Warrington, 1986, p.361).

However, some patients with fluent surface dyslexia appear to have only a partial impairment in the semantic pathway. In particular, among patients with semantic dementia whose reading has been tested in detail, the large majority also exhibit a surface dyslexic pattern such that severity of the reading disorder is correlated with the degree of semantic deterioration (Graham et al., 1994; Patterson & Hodges, 1992; but see Cipolotti & Warrington, 1995). A similar finding applies among patients with Alzheimer's type dementia (Patterson et al., 1994). Such cases have a natural interpretation in the current context in terms of the performance of the network with partial rather than complete elimination of the contribution of the putative semantic pathway. To illustrate this effect, Fig. 25 shows the performance of the network trained with semantics to Epoch 2,000, as the strength of the semantic contribution to the phoneme units — the parameter g in Equation 16 — was gradually reduced. As semantics degraded, performance on the low-frequency exceptions was the first to be affected, followed by the high-frequency exceptions. By contrast, performance on regular words and nonwords was relatively unaffected by semantic deterioration, although performance on low-frequency regular words was somewhat impaired as semantics was completely eliminated (for $g = 0.0$, the data are identical to those in Fig. 23 for Epoch 2,000). In fact, semantic

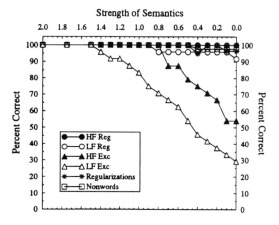

FIG. 25. The effect of gradual elimination of semantics on the correct performance of the network after 2,000 epochs of training with semantics, for Taraban and McClelland's (1987) high-frequency (HF) and low-frequency (LF) regular consistent words (Reg) and exception words (Exc), and for Glushko's (1979) nonwords, and the approximate percentage of errors on the exception words that were regularizations.

dementia patients also exhibit a drop in performance on low-frequency regular words when their semantic impairment becomes very severe (Patterson & Hodges, 1992). Of course, a patient with progressive dementia may also have some amount of deterioration within the phonological pathway itself. As Fig. 20 and Table 9 illustrate, such impairment would tend to degrade performance on exception words even further but would also affect performance on regular words and nonwords to some degree.

The observation of surface dyslexic reading in association with either degraded semantics or a disrupted mapping from semantics to phonology (which, by our account, should have the same effect) is common and indeed has been reported in several languages other than English, including Dutch (Diesfeldt, 1992), Italian (Miceli & Caramazza, 1993), and Japanese (Patterson, Suzuki, Wydell, & Sasanuma, 1995). It is important to note, however, that there are cases that suggest there may be individual differences in the extent to which the pronunciation of low-frequency exception words depends on contributions from semantics. The first is patient WLP (Schwartz, Saffran, & Marin, 1980), one of the most thoroughly studied

cases of neurodegenerative disease in the history of cognitive neuropsychology. Although WLP began to make regularization errors on low-frequency exception words at a later stage of her disease, there was a period of testing at which her semantic disorder was already marked but her exception-word reading was still largely intact. Even more dramatically, Cipolotti and Warrington (1995) recently reported a patient, DRN, with a substantial loss of meaning for low-frequency words, though his comprehension of high-frequency words (as measured by the difficult task of producing word definitions) was still intact. DRN's performance in reading low-frequency exception words was, however, almost perfectly intact, with only two or three reported regularization errors (CANOE ⇒ "kano", SHOE ⇒ "show"). By our account, these observations suggest that, in these individuals, the phonological pathway had developed a relatively high degree of competence without assistance from semantics; but this post hoc interpretation clearly requires some future, independent source of evidence.

One final comment with respect to phonological dyslexia seems appropriate. Recall that phonological dyslexic patients are able to read words much better than nonwords. In the current simulation, the external input to the phoneme units that represents the contribution of the semantic pathway was sufficient, on its own, to support accurate word reading (but not nonword reading). On the other hand, severe damage to the phonological pathway certainly impaired nonword reading (see Fig. 20 and Table 9). In the limit of a complete lesion between orthography and phonology, nonword reading would be impossible. Thus, a lesion to the network that severely impaired the phonological pathway while leaving the contribution of semantics to phonology (relatively) intact would replicate the basic characteristics of phonological dyslexia (although we do not claim that such a lesion provides the correct account of all phonological dyslexic patients — see the General Discussion).

Summary

The detailed patterns of behavior of acquired dyslexic patients provide important constraints on the nature of the normal word reading system. The most relevant patients in the current context are those with (fluent) surface dyslexia, because, like the networks, they seem to read without the aid of semantics. These patients read nonwords normally but exhibit a frequency by consistency interaction in word reading accuracy such that low-frequency exception words are particularly error prone and typically produce regularization errors. Patterson et al. (1989; Patterson, 1990) were relatively unsuccessful in replicating the surface dyslexia reading pattern by damaging the SM89 model. Although the current simulations used more appropriately structured representations, when damaged they too failed to produce surface dyslexia — particularly the more severe form exhibited by KT (McCarthy & Warrington, 1986). These findings call into question the interpretation of surface dyslexia as arising from a partial impairment of the phonological pathway in addition to extensive impairment of the semantic pathway. Rather, a better match to the surface dyslexic reading pattern — in both its mild and severe forms — was produced by the normal operation of an isolated phonological pathway that developed in the context of support from the semantic pathway. This finding supports a view of the normal word reading system in which there is a division of labor between the phonological and semantic pathways such that neither pathway alone is completely competent and the two must work together to support skilled word and nonword reading.

General discussion

The current work develops a connectionist approach to processing in quasi-regular domains as exemplified by English word reading. The approach derives from the general computational principles that processing is graded, random, adaptive, interactive, and nonlinear and that representations and knowledge are distributed (McClelland, 1991, 1993). When instantiated in the specific domain of oral reading, these principles lead to a view in which the reading system learns gradually to be sensitive to the statistical structure among

orthographic, phonological, and semantic representations and in which these representations simultaneously constrain each other in interpreting a given input.

In support of this view, we have presented a series of connectionist simulations of normal and impaired word reading. A consideration of the shortcomings of a previous implementation (Seidenberg & McClelland, 1989) in reading nonwords led to the development of orthographic and phonological representations that better capture the relevant structure among the written and spoken forms of words. In Simulation 1, a feedforward network that used these representations learned to pronounce all of a large corpus of monosyllabic words, including the exception words, and yet also pronounced nonwords as well as skilled readers.

An analysis of the effects of word frequency and spelling–sound consistency in a related but simpler system formed the basis for understanding the empirical pattern of naming latencies as reflecting an appropriate balance between these factors. In Simulation 2, a feedforward network trained with actual word frequencies exhibited good word and nonword reading and also replicated the frequency by consistency interaction in the amount of error it produced for words of various types.

In Simulation 3, a recurrent network replicated the effects of frequency and consistency on naming latency directly in the time required to settle on a stable pronunciation. More critically, the attractors that the network developed for words over the course of training had componential structure that also supported good nonword reading.

Finally, in Simulation 4, the role of the semantic pathway in oral reading was considered in the context of acquired surface dyslexia, in which patients read nonwords well but exhibit a frequency by consistency interaction in naming accuracy, typically regularizing low-frequency exception words. The view that these symptoms — particularly in their most severe form — reflect the operation of a partially impaired phonological pathway was not supported by the behavior of the attractor network after a variety of types of damage. A further simulation supported an alternative interpretation of surface dyslexia: that it reflects the normal operation of a phonological pathway that is not fully competent on its own because it learned to rely on support from the semantic pathway (which is subsequently impaired by brain damage).

Alternative perspectives on word reading

We can now raise, and then consider in the light of the results summarized above, several issues concerning the nature of the reading process. There is general agreement that (at least) two pathways contribute to reading words and nonwords aloud, but this still leaves open a number of fundamental questions. What are the underlying explanatory principles that determine the existence and the character of these different pathways? How does the operation of each arise from the fundamental principles, and what are the particular principles to which each pathway adheres? How do the different pathways combine to contribute to word and nonword reading? We consider here two very different approaches to these questions.

One view — the so-called dual-route view — holds that the fundamental explanatory principle in the domain of word reading is that distinctly different mechanisms are necessary for reading nonwords on the one hand and exception words on the other. The two mechanisms operate in fundamentally different ways. One assembles pronunciations from phonemes generated by the application of grapheme–phoneme correspondence rules. The other maps whole (orthographic) inputs to whole (phonological) outputs, using either a lexical lookup procedure or, in more recent formulations, an associative network (Pinker, 1991) or McClelland and Rumelhart's (1981) interactive activation model (Coltheart et al., 1993; Coltheart & Rastle, 1994).

The alternative view — our connectionist approach — holds that the fundamental explanatory principle in the domain of word reading is that the underlying mechanism uses a nonlinear, similarity-based activation process in conjunction with a frequency-sensitive connection weight adjustment process. Two pathways are necessary in reading, not because different principles apply to items of different types, but because different tasks must be performed. One pathway — here

termed the *phonological* pathway — performs the task of transforming orthographic representations into phonological representations directly. The other — the *semantic* pathway — actually performs two tasks. The first is specific to reading, namely, the transformation of orthographic representations into semantic representations. The second is a more general aspect of language, namely, the transformation of semantic representations into phonological representations.

At first glance, these two views may appear so similar that deciding between them hardly seems worth the effort. After all, both the lexical procedure in the dual-route account and the semantic pathway in the connectionist account can read words but not nonwords, and both the sublexical procedure and the phonological pathway are critical for nonword reading and work better for regular words than for exception words. It is tempting to conclude that these two explanatory perspectives are converging on essentially the same processing system. Such a conclusion, however, neglects subtle but important differences in the theoretical and empirical consequences of the two approaches.

As a case in point, the sublexical GPC procedure in the dual-route account cannot be sensitive to whole-word frequency, because it eschews storage of whole lexical items. By contrast, in the connectionist approach, the phonological pathway maintains an intrinsic and incontrovertible sensitivity to both word frequency and spelling–sound consistency (also see Monsell, 1991). This sensitivity is captured in approximate form by the frequency–consistency equation (Equation 12), which expresses the strength of the response of a simple two-layer network to a given test pattern in terms of the frequency and overlap of the training patterns. The connectionist approach, as reflected by this equation, predicts that there can never be a complete dissociation of frequency and consistency effects; the phonological pathway must always exhibit sensitivity to both. This sensitivity takes a specific form, however: Items that are frequent, consistent, or both will have an advantage over items that are neither frequent nor consistent, but items that are frequent and consistent may not enjoy a large additional advantage over those that are only frequent or only consistent; as either frequency or consistency increases, sensitivity to differences in the other decreases.[15]

This relationship, as we have previously discussed, is approximately characterized by the frequency–consistency equation, which we reproduce here in a form that is elaborated to include a term for the contribution of the semantic pathway, and by separating out the contributions of training patterns whose outputs are consistent with that of the test pattern (i.e. so-called *friends*; Jared et al., 1990) from those whose outputs are inconsistent (i.e. *enemies*). Accordingly, the state $s_j^{[t]}$ of an output (phoneme) unit j that should be on in test pattern t can be written as[16]

$$s_j^{[t]} = \sigma(S^{[t]} + \varepsilon(F^{[t]} + \sum_f F^{[f]}O^{[ft]}$$
$$- \sum_e F^{[e]}O^{[et]})), \qquad (17)$$

in which the logistic activation function $\sigma(\cdot)$ is applied to the contribution of the semantic pathway, $S^{[t]}$, plus the contribution of the phonological pathway, which itself is the sum of three terms (scaled by the learning rate, ε): (a) the cumulative frequency of training on the pattern itself, (b) the sum of the frequencies of the friends (indexed by f) times their overlap with the test pattern, and (c) the sum of the frequencies of the enemies (indexed by e) times their overlap with the test pattern. It must be kept in mind, however, that this equation is only approximate for networks with hidden units and trained by error correction. These two aspects of the implemented networks are critical in that they help to overcome interference from enemies (i.e. the negative terms in Equation 17), thereby enabling the networks to achieve correct performance on exception words — that is, words with many enemies and few if any friends — as well as on regular words and nonwords.

Many of the basic phenomena in the domain of word reading can be seen as natural consequences of adherence to this frequency–consistency equation. In general, any factor that serves to increase the summed input to the activation function, $\sigma(\cdot)$ in Equation 17, improves performance, as measured by naming accuracy, latency, or both. Thus, more frequent words are read better (e.g. Forster & Chambers, 1973; Frederiksen & Kroll, 1976) because they have higher values of $F^{[t]}$, and words with greater spelling–sound consistency are read better (Glushko, 1979; Jared et al., 1990) because the positive sum from friends outweighs the negative sum from enemies. The nonlinear, asymptotic nature of the activation function, however, dictates that the contributions of these factors are subject to "diminishing returns" as performance improves. Thus, as reading experience accumulates —thereby increasing $F^{[t]}$, $F^{[f]}$, and $F^{[e]}$ proportionally or, equivalently, increasing ε — the absolute magnitudes of the frequency and consistency effects diminish (see, e.g. Backman et al., 1984; Seidenberg, 1985). The same principle applies among different types of stimuli for a reader at a given skill level: Performance on stimuli that are strong in one factor is relatively insensitive to variation in other factors. Thus, regular words show little effect of frequency, and high-frequency words show little effect of consistency (as shown in Fig. 7). The result is the standard pattern of interaction between frequency and consistency, in which the naming of low-frequency exception words is disproportionately slow or inaccurate (Andrews, 1982; Seidenberg, 1985; Seidenberg et al., 1984; Taraban & McClelland, 1987; Waters & Seidenberg, 1985).

The elaborated version of the frequency–consistency equation also provides a basis for understanding the effects of semantics on naming performance. In the approximation expressed by Equation 17, the contribution of the semantic pathway for a given word, $S^{[t]}$, is simply another term in the summed input to each output (phoneme) unit. Just as with frequency and consistency, then, a stronger semantic contribution moves the overall input further along the asymptotic activation function, thereby diminishing the effects of other factors. As a result, words with a relatively weak semantic contribution (e.g. abstract or low-imageability words; Jones, 1985; Saffran, Bogyo, Schwartz, & Marin, 1980) exhibit a stronger frequency by consistency interaction — in particular, naming latencies and error rates are disproportionately high for items that are weak on all three dimensions: abstract, low-frequency exception words (Strain et al., 1995).

Of course, as the simulations demonstrate, networks with hidden units that are trained with error correction can learn to pronounce correctly all types of words without any help from semantics. In the context of the more general framework, however, full competence is required only from the combination of semantic and phonological influences. Thus, as the semantic pathway develops and $S^{[t]}$ increases, the contribution required from the other, phonological terms in Equation 17 to achieve the same level of performance is correspondingly reduced. With the additional assumption that the system has an intrinsic bias against unnecessary complexity (e.g. by limiting its effective degrees of freedom with weight decay), extended reading experience leads to a redistribution of labor. Specifically, as the semantic pathway improves, the phonological pathway gradually loses its ability to process the words it learned most weakly: those that are low in both frequency and consistency.

If, in this context, the contribution from semantics is severely weakened or eliminated (by brain damage), the summed input to each output unit will be reduced by as much as $S^{[t]}$. For output units with significant negative terms in their summed input — that is, for those in words with many enemies — this manipulation may cause their summed input (and hence their output) to change sign. The result is an incorrect response. Such errors tend to be regularizations because the reduced summed input affects only those output units whose correct activations are inconsistent with those of the word's neighbors. Furthermore, because frequency makes an independent positive contribution to the summed inputs, errors are more likely for low- than for high-frequency exception words. By contrast, a reduction in the contribution from semantics has little if any effect on correct performance on regular words because the positive contribution from their friends is sufficient on its own to give output units the appropriately signed summed input. The resulting pattern of behavior, corresponding to fluent surface dyslexia (Bub et al., 1985; McCarthy & Warrington, 1986; Shallice et al., 1983), can thus be seen as an exaggerated manifestation of the same influences

of frequency and consistency that give rise to the normal pattern of naming latencies.

The pattern of joint, nonlinear sensitivity to the combined effects of frequency and consistency in the connectionist account, along with assumptions about the contribution of semantics, leads to a number of predictions not shared by traditional dual-route accounts. First, frequency and consistency can trade off against each other, so that the detrimental effects of spelling–sound inconsistency can always be overcome by sufficiently high word frequency. Consequently, the connectionist account makes a strong prediction: There cannot be an (English-language) surface dyslexic patient who reads no exception words; if regular words can be read normally, there must also be some sparing of performance on high-frequency exceptions. By contrast, a dual-route framework could account for such a patient quite easily in terms of damage that eliminates the lexical route(s) while leaving the GPC route in operation. In fact, given the putative separation of these routes, the framework would seem to predict the existence of such patients. The connectionist account also differs from the dual-route account in claiming that consistency rather than regularity per se (i.e. adherence to GPC rules) is the determining variable in "regularization" errors (where, as formulated here, consistency depends on all types of orthographic overlap rather than solely on word bodies; cf. Glushko, 1979). Finally, the connectionist account predicts a close relationship between impairments in the contribution of semantics to phonology and the surface dyslexic reading pattern (Graham et al., 1994; Patterson & Hodges, 1992), although this relationship will be subject to premorbid individual differences in reading skill and division of labor between the semantic and phonological pathways. Thus, patients with highly developed phonological pathways may not exhibit the pattern unless the semantic impairment is very severe (Cipolotti & Warrington, 1995; Schwartz et al., 1980). By contrast, dual-route theories that include a lexical, nonsemantic pathway (e.g. Coltheart, 1978, 1985; Coltheart et al., 1993) predict that selective semantic damage should never affect naming accuracy.

Our connectionist account, we believe, also has an important advantage of simplicity over the dual-route approach. This advantage goes well beyond the basic point that it provides a single set of computational principles that can account for exception word and nonword reading whereas the dual-route model must rely on separate sets of principles. The additional advantage lies in the fact that the boundary between regular and exception words is not clear, and all attempts to draw such boundaries lead to unfortunate consequences. First, the marking of items as exceptions that must be looked up as wholes in the lexicon ignores the fact that most of the letters in these items will take their standard grapheme-phoneme correspondences. Thus, in PINT, three quarters of the letters take their regular correspondence. Second, the marking of such items as exceptions ignores the fact that even the parts that are exceptional admit of some regularity, so that, for example, the exceptional pronunciation of the I in PINT also occurs in many other words containing an I (e.g. most of those ending in _I * E, _IND or _ILD, where the "*" represents any consonant). Third, exceptions often come in clusters that share the same word body. Special word-body rules may be invoked to capture these clusters, but then any word that conforms to the more usual correspondence becomes exceptional. Thus, we could treat OO ⇒ /u/ when followed by K as regular, but this would make SPOOK, which takes the more common correspondence OO ⇒ /U/, an exception. The explicit treatment of virtually any word as an exception, then, neglects its partial regularity and prevents the word both from benefiting from this partial regularity and from contributing to patterns of consistency it enters into with other items. Our connectionist approach, by contrast, avoids the need to impose such unfortunate divisions and leaves a mechanism that exhibits sensitivity to all these partially regular aspects of so-called exception words.

The fact that exceptions are subject to the same processes as all other items in our system allows us to explain why there are virtually no completely arbitrary exceptions. On the other hand, the dual-route approach leaves this fact of the spelling-sound system completely unexplained. Nor, in fact, do some dual-route models even provide a basis for accounting for effects of consistency in reading words and nonwords. Recent dual-route theorists (e.g. Coltheart et al., 1993; Coltheart & Rastle, 1994) have appealed to partial activation of other lexical items as a basis for such effects. Such an assumption moves partway toward our view that consistency effects arise from the influence of all lexical items. We would only add that our connectionist model exhibits these effects as well as the requisite sensitivity to general grapheme-phoneme correspondences, without stipulating a separate rule system over and above the system that exhibits the broad range of consistency effects.

Additional empirical issues

Proponents of dual-route theories have raised a number of empirical issues that they believe challenge our connectionist account of normal and impaired word reading. For example, Coltheart et al. (1993; also see Besner et al., 1990) raise six questions concerning the reading process, all but one of which — exception word reading — they deem problematic for the SM89 framework. Two of the remaining five — nonword reading and acquired surface dyslexia — have been addressed extensively in the current work. Here we discuss how the remaining three issues — acquired phonological dyslexia, developmental dyslexia, and lexical decision — may be accounted for in light of these findings. We also consider three other empirical findings that have been interpreted as providing evidence against the current approach — pseudohomophone effects (Buchanan & Besner, 1993; Fera & Besner, 1992; McCann & Besner, 1987; Pugh, Rexer, & Katz, 1994), stimulus blocking effects (Baluch & Besner, 1991; Coltheart & Rastle, 1994; Monsell et al., 1992), and the recent finding that naming latencies for exception words are influenced by the position of the exceptional correspondence (Coltheart & Rastle, 1994).

Acquired phonological dyslexia. As mentioned earlier, the SM89 framework is straightforward in accounting for the central characteristic of acquired phonological dyslexia — substantially better word reading than nonword reading — in terms of a relatively selective impairment of the phonological pathway. The apparent difficulty arises when patients are considered who (a) are virtually unable to read nonwords, which suggests a complete elimination of the phonological pathway, and (b) have an additional semantic impairment that seems to render the semantic pathway insufficient to account for the observed proficiency at word reading. Two such patients have been described in the literature: WB (Funnell, 1983) and WT (Coslett, 1991). To explain the word reading of these patients, dual-route theorists claim that it is necessary to introduce a third route that is lexical but nonsemantic.

In point of fact, Coltheart et al. (1993) explicitly considered an alternative explanation and (we think too hastily) rejected it:

> Perhaps a patient with an impaired semantic system, who therefore makes semantic errors in reading comprehension and who also has a severely impaired nonsemantic reading system, could avoid making semantic errors in reading aloud by making use of even very poor information about the pronunciation of a word yielded by the nonsemantic reading system. The semantic system may no longer be able to distinguish the concept *orange* from the concept *lemon*; however, to avoid semantic errors in reading aloud, all the nonsemantic route needs to deliver is just the first phoneme of the written word, not a complete representation of its phonology. (p.596)

Coltheart and colleagues argued against this account entirely on the basis of two findings of Funnell (1983): WB did not pronounce correctly any of a single list of 20 written nonwords, and he did not give the correct phonemic correspondence to any of 12 single printed letters. Thus, Coltheart et al. (1993) claimed, "WB's nonsemantic reading route was not just severely impaired, it was completely abolished" (p.596).

This argument is unconvincing. First, it seems unwise to base such a strong theoretical claim on

so few empirical observations, especially given how little information is required of the phonological pathway in the above account. To pronounce a nonword correctly, by contrast, all of its phonemes must be derived accurately. Thus, WB's inability to read 20 nonwords cannot be taken as definitive evidence that his phonological pathway is completely inoperative. Furthermore, WB did, in fact, make semantic errors in oral reading (e.g. TRAIN ⇒ "plane", GIRL ⇒ "boy"; see Appendix 1 of Funnell, 1983). Although such errors were relatively rare, comprising only 7.5% (5/67) of all lexical error responses, there were no error responses that were completely unrelated to the stimulus. Thus, the effect of semantic relatedness in errors is difficult to ascribe to chance responding (see Ellis & Marshall, 1978; Shallice & McGill, 1978). More generally, fully 38.8% (26/67) of WB's lexical errors had a semantic component, typically in combination with visual/phonemic or morphological relatedness.

More critically, Coltheart and colleagues failed to take into account the fact that WB exhibited deficits on purely phonological tasks such as nonword repetition (Funnell, 1983) and phoneme stripping and blending (Patterson & Marcel, 1992), which suggests an additional impairment within phonology itself. Funnell had argued that such a phonological impairment could not explain WB's nonword reading deficit because (a) he repeated nonwords more successfully (10/20) than he read them (0/20), and (b) he achieved some success (6/10) in blending three-phoneme words from auditory presentation of their individual phonemes. We note, however, that the failure to repeat fully half of a set of simple, single-syllable, wordlike nonwords (e.g. COBE, NUST) certainly represents a prominent phonological deficit. Moreover, because Funnell's auditory blending test used only words as target responses, WB's partial success on this task is not especially germane to the issue. Patterson and Marcel (1992) assessed WB's blending performance with nonword targets and found that he was unable to produce a single correct response whether the auditory presentation consisted of the three individual phonemes of a simple nonword (such as COBE) or of its onset and rime. Patterson and Marcel argued that this phonological deficit in a nonreading task was sufficient to account for WB's complete inability to read nonwords.

Thus, the pattern of performance exhibited by WB can be explained within the SM89 framework in terms of a mildly impaired semantic reading pathway, possibly an impaired phonological reading pathway, but, in particular, an impairment within phonology itself. A similar explanation applies to WT (Coslett, 1991): Although this patient's performance on phonological blending tasks was not reported, she was severely and equally impaired in her ability to read and to repeat the same set of 48 nonwords.

We point out in passing that deep dyslexia (Coltheart et al., 1980), the remaining major type of acquired central dyslexia and one closely related to phonological dyslexia (see, e.g. Glosser & Friedman, 1990), can be accounted for in terms of the same computational principles that are used in the current work (see Plaut & Shallice, 1993).

Developmental dyslexia. Our focus in the current work has been on characterizing the computational principles governing normal skilled reading and acquired dyslexia following brain damage in premorbidly literate adults. Even so, we believe that the same principles provide insight into the nature of reading acquisition, both in its normal form and in developmental dyslexia, in which children fail to acquire age-appropriate reading skills.

There is general agreement that a number of distinct patterns of developmental dyslexia exist, although exactly what these patterns are and what gives rise to them are a matter of ongoing debate. A common viewpoint is that there are developmental analogues to the acquired forms of dyslexia (see, e.g. Baddeley, Ellis, Miles, & Lewis, 1982; Harris & Coltheart, 1986; Marshall, 1984). Perhaps the clearest evidence comes from Castles and Coltheart (1993), who compared 53 dyslexic children with 56 age-matched normal readers in their ability to pronounce exception words and nonwords. The majority (32) of the dyslexic children were abnormally poor on both sets of items. However, 10 were selectively impaired at exception word reading, which corresponds to developmental surface dyslexia, and 8 were selectively impaired at nonword reading, which corresponds

to developmental phonological dyslexia. Castles and Coltheart interpreted their findings as supporting a dual-route theory of word reading in which either the lexical or the sublexical procedure can selectively fail to develop properly (although they offered no suggestion as to why this might be).

More recently, Manis, Seidenberg, Doi, McBride-Chang, and Peterson (in press) compared 51 dyslexic children with 51 controls matched for age and 27 matched for reading level. They confirmed the existence of separate surface and phonological dyslexic patterns, although, again, most of the dyslexic children showed a general reading impairment. Critically, the performance of the developmental surface dyslexic children was remarkably similar to that of reading-level matched controls, which suggests a developmental delay. By contrast, the phonological dyslexic children performed unlike either set of controls, which suggests a deviant developmental pattern. Although these findings are not incompatible with the dual-route account, Manis and colleagues contend that they are more naturally accounted for in terms of different impediments to the development of a single (phonological) pathway. Specifically, they suggest (following SM89) that the delayed acquisition in developmental surface dyslexia may arise from limitations in the available computational resources within the phonological route. Consistent with this interpretation, SM89 found that a version of their network trained with only half the normal number of hidden units showed a disproportionate impairment on exception words compared with regular words (although performance on all items was poorer, consistent with finding that generalized deficits are most common). However, the nonword reading capability of the network was not tested, and Coltheart et al. (1993) pointed out that it was not likely to be very good given that overall performance was worse than in the normal network, which itself was impaired on nonword reading.

Just as for normal skilled reading, this limitation of the SM89 model stems from its use of inappropriately structured orthographic and phonological representations. To demonstrate this, we trained a feedforward network with only 30 hidden units in an identical fashion to the one with

100 hidden units from Simulation 4 (without semantics). This network was chosen for comparison simply because it is the only one for which the relevant acquisition data have already been presented, in Fig. 22 — the other networks would be expected to show similar effects. The corresponding data for the version with 30 hidden units are given in Fig. 26. As a comparison of the figures reveals, limiting the number of hidden units selectively impairs performance on exception words, particularly those of low frequency. By contrast, nonword reading is affected only very slightly. Notice that the performance of the dyslexic network at Epoch 500 is quite similar to that of the normal network at about Epoch 150. Thus, limiting the computational resources that are available for learning the spelling-to-sound task reproduces the basic delayed pattern of developmental surface dyslexia. Other manipulations that impede learning, such as weak or noisy weight changes, would be expected to yield similar results.

With regard to developmental phonological dyslexia, Manis et al. (in press) suggest that a selective impairment in nonword reading may arise from the use of phonological representations that are poorly articulated, perhaps because of more

peripheral disturbances (also see, e.g. Liberman & Shankweiler, 1985; Rack, Snowling, & Olson, 1992). A consideration of the normal SM89 model is instructive here. That network used representations that, we have argued, poorly capture the relevant structure within and between orthography and phonology. As a result, the model was over 97% correct at reading words, both regular and exception, but only 75% correct on a subset of Glushko's (1979) nonwords (when scored appropriately; see Seidenberg & McClelland, 1990). Thus, in a sense, the model behaved like a mild phonological dyslexic (see Besner et al., 1990, for similar arguments). In this way, the performance of the model provides evidence that a system with adequate computational resources, but which fails to develop appropriately componential orthographic and (particularly) phonological representations, will also fail to acquire normal proficiency in sublexical spelling–sound translation. It should also be kept in mind that, to whatever extent the semantic pathway develops and contributes during reading acquisition, the dissociation between word and nonword reading would be exacerbated.

A final point of contention with regard to the implications of developmental reading disorders for the SM89 framework concerns the existence of children whose oral reading ability, even on exception words, far surpasses their comprehension — as in so-called *hyperlexia* (Huttenlocher & Huttenlocher, 1973; Mehegan & Dreifuss, 1972; Metsala & Siegel, 1992; Silverberg & Silverberg, 1967). Typically, these children are moderately to severely retarded on standardized intelligence tests and may totally lack conversational speech. They also tend to devote a considerable amount of time and attention to reading, although this has not been studied thoroughly. We suggest that, perhaps owing to abnormally poor development in the semantic pathway, such children may have phonological pathways that are like our networks trained without semantics. In the limit, such networks learn to pronounce all types of words and nonwords accurately with no comprehension.

Lexical decision. The final of Coltheart et al.'s (1993) objections to the SM89 model concerns its ability to perform lexical decisions. Although

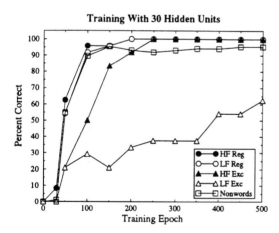

FIG. 26. Correct performance of a feedforward network with only 30 hidden units on Taraban and McClelland's (1987) high- (HF) and low-frequency (LF) exception words (Exc) and their regular consistent control words (Reg), and on Glushko's (1979) nonwords, as a function of training epoch. The network was trained exactly as the one whose corresponding data are shown in Fig. 22.

SM89 established that, under some stimulus conditions, the model can discriminate words from nonwords on the basis of a measure of its accuracy in regenerating the orthographic input, Besner and colleagues (Besner et al., 1990; Fera & Besner, 1992) demonstrated that its accuracy in doing so is worse than that of human readers in many conditions. Coltheart et al. (1993) mistakenly claimed that the SM89 orthographic error scores yielded a false-positive rate of over 80% on Waters and Seidenberg's (1985) nonwords when word error rates were equated with human readers' rates at 6.1% — in fact, these numbers result from using phonological error scores (Besner et al., 1990), which SM89 did not use (although they did suggest that learning phonological attractors for words might help). Although the actual false-positive rate was much lower — Besner and colleagues reported a rate of 28% when orthographic and phonological error scores were summed and orthographically strange words were excluded — it was still unsatisfactory.

Of course, SM89 never claimed that orthographic and phonological information was completely sufficient to account for lexical decision performance under all conditions, and they pointed out that "there may be other cases in which subjects must consult information provided by the computation from orthography to semantics" (p.552). Semantics is a natural source of information with which to distinguish words from nonwords, given that, in fact, a string of letters or phonemes is defined to be a word by virtue of it having a meaning. Coltheart et al. (1993) raised the concern that, in a full implementation of the SM89 framework, the presentation of an orthographically regular nonword (e.g. SARE) would activate semantics to the same degree as a word (e.g. CARE) and thereby preclude lexical decision.

Although further simulation work is clearly required to address the full range of lexical decision data adequately, a few comments may serve to allay this specific concern. We imagine that the semantic representations for words are relatively sparse, meaning that each word activates very few of the possible semantic features and each semantic feature participates in the meanings of a very small percentage of words.

Connectionist networks of the sort we are investigating learn to set the base activation level of each output unit to the expected value of its correct activations across the entire training corpus, because these values minimize the total error in the absence of any information about the input. In the case of sparse semantic representations, this means that semantic features would be almost completely inactive without specific evidence from the orthographic input that they should be active. Notice that the nature of this evidence must be very specific in order to prevent the semantic features of a word like CARE from being activated by the presentation of orthographically similar words like ARE, SCARE, CAR, and so forth. This extreme sensitivity to small orthographic distinctions would also prevent many semantic features from being activated strongly by a nonword like SARE. Thus, on this account, the computational requirements of a connectionist system that maps orthography to semantics veritably entail the ability to perform lexical decision.

Pseudohomophone and blocking effects. Two other, somewhat overlapping sets of empirical findings have been viewed as problematic for the current approach: pseudohomophone effects (Buchanan & Besner, 1993; Fera & Besner, 1992; McCann & Besner, 1987; Pugh et al., 1994) and blocking effects (Baluch & Besner, 1991; Coltheart & Rastle, 1994; Monsell et al., 1992). The first set involves demonstrations that, under a variety conditions, pseudohomophones (i.e. nonwords with pronunciations that match that of a word; e.g. BRANE) are processed differently than orthographically matched nonpseudohomophonic nonwords (e.g. FRANE). For example, readers are faster to name pseudohomophones and slower (and less accurate) to reject them in lexical decision (McCann & Besner, 1987). The second set of problematic findings involves demonstrations that readers' performance is sensitive to the context in which orthographic stimuli occur, usually operationalized in terms of how stimuli are blocked together during an experiment. For example, skilled readers are slower and make more regularization errors when pronouncing exception words intermixed with nonwords than when pronouncing pure blocks of exception words (Monsell et al., 1992).

Neither of these sets of phenomena is handled particularly well by the SM89 implementation, but both have natural formulations within the more general framework that includes semantics. Pseudo-homophone effects may stem from an articulatory advantage in initiating familiar pronunciations (Seidenberg, Petersen, MacDonald, & Plaut, 1996) or from interactions between phonology and semantics that do not occur for control nonwords. Blocking effects may reflect adjustments — either stimulus-driven or under the strategic control of readers — in the relative contribution of the semantic and phonological pathways in lexical tasks. These interpretations are supported by recent findings of Pugh et al. (1994), who investigated effects of spelling–sound consistency and semantic relatedness in lexical decision as a function of whether or not the nonword foils include pseudohomophones. They found faster latencies for consistent words than for inconsistent words only in the context of purely nonpseudohomophonic nonwords; there was no effect of consistency when pseudohomophones were present. Similarly, in a dual lexical decision paradigm, they obtained facilitation for visually similar word pairs that were phonologically consistent (e.g. BRIBE–TRIBE) and inhibition for those that were inconsistent (e.g. COUCH–TOUCH; Meyer et al., 1974) only when no pseudohomophones were present; the introduction of pseudohomophones eliminated the consistency effect. However, semantic relatedness (e.g. OCEAN-WATER) yielded facilitation regardless of nonword context. These findings suggest that readers normally use both the semantic and phonological pathways in lexical decision but avoid the use of the phonological pathway when this would lead to inappropriate semantic activity, as when pseudohomophones are included as foils.

Effects of position of exceptional correspondence. Coltheart and Rastle (1994) argued that one of the determinants of naming RT for exception words is the position — counting graphemes and phonemes from left to right — at which the word deviates from rule-governed correspondences. They claimed that such an effect is incompatible with any parallel approach to word naming, whereas the Dual-Route Cascaded (DRC) model of Coltheart et al. (1993) both predicts and simulates this effect, because the GPC procedure of the DRC model operates serially across an input string. The three monosyllabic words for which they provided simulation data from the DRC model are CHEF, TOMB, and GLOW. By their account, the critical factor is that CHEF — for which the model requires the largest number of processing cycles — is irregular at its first grapheme/phoneme, TOMB, requiring an intermediate number of cycles, breaks the rules at the second grapheme/phoneme; and GLOW, which yields the fastest time from the model, becomes only irregular at the third position.

By our account, the critical difference between these three words may not be the position of irregularity but rather the proportion of other known words with similar spelling patterns that agree or conflict with the target word's pronunciation (see Jared & Seidenberg, 1990, for an elaboration of this argument). The *Concise Oxford Dictionary* lists 72 monosyllabic words starting with CH_; 63 of these have the pronunciation /C/ as in CHAIR; 5 have the pronunciation /S/ as in CHEF; 4 are pronounced /k/ as in CHORD. CHEF is therefore a highly inconsistent word. For the word TOMB, it is somewhat difficult to know what neighborhood of words to choose for a similar analysis. If we take words beginning with TO_, although the two most common pronunciations are /a/ as in TOP and /O/ as in TONE, the third most likely pronunciation, with 7 exemplars, is /U/ as in TO, TOO, and TOMB; other pronunciations (as in TON, TOOK, and TOIL) are less common. At the body level, TOMB has one friend, WOMB, and two enemies, BOMB and COMB. TOMB is therefore a moderately inconsistent word. Finally, for words ending in _OW, although the GPC procedure of Coltheart et al. (1993) considers OW ⇒ /W/ (as in NOW) regular and OW ⇒ /O/ as in GLOW irregular, in fact 17 of the 29 monosyllabic words in English ending in _OW rhyme with GLOW, whereas only 12 have Coltheart and colleagues' "regular" pronunciation as in NOW. Thus, GLOW is inconsistent but has the more frequent correspondence. Consistent with this interpretation, the attractor network developed in Simulation 3 produced naming latencies of 2.00 for CHEF, 1.92 for TOMB, and 1.73 for GLOW.

The experiment with human readers performed by Coltheart and Rastle (1994) revealed their predicted relationship between position of irregularity and naming RT, with the slowest RTs to words like CHAOS with an irregular first grapheme–phoneme correspondence and fastest RTs to words like BANDAGE that do not become irregular until the fifth grapheme–phoneme correspondence. All of the stimulus words had two syllables, which prevents us from evaluating the performance of our networks on their materials. Inspection of these words in their appendix, however, again suggests a confounding between position and degree of consistency. Take the items which, by their analysis, become irregular at the fifth position; almost half of these words (6/14) were two-syllable words with first-syllable stress and with second syllables ending in silent E (e.g. BANDAGE and FESTIVE). Because the GPC procedure of Coltheart et al. (1993) applies the same rules independent of syllable position, it assigns the vowel /A/ to the grapheme A_E in the second syllable of BANDAGE and the vowel /I/ to the grapheme I_E in the second syllable of FESTIVE. Despite the fact that our model is not yet able to treat multisyllabic words, the nature of its operation ensures that it would be sensitive to the fact that words with this sort of pattern do not have tense (long) vowels in second syllable. The great majority of two-syllable words ending in _IVE (e.g. ACTIVE, PASSIVE, MOTIVE, NATIVE) have the same final vowel as FESTIVE, making FESTIVE a relatively consistent word. Whether this reinterpretation of the Coltheart and Rastle effect turns out to give an adequate account of their results remains to be seen from future empirical and modeling work. Furthermore, even if a position effect is found when properly controlled stimuli are used, it may very well be consistent with a parallel computation of phonology from orthography in which the decision to initiate articulation depends only on the initial phoneme(s) (Kawamoto, Kello, & Jones, 1994, in press). Thus, rather than being incompatible with our approach, Coltheart and Rastle's findings may in fact relate to simple properties of networks that develop representations over time.

Extensions of the approach

The approach we have taken can be extended in a number of different directions. The most obvious and natural extension is to the reading of multi-syllabic words. The pronunciation of these words exhibits the same kind of quasi-regular structure found at the level of monosyllables (Jared & Seidenberg, 1990), but these regularities now apply not just to grapheme–phoneme correspondences but to the assignment of stress as well, and they involve sensitivity to linguistic variables such as the form–class of the word, its derivational status, and several other factors (Smith & Baker, 1976).

One challenge that arises in extending our approach to multisyllabic words is finding a better method for condensing regularities across positions within a word. The representations we have used condense regularities within the onset or the coda of a monosyllabic word, but experience with particular correspondences in the onset does not affect processing of the same correspondence in the coda or vice versa. Indeed, our model has two completely separate sets of weights for implementing these correspondences, and most of its failures (e.g. with the consonant J in the coda) are attributable to the fact that its knowledge cannot be transferred between onsets and codas.

Ultimately, it seems likely that the solution to the problem of condensing regularities will involve sequential processing at some level. The paradigm case of this is the approach used in NETtalk (Sejnowski & Rosenberg, 1987; also see Bullinaria, 1995), in which the letters are processed sequentially, proceeding through a text from left to right. The input is shifted through a window that is several slots wide, and each letter is mapped to its corresponding phoneme when it falls in the central slot. This allows each successive letter to be processed by the same set of units, so the regularities extracted in processing letters in any position are available for processing letters in every other position. At the same time, the presence of other letters in the slots flanking the central slot allows the network to be context sensitive and to exhibit consistency effects.

One drawback of such a letter-by-letter approach is that the onset of pronunciation of a word is completely insensitive to the consistency of its vowel; consistency does affect the vowel correspondences, but these only come into play after the pronunciation of the onset has been completed. This presents a problem because the empirical finding of consistency effects in naming latencies is one of the main motivations of a connectionist approach to word reading. For this reason, and because there is a great deal of coarticulation of successive phonemes, we have taken the view that fluent, skilled reading involves a parallel construction of a pronunciation of at least several phonemes at a time. One possibility is that skilled readers attempt to process as much of the word as they can in parallel and then redirect attention to the remaining part and try again (see Plaut, McClelland, & Seidenberg, in press, for a simulation illustrating this approach). In this way, early on in learning, reading is strictly sequential, as in NETtalk, but as skill develops, it becomes much more parallel, as in the models we have presented here. The result is that the system can always fall back on a sequential approach, which allows the application of knowledge of regularities acquired in reading units of any size to be applied across the entire length of the utterance (Skoyles, 1991). The approach extends naturally to words of any length, with the size of the window of parallel computation being completely dependent on experience.

Moving beyond single word reading, the approach taken here is applicable, we believe, to a wide range of linguistic and cognitive domains — essentially to all those with quasi-regular structure in the sense that there is systematicity that coexists with some arbitrariness and many exceptions. The first domain to which the approach was applied was that of inflectional morphology (Rumelhart & McClelland, 1986). As stated in our introduction, this application certainly remains controversial; Pinker and his colleagues (Marcus et al., 1992; Pinker, 1991; Pinker & Prince, 1988) continue to maintain that no single mechanism can fully capture the behavior of the regular inflectional process and the handling of exceptions. Although we do not claim that the existing connectionist simulations have fully addressed all valid criticisms raised, at this point we see little in these criticisms that stands against the applicability of the connectionist approach in principle. Indeed, the arguments raised in these articles do not, in general, reflect a full appreciation of the capabilities of connectionist networks in quasi-regular domains. For example, Pinker (1991) did not acknowledge that connectionist models of both reading aloud (as shown here and in SM89) and of

inflectional morphology (Daugherty & Seidenberg, 1992) show the very frequency by regularity interaction that he takes as one of the key indicators of the operation of a (frequency-insensitive) rule system and a (frequency-sensitive) lexical lookup mechanism.

Indeed, there are several aspects of the empirical data in the domain of inflectional morphology that appear at this point to favor an interpretation in terms of a single, connectionist system that is sensitive to both frequency and consistency. We consider here one such aspect — namely, the historical evolution of the English past tense system. Hare and Elman (1995) have reviewed the pattern of change from the early Old English period (circa 870) to the present. In early Old English, there were two main types of verbs — strong and weak — each consisting of several subtypes. Over the period between 870 and the present, the different types of weak verbs coalesced into a single type: the current "regular" past. Many of the strong verbs "regularized," but several of them persist to this day as the various irregular verbs of modern English. The coalescence of the various types of weak verbs into a single type, the pattern of susceptibility to regularization among the strong verbs, and the occasional occurrence of "irregularization," in which a particular weak verb took on the characteristics of a cluster of strong verbs, are all traced to workings of a single connectionist system that is sensitive to both frequency and consistency. In Hare and Elman's approach, language change is cast as the iterative application of a new generation of learners (simulated by new, untrained networks) to the output of the previous generation of learners (simulated by old networks, trained on the output of even older networks). Each generation imposes its own distortions on the corpus: Among these are the elimination of subtle differences between variations of the weak past that apply to similar forms, and the regularization of low-frequency irregular forms with few friends. Gradually over the course of generations, the system is transformed from the highly complex system of circa 870 to the much simpler system that is in use today. The remaining irregular verbs are either highly consistent with their neighbors, highly frequent, or both; less frequent and less consistent strong verbs have been absorbed by the regular system. Crucially for our argument, both the "regular" (or weak) system and the "exception" (or strong) system show effects of frequency and consistency, as would be expected on a single-system account.

Derivational morphology presents another rich quasi-regular domain to which our approach would apply. First, there are many morphemes that are partially productive in ways that are similar to quasi-regular correspondences in inflectional morphology and reading aloud: That is, they appear to be governed by a set of "soft" constraints. Second, the meaning of a morphologically complex word is related to, but not completely determined by, its constituent morphemes; thus, there is partial, but not complete, regularity in the mapping from meaning to sound (see Bybee, 1985, for a discussion of these points).

Graded influences of frequency and consistency appear to operate not just at the level of individual words but also at the level of sentences, as evidenced by recent findings of lexical, semantic, and contextual effects in syntactic ambiguity resolution (see, e.g. MacDonald, 1994; Taraban & McClelland, 1988; Trueswell, Tanenhaus, & Garnsey, 1994). For example, consider the temporary main verb versus reduced relative ambiguity associated with the word EXAMINED in the sentence THE EVIDENCE EXAMINED BY THE LAWYER WAS USELESS (Ferreira & Clifton, 1986). The degree to which readers are slowed in sentence comprehension when encountering such ambiguities is subject to a number of influences, including a previous disambiguating context (Trueswell et al., 1994), the semantic plausibility of the head noun in the main-verb reading (cf. EVIDENCE vs. an animate noun like WITNESS), and the relative frequency with which the verb is used as a simple past tense (e.g. THE PERSON EXAMINED THE OBJECT) as opposed to a passivized past participle (e.g. THE OBJECT WAS EXAMINED BY THE PERSON; MacDonald, 1994). Verbs that are consistently used in the simple past tense lead to much stronger garden path effects when a reduced relative interpretation is required than do verbs that are more ambiguous in their usage. These effects have a natural interpretation in terms of a constraint-satisfaction process in which a variety of sources of lexical knowledge conspire to produce a coherent sentence interpretation, including graded influences whose strength depends on the consistency of a word-form's usage (see Juliano & Tanenhaus, 1994; MacDonald, Pearlmutter, & Seidenberg, 1994, for discussion, and Kawamoto, 1993; N. Pearlmutter, Daugherty, MacDonald, & Seidenberg, 1994; St. John & McClelland, 1990, for connectionist simulations illustrating some of these principles).

Even more generally, the domains encompassed by semantic, episodic, and encyclopedic knowledge are all quasi-regular in that facts and experiences are partially arbitrary but also partially predictable from the characteristics of other, related facts and experiences (see McClelland, McNaughton, & O'Reilly, 1995, for discussion). Consider the robin, for example. Its properties are largely predictable from the properties of other birds, but its color and exact size, the sound that it makes, the color of its eggs, and so forth are relatively arbitrary. Rumelhart (1990; Rumelhart & Todd, 1993) showed how a connectionist network can learn the contents of a semantic network, capturing both the shared structure that is present in the set of concepts — so as to allow generalization to new examples — while at the same time mastering the idiosyncratic properties of particular examples. As another example, consider John F. Kennedy's assassination. There were several arbitrary aspects, such as the date and time of the event. But our understanding of what happened depends on knowledge derived from other events involving presidents, motorcades, rifles, spies, and so on. Our understanding of these things informs, indeed pervades, our memory of Kennedy's assassination. And our understanding of other similar events is ultimately influenced by what we learn about Kennedy's assassination. St. John (1992) provided an example of a connectionist network that learned the characteristics of events and applied them to other, similar events, using just the same learning mechanism, governed by the same principles of combined frequency and consistency sensitivity, as our spelling-to-sound simulations.

In summary, quasi-regular systems like that found in the English spelling-to-sound system appear to be pervasive, and there are several initial indications that connectionist networks sensitive to frequency and consistency will provide insight into the way such systems are learned and represented.

Conclusions

At the end of their article, Coltheart et al. (1993) reached a conclusion that seemed to them "inescapable":

> Our ability to deal with linguistic stimuli we have not previously encountered . . . can only be explained by postulating that we have learned systems of general linguistic rules, and our ability at the same time to deal correctly with exceptions to these rules . . . can only be explained by postulating the existence of systems of word-specific lexical representations. (p.606)

We have formulated a connectionist approach to knowledge and processing in quasi-regular domains, instantiated it in the specific domain of English word reading, and demonstrated that it can account for the basic abilities of skilled readers to handle correctly both regular and exception items while still generalizing well to novel items. Within the approach, the proficiency of humans in quasi-regular domains stems not from the existence of separate rule-based and item-specific mechanisms, but from the fact that the cognitive system adheres to certain general principles of computation in neural-like systems.

Our connectionist approach not only addresses these general reading abilities but also provides insight into the detailed effects of frequency and consistency both in the naming latency of normal readers and in the impaired naming accuracy of acquired and developmental dyslexic readers. A mathematical analysis of a simplified system, incorporating only some of the relevant principles, forms the basis for understanding the intimate relationship between these factors and, in particular, the inherently graded nature of spelling–sound consistency.

The more general lexical framework for word reading on which the current work is based contains a semantic pathway in addition to a phonological pathway. In contrast to the lexical and sublexical procedures in dual-route theories, which operate in fundamentally different ways, the two pathways in the current approach operate according to a common set of computational principles. As a result, the nature of processing in the two pathways is intimately related. In particular, a consideration of the pattern of impaired and preserved abilities in acquired surface dyslexia leads to a view in which there is a partial division of labor between the two pathways. The contribution of the phonological pathway is a graded function of frequency and consistency; items weak on both measures are processed particularly poorly. Overt accuracy on these items is not compromised, however, because the semantic pathway also contributes to the pronunciation of words (but not nonwords). The relative capabilities of the two pathways are open to individual differences, and these differences may become manifest in the pattern and severity of reading impairments following brain damage.

Needless to say, much remains to be done. The current simulations have specific limitations, such as the restriction to uninflected monosyllables and the lack of attention paid to the development of orthographic representations, which need to be remedied in future work. Furthermore, the nature of processing within the semantic pathway has been characterized in only the coarsest way. Finally, a wide range of related empirical issues, including phonological dyslexia, developmental dyslexia, lexical decision, and pseudohomophone and blocking effects, have been addressed in only very general terms. Nonetheless, the results reported here, along with those of others taking similar approaches, clearly suggest that the computational principles of connectionist modeling can lead to a deeper understanding of the central empirical phenomena in word reading in particular and in quasi-regular domains more generally.

Notes

1. The findings of these studies have often been cast as effects of *regularity* rather than *consistency* — we address this distinction in the next section.

2. This is particularly true with respect to the distinction between regular inconsistent words and ambiguous words, which differ only in the degree of balance between friends and enemies. In fact, a number of previous studies, including that of Taraban and McClelland (1987), failed to make this distinction. As a result, some of the Taraban and McClelland regular inconsistent words contain bodies that we categorize as ambiguous (e.g. DEAR, GROW). This has the unfortunate consequence that, occasionally, words with identical bodies are assigned into different consistency classes. However, in the current context, we are not concerned with individual items but solely with using the pattern of means across classes to illustrate overall consistency effects. In this regard, the word classes differ in the appropriate manner in their average relative numbers of friends and enemies. Thus, for continuity with earlier work, we will continue to use the Taraban and McClelland stimuli.

3. Bullinaria (1995) has recently developed a series of networks of this form that exhibit impressive performance in reading nonwords, although only very weak effects of word frequency. Coltheart et al. (1993) also took a sequential approach to solving the dispersion problem in that a correspondence learned from one position is applied to all positions unless a different correspondence is learned elsewhere.

4. The Plaut and McClelland (1993; Seidenberg et al., 1994) network was also trained on 103 isolated CPCs, as an approximation to the explicit instruction many children receive in learning to read. These correspondences were not included in the training of any of the networks reported in this article.

5. This is not precisely true because the procedure for determining the pronunciation based on phoneme unit activities, soon to be described, does not consider these units independently, and their states are not determined independently but are based on the same set of hidden unit states. Nonetheless, the approximation is sufficient to make cross-entropy a more appropriate error measure than summed squared error.

6. The derivative of cross-entropy with respect to an output unit's total input is simply the difference between the unit's state and its target:

$$\frac{\partial C}{\partial x_j} = \frac{\partial C}{\partial s_j}\frac{ds_j}{dx_j} = \left(\frac{1-t_j}{1-s_j} - \frac{t_j}{s_j}\right)s_j(1-s_j)$$
$$= s_j - t_j.$$

7. The procedure for adjusting the connection-specific learning rates, called *delta-bar-delta* (Jacobs, 1988), works as follows. Each connection's learning rate is initialized to 1.0. At the end of each epoch, the error derivative for that connection calculated by back-propagation is compared with its previous weight change. If they are both in the same direction (i.e. have the same sign), the connection's learning rate is incremented (by 0.1 in the current simulation); otherwise, it is decreased multiplicatively (by 0.9 in the current simulation).

8. Actually, given the use of extreme targets and an asymptotic activation function, no set of finite weights will reduce the error to zero. In this case, a "solution" consists of a set of weights that produces outputs that are within some specified tolerance (e.g. 0.1) of the target value for every output unit in every training pattern. If a solution exists that produces outputs that all have the correct sign (i.e. tolerance of 1.0, given targets of ±1), then a solution also exists for any smaller tolerance because multiplying all the weights by a large enough constant will push the output of the sigmoid arbitrarily close to its extreme values without affecting its sign.

9. An alternative strategy for increasing the range of tasks that can be solved by a two-layer network is to add additional input units that explicitly code relevant combinations of the original input units (see Gluck & Bower, 1988; Marr, 1969; Rumelhart et al., 1986a, for examples). In the domain of word reading, such higher order units have been hand-specified by the experimenter as input units (Norris, 1994), hand-specified but activated from the input units as a separate pathway (Reggia, Marsland, & Berndt, 1988), or learned as hidden units in a separate pathway (Zorzi, Houghton, & Butterworth, 1995).

10. This characterization of the derivation of word meanings is necessarily oversimplified. Words with multiple, distinct meanings would map to one of a number of separate semantic attractors. Shades of meaning across contexts could be expressed by semantic attractors that are *regions* in semantic space instead of single points. Notice that these two conditions can be seen as ends of a continuum involving various degrees of similarity and variability among the semantic patterns generated by a word across contexts (also see McClelland, St. John, & Taraban, 1989).

11. These temporal dynamics are somewhat different from those of the Plaut and McClelland (1993; Seidenberg et al., 1994) network. In that network,

each unit's input was set instantaneously to the summed external input from other units; the unit's state was a weighted average of its current state and the one dictated by its instantaneous input.

12. This specific criterion was chosen because it gives rise to mean response times that are within the 2.0 units of time over which the network was trained; other criteria produce qualitatively equivalent results.

13. Final E was considered to be part of the orthographic vowel cluster.

14. To see why this should be the case, imagine a much larger network in which the role of each weight in a smaller network is accomplished by the collective influence of a large set of weights. For instance, we might replace each connection in the small network by a set of connections whose weights are both positive and negative and sum to the weight of the original connection. Randomly removing some proportion of the connections in the large network will shift the mean of each set of weights; this will have the same effect as adding a random amount of noise to the value of the corresponding weight in the small network.

15. Recently, Balota and Ferraro (1993) reported an apparent dissociation of frequency and consistency in the naming latencies of patients with Alzheimer's type dementia over increasing levels of severity of impairment. However, these patients made substantial numbers of errors, and the usual relationship of frequency and consistency held in their accuracy data (also see Patterson et al., 1994). Furthermore, the dissociation was not found in the naming latencies of younger or older normal readers.

16. For a unit with a target of −1, the signs would simply be reversed. Alternatively, the equation can be interpreted as reflecting the correlation of the activation of output unit j with its target, which may in that case be either +1 or −1.

References

Anderson, J. A., Silverstein, J. W., Ritz, S. A., & Jones, R. S. (1977). Distinctive features, categorical perception, and probability learning: Some applications of a neural model. *Psychological Review, 84,* 413–451.

Andrews, S. (1982). Phonological recoding: Is the regularity effect consistent? *Memory and Cognition, 10,* 565–575.

Backman, J., Bruck, M., Hébert, M., & Seidenberg, M. S. (1984). Acquisition and use of spelling–sound information in reading. *Journal of Experimental Child Psychology, 38,* 114–133.

Baddeley, A. D., Ellis, N. C., Miles, T. C., & Lewis, V. J. (1982). Developmental and acquired dyslexia: A comparison. *Cognition, 11,* 185–199.

Balota, D., & Ferraro, R. (1993). A dissociation of frequency and regularity effects in pronunciation performance across young adults, older adults, and individuals with senile dementia of the Alzheimer type. *Journal of Memory and Language, 32,* 573–592.

Baluch, B., & Besner, D. (1991). Visual word recognition: Evidence for strategic control of lexical and nonlexical routines in oral reading. *Journal of Experimental Psychology: Learning, Memory, and Cognition, 17,* 644–652.

Baron, J., & Strawson, C. (1976). Use of orthographic and word-specific knowledge in reading words aloud. *Journal of Experimental Psychology: Human Perception and Performance, 4,* 207–214.

Beauvois, M.-F., & Derouesné, J. (1979). Phonological alexia: Three dissociations. *Journal of Neurology, Neurosurgery, and Psychiatry, 42,* 1115–1124.

Behrmann, M., & Bub, D. (1992). Surface dyslexia and dysgraphia: Dual routes, a single lexicon. *Cognitive Neuropsychology, 9,* 209–258.

Besner, D., & Smith, M. C. (1992). Models of visual word recognition: When obscuring the stimulus yields a clearer view. *Journal of Experimental Psychology: Learning, Memory, and Cognition, 18,* 468–482.

Besner, D., Twilley, L., McCann, R. S., & Seergobin, K. (1990). On the connection between connectionism and data: Are a few words necessary? *Psychological Review, 97,* 432–446.

Brousse, O., & Smolensky, P. (1989). Virtual memories and massive generalization in connectionist combinatorial learning. In *Proceedings of the 11th Annual Conference of the Cognitive Science Society* (pp. 380–387). Hillsdale, NJ: Erlbaum.

Bub, D., Cancelliere, A., & Kertesz, A. (1985). Whole-word and analytic translation of spelling-to-sound in a non-semantic reader. In K. Patterson, M. Coltheart, & J. C. Marshall (Eds.), *Surface dyslexia* (pp. 15–34). Hove, UK: Erlbaum.

Bub, D. N., Black, S., Hampson, E., & Kertesz, A. (1988). Semantic encoding of pictures and words: Some neuropsychological observations. *Cognitive Neuropsychology, 5,* 27–66.

Buchanan, L., & Besner, D. (1993). Reading aloud: Evidence for the use of a whole word nonsemantic pathway. *Canadian Journal of Experimental Psychology, 47*, 133–152.

Bullinaria, J. A. (1995). *Representation, learning, generalization and damage in neural network models of reading aloud.* Manuscript submitted for publication.

Butler, B., & Hains, S. (1979). Individual differences in word recognition latency. *Memory and Cognition, 7*, 68–76.

Bybee, J. L. (1985). *Morphology: A study of the relation between meaning and form.* Philadelphia: John Benjamins.

Bybee, J. L., & Slobin, D. L. (1982). Rules and schemas in the development and use of the English past tense. *Language, 58*, 265–289.

Castles, A., & Coltheart, M. (1993). Varieties of developmental dyslexia. *Cognition, 47*, 149–180.

Cipolotti, L., & Warrington, E. K. (1995). Semantic memory and reading abilities: A case report. *Journal of the International Neuropsychological Society, 1*, 104–110.

Coltheart, M. (1978). Lexical access in simple reading tasks. In G. Underwood (Ed.), *Strategies of information processing* (pp.151–216). New York: Academic Press.

Coltheart, M. (1981). Disorders of reading and their implications for models of normal reading. *Visible Language, 15*, 245–286.

Coltheart, M. (1985). Cognitive neuropsychology and the study of reading. In M. I. Posner & O. S. M. Marin (Eds.), *Attention and performance XI* (pp.3–37). Hillsdale, NJ: Erlbaum.

Coltheart, M., Curtis, B., Atkins, P., & Haller, M. (1993). Models of reading aloud: Dual-route and parallel-distributed-processing approaches. *Psychological Review, 100*, 589–608.

Coltheart, M., Patterson, K., & Marshall, J. C. (Eds.). (1980). *Deep dyslexia.* London: Routledge & Kegan Paul.

Coltheart, M., & Rastle, K. (1994). Serial processing in reading aloud: Evidence for dual-route models of reading. *Journal of Experimental Psychology: Human Perception and Performance, 20*, 1197–1211.

Coslett, H. B. (1991). Read but not write "idea": Evidence for a third reading mechanism. *Brain and Language, 40*, 425–443.

Cottrell, G. W., & Plunkett, K. (1991). Learning the past tense in a recurrent network: Acquiring the mapping from meaning to sounds. In *Proceedings of the 13th Annual Conference of the Cognitive Science Society* (pp.328–333). Hillsdale, NJ: Erlbaum.

Daugherty, K., & Seidenberg, M. S. (1992). Rules or connections? The past tense revisited. In *Proceedings of the 14th Annual Conference of the Cognitive Science Society* (pp.259–264). Hillsdale, NJ: Erlbaum.

Derthick, M. (1990). Mundane reasoning by settling on a plausible model. *Artificial Intelligence, 46*, 107–157.

Diesfeldt, H. F. A. (1992). Impaired and preserved semantic memory functions in dementia. In L. Backman (Ed.), *Memory functioning in dementia* (pp.227–263). Amsterdam: Elsevier Science.

Ellis, A. W., & Marshall, J. C. (1978). Semantic errors or statistical flukes? A note on Allport's "On knowing the meanings of words we are unable to report". *Quarterly Journal of Experimental Psychology, 30*, 569–575.

Fera, P., & Besner, D. (1992). The process of lexical decision: More words about a parallel distributed processing model. *Journal of Experimental Psychology: Learning, Memory, and Cognition, 18*, 749–764.

Ferreira, F., & Clifton, C. (1986). The independence of syntactic processing. *Journal of Memory and Language, 25*, 348–368.

Fodor, J. A., & Pylyshyn, Z. W. (1988). Connectionism and cognitive architecture: A critical analysis. *Cognition, 28*, 3–71.

Forster, K. I. (1994). Computational modeling and elementary process analysis in visual word recognition. *Journal of Experimental Psychology: Human Perception and Performance, 20*, 1292–1310.

Forster, K. I., & Chambers, S. (1973). Lexical access and naming time. *Journal of Verbal Learning and Verbal Behavior, 12*, 627–635.

Frederiksen, J. R., & Kroll, J. F. (1976). Spelling and sound: Approaches to the internal lexicon. *Journal of Experimental Psychology: Human Perception and Performance, 2*, 361–379.

Friedman, R. B. (1996). Recovery from deep alexia to phonological alexia. *Brain and Language, 28.*

Funnell, E. (1983). Phonological processing in reading: New evidence from acquired dyslexia. *British Journal of Psychology, 74*, 159–180.

Glosser, G., & Friedman, R. B. (1990). The continuum of deep/phonological alexia. *Cortex, 26*, 343–359.

Gluck, M. A., & Bower, G. H. (1988). Evaluating an adaptive network model of human learning. *Journal of Memory and Language, 27*, 166–195.

Glushko, R. J. (1979). The organization and activation of orthographic knowledge in reading aloud. *Journal of Experimental Psychology: Human Perception and Performance, 5*, 674–691.

Graham, K. S., Hodges, J. R., & Patterson, K. (1994). The relationship between comprehension and oral reading in progressive fluent aphasia. *Neuropsychologia, 32,* 299–316.

Hanson, S. J., & Burr, D. J. (1990). What connectionist models learn: Learning and representation in connectionist networks. *Behavioral and Brain Sciences, 13,* 471–518.

Hare, M., & Elman, J. L. (1992). A connectionist account of English inflectional morphology: Evidence from language change. In *Proceedings of the 14th Annual Conference of the Cognitive Science Society* (pp.265–270). Hillsdale, NJ: Erlbaum.

Hare, M., & Elman, J. L. (1995). Learning and morphological change. *Cognition, 56,* 61–98.

Harris, M., & Coltheart, M. (1986). *Language processing in children and adults.* London: Routledge & Kegan Paul.

Henderson, L. (1982). *Orthography and word recognition in reading.* London: Academic Press.

Hinton, G. E. (1981). Implementing semantic networks in parallel hardware. In G. E. Hinton & J. A. Anderson (Eds.), *Parallel models of associative memory* (pp.161–188). Hillsdale, NJ: Erlbaum.

Hinton, G. E. (1989). Connectionist learning procedures. *Artificial Intelligence, 40,* 185–234.

Hinton, G. E. (1990). Mapping part-whole hierarchies into connectionist networks. *Artificial Intelligence, 46,* 47–76.

Hinton, G. E. (Ed.). (1991). *Connectionist symbol processing.* Cambridge, MA: MIT Press.

Hinton, G. E., McClelland, J. L., & Rumelhart, D. E. (1986). Distributed representations. In D. E. Rumelhart, J. L. McClelland, & the PDP Research Group (Eds.), *Parallel distributed processing: Explorations in the microstructure of cognition: Vol. 1. Foundations* (pp.77–109). Cambridge, MA: MIT Press.

Hinton, G. E., & Sejnowski, T. J. (1986). Learning and relearning in Boltzmann machines. In D. E. Rumelhart, J. L. McClelland, & the PDP Research Group (Eds.), *Parallel distributed processing: Explorations in the microstructure of cognition: Vol. 1. Foundations* (pp.282–317). Cambridge, MA: MIT Press.

Hinton, G. E., & Shallice, T. (1991). Lesioning an attractor network: Investigations of acquired dyslexia. *Psychological Review, 98,* 74–95.

Hoeffner, J. (1992). Are rules a thing of the past? The acquisition of verbal morphology by an attractor network. In *Proceedings of the 14th Annual Conference of the Cognitive Science Society* (pp.861–866). Hillsdale, NJ: Erlbaum.

Hoeffner, J. H., & McClelland, J. L. (1993). Can a perceptual processing deficit explain the impairment of inflectional morphology in developmental dysphasia? A computational investigation. In E. V. Clark (Ed.), *Proceedings of the 25th Annual Child Language Research Forum* (pp.38–49). Stanford, CA: Center for the Study of Language and Information.

Humphreys, G. W., & Evett, L. J. (1985). Are there independent lexical and nonlexical routes in word processing? An evaluation of the dual-route theory of reading. *Behavioral and Brain Sciences, 8,* 689–740.

Huttenlocher, P., & Huttenlocher, J. (1973). A study of children with hyperlexia. *Neurology, 26,* 1107–1116.

Jacobs, R. A. (1988). Increased rates of convergence through learning rate adaptation. *Neural Networks, 1,* 295–307.

Jared, D., McRae, K., & Seidenberg, M. S. (1990). The basis of consistency effects in word naming. *Journal of Memory and Language, 29,* 687–715.

Jared, D., & Seidenberg, M. S. (1990). Naming multisyllabic words. *Journal of Experimental Psychology: Human Perception and Performance, 16,* 92–105.

Jones, G. V. (1985). Deep dyslexia, imageability, and ease of predication. *Brain and Language, 24,* 1–19.

Jordan, M. I., & Rumelhart, D. E. (1992). Forward models: Supervised learning with a distal teacher. *Cognitive Science, 16,* 307–354.

Juliano, C., & Tanenhaus, M. K. (1994). A constraint-based lexicalist account of the subject/object attachment preference. *Journal of Psycholinguistic Research, 23,* 459–471.

Kawamoto, A. H. (1993). Nonlinear dynamics in the resolution of lexical ambiguity: A parallel distributed processing approach. *Journal of Memory and Language, 32,* 474–516.

Kawamoto, A. H., Kello, C., & Jones, R. (1994, November). Locus of the exception effect in naming. In *Proceedings of the 35th Annual Meeting of the Psychonomic Society* (p.51). Austin, TX: Psychonomic Society Publications.

Kawamoto, A. H., Kello, C., & Jones, R. (in press). Temporal and spatial loci of consistency effects in naming: Evidence based on articulatory characteristics of initial consonant. *Journal of Experimental Psychology: Human Perception and Performance.*

Kučera, H., & Francis, W. N. (1967). *Computational analysis of present-day American English.* Providence, RI: Brown University Press.

Kullback, S., & Leibler, R. A. (1951). On information and sufficiency. *Annals of Mathematical Statistics, 22,* 79–86.

Lachter, J., & Bever, T. G. (1988). The relation between linguistic structure and theories of language learning: A constructive critique of some connectionist learning models. *Cognition, 28*, 195–247.

Lacouture, Y. (1989). From mean squared error to reaction time: A connectionist model of word recognition. In D. S. Touretzky, G. E. Hinton, & T. J. Sejnowski (Eds.), *Proceedings of the 1988 Connectionist Models Summer School* (pp.371–378). San Mateo, CA: Morgan Kauffman.

Lass, R. (1984). *Phonology: An introduction to basic concepts.* Cambridge, England: Cambridge University Press.

Liberman, I. Y., & Shankweiler, D. (1985). Phonology and the problems of learning to read and write. *Remedial and Special Education, 6*, 8–17.

MacDonald, M. C. (1994). Probabilistic constraints and syntactic ambiguity resolution. *Language and Cognitive Processes, 9*, 157–201.

MacDonald, M. C., Pearlmutter, N. J., & Seidenberg, M. S. (1994). The lexical nature of syntactic ambiguity resolution. *Psychological Review, 101*, 676–703.

MacWhinney, B., & Leinbach, J. (1991). Implementations are not conceptualizations: Revising the verb learning model. *Cognition, 40*, 121–153.

Maddieson, I. (1984). *Patterns of sounds.* Cambridge, England: Cambridge University Press.

Manis, F. R., Seidenberg, M. S., Doi, L. M., McBride-Chang, C., & Peterson, A. (in press). On the bases of two subtypes of developmental dyslexia. *Cognition.*

Marcel, T. (1980). Surface dyslexia and beginning reading: A revised hypothesis of the pronunciation of print and its impairments. In M. Coltheart, K. Patterson, & J. C. Marshall (Eds.), *Deep dyslexia* (pp.227–258). London: Routledge & Kegan Paul.

Marchman, V. A. (1993). Constraints on plasticity in a connectionist model of the English past tense. *Journal of Cognitive Neuroscience, 5*, 215–234.

Marcus, G. F., Pinker, S., Ullman, M., Hollander, M., Rosen, J. T., & Xu, F. (1992). Overregularization in language acquisition. *Monographs of the Society for Research in Child Development, 57*, 1–165.

Marr, D. (1969). A theory of cerebellar cortex. *Journal of Physiology, 202*, 437–470.

Marshall, J. C. (1984). Toward a rational taxonomy of the developmental dyslexias. In R. N. Malatesha & H. A. Whitaker (Eds.), *Dyslexia: A global issue* (pp.211–232). The Hague: Martinus Nijhoff.

Marshall, J. C., & Newcombe, F. (1966). Syntactic and semantic errors in paralexia. *Neuropsychologia, 4*, 169–176.

Marshall, J. C., & Newcombe, F. (1973). Patterns of paralexia: A psycholinguistic approach. *Journal of Psycholinguistic Research, 2*, 175–199.

Massaro, D. W. (1988). Some criticisms of connectionist models of human performance. *Journal of Memory and Language, 27*, 213–234.

Massaro, D. W. (1989). Testing between the TRACE model and the fuzzy logical model of speech perception. *Cognitive Psychology, 21*, 398–421.

Masterson, J. (1985). On how we read non-words: Data from different populations. In K. Patterson, M. Coltheart, & J. C. Marshall (Eds.), *Surface dyslexia* (pp.289–299). Hove, UK: Erlbaum.

McCann, R. S., & Besner, D. (1987). Reading pseudohomophones: Implications for models of pronunciation and the locus of the word-frequency effects in word naming. *Journal of Experimental Psychology: Human Perception and Performance, 13*, 14–24.

McCarthy, R., & Warrington, E. K. (1986). Phonological reading: Phenomena and paradoxes. *Cortex, 22*, 359–380.

McClelland, J. L. (1987). The case for interactionism in language processing. In M. Coltheart (Ed.), *Attention and performance XII: The psychology of reading* (pp.3–36). Hove, UK: Erlbaum.

McClelland, J. L. (1991). Stochastic interactive processes and the effect of context on perception. *Cognitive Psychology, 23*, 1–44.

McClelland, J. L. (1993). The GRAIN model: A framework for modeling the dynamics of information processing. In D. E. Meyer, & S. Kornblum (Eds.), *Attention and performance XIV: Synergies in experimental psychology, artificial intelligence, and cognitive neuroscience* (pp.655–688). Hillsdale, NJ: Erlbaum.

McClelland, J. L., & Elman, J. L. (1986). The TRACE model of speech perception. *Cognitive Psychology, 18*, 1–86.

McClelland, J. L., McNaughton, B. L., & O'Reilly, R. C. (1995). Why there are complementary learning systems in the hippocampus and neocortex: Insights from the successes and failures of connectionist models of learning and memory. *Psychological Review, 102*, 419–457.

McClelland, J. L., & Rumelhart, D. E. (1981). An interactive activation model of context effects in letter perception: Part 1. An account of basic findings. *Psychological Review, 88*, 375–407.

McClelland, J. L., Rumelhart, D. E., & the PDP Research Group (Eds.). (1986). *Parallel distributed processing: Explorations in the microstructure of cognition: Vol. 2. Psychological and biological models.* Cambridge, MA: MIT Press.

McClelland, J. L., St. John, M., & Taraban, R. (1989). Sentence comprehension: A parallel distributed processing approach. *Language and Cognitive Processes, 4*, 287–335.

McCloskey, M. (1991). Networks and theories: The place of connectionism in cognitive science. *Psychological Science, 2*, 387–395.

Mehegan, C. C., & Dreifuss, F. E. (1972). Hyperlexia: Exceptional reading in brain-damaged children. *Neurology, 22*, 1105–1111.

Metsala, J. L., & Siegel, L. S. (1992). Patterns of atypical reading development: Attributes and underlying reading processes. In S. J. Segalowitz & I. Rapin (Eds.), *Handbook of neuropsychology* (Vol. 7, pp.187–210). Amsterdam: Elsevier Science.

Meyer, D. E., Schvaneveldt, R. W., & Ruddy, M. G. (1974). Functions of graphemic and phonemic codes in visual word recognition. *Memory and Cognition, 2*, 309–321.

Miceli, G., & Caramazza, A. (1993). The assignment of word stress in oral reading: Evidence from a case of acquired dyslexia. *Cognitive Neuropsychology, 10*, 273–296.

Minsky, M. (1975). A framework for representing knowledge. In P. H. Winston (Ed.), *The psychology of computer vision* (pp.211–277). New York: McGraw-Hill.

Minsky, M., & Papert, S. (1969). *Perceptions: An introduction to computational geometry.* Cambridge, MA: MIT Press.

Monsell, S. (1991). The nature and locus of word frequency effects in reading. In D. Besner & G. W. Humphreys (Eds.), *Basic processes in reading: Visual word recognition* (pp.148–197). Hillsdale, NJ: Erlbaum.

Monsell, S., Patterson, K., Graham, A., Hughes, C. H., & Milroy, R. (1992). Lexical and sublexical translation of spelling to sound: Strategic anticipation of lexical status. *Journal of Experimental Psychology: Learning, Memory, and Cognition, 18*, 452–467.

Morais, J., Bertelson, P., Cary, L., & Alegria, J. (1986). Literacy training and speech segmentation. *Cognition, 24*, 45–64.

Morais, J., Cary, L., Alegria, J., & Bertelson, P. (1979). Does awareness of speech as a sequence of phones arise spontaneously? *Cognition, 7*, 323–331.

Morton, J. (1969). The interaction of information in word recognition. *Psychological Review, 76*, 165–178.

Morton, J., & Patterson, K. (1980). A new attempt at an interpretation, Or, an attempt at a new interpretation. In M. Coltheart, K. Patterson, & J. C. Marshall (Eds.), *Deep dyslexia* (pp.91–118). London: Routledge & Kegan Paul.

Movellan, J. R., & McClelland, J. L. (1993). Learning continuous probability distributions with symmetric diffusion networks. *Cognitive Science, 17*, 463–496.

Mozer, M. C. (1990). Discovering faithful "Wickelfeature" representations in a connectionist network. In *Proceedings of the 12th Annual Conference of the Cognitive Science Society* (pp.356–363). Hillsdale, NJ: Erlbaum.

Mozer, M. C. (1991). *The perception of multiple objects: A connectionist approach.* Cambridge, MA: MIT Press.

Norris, D. (1994). A quantitative multiple-levels model of reading aloud. *Journal of Experimental Psychology: Human Perception and Performance, 20*, 1212–1232.

Olsen, A., & Caramazza, A. (1991). The role of cognitive theory in neuropsychological research. In S. Corkin, J. Grafman, & F. Boller (Eds.), *Handbook of neuropsychology* (pp.287–309). Amsterdam: Elsevier.

Paap, K. R., & Noel, R. W. (1991). Dual route models of print to sound: Still a good horse race. *Psychological Research, 53*, 13–24.

Parkin, A. J. (1982). Phonological recoding in lexical decision: Effects of spelling-to-sound regularity depend on how regularity is defined. *Memory and Cognition, 10*, 43–53.

Patterson, K. (1990). Alexia and neural nets. *Japanese Journal of Neuropsychology, 6*, 90–99.

Patterson, K., & Behrmann, M. (1995). *Frequency and consistency effects in a pure surface dyslexic patient.* Manuscript submitted for publication.

Patterson, K., Coltheart, M., & Marshall, J. C. (Eds.). (1985). *Surface dyslexia.* Hove, UK: Erlbaum.

Patterson, K., Graham, N., & Hodges, J. R. (1994). Reading in Alzheimer's type dementia: A preserved ability? *Neuropsychology, 8*, 395–412.

Patterson, K., & Hodges, J. R. (1992). Deterioration of word meaning: Implications for reading. *Neuropsychologia, 30*, 1025–1040.

Patterson, K., & Marcel, A. J. (1992). Phonological ALEXIA or PHONOLOGICAL alexia? In J. Alegria, D. Holender, J. Junça de Morais, & M. Radeau (Eds.), *Analytic approaches to human cognition* (pp.259–274). New York: Elsevier.

Patterson, K., & Morton, J. (1985). From orthography to phonology: An attempt at an old interpretation. In K. Patterson, M. Coltheart, & J. C. Marshall (Eds.), *Surface dyslexia* (pp.335–359). Hove, UK: Erlbaum.

Patterson, K., Seidenberg, M. S., & McClelland, J. L. (1989). Connections and disconnections: Acquired dyslexia in a computational model of reading processes. In R. G. M. Morris (Ed.), *Parallel distributed processing: Implications for psychology and neuroscience* (pp.131–181). London: Oxford University Press.

Patterson, K., Suzuki, T., Wydell, T., & Sasanuma, S. (1995). Progressive aphasia and surface alexia in Japanese. *Neurocase*, *1*, 155–165.

Pearlmutter, B. A. (1989). Learning state space trajectories in recurrent neural networks. *Neural Computation*, *1*, 263–269.

Pearlmutter, N. J., Daugherty, K. G., MacDonald, M. C., & Seidenberg, M. S. (1994). Modeling the use of frequency and contextual biases in sentence processing. In *Proceedings of the 16th Annual Conference of the Cognitive Science Society* (pp.699–704). Hillsdale, NJ: Erlbaum.

Phillips, W. A., Hay, I. M., & Smith, L. S. (1993). *Lexicality and pronunciation in a simulated neural net* (Tech. Rep. CCCN-14). Stirling, Scotland: Centre for Cognitive and Computational Neuroscience, University of Stirling.

Pinker, S. (1984). *Language learnability and language development*. Cambridge, MA: Harvard University Press.

Pinker, S. (1991). Rules of language. *Science*, *253*, 530–535.

Pinker, S., & Prince, A. (1988). On language and connectionism: Analysis of a parallel distributed processing model of language acquisition. *Cognition*, *28*, 73–193.

Plaut, D. C. (1995). Double dissociation without modularity: Evidence from connectionist neuropsychology. *Journal of Clinical and Experimental Neuropsychology*, *17*, 291–321.

Plaut, D. C., Behrmann, M., Patterson, K., & McClelland, J. L. (1993). Impaired oral reading in surface dyslexia: Detailed comparison of a patient and a connectionist network [Abstract 540]. *Psychonomic Society Bulletin*, *31*, 400.

Plaut, D. C., & Hinton, G. E. (1987). Learning sets of filters using back propagation. *Computer Speech and Language*, *2*, 35–61.

Plaut, D. C., & McClelland, J. L. (1993). Generalization with componential attractors: Word and nonword reading in an attractor network. In *Proceedings of the 15th Annual Conference of the Cognitive Science Society* (pp.824–829). Hillsdale, NJ: Erlbaum.

Plaut, D. C., McClelland, J. L., & Seidenberg, M. S. (in press). Reading exception words and pseudowords: Are two routes really necessary? In J. P. Levy, D. Bairaktaris, J. A. Bullinaria, & P. Cairns (Eds.), *Proceedings of the Second Neural Computation and Psychology Workshop*. London: UCL Press.

Plaut, D. C., & Shallice, T. (1993). Deep dyslexia: A case study of connectionist neuropsychology. *Cognitive Neuropsychology*, *10*, 377–500.

Plunkett, K., & Marchman, V. A. (1991). U-shaped learning and frequency effects in a multi-layered perceptron: Implications for child language acquisition. *Cognition*, *38*, 43–102.

Plunkett, K., & Marchman, V. A. (1993). From rote learning to system building: Acquiring verb morphology in children and connectionist nets. *Cognition*, *48*, 21–69.

Pugh, K. R., Rexer, K., & Katz, L. (1994). Evidence of flexible coding in visual word recognition. *Journal of Experimental Psychology: Human Perception and Performance*, *20*, 807–825.

Quinlan, P. (1991). *Connectionism and psychology: A psychological perspective on new connectionist research*. Chicago: University of Chicago Press.

Rack, J. P., Snowling, M. J., & Olson, R. K. (1992). The nonword reading deficit in developmental dyslexia: A review. *Reading Research Quarterly*, *27*, 29–53.

Reggia, J. A., Marsland, P. M., & Berndt, R. S. (1988). Competitive dynamics in a dual-route connectionist model of print-to-sound transformation. *Complex Systems*, *2*, 509–547.

Richardson, J. T. E. (1976). The effects of stimulus attributes upon latency of word recognition. *British Journal of Psychology*, *67*, 315–325.

Rumelhart, D. E. (1990). Brain style computation: Learning and generalization. In S. F. Zometzer, J. L. Davis, & C. Lau (Eds.), *An introduction to neural and electronic networks* (chap. 21, pp.405–420). New York: Academic Press.

Rumelhart, D. E., Durbin, R., Golden, R., & Chauvin, Y. (1995). Backpropagation: The basic theory. In D. E. Rumelhart & Y. Chauvin (Eds.), *Backpropagation: Theory and practice* (pp.1–34). Cambridge, MA: MIT Press.

Rumelhart, D. E., Hinton, G. E., & Williams, R. J. (1986a). Learning internal representations by error propagation. In D. E. Rumelhart, J. L. McClelland, & the PDP Research Group (Eds.), *Parallel distributed processing: Explorations in the microstructure of cognition: Vol. 1. Foundations* (pp.318–362). Cambridge, MA: MIT Press.

Rumelhart, D. E., Hinton, G. E., & Williams, R. J. (1986b). Learning representations by back-propagating errors. *Nature*, *323*, 533–536.

Rumelhart, D. E., & McClelland, J. L. (1982). An interactive activation model of context effects in letter perception: Part 2. The contextual enhancement effect and some tests and extensions of the model. *Psychological Review*, *89*, 60–94.

Rumelhart, D. E., & McClelland, J. L. (1986). On learning the past tenses of English verbs. In J. L. McClelland, D. E. Rumelhart, & the PDP Research

Group (Eds.), *Parallel distributed processing: Explorations in the microstructure of cognition: Vol. 2. Psychological and biological models* (pp.216–271). Cambridge, MA: MIT Press.

Rumelhart, D. E., McClelland, J. L., & the PDP Research Group (Eds.). (1986). *Parallel distributed processing: Explorations in the microstructure of cognition: Volume 1. Foundations.* Cambridge, MA: MIT Press.

Rumelhart, D. E., & Todd, P. M. (1993). Learning and connectionist representations. In D. E. Meyer & S. Kornblum (Eds.), *Attention and performance XIV: Synergies in experimental psychology, artificial intelligence, and cognitive neuroscience* (pp.3–30). Cambridge, MA: MIT Press.

Saffran, E. M., Bogyo, L. C., Schwartz, M. F., & Marin, O. S. M. (1980). Does deep dyslexia reflect right-hemisphere reading? In M. Coltheart, K. Patterson, & J. C. Marshall (Eds.), *Deep dyslexia* (pp.381–406). London: Routledge & Kegan Paul.

Schwartz, M. F., Marin, O. M., & Saffran, E. M. (1979). Dissociations of language function in dementia: A case study. *Brain and Language, 7,* 277–306.

Schwartz, M. F., Saffran, E. M., & Marin, O. S. M. (1980). Fractioning the reading process in dementia: Evidence for word-specific print-to-sound associations. In M. Coltheart, K. Patterson, & J. C. Marshall (Eds.), *Deep dyslexia* (pp.259–269). London: Routledge & Kegan Paul.

Seidenberg, M. S. (1985). The time course of phonological code activation in two writing systems. *Cognition, 19,* 1–10.

Seidenberg, M. S. (1993). Connectionist models and cognitive theory. *Psychological Science, 4,* 228–235.

Seidenberg, M. S., & McClelland, J. L. (1989). A distributed, developmental model of word recognition and naming. *Psychological Review, 96,* 523–568.

Seidenberg, M. S., & McClelland, J. L. (1990). More words but still no lexicon: Reply to Besner et al. (1990). *Psychological Review, 97,* 477–452.

Seidenberg, M. S., & McClelland, J. L. (1992). *Connectionist models and explanatory theories in cognition* (Tech. Rep. PDP.CNS.92.4). Pittsburgh, PA: Carnegie Mellon University, Department of Psychology.

Seidenberg, M. S., Petersen, A., MacDonald, M. C., & Plaut, D. C. (1996). Pseudohomophone effects and models of word recognition. *Journal of Experimental Psychology: Learning, Memory, and Cognition, 22,* 1–13.

Seidenberg, M. S., Plaut, D. C., Petersen, A. S., McClelland, J. L., & McRae, K. (1994). Nonword

pronunciation and models of word recognition. *Journal of Experimental Psychology: Human Perception and Performance, 20,* 1177–1196.

Seidenberg, M. S., Waters, G. S., Barnes, M. A., & Tanenhaus, M. K. (1984). When does irregular spelling or pronunciation influence word recognition? *Journal of Verbal Learning and Verbal Behavior, 23,* 383–404.

Sejnowski, T. J., Koch, C., & Churchland, P. S. (1989). Computational neuroscience. *Science, 241,* 1299–1306.

Sejnowski, T. J., & Rosenberg, C. R. (1987). Parallel networks that learn to pronounce English text. *Complex Systems, 1,* 145–168.

Shallice, T. (1988). *From neuropsychology to mental structure.* Cambridge, England: Cambridge University Press.

Shallice, T., & McCarthy, R. (1985). Phonological reading: From patterns of impairment to possible procedures. In K. Patterson, M. Coltheart, & J. C. Marshall (Eds.), *Surface dyslexia* (pp.361–398). Hove, UK: Erlbaum.

Shallice, T, & McGill, J. (1978). The origins of mixed errors. In J. Requin (Ed.), *Attention and performance VII* (pp.193–208). Hillsdale, NJ: Erlbaum.

Shallice, T., Warrington, E. K., & McCarthy, R. (1983). Reading without semantics. *Quarterly Journal of Experimental Psychology, 35A,* 111–138.

Silverberg, N. E., & Silverberg, M. C. (1967). Hyperlexia — Specific word recognition skills in young children. *Exceptional Children, 34,* 41–42.

Skoyles, J. (1991). Connectionism, reading and the limits of cognition. *Psychology, 2(8),* 4.

Smith, P. T., & Baker, R. G. (1976). The influence of English spelling patterns on pronunciation. *Journal of Verbal Learning and Verbal Behavior, 15,* 267–285.

Stanhope, N., & Parkin, A. J. (1987). Further exploration of the consistency effect in word and nonword pronunciation. *Memory and Cognition, 15,* 169–179.

St. John, M. F. (1992). The story Gestalt: A model of knowledge-intensive processes in text comprehension. *Cognitive Science, 16,* 271–306.

St. John, M. F., & McClelland, J. L. (1990). Learning and applying contextual constraints in sentence comprehension. *Artificial Intelligence, 46,* 217–257.

Stone, G. O. (1986). An analysis of the delta rule and the learning of statistical associations. In D. E. Rumelhart, J. L. McClelland, & the PDP Research Group (Eds.), *Parallel distributed processing: Explorations in the microstructure of cognition: Vol. 1.*

Foundations (pp.444–459). Cambridge, MA: MIT Press.

Stone, G. O., & Van Orden, G. C. (1989). Are words represented by nodes? *Memory and Cognition, 17,* 511–524.

Stone, G. O., & Van Orden, G. C. (1994). Building a resonance framework for word recognition using design and system principles. *Journal of Experimental Psychology: Human Perception and Performance, 20,* 1248–1268.

Strain, E., Patterson, K., & Seidenberg, M. S. (1995). Semantic effects in single word naming. *Journal of Experimental Psychology: Learning, Memory, and Cognition, 21,* 1140–1154.

Sutton, R. S. (1992). Adapting bias by gradient descent: An incremental version of Delta-Bar-Delta. *Proceedings of the 10th National Conference on Artificial Intelligence* (pp.171–176). Cambridge, MA: MIT Press.

Taraban, R., & McClelland, J. L. (1987). Conspiracy effects in word recognition. *Journal of Memory and Language, 26,* 608–631.

Taraban, R., & McClelland, J. L. (1988). Constituent attachment and thematic role assignment in sentence processing: Influences of content-based expectations. *Journal of Memory and Language, 27,* 597–632.

Treiman, R., & Chafetz, J. (1987). Are there onset- and rime-like units in printed words? In M. Coltheart (Ed.), *Attention and performance XII: The psychology of reading* (pp.281–327). Hove, UK: Erlbaum.

Treiman, R., Mullennix, J., Bijeljac-Babic, R., & Richmond-Welty, E. D. (1995). The special role of rimes in the description, use, and acquisition of English orthography. *Journal of Experimental Psychology: General, 124,* 107–136.

Trueswell, J. C., Tanenhaus, M. K., & Garnsey, S. M. (1994). Semantic influences on parsing: Use of thematic role information in syntactic disambiguation. *Journal of Memory and Language, 33,* 285–318.

Van Orden, G. C. (1987). A ROWS is a ROSE: Spelling, sound and reading, *Memory and Cognition, 15,* 181–198.

Van Orden, G. C., & Goldinger, S. D. (1994). Interdependence of form and function in cognitive systems explains perception of printed words. *Journal of Experimental Psychology: Human Perception and Performance, 20,* 1269.

Van Orden, G. C., Pennington, B. F., & Stone, G. O. (1990). Word identification in reading and the promise of subsymbolic psycholinguistics. *Psychological Review, 97,* 488–522.

Vellutino, F. (1979). *Dyslexia.* Cambridge, MA: MIT Press.

Venezky, R. L. (1970). *The structure of English orthography.* The Hague: Mouton.

Waters, G. S., & Seidenberg, M. S. (1985). Spelling–sound effects in reading: Time course and decision criteria. *Memory and Cognition, 13,* 557–572.

Wickelgren, W. A. (1969). Context-sensitive coding, associative memory, and serial order in (speech) behavior. *Psychological Review, 76,* 1–15.

Widrow, G., & Hoff, M. E. (1960). Adaptive switching circuits. *Institute of Radio Engineers, Western Electronic Show and Convention, Convention Record, Part 4* (pp.96–104). New York: IRE.

Williams, R. J., & Peng, J. (1990). An efficient gradient-based algorithm for on-line training of recurrent network trajectories. *Neural Computation, 2,* 490–501.

Zorzi, M., Houghton, G., & Butterwort, B. (1995). *Two routes or one in reading aloud? A connectionist "dual-process" model* (Tech. Rep. UCL.RRG.95.1). London: University of London, University College, Department of Psychology.

Appendix A
Stimuli used in simulation studies

High frequency					Low frequency				
Regular consistent	Regular inconsistent	Ambiguous	Exception	Nonword	Regular consistent	Regular inconsistent	Ambiguous	Exception	Nonword
BEST	BASE	BROWN	ARE	LARE	BEAM	BROOD	BLOWN	BOWL	NOWL
BIG	BONE	CLEAR	BOTH	FOTH	BROKE	COOK	BROW	BROAD	BOAD
CAME	BUT	DEAD	BREAK	DEAK	BUS	CORD	CONE	BUSH	FUSH
CLASS	CATCH	DOWN	CHOOSE	BOOSE	DEED	COVE	CROWN	DEAF	MEAF
DARK	COOL	FOUR	COME	POME	DOTS	CRAMP	DIVE	DOLL	FOLL
DID	DAYS	GONE	DO	MO	FADE	DARE	DREAD	FLOOD	BOOD
FACT	DEAR	GOOD	DOES	POES	FLOAT	FOWL	FLOUR	GROSS	TROSS
GOT	FIVE	HEAD	DONE	RONE	GRAPE	GULL	GEAR	LOSE	MOSE
GROUP	FLAT	HOW	FOOT	POOT	LUNCH	HARM	GLOVE	PEAR	LEAR
HIM	FLEW	KNOW	GIVE	MIVE	PEEL	HOE	GLOW	PHASE	DASE
MAIN	FORM	KNOWN	GREAT	REAT	PITCH	LASH	GOWN	PINT	PHINT
OUT	GO	LOVE	HAVE	MAVE	PUMP	LEAF	GROOVE	PLOW	CLOW
PAGE	GOES	LOW	MOVE	BOVE	RIPE	LOSS	HOOD	ROUSE	NOUSE
PLACE	GROW	NEAR	PULL	RULL	SANK	MAD	LONE	SEW	TEW
SEE	HERE	NOW	PUT	SUT	SLAM	MOOSE	PLEAD	SHOE	CHOE
SOON	HOME	ONE	SAID	HAID	SLIP	MOTH	POUR	SPOOK	STOOK
STOP	MEAT	OUR	SAYS	TAYS	STUNT	MOUSE	PRONE	SWAMP	DRAMP
TELL	PAID	OWN	SHALL	NALL	SWORE	MUSH	SHONE	SWARM	STARM
WEEK	PLANT	SHOW	WANT	BANT	TRUNK	PORK	SPEAR	TOUCH	MOUCH
WHEN	ROLL	SHOWN	WATCH	NATCH	WAKE	POSE	STOVE	WAD	NAD
WHICH	ROOT	STOOD	WERE	LERE	WAX	POUCH	STRIVE	WAND	MAND
WILL	SAND	TOWN	WHAT	DAT	WELD	RAVE	SWEAR	WASH	TASH
WITH	SMALL	YEAR	WORD	TORD	WING	TINT	THREAD	WOOL	BOOL
WRITE	SPEAK	YOUR	WORK	BORK	WIT	TOAD	ZONE	WORM	FORM

Note. The regular consistent words, regular inconsistent words, and exception words are from Experiments 1 and 2 of Taraban and McClelland (1987). In those studies, the regular consistent words are the control words for the exception words. In addition, each regular inconsistent word shares a body with some exception word. The ambiguous words contain bodies associated with two or more pronunciations, each of which occurs in many words. They were generated by Seidenberg and McClelland (1989) to be matched in frequency (Kuçera & Francis, 1967) with the Taraban and McClelland high- and low-frequency regular consistent and exception words. The nonwords were generated by altering the onsets of the exception words.

Appendix B
Accepted pronunciations of Glushko's (1979) nonwords

	Consistent nonwords		Inconsistent nonwords
Nonword	Pronunciation(s)	Nonword	Pronunciation(s)
BEED	/bEd/	BILD	/bIld/,/bild/
BELD	/beld/	BINT	/bInt/,/bint/
BINK	/biNk/	BLEAD	/blEd/,/bled/
BLEAM	/blEm/	BOOD	/bUd/,/bʌd/,/bud/
BORT	/bOrt/	BOST	/bOst/,/bʌst/,/bost/
BROBE	/brOb/	BROVE	/brOv/,/brUv/,/brʌv/
CATH	/k@T/,/kaT/	COSE	/kOs/,/kOz/,/kUz/
COBE	/kOb/	COTH	/kOT/,/koT/
DOLD	/dOld/,/dald/	DERE	/dAr/,/dEr/,/dur/
DOON	/dUn/	DOMB	/dOm/,/dUm/,/dam/,/damb/
DORE	/dOr/	DOOT	/dUt/,/dut/
DREED	/drEd/	DROOD	/drUd/,/drʌd/,/drud/
FEAL	/fEl/	FEAD	/fEd/,/fed/
GODE	/gOd/	GOME	/gOm/,/gʌm/
GROOL	/grUl/,/grul/	GROOK	/grUk/,/gruk/
HEAN	/hEn/	HAID	/h@d/,/hAd/,/hed/
HEEF	/hEf/	HEAF	/hEf/,/hef/
HODE	/hOd/	HEEN	/hEn/,/hin/
HOIL	/hYl/	HOVE	/hOv/,/hUv/,/hʌv/
LAIL	/lAl/	LOME	/lOm/,/lʌm/
LOLE	/lOl/	LOOL	/lUl/,/lul/
MEAK	/mAk/,/mEk/	MEAR	/mAr/,/mEr/
MOOP	/mUp/	MONE	/mOn/,/mʌn/,/mon/
MUNE	/mUn/,/myUn/	MOOF	/mUf/,/muf/
NUST	/nʌst/	NUSH	/nʌS/,/nuS/
PEET	/pEt/	PILD	/pIld/,/pild/
PILT	/pilt/	PLOVE	/plOv/,/plUv/,/plʌv/
PLORE	/plOr/	POMB	/pOm/,/pUm/,/pam/,/pamb/
PODE	/pOd/	POOT	/pUt/,/put/
POLD	/pOld/,/pald/	POVE	/pOv/,/pUv/,/pʌv/
PRAIN	/prAn/	PRAID	/pr@d/,/prAd/,/pred/
SHEED	/SEd/	SHEAD	/SEd/,/Sed/
SOAD	/sOd/,/sod/	SOOD	/sUd/,/sʌd/,/sud/
SPEET	/spEt/	SOST	/sOst/,/sʌst/,/sost/
STEET	/stEt/	SPEAT	/spAt/,/spEt/,/spet/
SUFF	/sʌf/	STEAT	/stAt/,/stEt/,/stet/
SUST	/sʌst/	SULL	/sʌl/,/sul/
SWEAL	/swEl/	SWEAK	/swAk/,/swEk/
TAZE	/tAz/	TAVE	/t@v/,/tAv/,/tav/
WEAT	/wAt/,/wEt/,/wet/	WEAD	/wEd/,/wed/
WOSH	/waS/	WONE	/wOn/,/wʌn/,/won/
WOTE	/wOt/	WULL	/wʌl/,/wul/
WUFF	/wʌf/	WUSH	/wʌS/,/wuS/

Note. /a/ in POT, /@/ in CAT, /e/ in BED, /i/ in HIT, /o/ in DOG, /u/ in GOOD, /A/ in MAKE, /E/ in KEEP, /I/ in BIKE, /O/ in HOPE, /U/ in BOOT, /W/ in NOW, /Y/ in BOY, /ʌ/ in CUP, /N/ in RING, /S/ in SHE, /C/ in CHIN, /Z/ in BEIGE, /T/ in THIN, /D/ in THIS. All other phonemes are represented in the conventional way (e.g. /b/ in BAT).

Appendix C
Regularizations of Taraban and McClelland's (1987) exception words

High-frequency exceptions			Low-frequency exceptions		
Word	Correct	Regularization(s)	Word	Correct	Regularization(s)
ARE	/ar/	/Ar/	BOWL	/bOl/	/bWl/
BOTH	/bOT/	/boT/	BROAD	/brod/	/brOd/
BREAK	/brAk/	/brEk/	BUSH	/buS/	/bʌS/
CHOOSE	/CUz/	/CUs/	DEAF	/def/	/dEf/
COME	/kʌm/	/kOm/	DOLL	/dal/	/dOl/
DO	/dU/	/dO/,/da/	FLOOD	/flʌd/	/flUd/,/flud/
DOES	/dʌz/	/dOz/,/dOs/	GROSS	/grOs/	/gros/,/gras/
DONE	/dʌn/	/dOn/	LOSE	/lUz/	/lOs/,/lOz/
FOOT	/fut/	/fUt/	PEAR	/pAr/	/pEr/
GIVE	/giv/	/gIv/	PHASE	/fAz/	/fAs/
GREAT	/grAt/	/grEt/	PINT	/pInt/	/pint/
HAVE	/hav/	/hAv/	PLOW	/plW/	/plO/
MOVE	/mUv/	/mOv/	ROUSE	/rWz/	/rWs/
PULL	/pul/	/pʌl/	SEW	/sO/	/sU/
PUT	/put/	/pʌt/	SHOE	/SU/	/SO/
SAID	/sed/	/sAd/	SPOOK	/spUk/	/spuk/
SAYS	/sez/	/sAz/,/sAs/	SWAMP	/swamp/	/sw@mp/
SHALL	/Sal/	/Sol/	SWARM	/swOrm/	/swarm/
WANT	/want/	/w@nt/	TOUCH	/tʌC/	/tWC/
WATCH	/waC/	/w@C/	WAD	/wad/	/w@d/
WERE	/wur/	/wEr/	WAND	/wand/	/w@nd/
WHAT	/wʌt/	/w@t/	WASH	/woS/	/w@S/
WORD	/wurd/	/wOrd/	WOOL	/wul/	/wUl/
WORK	/wurk/	/wOrk/	WORM	/wurm/	/wOrm/

Note. /a/ in POT, /@/ in CAT, /e/ in BED, /i/ in HIT, /o/ in DOG, /u/ in GOOD, /A/ in MAKE, /E/ in KEEP, /I/ in BIKE, /O/ in HOPE, /U/ in BOOT, /W/ in NOW, /Y/ in BOY, /ʌ/ in CUP, /N/ in RING, /S/ in SHE, /C/ in CHIN, /Z/ in BEIGE, /T/ in THIN, /D/ in THIS. All other phonemes are represented in the conventional way (e.g. /b/ in BAT).

Received August 16, 1994
Revision received February 27, 1995
Accepted March 27, 1995

7

High-level language and thought

7.1 SYNTAX AND SEMANTICS

In Chapter 6 we reviewed connectionist models of human word processing, dealing with the recognition and production of print and speech (in reading, listening, writing, and speaking tasks). However, as we outlined at the start of that chapter, human language processing involves far more than the reception and production of single words. Words are related to one another by the syntax of the language in order that the meaning of whole sentences can be derived. Thus models need to address how syntactic and semantic information is utilised in language processing ("high-level" language functions), if the models are to provide complete accounts of human language operations. It has also been argued that the major limitations of connectionist models concern such higher-levels of language function, for instance because the models fail to represent rules explicitly and so (for instance) are unable to represent combinatorial structures between words. For instance, language understanding may involve building forms of representation so that the similarity between sentences such as (1) "John loves Mary" and (2) "Mary loves John", can be readily derived.

In traditional linguistic models, this similarity is captured in various ways, such as in so-called

case role representations (cf. Fillmore, 1968) such as:

> For "John loves Mary":
> (V) loves: (actor) John, (object) Mary   (1)

> and for "Mary loves John":
> (V) loves: (actor) Mary, (object) John.   (2)

In terms of their case role assignments, John, in sentence (1), has the same role with respect to Mary as Mary does to John in sentence (2). As the syntactically determined roles for John and Mary in the two sentences are the same, and are linked to the same verb, it follows that there are close semantic relations between the sentences. Fodor and Pylyshyn (1988), in particular, have argued that connectionist models necessarily lack structures for combining words in ways that are syntactically appropriate and that go beyond the surface structure of sentences. Whether this point holds true is something we will review in this chapter. However, the difficulty that connectionist models have with so-called combinatorial structures can be illustrated as follows. Consider a connectionist representation of the sentence "John loves Mary", in which each term is locally represented in terms of its position in the sentence. Here "John" would be represented by particular values of units for word position 1; "loves" by particular values for units in word position 2; "Mary" by particular values for units in word position 3. Likewise for the sentence "Mary loves John", "Mary" would be represented by particular values of units for word in position 1 (which are different from those for "John" in position 1), and so forth. As the units and values for "John" in position 1 have nothing in common with those representing "Mary" in position 1, nor anything in common with those representing John in position 3, there is little similarity between the representations of the sentences. Such problems still occur even if position information is coarsely coded within sentences (e.g. if there were what we might term a "Wickelword" representation, so that units capture relationships such as John-loves, loves-Mary; see Chapter 6 for examples from the area of visual word recognition). If there are no means by which syntactically determined relationships can be derived from sentences, it becomes difficult to express underlying similarities in meaning.

The issue of how connectionist models might derive and express the underlying meaning in sentences by the application of syntactic operations runs throughout this chapter, and we will return to it at several junctures. In particular, in later sections we deal with such issues when we consider how some combinatorial structures in syntactic operations, as captured in traditional linguistic theories, can be built-in to connectionist models. However, we begin the chapter with an issue that has served as a test-bed for connectionist models of language processing: the learning and expression of the past tense of English verbs. Although the topic does not deal with how words are organised into sentences, it does concern the linguistic expression of one syntactic operation (forming the past tense of verbs). Additionally, the issue is one where psychological evidence has frequently been used to argue for explicit rule-based operations in human language. To the extent that the same data can be simulated by connectionist models that do not have this rule structure, we may start to review whether explicit rule-based operations are necessary to explain human language function.

7.2 LEARNING THE PAST TENSE

7.2.1 Psychological evidence

Noam Chomsky, in 1959, made a critical and influential attack on the idea that human language might be an example of a stimulus–response relationship, associatively learned by children (e.g. in this case, between hearing words and speaking them). Instead Chomsky posited the existence of an innate language acquisition device, operating on a set of explicit but unconscious rules. According to Chomsky, the language acquisition device would generate hypotheses for the expression of certain linguistic rules for the language the child was learning, with the rules being rejected and replaced by others if they proved inadequate.

Evidence for the existence of a language acquisition device can be drawn from several areas: the fact the language develops at about the same age in all children in all cultures; the similarity of the acquisition process across children and cultures, despite differences in the learning environments; the fact that language acquisition is very difficult to suppress, and so forth. However, some of the strongest evidence for its existence comes from reports that children make systematic errors during language acquisition, a characteristic one in English being in the expression of the past tense.

Ervin (1964), Brown (1973), and Kuczaj (1977) describe the development of expressions of the past tense of verbs in the following terms. First (in Stage 1), when the child's vocabulary is relatively small, the past tense (when it is expressed) tends to be produced correctly. This holds both for verbs with regular past tense forms and for verbs with irregular past tense forms, such as go → went; come → came; give → gave etc.

Second (in Stage 2), as children acquire a larger vocabulary, so they tend to make errors in expressing the past tense of irregular verbs, particularly by "regularising" the form (e.g. saying "goed" instead of "went"; "comed" instead of "came" etc.). On some occasions this can involve the children generating an incorrect, regularised form for a verb they produced correctly during Stage 1. During

Stage 2, children can also generate a plausible past tense form for an invented word (e.g. if children are told that "rick" describes an action, they will use the term "ricked" in the past tense form; Berko, 1958). They may also move from producing complete regularisations of irregular verbs (go → goed) to expressions that are a mixture (go → wented) (Kuczaj, 1977).

Finally, in Stage 3, the child begins to use both forms of verbs, sometimes using the incorrect, regularised form of irregular verbs, sometimes the correct form. At least for frequent words, the irregular form comes to dominate.

One interesting aspect of these systematic errors in expressing the past tense is that there is a type of "inverted-U"-shaped learning function. Children may initially do well on a small set of words; they then perform less well on those items while acquiring a large vocabulary (the dip in the U), before gradually coming back to learn the items. From this, linguists have argued for the child using explicit rules for generating past tense forms. It is difficult to account for such a function in straightforward associative learning terms, because, for example, the regularised form of an irregular verb is unlikely to be reinforced by any teacher. By Stage 1, children have learned a small vocabulary of words, and do not distinguish regular from irregular verb forms. By Stage 2, children have acquired the "past tense rule". This is applied to all past tense expressions, leading to regularisation errors on irregular verbs. In Stage 3, children may establish separate representations for regular and irregular verb forms. Irregular verbs are stored in the child's lexicon, and are not derived from the stem. These forms may also be identified because of having a "family resemblance" of phonological similarity. In contrast, regular verb forms are not stored as independent lexical items; rather their stems are stored and their past tense endings are derived on the fly, by application of the past tense rule (cf. Pinker & Prince, 1988, 1989). During Stage 3, the weight of the lexical relative to the rule-based procedure is adjusted, so that, for a time, both forms may be expressed by children.

7.2.2 Rumelhart & McClelland (1986)

Rumelhart and McClelland (1986) attempted to simulate the learning of the past tense of verb forms in a connectionist model. They used a two-layer, fully interconnected net (Fig. 7.1), which was trained using the standard "delta rule" algorithm (see Chapter 2). The units in the input and output representations could either be in an "on" or an "off" state, marking the presence or absence

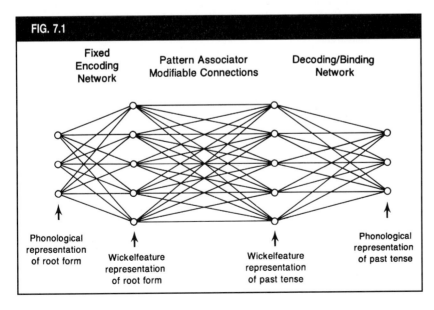

FIG. 7.1

Fixed Encoding Network

Pattern Associator Modifiable Connections

Decoding/Binding Network

Phonological representation of root form

Wickelfeature representation of root form

Wickelfeature representation of past tense

Phonological representation of past tense

Architecture of the past tense learning model of McClelland and Rumelhart (1986). Input went from the second level of the model (the Wickelfeature representations of the root form) to the third level, which was taken as the output (the Wickelfeature representations of the past tense).

of a particular property in a word. The representations were coded in terms of "Wickelfeatures" (see Chapter 6). Remember that Wickelgren (1969) introduced the idea that linguistic representations may be coded in terms of triplets of letters (or phonemes, or phonetic features etc.), to save an exponential increase in processing units as a function of the number of stimuli to be represented. A Wickelphone representation of a word such as *clap* would have units activated by the following phoneme triples: [/#cl/, /cla/, /lap/, /ap#/], where # corresponds to a word boundary. Rumelhart and McClelland used Wickelfeature rather than Wickelphone representations, so their units corresponded to triplets of phonetic features such as place and manner of articulation, voicing, the height and tenseness of vowels etc. By using Wickelfeature representations, a smaller set of units could be utilised to represent the words in the training and test vocabularies. Also, Wickelfeatures may capture generalisations to past tense forms in English better than Wickelphones. As Pinker and Prince (1989) note, English speakers asked to produce a past tense form for *Bach* (the composer's name), would generate *bacht* not *bachd* or *bached*. This "generalisation" occurs because of the similarity of ch (at the end of Bach) to p, k, s, all of which have their past tenses ending in the sound for /t/. The similarity is captured in terms of a shared phonetic feature: unvoiced. Hence Wickelfeatures may provide the appropriate form of representation for generalising past tense forms in English. Rumelhart and McClelland used a set of 460 Wickelfeature units, and argued that most English words could be uniquely identified in terms of the sets of units activated, even though common subsets of words would be activated by words with phonological similarities.

Rumelhart and McClelland argued that, during Stage 1 of learning the past tense, children have a small vocabulary which will comprise the most frequent verbs in English. As irregular verbs in English also tend to have a high frequency of occurrence, Rumelhart and McClelland used a high proportion of irregular verbs in their learning set when the model was initially trained. There was initially a set of 10 high-frequency verbs, 8 irregular, and 2 regular. Following the learning of these verbs, the

model was then trained on a larger vocabulary of words, containing 410 medium-frequency verbs in addition to the original 10 high-frequency verbs. By definition, in this larger population the majority of verbs had regular past tense expressions (334 out of 410). Following the learning of this larger set (about 200 cycles of the whole vocabulary), generalisation was tested by giving the model a set of 86 low-frequency verbs on which it had never been trained (there were 72 regular and 14 irregular verbs in this set). During training, inputs representing the root form of verbs were associated with outputs representing the past tense of the verbs. In addition, to produce better generalisation, Rumelhart and McClelland added noise to the model in two ways. First, units were placed into an on or off state probabilistically, where the relationship between the net activation coming into a unit and the likelihood that the unit was placed into an "on" state varied according to a particular parameter setting (the "temperature" of the system; as in a Boltzmann machine model, see Chapter 2, section 2.8). Second, the input representations were systematically "blurred" by randomly selecting a subset of the Wickelfeatures that encode the central phoneme in a target word correctly but the neighbouring (contextual) phonemes incorrectly (e.g. if the correct Wickelfeature unit corresponded to the central and contextual features $f1$, $f2$, $f3$, then in addition to this unit, units corresponding to $?$, $f2$, $f3$ and $f1$, $f2$, $?$, would also be activated, where $?$ indicates any feature). By "blurring" the input representation, Rumelhart and McClelland made learning less sensitive to the idiosyncrasies of what was a relatively small training set.

Rumelhart and McClelland found several interesting results. Perhaps most importantly, they found that regular and irregular verbs had different learning profiles. When performance was measured in terms of the proportions of the correct Wickelfeature representations that were switched on to a given input, then on the initial learning trials with the larger set of verbs, performance with both regular and irregular verbs improved at approximately the same rate. However, as learning progressed, performance on the irregular verbs deteriorated for a time before improving again as training on the word set continued; that is, there was a U-shaped learning function for these items. In contrast to the results with irregular verbs, the learning function for regular verbs showed a monotonic increase as training progressed. These results are illustrated in Fig. 7.2.

The nature of the errors made by the model was also assessed. One measure of this was based on the *relative response strengths* of regular and irregular past tense expressions, to an irregular verb input. A measures of the relative response strength for these expressions involves computing the residual error score between the output that the model generated to a given irregular verb input and what would have been the appropriate output either for the correct, irregular realisation of the verb or for the incorrect regularised form. The greater the response strength, the smaller the residual error between the observed and the expected output. The results are shown in Fig. 7.3. During the period between the initial learning trials

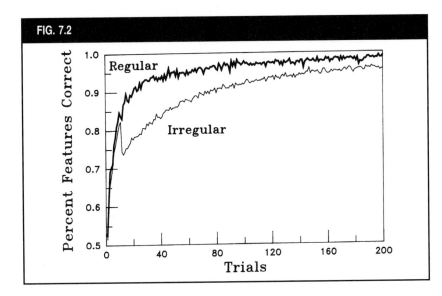

FIG. 7.2

Performance of Rumelhart and McClelland's (1986) past tense learning model, scored in terms of the number of output features correctly reproduced as a function of training. From McClelland and Rumelhart (1986).

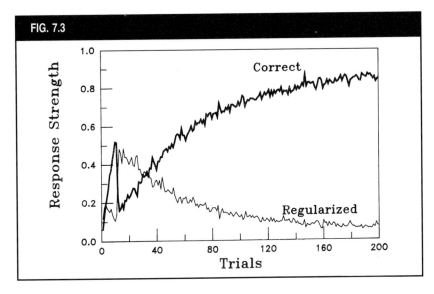

FIG. 7.3

Measures of the response strength for correct vs. regularised past tense expressions of irregular verbs, from Rumelhart and McClelland (1986).

and about 40 learning trials[1], there was a period in which the response strength for the (incorrect) regularised expression of the irregular verb was higher than that for the (correct) irregular expression. Rumelhart and McClelland suggested that, during this critical period, the model was likely to make regularisation errors when generating past tense forms for irregular verbs.

Rumelhart and McClelland's model is essentially a simple pattern associator, which learns to match root forms of verbs to their past tense forms. Their simulations show that, even with such an associative system, U-shaped learning functions can emerge. In their work, this learning function occurred because, after the model's initial learning with a small vocabulary, there was a change in the nature of the learning set; the set went from one with a majority of irregular verbs to one with a (large) majority of regular verbs. When the large training set was introduced, the weights initially set up as appropriate for the small word set needed to be changed, in order to capture the mappings between root and past tense forms for the majority of stimuli in the set. As these were (by definition) regular mappings, performance on irregular words declined. However, as learning continued to progress, so weights could be re-established to enable irregular as well as regular mappings to operate successfully. Thus, with more learning, irregular past tense forms were correctly expressed (Fig. 7.3).

In addition to capturing important aspects of the general profile in learning past tense forms for verbs, the simulation was also correct on some minor details. For example, Rumelhart and McClelland noted that, in English, there are some verbs that show no change between their past and present tense (particularly verbs ending in /t/ or /d/; e.g. hit, hurt, set etc.). They found that the correct (unchanged) past tense form was learned relatively quickly by their model, despite their being exceptions to the standard past tense rule. Similar results were reported by Bybee and Slobin (1982) with children. The facilitated learning in the model for these verbs may occur because there is a reasonably large group of verbs ending in /t/ or /d/ in the training set that undergo no change between their present and past tense forms; the

same also holds for English. The model is sensitive to such statistical regularities.

The model also generalised its learning relatively well. When presented with the set of low-frequency verbs after training (nonwords, as far as the model was concerned), over 90% of the correct past tense Wickelfeatures were activated for regular verbs, and 80% even for irregular verbs. Like children, the model would tend to produce a regular past tense ending when forced to express a novel word in the past tense.

From such results, Rumelhart and McClelland argued that the U-shaped learning function with irregular verbs does not necessarily reflect the operation of an innate language acquisition device, operating with explicit rules; it can reflect associative learning processes sensitive to changes in the frequencies of particular verb forms.

7.2.3 Criticisms

Following its initial publication, Rumelhart and McClelland's past tense learning model has been the subject of considerable interest as a direct challenge to rule-based accounts of language function. It has also been subject to a number of criticisms. For example, Bever (1992) noted that Rumelhart and McClelland presented individual words equally often within their training set, irrespective of the frequency of the words in English. The simulation was sensitive to word frequency only in the way in which high-frequency verbs comprised the initial learning set. This weighting of the initial learning set towards high-frequency verbs also biased initial learning to irregular past tense endings, as many of the high-frequency verbs in English are irregular. However, if high-frequency verbs were also presented more often during training than lower-frequency verbs when a larger vocabulary is acquired, then the bias towards regular verb endings during the second stage of training may not have occurred.

Pinker and Prince (1988, 1989) have made further charges. For instance, they argued that Wickelfeatures are inadequate because they fail to distinguish between sets of multisyllabic words (which can have common Wickelfeature representations). Also the simulation would fail with homographs in English (words that have the same spelling but different meanings, such as *ring*: the sound made by telephones and the action performed with one's hands), when the homographs have different past tense endings (e.g. rang and wrung, in the above example). This problem with homographs occurs because the model maps from one sound representation (Wickelfeatures for the present tense of verbs) to another (Wickelfeatures for the past tense of verbs), whereas the change from the present to the past tense for people is morphological, determined by the meaning of the sentence to be expressed. However, there would be problems in simulating human learning of the past tense of verbs, for a connectionist model that learns to map from meaning to a sound representation, because there would be fewer regularities in this mapping to support any generalisation when new words are presented. Generalisation in connectionist models typically occurs as a function of the similarity in the input representations for stimuli. As old and new words would not share meaning, in a model that maps semantics to sound, there is no reason for generalisation of past tense endings to take place. Pinker and Prince in fact argued that the regular past tense is produced in English for verbs that have little in common, and so generalisation of the regular past tense form cannot be based on similarity between items.

Perhaps the most damning criticism made by Pinker and Prince of Rumelhart and McClelland's work concerns the training set used. Pinker and Prince suggest that the U-shaped learning function for irregular verbs was a direct result of the discontinuity in the vocabulary structure and size, when the initial small training set was replaced by the larger training set. Performance on irregular verbs decreased because, in the larger training set, these items comprised the minority, and the weights within the network underwent change during training to reflect the majority of (regular) items present. However, such a discontinuity in the relative proportions of irregular to regular verbs does not occur in the vocabulary of children. Pinker and Prince proposed that the model was based on changes in a learning set that are not psychologically plausible. Hence the value of the model for simulating human language learning is thrown into doubt.

7.2.4 A response and extension to other linguistic expressions

Following on from the objections raised to Rumelhart and McClelland's model, other attempts have been made to learn the past tense of English verbs in connectionist models. Most noteworthily, Plunkett and Marchman (1991; also Marchman, 1993) trained both two- and three-layer networks using back-propagation to map from phonological representations of the present tense of verbs to phonological representations of past tenses. Each vowel and consonant in the words was represented by a pattern of features distributed across six units, where the units coded (i) whether there was a vowel or consonant, (ii) whether it was voiced or not, (iii) the manner of articulation, and (iv) the place of articulation (see Table 7.1). Training was carried out using a set of 700 verbs, in which the frequency of occurrence of words in the language was varied in terms of the number of times each verb was included in one run through the training set. Importantly, there were no discontinuities introduced into the training as learning progressed.

The two-layer networks without hidden units performed poorly in their learning, whereas the three-layer networks with hidden units performed relatively well and were able to learn the present–past tense mappings. Furthermore, as in the Rumelhart and McClelland simulation, irregular verbs manifested a U-shaped learning function, in which, after an initial period of learning, irregular verbs became less accurate in realising their past tense forms, before, with more learning, performance improved again. Also regularisation errors occurred in the expression of the past tense of irregular verbs. In this work, the U-shaped function did not occur because of an explicit change in the vocabulary of words being acquired by the model; rather it was due to the competition to establish appropriate weights for both regular and irregular verbs within a single network. Also like the Rumelhart and McClelland model, some forms of irregularity were learned more easily than others, with the "no change" form being particularly easy.

Plunkett and Marchman's simulation suggests that U-shaped learning may be a feature within

TABLE 7.1

Phonological representations used by Plunkett and Marchman (1991)

	Phonological feature					
	Cons./vowel *Unit 1*	*Voicing* *Unit 2*	*Manner* *Units 3 and 4*		*Place* *Units 5 and 6*	
Consonants						
/b/	0	1	1	1	1	1
/p/	0	0	1	1	1	1
/d/	0	1	1	1	1	0
/t/	0	0	1	1	1	0
/g/	0	1	1	1	0	0
/k/	0	0	1	1	0	0
/v/	0	1	1	0	1	1
/f/	0	0	1	0	1	1
/m/	0	1	0	0	1	1
/n/	0	1	0	0	1	0
/ŋ/	0	1	0	0	0	0
/ð/	0	0	1	0	1	0
/θ/	0	1	1	0	1	0
/z/	0	1	1	0	0	1
/s/	0	0	1	0	0	1
/w/	0	1	0	1	1	1
/l/	0	1	0	1	1	0
/r/	0	1	0	1	0	1
/y/	0	1	0	1	0	0
/h/	0	0	0	1	0	0
Vowels						
/i/ (eat)	1	1	1	1	1	1
/I/ (bit)	1	1	0	0	1	1
/o/ (boat)	1	1	1	0	1	1
/ɛ/ (but)	1	1	0	1	1	1
/u/ (boot)	1	1	1	1	0	1
/U/ (book)	1	1	0	0	0	1
/e/ (bait)	1	1	1	1	1	0
/ʌ/ (bet)	1	1	0	0	1	0
/ai/ (bite)	1	1	1	0	0	0
/æ/ (bat)	1	1	0	1	0	0
/au/ (cow)	1	1	1	1	0	0
/O/ (or)	1	1	0	0	0	0

networks that are attempting to learn regularities across word *types*, when those regularities compete with the learning required for a smaller set of irregular items which have relatively high *token* frequencies. The high token frequencies for irregular words make it likely that they are sampled early-on during learning, but, as learning proceeds, so their effects on the setting of the weights in the networks are reduced by the overall effects of the greater number of regular words.

Furthermore, variations in the microstructure of learning different verbs may reflect the statistical properties of the language environment, so that (for instance) not all verbs are equally irregular in their past tense expression. Connectionist models, employing association-based learning, can capture at least some forms of syntactic operation, such as expressing the past tenses of verbs. Plunkett and Marchman's paper is reproduced after this chapter.

Whether such accounts can be extended to cover other aspects of linguistic expression (e.g. pluralisation) is a matter of considerable debate. For example, Marcus et al. (1995) argued that the use of "default" rules gives linguistic systems not only productivity (as the rules can be applied to new examples) but also parsimony. They discuss the case of German plurals. Plurals in German can be created in as many as 60 ways, with many of these categories of pluralisation having only a single member. Nevertheless people take the plural form —s as the standard, even though it is a minority form, and apply this to sets of other forms including acronyms, proper names, quotations, and truncations. This enables what would otherwise be a heterogeneous set of different exemplars to be unified in a single rule. Marcus et al. suggested that pluralisation can be achieved through either of two processes: a lexical memory for known plural examples (which may be connectionist in nature, perhaps like a simple pattern associator) and a default rule (add "s") when retrieval from lexical memory fails. Although this account is attractive, Nakisa and Hahn (1996) tested a hybrid "associator + default rule" model on a task requiring German plural forms to be classified and found that it failed to outperform a pattern associator network alone. They presented as input to the models vector representations of the phonetic features of nouns, and as output the model represented the category of plural for the input noun (e.g. whether —s, —n, or — n is added). In one case, a three-layer network was trained to categorise each noun input into 1 of 15 most common types of plural change, using a relatively large set of German words (4000+ in the training set and a similar number in the test set). This training set included examples where

the —s change was valid. They compared the performance of this network with that of a hybrid network in which a network part was trained without examples from the —s class, but this form of plural was applied as a rule every time any output unit failed to be activated to a threshold level. The associative network alone (trained on the full set of common plurals) classified 83.5% of the new examples after training. The hybrid associative network + default rule only classified 81.4% of the new examples correctly. The reason why the model comprising both the network *and* the default rule fails to do better is because it starts to make false positive —s responses to some non-standard plural forms, and any gain in correct classification for a regular plural form is at the expense of these false positives. Nakisa and Hahn suggest that, in principle, there may be some languages whose statistical properties do not lead to such false positives occurring, but German is not one of these. This does not mean, of course, that a default plural rule is not used by German speakers — it could still be a parsimonious means of expressing other linguistic forms (acronyms, truncations etc.) — but use of such a rule does not guarantee improved performance for pluralisation of German nouns. Similar arguments have been made concerning Arabic, another language in which the default plural is a minority form, across the language; here Plunkett and Nakisa (1997) have shown how a connectionist model can learn to assign minority defaults. In essence, this occurs if the "exceptions", although comprising the majority of tokens in a training set, cluster into small parts of the input space (the space of possible values taken by input units). There can be "default" assignment of another category of response (such as the plural —s) to a new stimulus, if that category occupies the greater area of the input space — even if there are relatively few tokens for the default category in the training set. This occurs because the new stimulus is likely to fall into the "default" area of input space, and so be given the default response. Hare, Elman and Daugherty (1995) have made a similar point. An illustration of the kind of "input space" that would lead to this behaviour is shown in Fig. 7.4.

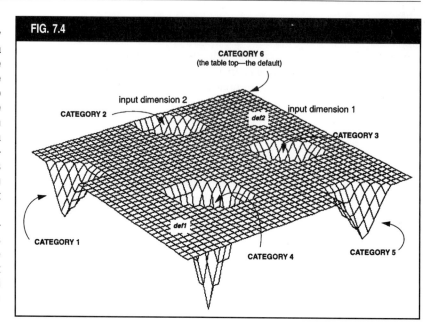

FIG. 7.4

Default minority assignment in a connectionist model. The majority of items in the training set cluster into categories 1–5, while exemplars of the sixth category — with a minority of exemplars — are drawn from positions across the remaining space of possible input values. In this instance, new (untrained) items — which fall in unfilled areas of the input space — are given a default assignment to the third (minority) category. From Hare et al. (1995).

7.3 CASE-ROLE ASSIGNMENTS IN SENTENCES

The conversion of present tense verb forms to past tenses at the single word level represents a minimal syntactic ability in networks. McClelland and Kawamoto (1986) attempted to accomplish a more complex syntactic procedure, concerned with assigning words in sentences to their appropriate case roles. By the term case role here we refer to the fact that words play particular thematic roles within sentences. In the sentence: "The boy broke the window with the hammer", the boy is the agent, the window is the patient, and the hammer is the instrument of the action. Language understanding depends on assigning the words their appropriate thematic case roles within sentences.

These case role assignments are determined by multiple factors, including the meaning of the words and their order in the sentence. For instance, take an ambiguous sentence such as: "The boy saw the girl with the binoculars". This sentence can be given one of two readings, with either the boy seeing the girl with the binoculars he was using, or the boy seeing a girl who was

carrying binoculars. Which of these two interpretations is taken by readers can be biased by giving different preceding contexts (Crain & Steedman, 1985). However, sometimes the semantic content of the words is not sufficient to overrule a given interpretation. For instance, even with an impossible sentence such as: "The chair kicked the boy", readers are likely to assign the agent role to the chair and the patient role to the boy, though semantic constraints suggest that the boy should be the agent. In this last case, word order is all important.

Connectionist models can handle this problem of case role assignment in terms of multiple constraint satisfaction between competing and/or cooperating influences: word order, semantics etc. (e.g. Cottrell & Small, 1983; Waltz & Pollack, 1985). This was the approach taken by McClelland and Kawamoto. Their stimuli comprised short sentences containing a verb and up to three noun phrases. The input to the model was meant to represent something like the surface form of a sentence, and the output represented the case structure interpretation. Each word activated a set of semantic "microfeatures". The particular microfeatures used were chosen because they were judged important in case role assignment, and corresponded to dimensions such as human/non-human; gender; soft/hard; breakable/unbreakable (for nouns); doer (did an agent instigate the event?); touch (did the agent or the instrument touch the patient?); and intensity (the force of the action)(for verbs). The surface form of the sentence was based on the activation of units coded for conjunctions of microfeatures (e.g. there might be one unit for human [yes] & gender [male], one for soft/hard [hard] & breakable/unbreakable [unbreakable] etc.). As sentences could contain words in up to four sentence roles (the verb and three noun phrases), there were four sets of units used, one for each sentence role (one for the verb, one for each noun phrase). Like Rumelhart and McClelland's past tense learning model, units were binary (either in an on or an off state), and their state was set probabilistically. If the two appropriate features for each unit were present in the input (e.g. if there was a human male, in the previous example), the probability that the unit entered an "on" state was 0.85; if one feature was present, the probability of being on was 0.5; if no features were present the probability of being on was 0.15. Thus there was some degree of noise in the model's operation (as on some occasions a unit would be active even if no appropriate features were present). In addition, because each feature was represented in relation to all others, there was also redundancy in the coding, so that (e.g.) human [yes] would be represented by a set of units being activated.

Output units took a related form to the input units, so that each unit corresponded to a conjunction of features. The syntactic relationship between the verb and each noun phrase was captured by having one part of the conjunction for each unit corresponding to the features for verbs and the other corresponding to the features for nouns. For example, a unit could represent: doer [agent instigated the event] & human [yes], or touch [the agent touched the patient] & gender [female] etc. Hence, distributed across the units would be an activation pattern that represented the particular verb (e.g. broke) in relation to particular noun phrases (boy, window, or hammer, for the sentence "The boy broke the window with a hammer"). The relationships between the verb

and noun phrases comprise the case roles for the words. To represent each case role, different sets of output units were involved, one set for each of the case roles allowed in the simulation (there were four, corresponding to agent, patient, instrument, and modifier[2]). The architecture of the model, and its case role assignments for the sentence "the boy broke the window with the hammer", are given in Fig. 7.5.

The model was trained using the delta rule algorithm to associate input with output patterns, using a corpus of sentences, and it was tested after different amounts of learning with either sentences drawn from the training set (familiar sentences) or new sentences. Overall the model performed relatively well. On average, after 50 training cycles through the sentence set, about 85% of the units that should have been turned on were, along with only about .6% of the units that should have been off. The model also manifested certain other interesting behaviours. For example, it was able to fill-in missing arguments in sentences. Given an input such as "The boy broke", there was activation for the features corresponding to some form of fragile object (non-human, neuter, breakable etc.) that could be inferred (filled-in) from the input words. This form of filling-in process also led to the model producing a shift in the meaning of some words under appropriate contextual conditions. An example of this was the model's response to the sentence: "The ball broke the window". In the training set, the noun "ball" involved the microfeature [soft]. For its output, however, the model activated practically all the correct output units except that for [soft] and instead activated features for [hard]. This shift in meaning occurred because all other examples of agents of the verb "break" were hard. In some sense, this shift in meaning captures some of the nuances of human language usage; it shows how, within systems of this sort, words do not have fixed meanings, as their meanings can be changed by the context.

The model was able to resolve case role assignments for ambiguous words by using the sentential context. Ambiguous words were represented in the input by having a 0.5 probability of activating each of the appropriate features. Thus for the

FIG. 7.5

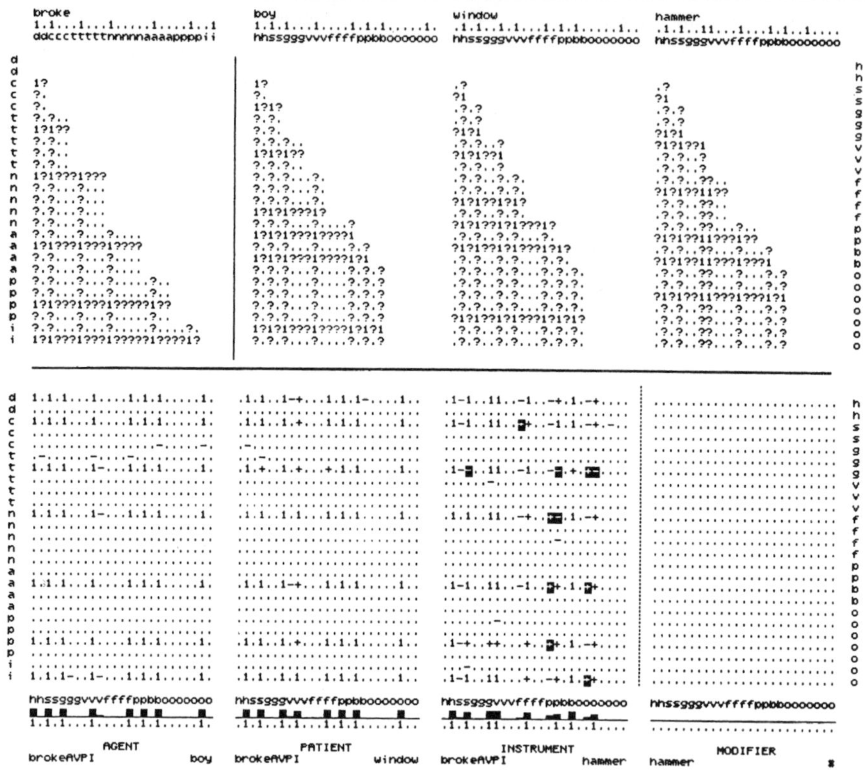

Architecture of the model for case role assignment, developed by McClelland and Kawamoto (1986). The letters listed at the top and sides are the initials for the features on which nouns and verbs were represented (h = human etc.) (note that the features to represent nouns, such as boy, differ from those to represent verbs, such as broke). 1 = unit has a probability of 1.0 of being in an "on" state. ? = unit has a 0.5 probability of being in an "on" state; . = unit has a 0.25 probability of being in an "on" state. The top units represent the input; the bottom units represent outputs. Output units capture conjunctions between a verb and a noun, and so the microfeatures on the left are for a verb while those at the bottom of the array are for nouns. The histograms at the foot of the figure indicate the units activated for the agent, patient, instrument and modifier case roles.

ambiguous word bat (as in flying creature or base-ball), the features for hard and soft were both set to be activated 0.5 of the time. However, in a sentence such as "The bat hit the ball", the output features activated corresponded to baseball bat, and the features corresponding to a flying bat were likely to be no more activated than those corres-ponding to other items activated by noise. In this case, the semantic content of the other words present in the input helped to constrain the case role assignment for the output.

McClelland and Kawamoto's model, then, achieved some success in case role assignment, and seems to mimic human langauge usage in some interesting aspects. However, the model is also clearly limited. For example, input units are locally coded for each of the noun or verb phrases in a sentence; output units are locally coded for each thematic case role. It is easy to see that the number of units required for case assignment in longer and more complex sentences could rapidly grow out of hand. In addition to this, the input given to the model does not really correspond to the surface structure of sentences. The ordering of the input units is not based on the order of occurrence for words in a sentence, but on whether the words are part of the subject or object noun phrase in the sentence. Hence, in a more complete model of language processing, the case role assignment system would need to be fed input from an earlier module that parses sentences into verb, subject, and object noun phrases. In McClelland and Kawamoto's simulation, this first stage was performed by the investigators. It could be argued that the most difficult part of the problem has been solved outside the model! We now turn to attempts to show how problems such as the parsing of sentences into noun and verb phrases may be solved in connectionist models.

7.4 PARSING VIA INTERACTIVE ACTIVATION AND COMPETITION

One connectionist approach to the parsing of sentences is exemplified by the model of Waltz and Pollack (1985), who used an interactive activation and competition architecture. Like other interactive activation and competition models (e.g. McClelland & Rumelhart's, 1981, model of visual word processing, Chapter 6), the network employed local representations in which one processing unit represented either a word or a particular linguistic form (e.g. a noun, verb, or adjective). Units were represented at one of three levels: a syntactic level, a lexical level, and a (semantic) contextual level. Units at the syntactic level represented relationships such as noun and verb phrases, and they were connected so as to preserve plausible syntactic structures for sentences. At the lexical level, units represented individual words and also their grammatical roles (noun, verb, determiner etc.). There were positive connections between units that were consistent with one other, and inhibitory connections between units that were inconsistent. For example, there were inhibitory connections between noun and verb units at the lexical level, so that an ambiguous word (e.g. hunt) could not be both a noun and a verb within a sentence; there were positive connections between contextual units

and lexical units consistent with the context; there were positive connections between lexical nodes representing grammatical roles and consistent units at the syntactic level. These connections were hardwired into the model, and so did not change with experience.

The model was used to generate predictions about the retrieval of word meanings over time. For instance, initially, after presentation of a sentence, there will be some activation for all meanings of words. However, over time, other activation within the system (from the other words, from activated context units etc.) can come to play a determining role, so that only one meaning remains active. The behaviour of the model over time captures aspects of human sentence comprehension, where evidence suggests that multiple meanings of words may initially be activated before one meaning becomes dominant (Seidenberg, Tanenhaus, Leiman, & Bienkowski, 1982; Swinney, 1979).

In Waltz and Pollack's (1985) model, syntactic parsing is performed implicitly, in that syntactic information is one influence brought to bear on the interpretation of the meaning of sentences and is reflected in the weights between units (similarly to effects of general contextual information and individual word meanings). However, the nature of the syntactic parse was determined by the investigators, who decided on the weights within the model. Also, as a general approach to sentence processing, the model is undoubtedly unwieldy, requiring many units to represent different words, contexts, and syntactic structures. A more satisfactory approach would be to develop models that learn to internalise syntactic structure in their representations of sentences. One example of how this might occur is provided by research using recurrent networks.

7.5 ELMAN'S (1990) RECURRENT NET REVISITED

In Chapter 5 we introduced Elman's (1990) work on learning in recurrent networks as an example of how connectionist models can learn structure in time as well as in spatial patterns. One experiment was particularly pertinent to arguments about how such models might learn to parse sentences into noun and verb phrases. Elman used a recurrent network as described in Chapters 2 and 5 (sections 2.8 and 5.6) in which hidden unit activation values on trial N were fed back and represented to the model along with new input on trial N + 1. The network was given the task of predicting which words followed which in a sentence (e.g. in the sentence "man eat bread" the model would be trained to output "eat" to the input "man", the output "bread" to the input "eat" and so forth). Thirteen classes of nouns and verbs were created (where a class corresponded to, for instance, NOUN-HUMAN or VERB-PERCEPT), which were occupied by 29 different lexical items (e.g. WOMAN, SEE). With these items 10,000 two- and three-word sentences were generated by combining appropriate classes of noun and verb. In the input to a network each word was represented by a 31-bit vector, with just one different bit set to 1 for each word. The input representations of the words were thus orthogonal to each other. The sentences were concatenated so as to create an input stream of 27,534 31-bit vectors. A network of 31 input units, 150 hidden units, 150 context units, and 31 output units was then trained with six passes through the sentences.

Determining the performance of this latter network is not straightforward, as the simple measures of error used thus far do not seem appropriate. For any particular input word there are a number of legal completions, so to label an output of "cookie" as an error to the input "eat" because the next item in the input stream was "bread" may underestimate the network's achievements. In fact if the network's outputs are regarded as indicating the likelihood of potential successor words, with the activity of each output component representing the probability of a given word appearing next, its error rate was low. That is, the outputs were, on average, a good approximation to the frequencies of successor words in the training corpus for a given word sequence. The network learned something about what words may occupy particular places in sentences from the co-occurrence statistics of the training data. Given this, we can ask how it represented those placement restrictions.

The network's representation of lexical class was analysed in terms of hidden unit activations as follows. After training the input sequence was again presented and each activation vector at the hidden unit level was noted for each of the words, averaging over the many different sentence contexts in which the words occurred. These "prototypical" representations were then the subject of an hierarchical cluster analysis in which items represented by similar vectors were grouped together. The results of this analysis are revealed in the tree structure shown in Fig. 7.6. The network appears to have discovered very sensible ways of representing categories of lexical items. Notably it has learned to distinguish between verbs and nouns! This classification can only have been extracted from word order regularities in the input stream. In addition, the network learned finer-grained distinctions between different classes of noun; between: animate and inanimate objects, human and non-human animate objects, food types and breakable items.

As we noted at the start of this chapter, one of the most comprehensive and profound critiques of the re-emergent connectionism has been to do with its limited ability to represent the structural properties of language (see especially Fodor & Pylyshyn, 1988). Natural language has a well defined syntactic structure which forms the basis of its "compositional semantics". The rules of grammar specify how the elements of language can be combined, and thereby define the (effectively unlimited) set of legal sequences of symbols or expressions. The meaning of an expression maps onto its grammatical structure so that components of semantics are in precise register with the components of syntax: semantic structure mirrors syntactic structure. It follows that language users must have representations that are faithful to this structure. It is these properties that make language both (i) generative, that is, an infinite set of expressions may be constructed, and (ii) systematic, so that, for example, knowing the meaning of "John loves Mary" entails knowing the meaning of "Mary loves John" (see section 7.1). Fodor and Pylyshyn (1988) argue that connectionist networks cannot develop representations that have the combinatorial structure necessary

FIG. 7.6

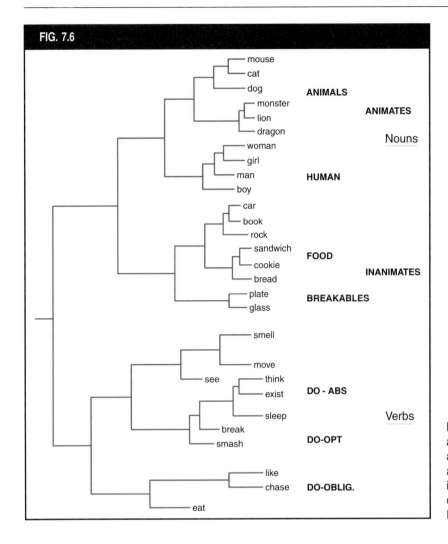

Results of the cluster analysis performed on averaged hidden unit activation values for each input word across different contexts, adapted from Elman's (1990) model.

for language processing. If this is the case, connectionist networks cannot be the basis of complete accounts of cognition.

Has Elman's (1990) network developed a combinatorial syntax? Probably not in the sense intended by Fodor and Pylyshyn (1988). Nevertheless, it does indicate that even very simple recurrent networks can learn surprisingly richly structured representations given an input population in which the critical relations extend over time. The recurrent connections from the context units allowed the network to learn patterns that span more than two inputs. The highly articulated representations that were learned were implicit in the sequence of inputs. Perhaps contrary to our initial intuitions, the simulation suggests the following: that a problem in representing fundamental linguistic classes in parallel computing devices may be resolved, at least in part, by the sequential nature of language behaviour. Interestingly this argument can be supported by statistical analyses of language which also suggest that syntactic relations covary with the co-occurrence statistics of words in sentences (see Finch & Chater, 1994). However, despite the promise of this work it is unlikely that word order alone is sufficient to account for our sensitivity to syntactic structure in sentences. A yet more sophisticated approach may thus be needed in models. We turn to one such approach next.

7.6 RECURSIVE AUTOASSOCIATIVE MEMORY (RAAM) MODELS

Pollack (1990) reported the first explorations of a form of connectionist model that enabled structured information to be represented. His ideas can be applied in order to represent sentences in an organised, hierarchical fashion, consistent with their decomposition into noun and verb phrases. Furthermore, this model need not be strictly bound to parsing on the basis of word order. The model, termed a RAAM (for recursive autoassociative memory), encodes the compositional structure of sentences implicitly. In simple terms, a RAAM model is based on autoassociative learning of patterns. For example, an input pattern is trained to map onto an identical output pattern, through a small set of hidden units (e.g. using the back-propagation learning algorithm). In doing this, the hidden units come to form a type of compressed representation of the patterns the model has learned.

Such a model can be trained to capture hierarchical sentence representations as follows. Take a sentence such as: "The boy broke the window". This can be represented in the following hierarchical form, where S = sentence, NP = noun phrase, VP = verb phrase and D = determiner.

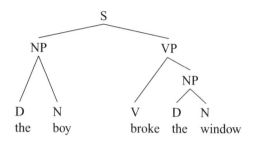

In this form, the sentence is represented as a tree structure, in which the first NP, the V, and the second NP are separate branches. A RAAM network can be trained to represent this tree and branch structure, a syntactically parsed representation for the sentence, if the input and output layers consist of sets of units, one set for each branch (see Fig. 7.7). A network is given the constituent parts of sentences sequentially; in our example, first the initial (subject) noun phrase (activating units for branch 1), then the verb (activating units for branch 2), then the final (object) noun phrase (activating units for branch 3). As the hidden layer contains only the same number of units as any branch, training must involve the network developing distributed representations of each branch, with each representation capable of being expanded to produce the original input on the output layer. For instance, the output

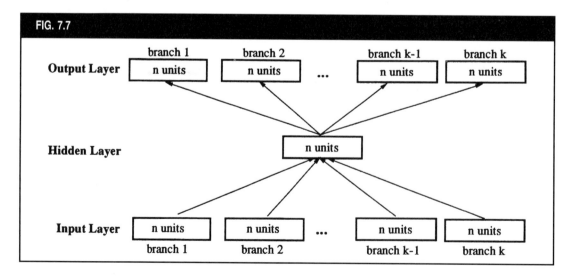

Architecture of a RAAM model for sentence representation. From Blank et al. (1992).

for branch 1 in the sentence will be re-created by re-activating the hidden unit values developed in autoassociative learning for that input, likewise for branches 2 and 3. Sentence structures can be retrieved by using the hidden unit activation values created during autoassociative learning as input later to the "back half" of the network (from the hidden units to the output units).

Something of the nested structure of sentences can be represented by recursively training the network through the tree-structure of the sentence, starting at the bottom nodes and working up to the full sentence. As noted in our example, the initial branches conform to the first NP, the V, and the second NP. Subsequently, the network would be trained on the VP (i.e. the V + the following NP), and then on the full sentence (first NP + VP). If these hidden units are stored, and then read back off a stack, then the first off the stack will re-create activation values for the whole sentence, the next for the first branch, the next for subsequent branches etc. The syntactic structure of the sentence can be recovered. In addition, if there is generalisation from learned to new sentences, then the structure of novel sentences will also be computed.

One problem with RAAM models of the form we have outlined is that their training needs to follow a syntactic parse of a sentence in order that this structure in turn becomes internalised via the hidden units and their connections to output units. Again, in presenting input for training

in the correct order, the modellers may be doing much of the hard work in sentence processing! Also such models need an off-line stack in order to store partial representations during training.

To address the problem of pre-parsing the input, Blank, Meeden, and Marshall (1992) used a further development of a RAAM model — a sequential RAAM (SRAAM), as shown in Fig. 7.8. In a SRAAM, a given input is again trained to autoassociate with a matching output representation, via a reduced set of hidden units. However, in addition, the network incorporated recurrency of the kind explored by Elman (1990). The activation values of hidden units on trial N were fed-back as new input on trial N + 1, and this part of the new input was trained to autoassociate with a matching output representation. Thus, with sentence inputs, the compressed representation formed at the hidden unit level was not only sensitive to each word or phrase, it was also sensitive to the preceding word or phrase. Just as in Elman's (1990) study, this recurrency in the network enabled it to learn sequential dependencies in word orders that correlate with syntactic roles.

Blank et al. trained a SRAAM network (of the size illustrated in Fig. 7.7) with a set of two- or three-word sentences generated from a set of 26 words (15 nouns, 11 verbs). Words were represented by arbitrary bit patterns in which one of the word units was active and the rest inactive. 100 sentences were used for training and a further

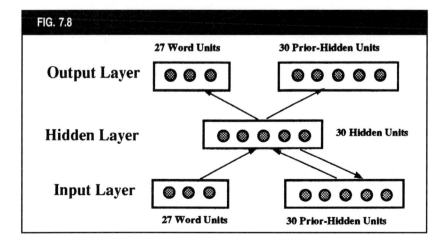

FIG. 7.8

Output Layer — 27 Word Units — 30 Prior-Hidden Units

Hidden Layer — 30 Hidden Units

Input Layer — 27 Word Units — 30 Prior-Hidden Units

The SRAAM architecture used by Blank et al. (1992). Here activation on the hidden units on trial N are fed-back as new input on trial N + 1, as in a standard recurrent network.

100 as tests of generalisation. An output was considered as correct if the correct word unit was activated above a value of 0.5 and no other word unit had a higher activation value. After training the model recalled 100% of its trained sentences correctly and generated correct output representations for 80% of the new sentences. Interestingly, when given ungrammatical sentences (an example here was "berries chase mice", which is ungrammatical because, in the sentence grammar used, chase had to be paired with an animate noun), only 30% were re-created correctly. Given its superior performance on novel grammatical sentences, the model appeared to have internalised differences between grammatical and ungrammatical sentences on its hidden unit representations.

The representations developed by the network were examined by means of a cluster analysis, using hidden unit activation values generated for each word averaged over the different contexts in which it appeared. Figure 7.9 illustrates the results from this analysis. Similarly to the recurrent network of Elman (1990), the cluster analysis revealed that the model developed representations that were generally distinct for nouns and verbs (there were some exceptions, such as for the words Jane, Tarzan, and tree). Something of the internal structure of the grammar has been captured by the model as it learned. Indeed, some finer-grained semantic distinctions were also assimilated, such as squashable (banana, berries) vs. non-squashable (coconut, meat). These fine-grained semantic distinctions likely reflect the pairings of nouns with particular verbs, and the noun vs. verb distinction likely reflects correlations in the word order on the training set. Thus we can conclude that not only something of the syntactic structure of language, but also its semantics, can be derived from models sensitive to temporal word order.

Now it can be argued that what this network has learned does not constitute any form of compositional structure about sentences, but simply constructions reflecting word order. If so, then the network should not serve as the useful basis for further training that changes the word order relations but maintains the grammatical roles of words. Blank et al. went on to explore this issue. First they showed that the hidden unit representations

could be decomposed back into separate word outputs. They trained a standard feed-forward network, using back-propagation, to map from the hidden unit values from the SRAAM net (as input) to output units representing individual words at specific positions in a sentence. Training was conducted using 50 sentences from the original training set, and generalisation was tested using the other 50 sentences in the SRAAM training set. Overall, 81% of the "new" sentences for the back-propagation network were produced correctly, and when mistakes were made, nouns were substituted for nouns and verbs for verbs. From this, it seems that the hidden unit representations formed when encoding sentences in a SRAAM network can also be used to produce sentences that are either grammatically correct or that generate plausible errors.

In a further simulation, Blank et al. used hidden unit values from the SRAAM network as input for a feed-forward network trained to transform the sentences from one form to their opposite (e.g. "cheetah chase Tarzan" to "Tarzan flee cheetah"), with the word order being transposed in the processs. Following learning, generalisation was again tested using either (a) sentences used in the original SRAAM training set but not in the training of the feed-forward network, or (b) novel sentences created using the same word set. Interestingly the outputs were correct for 100% of the SRAAM-trained sentences and for 75% of the completely novel sentences. Now the switch from one form of the sentence (X chase Y) to the opposite (Y flee X) can be considered syntactic in nature, because the switch can be performed by the application of rules that work irrespective of the external information about (e.g.) the meaning of the words. Blank et al. demonstrated that connectionist networks are not only able to learn such transformations but they can generalise on the basis of them to new inputs which follow similar syntactic structures. From this it can be argued that the SRAAM developed a structured representation concerned with the syntactic relationships between the words in the sentences (as generalisation occurred to new inputs occupying equivalent syntactic roles to the inputs in the training set). Also, the simulations show how structured information can be embodied implicitly in distributed representations, as the

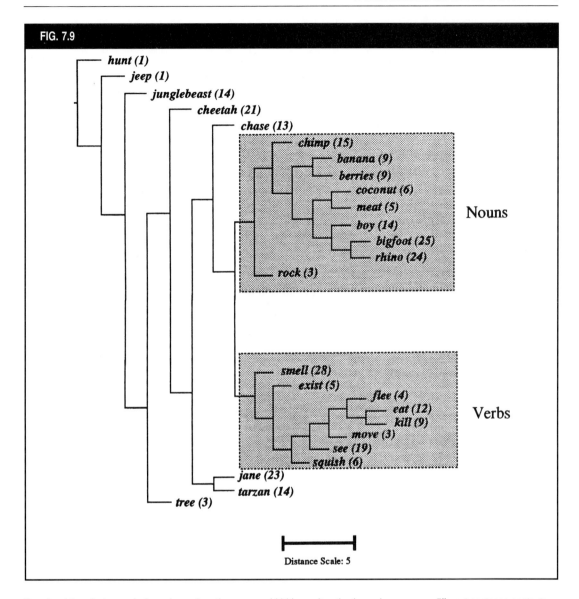

FIG. 7.9

Results of the cluster analysis performed on the averaged hidden unit activation values, across different sentence contexts, in the model of Blank et al. (1992).

hidden unit representations in such networks, being compressed, are typically highly distributed. Similar arguments can be made from simulations conducted by Callan and Palmer-Brown (1997) and Chalmers (1990), using RAAM and SRAAM nets to retrieve appropriate outputs to sentences transformed from the (trained) active form to novel passive forms.

7.7 THINKING AND REASONING

7.7.1 Reflexive reasoning

Traditionally psychologists interested in the processes of thought have been concerned with what Dewey (1910) termed reflective thought processes. That is, those processes that appear, to the thinker, to involve deliberate, conscious effort to reason or solve a problem, and to involve (serially) one thought at a time. Example tasks that may require this sort of activity are playing games such as draughts or chess, in which one line of logical argument may need to be "worked-through" at a time. Similarly to syntactic processes in language, connectionist models may be thought limited when applied to reflective reasoning, in which logical operators may need to be established with "fillers" for the particular problem ("if I do A, then C will follow, but if I do B then D will follow" — much as a syntactic frame of a sentence may be established, with word fillers that fill the frame for a particular sentence). We now consider whether connectionist models are necessarily limited in this domain.

Forms of reasoning can be said to underlie much of our everyday activity. Consider an example from a study by Rumelhart and Ortony (1977):

1. Mary heard the ice cream man coming.
2. She remembered the money.
3. She rushed into the house.

Our understanding of this scenario may be effectively immediate on seeing the events or on being told the events afterwards, yet such understanding depends on almost unbounded inferential reasoning. One assumes for example that the ice cream man wishes to sell ice cream; that Mary desires ice cream; that the money is hers to spend; that her money is to be found in the house; she intends to use at least some of the money to buy an ice cream; if she buys the ice cream she will be free to eat it and so forth. None of these propositions will be apparent in the events or mentioned in the three sentences but our understanding rests on our inferring their truth. Shastri and Ajjanagade (1993) describe a connectionist model that makes such inferences and which, thus, can be thought of as carrying out a form of reflective reasoning. The model is somewhat baroque in structure, and needs to be read carefully.

An obvious feature that any account of such reasoning must deal with is the remarkable efficiency of inferencing, despite the massive size of the knowledge base on which it draws. One

estimate of the order of the size of a typical human knowledge base is 10^8 items (Guha & Lenat, 1990) yet inferences drawing on this knowledge, such as in our example, take only some few hundred milliseconds. A model must therefore scale well: the time to retrieve knowledge and use it must not increase rapidly with the size of the knowledge base. Shastri and Ajjanagade (1993) show this to be the case for their connectionist model which has the following features or assumptions. Within a network of units whose activity oscillates in time, reasoning is identified with the propagation of a pattern of rhythmic activity. An item in working or dynamic memory is constituted by a phase within the pattern. The variable bindings needed for the representation of propositions are marked by synchronous firing of bound representational units (see Chapter 4, section 4.4, for a similar solution to a binding problem in visual representation). Items of knowledge are represented by subnetworks (each subnet representing a particular action or state — such as "give" — and nodes within the subnets representing objects that are the used in the action); rules are represented by interconnections which determine the propagation of rhythmic patterns of activity. Particular objects and individuals are represented by "filler" nodes, that are dynamically bound to the arguments. We will now describe in some detail these properties and their instantiation.

First consider the need for dynamic binding in the representation of facts such as "Bill gave Mary the ice-cream". A simple network that had active representations for the arguments "giver", "receiver", "object", and the fillers "Bill", "Mary", "ice-cream" would be ambiguous. It would not distinguish between the two situations in one of which Bill gave Mary the ice-cream and the other in which Mary gave the ice-cream to Bill. Worse still, in attempting to represent multiple facts in such a system, false conjunctions of arguments and fillers become possible: representing "Bill gave Mary the ice-cream" and "Mary gave John the toy" would result in activity whose interpretation could include the fact "Mary gave Bill the toy". The obvious solution is to bind together the representations of the appropriate arguments and entities (the fillers). Yet this would lead to an unmanageable network if bindings between the arguments and entities were hard-wired (with consequent duplication of filler units for different bindings — a unit for John as giver, for John as recipient and so forth). Representing knowledge of this sort in networks appears to require a dynamic binding mechanism, with a single unit for each "filler" (John, Mary etc.) that can be bound to different arguments. If one considers the activity of network units over time, the phase relationships among them provide just such a mechanism. Consider as an example the representation of the fact "John gave Mary the book" in a model having subnets standing for roles such as giver, recipient, and objects-which-may-be-given, along with filler units for entities such as Mary, John, and tokens of objects. The phase relations between these units may express the appropriate bindings as shown in Fig. 7.10a, in which the unit for "John" is repeatedly firing at the same time as the unit for "g-object" (an object-which-may-be-given, in the "give" subnet). The bindings of "Mary" with "recipient" and "book1" with "object" are similarly represented by each pair of units having different, synchronous firing patterns. Synchrony between appropriate nodes is established, in the simulated model, by a simple activation function which ensures that periodic activation of a node will lead to in-phase periodic activity in any node to which it is connected provided the latter's threshold is exceeded. The threshold is such that a unit will only fire when it receives n or more synchronous inputs, where n can range from one to many.

How does the representation of a fact lead to the chain of subsequent inferences observed in reflective reasoning? For instance, an understanding of the expression "John gave Mary the book" is constituted in part by the belief that Mary is now able to sell the book. The activations shown in Fig. 7.10a should lead to those in 7.10b in which the representation of Mary is bound, by phase synchrony, to "recipient", "owner", and "potential seller". The propagation of the appropriate bindings that underpin the reasoning is achieved by having connections between nodes which serve as arguments in an inference rule. For example the inference that Mary may sell something that she owns may be represented by two connections:

one between the representations of "owner" and "potential seller", and another between "own-object" and "can-sell-object". Appropriate connectivity for a small inference chain is illustrated in Fig. 7.11. In this network, nodes in an "ownership" subnet can be activated by nodes in both the "give" and "buy" subnets, and the "ownership" nodes themselves are connected on to "can sell" nodes, implying that an object, once owned (whether given or bought) can be sold. An important consequence of having this sort of inference mechanism is that inference time is a function of the length of the inference chain and not the size of the knowledge base.

With the addition of some further features the model is able to encode long-term facts and to perform reasoning over these facts. Figure 7.12 shows a network encoding of the fact that Mary gave John a book. The arguments and their fillers are linked by connections or static bindings as well as three other types of node (the c-give, e-give, and F1 nodes). Each of the latter acts as a temporal "and" gate, that is, it will fire if it receives an uninterrupted sequence of inputs and its threshold of n synchronous inputs is exceeded. One of these and-nodes, the e-node in Fig. 7.12, acts as a device for interrogating the system: if active in our example it would be equivalent to asking the system if John gave Mary the book. Another and-node, the c-node in Fig. 7.12, serves as a response to such an enquiry and will be active if long-term memory contains a set of static bindings that match the dynamic bindings represented in the query. The three-term predicate "give" is therefore represented by the two and-nodes (c and e) and the three argument nodes (give, recipient, and given-object).

Appropriate responses to queries are ensured by a set of inhibitory connections and a third and-node, labelled the fact node (F1) in Fig. 7.12. A query involving a particular predicate will cause the e-node to emit a set of consecutive activations (a pulse chain) to all appropriate fact nodes. In our example that would be to all fact nodes representing long-term memories for someone giving something to someone. Each fact node also receives inhibitory connections from the argument nodes in the predicate representation. These in

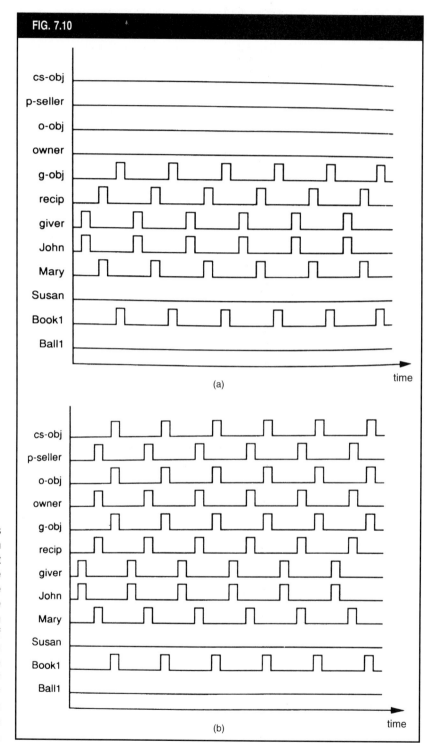

(a) The phase relations between units which together represent the fact "John gave Mary the book", and (b) the phase relations that might be expected to apply when the consequences of this fact have been propagated in the network; that is, "Mary owns the book" and "Mary may sell the book". From Shastri and Ajjanagade (1993).

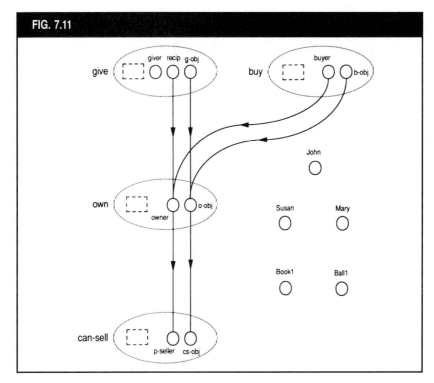

A network encoding for predicates and rules such as "owning and object" has the consequence of being able to sell that object. From Shastri and Ajjanagade (1993).

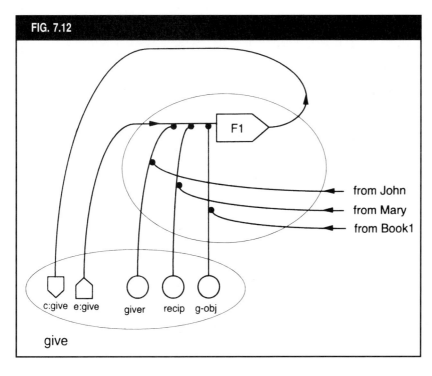

A network encoding of a long-term fact, that Mary gave John a book, as suggested by Shastri and Ajjanagade (1993).

turn have inhibitory connections, the static bindings, from entities in long-term memory. It follows that the fact node will receive an uninterrupted pulse chain if the fillers of the arguments specified by the long-term fact are firing in synchrony with the arguments (inhibiting the inhibition from the arguments). This will occur precisely when filler and arguments are dynamically bound as a result of the query. In these circumstances the fact node will be activated and lead to activation of the c-node for the appropriate predicate. Effectively the system has behaved as a pattern matcher: whenever the dynamic bindings representing a query match a long-term memory in the form of the static bindings, the c-node signals the match and confirms the query.

These mechanisms not only generate the inferences observed in reflexive reasoning but also serve as the foundation of episodes of reflective reasoning. Shastri and Ajjanagade describe the model's ability to perform backward reasoning tasks so that whenever the state of the system is initialised so as to represent some situation or query, as described earlier, it attempts to explain the situation or answer the query on the basis of its long-term knowledge. To illustrate these processes, Fig. 7.13 shows a network that encodes rules and long-term facts. The rules are: (1) if x gives z to y then y owns z (connections from the "give" subnet to the "own" subnet); (2) if x buys y then x owns y (connections from the "buy" subnet to the "own" subnet); and (3) if x owns y

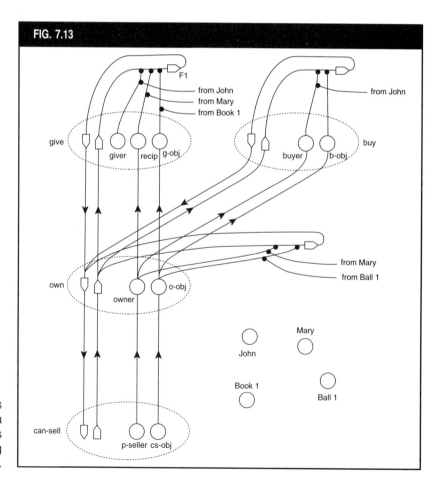

FIG. 7.13

Shastri and Ajjanagade's (1993) suggestion for a network that implements backward reasoning (see the text for details).

then x can sell y (connections from the "own" subnet to the "can-sell" subnet). The long-term facts are (1) John gave Mary book1 (connections into the "give" subnet); (2) John bought something (connections into the "buy" subnet); and (3) Mary owns book2 (connections into the "own" subnet). A rule is instantiated by the following connectivity. The c-node (see earlier) of the antecedent predicate, say "give" in rule (1), is connected to the c-node of the consequent predicate, "own" in rule (1). The e-node of the consequent predicate is connected to that of the antecedent predicate ("own" back to "give"). Finally, as this is a backward reasoning system, the arguments of the consequent predicate are connected appropriately to the arguments of the antecedent predicate; for example in the case of the rule (1) the "owner" and "own-object" nodes are connected to the "giver" and "give-object" nodes respectively (as well as vice versa).

Consider asking the network in Fig. 7.13 the question "can Mary sell book1?" Such a query would be represented by activation of (i) the e-node for the "can-sell" predicate, (ii) the argument nodes "p-seller" and "cs-object" (for a potential seller and an object that could be sold), and (iii) the filler nodes Mary and book1. Note that there will be two distinct phases within this pattern of activity for the two parts of the query: the nodes for Mary and p-seller will be synchronised as will those for book1 and cs-object. The connections described in the previous paragraph will ensure that in the second time period Mary, owner (in the "own" subnet) and p-seller will be firing together in one phase, with book1, cs-object and o-object firing together in another phase. Also the e-node for own is activated as a result of the connection from the e-node for can-sell. In the second period, then, the network has generated a representation of the question "does Mary own book1?". The reader should test their understanding of the model by confirming that the activation state in a third period will additionally represent the questions "did someone give Mary book1?" and "did Mary buy book1?". At this point the node for the long-term fact that John gave Mary book1 will become active as a result of uninterrupted input from the e-node for

give (see the section describing the behaviour of the network in Fig. 7.12 as a reminder of why this is so). The output of this fact node will then cascade down the network through the c-nodes for give and own to activate the c-node for can-sell and thereby confirm the original query (yes, yes and yes!!). The network has behaved very sensibly: it answered the question by asking if Mary owned book1, and confirmed that this was the case by asking if she had been given or sold the book. Most importantly the time to answer the question did not depend on the size of the knowledge base, but on the length of the derivation chain.

The model is very ambitious and inevitably fails to satisfy in a number of respects. Some aspects of it appear rather contrived or ad hoc. For instance in the model we have described thus far there is no way of having a predicate simultaneously bound within different facts. One cannot for example, represent "John gave Mary a book" and "Bill gave Jim a beer" at the same time. The authors overcome this difficulty by simply multiplying the number of subnetworks for each predicate. Clearly this threatens to undermine the economic efficiency of their form of representation. Perhaps more significantly the type of reasoning the system is capable of is very limited. The actual extent, in the human case, of the logic-based reasoning of the sort supported by the model may be narrow compared to other reasoning styles such as analogical reasoning, mental simulation, and associative recall (Touretzky & Fahlman, 1993).

Despite these obvious failings of the model the ingenious simulation is concerned with solving some central problems of connectionism. It appears to provide means by which networks can develop in principle the representational capacities of the type required for high-level cognition. It is therefore a further response to those (Fodor & Pylyshyn, 1988, being the best example) who claim that connectionist models are not able, in principle, to capture essential aspects of cognition because of their failure to capture the systematicity evident in human thought and language. We will be returning to these general issues in the concluding chapter, but will introduce some reflections on the nature of Shastri and Ajjanagade's

(1993) proposed solution at this point. Several commentators on this work have seen it as being haunted by the ghost of the classical symbolic approach. For instance, Dorfner (1993) points out that the network is contrived precisely to capture the syntactic structure reflected in classical representations of predicates such as Gave (Mary, John, Book1). In the latter case, binding is achieved by rules about the spatial proximity of arguments in a symbolic expression. In the oscillatory network, temporal relations replace these spatial patterns. Essentially, however, both representations achieve their powers of systematicity by having an explicit syntax (e.g. a subject and object node for each action). Also the network meets the syntactic requirements by having local representations, and thereby forgoes the many advantages of a distributed representations we have previously described (Chapter 3, sections 3.1 and 3.2). Shastri and Ajjanagade claim this classical flavour is inevitable if systematicity is to be captured and connectionism is to avoid the unstructured "associationist glob" that is such an easy prey for those advocating the classical approach. Yet in section 7.6 here we described recursive autoassociative memory networks which appear to possess properties akin to systematicity, but do so using distributed representations. We think that in the future much will turn on demonstrations of the representational powers of dynamic, recurrent networks of which RAAM is an early example.

7.7.2 Analogical reasoning

An attempt to capture analogical reasoning processes within a connectionist framework was made by Holyoak and Thagard (1989). Consider the classic "radiation problem", used originally by Duncker (1945) in a study of human problem solving:

> Suppose you are a doctor faced with a patient who has a malignant tumour in his stomach. To operate on the patient is impossible, but unless the tumour is destroyed the patient will die. A kind of ray, at a sufficiently high intensity, can destroy the tumour. Unfortunately, at this intensity the healthy tissue that the rays pass through on

the way to the tumour will also be destroyed. At lower intensities the rays are harmless to healthy tissue but will not affect the tumour either. How can the rays be used to destroy the tumour without injuring the healthy tissue?

Most people find this problem difficult to solve, and may only come up with solutions that are impractical. However, if sometime earlier you read a story that can be used as an analogy for the tumour problem, then you may quickly come to a practical solution. For example, consider the following story:

> This is about a general who wished to conquer a fortress in the middle of a country. Many roads came out from the fortress, but these were mined so that although small groups of men could pass over them to safety, a large group would detonate the mines. Still the general needed to get his entire army to the fortress to capture it. He did this by dividing his men into small groups, dispatching each to the head of a different road, and having the groups converge simultaneously on the fortress.

Having read this story, Gick and Holyoak (1980, 1983) showed that subjects were able to reason that the radiation problem could be solved if the tumour could be irradiated simultaneously from multiple directions with low-intensity rays. Psychologically, the feelings that people have when solving examples such as the radiation problem by analogy seem different from those involved when they solve (for example) problems in algebra, which rely on a reflective chain of reasoning. Metcalfe and Wiebe (1987) found that, when solving algebra problems, people stated that they were getting increasingly "warm" as they reached the solution. In contrast, when people solved a problem by analogy — often restructuring their representation of the problem — there was little feeling of increased warmth except when the solution was derived. Metcalfe and Wiebe described the latter as problem solving "by insight".

Holyoak and Thagard (1989) modelled problem solving by analogy using a parallel constraint satisfaction network. Units in the network stood for particular "mapping" relationships between the constituents in the analogies. For instance, for the radiation problem there might be a unit for "fortress as tumour" (the correct mapping) but also a unit for "fortress as radiation rays" (the incorrect mapping) and so forth. Units that would achieve a consistent mapping ("fortress as tumour" and "army as radiation rays") were positively connected, and there were inhibitory connections between units that would represent inconsistent mappings ("fortress as tumour" and "fortress as radiation rays"). Holyoak and Thagard suggest that this pattern of connectivity captures important "structural constraints" in the mapping process, Example units are shown in Fig. 7.14. Units were activated and activation allowed to cycle round the model. Consistent mappings support one another and inhibit inconsistent mappings.

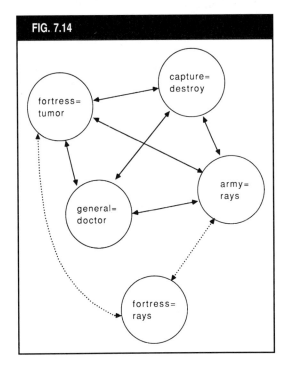

FIG. 7.14

A simplified constraint-satisfaction network for finding an analogical mapping between elements of the "fortress" and "radiation" problem (see the text for details). From Holyoak (1990).

Over time, then, the network tends to settle into a steady state in which units for consistent mappings are activated — and those mappings that are inconsistent with the "winning" interpretation are inhibited. Holyoak and Thagard showed that this approach could differentiate occasions when people found the mapping process easy or difficult.

Holyoak and Thagard's model was used (successfully) to account for the amount of time it took people to solve different analogies, although the question of how the mapping units are derived or initialised in the first place was bypassed. It is possible that structural constraints in mapping can be imposed by semantic and syntactic representations of the type modelled by Shastri and Ajjanagade (1993), so that only certain mappings are allowed (noun to noun, verb to verb, subject to subject etc.), but such steps have yet to be worked through. We only note that mutual constraint satisfaction procedures can provide one approach to human problem solving, and that, perhaps, such procedures can capture the feelings of sudden insight that arise in people, using the analogy of the network falling into a stable state.

7.8 HYBRID SYSTEMS AND HIGH-LEVEL COGNITION

So far we have discussed approaches to problem solving that are exclusively connectionist in flavour, reflecting the idea that connectionist models can provide complete accounts of cognition — a theme we return to in the final chapter. However, it is important to point out that connectionist and classical symbolic approaches to cognition are not necessarily mutually exclusive, and they may be combined to good effect. In such combined or hybrid models, a connectionist system is linked to a symbolic processor, with the idea being to capitalise on the virtues of each approach. In commercial environments such hybrid systems have had some success. As an example, Hammerstrom (1993) described a model financial system that attempted to predict the international bond market and planned investments on the basis of these predictions. Each country's market was modelled by a separate network, trained using back-propagation. The individual predictions provided the inputs to a conventional, rule-based expert system which made investment decisions on their basis. This hybrid system was more than three times better, in terms of returns, than homogeneous expert system investment software!

Is the utility of hybrid systems confined to applied problems? Might the notion of networks being components in a broader architecture which included classical elements be a fruitful approach to understanding biological systems? There are a number of hybrid models of different aspects of high-level cognition, although we confine the present discussion to two: Maes' (1989) account of planning problems and Lamberts' (1990) model of solving physics problems.

In abstract terms, planning involves finding a route from a present state to a goal state via a sequence of permissable intermediate states. For example, to find out what the approximate population of New York is one might decide to consult an atlas, but if this is on the top shelf a ladder may need to be fetched and, if this is in the basement and the basement is locked, one may need to find the key. Planning of this sort has been a central issue in classical symbolic artificial intelligence (see Charniak & McDermott, 1985, for an overview).

Maes' (1989) model of planning is inspired by Minsky's (1986) idea of a society of mind in which an intelligent system is constituted by a set of interacting, sub-intelligent entities or modules. Each module can do something to, or knows something about, a narrow aspect of their world. The global intelligence of the system arises as a result of local interactions between the competence modules. The system does not need a control structure or orchestration. Who does what at what moment does not require an explicit decision — the schedule is, in a sense, a byproduct of the interactions of modules with each other and the world. In the case of Maes' (1989) model these interactions are patterns of inhibition and excitation within a network, which we will now describe in some detail.

Each unit in the network is a competence module which may be described by a list of the preconditions that must apply before it may be executed, a set of things (states, objects, or functions) that its execution adds to the world, and a set of things that its execution deletes from the world. Call these lists pre_conditions, add_list, and del_list respectively. The units are linked by three sorts of connections. First, there is a successor connection from module x to module y, if members of the add_list for x are also members of the pre_conditions list for y. Second, there is a predecessor connection between x and y whenever members of pre_conditions for x are also members of add_list for y. Third, there is a conflict connection between x and y whenever the members of pre_conditions for x are members of del_list for y. Each module has an activation level associated with it at any given time and is executable only when this level exceeds a threshold.

The network behaviour unfolds over time as a result of the exchanges of activation and inhibition of the following types. Activity accrues to modules whose pre_conditions partially match the state of the world, thus the greater the number of pre-conditions that are currently true the greater the activity. Similarly the global goals of the agent will increase activity in those modules whose add_list includes some of those goals. Goals that have already been achieved will reduce the activity of modules that have them as part of their del_list. Modules also affect their neighbours. Executable modules will increase the activity of successor modules by a fraction of their activation, non-executable modules will have similar effects on predecessor modules, and all modules, whether executable or not, inhibit, again by a fraction of their activation, all other modules with which they share a conflict connection.

The network iterates, and at each time step the net change in a module's activation, resulting from the various effects described in the last paragraph, is calculated and a decay factor added in. The most active of the above-threshold, executable modules is executed, and the consequences of this enter into the calculations at the next time step, while the module's activation is reset to zero.

The authors described the network's performance in solving a hypothetical planning problem which involves a robot having to sand a board and spray paint itself. It has two arms, a paint sprayer, a vice, and a sander. The various options open to this system may be expressed as competence modules such as pick_up_sander. The latter has sander is somewhere and hand is empty as a pre_condition list; sander in hand as the add_list; and sander is somewhere and hand is empty as the del_list. Given suitable values for network parameters such as module thresholds, a schedule for the accomplishment of the tasks will be derived. For instance, in one particular simulation the authors report the following sequence of module executions. At time slice 3 the sander was picked up; at 5 the board was picked up; at 7 the board was sanded while held in a hand; at 17 the board was placed in the vice 9 (during this pause the activation to the spray paint itself module was accumulating); at 18 the paint sprayer was picked up by the newly free hand, and finally the robot sprayed itself.

There are several aspects of this performance worth noting. Although the schedule just described was not optimal (a smart solution would have the robot sanding the board while held in the vice and spray painting at the same time) it was potentially highly adaptive. A change in the environment will have immediate consequences for the spread of activation among modules. Similarly a change in goal states, for whatever reason, may lead to changes in the sequence of execution of modules. The system does not construct brittle, inflexible plans that are made ineffective by sudden changes. It is highly opportunist and will exploit whatever means are available to it. If the robot drops the sprayer, immediate remedies will result from the redirection of activation. Performance is also robust when modules are deleted. The system will do whatever it can with the modules that survive. This contrasts sharply with the brittle, but perhaps optimal, solutions found by classical techniques such as search in a problem space.

Lamberts' (1990) example is more psychologically oriented. He was concerned with the development of expertise in problem solving. Unlike novices, experts tend not to go through a painstaking process of reflective reasoning when solving problems (making backward inferences of the type examined by Shastri and Ajjanagade, 1993),

but rather move forward directly to a solution, using acquired knowledge. This shift in the mode of solving problems was simulated by using a hybrid model (see Fig. 7.15 for the architecture). One part of the model used a production system (the PS-component), and the other a distributed associative memory (the DM-component) of the type used by McClelland and Rumelhart (1985) and discussed in detail in Chapter 3 (section 3.1).

The model was used to find solutions to kinematic physics problems of the type:

> an object starts from rest and moves along a straight line with a uniform acceleration of a m/s^2. Find the distance x from the starting point at which the object will have a speed of speed of v m/s.

Let us suppose that the model only knows three principles of kinematics:

1. $v = v_0 + at$
2. $x = (v_0 + v)t/2$
3. $x = v_0 t + at^2/2$

If just these three principles are listed in the database of a production system, the problem will not be solved because the required unknown variable (x) is always part of a principle with another unknown factor (t). The solution requires that t is derived first, and then used to solve for x. Finding t is a necessary subgoal that must be achieved on the way to deriving the final goal. The DM-component of the model carries out this process of subgoal retrieval.

Units in the DM-component were arbitrarily labelled as belonging to one of three sets called the *data set*, the *final-goal set*, and the *subgoal set* (although all units in the network remained fully connected). Within each set, units corresponded to current speed (v), initial speed (v_0), acceleration (a), time (t), and distance (x). Units in the data set represented what is currently known in a problem. In the above example V, V$_0$, and A are known, and so these would all be set to +1; the other units in the data set (representing the unknown variables t and x) would be set to −1. In the final-goal set, the unit for x would be set to 1 (as this is the answer required) and the other units

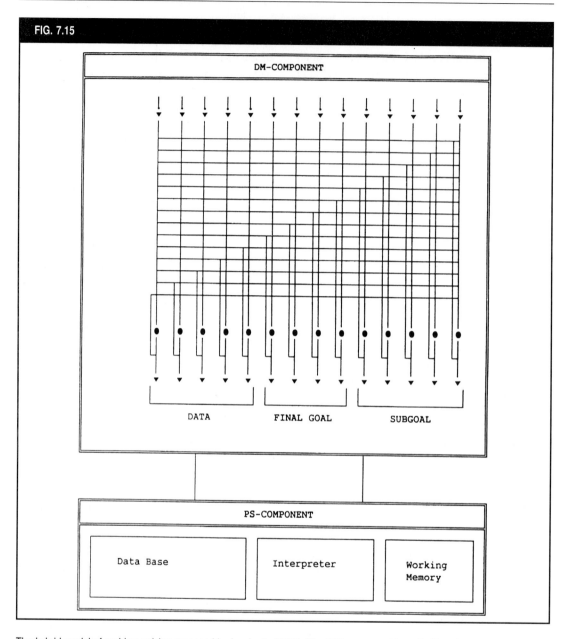

The hybrid model of problem solving proposed by Lamberts (1990). The DM-component is a distributed associative memory; the PS-component is a production system. Units in the DM component stand for the input data for a problem, the final goal for the problem, and any subgoal.

set to −1. The aim was to use the input (data set) and the final-goal to help retrieve a useful subgoal. Once retrieved, the subgoal was then used by the PS-component, to look-up a principle to solve for the subgoal.

To serve as a useful memory retrieval device, the DM-component was trained using sets of kinematic physics problems (the delta learning rule was used, as set out in equation 2 in section 3.1). When parts of problems were subsequently presented (i.e. a data set and a final-goal set but with no subgoal set), the DM-component showed pattern completion and generated the required subgoal item (in our example, the subgoal unit for t was activated close to 1 while the other subgoal units [v, v_0, a and x] maintained activations close to 0). The subgoal, find t, was thus retrieved. Search of the PS-component for a principle with only t was an unknown variable rendered "$v = v_0 + at$". t was calculated and a principle found for which only x was the unknown variable ($x = (v_0 + v)t/2$, and the solution was found. Following this, the DM-component was trained with an external input corresponding to the data and final-goal sets used plus also now a subgoal set (where unit t = 1 and the other units were −1).

In the DM-component of the model, subgoals are derived using both "forward" information specified in the data set of the problem and "backward" information concerning the final goal. Lamberts went on to assess whether experts in mechanics, like the model, did make use of "backward" information in solving problems. He gave two experts kinematic problems to solve which contained in the data set quantities that could be derived but which would not contribute to the final solution. In many classical expert systems, only forward reasoning is employed. If the human experts too use only forward reasoning from the problem statement, then they should often derive the unnecessary quantities on the way to solving the problems. Lamberts found that experts tended not to do this. This suggests that some form of constraint-satisfaction procedure, using final-goal information as well as the data-set, captures aspects of expert problem solving. The DM-component also has the useful attribute here of allowing generalisation to take place in learning, which may be less easily accomplished in a production system approach in which only known principles are listed in a database.

7.9 SOME SUMMARY POINTS

The work we have reviewed in this chapter attempts to simulate higher-level cognitive processes in connectionist models, including the processes involved in decomposing sentences using syntactic and semantic information, and the processes involved in reasoning and problem solving. Connectionist research in this area is in its relative infancy, and it remains unclear whether connectionist approaches will be completely successful in capturing all aspects of human performance, and particularly the compositional nature of linguistic operations. Nevertheless, we believe the work has been promising. Modellers have shown how simple syntactic operations, such as transforming present tense verbs to their past tense forms, can be learned in ways that are psychologically plausible. Research has also shown how networks can perform sentence parsing and case role assignment, although in many of the cases the applicability of the simulations is limited because the modellers have built syntactic structures into the models. More recent developments, using recurrent and RAAM networks show perhaps even more promise, because such networks can learn syntactic and semantic distinctions, and, in RAAM networks, the embodied knowledge can be used successfully for the subsequent learning of syntactic transformations. Although high-level language functions may represent some of the toughest problems for connectionist models, the problems may not be insurmountable.

NOTES

1. Here a learning trial involves one complete cycle of training through the learning set.
2. In a sentence such as: "The woman wanted the dress on the rack" the case role assignments are: woman = agent; dress = patient. "Rack" is a modifier of dress, in the sense that it is a particular dress (the one on the rack) that is desired. To avoid undue complexity, we have not given examples of modifiers in the text; the modifier "slot" in the case role representations used by McClelland and Kawamoto (1986) is presented in Fig. 7.5 only for completeness.

U-shaped learning and frequency effects in a multilayered perceptron: Implications for child language acquisition*

Kim Plunkett

University of Aarhus, Denmark

Virginia Marchman

Center for Research in Language, University of California, San Diego

Plunkett, K., and Marchman, V., 1991. U-shaped learning and frequency effects in a multi-layered perceptron: Implications for child language acquisition. Cognition, 38: 43–102.

A three-layer back-propagation network is used to implement a pattern association task in which four types of mapping are learned. These mappings, which are considered analogous to those which characterize the relationship between the stem and past tense forms of English verbs, include arbitrary mappings, identity mappings, vowel changes, and additions of a suffix. The degree of correspondence between parallel distributed processing (PDP) models which learn mappings of this sort (e.g. Rumelhart & McClelland, 1986, 1987) and children's acquisition of inflectional morphology has recently been at issue in discussions of the applicability of PDP models to the study of human cognition and language (Pinker & Mehler, 1989; Bever, in press). In this paper, we explore the capacity of a network to learn these types of mappings, focusing on three major issues. First, we compare the performance of a single-layered perceptron similar to the one used by Rumelhart and McClelland with a multilayered perceptron. The results suggest that it is unlikely that a single-layered perceptron is capable of finding an adequate solution to the problem of mapping stems and past tense forms in input configurations that are sufficiently analogous to English. Second, we explore the input conditions which determine learning in these networks. Several factors that characterize linguistic input are investigated: (a) the nature of the mapping performed by the network (arbitrary, suffixation, identity, and vowel change); (b) the competition effects that arise when the task demands simultaneous learning of distinct mapping types; (c) the role of the type and token frequency of verb stems; and (d) the influence of phonological sub-regularities in the irregular verbs. Each of these factors is shown to have selective consequences on both successful and erroneous performance in the network. Third, we outline several types of systems which could result in U-shaped acquisition, and discuss the ways in which learning in multilayered networks can be seen to capture several characteristics of U-shaped learning in children. In general, these models provide information about the role of input in determining the kinds of errors that a network will produce, including the conditions under which rule-like behavior and U-shaped learning will and will not emerge. The results from all simulations are discussed in light of behavioral data on children's acquisition of the past tense and the validity of drawing conclusions about the acquisition of language from models of this sort.

* This research was supported in part by grants from the Danish Humanities Research Council and the Danish Technical Research Committee, and by the Center for Neuro-developmental Studies at UCSD (NIH PHS NS22343). The authors sincerely thank an anonymous reviewer, Steven Pinker, and Alan Prince for insightful comments, and the members of the Center for Research in Language and the PDP Natural Language Processing Discussion Group at the University of California, San Diego, especially Elizabeth Bates and Jeffrey Elman, for their encouragement, patience, and thoughtful commentary. Reprints may be obtained from the first author at the Institute of Psychology, University of Aarhus, Asylvej 4, DK-8240 Risskov, Denmark.

Cognition, 38 (1991) 43–102

1. Introduction

It is a common finding in both naturalistic and experimental contexts that English-speaking children sometimes produce erroneous past tense forms, such as *goed* or *sitted*, in which /-ed/ is added to verb stems whose past tense forms are exceptions to the regular rule (Bowerman, 1982; Bybee & Slobin, 1982; Derwing & Baker, 1986; Kuczaj, 1977; Marchman, 1984). The occurrence of these errors is typically thought to illustrate that children are capable of going beyond their data to create novel lexical forms which they are not likely to hear in the input. Interestingly, overgeneralizations typically occur *after* children have been using correct forms of irregular verbs appropriately. With development, the organization of the linguistic system supports the correct production of both regular and irregular past tense forms. This apparent regression and subsequent improvement suggests that acquisition involves a stage-like reorganization of rules and representations (Bowerman, 1982; Karmiloff-Smith, 1979, 1986; Pinker & Prince, 1988) and is an oft-cited example of U-shaped development (see also Bever, 1982; Strauss, 1982). Taken together, the phenomena of overgeneralizations and U-shaped acquisition have been viewed as among the most persuasive pieces of behavioral evidence that language learning involves the process of organizing linguistic knowledge into a system in which rules and the exceptions to those rules must coexist.

Acquisitionists have not generally questioned whether children use rules in learning and producing language. Indeed, it would appear to be difficult to account for many phenomena of acquisition, most notably overgeneralizations, without some version of a rule system. Debate has instead focused on what rules are acquired, what form they must take, how and when children *do not* appear to utilize an adequate version of the rule system, as well as how and when the correct version is eventually attained. In addressing these questions, it is assumed that the input itself does not force the child to begin to produce overgeneralizations, nor to eliminate those errors from their output. Rather, endogenous factors trigger reorganizational processes that result initially in a performance decrement followed by gradual mastery of the system.

Recently, work within the connectionist perspective has promoted a re-evaluation of several of the basic assumptions about the constructs and processes guiding the acquisition of language. In an attempt to illustrate the applicability of parallel distributed systems to the "favored domain of non-associationist, higher-order structural cognition" (Maratsos, 1988, p.242), Rumelhart and McClelland (1986) set out to capture several of the facts of the acquisition of the English past tense. In general, the goal of this work was to suggest how a model of language processing and acquisition might be able to avoid reliance on rule-based mechanisms and discrete symbols, yet still capture what children do at various points in acquisition. Models such as this one characteristically utilize distributed representations and focus on elaborating the microstructure or sub-symbolic nature of cognition and language (Smolensky, 1988).

The performance of the Rumelhart and McClelland simulation is important because the learning curves and overgeneralizations generated by the simulation resemble many of the errors that children make and the stages of development that they pass through in the acquisition of past tense verb forms. More controversially, the Rumelhart and McClelland model (and the general class of models that it represents) does not rely in any obvious way on rules which are "assumed to be an essential part of the explanation of the past tense formation process" (Pinker & Prince, 1988, p.79). As Rumelhart and McClelland claim, "we have shown that a reasonable account of the acquisition of the past tense can be provided without recourse to the notion of a 'rule' as anything more than a *description* of the language" (1987, p.246). The ability of networks of this sort to mimic children's behavior when learning the past tense is intended to challenge the traditional view that acquisition is *necessarily* a process of organizing and reorganizing explicitly represented rules and principles, and their exceptions. These proposals have been met with enthusiasm in some circles, fueling many explorations of parallel distributed processing (PDP) models in other linguistic and non-linguistic domains (e.g. Churchland & Sejnowski, 1988; Elman, 1988, 1989; Elman & Zipser, 1988; Hare, 1990; Hare, Corina & Cottrell, 1989; MacWhinney, Leinbach, Taraban, & McDonald, 1989; Mozer, 1988; Seidenberg & McClelland, 1989; Smolensky, 1988). Elsewhere, these claims have undergone considerable scrutiny and have met with resistance (Pinker & Mehler, 1989). Several criticisms specifically address the details of the structure and/or success of this particular simulation. Others have been offered at a more general level, nominating it as the test case for evaluating the general potential of connectionist approaches (Fodor & Pylyshyn, 1988).

Clearly, the Rumelhart and McClelland simulation has several substantive limitations as a model of children's morphological acquisition. First, the model never achieves complete mastery of the task. The network continues to produce incorrect past tense forms at the end of training, even when the output from the learning component is evaluated using a binding system. Second, the task modeled by this simulation cannot be said to resemble the task of language learning in any real sense. It is clear that children do not hear stem and past tense forms side-by-side in the input in the absence of semantic information or outside of a larger communicative frame. Nor do children receive an explicit teacher signal as feedback about the relationship between the phonological form of their output and what the correct form should be. However, it is possible to characterize the Rumelhart and McClelland simulation at a more abstract level, as modeling a hypothetical, internal system-building process, such as *primary explicitation* outlined by Karmiloff-Smith (1986). Other criticisms have focused on the limitations of the phonological notation and the encoding/decoding processes used by Rumelhart and McClelland. For example, Lachter and Bever (1988) point out that Wickelfeature representations presuppose a theory of the phonological regularities present in the English past tense system. Lachter and Bever accuse Rumelhart and McClelland of using several "TRICS" (the representations that it crucially supposes) in order to ensure that the model is sensitive to the linguistic properties of past tense formation and, hence, performs in the way that it does.

More importantly for our purposes, these reviews point out that Rumelhart and McClelland misrepresent the input set within which children abstract and organize the regularities of the past tense system in three crucial ways. First, in the Rumelhart and McClelland simulation, one token each of the ten most frequent verbs in English (eight of which happen to be irregular) is presented to the simulation during the first ten training epochs. At that point in the learning process, the size of the input set is increased so that it is composed of a larger vocabulary of both frequent and infrequent verb forms. Pinker and Prince (1988) point out that the simulation's U-shaped developmental curve is a direct result of the *discontinuity* in vocabulary size and structure to which the network is exposed. It is no accident that the simulation's overusage of the /-ed/ ending and the related drop in performance on the irregular verbs coincides directly with the increase of the number of regular verbs in the vocabulary. While this vocabulary configuration does capture certain characteristics of the input to which children are exposed, generally accepted learnability conditions suggest it unwise to develop a model of acquisition which assumes that children experience substantive discontinuities in the available linguistic data early in development.

Second, in the Rumelhart and McClelland model, exemplars (i.e. tokens) of particular verbs are presented with equal frequency. Bever (in press) suggests that Rumelhart and McClelland:

> predigested the input for their model in much the same way a linguist does — by ignoring real frequency information. This is probably the most important trick of all — and it is absolutely clear why they did it. Irregular past tense verbs are by far and away the most frequently occurring tokens. Hence, if Rumelhart and McClelland had presented their model with data corresponding to the real frequency of occurrence of the verbs, the model would have learned

all the irregulars, and might never receive enough relative data about regulars to learn them (p.11).

Third, Rumelhart and McClelland's failure to capture basic categorical differences between regular and irregular verbs is interpreted as a significant and fatal shortcoming of the model. According to Pinker and Prince, symbolic and PDP models share several assumptions about linguistic systems. Both classes of models are theoretically capable of dealing with type-frequency sensitivity, graded strength of representations, and competition among candidate hypotheses. However, the approach embodied in the Rumelhart and McClelland simulation differs from a rule-based one in its treatment of regular and irregular verbs, in that phonological and morphological operations are applied uniformly to all verbs (in the formation of past tense forms) rather than differentially to regulars versus irregulars. The differential application of these operations to regular and irregular verbs is a crucial component of Pinker and Prince's model of past tense acquisition. In their view, membership in the regular class is not dependent on phonological characteristics of the stem or on the degree of phonological similarity among class members. The application of the regular rule occurs to verb stems regardless of phonological shape, and constitutes the default past tense formation procedure.

On the other hand, the stem and past tense forms of irregular (strong) verbs are stored independently in the lexicon. The past tense forms of irregular verbs are memorized as distinct lexical items, and are not derived from the stem. Further, most classes of strong verbs are characterized by family resemblances of phonological similarity, and are categorized as such with reference to lexical and morphological information. However, these phonological properties do not *guarantee* membership in a particular irregular class. Rather, the irregular verbs are

held together by phonologically-unpredictable hypersimilarities which are neither necessary nor sufficient criteria for membership in the classes (Pinker & Prince, p.122).

Thus, the acquisition and formation of regular and irregular past tense forms require two distinct mechanisms. However, the approach to past tense acquisition embodied in the Rumelhart and McClelland model incorporates only one of them: the abstraction of family resemblance clusters of phonological similarity. According to Pinker and Prince, this mechanism can only do half of the job, as it is neither necessary nor appropriate for the acquisition of verbs in the regular class, since the operation of the regular rule is not sensitive to phonological regularity. Missing from the Rumelhart and McClelland model are higher-level lexical representations manipulated by the past tense rule regardless of their lower-level phonological character.

Despite the detailed analysis and criticism focused on the Rumelhart and McClelland model in these and other reviews, a number of issues crucial to evaluating the adequacy of models of this type as explanatory accounts of language acquisition remain to be resolved. First, it is unclear whether the original model is appropriate for learning a system of mappings such as that constituting the past tense system of English. Rumelhart and McClelland used a binding network to determine the output performance of their system. They were not able to evaluate the exact output forms but instead forced the binding net to choose between a range of likely outputs. Given the well-discussed limitations of the perceptron convergence procedure used by Rumelhart and McClelland (Minsky & Papert, 1969), in combination with insufficient information about the output of the network, it is not known whether the global error minimum achieved in the simulation might be reduced to a level that constitutes a real solution to the overall mapping problem.

Second, although it is clear that discontinuous input to the network can lead to U-shaped learning, it cannot be concluded that discontinuous input is a necessary condition for the emergence of U-shaped learning curves. It is important to distinguish between two interpretations of the notion of U-shaped learning. In the first case, overgeneralizations emerge as the learning mechanism switches from a stage of rote learning to a stage of system building. This transition describes the classical interpretation of U-shaped development and is captured by Rumelhart and McClelland by requiring their network to learn initially only a few past tense forms and then increasing the total number of forms, that is, a discontinuity in vocabulary size. Of course, not all past tense forms are learned by rote, and overgeneralizations continue long after the child has passed into the period of system building. Thus, U-shaped learning may also result from the competition between different mapping types in the past tense system. Neural networks achieve multiple mappings by constructing a weight matrix that simultaneously satisfies the demands of each pair of mappings in the training set. If the mapping types within the set are mutually distinct (e.g. regular vs. irregular), then training the network on one input/output pair can lead to a decrement in performance on a previously trained input/output pair. Thus, the presence of distinct mapping types is the essential ingredient for obtaining U-shaped curves during the system-building period. The input discontinuity imposed on the network by Rumelhart and McClelland both exploits this conflict between mapping types and the property of neural networks to perform rote learning when the task domain is small and to generalize when the task domain is expanded. It is not yet known whether the conflicts inherent in the relationships between English verb stems and their past tense forms lead to plausible U-shaped reorganizations in networks in which input discontinuities are absent.

Third, Rumelhart and McClelland justify their introduction of a discontinuity in the input set by noting that certain verbs are more frequent than others and are, therefore, more likely to be heard by children. Pinker and Prince criticize Rumelhart and McClelland's particular operationalization of this fact on the grounds that input to children and what children actually process (i.e. intake) need not be the same. However, both pairs of authors fail to acknowledge that *two aspects* of a verb's frequency may influence its acquisition in a neural network and in children. First, individual tokens of verbs may be encountered with high or low frequency in the input. In English, many of the most commonly produced verbs are irregular and, thus, irregular verbs typically have a high *token*

frequency. Regular verbs, in contrast, fall anywhere along a continuum between very low and very high token frequency. Second, verbs can be grouped according to the type of transformation required to map a verb stem onto its past tense form. *Type frequency* (i.e. the number of verbs in the input that undergo a particular type of transformation) also varies across verb classes. In English, irregular verbs tend to have low type frequency, whereas regular verbs constitute a large, possibly infinite class. In the Rumelhart and McClelland simulation, these parameters are completely confounded. It is obvious that a verb with a high token frequency will be learned by a network, all other things being equal, faster than a verb with a low token frequency. The network will adjust its weight matrix to accommodate the constraints of one mapping more frequently than it will adjust its weight matrix for the other. However, all other things are not equal. Some verbs may be inherently easier for the network to map, both because of the number of verbs that undergo that type of mapping (i.e. the type frequency of that verb class in the problem set), and the relationship of that mapping to the total problem set (e.g. identity mapping may be easier than vowel change in the context of a dominant suffixation process). It is unlikely that all children are exposed to precisely the same distribution of type and token verb frequencies. Nevertheless, the great majority of English children succeed in mastering the English past tense. Thus, understanding the conditions under which these frequency parameters influence learning may help clarify their role in the acquisition of English verb morphology.

Overview

We will address all three of these unresolved issues. First, we compare the performance of single-layered and multi-layered perceptrons faced with learning a system of mappings analogous to English stem and past tense forms. Although the representational notation that we use for encoding verbs is different from the one used by Rumelhart and McClelland, the range of mapping types performed by the network is similar. Furthermore, we evaluate the actual (rather than probable) verbal output of the net for all verb stems in the training set.

Second, we describe several series of simulations in which type and token frequencies of the verb stems presented to the network are systematically varied. Here, the goal is to establish the input conditions under which more or less successful performance is achieved by the network, and the extent to which U-shaped development is sensitive to manipulations of type and token frequency. We relate these findings to what we know about the frequency of different types of verbs in natural languages and the role that frequency plays (if any) in the acquisition of English verb morphology. Further, we explore the manner in which phonological subregularities within verb class interact with the frequencies of verb stems to support the acquisition of both regular and irregular past tense forms.

Lastly, the performance of all of the simulations is evaluated when presented with a constant diet of input stems, rather than when discontinuity has been introduced in the input set across training. Our goal is to evaluate the degree to which the conflicting mapping relations between the various classes of English verbs, in and of themselves, give rise to reorganizational phenomena that can be interpreted to underlie U-shaped developments which are similar to those through which children pass during the system-building period in the acquisition of English verb morphology. In addition, we attempt to compare the performance of our simulations to the actual linguistic productions of young children who are in the process of acquiring the English past tense. We analyze several possible interpretations of the notion of U-shaped development and how those interpretations impact on theoretical and methodological issues relevant to development in children and artificial neural nets.

2. Method

2.1. Phonological representation

In order to avoid a number of theoretical and technical difficulties associated with Wickelphones, all of our simulations use an artificial language that consists of randomly generated, legal (i.e.

possible) English CVC, VCC and CCV strings. Each consonant and vowel is represented by a pattern of features distributed across 6 units, reflecting standard phonological contrasts such as voiced/unvoiced, front/central/back, etc., to which speakers are known to be sensitive when manipulating sound sequences in English. Assignments to feature categories do not attempt to be a completely accurate or exhaustive representation of English phonology. Rather, the representational system reflects a trade-off between accuracy and economy of representation, given the particular set of phonemes used in these simulations. It is also important to note that the use of a single, restricted set of nodes to represent both vowels and consonants requires the network to interpret features differently depending on whether the consonant/vowel unit is or is not activated (i.e. 0 or 1). For example, the manner and place units for the consonant /b/ indicate "stop" and "labial"; whereas, for the vowel /i/, these same banks of units indicate the features "high" and "front." Table 1 provides a complete listing of the phonemes used.

Since each verb in our language has a fixed length, a total of 18 units are required to uniquely identify each verb stem. The network's task is to learn mappings between these stems and their corresponding past tense forms. In many cases, the past tense form consists of the stem plus an appropriate suffix. The possible patterns of activation on the suffix units are analogous to the allomorphs of the past tense morpheme in English, to the extent that the choice of suffix depends upon whether the final phoneme in the input string is a voiced non-dental consonant or vowel, an unvoiced non-dental consonant, or a dental consonant. For example,

1. /tem/ $\Rightarrow$ /temd/   (i.e. tame $\Rightarrow$ tamed)
2. /ræp/ $\Rightarrow$ /ræpt/   (i.e. wrap $\Rightarrow$ wrapped)
3. /wet/ $\Rightarrow$ /wetʌd/   (i.e. wait $\Rightarrow$ waited)

Two units are used to distinguish three possible suffixes as well as the absence of a suffix (for all irregular verbs). Unlike the stem representations, suffix representations are not based on a phonological feature system. The network cannot, therefore, match phonological features of the

TABLE 1
Representation of phonemes

		Phonological feature					
		Cons./vowel Unit 1	Voicing Unit 2	Manner Units 3 and 4		Place Units 5 and 6	
Consonants							
/b/		0	1	1	1	1	1
/p/		0	0	1	1	1	1
/d/		0	1	1	1	1	0
/t/		0	0	1	1	1	0
/g/		0	1	1	1	0	0
/k/		0	0	1	1	0	0
/v/		0	1	1	0	1	1
/f/		0	0	1	0	1	1
/m/		0	1	0	0	1	1
/n/		0	1	0	0	1	0
/ŋ/		0	1	0	0	0	0
/ð/		0	0	1	0	1	0
/θ/		0	1	1	0	1	0
/z/		0	1	1	0	0	1
/s/		0	0	1	0	0	1
/w/		0	1	0	1	1	1
/l/		0	1	0	1	1	0
/r/		0	1	0	1	0	1
/y/		0	1	0	1	0	0
/h/		0	0	0	1	0	0
Vowels							
/i/	(eat)	1	1	1	1	1	1
/I/	(bit)	1	1	0	0	1	1
/o/	(boat)	1	1	1	0	1	1
/ʌ/	(but)	1	1	0	1	1	1
/u/	(boot)	1	1	1	1	0	1
/U/	(book)	1	1	0	0	0	1
/e/	(bait)	1	1	1	1	1	0
/ɛ/	(bet)	1	1	0	0	1	0
/ai/	(bite)	1	1	1	0	0	0
/æ/	(bat)	1	1	0	1	0	0
/au/	(cow)	1	1	1	1	0	0
/O/	(or)	1	1	0	0	0	0

suffix to those of the stem in order to decide which suffix units to activate, but is restricted to identifying correlations between features of the stem final phoneme and the pattern of activation on the suffix units.

For all stem/past tense form pairs, a total of 20 units are used to encode each stem (input) and

each past tense form (output). In the input, the final two units (i.e. the suffix) are always clamped off (i.e. at zero). This system of featural representations enable us to assess the performance of the network in a variety of ways. In particular, we can determine whether the network learned the correct transformation for every string in the training set (to some criterial level) and, if the output is incorrect, we assess the kind of error produced: that is, consonant miss(es), a vowel miss, or a suffix miss. We also compute the closest phonological representation for each output as an estimate of the actual verbal output of the network. The disadvantage of this architecture is that the model is restricted to processing strings of only three phonemes in length.

2.2. Mappings

With respect to the English past tense, verbs fall into two major categories: regular and irregular. In our simulations, the past tense forms of some verbs consist of the stem plus the appropriate suffix. For this set of regular verbs, the final two units in the output representation are activated depending on the phonological character of the stem final phoneme (described above). The remaining mapping types used in our simulations are analogous to the set of irregular verbs in English. For our purposes, irregular past tense forms can be grouped into three general subcategories according to the relationship they exhibit to their corresponding stem:[1] (a) *identity mapping* (or no marking — doing nothing to the stem, e.g. *hit* $\Rightarrow$ *hit*); (b) *vowel change* (transforming the vowel, e.g. *come* $\Rightarrow$ *came; see* $\Rightarrow$ *saw*); (c) *arbitrary* (there is no obvious structural relationship between the present and past tense form, e.g. *go* $\Rightarrow$ *went*). All three types of irregular verbs are represented in our artificial language, though within the constant length constraints imposed by the language. Identity mappings and arbitrary mappings are exemplified by the following input/output pairs:

Identity mapping: /tem/ $\Rightarrow$ /tem/
Arbitrary mapping: /rep/ $\Rightarrow$ /klo/

Approximately 32 vowel transformations occur in English, for example, /I/ $\Rightarrow$ /æ/, *ring* $\Rightarrow$ *rang*; /ʌ/ $\Rightarrow$ /e/, *come* $\Rightarrow$ *came*. A representative subset of 11 vowel transformations were chosen for inclusion in our language. (See Appendix for a complete listing of vowel changes used and analogous English examples.) It is important to note that the

vowel change transformations are rarely absolute, that is, a particular vowel can be transformed to one, two or three possible new vowels in the output.

In summary, the input/output pairs undergoing a vowel change, arbitrary, or identity mapping possess surface relationships similar to English irregular verbs. The strings (stem and past tense forms) in the suffixation class are similar in surface structure to verbs in the regular class. In the teacher signal, the last two suffix units are at zero for all irregular verbs, whereas at least one unit in the suffix portion of the string is activated for regular verbs.

2.3. Vocabulary

In the majority of simulations presented here, the network learns all four types of mappings. The same network that performs suffixation mappings must also be able to carry out the various irregular mappings. Thus, the network, like the child, must learn to deal with several different classes of transformations simultaneously. However, for all but one set of simulations, the network is at a disadvantage compared to the child in that strings are assigned to the different classes *randomly*; that is, there is no more phonological similarity between the members of a given class than between members of different classes. The only exception is the vowel change class in which class assignment is conditional upon the stem possessing the type of vowel that can undergo a legal transformation. However, a string containing a particular vowel can undergo several possible transformations whose relative frequency is not dependent on the phonological character of the stem.

Taking into account the restriction on the vowel change class, members of the four verb classes in each simulation are assembled from a source vocabulary of 700 legal strings. The exact number of strings in each class (type frequency) is varied from one simulation to another. In addition, the number of repetitions of a unique string (token frequency) is also manipulated so that the network experiences some items more frequently than others within a given sweep through the data. However, the total number of unique strings that the network must learn is held constant within a given set of simulations (in most simulations 500 unique strings are used).

2.4. Network configuration

All the simulations were run using the RLEARN simulator (Center for Research in Language, UCSD) using a back-propagation learning algorithm. Back-propagation involves the adjustment of weighted connections and unit biases when a discrepancy is detected between the actual output of the network and the desired output specified in a teacher signal. In multi-layered perceptrons (containing hidden units), error is assigned to non-output units in proportion to the weighted sum of the errors computed on the output layer. In a single-layered perceptron, back-propagation is equivalent to the perceptron convergence procedure, except that a logistic function is used to calculate the activity of the output units.

All networks contain 20 input units and 20 output units. In simulations using multi-layered perceptron architectures, 20 hidden units are included. There is no generally acknowledged criterion for selecting appropriate numbers of hidden units for an arbitrary problem. The modeller must, therefore, experiment with network capacities in order to find a configuration suited to the problem. In the current task, we varied the number of hidden units (when they were used) from 10 to 120. The final choice of 20 reflects a compromise between the attempt to achieve an optimal level of performance and the aim to maximize the generalization properties of the network. Minimizing the number of hidden units in a network encourages the system to search for regularities in the input stimuli.

Training in the simulations follows a pattern update schedule; that is, a pattern is presented to the net, a signal propagates through the net, the error is calculated, and the weights are adjusted. Learning rate and momentum are adjusted at various points during the simulation.[2] (As with the choice of network configuration, manipulations of this kind are typically determined through experimentation rather than principled criteria.) At the beginning of training, learning rate and momentum are high. Across learning, their values are gradually reduced.

2.5. Output analysis

On each presentation of an input pattern, any error on the output units is recorded and the weights adjusted accordingly. Verb stems are presented randomly to the network. The weight matrix for the network is saved at regular intervals: at the end of every epoch for the first 15 epochs,[3] every 5 epochs through epoch 30, and every 10 epochs through epoch 50. In this way, a total of 20 snapshots of the state of the network are saved from each simulation. These snapshots are used to evaluate the accuracy of the network in producing the correct past tense form for each unique stem at different points in the network's development. In order to perform correctly, an individual output unit must be within 0.5 of the value stipulated in the teacher set (which can be either 0 or 1). If all units are within criterion, the output is judged to be correct. In addition, the output units are categorized into sets corresponding to the vowel (1 set of 6 units), consonants (2 sets of 6 units each) and suffix (1 set of 2 units) phonemes. Each phoneme is then evaluated to see if all units meet criterion. For each class of stems, the error analysis procedures provide a calculation of the global error, an overall hit rate (i.e. percentage correct), as well as a breakdown of the type of error (e.g. consonant, vowel or suffix) and its frequency. Additional analyses determine the verbal output (closest fit in Euclidean space) of the network to each of the unique stems at different points in learning. Error types are also classified by verb class. Thus, stems which are incorrectly mapped by the network are categorized in terms of whether they are mistakenly treated as an identity stem, a vowel change stem, a blend, etc.

3. Results and discussion[4]

3.1. The role of network architecture

Rumelhart and McClelland use a single-layered perceptron in their simulation of the acquisition of the English past tense. In this section, we evaluate the adequacy of a single-layered perceptron to perform a mapping task in which the network is required to learn suffixations, vowel changes, identity mappings, and arbitrary changes.

Rosenblatt (1962) showed that the perceptron convergence procedure guarantees that a suitable configuration of weights will be found during learning, provided that a solution to the given mapping problem exists within the confines of a single-layered perceptron. Determining whether a solution exists to a given mapping problem in a perceptron involves solving a set of simultaneous equations. For a complex mapping problem, this procedure is computationally expensive and, in practice, is equivalent to running the problem in a perceptron network to determine whether or not a solution can be found. We, therefore, apply a single-layered perceptron to the task of learning the past tense forms of 500 verb stems and observe the trajectory of global error across training. If the global error is reduced to zero (or close to zero),[5] we may conclude that a single-layered perceptron is able to find a solution to the mapping problem. However, if the error function of the network asymptotes at a non-zero level, we must conclude that a single-layered perceptron is inadequate for obtaining solutions to such problems, and that a multi-layered network architecture using a generalized learning algorithm (e.g. back-propagation) is required.

We tested the performance of a single-layered perceptron on learning the past tense using two vocabulary configurations. These vocabulary configurations were chosen because they represent two reasonable relative distributions of regular to irregular verbs in English compiled from recent discussions (e.g. Pinker & Prince, 1988). In one, the vocabulary is composed of 10 arbitrary stems, 370 regular stems, 30 identity stems, and 90 vowel change stems, resulting in a 3:1 ratio of regular to irregular stems. In the second, the vocabulary is structured using 10 arbitraries, 250 regulars, 70 identities, and 170 vowel changes, resulting in a ratio of regulars to irregulars of 1:1.[6] Items in these vocabularies are presented to the network randomly such that the network sees each unique stem an average of once per training epoch (i.e. one pass through the entire vocabulary). Thus, token frequency is uniform across verb classes and vocabulary configurations.[7] Each network is trained for 250 epochs, and the total sum squared error is measured after every epoch of training. Total sum squared error provides a measure of error averaged across all output units for a given learning period (most typically per epoch). When the weights in the network are randomized, the averaged (non-squared) chance error across input stems is 10.0. In contrast, if all mappings are mastered by the network, the global error should be reduced to (or close to) zero.

The computation of total sum squared error in these two simulations suggests that it is highly unlikely that global error could ever be reduced to a near-zero value when solving this problem in a single-layered perceptron. For both simulations, learning curves asymptote at or near the 15th epoch of training at a non-squared error value of approximately 2.5. From that point in the training onward, average error proceeds on a near zero-gradient trajectory, and continues at this level until training was stopped after the 250th epoch. We may, therefore, conclude that a single-layered perceptron cannot solve the overall mapping problem presented by these vocabulary configurations. Of course, in principle, a definitive proof of this point would involve training these networks for infinite time. Nevertheless, these results provide reasonably convincing evidence that the mapping function required to solve the past tense problem demands the use of a multi-layered perceptron and a suitable learning algorithm. It is unlikely that the notational differences in the input/output representations used here and by Rumelhart and McClelland affects the character of the global mapping solution required of the perceptron. Since the set of mapping relationships required of both these simulations and Rumelhart and McClelland's were similar to those in English, we may conclude that it is improbable that the Rumelhart and McClelland simulation achieved a reasonable solution to the mapping problem. However, a completely stringent evaluation of the suitability of the perceptron for the Rumelhart and McClelland version of the past tense problem would involve computing global errors for Wickelfeature representations.

3.2. Effects of type and token frequency

All simulations described in the remainder of the paper use a multi-layered perceptron and a back-propagation learning algorithm. All network architectures contain 20 hidden units.

3.2.1. Evaluation of network performance under non-conflict and conflict conditions

The first set of simulations evaluate the capacity of a multi-layered perceptron to learn each of the four types of mappings between stems and past tense forms. This capacity is investigated in two basic conditions:

1. When the network has to learn only one type of mapping.
2. When the classes are in competition with each other for the network's resources.

Four simulations (the *independents*) explore the learning of each mapping type (arbitrary, suffix, identity and vowel change) independently of each other. 125 unique stems are randomly assigned to each class and the appropriate past tense forms are compiled into a corresponding teacher set. The network is trained on one and only one class of mappings for 50 epochs. In a fifth simulation (the *base*), the network is required to learn all four classes of mappings simultaneously, that is, a vocabulary consisting of 500 unique strings. The type frequency of the classes is the same for each of these simulations (i.e. 125). In general, these five baseline simulations allow the evaluation of (a) the relative difficulty of learning the various mapping types in this type of network, and (b) the effect of learning the mapping types in the context of other mapping types (i.e. in conflict) versus in isolation (i.e. in non-conflict situations).

3.2.1.1. Results of the independent and base simulations. Performance of the network, confronted with only a single class of transformations, is summarized in Fig. 1. Figure 1 plots the global error for each of the four classes of mappings across 50 epochs of learning. The arbitrary mappings have the highest global error, while the regular and identity mappings have the lowest error.

Figure 1 also provides a breakdown of the network's ability to output correctly the three phonemes and the suffix for each class of mappings.

Not unsurprisingly, a network that is required to map only arbitrary stems correctly outputs only past tense forms which do not have a suffix (no suffixed past tense forms are seen by the network); however, its ability to generate the correct consonants and vowels in the past tense form is rather poor ($\approx$25%). As a consequence, the network correctly generates the appropriate three-phoneme sequence for only about 2% (or two strings) of the total learning set. This poor performance can be contrasted with that of a network learning only regular mappings. In such a network, the entire set of regular mappings is learned correctly by the network within about 15 epochs. Fewer than 1% of the output patterns (one string) are generated with an incorrect suffix, and all consonants and vowels comprising the stem are reproduced correctly. Similarly, performance on the identity mappings is optimal within about 13 epochs. No suffix errors are produced throughout learning. Lastly, as suggested by the global error, the network has more difficulty learning the vowel changes than either the identity or regular mappings. After 50 epochs, only about 75% of the forms are mapped correctly. Most errors are due to inaccurate vowel representations on the output units. Over half of these vowel errors are a result of the network reproducing the same vowel from the input stem on the output, that is, performing an identity mapping. On only one occasion does the network attempt to perform a legal, but inappropriate vowel change from input to output. A small minority of the errors in the vowel change class are due to incorrectly mapped consonants, and the network correctly keeps the suffix units turned off at all times.

These simulations clearly demonstrate that the network learns some types of mappings more easily than it learns others. The ease with which the network can map a given class of verb stems can be best understood in terms of the degree to which a given set of mappings constitutes a single homogeneous class. For example, identity mappings are most quickly learned by the network because they all require the same type of mapping, that is, map each input activation to an equivalent activation on the corresponding output unit. In contrast, arbitrary mappings are the least well mapped

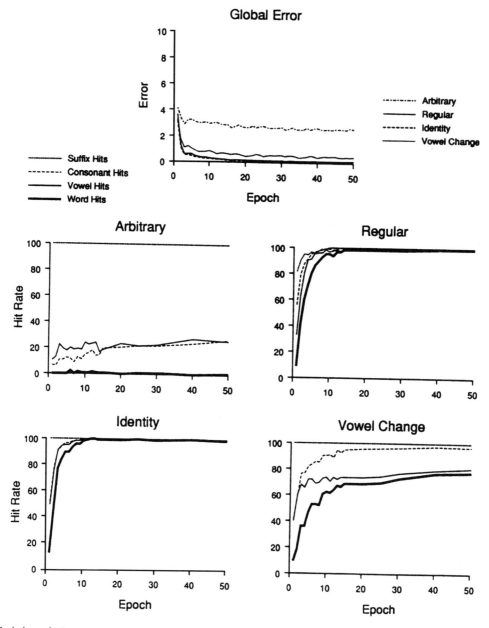

FIG. 1. Independents.

by the network since the input units are mapped to the output units in completely unpredictable ways. In fact, the arbitrary class might be thought of as several subclasses, each subclass having just one member represented by its own distinctive mapping relation. Regular and vowel change mappings are intermediate cases. The regular class consists of three subclasses, each corresponding to the allomorphs used in the suffixation process. Yet, for all regular verbs, the majority of output unit activations are related to their input unit activations in a completely coherent fashion; that is, all stem units are mapped to equivalent activation values of the corresponding output units. The vowel change class is comprised of 11 subclasses. For each of these, the input units representing the consonants are identity mapped to their corresponding output units; however, the vowel must undergo one of several possible transformations. As noted above, many errors on vowel-change verbs result from mapping the input vowels directly to output vowels, reflecting the underlying identity mapping characteristic of the majority of the phonemes in the learning set.

Since the type frequency of the different classes in these simulations is quite large, it is unlikely that the relative order of mappings is an artifact of the particular assignment of strings to a given class. Nevertheless, several replications of these simulations have been performed. The results are essentially identical to those just reported.

Figure 2 depicts the performance of the network in the conflict learning condition, that is, when it must learn a vocabulary of 500 words consisting of all four types of mappings.

In comparison to the *independents*, global error on this *base* simulation is increased for all classes. Thus, the network's ability to learn each of the four types of mappings is affected by the context in which those mappings must be performed. The arbitrary transformation is the most adversely affected. In the *base* simulation, the network is unable to learn arbitrary mappings, generating both incorrect vowels and consonants. However, as in the *independents*, the network rarely attempts to turn on the suffix units for those stems belonging to the arbitrary class. The ability of the network to produce all portions of the string correctly for regular verbs is also quite poor, in spite of their relatively low global error. Less than 10% of the stems are inflected with the correct suffix, and the relationship between overall hits and suffix hits is strong. That is, the network is able to correctly reproduce the stem on the output, but generally fails to activate the suffix units. Verbs in the regular class tend to be treated as if they belong to the identity class.

In contrast to arbitraries and regulars, however, identity mappings perform rather well ($\approx 65\%$ overall correct). Errors are mostly due to vowel misses. The network makes virtually no attempt to turn on the suffix units and few consonant errors

are generated after 10 epochs. Finally, mappings in the vowel change class display a low level of overall performance ($\approx 20\%$). Here, there is a strong relationship between overall hit rate and vowel hit rate. As with the regular class, many (52 or 42%) of the incorrectly mapped vowel changes stems are treated as though they belonged to the identity class; that is, stem identity is maintained in the output. Consonants are generally produced correctly throughout. As with the *independent* simulations, the *base* simulation has been replicated with essentially identical results using several randomly generated class assignments.

The pattern of results summarized in Fig. 2 is complex; however, some tendencies are apparent. First, the network appears to prefer to keep output suffix units shut off irrespective of the stem it transforms. This is an appropriate strategy for many of the input stems (75%); however, it is also the greatest source of error when generalized to the class of regular stems. In fact, the majority of errors for *all* stem classes can be accounted for by the degree to which that class of mappings diverges from identity mapping. That is, the network generates incorrect vowels and consonants on arbitrary stems, but not suffixes. The network generates incorrect suffixes on regular stems, but not incorrect vowels and consonants. Incorrect vowels are generated on the vowel change stems, but not suffixes or consonants. In general, then, the network appears to have adopted a single strategy in encoding the relationship between stems and past tense forms: identity map the input stem to the output. This strategy clearly makes sense given the vocabulary and transformations as we have defined them: identity mapping is the lowest common denominator that glues the different classes together into a coherent system.[8] (In several of the following sets of simulations, we explore the conditions under which the system does and does not adopt identity mapping as its most preferred strategy.)

In summary, a comparison of the general increase in global error from the *independent* to *base* simulations suggests that the network appears to have a limited capacity to learn input/output mappings when they are numerous and inhomogeneous. Furthermore, the network is able to map

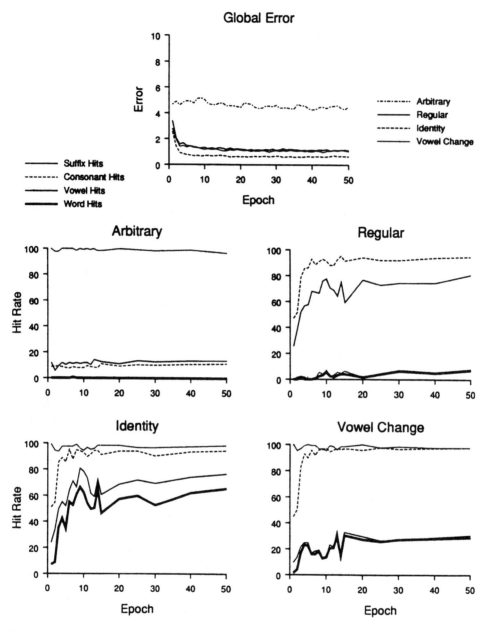

FIG. 2. Base.

some classes of transformations easier than others. This result could have been anticipated from the different error patterns in the four *independent* simulations. However, the rank order of performance from each individual simulation is not maintained in the conflict condition. For example, regular mappings are easily learned in an indi-

vidual simulation but poorly learned in the context of the three other classes of mapping. Hence, there is a clear *competition effect* that is not directly predictable from the ability of the network to perform the mappings in isolation. As mentioned above, the major impact of this competition can be described in terms of an identity mapping strategy, to the extent that the errors made by the network can be described as a result of an over-application of this strategy. However, while identity mapping can account for the majority of the *errors* generated by the network, there are still many cases in which the network generates a *correct* past tense form that does not involve pure identity mapping, for example, correct performance on 20% of the vowel change stems. In addition, stems in the identity class are not immune from competition or leakage from the vowel change class, as *within-class* errors also result (about 25% incorrect vowel mappings on identity stems). Therefore, for certain aspects of this network's performance, it is useful to summarize the source of the errors in terms of an over-application of a general strategy. However, other aspects of both correct and incorrect performance cannot be captured by this characterization.

The performance of these simulations is only partially analogous to the patterns observed in children's acquisition of the English past tense. This is not surprising given the unrealistic statistical properties of the set of forms that the network is required to learn, in particular, the *equal type frequency* of verbs across each of the four mapping classes. Nevertheless, these simulations provide a baseline against which to compare network performance on vocabulary configurations in which the frequency structure is increasingly analogous to English. Without an understanding of the general preferences of the network in baseline conditions, it would be impossible to evaluate the degree to which type and token frequency affects the occurrence and pattern of overgeneralization errors using more English-like vocabularies.

3.2.2 Evaluation of two vocabulary configurations: Dictionary and production simulations

From very early in acquisition, the vocabulary that a child learns contains examples of all types of past tense forms. It is difficult, however, to determine the relative numbers of verbs of each type that are relevant and/or salient for the child, and hence should be used for modeling past tense acquisition. Rumelhart and McClelland constructed their set of stimuli by consulting Kucera

and Francis' (1967) listing of English word frequencies. Pinker and Prince (1988) suggest that reports of children's actual productions provide a better foundation for determining the relative sizes of verb classes that are pertinent to models of early acquisition. Both proposals have their pitfalls. The Kucera and Francis frequencies were compiled from written texts and, hence, are highly unlikely to reflect the statistical properties of language to which children are exposed (i.e. input) or which children are able to process (i.e. intake). In addition, production measures disregard the documented precociousness of comprehension skills found in young children (e.g. Bates, Bretherton, & Snyder, 1988) — skills that might suggest yet another relative size configuration of verb classes in English.[9] Further, token frequency (i.e. the frequency with which a unique string is experienced by the child) varies across the irregular and regular verb classes in English. As discussed above, the past tense forms of irregular verbs tend to be commonly used (e.g. went); whereas, the class of regular verbs is comprised of both very frequently and very infrequently occurring forms.

In the following set of simulations, both type and token frequency are varied in order to investigate the effect of class size and the repetition of unique strings on learning. Four simulations are described in which a total of 500 unique input/output pairings are presented. Note that the total number of input/output pairings is identical to that in the *base* simulations. However, rather than having an equal number of verbs in each class, the vocabulary is structured such that it resembles two possible configurations of the English lexicon. For each of these type frequency configurations, learning is assessed given two token frequency configurations, In two *dictionary* simulations, the type frequency of the regular class greatly outnumbers that in all the irregular classes. In contrast, in the two *production* simulations, the size of the regular class equals the size of the combined irregular classes. One version of each of these (*production-type* and *dictionary-type*) holds the token frequency of strings constant across classes (i.e. one token). A second version (*production-token* and *dictionary-token*) varies token frequency across the four verb classes. These token frequencies were derived from anecdotal reports of the relative frequency of occurrence of the different types of verbs (e.g. Bever, 1992). As an example, in the *token* simulations, the network sees the arbitrary input/output pairings ten times more frequently than it sees any given regular pairing.

All strings are available to the system in each epoch; the token manipulation simply increases the number of times that the network sees a given identical string during a single pass through the input set. The type frequencies (class size) and token frequencies (number of unique stem repetitions per epoch) for each simulation are summarized in Table 2. This table also presents the percentage of stems in each class that were generated correctly by the network at the end of training, that is, after 50 epochs.

3.2.2.1. Results of the dictionary and production simulations.

In the *dictionary-type* simulation, verbs in the regular class occur most frequently and are the only verb type that is mastered by the network (90% correct). Verbs belonging to the other three classes are likely to be overgeneralized, that is, treated as if they are regular. In this simulation, the large class size of the regulars relative to the other classes results in correct performance on those verbs which should undergo suffixation. However, the tendency for the network to add a suffix is too general, thus interfering with performance on the irregular verbs. Performance on vowel change verbs, which have the second

largest type frequency, produces the fewest suffix errors of all of the irregular classes. The behavior of this network can be seen to illustrate one aspect of what is known about past tense acquisition at certain phases of development; that is, that children will tend to add a suffix to verbs in the irregular classes.

The *dictionary-token* simulation increases the number of tokens in each irregular class, within the same type frequency configuration. The impact of this manipulation on network performance is quite dramatic. First, the percentage of correct output on regular verbs drops to approximately 32%, while performance on the identity and vowel change classes improves substantially (≈90%). One arbitrary verb (10%) is mastered by the network. Further analyses reveal that errors on the regulars are due to suffix and vowel misses, and errors on the identity and vowel change classes are due almost entirely to vowel misses. Arbitrary errors are due primarily to consonant misses, although vowel misses contribute a substantial proportion of the error.

In general, a comparison of these two simulations suggests that an increase in token frequency in the irregular classes results in improved performance on those verbs, measured in terms of both hit rate and global error. When the network sees individual irregular stems *more often* than individual regular stems, the network no longer treats all stems as though they are regulars. On the contrary, this configuration results in the tendency to categorize stems into one of two irregular

TABLE 2
Type and token frequency distributions and hit rates in the dictionary and production simulations

| | *Type of mapping* | | | | | | | | | | | |
| | *Arbitrary* | | | *Regular* | | | *Identity* | | | *Vowel change* | | |
Simulation	*Type*	*Token*	*% hits*	*Type*	*Token*	*% hits*	*Type*	*Token*	*% hits*	*Type*	*Token*	*% hits*
Dictionary-type	10	1	0	370	1	90	30	1	23	90	1	3
Dictionary-token	10	10	10	370	1	32	30	8	87	90	8	91
Production-type	10	1	0	250	1	67	70	1	46	170	1	27
Production-token	10	10	8	250	1	25	70	8	87	170	8	83

classes, that is, identities and vowel changes. Thus, increasing the token frequency of the irregular classes results in a decrease in both (a) the performance on the regular verbs, and (b) the tendency of the network to overgeneralize the suffix to irregular verbs. Thus, by incorporating information about token frequency into the input configuration, we have *decreased* the degree to which the performance of the network resembles children's acquisition of the past tense. The generality of this result is further explored in the *production* simulations which use a vocabulary configuration based on estimates of the ratio of regular to irregular verbs in children's productive speech.

The *production-type* simulation maintains a constant token frequency across classes (tokens = 1); however, the number of items in each verb class follows the verb configuration outlined in Table 2. Compared to the *dictionary-type* simulation, the identity and vowel change mappings improve, while performance on the regulars deteriorates. This result can be partially, but not totally, predicted from changes in relative class size. In the *production* simulations, regular verbs are not as frequent as in the *dictionary* simulations and, not unexpectedly, the proportion of correct output for that class decreases. However, relative class size would also predict that vowel changes should be easier than identities. This is not the case. But recall that the baseline simulations confirm that identity mapping is one of the preferred strategies for this network in neutral conditions. Hence, because of the common input/output relationships inherent in these analogs to English verbs, identity mapping itself does rather well despite its small class size. In both vocabulary configurations, "add /-ed/" overgeneralizations to the arbitrary and identity classes are quite common. However, in the *production* simulations, where vowel changes have a type frequency of 170, the vowel change class is resistant to suffix overgeneralization. Class size, then, does appear to play an important role in determining the degree to which other class characteristics leak to a target class.

The fourth simulation in this set, *production-token*, maintains the same type frequency as the *production-type* simulation; however, token frequency is manipulated across classes (see Table 2).

As in the *dictionary-token* manipulation, changes in the relative token frequency of the irregular classes has a dramatic effect on performance for all verb classes. In particular, regulars decrease to a very low hit rate, while identities and vowel changes improve to near optimal performance. Most of the incorrect outputs on the regulars are due to errors on the suffix, while errors on identity and vowel change stems are due entirely to vowel misses. Again, the network tends to treat all stems as if they belong to one of two classes: identity mapping or vowel change.

These four simulations demonstrate that manipulations of class size and frequency of exemplars affect both the rate of learning and the final level of performance within that class, as Bever and others have suggested. These simulations also demonstrate that type frequency parameters affect the degree to which characteristics of the mapping in one class will be adopted by the network when forming the past tense forms of stems in other classes. However, varying the token frequency of a class (type $\Rightarrow$ token) has a *greater* effect on class performance than varying type frequency (dictionary $\Rightarrow$ production). The generality of this result is unclear.

What is clear is that overgeneralization errors can be observed in many directions, depending on which strategy is dominant in a given simulation. The dominance of a particular strategy is determined by the relative type and token frequencies of the competing classes, in interaction with the global characteristics of the total mapping function that the network is required to perform. In particular, there is a substantial tendency of the network to perform identity mapping even when the type frequency of this class is small. Note also that the arbitrary mappings never exceed a hit rate greater than 10%.

The *dictionary* and *production* simulations mimic the performance of real children learning the past tense of English in a limited sense. While the *dictionary-type* simulation produces suffix overgeneralizations to many verbs in the irregular classes, just as children have been observed to do, increasing the token frequency of irregular verbs in a realistic direction *reduces* the tendency of the system to make this standard overgeneralization error and interferes with its overall mastery of the regular mapping. While not as frequent as the standard regularization error, it has been noted that children occasionally do produce the type of overgeneralizations that predominate in these simulations, that is, treat verb stems as if they belonged to one of the irregular classes (e.g. identities). These findings suggest that the type and token configuration of a vocabulary that is to be learned by a child may play a crucial role in outlining the conditions under which one type of mapping will be adopted over another (albeit sometimes with erroneous results).

3.2.3. Token frequency and phonological predictability: Parent and phone simulations

The simulations discussed so far establish that type and token frequency have significant impact on learning outcomes in a network. In the following sets of simulations, the *parents* and the *phones*, we use yet another configuration of type frequencies in constructing our verb classes. On most accounts, English boasts a total of only about 150 irregular verbs, compared to regular verbs which number in the thousands. In the *dictionary* and *production* simulations, the total number of irregular stems presented to the network exceeded this number. Therefore, we construct our next set of vocabularies such that they more closely resemble the vocabulary configuration of English verbs. In so doing, we adopt the assumption that parents' speech to children is roughly representative of the general configuration of average English (Hayes & Ahrens, 1988).

Nineteen *parent* and 19 *phone* simulations were conducted in which the arbitrary, regular, identity and vowel change classes have type frequencies of 2, 410, 20 and 68, respectively. Although the type frequency distribution still does not reflect the absolute proportion of irregular to regular verbs in English, the *parent* and *phone* simulations provide a more realistic assessment of the *relative* class sizes that young children must learn. (In order to clarify the interpretation of the results, two additional *parent* simulations were conducted, *parent 24* and *parent 25*, in which slightly different type frequency configurations were used; see

section 3.2.3.1) Token frequency is then varied parametrically across simulations in an attempt to isolate the *combination* of type and token frequencies which achieves optimal learning for all four classes of verbs. One main goal of these simulations, then, is to examine systematically the effect of *token frequency* while type frequency is held constant.

In the *parent* simulations, as in all of the previously discussed simulations, the assignment of a stem to a particular verb class is performed randomly. Any stem can belong to any verb class, and hence can relate to its corresponding past tense form through an identity map, suffixation, vowel change, or arbitrary transformation. Thus, except for the conditions on vowel change class membership, stems are assigned to classes irrespective of their phonological character.

In the *phone* simulations, in contrast, we partially mimic the phonological characteristics of irregular verbs in English. Instead of random assignment, we impose the following constraints on class membership:

1. All identity stems must end in a dental.
2. All vowel change stems are restricted to 11 possible VC endings (i.e. stem final vowel–consonant clusters). Corresponding to each possible ending, the vowel change transformation that must be learned by the network maintains the identity of the final consonant, but transforms the vowel according to the same rules used in all of the previous simulations. The Appendix details the transformations involved.

In addition, we ensure that the regular class contains stems that fulfill the criteria for membership in these two irregular classes. Thus, as in English, the network cannot use phonological information to *define* an irregular class, although it can insist on the presence of specific phonological features as a *condition* for performing one of the irregular mappings.

Our aims in performing the *phone* simulations are twofold. First, we determine how the network exploits the phonological subregularities in the identity and vowel change classes. That is, in what conditions do constraints on class membership assist the network in discovering which stems should undergo the different mappings, leading to improved performance? Second, we explore the patterns of competition and overgeneralization that occur as a function of token frequency when phonological subregularities are available to the network. That is, are patterns of learning in the *phone* simulations similar to those observed in the *parents*, where phonological information is not useful to the network? Table 3 outlines the type and token frequencies for the different mapping classes in the *parent* and *phone* simulations. In addition, the percentage hit rates for the various verb classes at the end of training (50 epochs) are presented.

3.2.3.1. Results of the parent and phone simulations. In the *parent* and *phone* simulations, we observe a variety of results that have important implications for child language acquisition. We first report on the conditions under which arbitrary mappings are acquired by the network, and relate this pattern of acquisition to the acquisition of analogously structured forms in children. Second, we provide a detailed description of the complex interactions between type and token frequency in these networks. In particular, we demonstrate that type and token frequency effects must be interpreted in interaction with mapping type in order to predict patterns of learning and error production. Lastly, we discuss the role of phonological

TABLE 3
Token frequencies and hit rates after 50 epochs in the parent and phone simulations[a]

Sim.	Arbitrary			Regular			Identity			Vowel change		
	Token freq.	Parent % hit	Phone % hit	Token freq.	Parent % hit	Phone % hit	Token freq.	Parent % hit	Phone % hit	Token freq.	Parent % hit	Phone % hit
1	1	0	0	1	96	94	1	15	50	1	0	3
2	5	0	0	1	92	89	1	10	40	1	5	1
3	10	100	0	1	96	93	1	0	65	1	0	0
4	15	50	100	1	96	90	1	15	40	1	3	1
5	15	50	100	1	50	69	1	20	35	5	82	88
6	20	100	100	1	93	92	1	5	60	1	0	6
7	40	100	100	1	90	92	1	15	65	1	3	6
8	145	100	100	1	87	90	1	10	60	1	3	10
9	15	50	100	1	77	76	1	40	40	2	22	31
10	15	100	50	1	84	88	5	75	95	1	6	13
11	15	100	50	1	82	86	14	100	100	1	6	6
16	15	100	50	1	74	83	16	100	100	1	6	4
17	15	50	50	1	65	71	5	70	100	3	28	62
18	20	100	100	1	59	67	1	30	40	5	72	88
19	20	100	50	1	82	79	1	25	35	2	18	44
20	20	100	100	1	88	87	5	80	100	1	5	7
21	20	100	100	1	82	88	14	100	100	1	2	4
*24	20	100	—	1	79	—	1	37	—	16	95	—
*25	20	100	—	1	73	—	5	88	—	1	0	—
26	20	100	50	1	76	83	16	100	100	1	3	7
27	20	100	100	1	60	73	5	70	100	3	37	57
Mean	—	81	68	—	80	84	—	48	70	—	19	23

[a] The type frequency configurations are identical for all simulations reported in this table, except for those marked with an asterisk. See text for explanation.

subregularities in constraining these frequency effects, and providing the network with a more substantive basis upon which to learn the past tense.

The *parent* simulations illustrate that arbitrary mappings must be few in number (low type frequency) and high in token frequency (large number of repetitions) if a back-propagation network with a limited number of hidden units is to succeed in learning them while simultaneously mastering other mapping types. However, once the input provides enough exemplars so that the arbitrary mappings can be mastered (e.g. *parents 6–8, 10, 11, 16, 18–27*), they enjoy a protected existence unaffected by, and not affecting, other stem–past tense pairs which must be learned in the network. It is important that the low type frequency of arbitrary mappings is supported by a high token frequency. In the absence of the latter, performance on arbitrary mappings is extremely poor.

Natural languages also make little use of truly arbitrary relationships between stem and past tense forms of verbs. When natural languages do incorporate these types of relationships, they are generally highly frequent and constitute a relatively small class of items. For the young child acquiring language, the present and past tense forms of English verbs which belong to the arbitrary class are represented frequently in the input. It is highly likely that the relatively few arbitrary transformations in English, together with their high token frequency, contributes to children's early learning of these forms.

Table 3 also demonstrates that regular and vowel change mappings frequently compete with each other for network resources in such a manner that neither class can be fully and simultaneously mastered by the network. It is clear that increasing the token frequency of the vowel change class is responsible for both improved performance of the vowel change stems and deteriorated performance on regular mappings (see, for example, *parents 5* and *18*). Yet, the results of other simulations (e.g. *parent 6*) suggest that the token frequency of a given class *per se* does not necessarily predict poor performance in other classes of stems being mapped by the network. In many simulations, an increase in the token frequency of stems in the identity class has little influence on the learning of regular verbs. The nature of the interference between the vowel change and the regular class is worth considering further. The vowel change class in *parent 18* possesses characteristics that may make it particularly efficacious for disrupting the performance of the regular mappings. For example, the vowel change class has a type frequency of 68: over three times larger than the identity class. The probability that a vowel change stem closely resembles a regular stem, and hence distorts the mapping of that stem, is thus correspondingly larger. This property predicts two results:

1. If the type frequency of the vowel change class is decreased, then the resulting disruption to the regular mappings should be reduced substantially even if the total number of vowel change tokens is maintained relative to *parent 18*.
2. If the type frequency of any *other class* is increased, then the probability that a token of that class would resemble a regular stem (and hence influence the mapping of that stem) is increased. For example, a high type frequency of identity mappings should have the same effect on the regular mappings as a large vowel change type frequency.

Parent 24 investigates the first hypothesis. In this simulation, the type frequency of the vowel change class is reduced to 20 at the same time as the type frequency of the identity class is increased to 68. The total vocabulary that the network is required to learn is held constant at 500; however, the token frequency of the vowel change stems presented to the network is increased so that the network sees just as many vowel change tokens per epoch as it did in *parent 18*. The predictions of the first hypothesis are confirmed: the vowel change class performs at near optimum level without significantly altering the performance in either the arbitrary or regular class. Therefore, type frequency would appear to be a crucial factor in determining the *coexistence* of different types of mapping. In particular, when the type frequencies of classes that compete with the dominant class are kept at a fairly low level, *coexistence* of those classes is facilitated.

The second hypothesis is tested in *parent 25*. In this simulation, the type and token frequency of the identity mappings are the same as those of the vowel change class in *parent 18*. The main finding is that the increased type frequency of the identity class also affects the performance of the regular mappings. However, this deleterious impact on performance is less severe than that caused by vowel changes in a network with identical type and token frequencies. The great majority of errors (71%) for stems in the regular class are due to their being treated as identities. Furthermore, it is noteworthy that the percentage of suffix errors on the regulars in this simulation is very close to that found in *parent 18*. This finding enables us to attribute the lower level of overall performance on regular stems in *parent 18* to the additive effect of the vowel and the suffix misses. Thus, both our hypotheses concerning the role of type frequency of competing classes on the performance of the regular mappings are confirmed. However, it should be noted that this *type frequency effect* is seen only when supported by an adequately large token frequency for that class.

Both type and token frequency play an important role in determining the level of performance in a given class and the extent to which mapping characteristics leak across classes. When the type frequency (class size) of an irregular mapping is kept low, an increase in the token frequency of verbs in that class results in a high level of performance for that class without any deleterious effects on the dominant form (highest type frequency) of mapping. However, if the type frequency of the irregular class is relatively large and backed up by a high token frequency, then the performance in the dominant form of mapping deteriorates dramatically. This effect is further exaggerated in the case of the vowel change class because it differs in several respects from the regular class; that is, do not add a suffix but do change the vowel. Competition effects like these lead to situations in which leakage of mapping characteristics across classes is complex. For example, vowel change characteristics may leak to the regular class at the same time as suffixation

characteristics leak to the identity class. Indeed, even compound leakage across classes is observed, that is, blends.

In general, the larger the irregular class, the greater the likelihood of an irregular stem resembling and thus interfering with the mapping of a regular stem. As it happens, the class of irregular verbs in English is rather small. However, in studies of children's acquisition of past tense inflectional morphology in English, subregularities in the irregular system sometimes give rise to their own patterns of overgeneralization, albeit less frequently than the standard "add /-ed/" overgeneralization (e.g. Bybee & Slobin, 1982). Children will sometimes overgeneralize a vowel change or identity mapping to a regular or irregular stem, producing errors such as *sit* $\Rightarrow$ *sit*, or combine mapping types to produce blended responses, such as *ated*. In other languages, such as French, in which the class sizes of different verb mappings are more homogeneous, these results would suggest that a qualitatively different pattern of leakage of mapping characteristics would be observed. Furthermore, an analysis of the type and token frequency characteristics of verb classes in other languages should enable us to predict the profile of mastery and overgeneralizations through which children pass in the acquisition process.

In the *parent* simulations, assignment of stems to each of the four classes was randomized. While the representation of each string was based on phonological contrasts used in English, it is highly unlikely that these networks were able to access any phonological regularity in the input patterns in order to decide whether or not a given stem belongs to a particular class. Thus, the phonological character of the input stems could not be said to predict category membership. The knowledge encoded in the weight matrix cannot, therefore, be organized in terms of class definitions represented as phonological features. Furthermore, at no point did any of the *parent* simulations succeed in reaching adult-like performance in this task. Therefore, within the confines of this network architecture, these results suggest that: (a) the particular language and input configurations used in the *parent* simulations do not accurately reflect English, even though considerable care was taken to devise a valid representation of input to children; and/or (b) the information represented in the input to these networks is not sufficient to achieve perfect mastery in this task.

The *phone* simulations explore whether the addition of phonological predictability into the input set enables this system to master the past tense. Compared to the *parent* simulations, all *phone* simulations exhibit a higher level of performance (see Table 3) across mapping types, except for the arbitrary mappings. However, since we can *force* arbitrary mappings to perform at an optimal level simply by increasing their token frequency, without affecting the other classes, we will not consider arbitrary mappings further in this set of simulations. Of more central concern are the performances of the regular and two other irregular classes. First, note that the regulars perform minimally better under the *phone* condition than under the *parent* condition. The greatest differences in regular performance tend to occur when the token frequency of the *vowel change* class is relatively high (simulations 5, 17, 18 and 27). Since there are no differences between the two conditions other than the subregularities in the identity and vowel change classes, we can attribute the lower performance of the regulars in the *parent* condition to the absence of these subregularities. In the *phone* simulations, the phonological subregularities which characterize vowel change and identity stems conspire to protect the regulars from interference, despite the facts that (a) the regular class contains stems that resemble the vowel change and identity classes (similar vowel and final consonant), and (b) there are no explicit features of the representation which can tell the network which stems belong in the regular class.

Table 3 also depicts a clear-cut advantage for the identity mappings in the *phone* simulations. Given the well-defined subregularity that characterizes the identity class (all identity stems end in a dental), it is not surprising that the network is able to map this class successfully. However, many stems, both in the regular and vowel change classes, that possess the identity stem characteristics are not mapped as identities. In other words, though the network is able to make use of the subregularities detectable in the input, it is

not indiscriminate in its categorization of verbs into classes on the basis of these subregularities (though they are of course a source of error).

Finally, Table 3 depicts a moderate advantage for vowel change mappings in the *phone* condition. These advantages are particularly apparent in several simulations (17, 19 and 27). In simulations 17 and 27, both the vowel change class and the identity class have relatively large token frequencies. In the *parent* condition, the lack of phonological subregularities permits the tendency towards identity mapping to spill over into the vowel change class. However, in the *phones*, the phonological regularity of the identity class restricts the application of identity mapping to stems that possess these characteristics and hence reduces the level of interference with the vowel change class. Again, these simulations suggest that analyses of the phonological regularities that characterize the verb classes in languages other than English will contribute to our understanding of the profile of mastery and overgeneralization errors produced by children throughout acquisition. However, the precise effect of phonological subregularities on mastery and overgeneralization will interact, in complex but predictable ways, with factors such as type and token frequency.

We observed in the *parent* simulations that type frequency (class size) is an important parameter in determining the extent to which irregular classes interfere with the regular or dominant mapping. In particular, it was shown that a small class size (backed up with an appropriate token frequency) enables an irregular class to be learned at an optimal level without interfering with the dominant mapping. This suggests that keeping *all* the irregular classes small should improve performance in these classes without disrupting the regular mappings. We test this hypothesis in a final simulation: *phone 34*. The total vocabulary that the network is required to learn is held constant at 500. However, the size of the vowel change class is reduced to that of the identity class, and the regular class is increased in size. All characteristics of the *phone* mapping types are maintained, though only four vowel change clusters are represented instead of the usual 11, in order to achieve recognizable VC clusters given the reduced class size. Type and token frequencies for *phone 34* are summarized in Table 4 as well as the percentage hit rates for the various verb classes. This type frequency configuration is a more accurate reflection of the relative sizes of the regular and irregular classes in English. The inadequacy of this representation lies in the incorrect ratio of the vowel change and identity type frequencies.

All classes perform at the 80% level or above. The provision of phonological constraints on class membership enables the network to construct a cleaner partitioning of the mapping problem space. Competition effects between classes diminish and overall performance improves. Taking these results in light of the overall set, the constraining effect of the phonological subregularities is particularly apparent in those simulations which otherwise give rise to substantial competition effects in the network (compare with simulations 5, 17, 18 and 27 in the *parent* set). Phonological subregularities can, thus, serve to both *support* and *constrain* the type and token frequency effects observed throughout these simulations. *Phone 34* demonstrates that type/token frequency manipulations and phonological subregularities work together to support a high level of mapping performance across all classes. Just as the network manages to partition the arbitrary mappings so that they appear immune to various parameter manipulations, so does the introduction of phonological subregularities in the other irregular classes endow the system with mapping properties that are increasingly impervious to type and token manipulations of the input vocabulary. Note, however, that type and token frequency effects do not disappear. It is more appropriate to view these effects as being *modulated*

by the internal structure of the sets of items that the network is required to process across learning.

3.3. Conditions on U-shaped learning

3.3.1. Definitions
U-shaped learning refers to a pattern of acquisition in which performance is initially satisfactory, then deteriorates, and then improves again. With respect to the English past tense, U-shaped acquisition is typically used to describe the onset and subsequent elimination of the overgeneralization of the /-ed/ suffix to irregular stems, which results in forms such as *goed* and *hitted*. As we noted above, children typically make these errors *after* producing the correct past tense forms of the irregular stem (e.g. *went* and *hit*). The classical account of this developmental profile posits a three-stage progression: (1) the child memorizes the past tense forms of all verbs (and hence outputs both correct irregular and regular forms); (2) a rule is abstracted from the regularities observed in the input and is applied to all regular and irregular verb stems; (3) recovery from ensuing errors is achieved by restricting the application of the rule to only regular forms, and creating an alternative organization for irregular stems which do not undergo suffixation. This account predicts that the onset of overgeneralizations is sudden and massive. That is, once the child has abstracted the rule, overgeneralization errors occur for all irregular verbs, given every opportunity to produce that verb. In contrast, the recovery from these overgeneralization errors is gradual and protracted. One by one, the child learns which stems are not regularized and stores these irregular past tense

TABLE 4
Type and token frequency distributions and hit rates in phone 34

| | Type of mapping | | | | | | | | | | | |
| | Arbitrary | | | Regular | | | Identity | | | Vowel change | | |
Simulation	Type	Token	% hits	Type	Token	% hits	Type	Token	% hits	Type	Token	% hits
Phone 34	2	20	100	458	1	85	20	5	100	20	10	80

forms as separate lexical entries. We will refer to this mechanism as generating *macro* U-shaped development.

Alternatively, the over-application of the suffixation process might occur selectively, rather than globally. If so, errors would not emerge all of a piece, but some irregular stems would be more likely to be overgeneralized than others. The basis for this selective overgeneralization could be, for example, similarity of an irregular stem to a regular stem. In this case, errors occur more frequently across development because children are learning an increasing number of regular past tense forms, and the likelihood that a non-regular stem resembles and is thus confused with a regular stem also increases. Selective overgeneralizations may also result from the probabilistic application of the regular rule. Errors increase in frequency across development because the probability of adding a suffix increases as the child learns more regular past tense forms. In both of these accounts, the onset of regularization errors is predicted to be gradual and non-absolute in its manifestation. Nevertheless, it is still supposed that children abstract a generally applicable rule from the input which determines the past tense forms of those stems falling under (or close to) its domain. A mechanism which applies rules on the basis of the properties of individual verbs offers a principled basis for predicting which irregular stems will or will not be regularized. In contrast, a probabilistic device, insensitive to verb stem properties, results in selective but indiscriminate over-regularizations. Both of these mechanisms, however, serve to *constrain* the domain of application of the general rule. We will refer to either of these mechanisms as resulting in a behavioral profile characterized by *micro* U-shaped change.

Recent explanations of U-shaped development generally reject the first of these two views; that is, that children enter a period of development in which a rule is consistently applied to whole classes or systems of verbs. From the onset of erroneous output, children produce appropriate past tense forms of irregular stems at the same time as they regularize other irregular stems. Indeed, at all points in development, errors typically comprise a relatively small proportion of children's total output (Marchman, 1988). Further, children sometimes vacillate repeatedly, even within a short time, between the correct and incorrect past tense form of the same irregular stem (e.g. Bybee & Slobin, 1982; Kuczaj, 1977, 1978). The lack of a period in which errors occur on all irregular stems on all occasions of usage suggests that U-shaped development is best viewed as a micro (as opposed to a macro) phenomenon. Thus, explanations of micro U-shaped development typically seek an account of children's ability to abstract general regularities from the input, as well as the factors which govern their selective application of the resulting rule. With respect to stem characteristics, a range of properties may be relevant (i.e. phonological, morphological, or semantic), and can be seen to be specific to individual verbs, group stems into clusters, or comprise the basis for well-defined verb classes. If errors occur as the result of the application of some non-deterministic probability function, then mechanisms for setting and changing the arguments to this function, in a fashion that honors the behavioral data, must also be identified.

Taking an alternative connectionist perspective, micro U-shaped development might also be characteristic of a system where an explicit rule-based mechanism is absent. Here, *similarity relationships* are seen to carry the primary responsibility for determining the output of the system, both correct and incorrect. As with the above approach, similarity might be defined across a wide range of properties of the verb stems. However, patterns of interference (and hence the pattern of occurrence and timing of overgeneralization errors) may be qualitatively different. The absence of a general mapping rule allows for the possibility that interference effects (and thus errors) will be multilateral: just as irregular stems may be regularized, regular stems may take on the mapping properties of irregular stems which they resemble.

In an elicitation task similar to Bybee and Slobin (1982), Marchman (1988) categorized children's errors in the production of English past tense verbs.[10] While these children are considerably older than those discussed in the typical naturalistic study (aged 3;9 to 9;8 years), children across the entire age range had difficulty producing the correct past tense forms of common English verbs. Indeed, all of the 4-, 5- and 6-year-old children produced regularizations, ranging from a mean of 24% to 17% of their responses. Of greater interest, however, is the fact that within the same experimental session these children also produced many examples for *irregularizations*, including identity mapping, vowel change, or blending errors. Irregularization errors comprised a smaller mean proportion of responses (ranging from 13% to 7%); however, a clear majority of children produced these types of past tense errors: *every* child in the 4- to 6-year-old age range produced at least one example of a regularization *and* one example of an irregularization. These data suggest that children produce the standard "add /-ed/" error when forming the past tense of some verbs *at the same time* that they are applying identity mapping or a stem internal vowel change to stems which do not belong to those classes.

Bybee and Slobin (1982) also report that children produce identity mapping irregularizations. They note that the tendency to do so correlates with phonological characteristics of the stem; that is, stems treated as identities are likely to contain a stem final dental consonant. This pattern was also observed in Marchman (1988). In both studies, the tendency to identity map dental-final stems increased with age. However, about 20% of the 115 identity irregularizations reported in Marchman (1988) occurred with verbs that did not end in a dental consonant (e.g. *make* ⇒ *make*). Thus, it appears that possession of a stem-final dental consonant is not necessary for the overapplication of identity mapping. Further, the possession of a dental consonant in final position did not necessarily *predict* identity mapping: suffixation overgeneralizations were equally likely to occur with dental final as non-dental final verbs in all but the youngest children. In their discussion, Pinker and Prince (1988) point out that there are several possible explanations for the correlation between type of stem-final consonant and error produced. Whatever specific explanation is given, each must nevertheless be compatible with the hypothesis that past tense production is sensitive to characteristics of individual stems, and that patterns of both regularization and irregularization

are to some degree (but not always) guided by similarity relationships among and between stems and past tense forms. These empirical findings do not, of course, eliminate the possibility that identity irregularizations are subject to probabilistic processes. The tendency for identity irregularizations to apply to dental-final stems can result from an identity rule with a high probability of application in the presence of a dental-final cue and a low probability of application in the absence of such a cue.

In our view, a non-rule-based system founded on similarity relationships is a viable alternative to a standard or revisionist rule-based explanation of U-shaped acquisition, especially with respect to simultaneous regularization and irregularization effects. However, similarity cannot in itself predict specific patterns of interference between two mappings. If two stems, one irregular and one regular, are similar to each other, then additional information is required in order to predict whether the regular stem will be irregularized or the irregular stem will be regularized. In addition, similarity *per se* cannot offer insight into the mechanisms which guide recovery from erroneous mappings since the objective similarity between verbs is presumed not to change over the course of development. Thus, a system founded solely on similarity relationships lacks the organizational framework within which the child learns to constrain the processes of regularization and irregularization. We might assume, however, that analogous (as yet unspecified) properties of the learning mechanism permit the *perceived* similarity between verbs to change, and hence restrict the application of stem final /-ed/ to regular stems and the various non-regular transformations to irregular stems.

Indeed, the postulation of a default mapping rule and the creation of separate lexical entries for irregular stems are powerful proposals which offer solutions to precisely these problems. However, a single-default rule system would only predict that regularization errors would occur — there is no available mechanism to account for the irregularization errors observed in children. But, as Pinker and Prince (1988) point out, it is a simple matter to elaborate a rule-based system to explain the occurrence of both irregularizations and regularizations. The child may extract a range of hypotheses that capture both major regularities and subregularities in the input patterns. Thus, in addition to noting that many past tense forms undergo suffixation, the child also notes that many verbs which end in a dental have identical present and past tense forms. The latter results in irregularizations of nonidentity stems which end in a dental. Furthermore, we might suppose (as do Pinker & Prince) that these competing hypotheses have graded strengths which determine the probability that a particular rule will be applied. Hence, not all regular stems that end in a dental will be regularized nor all irregular stems regularized. Recovery from erroneous irregularization of regular stems occurs as the child discovers that the hypothesized subregularity is not a reliable predictor of appropriate past tense forms. The erroneous candidate hypothesis decreases in strength over time and is eventually eliminated as a possibility. Stems which do indeed undergo identity mapping are stored as separate lexical entries, outside the regular rule's domain of application.

We suggest that although this theoretical framework can, in principle, be elaborated to account for complex patterns of regularization and irregularization, this approach can be seen to incorporate *ad hoc* assumptions concerning the processes by which children abstract possible rule candidates from the input. This point can be substantiated by considering the conditions under which a child might abstract a candidate procedure for past tense formation. By definition, abstraction requires that a *pattern* of mapping relationships is extracted from *sets* of forms which undergo *transparent* processes of transformation. The arbitrary mapping relation *go* ⇒ *went* is unlikely to lead to the abstraction of a rule candidate for two reasons: (a) it constitutes a singular type pair in the verb system (i.e. it is unique); and (b) the transformation that results in the past tense form *went* is phonologically and morphologically opaque. In contrast, the stem/past tense pair *hit* ⇒ *hit* can be grouped together with a relatively large number of other pairs undergoing the same transformation (i.e. identity mapping), and which share a stem-final dental consonant. Thus, it is likely that a candidate hypothesis would be generated in this

case, given that (a) a relatively large number of dental-final verbs have identical stem and past tense forms, and (b) the phonological cue "dental-final" is a sufficiently salient and reliable predictor of this relationship.

To take another example, Marchman (1988), as well as Kuczaj (1978), report that children sometimes produce past tense forms in which the vowel is changed (e.g. *pick* ⇒ *pack*), or in which a stem-final dental is affixed and a vowel changed (i.e. blends, such as *eat* ⇒ *ated* or *feel* ⇒ *feld*). These errors can result from the application of a candidate hypothesis abstracted from subregularities present among irregular verb clusters. Interestingly, however, Pinker and Prince's detailed overview of the structure of the English strong verbs (i.e. irregular verbs) suggests that phonologically transparent clusters of vowel change verbs typically contain few members (generally less than 7). In order for these clusters to provide the basis for possible rule candidates, the mechanism responsible for generating candidate hypotheses must be sensitive to relatively abstract phonological or morphological relationships, and/or the mechanism is rather lenient in the case of small numbers of contingencies. We might expect, then, that the average English-speaking child would posit a potentially large number of rule candidate hypotheses, each of which would lead to erroneous forms and which must later be abandoned. This would predict two possible behavioral patterns:

1. At any given point in development, past tense errors would result from the concurrent application of many different candidate hypotheses (i.e. children simultaneously abstract and apply several rule candidates).
2. Across development, the total number of candidate hypotheses that are tested is quite large (i.e. every child tries out a great many potential candidate hypotheses at one point or another, each of which must be abandoned in favor of the "add /-ed/" rule).

The cross-sectional data from Marchman (1988) suggest that throughout much of development most children do indeed appear to be testing out more than one candidate hypothesis simultaneously. The majority of the children in this study produce both irregularizations and regularizations within a single experimental session. Nevertheless, those errors only constitute a minority of their output, as children get most verbs right most of the time. A rule-based approach could account for these patterns of results by either setting a limit on the number of hypotheses that a child is able to entertain at any given point in development (i.e. children can only handle two or three [five? six?] candidate hypotheses at a single time), or by severely restricting the domain of application of any single candidate hypothesis to a subset of the possible stems to which it could apply.

As in (2) above, a loose or lenient rule hypothesis mechanism might also predict that children continually posit and then subsequently abandon candidate hypotheses across development. While detailed longitudinal data would be necessary to adequately evaluate this prediction, current findings suggest that stems can be overgeneralized in a variety of different ways (e.g. *feeled, feld, felded*) sometimes by a single child, and there are tendencies for children in different age groups to make characteristic overgeneralization errors (e.g. older children are more likely to produce vowel change irregularizations). Clearly, however, the tendency to posit candidate hypotheses decreases over time. In models that incorporate competitions among explicitly represented rule candidates, the constraints on hypothesis generation, application, and their subsequent elimination must be identified.

Thus, all models must account for the potential range of candidate hypotheses that children can and sometimes do devise, while at the same time limiting the spurious application of candidate hypotheses both within and across periods of development. Within a rule-based account, the relevant parameters of set size, cue reliability, transparency of mapping, upper limits on the ability of the child to entertain a number of candidate hypotheses, domains of application, and so on, must be stipulated independently of the forms and mappings which are to be acquired. Although it may be *possible* to outline the relevant parameters in these terms, it may not be the case that such a description provides the most parsimonious account of the underlying mechanisms responsible for children's past tense production.

We propose that a single mechanism system which simultaneously incorporates evaluations of similarity between verbs guided by *mapping strength* is adequate to the task of accounting for these and other aspects of past tense acquisition in children. Such a system does not attribute explicit competing hypotheses or the formation of qualitatively different categories of lexical entries for regular and irregular verbs. In the next section, we outline the performance of a single mechanism system across the course of learning the English past tense. We show that such a system can provide the basis for an explanation of several of the phenomena reminiscent of micro U-shaped development in children, including selective overgeneralizations, multi-lateral interference effects, age-related patterns of output, and gradual recovery from errors.

3.3.2. U-shaped learning in networks

In the preceding sections, we charted the performance of a multi-layered perceptron in mapping verb stems to their corresponding past tense forms. Using various input configurations, we demonstrated that the type frequency of a verb class and the token frequency of a verb stem have a significant effect on learning. Although we have not yet discussed in detail the nature of the errors produced by the network en route to acquiring a large number of past tense forms, we have demonstrated how conflicts between the four mapping types lead to good performance on some forms and poor performance on other past tense forms.

At any point in training, the mapping of a given verb stem to its appropriate output form is determined by a complex nexus of factors, all of which are implicitly coded in the weight matrix of the network. In order to explicate the dynamics of these factors, the operation of the network can be described in terms of two component processes.[11] First, the mapping of a given stem will be partially determined by its *similarity* to the other stems on which the network has been previously trained. Mapping characteristics of stems which are highly similar undergo positive transfer, while stems which are dissimilar to other stems will not exert influence on the mapping of those stems. For the simulations that we have reported here, similarity can be defined entirely in terms of phonetic shape. The phonetic shape of each stem is characterized by an 18-dimensional vector (one for each input unit, excluding the suffix) which represents a particular configuration of standard phonetic features. Hence, the similarity between any two stems is simply the normalized dot product or cosine of the angle between the two vectors representing the stems. Weight matrices may encode several different types of similarity relationships. For example, similarity may be evaluated in terms of the distributed pattern of activation across the entire input vector (as in arbitrary mappings). At the same time, the network may learn to recognize feature clusters in specific sections of the input vector (as in identity or vowel change mappings). In addition, the network can also encode and utilize information indicating a *lack* of global or localized cues. The weight matrix may establish conditions for similarity, and hence for the application of a mapping, which operate in the absence of any other cues, that is, as a default mapping.

In the network models that we have discussed here, similarity relationships are relatively well defined, leading to interference effects with predictable consequences. Of course, it is assumed that the set of mappings comprising morphological systems such as the English past tense are organized around more than phonetic shape. In principle, the input vector representing the verb stem can be extended in a variety of ways, with the potential to incorporate a range of morphological, semantic and grammatical information. Thus, as we envision it is done by children, a neural network faced with the task of learning the past tense of English would take advantage of several categories or levels of information, creating outputs on the basis of complex interactions between phonology, morphology, syntax and semantics (among others) when computing the mapping relationship of a verb stem to its past tense form.[12]

The second major determinant of network performance is the layer of non-linear hidden units. The response of the network to a given verb stem is regulated by the network's internal representation of that stem, as specified by the pattern of activation across the array of hidden units. Verb stems with similar internal representations will be mapped to similar past tense forms. Thus, it is the vector of activation values at the hidden unit level which determines the ultimate fate of an input stem. Hidden unit activations are determined by the input vector, the weight matrix connecting the input and hidden units, and the biases on the hidden units themselves. Hidden unit activations encode information regarding the phonological shape of a verb stem, plus information regarding the mapping class to which the verb stem belongs. In order that two very similar verb stems (at the input level) may belong to distinct classes, and hence may be mapped in quite distinct ways, the network must construct distinctive internal representations of the two stems. To achieve this, the network must develop a sensitivity to potentially small differences between verb stems. As we have shown, two main factors contribute to the network's ability to develop such a sensitivity: (a) the number of other verbs in the training set that undergo similar mappings (i.e. type frequency); and (b) the frequency with which the network sees a given stem (i.e. token frequency). The type and token frequencies of the various mappings influence the network's ability to recognize particular patterns of activity and to successfully *modulate* the effects of stem similarity at the input level. Hidden units are an indispensable component of a network which manifests long-term token frequency effects (see footnote 7). We refer to the recognition and concurrent modulation of input vectors that is encoded in the hidden unit activations as the *mapping strength* of a given stem/past tense pair.

Across the course of training, the process of the accumulation of mapping strength over the entire set of verb stem/past tense pairings results in network performance which is characterized by complex patterns of interference. Hence, the output generated by the system is analogous to that produced by both the processes of regularization and irregularization in children. Further, given the localized nature of the computations performed in PDP systems, patterns of interference may operate on individual verb stem/past tense pairings. The errors generated by the system, then, may possess the qualities of a messy rule-user, resulting in selective error production, as opposed to errors spanning across categories or classes of verbs. However, with training (i.e. development), the erroneous output gradually diminishes as the network eventually organizes the weight matrix such that a solution to the entire mapping problem is found.

In the remainder of this section, we investigate in more detail the time course of the acquisition of past forms across training in these systems. In particular, we evaluate the verbal output of the network in response to individual stems with which it is presented. This is achieved by using the stored weight matrices (including unit biases) obtained during training in order to test the individual verb stems at different points in development. In this way, we evaluate how the network performs both in relation to individual stems and externally defined verb classes as a whole.

In our view, these date demonstrate that a neural network (which incorporates hidden units and hence is sensitive to token frequency effects) faced with the task of learning a system of mappings analogous to English verbs manifests a pattern of development and errors which resemble U-shaped acquisition in children in the following ways:

1. U-shaped development follows a micro rather than macro U-shaped pattern.
2. Overgeneralization effects are multi-lateral.
3. On the way to mastering the correct system of mappings, the errors generated by the network are explicable in terms of a complex interaction between the mapping strength and the similarity relationships between verb stems.

Manipulations of type and token frequency of verb stems influence patterns of error production in the network. Further, the addition of phonological subregularities into the input set (the *phone* simulations) serves to further constrain the nature of those errors in a realistic fashion. As noted above, both frequency and phonological predictability have also been posited as potential constraining factors in rule-based explanations. However, unlike traditional conceptualizations of past tense acquisition, these manipulations of input parameters are performed *within the confines of a single learning mechanism.*

The micro nature of U-shaped development in these networks is apparent in the learning curves of *phone 34* which most closely approximates both the frequency structure (see Table 4) and patterns of phonological subregularity that have been proposed to characterize the identity and vowel change classes of English verbs. Figure 3 overviews learning in the different verb classes for *phone 34.*

First, it should be noted that initial performance (the first few epochs) on mapping verbs to their past tense forms is inaccurate. This finding is inevitable given the random initialization of weights in the network prior to training. Thus, unlike children who have already acquired considerable knowledge about the phonology of their language before they begin to acquire the past tense, this network must extract the general characteristics of the phonological mappings to which it is exposed, at the same time as it is learning the morphological regularities of the task. However, once it has extracted the relations between consonants and vowels in the input and output strings, the majority of stems are mapped correctly.

Nevertheless, word hit rate for all classes of verbs undergo temporary decrements in performance during the course of training. In other words, for all classes of verbs, there are examples of several stems whose past tense forms are generated correctly by the network but subsequently undergo a temporary period of incorrect mapping. However, not all verbs in the class are incorrectly mapped. For example, consider the arbitrary stem /mid/ which has the correct past tense form /twɛ/. From epoch 2 until epoch 4, /mid/ is mapped by the network as /mid-D/; that is, it is regularized. At epochs 5, 6, 8, 9, 11 and onwards it is correctly mapped as /twɛ/. However, at epochs 7 and 10, /mid/ is mapped as /mid/ and /mid-D/, respectively; that is, it is treated first as an identity stem (irregularized) and then as a regular stem (regularized). The other arbitrary stem in the set, /nuf/, is correctly mapped as /sko/ from epoch 2 onward, apart from epoch 4 when it is regularized as /nuf-t/. Thus, we see that the system does not enter a phase where it categorically regularizes all arbitrary stems. One stem may be mapped correctly while the other stem is regularized or irregularized. Furthermore, a single mapping may

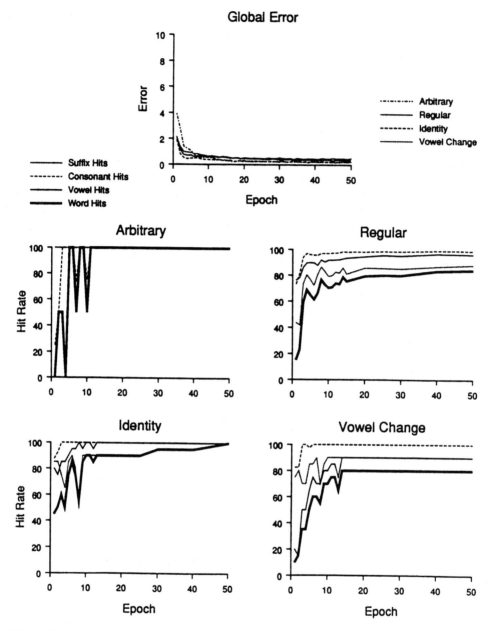

FIG. 3. Phone 34.

undergo repeated fluctuations before stabilizing at an optimum level. Thus, looking at this class alone, we observe that the onset of errors and then subsequent recovery does not follow a macro-shaped pattern.

Arbitrary stems are few in number and cannot be said to constitute a class in the same sense as, say, identity mapping stems (i.e. they have no characteristic features and share no common mapping relation). Nevertheless, similar micro U-shaped patterns of development are also observed in the other irregular classes. For example, at epoch 6, the identity stems /tud/ and /hUt/ are correctly mapped, while at epoch 8 they are regularized. However, at epoch 8, 11 other identity stems are correctly mapped by the network. Again, identity class stems undergo repeated successions of correct performance followed by incorrect performance. On each occasion, however, erroneous output is restricted to a subset of the identity mapping stems rather than the whole class. After epoch 13, the proportion of correct output for the identity mapping stems increases monotonically, though several stems continue to be regularized until the final stages of training. Vowel change stems also undergo a similar pattern of micro U-shaped development in which some stems are regularized or irregularized after having been correctly mapped by the network on previous epochs. These same stems are subsequently correctly mapped as vowel changes.

The erroneous mappings cited above illustrate that errors of arbitrary, identity, and vowel change stems undergo periods where some stems are mapped correctly, while others are not. Figure 3 also illustrates that regular stems in *phone 34* are also subject to erroneous mappings. For example, between epoch 4 and 6 the number of correctly mapped regular stems decreases from 320 to 288. Two of these incorrectly mapped stems are /sʌt/ and /pen/, both of which are irregularized as identity mappings. By epoch 10, these two stems are once again correctly mapped by the network. Hence, the same mechanism which results in the regularization of irregular stems causes the temporary irregularization of regular stems. Errors that result both from regularization and irregularization processes, then, undergo patterns of onset and recovery that are micro rather than macro in character.

Figure 3 also illustrates that U-shaped fluctuations are generally uncorrelated across the different mapping classes. Thus, it is not possible to predict overall decrements in performance in one class from overall patterns of improvement or decrement in other classes. In these simulations, decrements in performance result from the conflict between the diverse mappings demanded of the network. Such conflict is manifest in relation to the mapping of individual verb stem/past tense pairs rather than in relation to whole classes (in spite of the fact that frequency parameters were manipulated on a class-by-class basis). To the extent that it is empirically feasible to view profiles of U-shaped learning in children with respect to individual verbs rather than classes of verbs,

neural networks provide an appropriate medium for modeling micro U-shaped development.

We also observe in these examples that overgeneralization phenomena can emerge early in the training of the network. In contrast, overgeneralizations are not characteristic of children's earliest productions. However, the task facing the network in this simulation is rather different from that faced by the child in the very earliest stages of language acquisition. The child, presumably, is not attempting to learn large numbers of verbs early in development. Consequently, he or she is not forced to make generalizations about the relation between large numbers of verb stems and their past tense forms. In this simulation, the network is being asked to generate 500 past tense forms from the very beginning of training. Given the limited resources available, the network is forced to extract generalizable patterns from the input immediately. Hence overgeneralizations are a necessary consequence of early training. Rote learning could be induced in the network by reducing the size of the vocabulary to be acquired. Indeed, this was precisely the strategy used by Rumelhart and McClelland in their original simulation. However, the transition from rote learning to system building in the Rumelhart and McClelland simulation confounded a discontinuity in both the size of the vocabulary to be learned and the structure of the vocabulary in relation to the relative proportions of regular and irregular verbs. The current set of simulations do not exploit either of these types of discontinuity. Hence, the U-shaped learning phenomena observed in these simulations do not result from an externally imposed transition from rote learning to system building. Rather, overgeneralizations and recovery from erroneous mappings are a consequence of the inherent competition between the diverse set of mapping properties demanded of a single network. Furthermore, the prediction of the timing of decrements in performance on individual verb stems is particularly difficult in these simulations since there are no input discontinuities with which decrements can be correlated. Internal processes of reorganization are entirely responsible for the observed overgeneralization phenomena.

Tables 5 and 6 provide a more detailed picture of the error types during training for the arbitrary,

TABLE 5

Hit rates and distribution of error types on arbitrary and regular verbs sampled at 20 points across learning in phone 34

						Type of mapping			
	Arbitrary				Regular				
		Error type					Error type		
Epoch	Hits (%)	Suf	Iden	Hits (%)	Inap Suf	Iden	Inap Vow-S	Blend	Vow Chan
1	0	0	0	17	6	28	6	0	0
2	50	100	0	26	7	37	6	0	0
3	50	100	0	60	18	32	13	1	0
4	0	100	0	70	25	32	15	1	0
5	100	0	0	66	23	35	12	0	1
6	100	0	0	63	16	43	9	0	0
7	50	0	100	70	19	31	15	0	0
8	100	0	0	79	29	25	17	1	2
9	100	0	0	74	17	36	19	0	0
10	50	100	0	72	18	45	10	1	0
11	100	0	0	73	20	46	10	0	1
12	100	0	0	75	14	47	15	0	1
13	100	0	0	75	14	50	14	0	0
14	100	0	0	80	17	42	16	1	2
15	100	0	0	77	15	55	7	0	0
20	100	0	0	81	11	56	12	1	0
25	100	0	0	81	13	59	10	1	1
30	100	0	0	81	11	58	11	1	0
40	100	0	0	84	9	65	8	1	0
50	100	0	0	85	10	62	9	1	0

The error categories presented in Tables 5 and 6 are to be interpreted as follows:

Arbitrary errors:
Suf   The stem is treated as a regular stem.
Iden   The stem is treated as an identity stem.

Regular errors:
Inap Suf   The stem is suffixed but with the wrong suffix.
Iden   The stem is treated as an identity stem.
Inap Vow-S   The stem is appropriately suffixed and undergoes an illegal vowel transformation.
Blend   The stem is appropriately suffixed and undergoes a legal vowel transformation.
Vow Chan   The stem is treated as though it were a vowel change stem.

Identity errors:
Suf   The stem is treated as a regular stem.
Inap Suf   The stem is treated as a regular stem but inappropriately suffixed.
Inap Vow   The stem is treated as a vowel change; however, the transformation is inappropriate though it may or may not be illegal.

Vowel change errors:
Suf   The stem is treated as a regular stem.
Iden   The stem is treated as an identity stem.
Inap Vow-S   The stem is transformed as though it were a vowel change but the vowel change is illegal. The stem is appropriately suffixed.
Blend   The stem undergoes a legal vowel change but is also appropriately suffixed.
Inap Vow   The vowel change transformation is inappropriate though may or may not be illegal.

TABLE 6
Hit rates and distribution of error types on identity and vowel change verbs sampled at
20 points across learning in phone 34

					Type of mapping					
		Identity						Vowel change		
			Error type						Error type	
Epoch	Hits (%)	Suf	Inap Suf	Inap Vow	Hits (%)	Suf	Iden	Inap Vow-S	Blend	Inap Vow
1	45	18	0	27	30	7	21	7	0	35
2	55	33	0	33	30	7	14	14	0	28
3	70	83	0	16	35	15	23	7	23	30
4	60	50	37	12	45	18	27	0	27	18
5	80	75	0	25	60	0	25	12	25	25
6	85	66	0	33	70	0	16	0	50	33
7	75	40	40	20	60	0	37	0	25	37
8	55	88	11	55	0	11	11	11	22	22
9	85	66	0	33	70	0	16	16	33	33
10	90	100	0	0	75	0	20	0	40	40
11	90	100	0	0	75	0	20	0	40	40
12	85	66	0	33	75	0	20	0	40	40
13	90	100	0	0	65	0	14	0	28	57
14	90	100	0	0	80	0	25	0	50	25
15	90	100	0	0	80	0	25	0	50	25
20	90	100	0	0	80	0	25	0	50	25
25	90	100	0	0	80	0	25	0	50	25
30	95	100	0	0	80	0	25	0	50	25
40	95	100	0	0	80	0	25	0	50	25
50	100	0	0	0	80	0	25	0	50	25

See Table 5 for explanation of error categories.

regular, identity and vowel change stems. As discussed above, the only errors on arbitrary stems are suffixation and identity mapping. Each of the two arbitrary stems are mastered by epoch 11, and are correctly mapped throughout the remainder of the training period.

For the regular stems, the most common single error type is identity mapping. Approximately 50% of these identity irregularizations involve stems which end in a dental. Other major error types include inappropriate suffixation and inappropriate vowel change. Blends and vowel change irregularizations occur, but are rare for regular verbs. Furthermore, as overall performance improves, identity irregularization makes up an increasing proportion of the errors. Note that the overwhelm-

ing majority of errors at the end of training involve clearly identifiable irregularizations as indicated in Table 5. A small residue of errors on regular verbs (not shown in Table 5) involve illegal vowel changes and consonant errors. These errors too are explicable in terms of the interaction of similarity relations and mapping strengths of verb stems. Thus, the consonant and vowel errors result from similarity to other consonants and vowels in the pre-defined phonological space.

Performance on the identity stems improves rapidly and reaches 90% (18 correct past tense forms) by epoch 10. From early in training, the majority of errors are the result of regularization. Inappropriate vowel changes and suffixations also occur but these are restricted to the early epochs of training. It is noteworthy that identity mappings are not subject to irregularization, as neither vowel change nor blending irregularizations are observed.

Performance on vowel change stems in *phone 34* is at one of the highest levels for all simulations we have performed. This result is achieved by reducing their type frequency and increasing their token frequency. Early in training, a variety of error types occur. These include regularizations, identity irregularizations, regularizations conflated with an illegal vowel change, and illegal vowel changes alone. Across training, the error types become more circumscribed. Regularizations (both pure and conflated with illegal vowel changes) disappear and the proportion of errors due to identity irregularizations or illegal vowel changes tends to decrease. The single identity irregularization remaining from epoch 14 through 50 is the dental-final stem, /vit/. In contrast, after several epochs of training, blending errors are more likely to occur, comprising an increasing proportion of the total errors throughout the rest of training.

The patterns of regularization and irregularization across verb stem classes in *phone 34* demonstrates the multi-lateral nature of the interference effects produced by the network. The error types observed make the following predictions for children acquiring the English past tense:

1. Identity stems are the least prone to irregularization.
2. The most common irregularization of regular stems is identity mapping.
3. Identity mappings are often (though not exclusively) generalized to stems which end in a dental.
4. Of the irregular stems, vowel change stems are the least prone to suffixation.
5. Blends are a characteristic of late development and are restricted primarily to vowel change stems.

Further evaluation of these patterns of overgeneralization reveals that it is possible to predict errors in terms of the similarity structure of the verb stems mapped by the network (though not the *timing* of errors). For example, it is no accident that many identity irregularizations in the arbi-

rary, regular and vowel change classes involve stems which end in a dental. The pattern is a direct result of the phonological subregularity that characterizes the identity class. In the absence of such subregularities, errors are less predictable and less circumscribed (as illustrated by the comparison between the *parent* and *phone* simulations, sections 3.2.3 and 3.2.3.1). Similarly, vowel change irregularizations of regular verbs are infrequent since there are a limited set of VC clusters that characterize vowel change subregularities, and thus the possibility for irregularizing on the basis of vowel change subregularities is thereby constrained. The introduction of phonological subregularities is thus an important factor in predicting the type of error that is made in response to a given stem and in constraining the range of error types generated by the system.

However, as we have been at pains to elaborate, the introduction of phonological subregularities does not determine the fate of all stems which possess these characteristics, just as the mapping properties of the largest verb class does not determine the fate of all stems outside the class. The similarity relations between stems are modulated by the mapping strength of the verb stems involved. Thus, we observe that many regular stems ending in a dental are not irregularized while, at the same time, regular stems which do not end in a dental undergo identity irregularization. These complex interactions of similarity relations and mapping strength are inherent properties of a network system in which diverse sources of information are processed in parallel and the resultant representations are distributed.

4. Conclusion

This paper systematically explored the acquisition of mappings that are analogous to the English past tense by a multi-layered perceptron, given various input conditions. The goals of this work were threefold:

1. To evaluate the criticism that PDP systems are dependent on discontinuous manipulations of the input to achieve regressions in

performance and subsequent recovery from errors.

2. To test hypotheses regarding the role of type and token frequency and phonological predictability in determining the errors and patterns of learning produced by the network.

3. To outline several possible mechanisms guiding U-shaped learning in children and, more generally, to evaluate the degree to which a connectionist approach can contribute to explanations of morphological acquisition even though they do not integrate qualitative distinctions between the representational status of different categories of verb stems or postulate dual-mechanism architectures.

The results of these simulations reveal that U-shaped development can be implemented in a PDP network *without* introducing discontinuities into the size and structure of the set of forms that the system is required to learn. In many simulations, mastery of a stem mapping was followed by a period of erroneous performance. The erroneous mapping function, however, did not result in random output. Input stems were typically mapped in a fashion that was characteristic of another verb class (or some blend of verb classes). Subsequent learning resulted in the re-establishment of correct output, though stems frequently underwent several phases of correct performance followed by erroneous mapping before a stable state was achieved. The timing of these U-shaped regressions for a given stem or class revealed that the majority of reorganizations occur during the first 15–20 epochs of learning.

We attempted to sketch an outline of the conditions under which these models did and did not resemble what is known about the developmental patterns of children's acquisition of the past tense. Our primary focus was on variations of the input with respect to:

1. The structure of the vocabulary that the system was required to learn.

2. Token frequencies of individual items in the input set.

3. Phonological subregularities as a predictor of mapping type.

Given different input conditions, the network was observed to regularize the suffix to irregular stems, as well as produce identity mapping and vowel change irregularizations or blends. In some simulations, it was useful to describe the errors made by the network in terms of a general strategy or rule in order to provide an account of the frequency of errors and patterns of recovery. However, the complexities inherent in the behavior of these systems did not typically warrant the use of such constructs. Errors within any given simulation were rarely restricted to a single type. Nevertheless, as input configurations increasingly approximated those of English, patterns of erroneous output were increasingly constrained.

The degree to which these results are analogous to the acquisition patterns of children is not as yet totally clear. Some reports of children's past tense productions have provided examples of vowel change or identity irregularizations (Bybee & Slobin, 1982; Marchman, 1988). In addition, some analyses suggest that children's production repertoires reflect, at various points in development, a variety of general strategies which result in both correct and incorrect performance (Derwing & Baker, 1986). Children, like these networks, are not likely to be exclusively suffix generalizers, or identity mappers, but will produce several different types of errors in generating past tense forms throughout a substantial portion of the acquisition process. Rule-based models typically explicate this phenomenon via the competition between two (or more) discrete and explicitly representable candidate hypotheses which, at various points in development, undergo changes in how and when they are likely to apply (Pinker & Prince, 1988). In these simulations, in contrast, multilateral errors and fluctuations across learning are the by-product of the implicit encoding of similarity relationships in the weight matrix of the network. However, the likelihood that two similar stems from different mapping classes interfere with each other is modulated by their respective mapping strengths. In particular, high token frequencies tend to localize the zones of interference while high type frequencies tend to extend them. In general, type and token frequencies of the verb classes affect the nature of the network's definition and partitioning of the task.

The competition effects observed in the investigation suggest several hypotheses about the study of the acquisition of morphology. First, we would expect to find more varied patterns of U-shaped behavior and overgeneralization than is traditionally reported in the literature. Second, the results predict that the classes of verb stems are differentially susceptible to overgeneralization at various points in development. For example, arbitrary stems are most likely to be overgeneralized early on in learning while identity stems and vowel change stems continue to be overgeneralized during a more prolonged period. Furthermore, the different classes of verb stems are differentially susceptible to error types. For example, identity stems rarely undergo blending and are likely to be restricted to errors of suffixation. In contrast, regulars are likely to be treated as identity stems while vowel change stems experience all three error types: sufffixation, identity mapping and blending. Of course, these error patterns suggest only *trends* rather than categorical claims and are highly sensitive to the parameters that characterize the input.

The type–token ratios that we manipulated in these simulations led to performance patterns that were reminiscent of the structure of natural language. For example, successful learning of the arbitrary mappings occurred only when they were relatively few in number, and when the relative token frequency was substantially greater than all of the other classes. In many of the world's languages, sets of lexical items which share surface relationships that are considerably more obscure than other classes of items in the same system (i.e. the arbitraries) are typically relatively few in number and constitute the most frequently used items in the system. In addition, once performance of the arbitrary class reached ceiling, these mappings were not affected by manipulations of token frequencies in other classes. The arbitraries consistently emerged as a class unto themselves, relatively uninfluenced by the variable learning in the other classes. The system was able to master these forms at the same time that it was grappling to capture and generalize the regularities in the other three classes. Unlike rule-based systems, the mechanism guiding the memorization of arbitrary forms was the same as that guiding the rule-like overgeneralization behavior in the other classes.

In all but one set of simulations presented here, we purposefully eliminated the possibility that information inherent in the phonological encoding of stems could be a determinant of network performance. We did so by randomly assigning stems to verb classes and by replicating the performance of each simulation using several different vocabularies. The fact that overgeneralization errors and patterns of U-shaped learning were observed in all simulations suggests that differences in the phonological structure of regular and irregular verbs may not be a necessary prerequisite for a linguistic system to exhibit those phenomena. We cannot, of course, claim that phonological information has no role to play in the differentiation of the two categories of verbs in children learning English. On the contrary, the results from these simulations suggest that in systems in which phonological predictability can be used to characterize the different mapping classes, overall performance is improved and the patterns of errors become considerably more constrained. However, several behaviors characteristic of acquisition were exhibited in networks in which phonological information could not be used to determine a string's assignment into a particular class.

The class size ratios and token frequencies used in these systems were explicitly chosen to represent configurations analogous to those in the English language. Languages other than English will certainly present a new set of parameters within which to guide the predictions of learning rates and patterns of overgeneralization. It is expected that a system facing competitions between several types of transformations with another set of type and token configurations will manifest different competition effects. We have shown that a large vowel change class is particularly disruptive for the dominant, regular form of mapping. The *parent* simulations suggest that the network has considerable difficulties resolving this conflict in the absence of specific properties which characterize the stems of the irregular class. The improved performance in the *phone* simulations was a direct consequence of the provision of such characteristics. This result has important implications for the acquisition of inflectional morphology in languages where the irregular classes are larger than those of English. First, we would expect that large irregular classes, involving transformations such as vowel change or identity mapping, are more likely to posses properties that assist the acquisition system in partitioning the mapping space between surface forms. It is likely that several properties simultaneously characterize a class of forms and can be exploited by such a network in constructing a cleaner partitioning of the mapping space. Second, we anticipate that large irregular classes will require tight or homogeneous constraints on class membership. For example, in the *phone* simulations we observed a higher level of performance in the identity class than in the vowel change class. In the former, the phonological subregularity (end in a dental) was clearly delimited, while the vowel change class was more inhomogeneous in its characterization (VC family resemblance clusters). Again, these constraints need not be restricted to the phonological form of the stem. Third, we expect that the homogeneity of the properties that characterize stems will interact with the token frequency of the stems in that class. As was observed in the *phone* simulations, an optimal level of performance was achieved in the identity class with a low token frequency while the vowel change class required a higher degree of stem repetition.[13] In general, then, we predict that qualitatively similar *patterns* of overgeneralization and U-shaped learning will occur during the acquisition of most languages, although the *specific* timing and nature of error types will vary with typological variables such as class size, token frequency, mapping type and class characteristics.

These series of simulations reinforced our intuitions regarding the importance of taking the original biases of networks into account when interpreting the performance of simulations. Clearly, different mappings of input to output strings are not created equal for a network of this type. In the individual baseline simulations, some verb classes were learned more quickly and more completely than others. In conflict conditions, in contrast, the performance of the entire system deteriorated in ways that could not be directly predicted from

performance in the non-conflict simulations. These initial biases and competition effects can be viewed as idiosyncratic to a certain degree. However, this fact does not mitigate the importance of interpreting the results of simulations in light of adequate baseline or control conditions.

More generally, these simulations illustrate the potential to model the complex facts of the acquisition of the past tense of English within the confines of a single mechanism system. Standard approaches are committed to postulating evaluation metrics for eliminating rules, and constraints for restricting the domain of application of existing rules. The connectionist approach espoused here exploits the explanatory concepts of similarity and mapping strength which are characteristic properties of a multi-layered network utilizing back-propagation as a general learning algorithm. Mechanisms of this kind have been shown to be applicable to a wide range of problem domains, and hence one interpretation of our results is that these networks approximate the task of language acquisition too loosely. That is, within certain limits, these networks mimicked the behavior of children acquiring a morphological system, but patterns of overgeneralizations and regressions in learning were easily produced given mere manipulations in frequency and phonological predictability. Clearly, these simulations represent only an approximation of the task required of a child who is learning language. Even if we limit ourselves to the acquisition of inflectional verb morphology in English, it is clear that our representation of the input conditions is far from adequate. For example, we know that individual stems vary in their token frequency, rather than having a constant value for all members of the class. Further, we know that semantic considerations *must* play a role in the disambiguation of certain stem/past tense mappings. Neither can architectural considerations be ignored. Although the use of a back-propagation algorithm in a network with hidden units represents a step forward in the application of PDP systems to problems of language processing and acquisition, we do not suppose that this is the last word in the search for more efficient and suitable learning procedures. New architectures will themselves place their own stamp on patterns of organization and reorganization that characterize PDP systems. Similarly, while refinements in the assumptions of the input conditions led to only an approximation of complete mastery of the task as we defined it, the behavior of these systems revealed that there is much to be gained from careful study of the nature and structure of input, as well as processing and representational constraints, in the problem of the acquisition of language.

Appendix: Conditions for transformations

The artificial language used in all simulations consists of a randomly generated set of 700 CVC, CCV, and VCC legal English strings. In the baseline, dictionary, production and parent simulations, the strings are randomly assigned to one of four classes (i.e. the set of stem forms). The set of strings comprising the teacher file (i.e. set of past tense forms) are derived using the following criteria. English analogs are provided.

Vowel change

A set of 32 possible vowel changes are consolidated from available listings of English verbs, including Kucera and Francis (1967), Rumelhart and McClelland (1986), Pinker and Prince (1988), Bybee and Slobin (1982), Marchman (1984). A representative subset of 11 are chosen for use in these simulations. In the phonological simulations 11 VC endings are used as templates to define the vowel change similarity clusters. The corresponding VC mappings are also listed.

Parent simulation	Analog	Phone simulation
/o/ $\Rightarrow$ /u/	blow $\Rightarrow$ blew	/of/ $\Rightarrow$ /uf/
/i/ $\Rightarrow$ /e/	eat $\Rightarrow$ ate	/iz/ $\Rightarrow$ /ez/
/i/ $\Rightarrow$ /ɛ/	meet $\Rightarrow$ met	/it/ $\Rightarrow$ /ɛt/
/i/ $\Rightarrow$ /o/	freeze $\Rightarrow$ froze	/im/ $\Rightarrow$ /om/
/u/ $\Rightarrow$ /O/	lose $\Rightarrow$ lost	/us/ $\Rightarrow$ /Os/
/u/ $\Rightarrow$ /o/	choose $\Rightarrow$ chose	/ul/ $\Rightarrow$ /ol/
/e/ $\Rightarrow$ /o/	break $\Rightarrow$ broke	/er/ $\Rightarrow$ /or/
/ɛ/ $\Rightarrow$ /O/	wear $\Rightarrow$ wore	/ɛr/ $\Rightarrow$ /Or/
/ai/ $\Rightarrow$ /e/	rise $\Rightarrow$ raise	/ais/ $\Rightarrow$ /es/
/ai/ $\Rightarrow$ /O/	fight $\Rightarrow$ fought	/ail/ $\Rightarrow$ /Ol/
/ai/ $\Rightarrow$ /o/	arise $\Rightarrow$ arose	/aig/ $\Rightarrow$ /og/

Regulars (suffixation)

OFF $\Rightarrow$ /t/	(voiceless dental) following /p, k, f, s/ in final position.
OFF $\Rightarrow$ /d/	(voiced dental) following /b, g, v, f, m, n, ŋ, θ, ð, z, w, l, y, r/ and all vowels in final position.
OFF $\Rightarrow$ /ʌD/	(schwa + voiced dental) following /t/ or /d/ in final position.

Arbitrary mapping

any CVC, CCV, VCC string $\Rightarrow$ any CVC, CCV, VCC string (e.g. go/went, am/was)

Identity mapping

string XXX $\Rightarrow$ string XXX

Notes

1. Several, more detailed, classifications of the irregular verbs in English have been posited. These classifications are generally more fine-grained than the one we are offering here and capture combinations of transformations, as in *sleep* $\Rightarrow$ *slept*. However, all draw major distinctions between arbitrary, identity mapping and vowel change transformations as we do (see Bybee & Slobin, 1982; Pinker & Prince, 1988).

2. Learning rate is a term representing a constant of proportionality in the weight change algorithm. This constant can be adjusted so that larger (or smaller) weight changes will occur in response to a given error signal. Momentum is a factor in the weight change algorithm which determines the degree to which earlier weight changes contribute to current weight changes.

3. For all simulations, an epoch consists of one complete sweep through the learning set.

4. A more detailed presentation of many of the results can be found in Plunkett, K., & Marchman, V. *Pattern association in a back propagation network: Implications for child language acquisition* (CRL TR #8902, March, 1989).

5. The logistic activation function used by the backpropagation learning algorithm precludes unit activation values of precisely 1.0 or 0.0.

6. These vocabularies are identical in type frequency to the *dictionary* and *production* simulations discussed in the next section.

7. While manipulations of token frequency are of primary importance in the simulations discussed

in the next section, note that token frequency cannot have any long-term learning effects in single-layered perceptrons since there are no local minima of the error function into which the network can be attracted. In a multi-layered perceptron, in which local minima can be observed, token frequency plays an important role in the mapping characteristics of the network in that repeated training on a given stem may push the network into a position in state space where local minima occur.

8. The identity mapping strategy preferred by this network emerges from the artificial language and the system of stem and past tense forms that, in a way that is analogous to English, is biased heavily toward stem preservation. Interestingly, identity mapping, or preservation of the stem, is a typical characteristic of inflectional morphological systems in the world's languages (see Pinker & Prince, 1988, p.108).

9. It is known, for example, that 1-year-olds comprehend about 4 to 5 times as many verbs as they produce between the ages of 12 to 20 months. Clearly, a great deal of verb learning (and by implication, verb morphology) could be going on underground.

10. Children were shown magazine pictures of people and animals doing everyday activities ($N = 38$; 54 verbs, 18 regular), and were asked to "tell a story about what happened yesterday" (e.g. "This man is walking. He walks everyday, Yesterday, he __.").

11. Of course, in practice, these networks are complex and highly interactive systems in which component processes are difficult to tease apart.

12. Other current work within a connectionist framework has demonstrated the ability of networks to extract positional information from input representations across time (e.g. Elman, 1989), and simultaneous semantic and phonological information (e.g. Gasser & Lee, 1990).

13. Alan Prince (personal communication) has suggested that the plural system in Arabic might offer an important test case for evaluating the predictions generated by these networks. The non-phonologically determined mappings of the plural in Arabic have both a low type and token frequency, and hence should be relatively difficult for these types of networks to learn. However, the numerous exceptions to the default mapping, constituting the major part of the Arabic plural system, tend to be clustered around sets of relatively well-defined features. This is precisely the kind of featural distribution that these networks require in order to simultaneously master a small set of default mappings and large numbers of exceptions.

References

Bates, E., Bretherton, I., & Snyder, L. (1998). *From first words to grammar: Individual differences and dissociable mechanisms.* Cambridge, MA: Cambridge University Press.

Bever, T. G. (Ed.) (1982). *Regressions in mental development: Basic phenomena and theories.* Hillsdale, NJ: Erlbaum.

Bever, T. G. (1992). The demons and the beast: Modular and nodular kinds of knowledge. In R. G. Reilly and N. E. Sharkey (Eds.), *Connectionist approaches to natural language processing.* Hove, UK: Lawrence Erlbaum Associates Ltd..

Bowerman, M. (1982). Reorganizational process in lexical and syntactic development. In E. Wanner & L. Gleitman (Eds.), *Language acquisition: The state of the art.* Cambridge, UK: Cambridge University Press.

Bybee, J., & Slobin, D. I. (1982). Rules and schemas in the development and use of the English past tense. *Language, 58,* 265–289.

Churchland, P. S., & Sejnowski, T. J. (1988). Perspectives on cognitive neuroscience. *Science, 242,* 741–745.

Derwing, B. L., & Baker, W. J. (1986). Assessing morphological development. In P. Fletcher & M. German (Eds.), *Language acquisition: Studies in first language development* (2nd ed., pp.326–338). Cambridge, UK: Cambridge University Press.

Derwing, B. L., & Skousen, R. (1989). Real-time morphology: Symbolic rules or analogical networks. *Proceedings of the 15th Annual meeting of the Berkeley Linguistics Society,* Berkeley, CA, February.

Elman, J. L. (1988). *Finding structure in time.* Technical Report no. 8801, Center for Research in Language. University of California, San Diego.

Elman, J. L. (1989). *Representation and structure in connectionist models.* Technical Report no. 8903, Center for Research in Language. University of California, San Diego.

Elman, J. L., & Zipser, D. (1988). Learning the hidden structure of speech. *Journal of the Acoustical Society of America, 83,* 1615–1626.

Fodor, J., & Pylyshyn, Z. (1988). Connectionism and cognitive architecture: A critical analysis. *Cognition, 28,* 3–71.

Gasser, M., & Lee, C. D. (1990). *Networks and morphophonemic rules revisited*. Technical Report no. 307, Department of Computer Science, Indiana University.

Hare, M. (1990). The role of similarity in Hungarian vowel harmony: A Connectionist account. *Connection Science, 2(1–2)*, 123–150.

Hare, M., Corina, D., & Cottrell, G. W. (1989). A connectionist perspective on prosodic structure. *Proceedings of the 15th Annual meeting of the Berkeley Linguistics Society*, Berkeley, CA, February.

Hayes, D. P., & Ahrens, M. G. (1988). Vocabulary simplifications for children: A special case of "motherese"? *Journal of Child Language, 15*, 395–410.

Karmiloff-Smith, A. (1979). *A functional approach to child language*. Cambridge, UK: Cambridge University Press.

Karmiloff-Smith, A. (1986). From meta-processes to conscious access: Evidence from children's metalinguistic and repair data. *Cognition, 23*, 95–147.

Kucera, H., & Francis, W. N. (1967). *Computational analysis of present-day American English*. Providence. RI: Brown University Press.

Kuczaj, S. (1977). The acquisition of regular and irregular past tense forms. *Journal of Verbal Learning and Verbal Behavior, 16*, 589–600.

Kuczaj, S. (1978). Children's judgements of grammatical and ungrammatical irregular past tense verbs. *Child Development, 49*, 319–326.

Lachter, J., & Bever, T. G. (1988). The relations between linguistic structure and associative theories of language learning: A constructive critique of some connectionist learning models. *Cognition, 28*, 195–247.

MacWhinney, B. (1987). The competition model. In B. MacWhinney (Ed.), *Mechanisms of language acquisition* (pp.249–308). Hillsdale, NJ: Erlbaum.

MacWhinney, B., Leinbach, J., Taraban, R., & McDonald, J. (1989). Language learning: Cues or rules? *Journal of Memory and Language, 28*, 255–277.

Maratsos, M. (1988). Problems of connectionism: Review of S. Pinker & J. Mehler (Eds.), Connections and symbols. *Science, 242*, 1316–1317.

Marchman, V. (1984). Learning not to overgeneralize. *Papers and reports on child language development, 24*, 69–74.

Marchman, V. (1988). Rules and regularities in the acquisition of the English past tense. *Center for Research in Language Newsletter, 2*, April.

Minsky, M., & Papert, S. (1969). *Perceptrons*. Cambridge, MA: MIT Press.

Mozer, M. (1988). *A focused back-propagation algorithm for temporal pattern recognition*. Technical Report no. CRC-TR-88-3, University of Toronto, Canada.

Pinker, S., & Mehler, J. (1989). *Connections and symbols*. Cambridge, MA: MIT Press.

Pinker, S., & Prince, A. (1988). On language and connectionism: Analysis of a parallel distributed processing model of language acquisition. *Cognition, 28*, 59–108.

Rosenblatt, F. (1962). *Principles of neurodynamics*. New York: Spartan.

Rumelhart, D. E., & McClelland, J. L. (1986). On learning the past tense of English verbs. In D. E. Rumelhart, J. L. McClelland, & the PDP Research Group (Eds.), *Parallel distributed processing: Explorations in the microstructure of cognition*. (Vol. 2). Cambridge, MA: Bradford Books.

Rumelhart, D. E., & McClelland, J. L. (1987). Learning the past tenses of English verbs: Implicit rules or parallel distributed processing. In B. MacWhinney (Ed.), *Mechanisms of language acquisition*. Hillsdale, NJ: Erlbaum.

Seidenberg, M. S., & McClelland, J. (1989). A distributed, developmental model of word recognition and naming. *Psychological Review, 96*, 523–528.

Slobin, D. (1985). Crosslinguistic evidence for the language-making capacity. In D. I. Slobin (Ed.), *The cross-linguistic study of language acquisition, Volume II: Theoretical issues*. Hillsdale, NJ: Erlbaum.

Smolensky, P. (1988). *The constituent structure of connectionist mental states: A reply to Fodor & Pylyshyn*. Technical report, Department of Computer Science, University of Colorado, Boulder, CO.

Strauss, S. (1982). *U-shaped behavioral growth*. New York: Academic Press.

Received April 17, 1989, final revision accepted August 24, 1990

8

Modelling cognitive disorders

8.1 COGNITIVE NEUROPSYCHOLOGY

Over the past 20 years or so, some of the most important insights into the nature of human cognition have come from studying people with acquired disorders of cognition following brain damage. After brain damage, patients can lose the ability to perform certain cognitive tasks, such as reading or speaking words, recognising objects, orienting attention appropriately within visual scenes and so forth — tasks that are normally performed effortlessly by intact cognitive systems in the brain. The disorders can inform us about the nature of these cognitive systems, particularly about which processes can operate independently of others, and so which processes can be selectively spared when others are impaired. Cognitive neuropsychologists attempt to use data from cognitive disorders in order to test and refine normal models of cognition; they also attempt to understand cognitive disorders in terms of these models (Coltheart, 1984). Connectionist modelling is useful in this last regard, because the effects of brain lesioning can be simulated by removing "neurons" (processing units) from the models, by reducing the weights on connections, or by adding noise to either activation functions or to connection strengths. Also the patient data can provide strong

tests of the validity of the simulated models, as the models need to break down in a way that matches human performance (see Olson & Humphreys, 1997). In this chapter we review attempts to simulate cognitive disorders in such models.

8.2 READING DISORDERS (THE DYSLEXIAS)

8.2.1 The cognitive neuropsychology of reading

Theorists attempting to understand acquired disorders of reading have distinguished between so-called "peripheral" and "central" dyslexias, according to whether the breakdown affects reading prior to access to some form of stored knowledge taking place. Peripheral dyslexias are thought to be due to impairments prior to there being access to stored knowledge; central dyslexias arise after (or at a stage of) accessing stored knowledge (see Riddoch, 1990). We now consider each in turn.

8.2.2 Peripheral dyslexias

Three forms of peripheral dyslexia are *alexia* or *letter-by-letter reading* (Déjérine, 1892), *neglect dyslexia* (Ellis, Flude, & Young, 1987a), and *attentional dyslexia* (Shallice & Warrington, 1977). Alexic patients seem to have a disorder affecting the visual recognition of words as single objects, so that they may resort to reading words letter-by-letter. Thus the cardinal symptoms of alexia are that the patients show abnormally strong effects of word length on their word naming times, and that (sometimes) the patients read words by explicitly naming their letters aloud (Patterson & Kay, 1982; Warrington & Shallice, 1980). Several different accounts of the disorder have been proposed in the cognitive literature, including: difficulties in encoding letter identities efficiently (Arguin & Bub, 1994), problems in processing letters in parallel (Howard, 1989; Patterson & Kay, 1982), and the loss of stored visual memories (entries in an orthographic lexicon, see Chapter 6) for words (Warrington & Shallice, 1980). According to this last account, the abnormal effects of word length, and explicit letter-by-letter reading, may reflect some strategy on the part of patients to bypass their impaired visual word recognition system.

Interestingly, studies of alexia have shown that some patients can have access to some types of information about words, even when the words are presented too briefly for explicit identification (Coslett & Saffran, 1992; Shallice & Saffran, 1986). For instance, the patients may perform above chance at lexical decisions (deciding whether a letter string is a word or a nonword) and at semantic classification judgements (is the item living or non-living?). This so-called "covert knowledge" about words may reflect the residual word-based reading of the patients, in the absence of the letter-by-letter reading strategy.

Neglect dyslexia typically occurs as part of a more general syndrome of *unilateral neglect*, in which patients fail to respond appropriately to stimuli presented on one side of space (see section 8.8 for a fuller discussion) (Ellis, Flude & Young, 1987a; Riddoch, 1990), although in some cases a problem in reading is the only symptom (Patterson & Wilson, 1990). Neglect dyslexics have a spatial bias in reading so that (for example) they make errors to the letters on one side of the word, they miss words on one side of the page etc. The disorder is often attributed either to the patients failing to pay attention to one side of stimuli (Riddoch, Humphreys, Cleton, & Fery, 1990), or to their having sustained damage to one

side of a particular representation needed in reading (Caramazza & Hillis, 1990a).

Attentional dyslexia is a disorder in which patients can read aloud single letters and words relatively well, while being markedly impaired at reading aloud the letters in the word and in reading multiple words (e.g. in text; Saffran & Coslett, 1996; Shallice & Warrington, 1977; Price & Humphreys, 1993). Shallice and Warrington (1977) argued that the patients were impaired at processing in parallel multiple items from the same category (multiple letters, in the task of naming letters from words; multiple words in text) (see also Warrington, Cipolotti, & McNeil, 1993). An alternative proposal is that the patients have problems in narrowing visual attention to focus on single letters in words and single words in text, with the result that the multiple letters or words compete for the response; in reading single words, however, the letters map onto a single response and so do not compete in this manner (see Shallice, 1988).

8.2.3 Central dyslexias

Three forms of central dyslexia have been documented. *Phonological dyslexic* patients are relatively good at naming words but are severely impaired at naming nonwords (Beauvois & Derouesne, 1979; Funnell, 1983). The naming errors produced by the patients on nonwords are typically visual or lexical, involving replacement of the nonword with the name of a visually related word. *Surface dyslexics*, in contrast, are relatively good at naming nonwords and regular words while being impaired at reading exception words, which have irregular relationships between their spelling and their sound (see Chapter 6 for a discussion of the reading of regular and irregular words by normal subjects) (Patterson, Marshall, & Coltheart, 1985). Surface dyslexics make a variety of reading errors, including visual errors, incorrect applications of spelling-sound relations, and "regularisations" (in which an exception word is given its regular pronunciation; such as "pint" being named to rhyme with "hint"). In the cognitive neuropsychology literature, phonological and surface dyslexia have been interpreted in terms of dual-route models of reading (Chapter 6), which hold that there are separate lexical (word-based) and non-lexical (rule-based) routes to naming (e.g. Coltheart, 1987). According to such models, phonological dyslexics have an impaired non-lexical route to naming, although the lexical route is relatively intact. Surface dyslexics, on the other hand, have an intact non-lexical route (and can read regular words and nonwords, conforming to rule-based correspondences between spellings and sound) but they are impaired at lexical reading (and are hence impaired at reading exception words, which require word-based knowledge). There is thus an opposite pattern of performance in the two classes of patient: intact reading of exception words and poor nonword reading in phonological dyslexia; and poor reading of exception words but relatively good reading of nonwords in surface dyslexia. Such an opposite pattern of performance is known as a *double dissociation*, and is typically interpreted as indicating that the tasks depend on independent processes; in this case, on a lexical and a non-lexical reading route respectively.

In the third type of central dyslexia, *deep dyslexia*, the patients show a range of symptoms (see Coltheart, Patterson, & Marshall, 1980). Most notably, there are semantic errors, in which patients misname a word by giving the name of a semantically related item (e.g. sword → dagger). They also produce visual errors and errors that are both semantically and visually related to target words (e.g. shirt → skirt). Like phonological dyslexics, deep dyslexics are poor at reading nonwords; some words are also particularly difficult to read, including grammatical function words (this, and, but, etc.) and words low in imageability (e.g. thought, ideal, hope)[1]. Two main accounts of deep dyslexia have been offered. One suggests that the patients have multiple lesions of their reading system. One lesion affects the non-lexical reading route, so impairing the reading of nonwords. A second lesion affects a direct lexical route for reading, based on a direct association between a visual and a phonological lexicon (if this were intact, the patients would never make semantic errors). A third lesion must affect a semantic route to naming, involving access to semantic information after visual recognition of the word is achieved. Due to this last lesion, semantic errors occur.

A rather different account is that the symptoms of deep dyslexia are caused by the patients attempting to read with their right hemisphere, rather than by using the normal reading systems within the left hemisphere (Saffran, Bogyo, Schwartz, & Marin, 1980). The right hemisphere may have poor representation of low-imageability words, and poor phonological translation processes between spelling and sound. There may also be approximate access to word meaning within the right hemisphere, leading to semantic errors on some occasions.

8.3 CONNECTIONIST ACCOUNTS OF READING DISORDERS

Attempts have been made to simulate the majority of the dyslexic disorders within connectionist models of reading.

8.3.1 Alexia

Mayall and Humphreys (1996a, b) simulated the residual reading abilities of alexic patients in a model of a lexical (word-based) route to word naming. They trained a three-layer feed-forward network using the back-propagation algorithm to associate an arbitrary input pattern (representing the visual description of a whole word) with arbitrary output patterns corresponding to both the meaning of the words (the semantic representation) and to the pronunciation of the words (the phonological representation). As the stimuli used had no relationships between the substructures of the input and output patterns, the model involves the learning of stimulus-specific associations, as would be involved in a lexical (word-based) reading process. Differences between words high in imageability and words low in imageability were simulated by having "sparse" semantic representations for low-imageability words (patterns with many 0s and few 1s), and "richer" semantic representations for high-imageability words (patterns with many 1s and relatively few 0s). Also, for the semantic representations, stimuli from the same category activated a set of overlapping units. In addition, input units were trained to map onto a corresponding set of "visual lexical" output representations, for autoassociative learning[2]. The activation values of these "visual lexical" output units will be modulated by weights learned from the original training patterns, and so they reflect the orthographic properties of words known to the model. Such activation values provide some indication of whether a word is familiar, as they should match the input set on which the model was trained. The architecture of the model is shown in Fig. 8.1.

With output representations corresponding to the semantic, phonological, and visual lexical status of words, Mayall and Humphreys were able to simulate semantic decisions to words (based on the activation values of the semantic units), naming (based on activation values of the phonological units), and lexical decision. For lexical decision, responses were contingent on a comparison between the values of the visual lexical units when words were presented to the model relative to when nonwords were presented (patterns not in the original training set). Alexia was simulated by add-

ing noise to the weights from the input system to the hidden unit for each output response, and (in a second set of simulations) by selectively reducing the number of hidden units after training.

The effect of lesioning the model was to disrupt naming responses more than semantic classification and lexical decisions, mimicking the covert recognition effects apparent in some alexic patients (Coslett & Saffran, 1992). Also like some alexic patients, naming and semantic classification for high-imageability words was better than that for low-imageability words, presumably because the richer semantic representations for high-imageability words increased the probability that degenerate input activations would be recovered.

One interesting result with alexic patients is that they can be severely impaired at reading words presented in MiXeD CaSe (Price & Humphreys, 1995; Warrington & Shallice, 1980). This is something of a puzzle, because case mixing disrupts the wholistic shape of words but the identities of individual letters remain the same as when the

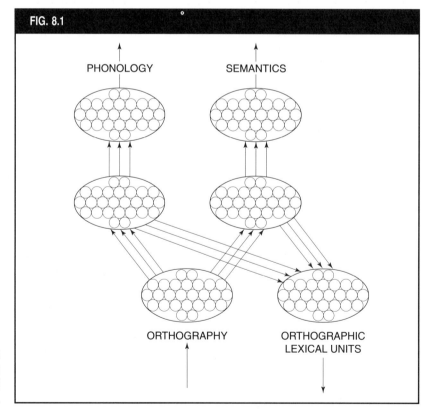

FIG. 8.1

PHONOLOGY   SEMANTICS

ORTHOGRAPHY   ORTHOGRAPHIC
LEXICAL UNITS

Architecture of the model of word recognition simulated by Mayall and Humphreys (1996a,b).

words are written in a single case. If the patients were literally reading letter-by-letter, mixed-case stimuli should be little harder to read than stimuli presented in a single case; this is not what happens. Instead the result is consistent with the patients trying to read using some residual word-based process which uses as input more wholistic visual descriptions, descriptions that at least are larger than single letters. This residual word-based recognition process is approximated by the Mayall and Humphreys (1996a, b) model. Mayall and Humphreys simulated the effects of case mixing by adding noise to the input patterns given to the model. The noise disrupted naming more than lexical decision, and lexical decision more than super-ordinate semantic classification, essentially because performance was a function of the specificity of the output representation required for the task. For correct naming the output representation needs to be more precise than for lexical decision (where there simply needs to be a difference between activation values generated by words and nonwords), and this needs to be more precise than for semantic classification (where values on the semantic units simply have to conform to those common to a number of members of the same category). In addition, weights to the semantic units, which are common to a set of category members, received more reinforcement during training than those used to map inputs to unique outputs, for naming and lexical decision; this again would lead to the preservation of semantic classification under noisy conditions. Consistent with this pattern of results in the model, Mayall and Humphreys (1996c) found that normal readers show a smaller effect of case mixing on lexical decision than on naming (see also Besner & McCann, 1987), and a smaller effect again on super-ordinate semantic classification. In studies of alexic patients, Arguin and Bub (1994) have also reported that the effects of case mixing are reduced on lexical decision compared with naming.

The Mayall and Humphreys simulation shows how "covert recognition" can emerge from a partially damaged recognition system. In the neuropsychological literature, covert recognition has sometimes been attributed to the operation of the right cerebral hemisphere, disconnected from speech output (Coslett & Saffran, 1992), or to disconnection of a system for conscious decision making from input "modules" for recognising stimuli from different modalities (e.g. a word recognition module; Schacter et al., 1988). The simulation shows that these last accounts are not *necessary* to explain covert recognition, as the model makes no distinction between the left and right hemispheres of the brain and no distinction between conscious and unconscious processes. The model also emphasises the role that residual word recognition may play in alexia, and this matches recent empirical data with patients (see Price & Humphreys, 1995). However, as the model only simulates word recognition processes, and not alternative means of reading by serial letter-by-letter analysis, it cannot capture the full pattern of alexic reading performance (in particular, those aspects concerned with letter-by-letter reading); the model deals only with residual word reading.

8.3.2 Neglect and attentional dyslexia: Lesioning MORSEL

Mozer and colleagues (Behrmann et al., 1991; Mozer, 1991; Mozer & Behrmann, 1992) have attempted to simulate neglect and attentional dyslexia by lesioning Mozer's MORSEL model of visual word recognition (section 6.4, Chapter 6). The MORSEL model has two main processing components: a word recognition module and an attentional module. In the word recognition module, letter cluster units are activated and are assembled into the correct spatial order by constraints from lexical/semantic knowledge. Letter clusters are placed into the correct spatial positions because they tend to occupy those positions in known words. The attentional module feeds down to early stages of letter coding, to activate letters at attended spatial positions. Activation in the attentional module changes dynamically over time, and units are updated according to certain constraints. For example, one constraint is that attention should spread over a contiguous region on the retina, but not over non-contiguous, separated regions[3]. With non-contiguous regions there is initial activation of both areas in a bottom-up manner, but the contiguity constraint then pushes attention to become narrowed on one region; as we shall see, these dynamics are important for simulating neglect and attentional dyslexia. When there are multiple words in the field, there is the possibility that multiple cluster units will be activated, leading to an increased probability that letter groups are miscombined. In this circumstance the attentional module enables activation to be biased only to the attended word, so that miscombinations of letter groups are reduced.

Aspects of neglect and attentional dyslexia can be simulated by this model by "lesioning" the attentional module. Behrmann et al. (1991) introduced a spatial lesion to the model, so that the left side of the attentional module was less likely to be activated in a bottom-up manner by low-level visual information. When this happened, the activation values for letters on the left side of the words tended to be relatively decreased, so that words were sometimes misidentified as another word with similar right-side letters (e.g. hand → sand). The likelihood of these spatial errors occurring was even larger if a nonword was presented, as then the lexical information used to assemble letter clusters may be even more likely to mismatch with the impoverished letter information. With such a mismatch, an incorrect word response may be produced to the nonword (tand → sand). This accords with neuropsychological data showing that neglect errors in reading are more likely with nonwords than with words (Riddoch et al., 1990; Sieroff, Pollatsek, & Posner, 1988).

Two other results from these simulations of neglect dyslexia are worthy of note. One is that, depending on the severity of the lesion, the model demonstrated the phenomenon of extinction. The term extinction is used by neuropsychologists to describe a situation in which report of a single stimulus (a word or letter say) is relatively good when that stimulus is presented alone in the impaired visual field (usually the field contralateral to the side of the brain lesion), but there is poor report of the same stimulus if a competing stimulus is presented at the same time in the unimpaired (ipsilateral) field. Sieroff and Posner (1988) showed that neglect dyslexics tend to "extinguish" the contralesional word (e.g. fail to report it) when two words are simultaneously presented separated by a single gap at fixation. In contrast,

report is much better if a single word is presented covering the same spatial area. When activation of the attentional module of MORSEL is reduced by lesioning, a similar pattern can emerge. A single word can sometimes be recovered and identified correctly, because only it matches lexical/semantic representations. Also, attention will tend to be driven to the target's location in a bottom-up fashion, because it is the only stimulus present. In contrast, with two words, attention is driven first to the ipsilateral item and is stopped from spreading to the contralateral item by the contiguity constraint, because there is a gap between the words. Consequently there is stronger activation for the letters in the ipsilateral word relative to those in the contralateral word. Under short presentation conditions, only the ispilateral word will be identified.

The second point to note is that Behrmann et al. (1991) introduced a spatial gradient in their lesioning, so that there was a gradual decrease in the probability of attentional units being activated from right to left[4]. One result of this is that some degree of neglect will be observed even when words are presented in the unimpaired (right) field, as the right-side letters will still receive a stronger attentional boost that the left-side letters. That is, the model generates a form of neglect that is somewhat "object-centred" rather than simply being based on the retinal location where stimuli fall. In this case, neglect is a function of the relative bias across the field. Again this matches the results from at least some neglect dyslexic patients (Young, Newcombe, & Ellis, 1991). However, MORSEL has little to say about other cases of neglect dyslexia, where it has been reported that patients show a form of neglect that can be completely detached from the positions of the letters in the visual field. Caramazza and Hillis (1990a) reported a left-hemisphere lesioned patient, NG, who neglected the last letters in words and nonwords (i.e. the letters falling at the right-hand end of the strings, when the stimuli are normally written in English; card → cart). Interestingly, NG still made errors to the last letters even when the words were mirror-reversed so that the last letters fell on the left-hand side (ꓷЯAƆ → cart). As Behrmann et al. simulated neglect dyslexia by lesioning the activation from retinal input, evidence for complete independence of neglect from visual field position cannot be accommodated. To accommodate such data either mirror-reversed words would need to be transformed into a retinotopic representation for subsequent word recognition, or there would need to be lesioning of some form of higher-order word representation (e.g. affecting letters falling at the end of stored word representations).

The syndrome of attentional dyslexia can be simulated by a different form of lesioning to the attentional module of MORSEL. Mozer and Behrmann (1992) examined performance when the attentional module was prevented from reaching equilibrium and settling down on one of two separated words, but instead remained in a first activated state, in which attentional activation involved both words. When there is attentional activation of both words, there is multiple activation of letter clusters, and an increased probability that clusters are combined incorrectly. This mimics the migration errors made by attentional dyslexics when reading text, when they mix-up the letters in words (sand lane → land, sane; Shallice & Warrington, 1977). Also if attention cannot be focused within a single word, then it may in turn be difficult to identify individual letters within words. In MORSEL, partial activation from the features in neighbouring letters can lead to some letter representations being activated incorrectly (e.g. features from V and L may activate the letter unit for N). This may not be problematic when whole words have to be identified, because the pull-out net is biased to select known letter combinations and unlikely letters will be rejected. In contrast, when the task is letter identification, responses from the pull-out net may not be used. In this instance, incorrect letter activations may be problematic as there is no means of distinguishing correct from incorrect letters. Partial activations of incorrect letters may be prevented in MORSEL by fixing attention sequentially to the location of each individual letter, to prevent cross-talk from neighbours. If the attentional module is prevented from focusing-in, however, then letter identification errors are made. For human patients, the consequence will be that they

are able to identify words in a word identification task but not the component letters in a letter identification task[5].

These studies of the effects of lesioning the MORSEL model show how a single model can capture a variety of neuropsychological disorders, and how important it is to understand the role of attention in tasks such as visual word recognition.

8.3.3 Surface dyslexia

The central dyslexic syndrome, surface dyslexia, has been simulated using the Seidenberg and McClelland (1989) connectionist model of word naming that we outlined in some detail in Chapter 6. This model took the form of a three-layer feed-forward network, trained to map orthographic input (based on coarsely coded letter clusters) to a phonological output representation (see section 6.7). The model has been of interest to reading researchers because it utilises a single (non-semantic) route to naming print, which operates for regular words, exception words, and nonwords alike; this contrasts with traditional dual-route models of naming, which propose independent lexical and non-lexical routes (for all words and for regular words and nonwords, respectively; see Coltheart, 1987).

Patterson, Seidenberg and McClelland (1989). Patterson et al. simulated the effects of brain damage on the model by (i) reducing the number of hidden units involved in mapping orthography to phonology, and (ii) adding noise to the weights connecting the hidden units from either the input or the output units. They found qualitatively similar results irrespective of the location or type of lesion. The performance of the model was measured in terms of an error score (the root mean square error, RMS_{error}), reflecting how far the actual phonemic output was from that expected. As the magnitude of the lesion increased, so there was an increase in the RMS_{error} score for each actual output, taken relative to what should have been the correct output. Patterson et al. also produced RMS_{error} scores in other ways; for example, by measuring the difference between the actual output and that expected from other words similar in spelling or sound to the input word. For exception words, one expected output might be the regularised pronunciation of the target (pint pronounced to rhyme with hint). For exception words the RMS_{error} score, relative to the correct pronunciation, was in some cases higher than the RMS_{error} score relative to the expected, but incorrect, regularised form; that is, the output was closer to the regularised pronunciation than to the correct pronunciation. If the phonemic output chosen is that with the lowest RMS_{error} score, then a regularisation error might sometimes be made. For regular words, the RMS_{error} associated with "other" (incorrect) pronunciations tended not to be lower than the RMS_{error} for the correct pronunciation, making an error less likely.

Patterson et al. also suggest that lesioning disrupted the identification of nonwords less than that of exception words. Before the lesion, the RMS_{error} scores for correct pronunciations of nonwords tended to be higher than those for both regular and exception words (see section 6.7). After lesioning the *increase* in the RMS_{error} score for nonwords was less in absolute terms than the magnitude of the increase with all words. Based on this, Patterson et al. propose that nonwords should be less affected by the lesion, particularly when compared with exception words that produce phonemic outputs close to those of words other than the target. They conclude that the model captures critical aspects of surface dyslexia — the selective impairment for exception words along with relatively preserved reading of regular words and nonwords.

The simulation of surface dyslexia within this model is interesting, because surface dyslexia has typically been attributed to a deficit within a lexical reading route, with the patients being left to use a non-lexical route (Coltheart, 1987). The Seidenberg and McClelland model does not have a lexical reading route, but rather a form of "mixed" route that translates orthography into phonology for words and nonwords alike. Thus the simulation suggests that independent "lexical" and "non-lexical" reading processes are not necessary to account for the data.

Can objections be raised against this last conclusion? The answer here is yes. For example, we have noted that, for exception words, the RMS_{error}

for the correct pronunciation was sometimes greater than that for the (incorrect) pronunciation of another word. Closer inspection of the RMS_{error} values by Patterson et al. revealed that the scores were a function of the number of phonemic features separating the actual output and that expected. Importantly however, the phonemic features changed in the output following damage to the model did not have to correspond to the regularised form of the pronunciation. For 31% of the errors on the exception words used in the simulations, the RMS_{error} score was lower for a word one phonetic feature away from the target than for the correct pronunciation. However, for only 19% of the errors were the RMS_{error} scores lowest for the regularised pronunciation. Hence, although the model was prone to making errors with exception words, these errors were not predominantly regularisations but rather were words that were phonemically close to the target (e.g. pint → paint). Patterson et al. went back to the neuropsychological data and assessed the nature of the pronunciation errors made by two surface dyslexic patients. Interestingly, they found that, like the model, the patients' errors tended to differ by a single phonemic feature from the target. In contrast to the model, however, the majority of the errors made by patients to exception words were regularisations (79 and 82% of the errors respectively).

At this closer level, the model fails to account for the neuropsychological data. Nevertheless, the model did prompt the finding that regularisations made by patients tend to be one rather than two phonemic features away from the correct pronunciation, suggesting that pronunciations by patients are influenced by phonemic relations between words. This indicates how modelling can be useful for empirical analyses of behaviour (even if the model turns out to be wrong at a fine-grained level!). For both the model and the patients, the distance between pronunciations in some space of phonemic features determines performance. However, distances in this space for humans also seem more strongly constrained than the model by the regularity of the relationship between spelling and sound. Although it is by no means certain, it is possible that the performance of the model in this respect may be improved by training it initially on a larger set of words (so the training set will tend to reflect the regularity of the spelling-to-sound relationships across the whole set) (see Seidenberg & McClelland, 1990). As we shall review later, performance may also be improved by using (i) an output representation that more closely resembles the space of phonemic features used by humans and, more particularly, and (ii) procedures that divide the mapping to phonology between semantic and orthographic inputs (cf. Plaut et al., 1996; see section 6.8, Chapter 6).

Before leaving the lesioned version of Seidenberg and McClelland, we should also note that, although the RMS_{error} scores for nonwords (relative to their correct pronunciations) were increased less than those for words after lesioning, they remained high in absolute terms. Again it is not clear that the model would produce the correct pronunciations for nonwords after lesioning, although this can be the case for surface dyslexic patients (however, see later). Modifications of the type we have suggested may be needed to better approximate the human data.

In general terms the effects of lesioning the Seidenberg and McClelland model were to: (i) generate worse performance across the board, although particularly for exception words; (ii) produce regularisation errors, although this was by no means the only error type produced, and (iii) leave nonword naming far from perfect. Patterson et al. point out, however, that surface dyslexia itself may not be a unitary syndrome, and that different classes of patient exist. In a first class (type 1 surface dyslexia): (a) the accuracy of naming for regular words is at or very close to normal levels and response latencies are within the normal range; (b) accuracy on naming nonwords is good; (c) most errors are regularisations; (d) access to semantic information from words is severely compromised. In a second class (type 2 surface dyslexia): (a) naming is affected for all words, although most profoundly for exception words, and naming latencies are slow; (b) nonword naming is impaired to some degree; (c) regularisation errors occur but they are only one of a number of different error types; and (d) there is no marked impairment of semantic knowledge. The lesioned

form of the Seidenberg and McClelland model most closely resembles type 2 surface dyslexic patients, but the model cannot accommodate type 1 surface dyslexia.

Plaut et al. (1996). This second form of surface dyslexia has been captured more accurately however, by Plaut et al.'s (1996) extension of the Seidenberg and McClelland model. As we discussed in Chapter 6 (section 6.8), Plaut et al. incorporated a different form of phonological representation into their model, with units corresponding to phonemes appearing in different "slots" in words, and they also used "attractors" at the phonological level (the notion of attractors is discussed more fully in the next section, 8.3.4; for now we simply note that, in such a system, the phonology initially activated in a first sweep through the model will be pushed towards the phonological representations for known words). Lesions were simulated either by removing a proportion of hidden units, by removing connections between groups of units, or by adding normally distributed noise values onto the weights between connecting units. Lesions affected the connections from grapheme to hidden units, from hidden units to phonemes, from phonemes to hidden units and the connections between phonemes (in the attractor part of the system). As in the study of Patterson et al. (1989), the same general pattern of results emerged irrespective of the lesion site. The results also resembled those reported by Patterson et al. Performance was relatively worse on exception words than on regular words, but (i) performance also tended to decrease on nonwords and (ii) the proportion of regularisation errors remained small when compared with those generated by at least some type 2 surface dyslexics (although patients with less extreme deficits in reading exception words could be modelled).

However, Plaut et al. point out that, for normal human subjects, phonology is addressed not only through orthography but also through semantics — as captured in models of object naming (Chapter 4) and speech production (Chapter 6). The models of spelling-to-sound translation that we have reviewed to date have only assessed the patterns of performance that emerge from a single process of mapping orthography to phonology. In a more complete model, this last process would co-exist with another route, for mapping semantics through to phonology. What might be the implications of learning in a system with a division of labour between semantic and orthographic procedures for word naming?

This is an interesting question, as it raises issues about how architectural constraints might influence processing within connectionist systems. Plaut et al. simulated a division of labour in the following way. In addition to having an orthographic route to phonology (see Fig. 6.16), they had a semantic pathway. As before, the model was trained to map orthography through to phonology. However, now during training a semantic input vector contributed to the activation values of the phonological units (the semantic input values themselves were fixed and not subject to learning). The contribution of the semantic input was set so that it increased as training

progressed (to capture the idea that initially reading development mainly involves learning the mapping between orthography and phonology but then involves naming through meaning), and it was set to influence high- relative to low-frequency words. The semantic vector for each word was simply a random pattern, so that the mapping involved in relating semantics to phonology for regular words was no different from that for exception words. After learning, lesioning involved removing the semantic input completely when the model tried to retrieve the phonology for a word. Now Plaut et al. found that the difference between performance on regular and exception words was enhanced (regular words being better preserved than previously and exception words being impaired), that nonword naming was maintained, and that the majority of errors on exception words were regularisations. That is, the model approximated the pattern of deficits found with type 2 surface dyslexics. These results are shown in Fig. 8.2.

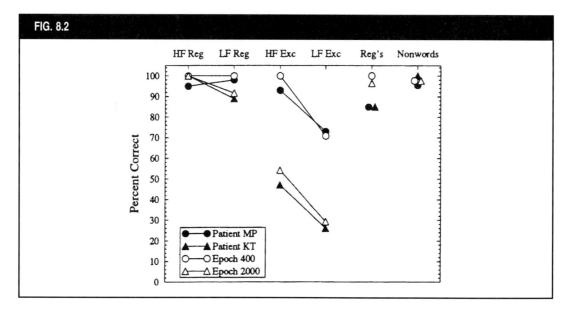

The effect of lesioning the model of word naming proposed by Plaut et al. (1996). In this version of the model, phonological output was addressed by two "routes" — from orthography and from semantics. Performance is shown after semantic input to word pronunciation has been eliminated, for networks with two levels of training (400 and 2000 epochs, or repeats of the training set). Performance is shown for high- and low-frequency regular words (HF Reg, LF Reg), for high- and low-frequency exception words (HL Exc, LF Exc), and for nonwords. In addition, "Reg's" indicates the percentage of errors on exception words that were regularisations. The model's performance is shown alongside that of two surface dyslexic patients, MP and KT.

These last simulations indicate that the learning of one function (mapping orthography to phonology) can differ according to whether a network computes only this function or whether there are contributions from other modules during learning (here from semantics as well as orthography). When phonological representations were activated from two sources, there seems to have been a division of learning according to the properties of each module. The semantic module provided equivalent inputs for regular and exception words, and in each case an arbitrary relationship had to be learned (between the "meaning" of the word and its phonology). The orthographic route, in contrast, was sensitive to the statistical relations between the orthographic and phonological representations, which favoured regular words. During training, then, it appeared that the semantic route learned to represent mappings for exception words while the orthographic route represented mainly the regular mappings. As a consequence, even when the semantic route was lesioned, the model remained able to pronounce regular words and nonwords, and the majority of its naming errors were regularisations. In this structured model, the route from orthography to phonology seems less competent for representing exception words than the same route when trained in isolation; when the semantic route was present, the model learned to rely on it for the naming of exception words.

Plaut et al. proposed that their second route was semantic in nature; however, they did not attempt to represent semantic knowledge in any plausible manner, and did not express differences between (for instance) high- and low-imageability words. Hence it may equally be argued that this route was lexical rather than semantic and that, in lesioning the model, they simulate operation of a non-lexical route in isolation from lexical reading processes — much as argued in dual-route accounts of reading. Future work needs to assess performance of the model when a semantic route is implemented more seriously. Moreover, recent case studies of putative type 2 surface dyslexics suggests that their reading of nonwords can be strongly affected by the consistency of the pronunciations given to orthographically similar words — that is, influenced by forms of lexical knowledge (Patterson & Behrmann, 1997). This is more consistent with a single procedure being used for reading, which is damaged in such cases.

Overall Plaut et al.'s attempt to assess the relations between different routes in reading is interesting not only as an attempt to capture surface dyslexia, but as an attempt to explore learning in more complex connectionist systems. It shows that having two routes in operation does not mean that the original route stays the same and a second route is simply added; rather the whole system is changed. In addition, it opens up the possibility of exploring individual differences in reading development and breakdown, which would emerge from differential involvement of a second route during learning. This issue has barely been touched on in prior connectionist models.

Where, then, does this leave the distinction, reinforced by the modelling enterprise, between type 1 and type 2 surface dyslexics? One suggestion is that type 1 patients have sustained more widespread damage, affecting the direct route between orthography and phonology in addition to the semantic route; hence such patients may be modelled by simulating damage to the direct route (as in Patterson et al., 1989). Another possibility is that there are individual differences between the patients in the way in which the semantic and direct reading routes are weighted, and consequent differences in the deficits suffered by the patients after brain damage. A more detailed understanding of individual differences in reading is needed before such claims can be evaluated.

8.3.4 Deep dyslexia

An attempt to model the mapping from orthography to semantics, and to assess performance after this process is damaged, was made by Hinton and Shallice (1991). They trained a network to learn a mapping between input units representing the orthography of words and output units representing word meanings. The architecture of the network is depicted in Fig. 8.3. Orthography was represented by having groups of position-specific letter units, with restrictions on which letters could appear in each position (the grapheme units).

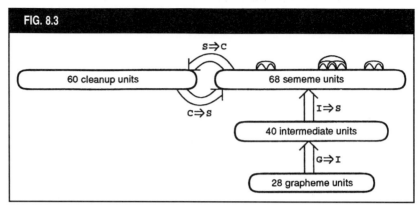

FIG. 8.3

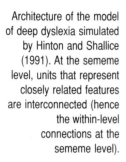

Architecture of the model of deep dyslexia simulated by Hinton and Shallice (1991). At the sememe level, units that represent closely related features are interconnected (hence the within-level connections at the sememe level).

Semantic information was represented by having "sememe" units, each standing for a semantic feature of a word. The letters and semantic features captured on the grapheme and sememe units are shown in Fig. 8.4. On average there were about 15 semantic features (out of 68) present for each word. The model had one set of hidden units connecting the grapheme to the sememe units (termed intermediate units by Hinton & Shallice), and a further set of "clean-up" units that connected back onto the sememe units (Fig. 8.3). The clean-up units enabled activity within the sememe layer to interact; this was also emphasised by adding connections between sememe units corresponding to closely related features. To reduce the total connectivity within the model, only a random 25% of the possible connections were implemented.

The model was trained using a variety of back-propagation, called back-propagation through time (Rumelhart et al., 1986a,b; Williams & Peng, 1990). In this procedure activation values were cycled around the network for seven iterations, with the values of the input units held constant ("clamped"). If the sememe units were not in the correct state for the last three iterations, they received a supervised error signal, and from this errors at other levels were calculated and back-propagated through the model. This was repeated for about 1000 sweeps through 40 words, after which the sememe units obtained activity states within 0.1 of the correct value for a given word. Note the mapping between orthography and semantics for words is arbitrary, and there is little in the substructure of the training set to facilitate learning.

After training the model was "damaged" in a variety of ways, including disconnecting or adding noise to connections between the grapheme and the intermediate units, doing the same to the connections between the intermediate units and the sememe units, or to the connections between the clean-up and the sememe units. The model was judged to make a particular semantic classification if either (a) the corrupted semantic representation was sufficiently close to the correct one, or (b) no other semantic representation, for another word, matched nearly so well. Using these criteria Hinton and Shallice found that the lesioned model made several types of error, which they categorised as:

1. visual: the retrieved meaning was that corresponding to a word that was visually but not semantically related to the target (e.g. cat → cot);
2. semantic: the model retrieved the meaning of a word semantically but not visually close to the target (cat → dog);
3. mixed (visual & semantic): the meaning retrieved was that of a word that was both visually and semantically related to the target (cat → rat);
4. other: responses were unrelated to the target (cat → mug).

Visual, semantic, and mixed (visual & semantic) errors were all produced at a rate greater than would be expected by chance (comparing each category of error to that of the other errors, under the assumption that errors are generated at

FIG. 8.4

The Words Used by Hinton and Shallice

(a) Letters Allowed in Each Position

Pos.	Letters
1	B C D G H L M N P R T
2	A E I O U
3	B C D G K M P R T W
4	E K

(b) Words in Each Category

Indoor Objects	Animals	Body Parts	Foods	Outdoor Objects
BED	BUG	BACK	BUN	BOG
CAN	CAT	BONE	HAM	DEW
COT	COW	GUT	HOCK	DUNE
CUP	DOG	HIP	LIME	LOG
GEM	HAWK	LEG	NUT	MUD
MAT	PIG	LIP	POP	PARK
MUG	RAM	PORE	PORK	ROCK
PAN	RAT	RIB	RUM	TOR

(a)

Semantic Features Used by Hinton and Shallice

1 max-size-less-foot	21 indoors	46 made-of-metal
2 max-size-foot-to-two-yards	22 in-kitchen	47 made-of-wood
3 max-size-greater-two-yards	23 in-bedroom	48 made-of-liquid
	24 in-livingroom	49 made-of-other-nonliving
4 main-shape-1D	25 on-ground	50 got-from-plants
5 main-shape-2D	26 on-surface	51 got-from-animals
	27 otherwise-supported	
6 cross-section-rectangular	28 in-country	52 pleasant
7 cross-section-circular	29 found-woods	53 unpleasant
	30 found-near-sea	
8 has-legs	31 found-near-streams	54 man-made
	32 found-mountains	55 container
9 white	33 found-on-farms	56 for-cooking
10 brown		57 for-eating-drinking
11 green	34 part-of-limb	58 for-other
12 colour-other-strong	35 surface-of-body	59 used-alone
13 varied-colours	36 interior-of-body	60 for-breakfast
14 transparent	37 above-waist	61 for-lunch-dinner
15 dark		62 for-snack
	38 mammal	63 for-drink
16 hard	39 wild	
17 soft	40 fierce	64 particularly-assoc-child
	41 does-fly	65 particularly-assoc-adult
18 sweet	42 does-swim	
19 tastes-strong	43 does-run	66 used-for-recreation
	44 living	
20 moves	45 carnivore	67 human
		68 component

Features within a block were considered "closely related" for the purposes of inter-connecting semantic units.

(b)

(a) Grapheme and (b) semantic representations used by Hinton and Shallice (1991). Grapheme representations were based on position-specific codings of letters. From Plaut and Shallice (1993a).

random). This held for all the lesions performed on the model. These different types of error match the errors made by deep dyslexic patients (Coltheart et al., 1980). Hinton and Shallice did find that the proportions of errors changed as a function of the lesion site; there tended to be proportionately more visual errors with "early" damage (close to the grapheme units), and proportionately more semantic errors with "late" damage (close to the sememes). However this too may correspond to observed differences across patients (Coltheart et al., 1987).

The occurrence of mixed (visual & semantic) errors is particularly of interest, as it is by no means obvious why these should arise after damage to any location in the model. Hinton and Shallice accounted for these errors in terms of the role of the clean-up units. When activation is first passed through this model from the grapheme to the sememe units, the semantic description retrieved may only be partially correct; the clean-up units then serve to modify the semantic description ("cleaning it up") until the sememe units achieve the correct state. The network can be said to be operating using "*attractors*" (see section 6.8, Chapter 6). The region in semantic space corresponding to the initial sememe activity is termed the *basin of attraction*, and basins of attraction are set up by the weights established within the network during training. Once words fall into their basin of attraction, the clean-up units tend to push the states of the sememe units towards the centre of their basins, corresponding to the correct semantic description. Now, in a task involving arbitrary input–output mappings, such as translating orthography into meaning, a model must learn not to produce similar outputs for words that are visually similar (e.g. cat and cot). This can be difficult, as similar inputs will tend to be mapped onto similar outputs. The learning of arbitrary mappings can be accomplished in an attractor network, however, if the model constructs large basins of attraction around each familiar meaning. Visually similar words may then be allowed to generate quite similar initial semantic states, as long as each state falls within the appropriate basin of attraction for each word (and not for the other, visually similar word). The clean-up units

will then push the semantic units into their correct state. Note now, however, that when lesioned, a property of such a network will be to generate relatively high proportions of mixed (visual & semantic) errors. After lesioning, the basins of attraction can be distorted, so that a target can fall into the basin of attraction of a visually similar word, and sometimes be pushed into the final semantic state for that word, leading to a mixed (visual & semantic) error. Figure 8.5 illustrates this notion.

Plaut and Shallice (1993a) extended Hinton and Shallice's initial simulations. They showed that the different error types, after lesioning, emerged from a variety of network architectures, and in networks trained with algorithms other than backpropagation (e.g. varieties of Boltzmann machine learning algorithms, see Chapter 2), although the high occurrence of mixed (visual & semantic) errors was confined to when intermediate units were used to develop attractors. They also showed that the different error types could be simulated in name production, in a model in which a further set of phonological units (with their own clean-up units) was added, to take activation from the sememe units (see Fig. 8.6). Thus these results appear quite general and are not confined to a particular architecture or learning algorithm.

Plaut and Shallice also simulated one characteristic of deep dyslexia not present in the Hinton and Shallice model; the effect of imageability. Deep dyslexic patients are able to read words high in imageability better than they read words low in imageability (Coltheart et al., 1987). Plaut and Shallice simulated the effects of imageability by having high-imageability words represented by more semantic features than low-imageability words (see also Mayall & Humphreys, 1996a,b). They found that high-imageability words were advantaged relative to low-imageability words, depending on the lesion site. For instance, lesions of the pathway leading to the activation of sememe units (i.e. lesions of the connections from the graphemes to the intermediate units, or of the connections from the intermediate units to the sememe units) generated a substantial benefit for high-imageability words. Incorrect responses made by the network also tended to be higher in

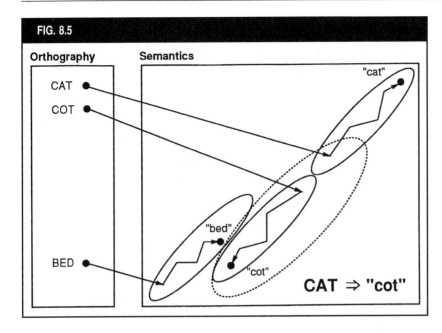

FIG. 8.5

Orthography | Semantics

CAT
COT

BED

"cat"
"bed"
"cot"

CAT ⇒ "cot"

Example of how damage to semantic attractors can cause visual errors in the model of Hinton and Shallice (1991). The solid ovals depict the normal "basins of attraction" for particular words within a semantic space; the dotted ovals depict an enlarged basin of attraction after brain damage. From Plaut and Shallice (1993a).

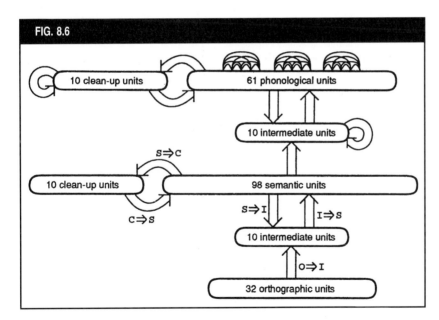

FIG. 8.6

10 clean-up units | 61 phonological units

10 intermediate units

s⇒c

10 clean-up units | 98 semantic units

c⇒s

s⇒I   I⇒s

10 intermediate units

o⇒I

32 orthographic units

Plaut and Shallice's (1993a) extension of the Hinton and Shallice (1991) model of deep dyslexia, to include phonological output units for naming.

imageability than the target words, matching neuropsychological data (Nolan & Caramazza, 1982). However, severe lesions of the clean-up units led to the opposite pattern. At least one patient with a selective advantage for reading abstract relative to concrete words has been documented (Warrington, 1981). It would appear to be the case that within models of this type, the clean-up units become more important for distinguishing between words with rich semantic representations (high-imageability words) than words with more impoverished semantic representations (low-imageability words); the low-imageability words may tend to have smaller basins of attraction than the high-imageability words. If so, lesions affecting the mapping through to semantic units will tend to "push" low-imageability words outside their basin of attraction, disrupting their identification (note the advantage for high-imageability words after lesioning affecting the mapping to the sememe units). In contrast, lesions of the clean-up units will affect low-imageability words less (generating an advantage for low-imageability words after such lesions).

The simulations conducted by Hinton and Shallice, and by Plaut and Shallice, show why it may be useful to employ connectionist models, with dynamic mapping between inputs and outputs, to simulate human performance. Specifically, in attractor networks such as they used, representations become sensitive not just to a single form of similarity between items (e.g. visual similarity, or semantic similarity), but to joint similarity even between arbitrary inputs and outputs (i.e. visual and semantic similarity between words). This accounts for the presence of mixed (visual & semantic) errors in deep dyslexia, a result that is difficult to explain in other frameworks. The work on the effects of imageability also show that it is possible to generate *opposite* effects from two different lesions to the same system; that is, it is possible to produce a double dissociation within a single, interactive network. In the models explored by these investigators, the double dissociation arises because the different components of the model are carrying out different computational jobs — for instance, mapping inputs into an appropriate part of semantic space and pushing initial semantic states into the centre of a bowl of attraction — and different variables (high and low imageability) impact in opposite ways on these computations. Finally, the work on imageability additionally shows that differences between performance with high- and low-imageability words, in human patients, do not have to be attributed to the separate anatomical localisation of low- and high-imageability words (cf. Warrington, 1981). The units mapping input into the semantic system, and the clean-up units in the model, all operate for both high- and low-imageability words, although they operate in different ways for the two word types. The double dissociation arises

out of the computational differences required to read the word types, not their anatomical localisation. These points, concerning double dissociations within models, will be returned to in Chapter 9, where we review the general utility of connectionist accounts of cognition.

8.3.5 Phonological dyslexia

Unlike the other dyslexias, there has to date been no attempt to simulate phonological dyslexia within a connectionist framework; nevertheless, the syndrome is important for connectionist models. The models of reading that we have reviewed here and in Chapter 6 have in the main concerned just one part of the reading system, such as mapping from orthography to phonology (Seidenberg & McClelland, 1989), or from orthography to semantics (Hinton & Shallice, 1991), although models such as those developed by Mayall and Humphreys (1996 a,b) and Plaut et al. (1996) have begun to incorporate both direct orthographic and semantic routes to phonology. In this framework, phonological dyslexia would arise from severe damage to the phonological reading route, forcing patients to read via semantics. This could produce successful naming of words but not nonwords, as found in this disorder.

One problem with this is that Funnell (1983) reported that, in addition to being unable to name nonwords, her phonological dyslexic patient (WB) could not read semantically either. Funnell found that WB could not point to which of two semantically related written words matched a spoken name, although he performed reasonably well when the words were unrelated. She proposed that WB showed poor discrimination between semantically related words, and therefore that he would have been unable to assign individual identities to words via a semantic route. If this holds, then there would appear to be a need for a third route, involving phonological translation for words alone, which is intact in phonological dyslexia and enables patients to read words correctly. Alternatively, within a connectionist account involving two routes it is possible that partial activation of the semantic route could be combined with partial activation of the phonological route to generate correct naming on at least some occasions.

Detailed testing of a model incorporating both orthographic and semantic reading routes is required here.

8.4 SPEECH DISORDERS: DYSPHASIA

Just as a variety of different disorders of reading can be observed after brain damage, so there can be a variety of speech disorders. Traditional distinctions have been drawn between patients with relative fluent speech output but poor content, and non-fluent patients who can convey basic meaning in sentences although often with impaired grammatical constructions and halting speech patterns (e.g. Goodglass & Kaplan, 1972). "Fluent" patients often produce nonword as well as word responses in their speech, leading to their being termed "jargon" aphasics. Patients may also present with an anomia, when there is good comprehension of the to-be-named stimuli, along with problems in word retrieval. Models of those anomias that are specific to certain classes of item are reviewed in section 8.6.2 here, where we deal with disorders of object recognition, as the models link such specific disorders to characteristics associated with processing certain kinds of object (Humphreys et al., 1995, see also section 4.6, Chapter 4). In this section we deal with attempts to simulate disorders that seem confined to the processing of spoken language.

Martin and colleagues (Martin, Dell, Saffran & Schwartz, 1994; Martin & Saffran, 1992) have examined the syndrome of *deep dysphasia*, in which patients have a variety of problems, including the following: nonwords cannot be repeated and there is impaired repetition of words (worse for low- than for high-imageability words); errors in word repetition involve the production of other phonologically similar words ("formal paraphrasias") and semantically related words; immediate verbal memory is impaired (e.g. measured in terms of digit span); object naming can be disrupted (with phonological and semantic errors resulting) (although see Howard & Franklin, 1988). Martin and Saffran (1992) proposed that these problems could be understood in terms of lesions to Dell's (1986) connectionist model of speech production, and this was simulated in Martin et al. (1994). We considered Dell's model in Chapter 6 (section 6.15). The model uses an interactive framework in which activation is mapped from semantic to lexical units, and from lexical to phoneme units, for speech production to occur. Normally, activation at the phoneme level is supported by continued activation of the target concept and word respectively at the semantic and lexical levels, so that the appropriate phonemes are maximally activated for output. However, if there is an abnormal decay of activation after lesioning, then the target concept and word may decay after their initial activation, being replaced either by a semantically related word (from spreading semantic activation) or a phonologically related word (from back-activation from the first activated phonemes). Repetition was simulated by initially activating the phoneme level and feeding this activation back to the lexical level, for the response. Again, due to abnormally rapid decay, repetition errors occurred which were typically either semantic in nature or were formal paraphrasias. Martin et al. also suggest fast decay of activation would lead to an impaired verbal memory span, and particularly poor repetition of nonwords which would not even be supported by initially strong lexical or semantic activation. Figure 8.7 gives examples of the error types generated by Dell's model when there was abnormally rapid decay of activation, compared with the error data from one deep dysphasic patient, NC.

Schwartz, Saffran, Bloch, and Dell (1994) proposed that another dysphasic disorder, jargon aphasia, could occur if there were a slow spread of activation between the levels of the model (rather than abnormal decay). Jargon aphasia is associated with high rates of speech errors, a tendency towards perseveratory responses (where previous responses, or related responses, are subsequently produced) and no bias to produce words rather than nonwords when production errors are made (i.e. there is no lexical bias, unlike normal subjects; see Chapter 6, section 6.15). When there is a slow spread of activation, there is a tendency to repeat prior responses, because their activation is not over-ridden by forthcoming (semantic and

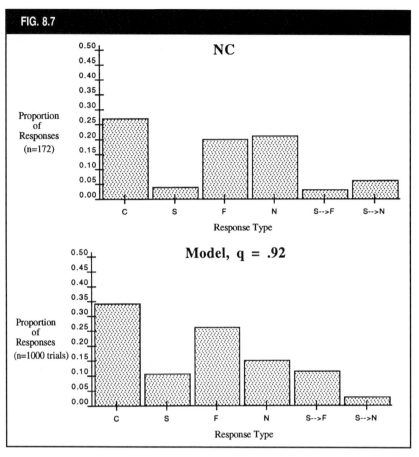

FIG. 8.7

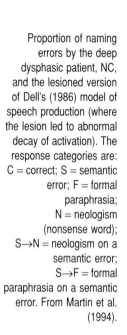

Proportion of naming errors by the deep dysphasic patient, NC, and the lesioned version of Dell's (1986) model of speech production (where the lesion led to abnormal decay of activation). The response categories are: C = correct; S = semantic error; F = formal paraphrasia; N = neologism (nonsense word); S→N = neologism on a semantic error; S→F = formal paraphrasia on a semantic error. From Martin et al. (1994).

lexical) speech signals. Also, the normal bias towards lexical errors is reduced because the slow spread of activation precludes strong top-down effects on phoneme selection. These simulations show how several of the characteristics of different dysphasias can be captured by contrasting lesions within a single model. Not all aspects of the syndromes have been simulated yet, however. For example, the effects of imageability found in deep dysphasia have not been modelled, although they may well occur if imageability reflects the number of semantic units activated by words.

Harley (1990) has also simulated aspects of jargon aphasia within his model of speech production (Chapter 6, section 6.15). Harley's model contrasts from that of Dell (1986) in having within-layer inhibitory connections at the lexical and phonological levels. At the lexical level, these connections serve to "damp-down" competition

between related words. The effect of lesioning lexical inhibitory connections is to increase lexical competition and associated phonological activation, with the result that phonological word errors and some "neologisms" (nonword responses) occur in speech production. At present there are few grounds to judge whether it is best to view brain damage as affecting the spread of activation, or affecting within-layer inhibitory connections, making it difficult to assess which model best accounts for jargon aphasia.

8.5 DISORDERS OF SPELLING: DYSGRAPHIA

In Chapter 6 we discussed three connectionist models of spelling, by Brown et al. (1994), by

Houghton et al. (1994), and by Olson and Caramazza (1994). The models of Brown et al. and Olson and Caramazza attempted to learn mappings from phonology to orthography (from sound to spelling) which would support the production of words with both regular and irregular sound–spelling correspondences. Each of these models was also "lesioned" by the experimenters (connections from the input to the hidden units, or from the hidden units to the output units were either set to zero or had random changes to their values). The results were quite similar. After lesioning spelling performance deteriorated overall, but more so for words with irregular sound–spelling correspondences than for words with regular correspondences. For example, Brown et al. measured performance in terms of RMS_{error} scores for the correct spelling output relative to that of either the regularised output or another near

alternative output, noting the number of "reversals" (when either the regularised or the alternative form had a lower RMS_{error} value than the correct output). The number of reversals are shown in Fig. 8.8. More reversals were made to irregular words than to regular words.

Olson and Caramazza also pointed that, when lesioned, their model tended to make phonologically plausible spelling errors (e.g. syntax → sintax). However, the model additionally made errors in which the incorrect letter produced was not phonologically plausible in the context in which the error occurred. For instance, *khaki* was misspelled as *cacy*, *kite* as *cit* and so forth. In these errors a "c" was produced in a way that was not bound by the other letters present. In English, "c" is pronounced differently according to the following vowels; if "c" precedes "i", "e", or "y" it is pronounced /s/, but it is pronounced /k/ if it

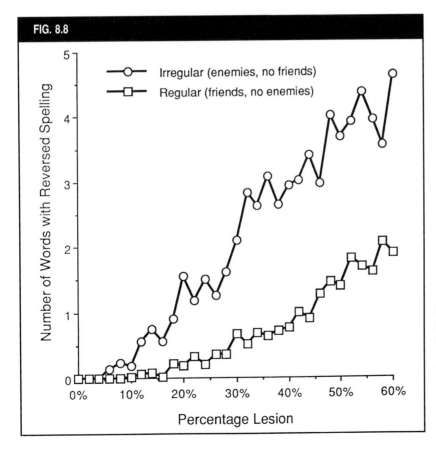

FIG. 8.8

Number of reversed spelling responses (where the RMS_{error} score for the correct spelling was higher than that for another word) in the lesioned version of the spelling model of Brown et al. (1994).

precedes other vowels. In the foregoing examples, "c" should not be substituted for a "k" if the following vowel gives "c" the pronunciation /k/. These phonologically implausible errors arise because the model is not sensitive to the graphemic context in which letters are produced; once a "c" has been selected for output, there are no constraints on the following vowels that are selected, and there are no constraints from the following vowels on the earlier selection of the "c". To eliminate such errors, the model would need to be made sensitive to larger graphemic contexts so that, for instance, a "c" would not be selected for the pronunciation /k/ if the following letter is a "y".

Several patients with acquired disorders of spelling, dysgraphia, have been documented, with the different forms of dysgraphia tending to mirror the reported forms of dyslexia. For example, in *surface dysgraphia*, patients make errors particularly on words with irregular sound–spelling correspondences, and it is this form of dysgraphia that the models of Brown et al. and Olson and Caramazza most resemble after lesioning. Surface dysgraphics tend to produce phonologically plausible errors when they mis-spell words and, like Olson and Caramazza's model, some also make errors that violate the graphemic context in which the letters are produced (e.g. Hatfield & Patterson, 1983). However, unlike the model, some surface dysgraphics make few such violations (Beauvois & Derouesne, 1981; Goodman & Caramazza, 1986). It may be that some form of "graphemic clean-up" procedure is needed to make the model sensitive to graphemic constraints in output, perhaps using an attractor network of the type used by Hinton and Shallice (1991) and Plaut and Shallice (1993a) to model deep dyslexia. Patients who remain sensitive to graphemic constraints may have such clean-up units intact. Whether this speculation turns out to be correct is obviously an empirical question.

What is clearer is that these models are only able to capture one form of dysgraphia. Other forms of dysgraphia reported in the neuropsychological literature are *phonological dysgraphia* and *deep dysgraphia* (e.g. Bub & Kertesz, 1982; Shallice, 1981), and dysgraphia due to damage to a supposed "graphemic buffer", specific to spelling. The

terms phonological and deep dysgraphia are used in a way that is analogous to the terms phonological and deep dyslexia, used to describe two reading disorders. The term phonological dysgraphia is applied to people who can spell words but not nonwords (i.e. who fail to spell phonologically), and deep dysgraphia to people who (i) make semantic errors in spelling, (ii) have difficulty spelling nonwords, and (iii) make more errors on low-imageability words and function words than on high-imageability words. To date no attempts have been made to model these two disorders, but one way in which it might be done would be to incorporate a second "route" for spelling, from sound through semantics to spelling. Phonological dysgraphics may spell through this semantic route but not through the phonological (sound–spelling) route (the route modelled by Brown et al. and by Olson & Caramazza); deep dysgraphics may also attempt this, but they additionally have lesions to the semantic route (cf. Hinton & Shallice, 1991). Relevant to this last proposal is the existence of relatively intact spelling to dictation in patients with so-called *word meaning deafness*. Patients with word meaning deafness are unable to comprehend the meaning of some words spoken to them, but, interestingly, they may be able to write the words down and then to comprehend them from their spelling. In one classic case reported by Bramwell (1897), a Scottish woman with this impairment was asked about the city Edinburgh; she failed to understand what the examiner said, but wrote down Edinburgh and then was able to say that she liked to visit it. For modern psycholinguists this example is telling because Edinburgh is a word with an irregular correspondence between its sound and its spelling. The fact that the patient was able to write it without comprehending it auditorily suggests that there is a non-semantic route to spelling that works for irregular words as well as for regular words. This may be the route modelled by Brown et al. and Olson and Caramazza.

Models of spelling used in cognitive neuropsychology typically suppose the involvement of a "graphemic buffer", after activation of stored orthographic knowledge about spellings; this buffer is used to hold letters temporarily until they are output in a variety of spelling tasks (e.g. including typing, handwriting, and oral spelling). This buffer is also assumed to have limited capacity. Patients with damage to the graphemic buffer should find it particularly difficult to spell long words, as the capacity of the buffer will be reduced by brain damage. However, such patients should not be strongly affected by linguistic factors, such as whether words have regular sound–spelling correspondences, because the buffer simply serves to maintain letters after stored knowledge about the spellings of words and letter sounds has been retrieved. Patients with this type of spelling disorder have been reported by Caramazza, Miceli, Villa, and Romani (1987), Caramazza and Miceli (1990), and Hillis and Caramazza (1990) (among others). In such cases patients have also been found to make substantial numbers of transposition errors (in which letters swap positions) and to show a bow-shaped serial position function, in which errors are more likely in the middle than at the ends of the words. Note that such bow-shaped functions are also found with normal spellers (Wing & Baddeley, 1980; see Chapter 6), but in the patients the overall level of performance is much worse.

Houghton et al. (1994) have assessed whether this last form of dysgraphia could be captured in their model of spelling, which deals essentially with how letters are output in a serial fashion after contacting stored knowledge about spellings (see also Shallice, Glasspool & Houghton, 1995). Houghton et al.'s model of spelling uses a competitive queuing mechanism to ensure that letters are output in their correct serial order in spelling. Letter nodes are activated from higher-level "control" units, which represent orthographic knowledge about respectively the beginnings and endings of words. Activation of the control unit for the beginning or end of a known word, for instance, leads to the activation of letter units, with the level of excitation in letter units a function of their serial position in the word (according to learned weights connecting the control units to the letter units). Control units for the beginnings of words activate the first letter most, the second letter less, the third letter less again and so forth, and there is a steep drop in activation values across the

serial positions; the opposite spread of activation is generated from control units for the ends of words (which activate the last letter most). Letters are output as a function of their activation values, via a competitive output filter which selects the most active unit and suppresses competitors (see Chapters 5 and 6). After selection, there is inhibition of the selected letter, allowing the next most active letter to be output. Control units for the beginnings of words are activated earlier in time than those for the ends of words, so that output starts at the beginnings of words. However, due to the non-linear variation in activation levels as a function of the serial positions of letters, differences in activation values between middle letters are much less than differences in activation values from first to second letter, or from final to next-to-final letter. Accordingly, transposition errors in spelling are more likely for middle than for end letters.

To simulate the effects of lesioning on the model, Houghton et al. added noise to the activation functions at the letter level. Under these conditions they showed that the model was less likely to identify long words relative to short words, and it was particularly prone to make errors at the centre of the words (the cause of these two effects is the same, reflecting the lack of discriminability between activation values at the centres of words, which is exacerbated in long words). They also simulated performance with words and nonwords, by contrasting effects with "word" stimuli that had been used to train the links between the control units and the letter units, and "nonword" stimuli, which had been used as the training set on just one previous trial. Performance was better for words than for nonwords, although the pattern of performance (e.g. as a function of string length) was the same. This is similar to data reported by Caramazza et al. (1987) with their patient. A final point concerns geminates (i.e. doubled letters in spellings). The model is able to produce geminates in its spelling by incorporating a special "geminate unit", which, when activated, ensures that activation in a letter unit is not reset after the letter is output so that the letter remains at a high activation level to be output a second time (section 6.14, Chapter 6).

One effect of adding noise to the activation functions at the letter level is that activation of the geminate can be misaligned in time with excitation in letter units; when this happens the geminate signal can be applied to the wrong letter and a "geminate error" occurs in which a letter other than the correct one is doubled (e.g. greed → grred). Interestingly, the same type of error occurs with human patients (Caramazza & Miceli, 1990).

The model of Houghton et al. demonstrates how "peripheral" problems in spelling (particularly in producing letters in the correct spatial order) can be captured in a connectionist model. Note that, in the cognitive neuropsychological literature, such problems have typically been assigned to impairment to a specific representation, the graphemic buffer. Houghton et al.'s model does away with such a representation; order in output is based not on a spatially ordered representation but on temporal variation in activation levels within letter units that are not spatially ordered. The model thus shows that theorists need to be cautious in interpreting data from patients as necessarily indicating the involvement of a particular form of representation in human performance. However, whether the model is able to capture all forms of peripheral spelling disorders remains open to question. For example, some patients have been documented with "*neglect dysgraphia*" in which their spelling disturbance is related to the lateral positions of letters in letter strings (Baxter & Warrington, 1983; Hillis & Caramazza, 1990; Katz, 1991); more errors might be made at the beginning or end of a word rather than in the middle (unlike the normal pattern of performance). Possibly lateral deficits may relate to lesions to the control units in Houghton et al.'s model, as these are separately represented for the beginnings and ends of words, but this needs thorough testing. In addition to this, in some dysgraphic patients spelling errors respect the consonant/vowel status of letters (McCloskey, Badecker, Goodman-Shulman, & Aliminosa, 1994). Houghton et al.'s model makes no distinction between representations of vowels and consonants, and so does not respect their status when errors are produced. It is possible that such effects might occur on a model trained with a large vocabulary, when learning in

the model may better reflect the statistical properties of the language (and if consonant–vowel status is correlated with the occurrences of letters in particular positions); alternatively there may need to be a change in the representations used so that they better reflect linguistic and/or phonological properties of the language (so distinguishing consonants and vowels).

8.6 DISORDERS OF OBJECT RECOGNITION AND NAMING: AGNOSIA AND CATEGORY-SPECIFIC ANOMIA

Damage to the posterior parts of the brain, and particularly to the areas running from the occipital lobe at the back of the brain to the temporal lobes on the side, can lead to selective problems in recognising and naming visually presented objects. Disorders of visual object recognition, or agnosia, do not seem to be due to a simple sensory loss. For instance, agnosic patients can show normal discrimination of patterns and shapes (e.g. Humphreys et al., 1992a) and they can often copy objects that they fail to recognise (see Humphreys & Riddoch, 1987, 1993; Warrington, 1985, for reviews). One long-standing distinction has been between patients whose agnosia seems due to a perceptual disturbance that prevents visual memories for objects from being accessed (apperceptive agnosics), and patients with intact perceptual processes but either impaired visual memories or impaired access from those memories to semantic knowledge (associative agnosics; Lissauer, 1890). For instance, in some cases patients are able to discriminate between pictures of real objects and those of artificial objects made up by interchanging the parts of real objects (e.g. a horse with a dog's head) (see for example, Hillis & Caramazza, 1995a; Riddoch & Humphreys, 1987b; Sheridan & Humphreys, 1993; Stewart, Parkin, & Hunkin, 1992). As the real and artificial objects are perceptually very similar, success at this task suggests that the patients do not have a perceptual disturbance and that they can access stored visual memories for objects (so can discriminate when an object is not real). Nevertheless, the patients may still have difficulty judging whether objects should be used together (e.g. when presented with pictures of a dog and a kennel), indicating a failure in accessing semantic information about the functions of objects. In such cases, the disturbance seems to be within the memory system for objects, so that visual but not semantic memories are evoked by objects. We now review models that have attempted to capture these different types of agnosia.

8.6.1 Apperceptive agnosia

Humphreys and Riddoch (1987) documented a patient, HJA, who was profoundly agnosic, failing to recognise most common objects by sight. Nevertheless, HJA was able to produce accurate copies of the objects he failed to recognise, and he could also reproduce drawings of the objects from memory (when asked to draw an object from its name). Humphreys and Riddoch argued that HJA's deficit lay in the processes leading to the activation of long-term memories from vision, and reflected a problem in grouping together form information in a spatially parallel manner. However his visual memories themselves were intact, and allowed him to draw from memory.

In one test of the grouping hypothesis, HJA was asked to search for an inverted T target defined by a conjunction of form elements (horizontal and vertical lines) relative to a set of homogeneous background stimuli sharing the same features (Ts). When the background items are homogeneous, normal subjects can search efficiently because they are able to group together the homogeneous distractors to segment them from the target. HJA was very impaired at this task; even after extensive practice his reaction times were slow and affected by the number of distractors present, and he made high proportions of errors (Humphreys et al., 1992a). However, his search was not impaired when grouping was not required. For instance, when the target was defined by a difference in orientation relative to the background (e.g. / target vs. 1 distractors), HJA performed normally; feature differences may be computed by early stages of visual processing prior to the grouping of form elements. HJA also performed normally in a difficult visual search

task, in which the target was a form conjunction (⊥) and the distractors were heterogeneous items each sharing features with the target (T, ⊢, ⊣). As heterogeneous distractors do not group efficiently, target detection here may be based on independent sampling of items and so be unaffected by impaired grouping. Representative data are shown in Fig. 8.9.

The performance of HJA on visual search tasks has been simulated by Humphreys, Freeman, and Müller (1992b) using the SERR model of visual search and attention (Chapter 4, section 4.5.3; see Fig. 4.18). SERR is a hierarchically organised model in which line orientations are first encoded in feature maps, these are then combined into conjunctions (e.g. to represent junctions at particular orientations), and the conjunctions are subsequently grouped together competitively (so that like conjunctions excite one another and inhibit other conjunctions at the same locations). Targets are detected on the basis of activation from conjunction maps collected by templates coded for the particular forms used in the display (e.g. ⊥, T, ⊢, and ⊣). SERR mimics the performance of normal subjects set to search for form conjunction targets amongst homogeneous and heterogeneous distractors. Homogeneous distractors group, and are quickly selected and then rejected as the target, enabling the target itself to be selected. Heterogeneous distractors compete to form stable groups and then have to be selected serially, leading to time penalties and effects of the number of distractors on search (see Chapter 4, section 4.5.3 for details).

SERR used a Boltzmann machine activation function (Chapter 2). Units were placed into an on or off state stochastically, according to a "temperature" parameter that altered the threshold for units throughout the model. In the simulations of search in agnosia, the temperature parameter was altered so that there was increased "noise" in the system; that is, there was an increased chance that units were placed into an on state even without strong supporting input, and that units were placed into an off state even if they had good supporting input. This meant that there was an increase in the probability of the incorrect conjunction unit coming on, as conjunctions were

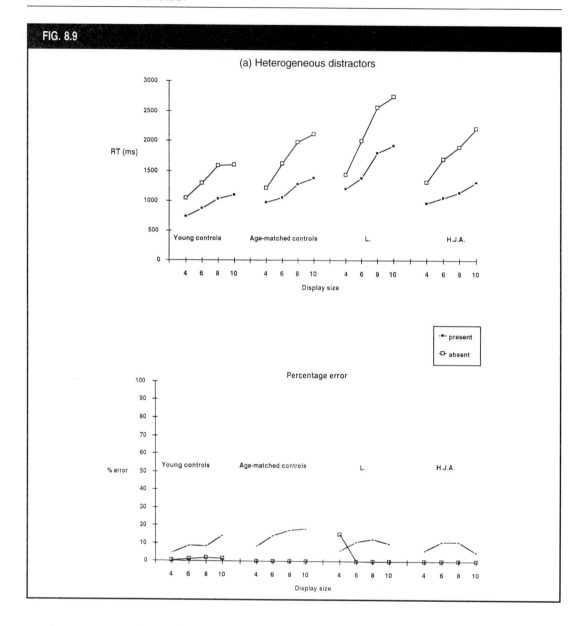

FIG. 8.9

(a) Heterogeneous distractors

encoded, breaking up grouping between similar conjunctions. The net result was that performance was particularly disrupted when conjunction search was among homogeneous distractors (which normally group), as was found with the agnosic patient HJA. With heterogeneous distractors, which normally form competing groups, incorrect coding of conjunctions had little impact; sometimes it hindered performance by disrupting a dominant group but sometimes it facilitated performance by (incorrectly) leading to dominant groups being formed. Figure 8.10 shows performance of the model in search with homogeneous and heterogeneous distractors as the temperature parameter of the system was varied. Humphreys et al. (1992b) also found that increases in the temperature had to affect particular levels in SERR, concerned with encoding and grouping form conjunctions (the conjunction and match–map units; see Fig. 4.18); changes just to the feature

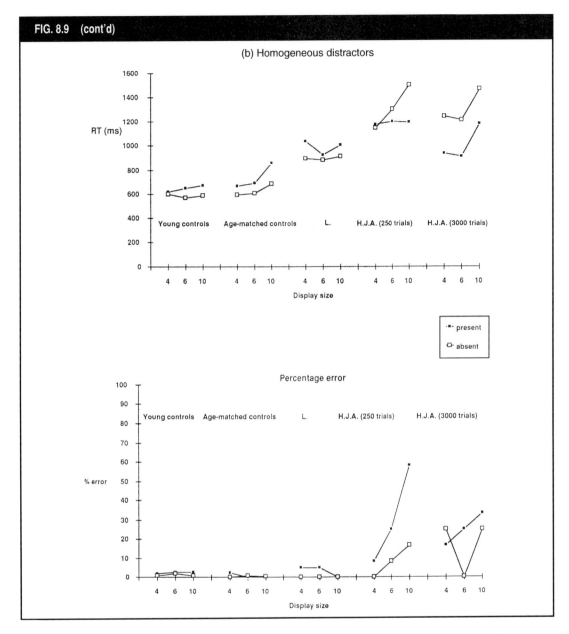

FIG. 8.9 (cont'd)

(b) Homogeneous distractors

RT (ms)

Young controls   Age-matched controls   L.   H.J.A. (250 trials)   H.J.A. (3000 trials)

Display size

present
absent

Percentage error

Young controls   Age-matched controls   L.   H.J.A. (250 trials)   H.J.A. (3000 trials)

% error

Display size

RT and error data for visual search for a form conjunction target (⊥) shown amongst either (a) heterogeneous (T, ⊢, and ⊣) or (b) homogeneous (T) distractors. Data are presented for young control subjects (university students), elderly subjects (over 60 years), an agnosic patient (L) without a problem in visual search and grouping, and HJA, an elderly agnosic patient with a selective problem in visual search and grouping. HJA is specifically impaired in the (easy) search task with homogeneous distractors, whereas he performs at a normal level for his age in the (difficult) search task with heterogeneous distractors. HJA's deficit with homogeneous distractors is not simply due to his having slow RTs; the agnosic patient L also has slow RTs but shows a normal pattern of performance. From Humphreys et al. (1992b).

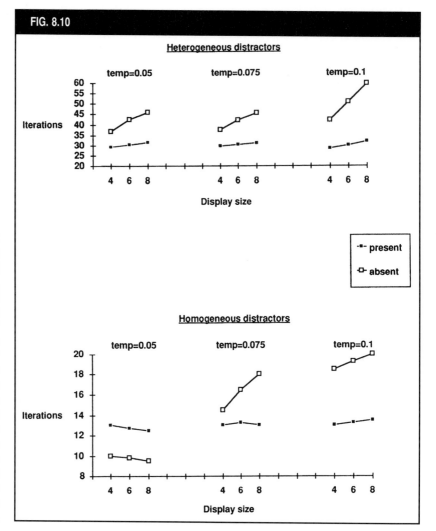

FIG. 8.10

Simulations of visual search performance with heterogeneous and homogeneous distractors, using the SERR model of visual search (Humphreys & Müller, 1993). "Normal" performance occurs when the temperature parameter is set to 0.05. As the temperature parameter is increased, there is more noise in the activation functions. Performance is more affected with homogeneous distractors than with heterogeneous distractors, as is found in some cases of agnosia (see Fig. 8.9).

encoding stage failed to produce differential effects in the search conditions. This is consistent with HJA having good feature detection (as shown in search for targets defined by an orientation difference relative to distractors) but poor parallel encoding of form conjunctions.

The simulations of HJA's performance are of interest not only because they capture a selective disturbance in coding and grouping form information, but because after lesioning the model performed in a somewhat counterintuitive fashion. The search task that was normally performed most efficiently, with homogeneous distractors, suffered most, and the more difficult search task, with

heterogeneous distractors, suffered less. This of course matches the human data (Humphreys et al., 1992a).

Neuropsychological evidence that the easier of two tasks can be the more impaired is important, because it shows that the breakdown in performance cannot simply be due to task difficulty. Task difficulty alone would count if performance depended on a certain level of resource (such as the number of neurons, or the amount of neurotransmitter present) and if this was depleted after brain damage. However, effects on the easier of two tasks indicate that the processing system must be organised into computationally distinct components, and that a particular component required for the easier task is affected differentially. In many of the simulations of neuropsychological disorders it is the more difficult of two processes that is the more affected after lesioning (e.g. in Patterson et al.'s 1989 study of surface dyslexia, where exception words were more affected by lesioning than regular words; note that the RMS$_e$ scores for exception words tended to be higher than those for regular words even in the unlesioned version of the model). In SERR the easier task, search with homogeneous distractors, is more affected because a factor important in search with these distractors — distractor grouping — is selectively disrupted. The research shows that component processes can be functionally isolatable even within highly interactive connectionist models.

One other point to note from this simulation is that, although lesioning affected pattern coding in the model, location coding (in the map of locations) was preserved. Thus, although the lesioned model was poor at grouping items, it nevertheless had information about where elements fell in the visual field and how many elements were present. This dissociation, between impaired pattern recognition and intact location and number judgements mirrors that found with agnosic patients (Humphreys & Riddoch, 1987). Other modelling work that distinguishes between pattern and location coding is taken up in Chapter 9.

8.6.2 Associative agnosia and category-specific anomia

Several connectionist models have attempted to deal with disorders affecting the retrieval of stored knowledge from objects and faces. Some of these models were developed in order to account for normal object and face identification (Burton et al., 1990; Humphreys et al., 1995) and so were introduced in Chapter 4 (sections 4.6 and 4.7); others have been used solely to simulate neuropsychological disorders (Farah & McClelland, 1991; Plaut & Shallice, 1993b). The models also differ in whether local representations were used within a modular architecture or whether more distributed representations were adopted. We review the models before returning to discuss these more general issues concerned with modularity

and distributed representations, beginning with models of object identification.

Humphreys et al. (1995). In Chapter 4 we discussed the interactive activation and competition model of object recognition and naming, implemented by Humphreys et al. (1995) (see Fig. 4.20 for the architecture). This model attempted to specify the processing stages and representations involved in object recognition and naming, including access to specific memorial systems for the structural descriptions (the visual memories of the structure of objects), the semantic memories, and the names of objects. Humphreys et al. also assessed the effects of lesioning on the model's performance. Lesioning was performed at several locations within the model, including the structural descriptions themselves, the weights mapping structural descriptions to semantic representations, and the weights mapping semantic to name representations. Humphreys et al. used input vectors for objects that reflected the similarity of an individual object to other objects in the set. In the normal (unlesioned) model, this variation in similarity across objects led to a general advantage for the identification of non-living things (which tend to be less similar as a class) and for the super-ordinate classification of living things (which tend to be similar as a class). When subject to "across the board" lesioning, affecting the weights and activation states of all objects, these differences between living and non-living things in identification became exaggerated. In general, lesioning had little effect on super-ordinate classification; as that requires that several exemplars are mapped through to a common set of semantic units, disrupting the activation states associated with individual exemplars had no great effect. Lesioning did affect naming, however, and this was particularly the case for living things, due to the high overlap in the input descriptions for these objects *a priori*. In studies of associative-type agnosic patients, who seem either to have impaired structural knowledge abut objects (Sartori & Job, 1988) or to have normal access to stored structural descriptions but not to semantic knowledge abut objects (Hillis & Caramazza, 1995a; Riddoch & Humphreys, 1987b; Sheridan

& Humphreys, 1993; Stewart et al., 1992), the identification of living things has largely been found to be worse than that of non-living things. Note also that, in such cases, patients typically remain able to make super-ordinate classification judgements to objects, as was also true of the lesioned model.

One other observation was that, even when lesioning affected only naming but not object recognition (i.e. the lesion was to the connections from semantic to name representations), identification performance was still differentially impaired for living relative to non-living things. This again matches neuropsychological evidence on so-called category-specific anomias. For instance, Hart, Berndt, and Caramazza (1985) and Farah and Wallace (1992) have both reported patients apparently with good retrieval of semantic knowledge about objects but with selectively impaired naming of living things (in both cases, fruits and vegetables). Such a deficit follows from an interactive model of object naming, such as that proposed by Humphreys et al., in which activation is transmitted through the system so that perceptual differences between living and non-living things are carried through to affect the naming process.

In contrast to the patients with impaired recognition or naming of living things, some reports have been made of the opposite pattern of disorder, with either access to semantic information being worse for non-living relative to living things (Warrington & McCarthy, 1983, 1987) or naming being worse for non-living things (Hillis & Caramazza, 1990; Sacchett & Humphreys, 1992). Within the interactive activation and competition model of Humphreys et al. (1995) such reports are difficult to explain, as the effects of differential perceptual overlap favour object identification for non-living things. However, the effects can be accounted for if the lesion is not global but more selective, affecting the stored units and connections for the representations of non-living relative to living things. This could occur if the semantic representations for living and non-living things tended also to be anatomically distinct (see Caramazza & Shelton, 1998; Sheridan & Humphreys, 1993).

One final piece of neuropsychological evidence that fits with the connectionist approach embodied in this model comes from work showing that patients can make different patterns of errors according to the modality of the response. For example, patients may make semantic errors when trying to name pictures, but produce the correct response in written naming (Caramazza & Hillis, 1990b), or vice versa (Caramazza & Hillis, 1991). Also, patients who make semantic errors in both output modalities may show little consistency in the two modalities across items — they will make a semantic error to one item in naming but not in writing, and a semantic error to another item in writing but not in naming (Miceli, Benvegnu, Capasso, & Caramazza, 1997). The fact that the patient produces the correct output when using one response modality suggests that they are able to access appropriate semantic information, and that the problem resides in accessing a particular response following semantic access. This in turn suggests that semantic information directly activates output responses (e.g. phonemic representations for naming, orthographic representations for writing), even before processing at the semantic level is completed — otherwise the incorrect response should not be semantically related to the stimulus. The reader will recall the debate in Chapter 6 about whether information for object naming is transmitted in a discrete or continuous fashion. The neuropsychological evidence here indicates a continuous process, which fits with interactive activation accounts of naming (and writing).

Farah and McClelland (1991). A somewhat different approach to the topic of category-specific object recognition disorders is that of Farah and McClelland (1991). They had normal subjects list the attributes associated with living and non-living things, and found that visual–perceptual attributes were frequently listed for living things, whereas functional attributes tended to be listed for non-living things. This difference between the attributes used to define living and non-living things had been noted before in the neuropsychological literature on category-specific recognition disorders (Warrington & Shallice, 1984). Farah and McClelland incorporated the assumption into a connectionist model of semantic memory using a distributed associative memory architecture (cf. Rumelhart & McClelland, 1985; see Chapter 3). They used three pools of processing units, one representing the names of items, one the visual properties of objects, and one the semantic memory representations of objects. These semantic units were coded according to whether they represented the visual–perceptual or functional attributes of objects, although all units within the semantic system were interconnected. Each item was represented as a pattern of +1 and −1s over the name and vision units, and by a subset of +1 and −1s in the semantic system.The proportion of visual–perceptual semantic units assigned a non-zero value in the coding of a stimulus, relative to the number of functional semantic units, differed for living and non-living things; for living things about seven times more visual–perceptual than functional units were involved, whereas for non-living things the proportions of visual–perceptual to functional units were about equal. The model was trained using the delta rule (Chapter 3, section 3.1) to associate the correct name and semantic units with a given visual input, and the correct visual and semantic units when given a name input. The architecture of the model is shown in Fig. 8.11.

To simulate the effect of lesioning on semantic memory, Farah and McClelland eliminated varying numbers of either visual–perceptual or functional units within the semantic system of their model. They then approximated a picture–word matching task, as might be performed with patients, by either presenting visual inputs to the model and monitoring for the recall of the name representations, or by presenting the name and monitoring the recall of the visual representation. Responses were scored as correct if outputs were closer to the target representation than to the representation of any other members of the training set. The results of the simulations are shown in Fig. 8.12. When visual–perceptual units within semantic memory were damaged, recall was worse for living things than for non-living things. In contrast, when functional units in semantic memory were damaged, recall was worse for non-living things than for living things. Farah and McClelland argued that, because they used a distributed associative memory system, their model is not functionally organised into distinct semantic stores for visual–perceptual or for functional attributes of objects (nor for living things as opposed to non-living things); nevertheless, there is a category-specific breakdown in performance. They also noted that, after damage to the visual–perceptual units in semantic memory, there was

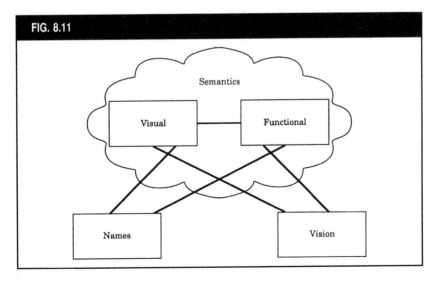

FIG. 8.11

Semantics

Visual   Functional

Names   Vision

Architecture of the model of semantic memory simulated by Farah and McClelland (1991).

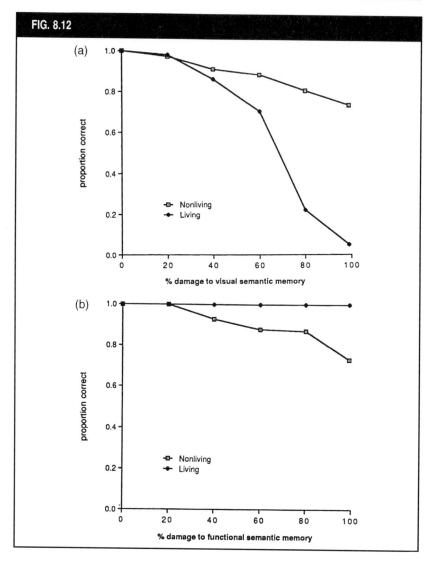

FIG. 8.12

(a) Effects of different degrees of damage to visual–perceptual units within the semantic system of Farah and McClelland's (1991) model. The task was to associate representations of names and pictures of either living things (diamonds) or non-living things (squares). (b) The effects of different degrees of damage to functional units within the semantic system of Farah and McClelland (1991). Performance with living things is shown in diamonds, and performance with non-living things is shown in squares.

impaired activation of functional units in the semantic system. This is a consequence of the interconnectivity between the visual–perceptual and functional units within the semantic system.

Farah and McClelland's model shows how apparent differences in picture–word matching for living and non-living things can be due to a contrast between the ways in which items from these categories are represented in memory, with either visual–perceptual or functional information being differentially important for different classes of object. A category-specific breakdown in recognition need not directly reflect a categorical organisation of semantic memory (see Warrington & Shallice, 1984, for an earlier rendition of this argument). Note however that to produce the more severe effect of lesioning on the recognition of living things, more visual–perceptual to functional semantic units had to be impaired. For this to occur within a real brain, there would need to be neurological localisation of the visual–perceptual and semantic units. Thus, to explain the neuro-psychological data, functional interactivity (as in Farah and McClelland's distributed associative semantic memory system) would need to operate on top of distinct neurological structures.

One problem with Farah and McClelland's interactive account is that some patients have been reported with severely impaired visual–perceptual memory for objects, but with intact functional information when probed with the names of objects (Hart & Gordon, 1992; Riddoch & Humphreys, 1993). Such dissociations are difficult to account for if visual–perceptual and functional attributes are both functionally interconnected and accessed in an identical manner from names and visual input alike — as in Farah and McClelland's model (remember that, in their model, there were always knock-on effects of lesioning perceptual units on the retrieval of functional as well as perceptual knowledge). The dissociations perhaps fit better with a model in which visual–perceptual and functional–semantic knowledge about objects is separable at a functional as well as at a neurological level, allowing visual–perceptual knowledge to be accessed directly from vision and functional knowledge to be accessed independently from object names; this would hold for the model proposed by Humphreys et al. (1995). In the last case, a patient with impaired visual–perceptual knowledge could still have intact access to functional information from an object's name. Because the model of Humphreys et al. has a differentiated structure, separating structural and semantic knowledge, it can also capture the opposite pattern of disorder; namely when a patient has intact access to structural knowledge but impaired access to functional knowledge from vision. We review this point again later, when we discuss the disorder "optic aphasia".

McCarthy and Warrington (1988) further documented a patient who had apparently impaired retrieval of semantic information about living things which was most severe when given the names of the stimuli. That is, the problem was not only category-specific but also modality-specific. In both the model of Farah and McClelland, and also that of Humphreys et al., a deficit that is most pronounced for living things can be traced to an impairment of visual–perceptual knowledge (the structural description system, in the terms used by Humphreys et al.). However, why should such a deficit occur only with name input? To account for this both Farah and McClelland and

Humphreys et al. propose that there would need to be a lesion affecting the connections either from object names to the visual–perceptual units or from the functional–semantic units to the structural description system (allowed only by the model of Humphreys et al.). Such a lesion from name information would lead to a deficit that is modality- as well as category-specific.

In summary, the models of Humphreys et al. (1995) and Farah and McClelland (1991) capture some aspects of category-specific recognition impairments in similar ways. For the model of Humphreys et al., a tendency for living things to be more difficult to identify than non-living things is inherent in the system, so that a deficit for living things can emerge from a lesion affecting performance across-the-board. A deficit for the recognition of non-living things would have to arise from a lesion specific to the units involved in recognising these stimuli. For the model of Farah and McClelland, both impairments (to living and to non-living things) would have to arise from lesions to the units that are differentially important for recognising each class of stimulus (visual–perceptual and functional units respectively). The model of Humphreys et al. is also structured, having separable pools of visual–perceptual and semantic units, which can be accessed independently from different modalities. This structure may capture patterns of strong dissociation (e.g. where there is intact retrieval of functional knowledge along with impaired visual–perceptual knowledge) better than an unstructured memory system accessed in the same way from different modalities. At the close of this chapter, we reproduce a paper from Farah (1994) that summarises her attempts to apply connectionist models to a number of neuropsychological disorders (including category-specific recognition problems). The paper illustrates one approach to modelling in this field.

Plaut and Shallice (1993b). In addition to frank disorders of object recognition and anomias that affect naming across different modalities of input, cases have been reported in which patients show a naming disorder that is more severe for one modality of presentation than for others. The term *optic aphasic* is applied to patients who find it particularly difficult to name visually presented objects (Gil et al., 1985; Hillis & Caramazza, 1995a; Lhermitte & Beauvois, 1973; Riddoch & Humphreys, 1987b). Optic aphasia has been distinguished from agnosia because optic aphasics are able to mime the use of seen objects that they cannot name. From this it has often been assumed that optic aphasics have intact access to semantic information from objects, and that the problem is solely one of naming. As we will show, there are grounds to dispute this argument.

To explain why a naming disorder should be confined to vision, theorists have argued that there may be two "routes" to naming for visually presented objects. These two routes are based on the activation of different forms of semantic knowledge. A direct route associates visual–semantic memory representations to names; a second, indirect route, associates verbal–semantic representations to names (see Davidoff & de Bleser, 1993). A functional architecture for such an account is illustrated in Fig. 8.13. On this account, optic aphasic patients have a lesion that disconnects the visual–semantic memory system from both the names of objects and from verbal–semantic knowledge. As a consequence, the ability of such patients to name from vision is impaired, although they can access visual–semantic information. The relatively intact ability of the patients to gesture to seen objects is taken as evidence for access to some form of semantic knowledge being preserved.

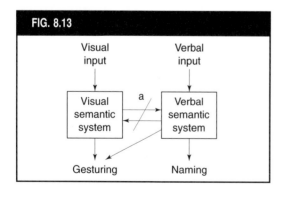

FIG. 8.13

A functional architecture to account for the disorder of optic aphasia. One possible site of lesion would be at "a".

However, it can also be argued that such patients do not have intact access to semantic information about objects from vision. For instance, in cases where access to semantic information from vision has been probed in some detail, patients have shown impairments (Hillis & Caramazza, 1995a; Riddoch & Humphreys, 1987b). Nevertheless, the same patients can demonstrate good access to stored visual knowledge/structural descriptions, as tested by means of difficult object decision tasks. These tasks are the equivalent of lexical decision tasks used frequently in studies of word recognition (Chapter 6). Patients are asked to differentiate between pictures of real objects and those of non-objects, made by combining the parts of real objects. Although such tasks can be difficult even for normal subjects, patients can perform at a high level and yet still show impaired access to detailed semantic knowledge about the objects. Thus there appears to be access to stored structural descriptions along with impaired access to semantic knowledge. As we noted earlier, this pattern of deficit can arise in the model of Humphreys et al. (1995) if the lesion affects the transmission of information from the structural descriptions to the semantic units, leaving object decision intact but naming impaired. The ability to mime may be relatively spared in these patients either if there are direct connections from the structural description to a set of associated actions (Riddoch & Humphreys, 1987b) or if the visual properties of objects, along with partially activated semantic knowledge, leads to appropriate gesturing (Hillis & Caramazza, 1995a). Models such as those of Farah and McClelland (1991), which do not separate different forms of stored knowledge, find it more difficult to account for such a pattern of dissociation in which one ability stays intact.

Plaut and Shallice (1993b) modelled the disorder of optic aphasia in some detail, being particularly concerned to generate the same types of errors in their model as are found with human patients. Optic aphasic patients make a variety of naming errors, including errors that are either (i) visually related to target objects, (ii) semantically related, (iii) mixed (visually and semantically related), and (iv) perseverative. Perseverative errors occur when the event (the stimulus, the response, or some combination) on a prior trial affects the response on the next; for example, when the response on a prior trial was "spoon" and on the next trial the patient makes an error of naming a fork as a "spoon". Plaut and Shallice (1993b) used a modified version of the attractor model originally developed by Hinton and Shallice (1991) to model deep dyslexia (section 8.3.4), but instead of the input representations conforming to graphemes (for words) they corresponded to the visual features of objects (e.g. units corresponded to the shape, size, colour, texture, and relative positions of parts). In addition, Plaut and Shallice used two forms of weights on the connections between units. The *long-term weights* corresponded to the standard weights used in connectionist modelling, and were subject to long-term learning, instantiated in this case by back-propagation through time (section 8.3.4). A further set of *short-term weights* were added however, the values of which corresponded to a rapidly decaying weighted average over stimulus presentations of the correlation between the states of the units that the weights connect. Thus if two connecting units tended to have correlated states, the short-term weight between them would have a high value; if two connecting units tended to have uncorrelated states, the short-term weight between them would have a low value. The activation values that were passed on from one unit to another were a function of the sum of the long-term weight plus the short-term weight value, multiplied by the activation value in the input unit. As we shall elaborate in the final chapter (Chapter 9), short-term weights may play a useful computational role in connectionist models. Plaut and Shallice did not use them for computational reasons, however, but in order to make the model sensitive to recently occurring events in a run of trials.

Plaut and Shallice trained their model to associate visual input representations for objects with states in a set of semantic "sememe" units (see Fig. 8.14 for the architecture of the model). After learning, the model was lesioned (a random set of connections was removed), with lesioning taking place at different locations within the model. Performance was most strongly affected if the lesion affected connections from the visual units to the intermediate units (Fig. 8.15), and then if it affected the connections from the intermediate units to the sememe units; performance was least affected by lesioning the connections between the sememe and the clean-up units. Perhaps more interestingly, the lesioned model generated high proportions of mixed (visual & semantic) errors when objects were misidentified, particularly if lesioning affected connections leading into the semantic system (visual → intermediate, or intermediate → semantic). The proportions of mixed errors were even higher than those observed in the simulations of deep dyslexia (Hinton & Shallice, 1991). This is because, unlike words, there are non-arbitrary mappings between the visual representations of objects and their semantics. In an attractor model, this has the following effect. When the model is lesioned, activation values for objects fall outside of their proper "basins of attraction", but because of the correlation between visual attributes and semantic properties of objects, neighbouring basins of attraction into which activation is mapped are likely to correspond to items that are both visually and semantically related to targets; mixed (visual & semantic) errors result. These high proportions of mixed (visual & semantic errors) are also found with optic aphasic patients.

Plaut and Shallice further examined the errors made by the model as a function of the item and the response on the previous trial. They found a reliable number of perseverative responses were made, and that these were most likely when the prior response and the subsequent target objects were semantically related. Perseverations were found after lesions to all tested locations, although they were mostly likely after lesions to connections between the clean-up and semantic units. This is because a high short-term weight at the clean-up unit level can override a weakened clean-up process for the correct semantics of the stimulus, leading to a perseveration.

Although Plaut and Shallice's model does not (and does not attempt to) capture all aspects of optic

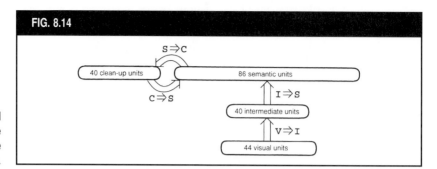

FIG. 8.14

Architecture of the model of Plaut and Shallice (1993b) used to simulate optic aphasia.

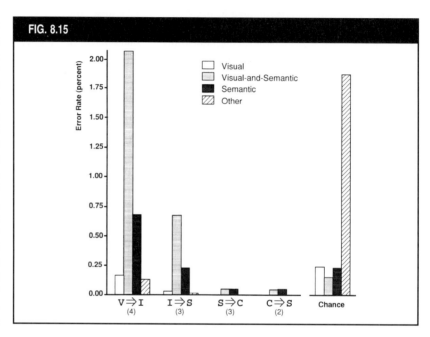

FIG. 8.15

The distribution of error types after lesioning to the model of object recognition proposed by Plaut and Shallice (1993b). Lesion sites: V→I, from visual units to the intermediate units; I→S, from the intermediate units to the semantic units; S→C, from the semantic units to the clean-up units; C→S, from the clean-up units to the semantic units. Also illustrated are the proportions of each category of error that would be expected by chance (in this case, primarily "other" errors).

aphasia (e.g. the relatively good ability to gesture to seen objects), it does again illustrate how variables affecting different levels of representation (the visual and semantic characteristics of objects) can be closely coupled within interactive connectionist models, leading to errors that do not reflect the locus of a lesion in any simple way. The model also demonstrates that access to any form of semantic information does not need to be intact to account for the naming errors in optic aphasic patients. Outside the specific application to optic aphasia, the model illustrates how short-term weights can lead to sensitivity to recent events in learning, and to an over-determining role of these recent events after lesioning.

8.7 FACE RECOGNITION DISORDERS: PROSOPAGNOSIA

8.7.1 Burton et al. (1991)

Visual agnosia in humans frequently co-occurs with disorders of face recognition, although it is possible for each to occur in isolation (De Renzi, 1986; Rumiati, Humphreys, Riddoch, & Bateman, 1994). Thus it is possible to model aspects of the visual recognition process that may be specific to faces, and that therefore show a selective pattern of impairment after brain damage: the neuro-psychological syndrome of prosopagnosia. Burton et al. (1991) applied the interactive activation and competition model of face recognition (Burton et al., 1990) to evidence on covert face recognition in prosopagnosia.

Some prosopagnosic patients, while showing profoundly impaired face recognition, have also been reported as showing "covert recognition" of faces (although this is by no mean true of all prosopagnosic patients; see McNeil & Warrington, 1991). Covert recognition has been demonstrated using face–name matching and face–name learning tasks. For example, when required to judge whether a written name is that of an actor or politician, performance is normally faster if the face of a related rather than an unrelated person is presented simultaneously. This has been shown in patients who are unable to identify the people involved from their faces. Similarly, the time for the patients to learn face–name pairings is less if the correct relative to the incorrect pairings are used (de Haan, Young, & Newcombe, 1987). However, there are limits on covert recognition even in patients who show some effects. For instance, Young and de Haan found that their patient did not learn correct face–occupation pairings more quickly than incorrect ones, although correct face–name pairs were learned more quickly than incorrect face–name pairs. It would appear that access to semantic information for face–occupation learning cannot be easily achieved, and that activation from name information (e.g. as in face–name learning) may be necessary to generate the effect.

The Burton et al. (1990) model of face recognition has independent pools of units for face recognition, person identification, and semantic/name information (the FRUs, PINs, and Semantic Units). Prosopagnosia has been simulated by reducing the weights on the connections from the FRUs to the PINs so that PIN units fail to become activated to an arbitrary threshold level (Burton et al., 1991). This means that faces may not be identified; also, if activation at the PIN level is used as the basis for familiarity judgements, then the model is unable to perform such tasks (as found with some prosopagnosics; de Haan et al., 1987). Nevertheless, sub-threshold activation of the PIN for a given face was still able to produce sufficient activation in the PINs of related faces (by inter-

actions with the semantic representations) to generate semantic priming when related faces are presented. To simulate effects with name inputs, Burton et al. introduced units corresponding to words that fed through to the PINs to enable familiarity decisions to words to be made. If a different (unrecognised) face was presented simultaneously with the name, decision times to the names were slowed. That is, the model showed covert recognition of faces.

8.7.2 Farah, O'Reilly, and Vecera (1993)

A contrasting model of covert recognition in prosopagnosia was proposed by Farah et al. (1993). They used a model with two sets of input units, corresponding to names and to visual descriptions of faces, and a set of semantic output units. The model was trained (using contrastive Hebbian learning, a form of learning similar to that used in Boltzmann machine models; Movellan, 1991; see Chapter 2) to associate names and visual descriptions of faces (presented together) with semantic representations of the faces (see Fig. 8.16 for the architecture of the model). There were 16 face and name units in each pool, and 18 semantic units, and each stimulus was represented by an arbitrary pattern of inputs and outputs. Following training, the model was damaged by the removal of varying numbers of face input or face-to-semantic hidden units; this severely reduced the ability of the model to produce the correct name to a face input (when given a choice out of 10 faces, taking as output the nearest vector to that produced by the lesioned model). It was then tested in two tasks shown to be sensitive to covert recognition in some prosopagnosics: face–name learning and occupation decisions to names. In Fig. 8.17, data are presented for the face–name learning task. The graphs show the percent correct retrieval of face names (to within 2 bits) when the lesioned model was retrained with either correct (previously trained) or incorrectly paired names, as a function of the re-learning trial (the epoch number). It is clear that, across different sizes of lesion, the model re-learns correct face–name pairings more quickly than incorrect ones; there is covert recognition. In addition, when the lesioned model was presented with the task of

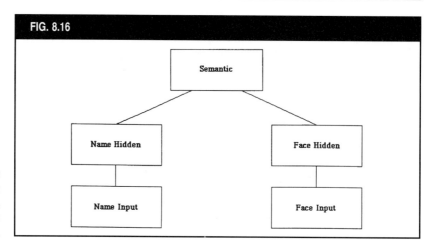

FIG. 8.16

Architecture of the model of face recognition proposed by Farah et al. (1993). From Farah (1994).

classifying the occupation of names (retrieving semantic representations from name inputs), performance was better when a face was presented simultaneously from the same occupation category as the name relative to when they belonged to different categories. This last result held for all but the most severely lesioned versions of the model.

In the Farah et al. model, face–name learning takes place more rapidly for correct than for incorrect pairings because, for correct pairings, the weights are already some way towards their correct values, even when learning takes place after damage to the model. For incorrect pairings, the model starts the re-learning phase with the weights not necessarily related to their final states. In addition, in the name–occupation decision task, even partial activation of semantic units, from faces, is sufficient to alter the efficiency of retrieving semantic information from names.

However, there are some problems for both the Burton et al. and the Farah et al. models in explaining the full pattern of data from prosopagnosic patients. Consider data on the limits on covert recognition in re-learning tasks (Young & de Haan, 1988). In both models semantic interference effects from semantically related faces on decisions to names is attributed to the faces partially activating semantic knowledge; however, if this is the case, then correct face–occupation relationships should also be learned more quickly than incorrect ones. As we have indicated, this is not necessarily true.

One other point concerns whether those patients who do and those who do not show covert recognition are simply differentiated in terms of the degree of damage to their face recognition system. In the Farah et al. simulations, covert recognition is manifest for all but the most damaged networks, and partial activation of stored knowledge should be a direct function of the amount of damage the network has sustained. However, McNeil and Warrington (1991) reported that the degree of prosopagnosia found in face matching tasks did not necessarily predict whether patients showed covert recognition. One patient with good face matching did not manifest covert recognition; two others with poor face matching did manifest covert recognition. McNeil and Warrington, like Burton et al., propose that patients with covert recognition have intact FRUs but access to the PINs is blocked. Hence such patients cannot judge the familiarity of faces. McNeil and Warrington argue that covert recognition is caused by top-down activation from names which enables sub-threshold activation in the FRUs to be accessed. Note that activation of the FRUs may be sub-threshold because of the poor perceptual processing in their patients who showed poor face matching. In contrast, their patient with good face matching without covert recognition may have lost the FRUs themselves. This kind of account explains the data on matching and covert recognition in terms of access to different types of knowledge store; such data are perhaps less easy to

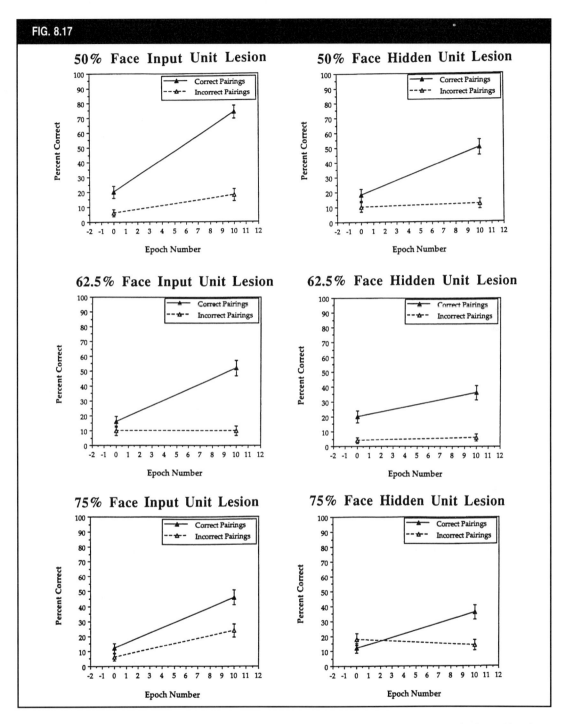

FIG. 8.17

Performance of the Farah et al. (1993) model of face recognition after lesioning different percentages of units at either the face input level or in the hidden units mapping from face inputs to semantic representations. The task was to learn face–name pairings. Note that, in all cases, correct face–name pairings were learned more rapidly than incorrect face–name pairings. From Farah (1994).

account for in terms of a unitary recognition network, such as that of Farah et al., which does not distinguish between different forms of stored representation.

Overall we conclude that models with modular structures, differentiating between different forms of stored representation, may be better able than unitary networks to capture the full pattern of human data. How networks may develop such modular structures is taken up in the final chapter.

8.8 UNILATERAL VISUAL NEGLECT

A type of visual processing disorder that is more common than agnosia and prosopagnosia is unilateral visual neglect. Visual neglect can be estimated as occurring in up to 50% of patients with right hemisphere damage (Fullerton, McSherry, & Stout, 1986). Patients with visual neglect typically fail to respond appropriately to stimuli presented on the side of space contralateral to their lesion (Heilman, 1979). Neglect is often thought of as a disorder of attention, as patients may improve performance when cued to attend to the affected side (Riddoch & Humphreys, 1983) and identification or even detection of the contralesional stimulus is particularly poor when a competing stimulus is presented simultaneously on the unaffected (ipsilesional) side (even when identification and detection of a single contralesional stimulus is relatively good; the phenomenon of "extinction"; see Karnath, 1988). Alternatively, theorists have argued that the disorder reflects distortion of a patient's internal representation of space, so that they have either "lost" the representation of the left side of space or there is some form of compression of the left side (e.g. Bisiach & Luzzatti, 1978; Halligan & Marshall, 1994). As we shall, these different accounts — of neglect as a disorder of attention or representation — are not necessarily incompatible, and connectionist modelling of neglect shows how the accounts may be reconciled. However, it should also be noted that visual neglect is probably not a unitary syndrome,

and subtly different disorders can be separated with careful study (see Robertson & Marshall, 1993). Models will need to be able to show how the different functional problems can arise.

8.8.1 MORSEL

We have already reviewed one attempt to simulate aspects of visual neglect, in Mozer's MORSEL model of reading (Mozer, 1991). In that model, neglect is attributed to a spatially selective lesion affecting an "attentional module" that acts to modulate early visual processing. Units in the attentional module compete to fix attention to one spatial region, and this competition can be influenced by reducing the effectiveness of units to favour on one side of space. In fact MORSEL has not only been applied to data on neglect dyslexia (section 8.3.2) but also to a task commonly used to measure neglect in clinical settings: line bisection (Mozer, Halligan, & Marshall, 1997). Here the patient is asked to mark the centre of a line, and, typically, their bisections are biased towards the "good" (ipsilesional) side of space (e.g. to the right of the true centre, in cases of left neglect). Line bisection in MORSEL was simulated by having the "attentional module" interact with retinal input until a stable state was reached, and then by assuming that the attended region (the region activated within the attentional module) is mapped onto a motor process for the bisection response. When a graded lesion was given to the model (more severe on the left than the right side of space), attention was biased towards the right end of the line. With a linear gradient, there was a linear relation between the amount of neglect of the line and the line length — a finding present in human neglect patients (Bisiach, Bulgarelli, Sterzi, & Vallar, 1983; Riddoch & Humphreys, 1983). Also, because the graded lesion was applied across the field, neglect in the model was largely independent of the line's location in the field; in each case, there was a bias towards the right end of the line.

Other connectionist simulations of aspects of the neglect syndrome have been carried out by Cohen et al. (1994), by Humphreys, Olson, Romani, and Riddoch (1996), and by Humphreys and Heinke (1997, 1998).

8.8.2 Cohen et al. (1994)

Cohen et al. modelled one classic finding with neglect patients: the so-called "attentional disengagement" problem under visual cueing conditions. We will describe the empirical result.

Neglect is classically associated with lesions to the right parietal lobe. Posner, Walker, Friedrich, and Rafal (1984) showed that patients with right parietal lesions demonstrated a particular pattern of deficit in an attentional cueing task. In the task, subjects are required to make a simple reaction time detection response to a light onset, which appears in one of two boxes presented respectively in the right and left visual fields. Prior to the target appearing, one of the boxes may be briefly illuminated to provide a spatial cue concerning the target's location. The target appears in the cued location on a majority of trials (75%); on the remaining 25% of the trials the target is in the uncued location (in the other visual field). Posner et al. found that patients with right parietal lesions were especially poor in a condition in which they were cued to attend to a box in their (good) right visual field and the target appeared in the uncued left visual field. They termed this a deficit in "disengaging" attention from a cued location in the ipsilesional field. They further suggested that a problem in disengaging attention could be an important component of the neglect syndrome. Patients with right parietal lesions may show neglect of stimuli in their left visual field because they fail to disengage attention from stimuli in the right visual field. In addition, Posner et al. concluded that a specific component of the attentional system, concerned with disengaging attention from attended spatial positions, was located in the parietal lobe.

Cohen et al. implemented a simple connectionist system (Fig. 8.18), for orienting attention to a spatial position. The model had inputs from two spatial positions, perhaps corresponding to the left and right visual fields. Activation from units in each position activated attentional units linked to each position, and both the information in each field and the attentional units activated a detection response system. The attentional units at a given location were mutually reinforcing and they were reciprocally connected to the perceptual units for each location, allowing attention to facilitate visual processing at attended locations. The attentional units at each location were also connected in an inhibitory fashion to those in the other location, forcing attention to be focused on one location. The weights on the connections were chosen by hand, and the number of cycles required by the network for the detection system to reach threshold was used as the measure of performance. The effects of attentional cueing on performance were assessed by pre-activating one location for a small number of cycles before presenting the target at either the same (cued) or the other (uncued) location. Reaction times (RTs) were faster to targets at cued relative to uncued locations. In addition, the effects of parietal lobe lesions were mimicked by removing some of the attentional units on the affected side. The result of this was to unbalance the competition between the attentional units under the cueing conditions. In particular, performance was very poor when the cue was presented at the unaffected location and the target at the affected location, because then the unimpaired attentional units were given an additional boost, inhibiting activation to the lesioned side. This is the pattern of performance linked to a problem in attentional disengagement by Posner et al. (1984). What is of interest is that the model does not have a specific processing mechanism for attentional engagement or disengagement; rather attentional engagement and disengagement are states of the attentional network as it operates to orient attention in space.

8.8.3 SERR

The model of Cohen et al. is extremely simple, and cannot be used to capture wider aspects of the neglect syndrome, especially those concerned with aspects of pattern or object coding, as it has no mechanisms for dealing with pattern information. Interestingly, recent work on neglect suggests that the performance of patients can be affected by grouping between elements at different parts of the visual field, and that, for some patients, the absolute positions of stimuli in the visual field may be less important than their relative positions (left or right of other objects). For instance, Ward, Goodrich, and Driver (1994)

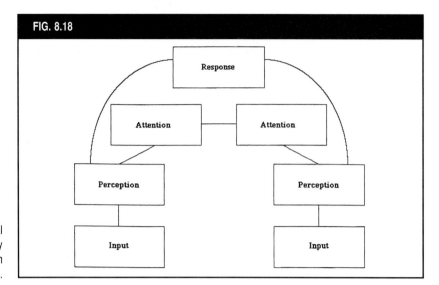

FIG. 8.18

The model of visual orienting proposed by Cohen et al. (1994). From Farah (1994).

used a so-called extinction paradigm, in which detection performance when a single stimulus was presented in the left or right visual field was contrasted with the detection of two stimuli (in the left and right fields respectively). The stimuli could either form a perceptual group (e.g. they might be two brackets positioned to have collinear side; [ ]) or they were unrelated and unlikely to form a perceptual group (e.g. [o). They reported data from two patients with parietal damage who were relatively good at detecting stimuli presented alone in their (impaired) left visual field; however the patients showed extinction with two unrelated stimuli, detecting only the right field stimulus. Interestingly, detection of both stimuli was much improved if the stimuli were grouped. Humphreys et al. (1996) reported similar effects, using a task in which the patient had to report a central target at fixation. Performance was again improved by grouping between stimuli; it was also affected by the position of the central target relative to the other stimuli in the field. Performance on the central target was much better when it was to the right of a distractor than when it was to the left of the distractor.

Humphreys et al. went on to simulate these effects in the SERR model of grouping and visual search (Chapter 4, Fig. 4.18). They introduced spatial lesions affecting either of two parts of the model: the map of locations or the maps coding

high-level form junctions (T junctions). In the model the map of locations contains units that respond solely to the location of stimuli in the field, and these units act to gate activity coming into the junction maps. The junction maps serve to group elements together. The lesions took the form of reducing the probability that units were placed in an active state on any given iteration of the model. Both lesions led to a pattern of extinction in which the model was able to detect a target presented alone in the impaired field, but there was poor detection of the same target when a distractor was presented simultaneously in the unimpaired field. This extinction effect is due to there being competition for selection between stimuli at the match map level. Strong activation for the distractor can lead to inhibition of units responding to the target, particularly when activation of the target units is impaired. Consequently there is a failure to detect the target if stimuli are only presented briefly to the model. A similar effect emerged if the target was maintained at the centre of the field and the distractor was presented either to the (impaired) left or (unimpaired) right of the target, and the lesion gradually became more severe across the visual field (i.e. there was a gradient rather than a step function for the lesion across space). With a gradient lesion there is always a bias for the item on the relatively unimpaired side, irrespective of the absolute spatial positions of the stimuli. This finding of a location-based bias that produces effects that are not fixed to one spatial position matches the results from Mozer et al. (1997), who also applied a lesion that was graded across space. What is important for models with internal competition is the relative rather than the absolute states of activation, and it is these relative states that are affected by a graded lesion.

In addition, Humphreys et al. noted two effects of grouping on selection after the model was lesioned, which depended on whether the distractor was encoded as a known object by the model. SERR has hard-wired representations for certain simple objects, Ts at varying locations. These items are individually represented at two levels: within the junction maps (and so form perceptual groups when there are identical forms in the field) and within the templates, that serve to detect the presence of targets (see Fig. 4.18). Humphreys et al. contrasted performance when the distractor had stored match map and template units (e.g. when the distractor was a T) and when it had no associated stored representations. Also, when the model had no associated stored representations the distractor either contained similar features to the target or it had dissimilar features (e.g. using ⌐ and ⌐ as the distractors respectively, for a target ⊥). When the distractor was not a known object but contained features present in the target, target detection was good; this held even when the target was in the lesioned part of the field and the distractor was in the unlesioned field. In this case similarity between the target and the distractor benefited target identification. In the model, this occurred because the similar "non-object" distractor activated features that became grouped with those of the target, supporting report of "weak" targets in the lesioned field. This result matches that found by Ward et al. (1994), where grouping between stimuli reduced extinction in human patients.

The second finding occurred when distractors could be represented as objects in the model (i.e. when distractors, like targets, had template representations). Now target identification was worse when targets and distractors had features in common. For the model, features shared between the target and distractor led to cross-activation of representations for both stimuli. However, this cross-activation was asymmetric, with the template for the item in the good field gaining the more activation, and inhibiting the template for the item in the impaired field. A similar distractor in the good field then provided even more competition for the selection of a target in the impaired field than when the distractor was dissimilar (and note that such template-based competition is eliminated when the distractor does not have a template, as in the first simulations of neglect in SERR). The net effect was that, when targets and distractors could be represented as objects in their own right, similarity between the stimuli was detrimental to target report. Interestingly, a similar result with neglect patients was documented by Baylis, Driver, and Rafal (1993), who found that extinction was increased when patients were presented with two identical letters relative to when they were presented with different letters, and simply had to report how many letters there were. SERR, when lesioned, directly mimics the two different effects of similarity on neglect that have been reported in the human literature. It does this in a unifying fashion, and predicts that the differing effects are a function of whether targets and distractors compete as separate objects (when similarity is harmful) or group to form a single object description (when similarity is beneficial).

Like the model of Cohen et al. (1994), SERR also simulates the "disengagement" deficit found after parietal lesions. Essentially, identification of a single target in the impaired field, or of a target preceded by a brief, valid spatial cue, is reasonable; identification of the same target when a second stimulus is placed in the unlesioned field is poor. This occurs because of the competition for selection between the stimuli, which becomes spatially biased due to the lesion. It seems likely that a disengagement deficit will arise in any model in which there is spatial competition for selection between stimuli at different regions of field, when activation from one region of field is weakened. What then becomes important in distinguishing the models is whether they can account for the variety of other effects found with neglect patients (such as the effects of grouping between visual elements).

8.8.4 SAIM

Models such as MORSEL and SERR account for aspects of neglect that are "field-independent" in terms of a graded lesion, so that there is a bias to the ipsilesional side irrespective of the absolute position of items in the field. Results that may be somewhat difficult for such models to accommodate have been reported by Driver, Baylis and Rafal (1992) and by Humphreys and Heinke (1998). These investigators have found that neglect patients can be better at reporting the right side of an object in their left field relative to when they have to report the left side of an object in their right field. In such cases, the effects of position within the object (left or right) over-rule effects of position in retinal or body-space. In models with a graded lesion, there should still be an overall tendency for parts that fall more to the right on the retina to be more strongly activated than parts falling more to the left, especially

when all the objects are presented together. However, such a result was captured by lesioning SAIM, the model of translation-invariant object recognition proposed by Humphreys and Heinke, which we reviewed in Chapter 4 (section 4.5.2; Fig. 4.16).

In SAIM, translation-invariant recognition was achieved by mapping input into a "focus of attention" (FOA) via a competitive "selection network". Units in the selection network represented possible mappings between locations on the retina and locations in the FOA, and, when multiple objects are present in the field, there is competition to establish the dominant mapping. Humphreys and Heinke "lesioned" the selection network in two ways; either a lesion affected the mapping of input from the retina into the selection network (a "vertical" lesion, shown in Fig. 8.19) or it affected the mapping of activations out from the selection network and into one side of the focus

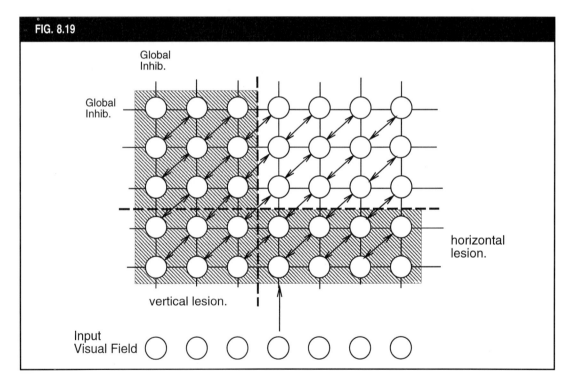

FIG. 8.19

"Vertical" and "horizontal" lesions applied to the selection network of SAIM (Humphreys & Heinke, 1998). The "vertical" lesion affects mapping from one side of the visual field into the selection network, the "horizontal" lesion affects mapping out of the selection network into one side of the focus of attention.

of attention (a "horizontal" lesion; Fig. 8.19). The two lesions produced different forms of neglect. The "vertical" lesion produced a field-dependent effect. For example, if the left side of the network was affected, then stimuli falling on the left of the retina tended to be neglected — elements on the left side would not be mapped into the FOA. However, performance improved as stimuli were presented further into the right visual field. In contrast, the "horizontal" lesion produced a form of object-based neglect, in which the elements on the left side were not mapped into the FOA irrespective of where the stimulus fell in the visual field. These effects are illustrated in

Fig. 8.20. The "vertical" lesion resulted in field-dependent neglect because it affected activation coming from one visual field into the selection network. The "horizontal" lesion produced object-based neglect because it affected units mapping into one side of the FOA from all across the visual field. These two patterns of neglect mirror human data demonstrating that some patients show effects that are dependent on where stimuli fall within the visual field, whereas, for others, there is neglect of the left sides of objects even when objects appear in the right field (Humphreys & Heinke, 1998). In the case of "pure" object-based neglect, report of the left side of objects in the

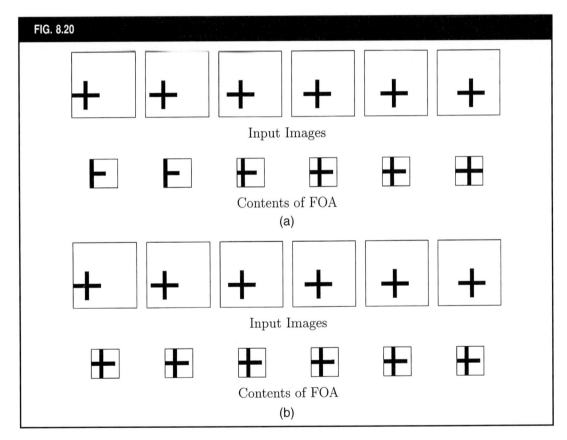

FIG. 8.20

Input Images

Contents of FOA

(a)

Input Images

Contents of FOA

(b)

Examples of "field-dependent" and "field-independent" neglect after, respectively, "vertical" and "horizontal" lesioning of the selection network in SAIM. In each case, the stimulus is a symmetrical cross, which is shifted from left to right across the model's retina. Activation is shown in the model's "focus of attention" (FOA). In field-dependent neglect, there is omission of the left-most pixels of the cross within the FOA when the cross appears in the left visual field, and this "neglect" decreases when the cross is moved into the right field (a). In field-independent neglect, the left side of the cross is omitted from the FOA wherever the stimulus appears in the field (b).

right field will be worse than report of the right side of objects in the left field.

As we pointed out at the start of this section, psychological accounts of visual neglect divide according to whether neglect is attributed to impaired attentional processes or to an impaired representation of space (Bisiach & Luzzatti, 1978; Riddoch & Humphreys, 1983). These studies with SAIM are interesting because they blur the distinction between attention and representation in visual processing. SAIM produces selective visual processing by mapping input through to a single FOA, but in doing this it also achieves different forms of spatial representation — moving from viewpoint-dependent to translation-independent codes. In this model, neglect can be conceptualised as a form of spatial distortion of an attended representation. In addition, although SAIM produces a form of object-based neglect, the representation coded within the FOA is not truly object-centred in the sense that we encountered in Chapter 4 (section 4.3.2) — that is, parts are not coded relative to some reference frame based on the objects. Rather parts are coded according to their positions in retinal space, relative to the centre of attention. The simulations indicate that experimenters should be cautious in their conclusions concerning the representations that may be affected in neglect. For example, forms of retinally based representation could still be involved even when patients show neglect of the left side of an object in the right field.

8.9 DISORDERS OF MEMORY

Cognitive neuropsychological studies have been very important for understanding the processes involved in human memory. For example, patients with damage to the inferior temporal lobes (at each side of the brain) and to the hippocampi (which lie just under the temporal lobes in each cerebral hemisphere) may have profound problems in laying down new long-term memories; they may fail to remember that they had been visited the previous day or even half an hour before. However, such "amnesic" patients can have normal immediate memory, when tested without

intervening activities taking place (Scoville & Milner, 1958). In contrast to this, lesions of the superior regions of the temporal lobe (particularly in the left hemisphere) can disrupt immediate verbal recall, so that patients may only be able to repeat back perhaps one or two words said to them; nevertheless, such patients may show good ability to recall over the longer term new events that have subsequently happened to them (see Vallar & Shallice, 1990, for reviews; although as we will discuss, there is some evidence for poor learning of certain things such as new words). This pattern of double dissociation provides a major reason for distinguishing between an immediate memory system and longer-term memories. In amnesia, the laying-down of new long-term memories can be impaired but immediate memory is left intact. In patients with deficits in immediate verbal memory, temporary representations of words may be disrupted but longer-term learning of other events is not.

In Chapter 5, we encountered simulations of immediate verbal memory as examples of how connectionist models can generate serial behaviour (in this case, serial recall of letters; see section 5.2). In such models, immediate memory is captured by temporarily coding associations — for example, associations between letter units and contextual units that signal temporal position in a list, and associations between phonological representations for speech input and output (e.g. Hitch et al., 1996). These associations typically decay over time unless actively refreshed by re-cycling activation through the model. Neuropsychological evidence indicates that this form of temporary representation may play a role in longer-term learning of phonological forms (e.g. new words; Baddeley, Papagno, & Vallar, 1988), but not in other forms of longer-term learning (see earlier). Longer-term learning of other events seems to depend on other processes. To date, connectionist models of immediate verbal memory have not been used to model cognitive neuropsychological disorders in detail, so we will not review this topic further. Nevertheless, we note that it will be important to do this, to help understand the nature of the disorders at a fine-grained level. Also, as neuropsychological evidence suggests some role for temporary verbal representations in longer-term learning, simulations of immediate memory disorders will force modellers to consider the relations between temporary and longer-term memory representations.

Some of the procedures involved in longer-term learning have been examined in simulations of the role of the hippocampus in establishing long-term memories, and possibly in overcoming one of the limitations in learning that has been found in connectionist models, namely *catastrophic interference*. In Chapter 3 we reviewed the work of McCloskey and Cohen (1989) which demonstrated that three-layer models trained using back-propagation were sensitive to catastrophic interference, in which old learning was interfered with by new learning. As we noted then, McClelland et al. (1995) have suggested that the hippocampus may be involved in preventing catastrophic interference in human learning. We now consider this proposal further.

McClelland et al. proposed that, during new learning, the hippocampus provides a temporally extended replay of events (recent input–output associations). By means of this replay process, recent associations (reinstated via the hippocampus) interleave with any new learning immediately taking place, presumably involving changing synaptic weights in the cortex. This temporal interleaving of recent and new associations helps reduce catastrophic interference, as weights set for the recent associations continue to be reinforced as the new associations are learned. McClelland et al. showed that recall of older associations was better preserved when interleaved learning regimes were used (in which the older associations continued to be reinforced) relative to when there was stepped training of first one and then another set of associations.

McClelland et al. also simulated some of the results found in the animal learning literature when damage to the hippocampus is imposed. For example, Kim and Fanselow (1992) placed rats in a novel environment and conditioned them to a tone paired with a footshock. After 1, 7, 14, or 28 days back in their home environment the rats received either bilateral lesions of the hippocampi or sham lesions (when the hippocampi were not lesioned but surgery was performed). Subsequently they

were placed in the novel environment again and their fear response was monitored (typically this involved the animals adopting freeze postures). The results are shown in Fig. 8.21a. The control animals (with sham lesions) showed a fear reaction irrespective of the number of days between the initial conditioning and the testing. The animals with hippocampal lesions, however, demonstrated a different pattern. Animals lesioned one day after the conditioning experience showed little fear response on retesting, and the level of the fear response increased in proportion to the days left after the conditioning before hippocampal lesioning took place. These data suggest that the hippocampus plays a role in "consolidating" long-term memories, even after the initial learning experience has taken place. Damaging the hippocampus leads to weak consolidation of memory.

McClelland et al. (1995) simulated these data by training a three-layer feed-forward network using back-propagation. The network had 16 input, 16 hidden, and 16 output units, and it was trained to make associations between 20 randomly determined input–output pairings. McClelland et al. proposed that these pairings would represent general prior learning by the animals. They then added an additional input–output pairing, to represent the experimental exposure of the shock and the tone in Kim and Fanselow's study. After the initial exposure to this in the overall training set (representing cortical learning), it was assumed that the experimental input–output pair would only be available for reinforcement via the hippocampus. Figure 8.21b illustrates the gradual build-up in learning of the new association as "hippocampal" reinforcement is continued as part of the model's learning (for the simulation, learning is measured in terms of the reduction in the average squared deviation from the correct output pattern). This experiment shows how the hippocampus may play a role in memory consolidation, even after the initial learning experience has finished. This notion is also supported by physiological data showing that neural activity associated with memory traces is reactivated in the rat hippocampus during "off line" activity, during rest or sleep (Wilson & McNaughton, 1994). For humans, the hippocampus also receives multiple sensory

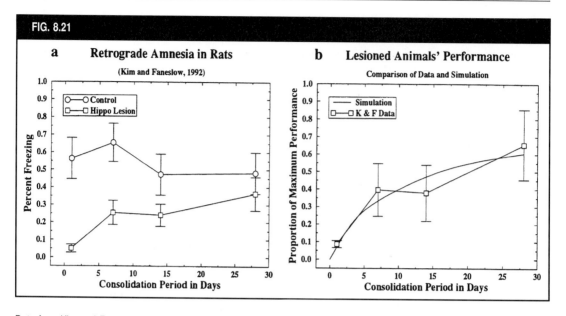

Data from Kim and Fanselow (1992) and from the simulation of McClelland et al. (1993). (a) The experimental data from experimental and control animals. (b) The simulation data along with the data from the animal experimental group (with hippocampal lesions). In (b) the experimental data are shown as a function of the amount of time spent "freezing" by each experimental group divided by the average amount of time spent freezing across the control groups at each delay. For the simulation the measure is the reduction in the mean square of the error on the output at each test point relative to the mean square of the error produced to the same pattern before any learning had taken place. From McClelland et al. (1995).

inputs from different areas of the cortex, so this reinstatement of reinforcement may play a particularly useful role in forming associations across modalities and in associating stimuli with their contexts (Teyler & Discenna, 1986).

From this work, it is possible to understand the effects of damage to the hippocampus. For example, without the hippocampus it should be difficult to absorb new learning experiences, as events would not continue to be "re-played" and consolidated into long-term memory; instead there would be a continued wash of short-term experiences linked to the constantly changing patterns presented to the cortical learning system. Such problems in new learning are known as anterograde amnesia. We also note that it is possible that an immediate verbal memory system plays a similar "reminding" role in longer-term learning of new phonological forms, so that deficits in this immediate memory system lead to deficits specifically in learning new words. This conjecture may be examined in future models that attempt to

link immediate verbal memory with longer-term learning.

The simulations of McClelland et al. further suggest that hippocampal damage should lead to impaired consolidation of events that took place shortly before a brain lesion, as these events would not continue to be reinforced in learning. The net result should be a form of "temporal gradient" of memory, in which recall of events in the long distant past is better than that in the near past. This temporal gradient is characteristic of so-called retrograde amnesia, in which memory for past events is disturbed in patients (e.g. Squire, Slater, & Chace, 1975).

Two somewhat different accounts of hippocampal function are suggested by Gluck and Myers (1993) and by Murre (1997). Gluck and Myers propose that learning in the cortex is limited, and equivalent only to that achieved in two-layer connectionist networks (see Chapter 2). In contrast, the hippocampus may accomplish more complex learning, equivalent to that present in networks with hidden units trained using back-propagation. They argue that hidden unit states achieved in the hippocampus can serve as an external "teacher" for cortical learning, enabling more complex relationships to be assimilated and providing a means for forms of supervised learning to operate in biological systems (see also Rolls, 1990, for a similar suggestion).

Murre (1997) proposes that learning can take place both within a cortical "trace" system, and in the connections between the cortical trace system and "link" system, analogous to the hippocampus. This suggestion was first considered in Chapter 3 (section 3.5), in the context of the distinction between implicit and explicit memory (see Fig. 3.15). There we postulated that implicit memories take the form of activations within the trace system, whereas explicit representations ("knowing" what the trace system represents) are based on the connections formed between the trace and link systems. A stimulus will initially activate the trace system. If there is sufficient excitation to activate the link system, then connections between the trace and link systems become strengthened, to help maintain activation in the trace system. This supports slower-acting learning that operates within the trace system, and it also helps associate together activation held in otherwise separate trace units (e.g. when stimuli are presented in different modalities). On this view, a lesion to the link system will impair new learning, although old memories may be preserved to some degree, as they are supported by established connections within the trace system. Nevertheless, some forms of implicit memory may operate, based on stimulus-driven activation within the trace system; difficulties are predicted in tasks requiring discrimination between already known target and distractor stimuli when targets only had previously been presented on one occasion (here the link system would be needed to help form an explicit representation of the occurrence of the target on a particular episode). This distinction, between relatively preserved implicit memory and poor explicit memory judgements is characteristic of amnesia (Schacter et al., 1993).

In the final chapter we will return to discuss neurophysiological evidence on the structure of the hippocampus, and speculate further on the role of the hippocampus using analogies to properties of neural networks learned from connectionist modelling. By means of such analogies, connectionist models may provide a level of functional description for real neural networks that sits above the operation of single cells but below that of whole-system behaviour.

8.10 REHABILITATION

For practical purposes it is of considerable importance to understand how cognitive problems might be rehabilitated after brain damage. This is of course of tremendous personal importance to those individuals who have sustained the damage, and it is also of economic importance due to the costs of health treatment and to loss of work time. Now, one of the important properties of connectionist networks is that they can be trained to learn new behaviours, and this also applies to networks that have been "lesioned". By examining which types of training regime are more successful for lesioned networks, and how training interacts with different types and locations of damage, we may begin to generate a principled account of neurological rehabilitation.

One relevant piece of work in this regard was reported by Plaut (1992). Plaut examined the effects of retraining on the model of deep dyslexia developed by Hinton and Shallice (1991) (section 8.3.4). Hinton and Shallice used an attractor network which was originally trained to associate orthographic input patterns with semantic output patterns; the network was then lesioned at various locations and, as we have seen, several of the symptoms of deep dyslexia were apparent. Plaut took words that the lesioned model either recognised correctly or incorrectly, and assigned half of each to a "treatment" condition and the other half to an "untreated" set. The lesioned model was then retrained with the treated words only, and performance after each learning cycle was measured for both the treated and the untreated words.

When this learning procedure was applied to a model with a lesion within the semantic system, the model not only learned the treated words but also generalised its learning to the untreated set. Correct performance on the untreated set improved from 20% after the lesion to 68% after 50 learning cycles. Training on the complete set of words also resulted in relatively rapid recovery of learning (see Fig. 8.22a).

Interestingly, rather a different pattern of performance emerged if damage had been sustained in the connections from the orthographic to the semantic units. In this case there was learning of the treated items but no generalisation to the untreated set. Also re-learning using the complete set of items led to relatively slow recovery (Fig. 8.22b).

This difference in recovery and generalisation can be understood in terms of the constraints operating on the different parts of the model. At the semantic level, the model operated with "clean-up" units, which push activation states in the semantic units towards learned "basins of attraction". Items that are semantically similar tend to be pushed towards similar basins of attraction.

Thus learning is structured on the basis of semantic similarity between the first state (the initial semantic activation) and the end state (the stable pattern left after the activity of the clean-up units). When retrained, there is generalisation due to this structure. A new item, which in a distributed scheme will share parts of its representation with old items, will tend to be pushed into an appropriate basin of attraction based on prior learning using sub-parts of its structure.

In contrast to this, the mapping from orthography to semantics is arbitrary, as similarity between orthographic representations is unrelated to that between semantic representations of words. In this case, effects of retraining on the lesioned weights lead to little generalisation from one word to another. Note also that the general pattern of recovery, when there is retraining of the complete word set, is slower, as the arbitrary learning task (retraining weights between orthography and semantics) is more difficult than the structured one (retraining weights at the semantic level). These results provide a means of understanding

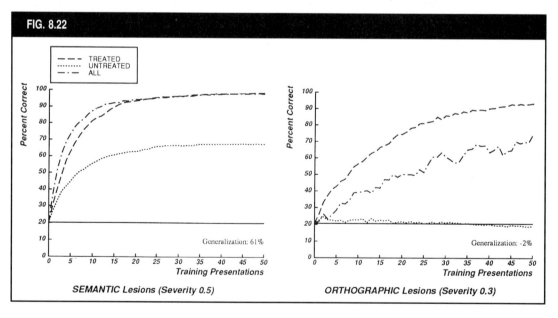

FIG. 8.22

SEMANTIC Lesions (Severity 0.5)

ORTHOGRAPHIC Lesions (Severity 0.3)

The effects of retraining the model of deep dyslexia proposed by Hinton and Shallice (1991). The left panel (a) shows performance after lesioning to the weights connecting the clean up units to the semantic units; the right panel (b) shows performance after lesioning to the weights connecting the orthographic input units to the intermediate units. The solid horizontal lines represent the levels of performance found at the onset of retraining. Generalisation of training is measured in terms of the ratio of improvement on the untreated relative to the treated items. From Plaut (1992).

when training effects might be specific, and when they might be generalisable, in patients with lesions to different parts of their reading system.

Plaut went on to assess the kinds of retraining programme that might lead to most success in rehabilitation. He tested between training using a "prototypical" and "non-prototypical" sets of stimuli. To create the prototypical and non-prototypical sets, Plaut based a training set around a single word, with the training words generated from random distortions of the vector patterns relative to the prototype. The "prototypical" set involved small distortions relative to the prototype; the "non-prototypical" set involved large distortions. Retraining was carried out on the Hinton and Shallice (1991) model after it had been lesioned on the connections between its intermediate and semantic units, training was conducted with half of the prototypical or half of the non-prototypical patterns (the treated sets), and generalisation was tested on the untreated items. The results are given in Fig. 8.23, scored according to a ratio of the improvement on untreated items after treatment had taken place relative to before it had taken place, using a criterion of best match between the input and the expected output relative to other possible outputs. Training on the prototypical set led to generalisation of learning to other (untreated) prototypical items, but not to untreated non-prototypical items; in contrast, training on non-prototypical items led to improvement on untreated prototypical and non-prototypical items alike.

Plaut interpreted his result using an analogy of randomly distributed points to represent items in the training sets. In a group of randomly distributed points, the average of the outliers (the non-prototypical items) will approximate the central points, which represent the prototype; if weights are affected both by the individual exemplars in the training set and by averaging across the set, then the effects of training on non-prototypical items should generalise to prototypical patterns. However, the average of the central points (the prototypes) may well fall quite far from any outliers (the non-prototypes). Thus training on the prototypes may fail to generalise to non-prototypical patterns.

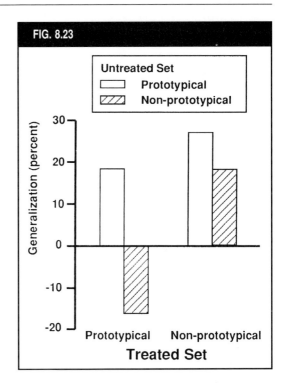

Generalisation of training from either prototypical or non-prototypical members of a training set, to untreated prototypical or non-prototypical items. From Plaut (1992).

Plaut's results provide some pointers concerning which types of training may, in general, give rise to improvements in the performance of brain-injured patients. Perhaps counterintuitively, the data suggest that training with non-prototypical members of a population might generate better overall learning than training with prototypical members. This point is not tied to a particular task domain, and in practical tasks the applications could include training on sets of words with varying spelling–sound regularity (from highly regular prototypes to less regular words), training on objects varying in the prototypicality of their shape relative to other category members, and so forth. To the best of our knowledge, the predictions that follow from the simulations have not been tested out (e.g. see papers in Riddoch & Humphreys, 1994), but such simulations should lead to the development of theoretically motivated therapies in the future.

8.11 SUMMARY

We have discussed attempts to model a wide variety of neuropsychological disorders by simulating the effects of brain lesions on connectionist models. The models have had some success in accounting for at least single disorders, and. in some cases the same model has captured several neurological disorders (e.g. the SERR model of grouping and visual attention, the MORSEL model of visual word recognition and attention). The models have also shown emergent properties that are of interest to neuropsychologists; for example, (i) similar error patterns can be generated even when there are different sites of lesion in a model (as in the models of deep dyslexia and optic aphasia; Hinton & Shallice, 1991; Plaut & Shallice, 1993a); (ii) problems in "attentional disengagement" can arise in lesioned models without a specific mechanism for disengaging attention (Cohen et al., 1994; Humphreys et al., 1996); (iii) there can be covert recognition in models that do not have hemispheric specialisation or impairments of conscious awareness (e.g. Burton et al., 1991; Farah et al., 1993; Mayall & Humphreys, 1996a,b); (iv) spelling errors associated with problems in a graphemic buffer can be generated even in a model where no such buffer exists (Houghton et al., 1994); and (v) damage to interactive networks can sometimes result in patterns of double dissociation or in instances in which the more difficult of two tasks is selectively impaired (Humphreys et al., 1992b; Plaut & Shallice, 1993a). In the final chapter we illustrate how these results question assumptions in neuropsychology, and in so doing they may lead to further empirical tests of the assumptions.

NOTES

1. The problem with function words may in turn be due to their being low in imageability.
2. This procedure, of autoassociative training of an input pattern back to itself is similar to the procedure used by Seidenberg and McClelland (1989), in their simulation of lexical decision performance in normal readers.
3. The contiguity constraint was implemented by having neighbouring units in the attention module support one another if they were both active, but units tended to shut-off if their activity was below a mean level.
4. At present there are not particularly strong neurological grounds for this, as patients typically have a unilateral lesion. However, neglect tends to be more common after right than left hemisphere lesions (Heilman, 1979), and there is evidence that the right hemisphere controls attention to both visual fields whereas the left only controls attention in the right field (Corbetta et al., 1993). A consequence of a right hemisphere lesion, then, may be to reduce the likelihood of attention being paid across the visual field, with the effect being stronger the further into the left field a stimulus is presented.
5. This account holds providing that patients do not use the strategy of identifying the whole word and then remembering the letters from the spelling.

Neuropsychological inference with an interactive brain: A critique of the "locality" assumption

Martha J. Farah

Department of Psychology, University of Pennsylvania, Philadelphia, PA 19104–6196
Electronic mail: mfarah@cattell.psych.upenn.edu

Abstract: When cognitive neuropsychologists make inferences about the functional architecture of the normal mind from selective cognitive impairments they generally assume that the effects of brain damage are local, that is, that the nondamaged components of the architecture continue to function as they did before the damage. This assumption follows from the view that the components of the functional architecture are modular, in the sense of being informationally encapsulated. In this target article it is argued that this "locality" assumption is probably not correct in general. Inferences about the functional architecture can nevertheless be made from neuropsychological data with an alternative set of assumptions, according to which human information processing is graded, distributed, and interactive. These claims are supported by three examples of neuropsychological dissociations and a comparison of the inferences obtained from these impairments with and without the locality assumptions. The three dissociations are: selective impairments in knowledge of living things, disengagment of visual attention, and overt face recognition. In all three cases, the neuropsychological phenomena lead to more plausible inferences about the normal functional architecture when the locality assumption is abandoned. Also discussed are the relations between the locality assumption in neuropsychology and broader issues, including Fodor's modularity hypothesis and the choice between top-down and bottom-up research approaches.

Keywords: brain lesions; cognitive architecture; face recognition; localization; modularity; neural nets; neuropsychology; semantics; vision

The fact that the various parts of the encephalon, though anatomically distinct, are yet so intimately combined and related as to form a complex whole, makes it natural to suppose that lesions of greater or lesser extent in any one part should produce such general perturbation of the functions of the organ as a whole as to render it at least highly difficult to trace any uncomplicated connection between the symptoms produced and the lesion as such. *Ferrier (1886).*

1. Introduction

Brain damage often has rather selective effects on cognitive functioning, impairing some abilities while sparing others. Psychologists interested in describing the "functional architecture" of the mind, that is, the set of relatively independent information-processing subsystems that underlies human intelligence, have recognized that patterns of cognitive deficit and sparing after brain damage are a potentially useful source of constraints on the functional architecture. In this target article I wish to focus on one of the assumptions that frequently underlies the use of neuropsychological data in the development of cognitive theories.

1.1. The locality assumption

Cognitive neuropsychologists generally assume that damage to one component of the functional architecture will have exclusively "local" effects. In other words, the nondamaged components will continue to function normally and the patient's behavior will therefore manifest the underlying impairment in a relatively direct and straightforward way. This assumption follows from a

Behavioral and Brain Sciences (1994) 17, 43–104

view of the cognitive architecture as "modular," in the sense of being "informationally encapsulated" (Fodor 1983; see also multiple book review, *BBS* 8(1) 1985).

According to this version of the modularity hypothesis, the different components of the functional architecture do not interact with one another except when one has completed its processing, at which point it makes the end product available to other components. Even these interactions are limited, so that a given component receives input from relatively few (perhaps just one) of the other components. Thus, a paradigm module takes its input from just one other component of the functional architecture (e.g. phonetic analysis would be hypothesized to take its input just from prephonetic acoustic analysis), carries out its computations without being affected by other information available in other components (even potentially relevant information, such as semantic context), and then presents its output to the next component in line, for which it might be the sole input (e.g. the auditory input lexicon, which would again be hypothesized to take only phonetic input).

In such an architecture, each component minds its own business and knows nothing about most of the other components. What follows for a damaged system is that most of the components will be oblivious to the loss of any one, carrying on precisely as before. If the components of the functional architecture were informationally encapsulated then the locality assumption would hold; the removal of one component would have only very local effects on the functioning of the system as a whole, affecting performance only in those tasks that directly call upon the damaged component. Indeed, one of Fodor's other criteria for modulehood, which he suggests will coincide with informational encapsulation, is that modules make use of dedicated hardware and can therefore be selectively impaired by local brain damage. In contrast, if the different components of the cognitive system were highly interactive, each one depending on input from many or most of the others, then damage to any one component could significantly modify the functioning of the others.

Several cognitive neuropsychologists have pointed out that informational encapsulation and the locality of the effects of brain damage are assumptions, and they have expressed varying degrees of confidence in them (Allport 1985; Caplan 1981; Humphreys & Riddoch 1987; Kinsbourne 1971; Kosslyn & Van Kleek 1990; Moscovitch & Umiltà 1990; Shallice 1988; von Klein 1977). For example, Shallice (1988, Ch. 2) endorses a weaker and more general version of modularity than Fodor's, according to which components of the functional architecture can be distinguished, (1) conceptually in terms of their specialized functions and (2) empirically by the relatively selective deficits that ensue upon damage to one of them. He likens this concept of modularity to Posner's (1978) "isolable subsystems" and offers the following criterion from Tulving (1983) for distinguishing modular systems with some mutual dependence among modules from fully interactive systems: components of a modular system in this weaker sense may not operate as efficiently when other components have been damaged but they will nevertheless continue to function roughly normally. According to this view, the locality assumption is not strictly true, but it is nevertheless roughly true: one would not expect *pronounced* changes in the functioning of nondamaged components.

Closely related to the locality assumption is the "transparency assumption" of Caramazza (1984; 1986). Although different statements of this assumption leave room for different interpretations, it is probably weaker than the locality assumption. Particularly in more recent statements (e.g. Caramazza 1992), it appears transparency requires only that the behavior of the damaged system be *understandable* in terms of the functional architecture of the normal system. Changes in the functioning of nondamaged components are not considered a violation of the transparency assumption so long as they are understandable. In particular, interactivity and consequent nonlocal effects are permitted; presumably only if the nonlocal interactions became unstable and chaotic would the transparency assumption be violated.

Unlike the weaker transparency assumption, the locality assumption licenses quite direct inferences from the manifest behavioral deficit to the identity of the underlying damaged cognitive component, inferences of the form "selective deficit in ability *A* implies a component of the functional architecture dedicated to *A*." Obviously such inferences can go awry if the selectivity of the deficit is not real, for example, if the tasks testing *A* are merely harder than the comparison tasks, if there are other abilities that are not tested but are also impaired, or if a combination of functional lesions is mistaken for a single one (see Shallice 1988, Ch. 10, for a thorough discussion of other possibilities for misinterpreting dissociations in a weakly modular theoretical framework). In addition, even simple tasks tap several components at once, and properly designed control tasks are needed to pinpoint the deficient component and absolve intact components downstream. However, assuming that the relevant ability has been experimentally isolated and that the deficit is truly selective, the locality assumption allows us to delineate and characterize the components of the functional architecture in a direct, almost algorithmic way.[1]

1.2. The locality assumption is ubiquitous in cognitive neuropsychology

At this point the reader may think that the locality assumption is naive and that the direct inferences that it licenses constitute a mindless reification of deficits as components of the cognitive architecture, something "good" cognitive neuropsychologists would not do. Note, however, that the locality assumption is justifiable in terms of informational encapsulation. Furthermore, whether or not this seems an adequate justification, many of the best-known findings in neuropsychology fit this form of inference. A few examples will be given here and three more will be discussed in detail later (perusal of recent journals and textbooks in cognitive neuropsychology will reveal many more examples).

With the domain of reading, phonological dyslexics show a selective deficit in tasks that require grapheme-to-phoneme translation; they are able to read real words (which can be read by recognizing the word as a whole), they can copy and repeat nonwords (demonstrating intact graphemic and phonemic representation), but they cannot read nonwords, which must be read by grapheme-to-phoneme translation. This has been interpreted as an impairment in a grapheme-to-phoneme translation mechanism and hence as evidence for the existence of such a mechanism in the normal

architecture (e.g. Coltheart 1985). Similarly, in surface dyslexia a selective deficit in reading irregular words with preserved regular word and nonword reading has been used to identify a deficit in whole-word recognition and hence to infer a whole-word reading mechanism distinct from the grapheme-to-phoneme route (e.g. Coltheart 1985).

In the production and understanding of spoken language, some patients are selectively impaired in processing closed class, or "function" words, leading to the conclusion that these lexical items are represented by a separate system, distinct from open class or "content" words (e.g. Zurif 1980).

In the domain of vision, some right hemisphere-damaged patients show an apparently selective impairment in the recognition of objects viewed from unusual perspectives. This has been taken to imply the existence of a stage or stages of visual information processing concerned specifically with shape constancy (e.g. Warrington 1985). Highly selective deficits in face recognition have been taken to support the existence of a specialized module for face recognition, distinct from more general-purpose recognition mechanisms (e.g. DeRenzi 1986).

In the domain of memory, the finding that patients can be severely impaired in learning facts and other so-called declarative or explicit knowledge while displaying normal learning of skills and other forms of implicit knowledge is interpreted as evidence for multiple learning systems, one of which is dedicated to the acquisition of declarative knowledge (e.g. Squire 1992).

Some of these inferences may well be proved wrong in the light of further research. For example, perhaps there is a confounding between the factor of interest and the true determinant of the deficit. In the case of aphasics who seem selectively impaired at processing closed class words, perhaps speech stress pattern, and not lexical class, determines the boundaries of the deficit. Critical thinkers may find reasons to question the inferences in any or all of the examples given above. However, note that in most cases the question will concern the empirical specifics of the case, such as stress pattern versus lexical class. In the course of scientific debate on these and other deficits, the *form* of the inference is rarely questioned. If we can truly establish a selective deficit in ability *A* then it seems reasonable to attribute the deficit to a lesion of some component of the functional architecture that is dedicated to *A*, that is, necessary for *A* and necessary only for *A*. We are, of course, thereby assuming that the effects of the lesion on the functioning of the system are local to the lesioned component.

1.3. Two empirical issues about the locality assumption

Although it is reasonable to assume that the effects of a lesion are confined to the operation of the lesioned components and the relatively small number of components downstream in a system with informationally encapsulated modules, we do not yet know whether the brain is such a system. There is, in fact, some independent reason to believe it is not. Neurologists have long noted the highly interactive nature of brain organization and the consequent tendency for local damage to unleash new emergent organizations or modes of functioning in the remaining system (e.g. Ferrier 1886; Jackson 1873). Of course, the observations that led to these conclusions were not primarily of cognitive disorders. Therefore, whether or not the locality assumption holds in the domain of cognitive impairments, at least to a good approximation, is an open empirical question.

Note that we should be concerned more about "good approximations" than precise generalizations to neuropsychological methodology. As already mentioned, Shallice (1988) has pointed out that modularity versus interactionism is a matter of degree. From the point of view of neuropsychological methodology, if nonlocal interactions were to modulate weakly the behavior of patients after brain damage, this would not necessarily lead to wrong inferences using the locality assumption. In such a case, in which the remaining parts of the system act ever-so-slightly differently following damage, the cognitive neuropsychologist would simply fail to account for 100% of the variance in the data (not a novel experience for most of us) but would make the correct inference about functional architecture. If deviations from locality were a first-order effect, however, then the best-fitting theory for the data using the locality assumption would be false.

There is a second question concerning the locality assumption: Is it really indispensable to cognitive neuropsychology? Must we abandon all hope of relating patient behavior to theories of the normal functional architecture if lesions in one part of the system can change the functioning of other parts? Like the first question, this one too is a matter of empirical truth or falsehood.

Nevertheless, unlike many empirical questions, these two are not of the type that lend themselves to single critical experiments. They concern very general properties of the functional architecture of cognition and our ability to make scientific inferences about complex systems using all the formal and informal methods and types of evidence available to us. The most fruitful approach to answering these two questions would therefore involve an analysis of the body of cognitive neuropsychological research, or at least an extensive sample of it.

As a starting point, I will describe three different neuropsychological dissociations that have been used to make inferences about the functional architecture of the mind. The aspect of cognition under investigation in each case is different: semantic memory, visual attention, and the relation between visual recognition and awareness. What all three have in common is the use of the locality assumption. For each I will explore alternative inferences about the functional architecture that are not constrained by the locality assumption.

How will such explorations answer the questions posed above? We can assess the empirical basis for the locality assumption by comparing the conclusions about functional architecture that are arrived at with and without it. Specifically, we can determine which conclusions are preferable, in the sense of being simpler and according better with other, independent evidence about the functional architecture. If the locality assumption generally leads to preferable conclusions, this suggests that we are probably justified in using it. However, if it often leads to nonpreferable conclusions, this suggests we should not assume that the effects of brain damage on the functioning of the cognitive architecture are local. The question of whether it is possible to draw inferences about the functional architecture from neuropsychological dissociations without the locality assumption will also be addressed by the degree to which sensible conclusions can be reached without it.

1.4. An architecture for interactive processing

Of course, comparisons between the results of inferences made with and without the locality assumption will be meaningful only if both types of inferences are constrained in principled ways. The locality assumption is one type of constraint on the kinds of functional architectures that can be inferred from a neuropsychological dissociation. It limits the elements in our explanation of a given neuropsychological deficit to just those in the normal functional architecture (minus the damaged component), operating in their normal fashion. If we simply eliminate that constraint without replacing it with other principled constraints on how local damage affects the remaining parts of the system then the comparison proposed above will not be fair to the locality assumption. We could, of course, pick the simplest, most appealing model of the normal functional architecture and say "the way in which the remaining parts of the system change their functioning after damage produces this deficit," without saying why we chose to hypothesize *that* particular change in functioning as opposed to some other that cannot explain the deficit.

The parallel distributed processing (PDP) framework will be used as a source of principled constraints on the ways in which the remaining parts of the system behave after local damage. Computer simulation will be used to test the sufficiency of the PDP hypotheses to account for the dissociations in question. Readers who would like a detailed introduction to PDP are referred to Rumelhart and McClelland's (1986) collection of readings. For present purposes, the relevant principles of PDP are:

Distributed representation of knowledge. In PDP systems, representations consist of patterns of activation distributed over a population of units. Different entities can therefore be represented using the same set of units, because the pattern of activation over the units will be distinctive. Long-term memory knowledge is encoded in the pattern of connection strengths distributed among a population of units.

Graded nature of information processing. In PDP systems processing is not all or none: representations can be partially active, for example, through partial or subthreshold activation of some of those units that would normally be active. Partial knowledge can be embodied in connection strengths, either before learning has been completed or after partial damage.

Interactivity. The units in PDP models are highly interconnected and thus mutual influence among different parts of the system is the rule rather than the exception. This influence can be excitatory, as when one part of a distributed representation activates the remaining parts (pattern completion), or it can be inhibitory, as when different representations compete with one another to become active or to maintain their activation. Note that interactivity is the aspect of the PDP framework that is most directly incompatible with the locality assumption. If the normal operation of a given part of the system depends on the influence of some other part, it may not operate normally after that other part has been damaged.

The psychological plausibility of PDP is controversial but it need not be definitively established here before proceeding. Instead, just as locality is being identified as an assumption and evaluated, so PDP is to be evaluated as a specific alternative assumption. In addition, as will be discussed further in the "General Discussion" (sect. 3), much of the controversy surrounding PDP concerns its adequacy for language and reasoning. It is possible that the arguments advanced here will not generalize to these cognitive domains.

2. Reinterpreting dissociations without the locality assumption: Three case studies

2.1. The functional architecture of semantic memory: Category-specific?

The existence of patients with apparent category-specific impairments in semantic memory knowledge has led to the inference that semantic memory has a categorical organization, with different components dedicated to representing knowledge from different categories. The best-documented forms of category-specific knowledge deficit (as opposed to pure naming or visual recognition deficits) are the deficits in knowledge of living and nonliving things.

2.1.1. Evidence for selective impairments in knowledge of living and nonliving things

Beginning in the 1980s, Warrington and her colleagues began to report the existence of patients with selective impairments in knowledge of either living or nonliving things (Warrington & McCarthy 1983; 1987; Warrington & Shallice 1984). Warrington and Shallice (1984) described four patients who were much worse at identifying living things (animals, plants) than nonliving things (inanimate objects); all four had recovered from herpes encephalitis and had sustained bilateral temporal lobe damage. Two of the patients were studied in detail and showed a selective impairment for living things across a range of tasks, both visual and verbal. Table 1 shows examples of their performance in a visual identification task (in which they were to identify by name or description the item shown in a colored picture) and in a verbal definition task (in which the names of these same items were presented auditorially and they were to define them). Examples of their definitions are shown in Table 2. Other cases of selective impairment in knowledge of living things

TABLE 2
Examples of definitions of living and nonliving things

Case	Definition
	Living Things
JBR	Parrot: don't know
	Daffodil: plant
	Snail: an insect animal
	Eel: not well
	Ostrich: unusual
SBY	Duck: an animal
	Wasp: bird that flies
	Crocus: rubbish material
	Holly: what you drink
	Spider: a person looking for things, he was a spider for his nation or country
	Nonliving things
JBR	Tent: temporary outhouse, living home
	Briefcase: small case used by students to carry papers
	Compass: tools for telling direction you are going
	Torch: hand-held light
	Dustbin: bin for putting rubbish in
SBY	Wheelbarrow: object used by people to take material about
	Towel: material used to dry people
	Pram: used to carry people, with wheels and a thing to sit on
	Submarine: ship that goes underneath the sea
	Umbrella: object used to protect you from water that comes

TABLE 1
An impairment in knowledge of living things: Performance on two tasks assessing knowledge of living and nonliving things

Case	Task	
	Picture identification	
	Living (%)	Nonliving (%)
JBR	6	90
SBY	0	75
	Spoken word definition	
	Living (%)	Nonliving (%)
JBR	8	79
SBY	0	52

include additional postencephalitic patients described by Pietrini et al. (1988), Sartori and Job (1988), and Silveri and Gianotti (1988), a patient with encephalitis and strokes described by Newcombe et al. (1994), two head injury patients described by Farah et al. (1991), and a patient with a focal degenerative disease described by Basso et al. (1988). In all these cases there was damage to the temporal regions, known to be bilateral except in Pietrini et al.'s case 1 and the case of Basso et al., where there was evidence only of left temporal damage.

The opposite dissociation, namely, impaired knowledge of nonliving things with relatively preserved knowledge of living things, has also been observed. Warrington and McCarthy (1983; 1987) described two cases of global dysphasia following large left-hemisphere strokes in which semantic knowledge was tested in a series of matching tasks. Table 3 shows the results of a matching task in which the subjects were asked to point to the picture in an array that corresponded to a spoken word. Their performance with animals and flowers was more reliable than with nonliving things. One subject was also tested with a completely nonverbal matching task in which different-looking depictions of objects or animals were to be matched to one another in an array; the same selective preservation of knowledge of animals relative to inanimate objects was found.

Although these patients are not entirely normal in their knowledge of the relatively spared category, they are markedly worse at recognizing, defining, or answering questions about items from the impaired category. The existence of a double dissociation makes it unlikely that a sheer difference in difficulty underlies the apparent selectivity of the deficits; some of the studies cited above tested several alternative explanations of the impairments in terms of factors other than semantic category (such as name frequency, familiarity, etc.) and failed to support them.

2.1.2. Interpretation of "living things" and "nonliving things" deficits relative to the functional architecture of semantic memory

Using the locality assumption, the most straight-forward interpretation of the double dissociation between knowledge of living and nonliving things is that they are represented by two separate category-specific components of the functional architecture of semantic memory. A related interpretation is that semantic memory is represented using semantic features such as "animate," "domestic," and so on, and that the dissociations described here result from damage to these features (Hillis & Caramazza 1991). In either case, the dissociations seem to imply a functional architecture for semantic memory that is organized along rather abstract semantic or taxonomic lines. Figure 1 represents a category-specific model of semantic memory and its relation to visual perception and language.

Warrington and colleagues, however, have suggested an alternative interpretation, according to which semantic memory is fundamentally modality-specific. They argue that selective deficits in knowledge of living and nonliving things may reflect the differential weighting of information from different sensorimotor channels in representing knowledge about these two categories. They have pointed out that living things are distinguished primarily by their sensory attributes, whereas nonliving things are distinguished primarily by their functional attributes. For example, our knowledge of an animal such as a leopard, by which we distinguish it from other similar creatures, is predominantly visual. In contrast, our knowledge of a desk, by which we distinguish it from other furniture, is predominantly functional

TABLE 3
An impairment in knowledge of nonliving things: Performance on two tasks assessing knowledge of living and nonliving things

Case	Task		
	Spoken word/picture matching		
	Animals (%)	Flowers (%)	Objects (%)
VER	86	96	63
YOT	86	86	67
	Picture/picture matching		
	Animals (%)	Objects (%)	
YOT	100	69	

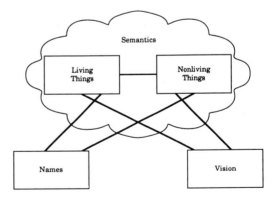

FIG. 1. Category-specific functional architecture for semantic memory.

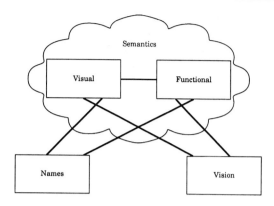

FIG. 2. Modality-specific functional architecture for semantic memory.

(i.e. what it is used for). Thus, the distinctions between impaired and preserved knowledge in the cases reviewed earlier may not be living/nonliving distinctions per se but sensory/functional distinctions, as illustrated in Figure 2.

The modality-specific hypothesis seems preferable to a strict semantic hypothesis for two reasons. First, it is more consistent with what is already known about brain organization. It is well known that different brain areas are dedicated to representing information from specific sensory and motor channels. Functional knowledge could conceivably be tied to the motor system. A second reason for preferring the sensory/functional hypothesis to the living/nonliving hypothesis is that exceptions to the latter have been observed in certain cases. For example, Warrington and Shallice (1984) report that their patients, who were deficient in their knowledge of living things, also had impaired knowledge of gemstones and fabrics. Warrington and McCarthy's (1987) patient, whose knowledge of most nonliving things was impaired, seemed to have retained good knowledge of very large outdoor objects such as bridges or windmills. It is at least possible that our knowledge of these aberrant categories of nonliving things is primarily visual.

Unfortunately, there appears to be a problem with the hypothesis that "living-thing impairments" are just impairments in sensory knowledge, and "nonliving-thing impairments" are just impairments in functional knowledge. This hypothesis seems to predict that cases of living-thing impairment should show good knowledge of the functional attributes of living things and cases of nonliving-thing impairment should show good knowledge of the visual attributes of nonliving things. The evidence available in cases of nonliving-thing impairment is limited to performance in matching-to-sample tasks, which does not allow us to distinguish knowledge of visual or sensory attributes from knowledge of functional attributes. However, there does appear to be adequate evidence in cases of living-thing impairment, and in at least some cases it disconfirms these predictions (for review see Farah & McClelland 1991). For example, although the definitions of living things shown in Table 2 contain little visual detail, in keeping with the sensory/functional hypothesis, they are also skimpy on functional information. If these cases had lost just their visual semantic knowledge, then why could they not retrieve functional attributes of living things, for example, the fact that parrots are kept as pets and can talk, that daffodils are a spring flower, and so on? A more direct and striking demonstration of the apparently categorical nature of the impairment is provided by Newcombe et al. (in press), whose subject was impaired relative to normal subjects in his ability to sort living things according to such nonsensory attributes as whether or not they were generally found in the United Kingdom, in contrast to his normal performance when the task involved nonliving things.

In sum, the sensory/functional hypothesis seems preferable to the living/nonliving hypothesis because it is more in keeping with what we already know about brain organization. However, it is not able to account for the impaired ability of these patients to retrieve nonvisual information about living things.

2.1.3. Accounting for category-specific impairments with an interactive modality-specific architecture

Jay McClelland and I have modeled the double dissociation between knowledge of living and nonliving things using a simple autoassociative memory architecture with modality-specific components (Farah & McClelland 1991). We found that a two-component semantic memory system, consisting of visual and functional components, could be lesioned to produce selective impairments in knowledge of living and nonliving things. More important, we found that such a model could account for the impairment of both visual and *functional* knowledge of living things.

The basic architecture of the model is shown in Fig. 2. There are three pools of units, representing the names of items, the perceived appearances of items, and the semantic memory representations of items. The semantic memory pool is subdivided into visual semantic memory and functional semantic memory. An item, living or nonliving, is represented by a pattern of +1 and −1 activations over the name and visual units, and a pattern of +1 and −1 activations over a *subset* of the semantic units. The relative proportion of visual and functional information comprising the semantic memory representation of living and nonliving things was derived empirically. Normal subjects identified terms in dictionary definitions of the living and nonliving items used by Warrington and Shallice (1984) as referring to either visual or functional properties. This experiment confirmed that visual and functional information was differentially weighted in the definitions of living and nonliving things and the results were used to determine the average proportions of visual and functional units in semantic memory representations of living and nonliving items. For the living items, about seven times as many visual semantic units than functional ones participated in the semantic memory pattern; for nonliving items the proportions were closer to equal. Units of semantic memory not involved in a particular item's representation took the activation value of 0.

The model was trained using the delta rule (Rumelhart et al. 1986) to associate the correct semantic and name portions of its pattern when presented with the visual portion as input, and the correct semantic and visual portions when presented with the name portion as input. It was then damaged by eliminating different proportions of functional or visual semantic units and its performance was assessed in a simulated picture-name matching task. In this task, each item's visual input representation is presented to the network and the pattern activated in the name units

is assessed, or each pattern's name is presented and the resultant visual pattern is assessed. The resultant pattern is scored as correct if it is more similar to the correct pattern than to any of the other 19 patterns.

Figure 3A shows the averaged picture-to-name and name-to-picture performance of the model for living and nonliving items under varying degrees of damage to visual semantics. With increased damage, the model's performance drops, and it drops more precipitously for living things, in effect showing an impairment for living things

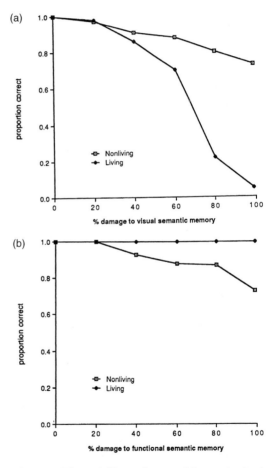

FIG. 3. (a) Effects of different degrees of damage to visual semantic memory units on ability of network to associate names and pictures of living things (diamonds) and nonliving things (squares). (b) Effects of different degrees of damage to functional semantic memory units on ability of network to associate names and pictures of living things (diamonds) and nonliving things (squares).

comparable in selectivity to that of the patients in the literature. Figure 3B shows that the opposite dissociation is obtained when functional semantics is damaged.

The critical challenge for a modality-specific model of semantic memory is to explain how damage could create an impairment in knowledge of living things that includes functional knowledge of living things. To evaluate the model's ability to access functional semantic knowledge, we presented either name or visual input patterns as before, but instead of assessing the match between the resulting output pattern and the correct output pattern, we assessed the match between the resulting pattern in functional semantics and the correct pattern in functional semantics. The normlized dot product of these two patterns, which provides a measure between 0 (completely dissimilar) and 1 (identical), served as the dependent measure.

Figure 4 shows the accuracy with which functional semantic memory information could be activated for living and nonliving things after different degrees of damage to visual semantics. At all levels of damage, the ability to retrieve functional semantic knowledge of living things is disproportionately impaired.

These dissociations can be understood as follows. In the case of picture-name matching, the

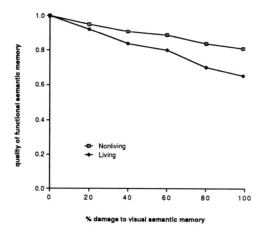

FIG. 4. Effects of different degrees of damage to visual semantic memory units on ability of network to activate correct pattern in functional semantic memory units for living things (diamonds) and nonliving things (squares).

ability of a given output unit (e.g. a name unit, in the case of picture-to-name matching) to attain its correct activation value depends on the input it receives from the units to which it is connected. These consist of other name units (collateral connections) and both visual and functional semantic units. Hence the more semantic units that have been eliminated, the more the output units are deprived of the incoming activation they need to attain their correct activation values. Because most of the semantic input to the name units of living things is from visual semantics, whereas the same is not true for nonliving things, damage to visual semantics will eliminate a greater portion of the activation needed to retrieve the name patterns for living things than nonliving things, and will therefore have a more severe impact on performance.

The same principle applies to the task of activating functional semantics, although in this case the units are being deprived of collateral activation from other semantic units. Thus, when visual semantic units are destroyed, one of the sources of input to the functional semantic units is eliminated. For living things, visual semantics comprises a proportionately larger source of input to functional semantic units than for nonliving things, hence the larger effect for these items.

2.1.4. Relevance of the locality assumption for architecture of semantic memory

Contrary to the locality assumption, when visual semantics is damaged the remaining parts of the system do not continue to function as before. In particular, functional semantics, which is part of the nondamaged residual system, becomes impaired in its ability to achieve the correct patterns of activation when given input from vision or language. This is because of the loss of collateral support from visual semantics. The ability of this model to account for the impairment in accessing functional knowledge of living things depends critically upon this nonlocal aspect of its response to damage.

2.2. The functional architecture of visual attention: A "disengage" module?

One of the best-known findings in cognitive neuropsychology concerns the "disengage" deficit that follows unilateral parietal damage. In an elegant series of studies, Posner and his colleagues have shown that parietally damaged patients have a selective impairment in their ability to disengage attention from a location in the spared ipsilesional hemifield in order to move it to a location in the affected contralesional hemifield (e.g. Posner et al. 1984). From this they have inferred the existence of a disengage component in the functional architecture of visual attention.

2.2.1. Evidence for the disengage deficit

Posner and colleagues inferred the existence of a disengage operation from experiments using a cued simple reaction time task. The typical task consists of a display, as shown in Fig. 5A, which the subject fixates centrally, and in which both "cues" and "targets" are presented. The cue is usually the brightening of one of the boxes, as depicted in Fig. 5B. This causes attention to be allocated to the region of space around the bright box. The target, usually a simple character such as an asterisk, is then presented in one of the boxes, as shown in Fig. 5C. The subject's task is to press a button as soon as possible after the appearance of the target, regardless of its location. When the target is "validly" cued, that is, when it occurs on the same side of the display as

the cue, reaction times to it are faster than with no cue, because attention is already optimally allocated for perceiving the target. When the target is "invalidly" cued, reaction times are slower than with no cue because attention is focused on the wrong side of space.

When parietally damaged patients are tested in this paradigm, they perform roughly normally on validly cued trials when the target appears on the side of space ipsilateral to their lesion. However, their reaction times are greatly slowed to invalidly cued contralesional targets. It is as if once attention has been engaged on the ipsilesional, or "good," side it cannot be disengaged to be moved to a target occurring on the contralesional, or "bad," side.

2.2.2. Interpretation of the disengage deficit relative to the functional architecture of visual attention

The disproportionate difficulty that parietally damaged patients have in disengaging their attention from the good side to move it to the bad side has led Posner and colleagues to infer the existence of a separate component of the functional architecture of disengaging attention. The resulting model of attention therefore postulates distinct components for engaging and disengaging attention, as shown in Fig. 6.

2.2.3. Accounting for the disengage deficit with an interactive architecture that has no "disengage" component

Jonathan Cohen, Richard Romero, and I (Cohen et al., in press) have modeled normal cuing effects and the disengage deficit using a simple model of visual attention that contains no "disengage" component.

The model is depicted in Fig. 7. The first layer consists of visual transducer, or input, units, through which stimuli are presented to the network. These units send their output to visual perception units, which represent the visual percept of a stimulus at a particular location in space. In this simple model there are only two locations in visual space. The visual perception units are connected to two other kinds of units. One is the response unit, which issues the detection response

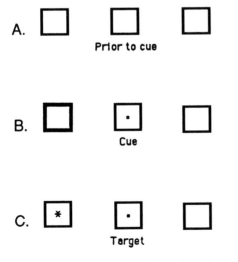

FIG. 5. Sequence of trial events in the lateralized simple reaction time task: (A) fixation display; (B) cue; (C) target.

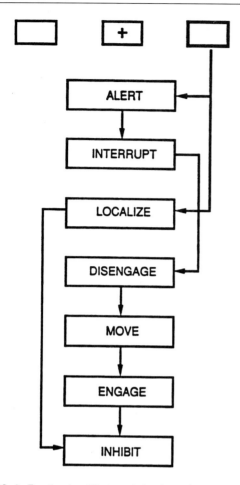

FIG. 6. Functional architecture of visual attention system derived by Posner et al. (1984) from the study of brain-damaged patients.

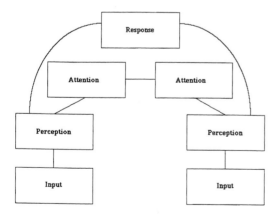

FIG. 7. Functional architecture of visual attention system as modeled by Cohen et al. (in press).

when it has gathered sufficient activation from the perception units to reach its threshold. We will interpret the number of processing cycles that intervene between the presentation of a target to one of the visual transducer units and the attainment of threshold activation in the response unit as a direct correlate of reaction time.

The visual perception units are also connected to a set of spatial attention units corresponding to their spatial location. The spatial units are activated by the visual unit at the corresponding location and reciprocally activate that same unit, creating a resonance that reinforces its activation. These reciprocal connections are what allow the spatial attention units to facilitate perception.

The spatial attention units are also connected to each other. For units corresponding to a given location, these connections are excitatory, that is, they reinforce each other's activation. The connections between units corresponding to different locations are inhibitory. In other words, if the units at one location are more active, they will drive down the activation of the other location's units. These mutually inhibitory connections are what give rise to attentional limitations in the model, that is, the tendency to attend to just one location at a time.

Connection strengths in this model were set by hand. Units in the model can take on activation values between 0 and 1, have a resting value of 0.1, and do not pass on activation to other units until their activation reaches a threshold of 0.9.

Before the onset of a trial, all units are at resting level activation except for the attention units, which are set to 0.5 to simulate the subject's allocation of some attention to each of the two possible stimulus locations. The presentation of a cue is simulated by clamping the activation value of one of the visual input units to 1 for the duration of the cuing interval. Presentation of the target is then simulated by clamping the activation value of one of the visual input units to 1. The target is validly cued if the same input unit is activated by both cue and target and invalidly cued if different input units are activated. We also simulated a neutral cuing condition in which no cue preceded the target. The number of processing cycles needed for the perception unit to raise the activation value of the response unit to threshold after target onset is the measure of reaction time. By regressing these numbers of cycles onto the data from normal subjects, we were able to fit the empirical data with our model.

Figure 8 shows the data from normal subjects obtained by Posner et al. (1984) and the model's best fit to the data. Why does our model show effects of valid and invalid cuing? In our model, attentional facilitation due to valid cuing is the result of both residual activation from the cue and top-down activation that the attention units give the perception unit at its corresponding location.

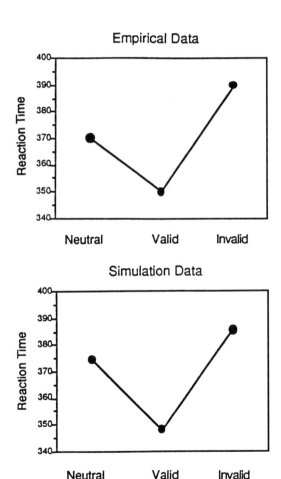

FIG. 8. Performance of normal subjects and network in lateralized cued simple reaction time task. Number of cycles needed for "response" unit to reach threshold has been regressed onto reaction times.

When the perception unit is activated by the cue, it activates the attention units on that side, which feed activation back to the perception unit, establishing a resonance that strengthens the activation of the target representation. Attentional inhibition due to invalid cuing is the result of the activated attention unit at the cued location suppressing the activation of the attention unit at the target location, leading to diminished top-down activation of the target perception unit. That is, the attention units on the cued side inhibit the attention units on the opposite side. As a result, when the target is presented to the opposite side, the attention unit on that side must first overcome the inhibition of the attention unit on the cued side before it can establish a resonance with its perception unit, and response time is therefore prolonged.

This very simple model of attention, which has no disengage component, captures the qualitative relations among the speeds of response in the three different conditions and can be fitted quantitatively to these average speeds with fairly good precision. In this regard, it seems preferable to a model that postulates separate components for orienting, engaging, and disengaging attention. The disengage component, however, was postulated on the basis of the behavior of parietally damaged subjects, not normal subjects. The critical test of this model, therefore, is whether it produces a disengage deficit when damaged.

A subset of the attention units on one side was eliminated and the model was run in the valid and invalid cuing conditions. (No patient data were available for the neutral condition.) Figure 9 shows the data of Posner et al. (1984) from parietally damaged patients and the simulation results, fitted to the data in the same way as before. Both sets of results show a disengage deficit: a disproportionate slowing from invalid cuing when the target is on the damaged side.

Why does the model show a disengage deficit when its attention units are damaged? The answer lies in the competitive nature of attentional allocation in the model and the imbalance introduced into the competition by unilateral damage. Attentional allocation is competitive, in that once the attention units on one side have been activated, they inhibit attentional activation on the other side.

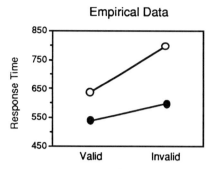

O Damaged
● Undamaged

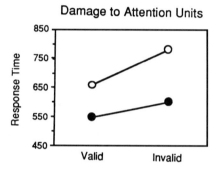

FIG. 9. Performance of parietally damaged patients and damaged network in lateralized cued reaction time task. Number of cycles needed for "response" unit to reach threshold has been regressed onto reaction times.

When there are fewer attention units available on the newly stimulated side, the competition is no longer balanced and much more bottom-up activation will be needed on the damaged side before the remaining attention units can overcome the inhibition from the attention units on the intact side to establish a resonance with the perception unit.

One might wonder whether we have really succeeded in simulating the disengage deficit without a disengage component, or whether some part of the model with a different label, such as the attention units or the inhibitory connections between attention units, is actually the disengage component. To answer this question, consider some of the attributes that would define a disengage component. First, it should be brought into play by perception of the target, and not the cue, on a

given trial. Second, it should be used to disengage attention and not for any other function. By these criteria, there is no part of the model that is a disengager. The attention units as well as their inhibitory connections are brought into play by both cue and target presentations. In addition, the attention units are used as much for engaging attention as for disengaging it. We therefore conclude that the disengage deficit is an emergent property of imbalanced competitive interactions among remaining parts of the system that do not contain a distinct component for disengaging attention.

Humphreys and Riddoch (1993) have independently proposed an account of the disengage deficit that does not include a disengage component in the normal architecture. Instead, they suggest that the deficit could be secondary to an impairment in orienting attention or to an overly strong engagement of attention ipsilesionally.

2.2.4. Relevance of the locality assumption for architecture of visual attention
After damage to the attention units on one side of the model, the nondamaged attention units on the other side function differently. Specifically, once activated they show a greater tendency to maintain their activation. This is because of the reduced ability of the attention units on the damaged side to recapture activation from the intact side, even when they are receiving bottom-up stimulus activation. The ability of this model to account for the disengage deficit depends critically upon this nonlocal aspect of its response to damage.

2.3. The functional architecture of visual face recognition: Separate components for visual processing and awareness?
Prosopagnosia is an impairment of face recognition that can occur relatively independently of impairments in object recognition and is not caused by impairments in lower-level vision or memory. Prosopagnosic patients are impaired in tests of face recognition such as naming faces or classifying them according to semantic information (such as occupation); they are also impaired in everyday life situations that call for face recognition.

Furthermore, based on their own introspective reports, prosopagnosics do not feel as though they recognize faces; however, when tested using certain indirect techniques, some of these patients do show evidence of face recognition. This has been taken to imply that their impairment lies not in face recognition per se, but in the transfer of the products of their face-recognition system to another system required for conscious awareness. This in turn implies that different components of the functional architecture of the mind are needed to produce perception and awareness of perception.

2.3.1. Evidence for dissociated recognition and awareness of recognition

Three representative types of evidence will be summarized here. The most widely documented form of "covert" face recognition occurs when prosopagnosics are taught to associate names with photographs of faces. For faces and names that were familiar to the subjects prior to their prosopagnosia, correct pairings are learned faster than incorrect ones (e.g. de Haan et al. 1987b). An example of this type of finding is shown in Table 4. It seems to imply that, at some level, the subject must have preserved knowledge of the faces' identities. The other two types of evidence come from reaction time tasks. One measures speed of visual analysis of faces, in which subjects must respond as quickly as possible to whether two photographs depict the same face or different faces. Normal subjects perform this task faster with familiar than unfamiliar faces. Surprisingly, as shown in Table 5, a prosopagnosic subject showed the same pattern, again implying that he was able to recognize them (de Haan et al. 1987b).

TABLE 4
Performance on correct and incorrect face-name pairings in a face-name relearning task

Trial:	1	2	3	4	5	6	7	8
Correct pairings	2	1	1	2	1	2	0	3
Incorrect pairings	0	0	0	1	1	0	0	0

Trial:	9	10	11	12
Correct pairings	2	3	2	2
Incorrect pairings	1	1	0	0

TABLE 5
Speed of visual matching for familiar and unfamiliar faces (in msec)

	Familiar	Unfamiliar
Prosopagnosic subject	2,795	3,297
Normal subjects	1,228	1,253

The last task to be reviewed is a kind of semantic priming task. Subjects must classify printed names as actors or politicians as quickly as possible, while on some trials photographs of faces are presented in the background. Even though the faces are irrelevant to the task subjects must perform, they influence reaction times to the names. Specifically, normal subjects are slowed in classifying the names when the faces come from the other occupation category. As shown in Table 6, the prosopagnosic patient who was tested in this task showed the same pattern of results, implying that he was unconsciously recognizing the faces fully enough to derive occupation information from them (de Haan et al. 1987a; 1987b).

2.3.2. Interpretation of covert recognition relative to the functional architecture of visual recognition and conscious awareness

The dissociation between performance on explicit tests of face recognition and patients' self-reporting of their conscious experience of looking at faces, on the one hand, and performance on implicit tests of face recognition on the other, has suggested to many authors that face recognition and the ability to make conscious use of it depend on different components of the functional architecture. For example, de Haan et al. (1992) interpret covert recognition in terms of the components shown in Fig. 10, in which separate components

TABLE 6
Priming of occupation judgments (in msec)

	Baseline	Unrelated	Related
Prosopagnosic subject	1,565	1,714	1,560
Normal subjects	821	875	815

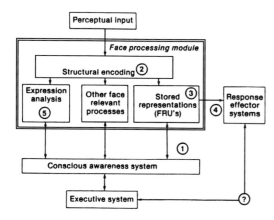

FIG. 10. Functional architecture of perception and awareness, proposed by de Haan et al. (1992).

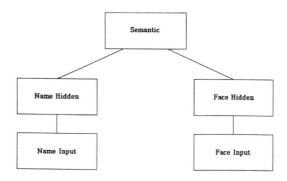

FIG. 11. Functional architecture of face perception as modeled by Farah et al. (1993).

of the functional architecture subserve face recognition and conscious awareness thereof. According to their model, the face-specific visual and mnemonic processing of a face (carried out within the "face processing module") proceeds normally in covert recognition, but the results of this process cannot access the "conscious awareness system" because of a lesion at location number 1.

2.3.3. Accounting for dissociated covert and overt recognition with an interactive architecture

Randy O'Reilly, Shaun Vecera, and I (Farah et al. 1993) have modeled overt and covert recognition using the five-layer recurrent network shown in Fig. 11, in which the same set of so-called face units subserves both overt and covert recognition. The face input units subserve the initial visual representation of faces, the "semantic" units represent the semantic knowledge of people that can be evoked either by the person's face or by the name, and the "name" units represent names. Hidden units were used to help the network learn the associations among patterns of activity in each of these three layers. These are located between the "face" and "semantic" units (called the "face" hidden units) and between the "name" and "semantic" units (the "name" hidden units). Thus, there are two pools of units that together comprise the visual face-recognition system in our model in that they represent visual information about faces: the "face input" units and the "face hidden" units.

The connectivity among the different pools of units was based on the assumption that in order to name a face, or to visualize a named person, one must access semantic knowledge of that person. Thus, face and name units are not directly connected but send activation to one another through hidden and semantic units. All connections shown in Fig. 11 are bidirectional.

Faces and names are represented by random patterns of 5 active units out of the total of 16 in each pool. Semantic knowledge is represented by 6 active units out of the total of 18 in the semantic pool. The only units for which we have assigned an interpretation are the "occupation units" in the semantic pool: one represents the semantic feature "actor," and the other, "politician." The network was trained to associate an individual's face, semantics, and name whenever one of these was presented, using the Contrastive Hebbian Learning algorithm (Movellan 1990). After training, the network was damaged by removing units.

Figure 12 shows the performance of the model in a 10-alternative, forced-choice naming task for face patterns after different degrees of damage to the "face input" and "face hidden" units. At levels of damage corresponding to removal of 62.5% and 75% of the face units in a given layer, the model performs at or near chance on this overt-recognition task. This is consistent with the performance of prosopagnosic patients who manifest covert recognition. Such patients perform poorly, but not invariably at chance, on overt tests of face recognition.

In contrast, the damaged network showed faster learning of correct face-name associations. When

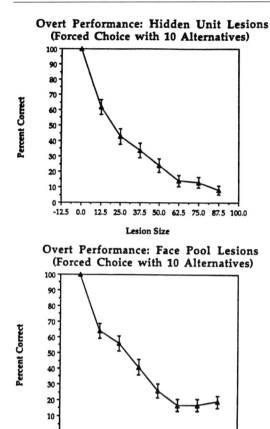

FIG. 12. Effect of different amounts of damage to face units on the network's ability to perform 10-alternative forced choice naming of faces, an overt face recognition task.

retrained after damage, it consistently showed more learning for correct pairings than incorrect ones in the first 10 training epochs, as shown in Fig. 13. The damaged network also completed visual analysis of familiar faces faster than unfamiliar ones. When presented with face patterns after damage, the face units completed their analysis of the input (i.e. the face units settled) faster for familiar than unfamiliar faces, as shown in Fig. 14. And finally, the damaged network showed semantic interference from faces in a name classification task. Figure 15 shows that when the network was presented with name patterns and the time it took to classify them according to occupation (i.e. the number of processing cycles

for the occupation units to reach threshold) was measured, classification time was slowed when a face from the incorrect category was shown, relative to faces from the correct category and, in some cases, to a no-face baseline.

Why does the network retain "covert recognition" of the faces at levels of damage that lead to poor or even chance levels of overt recognition? The general answer lies in the nature of knowledge representation in PDP networks. As already mentioned, knowledge is stored in the pattern of weights connecting units. The set of the weights in a network that cannot correctly associate patterns because it has never been trained (or has been trained on a different set of patterns) is different in an important way from the set of weights in a network that cannot correctly associate patterns because it has been trained on those patterns and then damaged. The first set of weights is random with respect to the associations in question, whereas the second is a subset of the necessary weights. Even if it is an inadequate subset for performing the overt association, it is not random; it has "embedded" in it some degree of knowledge of the associations. Furthermore, consideration of the tasks used to measure covert recognition suggest that the covert measures should be sensitive to this embedded knowledge.

A damaged network would be expected to relearn associations that it originally knew faster than novel associations because of the nonrandom starting weights. The faster settling with previously learned inputs can be attributed to the fact that the residual weights come from a set designed to create a stable pattern from that input. Finally, to the extent that the weights continue to activate partial and subthreshold patterns over the non-damaged units in association with the input, these resultant patterns will contribute activation toward the appropriate units downstream, which are simultaneously being activated by intact name units.

2.3.4. Relevance of the locality assumption for architecture of perception and awareness

The role of the locality assumption is less direct in the foregoing example than in the previous two, but it is nevertheless relevant. Many authors have reasoned according to the locality assumption that

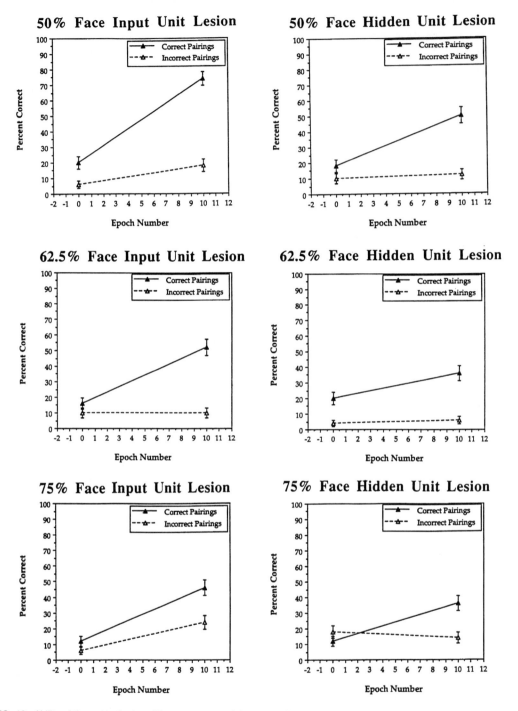

FIG. 13. Ability of the network after different amounts of damage to face units to produce the name associated to a face (to within 2 bits), for correctly and incorrectly paired names and faces, immediately after damage and following 10 epochs of further training. Note that learning occurs more quickly for correctly paired names and faces.

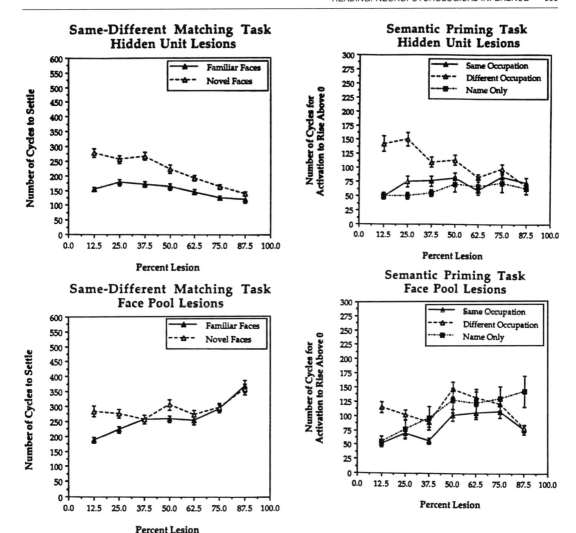

FIG. 14. Effect of different amounts of damage to face units on the time needed for the face units to settle, for familiar input patterns (closed triangles) and for unfamiliar input patterns (open triangles). Note that familiar patterns tend to settle more quickly.

FIG. 15. Effect of different amounts of damage to face units on the number of cycles needed for the "actor" and "politician" units to reach threshold when presented with name and face input patterns. When the face is from a different occupation category, it takes longer for the name to push the correct occupation unit over threshold.

the selective loss of overt recognition and the preservation of covert recognition implies that there has been localized damage to a distinct component of the functional architecture needed for overt, but not covert, recognition. The alternative account, proposed here, suggests that partial damage to the visual face-recognition component changes the relative ability of the remaining parts of the system (i.e. the remaining parts of the face-

recognition component along with the other components) to perform the overt and covert tasks. Specifically, the discrepancy between the difficulty of the overt and covert tasks is increased, as can be seen by comparing the steep drop in overt performance as a function of damage shown in Fig. 12 with the relatively gentle fall-off in the magnitude of the covert recognition effects shown in Figs. 13–15. According to the model, this is because the information processing required by the covert tasks can make use of partial knowledge encoded in the weights of the damaged network and is therefore more robust to damage than the information processing required by the overt task. In other words, with respect to the relative ability of the remaining system to perform overt and covert tasks, the effects of damage were nonlocal. The ability of the model to account for the dissociation between overt and covert recognition depends critically on this violation of the locality assumption.

3. General discussion

3.1. Evaluating the truth and methodological necessity of the locality assumption

The foregoing examples were intended as a small "data base" with which to test two empirical claims about the locality assumption. First, that it is true, namely, that after local brain damage the remaining parts of the system continue to function as before. Second, that it is necessary, in other words, that there is no other way to make principled inferences from the behavior of brain-damaged subjects to the functional architecture of the mind, and that the only alternative is therefore to abandon cognitive neuropsychology.

The examples allow us to assess the likely truth of the locality assumption by assessing the likely truth of the different inferences made with and without it. Of course, each such pair of inferences was made on the basis of the same data and fits those data equally well, so the choice between them rests on considerations of parsimony and consistency with other information about brain organization. On the basis of these considerations, the inferences made without the locality assumption seem preferable. In the case of semantic memory, the model obtained without the locality assumption is consistent with an abundance of other data implicating modality-specificity as a fundamental principle of brain organization and with the lack of any other example of a purely semantic distinction determining brain organization. In the case of visual attention, the model obtained without

the locality assumption has fewer components: although the overviews of the models presented in Figs. 6 and 7 are not strictly comparable (Fig. 6 includes components postulated to account for other attentional phenomena and Fig. 7 includes separate depictions of the left and right hemispheres' attentional mechanisms as well as two different levels of stimulus representation), it can be seen that the same "attention" component shown in Fig. 7 does the work of both the "engage" and "disengage" components in Fig. 6. Similarly, setting aside the irrelevant differences in the complexity of Figs. 10 and 11 arising from factors such as the greater range of phenomena to be explained by Fig. 10, it is clear that the same visual "face" components in Fig. 11 do the work of the visual "face" components and "conscious awareness system" in Fig. 10, at least as far as explaining performance in overt and covert tasks is concerned.

It should be noted that the success of these models is a direct result of denying the locality assumption, as explained in subsections on the relevance of the locality assumption (sects. 2.1.4, 2.2.4, 2.3.4). In linking each neuropsychological dissociation to the more parsimonious functional architecture, a key explanatory role is played by the nonlocal effects that damage to one component of the architecture has on the functioning of other components. Hence the weight of evidence from the three cases discussed here suggests that the locality assumption is false. Finally, with respect to its necessity, the examples provide existence proofs that principled inferences can be made in cognitive neuropsychology without the locality assumption.

3.2. Possible objections

In this section I consider some possible objections to these conclusions, with the hope of clarifying what has and has not been demonstrated here.

3.2.1. PDP and box-and-arrow: Apples and oranges?

One kind of objection concerns the comparability of the hypotheses that were derived with and without the locality assumption. The two types of hypotheses do indeed differ in some fundamental ways, and comparing them may be a bit like comparing apples and oranges. Nevertheless, apples and oranges do share some dimensions that afford meaningful comparisons, and I argue that the hypotheses under consideration here are likewise comparable in the ways discussed above.

For example, it might be objected that the computer models denying the locality assumption can only demonstrate the sufficiency of a theory, not its empirical truth, whereas the alternative hypotheses are empirically grounded. It is true that the models presented here have only been shown to be sufficient to account for the available data, but this is also true of the alternative hypotheses, and indeed of *any* hypothesis. It is always possible that a hypothesis can fit all the data collected so far, but that some other, as yet undiscovered, data could falsify it. The reason this may seem more problematic for PDP models is that there is a research tradition in computer modeling that takes as its primary goal the accomplishment of a task rather than the fitting of psychological data (e.g. Rosenberg & Sejnowski 1986), relying exclusively on computational constraints rather than empirical constraints to inform the models. This is not a necessary feature of modeling, however, and the models presented here are constrained as much as the alternative hypotheses are by the empirical data.

Furthermore, the computational models presented here and the alternative hypotheses are on equal footing with respect to the distinction between prediction and retrodiction of data. In all three cases, the locality assumption has been used to derive a hypothesis, post hoc, from the observed neuropsychological dissociation. It was not the case that researchers had already formulated hypotheses to the effect that semantic memory was subdivided by taxonomic category or that there was a distinct component of the attention system for disengaging attention, or that awareness of face recognition depended on distinct parts of the mental architecture from face recognition; nor did they then go looking for the relevant dissociations to test those hypotheses. Rather, they began with the data and inferred their hypotheses just as we have done with the models presented

earlier. Both the hypotheses derived using the locality assumption and the PDP models presented here await further testing with new data. An example of the way in which new data can be used to distinguish between the competing hypotheses comes from the work of Verfaellie et al. (1990) with a bilateral parietally damaged patient. They found that, contrary to their expectation of a bilateral disengage deficit, their subject showed diminished effects of attentional cuing. When attention units are removed bilaterally from the Cohen et al. (in press) model, which was developed before the authors knew of the Verfaellie et al. finding, the model also shows reduced attentional effects rather than a bilateral disengage deficit. This is because the disengage deficit in our model is caused by the imbalance in the number of attention units available to compete with one another after unilateral damage; bilateral damage does not lead to an imbalance but it does, of course, reduce the overall number of attention units and therefore the magnitude of the attentional effects.

Another way the comparisons presented above might seem mismatched is in their levels of description. The hypotheses derived using the locality assumption concern "macrostructure," that is, the level of description that identifies the components of the functional architecture, as shown in the so-called box-and-arrow models. In contrast, the hypotheses that deny the locality assumption appear to concern "microstructure," that is, the nature of the information processing that goes on within the architectural components. However, the latter hypotheses concern both microstructure and macrostructure, as should be clear from the macrostructures depicted in Figs. 2, 7, and 11. We can therefore compare the two types of hypotheses at the level of macrostructure.

3.2.2. The locality assumption can be saved with more fine-grained empirical analysis of the deficit

Perhaps the prospects for the locality assumption look so dim because the types of data considered so far are unduly limited. The arguments and demonstrations presented above concern a relatively simple type of neuropsychological observation, namely, a selective deficit in some previously normal ability. I have focused on this type of observation for two reasons; the first is its very simplicity, and the seemingly straightforward nature of the inferences that follow from it. At first glance, a truly selective deficit in *A* does seem to demand the existence of an *A* component, and this inference is indeed sound under the assumption that the *A* component is informationally encapsulated. The second reason is that this is still the most common form of inference in cognitive neuropsychology, as argued earlier in the section on ubiquity (sect. 1.2).

Nevertheless, other, finer-grained ways of analyzing patient performance are used increasingly by cognitive neuropsychologists to pinpoint the underlying locus of impairment in a patient's functional architecture. The two most common are qualitative error analyses, and selective experimental manipulations of difficulty of particular processing stages. Can the use of the locality assumption be buttressed by the additional constraints offered by these methods? Several recent PDP simulations of patient performance suggest that these finer-grained analyses are just as vulnerable to nonlocal effects of brain damage as are the more brute-force observations of deficit per se.

For example, semantic errors in single-word reading (e.g. pear → "apple") have been considered diagnostic of an underlying impairment in the semantic representations used in reading, and visual errors (pear → "peer") are generally taken to imply a visual processing impairment (e.g. Coltheart 1985). Hinton and Shallice (1991) showed how a PDP simulation of reading could produce both kinds of errors when lesioned either in the visual or the semantic components of the model. Humphrey et al. (1992) make a similar point in the domain of visual search: error patterns suggestive of an impairment in gestalt-like grouping processes can arise either from direct damage to the parts of the system that accomplish grouping or by adding noise to earlier parts of the system. In both cases, the nondiagnosticity of error types results from the interactivity among the different components of the model.

Another well-known example of the use of error types to infer the locus of impairment is the occurrence of regularization errors in the reading performance of surface dyslexics (e.g. Coltheart 1985). As mentioned earlier, surface dyslexics fail to read irregular words; this has been interpreted, using the locality assumption, as the loss of a whole-word reading route with preservation of the sublexical grapheme-phoneme translation route. The inference that these patients are relying on the latter route seems buttressed by a further analysis of the nature of their errors, which are typically regularizations (e.g. *pint* is pronounced like "lint"). Patterson et al. (1989), however, showed that a single-route architecture, comprised only of whole-word spelling-sound correspondences, produced, when partially damaged, both a selective impairment in the reading of irregular words and a tendency to regularize them. With the distributed representations used in their model, similar orthographies and phonologies have similar representations at each of these levels and there is consequently a tendency toward generalization. Although with training the system learns not to generalize the pronunciation of, say, *pint* to the pronunciation of most other *-int* words (such as *lint*, *mint*, *hint*), this tendency is unmasked at moderate levels of damage. The model's regularization errors are probably best understood as a result of the distributed nature of the word representations in their model. The principles of PDP are closely interrelated, however, and the regularization effects can also be viewed as the result of interactions among different word representations, with the less common pronunciations losing their "critical mass" and therefore being swamped by the remaining representations of more common pronunciations.

Analyses of selective deficits and of the nature of the errors produced have in common the use of a purely observational method. Perhaps experimental manipulations designed to tax the operation of specific components offer a more powerful way of pinpointing the locus of impairment. Two recent models speak to this possibility and show that direct manipulations of particular processing stages are no more immune to nonlocal effects than are the previous methods. Mozer and Behrmann's (1990) model of visual-spatial neglect shows how the manipulation of a stimulus property designed to affect postvisual processing, namely the lexicality of a letter string (word, pseudoword, nonword), can have pronounced effects on the performance of a model whose locus of damage is visual. Interactions between attended visual information and stored lexical representations allow letter strings to be reconstructed more efficiently the more they resemble familiar words. Tippett and Farah (in press) showed how apparently conflicting results in the literature on the determinants of naming difficulty in Alzheimer's disease can be accounted for with a single hypothesis. Although most researchers believe that the naming impairment in Alzheimer's disease results from an underlying impairment of semantic knowledge, manipulations of visual difficulty (degraded visual stimuli) and lexical access difficulty (word frequency) have pronounced effects on patients' likelihood of naming, leading to alternative hypotheses of visual agnosia or anomia (Nebes 1989). When semantic representations were damaged, a PDP model of visual naming showed heightened sensitivity to visual degradation and word frequency. Thus, when one component of an interactive system is damaged, the system as a whole becomes more sensitive to manipulations of the difficulty of any of its components.

In sum, the problem of nonlocal effects of brain damage is not limited to inferences based on the range and boundaries of the impairment; it also affects inferences based on the qualitative mode of failure and the sensitivity of the system to manipulations designed to affect specific components directly.

3.2.3. PDP could be false

A different type of objection concerns the assumptions of the PDP framework. As already acknowledged, PDP is controversial. How can one be convinced, through comparisons involving PDP models, that the locality assumption is false, if it has not been established first that PDP is a correct way of characterizing human information processing? First, it should be pointed out that much of the controversy concerning PDP involves the adequacy of PDP models of language and reasoning, which are not relevant here. Few vision researchers would deny that the basic prin-

ciples of PDP are likely to apply to visual attention and pattern recognition (e.g. see the recent textbook overviews of these topics by Allport 1989; Biederman 1990; Hildreth & Ullman 1989; Humphreys & Bruce 1989; and even Pinker 1985, who has been critical of PDP models of language). Semantic memory may be a more controversial case. Second, and perhaps more important, one can remain agnostic about PDP as a general framework for human information processing and still appreciate that the particular models presented here are credible alternatives to those derived using the locality assumption. PDP, like the locality assumption, is ultimately an empirical claim that will gain or lose support according to how well it helps explain psychological data. The ability of PDP to provide parsimonious accounts for neuropsychological dissociations such as the ones described here counts in its favor. Finally, even if PDP were false, there would remain other ways of conceptualizing human information processing that would provide explicit, mechanistic alternatives to modularity. For example, in production system architectures (see Klahr et al. 1987) working memory is highly nonencapsulated. Kimberg and Farah (in press) found that weakening association strengths in working memory produced an array of specific and characteristic frontal impairments that were in no transparent way related to working memory. Although interactive computation is at the heart of PDP, which makes PDP the natural architecture to contrast with the locality assumption, other architectures are also capable of accommodating high degrees of interactivity.

3.3. General implications of denying the locality assumption

3.3.1. Modularity

The truth of the locality assumption has implications for issues in psychology beyond how best to infer functional architecture from the behavior of brain-damaged patients. As discussed at the outset, the locality assumption follows from a view of the mind and brain according to which the components of the functional architecture are informationally encapsulated, that is, their inputs and outputs are highly constrained. Components interact only when one has completed its processing, at which point it makes the end product available to a relatively small number of other components. If this were true, then the effects of damaging one component should be relatively local. Alternatively, if we judge that the best interpretation of various neuropsychological deficits (on the grounds of parsimony or consistency with other scientific knowledge, not on the grounds of a priori preferences for encapsulation or interactivity) involves denying the locality assumption, then this counts as evidence against modularity.

The term "modularity" is often used in a more general sense than I have used it so far, and this more general sense is not challenged by the failure of the locality assumption. Specialized representations are sometimes called "modules," so that the model in Fig. 2 could be said to contain "visual knowledge" and "functional knowledge" modules. In this more general sense, the "modularity hypothesis" is simply that there is considerable division of labor among different parts of functional architecture with, for example, knowledge of language represented by a separate part of the system (functionally, and possibly anatomically), compared with other knowledge. Of course, if such a system is highly interactive, it may be difficult to delineate and characterize the different modules, but this is a problem of *how* you find something out, not of what it is or whether it exists.

3.3.2. Top-down versus bottom-up research strategies

Denying the locality assumption also has a more general implication for research strategy in cognitive neuroscience. Most researchers in neuroscience and cognitive science acknowledge that there are multiple levels of description of the nervous system, from molecules to thoughts, and that one of the goals of science is a complete description of the nervous system at all of these levels. However, such researchers may differ in their opinions as to the most efficient way to arrive at this complete description. The bottom-up, or reductionist, approach is to begin with the most elementary levels of description, such as the biophysics of neurons, believing that it will be impossible to

understand higher levels of organization if one does not know precisely *what* is being organized. This approach is anathema to cognitive neuroscience, which is, by definition, forging ahead with the effort to understand such higher-level properties of the brain as perception, memory, and so forth, while acknowledging that our understanding of the more elementary level of description is far from complete.

The main alternative, explicitly endorsed by many cognitive neuroscientists, is the top-down approach, according to which the most efficient way to understand the nervous system is by successive stages of analysis of systems at higher levels of description in terms of lower levels of description. It is argued that our understanding of lower levels will be facilitated if we know what higher-level function they serve. It is also argued that the complexity of the task of understanding the brain will be reduced by the "divide and conquer" aspect of this strategy, in which the system is analyzed into simpler components that can then be further analyzed individually (e.g. Kosslyn et al.'s 1990 "hierarchical decomposition constraint"). In the context of the three examples discussed earlier, this corresponds to first deriving the macrostructural hypotheses, in which the relevant components of the functional architecture are identified, and then investigating the microstructure of each component's internal operation. Unfortunately, to derive a macrostructure from neuropsychological data requires either making the locality assumption or considering the system's microstructure, as was done in the foregoing examples. If the locality assumption is false, the microstructure has implications for the macrostructure, and one cannot be assured of arriving at the correct macrostructural description without also considering hypotheses about microstructure.

Thus, even if one's only goal is to arrive at the correct macrostructural description of the functional architecture, as is the case for most cognitive neuropsychologists, the three examples presented here suggest that one must nevertheless consider hypotheses about microstructure. This points out a correspondence between theories of functional architecture and the methodologies for studying it. If one holds that the components of the functional architecture are informationally encapsulated, one can take a strictly top-down approach to the different levels of description, "encapsulating" one's investigations of the macrostructure from considerations of microstructure. In contrast, if one views the functional architecture as a highly interactive system, with each component responding directly or indirectly to the influences of many others, then one must adopt a more interactive mode of research, in which hypotheses about macrostructure are influenced by constraints imposed simultaneously at both the macrostructural and the microstructural levels.

3.3.3. Implications for cognitive neuropsychology

The conclusion that the locality assumption may be false is a disheartening one. It undercuts much of the special appeal of neuropsychological dissociations as evidence about the functional architecture. Although perhaps naive in hindsight, this special appeal came from the apparent directness of neuropsychological data. Conventional methods of cognitive psychology are limited to what Anderson (1978) has called "input-output" data: manipulation of stimuli and instructions on the input end and the measurement of responses and response latencies at output. From the relations between these, the nature of the intervening processing must be inferred. Such inferences are indirect, and as a result often underdetermine choices between competing hypotheses. In contrast, brain damage directly affects the intervening processing, constituting a direct manipulation of the "black box."

Unfortunately, the examples presented here suggest that even if the manipulation of the intervening processing is direct, the inferences by which the effects of the manipulations must be interpreted are not. In Ferrier's (1886) words, it may well be "at least highly difficult to trace any uncomplicated connection between the symptoms produced and the lesion as such." The locality assumption, which constitutes the most straightforward way of interpreting neuropsychological impairments, does not necessarily lead to the correct interpretation. If the locality assumption is indeed false, then dissociations lose their special status as particularly direct forms of evidence about the functional architecture.

Even for cognitive neuropsychologists who would not claim any special status for neuropsychological data, abandoning the locality assumption would make their work harder. The interpretation of dissociations without the locality assumption requires exploring a range of possible models that, when damaged, might be capable of producing that dissociation. What makes this difficult is that the relevant models would not necessarily have components corresponding to the distinctions between preserved and impaired abilities and we therefore lack clear heuristics for selecting models to test.

The foregoing demonstrations and arguments are not intended to settle decisively the issue of whether the locality assumption is correct. As already acknowledged, this is not the type of issue that can be decided on the basis of a single study or even a small number of studies. Instead, my goal has been to call attention to the fact that we do not have any firm basis for an opinion one way or the other, despite the widespread use of the locality assumption. Furthermore, at least in a few cases the best current interpretation seems to involve denying the locality assumption.

It is possible that some cognitive domains will conform more closely to the locality assumption than others; if so, this would have interesting theoretical as well as methodological implications concerning the degree of informational encapsulation in different subsystems of the functional architecture. However, until we have a broad enough empirical basis for deciding when the locality assumption can safely be used and when it will lead to incorrect inferences, we cannot simply assume it to be true, as has been done almost universally in the past.

Acknowledgments

The writing of this paper was supported by ONR grant N00014–91-J1546, NIMH grant R01 MH48274, NIH career development award K04-NS01405, and a grant from the McDonnell-Pew Program in Cognitive Neuroscience. I thank my coauthors on the projects described herein for their collaboration and tutelage in PDP modeling: Jonathan Cohen, Jay McClelland, Randy O'Reilly, Rick Romero, and Shaun Vecera. Special thanks to Jay McClelland for his encouragement and support. I thank several colleagues for discussions of the ideas in this paper: John Bruer, Alfonso Caramazza, Clark Glymour, Mike McCloskey, Morris Moscovitch, Edmund Rolls, and Larry Squire. I also thank Larry Weiskrantz for calling my attention to the passage from Ferrier quoted at the beginning. Finally, I thank the reviewers and editor of *BBS* for useful comments and criticisms of a previous draft: C. Allen, S. Harnad, G. Humphreys, M. McCloskey, M. Oaksford, T. Van Gelder, and four anonymous reviewers.

Note

1. There are, of course, many other ways to make a wrong inference using the locality assumption, even with the foregoing conditions satisfied, but these have to do with the particular content of the hypothesis being inferred and its relation to the data, not the use of the locality assumption per se. For example, Caramazza et al. (1990) have pointed out that selective impairments in modality-specific knowledge do not imply that knowledge of different modalities is represented in different formats; dissociability will not, in general, tell us about representational formats.

References

Allport, D. A. (1985). Distributed memory, modular subsystems, and dysphasia. In: *Current perspectives in dysphasia*, ed. S. K. Newman & R. Epstein. Churchill Livingstone.

Allport, D. A. (1989). Visual attention. In: *Foundations of cognitive science*, ed. M. I. Posner. MIT Press.

Anderson, J. R. (1978). Arguments concerning representation for mental imagery. *Psychological Review, 85*, 249–77.

Basso, A., Capitani, E. & Laiacona, M. (1988). Progressive language impairment without dementia: A case with isolated category specific semantic defect. *Journal of Neurology, Neurosurgery and Psychiatry, 51*, 1201–7.

Biederman, I. (1990). Higher-level vision. In: *Visual cognition and action*, ed. D. N. Osherson, S. M. Kosslyn & J. M. Hollerbach. MIT Press.

Caplan, D. (1981). On the cerebral localization of linguistic functions: Logical and empirical issues surrounding deficit analysis and functional localization. *Brain and Language, 14*, 120–37.

Caramazza, A. (1984). The logic of neuropsychological research and the problem of patient classification in aphasia. *Brain and Language, 21*, 9–20.

Caramazza, A. (1986). On drawing inferences about the structure of normal cognitive systems from the analysis of patterns of impaired performance: The case for single-patient studies. *Brain and Cognition, 5*, 41–66.

Caramazza, A. (1992). Is cognitive neuropsychology possible? *Journal of Cognitive Neuroscience, 4*, 80–95.

Caramazza, A., Hillis, A. E., Rapp, B. C. & Romani, C. (1990). The multiple semantics hypothesis: Multiple confusions? *Cognitive Neuropsychology, 7*, 161–90.

Cohen, J. D., Romero, R. D. & Farah, M. J. (in press). Disengaging from the disengage function: The relation of macrostructure to microstructure in parietal attentional deficits. *Journal of Cognitive Neuroscience*.

Coltheart, M. (1985). Cognitive neuropsychology and the study of reading. In: *Attention and performance XI*, ed. M. I. Posner & O. S. M. Marin. Erlbaum.

de Haan, E. H. F., Bauer, R. M. & Greve, K. W. (1992). Behavioural and physiological evidence for covert face recognition in a prosopagnosic patient. *Cortex, 28*, 77–95.

de Haan, E. H. F., Young, A. & Newcombe, F. (1987a). Faces interfere with name classification in a prosopagnosic patient. *Cortex, 23*, 309–16.

de Haan, E. H. F., Young, A. & Newcombe, F. (1987b). Face recognition without awareness. *Cognitive Neuropsychology, 4*, 385–416.

DeRenzi, E. (1986). Current issues in prosopagnosia. In: *Aspects of face processing*, ed. H. D. Ellis, M. A. Jeeves, F. Newcombe & A. Young. Martinus Nijhoff.

Farah, M. J. & McClelland, J. L. (1991). A computational model of semantic memory impairment: Modality-specificity and emergent category-specificity. *Journal of Experimental Psychology: General, 120(4)*, 339–57.

Farah, M. J., McMullen, P. A. & Meyer, M. M. (1991). Can recognition of living things be selectively impaired? *Neuropsychologia, 29*, 185–93.

Farah, M. J., O'Reilly, R. C. & Vecera, S. P. (1993). Dissociated overt and covert recognition as an emergent property of lesioned neural networks. *Psychological Review, 100*, 571–88.

Ferrier, D. (1886). *The functions of the brain*. Smith, Elder.

Fodor, J. A. (1983). *The modularity of mind.* Bradford Books/MIT Press.

Hildreth, E. C. & Ullman, S. (1989). The computational study of vision. In: *Foundations of cognitive science*, ed. M. I. Posner, MIT Press.

Hillis, A. E. & Caramazza, A. (1991). Category-specific naming and comprehension impairment: A double dissociation. *Brain, 114*, 2081–94.

Hinton, G. E., McClelland, J. L. & Rumelhart, D. E. (1986). Distributed representations. In: *Parallel distributed processing: Explorations in the micro-structure of cognition*, ed. D. E. Rumelhart & J. L. McClelland. MIT Press.

Hinton, G. E. & Shallice, T. (1991). Lesioning an attractor network: Investigations of acquired dyslexia. *Psychological Review, 98(1)*, 74–95.

Humphreys, G. W. & Bruce. V. (1989). *Visual cognition: Computational, experimental and neuropsychological perspectives.* Hove, UK: Lawrence Erlbaum.

Humphreys, G. W., Freeman, T. & Muller, H. J. (1992). Lesioning a connectionist model of visual search: Selective effects of distractor grouping. *Canadian Journal of Psychology, 46*, 417–60.

Humphreys, G. W. & Riddoch, M. J. (1987). *Visual object processing: A cognitive neuropsychological approach.* Hove, UK: Lawrence Erlbaum.

Humphreys, G. W. & Riddoch, M. J. (1993). Interactions between object- and space-vision revealed through neuropsychology. In: *Attention and performance XIV*, ed. D. E. Meyer & S. Kornblum. MIT Press.

Jackson, J. H. (1873). On the anatomical and physiological localization of movements in the brain. *Lancet, 1*, 84–85, 162–64, 232–34.

Kimberg, D. Y. & Farah, M. J. (in press). A unified account of cognitive impairments following frontal lobe damage: The role of working memory in complex, organized behavior. *Journal of Experimental Psychology, General.*

Kinsbourne, M. (1971). Cognitive deficit: Experimental analysis. In: *Psychobiology*, ed. J. L. McGaugh. Academic Press.

Kinsbourne, M. (1977). Hemi-neglect and hemispheric rivalry. In: *Advances in neurology*, ed. E. A. Weinstein & R. P. Friedland. Raven Press.

Klahr, D., Langley, P. & Neches, R. (1987). *Production system models of learning and development.* MIT Press.

Kosslyn, S. M., Flynn, R. A., Amsterdam, J. B. & Wang, G. (1990). Components of high-level vision: A cognitive neuroscience analysis and accounts of neurological syndromes. *Cognition, 32*, 203–77.

Kosslyn, S. M. & Van Kleek, M. (1990). Broken brains and normal minds: Why Humpty Dumpty needs a skeleton. In: *Computational neuroscience*, ed. E. Schwartz. MIT Press.

Moscovitch, M. & Umiltà, C. (1990). Modularity and neuropsychology: Modules and central processes in attention and memory. In: *Modular deficits in Alzheimer-type dementia*, ed. M. F. Schwartz. MIT Press.

Movellan, J. R. (1990). Contrastive Hebbian learning in the continuous Hopfield model. In: *Proceedings of the 1989 Connectionist Models Summer School*, ed. D. S. Touretzky, G. E. Hinton & T. J. Sejnowski. Morgan Kaufmann.

Mozer, M. C. & Behrmann, M. (1990). On the interaction of selective attention and lexical knowledge: A connectionist account of neglect dyslexia. *Journal of Cognitive Neuroscience, 2(2)*, 96–123.

Nebes, R. D. (1989). Semantic memory in Alzheimer's disease. *Psychological Bulletin, 106*, 377–94.

Newcombe, F., Mehta, Z. & de Haan, E. F. (1994). Category-specificity in visual recognition. In: *The neuropsychology of high-level vision: Collected tutorial essays*, ed. M. J. Farah & G. Ratcliff. Hillsdale, NJ: Erlbaum.

Patterson, K. E., Seidenberg, M. S. & McClelland, J. L. (1989). Connections and disconnections: Acquired dyslexia in a computational model of reading processes. In: *Parallel distributed processing: Implications for psychology and neurobiology*, ed. R. G. M. Morris. Oxford University Press.

Pietrini, V., Nertimpi, T., Vaglia, A., Revello, M. G., Pinna, V. & Ferro-Milone, F. (1988). Recovery from herpes simplex encephalitis: Selective impairment of specific semantic categories with neuroradiological correlation. *Journal of Neurology, Neurosurgery, and Psychiatry, 51*, 1284–93.

Pinker, S. (1985). Visual cognition: An introduction. In: *Visual cognition*, ed. S. Pinker. MIT Press.

Posner, M. I. (1978). *Chronometric explorations of mind.* Erlbaum.

Posner, M. I., Walker, J. A., Friedrich, F. J. & Rafal, R. D. (1984). Effects of parietal lobe injury on covert orienting of visual attention. *Journal of Neuroscience, 4*, 1863–74.

Rosenberg, C. R. & Sejnowski, T. K. (1986). NETtalk: A parallel network that learns to read aloud. *EE & CS Technical Report #JHU-EECS-86/01.* Johns Hopkins University Press.

Rumelhart, D. E., Hinton, G. E. & McClelland, J. L. (1986). A general framework for parallel distributed processing. In: *Parallel distributed processing:*

Explorations in the microstructure of cognition, ed. D. E. Rumelhart & J. L. McClelland. MIT Press.

Rumelhart, D. E. & McClelland, J. L. (1986). *Parallel Distributed Processing: Explorations in the microstructure of cognition*. Vol. 1: *Foundations*. MIT Press.

Sartori, G. & Job, R. (1988). The oyster with four legs: A neuropsychological study on the interaction of visual and semantic information. *Cognitive Neuropsychology*, *5*, 105–32.

Shallice, T. (1988). *From neuropsychology to mental structure*. Cambridge University Press.

Silveri, M. C. & Gainotti, G. (1988). Interaction between vision and language in category-specific semantic impairment. *Cognitive Neuropsychology*, *5*, 677–709.

Squire, L. R. (1987). *Memory and brian*. Oxford University Press.

Squire, L. R. (1992). Memory and the hippocampus: A synthesis from findings with rats, monkeys, and humans. *Psychological Review*, *99*, 195–231.

Tippett, L. J. & Farah, M. J. (in press). A computational model of naming in Alzheimer's disease: Semantic, visual, and lexical factors. *Neuropsychology*.

Tulving, E. (1972). Episodic and semantic memory. In: *Organization of memory*, ed. E. Tulving & W. Donaldson. Academic Press.

Tulving, E. (1983). *Elements of episodic memory*. Oxford University Press.

Verfaellie, M., Rapcsak, S. Z. & Heilman, K. M. (1990). Impaired shifting of attention in Balint's syndrome. *Brain and Cognition*, *12*, 195–204.

von Klein, B. E. (1977). Inferring functional localization from neurological evidence. In: *Explorations in the biology of language*, ed. E. Walker. Bradford Books/MIT Press.

Warrington, E. K. (1985). Agnosia: The impairment of object recognition. In: *Handbook of clinical neurology*, ed. P. J. Vinken, G. W. Bruyn & H. L. Klawans. Elsevier.

Warrington, E. K. & McCarthy, R. (1983). Category specific access dysphasia. *Brain*, *106*, 859–78.

Warrington, E. K. & Shallice, T. (1984). Category specific semantic impairments. *Brain*, *107*, 829–54.

Zurif, E. B. (1980). Language mechanisms: A neuropsycholinguistic perspective. *American Scientist*, *68*, 305–34.

9

A reckoning

We hope that the contents of the previous chapters have been sufficient to persuade the reader that connectionism has much to offer the science of mental life. Models have been described that offer useful insights into often-puzzling phenomena over a wide range of behaviours. There seems little doubt that connectionism has found a place among the competing schools of psychology, in that a significant group of scientists find it fruitful. But does connectionism provide a view on human cognition that is radically different from other approaches? Do connectionist models simply implement accounts previously expressed in other forms (e.g. as "box and arrow" diagrams), or do they offer something in addition? Even if viewed as "mere" implementations (a view that we will question), should such models be thought of as capturing real neuronal processes or as being functional accounts that "sit" above neuronal theories of behaviour? This final chapter will attempt to evaluate the successes and failures of the models with regard to these wider issues.

9.1 SYMBOLIC AND SUBSYMBOLIC COMPUTATION

At several places in this book the contrast between so-called symbolic and subsymbolic models of cognition has been mentioned but a detailed discussion of it has been avoided. This is the place for that discussion.

Smolensky (1988) has developed the most clear distinction between connectionism and the classical approach which turns on the differences between symbolic and subsymbolic models. Smolensky observed that an evaluation of the potential of connectionism requires a clear description of its foundations, or the development of what he refers to as the proper treatment of connectionism (PTC). On his account the connectionist endeavour is an attempt to explain processes that are specifically "cognitive". A cognitive system is characterised in terms of the repertoire of goals it maintains over a range of environmental conditions. The number of goals and the extent of the range of environments determine whether a system is to be regarded as cognitive or not. A thermostat, which has only one goal, fails the test, whereas a fruit-fly, which has a set of goals that it can maintain over different environments, passes.

Cognitive systems, so conceived, are the subject of two major competing types of explanation: traditional symbolic models and the form of connectionism described by the PTC. In symbolic models there are entities that are properly described as symbols, in that they refer to other things and that they participate in operations governed by rules of syntax. For example there will be rules for forming legal or well formed combinations of symbols. Particular types of behaviour, in a symbolic model, are explained by reference to particular types of operation on symbol structures. In contrast, connectionism, according to Smolensky, seeks to explain those same behaviours by finer-grain descriptions in which the entities do not themselves refer but are constituents of symbols. These entities are subsymbols. They participate in numerical rather than general, syntactic operations.

Given this way of contrasting connectionist and symbolic accounts, two fundamental, related questions arise. First, how are the two views related in terms of their level of analysis? The talk of symbols being constituted by subsymbols may suggest, for instance, that connectionist architectures should be regarded as implementing symbolic cognitive systems. This issue of levels of analysis or explanation will be considered in detail in section 9.2. The second fundamental question is whether either account could be complete. Various answers to this question will be considered here, first that of Fodor and Pylyshyn (1988) which we briefly summarised in Chapter 6.

Fodor and Pylyshyn (1988) argued that connectionist theories cannot be cognitive theories. This is so because connectionist architectures do not provide the sorts of representations needed to account for a fundamental aspect of cognition: the systematicity of thought and language. To understand or produce the sentence or thought "John loves the girl", entails an understanding of "The girl loves John". It is simply impossible to understand or think one such proposition without being able to understand or think the other. This can only be the case, the authors contend, because of the structural or syntactic relationship between the two. The shared structure results from the rules of combination of the elements of language that determine the well formed or legal expressions in that language — the syntax. Meaning must map onto the syntactic structure, so one can also talk of a combinatorial semantics. If the expressions possess combinatorial syntax and semantics then so must their mental representations.

If these observations are accepted (and the systematicity of language seems difficult to deny),

then only symbolic models can provide a psychological theory of language use and thought. Such models have precisely the representational formalisms needed. Connectionist models, on the other hand, only seem to. To see that this is so consider the example, from propositional logic, of the well formed formula: $(A \& B) \rightarrow A$. A can be derived from $(A \& B)$ because of the rules of combination and derivation that are the propositional calculus. The derivation depends on the syntax of the expression not its content, so it remains valid whatever is substituted for A and B. In a symbolic model the representation would mirror the syntax: mental representations have a constituent structure that arises from rules of combination of elements just as in the propositional calculus (only vastly more complex and elaborate). Moreover, according to Fodor and Pylyshyn, processes that use these representations are sensitive to their structure. In the case of our example, there will be an operation that takes any expression of the form $(P \& Q)$ and produces an expression of the form P. These properties of mental representations are physically realised. For example, the relationship between A and $(A \& B)$ is that of A being part of $(A \& B)$ and this would be reflected in the relationships among the brain states representing those expressions. The brain is, under this description, a physical symbol system (Newell, 1980). This is important because it ensures that the state transitions of the brain result from the structural or syntactic properties of the represented expressions. A is derived from $(A \& B)$ because of the relations and rules that apply to the expressions.

Now consider a connectionist model of the derivation of A from $(A \& B)$. This seems straightforward: a network of just three units, one of which encodes $(A \& B)$ and has excitatory connections to two units that encode A and B respectively. Activation in the $(A \& B)$ unit will lead to activation in the A unit, thus the network can be said to derive A from $(A \& B)$ in just the same way as the symbolic representational system. This conclusion is a misunderstanding. The labels associated with the units are in fact just that: labels. They play no part in the behaviour of the network, which is explicable only in terms of activation, weights, and their like. If the label $(A \& B)$

were replaced by (A or B) the network's behaviour would not be changed. The equivalent symbols play a very different role in the physical symbol system case. Changing (A & B) to (A or B) would, by definition, change the behaviour of the system, because the syntax of expressions causes that behaviour.

It is the constituent structure of mental representations and the sensitivity to that structure of the processes using the representations that provides the basis of the mind's systematicity. Understanding "John loves the girl" is intrinsically linked to "The girl loves John" because the representations, like the sentences, contain the same parts. As connectionist representations do not have constituent structure, the mind cannot be a connectionist network.

If the preceding arguments are accepted then connectionism has no role in the explanation of cognitive processes. Cognitive explanations must use the language of symbol systems, and connectionism is confined to accounting for the implementation of the systems (see the next section). Before turning to Smolensky's (1988) radical rebuttal of this view, and his claims that connectionism can be complete, we will consider an ecumenical position.

Clark (1989) makes the perfectly reasonable suggestion that the computational architecture of the brain may not be uniform. That is, it may support a variety of virtual machines: symbolic, connectionist, and, presumedly, others as yet unsuspected. The behaviours that provide connectionism with their greatest challenges, as outlined earlier, may well depend on a non-connectionist virtual architecture. Clark (1989) argues that in fact, for some evolutionary recent behaviours such as logical inference and arithmetic, the mind simulates a classical von Neumann architecture. Following the speculations of Rumelhart, Smolensky, McClelland, and Hinton (1986b), the von Neumann virtual architecture is said to be the product of learning to represent possible states of the world using external artefacts. Take the case of multiplication. For simple cases, learning can result in pattern-matching skills that allow one to recognise, for example, that the product of 9 and 5 is 45. It would not be hard to construct a network account

of this form of pattern recognition. But what of more difficult cases? Most of us cannot multiply 2347 by 3458 in our heads. Faced with such a problem we might use paper and pen and arrange the problem so as to apply the rules of long multiplication. The latter effectively breaks the problem down into a series of simple pattern-matching stages, with the results of intermediate stages being represented on paper. This is undeniably a symbol-manipulating process, but the symbols are in the world, not the head! However it is clearly possible to learn to do long multiplication in the head. We do so, according to Rumelhart et al. (1986b), by developing a mental model of the in-the-world symbol manipulation involved in doing long multiplication with pen and paper. Similar explanations are meant to apply to those other behaviours that are best characterised by rule-governed, sequential processes. On this account, symbolic representations in the world are the germ of mental symbolic representation.

For Clark (1989) the foregoing implies that the behaviours in question are best explained by the operations of a von Neumann virtual machine implemented on a connectionist machine. The mind is not uniform, it is hybrid. For some behaviours, such as seeing and remembering, the appropriate psychological models will be connectionist. For other behaviours, such as mental arithmetic and logic, the appropriate models will be variants of physical symbol systems.

Smolensky (1988) acknowledges a similar distinction between types of mental process or behaviour. The intuitive processor is involved with those behaviours that do not require the conscious application of rules, such as perception, skilled motor actions, and word comprehension. There are also good psychological grounds for arguing this. These behaviours, for instance, are typically fast acting, difficult to prevent once initiated, and relatively immune to effects of other ongoing tasks. The other class of behaviours are those that do involve conscious rule application — such as reasoning and higher-level language operations (beyond single words). Some behaviours, but particularly the latter sort, may be captured with a high degree of validity by traditional, symbolic models. For Smolensky (1988), and others such as Rumelhart et al. (1986b), these remain an approximation to the actual psychological mechanisms, however. The sense of approximation is often hinted at by analogy with the distinction between Newtonian mechanics and quantum theory in physics. The two sorts of explanation make exactly the same sorts of prediction in most circumstances, but in some exceptional cases the Newtonian account breaks down and the microstructural quantum theory is thereby shown to be more complete.

What are we to make of these contending views on the adequacy or completeness of connectionism? They range from a uniform theory which holds that only symbolic models can account for cognitive processes, through hybrid theories which resort to both connectionist and symbolic accounts for the differing aspects of cognition, to a uniform theory which seeks purely connectionist accounts of the fundamental aspects of cognition. Where in this range is the truth?

There are sufficient examples, described in this book, to convince us that a uniform symbolic theory is unlikely. In learning, memory, perception, and some aspects of language use, connectionist accounts have been shown to have considerable virtues and power. It seems now difficult to conceive of at least some of these behaviours being convincingly accounted for without some mention of connectionist notions. We have also seen, however, during our discussions of serial order in behaviour and of high-level language operations, several instances in which connectionist models are faced with deep problems. Connectionist solutions to these have often resulted in models that are hybrid in some sense, as for example in Shastri and Ajjanagade's (1993) reasoning network (see Chapter 7). In the latter model, temporal relations among the oscillating output of units achieved the variable binding required for the compositionality that leads to systematicity in reasoning, but the point is that, in doing so, the network replicated the explicit syntax of symbolic models. This syntax enters into the explanation of the behaviour. If no other method of obtaining systematicity were to be discovered, the non-uniformity position would be reinforced and a uniform connectionist theory would not be tenable. However,

some glimpses of purely connectionist approaches to compositionality have also been described, in particular in the form of recurrent and RAAM networks (see Chapters 2, 5 and 7). We assess in section 9.4 the possibility that the distinctive form of representation that such networks develop does provide compositionality, and therefore makes possible a uniform connectionist account. Before we do so however, we return to the second fundamental issue mentioned at the beginning of this section. That is, what level of explanation are connectionist models concerned with, and, in particular, should they be regarded as mere implementations of higher-level symbolic models?

9.2 LEVELS OF EXPLANATION: MODELS AT THE ALGORITHMIC LEVEL

Marr (1982) introduced a highly influential set of distinctions between three levels of explanation of information processing systems. At the highest, most abstract level, a computational theory described the fundamental problem the system was solving. An intermediate algorithmic level described one solution to that problem, particularly in terms of the representations and operations required for the solution. The lowest-level description was concerned with the physical implementation of the algorithm (the theory as implemented in the hardware). According to some observers, the proper place for connectionism is at this implementational level, but we need to be careful to define what we mean here; researchers have used the term "implementation" in at least two ways, only one of which conforms to Marr's usage.

Broadbent (1985) illustrates the two types of "implementation" view by reference to McClelland and Rumelhart's (1985) model of memory which we described in Chapter 3 (section 3.1). This, the reader will remember, consisted of a simple autoassociative network which was shown to be capable of storing several prototype patterns, in a single set of weights, by being trained with exemplars of those prototypes. The trained network appeared to show the same sort of familiarity and repetition effects that have been reported in the human experimental literature. In particular, it showed a graded response to repeated stimuli: its response was strongest to patterns that were identical to preceding ones, intermediate to ones related to a previous presentation, and weakest to those that bore no relationship to a previous presentation. This appears to be a rather elegant account of the experimental findings, in that the effects are an intrinsic property of a network that is constantly adapting to a stream of inputs. Earlier psychological models, in which there is an internal unit (or "logogen") activated by the presence of each known pattern (e.g. Morton, 1969, 1979), appear contrived by comparison, needing to make additional assumptions about the effects of active logogens on logogens for related items or needing to proliferate logogens to account for the differing priming effects observed.

Broadbent (1985, p.190) rejects the comparison between the network and the logogen account as a confusion about levels of explanation and says that it:

> . . . misses the point of Morton's contribution. A single logogen is a system responding to one pattern rather than to others: to say that there are two logogens is to say that there are two patterns each of which is a prototype for discrimination. There is no implication whatsoever that the mechanisms of discrimination are physically specific [1], nor alternatively that they are distributed over a common set of multiple codes [2]. Such statements belong to a different realm of theory. [numerals are inserted by us.]

In this statement, one view is that the network is a description of the physical implementation of a logogen system (view 1). Another view, however, is that the network is a functional realisation, using distributed representations, of a psychological theory in which there are local representations ("logogens") (view 2). Note that a theory of the latter kind makes no commitment to the nature of the hardware on which the distributed representations are formed. Indeed, it can be argued that the

distributed model of memory, and many of the other connectionist schemes described in this book, were *not* intended as theories of the hardware in the sense outlined by Marr (1982). As we discuss in section 9.3, the connectionist models we have reviewed are a long way from models of real neurons. Rather such connectionist theories may form a second type of algorithmic account of cognition, albeit at a somewhat lower level than the more typical "psychological" description. Are such models, then, direct competitors of other algorithmic accounts, including symbolic models such as logogen theories? Our answer to this is both no and yes, as we will explain.

Let us first consider the argument that connectionist and symbolic accounts are not competitive. As noted earlier, algorithmic processes may be described at a number of different levels of abstraction. By analogy with programming languages, a specific algorithm may be composed of high-level commands in a language such as LISP or as a set of machine routines, yet neither of these describes actual hardware operations. Similarly between the computational and implementational level descriptions there may be several levels of analysis. The question is: what is the most fruitful description for psychological research? Staying with the computer analogy, we can argue that connectionist models provide a kind of machine code account of symbolic theories that use high-level descriptions — this may be the "different realm of theory" supposed by Broadbent (1985, see earlier). Connectionist models are concerned with the "microstructure", and symbolic models the "macrostructure", of cognition. On this account, the different views are complementary, not competitive.

However, we suggest that the situation is somewhat more complex. Our view is that, at one stage in the evolution of theories, the macro- and microstructural accounts can indeed be complementary. But, as theories at the microstructural level become more detailed, so they will serve to drive psychological prediction. Macrostructure theories may still be useful to provide broad-brush sketches of behaviour, but microstructural accounts will be "where the action is" — and for "scientific action" here, read the generation and testing of new predictions. Microstructural accounts may then gradually supersede macrostructural accounts as psychological models of cognition.

What are the grounds for this argument — that over time, connectionist accounts will indeed become true competitors to higher-level models? The more cynical view of connectionist modelling is that it only simulates known data, but it is not productive in the sense of generating new predictions. If such models are "mere" simulations, then they are not competitors to higher-level psychological theories but serve only as instantiations. Certainly there is something to the argument that models are not productive. In Chapters 3–8 of this book we have reviewed numerous models — of perception, memory, language, attention, and serial behaviour — which have reproduced psychological data, yet the number of cases where the models have then been used to generate new predictions is much smaller. Even so, examples where models have been productive have been given at several junctures, and we expect that this close coupling of modelling to experimentation is something that will become ever more salient — once models have been shown to be capable of capturing basic phenomena. We now outline how predictions can arise both from the properties of specific models and from the more general properties of connectionist networks.

9.2.1 Predictions generated from general properties of networks

Connectionist models can be divided into several classes, according to whether they use local or distributed representation, whether they are interactive or only feed-forward, whether they are "hard-wired" or exhibit learning, and so forth. It can be argued that these different classes of model exhibit characteristics that can be evaluated using psychological data. Predictions emerge from the general properties of such networks.

Consider the issue of interactivity. Models that use either interactive activation and competition, or recurrent feedback on-line during processing, make several overarching predictions. One is that performance in a given task should be determined by a particular form of interaction between bottom-up and top-down processes: top-down effects should vary as a function of the quality of

information given "bottom-up" to the system. When bottom-up information is degraded, top-down knowledge will have a greater time to operate and to influence performance. When bottom-up information is not degraded, top-down knowledge will exert a lesser influence. We have discussed several examples of such interactions in the psychological literature. For example, we reviewed evidence on the "word superiority effect" (WSE) in Chapter 6 (section 6.2), where letters are identified more accurately within words than within nonwords. This effect with skilled readers is most pronounced under conditions in which target words are followed by pattern masks, which disrupt letter processing (McClelland & Rumelhart, 1981). Within the interactive activation model of word recognition, the effect is produced by the features in masks activating letter representations; top-down feedback for words leads to their letters being less affected by "noise" than the letters of nonwords (which enjoy weaker feedback).

This issue, of top-down effects in perception, has been much researched in studies of speech recognition, with much of the debate fuelled by the predictions derived from interactive connectionist models. As we discussed in sections 6.11–6.13 of Chapter 6, some of the predictions have not been borne out and this has led to further refinement of the models so that, for instance, stochastic rather than deterministic activation functions are used (e.g. McClelland, 1993). Although it may turn out to be the case that interactive models fail to explain the minutiae of data, and that forms of non-interactive model are best supported, this is not the point; the point is that explicit models can give rise to experimental tests that help to advance our understanding of cognition, and this holds even if the model subsequently turns out to be wrong.

A second general prediction that can be derived from interactive models is that effects arising at early stages in a model may interact with effects arising at later stages, so that the early effect is modified. This contrasts with predictions of more discrete (often symbolic) models, in which effects at early and later stages of processing may simply add together in performance. A concrete example arises in studies of object naming. Human object naming is influenced by several factors, including whether objects belong to categories with perceptually similar exemplars, and the frequency of the object's name. Naming times tend to be faster for objects belonging to categories with perceptually dissimilar exemplars, and they tend to be faster for objects with high- rather than low-frequency names. Now, perceptual similarity between category exemplars ought to influence early stages of object recognition, concerned with accessing stored structural memories for objects (see Chapter 4, section 4.6). The frequency of an object's name, however, should influence a late stage of name retrieval rather than visual aspects of object recognition. Despite the two variables — perceptual similarity within a category and name frequency — appearing to affect different stages of object naming, the evidence shows that they interact; effects of name frequency are larger for objects belonging to perceptually dissimilar categories (Humphreys et al., 1988). In Chapter 4 we showed how an interactive model of object naming could capture such effects. Essentially, the influence of the late-acting variable (name frequency) can be overridden when the earlier factor (perceptual similarity within a category) leads to many competitors being activated at the late stage. In Chapter 6 (section 6.15), we also discussed how the issue of discrete or interacting processing stages has been hotly debated within the psychological community working on speech production. In such instances, general properties of network models provide useful frameworks for experimental tests.

In other instances, it is less the general properties of models that are important, and more the issues that the models highlight that can form the focus of experimental analyses. For example, connectionist models of visual word recognition have demonstrated that coding position information in words is a non-trivial problem and, in some of the solutions suggested, particular problems are encountered when multiple words are presented (PABLO and BLIRNET; see sections 6.3 and 6.4, Chapter 6). Although they have not been used to formulate specific predictions, such models have formed the backdrop for studies into letter-position coding in reading (Humphreys et al., 1990) and for studies of how we read multiple-word displays

(McClelland & Mozer, 1986). Likewise, connectionist models of language acquisition (e.g. the past tense learning models of Plunkett & Marchman, 1991, and Rumelhart & McClelland, 1986), and the acquisition of syntactic representations (e.g. Elman, 1990) emphasise the importance of understanding the statistical properties of languages in order for models to be evaluated (e.g. the relative balance of regular to irregular verb forms, or the statistical relations between word order and syntax). These topics have subsequently stimulated psychological research (Finch & Chater, 1994; Pinker & Prince, 1988, 1989).

9.2.2 Predictions from specific models

In other instances it has been possible to derive predictions from the properties of specific models, allowing these models to be pitted and tested against competitor accounts. One example here is the SERR model of visual search, proposed by Humphreys and Müller (1993). This model was discussed in detail in Chapter 4 (section 4.5.3), where we reported on how one prediction (concerning grouping between multiple targets in search) had been tested and shown to support this model (in which there is parallel grouping of visual elements) rather than a model supposing serial visual search (Müller et al., 1994). Several other such predictions were outlined and tested by Humphreys and Müller, also with broad support for the model. Some of these predictions could only be formulated by implementing and running the model. For instance, when running SERR Humphreys and Müller observed that, in search displays containing multiple distractor groups, there was some chance of missing a target when it was present. The probability of a miss occurring grew exponentially as the number of distractors increased in the displays (as the "display size" increased). Error rates only decreased by having the model repeat its searches ("re-check") on a certain proportion of trials. Following this, they tested human detection of targets in similar displays when subjects had to respond to a short deadline to prevent any re-checking process. Like the model, error rates increased exponentially with display size.

Another example of specific predictions derived by running a model concerns the effects of phonemic similarity on errors in word naming, as found after lesioning the model of word naming proposed by Seidenberg and McClelland (1989). In Chapter 8 (section 8.3.3) we noted that, when lesioned, many errors generated by this model differed by a single phoneme from target words and that errors differing by two phonemes or more were relatively rare. Re-examination of the errors made by surface dyslexic patients supported this finding, illustrating that phonemic similarity can influence surface dyslexic reading.

It also turned out, however, that the lesioned version of Seidenberg and McClelland's model failed to account for other aspects of surface dyslexia in important respects. We have suggested that, to some degree, this may reflect a difference between subgroups of patients (section 8.3.3); in addition, however, it indicates that the model was incomplete in many respects — it failed to capture the full detail of the procedures mediating word naming in human subjects. Subsequent revisions of the model, using different forms of phonological representation and a semantic influence on word naming during learning, have proved more successful (Plaut et al., 1996). The work demonstrates that full models of reading will need to incorporate multiple routes (at least a semantic as well as a direct route between orthography and phonology), and that it will be important to understand what we term "interactive learning" in networks. This form of interactivity is different of course from the kind of interactive effects that take place in interactive activation models, which we discussed in section 9.2.1. Those effects involve dynamic, top-down changes in activation states during a single perceptual event. In interactive learning, we witness evolutionary changes in the characteristics of one processing route when it operates in conjunction with another route. Plaut et al.'s work shows that learning within a given route is clearly not the same when it operates in partnership with another route, but the full implications of this for other areas of cognition have not been fully explored yet.

These two examples illustrate how connectionist models can be used to generate specific predictions, predictions that could not have been generated without implementing and running the models. Also, in these examples, the predictions derived from the models reflect properties that are inherently "connectionist". In the case of SERR, the predictions follow from there being parallel perceptual grouping operations. In the case of word naming, the predictions concerning naming errors emerge because the models allow approximate addressing of output units even when input representations are impaired, and so phonological approximations result after lesioning. These models go beyond being mere simulations of higher-level theories and become competitor theories in their own right.

9.3 LEVELS OF EXPLANATION: MODELS AT THE HARDWARE LEVEL

The vast majority of the connectionist models that we have considered are not theories of neural hardware; real neural networks differ in many important respects (see Crick & Asanuma, 1986 for one summary). Perhaps most critically, learning algorithms such as back-propagation have no known neural counterpart. For back-propagation to operate, neurons must compute exact differences in activation value between their current state and a desired state (set up by the "supervisor"), store these differences, and use them to compute differences in other units at earlier stages of processing. There is no evidence for transportation of exact activation values in the brain. Also, the weights used in the feed-forward of activation need to be the same as those used in calculating the error signal during the feed-back process. In real neural systems there are typically as many back projections as there are forward ones[1], but the two forms of projection are physically separated. There would be no way for the feed-back system to know the weights utilised in the feed-forward system (see Grossberg, 1987).

There are numerous other ways in which the real and artificial systems can differ. For example, the processing units in most connectionist models can have both positive (excitatory) and negative (inhibitory) connections to other units. This is not the case in the brain, where neurons either serve an excitatory or inhibitory role. Inhibitory neurons in the brain can also operate as "veto cells", preventing the firing of connecting cells irrespective of the strength of the input signal into those cells; in many connectionist models, positive and negative inputs are simply summed to determine output values. Real neurons are typically sparsely connected; in contrast many of the models we have reviewed have had units at each level fully interconnected, and precise connectivity is particularly important in models using local representations.

9.3.1 From models to brains

Nevertheless, despite the many differences we have documented, a dialogue is possible between connectionist theorists and theorists interested in real brain processes. In Chapter 3 we discussed Marr's (1969) account of the cerebellum as a type of associative network (section 3.1). This model makes a clear link between the operation of its processing units and the operation of different cerebellum neurons, and it provides a functional account of how the cerebellum interacts with the cerebral cortex during learning. This model is pitched at the level of how particular cell types operate.

Other levels of analogy are also possible. Consider the studies that have trained networks to learn shape codes from continuous patterns of shading as input (the "shape-from-shading" problem — see Lehky & Sejnowski, 1988; section 4.2.3). In these simulations modellers have used the back-propagation learning algorithm, and so have not attempted to capture exactly how learning takes place in the brain (see earlier). Even so, analyses of the representations developed by the models are useful because these representations can be related to the stimulus preferences found in real neurons: the hidden units appear to show preferences for stimuli at particular orientations, similar to real neurons in the visual cortex that are activated by an edge at a particular orientation (cf. Hubel & Wiesel, 1959). However, the fact that the models are trained not on edge-detection but on interpreting shape from shading throws open the question of the role played by the neurons in the brain. Note that, for the analogy to be made to real neurons here, it matters little that

the models were trained using a learning algorithm that is not neurally plausible; in the real brain, the structure of the network may be established by evolution or by a form of learning other than back-propagation. Whatever the case, the models serve as an existence proof that neurons that resemble "edge-detectors", when probed using single-cell recording techniques, could play a different computational role in vision. What the model does here is provide a functional account of neurons in a larger-scale computational process. Such functional accounts may enable neurophysiological researchers to map single-cell operations to accounts of networks of cells.

Another example of deductions being made about real brain processes from the functional properties of connectionist networks comes from research into the hippocampus and into spatial representations in the parietal cortex (see Fig. 9.1). In Chapter 8 (section 8.9) we introduced modelling work that has attempted to capture the functional role of the hippocampus in human learning, but we did not analyse the structure of this memory system. The hippocampi sit under the temporal lobes, one at the side of each cerebral hemisphere (see Fig. 9.2) and each hippocampus receives input from many cortical areas, including those concerned with coding visual, auditory, tactile, and olfactory stimuli. Each is thus a site in which information may be combined across modalities. Studies of the real hippocampus have shown that it has a clear and elegant structure (see Rolls, 1989, for one review). There are distinct sets of cells, the FD_{gc} cells, the CA3 cells, and the CA1 cells, that are activated in series, without the presence of back-projections from cells later in the path to cells that occur earlier (see Fig. 9.3). Each set of cells has a particular structure. For example, the first set of cells, termed the FD_{gc} cells, form a kind of matrix, while units that input into these cells are connected by inhibitory neurons to the cells receiving output from the FD_{gc} cells. In the connectionist literature, associative memory models have used similar inhibitory links from input units to output units in order to scale the outputs from the associative memory (see Fig. 9.4 and McNaughton & Morris, 1987, for one example). Rolls (1989) suggests that inhibitory

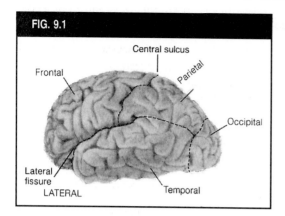

FIG. 9.1

Lateral view of the cerebral cortex, illustrating the occipital, parietal, temporal, and frontal lobes, along with major sulci. From Kolb and Wishaw (1980).

neurons at the FD$_{gc}$ stage may play a similar computational role. These inhibitory neurons may also effect a form of competition between output units, as is found in competitive learning in connectionist networks (section 2.9, Chapter 2). Competitive learning serves to "orthogonalise" inputs, so that patterns are represented by just a few output neurons. Activation from the FD$_{gc}$ stage is transmitted on to the CA3 stage. Cells at this stage have strong recurrent collateral connections, which connect on to other cells at the same stage. This is similar to the connectivity found in autoassociative distributed memory systems (section 3.1, Chapter 3), suggesting that such cells are involved in creating autoassociative memories. Such autoassociative memories would help form cross-modal associations between stimuli brought by different sensory systems into the hippocampus. Now, connectionist research has shown that distributed associative memories are subject to interference in recall if too many patterns with similar representations are stored. The storage capacity of such systems is helped by orthogonalising the input, so that patterns are less similar. This may be done by competitive learning at the FD$_{gc}$ stage in the hippocampus. Finally, activation from the CA3 stage is passed on to CA1 neurons. These neurons may detect conjunctive firing from CA3 cells, again helping the formation of cross-modal associations.

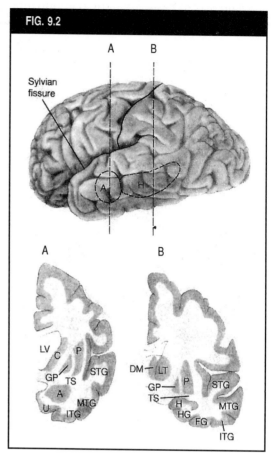

FIG. 9.2

Lateral view of the cerebral cortex illustrating the position of the hippocampus (H) along with another forebrain structure, the amygdala (A). The dashed lines A and B give the approximate locations of the sections in the bottom figures, where specific structures within the temporal lobes are located. A = amygdala; C = caudate nucleus; DM = dorsomedial nucleus of the thalamus; FG = fusiform gyrus; GP = globus pallidus; H = hippocampus; HG = hippocampal gyrus; ITG = inferior temporal gyrus; LT = lateral thalamus; LV = lateral ventricle; MTG = middle temporal gyrus; P = putamen; STG = superior temporal gyrus; TS = temporal stem; U = uncus. For current purposes, only the hippocampus is relevant.

Overall, then, details of the organisation of cells in the hippocampus, when combined with our knowledge of the properties of connectionist models, suggest a functional account of stimulus coding in this brain structure. On this account, the hippocampus is the site of unsupervised learning

FIG. 9.3

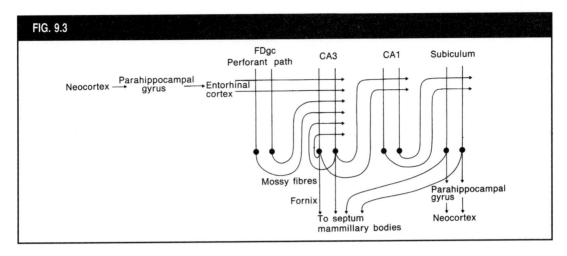

Schematic illustration of the network of cells in the hippocampus. Input is received from the (neo)cortex and output given back to the (neo)cortex. From Rolls (1989).

FIG. 9.4

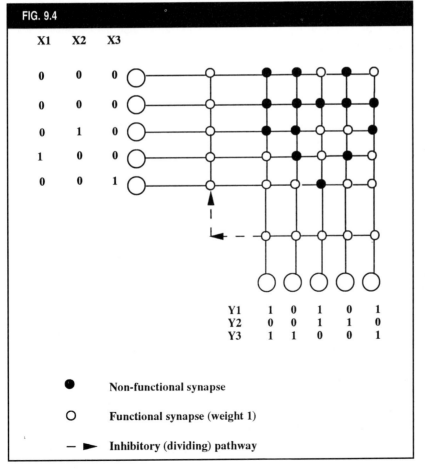

Scaling of output in an association memory by inhibitory connections from input units. Events are represented as input vectors (X1, X2, X3, for X patterns; Y1, Y2 and Y3, for Y patterns). Associations between these vectors are stored as a weight matrix. Recall of an X pattern can be generated by giving a Y pattern as input. For a given input, the output pattern is generated by multiplying each input value by the value of the connecting weight (in this instance 0 or 1); by summing along each row and then by (integer) dividing the elements of the resulting vector by the number of 1s in the input pattern. This form of scaling was first suggested by Marr (1969).

615

which serves first to orthogonalise input stimuli, and then to form associations between stimuli converging from different modalities (Rolls, 1989). Note that these cross-modal memories may be formed in the hippocampus in order either to interleave with future learning in the cortex, to prevent catastrophic interference (the view of the hippocampus proposed by McClelland et al., 1995), to serve as an "external supervisor" for learning within the cortex (the view proposed by Gluck & Myers, 1993), or to provide links with cortical activation that help consolidate cortical learning over the longer term (Murre, 1997; see Chapter 8, section 8.9). In each case, the representations provided by the hippocampus to the cortex will be enriched by cross-modal associations.

Zipser and Anderson (1988) examined the nature of the spatial codes that may be formed in the parietal cortex. They employed a network with three layers of processing units: two sets of input units (one for the position of a stimulus on the retina, the other for the position of the eye), a set of hidden units, and a set of output units coding "egocentric" position (the position of the stimulus relative to the observer, rather than the retina). Using back-propagation, they trained a network to map from a retinotopic location to a set of egocentric coordinates. Input at one retinal location generated a Gaussian activation profile across the surrounding cells. Eye position was coded in terms of the magnitude of the eye deviation in x and y coordinates. Following this, the properties of the hidden units were assessed. They found that the hidden units carried a distributed representation of the egocentric position of the stimulus — with no single unit unambiguously coding the stimulus position. The "receptive fields" of the hidden units were also assessed by holding eye position input constant and presenting stimuli at different retinal positions. When this was done, there was remarkable agreement between the profiles for these units and the activation profiles found by recording from single cells in the parietal cortex. From this Zipser and Andersen speculate that the parietal cortex has a distributed representation of egocentric position, perhaps learned by associating body position with the visual position of a stimulus on the retina. The model here enables us to interpret the functional role of cells in this brain area.

9.3.2 From brains to models

In the examples on modelling the cerebellum, the "shape from shading" problem, and on understanding the hippocampus, we have stressed the implications of modelling for neurophysiological research. This is a two-way process, however. Modellers can also learn a good deal from studies that deal with the properties of both individual neurons and networks of neurons. In Chapter 4, we discussed how models such as SLAM (Phaf et al., 1990) relate to single-cell studies of visual attention. In SLAM visual selection when multiple stimuli are present is achieved by activating units that code target properties (e.g. red, round), so that the target then wins the competition for selection, relative to the other items that fall in the visual field. This mimics the behaviour of individual cells in the inferotemporal cortex during search selection tasks (Chelazzi et al., 1993). We suggest that the analogy here heightens interest in the model.

At a network rather than the single-cell level, much neurophysiological (and also neuropsychological) research indicates that real neural systems have some degree of modularity. For example, when we discussed the SERR model of visual search, in Chapters 4 and 8 (sections 4.5.3 and 8.6.1), we alluded to neurophysiological data distinguishing between the coding of pattern and location information ("what" and "where") in the brain. In SERR this distinction is found because there are separate sets of units for coding the locations of stimuli (irrespective of their identity) and for coding the identity of stimuli (irrespective of their locations) (the "location" and "template" units). A good deal of biological data support this distinction, suggesting that (i) pattern information is coded in pathways running from the primary visual area (the occipital cortex) to the temporal lobes, and (ii) location information is coded in pathways running from the occipital cortex to the parietal lobes at the top of the brain. Thus monkeys with damage to the parietal cortex find it difficult to learn location discrimination tasks but can learn pattern discrimination tasks; monkeys with damage to the temporal lobe, on the other hand, find it easy to learn location discrimination tasks but find pattern discrimination tasks difficult (Ungerleider & Mishkin, 1982). Similarly damage to the occipital-temporal pathways in humans produces problems in pattern recognition — visual agnosia; damage to the occipital-parietal pathways produces spatial problems such as unilateral neglect (sections 8.6 and 8.8, Chapter 8). This suggests that there is some degree of modularity in visual processing, with the neural structures subserving pattern recognition being separate from those subserving forms of location coding.

There may well be good computational reasons for this separation between coding "what" and "where" stimuli are. For example, object recognition requires viewpoint invariance, and so memory representations should not be tied to locations. Indeed, in the models of object recognition reviewed in Chapter 4, attempts were made to achieve viewpoint invariance by having inputs map onto stored representations that responded irrespective of where the objects fell in the visual field (see particularly the model of Hinton, 1981b, section 4.3.2, and the "shifter circuit" models of visual attention, Humphreys & Heinke, 1997, 1998; Olshausen et al., 1993, section 4.5.2). Rueckl, Cave, and Kosslyn (1989) explored the utility of the "what" and "where" distinction in modelling pattern recognition and location discrimination tasks. A three-layer feed-forward network with a total of 18 hidden units was presented with patterns on its retina and trained using back-propagation to discriminate both the identity of the pattern and its location. Some output units coded pattern identity (irrespective of the retinal position of the pattern) and others coded location (and were activated irrespective of which pattern fell at that location). Rueckl et al. compared learning within a "fully connected" net, in which the hidden units connected to all the output units, with that in "split" nets, in which one group of hidden units connected to the "pattern" units and one group of hidden units connected to the "location" units at the output level. These "split" nets are of interest because they have a form of modular structure in which some hidden units will be devoted to computing "what" a pattern is and others to computing "where" it is. Figure 9.5 illustrates the nature of the problem and the architecture of the model.

Several different "splits" were tried, which varied in the numbers of hidden units that were given over to either the pattern recognition task or the location discrimination task — the complexity of these two tasks differed and so, for learning to be successful, relatively more hidden units had to be devoted to the pattern recognition task. The results are shown in Fig. 9.6, plotted in terms of the total error scores (summed over the "pattern" and the "location" output units) across learning trials (where one block equals one presentation of each stimulus in the training set). With some "splits" of the hidden units the networks performed poorly — essentially when insufficient hidden units were allocated to either the pattern task (e.g. the 9–9 split) or the location task (the 15–3 "pattern to location" split of hidden units; see Fig. 9.6). However, other split networks outperformed the fully connected network (particularly the 14–4 "pattern to location" split network). Thus, providing enough computational resources (hidden units) are available to each "module", networks with modular structures can learn two concurrent problems more efficiently than non-modular networks with fully connected structures. A network that allocates separate units to coding "what" and "where" a pattern is outperforms a network that does not. For the model, this is probably because the two tasks are independent of one another. Thus the weight changes that are involved in learning where a pattern is may conflict with those involved in learning what the pattern is, slowing learning within a fully connected network. Modular networks do not suffer such conflict. It would appear that the brain has reached a similar modular solution, although presumably through evolution rather than via learning within the lifetime of one individual.

Rueckl et al.'s study illustrates how knowledge of neural structures can influence and help optimise network design. It also shows how interactivity can take place between modelling and empirical studies, because, in this instance, the modelling work provides a computational account of why modularity might be useful for neural structures — modularity is useful when independent problems must be learned from common inputs (in this case, patterns on the retina).

Other network modellers have proposed learning algorithms that can lead to networks developing modular structures during learning, rather than having them imposed by the modeller. For

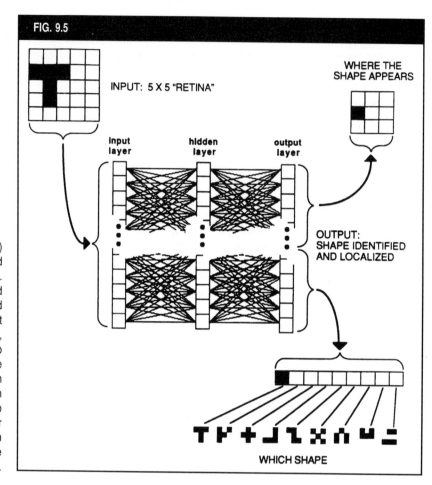

FIG. 9.5

INPUT: 5 X 5 "RETINA"

WHERE THE
SHAPE APPEARS

input
layer

hidden
layer

output
layer

OUTPUT:
SHAPE IDENTIFIED
AND LOCALIZED

WHICH SHAPE

The Rueckl et al. (1990) model of pattern and location discrimination. The hidden units could either be fully connected to all input and all output units (the "unsplit" model), or they could be split so that some fed into the output units for pattern recognition (which shape?) and others into the output units for location discrimination (where the shape appears).

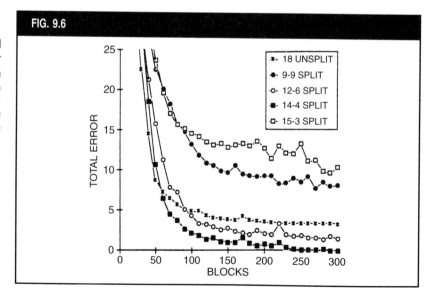

FIG. 9.6

Total error score (summed across output units for both pattern and location discrimination) for the Rueckl et al. (1990) model, as a function of training blocks (repeats of the training set). Data are shown as a function of the split between the pattern and location units (e.g. 15–3 means that 15 hidden units were devoted to the pattern discrimination task and 3 to the location discrimination task).

instance, adaptions of back-propagation exist that lead to weight decay or elimination if connections only develop small weights during learning (see Hinton, 1987; le Cun, 1989; Weigend, Huberman, & Rumelhart, 1990). When trained using such "pruning" algorithms, networks can develop modular structures in which connections remain only if there are strong weights between input and hidden units, or between hidden and output units. This too may mimic real brain processes. In the brain, an excess of axons may initially be sent to a target area, which are selectively eliminated during learning (e.g. Brown, Hulme, Hyland & Mitchell, 1994).

Jacobs and Jordan (1992) used a "pruning" approach in which learning was influenced not only by weight strength but also by the distance between units within the network. Units in the network were assigned a "location", and the learning algorithm acted to favour large weights between nearby units in the network and small weights between distant units. Thus this network

was biased towards developing strong local connections. The network was applied to the "what" and "where" tasks used by Rueckl et al. (1989). Interestingly, as learning took place, a modular structure was developed. This is shown in Fig. 9.7. This figure illustrates the weights on the connections into the output units from the hidden units. There are 18 rows, corresponding to 18 output units used in the model, and 36 columns corresponding to the 36 hidden units that were used. The first nine rows correspond to the output units for the "what" task, and the last nine rows correspond to the output units for the "where" task. Positive weights are depicted with a plus sign (+) and negative weights have a minus sign (−); weights near zero have a full stop (.). Figure 9.7 indicates that, for the "what" task (the first nine rows), there are strong weights (both positive and negative) from the first 18 or so hidden units and weak weights from the remaining hidden units. In contrast, for the "where" task (the second nine rows), there are strong weights from the last 18

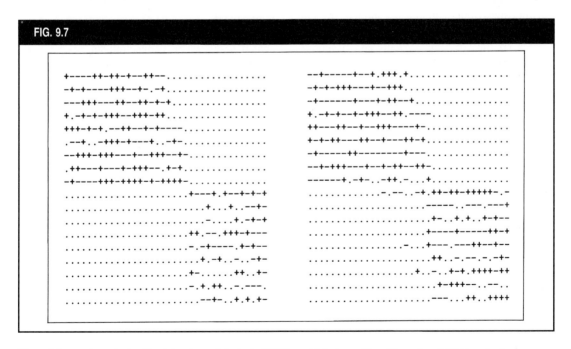

FIG. 9.7

The weights on the output units of Jacobs and Jordan's (1992) model that was biased towards establishing short connections. The 18 rows correspond to 18 output units and the 36 columns to 36 hidden units. The first nine rows show the weights of the output units for the "what" task and the last nine rows show the weights of the output units for the "where" task.

or so hidden units and weak weights from the earlier hidden units. The model has divided itself, having one set of units discriminate "what" the pattern is and another "where" it is.

The simulations of Jacobs and Jordan now turn the circle again. They show how a physical constraint of the hardware — a bias towards short connections — can influence network structure, but in a way that interacts with the computational task at hand. For example, the "what" and "where" tasks are functionally independent of one another. In a network with a bias to short connections, the representation learned by a unit will be influenced by those of its neighbours. Units that are strongly connected to the output units for the "what" task will come to be devoted to that task, and separate from those initially strongly connected to the "where" units at output, especially when a unit is reinforced for its role in solving the "what" task but not the "where" task (and vice versa, given the independence of these tasks). Such examples demonstrate how connectionist models can link neurophysiological data to functional accounts of network behaviour. Through the models, we can also begin to realise the relations between hardware properties of brain systems and psychological accounts of the macrostructure of cognition. Brain can be related to mind, and vice versa (see Jacobs, 1997). As an example of a neurally inspired approach to connectionist modelling, Jacobs and Jordan's paper is included at the end of the chapter.

It is also possible to develop connectionist models pitched directly at the neural level, which attempt to simulate in detail the properties of single cells (see Jefferys, Traub, & Whittington, 1996). Although undoubtedly this is an important line of work, such low-level models at present do not speak to psychological data that likely reflect properties of large networks of units. It is in their ability to capture such data that the more abstract models we have covered here have their value.

9.4 LEARNING AND REPRESENTATION

We have suggested that connectionist modelling can provide a functional account of behaviour that can serve as the "glue" to link descriptions at the level of the hardware to psychological descriptions that deal with processing algorithms. For hardware accounts, connectionist theories are "high-level"; for algorithmic accounts, connectionist theories are "low-level". The "glue" sits neatly between the linking levels of theory. Moreover we have also argued that connectionist theories not only complement the algorithmic accounts, but can also supersede them. How general is this argument? Is it limited to certain areas of application — for instance, where behaviour seems based on prior associations rather than on thinking through new problems? On pattern recognition rather than language functions? In section 9.1 we noted that the potential for a uniform connectionist account covering the whole of cognition was related to the possibility of a purely connectionist, that is, non-hybrid, account of compositionality. This was seen to depend on the ability of networks to develop appropriate, structured representations. If this enterprise is not possible, then, at least for some areas of investigation, connectionist theories will remain constrained.

Contrary to this last argument, we have presented cases where connectionism has certainly done enough to show it does not have to be confined to an associationist glob! Hinton's (1989a) family tree network, described in Chapter 3 (section 3.2), illustrated the ability to learn tree structures for example. But more is needed for the compositionality demanded, rightly, by Fodor and Pylyshyn (1988). A glimpse of what might be possible was seen in the discussions of simple recurrent networks at various places in this book (sections 5.6.2, 7.5 and 7.6 in Chapters 5 and 7). Pollack's (1990) ingenious network implementation of a stack, for example, showed how a tree structure, as in a phrase structure diagram, could be encoded on a set of hidden units and, most importantly, recovered by a recursive process.

Van Gelder (1990) has suggested that work like this shows how connectionism may provide compositionality effectively equivalent to that of symbolic models, but by different means. He distinguishes concatenative compositionality, used in symbolic approaches, and functional compositionality, which some connectionist models, such as Pollack's (1990), adopt. As illustration of this distinction consider again the well formed formula of propositional logic: "A & B". This counts as a well formed formula precisely because it combines three legitimate tokens of the logic by means of a legitimate rule, which, in this case, amounts to spatial concatenation. The rules of the logic result in tokens being arranged as a series chained together in a one-dimensional spatial array. Similarly the grammar of a natural language specifies lawful ways of combining language tokens in, for written expressions, a spatial series or, for utterances, a temporal series. An essential feature of this mode of combination is that the constituents are not altered by their combination. For instance "A" is not changed by being combined with "B" in the compound expression "A & B". In these cases the constituent structure of the expression is transparent because the constituents are preserved within the expression. The constituent or syntactic structure is expressed directly in the physical structure of the expression. As we pointed out in section 9.1, Fodor and Pylyshyn (1988) assert that these syntactic properties map onto physical properties of the brain in a manner that ensures that its state transitions result from the structural properties of the represented expressions.

Now consider an alternative to concatenative compositionality. The representation of the tree structure in Pollack's (1990) network does not contain elements of the tree structure as constituents. The syntax of the tree is not transparent as in the concatenative schemes just discussed. Yet the syntactic structure, indeed the tree, is recoverable by the recursive procedure we described earlier in this book. Van Gelder (1990) refers to this sort of connectionist representation as possessing a functional compositionality, and provides a flavour of a purely connectionist solution to the problems of systematicity in thought and language. It has to be admitted that functional compositionality offers no more than a glimpse of what might be possible, and it does not constitute a solution at present. In particular what is needed is work that shows how the non-concatenative representations can enter directly into processes that provide for systematicity. It is not enough that processes form a compressed representation that can be uncom-

pressed into syntactically transparent representations, which then form the basis of systematicity. Such a scheme would be clearly symbolic in essence. No, a uniform connectionist account of the mind must show how network representations like those in Pollack's (1990) network, in which syntactic structure is not manifest, can result in structure-sensitive operations like language use. In Chapter 7 we described the results of a network which seemed to demonstrate precisely these effects. Blank et al. (1992) found that the hidden unit representations of sentences, in a sequential RAAM, could be used to train a further network to transform the sentences: from, for example, "cheetah chase Tarzan" to "Tarzan flee cheetah". In this case the non-concatenative representation formed the basis of compositionality without any need to decode it into a transparently structured expression (see also Chalmers, 1990).

The requirement of compositionality is clearly a considerable challenge for connectionism, but the discussions here, and in Chapter 7, of the use of simple recurrent networks in language processing show that the challenge is not an impossible one in principle, contrary to Fodor and Pylyshyn (1988)!

9.5 VARIABLE BINDING AND THE CURSE OF VON NEUMANN

At several places in this book we have discussed a version of the variable binding problem. In Chapter 4 we discussed it in relation to the problem of grouping visual features. In Chapter 7 the assignment of roles to individuals in reasoning tasks was seen to be a case of variable binding. The property of compositionality discussed in Chapters 6 and 7 on language, and in this final chapter, arises because of an ability to have variable assignments to syntactic elements. It turns out that the solution to many interesting problems in psychology amounts to a requirement to solve some variety of the variable binding problem. It might be thought that this observation adds greatly to the explanatory adequacy of the symbolic approach as, in some senses, variable binding is simply not a problem for the approach. One of the great strengths, and characteristic features, of von Neumann-style computation is precisely the ability to assign values to variable slots. The symbolic tradition inherits this strength: the expression Loves(x,y), for example, permits the representation of an unbounded set of propositions, given appropriate fillers for the variables x and y.

This apparent strength of symbolic models may be also construed as a major weakness however. It may be a symptom of what we term the curse of von Neumann! To see this, consider again the Church–Turing thesis discussed in the first chapter. Any effective procedure can be computed by some Turing machine or other, and a Universal Turing machine can compute any effective procedure. By extension, a von Neumann computer can compute any effective procedure. Now consider the (science fiction) solutions to the problem of understanding the basis of, say, natural language use, and imagine these solutions represented as points in multidimensional space. Each point would represent a possible solution, with the value at that point on each dimension representing some feature of the solution. Given the paucity of language-using systems, it seems reasonable to suppose that the space is thinly populated with solutions. The problem faced by scientists is to effectively search this thinly populated feature space. The point is that von Neumann computation allows access to all regions of the space. And this is its curse. Given the unlimited access, we are able to carve elegant but, almost certainly, off-target pathways through this space. What is badly needed is a set of constraints that limit the search to the neighbouring regions of solution points. Connectionism may be just such a set of constraints.

To return to the problems of variable binding: the readily available solutions of symbolic systems could result in a neglect of some very important general principles that need to be understood to account for language use, reasoning, and visual object representation. It may turn out, for example, that the phase relations in oscillatory elements are vital to any explanation of such mental functions. Such an outcome would not have even been suspected from a symbolic perspective. Perhaps there are many such principles which are currently

concealed by the great power of general-purpose, universal computing architectures!

9.6 KEY PROBLEMS FOR CONNECTIONISM

We complete this evaluation by listing key issues for which developments are required for the future health of connectionist modelling. Some of these issues have been discussed elsewhere in this book, at some length; others have been merely mentioned; some are new. We separate the arguments into two sets — those dealing with empirical applications of the models to provide fuller accounts of psychological data, and those dealing with the development of better analytical tools.

9.6.1 Empirical developments

Models that cover multiple tasks. Many of the connectionist models that we have reviewed have simulated single tasks. For example, just consider the task of naming. We have described models of object naming, face naming, word naming, and naming in sentence production. Each behaviour has been dealt with in isolation. There are reasons for this. As we discussed in Chapter 4 (sections 4.6 and 4.7), the kinds of descriptions extracted by the visual system for object, face, and word naming may be quite different, given the contrasting computational problems presented by these different stimuli (see Biederman & Kalocsai, 1997; Bruce & Humphreys, 1994; Farah, 1990). It would be incorrect to gloss over such differences when modelling visual aspects of the tasks. Nevertheless, there is also little evidence that phonological descriptions differ across the stimuli, and there is no reason why aspects of name retrieval could not be compared[2]. When two or more tasks are simulated in conjunction, interesting new questions emerge, for instance concerning the effects of what we have termed "interactive learning" (section 9.2.2). To date very few models have tackled such issues. One initial attempt is the model of word naming proposed by Plaut et al. (1996), which incorporates a semantic influence on name retrieval when the model is learning to map orthography onto phonology (for word naming). Even here, however, the issue is not explored fully. Thus the semantic route simply provided a constant input (varying for each phoneme in each word), but it did not itself adapt over time; the joint effect of interactive learning on both semantic and orthographic naming routes was not assessed. Nevertheless, one of the lessons from such work is that the content of learning in one route is not the same when this route operates in conjunction with other processes — there are emergent properties from the operation of the whole network. Such interactions need to be examined in further detail, across a broad number of areas of cognition where different inputs converge on a common response. Only then may we begin to understand more fully the relations between (say) object and word naming; only then may new predictions arise concerning interactions and carry-over effects between tasks.

Models that produce double as well as single dissociations. A point related to the argument for broader-ranging models of multiple tasks concerns the need for models to capture double as well as single dissociations. A single dissociation occurs when behaviour on one task is selectively disrupted after a brain lesion. Many of the models of cognitive pathology that we have reviewed have dealt with single dissociations, and in many of the examples it is the more difficult task for a network that breaks down first, after lesioning (as when models of word naming encounter difficulties with exception words; Patterson et al., 1989). However, often inferences drawn from neuropsychology are based on *double* rather than single dissociations, and for this, evidence of only the more difficult process being impaired is not good enough. Double dissociations arise where two patients show opposite patterns of impairment — one patient may be impaired on ability 1 but relatively good on ability 2, while the second patient may be impaired on ability 2 but relatively good on ability 1 (see Shallice, 1988, for discussion). In one concrete example, surface dyslexics are impaired at reading irregular words but can be relatively good at reading nonwords, whereas phonological dyslexics are poor at reading nonwords

but can read irregular words (see sections 8.3.3 and 8.3.5 in Chapter 8). Similar double dissociations are found for many other behaviours. Neuropsychologists have used double dissociations to argue for the involvement of at least some separable processing components in task performance — for instance, for a "lexical" and a "non-lexical" route in reading (e.g. Coltheart et al., 1993). Such evidence has played an important role in structuring psychological thinking about the cognitive architecture underlying many of the behaviours that we have reviewed.

Double dissociations based on evidence from different tasks obviously cannot be captured in models that perform only single tasks. To begin to address such evidence, multi-task models are needed. Nevertheless, not all double dissociations involve different tasks, and in many instances double dissociations exist between patients performing the same task on contrasting stimuli (as in the examples of reading different types of word). Work such as that of Plaut et al. (1996) suggests that multi-task models can be useful here too. For example, in that simulation evidence was provided for more "specialisation" in learning direct spelling–sound correspondences when this direct route was paired with a semantic route to naming; when paired, the direct route catered more for regular correspondences and less for irregular correspondences (which were supported via the semantic route). Selective lesioning of the semantic route was shown to approximate aspects of surface dyslexia, and we can assume that lesioning of the direct route would reproduce aspects of phonological dyslexia — there would be preserved reading of known words through the semantic route along with impaired reading of nonwords via the lesioned direct route[3]. A multi-task model may develop representations that function in a modular way, once a form of structure is imposed by "adding on" processing routes that accomplish additional tasks. Here functional modularisation may be generated once structural modularisation is imposed. Models that have a modular functional organisation will show a pattern of double dissociation when damage occurs.

An interesting parallel with this may be drawn with networks that do not start with separate structures for different tasks, but develop them because of physical constraints on network development and because of the nature of the tasks. Here tasks that are functionally independent can lead to the development of a modular structure in a model — as in the models where "pruning" of the weights takes place (section 9.3.2). In Rueckl et al.'s (1989) model of pattern and location learning, for example, damage to one set of hidden units would disrupt pattern recognition but not stimulus localisation; damage to the other set of hidden units would produce the opposite result. It would appear that certain tasks, when performed in combination, may lend themselves to better solutions by modular networks (see also Jacobs & Jordan, 1992). Such lessons may well have been imposed on real neural networks by evolution.

So it would seem that connectionist models can generate double dissociations when they incorporate structural divisions — both when the division is imposed by the modeller and when it develops during learning. In such cases, the modelling effort reinforces the standard neuropsychological inference — that the double dissociation indicates functional independence between two tasks or abilities. However, can models without such divisions also produce double dissociations? This last result would have implications for neuropsychology, as it would indicate that theorists should be cautious when making inferences about the modular structure of a processing system from this pattern of data.

Woods (1978) examined this issue in an early simulation. He trained a simple associative memory system with eight input units to learn sets of patterns. In one example, two sets of patterns were distinguished from each other just by activity in two of the input units, and the other input units had identical values for the patterns. Perhaps not surprisingly, lesioning one of the two distinguishing units disrupted recognition of one of the patterns, while lesioning the other distinguishing unit disrupted recognition of the other pattern. Woods suggested that, even though all of the associative memory participated in the representation of each pattern, and so the memory was distributed across units, a double dissociation could still emerge —

lesion 1 affecting pattern 1 but not pattern 2, lesion 2 having the opposite effect. In this example, however, it may be false to make the standard neuropsychological assumption that pattern 1 was represented in a way that was functionally independent of pattern 2, as the same units were involved in the representation of both patterns.

More recently, however, Bullinaria and Chater (1995) have assessed whether double dissociations can occur when random lesions are applied to larger-scale models, trained to learn larger-scale data sets through back-propagation. They found that the chances of observing double dissociations within fully connected models reduced as the network size increased. One reason for this may be that, with small networks and small training sets, representations may not be fully distributed. Consequently, performance may be strongly affected in opposite directions by different random lesions, so generating double dissociations. With larger networks and training sets, more distributed forms of representation may be enforced, making it harder for double dissociations to emerge. This largely negative result supports the standard neuropsychological assumption, that a double dissociation does indicate functional independence.

Even so, our review has provided some examples where double dissociations occur even within distributed and interactive processing systems. The "attractor" model of Plaut and Shallice (1993a) is a case in point. That model mapped graphemic input through to a set of semantic classification units, and incorporated into this semantic layer were "basins of attraction", produced by a feedback loop (the "clean-up" units), that forced semantic activation into states corresponding to known words. High-imageability (concrete) words were given "richer" representations than low-imageability (abstract) words at the semantic level (having more active units). Lesions affecting access from graphemic input into the semantic units generally disrupted the recognition of abstract words more than concrete words. In contrast, lesions to the semantic "clean-up" units affected the recognition of concrete words more than abstract words. Plaut and Shallice accounted for this in terms of functional specialisation within their model. The clean-up units may play an important role in the recognition of concrete words that fall in broad basins of attraction (and that continue to do so even when lesions affect input into the semantic system); lesioning the clean-up units is thus disruptive. Abstract words have small basins of attraction, so that the clean-up of activation is less important for their final recognition. In contrast, an "input" lesion may push an abstract word into the wrong basin (e.g. the basin for a concrete word), disrupting recognition. Irrespective of whether this interpretation is valid, the simulation does show that models can develop some functional specialisation when they have a sufficiently complex architecture (here involving a recurrent feedback loop), and this can occur even when they use a distributed representation scheme and are trained using a learning algorithm that does not involve "pruning" (e.g. standard back-propagation). What are the consequences of this for neuropsychology? At present, it is not clear. On the one hand, the double dissociation reflects lesioning to different components of the model, which is consistent with the standard neuropsychological inference of a modular system; on the other hand, the components in the model are highly interactive and cannot be properly considered in isolation from each other. Perhaps at the very least, we should refrain from using a double dissociation to argue that modules do not interact. Understanding how the nature of the learning task interacts with network architecture even in dynamic, interactive models is a major question for future research, the answers to which should inform neuropsychology. Again we can also point to a two-way process between modelling and experimentation. For example, in attempting to account for double dissociations, modellers will need to develop better analytic tools for evaluating internal representations in models.

Models that account for associations as well as dissociations. Although neuropsychologists often make inferences about cognitive architecture from dissociations, they are typically more cautious in interpreting associations — that is, patterns of deficit that co-occur together. One reason for being cautious with data from associations is that they can reflect anatomical rather than functional prop-

erties of processing systems. For example, as we discussed in Chapter 8 (section 8.7), patients with damage to the posterior cerebral cortex can have problems in recognising faces ("prosopagnosia"). Meadows (1974) noted that prosopagnosia was frequently associated with the condition of "cerebral achromatopsia", in which patients can no longer perceive colour (due to the brain lesion). That is, there is an association between impaired face recognition and cortical colour blindness. Does this mean that these two deficits are related in some way? Does colour blindness impair face recognition? Most theorists would answer this question with a resounding "no"! After all, we can recognise faces from black and white photographs! A different view is that these deficits are associated because the two functions — face recognition and colour perception — are carried out in anatomically close areas of the brain; their association tells us about the anatomical localisation of these abilities but little about their functional properties.

Interestingly, connectionist models may provide the investigator with a principled way of assessing associated deficits. Again consider the model of reading implemented by Plaut and Shallice (1993a). When lesioned, this model produced a pattern of associated visual and semantic errors, and this was so even when the model was lesioned at different sites (e.g. the hidden units from orthography to semantics, the semantic units, the clean-up units). Mixed visual and semantic errors arise because visual and semantic factors interact in determining the final activation states of words at the semantic level. Visual factors influence the initial semantic state; semantic feedback (via the clean-up units) influences the final semantic state. The net result is that whether lesions affect the activation of semantic or orthographic features, the error is likely to be both visually and semantically related to the target word. Prior to the model, the occurrence of these "mixed" errors was something of a puzzle, especially as they could occur in some patients who seemed to have a semantic rather than a visual deficit (e.g. Morton & Patterson, 1980). For the model, however, mixed errors are a natural consequence of the interactions that take place between levels of processing, and they are predicted following "late" (semantic) as well as "early" (visual) lesions.

Connectionist models, then, can predict when associated deficits can be expected, and so provide a way of assessing whether such deficits are informative about the functional properties as well as the anatomical properties of the system. Tests of associations, however, will be most powerful when models incorporate several tasks, so associations between deficits on different tasks can be analysed — another reason why multi-task models would be useful.

Before leaving this point concerning associated deficits, we highlight one other issue. This concerns the use of error types in neuropsychology to diagnose the functional site of a lesion. When patients make semantic errors, for instance, it is tempting to conclude that they have some form of semantic deficit; when they make visual errors, a visual deficit may be presumed (although see Caramazza & Hillis, 1990b, 1991; Miceli et al., 1997). Models such as that of Plaut and Shallice, however, produce visual errors even from lesions at the semantic level, and semantic errors even from lesions at the visual level. Once more this reflects the interactivity of the model. For example, semantic errors could arise from an "early" lesion (affecting orthographic input) if the lesion led to incorrect semantic features being activated and the clean-up units then push the word into the wrong basin of attraction. For neuropsychologists there is a salutary lesson — the nature of the error alone is not diagnostic of the functional site of a lesion. Nevertheless, Plaut and Shallice did find that the proportions of the different error types varied according to the lesion site; there were proportionately more visual than semantic errors after "early" lesions and the opposite pattern for "later" lesions. There is another lesson here. The model suggests that neuropsychologists need to attend to the *distribution* as well as the occurrence of particular error types. Distribution data may then be used in conjunction with converging evidence from other tasks to verify the locus of impairment — for instance, if there is a semantic locus, then the patient may be impaired at semantic judgements when tested with stimuli other than printed words.

Neuropsychiatry and forms of lesioning. We have evaluated connectionist models of neuropsychological impairments in some detail (Chapter 8 and also here), and we have argued that such models can provide useful frameworks both for understanding the impairments and for directing empirical research in this field. It may also be possible for the models to provide similar frameworks for psychiatric disorders, such as schizophrenia and manic depression. Psychiatric disturbances can differ from neuropsychological ones in several important ways — for example, cognitive deficits tend to be less severe and they can be transitory. Frequently psychiatric problems are attributed to imbalances in chemical transmitters in the brain, rather than to organic brain injury (Swerdlow & Koob, 1987), although it seems likely that long-term neural changes can be established too, at least after the illness progresses (Selemon, Rajowska, & Goldman-Rakic, 1993). Putting this crudely, psychiatric impairments may initially reflect differences in the operation of the processing system rather than hardware changes, although hardware changes may follow. Can such processing differences be captured by connectionist models?

Attempts to model psychiatric disorders using connectionist models are currently in their infancy. Even so, some attempts have been made, with quite promising results. We present just two. Cohen, Servan-Schreiber, and colleagues (Cohen, Braver, & O'Reilly, 1996; Cohen & Servan-Schreiber, 1992, 1993; Servan-Schreiber & Cohen, 1996; Servan-Schreiber, Printz, & Cohen, 1990) have modelled some schizophrenic symptoms in terms of alterations to the "gain control" of the normal sigmoid activation function used in networks trained with back-propagation. For instance, in modelling performance on the Stroop task (Chapter 5, section 5.5), they decreased the gain control of the task demand units that modulate learned processing according to the context of the task, so that these units functioned less efficiently. They found consequent increases in the magnitude of Stroop interference, which matched with those found in schizophrenic subjects. They suggested that, in schizophrenia, decreases in the gain control of activation may be related to changes in dopamine transmitter levels. Also, if this change is localised with neural systems concerned with task control, most likely located within the frontal lobes of the brain (Cohen et al., 1996), then performance deficits in schizophrenic patients should be most pronounced when tasks stress control processes (e.g. when overlearned responses need to be overridden).

Horn and Ruppin (1995), in contrast, propose that schizophrenia is linked to changes in memory retrieval processes when frontal lobe retrieval systems receive reduced input from recognition systems in the temporal lobes. This was simulated by using Hopfield networks (Chapter 2) in which (i) external inputs were reduced, and (ii) internal weights and noise levels were increased during Hebbian learning (the latter may reflect compensatory synaptic changes within frontal lobe structures). Horn and Ruppin found that such networks often retrieved memory patterns erroneously, even in the absence of external input! Also, as learning progressed, so networks could become dominated by a single attractor state, from which the network could not be moved. These behaviours of the network are reminiscent of some of the so-called "positive" symptoms of schizophrenia, such as hallucinations. In addition, the shift towards networks maintaining only a single state may mirror clinical changes as schizophrenia progresses.

These two examples take quite different approaches to capturing schizophrenia, and to where the underlying pathology might lie within the brain. Of course, it may be that both approaches are correct, and that the syndrome of schizophrenia needs to be further divided according to the particular symptoms shown by individual patients, which may reflect deficits in different parts of a complex network. Further research will be needed here. Nevertheless, the work done so far indicates that connectionist models may help to link brain processes to disordered psychological states in a way that has not been possible hitherto. For additional developments to take place, several factors are needed. On the modelling side, the simulations may need to become more refined, and perhaps also closer to modelling real neurons, to capture both different forms of neurochemical imbalance and how different neurochemicals interact. On the empirical side too, work is needed. One current restriction is that, relative to studies of neuropsychological patients, few tests of psychiatric patients have been conducted using standard cognitive tasks to which models can be applied. Having additional behavioural data to constrain models can never be a bad thing, and more psychiatric data are required in order to test models to the full.

The research into psychiatric problems also throws into question the most appropriate way to simulate neural damage using connectionist models. In simulations of neuropsychological disorders (Chapter 8), different types of "lesions" have been applied in an almost promiscuous manner. Processing units have been removed, weights connecting units have been removed or they have had noise added, noise has been added to activation functions, or the probability that units fire has simply been reduced. Some of these changes are close to those used to model psychiatric disorders (e.g. altering the "temperature" parameter in models using Boltzmann machine activation functions, as used by Humphreys et al., 1992b, in their simulations of agnosia), others are not (e.g. removing units). Which approach is the most valid? At present we just do not know. To answer this question, we will need to have a better understanding of how changes in brain states affect real neuronal processes, and also an understanding of how changes in real neuronal processes map onto connectionist models. These are major issues for this field.

Mixed architectures and weights. Nearly all of the models that we have considered have used unitary networks, where there has been a single type of unit and a single learning rule. In real neural systems, this need not be the case. For example, our brief review of the hippocampus (section 9.3.1) suggests that contrasting types of learning may be performed by different brain regions — perhaps competitive learning in the hippocampus itself, supervised learning within the cortex. The utility of heterogeneous models, with different forms of learning, has barely been explored.

At several points in the book, we have also discussed the utility of varying the rate of change of weights across different units during learning.

For example, Plaut and Shallice (1993b) used "fast" as well as "slow" weights to model perseverative behaviour in the neuropsychological syndrome optic aphasia (section 8.6.2, Chapter 8), and Murre (1997) proposed that "fast" changes within one system (the "link" system) support slower changes within a second system (the "trace" system). The use of weights with different rates of change may also be useful for overcoming catastrophic interference (section 3.3, Chapter 3). In this last case, fast weights may be rapidly overwritten as new learning takes place, whereas slow weights may be more stable and help to preserve prior learning despite new learning taking place. Further empirical work is required before these assertions can be evaluated (see Levy & Bairaktaris, 1995, for further discussion).

Issues in cognitive development. One of the great attractions of connectionist models is that they can learn. This makes such models useful for modelling aspects of human cognitive development. Yet, despite the potential of connectionist models for developmental psychology, their application to

developmental issues remains underexplored. We have certainly covered some applications — the acquisition of the past tense of English verbs being one (Chapter 7), but the area remains ripe for further studies. One example of how connectionist models may be beneficial in this area comes from the work of McClelland (1989), who modelled the "balance beam" problem. In this problem, children are shown a balance beam with weights of different size placed at different distances from the fulcrum (see Fig. 9.8), and they have to judge whether the beam will tip to the right or left. Siegler (1981) reported that children pass through a series of stages when learning to make correct judgements. Initially they focus almost exclusively on the heavier object and ignore the relative distances of the objects from the fulcrum. Subsequently they incorporate distance information in their judgements, but only when the weights are equal. Then, in a third stage, they take distance into account but make errors when the distances and the weights both differ.

McClelland simulated this developmental progression using the network presented in Fig. 9.8.

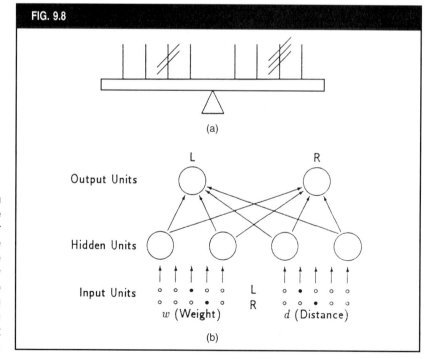

FIG. 9.8

(a)

Output Units   L   R

Hidden Units

Input Units   L / R w (Weight) d (Distance)

(b)

(a) A balance beam problem — a child may be asked to decide whether the beam would tip to the left or right. (b) The network used by McClelland (1989) to simulate children learning the balance beam problem. From Plunkett and Sinha (1992).

The model had separate input units corresponding to the weight and its distance. These units fed into two independent groups of two hidden units (one pair for the weight dimension and one for the distance), and activation from the hidden units fed into output units that coded whether the beam tipped left or right. The model was trained to make a judgement as to which side of the beam would tip (i.e. which output unit would come on) according to the weights placed at different distances, in the input. McClelland assumed that, early on in development, children attend primarily to the weight dimension. To capture this, the training set was uneven, with there being more weight variations than distance variations. McClelland justified this last step by arguing that children have more experience with weight than distance when determining whether one item is heavier than another. With this assumption, McClelland found that, after a small amount of training, the model was biased to respond to the weight dimension. With more training, however, there was a sudden transition to the second and third stages, in which distance was taken into account.

What is of interest here is not that the model can learn the problem, but more that discrete stages emerged in performance despite learning being continuous. An analysis of the connection strengths on the hidden units is helpful in understanding this. Figure 9.9 presents these connection strengths, from input to hidden and from hidden to output units. Figure 9.9 reveals that, at first, there is an increase in the connection strengths for units responding to the weight dimension. Early on in training, the model is reinforced by increasing connection strengths for this dimension, because, across the whole training set, it is more predictive of the outcome of the task. At this "stage", the model appears to have mastered the weight dimension, and responses will be swayed only by this factor. However during the following training epochs (20–40) the weights on the distance dimension continue to be strengthened, although they remain too weak to influence activity on the output units. The transition to the next "stage" occurs when the weights on the distance units are sufficiently strong to influence the output units, and the network then uses distance information

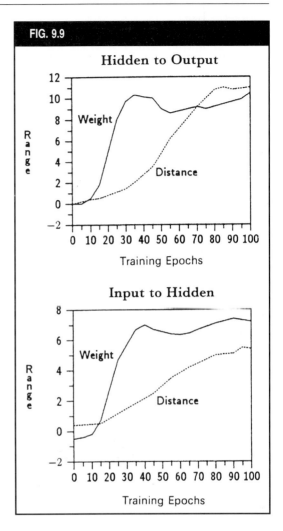

The relative magnitude of the connections in McClelland's (1989) network that encode either the weight or distance of the stimulus from the fulcrum, as a function of the number of training epochs. Note that the network learns first to place strong connections on the units coding weight, before subsequently placing strong connections on the units coding distance. From Plunkett and Sinha (1992).

when the weights are equal on the left and right sides of the beam. This situation then remains stable until the connections on the distance dimension approximate those on the weight dimension, when the network then uses each dimension equally for decision making.

In this simulation, distinct "stages" of development arise for at least two reasons. One is that the network is structured to process the weight and distance dimensions separately, so that these dimensions contribute independently to the decision. A second is that the training set is biased towards the weight dimension. This leads to early gains on the units encoding this dimension, although the model only improves performance subsequently by developing weights on the distance dimension. Provided that stimulus coding is structured to occur along independent dimensions, and there are initial biases in learning, "stage"-like performance can be generated by a continuous learning process. Clearly such a conclusion is relevant to developmental psychologists, who have long held that cognitive development in children proceeds through a series of discrete stages (Piaget, 1975). It would be of considerable interest to explore how far this approach can be extended to cover other examples of apparently discontinuous cognitive development. In this arena connectionism can help us probe beneath the observed performance, so we can understand the underlying processes taking place.

Another example of a continuous pattern of training within a connectionist model leading to apparent discontinuities in learning comes from studying the growth of vocabularies. Plunkett et al. (1992) trained a model autoassociatively to represent both a visual image and a label (one set of input units corresponding to the image, the other to the label; these input units had corresponding output units, for autoassociation). At various stages during learning both "production" and "comprehension" were tested. "Production" corresponded to generating a label when the image was presented as input. "Comprehension" corresponded to generating an image when the label was presented as input. Plunkett et al. found that comprehension was achieved earlier than production, as occurs with children. In addition, performance improved non-linearly with learning. Initially learning was slow and both comprehension and production measures of vocabulary barely improved. However, with further learning there was a "spurt" in the model's vocabulary, so that the vocabulary made sudden rapid increases before reaching a subsequent asymptote. A similar "spurt" in vocabulary growth can be observed in children, and has

often been attributed to maturation of the language system in the brain. In contrast, the modelling approach suggests that it is entirely consistent with gradual, experience-driven learning. In this field, modelling may help us to understand which forms of training profile may be expected from environmental learning alone.

Having considered areas for the future empirical development of connectionist modelling, let us now assess the kinds of analytical developments needed.

9.6.2 Analytic developments

A computational theory. A computational-level theory of learning is needed. That is computational-level in Marr's (1982) sense. At the present most network simulations demonstrate the effects of a particular learning technique with a particular set of inputs. Success is measured in terms of the ability of the trained networks to generalise to new cases. In such cases the learning technique is demonstrated to be adequate for producing generalisations in particular domains. As we pointed out in Chapter 2 however, this very pragmatic approach has so far failed to provide any general, domain-independent theory of learning. The development of such a computational-level theory of learning is highly desirable, as it might be expected to constrain and aid theory construction at the algorithmic and implementation levels. Also, theories at the computational level are required for a satisfactory response to the criticisms of Minksy and Papert (1969), summarised in Chapter 2, which questioned whether the discovery of learning rules for multilayer networks truly escape the limitations of perceptron learning.

Principles of network architecture. Principles of network architecture need to be established. Just as with learning, the principles that govern the choice of network architecture for particular models appear highly pragmatic: effective architectures are ones that meet the goals of a particular simulation. Connectionism turns out to be a highly empirical science and we are now faced with a bewildering range of alternatives! How do we decide between a three-layer feed-forward network, a fully connected Hopfield net, or a network with recurrency and "basins of attraction"? As with learning, theoretical developments are required which allow statements about the properties of network architecture independent of their domain of application.

One way out of this problem, however, may be to finesse it. The problem of how to choose the appropriate network architecture may be solved by learning algorithms that alter the structure of the network as they operate — for example, that "prune" low weights. On this approach there is no "principle of the architecture" that needs to be established — this will be solved by the interactions of some constraint on the model and the nature of the task to be accomplished. Note that the constraint on the model could be either high- or low-level — at a high level it could be the principle of eliminating (re-allocating?) low weights during learning, at a low level it could be the principle of maintaining short connections (Jacobs & Jordan, 1992). What matters is how this interacts with the task. Another empirical solution!

The scale of models. The problems of scale in connectionist modelling remain largely unassessed. The absence of computational theories of learning and of theories of the network architecture make it difficult to determine to what extent Minksy and Papert's (1969) description of the scaling problems of perceptrons apply to the new forms of multilayer networks. The reader will recall that Minksy and Papert showed that, of those functions that could be learned by single-layer networks, some were effectively unrealisable. They could be overwhelmed by problems of scale: either the number and magnitude of the weights became absurdly large or learning time became hopelessly long. The same may be true of multilayer networks. For instance Rumelhart et al. (1986a) demonstrated that back-propagation could train a network to compute parity on four input units. But Minsky and Papert (1988, pp.254–255 of the epilogue to the second edition of *Perceptrons*; our emphasis) comment on this seeming success thus:

To learn these coefficients, the procedure described in PDP required 2,825 cycles through the 16 possible input patterns, thus consuming 45,200 trials for the network to learn to compute the parity predicate for only four inputs. Is this a good result or a bad result? We cannot tell without more knowledge about why the procedure requires so many trials. Until one has some *theory* of that, there is no way to assess the significance of any such experimental result . . .

How easily many of the models of single tasks that we have reviewed will scale-up when faced with larger (more realistic?) training sets, and/or more variable inputs (when noise is added, as is likely in real biological systems), remains an open question. More to the point, at present it is a question that can only be solved empirically.

The analysis of networks. Techniques are needed for the analysis of network solutions and dynamics, and also for analysing how well networks simulate data.

Increasingly the significant results in network simulations are concerned not just with their ability to learn certain functions, but also *how* this is achieved. Given this, methods of understanding the weight and activation structure of networks have become important (see for examples our description of the representations formed by simple recurrent networks in Chapter 7). Typically this will involve the analysis of high-dimensional spaces, which is a far from trivial mathematical task. Efforts in this direction include the use of dimension-reduction techniques, such as principal components analysis or canonical discriminant analysis, which attempt to understand the structure of high-dimensional spaces by examining low-dimensional transformations of them (see Bloesch & Wiles, 1991, for a review of such techniques).

In the longer term, entirely novel ways of describing network dynamics may be needed. We have suggested, in section 9.4, that the solution to the representational limitations of networks may be found by the study of the behaviour of recurrent networks. The problem with this proposal is that the behaviour of recurrent networks of any complexity is not well described by existing formalisms. Such highly dynamic systems, in which small changes can have quite dramatic effects, are the subject matter of the, relatively new, mathematics of chaotic systems. It is possible that some of the most exciting future developments in understanding cognition will flow from the integration of theories of highly dynamic networks and chaos.

Finally, we need heuristics that will allow us to judge when models are successful, when applied to psychological data, and conversely, when they are unsuccessful. In Chapter 6 (section 6.2.1) we used the example of the interactive activation model of reading to raise issues concerning how simulations should be evaluated. Any model is likely to be based on a mixture of assumptions, some that may be critical to its operation and some that are tangential, perhaps reflecting a detail of the implementation. For the interactive activation model, the adoption of a vocabulary of only four-letter words was taken to be an implementational detail, whereas the use of position-specific letter detectors was taken as critical to the way in which the model operated. If a different form of letter representation had been used, the operation of the model would have differed greatly — for instance, the basis on which similarity between words would be computed would differ if the model used a distributed rather than a local, position-specific representation; consequently different predictions would be made about similarity effects in reading and so forth. In contrast, the number of units could have been increased to allow five- or six-letter words also to be recognised and the basic nature of the representations in the model would not have changed. From this we conclude that the model cannot be judged negatively simply because it cannot recognise words containing more than four letters. On the other hand, the model can be judged on the basis of making the wrong predictions about effects of orthographic similarity between words in reading tasks (section 6.2.1, Chapter 6).

What is important here is to distinguish between assumptions that are critical and those that are of secondary importance to the way a model operates. Evaluations (both positive and negative) should be based on critical rather than secondary

assumptions. In reviewing models, we have aimed always to highlight what we believe are critical assumptions, but this is a matter of heuristics and judgement, and an area where scientists can justifiably differ in opinion. Our aim, in raising the issue, is to provide a framework within which models can be usefully assessed.

9.7 CONNECTIONIST MODELLING AND PSYCHOLOGY

We have covered a diverse set of topics, linked by the application of connectionist models to the problems at hand. We hope to have conveyed what we believe is the continuing challenge of this form of modelling to psychological theorising, and to have indicated issues that modellers will need to address to maintain progress in the field. We close with a final point concerning how data and models may interact.

We have suggested that experimenters need to distinguish between critical assumptions and assumptions made simply to implement a model. Experimental tests can be applied to both types of assumption, but only tests of critical assumptions may be crucial for rejecting a model. For instance, interactive activation and competition models, as a general class, make the critical assumption that information is transmitted continuously (in cascade) between processing levels. If this assumption proves incorrect for some behaviours (and see section 6.15, Chapter 6, for an analysis of whether information is transmitted in cascade in speech production), then this form of model may be rejected.

In other instances, however, the model may generate an incorrect prediction but this may reflect a more arbitrary property. Take the performance of the Seidenberg and McClelland (1989) model of word naming as an example. This model did not fare particularly well at retrieving the appropriate phonology for nonwords, and, when lesioned, it failed to produce substantial numbers of regularisation errors when presented with irregular words (Patterson et al., 1989). Some of the problems encountered by the model were probably because the forms of phonological representation used ("Wickelfeatures") fail to capture the nature of phonological representations in people. Other problems seem to be due to the direct spelling-to-sound route in the model being insufficiently biased towards regular correspondences. As we have documented, these problems were modified, with some degree of success by Plaut et al. (1996). What we see here is not the rejection of a theory when its specific predictions are incorrect, but rather an evolutionary process in which the theory is modified in the light of the empirical data. The skeleton theory maintains critical properties such as: learning based on the statistical properties of the training set, and performance based on distributed representations and on properties of the network rather than single units; modelling is conducted within those constraints, although the architecture of the model is modified. In this modification, we also come to understand about general aspects of network function, such as how interactive learning changes the functional properties of the model. In this cycle of modelling and experimentation lies the future.

NOTES

1. As we discuss later, the hippocampus appears to be one exception to this.
2. Indeed, many of the models we have evaluated have used very abstract input descriptions to represent objects, faces, and words, so the models do not in any case capture the different visual descriptions for the different stimuli.
3. Note that we are *not* claiming here that Plaut et al.'s (1996) model will be able to account for all aspects of phonological dyslexia when the direct spelling–sound route is lesioned. For instance, as we noted in Chapter 8 (section 8.3.5), there is some evidence that preserved word naming in phonological dyslexia can co-occur with a semantic impairment (Funnell, 1983). Such a result suggests that phonological dyslexics can read using a direct "lexical" reading route, which is specific to known words but non-semantic in nature. Whether the model would be able to account for such results is an empirical question. Here we mean only to emphasise that the structural properties of the model biased it towards developing a modular functional organisation which can accommodate double dissociations.

Computational consequences of a bias toward short connections

Robert A. Jacobs and Michael I. Jordan
Massachusetts Institute of Technology

A fundamental observation in the neurosciences is that the brain is a modular system in which different regions perform different tasks. Recent evidence, however, raises questions about the accuracy of this characterization with respect to neonates. One possible interpretation of this evidence is that certain aspects of the modular organization of the adult brain arise developmentally. To explore this hypothesis we wish to characterize the computational principles that underlie the development of modular systems. In previous work we have considered computational schemes that allow a learning system to discover the modular structure that is present in the environment (Jacobs, Jordan, & Barto, 1991). In the current paper we present a complementary approach in which the development of modularity is due to an architectural bias in the learner. In particular, we examine the computational consequences of a simple architectural bias toward short-range connections. We present simulations that show that systems that learn under the influence of such a bias have a number of desirable properties, including a tendency to decompose tasks into subtasks, to decouple the dynamics of recurrent subsystems, and to develop location-sensitive internal representations. Furthermore, the system's units develop local receptive and projective fields, and the system develops characteristics that re typically associated with topographic maps.

Introduction

A common assumption of many investigations in the cognitive and brain sciences is that the brain is a collection of modules, in which different regions perform different tasks. Occasionally this assumption has been made explicit and used as the foundation of a theory about the brain's underlying structure (e.g. Fodor, 1983; Gazzaniga, 1989). However, even if the hypothesis of a modular organization is a correct characterization of the adult human brain, recent evidence raises questions about its accuracy with respect to newborns and young children (e.g. Greenfield, 1991; O'Leary, 1989). The evidence suggests that cognitive processes are less localized in newborns than in adults, and that newborns' neocortices are less structurally differentiated. Consequently it may be that some aspects of the modular organization of the adult brain arise developmentally.

From a computational point of view it is important to characterize the principles that govern the development of modular systems. In previous work we have investigated computational schemes whereby modularity can arise in an adaptive system if the environment provides training data that are decomposable (Jacobs, Jordan, & Barto, 1991; Jacobs, Jordan, Nowlan, & Hinton, 1991). In that framework the main problem for the learning algorithm is to discover the modularity that is present in the environment. In the current paper we present a complementary approach in which the development of modularity is due to an architectural bias in the learner. Specifically, we consider a simple architectural bias that leads developing systems to eliminate the connections between distantly located units and to make use of the connections between nearby units. We show that systems that learn under the influence of such a bias have a number of desirable properties. The most important property of these systems is that they are capable of decomposing tasks into subtasks. That is, they can eliminate connections so as to dedicate different portions of the system to learn different tasks. A related property is that systems containing recurrent loops can eliminate

Journal of Cognitive Neuroscience Volume 4, Number 4

connections so as to decouple their dynamics. An additional property is that the representation learned by each unit of the system is dependent on the representations learned by neighboring units and, thus, is a function of the unit's location. Furthermore, the system's units develop local receptive and projective fields, and the system develops characteristics that are typically associated with topographic maps.

Previous computational investigations have considered the use of locality information within an *unsupervised* learning setting.[1] Kohonen (1982) and Durbin and Mitchison (1990) studied learning rules that combine unsupervised competitive learning with a locality constraint. They show that artificial neural networks trained with these rules develop representations that resemble the topographic maps found in the cortex. In contrast, we consider the use of locality information within a *supervised* learning setting. We show that an implicit form of competition arises from the interaction between the supervised error-correction process and the locality constraint and that this competition leads to modular specialization.

The second section reviews the relevant developmental neurobiology and discusses previous theories relating functional localization and a bias toward short connections in the cortex. The third section lists computational advantages of a system that is biased toward short connections. The fourth section presents the learning algorithm used to train several artificial neural networks. This algorithm is a modification of a weight-elimination procedure originally proposed by Rumelhart (1988). The fifth section reports the results of training these networks to perform a variety of tasks.

Biological background

Neuroscience is often concerned with delineating and characterizing the areas of the adult mammalian neocortex based on morphological or functional distinctions. However, the developing neocortex lacks many of the area-specific properties. How do these area-specific features emerge from a developing neocortex that lacks such features?

To highlight its relative uniformity, O'Leary (1989) refers to the developing neocortex as a "protocortex." This term also serves to emphasize the considerable flexibility that appears to exist in the determination of which portions of the developing neocortex develop into which areas of the adult neocortex. Several recent experiments suggest that neocortical areas are not strictly predetermined. Sur and his colleagues (e.g. Sur, Pallas, & Roe, 1990) induced retinal afferents to project to the medial geniculate nucleus (MGN), also referred to as auditory thalamus. Consequently, visually responsive cells were recorded in MGN. Because MGN projects to primary auditory cortex, visually responsive cells were also found in this region. These cells tended to have large receptive fields with roughly one-third of the fields being orientation–selective and a similar proportion being direction–selective. Similar to the fields of simple or complex cells in normal visual cortex, the oriented receptive fields had either separate or coextensive ON and OFF zones. In addition, many cells were driven binocularly. These results support the hypothesis that "primary sensory areas arise from regions of developing neocortex that are initially similar or to some extent pluripotent" (O'Leary, 1989, p.401).

If neocortical areas are not strictly predetermined, then the location of a region of developing neocortex may play a critical role in its acquisition of area-specific properties. O'Leary and Standfield (1989) transplanted pieces of late fetal neocortex to heterotopic positions within the neocortex of newborn rodents. It was found that visual cortical neurons transplanted to the sensorimotor region extended and retained axons to the spinal cord, a subcortical target of sensorimotor cortex. Conversely, sensorimotor cortical neurons transplanted to the visual region extended but did not retain spinal axons, although they did retain a projection to a subcortical target of visual cortex, the superior colliculus.

Although location appears to be important, the factors that directly influence the differentiation of the developing neocortex are not currently known. During development, the vertebrate nervous system undergoes a number of progressive and regressive events. The progressive events include the proliferation of cells, their migration from the proliferation zones in which they are generated to their definitive locations, their aggregation with other cells of similar type, the establishment of phenotypic diversity, and the formation of connections. The regressive events include the restriction of cellular potential, neuronal death, and the elimination of synapses and axon collaterals (Cowan, Fawcett, O'Leary, & Stanfield, 1984). In the discussion below, we restrict our attention to regressive events, particularly regressive events that have a competitive nature.

The development of ocular dominance columns in the visual cortex illustrates the competitive nature of regressive events. In cats and monkeys, axons from each eye initially terminate in an intermixed manner in layer IV of the primary visual cortex. During postnatal development, the axons segregate into ocular dominance columns meaning that each column contains cells especially responsive to one or the other eye. A selective loss then occurs of the axons that terminate in inappropriate columns (Wiesel, 1982). If a kitten is deprived of vision in one eye in early life, then its cortical cells subsequently become relatively unresponsive to the deprived eye (Wiesel & Hubel, 1965). The axon terminals bringing input from the normal eye to the cortex occupy a large portion of the space that ordinarily would have been filled by terminals from the deprived eye. Because binocular deprivation does not result in unresponsive cells to the same extent as following monocular deprivation, this change is not a simple consequence of disuse. These results suggest that the axons representing the input from each eye compete for control of the potentially binocular cortical neuron.

One possible mechanism underlying the development of ocular dominance columns is that axon terminals move from inappropriate columns to appropriate columns. A second possible mechanism is that axons terminating in inappropriate columns are selectively eliminated. According to Rakic (1986), both mechanisms are important in the development of ocular dominance columns in both the cortex and the lateral geniculate nucleus (LGN), although available evidence suggests that the latter mechanism plays the dominant role

in the LGN. Consequently, Rakic (1986) proposed the *competitive elimination hypothesis*, which states that (1) an excess number of axons is sent to a target area, (2) the elimination of excess axons coincides with segregation, and (3) the loss of axons primarily involves those axons terminating in inappropriate locations. Rakic suggested that competitive elimination is important in LGN and that it may play a significant role in the development of other neural systems of the mammalian brain.

If axon or synapse elimination is based on a competitive process, then it is important to know what resource the competitors are competing to obtain, and to know what determines the winners and losers of the competition. According to the trophic theory of neural connections, "synaptic connections form and are maintained by interactions in which nerve terminals compete for target-derived molecules available in limited supply" (Purves, 1986, p.486). That is, postsynaptic cells or target areas release limited amounts of trophic factors, such as nerve growth factor (NGF), that presynaptic cells compete to acquire. Experimental evidence indicates that this competitive mechanism is capable of modulating the size of axonal and dendritic arbors as well as the size of neuronal populations (e.g. Purves, 1986). One interesting hypothesis is that the competition for trophic factors is Hebbian, meaning that the amount of trophic factor available to a presynaptic cell is increased by the near synchronous activity of presynaptic and postsynaptic cells (e.g. Cowan, Fawcett, O'Leary, & Stanfield, 1984; Purves & Lichtman, 1985). In the case of the central projections of the retina, where neighboring presynaptic cells are expected to have a high probability of simultaneous activation, this mechanism favors the survival of axons from neighboring ganglion cells and the elimination of axons from more distantly located cells. In this regard, it is interesting to note that simulations have shown that a Hebb-like learning rule can result in the formation of topographic maps in which neighboring presynaptic cells connect with neighboring postsynaptic cells (Willshaw & von der Malsburg, 1976).

In this article, we study the possibility that the competitive elimination process may include a bias to maintain neural connections between presynaptic and postsynaptic cells that are physical neighbors. The hypothesis that the nervous system is biased to utilize short connections has been proposed by several researchers. However, of greatest interest to us is that theorists have speculated that this bias may account for the large number of functionally distinct cortical areas.

Cowey (1981) suggested that if the cortex uses lateral inhibition to sharpen various visual attributes, such as edges, orientation, color, disparity, spatial frequency, size, and movement, then a retinotopic representation of these attributes is preferable because such a representation places the interneurons necessary for receptive-field tuning in relative proximity (Kohonen, 1982; Durbin & Mitchison, 1990). Moreover, if neurons for all the different attributes were represented in a single retinotopic map, the connections needed to sharpen the tuning of individual neurons for each of these attributes would be unnecessarily long. The existence of multiple retinotopic maps, each in a separate cortical area, allows the cortex to highlight several attributes using short local connections.

Similarly, Barlow (1986) suggested that to detect various visual attributes using neurons whose connections are of minimal length, the cortex must employ multiple representations. He argued that because the brain primarily contains local connections, it is difficult, using a retinotopic representation, to detect similarities among noncontiguous locations of the visual field. To detect such similarities, it is necessary to map the information in the retinal image so that similar events are represented close to each other independently of the retinal coordinates of the events. For example, using a retinotopic representation and neurons with local connections, it is difficult to detect the colinearity of line segments located at different places in the retinal image. However, in a different, nonretinotopic representation [e.g. the Hough transform (Duda & Hart, 1973; Ballard, 1984)] nearly colinear line segments can be represented by neighboring neurons. In general, the existence of multiple representations, each in a separate area, allows the brain to detect several attributes using short connections.

Computational advantages of a bias toward short connections

A bias toward short connections, and the local connectivity among processing units that such a bias produces, may result in several computational advantages in natural and artificial neural networks.

Real-time processing

Compared to processors in modern computers, neurons are slow. Electrical impulses propagate along axons at speeds from 0.5 to 130 m/sec, depending on factors such as the diameter of the axon and the degree of myelination. As a result of these slow rates of propagation, sensory inputs cannot be processed in real time. Consequently, an advantage of short connections is that they permit relatively rapid information processing.[2]

Reduced spatial requirements

The maintenance of connections between neighboring cells and the elimination of connections between distant cells result in a connectivity pattern that is space efficient. The importance of this efficiency is apparent when it is contrasted with the space inefficiency of a global connectivity pattern. According to Nelson and Bower (1990, p.408), "if the brain's estimated 10^{11} neurons were placed on the surface of a sphere and fully interconnected by individual axons 0.1 μm in radius, the sphere would have to have a diameter of more than 20 km to accommodate the connections." Ringo (1991) argued that due to spatial constraints, increases in brain size must be accompanied by decreases in the average percentage of cells with which any one cell directly communicates. Consequently, larger brains tend to show more local connectivity, which, as argued by Cowey (1981) and Barlow (1986), results in greater specialization.

Reduced spatial crosstalk and task decomposition

An artificial neural network may show slow learning because it is being trained to simultaneously perform two or more tasks. For example, suppose that the mappings from the input units to each output unit constitute separate tasks and that the network is trained with the backpropagation algorithm. During training, each output unit provides error information to the hidden units from which it receives a projection. It is possible that the error information from one output unit may indicate that a hidden unit's activation should be larger and, at the same time, the error information from another output unit may indicate that the same hidden unit's activation should be smaller (Jordan, 1986; Plaut & Hinton, 1987). This conflict in error information is called spatial crosstalk. Although spatial crosstalk is clearly seen in terms of the backpropagation algorithm, it is not limited to networks trained using this algorithm. A network trained using any algorithm that approximates gradient descent [e.g. the A_{R-P} algorithm of Barto and Anandan (1985) and Barto & Jordan (1987)] is susceptible to spatial crosstalk. Therefore, spatial crosstalk may be considered as resulting from the connectivity of the network and not from the learning algorithm used to train the network.

By maintaining short connections and eliminating long connections, spatial crosstalk can be reduced and tasks can be decomposed into subtasks. Although the three systems shown in Fig. 1 can be trained to perform the same mappings, the system in Fig. 1A has its hidden units fully interconnected with its output units and is most susceptible to spatial crosstalk. The system in Fig. 1B has its hidden units on the top fully interconnected with its top output units and its hidden units on the bottom fully interconnected with its bottom output units. Thus, it consists of two separate networks (two $4 \rightarrow 4 \rightarrow 2$ networks). If the mapping that this system is trained to perform can be decomposed so that the mapping from the input units to the top set of output units may be thought of as one task and the mapping from the input units to the bottom set of output units may be thought of as a second task, then this system has dedicated different networks to learn the different tasks. Because there is no spatial crosstalk between the two tasks, such a system may show rapid learning. The system in Fig. 1C has each hidden unit project to only a single output unit. It therefore consists of a separate network for each

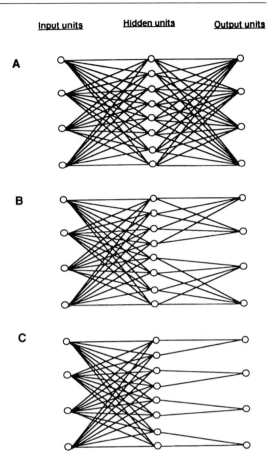

FIG. 1. (**A**) One $4 \rightarrow 8 \rightarrow 4$ network. (**B**) Two $4 \rightarrow 4 \rightarrow 2$ networks. (**C**) Four $4 \rightarrow 2 \rightarrow 1$ networks.

output unit (four $4 \rightarrow 2 \rightarrow 1$ networks) and is immune to spatial crosstalk (Plaut & Hinton, 1987).

Decoupling of dynamics in recurrent networks

Recurrent networks are often designed so that each unit is connected to itself and to many or all of the other units of the network (see Fig. 2A). The loops formed by the connections provide the network with high-order nonlinear dynamics that allow it to perform complex temporal processing. Unfortunately, a global connectivity pattern may make a recurrent network slow to train and difficult to analyze (Mozer, 1989). Moreover, networks with global connectivity have increased susceptibility to instabilities. By maintaining short

A

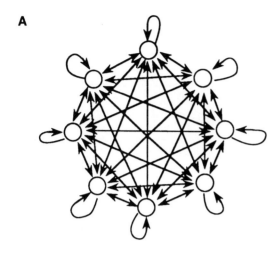

B

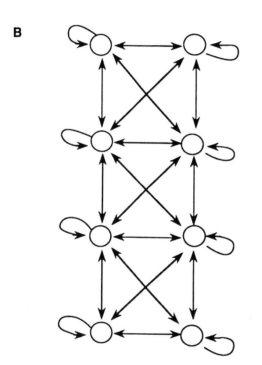

FIG. 2. (**A**) A fully connected recurrent network.
(**B**) A recurrent network with restricted connectivity.

tance from unit A to unit B is the same as the distance from B to A, if A maintains a projection to B, then it is likely that B will maintain a projection back to A.

Improved generalization

Artificial neural networks with many adjustable weights may learn the training data quickly and accurately, but generalize poorly to novel data. One method of improving the generalization abilities of networks with too many "degrees of freedom" is to decay or eliminate weights during training (e.g. Hinton, 1987; le Cun, 1989; Rumelhart, 1988; Weigend, Huberman, & Rumelhart, 1990). A second method is to match the structure of the network with the structure of the task. For example, networks whose units have local receptive fields can learn to reliably detect the local structure that is often present in pattern recognition tasks (Hinton, 1987; le Cun, 1989). A system that maintains short connections and eliminates long connections should generalize well because its degrees of freedom are reduced and because its units develop local receptive fields.

Improved interpretability of representations

Artificial neural networks often develop relatively uninterpretable representations for at least two reasons. Networks whose units are densely connected tend to develop representations that are distributed over many units and, thus, are difficult to interpret. In addition, uninterpretable representations often develop in networks that are trained to simultaneously perform multiple tasks (Rueckl, Cave, & Kosslyn, 1989). In contrast, a system with a bias toward short connections may develop interpretable representations. Its units tend to have local receptive fields and, thus, develop relatively local representations. Furthermore, as was discussed above, such a system may be capable of eliminating connections so that different networks learn different tasks.

A learning algorithm

To study the computational consequences of a bias toward short connections we performed a

connections and eliminating long connections, the dynamics of the network can, at least in part, be decoupled. As illustrated in Fig. 2B, the bias toward short connections tends to maintain short local loops, either from a unit to itself or between neighboring units. Furthermore, because the distance from unit A to unit B is the same as the series of simulation experiments. In each of the simulations an artificial neural network learned to perform a task under a connectivity constraint. The constraint acted to favor weights of large magnitude on connections between nearby units and weights of small or zero magnitude on connections between distant units. The weight values learned by any particular network can be viewed as a compromise between the constraint favoring local connections and the constraint that the network perform the task correctly.

The locality constraint was achieved by using a modification of the weight-elimination procedure originally proposed by Rumelhart (1988) and studied by Chauvin (1989), Hanson and Pratt (1989), and Weigend, Huberman, and Rumelhart (1990), among others. Specifically, the weights of the networks were adjusted using the backpropagation algorithm (le Cun, 1985; Parker, 1985; Rumelhart, Hinton, & Williams, 1986; Werbos, 1974) so as to minimize the cost function

$$J = \frac{1}{2}\sum_{i=1}^{n}(y_i^* - y_i)^2 + \lambda\sum_{i,j}\frac{d_{ji}w_{ji}^2}{1 + w_{ji}^2} \qquad (1)$$

where n is the number of output units, y_i^* is the desired activation for the ith output unit, y_i is the ith output unit's actual activation, d_{ji} is the distance from unit i to unit j, w_{ji} is the weight on the connection from unit i to unit j, and λ is a regularization parameter that determines the relative importance of minimizing the second term in the cost function.

The first term in the cost function is the sum of squared error and is minimal when the network produces the target output vector corresponding to each input vector. The second term in the cost function is a term that causes the magnitude of each weight of the network to decay toward zero. The strength of this decay is proportional to the length of the connection d_{ji}. That is, weights on connections between nearby units are only mildly decayed, whereas weights on connections between distant units are more strongly decayed.

To clarify the role of the weight-elimination term, Fig. 3 shows the relationship between the length of a connection, the magnitude of the con-

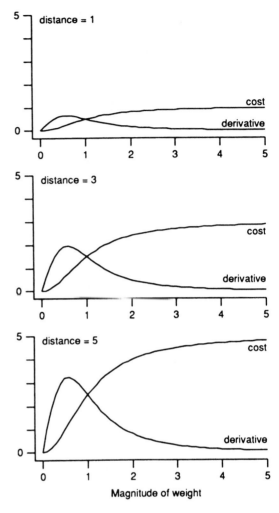

FIG. 3. Each graph shows the cost of an individual weight and the derivative of the cost. The derivative specifies how strongly the weight is decayed. The three graphs are for weights whose corresponding presynaptic and postsynaptic units are 1, 3, and 5 metric units apart.

nection's corresponding weight, and the strength of the decay. Each graph shows the cost of an individual weight [that is, cost = $(d_{ji}w_{ji}^2/1 + w_{ji}^2)$] and the derivative of the cost. The derivative specifies how strongly the weight is decayed. The three graphs are for weights whose corresponding presynaptic and postsynaptic units are 1, 3, and 5 metric units apart. Two properties of the algorithm are apparent in this figure. First, weights on long connections are more strongly decayed than weights on short connections. Second, relatively small weights (roughly those whose magnitude is less than 1) are more strongly decayed than large weights. Because the weights that play an important role in a network's computation tend to be large, this has the desirable consequence that important weights are not strongly decayed.

Each unit of a network was assigned a location in a three-dimensional space. If $\mathbf{r}i = [x_i y_i z_i]^T$ is the location of unit i with respect to the unit basis vectors, then the distance from unit i to unit j is given by

$$d_{ji} = \|\mathbf{r}_j - \mathbf{r}_i\|_p^p$$
$$= |x_j - x_i|^p + |y_j - y_i|^p + |z_j - z_i|^p \qquad (2)$$

Based on initial experiments with several different values of p, we chose $p = 10$.[3] The regularization parameter λ was initialized to zero. During the course of a simulation it was increased until the network's performance began to decline, and thereafter increased or decreased so that the performance improved at a steady rate (Weigend, Huberman, & Rumelhart, 1990).

The locality constraint obtained by minimizing the second term in Eq. (1) is related to the locality constraint obtained in the unsupervised learning procedures of Kohonen (1982) or Durbin and Mitchison (1990). Those algorithms incorporate a topological constraint such that nearby postsynaptic units tend to develop similar response properties. As a result of this constraint, nearby postsynaptic units tend to be activated by nearby presynaptic units.[4] However, because there is no distance metric that relates presynaptic and postsynaptic units, it cannot be said that the presynaptic units that activate a postsynaptic unit are physically close to that unit. In contrast, the networks described here are characterized by the constraint that presynaptic units project to postsynaptic units that are their physical neighbors. Consequently, nearby presynaptic units project to nearby postsynaptic units, and nearby postsynaptic units have related response properties.

The weight-elimination term in the cost function has an interpretation in terms of competition. Whereas derivatives stemming from the sum of squared error make a network's weights more useful in correcting the errors between the desired output and the actual output, derivatives stemming from the weight-elimination term decay the magnitudes of the weights toward zero. Thus, two possibly conflicting influences determine how a weight is adapted during the learning process. We may consider the network's connections as competing for the right to be used in the network's computation. The winners of this competition are connections whose associated weights play a role in the network's computation; that is, those whose weights are nonzero. The weights associated with the losing connections are driven to zero, and these connections are essentially eliminated from the network. Because weights on long connections are decayed faster than those on short connections, the winners tend to be short, and the losers long.

Simulations

In this section we describe simulations in which networks with a bias toward short connections were applied to a "what" and "where" vision task originally studied by Rueckl, Cave, and Kosslyn (1989), a shift detection task that requires recurrent connections, and a dimensionality reduction task originally studied by Saund (1987).

The "what" and "where" vision tasks
Despite the fact that a variety of images are projected on the retina of a person watching a rotating or translating object, people recognize that the same object is depicted in each of the images. One hypothesis about how such insensitivity to translation and orientation is achieved is that a canonical representation of each familiar object is stored, and the retinal image of an object is transformed so that the image and the representations can be compared. As a result of this transformation, information relevant to determining an object's spatial location is lost. This suggests that the process performing object recognition does not also perform spatial localization. It has been suggested that distinct cortical pathways of the primate visual system compute object identity and

spatial location. Mishkin, Ungerleider, and Macko (1983) reviewed evidence that a pathway running ventrally, interconnecting the striate, prestriate, and inferior temporal areas, computes object identity, whereas a pathway running dorsally, interconnecting the striate, prestriate and inferior parietal areas, computes spatial location.

To investigate the computational advantages of employing distinct systems to perform these two tasks, Rueckl, Cave, and Kosslyn (1989) applied several connectionist systems to an object recognition task (henceforth referred to as the "what" task) and a spatial localization task (henceforth referred to as the "where" task). The retina was represented as a 5×5 binary matrix. Each object was a specific pattern of binary entries in a 3×3 matrix. At each time step of the training period, one of nine object matrices was centered at one of nine locations on the retinal matrix. The entries of the retinal matrix that lie outside the object matrix were set to zero. The "what" task is to identify the object; the "where" task is to identify its location.

Systems that are biased toward short connections can eliminate connections so as to dedicate different networks to learn different tasks.[5] To test the conditions under which this may occur, we trained three systems to perform the "what" and "where" vision tasks. The systems had 25 input units, 36 hidden units, and 18 output units. They were initialized so that all input units projected to all hidden units, and all hidden units projected to all output units. System 1 was trained to minimize only the sum of squared error between the targets and the outputs [i.e. the first term of the cost function in Eq. (1)] and, thus, incurred no cost for long connections. In contrast, systems 2 and 3 were biased to use short connections between their hidden and output layers. Whereas the output units for the "what" and "where" tasks in system 2 were placed relatively far apart, they were placed close together in system 3 (see Fig. 4A and B).

Figures 5, 6, and 7 show the matrices of weights corresponding to the connections between the hidden and output layers in systems 1, 2, and 3, respectively. Each figure presents the weight matrices for two typical simulations. Each matrix

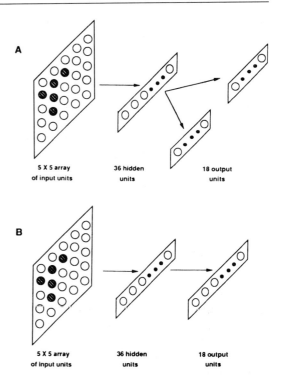

FIG. 4. (**A**) The output units of system 2 are relatively far apart. (**B**) The output units of system 3 are close together.

has 18 rows corresponding to the 18 output units, and 36 columns corresponding to the 36 hidden units. Whereas the first 9 rows show the weights of the output units for the "what" task, the last 9 rows show the weights of the output units for the "where" task. Weights that were positive are shown by a plus sign ("+"), weights that were negative are shown by a minus sign ("−"), and near-zero weights are shown by a period ("."). For example, the weight on the connection from the first hidden unit to the first output unit in the first simulation of system 1 (see Fig. 5) was negative, the weight between the second hidden unit and the first output unit was positive, and the weight between the first hidden unit and the second output unit was near-zero.

The results support two important hypotheses. First, systems that are biased toward short connections are, at least in some circumstances, capable of task decomposition. That is, they can eliminate connections so as to dedicate different

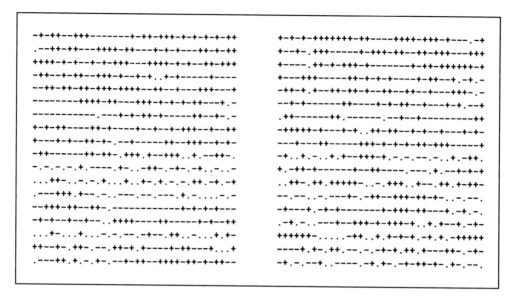

FIG. 5. Output units' weights at the end of two typical simulations of system 1.

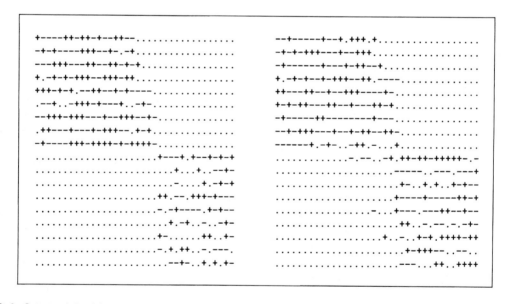

FIG. 6. Output units' weights at the end of two typical simulations of system 2.

networks to learn different tasks. Second, the representation learned by a unit in a system that is biased toward short connections is dependent on the representations learned by neighboring units and, thus, is a function of the unit's location. The

hidden units of system 1, the only system that was not biased toward short connections, were fully interconnected with the output units for both the "what" and "where" tasks (see Fig. 5). Consequently, each of these hidden units learned

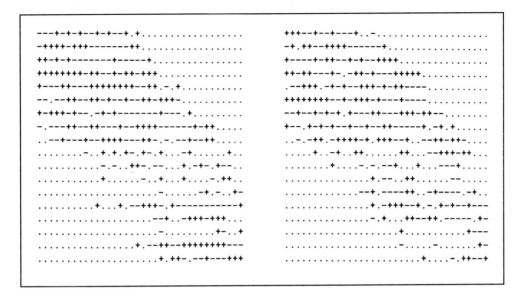

FIG. 7. Output units' weights at the end of two typical simulations of system 3.

representations that are useful for performing both tasks.[6] In contrast, the hidden units toward the left of system 2 were almost exclusively interconnected with the output units on the left (those for the "what" task), whereas the hidden units toward the right were almost exclusively interconnected with the output units on the right (those for the "where" task). System 2 eliminated connections so as to dedicate different networks to learn the different tasks (see Fig. 6). Note that the "what" task is more difficult than the "where" task (the "where" task, but not the "what" task, is linearly separable), and that the network dedicated to the "what" task is larger than the network dedicated to the "where" task. This means that system 2 dedicated some hidden units to the "what" task despite the fact that these units were closer to the "where" output units. Not surprisingly, the hidden units toward the left developed representations that are useful for performing the "what" task, whereas the hidden units toward the right developed representations that are useful for performing the "where" task. In system 3, the leftmost hidden units were exclusively interconnected with the "what" output units, the rightmost hidden units were exclusively interconnected with the "where"

output units, and the middle hidden units maintained connections to both sets of output units (see Fig. 7).

The shift detection task

In the shift detection task, a system is shown a binary pattern at time t and the same pattern shifted one bit to the left or to the right at time $t + 1$. The system must detect the direction of the shift. The recurrent network that we applied to this task had 10 input units, two layers of 10 hidden units each, and a single output unit (see Fig. 8). The network was initialized so that the units in the first hidden layer received projections from all of the input units as well as recurrent connections from all of the units in the first and second hidden layers. If the input layer is considered to be a one-dimensional retina, then the patterns were formed by placing one of 8 shapes at one of 4 locations on the retina. The shapes were 5 bits long, and the first and last bits were set to one (Hinton, 1987).

Figure 9 shows the weight matrices at the end of two typical simulations of the recurrent network. The weight matrices corresponding to the connections from each of hidden layer 1's units to

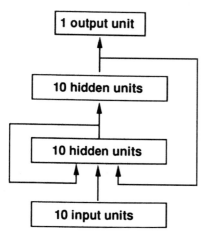

FIG. 8. Recurrent network applied to the shift detection task.

all the other units of this layer are roughly diagonal. This means that each unit tended to maintain projections to itself or to its neighbors within the layer. The weight matrices corresponding to the connections between hidden layers 1 and 2 are also roughly diagonal indicating that if unit A in hidden layer 1 maintained a projection to unit B in hidden layer 2, then B tended to maintain a projection back to A. These results provide support for the hypothesis that recurrent networks that are biased toward short connections tend to maintain short local loops, either from a unit to itself or between neighboring units. The locality of the network's recurrent loops and the fact that many recurrent connections were eliminated suggests that the system's dynamics were decoupled by the learning process.

	First hidden layer's weights			Second hidden layer's weights	Output unit's weights
	from input units	from hidden layer 1	from hidden layer 2		
	. . . .	.⁻.	. . . .	---.	. . .+++++. .
	. . . .	. .⁻.	-.	----.	
	++++-.	.----.	. . .+.	-----.	
R	++----. . . .	.+----. . . .	. .++++. . . . ·	. .----. . . .	
u	. .+---. . . .	.----+-. . .	. .+++++. . .	. .+----. . .	
n	. . .+----. .	. . . .----. .	. . .+++++. .	. . .----. .	
1	. . .+.+----	. . . .-+---.	. . . .++++. .	. . . .---. .	
	. . . . .-----	. . . . .-----	. . . . .+++--	. . . . .----	
	. . . . . .----	. . . . . .---.	. . . .	. . . . . .----	
	. . . .--	. . . .--	. . . .-	. . . .---	
	-.	-.	. . . .	---.	. . .++++. . .
	+++.	. . . .	. . . .	----.	
	.+++.	.-.	. . . .	.----.	
R	++----. . . .	.-----. . . .	. .++++. . . .	. .----. . . .	
u	. .+----. . .	. .---+-. . .	. .+++++. . .	. .+----. . .	
n	. . .-----. .	. . .-----. .	. . .+++++. .	. . .----. .	
2	. . .+. . .---	. . . .-+--+.	. . . .++++. .	. . . .---. .	
	. . . . . .----	. . . . .---. .	. . . . .+++. .	. . . . .-----	
	. . . .+.+	. . . .+++	. . . .+.	. . . . . .----	
	. . . .--.	. . . .--	. . . .-	. . . .---	

FIG. 9. Weight matrices at the end of two typical simulations of a recurrent network on the shift detection task.

A dimensionality reduction task

Saund (1987) studied a dimensionality reduction task in which the input patterns lie along a one-dimensional manifold embedded in a two-dimensional space. Given the input patterns' two-dimensional coordinates, the system must discover a one-dimensional representation that preserves the patterns' topological order. For example, a pattern that lies at the beginning of the one-dimensional manifold should be assigned a smaller coordinate than a pattern that lies at the manifold's end. Durbin and Mitchison (1990) argued that cortical maps, such as those for ocular dominance, orientation, and retinotopic position in primary visual cortex, can be understood in terms of dimension-reducing mappings from many-dimensional parameter spaces to the surface of the cortex.

As is illustrated in Fig. 10, the network that we applied to this task had 64 input units, 8 hidden units, and 64 output units. The input and output units were arranged into 8×8 arrays. The network was an "autoassociator," meaning that the target values for the output units and the activations of the input units are the same. The input units had gaussian receptive fields that uniformly covered the two-dimensional input space. To increase the interpretability of the network's representations, the hidden and output units were constrained to have nonnegative weights on all connections and to have nonpositive bias weights. The network was initialized so that all input units projected to all hidden units which, in turn, projected to all output units. Figure 11A shows the 100 input patterns that were used in the first set of experiments. Note that the 5th, 15th, . . . , 95th patterns are numbered.

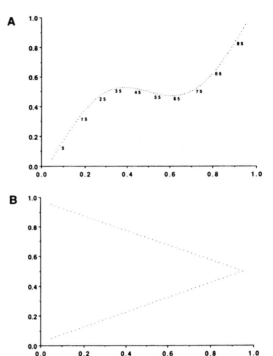

FIG. 11. (A) The input patterns used in the first set of experiments. The 5th, 15th, . . . , 95th patterns are numbered. (B) The input patterns used in the second set of experiments.

Figure 12 shows the hidden units' activations for a typical simulation. The hidden units successfully converted each input pattern's location in the two-dimensional space into an appropriate coordinate along the one-dimensional manifold. That is, the hidden units learned a topographic map of the patterns. Whereas hidden units toward the left responded to input patterns toward the manifold's beginning, hidden units toward the right responded to patterns toward the manifold's end. Figure 13 shows the weights for some of the units of the network. Each hidden unit had 64 weights, and the display of these weights are arranged in an 8×8 array to reflect the spatial arrangement of the input layer. Clearly, each hidden unit developed a local receptive field. This figure also shows two blocks of output weights. Each block has eight rows corresponding to the eight output units in a single row of the array of output units, and eight columns corresponding to the eight

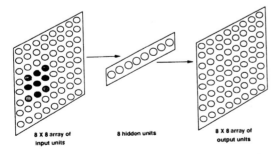

FIG. 10. The network applied to the dimensionality reduction task.

Data Point   Activations of Hidden Units

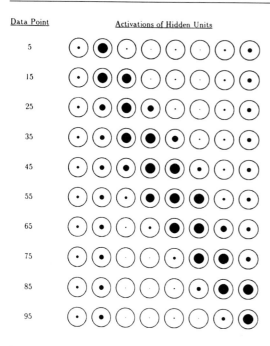

FIG. 12. Hidden units' activations in response to some of the input patterns.

```
Hidden unit 3                    Hidden unit 6
........                         ........
........                         ........
.+......                         ........
.+++....                         ....+..
.+......                         ....+++.
........                         ......+.
........                         ........
........                         ........

Output units 25–32               Output units 33–40
.+......                         .+......
..+.....                         .++.....
..++....                         ..++....
..+++...                         ..+++...
...+++..                         ...+++..
....+++.                         .....+..
.....++.                         .....+++
......++                         ......+.
```

FIG. 13. Weight matrices for some of the units of the network trained to perform the dimensionality reduction task.

weights of each unit. Output units toward the left received projections from hidden units toward the left, whereas output units toward the right received projections from hidden units toward the right. The leftmost hidden unit was eliminated from the network.

It should be emphasized that the weight-elimination technique is an extremely simple mechanism for obtaining a topographic map at the hidden layer. A network using this technique is not able to learn arbitrary topologies. For example, the input patterns shown in Fig. 11B lie on a manifold that doubles back on itself. In this case, the network mistakenly uses the same set of hidden units to represent the patterns both at the manifold's beginning and at its end. Thus, the hidden units' activations do not preserve the topological order of the input patterns, and the network does not successfully learn to perform the task. To construct a topographic map of these patterns requires more sophisticated techniques (e.g. Kohonen, 1982; Durbin & Mitchison, 1990).

Conclusions

This article has reviewed evidence that the developing neocortex is relatively uniform in its morphological and functional properties, and that there is considerable flexibility in the determination of which portions of the developing neocortex develop into which areas of the adult neocortex. Though the location of a region of developing neocortex appears to play a critical role in its acquisition of area-specific properties, the factors that directly influence the differentiation of the developing neocortex are not currently known. We have focused our attention on the regressive events that occur during development, particularly on those that have a competitive nature.

According to the competitive elimination hypothesis of Rakic (1986), competitive regressive events play a dominant role in the development of ocular dominance columns in the lateral geniculate nucleus and the cortex, and may play a significant role in the development of other properties of the mammalian brain. The trophic theory of neural connections (e.g. Purves, 1986) posits that presynaptic cells compete to acquire trophic factors that are released in limited amounts by postsynaptic cells or target areas. One possibility is that the competition for trophic factors is Hebbian, meaning that it favors presynaptic cells whose activity is positively correlated with that of the postsynaptic cell. In this article, we have pursued the alternative possibility that the competition is biased to favor presynaptic cells that are physically near to the postsynaptic cell. This hypothesis is particularly attractive because several researchers (e.g. Barlow, 1986; Cowey, 1981) have speculated that a bias toward short connections may account for the large number of functionally distinct cortical areas. Indeed, our simulations have shown that such a bias in artificial neural networks allows these systems to eliminate connections so as to dedicate different portions of the system to learn different tasks.

If biological neural systems are biased to use short connections, then it is important to know how neurons determine their relative positions. Positional information plays a role in many events during neural development including regional differentiation of tissues, stereotyped movements of cells, the emergence of the characteristic shape of various parts of the embryo, and the organized outgrowth of nerves to targets (Purves & Lichtman, 1985). One mechanism that is often hypothesized to allow positional information to operate is that gradients of a chemical signal influence developmental events. It is not difficult to imagine how a mechanism of this type would allow presynaptic and postsynaptic neurons to determine their relative positions.

A possible alternative to a system that is biased to eliminate long connections is a system that is constructed from the outset with only short connections. An advantage of the former system is that it can selectively adapt its structure to the nature of the tasks that it must learn. For example, one region may learn to perform a function that requires only comparing local sources of information (e.g. via lateral inhibition). This region can restrict its structure to only include very short connections. However, a different region may need to combine more distant sources of information and would

need access to relatively longer connections. The fact that regressive events during neural development show activity dependence is consistent with our hypothesis that the fate of a connection is determined both by its length and by its role in the computation the network performs.

Appendix

This appendix contains details of the simulations that were not included in the main body of the article.

Network topographies

We define a three-dimensional space whose x axis is orthogonal to the page, y axis is horizontal along the page, and z axis is vertical along the page. Each network's layers were centered along the y axis, and each layer was one unit away from its neighboring layers. If a layer was two-dimensional, then its units were uniformly distributed along the x and z axes from -3 to $+3$ along each axis. If a layer was one-dimensional, then its units were uniformly distributed along the x axis from -3 to $+3$. One exception to this rule was the recurrent network trained to perform the shift detection task. Each layer's units in this network were uniformly distributed along the x axis from -5 to $+5$. A second exception is system 2 trained to perform the "what" and "where" tasks. The output units for the "what" task were uniformly distributed along the x axis from -2 to -3, whereas those for the "where" task were uniformly distributed from $+2$ to $+3$.

Training time and step sizes

In all simulations, networks were trained for 1000 epochs. Within each epoch, training patterns were presented in a random order, and each network's weights were updated after each pattern. On the "what" and "where" tasks, the step size was 3. Otherwise, the step size was 1. In all simulations, the step size was gradually decreased to zero during the last 10 epochs.

Miscellaneous

Units used the logistic activation function with asymptotes at 0 and 1. If target output values were binary, then the actual targets used were 0.1 and 0.9. Networks were initialized with weights selected from a uniform distribution over the interval $(-0.1, 0.1)$. The only exception is the network trained to perform the dimensionality reduction task. In this case, the weights on connections were selected from the interval $(0, 0.1)$, and the bias weights were selected from $(-0.1, 0)$. In the displays of networks' weights, a weight is considered to be near zero if it lies in the interval $(-0.1, 0.1)$.

Notes

1. An unsupervised learner attempts to discover the underlying structure in the input in the absence of explicit feedback about desired outputs. In contrast, a supervised learner attempts to recover structure in the input by associating a desired output with each input.

2. Helmholtz wrote, "Happily, the distances our sense-perceptions have to traverse before they reach the brain are short, otherwise our consciousness would always lag far behind the present" (Helmholtz, quoted in Resnikoff, 1989).

3. The selection of a good value for p is dependent, at least in part, on the placement of the units of the network. As discussed below, the task that a network is trained to perform constrains the placement of many of the network's units. However, the task does not determine the placement of every unit (particularly the units of hidden layers) and, thus, we have often been forced to make arbitrary (though hopefully reasonable) selections for the placements of units.

4. Strictly speaking, Kohonen's learning procedure constrains nearby postsynaptic units to respond to nearby input vectors, not nearby presynaptic units. Because nearby input vectors are typically represented by patterns of activation on nearby presynaptic units, however, this distinction it not important for present purposes.

5. For an alternative approach to the problem of dedicating different networks to different tasks, see Jacobs, Jordan, and Barto (1991) and Jacobs, Jordan, Nowlan, and Hinton (1991).

6. See Rueckl, Cave, and Kosslyn (1989) for a discussion of the hidden unit representations that are useful for performing the "what" and "where" tasks.

Acknowledgements

We are grateful to David Rumelhart for discussions of his weight-elimination learning procedure, and to Daphne Bavelier and Stephen Kosslyn for commenting on an earlier version of this manuscript. This research was supported by the Mc-Donnell-Pew Program in Cognitive Neuroscience through JSMF Grant 90-33 awarded to the first author, by funding provided to the second author from Siemens Corporation and the Human Frontier Science Program, and by NSF Grant IRI-9013991 awarded to both authors.

Reprint requests should be sent to Dr. Robert Jacobs, Department of Brain and Cognitive Sciences, Massachusetts Institute of Technology, Cambridge, MA 02139.

References

Ballard, D. H. (1984). Parameter nets. *Artificial Intelligence*, 22, 235–267.

Barlow, H. B. (1986). Why have multiple cortical areas? *Vision Research*, 26, 81–90.

Barto, A. G., & Anandan, P. (1985). Pattern-recognizing stochastic learning automata. *IEEE Transactions on Systems, Man, and Cybernetics*, 15, 360–375.

Barto, A. G., & Jordan, M. I. (1987). Gradient following without back-propagation in layered networks. *Proceedings of the IEEE First Annual Conference on Neural Networks*, 2, 629–636.

Chauvin, Y. (1989). A back-propagation algorithm with optimal use of hidden units. In D. Touretzky (Ed.), *Advances in neural information processing systems 1*. San Mateo, CA: Morgan Kaufmann.

Cowan, W. M., Fawcett, J. W., O'Leary, D. D. M., & Stanfield, B. B. (1984). Regressive events in neurogenesis. *Science*, 225, 1258–1265.

Cowey, A. (1981). Why are there so many visual areas? In F. O. Schmidt, F. G. Warden, G. Adelman, & S. G. Dennis (Eds.), *The organization of the cerebral cortex*. Cambridge, MA: MIT Press.

Cowey, A. (1985). Aspects of cortical organization related to selective attention and selective impairments of visual perception: A tutorial review. In M. I. Posner & O. S. M. Marin (Eds.), *Attention and performance XI*. Hillsdale, NJ: Lawrence Erlbaum.

Duda, R. O., & Hart, P. E. (1973). *Pattern classification and scene analysis*. New York: John Wiley.

Durbin, R., & Mitchison, G. (1990). A dimension reduction framework for understanding cortical maps. *Nature (London)*, 343, 644–647.

Durbin, R., & Willshaw, D. (1987). An analogue approach to the travelling salesman problem using an elastic net method. *Nature (London)*, 326, 689–691.

Fodor, J. A. (1983). *The modularity of mind.* Cambridge, MA: MIT Press.

Gazzaniga, M. S. (1989). Organization of the human brain. *Science, 245,* 947–952.

Greenfield, P. M. (1991). Language, tools, and brain: The ontogeny and phylogeny of hierarchically organized sequential behavior. *Behavioral and Brain Sciences, 14,* 531–595.

Hanson, S. J., & Pratt, L. Y. (1989). Some comparisons of constraints for minimal network construction with back-propagation. In D. Touretzky (Ed.), *Advances in neural information processing systems 1.* San Mateo, CA: Morgan Kaufmann.

Hinton, G. E. (1987). Learning translation invariant recognition in a massively parallel network. In J. W. deBakker & P. C. Treleaven (Eds.), *PARLE: Parallel architectures and languages europe.* Berlin: Springer-Verlag.

Jacobs, R. A., Jordan, M. I., & Barto, A. G. (1991). Task decomposition through competition in a modular connectionist architecture: The what and where vision tasks. *Cognitive Science, 15,* 219–250.

Jacobs, R. A., Jordan, M. I., Nowlan, S. J., & Hinton, G. E. (1991). Adaptive mixtures of local experts. *Neural Computation, 3,* 79–87.

Jordan, M. I. (1986). Serial order: A parallel, distributed processing approach. Technical Report ICS-8604, University of California at San Diego, La Jolla, CA.

Kohonen, T. (1982). Self-organized formation of topologically correct feature maps. *Biological Cybernetics, 43,* 56–69.

le Cun, Y. (1985). Une procedure d'apprentissage pour reseau a sequil assymetrique [A learning procedure for asymmetric threshold network]. *Proceedings of Cognitiva, 85,* 599–604.

le Cun, Y. (1989). Generalization and network design strategies. Technical Report CRG-TR-89-4, University of Toronto, Toronto, Ontario.

Mishkin, M., Ungerleider, L. G., & Macko, K. A. (1983). Object vision and spatial vision: Two cortical pathways. *Trends in Neurosciences, 6,* 414–417.

Mozer, M. C. (1989). A focused backpropagation algorithm for temporal pattern recognition. *Complex Systems, 3,* 349–381.

Nelson, M. E., & Bower, J. M. (1990). Brain maps and parallel computers. *Trends in Neurosciences, 13,* 403–408.

O'Leary, D. D. M. (1989). Do cortical areas emerge from a protocortex? *Trends in Neurosciences, 12,* 400–406.

O'Leary, D. D. M., & Stanfield, B. B. (1989). Selective elimination of axons extended by developing cortical neurons is dependent on regional locale: Experiments utilizing fetal cortical transplants. *Journal of Neuroscience, 9,* 2230–2246.

Parker, D. B. (1985). Learning logic. Technical Report TR-47, Massachusetts Institute of Technology, Cambridge, MA.

Plaut, D. C., & Hinton, G. E. (1987). Learning sets of filters using back-propagation. *Computer Speech and Language, 2,* 35–61.

Purves, D. (1986). The trophic theory of neural connections. *Trends in Neurosciences, 9,* 486–489.

Purves, D., & Lichtman, J. W. (1980). Elimination of synapses in the developing nervous system. *Science, 210,* 153–157.

Purves, D., & Lichtman, J. W. (1985). *Principles of neural development.* Sunderland, MA: Sinauer Associates.

Rakic, P. (1986). Mechanism of ocular dominance segregation in the lateral geniculate nucleus: Competitive elimination hypothesis. *Trends in Neurosciences, 9,* 11–15.

Rakic, P. (1989). Competitive interactions during neuronal and synaptic development. In A. M. Galaburda (Ed.), *From reading to neurons.* Cambridge, MA: MIT Press.

Resnikoff, H. L. (1989). *The illusion of reality.* New York: Springer-Verlag.

Ringo, J. L. (1991). Neuronal interconnection as a function of brain size. *Brain, Behavior, and Evolution, 38,* 1–6.

Rueckl, J. G., Cave, K. R., & Kosslyn, S. M. (1989). Why are "what" and "where" processed by separate cortical visual systems? A computational investigation. *Journal of Cognitive Neuroscience, 1,* 171–186.

Rumelhart, D. E. (1988). Lecture at the 1988 Connectionist Models Summer School, Carnegie Mellon University, Pittsburgh, PA.

Rumelhart, D. E., Hinton, G. E., & Williams, R. J. (1986). Learning internal representations by error propagation. In D. E. Rumelhart, J. L. McClelland, & the PDP Research Group, *Parallel distributed processing: Explorations in the microstructure of cognition. Volume 1: Foundations.* Cambridge, MA: MIT Press.

Saund, E. (1987). Dimensionality-reduction using connectionist networks. A.I. Memo 941, Artificial Intelligence Laboratory, Massachusetts Institute of Technology, Cambridge, MA.

Sur, M., Pallas, S. L., & Roe, A. W. (1990). Cross-modal plasticity in cortical development: Differentiation and specification of sensory neocortex. *Trends in Neurosciences, 13,* 227–233.

Weigend, A. S., Huberman, B. A., & Rumelhart, D. E. (1990). Predicting the future: A connectionist

approach. *International Journal of Neural Systems,*
1, 193–210.

Werbos, P. J. (1974). *Beyond regression: New tools for*
prediction and analysis in the behavioral sciences.
Ph.D. thesis, Harvard University, Cambridge, MA.

Wiesel, T. N. (1982). Postnatal development of the
visual cortex and the influence of environment.
Nature (London), 299, 583–591.

Wiesel, T. N., & Hubel, D. H. (1965). Comparison of
the effects of unilateral and bilateral eye closure on
cortical unit responses in kittens. *Journal of Neuro-*
physiology, 28, 1029–1040.

Willshaw, D. J., & von der Malsburg, C. (1976). How
patterned neural connections can be set up by self-
organization. *Proceedings of the Royal Society of*
London B, 194, 431–445.

Glossary

Activation: A value associated with each unit or element in a network, usually interpreted as its level of activity, and propagated to other units to which it is connected. Values may be either binary, 0 or 1, or vary within a range of (positive or negative) real numbers. The actual values are determined by an activation rule or function (see below).

Activation function or rule: A means of calculating the levels of activation of the units of a network at an instant. The precise form of the rule varies between different sorts of network, but in all cases the activation of any given unit is some function of the sum of the inputs from the other units to which it is connected. For example, in a network of so-called linear threshold units, activation is 1 if the summed input is greater than some threshold value, and 0 otherwise. Alternatively activation may be a continuous function of the input, expressed as a simple equation. The timing of the activation changes may be synchronous, in that all units have their activation updated simultaneously; or asynchronous, for instance each unit may adjust its activation randomly in time at some average attempt rate.

Activation patterns: The set of activation values over some or all of the units in a network. In some circumstances the pattern may be said to represent things such as visual objects, concepts, memory items, elements of a natural language and so forth (see distributed representation, local representation, and units, below).

Attactor models: Models that operate iteratively, cycling activation around the network until a stable pattern is reached. The learned weights in the model can push activation into one stable form, depending on the input given; these weights are said to form *basins of attraction* within the model's weight space. A Hopfield net is one form of attractor model.

Binding: The problem of coding which elements go with which, in which spatial or temporal order. This can represent a problem for networks using distributed representations of microfeatures, where the relations between the microfeatures are not necessarily coded.

Competitive queuing: A procedure for coding temporal order in networks. Units are given an activation level that reflects the temporal order of output (like the order in a queue), and units compete to gain access to output units (only one unit wins at a time). After a unit has "won" the competition, it enters a refractory state, when it no longer competes to form the next output; this enables different outputs to be made on the next iteration of the network.

Compositionality: The property of a formal system such as a logic or number system which allows the generation of legal expressions by rules that combine the basic or atomic elements to form compound structures. The rules of the number system, for example, determine the generation of expressions such as "1 + 1 = 2". Such systems are productive in that an infinite set of legal expressions may be derived from a finite set of basic elements. It has been argued that natural language exhibits compositionality and is productive in the same sense.

Connection: A link between two units in a network, through which activation is passed, either in both directions or in one direction. The activation value passed is modulated by a weight associated with each connection (see weights, below), and a connection may be excitatory or inhibitory.

Distributed representation: A network in which the joint activity of a set of units may be interpreted as standing for a concept or an external object or event. Each unit may be taken as encoding some microfeature of the item in whose representation it participates. Each unit may, therefore, play a role in more than one item, so the representations of cats and dogs may both involve a unit that stands for "furry things". In contrast local representations have just one unit standing for each concept or object.

Error score: This is the difference between the values of an output produced by a network and the output that is expected if the network classifies a pattern correctly, and is used in *supervised learning* schemes (see below). A common error measure is the root mean error (RMS_e), in which differences between obtained and expected output values are squared (to equate positive and negative differences) and averaged, and then the square root is taken.

Feed-forward network: A network that has a layer of input units, a layer of output units, and, typically, one layer or more of intermediate units, often referred to as hidden (see below). Activity passes in one direction only: from input units to the output units via the intermediate layers. Notice that this architecture entails a one-shot activation rule (see above), in which activations are updated once only for each new input, rather than converge to some stable state via a series of applications of an activation, as in a relaxation network (see relaxation in a network, below).

Hidden units: See units, below.

Hybrid models: Models that have both a connectionist component and a symbol-processing component (e.g. a production system).

Input units: See units, below.

Interactive activation and competition models: Models typically with local representations which compete to form a representation of the input. Activation is also typically transmitted in a top-down as well as a bottom-up fashion to determine network performance.

Learning rule: A procedure for determining the weight values associated with the connections between units in a network (see weights, below). Typically it consists of an arithmetic rule which is applied after the activation states of the units have been determined and has the effect of reducing the difference between the actual activation pattern and some desired pattern. For instance in feed-forward networks (see above) the distance between actual outputs and some set of target outputs is typically reduced in a progressive manner by the repeated application of a rule for adjusting the weights. When a set of target outputs are used for training, this is known as *supervised learning*. In *unsupervised learning*, weights are adjusted without comparison to a set of target outputs. An important feature of all the various learning procedures is that they depend only on local information, for instance the activations of the units at either end of the connection, rather than any global property of the network or distant parts of it.

Local representation: See distributed representation, above.

Multilayer network: A feed-forward network that has intermediate units mediating between input and output units, and therefore has at least two layers of adaptable connections, in contrast to single-layer networks which have only one such layer linking input and output units. There are significant limitations to single-layer networks, which may be overcome by the move to multiple layers of adaptive connections.

Output units: See units, below.

Recurrent networks: In contrast to feed-forward networks (see above) there are no restrictions on connectivity in recurrent networks: units may be connected to others in the same layer, to units in higher and lower layers, and to themselves. The rich interconnectivity makes such networks highly dynamic, and stable patterns of activation usually result only from the repeated application of an activation rule (see above). The process of arriving at a stable pattern of activations is referred to as relaxation in a network (see below).

Relaxation in a network: Describes the convergence of the activation states of the units of a recurrent network (see above) from some unstable pattern to to a stable one, in that further application of the activation rule (see above) would produce no change in the activation levels of any of the units. The convergence usually involves a sequence of cycles, with the activation rule being applied at each cycle, through a series of unstable activation pattern until the network settles on the final stable set of activation levels.

Simultaneous multiple constraint satisfaction: A solution to a problem may have to fulfil certain requirements in order to be acceptable. The solution may be said to satisfy constraints. May cognitive processes can be seen to depend on the simultaneous satisfaction of multiple constraints. For example, a word in a sentence must simultaneously satisfy grammatical and semantic restrictions. Networks provide very natural ways of optimising satisfaction among multiple constraints.

Single-layer networks: Networks that have only one layer of modifiable connections (see above) between input units and output units (see below).

Stochastic networks: Networks in which the states of the units are determined probabilistically, with the probability that a unit takes a given state being a function of the input activation and connection weight. The probabilistic functions add "noise" to the operations of the networks, which in some cases can aid learning. Stochastic networks contrast with *deterministic networks*, where the states of units are absolutely determined by the product of the input activation and connection weight.

Subsymbolic models: These are said to characterise the connectionist approach in psychology, in contrast to those traditional theories that have symbol systems, and operations on them, at their heart. The microfeatures represented by the units in a distributed network are subsymbolic in the sense intended here: they are finer-grained than the entities referred to in symbolic models and may not be open to semantic interpretation. The behaviour described by the symbolic models emerges from the interaction of the subsymbolic elements. The subsymbolic level of explanation is said to be a more exact account of behaviour by some in the connectionist community.

Supervised learning: Many learning rules (see above) require an estimate of the distance between a current response and a desired one. The learning is therefore supervised in that knowledge of the target response is required. In contrast unsupervised learning procedures

may be applied to some networks which, given a set of training examples, with discover its statistical structure, for example dividing the set into distinct categories and, after learning, classifying new inputs in terms of these categories. Examples include the *delta rule* and *back-propagation*.

Units: The elementary, computational components of a network. Each is a relatively simple device which receives numerical inputs from other units via connections (see above) or from sources outside the network, effectively the world relative to the network. A unit also sends numerical values to other units within the network or to the outside world, with the actual value being determined by its total input (see activation rule, above). Units may be categorised as input, that is, those that receive inputs from the world; output, that is, those that send values to the world; and hidden, that is, those units that communicate only with other units in the network.

Unsupervised learning: Forms of learning determined by patterns of correlated firing between units (*Hebbian learning*) or by whichever units take the highest activation level (as in *competitive learning*). Critically, there is no predetermined correct output state for networks; rather networks adapt to a combination of the input patterns and the initial weight structure of the network.

Weights: These are associated with the connections (see above) in a network. For each connection there is a positive or negative numerical value, the size of which determines the extent of the influence one unit has over the activity of the unit to which the connection links it. Negative values result in inhibitory influence, and positive values have excitatory effects. In an adaptive network the values are variables that are assigned by the application of a learning rule (see above).

Wickelphones and Wickelfeatures: Forms of distributed coding used in some studies of learning the past tense, and of word naming. In this form of coding, units code triplets of features, with the start and end triplets demarked by one part of the triplet standing for a space. Other triplets can appear in words of different length, so helping to solve the problem of having different units representing the same letters/graphemes/phonemes in different positions across words.

References

Aaronson, D. (1968). Temporal course of perception in an immediate recall task. *Journal of Experimental Psychology, 76,* 129–140.

Ackley, D. H., Hinton, G. E., & Sejnowski, T. J. (1985). A learning algorithm for Boltzmann machines. *Cognitive Science, 9,* 147–169.

Amari, S. A. (1977). A mathematical approach to neural systems. In J. Metzler (Ed.), *Systems neuroscience.* New York: Academic Press.

Anderson, J. A. (1970). Two models for memory organization using interacting traces. *Mathematical Biosciences, 8,* 137–160.

Arbib, M. A. & Hanson, A. R. (1987). Vision, brain and cooperative computation: An overview. In M. A. Arbib & A. R. Hanson (Eds.), *Vision, brain and cooperative computation.* London: MIT Press.

Arguin, M. & Bub, D. N. (1994). Functional mechanisms in pure alexia: Evidence from letter processing. In M. J. Farah & G. Ratcliff (Eds.), *The neuropsychology of high-level vision* (pp.149–172). Hillsdale, NJ: Lawrence Erlbaum Associates Inc.

Baars, B. J., Motley, M. T., & Mackay, D. G. (1975). Output editing for lexical status from artificially elicited slips of the tongue. *Journal of Verbal Learning and Verbal Behavior, 14,* 382–391.

Baddeley, A. D. (1968). How does acoustic similarity influence short-term memory? *Quarterly Journal of Experimental Psychology, 20,* 249–264.

Baddeley, A. D. (1986). *Working memory.* Oxford: Oxford University Press.

Baddeley, A. D., Papagno, C., & Vallar, G. (1988). When long-term learning depends on short-term storage. *Journal of Memory and Language, 27,* 586–595.

Baddeley, A. D., Thomson, N., & Buchanan, M. (1975). Word length and the structure of short-term memory. *Journal of Verbal Learning and Verbal Behavior, 14,* 575–589.

Baldi, P. & Meir, R. (1990). Computing with arrays of coupled oscillators: An application to preattentive texture discrimination. *Neural Computation, 2,* 458–471.

Ballard, D. H. (1986). Cortical connections and parallel processing: Structure and function. *Behavioral and Brain Sciences, 9,* 67–120.

Ballard, D. H. (1991). Animate vision. *Artificial Intelligence, 48,* 57–86.

Ballard, D. H. & Brown, C. M. (1982). *Computer vision.* Englewood Cliffs, NJ: Prentice-Hall.

Barnes, J. M. & Underwood, B. J. (1959). "Fate" of first-list associations in transfer theory. *Journal of Experimental Psychology, 58,* 97–105.

Barrow, H. G. & Tennenbaum, J. M. (1978). Recovering intrinsic scene characteristics from images. In A. R. Hanson & E. M. Riseman (Eds.), *Computer vision systems.* New York: Academic Press.

Bartlett, F. C. (1932). *Remembering: A study in experimental and social psychology.* Cambridge: Cambridge University Press.

Baxter, D. M. & Warrington, E. K. (1983). Neglect dyslexia. *Journal of Neurology, Neurosurgery and Psychiatry, 46,* 1073–1078.

Baylis, G. & Driver, J. (1993). Visual attention and objects: Evidence for hierarchical coding of location. *Journal of Experimental Psychology: Human Perception and Performance, 19*, 451–470.

Baylis, G., Driver, J., & Rafal, R. D. (1993). Visual extinction and stimulus repetition. *Journal of Cognitive Neuroscience, 5*, 453–466.

Beatty, J. (1995). *Principles of behavioral neuroscience*. London: Brown & Benchmark Publishers.

Beauvois, M.-F. & Derouesné, J. (1979). Phonological alexia: Three dissociations. *Journal of Neurology, Neurosurgery and Psychiatry, 42*, 1115–1124.

Beauvois, M.-F. & Derouesné, J. (1981). Lexical or orthographic alexia. *Brain, 104*, 21–49.

Behrmann, M., Moscovitch, M., & Mozer, M. C. (1991). Directing attention to words and nonwords in normal subjects and in a computational model: Implications for neglect dyslexia. *Cognitive Neuropsychology, 8*, 213–248.

Berent, I. & Perfetti, C. A. (1995). A rose is a REEZ: The two-cycles model of phonology assembly in reading English. *Psychological Review, 102*, 146–184.

Berko, J. (1958). The child's learning of English morphology. *Word, 14*, 150–177.

Besner, D. (1996). Basic processes in reading: Multiple routines in localist and connectionist models. In P. A. McMullen & R. M. Klein (Eds.), *Converging methods for understanding reading and dyslexia*. Cambridge, MA: MIT Press.

Besner, D. & McCann, R. S. (1987). Word-frequency and pattern distortion in visual word identification and production. In M. Coltheart (Ed.), *Attention and performance XII*. Hove, UK: Lawrence Erlbaum Associates Ltd.

Besner, D., Twilley, L., McCann, R. S., & Seergobin, K. (1990). On the connection between connectionism and data: Are a few words necessary? *Psychological Review, 97*, 432–446.

Bever, T. G. (1992). The demons and the beast: Modular and nodular kinds of knowledge. In R. G. Reilly & N. E. Sharkey (Eds.), *Connectionist approaches to natural language processing*. Hove, UK: Lawrence Erlbaum Associates Ltd.

Biederman, I. & Kalocsai, P. (1997). Neurocomputational bases of object and face recognition. *Philosophical Transactions of the Royal Society, 352*, 1203–1220.

Bisiach, E., Bulgarelli, C., Sterzi, R., & Vallar, G. (1983). Line bisection and cognitive plasticity of unilateral neglect of space. *Brain and Cognition, 2*, 32–38.

Bisiach, E. & Luzzatti, C. (1978). Unilateral neglect of representational space. *Cortex, 14*, 129–133.

Blank, D. S., Meeden, L. A., & Marshall, J. B. (1992). Exploring the symbolic/subsymbolic continuum: A case study of RAAM. In J. Dinsmore (Ed.), *The symbolic and connectionist paradigms: closing the gap*. Hillsdale, NJ: Lawrence Erlbaum Associates Inc.

Bloesch, A. & Wiles, J. (1991). Data representation and display techniques for representations in hidden unit space. *First Indiana conference on dynamics in cognition*. Indiana University.

Brachman, R. J. & Levesque, H. J. (Eds.). (1985). *Readings in knowledge representation*. Los Altos, CA: Morgan Kaufman.

Bramwell, B. (1897). Illustrative cases of aphasia. *The Lancet, i*, 1256–1259.

Bransford, J. D. & Johnson, M. K. (1973). Consideration of some problems of comprehension. In W. G. Chase (Ed.), *Visual information processing*. New York: Academic Press.

Bredart, S., Brennen, T., & Valentine, T. (1997). Dissociations between the processing of proper and common names. *Cognitive Neuropsychology, 14(2)*, 209–217.

Breitmeyer, B. G. (1988). *Visual masking*. Oxford: Oxford University Press.

Broadbent, D. E. (1985). A question of levels: Comment on McClelland and Rumelhart (1985). *Journal of Experimental Psychology: General, 114*, 189–192.

Brown, G. D. A., Hulme, C. A., Hyland, P., & Mitchell, I. J. (1994). Programmed cell death in the developing nervous system: A functional neural network model. *Neuroscience, 63*, 881–894.

Brown, G. D. A. & Loosemore, R. P. W. (1994). Computational approaches to normal and impaired spelling. In G. D. A. Brown & N. C. Ellis (Eds.), *Handbook of spelling*. Chichester: Wiley.

Brown, G. D. A., Loosemore, R. P. W., & Watson, F. L. (1994). Normal and dyslexic spelling: A connectionist approach.

Brown, R. (1973). *A first language*. Cambridge, MA: MIT Press.

Bruce, V. & Green, P. R. (1990). *Visual perception: Physiology, psychology and ecology (2nd Edn)*. Hove: Lawrence Erlbaum Associates Ltd.

Bruce, V. & Humphreys, G. W. (1994). Recognizing objects and faces. *Visual Cognition, 1*, 141–180.

Bruce, V. & Valentine, T. (1986). Semantic priming of familiar faces. *Quarterly Journal of Experimental Psychology, 38A(1)*, 125–150.

Bruce, V. & Young, A. (1986). Understanding face recognition. *British Journal of Psychology, 77*, 305–327.

Bub, D. & Kertesz, A. (1982). Deep agraphia. *Brain and Language, 17,* 146–165.

Bullinaria, J. A. & Chater, N. (1995). Connectionist modelling: Implications for cognitive neuropsychology. *Language and Cognitive Processes, 10,* 227–264.

Burgess, N. (1995). A solvable connectionist model of immediate recall of ordered lists. In G. Tesauro, D. Touretzky, & T. K. Leen (Eds.), *Neural information processing systems. Vol. 7.* Cambridge, MA: MIT Press.

Burgess, N. & Hitch, G. J. (1992). Toward a network model of the articulatory loop. *Journal of Memory and Language, 31,* 429–460.

Burton, A. M. (1994). Learning new faces in an interactive activation and competition model. *Visual Cognition, 1,* 313–348.

Burton, A. M. & Bruce, V. (1993). Naming faces and naming names: Exploring an interactive activation model of person recognition. *Memory, 1,* 457–480.

Burton, A. M., Bruce, V., & Johnston, R. A. (1990). Understanding face recognition with an interactive activation model. *British Journal of Psychology, 81,* 361–380.

Burton, A. M., Young, A. W., Bruce, V., Johnston, R. A., & Ellis, A. W. (1991). Understanding covert recognition. *Cognition, 39,* 129–166.

Bybee, J. L. & Slobin, D. L. (1982). Rules and schemas in the development and use of the English past tense. *Language, 58,* 265–289.

Callan, R. E. & Palmer-Brown, D. (1997). (S)RAAM: An analytic technique for fast and reliable derivation of connectionist symbol structure representations. *Connection Science, 9,* 139–160.

Caramazza, A. & Hillis, A. E. (1990a). Levels of representation, co-ordinate frames, and unilateral neglect. *Cognitive Neuropsychology, 7(5–6),* 391–445.

Caramazza, A. & Hillis, A. E. (1990b). Where do semantic errors come from? *Cortex, 26,* 95–122.

Caramazza, A. & Hillis, A. E. (1991). Lexical organization of nouns and verbs in the brain. *Nature, 349,* 788–790.

Caramazza, A. & Miceli, G. (1990). The structure of graphemic representations. *Cognition, 37,* 243–297.

Caramazza, A., Miceli, G., Villa, G., & Romani, C. (1987). The role of the graphemic buffer in spelling: Evidence from a case of acquired dysgraphia. *Cognition, 26,* 59–85.

Caramazza, A. & Shelton, J. R. (1998). Domain-specific knowledge systems in the brain: The animate–inanimate distinction. *Journal of Cognitive Neuroscience, 10,* 1–34.

Carlson, N. R. (1986). *Physiology of behavior: Second edition.* Hemel Hempstead, UK: Allyn & Bacon.

Carpenter, G. A. & Grossberg, S. (1987a). A massively parallel architecture for a self-organizing neural pattern recognition machine. *Computer Vision, Graphics and Image Processing, 37,* 54–115.

Carpenter, G. A. & Grossberg, S. (1987b). ART2: Stable self-organization of pattern-recognition codes for analog input patterns. *Applied Optics, 26,* 4919–4930.

Carr, T. H. & Pollatsek, A. (1985). Recognizing printed words: A look at current models. In D. Besner, T. G. Waller, & G. E. MacKinnon (Eds.), *Reading research: Advances in theory and in practice, V.* New York: Academic Press.

Cattell, J. M. (1886). The time taken up by cerebral operations. *Mind, 11,* 220–242, 377–392.

Chalmers, D. J. (1990). Syntactic transformations on distributed representations. *Connection Science, 2,* 53–62.

Charniak, E. & McDermott, D. (1985). *Introduction to artificial intelligence.* Reading, MA: Addison-Wesley.

Chelazzi, L., Miller, E. K., Duncan, J., & Desimone, R. (1993). A neural basis for visual search in inferior temporal cortex. *Nature, 363,* 345–347.

Chomsky, N. (1957). *Syntactic structures.* The Hague: Mouton.

Chomsky, N. (1959). Review of B. F. Skinner's "Verbal behavior". *Language, 35,* 16–58.

Clark, A. (1989). *Microcognition: Philosophy, cognitive science and parallel distributed processing.* Cambridge, MA: MIT Press.

Clark, A. (1992). The presence of a symbol. *Connection Science, 4,* 193–205.

Cohen, G. & Burke, D. M. (1993). Memory for proper names: A review. *Memory, 1,* 249–264.

Cohen, J. D., Braver, T. S., & O'Reilly, R. C. (1996). A computational approach to prefrontal cortex, cognitive control and schizophrenia: Recent developments and current challenges. In A. C. Roberts, T. W. Robbins, & L. Weiskrantz (Eds.), *Executive and cognitive functions of the prefrontal cortex.* Oxford: Oxford University Press.

Cohen, J. D., Dunbar, K., & McClelland, J. L. (1990). On the control of automatic processes: A parallel distributed processing account of the Stroop Effect. *Psychological Review, 97(3),* 332–361.

Cohen, J. D., Farah, M. J., Romero, R. D., & Servan-Schreiber, D. (1994). Mechanisms of spatial attention: The relation of macrostructure to microstructure in parietal attentional deficits. *Journal of Cognitive Neuroscience, 6,* 377–387.

Cohen, J. D. & Servan-Schreiber, D. (1992). Context, cortex and dopamine — A connectionist approach to behavior and biology in schizophrenia. *Psychological Review, 99(1)*, 45–77.

Cohen, J. D. & Servan-Schreiber, D. (1993). A theory of dopamine function and its role in cognitive deficits in schizophrenia. *Schizophrenia Bulletin, 19(1)*, 85–104.

Cohen, M. A. & Grossberg, S. G. (1983). Absolute stability of global pattern formation and parallel memory storage by competitive neural networks. *IEEE Transactions on Systems, Man and Cybernetics, 13*, 815–826.

Coltheart, M. (1984). [Editorial.] *Cognitive Neuropsychology, 1*, 1–8.

Coltheart, M. (1987). Cognitive neuropsychology and the study of reading. In M. I. Posner & O. S. M. Marin (Eds.), *Attention and performance XI*. Hillsdale, NJ: Lawrence Erlbaum Associates Inc.

Coltheart, M., Curtis, B., Atkins, P., & Haller, M. (1993). Models of reading aloud: Dual-route and parallel-distributed-processing approaches. *Psychological Review, 100*, 589–608.

Coltheart, M., Patterson, K. E., & Marshall, J. C. (Eds.). (1980). *Deep dyslexia*. London: Routledge & Kegan Paul.

Coltheart, M., Patterson, K. E., & Marshall, J. C. (1987). *Deep dyslexia* (2nd Edn.) London: Routledge & Kegan Paul.

Conrad, R. (1964). Acoustic confusion in immediate memory. *British Journal of Psychology, 55*, 75–84.

Corbetta, M., Miezin, F. M., Shulman, G. L., & Petersen, S. E. (1993). A PET study of visuospatial attention. *The Journal of Neuroscience, 13*, 1202–1226.

Coslett, H. B. & Saffran, E. M. (1992). Optic aphasia and the right-hemisphere: A replication and extension. *Brain and Language, 43(1)*, 148–161.

Cottrell, G. & Small, S. (1983). A connectionist scheme for modelling word sense disambiguation. *Cognition and Brain Theory, 1*, 89–120.

Crain, S. & Steedman, M. (1985). On not being led up the garden-path: The use of context by the psychological parser. In D. Dowty, L. Karttunen, & A. Zwicky (Eds.), *Natural language parsing*. Cambridge: Cambridge University Press.

Crick, F. (1984). The function of the thalamic reticular spotlight: The searchlight hypothesis. *Proceedings of the National Academy of Sciences, 81*, 4586–4590.

Crick, F. & Asanuma, C. (1986). Certain aspects of the anatomy and physiology of the cerebral cortex. In J. L. McClelland & D. E. Rumelhart (Eds.), *Parallel distributed processing: Explorations in the microstructure of cognition. Vol. 2*. Cambridge, MA: MIT Press.

Cutler, A., Mehler, J., Norris, D., & Segui, J. (1987). Phonemic identification and the lexicon. *Cognitive Psychology, 19(2)*, 141–177.

Cutler, A. & Norris, D. (1979). Monitoring sentence comprehension. In W. E. Cooper & E. C. T. Walker (Eds.), *Sentence processing: Psycholinguistic studies presented to Merrill Garrett*. Hillsdale, NJ: Lawrence Erlbaum Associates Inc.

Cutler, A. & Norris, D. (1988). The role of strong syllables in segmentation for lexical access. *Journal of Experimental Psychology: Human Perception and Performance, 14*, 113–121.

Davidoff, J. & De Bleser, R. (1993). Optic Aphasia: A review of past studies and reappraisal. *Aphasiology, 7(2)*, 135–154.

De Haan, E. H. F., Young, A. W., & Newcombe, F. (1987). Face recognition without awareness. *Cognitive Neuropsychology, 4(4)*, 385–415.

De Renzi, E. (1986). Current issues in prosopagnosia. In H. Ellis, M. A. Jeeves, F. Newcombe, & A. W. Young (Eds.), *Aspects of face processing*. Dordrecht: Martinus Nijhoff.

Déjérine, J. (1892). Contribution a l'étude anatomoclinique et clinique des différentes variétés de cécité verbale. *Memoires de la Société de Biologie, 4*, 61–90.

Dell, G. S. (1985). Positive feedback in hierarchical connectionist models: Applications to language production. *Cognitive Science, 9*, 3–24.

Dell, G. S. (1986). A spreading-activation theory of retrieval in sentence production. *Psychological Review, 93*, 283–321.

Dell, G. S. (1988). The retrieval of phonological forms in production: Tests of predictions from a connectionist model. *Journal of Memory and Language, 27*, 124–142.

Dell, G. S. (1989). The effect of practice on speech production errors. *Bulletin of the Psychonomic Society, 27*, 527.

Dell, G. S. (1990). Effects of frequency and vocabulary type on phonological speech errors. *Language and Cognitive Processes, 5*, 313–349.

Dell, G. S., Juliano, C., & Govindjee, A. (1995). Structure and content in language production: A theory of frame constraints in phonological speech errors. *Cognitive Science, 17*, 149–195.

Dell, G. S. & Reich, P. A. (1981). Stages in sentence production: An analysis of speech error data. *Journal of Verbal Learning and Verbal Behavior, 20*, 611–629.

Desimone, R. & Ungerleider, L. G. (1989). Neural mechanisms of visual processing in monkeys. In F. Boller & J. Grafman (Eds.), *Handbook of neurophysiology. Vol. 2* (pp.267–299). New York: Elsevier Science.

Dewey, J. (1910). *How we think*. London: D. C. Heath.

Dienes, Z. (1992). Connectionist and memory-array models of artificial grammar learning. *Cognitive Science, 16(1)*, 41–79.

Dienes, Z. & Perner, J. (1994). Dissociable definitions of consciousness. *Behavioral and Brain Sciences, 17(3)*, 403–404.

Donnelly, N., Humphreys, G. W., & Riddoch, M. J. (1991). Parallel computation of primitive shape descriptions. *Journal of Experimental Psychology: Human Perception and Performance, 17(2)*, 561–570.

Dorfner, G. (1993). Connectionism and syntactic binding of concepts. *Behavioral and Brain Sciences, 16*, 456–457.

Driver, J., Baylis, G. C. & Rafal, R. D. (1992) Preserved figure-ground segregation and symmetry perception in visual neglect. *Nature, 360*, 73–75.

Duncan, J. (1984). Selective attention and the organization of visual information. *Journal of Experimental Psychology: General, 113*, 501–517.

Duncan, J. & Humphreys, G. W. (1989). Visual search and stimulus similarity. *Psychological Review, 96(3)*, 433–458.

Duncker, K. (1945). On problem solving. *Psychological Monographs, 58, (Whole number 270)*.

Eckhorn, R., Bauer, R., Jordan, W., Brosch, M., Kruse, W., Munk, M., & Reitbock, H. J. (1988). Coherent oscillations: A mechanism of feature linking in the visual cortex? *Biological Cybernetics, 60*, 121–130.

Eckhorn, R., Reitbock, H. J., Arndt, M., & Dicke, P. (1990). Feature linking via synchronization among distributed assemblies: Simulations of results from cat visual cortex. *Neural Computation, 2*, 293–307.

Ellis, A. W. (1980). On the Freudian theory of speech errors. In V. A. Fromkin (Ed.), *Errors in linguistic performance* (pp.123–132). New York: Academic Press.

Ellis, A. W., Flude, B. M., & Young, A. W. (1987a). "Neglect dyslexia" and the early visual processing of letters in words and nonwords. *Cognitive Neuropsychology, 4*, 439–464.

Ellis, A. W., Young, A. W., Flude, B. M., & Hay, D. C. (1987b). Repetition priming of face recognition. *Quarterly Journal of Experimental Psychology, 39A(2)*, 193–210.

Elman, J. L. (1990). Finding structure in time. *Cognitive Science, 14*, 179–211.

Elman, J. L. & McClelland, J. L. (1986). Exploring lawful variability in the speech waveform. In S. Perkell & D. H. Klatt (Eds.), *Invariance and variability in speech processing* (pp.360–385). Hillsdale, NJ: Lawrence Erlbaum Associates Inc.

Elman, J. L. & McClelland, J. L. (1988). Cognitive penetration of the mechanisms of perception: Compensation for coarticulation of lexically restored phonemes. *Journal of Memory and Language, 27*, 143–165.

Eriksen, C. W. (1995). The flankers task and response competition: A useful tool for investigating a variety of cognitive problems. *Visual Cognition, 2*, 101–118.

Ervin, S. (1964). Imitation and structural change in children's language. In E. Lenneberg (Ed.), *New directions in the study of language*. Cambridge, MA: MIT Press.

Evett, L. J. & Humphreys, G. W. (1981). The use of abstract graphemic information in lexical access. *Quarterly Journal of Experimental Psychology, 33A*, 325–350.

Fahlman, S. E. (1981). Representing implicit knowledge. In G. E. Hinton & J. A. Anderson (Eds.), *Parallel models of associative memory*. Hillsdale, NJ: Lawrence Erlbaum Associates Inc.

Farah, M. J. (1990). *Visual agnosia*. Cambridge, MA: MIT Press.

Farah, M. J. (1994). Neuropsychological inference with an interactive brain: A critique of the "locality" assumption. *Behavioral and Brain Sciences, 17*, 43–104.

Farah, M. J. & McClelland, J. L. (1991). A computational model of semantic memory impairment: Modality specificity and emergent category specificity. *Journal of Experimental Psychology: General, 120(4)*, 339–357.

Farah, M. J., O'Reilly, R. C., & Vecera, S. P. (1993). Dissociated overt and covert recognition as an emergent property of a lesioned neural network. *Psychological Review, 100*, 571–588.

Farah, M. J. & Wallace, M. A. (1992). Semantically-bounded anomia: Implications for the neural implementation of naming. *Neuropsychologia, 30(7)*, 609–621.

Fay, D. & Cutler, A. (1977). Malapropisms and the structure of the mental lexicon. *Linguistic Inquiry, 8*, 505–520.

Feldman, J. A. (1981). A connectionist model of visual memory. In G. E. Hinton & J. A. Anderson (Eds.), *Parallel models of associative memory*. Hillsdale, NJ: Lawrence Erlbaum Associates Inc.

Feldman, J. A. & Ballard, D. H. (1982). Connectionist models and their properties. *Cognitive Science*, *6*, 205–254.

Feustel, T. C., Shiffrin, R. M., & Salasoo, A. (1983). Episodic and lexical contributions to the repetition effect in word identification. *Journal of Experimental Psychology: General*, *112*, 309–346.

Fillmore, C. J. (1968). The case for case. In E. Bach & R. T. Harms (Eds.), *Universals in linguistic theory*. New York: Holt, Rinehart & Winston.

Finch, S. & Chater, N. (1994). Learning syntactic categories: A statistical approach. In M. Oaksford & G. D. A. Brown (Eds.), *Neurodynamics and psychology*. London: Academic Press.

Fodor, J. A. & Pylyshyn, Z. W. (1988). Connectionism and cognitive architecture: A critical analysis. *Cognition*, *28*, 3–71.

Frauenfelder, U. H., Segui, J., & Dijkstra, T. (1990). Lexical effects in phonemic processing: Facilitatory or inhibitory? *Journal of Experimental Psychology: Human Perception and Performance*, *16(1)*, 77–91.

Frederiksen, J. R. & Kroll, J. F. (1976). Spelling and sound: Approaches to the internal lexicon. *Journal of Experimental Psychology: Human Perception and Performance*, *1*, 361–379.

French, R. M. (1992). Semi-distributed representations and catastrophic forgetting in connectionist networks. *Connection Science*, *4*, 365–377.

Freud, S. (1901/1958). *The psychopathology of everyday life* [Trans. A. Tyson]. Harmondsworth, UK: Penguin.

Frisby, J. (1979). *Seeing: Illusion, brain and mind*. Milton Keynes, UK: Open University Press.

Fruzzetti, A. E., Toland, K., Teller, S. A., & Loftus, E. F. (1992). Memory and eyewitness testimony. In M. M. Gruneberg & P. E. Morris (Eds.), *Aspects of memory, Vol. 1: The practical aspects (2nd edn)*. London: Routledge & Kegan Paul.

Fullerton, K. J., McSherry, D., & Stout, R. W. (1986). Albert's test: A neglected test of visual neglect. *The Lancet*, *334*, 430–432.

Funnell, E. (1983). Phonological processing in reading: New evidence from acquired dyslexia. *British Journal of Psychology*, *74*, 159–180.

Ganong, W. F. III (1980). Phonetic categorization in auditory word perception. *Journal of Experimental Psychology: Human Perception and Performance*, *6*, 110–125.

Garrett, M. F. (1975). The analysis of sentence production. In G. H. Bower (Ed.), *The psychology of learning and motivation* (pp.133–177). New York: Academic Press.

Garrett, M. F. (1980). Levels of processing in sentence production. In B. Butterworth (Ed.), *Language production. Vol. 1*. London: Academic Press.

Gentner, D. R., Grudin, J., & Conway, E. (1980). *Finger movements in transcription typing. Technical Report 8001*. San Diego, CA: Center for Human Information Processing.

Gibson, E. J. & Walk, R. D. (1956). The effect of prolonged exposure to visually presented patterns on learning to discriminate them. *Journal of Comparative and Physiological Psychology*, *49*, 239–242.

Gick, M. L. & Holyoak, K. J. (1980). Analogical problem solving. *Cognitive Psychology*, *12*, 306–355.

Gick. M. L. & Holyoak, K. J. (1983). Schema induction and analogical transfer. *Cognitive Psychology*, *15(1)*, 1–38.

Gil, R., Pluchon, C., Toullat, G., Michenau, D., Rogez, R., & Levevre, J. P. (1985). Disconnexion visuo-verbale (aphasie optique) pour les objets, les images, les couleurs et les visages avec alexie "abstractive". *Neuropsychologia*, *23*, 333–349.

Gluck, M. A. & Bower, G. H. (1988). From conditioning to category learning: An adaptive network model. *Journal of Experimental Psychology: General*, *117*, 227–247.

Gluck, M. A. & Bower, G. H. (1990). Component and pattern information in adaptive networks. *Journal of Experimental Psychology: General*, *119*, 105–109.

Gluck, M. A. & Myers, C. E. (1993). Hippocampal mediation of stimulus representation: A computational theory. *Hippocampus*, *3(4)*, 491–516.

Glushko, R. J. (1979). The organisation and activation of orthographic knowledge in reading aloud. *Journal of Experimental Psychology: Human Perception and Performance*, *5*, 674–691.

Goodglass, H. & Kaplan, E. (1972). *The assessment of aphasia and related disorders*. Philadelphia: Lea & Febiger.

Goodman, R. A. & Caramazza, A. (1986). Aspects of the spelling process: Evidence from a case of acquired dyslexia. *Language and Cognitive Processes*, *1*, 263–296.

Grainger, J. (1990). Word-frequency and neighborhood frequency: Effects in lexical decision and naming. *Journal of Memory and Language*, *29(2)*, 228–244.

Grainger, J. & Segui, J. (1990). Neighborhood frequency-effects in visual word recognition: A comparison of lexical decision and masked identification latencies. *Perception & Psychophysics, 47(2)*, 191–198.

Gray, C. M., Konig, P., Engel, A. E., & Singer, W. (1989). Oscillatory responses in cat visual cortex exhibit inter-column synchronization which reflects global stimulus properties. *Nature, 338*, 334–337.

Gray, C. M. & Singer, W. (1989). Stimulus-specific neuronal oscillations in orientation columns of cat visual cortex. *Proceedings of the National Academy of Science, 86*, 1698–1702.

Grossberg, S. (1969). Some networks that can learn, remember and reproduce any number of complicated space–time patterns, I. *Journal of Mathematics and Mechanics, 19*, 53–91.

Grossberg, S. (1970a). Neural pattern discrimination. *Journal of Theoretical Biology, 27*, 291–337.

Grossberg, S. (1970b). Some networks that can learn, remember and reproduce any number of complicated space–time patterns, II. *Studies in Applied Mathematics, 49*, 135–166.

Grossberg, S. (1973). Contour enhancement, short term memory and constancies in reverberating neural networks. *Studies in Applied Mathematics, 52*, 217–257.

Grossberg, S. (1976a). On the development of feature detectors in the visual cortex with applications to learning and reaction-diffusion systems. *Biological Cybernetics, 21*, 145–159.

Grossberg, S. (1976b). Adaptive pattern classification and universal recoding, I: Parallel development and coding of neural feature detectors. *Biological Cybernetics, 23*, 121–134.

Grossberg, S. (1978). A theory of human memory: Self-organization and performance of sensory-motor codes, maps, and plans. In R. Rosen & F. Snell (Eds.), *Progress in theoretical biology, Vol. 5.* (pp.233–374). New York: Academic Press.

Grossberg, S. (1982). *Studies of mind and brain: Neural principles of learning, perception, development, cognition and motor control.* Amsterdam: Reidel Press.

Grossberg, S. (1987). Competitive learning: From interactive activation to adaptive resonance. *Cognitive Science, 11*, 23–63.

Grossberg, S. (1988). *Neural networks and natural intelligence.* Cambridge, MA: MIT Press.

Grossberg, S. & Somers, D. (1991). Synchronized oscillations during cooperative feature linking in a cortical model of visual perception. *Neural Networks, 4*, 453–466.

Grossberg, S. & Stone, G. (1986). Neural dynamics of word recognition and recall: Attentional priming, learning and resonance. *Psychological Review, 93(1)*, 46–74.

Guha, R. V. & Lenat, D. B. (1990). Cyc: A mid-term report. *AI Magazine, 11.*

Halligan, P. W. & Marshall, J. C. (1994). Toward a principled explanation of unilateral neglect. *Cognitive Neuropsychology, 11*, 1667–206.

Hammerstrom, D. (1993). Neural networks at work. *IEEE Spectrum, 30*, 26–32.

Hare, M., Elman, J. L., & Daugherty, K. G. (1995). Default generalization in connectionist networks. *Language and Cognitive Processes, 10(6)*, 601–630.

Harley, T. (1984). A critique of top-down independent levels models of speech production: Evidence from non-plan-internal speech errors. *Cognitive Science, 8*, 191–219.

Harley, T. (1993). Phonological activation of semantic competitors during lexical access in speech production. *Language and Cognitive Processes, 8*, 291–309.

Harley, T. & MacAndrew, S. B. G. (1992). Modelling paraphasias in normal and aphasic speech. *Proceedings of the 14th Annual Conference of the Cognitive Science Society* (pp.378–383). Hillsdale, NJ: Lawrence Erlbaum Associates Inc.

Harley, T. & MacAndrew, S. B. G. (1995). Interactive models of lexicalisation: Some constraints from speech error, picture naming and neuropsychological data. In J. Levy, D. Bairaktaris, J. Bullinaria, & D. Cairns (Eds.), *Connectionist models of memory and language.* London: UCL Press.

Harley, T. A. (1990). Paragrammatisms: Syntactic disturbance or failure of control? *Cognition, 34*, 85–91.

Hart, J., Berndt, R. S., & Caramazza, A. (1985). Category-specific naming deficit following cerebral infarction. *Nature, 316*, 439–440.

Hart, J. & Gordon, B. (1992). Neural subsystems for object knowledge. *Nature, 359*, 60–64.

Hartley, T. & Houghton, G. (1996). A linguistically constrained model of short-term memory for nonwords. *Journal of Memory and Language, 35*, 1–31.

Hatfield, F. M. & Patterson, K. E. (1983). Phonological spelling. *Quarterly Journal of Experimental Psychology, 35A*, 451–468.

Haugeland, J. (1985). *Artificial intelligence.* Cambridge, MA: MIT Press.

Hawkins, H. L., Reicher, G. M., Rogers, M., & Peterson, L. (1976). Flexible coding in word recognition. *Journal of Experimental Psychology: Human Perception and Performance, 2*, 380–385.

Heathcote, A., Popiel, S. J., & Mewhort, D. J. K. (1991). Analysis of response time distributions: An example using the Stroop task. *Psychological Bulletin, 109,* 340–347.

Hebb, D. O. (1949). *The organization of behavior.* New York: Wiley.

Heilman, K. M. (1979). Neglect and related disorders. In K. M. Heilman & E. Valenstein (Eds.), *Clinical neuropsychology.* Oxford: Oxford University Press.

Heinke, D. & Humphreys, G. W. (1997). SAIM: A model & visual attention and neglect. *Proceedings of the 7th International Conference on Artificial Neural Networks,* 913–918.

Henson, R. N. A., Norris, D. G., Page, M. P. A., & Baddeley, A. D. (1996). Unchained memory: Error patterns rule out chaining models of immediate serial-recall. *Quarterly Journal of Experimental Psychology, 49A(1),* 80–115.

Herdman, C. M. & Beckett, B. L. (1996). Code-specific processes in word naming: Evidence supporting a dual-route model of word recognition. *Journal of Experimental Psychology: Human Perception and Performance, 22(5),* 1149–1165.

Hillis, A. E. & Caramazza, A. (1990). The effects of attentional deficits on reading and spelling. In A. Caramazza (Ed.), *Cognitive neuropsychology and neurolinguistics: Advances in models of cognitive function and impairment.* Hillsdale, NJ: Lawrence Erlbaum Associates Inc.

Hillis, A. E. & Caramazza, A. (1995a). Cognitive and neural mechanisms underlying visual and semantic processing: Implications from optic aphasia. *Journal of Cognitive Neuroscience, 7(4),* 457–478.

Hillis, A. E. & Caramazza, A. (1995b). A framework for interpreting distinct patterns of hemispatial neglect. *Neurocase, 1(3),* 189–207.

Hillis, A. E. & Caramazza, A. (1995c). Spatially specific deficit in processing graphemic representations in reading and writing. *Brain and Language, 48(3),* 263–308.

Hinton, G. E. (1981a). A parallel computation that assigns canonical object-based frames of reference. *Proceedings of the International Joint Conference on Artificial Intelligence,* Vancouver, Canada.

Hinton, G. E. (1981b). Implementing semantic networks in parallel hardware. In G. E. Hinton & J. A. Anderson (Eds.), *Parallel models of associative memory.* Hillsdale, NJ: Lawrence Erlbaum Associates Inc.

Hinton, G. E. (1984). Parallel computations for controlling an arm. *Journal of Motor Behaviour, 16,* 171–194.

Hinton, G. E. (1987). Learning translation invariant recognition in a massively parallel network. In J. W. deBakker & P. C. Treleaven (Eds.), *PARLE: Parallel architectures and languages europe.* Berlin: Springer-Verlag.

Hinton, G. E. (1989a). Learning distributed representations of concepts. In R. G. M. Morris (Ed.), *Parallel distributed processing: Implications for psychology and neurobiology.* Oxford: Oxford University Press.

Hinton, G. E. (1989b). Connectionist learning procedures. *Artificial Intelligence, 40,* 185–234.

Hinton, G. E. & Anderson, J. A. (1981). *Parallel models of associative memory.* Hillsdale, NJ: Lawrence Erlbaum Associates Inc.

Hinton, G. E. & Lang, K. (1985). Shape recognition and illusory conjunctions. *Proceedings of the International Joint Conference on Artificial Intelligence,* San Francisco, CA.

Hinton, G. E., McClelland, J. L., & Rumelhart, D. E. (1986). Distributed representations. In D. E. Rumelhart & J. L. McClelland (Eds.), *Parallel disributed processing: Explorations in the microstructure of cognition, Vol. 1,* (pp.77–109). Cambridge, MA: MIT Press.

Hinton, G. E. & Sejnowski, T. J. (1986). Learning and relearning in Boltzmann machines. In D. E. Rumelhart, & J. L. McClelland (Eds.), *Parallel distributed processing: Explorations in the microstructure of cognition, Vol. 1,* (pp.282–317). Cambridge, MA: MIT Press.

Hinton, G. E. & Shallice, T. (1991). Lesioning an attractor network. Investigations of acquired dyslexia. *Psychological Review, 98,* 74–96.

Hintzman, D. (1986). "Schema abstraction" in a multiple-trace memory model. *Psychological Review, 93,* 411–428.

Hirsch, H. V. B. & Spinelli, D. N. (1970). Visual experience modifies distribution of horizontally and vertically oriented receptive fields in cats. *Science, 168,* 869–871.

Hitch, G. J., Burgess, N., Towse, J. N., & Culpin, V. (1996). Temporal grouping effects in immediate recall: A working-memory analysis. *Quarterly Journal of Experimental Psychology, 49A(1),* 116–139.

Hollerbach, J. M. (1982). Computers, brains and the control of movement. *Trends in Neurosciences, 5(6),* 189–192.

Holyoak, K. J. (1990). Problem solving. In D. N. Osherson & E. E. Smith (Eds.), *Thinking: An Invitation to cognitive science, Vol. 3.* Cambridge, MA: MIT Press.

Holyoak, K. J. & Thagard, P. (1989). Analogical mapping by constraint satisfaction. *Cognitive Science, 13(3)*, 295–355.

Hopfield, J. J. (1982). Neural networks and physical systems with emergent collective computational abilities. *Proceedings of the National Academy of Science, 79*, 2554–2558.

Horn, D. & Ruppin, E. (1995). Compensatory mechanisms in an attractor neural-network model of schizophrenia. *Neural Computation, 7(1)*, 182–205.

Houghton, G. (1990). The problem of serial order: A neural model of sequence learning and recall. In R. Dale, C. Mellish, & M. Zock (Eds.), *Current research in natural language generation*. London: Academic Press.

Houghton, G., Glasspool, D., & Shallice, T. (1994). Spelling and serial recall: Insights from a competitive queueing model. In G. D. A. Brown & N. C. Ellis (Eds.), *Handbook of spelling: Theory, process and intervention*. Chichester, UK: John Wiley.

Howard, D. (1989). Letter-by-letter readers: Evidence for parallel processing. In D. Besner & G. W. Humphreys (Eds.), *Basic processes in reading: Visual word recognition*. Hillsdale, NJ: Lawrence Erlbaum Associates Inc.

Howard, D. & Franklin, S. (1988). *Missing the meaning? A cognitive neuropsychological analysis of single word processing in an aphasic patient*. Cambridge, MA: MIT Press.

Hubel, D. H. & Wiesel, T. N. (1959). Receptive fields of single neurons in the cat's striate cortex. *Journal of Physiology, 148*, 574–591.

Hubel, D. H. & Wiesel, T. N. (1968). Receptive fields and functional architecture of monkey striate cortex. *Journal of Physiology, 195*, 215–243.

Hummel, J. E. & Biederman, I. (1992). Dynamic binding in a neural network for shape-recognition. *Psychological Review, 99(3)*, 480–517.

Humphreys, G. W. (1981). Flexibility of attention between stimulus dimensions. *Perception & Psychophysics, 30*, 291–302.

Humphreys, G. W. (1993). Prospects for connectionism: Science and engineering. In A. Sloman et al. (Eds.), *Prospects for artificial intelligence*. Amsterdam: IOS Press.

Humphreys, G. W. & Boucart, M. (1997). Selection by color and form in vision. *Journal of Experimental Psychology: Human Perception and Performance, 23(1)*, 136–153.

Humphreys, G. W. & Bruce, V. (1989). *Visual cognition: Computational, experimental and neuropsychological perspectives*. Hove, UK: Lawrence Erlbaum Associates Ltd.

Humphreys, G. W. & Evett, L. J. (1985). Are there independent lexical and nonlexical routes in word processing? An evaluation of the dual-route theory of reading. *Behavioral and Brain Sciences, 8*, 689–740.

Humphreys, G. W., Evett, L. J., & Quinlan, P. T. (1990). Early orthographic processing in visual word recognition. *Cognitive Psychology, 22*, 517–560.

Humphreys, G. W., Freeman, T. A. C., & Müller, H. J. (1992b). Lesioning a connectionist network of visual-search: Selective effects on distractor grouping. *Canadian Journal of Psychology, 46(3)*, 417–460.

Humphreys, G. W. & Heinke, D. (1997). Selection for object identification: Modelling emergent attentional processes in normality and pathology. In J. A. Bullinaria, D. W. Glasspool, & G. Houghton (Eds.), *Connectionist representations*. London: Springer-Verlag.

Humphreys, G. W. & Heinke, D. (1998). Spatial representation and selection in the brain: Neuropsychological and computational constraints. *Visual Cognition, 5*, 9–47.

Humphreys, G. W., Lamote, C., & Lloyd-Jones, T. J. (1995). An interactive activation approach to object processing: Effects of structural similarity, name frequency and task in normality and pathology. *Memory, 3*, 535–586.

Humphreys, G. W. & Müller, H. J. (1993). Search via recursive rejection (SERR): A connectionist model of visual search. *Cognitive Psychology, 25(1)*, 43–110.

Humphreys, G. W., Olson, A., Romani, C., & Riddoch, M. J. (1996). Competitive mechanisms of selection by space and object: A neuropsychological approach. In A. F. Kramer, M. G. H. Coles, & G. D. Logan (Eds.), *Converging operations in the study of visual attention*. Washington, DC: American Psychological Association.

Humphreys, G. W., Quinlan, P. T., & Riddoch, M. J. (1989). Grouping processes in visual search: Effects with single-feature and combined-feature targets. *Journal of Experimental Psychology: General, 118(3)*, 258–279.

Humphreys, G. W. & Riddoch, M. J. (1987). *To see or not to see: A case study of visual agnosia*. Hove: Lawrence Erlbaum Associates Ltd.

Humphreys, G. W. & Riddoch, M. J. (1993). Object agnosias. In C. Kennard (Ed.), *Balliere's clinical neurology: Visual perceptual deficits*. London: Balliere Tindall.

Humphreys, G. W., Riddoch, M. J., & Quinlan, P. T. (1988). Cascade processes in picture identification. *Cognitive Neuropsychology, 5(1)*, 67–103.

Humphreys, G. W., Riddoch, M. J., Quinlan, P. T., Price, C. J., & Donnelly, N. (1992a). Parallel pattern processing in visual agnosia. *Canadian Journal of Psychology, 46*, 377–416.

Jacobs, A. M. & Grainger, J. (1992). Testing a semi-stochastic variant of the interactive activation model in different word recognition experiments. *Journal of Experimental Psychology: Human Perception and Performance, 18(4)*, 1174–1188.

Jacobs, R. A. (1988). Increased rates of convergence through learning rate adaptation. *Neural Networks, 1*.

Jacobs, R. A. (1997). Nature, nurture, and the development of functional specializations: A computational approach. *Psychonomic Bulletin & Review, 4(3)*, 299–309.

Jacobs, R. A. & Jordan, M. I. (1992). Computational consequences of a bias towards short connections. *Journal of Cognitive Neuroscience, 4(4)*, 323–336.

Jeannerod, M. (1996). *The cognitive neuroscience of action*. Oxford: Oxford University Press.

Jefferys, J. G. R., Traub, R., & Whittington, M. A. (1996). Neuronal networks for induced "40 Hz" rhythms. *Trends in Neurosciences, 19*, 202–208.

Johnson-Laird, P. N. (1989). *The computer and the mind: An introduction to cognitive science*. London: Fontana.

Johnston, J. C. & McClelland, J. L. (1974). Perception of letters in words: Seek not and ye shall find. *Science, 184*, 1192–1194.

Jones, G. V. (1989). Back to Woodworth: Role of interlopers in the tip-of-the-tongue phenomenon. *Memory and Cognition, 17*, 69–76.

Jordan, M. I. (1986). *Serial order: A parallel distributed approach. ICS Report 8604*. San Diego, CA: University of California, Institute for Cognitive Science.

Julesz, B. (1971). *Foundations of cyclopean perception*. Chicago: University of Chicago Press.

Kahneman, D. & Tversky, A. (1973). On the psychology of prediction. *Psychological Review, 80*, 237–251.

Kamin, L. J. (1969). Predictability, surprise, attention, and conditioning. In B. A. Campbell & R. M. Church (Eds.), *Punishment and aversive behavior*. New York: Appleton Century Crofts.

Kammen, L. J., Koch, C., & Holmes, P. J. (1990). Collective oscillations in the visual cortex. In D. S. Touretzky (Ed.), *Advances in neural information processing systems, Vol. 2*. San Mateo, CA: Morgan Kaufman.

Karnath, H. O. (1988). Deficits of attention in acute and recovered visual hemi-neglect. *Neuropsychologia, 26(1)*, 27–43.

Katz, R. (1991). Limited retention of information in the graphemic buffer. *Cortex, 27*, 111–119.

Kawamoto, A. H. & Kitzis, S. N. (1991). Time course of regular and irregular pronunciations. *Connection Science, 3*, 207–217.

Kay, J. & Marcel, A. (1981). One process, not two, in reading aloud: Lexical analogies do the work of non-lexical rules. *Quarterly Journal of Experimental Psychology, 33A*, 397–413.

Kim, J. J. & Fanselow, M. S. (1992). Modality-specific retrograde amnesia of fear. *Science, 256*, 675–677.

Kirkpatrick, S., Gellat, C. D., & Vecchi, M. D. (1983). Optimisation by simulated annealing. *Science, 220*, 671–680.

Klar, D. (1973). Quantification processes. In W. G. Chase (Ed.), *Visual information processing*. San Diego, CA: Academic Press.

Kohonen, T. (1982a). Clustering, taxonomy, and topological maps of patterns. In M. Lang (Ed.), *Proceedings of the 6th International Conference on Pattern Recognition*. Silver Spring, MD: IEEE Computer Society Press.

Kohonen, T. (1982b). Self-organized formation of topologically correct feature maps. *Biological Cybernetics, 43*, 59–69.

Kohonen, T. (1984a). *Associative memory: A system-theoretical approach*. Berlin: Springer-Verlag.

Kohonen, T. (1984b). *Self-organization and associative memory*. Berlin: Springer-Verlag.

Kohonen, T. (1988). The neural phonetic typewriter. *IEEE Computer, 21*, 11–22.

Kohonen, T. (1990). The self-organizing map. *Proceedings of the IEEE, 78*, 1464–1480.

Kolb, B. & Wishaw, I. Q. (1980). *Fundamentals of human neuropsychology: Fourth edition*. New York: W. H. Freeman.

Kremin, H. (1986). Spared naming without comprehension. *Journal of Neurolinguistics, 2*, 131–150.

Kruschke, J. K. (1992). ALCOVE: An exemplar-based connectionist model of category learning. *Psychological Review, 99*, 22–44.

Kruschke, J. K. (1993). Human category learning: Implications for backpropagation models. *Connection Science, 5*, 3–36.

Kuçera, H. & Francis, W. N. (1967). *Computational analysis of present-day American English*, Providence, RI: Brown University Press.

Kuczaj, S. A. (1977). The acquisition of regular and irregular past tense forms. *Journal of Verbal Learning and Verbal Behavior, 16*, 589–600.

Lamberts, K. (1990). A hybrid model of learning to solve physics problems. *European Journal of Cognitive Psychology, 2(2)*, 151–170.

Lashley, K. (1951). The problem of serial order in behavior. In L. A. Jeffreys (Ed.), *Cerebral mechanisms in behaviour: The Hixon symposium.* New York: Hafner Publishing.

le Cun, Y. (1985). A learning scheme for asymmetrical threshold networks. *Proceedings of Cognitiva, 85*, 599–604.

le Cun, Y. (1989). *Generalization and network design strategies. Technical report CRG-TR-89-4.* University of Toronto, Ontario.

Lehky, S. R. & Sejnowski, T. J. (1988). Network model of shape-from-shading: Neural function arises from both receptive field and projective fields. *Nature, 333*, 452–454.

Levelt, W. J. M. (1989). *Speaking: From intention to articulation.* Cambridge, MA: MIT Press.

Levelt, W. J. M., Schriefers, H., Vorberg, D., Meyer, A. S., Pechmann, T., & Havinga, J. (1991). The time course of lexical access in speech production: A study of picture naming. *Psychological Review, 98.* 122–142.

Levy, J. P. & Bairaktaris, D. (1995). Connectionist dual-weight architectures. *Language and Cognitive Processes, 10*, 265–284.

Lhermitte, F. & Beauvois, M. F. (1973). A visual speech disconnection syndrome: Report of a case with optic aphasia, agnosic alexia and colour agnosia. *Brain, 96*, 695–714.

Lindsay, P. H. & Norman, D. A. (1977). *Human information processing: Second edition.* London: Academic Press.

Linkser, R. (1986). From basic network principles to neural architecture: Emergence of spatial-opponent cells. *Proceedings of the National Academy of Science, 83*, 7508–7512.

Lissauer, H. (1890). Ein Fall von Seelenblindheit nebst einem Beitrage zue Theorie derselben. *Archiv für Psychiatrie und Nervenkrankheiten, 21*, 222–270.

Livingstone, M. & Hubel, D. (1988). Segregation of form, color, movement and depth: Anatomy, physiology and perception. *Science, 240*, 740–749.

Lloyd-Jones, T. J. & Humphreys, G. W. (1997). Perceptual differentiation as a source of category effects in object processing: Evidence from naming and object decision. *Memory and Cognition, 25*, 18–35.

Loftus, E. F. & Palmer, J. C. (1974). Reconstruction of automobile deconstruction: An example of the interaction between language and memory. *Journal of Verbal Learning and Verbal Behavior, 13*, 585–589.

Lubrow, R. E. (1973). Latent inhibition. *Psychological Bulletin, 79*, 398–407.

Mackay, D. G. (1970). Spoonerisms: The structure of errors in the serial order of speech. *Neuropsychologia, 8*, 323–350.

Macleod, C. M. (1992). The Stroop task: The gold standard of attentional measures. *Journal of Experimental Psychology: General, 121(1)*, 12–14.

Macleod, C. M. (1993). Complex information processing: The impact of Simon, Herbert, A., Klahr, D., Kotovsky, K. *Contemporary Psychology, 38(1)*, 14–15.

Maes, P. (1989). How to do the right thing. *Connection Science, 1*, 291–323.

Marchman, V. A. (1993). Constraints on plasticity in a connectionist model of the English past tense. *Journal of Cognitive Neuroscience, 5*, 215–234.

Marcus, G. F., Brinkman, U., Clahsen, H., Wiese, R., & Pinker, S. (1995). German inflection: The exception that proves the rule. *Cognitive Psychology, 29(3)*, 189–256.

Marr, D. (1969). A theory of cerebellar cortex. *Journal of Physiology, 202*, 437–470.

Marr, D. (1971). Simple memory: A theory for archicortex. *Philosophical Transactions of the Royal Society, London, B262.*

Marr, D. (1982). *Vision.* San Francisco, CA: W. H. Freeman.

Marr, D. & Hildreth, E. (1982). Theory of edge detection. *Proceedings of the Royal Society, London, B207*, 187–216.

Marr, D. & Poggio, T. (1976). Cooperative computation of stereo disparity. *Science, 194*, 283–287.

Marr, D. & Ullman, S. (1981). Directional selectivity and its use in early visual processing. *Proceedings of the Royal Society, London, B211*, 151–180.

Marslen-Wilson, W. (1984). Function and process in spoken word recognition: A tutorial review. In H. Bouma & D. Bouwhuis (Eds.), *Attention and performance X.* Hove, UK: Lawrence Erlbaum Associates Ltd.

Marslen-Wilson, W. D. & Tyler, L. (1980). The temporal structure of spoken language understanding. *Cognition, 8*, 1–71.

Martin, N., Dell, G. S., Saffran, E. M., & Schwartz, M. F. (1994). Origins of paraphasias in deep dysphasia:

Testing the consequences of a decay impairment to an interactive spreading activation model of lexical retrieval. *Brain and Language, 47(4),* 609–660.

Martin, N. & Saffran, E. M. (1992). A computational account of deep dyslexia: Evidence from a single case-study. *Brain and Language, 43*(2), 240–274.

Martinez, T. M., Ritter, H. J., & Schulten, K. J. (1990). Three-dimensional neural net for learning visuomotor coordination of a robot arm. *IEEE Transactions on Neural Networks, 1,* 131–136.

Massaro, D. (1989). Testing between TRACE and the fuzzy logical model of speech perception. *Cognitive Psychology, 21,* 398–421.

Masson, M. E. J. (1991). A distributed memory model of context effects in word identification. In D. Besner & G. W. Humphreys (Eds.), *Basic processes in reading: Visual word recognition.* Hillsdale, NJ: Lawrence Erlbaum Associates Inc.

Maunsell, J. H. R. & Van Essen, D. (1986). The topographic organization of the middle temporal visual area in the macaque monkey: Representational biases and the relationship to callosal connections. *Journal of Comparative Neurology, 266,* 535–555.

Mayall, K. A. & Humphreys, G. W. (1996a). A connectionist model of alexia: Covert recognition and case mixing effects. *British Journal of Psychology, 87,* 355–402.

Mayall, K. A. & Humphreys, G. W. (1996b). Covert recognition in a connectionist model of pure alexia. In J. Reggia, E. Ruppin, & R. S. Berndt (Eds.), *Neural modeling of brain and cognitive disorders.* London: World Scientific.

Mayall, K. & Humphreys, G. W. (1996c). Case mixing and the task-sensitive disruption of lexical processing. *Journal of Experimental Psychology: Learning, Memory and Cognition, 22*(2), 278–294.

Mayhew, J. E. W. & Frisby, J. P. (1984). Computer vision. In T. O'Shea & M. Eisenstadt (Eds.), *Artificial intelligence: Tools, techniques and applications.* New York: Harper Row.

McCann, R. S. & Besner, D. (1987). Reading pseudohomophones: Implications for models of pronunciation assembly and the locus of word frequency effects in naming. *Journal of Experimental Psychology: Human Perception and Performance, 13,* 14–24.

McCarthy, R. & Warrington, E. K. (1988). Evidence for modality-specific meaning systems in the brain. *Nature, 334,* 428–430.

McClelland, J. L. (1985). Putting knowledge in its place: A scheme for programming parallel processing structures on the fly. *Cognitive Science, 9,* 113–146.

McClelland, J. L. (1986). The programmable blackboard model of reading. In J. L. McClelland & D. E. Rumelhart (Eds.), *Parallel distributed processing: Explorations in the microstructure of cognition, Vol. 2.* Cambridge, MA: MIT Press.

McClelland, J. L. (1987). The case for interactionism in language processing. In M. Coltheart (Ed.), *Attention and performance XII.* Hove, UK: Lawrence Erlbaum Associates Ltd.

McClelland, J. L. (1989). Parallel distributed processing: Implications for cognition and development. In R. G. M. Morris (Ed.), *Parallel distributed processing: Implications for psychology and neurobiology.* Oxford: Oxford University Press.

McClelland, J. L. (1991). Stochastic interactive processes and the effect of context on perception. *Cognitive Psychology, 23,* 1–44.

McClelland, J. L. (1993). The GRAIN model: A framework for modelling the dynamics of information processing. In D. E. Myer & S. Kornblum (Eds.), *Attention and performance XIV.* Hillsdale, NJ: Lawrence Erlbaum Associates Inc.

McClelland, J. L. & Elman, J. L. (1986). The TRACE model of speech perception. *Cognitive Psychology, 18,* 1–86.

McClelland, J. L. & Kawamoto, A. H. (1986). Mechanisms of sentence processing: Assigning roles to constituents. In J. L. McClelland & D. E. Rumelhart (Eds.), *Parallel distributed processing: Explorations in the microstructure of cognition, Vol. 2.* Cambridge, MA: MIT Press.

McClelland, J. L., McNaughton, B. L., & O'Reilly, R. C. (1995). Why there are complementary learning systems in the hippocampus and neocortex: Insights from the successes and failures of connectionist models of learning and memory. *Psychological Review, 102,* 419–457.

McClelland, J. L. & Mozer, M. C. (1986). Perceptual interactions in two-word displays: Familiarity and similarity effects. *Journal of Experimental Psychology: Human Perception and Performance, 12,* 18–35.

McClelland, J. L. & Rumelhart, D. E. (1981). An interactive activation model of context effects in letter perception: Part 1. An account of basic findings. *Psychological Review, 88,* 375–407.

McClelland, J. L. & Rumelhart, D. E. (1985). Distributed memory and the representation of general and specific information. *Journal of Experimental Psychology: General, 114,* 159–188.

McClelland, J. L. & Rumelhart, D. E. (1986). A distributed model of human learning and memory. In

J. L. McClelland & D. E. Rumelhart (Eds.), *Parallel distributed processing: Explorations in the microstructure of cognition, Vol. 2*. Cambridge, MA: MIT Press.

McClelland, J. L., Rumelhart, D. E., & Hinton, G. E. (1986). The appeal of parallel distributed processing. In D. E. Rumelhart & J. L. McClelland (Eds.), *Parallel distributed processing: Explorations in the microstructure of cognition, Vol. 1*. Cambridge, MA: MIT Press.

McCloskey, M., Badecker, W., Goodman-Schulman, R. A., & Aliminosa, D. (1994). The structure of graphemic representation in spelling: Evidence from a case of acquired dysgraphia. *Cognitive Neuropsychology, 11(3)*, 341–392.

McCloskey, M. & Cohen, N. J. (1989). Catastrophic interference in connectionist networks: The sequential learning problem. In G. H. Bower (Ed.), *The psychology of learning and motivation, 24*. New York: Academic Press.

McCulloch, W. S. & Pitts, W. (1943). A logical calculus of the ideas imminent in nervous activity. *Bulletin of Mathematical Biophysics, 9*, 127–147.

McLaren, I. P. L., Kaye, H., & Mackintosh, N. J. (1989). An associative theory of the representation of stimuli: Applications to perceptual learning and latent inhibition. In R. G. M. Morris (Ed.), *Parallel distributed processing: Implications for psychology and neurobiology*. Oxford: Oxford University Press.

McNaughton, B. L. & Morris, R. G. M. (1987). Hippocampal synaptic enhancement and information storage within a distributed memory system. *Trends in Neurosciences, 10*, 408–415.

McNeil, J. E. & Warrington, E. K. (1991). Prosopagnosia: A reclassification. *Quarterly Journal of Experimental Psychology, 43A*, 267–287.

McQueen, J. M. (1991). The influence of the lexicon on phonetic categorization: Stimulus quality in word-final ambiguity. *Journal of Experimental Psychology: Human Perception and Performance, 17(2)*, 433–443.

McRae, K. & Hetherington, P. A. (1993). Catastrophic interference is eliminated in pretrained networks. *Proceedings of the Fifteenth Annual Meeting of the Cognitive Science Society* (pp.723–728). Hillsdale, NJ: Lawrence Erlbaum Associates Inc.

Meadows, J. C. (1974). Disturbed perception of colours associated with localised cerebral lesions. *Brain, 97*, 615–632.

Medin, D. L. & Schaffer, M. M. (1978). Context theory of classification learning. *Psychological Review, 85*, 207–238.

Metcalfe, J. & Wiebe, D. (1987). Intuition in insight and noninsight problem-solving. *Memory and Cognition, 15(3)*, 238–246.

Meyer, A. S. & Dell, G. S. (1993). An experimental analysis of positional and phonotactic constraints on phonological speech errors. (*Manuscript in preparation*)

Meyer, D. E. & Schvaneveldt, R. W. (1971). Facilitation in recognizing pairs of words: Evidence of a dependence between retrieval operations. *Journal of Experimental Psychology, 90*, 227–234.

Miceli, G., Benvegnu, B., Capasso, R., & Caramazza, A. (1997). The independence of phonological and orthographic lexical forms: Evidence from aphasia. *Cognitive Neuropsychology, 14*, 35–70.

Miller, G. A. (1956). The magical number seven, plus or minus two: Some limits on our capacity for processing information. *Psychological Review, 63*, 81–97.

Miller, J. L. & Eimas, P. D. (1995). Speech perception: From signal to word. *Annual Review of Psychology, 46*, 467–492.

Milner, D. & Goodale, M. (1995). *The visual brain in action*. London: Academic Press.

Minsky, M. (1975). A framework for representing knowledge. In P. H. Winston (Ed.), *The psychology of computer vision*. New York: McGraw-Hill.

Minsky, M. (1986). *The society of mind*. New York: Simon & Schuster.

Minsky, M. & Papert, S. (1969). *Perceptrons: An introduction to computational geometry*. Cambridge, MA: MIT Press.

Minsky, M. & Papert, S. (1988). *Perceptions: An introduction to computational geometry. Expanded edition*. Cambridge, MA: MIT Press.

Moran, J. & Desimone, R. (1985). Selective attention gates visual processing in the extrastriate cortex. *Science, 229*, 782–784.

Morton, J. (1969). The interaction of information in word recognition. *Psychological Review, 76*, 165–178.

Morton, J. (1979). Facilitation in word recognition: Experiments causing change in the logogen model. In P. A. Kolers, M. A. Wrolstad, & H. Bouma (Eds.), *Processing of visible language*. New York: Plenum Press.

Morton, J. & Patterson, K. (1980). A new attempt at an interpretation, or, an attempt at a new interpretation. In M. Coltheart, K. Patterson, & J. C. Marshall (Eds.), *Deep dyslexia*. London: Routledge & Kegan Paul.

Movellan, J. (1991). Contrastive Hebbian learning in the continuous Hopfield model. In D. Touretzky, J. Elman, T. Sejnowski, & G. E. Hinton (Eds.),

Connectionist models: Proceedings of the 1990 summer school. San Mateo, CA: Morgan Kaufman.

Mozer, M. C. (1983). Letter migration in word perception. *Journal of Experimental Psychology: Human Perception and Performance, 9,* 531–546.

Mozer, M. C. (1987). Early parallel processing in reading: A connectionist approach. In M. Coltheart (Ed.), *Attention and performance XII.* Hove, UK: Lawrence Erlbaum Associates Ltd.

Mozer, M. C. (1991). *The perception of multiple objects: A connectionist approach.* Cambridge, MA: MIT Press.

Mozer, M. C. & Behrmann, M, (1990). On the interaction of selective attention and lexical knowledge: A connectionist account of neglect dyslexia. *Journal of Cognitive Neuroscience, 2,* 96–123.

Mozer, M. C. & Behrmann, M. (1992). Reading with attentional impairments: A brain-damaged model of neglect and attentional dyslexias. In R. G. Reilly & N. E. Sharkey (Eds.), *Connectionist approaches to natural language processing.* Hove, UK: Lawrence Erlbaum Associates Ltd.

Mozer, M. C., Halligan, P. W., & Marshall, J. C. (1997). The end of the line for a brain-damaged model of unilateral neglect. *Journal of Cognitive Neuroscience, 9,* 171–190.

Mozer, M. C., Zemel, R. S., & Behrmann, M. (1991). *Learning to segment images using dynamic feature binding. Technical report CU-CS-540-91.* University of Colorado, USA.

Müller, H. J., Humphreys, G. W., & Donnelly, N. (1994). Search via recursive rejection (SERR): Visual search for single and dual form-conjunction targets. *Journal of Experimental Psychology: Human Perception and Performance, 20(2),* 235–258.

Murray, D. J. (1968). Articulation and acoustic confusability in short-term memory. *Journal of Experimental Psychology, 78,* 679–684.

Murre, J. M. J. (1992). *Categorization and learning in modular neural networks.* Hemel Hempstead, UK: Harvester Wheatsheaf.

Murre, J. M. J. (1997). Implicit and explicit memory in amnesia: Some explanations and predictions by the TraceLink model. *Memory, 5,* 213–232.

Nakisa, R. C. & Hahn, U. (1996). Where defaults don't help: The case of the German plural system. In G. W. Cottrell et al. (Eds.), *Proceedings of the 18th Annual Conference of the Cognitive Science Society* (pp.177–182). Hillsdale, NJ: Lawrence Erlbaum Associates Inc.

Navon, D. (1977). Forest before trees: The precedence of global features in visual perception. *Cognitive Psychology, 9,* 353–383.

Neely, J. H. (1977). Semantic priming and retrieval from lexical memory: The roles of inhibitionless spreading activation and limited-capacity attention. *Journal of Experimental Psychology: General, 106,* 226–254.

Neely, J. H. (1991). Semantic priming effects in visual word recognition: A selective review of current findings and theories. In D. Besner & G. W. Humphreys (Eds.), *Basic processes in reading: Visual word recognition.* Hillsdale, NJ: Lawrence Erlbaum Associates Inc.

Neisser, U. (1976). *Cognition and reality: Principles and implications of cognitive psychology.* San Francisco: W. H. Freeman.

Newell, A. (1980) Physical symbol systems. *Cognitive Science, 4,* 135–183.

Newell, A. & Simon, H. A. (1980). Computer science as empirical enquiry. In J. Haugeland (Ed.), *Mind design: Philosophy, psychology, artificial intelligence.* Cambridge, MA: MIT Press.

Nilsson, N. J. (1965). *Learning machines.* New York: McGraw-Hill.

Nolan, K. A. & Caramazza, A. (1982). Modality independent impairments in word-processing in a deep dyslexic patient. *Brain and Language, 16(2),* 237–264.

Norris, D. (1990). A dynamic net model of human speech recognition. In G. Altmann (Ed.), *Cognitive models of speech processing.* Cambridge, MA: MIT Press.

Norris, D. (1993a). Connectionism: A case for modularity. In D. Balota, G. B. Flores d'Arcais, & K. Rayner (Eds.), *Comprehension processes in reading.* Hillsdale, NJ: Lawrence Erlbaum Associates Inc.

Norris, D. (1993b). Bottom-up connectionist models of interaction. In R. Shillcock & G. Altmann (Eds.), *Cognitive models of speech processing: Sperlonga II.* Hove: Lawrence Erlbaum Associates Ltd.

Norris, D. (1994a). A quantitative multiple-levels model of reading aloud. *Journal of Experimental Psychology: Human Perception and Performance, 20,* 1212–1232.

Norris, D. (1994b). Shortlist: A connectionist model of continuous speech recognition. *Cognition, 52,* 189–234.

Olshausen, B. A., Anderson, C. H., & Van Essen, D. C. (1993). A neurobiological model of visual attention and invariant pattern recognition based on dynamic routing of information. *Journal of Neuroscience, 13,* 4700–4719.

Olson, A. & Caramazza, A. (1994). Representation and connectionist models: The NET spell experience. In G. D. A. Brown & N. C. Ellis (Eds.), *Handbook of spelling: Theory, process and intervention.* Chichester, UK: John Wlley.

Olson, A. & Humphreys, G. W. (1997). Connectionist models of neuropsychological disorders. *Trends in Cognitive Science, 1,* 222–228.

O'Regan, J. K. & Levy-Schoen, A. (1987). Eye-movement strategy and tactics in word recognition and reading. In M. Coltheart (Ed.), *Attention and performance XII.* Hove, UK: Lawrence Erlbaum Associates Ltd.

Paap, K. R. & Noel, R. W. (1991). Dual route models of print to sound: Still a good horse race. *Psychological Research, 53,* 13–24.

Parker, D. B. (1985). *Learning logic. Technical Report 47.* MIT Center for Computational Research in Economics and Management Science, Cambridge, MA.

Patterson, K. E. & Behrmann, M. (1997). Frequency and consistency effects in a pure surface dyslexic patient. *Journal of Experimental Psychology: Human Perception and Performance, 23,* 1217–1231.

Patterson, K. E. & Kay, J. (1982). Letter-by-letter reading: Psychological descriptions of a neurological syndrome. *Quarterly Journal of Experimental Psychology, 34A,* 411–441.

Patterson, K. E., Marshall, J. C., & Coltheart, M. (Eds.) (1985). *Surface dyslexia.* Hove, UK: Lawrence Erlbaum Associates Ltd.

Patterson, K. E., Seidenberg, M. S., & McClelland, J. L. (1989). Connections and disconnections: Acquired dyslexia in a computational model of reading processes. In R. G. M. Morris (Ed.), *Parallel distributed processing: Implications for psychology and neuroscience.* London: Oxford University Press.

Patterson, K. E. & Wilson, B. (1990). A ROSE is a ROSE or a NOSE: A deficit in initial letter misidentification. *Cognitive Neuropsychology, 7,* 447–477.

Pawlicki, T. (1988). NORA: Neural-network object recognition architecture. In D. Touretzky, G. E. Hinton, & T. J. Sejnowski (Eds.), *Proceedings of the 1988 Connectionist Models Summer School.* San Mateo, CA: Morgan Kaufman.

Pearlmutter, B. A. (1989). Learning state space trajectories in recurrent neural networks. *Neural Computation, 1,* 263–269.

Peterhans, E. & von der Heydt, R. (1989). Mechanisms of contour perception in monkey visual cortex 1: Contours bridging gaps. *Journal of Neuroscience, 9,* 1749–1763.

Peterson, R. R. & Savoy, P. (in press) Lexical selection and phonological encoding during language production: Evidence for cascaded processing. *Journal of Experimental Psychology: Learning, Memory and Cognition.*

Phaf, R. H., Van der Heijden, A. H. C., & Hudson, P. T. W. (1990). SLAM: A connectionist model for attention in visual selection. *Cognitive Psychology, 22(3),* 273–341.

Piaget, J. (1975). *The development of thought: Equilibration of cognitive structures.* Oxford: Oxford University Press.

Pineda, F. J. (1987). Generalisation of back-propagation to recurrent neural networks. *Physics Review Letters, 59,* 2229–2232.

Pinker, S. & Prince, A. (1988). On language and connectionism: Analysis of a parallel distributed processing model of language acquisition. *Cognition, 28,* 59–108.

Pinker, S. & Prince, A. (1989). Rules and connections in human language. In R. G. M. Morris (Ed.), *Parallel distributed processing: Implications for psychology and neurobiology.* Oxford: Oxford University Press.

Pitt, M. A. & Samuel, A. G. (1993). An empirical and meta-analytic evaluation of the phoneme identification task. *Journal of Experimental Psychology: Human Perception and Performance, 19(4),* 699–725.

Plaut, D. C. (1992). *Relearning after damage in connectionist networks: Implications for patient rehabilitation.* Paper presented to the Cognitive Science Society, March.

Plaut, D. C., McClelland, J. L., Seidenberg, M. S., & Patterson, K. (1996). Understanding normal and impaired word reading: Computational principles in quasi-regular domains. *Psychological Review, 103(1),* 56–115.

Plaut, D. C. & Shallice, T. (1993a). Deep dyslexia: A case study of connectionist neuropsychology. *Cognitive Neuropsychology, 10,* 377–500.

Plaut, D. C. & Shallice, T. (1993b). Perseverative and semantic influences on visual object naming errors in optic aphasia: A connectionist account. *Journal of Cognitive Neuroscience, 5,* 89–117.

Plunkett, K. & Marchman, V. A. (1991). U-shaped learning and frequency effects in a multi-layered perceptron. *Cognition, 38,* 43–102.

Plunkett, K. & Nakisa, R. C. (1997). A connectionist model of the Arabic plural system. *Language and Cognitive Processes, 12,* 807–836.

Plunkett, K. & Sinha, C. (1992). Connectionism and developmental theory. *British Journal of Developmental Psychology, 10,* 209–254.

Plunkett, K. Sinha, C., Moller, M. F., & Strandsby, O. (1992). Symbol grounding or the emergence of symbols? Vocabulary growth in children and in a connectionist net. *Connection Science, 4,* 293–312.

Poggio, T. & Edelman, S. (1990). A network that learns to recognise three-dimensional objects. *Nature, 343*, 263–266.

Pollack, J. B. (1989a). Implications of recursive distributed representations. In D. Touretzky (Ed.), *Advances in neural information processing systems*. San Mateo, CA: Morgan Kaufman.

Pollack, J. B. (1989b). Recursive auto-associative memory: Devising compositional representations. In D. Touretzky (Ed.), *Advances in neural information processing systems*. San Mateo, CA: Morgan Kaufman.

Pollack, J. B. (1990). Recursive distributed representations. *Artificial Intelligence, 46*, 151–176.

Posner, M. I. (1980). Orienting of attention. *Quarterly Journal of Experimental Psychology, 32*, 3–25.

Posner, M. I., Walker, J. A., Friedrich, F., & Rafal, R. D. (1984). Effects of parietal injury on the covert orienting of attention. *Journal of Neuroscience, 4*, 1863–1874.

Prager, J. M. (1980). Extracting and labelling boundary segments in natural scenes. *IEEE Transactions, PAMI2, 1*, 16–27.

Price, C. J. & Humphreys, G. W. (1993). Attentional dyslexia: The effect of co-occurring deficits. *Cognitive Neuropsychology, 10(6)*, 569–592.

Price, C. J. & Humphreys, G. W. (1995). Contrasting effects of letter-spacing in alexia: Further evidence that different strategies generate word-length effects in reading. *Quarterly Journal of Experimental Psychology, 48A(3)*, 573–597.

Qian, N. & Sejnowski, T. J. (1988). Learning to solve random-dot stereograms of dense and transparent surfaces with recurrent backpropagation. In D. Touretzky, G. E. Hinton, & T. J. Sejnowski (Eds.), *Proceedings of the 1988 Connectionist Models Summer School*. San Mateo, CA: Morgan Kaufman.

Rapp, B., Benzing, L., & Caramazza, A. (1997). The autonomy of lexical orthography. *Cognitive Neuropsychology, 14*, 71–104.

Ratcliff, R. (1990). Connectionist models of recognition memory: Constraints imposed by learning and forgetting functions. *Psychological Review, 97*, 285–308.

Rayner, K. & Pollatsek, A. (1987). Eye-movements in reading — A tutorial review. In M. Coltheart (Ed.), *Attention and Performance XII*. Hove, UK: Lawrence Erlbaum Associates Ltd.

Reason, J. T. (1984). Lapses of attention in everyday life. In R. Parasuramen & D. R. Davies (Eds.), *Varieties of attention*. London: Academic Press.

Reber, A. S. (1967). Implicit learning of artificial grammars. *Journal of Verbal Learning and Verbal Behavior, 5*, 855–863.

Reicher, G. M. (1969). Perceptual recognition as a function of meaningfulness of stimulus material. *Journal of Experimental Psychology, 81*, 274–280.

Rescorla, R. A. & Wagner, A. R. (1972). A theory of Pavlovian conditioning: Variations in the effectiveness of reinforcement and nonreinforcement. In A. H. Black & W. F. Protasy (Eds.), *Classical conditioning: II. Current research and theory*. New York: Appleton Century Crofts.

Riddoch, M. J. (1990). Neglect and the peripheral dyslexias. *Cognitive Neuropsychology, 7*, 369–389.

Riddoch, M. J. & Humphreys, G. W. (1983). The effect of cueing on unilateral neglect. *Neuropsychologia, 21*, 589–599.

Riddoch, M. J. & Humphreys, G. W. (1987a). Picture naming. In G. W. Humphreys & M. J. Riddoch (Eds.), *Visual object processing: A cognitive neuropsychological approach*. Hove: Lawrence Erlbaum Associates Ltd.

Riddoch, M. J. & Humphreys, G. W. (1987b). Visual object processing in optic aphasia: A case of semantic access agnosia. *Cognitive Neuropsychology, 4(2)*, 131–185.

Riddoch, M. J. & Humphreys, G. W. (1993). The smiling giraffe: An illustration of a visual memory disorder. In R. Campbell (Ed.), *Mental lives*. Oxford: Blackwell.

Riddoch, M. J. & Humphreys, G. W. (Eds.) (1994). *Cognitive neuropsychology and cognitive rehabilitation*. Hove, UK: Lawrence Erlbaum Associates Ltd.

Riddoch, M. J., Humphreys, G. W., Cleton, P., & Fery, P. (1990). Interaction of attentional and lexical processes in neglect dyslexia. *Cognitive Neuropsychology, 7(5–6)*, 479–517.

Robertson, I. & Marshall, J. C. (Eds.) (1993). *Unilateral neglect: Clinical and experimental studies*. Hove, UK: Lawrence Erlbaum Associates Ltd.

Robins, A. (1995). Catastrophic forgetting, rehearsal and pseudorehearsal. *Connection Science, 7*, 123–146.

Rolls, E. T. (1989). Parallel distributed processing in the brain: Implications of the functional architecture of neuronal networks in the hippocampus. In R. G. M. Morris (Ed.), *Parallel distributed processing: Implications for psychology and neurobiology*. Oxford: Oxford University Press.

Rolls, E. (1990). Principles underlying the representation and storage of information in neuronal networks in the primate hippocampus and cerebral cortex. In S. F. Zornetzer, J. L. Davis, & C. Lau

(Eds.), *An introduction to neural and electronic networks*. San Diego, CA: Academic Press.

Rosch, E., Mervis, C. B., Gray, W. D., Johnson, D. M., & Boyes-Bream, P. (1976). Basic objects in natural categories. *Cognitive Psychology, 8*, 382–439.

Rosenblatt, F. (1958). The perceptron: A probabilistic model for information storage and organisation in the brain. *Psychological Review, 65*, 386–408.

Rosenblatt, F. (1962). *Principles of neurodynamics*. Washington, DC: Sparton Books.

Rosson, M. B. (1983). From SOFA to LOUCH: Lexical contributions to pseudoword pronunciation. *Memory and Cognition, 11*, 152–160.

Rueckl, J. G., Cave, K. R., & Kosslyn, S. M. (1989). Why are "what" and "where" processed by separate cortical visual systems? A computational investigation. *Journal of Cognitive Neuroscience, 1*, 171–186.

Rumelhart, D. E. (1977). Toward an interactive model of reading. In S. Dornic (Ed.), *Attention and performance VI*. Hillsdale, NJ: Lawrence Erlbaum Associates Inc.

Rumelhart, D. E., Hinton, G. E., & McClelland, J. L. (1986a). A general framework for parallel distributed processing. In D. E. Rumelhart & J. L. McClelland (Eds.), *Parallel distributed processing: Explorations in the microstructure of cognition, Vol. 1*, (pp.45–76). Cambridge, MA: MIT Press.

Rumelhart, D. E., Hinton, G. E., & Williams, R. J. (1986). Learning internal representations by error propagation. In D. E. Rumelhart & J. L. McClelland (Eds.), *Parallel distributed processing: Explorations in the microstructure of cognition, Vol. 1*. Cambridge, MA: MIT Press.

Rumelhart, D. E. & McClelland, J. L. (1982). An interactive activation model of context effects in letter perception: Part 2. The contextual enhancement effect and some tests and extensions of the model. *Psychological Review, 89*, 60–94.

Rumelhart, D. E. & McClelland, J. L. (1985). Levels indeed! A response to Broadbent. *Journal of Experimental Psychology: General, 114*, 193–197.

Rumelhart, D. E. & McClelland, J. L. (1986). On learning the past tenses of English verbs. In J. L. McClelland & D. E. Rumelhart (Eds.), *Parallel distributed processing: Explorations in the microstructure of cognition. Vol. 2*. Cambridge, MA: MIT Press.

Rumelhart, D. E. & Norman, D. A. (1982). Simulating a skilled typist: A study of skilled motor performance. *Cognitive Science, 6*, 1–36.

Rumelhart, D. E. & Ortony, A. (1977). The representation of knowledge in memory. In R. C. Anderson, R. J. Spiro, & W. E. Montague (Eds.), *Schooling and the acquisition of knowledge*. Hillsdale, NJ: Lawrence Erlbaum Associates Inc.

Rumelhart, D. E., Smolensky, P., McClelland, J. L., & Hinton, G. E. (1986b). Schemata and sequential thought processes in PDP models. In J. L. McClelland & D. E. Rumelhart (Eds.), *Parallel distributed processing: Explorations in the microstructure of cognition, Vol. 2*, (pp.7–57). Cambridge, MA: MIT Press.

Rumelhart, D. E. & Todd, P. M. (1993). Learning and connectionist representations. In D. E. Meyer & S. Kornblum (Eds.), *Attention and performance XIV*. Cambridge, MA: MIT Press.

Rumelhart, D. E. & Zipser, D. (1985). Feature discovery by competitive learning. *Cognitive Science, 9*, 75–122.

Rumiati, R. I., Humphreys, G. W., Riddoch, M. J., & Bateman, A. (1994). Visual object agnosia without prosopagnosia or alexia: Evidence for hierarchical theories of visual recognition. *Visual Cognition, 1*, 181–226.

Ryan, J. (1969). Grouping and short-term memory: Different means and patterns of grouping. *Quarterly Journal of Experimental Psychology, 21*, 137–147.

Sacchett, C. & Humphreys, G. W. (1992). Calling a squirrel a squirrel but a canoe a wigwam: A category-specific deficit for artefactual objects and body parts. *Cognitive Neuropsychology, 9(1)*, 73–86.

Saffran, E. M., Bogyo, L. C., Schwartz, M. F., & Marin, O. S. M. (1980). Does deep dyslexia reflect right-hemisphere reading? In M. Coltheart, K. Patterson, & J. C. Marshall (Eds.), *Deep dyslexia*. London: Routledge & Kegan Paul.

Saffran, E. M. & Coslett, H. B. (1996). Attentional dyslexia in Alzheimer's disease: A case study. *Cognitive Neuropsychology, 13(2)*, 205–228.

Salasoo, A., Shiffrin, R. M., & Feustel, T. C. (1985). Building permanent memory codes: Codification and repetition effects in word identification. *Journal of Experimental Psychology: General, 114*, 50–77.

Samuel, A. L. (1963). Some studies in machine learning using the game of checkers. In E. A. Feigenbaum & J. Feldman (Eds.), *Computers and thought*. New York: McGraw-Hill.

Sartori, G. & Job, R. (1988). The oyster with four legs: A neuropsychological study on the interaction of visual and semantic information. *Cognitive Neuropsychology, 5(1)*, 105–132.

Scarborough, D. L., Cortese, C., & Scarborough, H. S. (1977). Frequency and repetition effects in lexical memory. *Journal of Experimental Psychology: Human Perception and Performance, 3*, 1–17.

Schacter, D. L., Chiu, C. Y., & Ochsner, K. N (1993). Implicit memory: A selective review. *Annual Review of Neuroscience, 16,* 159–182.

Schacter, D. L., McAndrews, M. P., & Moscovitch, M. (1988). Access to consciousness: Dissociations between implicit and explicit knowledge in neuropsychological syndromes. In L. Weiskrantz (Ed.), *Thought without language.* Oxford: Oxford University Press.

Schank, R. C. & Abelson, R. P. (1977). *Scripts, plans, goals and understanding.* Hillsdale, NJ: Lawrence Erlbaum Associates Inc.

Schriefers, H. (1996). *Language production: Some evidence concerning the discrete stages question and the advance planning question.* Paper presented to the Experimental Psychology Society, London, January.

Schwartz, M. F., Saffran, E., Bloch, D., & Dell, G. S. (1994). Disordered speech production in aphasic and normal speakers. *Brain and Language, 47,* 52–88.

Scoville, W. B. & Milner, B. (1958). Loss of recent memory after bilateral hippocampal lesions. *Journal of Neurology, Neurosurgery and Psychiatry, 20,* 11–21.

Seidenberg, M. S. (1992). Beyond orthographic depth in reading: Equitable division of labour. In R. Frost & L. Katz (Eds.), *Orthography, phonology, morphology and meaning.* Amsterdam: Elsevier Science.

Seidenberg, M. S. & McClelland, J. L. (1989). A distributed, developmental model of word recognition and naming. *Psychological Review, 96,* 523–568.

Seidenberg, M. S. & McClelland, J. L. (1990). More words but still no lexicon: Reply to Besner et al. (1990). *Psychological Review, 97,* 447–452.

Seidenberg, M. S., Tanenhaus, M. K., Leiman, J. M., & Bienkowski, M. (1982). Automatic access of the meanings of ambiguous words in context: Some limitations of knowledge-based processing. *Cognitive Processing, 14,* 489–537.

Seidenberg, M. S., Waters, G. S., Barnes, M. A., & Tanenhaus, M. K. (1984). When does irregular spelling or pronunciation influence word recognition? *Journal of Verbal Learning and Verbal Behavior, 23,* 383–404.

Sejnowski, T. J. (1981). Skeleton filters in the brain. In G. E. Hinton & J. A. Anderson (Eds.), *Parallel models of associative memory.* Hillsdale, NJ: Lawrence Erlbaum Associates Inc.

Sejnowski, T. J. (1986a). Computational neuroscience. *Behavioral and Brain Sciences, 9,* 104–105.

Sejnowski, T. J. (1986b). Open questions about computation in the cerebral cortex. In J. L. McClelland & D. E. Rumelhart (Eds.), *Parallel distributed processing: Explorations in the microstructure of cognition, Vol. 2.* Cambridge, MA: MIT Press.

Sejnowski, T. J., Koch, C., & Churchland, P. (1988). Computational neuroscience. *Science, 241,* 1299–1306.

Sejnowski, T. J. & Rosenberg, C. R. (1987). Parallel networks that learn to pronounce English text. *Complex Systems, 1,* 145–168.

Selemon, L. D., Rajowska, G., & Goldman-Rakic, P. S. (1993). A morphometric analysis of prefrontal areas 9 and 46 in the schizophrenic and normal human brain. *Schizophrenia Research, 9,* 151.

Semenza, C. & Zettin, M. (1988). Generating proper names: A case of selective inability. *Cognitive Neuropsychology, 5(6),* 711–721.

Semenza, C. & Zettin, M. (1989). Evidence from aphasia for the role of proper names as pure referring expressions. *Nature, 342,* 678–679.

Servan-Schreiber, D. & Cohen, J. D. (1996). Dopamine, frontal cortex and schizophrenia: Model and data. In J. R. Reggia, E. Ruppin, & R. S. Berndt (Eds.), *Neural modeling of brain and cognitive disorders.* New York: World Scientific.

Servan-Schreiber, D., Printz, H., & Cohen, J. D. (1990). A network model of catecholamine effects — Gain, signal-to-noise ratio, and behavior. *Science, 249,* 892–895.

Shaffer, L. H. (1975). Multiple attention in continuous verbal tasks. In P. M. A. Rabbitt & S. Dornic (Eds.), *Attention and performance V.* New York: Academic Press.

Shaffer, L. H. (1978). Timing in the motor programming of typing. *Quarterly Journal of Experimental Psychology, 30,* 333–345.

Shallice, T. (1981). Phonological agraphia and the lexical route in writing. *Brain, 104,* 413–429.

Shallice, T. (1988). *From neuropsychology to mental structure.* Cambridge: Cambridge University Press.

Shallice, T., Glasspool, D. W., & Houghton, G. (1995). Can neuropsychological evidence inform connectionist modelling? Analyses of spelling. *Language and Cognitive Processes, 10(3/4),* 195–225.

Shallice, T. & Saffran, E. (1986). Lexical processing in the absence of explicit word identification: Evidence from a letter-by-letter reader. *Cognitive Neuropsychology, 3(4),* 429–458.

Shallice, T. & Warrington, E. K. (1977). The possible role of selective attention in acquired dyslexia. *Neuropsychologia, 15,* 31–41.

Shanks, D. (1990). Connectionism and human learning: Critique of Gluck and Bower (1988). *Journal of Experimental Psychology: General, 119,* 101–104.

Shastri, L. & Ajjanagade, V. (1993). From simple associations to systematic reasoning: A connectionist representation of rules, variables, and dynamic bindings using temporal synchrony. *Behavioral and Brain Sciences, 16*, 417–451.

Shepherd, G. M. (1979). *The synaptic organization of the brain.* New York: Oxford University Press.

Shepherd, G. M. (1988). *Neurobiology.* New York: Oxford University Press.

Sheridan, J. & Humphreys, G. W. (1993). A verbal-semantic category-specific deficit. *Cognitive Neuropsychology, 10*, 143–184.

Shulman, H. G., Hornak, R., & Sanders, E. (1978). The effect of graphemic, phonetic and semantic relationships on access to lexical structures. *Memory and Cognition, 6*, 115–123.

Siegler, R. S. (1981). Developmental sequences within and between concepts. *Monographs of the Society for Research in Child Development, 46.*

Sieroff, E., Pollatsek, A., & Posner, M. I. (1988). Recognition of visual letter strings following injury to the posterior visual spatial attention system. *Cognitive Neuropsychology, 5(4)*, 427–449.

Sieroff, E. & Posner, M. I. (1988). Cueing spatial attention during processing of words and letter strings in normals. *Cognitive Neuropsychology, 5*, 451–472.

Smolensky, P. (1988). On the proper treatment of connectionism. *Behavioral and Brain Sciences, 11*, 1–74.

Squire, L. R., Slater, P. C., & Chace, P. (1975). Retrograde amnesia: Temporal gradient in very long-term memory following electroconvulsive therapy. *Science, 187*, 77–79.

Starreveld, P. A. & La Heij, W. (in press). Error analyses of context effects in picture naming. *American Journal of Psychology.*

Stemberger, J. P. (1984). Structural errors in normal and agrammatic speech. *Cognitive Neuropsychology, 1*, 281–313.

Stewart F., Parkin A. J., & Hunkin, N. M. (1992). Naming impairments following recovery from herpes-simplex encephalitis: Category specific? *Quarterly Journal of Experimental Psychology, 44A(2)*, 261–284.

Strain, E., Patterson, K. E., & Seidenberg, M. S. (1995). Semantic effects in single-word naming. *Journal of Experimental Psychology: Learning, Memory and Cognition, 21(5)*, 1140–1154.

Stroop, J. R. (1935). Studies of interference in serial verbal reactions. *Journal of Experimental Psychology, 18*, 643–662.

Sutton, R. S. & Barto, A. G. (1981). Toward a modern theory of adaptive networks: Expectation and prediction. *Psychological Review, 88*, 135–170.

Swerdlow, N. R. & Koob, G. F. (1987). Dopamine, schizophrenia, mania and depression: Toward a unified hypothesis of cortico-striato-pallido-thalamic function. *Behavioral and Brain Sciences, 10(2)*, 197–207.

Swinney, D. A. (1979). Lexical access during sentence comprehension: (Re)consideration of context effects. *Journal of Verbal Learning and Verbal Behavior, 18*, 545–569.

Teyler, T. J. & Discenna, P. (1986). The hippocampal memory indexing theory. *Behavioural Neuroscience, 100(2)*, 147–154.

Touretzky, D. S. & Fahlman, S. E. (1993). Should first-order logic be neurally plausible? *Behavioral and Brain Sciences, 16*, 474–475.

Touretzky, D. S. & Geva, S. (1987). A distributed connectionist representation for concept structures. *Proceedings of the 9th Annual Conference of the Cognitive Science Society* Seattle, Washington.

Treiman, R. & Danis, C. (1988). Short-term-memory errors for spoken syllables are affected by the linguistic structure of the syllables. *Journal of Experimental Psychology: Learning, Memory and Cognition, 14(1)*, 145–152.

Treisman, A. (1988). Features and objects: The 14th Bartlett memorial lecture. *Quarterly Journal of Experimental Psychology, 40A(2)*, 201–237.

Turing, A. (1937). On computable numbers with an application to the Entscheidungs problem. *Proceedings of the London Mathematical Society, 42*, 230–265.

Turing, A. (1950). Computing machinery and intelligence. *Mind, 59*, 433–460.

Ungerleider, L. G. & Mishkin, M. (1982). Two cortical visual systems. In D. J. Ingle, M. A. Goodale, & R. J. W. Mansfield (Eds.), *Analysis of visual behavior.* Cambridge, MA: MIT Press.

Vallar, G. & Shallice, T. (Eds.) (1990). *Neuropsychological impairments of short-term memory.* Cambridge: Cambridge University Press.

Van Gelder, T. (1990). Compositionality: A connectionist variation on a classical theme. *Cognitive Science, 14*, 355–384.

Van Orden, G. C. (1987). A ROWS is a ROSE: Spelling, sound and reading. *Memory and Cognition, 15*, 181–198.

Vitkovitch, M. & Humphreys, G. W. (1991). Perseverative responding in speeded naming to pictures: Its in the links. *Journal of Experimental Psychology: Human Perception and Performance, 17*, 664–680.

Vitkovitch, M., Humphreys, G. W., & Lloyd-Jones, T. J. (1993). On naming a giraffe a zebra: Picture naming errors across different categories. *Journal of Experimental Psychology: Learning, Memory and Cognition, 19*, 243–259.

von der Malsburg, C. (1973). Self-organization of orientation sensitive cells in the striate cortex. *Kybernetik, 14*, 85–100.

von der Malsburg, C. (1981). *The correlation theory of brain function. Internal Report 81–2* Department of Neurobiology, Max-Planck-Institute for Biophysical Chemistry.

von Neumann, J. (1958). *The computer and the brain*, New Haven, CT: Yale University Press.

Wagner, A. R. & Rescorla, R. A. (1972). Inhibition in Pavlovian conditioning: Applications of a theory. In R. A. Boakes & M. S. Halliday (Eds.), *Inhibition and learning*. London: Academic Press.

Waltz, D. L. & Pollack, J. B. (1985). Massively parallel parsing: A strongly interactive model of natural language interpretation. *Cognitive Science, 9*, 51–74.

Ward, R., Goodrich, S., & Driver, J. (1994). Grouping reduces visual extinction: Neuropsychological evidence for weight-linkage in visual selection. *Visual Cognition, 1*, 101–130.

Warren, C. & Morton, J. (1982). The effects of priming on picture recognition. *British Journal of Psychology, 73*, 117–129.

Warrington, E. K. (1981). Concrete word dyslexia. *British Journal of Psychology, 72*, 175–196.

Warrington, E. K. (1985). Agnosia: the impairment of object recognition. In J. A. M. Frederiks (Ed.), *Handbook of clinical neurology, Vol. 1: Clinical neuropsychology*. London: Elsevier Science.

Warrington, E. K., Cipolotti, L., & McNeil, J. (1993). Attentional dyslexia: A single case study. *Neuropsychologia, 31*, 871–885.

Warrington, E. K. & McCarthy, R. (1983). Category-specific access dysphasia. *Brain, 106*, 859–878.

Warrington, E. K. & McCarthy, R. (1987). Categories of knowledge: Further fractionations and an attempted integration. *Brain, 110*, 1273–1296.

Warrington, E. K. & Shallice, T. (1980). Word form dyslexia. *Brain, 103*, 99–112.

Warrington, E. K. & Shallice, T. (1984). Category-specific semantic impairment. *Brain, 107*, 829–854.

Wasserman, P. D. (1988). Experiments in translating Chinese characters using back-propagation. *Proceedings of the 33rd IEEE Computer Society International Conference*. Washington DC: Computer Society Press of the IEEE.

Wasserman, P. D. (1989). *Neural computing: Theory and practice*. New York: Van Nostrand Reinhold.

Waters, G. S. & Seidenberg, M. S. (1985). Spelling–sound effects in reading: Time course and decision criteria. *Memory and Cognition, 13*, 557–572.

Weigend, A. S., Huberman, B. A., & Rumelhart, D. E. (1990). Predicting the future: A connectionist approach. *International Journal of Neural Systems, 1*, 193–210.

Wermter, S. & Lehnert, W. G. (1989). A hybrid/connectionist model for noun phrase understanding. *Connection Science, 1*, 255–272.

Wheeldon, L. R. & Monsell, S. (1994). Inhibition of spoken word production by priming a semantic competitor. *Journal of Memory and Language, 33*, 332–356.

Wheeler, D. D. (1970). Processes in word recognition. *Cognitive Psychology, 1*, 59–85.

Wickelgren, W. A. (1965). Short-term memory for acoustically similar lists. *American Journal of Psychology, 78*, 567–574.

Wickelgren, W. A. (1969). Context-sensitive coding, associative memory, and serial order in (speech) behavior. *Psychological Review, 76*, 1–15.

Williams, R. J. & Peng, J. (1990). An efficient gradient-based algorithm for on-line training of recurrent network trajectories. *Neural Computation, 2*, 490–501.

Willshaw, D. J., Buneman, O. P., & Longuet-Higgins, H. C. (1969). Nonholographic associative memory. *Nature, 222*, 960–962.

Wilson, M. A. McNaughton, B. L. (1994). Reactivation of hippocampal ensemble memories during sleep. *Science, 265*, 676–679.

Wing, A. & Baddeley, A. D. (1980). Spelling errors in handwriting: A corpus and a distributional analysis. In U. Frith (Ed.), *Cognitive processes in spelling*. London: Academic Press.

Winograd, T. (1972). *Understanding natural language*. New York: Academic Press.

Winston, P. H. (1975). *The psychology of computer vision*. New York: McGraw-Hill.

Woods, C. C. (1978). Variations on a theme by Lashley: Lesion experiments on the neural model of Anderson, Silverstein, Ritz and Jones. *Psychological Review, 85*, 582–591.

Young, A. W. & de Haan, E. H. F. (1988). Boundaries of covert recognition in prosopagnosia. *Cognitive Neuropsychology, 5*, 317–336.

Young, A. W., Newcombe, F., & Ellis, A. W. (1991). Different impairments contribute to neglect dyslexia. *Cognitive Neuropsychology, 8(3–4)*, 177–191.

Zemel, R. S., Mozer, M. C., & Hinton, G. E. (1988). TRAFFIC: A model of object recognition based on transformations of feature instances. In D. Touretzky, G. E. Hinton, & T. J. Sejnowski (Eds.), *Proceedings of the 1988 Connectionist Models Summer School*. San Mateo, CA: Morgan Kaufman.

Zipser, D. & Anderson, R. A. (1988). A back-propagation programmed network that simulates response properties of a subset of posterior parietal neurons. *Nature, 331*, 679–684.

Zucker, S. W., Hummel, R. A., & Rosenfeld, A. (1977). An application of relaxation labelling to line and curve enhancement. *IEEE Trans. Computers, 26*.

Author Index

Subject Index